The British
BOXING
Board of Control
YEARBOOK
1995

Edited by
Barry J. Hugman

Published by Tony Williams Publications,
24a Queen Square, North Curry, Taunton, Somerset TA3 6LE

ISBN 1 869833 33 3

Distributed by Little Red Witch Book Distribution,
Helland Cottage, Helland, North Curry, Taunton, Somerset TA3 6DU
Telephone 0823 490080, Fax 0823 490281

Typesetting & Artwork by Typecast (Artwork & Design), 8 Mudford Road, Yeovil, Somerset BA21 4AA
Printed & Bound by Hillman Printers (Frome) Ltd,
Handlemaker Road, Marston Trading Estate, Frome, Somerset BA11 4RW

All sales enquiries should be referred to The Little Red Witch Book Distribution Co.

Contents

NOBLE ART PROMOTIONS LTD
GREG STEENE & BRUCE BAKER
INTERNATIONAL PROMOTERS, MANAGERS, MATCHMAKERS AND AGENTS

BOXERS MANAGED BY GREG STEENE:

JOHNNY NELSON ....WBF WORLD HEAVYWEIGHT CHAMPION

DEVON RHOOMS ...............CRUISERWEIGHT

HUNTER CLAY....................WBC INTERNATIONAL SUPER-MIDDLEWEIGHT CHAMPION

ANDY WRIGHT....................FORMER UNDEFEATED SOUTHERN AREA SUPER-MIDDLEWEIGHT CHAMPION

HORACE FLEARY ....GERMAN INTERNATIONAL SUPER-MIDDLEWEIGHT CHAMPION

DAVID CRANSTON ..............MIDDLEWEIGHT

JASON HART ......................MIDDLEWEIGHT

ANTHONY WANZA..............SUPER-FEATHERWEIGHT

IAN REID............................BANTAMWEIGHT

TRAINERS

CASEY MCCULLUM, TREVOR CATTOUSE, REG DAVIS AND GERRY CONTEH (USA)

ANY UNATTACHED PROFESSIONALS OR SERIOUS AMATEURS SEEKING FIRST CLASS TRAINING AND MANAGEMENT, PLEASE CONTACT THE BELOW NUMBER

22 Welbeck Street, London, W1M 7PG Telephone: 081 830 0720 Fax: 081 830 0932
Company Reg. No. 02840916

Acknowledgements

I would like to start this edition off by thanking all the readers of the *British Boxing Yearbook* for their continued support over the years. Support which has helped to make this book an eagerly anticipated pre-Christmas item, that is if my mail bag is anything to go by.

Even after all these years one should never become complacent, and I must say that I value my excellent relationship with the General Secretary, John Morris, and the majority of license holders as much now as I did when setting out on the first *Yearbook* back in 1983. I have always felt privileged to be producing a book which has become a public relations tool for boxing in general and, just like John, I am a great believer in the amateur and professional codes working together ethic. Without digressing too far from acknowledging all those at the BBBoC, whose help is crucial in keeping this book on the road, I would once again like to publicly thank John Morris, Simon Block (Assistant Secretary), Paula Gibson, Mary Farnan, Joanne Landers and Karyn Locke, for all their help. As you can imagine, a lot of hard work goes into keeping the *British Boxing Yearbook* abreast of the times and the Board certainly plays its part.

Ron Olver has been with me every step of the way. Eleven *British Boxing Yearbooks*, three *International Boxing Annual's* and a one off *George Wimpey Amateur Boxing Yearbook*, plus giving me a shoulder to lean on when I first launched *Boxing Monthly* and *Boxing Weekly* and later, *Boxing Outlook*. He has been involved in boxing for more years than he cares to remember, having been a former Assistant Editor of *Boxing News*; former Assistant Editor of *Boxing World*; British correspondent for *The Ring*; author of *The Professionals*; author of the boxing section within *Encyclopedia Britannica*; author of *Boxing*, Foyles' Library Service; former co-Editor of the *Boxing News Annual*; Chairman of the BBBoC Benevolent Fund Grants Committee; Vice President of many ex-boxers' associations; Public Relations Officer of the London Ex-Boxers' Association; writer of the "Old Timers'" feature in *Boxing News* for 27 years; member of the Commonwealth Boxing Council and a member of the International Hall of Fame Election Committee.

It is always nice to introduce fresh faces to the *Yearbook*, but in passing on to pastures new I would like to thank Chris Kempson for all the hard work he put in over the years. This year I am most fortunate to have been joined by Bob Lonkhurst, currently looking to publish his much researched book on the life and times of Tommy Farr; Ralph Oates, of boxing quiz book fame and with *Boxing Clever* on sale at present; and David Prior, who writes on amateur boxing for *Boxing News* and who has pieced together Highlights from the 1993-94 Amateur Season for this edition. David is also in the process of looking to publish his book on an in-depth history of amateur boxing in this country. As a Licensed Inspector, Bob Lonkhurst's Eyes and Ears of the Board is written from first-hand experience, while his piece on The Journeymen: Saviours of the Sport gives an excellent insight into just what makes these men tick. Another area of interest right now is the role of women in boxing and Ralph Oates gets right to the heart of the matter as he interviews Carol Polis, Jackie Kallen, Tania Follett, Lisa Budd and Kathy Morrison.

The biggest single area of research in the book this year is contained in the 36 pages that are World Title Bouts (M. Flyweight to Lightweight), 1891-1993. As I have said elsewhere in the book, without the expert help of Professor Luckett Davis, Bob Soderman and Hy Rosenberg (America), and Harold Alderman, Bill Matthews (author of *The English Boxing Champions*), and Derek O'Dell, at home, I could not have started, let alone completed, what has been such a complex area of research down the ages. Certainly, without the tremendous help in the shape of Luckett Davis, in hours upon hours of detailed research, early day boxing in America would have remained a mystery. Luckett has always been in demand and I am not surprised. He supplied a large amount of information for the revision of champions' records in the 1986-87 *Ring Record Book* and earlier editions, and also helped Giuseppe Ballarati revise records of European fighters included in the "The Golden Pages" section of several editions of *Pugilato*. An elector for the Boxing Hall of Fame (Old Timers section, pre 1930), Luckett has also contributed articles on boxers for the *Biographical Dictionary of American Sports*, edited by David L. Porter and published by the Greenwood Press (1989) and is at present preparing biographies for the *American National Biography* to be published by the Oxford University Press. He was also a major contributor to the now defunct IBRO newsletter. Harold Alderman is another unsung hero, who has spent the last 30 odd years researching boxing at the National Newspaper Library, and he too put in many hours of work on the British side of the project.

I must once again thank John Jarrett, who wrote Home and Away with British Boxers during 1993-94 and Eric Armit for producing the A-Z of Current World Champions. Others who help keep me up-to-date include Patrick Myler (Irish amateur boxing), Neil Blackburn (world-wide obituaries), Bob Yalen (seasonal world title data), Mrs Enza Merchione Jacoponi (EBU data), Cai Corp, Jim Paull, Paul Thomas and Harry Warner (BBBoC area title bout information), Frank Hendry, Arthur Atherton, Bert Pontremoli, Roy Smith, Bill Evans and Peter Rafferty (amateur boxing) and David Roake, Fred Snelling and Derek O'Dell. Due to a space problem, Derek's excellent article about "Jersey" Joe Walcott and Rocky Marciano, namely the "Old Man and the Rock", will appear in next year's edition. However, it is well worth the wait.

As I said last year, the *British Boxing Yearbook* relies heavily on Les Clark for its photos and 1994 is no exception. Les continues to take action photos and poses from venues around the country and is an invaluable asset. If anyone requires a photo that has been used in the book, he can be reached at 352 Trelawney Avenue, Langley, Bucks SL3 7TS. Other photos were supplied by Chris Bevan, George Ashton, of Sportapics Ltd, Pennie Cattle, and my old mate from Manchester, Harry Goodwin.

Before signing off, I would also like to mention Bernard Hart, the Managing Director of Lonsdale Sports Equipment Ltd, who sponsors the BBBoC Awards that coincide with the launch of the *Yearbook*; Jean Bastin, of Typecast (Artwork & Design), for her patience with the typesetting and design, and the publisher, Tony Williams, whose continued support has helped to keep the *British Boxing Yearbook* at the forefront of boxing publications.

B. J. Hugman (Editor)

Introduction

by Barry J. Hugman

In this, the 11th edition of the *British Boxing Yearbook,* I am happy to think that it continues to present fresh new articles and opinions, and additional records, where worthy of space. That has not been done at the expense of regular features, but in a form complimentary, hopefully, to what the reader has come to expect. Also, we try hard not to get too involved in politics, leaving that to others, but concentrate more on presenting the positive side of the sport.

This year, as in others, I feel we have done just that. Full records of British boxers remain, while I have introduced a brand new section, World Title Bouts (mini-flyweight to lightweight), 1891-1993. Part two will follow in the 1996 *Yearbook* and will contain the light-welterweight division through to the heavyweights.

There is no doubt in my mind that this has been the biggest area of boxing research I have ever undertaken and with magnificent back-up from men like Professor Luckett Davis in America and Harold Alderman and Bill Matthews, here in Britain, this task would have probably been insurmountable. Along with other's, such as Bob Soderman and Hy Rosenberg and the unstinting support of Derek O'Dell, my task was made easier. As it was, I spent many, many hours at the National Newspaper Library in Colindale pouring over papers such as *The San Francisco Chronicle*, *Los Angeles Times*, *New Orleans Daily Picayune*, *Chicago Tribune*, *Boston Post* and *New York Times* and *The Herald*, to name just a few.

I think it is fair to say that by reading the newspapers of the day one developed a fair idea of how boxing was not controlled in America prior to the 1920s. The biggest single problem has been that over the years the history of boxing has been portrayed inaccurately, to say the least. The reason appears to have been the historian's penchant for showing early day claimants, at a variety of weights, as representing the divisions we know so well today.

For example, there has always been a contradiction in terms as to when George Dixon moved between bantam and feather. Later, Jimmy Barry claimed the world title at 106 lbs, while, at the same time, Billy Plimmer was recognised at 110 lbs before moving his weight up to 112. Following on from that, Johnny Coulon claimed the 105 lbs title in 1908, which he eventually moved to 112, while in England, Digger Stanley was acclaimed the world's 118 lbs bantamweight champion.

Anybody who has even thought of delving thus deep would soon have been disuaded from doing so. That might explain why the exercise has only just begun to be carried out. Only recently, Herb Goldman, the former editor of the *Ring* and now with *Boxing Illustrated*, discovered that several fights attributed to George Dixon, as being over the weight, were, in fact, recognised as being for the championship. This incorrect version of history, according to Herb, was passed down to Nat Fleischer some 30 year's after the events by Tom O'Rourke, who just happened to be Dixon's manager.

Just by using this weight class as an example, you can see that different historians took their pick as to who they thought was the world champion of the day, leaving the unlucky ones out. In truth, men who were recognised as world champions up to the time that weights were regulated, should really be shown under their actual weight they defended at, not by class. That would reflect the situation more accurately. At present, though, I have left all the fights in their so-called weight divisions with notes attached. You takes your pick!

Before signing off, I would just like to mention my old mate, Mickey Moynihan, an avid reader of the *Yearbook* and recognised by many as Britain's number one fight fan. Mickey sadly passed away recently, but he will not be forgotten. Here's to his memory, may he rest in peace.

Abbreviations and Definitions used in the record sections of the Yearbook: PTS (Points), CO (Count Out), RSC (Referee Stopped Contest), RTD (Retired), DIS (Disqualified), NC (No Contest), ND (No Decision).

British Boxing Board of Control Ltd: Structure

(Members of the World Boxing Council, World Boxing Association, International Boxing Federation, World Boxing Organisation, Commonwealth Boxing Council and European Boxing Union)

PRESIDENT	Sir David Hopkin
VICE PRESIDENT	Leonard E. Read, QPM
CHAIRMAN	Sir David Hopkin
VICE CHAIRMAN	Leonard E. Read, QPM
GENERAL SECRETARY	John Morris

ADMINISTRATIVE
STEWARDS

Dr Adrian Whiteson, OBE
Dr Oswald Ross
William Sheeran
Dennis Lockton
Lincoln Crawford
Frank Butler, OBE
Tom Pendry, MP
Cliff Curvis
Bill Martin
Robert Graham, BEM
Lord Brooks of Tremorfa
Gerald Woolard
Charles Giles
Sebastian Coe, OBE, MP
Judge Alan Simpson

HONORARY STEWARD*   Dr James Shea

STEWARDS OF APPEAL*

Robin Simpson, QC
John Mathew, QC
Nicholas Valios, QC
Robert Harman, QC
William Tudor John
Geoffrey Finn
Judge Brian Capstick, QC
Colin Ross Munro, QC
Peter Richards
Lord Meston

HONORARY
CONSULTANT*   Ray Clarke, OBE

HEAD OFFICE

Jack Petersen House
52a Borough High Street
London SE1 1XW
Tel. 071 403 5879
Fax. 071 378 6670
Telegrams:
BRITBOX, LONDON

* Not directors of the company

AREA COUNCILS - AREA SECRETARIES

AREA NO 1 (SCOTLAND)
Brian McAllister
11 Woodside Crescent, Glasgow G3 7UL
Telephone 041 332 0932

AREA NO 2 (NORTHERN IRELAND)
Stanley Anderson
5 Ardenlee Avenue, Ravenhill Road, Belfast,
Northern Ireland BT6 0AA
Telephone 0232 453829

AREA NO 3 (WALES)
Dai Corp
113 Hill Crest, Brynna, Llanharan, Mid Glamorgan
Telephone 0443 226465

AREA NO 4 (NORTHERN)
(Northumberland, Cumbria, Durham, Cleveland, Tyne and Wear, North Yorkshire [north of a line drawn from Whitby to Northallerton to Richmond, including these towns].)
John Jarrett
5 Beechwood Avenue, Gosforth, Newcastle
Telephone 091 2856556

AREA NO 5 (CENTRAL)
(North Yorkshire [with the exception of the part included in the Northern Area - see above], Lancashire, West and South Yorkshire, Greater Manchester, Merseyside and Cheshire, Isle of Man, North Humberside.)
Harry Warner
14 St Christopher's Road,
The 18th Fairway, Ashton under Lyme, Lancashire
Telephone 061 330 4572

AREA NO 6 (SOUTHERN)
(Bedfordshire, Berkshire, Buckinghamshire, Cambridgeshire, Channel Islands, Isle of Wight, Essex, Hampshire, Kent, Hertfordshire, Greater London, Norfolk, Suffolk, Oxfordshire, East and West Sussex.)
Simon Block
British Boxing Board of Control
Jack Petersen House, 52a Borough High Street, London
SE1 1XW
Telephone 071 403 5879

AREA NO 7 (WESTERN)
(Cornwall, Devon, Somerset, Dorset, Wiltshire, Avon, Gloucestershire.)
Jim Paull
The Coach House, Clarence Court, Kent Road,
Congresbury, Bristol BS19 5BE
Telephone 0934 876036

AREA NO 8 (MIDLANDS)
(Derbyshire, Nottinghamshire, Lincolnshire, Salop, Staffordshire, Herefordshire and Worcestershire, Warwickshire, West Midlands, Leicestershire, South Humberside, Northamptonshire.)
Alec Kirby
105 Upper Meadow Road, Quinton, Birmingham B32
Telephone 021 421 1194

Foreword

by John Morris *(General Secretary, British Boxing Board of Control)*

The *British Boxing Yearbook* moves into its second decade with editor Barry Hugman firing on top form, producing yet another superb volume. It is a record book that moves way beyond the bare statistics and includes in-depth articles that get to the heart of our sport to reflect the way professional boxing has caught the public imagination with an array of colourful champions. Indeed, champions of the present to rival those of a glorious past.

Britain had, at the time of going to press, two world heavyweight champions in Lennox Lewis (WBC) and Herbie Hide (WBO), Nigel Benn (WBC) and Chris Eubank (WBO) reign at super-middleweight, while the brash, extrovert Prince Nassem Hamed has taken the EBU bantamweight title by storm. Whether he has stolen hearts remains to be seen and perhaps he needs to tone down some of his antics a trifle as he matures as both fighter and person.

Then we have Steve Robinson, the "Cinderella Man" from Cardiff. Steve's performances as WBO featherweight champion have been an example to all professionals in any sport and his hometown clash with Paul Hodkinson provided the sort of domestic classic that keeps boxing so high in the TV ratings.

But the year has also brought great sadness. Boxing lost Bradley Stone, who collapsed a few hours after his stirring British super-bantamweight championship match against Richie Wenton at York Hall, marring the first ever title contest in this new division with tragedy. Bradley was a dedicated pro and true sportman and his death, the day after the contest, was a terrible loss.

Not only do I offer sympathy on behalf of everyone associated with British boxing to Bradley's family and to his fiancee Donna and her family, but I thank them all for the dignity they showed in their grief and tremendous support they have given to boxing. Donna's drive to create a Bradley Stone Memorial Fund to assist young boxers with their medical payments is a great idea and has been fully supported by the Board with a sizeable donation.

Bradley's death also brought the inevitable and immediate attacks on the sport, but the onslaught was muted within days following the deaths of two Grand Prix drivers, one the great Ayrton Senna, and a young jockey. The comparative risks run by so many in all sports were thus put into perspective.

While the last two years have been good for boxing in a variety of ways, many problems remain, not least the involvement of television in a way that makes the sport more and more dependent on this section of the entertainment industry for its finances. Unless a sensible balance is kept the TV men will rule us and, possibly, leave a dangerous void if at some stage in the future they decide to remove their investment.

As we move nearer to the 21st Century, my aims for boxing are legion both domestically and on the confused international scene, but they have to be narrowed down to specific objectives.

Here in Britain we must achieve an acceptance that boxing is one sport, amateur and professional, even if the controlling organisations remain entirely independent. The creation of an umbrella body with real powers and with representation from all aspects of boxing still seems to me the most sensible of objectives.

World boxing remains, quite frankly, a mess. With so many so-called world championships available, the commercial prospects may for a time be increased, but credibility will fast slip away.

Boxing urgently needs a world controlling body on a par with FIFA's influence on football. In the United States an association of State Commissions has been formed and is slowly flexing its muscles. This must be extended to take in the national board's commissions and federations all over the world. I realise I am riding a hobby horse, but more and more I become convinced that action has to be taken now to retain respect for boxing in the world corridors of power. Without that respect our sport may soon be in dire trouble.

International Boxing Corporation

The Penthouse Suite
Duke Street House
50 Duke Street
London W1M 5DS
Tel: 0171 495 6916
Fax: 0171 495 6918

ALFRED "COBRA" KOTEY
(Ghana)
WBO Bantamweight Champion

TONY "KID" PEP
(Canada)
Commonwealth Super-Featherweight
Champion

RICHARD BANGO
(Nigeria/London)
Undefeated Heavyweight. Olympic Silver
Medalist 1992

JACKLORD JACOBS
(Nigeria/London)
Undefeated Cruiserweight. World
Championship Silver Medalist 1993

KEVIN "THE LOOK" LUESHING
(London)
Welterweight. Former Southern Area
Light-Middleweight Champion

SEAN KNIGHT
(New York/London)
Light-Welterweight
Twice Golden Gloves Champion

J T WILLIAMS
(Wales)
Super-Featherweight Champion of Wales

SPENCER OLIVER
(London)
ABA Bantamweight Champion 1994.
Commonwealth Games Silver Medalist
1994

Promoters Of
ROCKY MILTON "CYPRUS CYCLONE"
(Cyprus/London)

The KOPRO Fight Team

ALFRED "COBRA" KOTEY
World Bantamweight Champion
KOPRO is the worldwide marketing division of International Boxing Corporation

John Spensley - Promoter

Mike Jacobs - Manager

Roger Levitt - Media Consultant

British Boxing Board of Control Awards, 1994

The Awards, inaugurated in 1984, in the form of statuettes of boxers, were originally designed by Morton T. Colver, the manufacturer of the Lonsdale Belt and the winners for 1994 were selected by an Awards' Committee, comprising John Morris, Simon Block, Frank Butler OBE, Bill Martin, Doctor Adrian Whiteson OBE and Barry J. Hugman, the editor of the *British Boxing Yearbook*.

British Boxer of the Year – Steve Robinson

Other nominations: Herbie Hide, for winning the WBO heavyweight title from Michael Bentt, Lennox Lewis, who successfully defended his WBC heavyweight belt against Frank Bruno and Phil Jackson, and Eamonn Loughran, who won the vacant WBO welterweight title, beating Lorenzo Smith, before holding off the challenge of Italy's Alessandro Duran.

Known as the "Cinderella Man" for good reason, Steve started his pro career off early in 1989 at the age of 20. There were no fanfares for him and by the end of 1992 his record showed eight losses in 21 contests. However, during that period he had beaten men of the calibre of Russell Davison (twice), Neil Haddock, Colin Lynch, Peter Harris, for the Welsh featherweight title, and, more recently, Stephane Haccoun, in France. The following year, 1993, was to be his year of destiny. He began by winning the vacant WBA Penta-Continental title after outpointing Paul Harvey, but then became the victim of a debatable points loss at the hands of French-Algerian, Mehdi Labdouni. Not deterred, Steve, through his manager, Dai Gardiner, stated that he would now be concentrating on the British title scene.

Nobody could have guessed what was next in store (no pun intended) for the Welshman. In training for a British title eliminator, the news broke that Ruben Palacio, who was due to defend his WBO title against John Davison, had failed an HIV medical. With the fight less than 48 hours away, the promoters frantically searched around for an opponent and came up with Robinson, a man not even in the WBO ratings. Steve had only just given up his day job as a lowly paid storeman and two weeks later was now fighting for his biggest ever purse and a version of the world title.

The rest is history. In a fight that swung first one way and then the other, Steve finally convinced two of the judges with a sustained last minute attack. Following that, his first defence, a ninth round kayo win against Sean Murphy, last July, was fairly predictable. However, his wins over former world champions, Colin McMillan and Paul Hodkinson, who were still highly rated, were not. Nevertheless, Robinson's constant aggression was all too much for McMillan, who was unfortunate to sustain a damaged right-hand during the middle rounds as he slumped to a points defeat, but his defeat of Hodkinson was emphatic. The Liverpudlian, who was reckoned to be the best featherweight in the world 12 months earlier, was battered and halted in the final round of a fight that was also deemed to be the Best British Contest of the Year.

Since those victories, Robinson has outpointed the Dominican Republic's Freddy Cruz to bring his tally of successful title defences in 1993-94 to four and at the time of going to press was confidently expected to retain his crown against Duke McKenzie, before seeking to unify the division. That would mean taking on the world's number one, Kevin Kelley, but after the events of the last 18 months who would bet against him!

Previous winners:- 1984: Barry McGuigan. 1985: Barry McGuigan. 1986: Dennis Andries. 1987: Lloyd Honeyghan. 1988: Lloyd Honeyghan. 1989: Dennis Andries. 1990: Dennis Andries. 1991: Dave McAuley. 1992: Colin McMillan. 1993: Lennox Lewis.

Steve Robinson, the WBO featherweight champion

Les Clark

Best British Contest of the Year: Steve Robinson v Paul Hodkinson

Other nominations: Michael Driscoll v Ross Hale and Felix Kelly v Shaun Shinkwin.

This was the fight that finally convinced the boxing public that Steve Robinson was no flash-in-the-pan. Prior to the action, there were still those who thought that his victories over Davison, Murphy and McMillan, lacked credence for a number of reasons, but against Hodkinson he answered the doubters the best way possible.

Robinson made a good start, marking up the former WBC champion's face with the jab, while Hodkinson bobbed and weaved and looked to get his left-hook working. Continuing at a hectic pace, it was becoming more and more noticeable that Hodkinson was being caught too often standing square where he was forced to take stick. He certainly looked in trouble in the fifth, although he somehow got off the hook to come back with some of his own medicine. But, from then on, the writing seemed to be on the wall.

Throughout, Robinson's defence proved sound and even when Hodkinson found the target, the champion never flinched. Meanwhile, the challenger was still giving it his best shot, still believing he had the tools to finish the job. However, the pro-Welsh crowd, although enthralled by the spectacle, were now beginning to realise that Robinson could finish his man off inside the distance. It certainly looked that way in the eighth round as Hodkinson was belted into the ropes, his right eye closing fast and his nose bleeding profusely. Somehow, he kept going, but every time he threatened to work Robinson over, the champion appeared capable of moving up a gear or two.

The sands of time finally ran out for Hodkinson in the 12th and final round. After hurting his man with a left-hook, Robinson followed up his advantage, both hands pumping away until Hodkinson sunk to the floor. Incredibly, he managed to rise at the count of six, only to be met by a three punch combination which dumped him yet again. This time there was to be no reprieve and, although trying desperately to raise himself, he was counted out with 1.40 of the round completed.

It had been a gripping spectacle, with Hodkinson showing unlimited courage, matched only by Robinson's game plan and his ability to carry it out. That and his superb conditioning was just too much for Hodkinson.

Previous winners:- 1984: Jimmy Cable v Said Skouma. 1985: Barry McGuigan v Eusebio Pedroza. 1986: Mark Kaylor v Errol Christie. 1987: Dave McAuley v Fidel Bassa. 1988: Tom Collins v Mark Kaylor. 1989: Michael Watson v Nigel Benn. 1990: Orlando Canizales v Billy Hardy. 1991: Chris Eubank v Nigel Benn. 1992: Dennis Andries v Jeff Harding. 1993: Andy Till v Wally Swift Jnr.

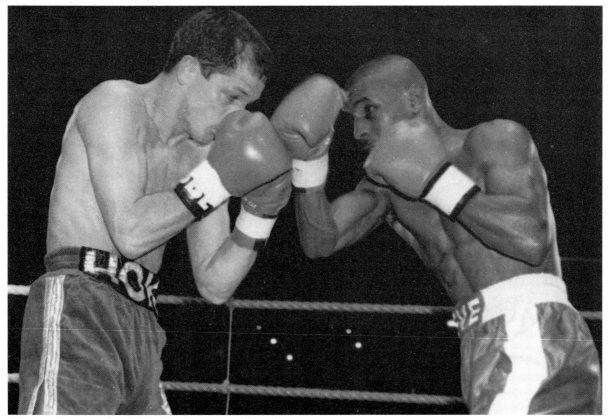

Steve Robinson (right) and Paul Hodkinson spar for an opening   Les Clark

Best Overseas Boxer of the Year: Juan "John-John" Molina

Other nominations: Jacob Matlala.

When Molina dismantled Floyd Havard in Cardiff last January, he proved himself one of the classiest operators to visit these shores. Floyd was challenging for the IBF super-featherweight title, and was ambitious to succeed, but after his retirement at the end of six completed rounds there was no doubt as to who was the better man.

We had seen the Puerto Rican on TV over the years, but to see him in the flesh was a new experience. And with a full range of sharp punches in his repertoire, plus the ability to go up a gear when required, to my mind, Molina is the outstanding nine stone, four pounds man in the world right now.

Prior to meeting Havard, he had been beaten just three times (Tony Lopez, twice, and Lupe Suarez) in 36 contests, in a career that began in 1986. He won his first major title on becoming WBO champion at the weight in 1989, but decided to relinquish that belt almost immediately, in order to take on Lopez for the IBF version. Despite winning the title from Lopez in October 1989, and making a successful defence against Suarez, he was beaten by the former in a return some eight months later. However, when the then IBF champion, Brian Mitchell, retired, Molina stopped South Africa's Jackie Gunguluza on 22 February 1992, to win the vacant title and successfully defended against Fernando Caicedo, Francisco Segura, Manuel Medina and Bernard Taylor, before making his trip to Britain.

Previous winners:- 1984: Buster Drayton. 1985: Don Curry. 1986: Azumah Nelson. 1987: Maurice Blocker. 1988: Fidel Bassa. 1989: Brian Mitchell. 1990: Mike McCallum. 1991: Donovan Boucher. 1992: Jeff Harding. 1993: Crisanto Espana.

Juan Molina holds up the IBF super-featherweight belt after his defeat of Floyd Havard   Les Clark

Special Award: Ron Olver

Like all the previous winners, Ron has done much for boxing over the years, but it is his unstinting work on behalf of the ex-boxers of this country that wins him this coveted Award.

You can get some idea of Ron's involvement in boxing by taking a glance through the acknowledgement page of this book, but it goes much deeper than that. From the day he joined the trade paper, *Boxing News*, just after the last war, his life has revolved around boxing, and those of us who have been privileged to know the man have been enriched. Incidentally, Ron was the first man to rate more than 1,000 active British boxers, which he did in 1950.

His interest in Ex-boxers' Associations, however, came about in 1967 when he realised just how little information and news there was regarding men whose careers had ended. He noted that from time-to-time *Boxing News* published complete records of former stars and how surprised he was to receive many letters from appreciative fans. Some wrote that the boxers so featured lived near them and were able to confirm that they were well or otherwise. That gave him the idea that there should be a

Ron Olver (left), this year's winner, presents last year's Special Award to the late Phil Martin   Les Clark

regular column on the subject and, in August of that year, "Old Timers' Corner" appeared.

At that time there were no more than six Ex-Boxers' Associations in existence, but with Ron's active encouragement and skilled use of his column, which is now called Time for Old-Timers, there are now close on 40 right across the country. Unless you have paid a visit to one of these groups you will have little idea as to how important they are in the everyday lives of men who boxed many years ago. Once a month they meet and talk over old times, forgetting their problems and disabilities, and many

in need are helped both financially and physically from within the group.

Ron is always ready to help and is a tower of strength to those seeking advice. He is extremely supportive and, I for one, am delighted that his good works over the years has been recognised at this level.

Previous winners:- 1984: Doctor Adrian Whiteson. 1985: Harry Gibbs. 1986: Ray Clarke. 1987: Hon. Colin Moynihan. 1988: Tom Powell. 1989: Winston Burnett. 1990: Frank Bruno. 1991: Muhammad Ali. 1992: Doctor Oswald Ross. 1993: Phil Martin.

Sportsmanship Award: Francis Ampofo

Due to challenge Salvatore Fanni for the European flyweight title, Francis' whole world crumbled on being told that there had been an irregularity on his brain scan and that his license was suspended pending further medicals. That was in August 1993 and many a man would have taken the decision badly, especially after recently winning the Commonwealth title and looking forward to garnering more championship belts and the pay days that go with them. Not so Francis.

While others worried for him, he resolutely got on with the task of proving himself fit and passing a whole range of tests, before being declared able to box-on by the doctors. That was the moment he had been waiting for and manager and promoter, Barry Hearn, celebrated by announcing a match between "Baby Jake" Matlala and Francis for the WBO flyweight crown.

Unfortunately, for the Ghanaian-born, Ampofo, 12 months away from the ring proved too much of an obstacle

as he went down to a ninth round retirement defeat, but he had given of his best against a hard-hitting champion. Afterwards, Francis claimed it was more from exhaustion than anything else that he had taken a count in the ninth and said he would continue his ring career after a good rest.

Boxing can ill afford to lose men of the calibre of Francis Ampofo. Not so much for his qualities as a fighter, but more so for the bubbly cheerfulness and honesty he brings to a sport that is more often than not tinged with bitterness and rivalries. For his ability to smile and shrug off bad fortune, he is a most deserving ninth winner of the Sportmanship Award.

Previous winners:- 1986: Frank Bruno. 1987: Terry Marsh. 1988: Pat Cowdell. 1989: Horace Notice. 1990: Rocky Kelly. 1991: Wally Swift Jnr. 1992: Duke McKenzie. 1993: Nicky Piper.

Francis Ampofo (right) celebrates winning the British flyweight title with the loser, Robbie Regan   Les Clark

Eyes and Ears of the Board

by Bob Lonkhurst

One of the most important positions within the British Boxing Board of Control is that of the inspector. It is a role often not appreciated or understood except by those people closely connected with the sport, yet it is one which places tremendous responsibility on those holding office.

An inspector needs to be a dedicated lover of boxing, and possess a willingness to work with everyone within the sport. Discipline, understanding, compassion, and a sense of humour are all esential ingredients, if he is to carry out his duties effectively. Boxing is a tough sport, but politeness and understanding will serve him well whenever problems arise. The Board of Control place a great deal of trust and reliance in their inspectors because they are the eyes and ears of that controlling body, acting as liaison officers between promoters and the Board or Area Council. When rules are broken, it is their duty to inform the Board, but, just as importantly, they should consider the well being of the boxers at all times.

Two areas where the inspector must be especially vigilant, involves the licensing and medical requirements. Before any boxer can take part in a contest, he must have a current license and have reached the required medical standards. Yet these are two areas in which disputes often arise. Every boxer is required to pay an annual fee, and failure to do so effectively means he is not licensed. The Board of Control notify inspectors in advance of shows as to whether boxers are licensed. Those who are not must pay the annual fee before they box. Frequently, boxers claim to have paid the fee at some previous venue, or by post, or other means, and the inspector will be required to investigate the position and act accordingly. When fees are collected, a receipt is issued, so the onus is clearly on the boxer to prove he is currently licensed. A similar situation applies to medical certificates, because if a boxer has not received medical clearance, he must not under any circumstances be allowed to box. The rules must be rigorously adhered to, and it is the responsibility of the inspector to enforce them.

Disputes will inevitably occur when such situations arise because the boxer's livelihood is in jeopardy, and the promoter is faced with the prospect of having the size of his show cut down. The inspector therefore has not only to administer the rules, but do so in such a way as to make it clear to all parties that he is doing so in the interests of the boxer and the sport in general. Boxing is constantly under the spot-light as its opponents continuously seek to denigrate it and have it banned. It is therefore of paramount importance that all participants are properly licensed and certified fit to box, and rules in these areas are strictly enforced.

The day of any promotion can be extremely busy for the Board's inspector, and as a variety of problems can arise, no two shows are the same. It is his responsibility to conduct the weigh-in, which usually takes place at around 12 noon, either at the venue or another establishment selected by the promoter. In respect of major contests, a certificate that the scales have been calibrated must be produced before the weigh-in commences. Also, he must record the weights of all boxers, and deal with any license or medical queries raised by the Board. In the event of a boxer being over the stipulated weight, the inspector must ensure steps are taken to reduce it within a given period of time. He must also enquire of all boxers as to the colour of the trunks they will wear during the contests. All boxers are required to carry two pairs, and should their chosen colour clash, one or other will be required to change. Any other queries raised by the Board will have to be discussed with the boxers, managers, or the promoter. If they cannot be resolved amicably, direct contact will have to be made with the Board of Control. In the event of a boxer being pronounced unfit to box, it is the inspector's duty to advise the promoter. And when a substitute boxer is used by the promoter for any contest, the inspector will need to satisfy himself that he is properly licensed and have medical clearance. Immediately after the weigh-in, the inspector is required to contact the Board and advise them of the weights of all participating boxers, and details of any changes to the advertised bill. It will also give him the opportunity to discuss any difficulties that have arisen, and to obtain last minute instructions involving the evening promotion.

During the course of any promotion, it is the inspector's duty to ensure that all relevant medical controls and safeguards are implemented. There is a need for close liaison with the appointed doctors to ensure that all boxers

All in a night's work. BBBoC Inspector, Bob Lonkhurst (left), and agent, Pepe Forbes, sift through the relevant paperwork   Pennie Cattle

15

are examined, and a certificate issued to that effect. Checks must be made to ensure that an ambulance manned by fully trained paramedics, is at the venue, and that an adequate medical room has been prepared. It is essential that all parties know the whereabouts of medical equipment, particularly a stretcher. Should an accident occur, time is of the utmost importance, and the inspector's attention to details in those areas before a show are therefore essential. In advance of the opening contest, he must check that the ring has been erected in accordance with regulations, particularly regarding size, tightness of ropes, centre ties, underlay, padding, lighting, and safety of corner steps. Any defect must be drawn to the attention of the promoter or his representative, and rectified before boxing can commence.

Two inspectors are on duty at most shows, and whilst the boxing is in progress, position themselves adjacent to the fighters' corners where they can supervise the proceedings. They should have a clear view at all times, and be in a position to liaise with doctors, referees, the master of ceremonies, and security men. Corners must be kept clear from obstruction, and cornermen made to comply with the Board of Control rules. Water, vaseline, and adrenalin are the only substances allowed in the corner to treat injuries and revive boxers and any other substance must be confiscated and submitted to the Board with a full report.

Coaching from the corners is prohibited, and inspectors must advise seconds to keep this to a minimum, but, at the same time, have an understanding of the trainer who has spent countless hours in the gym coaching his boxer. Most cornermen have good working relationships with the inspectors and comply with the request. There are, of course, always odd exceptions to the rule, and persistent offenders should be reported to the Board only as a last resort.

Whilst ensuring good behaviour by cornermen, inspectors must also extend them every assistance, as they have important roles to play, particularly between rounds, and need room in which to work. It is the inspector's responsibility to make sure they are not impeded by cameramen, or those operating video equipment on behalf of television companies.

There are many other duties to perform, including checking that a boxer's hands have been properly taped, examining the condition of gloves, and checking referees' score sheets for accuracy. Vigilance is essential, and constant checks must be made to ensure that at least one doctor is present at ringside during a contest. In the event that both are treating boxers, the master of ceremonies must be instructed to delay the boxing until they return.

Whenever a boxer is knocked out or stopped for any reason, it is the duty of the inspector to automatically suspend him for a minimum period of 28 days and a document must be served on the boxer, or his manager, immediately after the contest. A section of this is forwarded to the Board of Control and the boxer will be required to undergo a rigorous medical examination before being allowed to fight again.

There are even more duties for inspectors to perform at promotions involving championship contests. The taping of contestants hands, and the gloving up must be carefully supervised and as this all takes place in the dressing room, whilst supporting contests are in progress, it is often necessary for additional inspectors to be appointed for such promotions. Between rounds, the work of corner-men must be carefully supervised from the ring apron during all championship contests. It is also the responsibility of the inspector to take the referee to the dressing rooms to meet the contestants prior to a title bout, and be present when he explains the rules.

Whenever overseas boxers appear on a promotion in Britain, documents produced by them or their agents must be carefully examined. Medical certificates, licenses, and foreign boxing commission authorities to box, must be in order, and, on most occasions, these will be handed over to an inspector at the weigh-in. Before an overseas boxer actually fights, the referee must meet him and explain the rules of the British Boxing Board of Control, and again the responsibility falls on the inspector to ensure that this is done.

At any promotion, the inspector will be the busiest person around. Referees, doctors, time-keepers, trainers, broadcasting representatives, Board of Control stewards, the whip, and master of ceremonies, will frequently require information and advice. Everyone relies to a certain extent on the inspector, and he will be expected to find a solution to every problem and provide answers to every query. At every promotion, one inspector records material details relating to each contest. The doctors are required to personally itemize the extent of injuries sustained by boxers, the treatment given, and any recommendations. These records are designed for the well being of the boxers, and to assist the Board of Control to operate efficiently. The inspector is also required to notify the Board the following morning of details of all injuries sustained by boxers. A full report must also be submitted as soon as possible after each promotion, and the inspector should address all matters which, in his opinion, require the attention of the Board. The quality of dressing rooms and the medical room, crowd problems and the effectiveness of security, insufficient numbers of fire exits, are all important aspects which may need to be taken up with the promoter before a venue is approved for boxing again. Failure by an inspector to report his concerns, effectively means that the Board cannot take steps to improve the standard of venues.

For decades, boxing has provided a life line for many men, and will continue to do so as long as it is strictly supervised. Although he is an unpaid official, the Board of Control inspector plays an important role in a sport which is constantly under scrutiny. His job is demanding, sometimes difficult and frustrating, often rewarding, but never dull. Carried out with effectiveness, enthusiasm, and understanding, he will gain the respect of most people with whom he works. For the well being of the sport, it is important therefore, that the man in the street is aware of the precautions and supervision in place at every boxing promotion in Great Britain which comes under the control of the British Boxing Board.

Home and Away with British Boxers during 1993-94

by John Jarrett

JULY

Boxing's new "Cinderella Man", Steve Robinson, stepped out for the first time as WBO featherweight champion in front of his Cardiff fans and turned on an immaculate performance as he crushed British champion Sean Murphy inside nine rounds.

The man from St Albans was fired up for this one and carried the fight to Robinson in the early rounds, but Steve's defence was sound and his countering punches deadly accurate. After eight rounds Murphy was looking shopworn and round nine saw the end.

Sean tumbled to the canvas after missing with a right hand, then was punched to his knees, bleeding from the mouth and looking like he wished he was somewhere else. He just failed to beat the count and the experts went away thinking maybe Robinson's substitute victory over John Davison wasn't such a fluke after all.

Defeat also cost Murphy his British title, with the Board declaring it vacant, to be contested by Sean and John Davison. Former WBO champion, Colin McMillan, was lined up as Robinson's next challenger, but his comeback was put on hold when a proposed fight in France was cancelled.

On the undercard, British super-featherweight champion, Neil Haddock, warmed up for his title defence against Steve Walker with a tough five rounds stoppage of Alan Levene.

Two weeks later the Welshman broke the jinx on the title, beating off Walker's challenge inside seven rounds. Since 1986, 13 champions had failed in their first defence and, on this night at Oldham, Walker must have thought he was going to add Haddock to the list. However, the champion turned the fight around in the seventh to end Steve's gutsy challenge.

Haddock was one of five British champions on a bill promoted by Walker's manager, Phil Martin. Phil's four champs all notched wins, with cruiserweight, Carl Thompson, lightweight king, Paul Burke, and middleweight boss, Frank Grant, winning over American opposition and light-heavyweight leader, Maurice Core, beating John Kaighin.

Glenn McCrory was the first (and only) north-east fighter to-date to win a world crown and the big lad from Annfield Plain jumped at the chance to box in the first world title bout to be held in Moscow. He was out of luck, however, when he tried to take his old IBF cruiserweight crown off the head of Al "Ice" Cole, the rangy American coming out with the decision. But McCrory surprised a lot of people with a gritty performance, climbing off the deck twice in round six to finish on his feet.

At York, local favourite Henry Wharton thrilled his fans when he blitzed American, Royan Hammond, and served notice on WBC champ, Nigel Benn, that their forthcoming title bout would be no picnic. The Commonwealth super-middleweight champion proved that his right hand had recovered from recent surgery when he blasted the visitor to the deck in round three. Hammond made it to his feet, but Mickey Vann called it off.

Former British and WBC International light-middleweight champ, Gary Stretch, found it tough on the comeback trail as he struggled to beat Midlands titleholder, Steve Goodwin, in a six-rounder at Brixton.

Former world champion, Mike McCallum, beat fellow-American, Glenn Thomas, in London during August

Les Clark

AUGUST

The World Boxing Federation landed in England and a sellout crowd of 1,200 packed the Mansfield Leisure Centre to see what all the fuss was about. And when I tell you that Johnny Nelson was top of the bill you had to figure there was nothing on the telly that night and the local bingo palace was closed for refurbishment.

In two shots at legitimate world titles, against WBC champion, Carlos DeLeon, and IBF titleholder, James

Warring, the reluctant Nelson had performed abysmally, but Brendan Ingle never gives up. He toted his pacific puncher off to the South Pacific (where else!) and Nelson finally did his duty for England, beating the shopworn Dave Russell to become WBF cruiserweight champion.

At Mansfield, Johnny was to defend his title against another fighter past his sell-by date in Tom Collins, the 38-year-old Leeds' veteran who had also failed in his two world title shots, albeit at light-heavy. Collins failed again this night as Nelson punched him to the canvas three times, before John Coyle stopped it at the 2.15 mark of round one. Johnny Nelson went home a happy man and so did manager Trevor Callighan when Tom Collins agreed that it was time to retire.

At the Hammersmith Apollo, on a show topped by Jamaican former double world champion, Mike McCallum, who took a decision from American, Glenn Thomas, former British super-middleweight champion, Fidel Castro Smith, had a comfortable victory over Karl Barwise, the referee saving the tough guy from Tooting in the sixth and final round. In taking his pro log to 22-5, Fidel had a good workout as he looked forward to meeting James Cook with his old title in the pot.

On the same bill, Southern Area welterweight champion, Gary Logan, took his record to 24 wins in 25 fights with a two-rounds knockout over Paul King, the Geordie becoming Gary's 13th victim to go home early. Aiming to get back into title contention, light-middleweight, Ensley Bingham, hit too hard and too often for Robert Peel, who was stopped in round three.

With most home rings closed for the summer season, some of the boys chanced their arm overseas and some of them even had their arms raised in victory! Former British welterweight champion, Delroy Bryan, made the long trek to Durban to face former South African champ, Sidney Msutu, over ten rounds and hammered his way a unanimous decision.

Birmingham light-welterweight, Mark Ramsey, did the business in Italy, not an easy trick, when he stopped Jean Chiarelli inside four rounds, albeit on a cut eye. It was Ramsey's ninth win in 14 pro fights. Camberley light-welter, Lee Tonks, continued his Californian campaign with a third round knockout of Robert Rivera in Hollywood, but picked up a cut left eye which took 12 stitches and stuck Lee on the shelf for a couple of months.

Heavyweight Julius Francis is 6' 2" in his socks, and flyweight Darren Fifield stands 5' 2". Both Brits measured up in Bismark, North Dakota, winning their fights on a card topped by local idol Virgil Hill, who retained his WBA light-heavy title for the umpteenth time. Fifield licked Eric Burton by first round kayo, while Francis did a number on Don Sargent in two.

Outside the ring, British and Commonwealth flyweight champion, Francis Ampofo, had his licence suspended for further medical tests, which put paid to his challenge for Salvatore Fanni's European title. And, just over two years after Lennox Lewis hammered him into retirement, former British heavyweight champion, Gary Mason, announced his first comeback fight would be in America.

Fidel Castro (left) was yet again on the wrong end of a close decision as another former champion, James Cook, won their vacant British super-middleweight title clash

Les Clark

SEPTEMBER

Glasgow's Gary Jacobs had to beat Ludovic Proto twice in France to get his southpaw mitts on the European welterweight title so you couldn't blame manager Mickey Duff for taking precautions when Gary's first defence came up. His mandatory challenger was another Frenchman, Daniel Bicchieray, so Duff staged the fight himself at Wembley Grand Hall. The Scot was well in command when a cut over the Frenchman's left eye brought the referee's intervention in round five.

On the same night in London, the vacant British welterweight title was contested at York Hall between former champion, Delroy Bryan, and ex-light-welter boss, Pat Barrett, with the Nottingham southpaw outworking his Manchester rival to take his old title and put his third notch on that coveted Londale Belt. Like Johnny Nelson, Barrett is a fighter who, for reasons best known to himself, has squandered his enormous talent. Maybe the "Black Flash" should now be called the "Black Flash in the Pan"!

Already standing in line for a crack at Bryan was former British and European champion, Kirkland Laing, at

39, still proving he was too good for the likes of David Maj as he stopped the Liverpool lad inside two rounds at Ashford.

At Leicester, local hero Chris Pyatt retained his WBO middleweight title with a convincing sixth round knockout over Argentina's, Hugo Corti. In taking his excellent record to 41-3, Chris had to survive a right-hand bomb in the opening round that exploded on his chin and shook the Pyatt building to its foundations! But by round three the champion was back on top and he wrapped it up in the sixth with a left-hook and right to the jaw and Senor Corti had no further interest in the proceedings.

Fidel Castro Smith couldn't believe they had done it to him again! Twelve months after losing his British super-middleweight title to Henry Wharton on a controversial decision, Fidel looked a good winner against James Cook in their fight for the vacant British title at Southwark, only to see John Coyle hand the title and the decision to the 34-year-old veteran. It wasn't much of a fight, but Smith appeared to have done the better work and he came out of the ring thinking maybe, unlike Rocky Graziano, somebody up there did not like him!

Heavyweight action, saw Herbie Hide taken the distance for the first time in his 23-fight career, when Everett Martin soaked it up for ten rounds. The overweight American took all the punches, took his money, and took the next plane home. Good riddance!

Big bad James Oyebola, all 6' 9" of him, returned to the ring after almost two-and-a-half years out with a predictable victory over former victim, Denroy Bryan, at Bethnal Green's York Hall. James stopped his man in five, one round better than his 1988 performance. Top of the bill that night saw little Mickey Cantwell reach for the vacant WBC International light-flyweight championship, only to fall short. Mexican, Pablo Tiznado, had too much of everything, but Mickey earned his coppers.

Olympic silver medallist, Wayne McCullough, had them dusting off the SRO signs in Dublin after seven straight pro wins in America. Providing the opposition was tough Algerian, Boulem Belkif, for the best part of five rounds anyway. By then the referee had seen enough and the fans wanted to see more of the man they were calling the "Pocket Rocket". Many would like to see him against Nassem Hamed, who made a tremendous impression on the show, knocking out Chris Clarkson in two rounds.

OCTOBER

Lennox Lewis keeps on winning fights, yet he can't win. On a cold night in Cardiff, the British-born WBC heavyweight champion managed only a luke-warm performance against Frank Bruno and when it was over pundits and punters were asking the same question . . . is Lewis the goods, or is he just good? For the best part of six rounds big Frank fought out of his skin and it was looking like third time lucky in his world title quest.

But in the seventh, Lewis dropped the bomb on Bruno, when a big left-hook sent him to the ropes where he stood defenceless as Lewis ripped in vicious punches until Mickey Vann stopped it 70 seconds into the round. At that time, most judges, including one of the official ones, had Bruno ahead on points.

American fight traders were still not sold on Lewis. "He fought like an amateur", said Lou Duva. "I was amazed how bad Lewis looked," said Tommy Virgits, trainer of WBO champion, Tommy Morrison, who was next on the list for Lennox. Four weeks later, Morrison forfeited the fight when London-born, Michael Bentt, sent him crashing to sensational defeat in 93 seconds!

When WBO super-middleweight champion, Chris Eubank, and WBC kingpin, Nigel Benn, finally climbed through the ropes for their long-awaited return bout, a tremendous crowd of 41,000 paid their way into Manchester's Old Trafford. They saw a good fight that was only spoiled by a draw decision, most people thinking that this time Benn had done enough to win. In fact, it was only the deduction of a point for a sixth round low blow that cost Nigel the decision on the scorecards.

Benn's official challenger, Henry Wharton, honed his fighting tools on Chicago tough guy, Ron Amundsen, hammering his way to an eighth round stoppage victory before his hometown fans at York.

Steve Robinson did it again! Going from strength to strength, the WBO featherweight champion delighted his Cardiff fans as he outpunched and outboxed former champion, Colin McMillan, to come out with the decision and retain his title for the second time. The brilliant future of McMillan now seems all behind him and the decision to go straight into the championship ring without benefit of a warm-up bout, some 13 months after losing to the ill-fated Ruben Palacio, seemed unwise in retrospect.

Like them or not, the WBO titles have proved a boon for British promoters, and we hooked another one in Belfast when Eamonn Loughran outpunched elusive American, Lorenzo Smith, to come out with the unanimous decision and the welterweight title given up by Gert Bo Jacobsen.

In Glasgow, local favourite Paul Weir hung on to his WBO straw-weight title as he contained the aspirations of South African challenger, Lindi Memani, in a good scrap. Paul took all three votes at the final bell.

It was Weir's seventh win in as many fights. A champion yes, but not a world champion, no more than Steve Robinson is or Chris Eubank or Nigel Benn. Surely it is time to stop fights being announced as for the world title when they are only for the WBO title, or the WBA crown, or whatever. In boxing, champion of the world used to mean just that. Sadly, this is no longer so.

Over in Belgium, Johnny Nelson's WBF "world title" label washed off when he was ruled out for illegal use of the shoulder in the tenth round against Francis Wanyama. Here at home, the little and large show played York Hall as Darren Fifield licked Danny Porter for the vacant Commonwealth flyweight title and towering James Oyebola exploded Roger McKenzie's Southern Area title claims in just 37 seconds!

NOVEMBER

Revenge was sweet for Billy Schwer as he took the

British and Commonwealth lightweight titles back from Preston's Paul Burke on a decision at Watford Town Hall. This was an excellent contest, with Schwer establishing an early lead and Burke battling back from three knockdowns to put in a strong finish, but not quite strong enough.

Maybe Burke missed manager Phil Martin in his corner. Martin was at York Hall that night with Frank Grant, but the magic ran out for them too as Neville Brown outboxed Grant and forced a cut eye stoppage in round seven to take the British middleweight championship.

The west country revival continued, spearheaded by lethal light-welterweight, Ross Hale. The Bristol bomber smashed unbeaten Colombian, Regino Caceres, to a second-round knockout and promoter, Frank Maloney, started talking world titles. Flyweight Mickey Cantwell took a decision from substitute Anthony Hanna and was named number one for European titleholder, Luigi Camputaro.

Commonwealth featherweight champion, Billy Hardy, saw his promised shot at the European title disappear when he lost a points verdict to Algerian, Mustapha Hame, in Marseille, finishing with a damaged rib and a cut eye.

Belfast's "Pocket Rocket", Wayne McCullough, being fired from a Las Vegas base, landed on Fargo and Pensacola and wiped out Andres Gonzalez and Jerome Coffee, respectively, with pin-point accuracy to strengthen his claim for a bantamweight title shot. Dublin middleweight, Steve Collins, another Irishman chasing a world title, retained his WBO Penta-Continental title when he stopped gutsy Wayne Ellis in nine rounds at Cardiff.

James Drummond refuses to go away. The Kilmarnock flyweight has come unstuck in three title challenges in his 16-fight career, losing to Fanni for the European title, after having him on the deck, and dropping verdicts to Robbie Regan and Francis Ampofo in British title bouts. James kept the spark alive in Glasgow when he beat Louis Veitch over eight heats.

Another fighter still chasing his tail is Commonwealth light-middleweight champion and former world welter boss, Lloyd Honeyghan. At 33, Lloyd still had enough left for the likes of Steve Goodwin, stopping the Midlands champion in six rounds at Southwark.

British heavyweight champion, Herbie Hide, remained undefeated at 24-0 and kept tight hold of his WBO Penta-Continental title with a ninth-round stoppage of Mike Dixon at York Hall, but the American's non-aggression pact bored the fans witless.

European boss, Henry Akinwande, is another heavyweight whose sleep-inducing qualities are not confined to his massive fists. Making his debut on the African continent, Henry was too big and awkward for American journeyman, Frankie Swindell, and won over ten tedious rounds at Sun City.

Sticking with the big fellows, Johnny Nelson stepped up to heavyweight to challenge Jimmy Thunder for his WBF title in Jimmy's own backyard, Auckland, New Zealand. Having previously held the WBF cruiser crown, Nelson turned in one of his better performances this time and won handily over his muscular opponent. If only . . .

While we are busy with the WBF, that other enigma of the British boxing business, Pat Barrett, lost a crack at their vacant light-middleweight title, when Belgian Patrick Vungbo outlasted him over 12 dreary rounds to come out with a split decision. Years from now someone may remember Barrett and ask, where did it all go wrong?

The British middleweight title changed hands as Neville Brown (left) stopped Frank Grant inside seven rounds

Les Clark

DECEMBER

It didn't come from the Mafia, but it was an offer Andy Holligan couldn't refuse. It came from the Godfather of the global fight business, Don King, with whom Frank Warren, Holligan's new manager, had connections. The British and Commonwealth light-welterweight champion was offered a crack at the WBC version of the world title held by the man reckoned as the world's greatest fighter, Julio Cesar Chavez, in Mexico!

Andy was undefeated in 21 fights, while Chavez had recently scraped a draw against Pernell Whitaker to hang on to his unbeaten certificate in 89 professional fights. It was an impossible task, but the lad from Liverpool gave it his best shot. He lasted five rounds, retiring in his corner with a damaged nose and a cut on his right eye. Christmas was just a week away, but there was no happy ending for Holligan.

That same night in Manchester another dream died, as Geordie warrior, John Davison, reached into his locker and found it empty. John had looked forward to fighting old amateur rival, Paul Hodkinson, for the vacant British featherweight title, but "Hoko" pulled out with a training injury and Duke McKenzie came in as substitute.

The former holder of the IBF flyweight, WBO bantam and super-bantam titles, was looking for another belt to hold his pants up and the Lonsdale trophy suited him just fine. After four painfully one-sided rounds, the Duke was a "King" again as a heartbroken Davison said a tearful farewell to the fans who had followed him from Newcastle.

British heavyweight champion, Herbie Hide, took his

Ojay Abrahams (right) shown sinking in a right to the body of Nick Appiah on his way to a six round points win at Watford on 9 December 1993   Les Clark

WBC International title to Sun City for a reluctant Jeff Lampkin to shoot at. The Yank was out of there inside two rounds and went home to retire.

Big Henry Akinwande retained his unbeaten record in 23 fights (1 draw) and turned in his best performance against the huge Italian challenger for his European title, Biagio Chianese. The referee pulled Chianese out in round four with blood cascading down his face from a nasty cut between the eyes, ending a bout that had become a rout.

That other elongated heavyweight, Southern Area champion, James Oyebola, received an early Christmas present with a decision over veteran Jimmy Bills, who looked to have done enough to go home a winner. This was one of an incredible TEN fights promoted by Frank Maloney at York Hall with Maurice Core on top, keeping his British light-bantamweight title against the game challenge of Simon Harris, when stopping the Hanwell man in 11 rounds.

The remarkable career of local favourite, Dean Bramhald, had a happy ending at Doncaster when he beat Jamie Morris in three rounds for his 32nd win (95 defeats and 14 draws) in 141 fights. Dean received a deserved ovation, and a shower of nobbins, as he bid goodbye to the glove game.

Winning fights abroad is never easy, which made the British hat-trick in Dusseldorf even more unbelievable. But Ross Hale, Gary Logan, and Roger McKenzie pulled it off, defeating Stephan Schramm, Horace Fleary, and Bernd Friedrich, respectively. But a trip to Italy proved fruitless for Gary de Roux, as the former British featherweight champion lost in six rounds to Swiss-based Tunisian, Hichem Dahmani, and Gloucester veteran, Johnny Melfah, came up empty in Finland, losing to Roland Ericsson.

Manchester light-heavyweight, Bobbi Joe Edwards, is one of those unfortunate people whose birthday falls on Christmas Day . . . just one lot of presents! They couldn't even give him the decision when he travelled to Belgium on the big day, losing to Francis Wanyama at Izegem.

JANUARY

Two Welsh boxers hoping for a Happy New Year had those same hopes dashed in the reality of the ring. Former British super-featherweight champion, Floyd Havard, had a 26-1 record, but had boxed only twice in two years and in no way deserved a shot at "John John" Molina's IBF title. That was soon apparent when the bell rang and the classy Puerto Rican started hitting Havard. Floyd retired after six rounds with a broken nose.

A week later, again in Cardiff, "Mensa Man", Nicky

Piper, fought out of his skin against WBO light-heavy-weight champion, Leonzer Barber, and going into the ninth round the Welsh boy had the look of a winner. The American had the look of a mugging victim with his right eye redundant, but saw enough of an opening to smash in a tremendous left-hook that poleaxed Piper. The Welshman struggled up at seven, but that punch had done its job and he was an easy mark for the big right hand that finished it.

Former British and European flyweight champion, Robbie Regan, managed to win one for Wales on the undercard when he took a decision over Italian, Michele Poddighe, in a tough ten. British featherweight titleholder, Duke McKenzie, had an easier ride against Mexican, Marcelo Rodriguez, over eight heats; old war-horse Dennis Andries fell down and was knocked down in round two against Crawford Ashley, but got back into it and forced the former British champion to retire after four rounds; and the new kid on the block, Prince Nassem Hamed, turned in another dazzling display to beat Pete Buckley in four rounds.

In Birmingham, new British middleweight champion, Neville Brown, had his hands full with Andrew Flute, before the gritty challenger was forced to pack it in after seven rounds with facial injuries.

Bristol light-welterweight, Ross Hale, came out of the Cardiff ring with cuts on both eyes that took seven stitches each and a badly swollen right hand. And he was the winner! Portsmouth's Mickey Driscoll had staged a war of attrition, with southpaw Hale, to see who would challenge Holligan, and in a fight that almost eliminated both of them, Driscoll finally succumbed in the seventh round.

Never mind the rhino becoming extinct in Africa, who's looking out for the bantamweights? Johnny Armour won his fourth Commonwealth title fight against a warrior from the African continent when he stopped Rufus Adebayo in seven rounds and a few hours later manager, Mickey Duff, was seen packing his bush hat, khaki shorts, and a small net, with Davey Jones on the phone asking Heathrow to hold the flight for Nairobi.

A bruising battle in Belfast, saw Eamonn Loughran retain his WBO welterweight title over Alessandro Duran with a lopsided decision that failed to recognise the stubborn resistance of the Italian hard man. And across the Atlantic, Belfast's Wayne McCullough punched his way to his first pro title at Omaha, crushing Javier Medina in seven rounds to win the vacant NABF bantamweight bauble.

Opportunity knocked for Hull light-heavyweight, Tony Booth, when he was offered a shot at the vacant Commonwealth cruiserweight title in Waregem, Belgium, against Ugandan-born, Francis Wanyama, who had already accounted for one of the 18 defeats on Tony's 39-fight record. This time Francis improved to stop the Englishman inside two rounds.

Former British heavyweight champion, Gary Mason, kicked off his comeback in Grand Forks, North Dakota, where he blasted out loser K. P. Porter in two rounds, while in London, Michael Bentt brawled in the street with Herbie Hide at a press conference to hype their coming WBO title bout.

The Irish wonder boy, Wayne McCullough, pictured in training for his coming NABF bantamweight title clash with Javier Medina   Les Clark

FEBRUARY

The 13-fight Earls Court supershow staged by Frank Warren and Don King was cut to nine fights, and the final contest was cut from six to four rounds when the local licensing authority insisted everyone go home at 11.45pm. That decision did not suit American cruiserweight, Mike Peak, who would have liked to slug Dennis Andries for another couple of rounds and maybe go on to win their fight. But the former triple WBC light-heavy champion got the nod.

Top of the bill saw Nigel Benn turn in an excellent performance to retain his WBC super-middleweight title against Henry Wharton, handing the Yorkshire lad his first pro defeat in 20 fights. Benn's experience and ring savvy won the fight for him against a strong rival who had the punch to beat him (Henry scored an official knockdown in round five), but one who let the occasion get to him and by the time he started to fight it was too late.

In another fight that saw an old head, allied to a pair of old fists, win through, Lloyd Honeyghan retained his Commonwealth light-middleweight title against the southpaw challenge of Kevin Adamson, who was rescued by the referee in round six. British light-welterweight champion, Andy Holligan, rebounded from his world title defeat by Chavez with a five rounds kayo of Massimo Bertozzi, and heavyweight hope, Clifton Mitchell, put a good name on his record when scoring his eighth stoppage in nine fights over former European champion, Jean Chanet.

WBO super-middleweight champion, Chris Eubank, took his show to Berlin where the local hero, Graciano Rocchigiani, gave him an uncomfortable evening and his first pro defeat in the eyes of many. However, the WBO officials decided that it was the German tough guy who had suffered his first defeat.

British cruiserweight champion, Carl Thompson, does

Although successfully defending his WBO super-middle-weight title in Berlin against Graciano Rocchigiani, the ubiquitous Chris Eubank was yet again deemed by his detractors to have been fortunate   Les Clark

not trust judges, especially when fighting in Italy, where he was going against Massimiliano Duran for his European title. Carl took his own judge and referee in his two heavy fists and Duran was down and out in round eight, giving the man from Manchester a tremendous victory.

The night before, in Paris, European welterweight champion, Gary Jacobs, beat off the challenge of Tek Nkalankete to come out with the decision, but the 35-year-old French-African gave the Glasgow southpaw a stubborn argument all the way.

Veteran Italian, Vincenzo Belcastro, returned the compliment when he turned up in Glasgow and gave British bantam boss, Drew Docherty, a beating to hang on to his European title. Drew's stablemate, Paul Weir, fared no better when he lost a dismal affair against WBO light-flyweight champion, Josue Camacho. Incredibly, Weir had already held the WBO strawweight title and this was only his EIGHTH professional contest!

Yet another WBO title was on the line when middleweight champion, Chris Pyatt, faced an easy challenger in Mark Cameron at Brentwood. Two big rights to the head smashed the South African to the canvas as the

first round was ending and he was counted out two seconds after the bell. Pyatt's next defence against the Irish veteran, Steve Collins, who beat Paul Wesley on the undercard, would be tougher.

At Watford, Mickey Duff stuck another champion in his stable when undefeated Robert McCracken took the British light-middleweight title off Andy Till in a brawl of a fight that inspired similar behaviour from several mindless spectators. Andy announced his retirement afterwards. British and Commonwealth lightweight champion, Billy Schwer, had an easy night at Stevenage, stopping challenger Sean Murphy in three rounds.

MARCH

The quality fight of the month had to be Steve Robinson's punch-perfect performance in retaining his WBO featherweight title for the third time against former WBC titleholder, Paul Hodkinson, who just couldn't hold out to the final bell. Robinson didn't put a glove wrong and went into the final round with a commanding lead on the scorecards. "Hoko" had the look of a beaten man, and suddenly came apart under fierce hooks from the champion, dropping for a six count. Somehow he got up, but had nothing left and ruthless "Robbo" dumped him again for the full count. As the little man from Cardiff said afterwards, "I just get better and better." He does that.

Major upset of the month saw Herbie Hide completely shatter Michael Bentt, taking his WBO heavyweight title with a seventh round knockout at Millwall's New Den, to put himself into boxing's big league. But while Hide's showing was his best yet in an unbeaten run of 26 fights, the abject performance of the London-born Bentt left a lot of questions hanging in the cold night air. Some of them were answered when he was taken to hospital suffering from concussion and reports surfaced of a similar collapse in his American training camp. Whatever, Herbie Hide has arrived even if he isn't as good as Barry Hearn says he is. Nobody could be that good!

Another upset that almost got lost in the shuffle saw Middlesbrough middleweight, Cornelius Carr, grab the chance to fight stablemate, James Cook, for his British super-middleweight title at York Hall. Carr, with a 22-1 log, boxed and punched his way to victory over the veteran Cook.

British and Commonwealth lightweight champion, Billy Schwer, kept busy with two fights at York Hall, stopping the American, John Roby, in two and a couple of weeks later knocking out Venezuelan, Edgar Castro, in five.

The British super-featherweight title changed hands yet again when former champion, Floyd Havard, regained the belt from fellow-Welshman, Neil Haddock, at Cardiff. It was a fine comeback by Havard after being dismantled by IBF champ, John-John Molina, two months previously and he was well on top when Haddock's cut right eye brought a tenth round stoppage.

Newcastle journeyman, Paul King, got a nice break when fighting Hughie Davey for the Northern Area welterweight title and used his experience to come out a

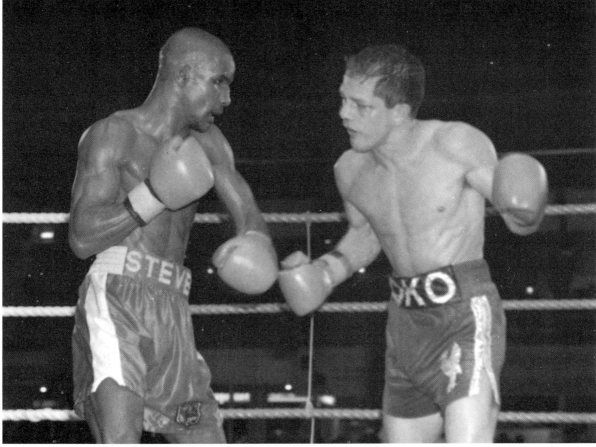

In the contest voted "Fight of the Year", Steve Robinson (left) kayoed Paul Hodkinson in the 12th round to retain his WBO featherweight title
Les Clark

handy winner and a champion. And at Southwark, Ali Forbes won the Southern Area super-middleweight title at the second attempt with a hard-fought victory over Richard Bustin.

It wouldn't be right to say that Jesse Ferguson fought like a "big Jesse" against Frank Bruno in Birmingham, because the veteran American didn't fight at all. Pushing 37, Ferguson was on his way to the showers after just 2.22 of round one, having been clubbed to the canvas twice before John Coyle figured he and the customers had suffered enough.

Life among the little man saw Glasgow veteran, Donnie Hood, emerge from 14-month exile to battle bravely against Kid McAuley, giving the Doncaster Irishman half-a-stone and a points beating . . . former British and European flyweight champ, Robbie Regan, kept his hopes alive with a workmanlike performance over Columbian, Mauricio Bernal . . . James Drummond started climbing the flyweight ladder again when he faced fellow Scot, Neil Armstrong, in a British title eliminator. However Drummond had to get off the deck to stop Armstrong in round five.

A little guy with a big future is Belfast bantamweight, Wayne McCullough, who came to London from his base in Las Vegas to fight on the Hide-Bentt card. Facing substitute, Mark Hargreaves, Mac stopped a few punches himself before he stopped the Burnley man in round three.

APRIL

The tragic death of Bradley Stone, two days after his fight with Richie Wenton for the inaugural British super-bantamweight championship at York Hall, cast a dark shadow over the sport. It had been a good, competitive contest and if Wenton was leading going into the tenth round, the lad from Canning Town was not far behind. But, for Bradley Stone, this was to be the last round. Wenton hurt him with a right and left and his follow-up attack brought the referee's intervention at the 1.15 mark.

Bradley appeared to have recovered normally from only his second pro defeat and talked to doctors, officials, and reporters, before leaving the arena. But he collapsed at 2.30am, was taken to hospital where he had an operation to remove a blood clot, and died the following day. Bradley's death came in a week when two racing drivers were killed

Bradley Stone (left) covers up against Richie Wenton. Unfortunately, the inaugural British super-bantamweight title fight
will be remembered more for the demise of Bradley than for the action itself   Les Clark

and a top jockey suffered serious injury, reminding us that sport sometimes demands the ultimate price from those who choose to play.

In Glasgow, Gary Jacobs retained his European welterweight title with a stunning eighth round knockout of Italian challenger, Alessandro Duran, but Duran's compatriot, flyweight, Luigi Camputaro, restored the balance as he fought off the determined attacks of Mickey Cantwell at York Hall to keep his European title on a close but unanimous decision.

Former British and Commonwealth lightweight champion, Paul Burke, was unlucky when going for the vacant European title against Racheed Lawal in Denmark, coming a cropper in round four, having decked the local favourite and looking good right up to the finish. In Glasgow, another former champion trying to get back on top finished on the bottom as ex-WBO fly-weight titleholder, Pat Clinton, was upset by unheralded Ady Benton in the very first round.

Prince Nassem Hamed is not everyone's cup of tea, but he is still too strong a brew for the other little guys out there. Former Belgian champion, John Miceli, had the bitter taste of defeat in his mouth before the first round had

run its course, being counted out on the third knockdown of their meeting in Mansfield.

West Ham light-heavyweight, Garry Delaney, kept his unbeaten certificate along with his WBO Penta-Continental and Southern Area titles when he outboxed and outpunched Simon Harris, before knocking the Hanwell man out in round six. Delaney took his record to 16 wins (11 inside) and a draw. In a preliminary on the York Hall card, Garry's younger brother, Mark, took his log to 6-0, all inside, when he stopped Tim Robinson in round two of their super-middleweight bout.

Birmingham's Karl Taylor got it right on his big night, taking a well-earned decision and the Midlands Area lightweight title at the second time of asking from Peter Till in a gruelling battle at Walsall, and at Hull, 35-year-old veteran, Cordwell Hylton, regained the Midlands cruiserweight title when he stopped Albert Call inside four rounds. Northern Area light-heavyweight champion, Terry French, hung on to his title in a gruelling battle with Ian Henry at Gateshead, coming out with a decision that could have gone either way.

It was one of those good news, bad news, situations. The good news was that the Board of Control rightly decided that former WBA heavyweight champion, James "Bonecrusher" Smith, was not medically fit to face Henry Akinwande at York Hall and sent him back home. The bad news was that Johnny Nelson would face Akinwande instead in a bout you couldn't give tickets away for. This was a fight that lived up to its promise . . . it promised to be boring and it was. For the record, Akinwande won points.

The bowler hatted Clifton Mitchell, who once sported the monicker, Paddy Reilly, recorded two fights in May, the first lasting just 35 seconds and the second being timed at 73   Les Clark

MAY

The big fella did it again! Lennox Lewis chastised another challenger for his WBC title over in Atlantic City, stopping Phil Jackson inside eight rounds to keep his crown and remain undefeated, and one of these days the Americans are going to admit that Lewis is a damn good fighter.

Going in, Jackson had only one defeat in 31 outings. Now he has two on his slate. He was on his backside in the first minute of the fight, down again in the fifth, and when he got up Lewis dropped him again, just after the bell had ended the round. Lewis got away with it and finished it in round eight, dumping Jackson a fourth time to bring the referee's intervention.

Another fellow to whom winning is a way of life is Chris Eubank. In Belfast, Chris put the tenth notch on his WBO super-middleweight belt with a hairline decision over Ray Close, the man who held him to a draw last year in their Glasgow fight. Like the first bout, this one was too close for comfort, and next time they meet it could again be "Close", this time the winner! Pun intended.

One Irishman did manage to win a WBO belt when Steve Collins stopped Chris Pyatt in five rounds to take his middleweight title at Sheffield. It was a case of third time lucky for the Dublin fighter after failing against Mike McCallum and Reggie Johnson. He dropped Pyatt in round five and kept the pressure on when Chris got up. Although Pyatt did not appear in too much trouble he was not firing back when the third man stopped it.

Prince Nassem Hamed quite literally boxed Vincenzo Belcastro to a standstill to win the European bantamweight title, but once again his show-boating tactics spoiled a brilliant performance in only his 12th pro fight.

Ross Hale, the man responsible for the west country revival, powered his way to the British and Commonwealth light-welterweight titles with a three rounds demolition job on Andy Holligan, who had lost only to the great Chavez in a 24-fight career. Hale sent the 2,000 crowd crazy as he hammered Holligan loose from his titles to give Bristol its first British boxing champion.

Another man to set his local fans alight was former British bantamweight champion, Billy Hardy, who added the vacant British featherweight title to his Commonwealth belt with a relentless pounding of Alan McKay in Sunderland. McKay was under the gun in round eight when it was stopped and Hardy was back in business.

With manager Mickey Duff talking world titles, British and Commonwealth lightweight champion, Billy Schwer, didn't put a glove wrong in retaining the latter title against Canada's former Olympian, Howard Grant, at Stevenage. The visitor brought an undefeated run of 16 fights into the ring and enjoyed height and reach advantages which enabled him to open cuts to both of Billy's eyes. But Schwer pressured his way to a fine victory inside nine rounds to keep his world title hopes alive.

It was a tall order for Neil Haddock to fill, but he took his chance, challenging Jacobin Yoma for his European super-featherweight title in Cayenne, French Guyana, just a couple of months after losing his British title. Something of a local idol, Yoma turned in a flawless performance and Haddock didn't come off his stool for round seven, claiming a nose injury. Haddock's brother Nigel was also out of luck when going for the Welsh featherweight title against former British champion, Peter Harris, at Neath. Although Harris was cut on both eyes, he outboxed and outpunched Nigel to come out a winner.

The perils of fighting abroad were painfully brought home to the Birmingham brothers Mark and Paul Ramsey when they journeyed to the Ukraine. Mark lost to Andrei Sinepupov for the vacant WBO Penta-Continental lightweight championship, despite having him cut badly around both eyes and looking a good winner to trainer John Ingle. However, the local hero got the decision, one judge giving him every round! Paul had no more luck than his brother when the local fighter flopped on to his stool totally exhausted after six rounds and the fight, scheduled for eight, was suddenly ended with, you guessed it, a points win for the local man!

Heavyweight business. Derby's Clifton Mitchell notched a couple of easy victories, beating Camargo from Brazil on a cut eye in just 35 seconds at Sheffield, and knocking out Steve Garber in 73 seconds in Belfast. Mitchell comes into the ring wearing a bowler hat and black cape and has a record of 12-0, and who knows?

Two British heavyweights fighting each other abroad for a title? Yes, it happened in Atlantic City on the Lewis card, and James Oyebola added the WBC International title to his Southern Area belt with a fifth round kayo of Scott Welch.

JUNE

The history of British boxers contesting European titles on the continent is steeped in tales of hometown decisions and myopic officials, something Manchester blaster, Carl Thompson, is well aware of. The big fellow takes no prisoners! Four months after knocking out Duran in Italy to win the European cruiserweight title, Thompson turned it on again when he gave Akim Tafer a shot in France.

Just as well really, as Carl had suffered two knockdowns against the WBC's number two contender and was trailing at the end of round five. In round six, Carl was a winner, having exploded a left-right on Tafer's chin that sent him crashing to the floor. The Frenchman got up but was still in a fog and was counted out. Winner, and still champion, Carl Thompson!

In Cardiff it was again winner, and still champion, Steve Robinson. Yes, the little guy did it again, retaining his WBO featherweight title for the fourth time with a unanimous decision over Dominican, Freddy Cruz, who was brought in when Duke McKenzie suffered a perforated eardrum in training. Watching from ringside, the Duke was confident he could fashion a sad ending to the little Welshman's "Cinderella" story when they meet in September, but he was about the only person in the arena that Saturday night who thought so.

Another little guy to hang on to his WBO title was

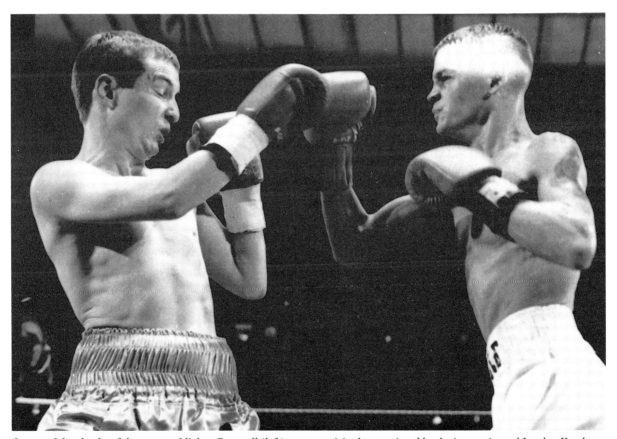

In one of the shocks of the season, Mickey Cantwell (left) was surprisingly outpointed by the inexperienced Lyndon Kershaw

Les Clark

27

flyweight boss, Jake Matlala, who turned back the challenge of British champion, Francis Ampofo, at York Hall, the latter being retired at the end of round nine. Ampofo had waged a good battle for five rounds and the South African had a bad swelling over his left eye, but "Baby" Jake then stepped up a gear and Ampofo couldn't keep up with him and was eventually pulled out by his corner.

Belfast's Wayne McCullough travelled from his Las Vegas base to Atlantic City to fight former WBC bantamweight champion, Victor Rabinales, in an official eliminator for the Mexican's old belt, but after 12 gruelling rounds it was the little Irishman who had the inside track on a title bout.

Wayne had stopped 11 of his 12 victims since he won Olympic silver and started chasing the green, but there was no way he was going to get Rabinales out of there in a hurry. The 52-fight veteran still had some mileage on him and he showed the kid a thing or two, but to his credit, McCullough fought back well enough to convince all three officials he was worth a unanimous decision.

At the Elephant & Castle Leisure Centre in London, 21-year-old Lyndon Kershaw tossed a major shock into flyweight contender, Mickey Cantwell, when coming out a points winner after eight rounds.

On the same bill, Darren Fifield's proposed Commonwealth flyweight title defence against Jamaican, Richard Clarke, fell through when the latter pulled out, and Fifield had a tough time with substitute, Ladislao Vazquez, before the Mexican was stopped with a cut eye in round four.

It was a night, and a fight, to remember for 33-year-old Des Gargano, as he climbed into a professional boxing ring for the 100th time. Des sold £2,000 worth of tickets to ensure a sell-out for his hometown fight with Marty Chestnut at Middleton and you knew he meant business when he left his running pumps in the dressing room and wore his boxing boots into the ring. Yes, Gargano fought this one and he won it too, taking Mickey Vann's decision after six nip-and-tuck rounds, along with a nice belt to commemorate reaching his century.

Boys to watch for the future are Robin Reid, a Runcorn middleweight who racked up Hammersmith southpaw Andy Furlong inside two rounds at Cardiff. . . Light-middleweight, Adrian Dodson, who wrecked Andrew Jervis of Liverpool in the second round . . . Welsh super-middleweight, Joe Calzaghe, who beat veteran Karl Barwise in one round for his sixth straight stoppage win . . . Scottish super-middle hope, Willie Quinn, who chalked up his 12th win in 13 outings at Glasgow when stopping Marvin O'Brien in round four . . . Liverpool light-welterweight, Shea Neary, who made it nine straight wins (7 inside) when he stopped Mark Pearce inside four rounds to keep his local fans happy.

Punch of the month? Take the big left-hook thrown by Watford welterweight, Ojay Abrahams, that wrecked the comeback of Darren Dyer in just 42 seconds of round one at the old York Hall. It'll do for me.

Facts and Figures, 1993-94

There were 712 British-based boxers who were active between 1 July 1993 and 30 June 1994, spread over 222 promotions held in Britain during the same period. The above figure comprised 573 boxers already holding licenses or having been licensed previously, three foreign-born boxers (Roland Ericsson, Chris Peters and Anthony Wanza) who started their careers elsewhere and 136 new professionals.

Unbeaten during season (minimum qualification: 6 contests) 7: Mark Delaney. 6: Joe Calzaghe, Hugh Collins, Adrian Dodson, Darren Dorrington (2 draws), P. J. Gallagher, Gilbert Jackson, Paul Lawson, Kevin McBride, Justin Murphy, Mark Prince, Peter Waudby.

Most wins during season (minimum qualification: 6 contests) 7: Mark Delaney, Scott Welch. 6: Joe Calzaghe, Glenn Catley, Hugh Collins, Adrian Dodson, P. J. Gallagher, Gilbert Jackson, John Keeton, Paul Lawson, Kevin McBride, Justin Murphy, James Murray, Mark Prince, Peter Waudby.

Most contests during season (minimum qualification: 10 contests) 16: Graham McGrath. 13: Pete Buckley, Miguel Matthews. 12: Brian Coleman, Julian Eavis. 11: Phil Found, Art Stacey. 10: Shamus Casey, Rick North, Nigel Rafferty, Warren Stephens.

Most contests during career (minimum qualification: 50 contests) 141: Dean Bramhald. 125: Shamus Casey. 100: Des Gargano. 90: Paul Murray. 78: Julian Eavis. 75: Miguel Matthews. 68: Cordwell Hylton. 63: Steve Pollard. 61: John Smith. 58: Dennis Andries, Pete Buckley. 57: Dave Owens. 54: Kirkland Laing, Trevor Meikle. 53: Sugar Gibiliru. 50: Tom Collins, Tony Foster, Ronnie Stephenson.

Longest unbeaten sequence (minimum qualification: 10 contests) 39: Chris Eubank (2 draws). 26: Herbie Hide. 25: Lennox Lewis. 23: Henry Akinwande (1 draw). 20: Darron Griffiths (3 draws). 19: Robert McCracken. 17: Garry Delaney (1 draw). 16: Richie Woodhall. 15: John Armour. 14: Cornelius Carr, Maurice Core (1 draw), Jason Rowland. 13: Clay O'Shea (2 draws). 12: Nigel Benn (1 draw), John Bosco, Prince Nassem Hamed, Clifton Mitchell, Paul Ryan, Michael Smyth. 11: Marco Fattore (4 draws), Gilbert Jackson, Paul Lloyd, Kevin Mabbutt, Spencer McCracken (1 draw), Alan McDowall (1 draw), Willie Quinn, Bruce Scott. 10: Denzil Browne (1 draw), Barry Jones, Dave McHale, Jamie Robinson.

The Journeymen: Saviour's of the Sport

by Bob Lonkhurst

Not surprisingly, the sports pages of our national newspapers invariably highlight the big names; goal scorers, wicket takers and run makers, top golfers and the like. Big names sell newspapers and, when it comes to boxing, focus is often centred on men like Lennox Lewis, Frank Bruno, Chris Eubank and Nigel Benn. Inevitably, stories about the sport relate to champions, hot prospects and those with the right connections. Yet there is rarely a mention of the men who for decades have been the back-bone of the fight game.

The journeyman fighter is recognized and appreciated only by the most ardent boxing fans and those working within the sport. They come from all part of the country and all walks of life. Yet without them, champions would never be crowned and the sport of boxing would die. They are men of great courage and tremendous pride, willing to meet anyone, anywhere, for the right price.

Prepared to fight at as little as 24 hours notice, they are a godsend to any promoter or match-maker seeking to push their bright young prospects up the championship ladders. The journeymen travel the length and breadth of the country and, while often outweighed and outgunned, they are rarely outgamed. Although not expected to win, they will sometimes cause an upset, but more likely be on the wrong end of a close decision.

For decades, boxers from Wales have been forced to travel to venues all over Britain in order to get regular work. Miguel Matthews, a featherweight from Ystalyfera, is a typical example of the modern day Welsh journeyman. After an amateur career of just 12 contests in nine months, the last against a welterweight, he turned professional in September 1988. In less than six years, he is a veteran of more than 70 contests, but only seven have taken place in his native Wales.

Incredibly, Miguel has won just eight and drawn ten, yet his record does not portray his true ability. Richie Wenton in 1988, Colin McMillan (1989), Bradley Stone and Moussa Sangare (1991), Prince Nassem Hamed (1992) and Dave McHale (1993), are the only men to have beaten him inside the distance. Of those, Wenton is the only man to have knocked out Matthews, just three months after he turned pro. Even then, Miguel may have an excuse because determined to get down to the agreed weight, he had hardly eaten for almost four days and was thoroughly drained.

Having fought all over Britain, in France and Denmark, the only other time that Miguel didn't do himself justice was when halted by Bradley Stone at Basildon in March 1991. Although he was just getting over an injury, he didn't want to let the promoter down and Stone's body shots took their toll, stopping him in the fourth. When they met again six weeks later, Matthews was fit and took the up-and-coming Londoner to a close points decision.

At least a dozen of Miguel's defeats have been by a mere half point and always in the other man's backyard.

With ten draws to his credit as well, it is reasonable to assume that he has not been getting the breaks when it comes to a close contest. Many men would have quit long ago, disillusioned and wondering if it was all worth it, but not Miguel, who loves travelling up and down the country meeting people. "I just love everything about boxing," he once told me, "The travelling, talking to people, the fighters, everything."

He likes to be friends with everyone, and this was typified at Brentwood one night in January 1993 when I came across him and Tim Yeates chatting in the corridor outside the dressing rooms. They were like a couple of old school chums, laughing and genuinely enjoying each others conversation. Yet only half an hour earlier they had hammered away at each other for six rounds in a contest Matthews had taken at short notice.

Not many people knew it, but while Miguel was battling away against Yeates, his wife was in hospital giving birth to their first child. Word reached Master of Ceremonies, Alan Hughes, and after the fight he called Miguel back into the ring and revealed the popular Welshman's secret. The east-end crowd gave him a warm ovation.

Miguel never ducks anyone, and has taken many contests on a phone call the same day, or with just 24 hours notice. Apart from McMillan, Hamed and Stone, he has shared the ring with quality opponents including WBO super-flyweight champion, Johnny Bredahl (Denmark), Paul Harvey, John Armour, Danny Porter, Tony Silkstone, Pete Buckley (four times), and east-end prospects Jimmy Clark (twice), Kevin Middleton (twice) and Mark Bowers.

He always gives value for money and invariably fights hard during the last two rounds in the hope that the occasional referee will be influenced. Although Dave McHale beat him on a cut eye, only the talented Hamed gunuinely stopped him during that time.

One of Miguel's best fights was at Kettering in February 1990 when he lost on points to Mickey Markie, with whom he had drawn three months earlier. They had an absolute war, but at the end were all smiles, hugs and handshakes, as "nobbins" showered into the ring from the crowd who gave them a standing ovation.

Away from the ring, Miguel is a devoted husband and father. For the past couple of years, he has had his own business as a coal merchant, and the money he earned from boxing helped him to get established. He trains five days a week in a gym above Cwmgors Rugby Club and, in his leisure time, loves shooting and fly fishing.

Miguel's ambition before leaving the fight game, is to get a shot at a Welsh title. "I'd love to leave the game with something after all the close calls," he told me. At the beginning of 1994, he actually got a backer, but the Welsh Area Council turned him down flat. They would not approve a persistent loser as a title contender.

The fact that he survives so well is a tribute to his skill, toughness, and attitude and he is a fighter who could easily qualify as the role model of a journeyman. As a dedicated professional, he is much better than his record suggests. Sadly, that is often the case with the journeyman, but when he leaves the game, Miguel Matthews will do so with respect from all who knew him.

Welsh boxers are frequently found on the undercards of promotions all over Britain. Men such as John Kaighin, Russell Washer and Andrew Bloomer, to name just three, are always at the beck and call of promoters.

Kaighin, a super-middleweight from Swansea, has had more than 40 contests, but only one in his home town. Although he has won just ten, he has created problems for a number of good pro's. He became the first man to take the hard-hitting Garry Delaney the distance, drew with Joey Peters, and lost on points to Maurice Core. His finest hour was undoubtedly in November 1991 at the Royal Albert Hall when he stopped the former ABA heavyweight champion, Keith Inglis, in the first round.

Several times, the likeable Kaighin has announced his retirement, only to return and try again. Unfortunately, his latest set-back, a broken jaw sustained at the hands of Shaun Cummins at Stevenage early this year, may prove too much to come back from.

Seven wins from just 39 contests caused the Welsh Area Council to suspend Swansea middleweight, Russell Washer. Yet he is a man who has provided tough opposition for many a bright prospect. Men such as Dean Cooper, Andrew Flute, Gilbert Jackson, Kevin Sheeran (twice), Adrian Dodson, Kevin Adamson (twice) and Jamie Robinson, have all failed to stop him. He has fought all over Britain, but, like Kaighin, only once in Swansea.

The shaven headed warrior with a roly poly physique is a tough man who is rarely floored. His main weakness is that he tends to cut easily and this caused his downfall against Tony Collins, John Bosco and, more recently, the talented American, Robert Allen.

Super-bantamweight, Andrew Bloomer, from Ynysybwl is another Welsh traveller to cause concern to the Area Council. By the end of 1993, he had engaged in 19 contests in two-and-a-half-years, losing them all, yet Nassem Hamed was the only man to stop him. He has boxed in London, Glasgow, Bristol and Liverpool, but only three times at venues in Wales.

Mike Morrison, a 31-year-old lightweight from Pembroke, was another persistent Welsh loser, but a typical journeyman fighter. When he first announced his retirement in July 1991, he had won just one of 29 contests, yet Mark Tibbs (cut eye) and Michael Smyth were the only men to have stopped him.

The rugged, shaven headed battler was a genuine hard man who stood toe-to-toe with many a good prospect. Jason Rowland (twice), Mo Hussein, Eamonn Loughran and Mark Tibbs were all promising London-based fighters who failed to halt Mike, and he met them all at venues in the capital, often at very short notice. He had no respect for reputations and, although many of his fights appeared on paper to be mismatches, his fitness and professionalism ensured they were not.

Mike Morrison (left) head-to-head with top prospect, P. J. Gallagher, at York Hall, Bethnal Green

Les Clark

Mike was often discussed by the Welsh Area Council, concerned about his long losing streak, but in reality he rarely took a hiding. After a year away, he found the lure of the ring too much and, in July 1992, returned with a third round knock-out of Steve Howden.

He had a further 14 fights in 18 months before finally calling it a day, but had carried on exactly where he left off. Good prospects Paul Ryan, Cham Joof, P. J. Gallagher and Bobby Guynan all beat him, but none could stop him. When he finally hung up his gloves in early 1994, following yet another points defeat, Mike had won just four of 44 contests. Had he faced more men in his own class, that final score would have looked much healthier.

Back in the 1930s it was not unusual for boxers to have well over 100 contests because many fought several times a week. Although nowadays this is something of a rarity, there are a group of modern day "centurions".

When Doncaster light-welterweight, Dean Bramhald, brought the curtain down on his career after stopping Jamie Morris in three rounds at the Doncaster Moat House in December 1993, he had taken part in 141 contests. It was an emotional occasion and the 30-year-old received a standing ovation from the packed house as he made his way to the ring. After Dean was declared the winner, "nobbins" showered into the ring, not because of the quality of the fight, but in appreciation of his service to the sport.

Turning professional in 1984, Dean packed 20 fights into his first year and was a credit to himself and the sport. Although he lost 95 contests, he won the Central Area lightweight title in his 127th, beating Kevin Toomey on points over ten rounds at Hull in November 1992. Despite losing it in a return just three months later, the former ladies' hair-dresser had accomplished something that most journeymen merely dream about.

Shamus Casey, a 34-year-old miner from Alfreton, is still going strong despite being a veteran of more than 120 contests. He turned pro in 1984 after an amateur career of about 40 fights, but got into boxing by way of a fluke. He tells a story about going football training one evening only to find that his team had not turned up. When another group of lads arrived at the recreation ground and asked him to join them in a run, he did so, believing them to be footballers. He later discovered they were from a local boxing club and, being a rough and ready lad, decided to give the game a try.

Casey is an incredible character. Not only has he come off an early shift in the pits to fight the same evening, but has boxed on his birthday and those of his wife and children, and even when his wife was in hospital having an operation. Despite frequently getting up at 4 a.m. for the early shift as a coal face worker, he will never refuse a fight, describing pit work as being much harder than boxing. "It's red hot down there," he remarked, "often like a sauna."

Although he has won only 26 contests, Casey has had his opportunities. In 1985 he boxed for the Midlands Area light-middleweight title, losing on points to Dennis Sheehan. In 1987 he was knocked out in seven rounds by Terry Magee for the vacant Irish light-middleweight crown, and, in 1992, was stopped in five rounds by Gary Osborne for the vacant Midlands Area title. That was his 107th

contest and he fought with a desire that belied his record. He badly wanted the belt, but a wicked left-hook to the body sent him home empty handed.

A perennial loser, Shamus had won just two of his last 20 fights at the end of 1993, but he ducked nobody. Neville Brown, Richie Woodhall, Ray Close, Cornelius Carr, John Graham, Derek Wormwald, Shaun Cummins, W. O. Wilson and Adrian Dodson all appear on his record. All are champions or leading contenders.

Casey is a typical tough miner and has been working at the coal-face since he was about 16. "Nobody's really hurt me yet," he claims, although he admits that his pride is always hurt whenever he fails to last the distance.

Des Gargano, a 33-year-old self-managed bantam-weight from Manchester, is another "centurion". After winning 29 out of 42 amateur contests, he turned pro in 1985, and is one of the most frustrating men in the British ring today. He is a known "runner" who has lost only four contests inside the distance. He has never avoided anyone or turned down the chance of a fight and, apart from boxing all over Britain, has travelled to Europe on four occasions. He has gone the distance with men such as John Davison (twice), Pat Clinton (twice), Sean Murphy, Danny Porter, Jimmy Bredahl, Bradley Stone, Eyup Can, Joe Kelly, Tim Driscoll, Wilson Docherty and Richie Wenton. A tribute to his elusiveness is demonstrated by the fact that he was not stopped until his 60th contest, having been a pro for six years. Although he has met many good men, the nearest Des ever got to a professional title was in February 1989 when he was outpointed by Nigel Crook in an eliminator for the Central Area bantamweight crown.

Boxing is just another job to Des and he is grateful to it for giving him some of the luxuries in life. At weekends he loves match fishing, and goes out regularly in all weathers. When he was on the dole a few years ago, he couldn't afford the expensive tackle and the cost of bait, but his earnings from boxing helped. Now he is the owner of a £1,000 carbon fibre roach pole and a car. He can pay his bills and afford a holiday abroad every year. While he will never earn the money of champions, boxing has been good to Des.

Although he has not fought since April 1993, Jamaican-born Winston Burnett, is another modern day "centurion" and a classic example of the journeyman fighter. Boxing out of Cardiff, he ran up a total of 99 contests before the Board of Control took away his license when he sustained a detached retina. The following year, he was presented with a special award for his outstanding contribution to British boxing.

Winston wasn't prepared to quit on 99, and after two operations on his damaged eye, he appealed to the Welsh Area Council. In April 1990, he even turned up at an Area Council Meeting armed with reports from three leading eye specialists declaring him fit to box again. He was working as a sales representative and promised to retire for good once he had reached the magical century. The Board, however, weren't prepared to take a chance and flatly refused to give him his license back.

During 1989, Burnett had worked in the United States, coaching boxing, rugby and soccer at a sports centre in the Catskill Mountains. He had an agreement to return in 1990, and again in 1991, and it was in the States that he resumed

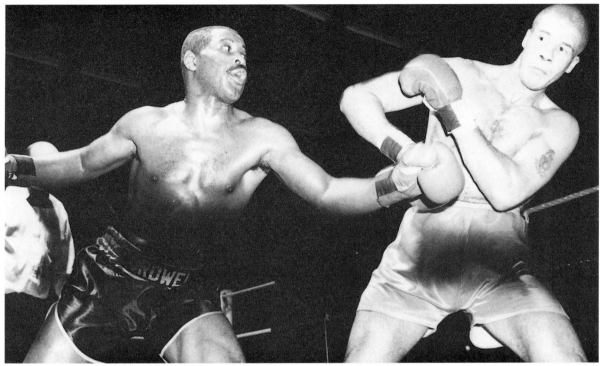

Cordwell Hylton (left) shown in the first of two losing fights against Wayne Llewelyn   Les Clark

his boxing career and passed the 100 mark. When he eventually quit, Winston had won just 20 of 119 contests, with the majority of his defeats coming on points. In 13 years as a professional he boxed all over the world, but only once in his home town of Cardiff.

There are good journeymen in most big cities around the country. Men like Paul Murray of Birmingham, a veteran of 90 contests since 1980. Heavyweight Denroy Bryan from Swindon has won just seven of almost 40 contests since 1983, but has mostly been up against young British heavyweight prospects during that time.

Newton Barnett, a 35-year-old Jamaican, boxes out of Camberwell in South London and has been a professional since 1983. He has won just 11 of 52 contests, but has fought the likes of Crisanto Espana, Kirkland Laing, Robert McCracken, Kevin Lueshing and Derek Grainger, to name just a few.

Liverpudlian, John Smith, is another man who is rarely stopped unless by cuts. The 34-year-old has had more than 60 contests since 1986 and when beating Kris McAdam at Glasgow in April 1994, he ended a losing run of 29 fights going back to October 1990.

Trevor Meikle from Scunthorpe turned pro in 1989 and packed 44 fights into his first two-and-a-half-years. He is a typical journeyman who has won fewer than a third of his fights and has never boxed in his home town.

Cordwell Hylton, a cruiserweight from Walsall, has had 68 contests, losing more than he has won. Yet he is the Midlands Area champion and had caused a few upsets along the way. A pro since 1980, he is an unpredictable,

often lazy looking fighter, but has tremendous power and is capable of changing the course of a fight with a single shot.

In 1988 he caused a sensation when he knocked out former ABA heavyweight champion, Eric Cardouza, in the fifth round. Two year's later, in 1990, he stopped Jim Peters in four and then, the following year, after two stoppage wins in ten days, won the Midlands Area title by halting Roy Smith in seven. Incredibly, Cordwell would win just one of his next 15 contests over the next three years. It looked as though the likeable Cordwell had reached the end of the road, but on 15 April 1994 at the Ennardale Sports Centre, Hull, his incredible punch once again brought him victory. A vicious right to the jaw of Albert Call in the fourth round, ensured that Hylton regained the Midlands Area cruiserweight title he had lost more than three years earlier.

A frequent visitor to Europe, Hylton has boxed in Germany on four occasions, France and Italy three each and in Denmark. In 1992 he caused an upset by stopping Jean-Marie Emebe in three rounds at Criel.

Outside boxing, Cordwell is a man of many talents and a fine all-round sportsman. He became the Midland's region shot putt champion at the age of 16 and at 21 had a soccer trial for Aston Villa. Although he failed to make it as a professional, he continued to play a good standard of football. Basketball is another of his sports and when trying his hand at karate, he was successful to the extent of winning a British junior title in 1985. Away from the sports field he is a married man who loves nature and the countryside. One of his hobbies is wild life photography and he has a fine collection of pictures proudly presented in his albums.

Boxing gave Cordwell Hylton a life line and in 1986 he was the subject of a Yorkshire Television documentary, entitled "Way Out of Walsall". It highlighted the grim picture of unrest and dole queues that exist in many under-privileged areas of Britain, reasons which cause many young men to turn to boxing.

One of the most unique men currently gracing British rings must be Steve Pollard of Hull. A professional since 1980, he has the distinction of being the only man to currently hold four British Boxing Board of Control licenses; boxer, second, manager and promoter.

Steve was just 12-years-old when he started and had over 80 contests as an amateur. Boxing with the Kingston ABC, he reached the 1976 North-Eastern Counties featherweight final, and the lightweight final in 1977 and 1980. He remembers the latter only too well, being thrown out for butting in the first round. "I was forced to turn pro after that," he told me. "They said I was butting, but I think of it as dangerous use of the head."

Turning pro in 1980, Steve started well, winning his first eight fights. In March 1983, he took the Central Area featherweight title by stopping Steve Farnsworth in two rounds. When he lost it to John Doherty in December the following year, it was to be his last shot at a title. Since then he has boxed up and down the country and occasionally abroad, but seldom in his home town.

Although he has won just 20 of 63 contests, Steve is a typical dour journeyman capable of testing the best. Nowadays his fights are few and far between, but he has met his share of good men. Jim McDonnell (twice), Pat Doherty, Jean-Marc Renard, Alex Dickson, Gary de Roux and Carl Crook appear on his record. Now at the age of 36, Steve is concentrating on training and managing his own group of boxers.

Boxing is Steve Pollard's life and, although he claims not to have made a lot of money from the sport, it did help him to set up his own sports shop business. He lives life to the full and, apart from running his shop which he has had for six-years, he trains his fighters six-days a week. He also formed the "Knock-Out" Executive Club at the Willerby Manor Hotel in Hull, where he promotes about four shows a year.

Steve is married to Diane, and they have three children, Sonny aged 16, Billy 12 and Laura nine. He comes from a sea-faring family and, not surprisingly, has spent plenty of time on the boats himself. At the age of 16 he went on the trawlers out to Norway and Iceland and had it not been for his boxing would have embarked on a career at sea.

Soon after turning pro, Steve met the owner of a cargo company operating out of Southampton. The man was a boxing lover and gave him work as a deck-hand every summer for ten years. He travelled all over Europe and often spent up to three weeks away from home, but only outside the boxing season. He kept in shape while away and even did bag training in a force ten gale. "I thought it would help improve my balance," he remarked dryly. It has to be good for the sport that a man of Steve Pollard's

dedication is staying in boxing and passing his knowledge on to youngsters.

Julian Eavis from Gillingham in Dorset is another dedicated professional prepared to travel anywhere for a fight at just 24 hours notice. After an amateur career or more than 150 contests, he turned pro in 1988 and has packed in more than 70 fights, winning just 14.

Even as an amateur, Julian had to travel all over the country to get fights and this forced him to go professional. The final straw came when he travelled to London to meet an opponent with more than 60 contests behind him. When he got there the man pulled out claiming that Eavis was too experienced. He was captain of the Western Counties team and in 1987 reached the area welterweight final.

Eavis is a tough, awkward southpaw whose record is deceptive and, although he has been stopped on occasions, nobody has knocked him out. In 1990 he had 18 fights and, despite failing to win any, he was only stopped once. He is elusive and the perfect spoiler for any young prospect. This was aptly demonstrated earlier this year when he took Dean Cooper the distance at Bristol on 31 March and, just nine days later, did the same to big-punching Darren Dyer at Bethnal Green.

His willingness and dedication were borne out by the fact that he took the Cooper fight at 3 p.m. the same day, having just 36 hours notice before meeting Dyer. Many pundits thought Darren was in for an early night, but Eavis made sure that he was not hit cleanly. That night Dyer had the experience of almost 140 fights against him, with Steve Pollard working in Julian's corner.

Many good names appear on the Eavis record and he has gone the distance with Eamonn Loughran, Gary Logan,

Julian Eavis   Pennie Cattle

Lindon Scarlett, Paul Wesley (twice) and Dean Cooper (twice). He has also had his Western Area title chances, losing to Mark Purcell (five rounds) in 1989 and to Ross Hale (eight rounds) in 1992 at welterweight, before being defeated on points by Cooper in July 1993 at light-middleweight.

Julian, who attended school at Gillingham and achieved nine GCE's, is a bricklayer by trade and works five or six days a week. Living in rural Dorset, however, is a handicap for the journeyman fighter because there are no gyms where he can get sparring. Instead, he cycles to work some 18 miles each way in order to keep fit and then, during the evenings, does at least half an hour on floor exercises. He keeps fighting regularly to use some of the contests virtually as sparring sessions.

Married for seven years, Julian has a five-year-old daughter and two sons aged four and one, and the family live in a semi-detached house over-looking picturesque lakes. Although he plays good class football in the Dorset Combination League, boxing is his main sport. "Why do you box?" I asked him. "Because I love it," he replied swiftly, "and it helps provide one or two luxuries in life. We've now got a carpet."

Eavis is a deceptive character; no broken nose, very little scar tissue, with a soft pleasant personality and nothing about him to indicate that he is a veteran of more than 70 professional fights, and 150 as an amateur. Whenever he is cut, he refuses to have stitches. Instead, he allows the Board of Control doctor to patch up the injury and when he gets home, his wife treats it with natural honey. "It's an old country remedy which works well for me," he remarked.

A natural welterweight, Eavis frequently gives away weight and is another of the courageous men on whom the sport relies so heavily. After the Dyer fight, he sat in the audience for the rest of the evening and it was fitting that there was the odd occasion when a fan walked up and asked for an autograph.

Pete Buckley is one of a number of fighters from the Nobby Nobbs' stable in Birmingham who are prepared to take a fight anywhere at short notice. Less fortunate than some small hall boxers, Pete has been unemployed for more than 12 months, but has now clocked up 58 contests since turning pro in October 1989 and, although he won only a third of them, is much better than his record suggests.

Buckley had a promising start to his career, losing only nine of his first 29 fights and won the vacant Midlands Area super-featherweight title by outpointing Brian Robb over ten rounds in June 1991. He successfully defended it by stopping Robb in February the following year and, 12 months later, travelled to Austria where he extended local favourite, Harald Geier, for the vacant WBA Penta-Continental title. Although all three judges gave it to the Austrian by a wide margin, the *Boxing News* correspondent had Peter just three rounds behind.

Nobody has knocked Pete out and his undoubted skill and toughness are demonstrated by the fact that only Duke McKenzie (twice) and Nassem Hamed have succeeded in stopping him. Drew Docherty (three times), Johnny Bredahl, Alan McKay (draw), Donnie Hood, Hamed (points) and Bradley Stone, have all been extended by the skilful Midland's journeyman.

Another man who is a classic modern day journeyman is the likeable Londoner, Karl Barwise. This amiable, soft-spoken man from Tooting, is a match-maker's dream, with a willingness to meet anybody at short notice. Three trips to Belfast, one each to Paris and Italy, as well as others outside London, have gained him tremendous respect wherever he has boxed.

By the time he became a professional in 1984, Karl had engaged in more than 100 amateur bouts, firstly with Harlow ABC, and then Norwood. As a pro, he lost only seven of his first 20 fights between September 1984 and October 1986, but was then out of the ring for almost four years due to illness. Doctors diagnosed it as delayed depression and anxiety brought about by the death of his father and brother in a horrific fire back in 1982. Karl was an amateur at the time, but, incredibly, he kept on with his boxing.

He bravely battled back to fitness and it is a tribute to his will-power and determination that he ever fought again. Since returning to the ring in 1990, Barwise has met good men such as Errol Christie, Andrew Flute, Lou Gent, Neville Brown, James Cook (twice) and Fidel Castro Smith. The names of Michael Watson and Christophe Tiozzo also appear on his earlier record.

Currently self-managed, Karl is a difficult man to hurt. Although he has been stopped on occasion, nobody has yet put him down for the full count, despite the fact that he frequently gives away weight to younger opponents.

Outside boxing, Karl works full-time as a scaffolder, but finds enough energy to train for a couple of hours at least four times a week. He has a nice home at Roehampton where he now lives with his girl friend and their four daughters and keeps very fit, often doing charity runs and even half marathons.

Karl Barwise may never become a champion but he carries on boxing because he really loves it. When he does decide to quit he should be given every encouragement to stay in the game because he has so much to offer. His bravery, dedication and discipline, are essential ingredients to pass on to future generations of boxers.

To climb into a boxing ring at any time requires a tremendous degree of courage, but to continue to do so and keep losing is beyond the call of duty. The majority of journeymen know they will never reach the top, or even get that one big pay-day. Yet to understand these men, one has to sit and talk to them. Having done so, I have nothing but admiration and respect for their courage. Their contribution to the hard sport of professional boxing is worthy of recognition, not only from everyone within the sport, but many outside it as well.

The journeymen fighters are men of dignity and, I confess, that while sitting at ringside I frequently long to see the likes of Karl Barwise, Miguel Matthews and Julian Eavis cause an upset. For what they put into boxing, they deserve that occasional good fortune.

Women in Boxing

by Ralph Oates

I don't believe that anyone could have failed to have noticed the increased participation of women in professional boxing. The trend of female involvement has developed at a steady and most progressive rate over a period of years. Today, a number of women play a vital role in the sport at various levels. So what made them step into the tough ringside shape world of boxing?

I decided to find out on behalf of the British Boxing Yearbook and in so doing I selected five ladies to interview.

These being:

Carol Polis	(First American female boxing judge)
Lisa Budd	(First British woman MC)
Tania Follett	(Britain's first woman to be licensed as a second)
Katherine Morison	(First Scottish lady promoter)
Jackie Kallen	(Manager of a stable that includes James Tooney).

Carol Polis (Boxing Judge)

Ralph Oates.   Where were you born?

Carol Polis.   Philadelphia, Pennsylvania.

RO.   When did you first become interested in boxing?

CP.   In the early 1970s my ex-husband Bob Polis (but husband at the time) was both a stockbroker and a boxing referee.

RO.   Are there any other members of your family involved in the Sport?

CP.   No, there is no other family involvement.

RO.   What made you become a boxing judge?

CP.   Well, to be honest, it was through the urging of my then husband Bob, he often took me to the fights with him, then one evening taught me how to keep score on the back of a programme. At that point in time, we worked on a five point must system in Pennsylvania. Then, at the end of my first evening of scoring on the back of a programme, Bob turned my scores into the then commissioner, Zack Clayton.

Zack said he liked my scoring and advised me to keep on doing it. I then studied the rules and regulations book (little but thick) for a year and a half. During that period of time I turned in sporadic scores to Zack, which he compared to the male judges. He would then ask me on the spot questions of which I really had to know the answers.

In fact, you could say that this was both the written and oral part of my examination.

RO.   When were you first appointed a judge?

CP.   One evening at the fights before the wind-up, Zack came over to me and said "Lady, I've both good and bad news for you". The bad news was that Bob and I had to drive up to Harrisburg, the capital of Pennsylvania. This wasn't really so bad, since it was only a two hour ride from my home in Fort Washington, a suburb of Philadelphia. However, the good news was, that I was to be sworn in by the then governor, Milton Shapp, as the first lady professional judge in the United States. This event took place on 1 February 1973 and as the saying goes the rest is history.

RO.   Can you remember the first fight you officiated at?

CP.   Yes, it was a contest between Earnie Shavers and Jimmy Young. This fabulous first fight took place at the Spectrum in Philadelphia on 18 February 1973.

RO.   Can you remember the first world title fight you officiated at?

CP.   Yes, this was on 8 April 1979, when Jorge Lujan defended his bantamweight title against Cleo Garcia in Las Vegas. Lujan retained his crown with a 15 round stoppage.

RO.   How many world title fights have you judged to date?

CP.   At this moment in time 25.

RO.   You once judged a world title fight in Britain, can you remember the fighters?

CP.   Yes I can. The contest was for the WBA Junior-lightweight title, with Brian Mitchell defending his crown against Jim McDonnell. This took place on 2 November 1988 at a very quaint and charming place, the Elephant & Castle. Mitchell retained the championship on points over 12 rounds.

RO.   Do you have any special memories about that night?

CP.   Yes, because there was a South African boxer fighting, in the shape of Brian Mitchell, a large group gathered outside to protest against apartheid. However, I must say that I felt very safe while this commotion was going on.

RO.   Did you notice much of a difference in the way things are done in America, when compared to Britain?

CP.   Yes I did, for as strict as things are in the United States with regards to a title fight, Great Britain appeared to be even stricter.

RO.   Did you form any opinion about the officials you met from the Board of Control?

CP.   I found them to be very formal, professional and charming. The word that best describes the British Boxing Board is austere. I respect them greatly.

RO. Did you encounter any problems when you first became a judge?

CP. The main problem was extreme scepticism among the "Old Timers". I did understand it though, as I was the first lady to enter a totally male dominated field. It must be remembered that in the early 1970s it was even harder for a woman to break in anywhere.

RO. Do you have any ambitions in boxing?

CP. The only ambition I have with regards to boxing is to keep judging at least one, preferably two, title fights a year. At one time, however, I thought it would be interesting to be the boxing commissioner here in Philadelphia, but it was a job that requires oodles of political connections, and I have very few. Plus the fact that I would miss, terribly, travelling throughout the world and making more wonderful friends.

RO. Do you have a favourite weight division?

CP. My personal favourite is the middleweight poundage.

RO. Who is your favourite boxer?

CP. Without a doubt, Roberto Duran.

RO. Do you find time for any kind of hobby?

CP. Well, my hobbies include playing the piano, writing a book based on my experiences over the past 21 years in boxing, the racetrack and going to every flea market and garage sale that I can find. I also love music, dancing and animals.

RO. What changes if any would you like to see with regards to boxing judges?

CP. The only change I would like to see is a rotation system installed when it comes to assigning the officials. In this way I feel I would then profit from more assignments. The more the merrier.

RO. Who has been your main influence in boxing?

CP. I have had many. Zack Clayton, Howard McCall, Jimmy Binns, Georgie Benton, George Katz, etc, etc, and the list goes on and on.

RO. What advice would you give to any woman considering a career in boxing?

CP. For any woman, or women considering a career in boxing, my advice would be three-fold.

(a) Have a fabulous sense of humour.

(b) Always be a lady, and most of the time you are treated as one.

(c) As Zack Clayton told me from day one, try not to even score a round, make a decision and be a man, plus, don't worry what they say about you in the newspaper – just make sure they spell your name right.

Carol Polis (left) seen at ringside as "Rocky", Sylvester Stallone, the famous screen-star, takes a bow

Lisa Budd (Boxing MC)

Ralph Oates. Where were your born?

Lisa Budd. I was born in Bristol, but I moved with my parents to Devon when I was 14 years of age.

RO. When did you first become interested in boxing?

LB. My grandfather, father and mother held season tickets at the Colston Hall in Bristol, which ran boxing shows every fortnight on a Saturday afternoon. This was about 1950. Even though they stopped holding tournaments there, the boxing bug never left the family and we continued to follow the sport on television. Therefore, from an early age, I had a keen interest and understanding of boxing.

I was about eight-years-old when my father took me to see a live fight (perhaps not quite the thing for a young lady, but I was more of a tom-boy).

RO. Are there any other members of your family involved in boxing?

LB. No, I am the only one.

RO. What made you become an MC?

LB. When I applied for my licence with the BBBoC, I was employed by a boxing manager and promoter. Obviously, my whole life revolved around boxing and I wanted to become more involved in the sport I loved. After some discussions with various individuals in the game, we agreed that only a few avenues were open to me, mainly due to the fact that as a woman it would not be appropriate for me to apply for certain categories, i.e. Whip – because it would involve me going in and out of boxers' dressing rooms when they might not be suitably attired. Not that I would have minded, but we felt it might not be quite the thing, being British.

Therefore, MC was a category we felt would be acceptable to the BBBoC, boxing fans, and the fighters themselves. It was also a role which could be carried out by either sex, since no male elements were required, i.e. strength.

However, in plain and simple terms, I became an MC because I wanted to take a real and positive role in a sport I loved and lived for.

RO. Can you remember the date of the first promotion you appeared on and the names of the main event fighters?

LB. The date of my first fight was 17 September 1992 at Watford Town Hall. The main fight was Wally Swift v Andy Till for the British Light-midlewight title. I was so nervous while I waited to go into the ring, that I sat with Billy Schwer and made him ask me anything he could think of so I kept talking. I thought that if I stopped my throat would seize up and I would never speak again. I have a great deal to thank Billy for, since I may not have made it into the ring without his help. However, once through those ropes all my nerves disappeared and I got on with the job I was employed to do.

RO. Have you ever had any problems with the crowds?

LB. No, I haven't had any trouble with the crowds, such as cat calling etc – I'm not sure if that's a compliment or not, but I feel that they respect the job I'm doing and therefore let me get on with it.

RO. Have you had any awkward moments to date?

LB. Only one. I had MC'd a show for Frank Maloney at Bethnal Green and he wanted me to call two boxers into the ring during the interval to help publicise their up-and-coming contest. However, when I announced the fight and called them into the ring, neither man materialised. After several moments I called them again – still no sign. In the end it became obvious that they had either gone home or were elsewhere. I was left in the ring feeling a bit stupid and ended up making the crowd smile by saying that I hoped they would not be that shy to get into the ring on the night of the fight.

RO. Do you have any ambitions in boxing?

LB. Yes. Ultimately, I would love to become a manager and was hoping to go to the States this summer to work with an American manager. However, this plan has had to be put on hold due to the arrival this December of a baby, but the ambition is still there – I'll be back.

RO. Who is your favourite boxer?

LB. All-time is Mike Tyson. He gave so much excitement to the sport, dominating the ring and taking no prisoners. There was no one like Mike, nor has there been since. However, my love for Tyson does not extend into his private life, which I disagree with completely and blame not only him but those who were there to support and take care of his well being. After they built Mike's career up they couldn't wait to knock him down, all to prove themselves powerful. It wouldn't be fair of me if I didn't mention the other boxers whom I admire, such as Jack Dempsey, Muhammad Ali, Jim Watt, Sugar Ray Leonard, Chris Eubank, Nigel Benn and of course, Michael Watson.

RO. Do you have a favourite weight division?

LB. Not really. I enjoy watching all weight classes and think that as long as both fighters have put in their gym and road work, are well matched and hungry for a win, then you have the right combination for an exciting contest which ever weight it its. It's a bone of contention of mine that the lower weight divisions have far less earning power, yet they give just as much to the sport as the heavyweights. An example of this is Duke McKenzie, who has held versions of the world title in three different weight divisions, which has made him a British record maker but very little money. Had Duke been born a heavyweight, I'm sure he would have been a millionaire by now. This does seem a little unfair, since the lighter weights can be just as exciting, if not more so. Often with the heavyweights, we have to put up with the sight of two big fat overweight boxers, completely out of condition, wrestle around the ring.

RO.   Do you find time for any kind of hobby?

LB.   No. When you are involved in boxing it becomes your life and nothing else gets a look-in.

RO.   Do you have any views about the safety of boxers?

LB.   I think that as far as health and safety for the boxers go, the BBBoC are doing as much as they can to make the sport as safe as possible. Obviously, the main aim of the sport is to hit your opponent – dangerous, yes, but when you take into account the number of deaths in boxing against that of motor racing and horse riding then I feel that the BBBoC have a record to be proud of.

RO.   What changes, if any, would you like to see in boxing?

LB.   I would like to see the authorities stand by certain decisions they make, rather than back down when a manager or promoter moans. Also, I would like to see a fairer pay scale for the weight divisions.

RO.   Who has been your main influence in boxing?

LB.   I didn't really have anyone as such, but Harry Holland has been a tower of strength and a great help in my boxing career. I owe him much.

RO.   What advice would you give to any woman considering a career in boxing?

LB.   Don't give up just because you get one turn down or bad comment. Remember, there are another 20 ready to say yes and have a kind word. You cannot expect to enter a male dominated sport without the odd MC resenting the fact that you are there and successful. Take it slowly and give it time – not for yourself but for those men who need time to get used to us and realise that we can do more than wash up.

Tania Follett (left), the first woman ever licensed by the BBBoC as a second, and Lisa Budd, likewise, in her capacity as a "Master of Ceremonies", captured together at ringside   Les Clark

Tania Follett (Boxing Second)

Ralph Oates. Where were your born?

Tania Follett. At the Canadian Redcross in Taplow, Buckinghamshire.

RO. When did you first become interested in boxing?

TF. Coming from a boxing family, the interest in the sport has always been apparent in my life. In fact, as a child, I was interested in boxing and as I have grown older I seem to have fallen even deeper in love with the sport.

RO. Are there any other members of your family involved in boxing?

TF. Yes. My father used to box for the North Hammersmith Boxing Club and also turned out for the 101 Medium Workshop Reme Territorial Army. As Lance Corporal 23739776, he boxed in the Territorial Army Championships at Welterweight.

My great great uncle, 8181 private Denis Regan, was a Regimental boxer. He was welterweight champion in India and boxed for the Kings Royal Rifle Corps between 1904-1914.

On my mothers side, my grandfather was a fitness instructor in the Army and boxed as an amateur. My grandmother's two brothers, the Rooneys, also boxed. One was in the Border Regiment and the other one was in the Air Force. Great grandfather also donned the gloves. They were all very successful in the amateur ranks, with the Rooney brothers winning a few trophies.

RO. What made you become a second?

TF. When most girls were playing house or holding tea parties for their dolls, I was glued to the TV watching boxing and it was after watching Leon Spinks defeat Muhammad Ali for the world heavyweight title in 1978 that I decided I wanted to become a second. I was nine years of age at the time. Where else can you get a better seat in the house, but in the corner where the action is.

RO. Can you remember the first fighter you became a second to?

TF. Yes, it was on a Frank Maloney Promotion called "A Hard Days Night". The date was 1 December 1993 and the show featured Maurice "Hard" Core defending his British Light-heavyweight title against Simon Harris. Other fighters on the ten fight boxing bonanza at the York Hall, Bethnal Green were: P. J. Gallagher (lightweight), Julius Francis (Heavyweight), Rocky Milton (light-weight), Manny Burgo (heavyweight), Kevin McBride (heavyweight), James Oyebola (heavy-weight), Floyd Havard (super-featherweight), Justin Murphy (featherweight) and Paul Lawson (heavyweight).

I cornered for every fighter on the bill with the exception of Maurice Core, so all nine boxers were in fact my first.

RO. How did people in general react to you when you were appointed a lady second?

TF. I encountered Scepticism at first from people who had never seen me work, but then, with everything that's new, there are both negative and positive comments. The more I work, the more I encounter positive reactions. I have received tremendous support from people who come and watch boxing shows and always receive comments from men, congratulating me on my achievement becoming the first woman second, which really explodes the theory that there is no place in the corner for women.

RO. What problems did you encounter in the beginning?

TF. Once again scepticism was my main problem. In the beginning, various people would ask why would a girl want to work in the corner where she could have blood and spit fall on her. Another problem was lack of communication and guidance, since people never had the time for me when I asked questions. Therefore, I had to work that much harder to prove I was worthy of being in the corner, or, if you like, being spat on and blooded. I also feel that I cannot just be good at what I do, I have to be better.

RO. Have you had any awkward moments to date?

TF. No, not really, but awkward moments are always around the corner.

RO. Do you have any ambitions in boxing?

TF. Yes. However, in this sport you always have to prove yourself time and time again. At present, I have to prove myself as a trainer and then one day as a manager. I realise that I still have a great deal to learn and I am taking one step at a time, because I would not want to be in a position of having to ask people to do things I cannot do myself. Many would say that I should start out as a cut's woman, but I know that I would not get the chance to do that in boxing. Then, again, many would say there is no way I could train a boxer, but I have a deep desire to learn about conditioning and boxing training methods.

RO. Do you have any views about training?

TF. I am not short of having my own ideas regarding training and management. To be honest, I feel there is too much talk and not enough action with regard to changes in boxers training routines. There is too much talk about the old days, rather than any concentrated effort to bring things up to date with new ideas. Why else do we send boxers to the States to train. The fighters here are clearly not given enough motivation and are in need of mental support leading up to their bouts. Lennox Lewis said "boxing is 70% mental and 30% physical". You have to have that mental edge. I believe that you need a strong mind in order to deal with getting up to train, plus having the guts to go into the ring and putting everything you have learnt during training into the fight. Mental support helps a boxer to learn and keep himself calm and not to panic in certain situations. That's what I think, anyway.

RO. Who are your favourite boxers?

TF. James Toney and Evander Holyfield.

RO. Which are your favourite weight divisions?

TF. Bantamweight and featherweight.

RO. Do you find time for any kind of hobby?

TF. I have a big interest in wildlife and conservation. In fact, I once ran my own rescue service for injured wildlife.

My other interest is Bull Terriers and, when I can, in helping the National Bull Terrier Welfare Rescue to find homes for the unwanted. This charity has brought me a great deal of enjoyment. My other love is music. I write and sing, and spend a lot of time in the recording studio and I love to perform live. However, boxing has taken over my life and I now find less time for my hobbies.

RO. What changes if any would you like to see in boxing?

TF. Too much emphasis has been put on the heavyweight division and not enough attention on the lower weight divisions, of which some of the most explosive and skilful boxing is provided. I would like to see more boxing from the lighter division on TV and more of these bouts on top of the bill.

I would also like to see training courses set up for both trainers and seconds to learn first aid training aspects, weight control, sports injuries and nutrition. The list can go on, but I feel a lot could be gained and change can only be good for the sport.

May I add that I would like to see surgical gloves used more often than they are at the moment in the various corners.

RO. Who has been your main influence in boxing?

TF. In truth, everyone I meet is an influence, because I never stop learning from people around me, but my main inspiration has been the American manager, Jackie Kallen, who has given me both support and encouragement, and Frank Maloney, who believed in me and gave me a chance to become involved in boxing. And, without the help of the boxers themselves, I could never have become a second.

RO. What advice would you give to a woman considering a career in boxing?

TF. This question always poses a difficult answer. I believe everyone is different, therefore, they have different ideas and ways of doing things. My advice would be to have dedication in the field you decide to embark upon, be objective, open minded, retain a good sense of humour, and, most importantly, whatever your actions in boxing, remember you represent the sport and everybody involved. Last, but not least, enjoy boxing.

Kathleen Morrison, Scotland's first lady boxing promoter

Katherine Morrison (Boxing Promoter)

Ralph Oates. In which part of Scotland were you born?

Katherine Morrison. Glasgow.

RO. When did you first become interested in boxing?

KM. It first developed in 1987. My father Alex promoted regular public shows at the Plaza Ballroom in Glasgow and I assisted him by selling programmes.

RO. Are there any other members of your family involved in the fight game?

KM. My father boxed as an amateur and at the age of 44 he won the Western District heavyweight title. The following year he won the Scottish title at super-heavyweight. Shortly after this he built his own gymnasium and began promoting professional boxing.

RO. What made you take up promoting?

KM. My father had been managing and promoting professional boxing for several years before I began to work for him. As I have already said, my early involvement started with me selling programmes, but I quickly graduated to selling tickets and advertising. Before long, I was helping to arrange fights and helping to look after the financial side of things. During this time, we promoted three WBC International title fights and various bouts which involved Scottish titles. It was about this time that I decided to apply for my own promoters license.

RO. Did you encounter any problems?

KM. Yes I did. I put my application forward to the Scottish Area Council and thus went along expecting to be interviewed. However, I was told by the Area Secretary that my application had been turned down and that the Council were not obliged to see me or even give a reason as to why it had been refused. This event happened three times before I contacted the head office in London. An appointment was arranged and, after a meeting, I was eventually granted a license.

RO. When did you get your promoters license?

KM. In March 1993.

RO. How many shows have you promoted to date?

KM. Approximately 20, both wine and dine and public.

RO. Have you had any awkward moments during your career?

KM. I am pleased to say that I haven't had too many. However, on one occasion I had a problem with the paramedics arriving late at one of my shows. The steward in charge was adamant that the show would not go ahead without them, but much to my relief they eventually arrived and the boxing was able to go on. It seemed that the paramedics had problems parking.

RO. What is your main ambition in boxing?

KM. I have only been promoting a short while so it is to keep working and to promote regular shows which please the public. I am learning all the time, my shows are well attended, and I am very pleased with the feed-back which I receive.

RO. Who is your favourite boxer?

KM. Gary Jacobs, who is totally dedicated. I also feel that Gary is a good ambassador for Scotland.

RO. Which is your favourite weight division?

KM. Bantamweight, since this poundage provides plenty of action.

RO. Do you find time for any kind of hobby?

KM. I do try and make time for my other interests, which include hill walking, horse riding and cooking. I also like to make time for both my family and friends.

RO. What changes, if any, would you like to see in boxing?

KM. I would like to see weigh-in times put back and not held on the day of the fight. Furthermore, I feel that when a boxer is knocked out he should be kept in hospital overnight for observation. I also feel that managers should have some ring experience themselves, be it either amateur or professional. There is nothing that annoys me more than a brave manager.

RO. You have the honour of being the first lady promoter in Scotland, are you involved in any other capacity?

KM. Yes, I am also on the Scottish Area Council.

RO. What advice would you give to any other woman who may be considering a career in boxing?

KM. I think it would be very difficult for a female, who may be considering a career on the promotional side of boxing, if she has no contacts in the business. I am quite sure that had my father not been involved I wouldn't have realised my ambition in becoming a promoter. It would be a good idea for any female who wanted to become involved in promoting to first gain some experience by going to work for a promoter/manager. This would prove to be of great value.

Jackie Kallen (Boxing Manager)

Ralph Oates. Where were you born?

Jackie Kallen. Detroit.

RO. When did you first become interested in boxing?

JK. I became interested when I was about 13 or 14-years-old. My mother was an amateur actress who played a role in a musical called "Kid Broadway". Her part was of a woman who inherited a boxer when her father (a boxing manager) died.

RO. Are there any other members of your family involved in boxing?

JK. My sons both work with me. Bryan, 25, is a sports entertainment lawyer and Brad, 24, assists me in the gym.

RO. What made you become a manager?

JK. After ten years as Thomas Hearns' publicist, I decided to try my hand at managing. I felt that I would be pretty good at it, because I am a very organized, even tempered person and very nurturing.

RO. What problems did you encounter in the beginning?

JK. Mostly a lack of respect. I don't think people took me seriously because they weren't sure when or where I was coming from and I had to prove that I knew my business.

RO. Have you had any awkward moments to date?

JK. Only when a bigoted, ignorant person has made a stupid or inappropriate comment to me.

RO. Do you have any ambitions in boxing?

JK. Yes. To have the hottest stable in boxing, with several world champions. I would also like to be named "Manager of the Year" one day.

RO. Who is your favourite boxer?

JK. I love all my boxers, but my favourite of all time (not including my current stable) is Thomas Hearns.

RO. Which is your favourite weight class?

JK. I like the middleweight and the super-middleweight division right now.

RO. Do you find time for any kind of hobby?

JK. I write two entertainment columns a week for a daily paper, I knit sweaters and I read a lot.

RO. What changes if any would you like to see in boxing?

JK. I would like to see better regulations and a national commission that would accurately list all boxers and their true ages and records.

RO. Who has been your main influence in boxing?

JK. My mentor was Emanuel Steward. I learned a great deal watching him over the years.

RO. What advice would you give a woman considering a career in boxing?

JK. To any woman seeking a future in boxing, keep your chin up, disregard sexist or insensitive remarks, always maintain your professionalism, never use profane language, don't smoke or drink around your boxers, go to the gym with them everyday, always give them a true and accurate accounting of the money and never lie to them.

Without doubt, I am of the view that these ladies have a real contribution to make to boxing. They are intelligent, strong minded, and have valuable input which can only benefit the game. It is also very clear that each one of them has the vitality to overcome any obstacles which may stand in their way and thus climb the ladder to success.

However, perhaps the most important factor of all is that they care and love the sport of boxing.

I wish them all the very best of luck for the future.

Jackie Kallen, manager of IBF super-middleweight champion, James Toney

---

Boxing Clever
by
Ralph Oates

A quiz book based on every world heavyweight champion from John L. Sullivan to Herbie Hide.

From Brooklyn Publishing Group, Moulton Park Business Centre, Northampton NN3 1AQ.

£5.95 + £1.15 p&p.

Diary of British Boxing Tournaments, 1993-94

Tournaments are listed by date, town, venue, and promoter and cover the period 1 July 1993 - 30 June 1994

Code: SC = Sporting Club

Date	Town	Venue	Promoters
01.07.93	York	Barbican Centre	National Promotions
02.07.93	Liverpool	Everton Park Sports Centre	Vaughan
10.07.93	Cardiff	National Ice Rink	Matchroom
25 07.93	Oldham	Sports Centre	Gorton
28.07.93	Brixton	Academy	Ringmaster Productions
11.08.93	Mansfield	Leisure Centre	Ingle/Brogan
14.08.93	Hammersmith	Apollo	Gee
31 08.93	Croydon	Fairfield Hall	Holdsworth
06.09.93	Liverpool	Devonshire House Hotel	Snagg
07.09.93	Stoke	Moat House Hotel	Brogan
09.09.93	Glasgow	Hospitality Inn	Morrison
13.09.93	Middleton	Civic Hall	Tara Boxing Promotions
13.09.93	Bristol	Odyssey Nightclub	McMahon Promotions
15.09.93	Newcastle	Mayfair Club	Fawcett
15.09.93	Ashford	Stour Centre	Uppercut Promotions
15.09.93	Bethnal Green	York Hall	Maloney
16.09.93	Southwark	Elephant & Castle Leisure Centre	National Promotions
16.09.93	Hull	Willerby Manor Hotel	Edwards
18.09.93	Leicester	Granby Halls	Matchroom
20.09.93	Northampton	Glenville's Club	Cox
20.09.93	Glasgow	Forte Crest Hotel	St Andrew's SC
20.09.93	Cleethorpes	Winter Gardens	Gray
22.09.93	Wembley	Grand Hall	National Promotions
22.09.93	Bethnal Green	York Hall	Warren
22.09.93	Chesterfield	Aquarius Club	Shinfield
27.09.93	Manchester	Piccadilly Hotel	Trickett
28.09.93	Liverpool	Ferrari's Nightspot	Vaughan
28.09.93	Bethnal Green	York Hall	Matchroom
30.09.93	Hayes	Stadium Leisure Centre	Evans
30.09.93	Walsall	Town Hall	Cowdell
01.10.93	Cardiff	Arms Park	Maloney
04.10.93	Bradford	Norfolk Gardens Hotel	Yorkshire Executive SC
04.10.93	Mayfair	Marriott Hotel	National Promotions
05.10.93	Mayfair	Grosvenor House	Matchroom
06.10.93	Glasgow	Forte Crest Hotel	St Andrew's SC
06.10.93	Solihull	Conference Centre	Midlands SC
07.10.93	York	Barbican Centre	National Promotions
07.10.93	Hull	Willerby Manor Hotel	Hull & District SC
09.10.93	Manchester	Old Trafford	Matchroom
12.10.93	Wolverhampton	Park Hall Hotel	Wolverhampton SC
13.10.93	Bethnal Green	York Hall	Maloney
13.10.93	Watford	Leisure Centre	Holdsworth
13.10.93	Stoke	Trentham Gardens	North Staffs SC
16.10.93	Belfast	King's Hall	Matchroom
19.10.93	Cleethorpes	Beachcomber Club	Frater
21.10.93	Glasgow	Hospitality Inn	Morrison
21.10.93	Bayswater	Royal Lancaster Hotel	Nordoff/Robbins Trust
23.10.93	Cardiff	National Ice Rink	Warren
25.10.93	Glasgow	Forte Crest Hotel	St Andrew's SC
25.10.93	Liverpool	Devonshire House Hotel	Snagg
27.10.93	West Bromwich	Gals Baths	National Promotions
27.10.93	Stoke	Moat House Hotel	Brogan

Date	Town	Venue	Promoters
28.10.93	Walsall	Saddler's Club	Gray
28.10.93	Torquay	Riviera Centre	Bousted
30.10.93	Chester	Northgate Arena	Vaughan
02.11.93	Southwark	Elephant & Castle Leisure Centre	National Promotions
03.11.93	Worcester	Northwick Theatre	Shinfield
03.11.93	Bristol	Whitchurch Sports Centre	Maloney
04.11.93	Stafford	Colosseum	Gray
06.11.93	Bethnal Green	York Hall	Matchroom
07.11.93	Glasgow	Forte Crest Hotel	St Andrew's SC
08.11.93	Bradford	Norfolk Gardens Hotel	Yorkshire Executive SC
10.11.93	Watford	Town Hall	National Promotions
10.11.93	Ystrad	Rhondda Sports Centre	Gardiner
10.11.93	Bethnal Green	York Hall	Warren
11.11.93	Burnley	William Thompson Leisure Centre	Tara Boxing Promotions
12.11.93	Hull	Ennardale Leisure Centre	Edwards/Pollard
13.11.93	Cullompton	Culm Valley Sports Centre	Van Bailey
22.11.93	Glasgow	Forte Crest Hotel	St Andrew's SC
23.11.93	Kettering	Reflection's Nightspot	Hall
24.11.93	Solihull	Conference Centre	Midlands SC
25.11.93	Tynemouth	Park Hotel	St Andrew's SC
25.11.93	Newcastle	Mayfair Club	Fawcett
28.11.93	Southwark	Elephant & Castle Leisure Centre	Gee
29.11.93	Manchester	Piccadilly Hotel	Trickett
29.11.93	Ingatestone	Moat House Hotel	Matchroom
30.11.93	Wolverhampton	Park Hall Hotel	Wolverhampton SC
30.11.93	Cardiff	Welsh Institute of Sport	Matchroom
30.11.93	Leicester	Colloseum	Griffin
01.12.93	Bethnal Green	York Hall	Maloney
01.12.93	Stoke	Moat House Hotel	Brogan
01.12.93	Kensington	Albert Hall	National Promotions
02.12.93	Evesham	Public Halls	Evesham SC
02.12.93	Sheffield	City Hall	Hobson
02.12.93	Walsall	Town Hall	Cowdell
02.12.93	Hartlepool	Borough Hall	Robinson
06.12.93	Bradford	Norfolk Gardens Hotel	Yorkshire Executive SC
06.12.93	Birmingham	Grand Hotel	Cowdell
07.12.93	Bethnal Green	York Hall	National Promotions
08.12.93	Stoke	Trentham Gardens	North Staffs SC
08.12.93	Hull	Willerby Manor Hotel	Hull & District SC
09.12.93	Watford	Town Hall	Evans
11.12.93	Liverpool	Everton Park Sports Centre	Vaughan
13.12.93	Doncaster	Moat House Hotel	Rushton
13.12.93	Cleethorpes	Winter Gardens	Gray
13.12.93	Bristol	Odyssey Nightclub	Sanigar
16.12.93	Newport	Leisure Centre	National Promotions
16.12.93	Walsall	Saddler's Club	Gray
18.12.93	Manchester	Wythenshawe Forum	Warren
19.12.93	Glasgow	Hospitality Inn	Morrison
19.12.93	Northampton	Moat House Hotel	Cox
21.12.93	Mayfair	Grosvenor House	Matchroom
11.01.94	Bethnal Green	York Hall	Matchroom
14.01.94	Bethnal Green	York Hall	National Promotions
19.01.94	Stoke	Moat House Hotel	Brogan
19.01.94	Solihull	Conference Centre	Midlands SC
20.01.94	Battersea	Town Hall	Sanigar/Carew
22.01.94	Cardiff	National Institute of Sport	Maloney
22.01.94	Belfast	King's Hall	Matchroom
24.01.94	Glasgow	Forte Crest Hotel	St Andrew's SC

Date	Town	Venue	Promoters
25.01.94	Mayfair	Cafe Royal	Maloney
26.01.94	Birmingham	Aston Villa Leisure Centre	National Promotions
26.01.94	Stoke	Trentham Gardens	North Staffs SC
29.01.94	Cardiff	National Ice Rink	Warren
02.02.94	Glasgow	Kelvin Hall	St Andrew's SC/Matchroom
07.02.94	Bradford	Norfolk Gardens Hotel	Yorkshire Executive SC
08.02.94	Wolverhampton	Park Hall Hotel	Wolverhampton SC
09.02.94	Brentwood	International Hall	Matchroom
09.02.94	Bethnal Green	York Hall	Maloney
10.02.94	Glasgow	Hospitality Inn	Morrison
10.02.94	Hull	Willerby Manor Hotel	Pollard
16.02.94	Stevenage	Ice Bowl	National Promotions
17.02.94	Dagenham	Goresbrook Leisure Club	Warren
17.02.94	Bury	Castle Leisure Centre	Tara Boxing Promotions
17.02.94	Walsall	Saddler's Club	Gray
18.02.94	Leicester	Colloseum	Griffin
21.02.94	Glasgow	Forte Crest Hotel	St Andrew's SC
23.02.94	Watford	Town Hall	Holland H./National Promotions
24.02.94	Hull	Royal Hotel	Hull & District SC
24.02.94	Walsall	Town Hall	Cowdell
25.02.94	Chester	Northgate Arena	Vaughan
26.02.94	Earls Court	Arena	Warren
28.02.94	Marton	Country Club	Spensley
28.02.94	Manchester	Piccadilly Hotel	Trickett
01.03.94	Dudley	Town Hall	National Promotions
02.03.94	Glasgow	Forte Crest Hotel	St Andrew's SC
02.03.94	Solihull	Conference Centre	Midlands SC
03.03.94	Ebbw Vale	Leisure Centre	Gardiner
03.03.94	Newcastle	Mayfair Club	Fawcett
04.03.94	Bethnal Green	York Hall	National Promotions
04.03.94	Irvine	Volunteer Rooms	St Andrew's SC
04.03.94	Weston super Mare	Winter Gardens	Queensberry SC
06.03.94	Southwark	Elephant & Castle Leisure Centre	Gee
07.03.94	Doncaster	Moat House Hotel	Rushton
08.03.94	Kettering	Reflection's Nightspot	Hall
08.03.94	Edgbaston	Tower Ballrooms	Cowdell
10.03.94	Watford	Town Hall	Holdsworth
10.03.94	Bristol	Whitchurch Sports Centre	Sanigar
11.03.94	Bethnal Green	York Hall	National Promotions
11.03.94	Glasgow	Hospitality Inn	Morrison
12.03.94	Cardiff	National Ice Rink	Warren
14.03.94	Mayfair	Marriott Hotel	National Promotions
15.03.94	Mayfair	Grosvenor House	Matchroom
15.03.94	Stoke	Moat House Hotel	Brogan
16.03.94	Birmingham	National Exhibition Centre	National Promotions
17.03.94	Lincoln	Drill Hall	Gray
19.03.94	Millwall	Football Ground	Matchroom
21.03.94	Glasgow	Forte Crest Hotel	St Andrew's SC
21.03.94	Bradford	Norfolk Gardens Hotel	Yorkshire Executive SC
22.03.94	Bethnal Green	York Hall	National Promotions
23.03.94	Cardiff	Star Leisure Centre	Maloney
23.03.94	Stoke	Trentham Gardens	North Staffs SC
28.03.94	Cleethorpes	Beachcomber Club	Frater
28.03.94	Musselburgh	Brunton Hall	St Andrew's SC
28.03.94	Birmingham	Grand Hotel	Cowdell
29.03.94	Bethnal Green	York Hall	Maloney
29.03.94	Wolverhampton	Park Hall Hotel	Wolverhampton SC
31.03.94	Bristol	Marriott Hotel	Sanigar

Date	Town	Venue	Promoters
05.04.94	Bethnal Green	York Hall	National Promotions
07.04.94	Walsall	Saddler's Club	Gray
09.04.94	Mansfield	Leisure Centre	Warren
09.04.94	Bethnal Green	York Hall	Matchroom
10.04.94	Glasgow	Forte Crest Hotel	St Andrew's SC
13.04.94	Glasgow	Kelvin Hall	National Promotions
14.04.94	Battersea	Town Hall	Carew
15.04.94	Hull	Ennardale Sports Centre	Gray
18.04.94	Walsall	Town Hall	Cowdell
18.04.94	Manchester	Piccadilly Hotel	Trickett
21.04.94	Hull	Willerby Manor Hotel	Pollard
21.04.94	Gateshead	Leisure Centre	Team Promotions
25.04.94	Bury	Castle Leisure Centre	Tara Boxing Promotions
25.04.94	Glasgow	Forte Crest Hotel	St Andrew's SC
26.04.94	Bethnal Green	York Hall	National Promotions
27.04.94	Bethnal Green	York Hall	Maloney
27.04.94	Solihull	Conference Centre	Midlands SC
28.04.94	Mayfair	Hilton Hotel	National Promotions
28.04.94	Hull	Royal Hotel	Hull & District SC
06.05.94	Liverpool	Everton Park Sports Centre	Vaughan
09.05.94	Bradford	Norfolk Gardens Hotel	Yorkshire Executive SC
10.05.94	Doncaster	Dome	Matchroom/Rushton
11.05.94	Sheffield	Ponds Forge Arena	Warren
11.05.94	Stevenage	Ice Bowl	National Promotions
13.05.94	Kilmarnock	Leisure Centre	Morrison
16.05.94	Cleethorpes	Winter Gardens	Gray
16.05.94	Morecambe	Carlton Club	Tara Boxing Promotions
16.05.94	Heathrow	Park Hotel	Holland H.
17.05.94	Kettering	Reflection's Club	Hall
20.05.94	Acton	Town Hall	Cameron
20.05.94	Neath	Glyn Clydach Hotel	Sporting Club of Wales
21.05.94	Belfast	King's Hall	Warren/Eastwood
22.05.94	Crystal Palace	National Sports Centre	Carew
23.05.94	Walsall	Town Hall	Cowdell/Gray/Matchroom
24.05.94	Sunderland	Crowtree Leisure Centre	St Andrew's SC/Matchroom
24.05.94	Leicester	Colloseum	Griffin
25.05.94	Stoke	Moat House Hotel	Brogan
25.05.94	Bristol	Colston Hall	Sanigar/Maloney
27.05.94	Ashford	Stour Centre	Uppercut Promotions
28.05.94	Queensway	Porchester Hall	Gee
02.06.94	Middleton	Civic Centre	Tara Boxing Promotions
02.06.94	Tooting	Leisure Centre	Anglo Swedish Promotions
04.06.94	Cardiff	National Ice Rink	Warren
06.06.94	Manchester	New Charity Hall	Jewish Blind Society
06.06.94	Glasgow	Forte Crest Hotel	St Andrew's SC
10.06.94	Glasgow	Hospitality Inn	Morrison
11.06.94	Bethnal Green	York Hall	Matchroom
13.06.94	Bradford	Norfolk Gardens Hotel	Yorkshire Executive SC
13.06.94	Liverpool	Devonshire House Hotel	Snagg
15.06.94	Southwark	Elephant & Castle Leisure Centre	Maloney
17.06.94	Plymouth	Mayfair Leisure Centre	Round One Boxing Promotions
25.06.94	Cullompton	Culm Valley Sports Centre	Van Bailey
28.06.94	Mayfair	Grosvenor House	Matchroom
28.06.94	Edgbaston	Tower Ballroom	Cowdell

Current British-Based Champions: Career Records

Shows the complete record of all British champions, or British boxers holding international championships, who have been active between 1 July 1993 and 30 June 1994. Names in brackets are real names, where they differ from ring names. The first place name given is the boxer's domicile. Boxers are either shown as self managed, or with a named manager. This information has been supplied by the BBBoC and is in accordance with their records at the time of going to press.

Henry Akinwande   Les Clark

Henry Akinwande
Lewisham. *Born* London, 12 October, 1965
European & Commonwealth Heavyweight
Champion. Ht. 6'7"
Manager M. Duff

04.10.89	Carlton Headley W CO 1 Kensington
08.11.89	Dennis Bailey W RSC 2 Wembley
06.12.89	Paul Neilson W RSC 1 Wembley
10.01.90	John Fairbairn W RSC 1 Kensington
14.03.90	Warren Thompson W PTS 6 Kensington
09.05.90	Mike Robinson W CO 1 Wembley
10.10.90	Tracy Thomas W PTS 6 Kensington
12.12.90	Francois Yrius W RSC 1 Kensington
06.03.91	J. B. Williamson W RSC 2 Wembley
06.06.91	Ramon Voorn W PTS 8 Barking
28.06.91	Marshall Tillman W PTS 8 Nice, France
09.10.91	Gypsy John Fury W CO 3 Manchester *(Elim. British Heavyweight Title)*
06.12.91	Tim Bullock W CO 3 Dussledorf, Germany
28.02.92	Young Joe Louis W RSC 3 Issy les Moulineaux, France
26.03.92	Tucker Richards W RSC 2 Telford
10.04.92	Lumbala Tshimba W PTS 8 Carquefou, France
05.05.92	Kimmuel Odum W DIS 6 Marseille, France
18.07.92	Steve Garber W RTD 2 Manchester

19.12.92	Axel Schulz DREW 12 Berlin, Germany *(Vacant European Heavyweight Title)*
18.03.93	Jimmy Thunder W PTS 12 Lewisham *(Vacant Commonwealth Heavyweight Title)*
01.05.93	Axel Schulz W PTS 12 Berlin, Germany *(Vacant European Heavyweight Title)*
06.11.93	Frankie Swindell W PTS 10 Sun City, South Africa
01.12.93	Biagio Chianese W RSC 4 Kensington *(European Heavyweight Title Defence)*
05.04.94	Johnny Nelson W PTS 10 Bethnal Green

Career: 24 contests, won 23, drew 1.

Francis Ampofo   Les Clark

Francis Ampofo
Bethnal Green. *Born* Ghana, 5 June, 1967
British Flyweight Champion. Former
Undefeated Commonwealth Flyweight
Champion. Ht. 5'1½"
Manager B. Hearn

30.01.90	Neil Parry W PTS 6 Bethnal Green
06.03.90	Robbie Regan L PTS 6 Bethnal Green
29.05.90	Eric George W RSC 3 Bethnal Green
12.09.90	Eric George W CO 2 Bethnal Green
26.03.91	Ricky Beard W PTS 8 Bethnal Green
22.06.91	Neil Johnston W RSC 2 Earls Court
03.09.91	Robbie Regan W RSC 11 Cardiff

	(British Flyweight Title Challenge)
17.12.91	Robbie Regan L PTS 12 Cardiff *(British Flyweight Title Defence)*
25.02.92	Ricky Beard W PTS 8 Crystal Palace
16.06.92	Shaun Norman RSC 4 Dagenham
12.12.92	James Drummond W PTS 12 Mayfair *(Vacant British Flyweight Title)*
17.02.93	Alberto Cantu W RSC 5 Bethnal Green
29.06.93	Albert Musankabala W RSC 3 Mayfair *(Vacant Commonwealth Flyweight Title)*
11.06.94	Jacob Matlala L RTD 9 Bethnal Green *(WBO Flyweight Title Challenge)*

Career: 14 contests, won 11, lost 3.

John Armour   Les Clark

John Armour
Chatham. *Born* Chatham, 26 October, 1968
Commonwealth Bantamweight Champion.
Ht. 5'4¾"
Manager Self

24.09.90	Lupe Castro W PTS 6 Lewisham
31.10.90	Juan Camero W RSC 4 Crystal Palace
21.01.91	Elijro Mejia W RSC 1 Crystal Palace
30.09.91	Pat Maher W CO 1 Kensington
29.10.91	Pete Buckley W PTS 6 Kensington
14.12.91	Gary Hickman W RSC 6 Bexleyheath
25.03.92	Miguel Matthews W PTS 6 Dagenham
30.04.92	Ndabe Dube W RSC 12 Kensington *(Vacant Commonwealth Bantamweight Title)*
17.10.92	Mauricio Bernal W PTS 8 Wembley
03.12.92	Albert Musankabala W RSC 6 Lewisham *(Commonwealth Bantamweight Title Defence)*

47

28.01.93 Ricky Romero W CO 1 Southwark
10.02.93 Morgan Mpande W PTS 12 Lewisham
(Commonwealth Bantamweight Title Defence)
09.06.93 Boualem Belkif W PTS 10 Lewisham
01.12.93 Karl Morling W CO 3 Kensington
14.01.94 Rufus Adebayo W RSC 7 Bethnal Green
(Commonwealth Bantamweight Title Defence)

Career: 15 contests, won 15.

Nigel Benn

Ilford. *Born* Ilford, 22 January, 1964
WBC S. Middleweight Champion. Former WBO & Commonwealth Middleweight Champion. Ht. 5'9½"
Manager Self

28.01.87 Graeme Ahmed W RSC 2 Croydon
04.03.87 Kevin Roper W RSC 1 Basildon
22.04.87 Bob Niewenhuizen W RSC 1 Kensington
09.05.87 Winston Burnett W RSC 4 Wandsworth
17.06.87 Reggie Marks W RSC 1 Kensington
01.07.87 Leon Morris W CO 1 Kensington
09.08.87 Eddie Smith W CO 1 Windsor
16.09.87 Winston Burnett W RSC 3 Kensington
13.10.87 Russell Barker W RSC 1 Windsor
03.11.87 Ronnie Yeo W RSC 1 Bethnal Green
24.11.87 Ian Chantler W CO 1 Wisbech
02.12.87 Reggie Miller W CO 7 Kensington
27.01.88 Fermin Chirinos W CO 2 Bethnal Green
07.02.88 Byron Prince W RSC 2 Stafford
24.02.88 Greg Taylor W RSC 2 Aberavon
14.03.88 Darren Hobson W CO 1 Norwich

20.04.88 Abdul Amoru Sanda W RSC 2 Muswell Hill
(Vacant Commonwealth Middleweight Title)
28.05.88 Tim Williams W RSC 2 Kensington
26.10.88 Anthony Logan W CO 2 Kensington
(Commonwealth Middleweight Title Defence)
10.12.88 David Noel W RSC 1 Crystal Palace
(Commonwealth Middleweight Title Defence)
08.02.89 Mike Chilambe W CO 1 Kensington
(Commonwealth Middleweight Title Defence)
28.03.89 Mbayo Wa Mbayo W CO 2 Glasgow
21.05.89 Michael Watson L CO 6 Finsbury Park
(Commonwealth Middleweight Title Defence)
20.10.89 Jorge Amparo W PTS 10 Atlantic City, USA
01.12.89 Jose Quinones W RSC 1 Las Vegas, USA
14.01.90 Sanderline Williams W PTS 10 Atlantic City, USA
29.04.90 Doug de Witt W RSC 8 Atlantic City, USA
(WBO Middleweight Title Challenge)
18.08.90 Iran Barkley W RSC 1 Las Vegas, USA
(WBO Middleweight Title Defence)
18.11.90 Chris Eubank L RSC 9 Birmingham
(WBO Middleweight Title Defence)
03.04.91 Robbie Sims W RSC 7 Bethnal Green
03.07.91 Kid Milo W RSC 4 Brentwood
26.10.91 Lenzie Morgan W PTS 10 Brentwood
07.12.91 Hector Lescano W CO 3 Manchester
19.02.92 Dan Sherry W RSC 3 Muswell Hill
23.05.92 Thulani Malinga W PTS 10 Birmingham

03.10.92 Mauro Galvano W RTD 3 Marino, Italy
(WBC S. Middleweight Title Challenge)
12.12.92 Nicky Piper W RSC 11 Muswell Hill
(WBC S. Middleweight Title Defence)
06.03.93 Mauro Galvano W PTS 12 Glasgow
(WBC S. Middleweight Title Defence)
26.06.93 Lou Gent W RSC 4 Earls Court
(WBC S. Middleweight Title Defence)
09.10.93 Chris Eubank DREW 12 Manchester
(WBC S. Middleweight Title Defence. WBO S. Middleweight Title Challenge)
26.02.94 Henry Wharton W PTS 12 Earls Court
(WBC S. Middleweight Title Defence)

Career: 41 contests, won 38, drew 1, lost 2.

Neville Brown   Les Clark

Neville Brown

Burton. *Born* Burton, 26 February, 1966
British Middleweight Champion. Ht. 5'10"
Manager M. Duff

08.11.89 Spencer Alton W RSC 4 Wembley
10.01.90 Colin Ford W RTD 4 Kensington
27.03.90 Jimmy McDonagh W RSC 2 Mayfair
09.05.90 William Pronzola W RSC 3 Wembley
13.09.90 Anthony Campbell W RSC 2 Watford
10.10.90 Nigel Moore W CO 1 Kensington
13.12.90 Chris Richards W RSC 2 Dewsbury
17.01.91 Shamus Casey W RSC 4 Alfreton
13.02.91 Jimmy Thornton W RSC 1 Wembley
28.03.91 Tony Booth W PTS 6 Alfreton
12.04.91 Winston Wray W RSC 1 Willenhall
04.07.91 Paul Wesley L RSC 1 Alfreton
29.08.91 Paul Smith W RSC 3 Oakengates
03.10.91 Paul Wesley W PTS 8 Burton
21.11.91 Colin Pitters W RSC 3 Burton
26.03.92 Paul Murray W CO 3 Telford
01.10.92 Ernie Loveridge W CO 4 Telford
02.11.92 Horace Fleary W PTS 8 Wolverhampton
04.12.92 Karl Barwise W RSC 6 Telford
20.01.93 Graham Burton W CO 4 Wolverhampton
16.03.93 Paul Busby W PTS 10 Wolverhampton
(Elim. British Middleweight Title)

Nigel Benn   Les Clark

10.11.93 Frank Grant W RSC 7 Bethnal Green
(British Middleweight Title Challenge)
26.01.94 Andrew Flute W RTD 7 Birmingham
(British Middleweight Title Defence)
16.03.94 Wallid Underwood W PTS 10
Birmingham
Career: 24 contests, won 23, lost 1.

Del Bryan   Les Clark

(Delroy) Del Bryan

Birmingham. *Born* Nottingham, 16 April, 1967
British Welterweight Champion. Former Undefeated Midlands Area Welterweight Champion. Ht. 5'8"
Manager W. Swift

21.04.86 Wil Halliday W PTS 6 Birmingham
15.05.86 Gary Sommerville L PTS 6 Dudley
28.05.86 Trevor Hopson W RTD 4 Lewisham
26.06.86 Gary Sommerville L PTS 8 Edgbaston
26.09.86 Gary Cass W PTS 6 Swindon
06.10.86 Gary Sommerville W PTS 8
Birmingham
14.10.86 Mickey Lerwill W PTS 8
Wolverhampton
04.11.86 George Collins L RSC 4 Oldham
16.12.86 Ray Golding W PTS 6 Alfreton
08.01.87 Darren Dyer W PTS 6 Bethnal Green
17.02.87 Tommy Shiels L RSC 2 Alfreton
30.09.87 Peter Ashcroft W PTS 8 Solihull
26.10.87 Gary Sommerville W RSC 7
Birmingham
(Vacant Midlands Area Welterweight Title)
03.12.87 Mickey Hughes W PTS 8 Southend
15.12.87 Lloyd Christie W PTS 8 Bradford
24.02.88 Gary Jacobs L PTS 10 Glasgow
(Final Elim. British Welterweight Title)
09.03.88 Michael Justin DREW 8 Wembley
20.04.88 Kelvin Mortimer W RSC 4 Stoke
04.05.88 Gary Sommerville W PTS 8 Solihull
09.08.88 Jimmy Thornton W PTS 6 St Helier
28.09.88 Ossie Maddix W PTS 8 Solihull
12.12.88 Michael Justin W RSC 8 Nottingham
(Midlands Area Welterweight Title Defence)

22.03.89 Lenny Gloster W PTS 8 Solihull
10.05.89 Crisanto Espana L PTS 8 Kensington
19.08.89 Javier Castillejos W PTS 8 Benidorm, Spain
04.09.89 Joni Nyman L PTS 8 Helsinki, Finland
30.01.90 Simon Eubank L PTS 8 Battersea
16.02.90 Arvey Castro W RSC 1 Bilbao, Spain
17.04.90 Damien Denny W PTS 10 Millwall
(Final Elim. British Welterweight Title)
30.09.90 Phumzile Madikane L RSC 6
Capetown, South Africa
16.01.91 Kirkland Laing W PTS 12
Wolverhampton
(British Welterweight Title Challenge)
16.04.91 Anthony Ivory W PTS 10 Nottingham
26.11.91 Mickey Hughes W RSC 3 Bethnal Green
(British Welterweight Title Defence)
20.02.92 Gary Jacobs L PTS 12 Glasgow
(British Welterweight Title Challenge)
12.05.92 Darren Dyer L RSC 10 Crystal Palace
29.09.92 Chris Peters W PTS 10 Stok
02.01.93 Godfrey Nyakana L PTS 8
Differdange, Luxembourg
05.05.93 Oscar Checca W CO 2 Belfast
11.08.93 Sidney Msutu W PTS 10 Durban,
South Africa
22.09.93 Pat Barrett W PTS 12 Bethnal Green
(Vacant British Welterweight Title)
17.02.94 Derek Grainger W CO 7 Dagenham
(British Welterweight Title Defence)
11.05.94 Paul Lynch W PTS 8 Sheffield
Career: 42 contests, won 30, drew 1, lost 11.

Cornelius Carr

(John) Cornelius Carr

Middlesbrough. *Born* Middlesbrough, 9 April, 1969
British S. Middleweight Champion. Ht. 5'9½"
Manager M. Duff

22.09.87 Paul Burton W RSC 5 Bethnal Green
28.11.87 Dave Heaver W RSC 2 Windsor
12.01.88 Shamus Casey W RSC 6 Cardiff
27.01.88 Kesem Clayton W PTS 6 Bethnal Green
29.03.88 Darren Parker W RSC 1 Bethnal Green

12.04.88 Franki Moro W PTS 6 Cardiff
10.05.88 Andy Catesby W RSC 5 Tottenham
15.11.88 Skip Jackson W CO 1 Norwich
20.12.88 Kevin Hayde W PTS 6 Swansea
22.03.89 Bocco George L RSC 3 Reading
24.10.89 Carlo Colarusso W RTD 4 Watford
20.02.90 Peter Gorny W RSC 4 Millwall
21.04.90 Franki Moro W PTS 8 Sunderland
26.09.90 John Maltreaux W CO 1 Metairie,
USA
27.10.90 Jerry Nestor W CO 1 Greenville, USA
16.02.91 Frank Eubanks W RSC 5 Thornaby
02.03.91 Carlo Colarusso W PTS 8 Darlington
18.05.91 Paul Burton W RSC 3 Verbania, Italy
06.09.91 Marvin O'Brien W RSC 7 Salemi,
Italy
29.10.92 Alan Richards W PTS 8 Bayswater
24.04.93 Graham Burton W PTS 6 Birmingham
19.05.93 Stan King W PTS 8 Sunderland
22.09.93 Horace Fleary W PTS 8 Wembley
11.03.94 James Cook W PTS 12 Bethnal Green
(British S. Middleweight Title Challenge)
Career: 24 contests, won 23, lost 1.

Steve Collins

Dublin. *Born* Dublin, 21 July, 1964
WBO Middleweight Champion. Former Undefeated USBA, WBO, Penta-Continental & All-Ireland Middleweight Champion. Ht. 5'11"
Manager Self

24.10.86 Julio Mercado W RSC 3 Lowell, USA
26.11.86 Mike Bonislawski W PTS 4
Dorchester, USA
20.12.86 Richard Holloway W RSC 2
Dorchester, USA
10.10.87 Jim Holmes W CO 1 Attleboro, USA
29.10.87 Harold Souther W PTS 8 Lowell, USA
20.11.87 Mike Williams W PTS 6 Atlantic City,
USA
09.12.87 Benny Sims W PTS 8 Atlantic City,
USA
18.03.88 Sammy Storey W PTS 10 Boston,
USA
(Vacant All-Ireland Middleweight Title)
26.05.88 Lester Yarborough W PTS 10 Boston,
USA
30.07.88 Mike Dale W PTS 8 Brockton, USA
22.10.88 Muhammad Shabbaz W RSC 4 Salem,
USA
10.12.88 Jesse Lanton W PTS 10 Salem, USA
07.02.89 Paul McPeek W RSC 9 Atlantic City,
USA
09.05.89 Kevin Watts W PTS 12 Atlantic City,
USA
(USBA Middleweight Title Challenge)
16.07.89 Tony Thornton W PTS 12 Atlantic
City, USA
(USBA Middleweight Title Defence)
21.11.89 Roberto Rosiles W RSC 9 Las Vegas,
USA
03.02.90 Mike McCallum L PTS 12 Boston,
USA
(WBA Middleweight Title Challenge)
16.08.90 Fermin Chirino W RSC 6 Boston, USA
24.11.90 Eddie Hall W PTS 10 Boston, USA
11.05.91 Kenny Snow W RSC 3 Belfast
22.05.91 Jean-Noel Camara W CO 3 Brest,
France
11.12.91 Danny Morgan W RSC 3 Dublin

22.04.92 Reggie Johnson L PTS 12 East Rutherford, USA
(Vacant WBA Middleweight Title)
22.10.92 Sumbu Kalambay L PTS 12 Verbania, Italy
(European Middleweight Title Challenge)
06.02.93 Johnny Melfah W RSC 3 Cardiff
20.02.93 Ian Strudwick W RSC 7 Kensington
26.06.93 Gerhard Botes W RSC 7 Kensington
(Vacant WBO Penta-Continental Middleweight Title)
30.11.93 Wayne Ellis W RSC 9 Cardiff
(WBO Penta-Continental Middleweight Title Defence)
22.01.94 Johnny Melfah W RSC 4 Belfast
09.02.94 Paul Wesley W PTS 8 Brentwood
11.05.94 Chris Pyatt W RSC 5 Sheffield
(WBO Middleweight Title Challenge)
Career: 31 contests, won 28, lost 3.

Steve Collins   Les Clark

Maurice Core (Coore)

Manchester. *Born* Manchester, 22 June, 1965
British L. Heavyweight Champion. Ht. 6'5"
Manager F. Warren

15.01.90 Dennis Banton W PTS 6 Mayfair
03.05.90 Everton Blake W PTS 8 Kensington
22.05.90 Nicky Piper DREW 6 St Albans
22.02.91 Everton Blake W RSC 8 Manchester
12.04.91 Glazz Campbell W CO 2 Manchester
31.05.91 Rodney Brown W RSC 6 Manchester
29.11.91 Steve Osborne W PTS 6 Manchester
31.01.92 Denroy Bryan W RSC 1 Manchester
05.04.92 Willie Ball W RSC 3 Bradford
18.07.92 Tony Booth W PTS 6 Manchester
28.09.92 Noel Magee W RSC 9 Manchester
(Vacant British L. Heavyweight Title)
05.02.93 Larry Prather W PTS 10 Manchester
25.07.93 John Kaighin W PTS 6 Oldham
01.12.93 Simon Harris W RSC 11 Bethnal Green
(British L. Heavyweight Title Defence)
Career: 14 contests, won 13, drew 1.

Maurice Core   Les Clark

(Andrew) Drew Docherty

Croy. *Born* Glasgow, 29 November, 1965
British Bantamweight Champion. Ht. 5'6"
Manager T. Gilmour

14.09.89 Gordon Shaw W PTS 6 Motherwell
23.11.89 Chris Clarkson W PTS 6 Motherwell
09.05.90 Rocky Lawlor DREW 8 Solihull
03.10.90 Steve Robinson W PTS 8 Solihull
21.11.90 Pete Buckley W PTS 8 Solihull
14.11.91 Stevie Woods W RSC 1 Edinburgh
27.01.92 Neil Parry W RSC 4 Glasgow
27.04.92 Pete Buckley W PTS 8 Glasgow
01.06.92 Joe Kelly W RSC 5 Glasgow
(British Bantamweight Title Challenge)
25.01.93 Donnie Hood W PTS 12 Glasgow
(British Bantamweight Title Defence)
26.04.93 Russell Davison W PTS 8 Glasgow

25.10.93 Pete Buckley W PTS 8 Glasgow
02.02.94 Vincenzo Belcastro L PTS 12 Glasgow
(European Bantamweight Title Challenge)
Career: 13 contests, won 11, drew 1, lost 1.

Chris Eubank

Brighton. *Born* Dulwich, 8 August, 1966
WBO S. Middleweight Champion. Former Undefeated WBO Middleweight Champion. Former Undefeated WBC International Middleweight Champion. Ht. 5'10"
Manager Self

03.10.85 Tim Brown W PTS 4 Atlantic City, USA
07.11.85 Kenny Cannida W PTS 4 Atlantic City, USA
08.01.86 Mike Bragwell W PTS 4 Atlantic City, USA
25.02.86 Eric Holland W PTS 4 Atlantic City, USA
25.03.87 James Canty W PTS 4 Atlantic City, USA
15.02.88 Darren Parker W RSC 1 Copthorne
07.03.88 Winston Burnett W PTS 6 Hove
26.04.88 Michael Justin W RSC 5 Hove
04.05.88 Greg George W RSC 5 Wembley
18.05.88 Steve Aquilina W RSC 4 Portsmouth
31.01.89 Simon Collins W RSC 4 Bethnal Green
08.02.89 Anthony Logan W PTS 8 Kensington
01.03.89 Franki Moro W PTS 8 Bethnal Green
26.05.89 Randy Smith W PTS 10 Bethnal Green
28.06.89 Les Wisniewski W RSC 2 Brentwood
04.10.89 Ron Malek W RSC 5 Basildon
24.10.89 Jean-Noel Camara W RSC 2 Bethnal Green
05.11.89 Johnny Melfah W CO 4 Kensington
20.12.89 Jose da Silva W RTD 6 Kirkby
16.01.90 Denys Cronin W RSC 3 Cardiff
06.03.90 Hugo Corti W RSC 8 Bethnal Green
(WBC International Middleweight Title Challenge)
25.04.90 Eduardo Contreras W PTS 12 Brighton
(WBC International Middleweight Title Defence)

Drew Docherty   George Ashton

05.09.90 Kid Milo W RSC 8 Brighton
(WBC International Middleweight Title Defence)
22.09.90 Reginaldo Santos W CO 1 Kensington
18.11.90 Nigel Benn W RSC 9 Birmingham
(WBO Middleweight Title Challenge)
23.02.91 Dan Sherry W TD 10 Brighton
(WBO Middleweight Title Defence)
18.04.91 Gary Stretch W RSC 6 Earls Court
(WBO Middleweight Title Defence)
22.06.91 Michael Watson W PTS 12 Earls Court
(WBO Middleweight Title Defence)
21.09.91 Michael Watson W RSC 12 Tottenham
(Vacant WBO S. Middleweight Title)
01.02.92 Thulani Malinga W PTS 12 Birmingham
(WBO S. Middleweight Title Defence)
25.04.92 John Jarvis W CO 3 Manchester
(WBO S. Middleweight Title Defence)
27.06.92 Ronnie Essett W PTS 12 Quinta do Lago, Portugal
(WBO S. Middleweight Title Defence)
19.09.92 Tony Thornton W PTS 12 Glasgow
(WBO S. Middleweight Title Defence)
28.11.92 Juan Carlos Giminez W PTS 12 Manchester
(WBO S. Middleweight Title Defence)
20.02.93 Lindell Holmes W PTS 12 Earls Court
(WBO S. Middleweight Title Defence)
15.05.93 Ray Close DREW 12 Glasgow
(WBO S. Middleweight Title Defence)
09.10.93 Nigel Benn DREW 12 Manchester
(WBO S. Middleweight Title Defence, WBC S. Middleweight Title Challenge)
05.02.94 Graciano Rocchigiani W PTS 12 Berlin, Germany
(WBO S. Middleweight Title Defence)
21.05.94 Ray Close W PTS 12 Belfast
(WBO S. Middleweight Title Defence)
Career: 39 contests, won 37. drew 2.

Chris Eubank   Les Clark

Ross Hale (centre), with Frank Maloney (left) and Chris Sanigar (right), proudly holds the Lonsdale Belt   Les Clark

Darren Fifield

Henley. *Born* Wantage, 9 October, 1969
Commonwealth Flyweight Champion. Ht. 5'2"
Manager F. Maloney

22.10.92 Glyn Shepherd DREW 4 Bethnal Green
10.12.92 Anthony Hanna W RSC 6 Bethnal Green
14.01.93 Graham McGrath W PTS 4 Mayfair
17.02.93 Kevin Jenkins DREW 6 Bethnal Green
14.04.93 Mickey Cantwell L PTS 10 Kensington
(Vacant Southern Area Flyweight Title)
28.08.93 Eric Burton W CO 1 Bismark, USA
13.10.93 Danny Porter W RSC 9 Bethnal Green
(Vacant Commonwealth Flyweight Title)
09.02.94 Danny Porter W RSC 6 Bethnal Green
(Commonwealth Flyweight Title Defence)
15.06.94 Ladislao Vazquez W RSC 4 Southwark
Career: 9 contests, won 6, drew 2, lost 1.

Darren Fifield   Les Clark

Ross Hale

Bristol. *Born* Bristol, 28 February, 1967
British & Commonwealth L. Welterweight Champion. Former Undefeated Western Area Welterweight Champion. Ht. 5'9"
Manager C. Sanigar

16.11.89 Dave Jenkins W PTS 6 Weston super Mare
30.11.89 Tony Gibbs W PTS 6 Mayfair
12.12.89 Chris McReedy W RSC 4 Brentford
13.03.90 Davey Hughes W RSC 3 Bristol
30.04.90 Andy Robins W RSC 4 Bristol
12.09.90 Derrick Daniel W PTS 6 Bethnal Green
21.11.90 Mark Kelly W PTS 8 Chippenham
29.11.90 Chris Saunders W PTS 6 Bayswater
24.10.91 Greg Egbuniwe W RSC 4 Bayswater
22.01.92 Tony Borg W PTS 6 Cardiff
30.04.92 Jason Matthews W RSC 3 Bayswater
12.05.92 John Smith W CO 1 Crystal Palace
07.07.92 Julian Eavis W RSC 8 Bristol
(Vacant Western Area Welterweight Title)
05.10.92 Malcolm Melvin W PTS 10 Bristol
(Elim. British L. Welterweight Title)
01.12.92 Sugar Gibiliru W RSC 1 Bristol
27.01.93 Andreas Panayi L RSC 3 Cardiff
26.06.93 Mark Antony W RSC 1 Keynsham
28.07.93 Gary Barron W CO 2 Brixton
01.10.93 Carlos Chase W RTD 8 Cardiff
(Elim. British L. Welterweight Title)
03.11.93 Regino Caceres W CO 2 Bristol
11.12.93 Stephen Schramm W RSC 4 Dusseldorf, Germany
22.01.94 Michael Driscoll W RSC 7 Cardiff
(Elim. British L. Welterweight Title)
25.05.94 Andy Holligan W RSC 3 Bristol
(British & Commonwealth L. Welterweight Title Challenge)
Career: 23 contests, won 22, lost 1.

Prince Nassem Hamed

Sheffield. *Born* Sheffield, 12 February, 1974
European Bantamweight Champion. Ht. 5'3"
Manager B. Ingle

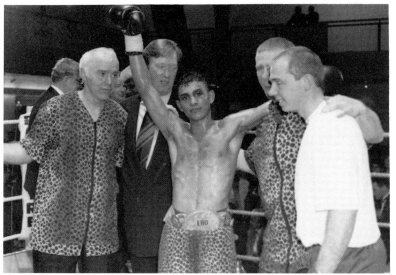

Prince Nassem Hamed acknowledges the crowd after winning the European Bantamweight title
Les Clark

14.04.92 Ricky Beard W CO 2 Mansfield
25.04.92 Shaun Norman W RSC 2 Manchester
23.05.92 Andrew Bloomer W RSC 2 Birmingham
14.07.92 Miguel Matthews W RSC 3 Mayfair
07.10.92 Des Gargano W RSC 4 Sunderland
12.11.92 Pete Buckley W PTS 6 Liverpool
24.02.93 Alan Ley W CO 2 Wembley
26.05.93 Kevin Jenkins W RSC 3 Mansfield
24.09.93 Chris Clarkson W CO 2 Dublin
29.01.94 Pete Buckley W RSC 4 Cardiff
09.04.94 John Miceli W CO 1 Mansfield
11.05.94 Vincenzo Belcastro W PTS 12 Sheffield
(European Bantamweight Challenge)
Career: 12 contests, won 12.

Billy Hardy
Les Clark

Billy Hardy

Sunderland. *Born* Sunderland, 15 September, 1964
British & Commonwealth Featherweight Champion. Former Undefeated British Bantamweight Champion. Ht. 5'6"
Manager T. Gilmour

21.11.83 Kevin Downer W PTS 6 Eltham
03.12.83 Brett Styles W PTS 6 Marylebone
27.01.84 Keith Ward W PTS 6 Longford
13.02.84 Johnny Mack W RSC 6 Eltham
01.03.84 Graham Kid Clarke W PTS 8 Queensway
27.03.84 Glen McLaggon W PTS 6 Battersea
06.04.84 Graham Kid Clarke W RSC 7 Watford
25.04.84 Anthony Brown W RSC 5 Muswell Hill
04.06.84 Roy Webb L PTS 6 Mayfair
06.09.84 Les Walsh W PTS 6 Gateshead
10.10.84 Jorge Prentas L RSC 5 Shoreditch
12.02.85 Ivor Jones W PTS 8 Kensington
17.04.85 Ivor Jones W PTS 10 Bethnal Green
08.06.85 Valerio Nati L RSC 4 Florence, Italy
10.10.85 Keith Wallace W RSC 7 Alfreton
(Final Elim. British Bantamweight Title)
02.06.86 Rocky Lawlor W PTS 8 Mayfair
19.02.87 Ray Gilbody W RSC 3 St Helens
(British Bantamweight Title Challenge)
23.04.87 Rocky Lawlor W RSC 7 Newcastle
04.06.87 Brian Holmes W PTS 10 Sunderland
17.03.88 John Hyland W CO 2 Sunderland
(British Bantamweight Title Defence)
11.05.88 Luis Ramos W RSC 2 Wembley
29.09.88 Jose Gallegos W RSC 4 Sunderland
02.11.88 Vincenzo Belcastro L PTS 12 Paolo, Italy
(European Bantamweight Challenge)
14.02.89 Ronnie Carroll W PTS 12 Sunderland
(British Bantamweight Title Defence)
29.03.89 Jose Soto W PTS 8 Wembley
28.06.89 Vincenzo Belcastro DREW 12 Pavia, Italy
(European Bantamweight Title Challenge)

10.10.89 Brian Holmes W CO 1 Sunderland
(British Bantamweight Title Defence)
24.01.90 Orlando Canizales L PTS 12 Sunderland
(IBF Bantamweight Title Challenge)
22.05.90 Miguel Pequeno W RSC 4 Stockton
29.11.90 Ronnie Carroll W RSC 8 Sunderland
(British Bantamweight Title Defence)
28.02.91 Francisco Ortiz W RSC 7 Sunderland
04.05.91 Orlando Canizales L RSC 8 Laredo, USA
(IBF Bantamweight Title Challenge)
03.03.92 Chris Clarkson W RSC 5 Houghton le Spring
07.10.92 Ricky Raynor W RSC 10 Sunderland
(Vacant Commonwealth Featherweight Title)
19.05.93 Barrington Francis W PTS 12 Sunderland
(Commonwealth Featherweight Title Defence)
15.06.93 Angel Fernandez W PTS 10 Hemel Hempstead
30.11.93 Mustapha Hame L PTS 8 Marseilles, France
24.05.94 Alan McKay W RSC 8 Sunderland
(Vacant British Featherweight Title)
Career: 38 contests, won 30, drew 1, lost 7.

Floyd Havard
Les Clark

Floyd Havard

Swansea. *Born* Swansea, 16 October, 1965
British S. Featherweight Champion.
Ht. 5'8"
Manager C. Breen

30.11.85 Dean Brahmald W RSC 3 Cardiff
22.01.86 Sugar Gibiliru W PTS 6 Muswell Hill
20.02.86 Dean Brahmald W PTS 6 Halifax
10.03.86 Russell Jones W PTS 8 Cardiff

28.04.86	Tony McLaggon W CO 2 Cardiff	
24.05.86	Sugar Gibiliru W PTS 8 Manchester	
20.09.86	George Jones W RSC 4 Hemel Hempstead	
25.10.86	Joe Duffy W RSC 3 Stevenage	
29.11.86	Marvin P. Gray W RSC 2 Wandsworth	
14.03.87	Nigel Senior W RSC 5 Southwark	
14.04.87	Ray Newby W RSC 7 Cumbernauld	
28.04.87	Hector Clottey W RSC 5 Halifax	
19.05.87	Kid Sumali W RTD 2 Cumbernauld	
22.09.87	Frank Loukil W RSC 4 Bethnal Green	
11.11.87	Cedric Powell W PTS 8 Usk	
12.01.88	Mario Salazar W RSC 2 Cardiff	
24.02.88	Richard Fowler W RSC 1 Aberavon	
20.04.88	Benji Marquez W PTS 8 Muswell Hill	
18.05.88	Pat Cowdell W RSC 8 Aberavon *(British S. Featherweight Title Challenge)*	
15.11.88	John Kalbhenn W PTS 10 Norwich	
11.04.89	Idabeth Rojas W PTS 10 Aberavon	
06.09.89	John Doherty L RTD 11 Aberavon *(British S. Featherweight Title Defence)*	
05.03.91	Tony Foster W PTS 8 Millwall	
29.10.91	Thunder Aryeh W RTD 6 Cardiff	
17.12.91	Patrick Kamy W DIS 5 Cardiff	
17.03.92	Harry Escott W RSC 7 Mayfair	
01.12.93	Harry Escott W PTS 8 Bethnal Green	
22.01.94	Juan Molina L RSC 6 Cardiff *(IBF S. Featherweight Title Challenge)*	
23.03.94	Neil Haddock W RSC 10 Cardiff *(British S. Featherweight Title Challenge)*	

Career: 29 contests, won 27, lost 2.

Herbie Hide

Norwich. *Born* Nigeria, 27 August, 1971
WBO Heavyweight Champion. Former
Undefeated British, WBC International &
WBA Penta-Continental Heavyweight
Champion. Ht. 6'1½"
Manager B. Hearn

24.10.89	L. A. Williams W CO 2 Bethnal Green
05.11.89	Gary McCrory W RTD 1 Kensington
19.12.89	Steve Osborne W RSC 6 Bethnal Green

Herbie Hide proudly displays his title belts   Les Clark

27.06.90	Alek Penarski W RSC 3 Kensington
05.09.90	Steve Lewsam W RSC 4 Brighton
26.09.90	Jonjo Greene W RSC 1 Manchester
17.10.90	Gus Mendes W RSC 2 Bethnal Green
18.11.90	Steve Lewsam W RSC 1 Birmingham
29.01.91	Lennie Howard W RSC 1 Wisbech
09.04.91	David Jules W RSC 1 Mayfair
14.05.91	John Westgarth W RTD 4 Dudley
03.07.91	Tucker Richards W RSC 3 Brentwood
15.10.91	Eddie Gonzalez W CO 2 Hamburg, Germany
29.10.91	Chris Jacobs W RSC 1 Cardiff
21.01.92	Conroy Nelson W RSC 2 Norwich *(Vacant WBC International Heavyweight Title)*
03.03.92	Percell Davis W CO 1 Amsterdam, Holland
08.09.92	Jean Chanet W RSC 7 Norwich

06.10.92	Craig Peterson W RSC 7 Antwerp, Belgium *(WBC International Heavyweight Title Defence)*
12.12.92	James Pritchard W RSC 2 Muswell Hill
30.01.93	Juan Antonio Diaz W RSC 3 Brentwood *(Vacant WBA Penta-Continental Heavyweight Title)*
27.02.93	Michael Murray W RSC 5 Dagenham *(Vacant British Heavyweight Title)*
11.05.93	Jerry Halstead W RSC 4 Norwich *(Penta-Continental Heavyweight Title Defence)*
18.09.93	Everett Martin W PTS 10 Leicester
06.11.93	Mike Dixon W RSC 9 Bethnal Green *(WBA Penta-Continental Heavyweight Title Defence)*
04.12.93	Jeff Lampkin W RSC 2 Sun City, South Africa *(WBC Heavyweight Title Defence)*
19.03.94	Michael Bentt W CO 7 Millwall *(WBO Heavyweight Title Challenge)*

Career: 26 contests, won 26.

Lloyd Honeyghan

Bermondsey. *Born* Jamaica, 22 April, 1960
Commonwealth L. Middleweight
Champion. Former WBC Welterweight
Champion. Former Undefeated WBA, IBF,
British, European, Commonwealth &
Southern Area Welterweight Champion.
Ht. 5'8½"
Manager Self

08.12.80	Mike Sullivan W PTS 6 Kensington
20.01.81	Dai Davies W RSC 5 Bethnal Green
10.02.81	Dave Sullivan W PTS 6 Bethnal Green
16.11.81	Dave Finigan W RSC 1 Mayfair
24.11.81	Alan Cooper W RSC 4 Wembley
25.01.82	Dave Finigan W CO 2 Mayfair
09.02.82	Granville Allen W RSC 5 Kensington
02.03.82	Tommy McCallum W PTS 6 Kensington

Lloyd Honeyghan (left), the current Commonwealth light-middleweight champion   Les Clark

53

15.03.82 Derek McKenzie W RSC 3 Mayfair
23.03.82 Dave Sullivan W RSC 3 Bethnal Green
18.05.82 Kostas Petrou W PTS 8 Bethnal Green
22.09.82 Kid Murray W RSC 3 Mayfair
22.11.82 Frank McCord W CO 1 Mayfair
18.01.83 Lloyd Hibbert W PTS 10 Kensington
 (*Elim. British Welterweight Title*)
01.03.83 Sid Smith W CO 4 Kensington
 (*Southern Area Welterweight Title Challenge & Elim. British Welterweight Title*)
05.04.83 Cliff Gilpin W PTS 12 Kensington
 (*Vacant British Welterweight Title*)
09.07.83 Kevin Austin W RSC 10 Chicago, USA
24.10.83 Harold Brazier W PTS 10 Mayfair
06.12.83 Cliff Gilpin W PTS 12 Kensington
 (*British Welterweight Title Defence*)
05.06.84 Roberto Mendez W PTS 8 Kensington
05.01.85 Gianfranco Rosi W CO 3 Perugia, Italy
 (*European Welterweight Title Challenge*)
12.02.85 R. W. Smith W RTD 6 Kensington
06.03.85 Roger Stafford W RSC 9 Kensington
30.08.85 Danny Paul W PTS 10 Atlantic City, USA
01.10.85 Ralph Twinning W RSC 4 Wembley
27.11.85 Sylvester Mittee W RSC 8 Muswell Hill
 (*European Welterweight Title Defence. British & Commonwealth Welterweight Title Challenge*)
20.05.86 Horace Shufford W RSC 8 Wembley
 (*Final Elim. WBC Welterweight Title*)
27.09.86 Don Curry W RTD 6 Atlantic City, USA
 (*World Welterweight Title Challenge*)
22.02.87 Johnny Bumphus W RSC 2 Wembley
 (*IBF Welterweight Title Defence*)
18.04.87 Maurice Blocker W PTS 12 Kensington
 (*WBC Welterweight Title Defence*)
30.08.87 Gene Hatcher W RSC 1 Marbella, Spain
 (*WBC Welterweight Title Defence*)
28.10.87 Jorge Vaca L TD 8 Wembley
 (*WBC Welterweight Title Defence*)
29.03.88 Jorge Vaca W CO 3 Wembley
 (*WBC Welterweight Title Challenge*)
29.07.88 Yung-Kil Chung W RSC 5 Atlantic City, USA
 (*WBC Welterweight Title Defence*)
05.02.89 Marlon Starling L RSC 9 Las Vegas, USA
 (*WBC Welterweight Title Defence*)
24.08.89 Delfino Marin W PTS 10 Tampa, USA
03.03.90 Mark Breland L RSC 3 Wembley
 (*WBA Welterweight Title Challenge*)
10.01.91 Mario Olmedo W RSC 4 Wandsworth
12.02.91 John Welters W RSC 1 Basildon
08.05.91 Darryl Anthony W CO 2 Kensington
22.04.92 Alfredo Ramirez W PTS 8 Wembley
13.05.92 Mick Duncan W RSC 2 Kensington
28.10.92 Carlo Colarusso W RSC 6 Kensington
30.01.93 Mickey Hughes W RSC 5 Brentwood
 (*Commonwealth L. Middleweight Title Challenge*)
26.06.93 Vinny Pazienza L RTD 10 Atlantic City, USA
02.11.93 Steve Goodwin W RSC 6 Southwark
26.02.94 Kevin Adamson W RSC 6 Earls Court
 (*Commonwealth L. Middleweight Title Defence*)

Career: 47 contests, won 43, lost 4.

Gary Jacobs

Glasgow. *Born* Glasgow, 10 December, 1965
European Welterweight Champion. Former Commonwealth Welterweight Champion. Former Undefeated British, WBC International & Scottish Welterweight Champion. Ht. 5'7½"
Manager M. Duff

20.05.85 John Conlan W PTS 6 Glasgow
03.06.85 Nigel Burke W PTS 6 Glasgow
12.08.85 Mike McKenzie W PTS 6 Glasgow
07.10.85 Albert Buchanan W PTS 6 Cambuslang
11.11.85 Tyrell Wilson W CO 5 Glasgow
02.12.85 Dave Heaver W PTS 6 Glasgow
10.02.86 Courtney Phillips W RSC 5 Glasgow
10.03.86 Alistair Laurie W PTS 8 Glasgow
14.04.86 Billy Cairns W PTS 8 Glasgow
24.06.86 Dave Douglas L PTS 10 Glasgow
 (*Vacant Scottish Welterweight Title*)
15.09.86 Jeff Connors W RSC 3 Glasgow
20.10.86 Kelvin Mortimer W RSC 5 Glasgow
27.01.87 Dave Douglas W PTS 10 Glasgow
 (*Scottish Welterweight Title Challenge*)
24.02.87 Gary Williams W CO 7 Glasgow
06.04.87 Robert Armstrong W RTD 5 Glasgow
19.05.87 Gary Williams W RSC 3 Cumbernauld
08.06.87 Tommy McCallum W RSC 5 Glasgow
 (*Scottish Welterweight Title Defence*)
26.11.87 Jeff Connors W PTS 8 Fulham
24.02.88 Del Bryan W PTS 10 Glasgow
 (*Final Elim. British Welterweight Title*)
19.04.88 Wilf Gentzen W PTS 12 Glasgow
 (*Commonwealth Welterweight Title Challenge*)
06.06.88 Juan Alonzo Villa W RSC 5 Mayfair
16.09.88 Javier Suazo W CO 10 Las Vegas, USA
 (*Vacant WBC International Welterweight Title*)
29.11.88 Richard Rova W CO 4 Kensington
 (*Commonwealth Welterweight Title Defence*)
14.02.89 Rocky Kelly W RTD 7 Wandsworth
 (*Commonwealth & WBC International Welterweight Title Defence*)
05.04.89 George Collins W PTS 12 Kensington
 (*Commonwealth & WBC International Welterweight Title Defence*)
27.06.89 Rollin Williams W RSC 1 Kensington
27.08.89 James McGirt L PTS 10 New York, USA
23.11.89 Donovan Boucher L PTS 12 Motherwell
 (*Commonwealth Welterweight Title Defence*)
26.04.90 Pascal Lorcy W RSC 2 Wandsworth
09.05.90 Mike Durvan W CO 1 Kensington
17.10.90 Mickey Hughes L CO 8 Bethnal Green
05.03.91 Kenny Louis W CO 2 Glasgow
20.11.91 Peter Eubank W PTS 8 Kensington
20.02.92 Del Bryan W PTS 12 Glasgow
 (*British Welterweight Title Challenge*)
25.03.92 Tommy Small W RSC 2 Kensington
22.04.92 Cirillo Nino W PTS 10 Wembley
09.07.92 Robert Wright W RSC 6 Glasgow
 (*British Welterweight Title Defence*)
16.10.92 Ludovic Proto L PTS 12 Paris, France
 (*Vacant European Welterweight Title*)
06.02.93 Ludovic Proto W RTD 9 Paris, France
 (*European Welterweight Title Challenge*)
19.05.93 Horace Fleary W RTD 4 Sunderland
22.09.93 Daniel Bicchieray W RSC 5 Wembley
 (*European Welterweight Title Defence*)
01.02.94 Tek Nkalankete W PTS 12 Paris, France
 (*European Welterweight Title Defence*)
13.04.94 Alessandro Duran W CO 8 Glasgow
 (*European Welterweight Title Defence*)

Career: 43 contests, won 38, lost 5.

Gary Jacobs

Lennox Lewis

Crayford. *Born* London, 2 September, 1965
WBC Heavyweight Champion. Former Undefeated British, European & Commonwealth Heavyweight Champion. Ht. 6'4¾"
Manager F. Maloney

27.06.89 Al Malcolm W CO 2 Kensington
21.07.89 Bruce Johnson W RSC 2 Atlantic City, USA
25.09.89 Andrew Gerrard W RSC 4 Crystal Palace
10.10.89 Steve Garber W CO 1 Hull
05.11.89 Melvin Epps W DIS 2 Kensington
18.12.89 Greg Gorrell W RSC 5 Kitchener, Canada
31.01.90 Noel Quarless W RSC 2 Bethnal Green
22.03.90 Calvin Jones W CO 1 Gateshead
14.04.90 Mike Simwelu W CO 1 Kensington
09.05.90 Jorge Dascola W CO 1 Kensington
20.05.90 Dan Murphy W RSC 6 Sheffield
27.06.90 Ossie Ocasio W PTS 8 Kensington
11.07.90 Mike Acey W RSC 2 Mississuaga, Canada
31.10.90 Jean Chanet W RSC 6 Crystal Palace
 (*European Heavyweight Title Challenge*)
06.03.91 Gary Mason W RSC 7 Wembley
 (*British Heavyweight Title Challenge. European Heavyweight Title Defence*)
12.07.91 Mike Weaver W CO 6 Lake Tahoe, USA
30.09.91 Glenn McCrory W CO 2 Kensington
 (*British & European Heavyweight Title Defence*)
23.11.91 Tyrell Biggs W RSC 3 Atlanta, USA
01.02.92 Levi Billups W PTS 10 Las Vegas, USA

Lennox Lewis   Les Clark

30.04.92 Derek Williams W RSC 3 Kensington
*(British & European Heavyweight Title
Defence. Commonwealth Heavyweight
Title Challenge)*
11.08.92 Mike Dixon W RSC 4 Atlantic City,
USA
31.10.92 Razor Ruddock W RSC 2 Earls Court
*(Final Elim. WBC Heavyweight Title &
Commonwealth Heavyweight Title
Defence)*
08.05.93 Tony Tucker W PTS 12 Las Vegas,
USA
(WBC Heavyweight Title Defence)
01.10.93 Frank Bruno W RSC 7 Cardiff
(WBC Heavyweight Title Defence)
06.05.94 Phil Jackson W RSC 8 Atlantic City
(WBC Heavyweight Title Defence)
Career: 25 contests, won 25.

Eamonn Loughran
Ballymena. *Born* Ballymena, 5 June, 1970
WBO Welterweight Champion. Former

Undefeated Commonwealth Welterweight
Champion. Ht. 5'9"
Manager B. Hearn

03.12.87 Adam Muir W DIS 4 Belfast
08.06.88 Tony Britland W RSC 1 Sheffield
25.06.88 Antonio Campbell DREW 4 Panama
City, Panama
19.10.88 Stan King W PTS 6 Belfast
19.09.89 Ricky Nelson W RSC 3 Belfast
31.10.89 Mark Pearce W PTS 6 Belfast
29.11.89 Ronnie Campbell W RSC 1 Belfast
24.11.90 Parrish Johnson W RSC 2
Benalmadena, Spain
12.12.90 Mike Morrison W PTS 6 Basildon
12.02.91 Nick Meloscia W CO 1 Cardiff
05.03.91 Julian Eavis W PTS 6 Cardiff
26.03.91 Stan Cunningham W RSC 2 Bethnal
Green
24.04.91 Kevin Plant W RTD 1 Preston
28.05.91 Terry Morrill W CO 1 Cardiff
03.09.91 Marty Duke W PTS 6 Cardiff

21.09.91 Glyn Rhodes W PTS 8 Tottenham
15.10.91 Juan Carlos Ortiz W PTS 8 Hamburg,
Germany
13.03.92 Tony Ekubia L DIS 5 Bury
(Elim. British Welterweight Title)
19.05.92 Kelvin Mortimer W RSC 1 Cardiff
29.09.92 Judas Clottey W PTS 8 Hamburg,
Germany
24.11.92 Donovan Boucher W RSC 3 Doncaster
*(Commonwealth Welterweight Title
Challenge)*
18.12.92 Desbon Seaton W RSC 2 Hamburg,
Germany
06.02.93 Michael Benjamin W RSC 6 Cardiff
*(Commonwealth Welterweight Title
Defence)*
16.10. 93 Lorenzo Smith W PTS 12 Belfast
(Vacant WBO Welterweight Title)
22.01.94 Alessandro Duran W PTS 12 Belfast
(WBO Welterweight Title Defence)
Career: 25 contests, won 23, drew 1, lost 1.

Eamonn Loughran   Pennie Cattle

Robert McCracken
Birmingham. *Born* Birmingham, 31 May,
1968
British L. Middleweight Champion. Ht.
6'0"
Manager M. Duff

24.01.91 Mick Mulcahy W RSC 1 Brierley Hill
13.02.91 Gary Barron W RTD 2 Wembley
06.03.91 Tony Britland W RSC 2 Wembley
12.04.91 Dave Andrews W RSC 4 Willenhall
08.05.91 Tony Gibbs W CO 1 Kensington
30.05.91 Paul Murray W RSC 2 Birmingham
04.07.91 Marty Duke W RSC 1 Alfreton
25.07.91 John Smith W RTD 1 Dudley
31.10.91 Newton Barnett W DIS 2 Oakengates
28.11.91 Michael Oliver W RSC 3 Liverpool
12.02.92 Paul Lynch W RSC 4 Wembley
01.10.92 Horace Fleary W PTS 8 Telford
02.11.92 Ensley Bingham W RSC 10
Wolverhampton
(Elim. British L. Middleweight Title)
20.01.93 Leigh Wicks W PTS 8 Wolverhampton

55

17.02.93 Ernie Loveridge W CO 4 Bethnal Green
24.04.93 Martin Smith W RSC 10 Birmingham
(Final Elim. British L. Middleweight Title)
29.06.93 Steve Langley W RSC 4 Edgbaston
01.12.93 Chris Peters W PTS 8 Kensington
23.02.94 Andy Till W PTS 12 Watford
(British L. Middleweight Title Challenge)
Career: 19 contests, won 19.

Robert McCracken   Les Clark

Steve Robinson

Cardiff. *Born* Cardiff, 13 December, 1968
WBO Featherweight Champion. Former
Undefeated Welsh Featherweight
Champion. Ht. 5'8"
Manager D. Gardiner

01.03.89 Alan Roberts W PTS 6 Cardiff
13.03.89 Terry Smith W RTD 4 Piccadilly
06.04.89 Nicky Lucas L PTS 8 Cardiff
04.05.89 John Devine W PTS 6 Mayfair
19.08.89 Marcel Herbert L PTS 6 Cardiff
13.11.89 Shane Silvester W RSC 2 Brierley Hill
10.07.90 Mark Bates L PTS 6 Canvey Island
12.09.90 Tim Driscoll L PTS 8 Bethnal Green
26.09.90 Russell Davison W PTS 8 Manchester
03.10.90 Drew Docherty L PTS 8 Solihull
22.10.90 Alan McKay L PTS 6 Mayfair
19.11.90 Neil Haddock W RSC 9 Cardiff
19.12.90 Brian Roche DREW 6 Preston
24.04.91 Russell Davison W RTD 6 Preston
28.05.91 Colin Lynch W RSC 6 Cardiff
18.07.91 Peter Harris W PTS 10 Cardiff
(Welsh Featherweight Title Challenge)
31.01.92 Henry Armstrong L PTS 6 Manchester
11.05.92 Neil Haddock L PTS 10 Llanelli
(Vacant Welsh S. Featherweight Title)
07.10.92 Edward Lloyd W RTD 8 Barry
30.10.92 Stephane Haccoun W PTS 8 Istres, France
01.12.92 Dennis Oakes W RTD 2 Liverpool
19.01.93 Paul Harvey W PTS 12 Cardiff
(Vacant WBA Penta-Continental Featherweight Title)

13.02.93 Medhi Labdouni L PTS 8 Paris, France
17.04.93 John Davison W PTS 12 Washington
(Vacant WBO Featherweight Title)
10.07.93 Sean Murphy W CO 9 Cardiff
(WBO Featherweight Title Defence)
23.10.93 Colin McMillan W PTS 12 Cardiff
(WBO Featherweight Title Defence)
12.03.94 Paul Hodkinson W CO 12 Cardiff
(WBO Featherweight Title Defence)
04.06.94 Freddy Cruz W PTS 12 Cardiff
(WBO Featherweight Title Defence)
Career: 28 contests, won 18, drew 1, lost 9.

Steve Robinson   Les Clark

Billy Schwer

Luton. *Born* Luton, 12 April, 1969
British & Commonwealth Lightweight
Champion. Ht. 5'8½"
Manager M. Duff

04.10.90 Pierre Conan W RSC 1 Bethnal Green

31.10.90 Mark Antony W RSC 2 Wembley
12.12.90 Sean Casey W RSC 1 Kensington
16.01.91 Dave Jenkins W PTS 6 Kensington
07.02.91 John Smith W RSC 2 Watford
06.03.91 Chubby Martin W RSC 3 Wembley
04.04.91 Andy Robins W RSC 2 Watford
17.04.91 Chris Saunders W RSC 1 Kensington
02.05.91 Karl Taylor W RSC 2 Northampton
30.06.91 Chris Saunders W RSC 3 Southwark
11.09.91 Tony Foster W PTS 8 Hammersmith
26.09.91 Felix Kelly W RSC 2 Dunstable
24.10.91 Patrick Kamy W CO 1 Dunstable
20.11.91 Marcel Herbert W PTS 8 Kensington
12.02.92 Tomas Quinones W CO 8 Wembley
25.03.92 Bobby Brewer W RSC 4 Kensington
03.09.92 Wayne Windle W CO 1 Dunstable
28.10.92 Carl Crook W RTD 9 Kensington
(British & Commonwealth Lightweight Title Challenge)
17.12.92 Mauricio Aceves W RSC 3 Wembley
24.02.93 Paul Burke L RSC 7 Wembley
(British & Commonwealth Lightweight Title Defence)
15.06.93 Farid Benredjeb W PTS 8 Hemel Hempstead
10.11.93 Paul Burke W PTS 12 Watford
(British & Commonwealth Lightweight Title Challenge)
16.02.94 Sean Murphy W RSC 3 Stevenage
(British & Commonwealth Lightweight Title Defence)
04.03.94 John Roby W RSC 2 Bethnal Green
22.03.94 Edgar Castro W CO 5 Bethnal Green
11.05.94 Howard Grant W RSC 9 Stevenage
(Commonwealth Lightweight Title Defence)
Career: 26 contests, won 25, lost 1.

(Adrian) Carl Thompson

Manchester. *Born* Manchester, 26 May, 1964
European Cruiserweight Champion. Former
Undefeated British & WBC International
Cruiserweight Champion. Ht. 6'0"
Manager N. Basso

06.06.88 Darren McKenna W RSC 2 Manchester
11.10.88 Paul Sheldon W PTS 6 Wolverhampton

Billy Schwer (left), shown here beating Carl Crook, regained the British and Commonwealth lightweight titles from Paul Burke during 1993-94   Les Clark

Carl Thompson   Harry Goodwin

13.02.89	Steve Osborne W PTS 6 Manchester	
07.03.89	Sean O'Phoenix W RSC 4 Manchester	
04.04.89	Keith Halliwell W RSC 1 Manchester	
04.05.89	Tenko Ernie W CO 4 Mayfair	
12.06.89	Steve Osborne W PTS 8 Manchester	
11.07.89	Peter Brown W RSC 5 Batley	
31.10.89	Crawford Ashley L RSC 6 Manchester	
	(Vacant Central Area L. Heavyweight Title)	
21.04.90	Francis Wanyama L PTS 6 St Amandsberg, Belgium	
07.03.91	Terry Dixon W PTS 8 Basildon	
01.04.91	Yawe Davis L RSC 2 Monaco, Monte Carlo	
04.09.91	Nicky Piper W RSC 3 Bethnal Green	
04.06.92	Steve Lewsam W RSC 8 Cleethorpes	
	(Vacant British Cruiserweight Title)	
17.02.93	Arthur Weathers W CO 2 Bethnal Green	
	(Vacant WBC International Cruiserweight Title)	
31.03.93	Steve Harvey W CO 1 Bethnal Green	
25.07.93	Willie Jake W CO 3 Oldham	

02.02.94	Massimiliano Duran W CO 8 Ferrara, Italy	
	(European Cruiserweight Title Challenge)	
14.06.94	Akim Tafer W RSC 6 Epernay, France	
	(European Cruiserweight Title Defence)	

Career: 19 contests, won 16, lost 3.

Richie Wenton

Liverpool. *Born* Liverpool, 28 October, 1967
British S. Bantamweight Champion. Ht. 5'8"
Manager F. Warren

14.12.88	Miguel Matthews W CO 2 Kirkby	
25.01.89	Sean Casey W PTS 4 Belfast	
10.04.89	Stuart Carmichael W RSC 2 Mayfair	
13.12.89	Joe Mullen W RSC 5 Kirkby	
21.02.90	Ariel Cordova W PTS 6 Belfast	
17.03.90	Mark Johnston W PTS 4 Belfast	

28.03.90	Jose Luis Vasquez W PTS 6 Manchester	
23.05.90	Graham O'Malley W PTS 6 Belfast	
09.07.90	Eugene Pratt W CO 1 Miami Beach, USA	
15.09.90	Graham O'Malley W PTS 6 Belfast	
30.10.90	Alejandro Armenta W RSC 2 Belfast	
12.02.91	Sean Casey W PTS 4 Belfast	
31.03.92	Graham O'Malley W PTS 6 Stockport	
25.07.92	Ramos Agare W RSC 3 Manchester	
26.09.92	Floyd Churchill L RSC 2 Earls Court	
28.04.93	Kelton McKenzie W PTS 8 Dublin	
13.11.93	Des Gargano W PTS 8 Cullompton	
26.04.94	Bradley Stone W RSC 10 Bethnal Green	
	(Vacant British S. Bantamweight Title)	

Career: 18 contests, won 17, lost 1.

Richie Wenton   Les Clark

Henry Wharton

York. *Born* Leeds, 23 November, 1967
Commonwealth S. Middleweight
Champion. Former Undefeated British S.
Middleweight Champion. Ht. 5'10½"
Manager M. Duff

21.09.89	Dean Murray W RSC 1 Harrogate	
25.10.89	Mike Aubrey W PTS 6 Wembley	
05.12.89	Ron Malek W RSC 1 Dewsbury	
11.01.90	Guillermo Chavez W CO 1 Dewsbury	
03.03.90	Joe Potts W CO 4 Wembley	
11.04.90	Juan Elizondo W RSC 3 Dewsbury	
18.10.90	Chuck Edwards W RSC 1 Dewsbury	
31.10.90	Dino Stewart W PTS 8 Wembley	
21.03.91	Francisco Lara W CO 1 Dewsbury	
09.05.91	Frankie Minton W CO 7 Leeds	
27.06.91	Rod Carr W PTS 12 Leeds	
	(Vacant Commonwealth S. Middleweight Title)	
30.10.91	Lou Gent DREW 12 Leeds	
	(Commonwealth S. Middleweight Title Defence)	
23.10.92	Nicky Walker W PTS 10 York	
19.03.92	Kenny Schaefer W CO 1 York	
08.04.92	Rod Carr W RSC 8 Leeds	
	(Commonwealth S. Middleweight Title Defence)	

23.09.92 Fidel Castro W PTS 12 Leeds
*(Commonwealth S. Middleweight Title
Defence. British S. Middleweight Title
Challenge)*
07.04.93 Ray Domenge W RSC 3 Leeds
01.07.93 Royan Hammond W RSC 3 York
07.10.93 Ron Amundsen W RSC 8 York
26.02.94 Nigel Benn L PTS 12 Earls Court
(WBC S. Middleweight Title Challenge)
Career: 20 contests, won 18, drew 1, lost 1.

Henry Wharton   Les Clark

Richie Woodhall

Telford. *Born* Birmingham, 17 April, 1968
Commonwealth Middleweight Champion.
Ht. 6'2"
Manager M. Duff

18.10.90 Kevin Hayde W RSC 3 Birmingham
30.11.90 Robbie Harron W RSC 2 Birmingham
16.01.91 Chris Haydon W RSC 3 Kensington
21.02.91 Shamus Casey W RSC 3 Walsall
30.05.91 Marty Duke W RSC 4 Birmingham
29.08.91 Nigel Moore W RSC 1 Oakengates
31.10.91 Colin Pitters W PTS 8 Oakengates
04.02.92 Graham Burton W RSC 2 Alfreton
26.03.92 Vito Gaudiosi W CO 1 Telford
*(Vacant Commonwealth Middleweight
Title)*
01.10.92 John Ashton W PTS 12 Telford
*(Commonwealth Middleweight Title
Defence)*
04.12.92 Horace Fleary W PTS 8 Telford
16.03.93 Carlo Colarusso W PTS 8
Wolverhampton
24.04.93 Royan Hammond W PTS 10
Birmingham
27.10.93 Garry Meekison W PTS 12 West
Bromwich
*(Commonwealth Middleweight Title
Defence)*
01.03.94 Heath Todd W RSC 7 Dudley
16.03.94 Greg Lonon W RSC 6 Birmingham
Career: 16 contests, won 16.

Richie Woodhall   Les Clark

Active British-Based Boxers: Career Records

Shows the complete record for all British-based boxers, excluding current champions, who have been active between 1 July 1993 and 30 June 1994. Names in brackets are real names, where they differ from ring names. The first place name given is the boxer's domicile. Boxers are either shown as self managed, or with a named manager. This information has been supplied by the BBBoC and is in accordance with their records at the time of going to press. Also included are foreign-born fighters who made their pro debuts in Britain, along with Roland Ericsson (Sweden), Chris Peters (South Africa) and Anthony Wanza (Trinidad), who although starting their careers elsewhere, now hold current BBBoC licenses.

Ojay Abrahams
Watford. *Born* Lambeth, 17 December, 1964
Welterweight. Ht. 5'8½"
Manager Self

21.09.91 Gordon Webster W RSC 3 Tottenham
26.10.91 Mick Reid W RSC 5 Brentwood
26.11.91 John Corcoran W PTS 6 Bethnal Green
21.01.92 Dave Andrews DREW 6 Norwich
31.03.92 Marty Duke W RSC 2 Norwich
19.05.92 Michael Smyth L PTS 6 Cardiff
16.06.92 Ricky Mabbett W PTS 6 Dagenham
13.10.92 Vince Rose L RSC 3 Mayfair
30.01.93 Vince Rose DREW 6 Brentwood
19.05.93 Ricky Mabbett L RSC 4 Leicester
18.09.93 Ricky Mabbett L PTS 6 Leicester
09.12.93 Nick Appiah W PTS 6 Watford
24.01.94 Errol McDonald W RSC 2 Glasgow
09.02.94 Vince Rose W PTS 6 Bethnal Green
23.05.94 Spencer McCracken L PTS 6 Walsall
11.06.94 Darren Dyer W RSC 1 Bethnal Green
Career: 16 contests, won 9, drew 2, lost 5.

Kevin Adamson
Walthamstow. *Born* Hackney, 19 February, 1968
L. Middleweight. Ht. 6'0½"
Manager Self

17.07.89 Carlton Myers W RSC 1 Stanmore
04.12.90 Darron Griffiths L RSC 4 Southend
12.11.91 Danny Shinkwin W RSC 4 Milton Keynes
30.04.92 Wayne Appleton W RSC 2 Bayswater
03.02.93 Joel Ani W RSC 6 Earls Court
27.02.93 Robert Whitehouse W RSC 1 Dagenham
31.03.93 Russell Washer W PTS 6 Barking
07.09.93 Bullit Andrews W PTS 6 Stoke
22.09.93 Russell Washer W PTS 6 Bethnal Green
27.10.93 Mick Duncan W RSC 3 Stoke
10.11.93 Clayon Stewart W RSC 1 Bethnal Green
01.12.93 Dave Maj W RSC 2 Stoke
19.01.94 Spencer Alton W RSC 1 Stoke
26.02.94 Lloyd Honeyghan L RSC 6 Earls Court
(Commonwealth L. Middleweight Title Challenge)
25.05.94 Chris Richards W RSC 2 Stoke
Career: 15 contests, won 13, lost 2.

Tanver Ahmed (Niazi)
Glasgow. *Born* Glasgow, 25 October, 1968
Lightweight. Ht. 5'10"
Manager T. Gilmour

22.10.92 John T. Kelly W PTS 6 Glasgow
01.12.92 Shaun Armstrong L PTS 6 Hartlepool
26.03.93 David Thompson W PTS 6 Glasgow

14.05.93 Dean Bramhald W PTS 6 Kilmarnock
09.09.93 Brian Wright W RTD 5 Glasgow
21.10.93 Martin Campbell W PTS 6 Glasgow
21.03.94 Chris Aston W CO 5 Glasgow
06.06.94 Chris Aston W CO 4 Glasgow
Career: 8 contests, won 7, lost 1.

Michael Alexander
Doncaster. *Born* Doncaster, 31 August, 1971
L. Welterweight. Ht. 5'9"
Manager T. Petersen

25.01.93 Tim Hill W PTS 6 Bradford
09.03.93 J. T. Kelly L PTS 6 Hartlepool
29.04.93 Pete Roberts W RSC 2 Hull
06.05.93 Ian Noble W PTS 6 Hartlepool
28.06.93 Mick Hoban W PTS 6 Morecambe
04.10.93 Micky Hall L CO 1 Bradford
28.11.93 Everald Williams L PTS 6 Southwark
28.02.94 Paul Hughes W PTS 6 Manchester
28.03.94 Laurence Roche W PTS 6 Cleethorpes
20.05.94 Andrew Morgan W PTS 6 Neath
13.06.94 Laurence Roche L PTS 6 Bradford
Career: 11 contests, won 7, lost 4.

Raziq Ali
Bradford. *Born* Wakefield, 14 September, 1972
L. Middleweight. Ht. 6'0"
Manager K. Tate

08.09.92 Wayne Panayiotiou W PTS 6 Doncaster
05.10.92 Sean Baker L PTS 6 Bristol
24.05.93 David Sumner W PTS 6 Bradford
25.04.94 Billy Collins L PTS 6 Glasgow
Career: 4 contests, won 2, lost 2.

Michael Alldis
Crawley. *Born* London, 25 May, 1968
S. Bantamweight. Ht. 5'6"
Manager B. Hearn

15.09.92 Ceri Farrell W RSC 3 Crystal Palace
10.11.92 Kid McAuley W PTS 6 Dagenham
12.12.92 Kid McAuley W CO 1 Muswell Hill
16.02.93 Ceri Farrell W CO 1 Tooting
29.06.93 Ady Benton L DIS 3 Mayfair
28.09.93 Alan Ley W PTS 6 Bethnal Green
06.11.93 Pete Buckley W PTS 8 Bethnal Green
09.04.94 Fernando Lugo W CO 1 Bethnal Green
11.06.94 Conn McMullen W PTS 8 Bethnal Green
Career: 9 contests, won 8, lost 1.

Adey Allen
Leicester. *Born* Leicester, 12 December, 1958
Welterweight. Former Midlands Area L.

Welterweight Champion. Ht. 5'8"
Manager J. Griffin

06.03.78 George Metcalf W RSC 3 Manchester
15.03.78 Gary Collins W PTS 6 Solihull
31.03.78 Brian Snagg W RSC 4 Liverpool
12.04.78 George Metcalf W PTS 4 Evesham
17.04.78 Steve Ward W PTS 6 Mayfair
08.05.78 Kevin Quinn W PTS 6 Manchester
07.09.78 Brian Snagg L PTS 6 Liverpool
18.09.78 George O'Neill L DIS 3 Wolverhampton
02.10.78 Granville Allen L PTS 8 Nantwich
27.11.78 Hugh Smith L PTS 8 Govan
11.09.79 Chris Sanigar L PTS 6 Wembley
15.10.79 Billy Ahearne W PTS 8 Manchester
15.11.79 Kevin Quinn W PTS 8 Caister
07.01.80 John Mount W PTS 8 Manchester
10.03.80 Jarvis Greenidge L PTS 6 Wolverhampton
21.04.80 Barry Price W PTS 8 Nottingham
08.05.80 Granville Allen L PTS 8 Solihull
08.07.80 Roger Guest W PTS 8 Wolverhampton
19.10.80 Roger Guest W PTS 10 Birmingham
(Midlands Area L. Welterweight Title Challenge)
13.11.80 Kevin Walsh W PTS 8 Caister
26.01.81 Kid Murray L PTS 8 Edgbaston
09.02.81 George Peacock L PTS 8 Glasgow
09.07.81 Mickey Baker W RSC 7 Dudley
(Midlands Area L. Welterweight Title Defence)
19.11.81 Alan Lamb W RSC 3 Morecambe
21.02.82 Chris Sanigar L RSC 7 Birmingham
05.10.83 Steve Early L PTS 10 Solihull
(Midlands Area L. Welterweight Title Defence)
14.02.84 Gerry Beard DREW 8 Wolverhampton
26.03.84 Lee McKenzie L PTS 8 Glasgow
19.10.93 Peter Reid L PTS 6 Cleethorpes
30.11.93 Kenny Scott W PTS 6 Leicester
Career: 30 contests, won 15, drew 1, lost 14

Mark Allen (Hodgson)
Denaby. *Born* Mexborough, 11 January, 1970
L. Welterweight. Ht. 5'11"
Manager J. Rushton

24.03.92 Jamie Morris L PTS 6 Wolverhampton
04.06.92 Blue Butterworth L RSC 5 Burnley
10.11.92 Bobby Guynan L RSC 2 Dagenham
09.12.92 Simon Hamblett DREW 6 Stoke
09.02.93 Simon Hamblett W PTS 6 Wolverhampton
23.02.93 Simon Hamblett L PTS 6 Doncaster
11.03.93 Jamie Morris DREW 6 Walsall
20.04.93 Paul Knights L PTS 6 Brentwood
06.05.93 Brian Coleman L PTS 6 Walsall
28.05.93 Nick Boyd L CO 2 Middleton
29.06.93 Robbie Sivyer W PTS 6 Edgbaston
14.08.93 Cham Joof L RSC 3 Hammersmith

59

28.10.93 Paul Bowen L RSC 2 Walsall
09.02.94 Paul Knights L RSC 2 Brentwood
18.04.94 Patrick Parton L PTS 6 Walsall
23.05.94 Patrick Parton L PTS 6 Walsall
13.06.94 James Jiora L PTS 6 Bradford
Career: 17 contests, won 2, drew 2, lost 13.

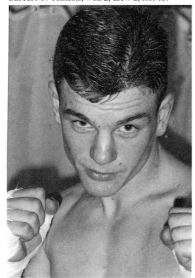

Mark Allen   Les Clark

Jimmy Alston

Preston. *Born* Preston, 2 February, 1967
L. Middleweight. Ht. 5'9"
Manager M. Chapman

07.12.92 Spencer Alton W PTS 6 Manchester
25.02.93 Crain Fisher L RTD 2 Burnley
22.04.93 Crain Fisher L PTS 6 Bury
02.12.93 Japhet Hans W PTS 6 Sheffield
18.02.94 Stuart Dunn L RSC 1 Leicester
18.04.94 Carl Smith W PTS 6 Manchester
06.06.94 Carl Smith DREW 6 Manchester
Career: 7 contests, won 3, drew 1, lost 3.

Spencer Alton

Derby. *Born* Derby, 4 October, 1966
S. Middleweight. Ht. 5'11"
Manager M. Shinfield

13.06.88 Ian Midwood-Tate W PTS 6 Manchester
10.07.88 Lou Ayres L PTS 6 Eastbourne
31.08.88 Ian Midwood-Tate L PTS 6 Stoke
30.09.88 Steve West L CO 3 Battersea
19.10.88 Wil Halliday W CO 6 Evesham
31.10.88 Michael Oliver W RSC 2 Leicester
14.11.88 G. L. Booth L RSC 7 Manchester
13.12.88 Paul Dolan W RTD 4 Glasgow
20.12.88 Wayne Ellis L RTD 4 Swansea
27.01.89 Neil Patterson W CO 1 Durham
31.01.89 Brian Robinson L PTS 6 Reading
15.02.89 Mark Holden DREW 6 Stoke
06.03.89 Mark Howell L PTS 8 Manchester
21.03.89 Ricky Nelson L PTS 6 Cottingham
04.04.89 Graham Burton L RSC 3 Sheffield
09.05.89 Wayne Ellis L RSC 3 St Albans
20.06.89 Peter Vosper L PTS 6 Plymouth
06.07.89 Ian Strudwick L PTS 8 Chigwell
26.09.89 Frank Eubanks W PTS 6 Oldham

10.10.89 Terry Morrill L PTS 6 Hull
17.10.89 Peter Vosper DREW 8 Plymouth
08.11.89 Neville Brown L RSC 4 Wembley
20.12.89 Mickey Morgan W RSC 5 Swansea
15.01.90 Andy Marlow DREW 6 Northampton
30.01.90 Darren Pilling L PTS 6 Manchester
13.02.90 Colin Pitters W PTS 6 Wolverhampton
26.02.90 Antoine Tarver L PTS 4 Crystal Palace
22.03.90 Richard Carter L PTS 6 Wolverhampton
24.05.90 Andrew Flute W RSC 1 Dudley
21.06.90 Paul Murray W PTS 6 Alfreton
10.09 92 Dave Johnson L PTS 6 Sunderland
23.10.92 Terry French L PTS 6 Gateshead
07.12.92 Jimmy Alston L PTS 6 Manchester
02.02.93 Chris Mulcahy W RSC 3 Derby
09.03.93 Mark Jay L RSC 4 Hartlepool
08.06.93 Eddie Collins W PTS 6 Derby
20.09.93 Sean Byrne L PTS 6 Northampton
03.11.93 Paul Busby L RTD 4 Worcester
16.12.93 Joe Calzaghe L RSC 2 Newport
19.01.94 Kevin Adamson L RSC 1 Stoke
28.03.94 Willie Quinn L RTD 3 Musselburgh
13.06.94 Craig Joseph L PTS 6 Bradford
Career: 42 contests, won 12, drew 3, lost 27.

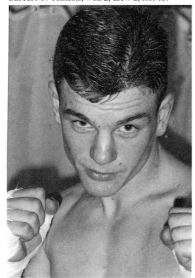

Trevor Ambrose   Les Clark

Trevor Ambrose

Leicester. *Born* Leicester, 8 September, 1963
S. Middleweight. Ht. 5'11"
Manager J. Bishop

19.02.90 Ian Thomas L RSC 3 Kettering
06.04.90 Colin Pitters W PTS 6 Telford
24.04.90 Barry Messam W RSC 4 Stoke
14.05.90 Gordon Blair L CO 5 Northampton
12.09.90 Dave Fallon W CO 3 Battersea
23.10.90 David Lake W PTS 6 Leicester
04.11.90 Eddie King W RSC 3 Doncaster
21.11.90 Andreas Panayi W RSC 5 Solihull
14.02.91 Adrian Riley W CO 6 Southampton
28.03.91 Richard O'Brien W RSC 1 Alfreton
25.04.91 Gary Logan L PTS 8 Mayfair
03.07.91 Darren Dyer L PTS 6 Brentwood
24.09.91 Willie Beattie L PTS 8 Glasgow
11.03.92 John Davies L RSC 5 Cardiff

19.05.92 Paul Jones L PTS 6 Cardiff
19.03.93 Errol Christie W CO 2 Manchester
10.07.93 Nicky Piper L RSC 5 Cardiff
30.09.93 Simon Harris L PTS 6 Hayes
27.11.93 Cesar Kazadi L CO 4 Echirofles, France
23.02.94 W. O. Wilson W RSC 5 Watford
06.03.94 Ray Webb L RSC 6 Southwark
14.05.94 Bernard Bonzon L PTS 8 Sierre, Switzerland
04.06.94 Zdravco Kostic L RSC 4 Paris, France
Career: 23 contests, won 10, lost 13.

Dean Amory

Birmingham. *Born* Marston Green, 2 July, 1969
Lightweight. Ht. 5'7"
Manager W. Swift

21.10.92 Brian Hickey W PTS 6 Stoke
20.01.93 Dean Bramhald W PTS 6 Solihull
28.04.93 Elvis Parsley W PTS 6 Solihull
19.05.93 Neil Smith W PTS 6 Leicester
19.12.93 Alan McDowall L PTS 8 Glasgow
26.01.94 Kevin McKillan L PTS 8 Stoke
Career: 6 contests, won 4, lost 2.

Derek Amory

Birmingham. *Born* Birmingham, 12 January, 1966
S. Featherweight. Ht. 5'5"
Manager Self

25.09.86 Roy Williams W CO 2 Wolverhampton
23.10.86 Shane Porter DREW 6 Birmingham
03.11.86 Mark Bignell W RSC 1 Edgbaston
18.11.86 Carl Parry L PTS 6 Swansea
26.01.87 Tony Heath W PTS 8 Nottingham
10.03.87 Mike Whalley L RSC 2 Manchester
09.05.87 Sean Murphy L RSC 2 Wandsworth
30.09.87 Lambsy Kayani DREW 8 Solihull
18.11.87 Carl Parry W PTS 8 Solihull
07.12.87 Graham O'Malley W PTS 8 Birmingham
14.12.87 Craig Windsor L PTS 6 Edgbaston
20.01.88 Lambsy Kayani W PTS 8 Solihull
24.02.88 Tony Heath W PTS 8 Leicester
17.06.88 John Hyland W RSC 3 Edgbaston
28.09.88 Colin Lynch L PTS 10 Solihull
(Vacant Midlands Area Featherweight Title)
27.10.88 Dave George W PTS 8 Birmingham
15.11.88 Joe Donohoe L PTS 8 Piccadilly
23.11.88 Patrick Kamy L RSC 2 Solihull
25.01.89 Russell Davison L PTS 8 Solihull
01.03.89 Henry Armstrong L PTS 8 Stoke
10.05.89 Peter English L PTS 8 Solihull
04.10.89 Mark Holt L PTS 10 Solihull
(Midlands Area Featherweight Title Challenge)
30.04.90 Peter Judson W PTS 6 Brierley Hill
03.09.90 Miguel Matthews W PTS 6 Dudley
24.09.90 Noel Carroll L PTS 8 Manchester
08.10.90 James Drummond W PTS 8 Cleethorpes
15.10.90 Jamie McBride W RTD 4 Brierley Hill
13.12.90 Darren Elsdon L PTS 6 Hartlepool
29.01.91 Carl Roberts W PTS 4 Stockport
18.03.91 Joe Donohoe L PTS 8 Piccadilly
17.06.91 Kelton McKenzie L RSC 6 Edgbaston
07.10.91 Ervine Blake L PTS 6 Birmingham
22.01.92 J. T. Williams L PTS 6 Cardiff
11.02.92 Jimmy Clark L PTS 6 Barking

09.05.92 Luis Ramon Rolon L CO 7 Madrid, Spain
28.10.92 Barrie Kelley L PTS 6 Cardiff
29.01.93 Edward Cook W PTS 6 Glasgow
20.02.93 Tim Driscoll L PTS 8 Earls Court
04.03.93 Edward Cook W RSC 4 Glasgow
26.04.93 Henry Armstrong L PTS 6 Manchester
28.11.93 Justin Juuko L RSC 1 Southwark
22.01.94 Jonjo Irwin W RSC 2 Belfast
04.03.94 Yifru Retta L RSC 1 Bethnal Green
06.05.94 Gary Thornhill L RSC 1 Liverpool

Career: 44 contests, won 17, drew 2, lost 25.

Colin Anderson

Leicester. *Born* Leicester, 7 June, 1962
Welterweight. Ht. 5'9"
Manager J. Griffin

30.09.83 Wayne Trigg W PTS 4 Leicester
14.02.84 Peter Bowen W PTS 6 Wolverhampton
20.02.84 Nicky Day DREW 6 Mayfair
15.03.84 Wayne Trigg L RSC 2 Leicester
01.10.84 Joey Morris L PTS 6 Leicester
02.12.92 Chris Mulcahy L PTS 6 Bardon
26.04.93 Warren Bowers L RSC 5 Cleethorpes
22.09.93 Kenny Scott W PTS 6 Chesterfield
30.11.93 Steve Howden L PTS 6 Leicester

Career: 9 contests, won 3, drew 1, lost 5.

Dave Anderson

Bellahouston. *Born* Glasgow, 23 December, 1966
Lightweight. Ht. 5'8"
Manager Self

25.09.90 Junaido Musah W RSC 3 Glasgow
09.10.90 Alan Peacock W RSC 3 Glasgow
10.12.90 Chris Bennett W RSC 7 Glasgow
11.02.91 Steve Pollard W PTS 6 Glasgow
15.04.91 Tony Foster W PTS 8 Glasgow
24.09.91 Ian Honeywood W PTS 8 Glasgow
28.11.91 Pete Roberts W RSC 3 Glasgow
11.09.92 Kevin Toomey W PTS 8 Glasgow
22.10.92 Kevin McKenzie W RSC 3 Glasgow
10.06.94 Peter Till W PTS 6 Glasgow

Career: 10 contests, won 10.

Shaun Anderson

Maybole. *Born* Girvan, 20 September, 1969
Bantamweight. Ht. 5'5"
Manager A. Melrose

29.05.92 Tucker Thomas W RSC 1 Glasgow
11.09.92 Mark Hargreaves W PTS 6 Glasgow
10.12.92 Graham McGrath W PTS 6 Glasgow
29.01.93 Graham McGrath W PTS 6 Glasgow
26.03.93 Dave Campbell W RSC 5 Glasgow
30.04.93 Paul Kelly W RSC 5 Glasgow
14.05.93 Kid McAuley W PTS 8 Kilmarnock
29.05.93 Ronnie Stephenson W PTS 6 Paisley
09.09.93 Graham McGrath W PTS 6 Glasgow
19.12.93 Pete Buckley W PTS 6 Glasgow
13.04.94 Paul Wynn DREW 6 Glasgow
13.05.94 Paul Wynn L PTS 8 Kilmarnock

Career: 12 contests, won 10, drew 1, lost 1.

(Alfie) Bullit Andrews

Birmingham. *Born* Birmingham, 29 April, 1964
S. Middleweight. Ht. 5'10"
Manager Self

11.10.88 Mohammed Ayub W PTS 6 Wolverhampton

22.11.88 Frank Graham L RSC 6 Wolverhampton
01.03.89 Peter Reid L RSC 2 Stoke
08.05.89 Ernie Loveridge L PTS 6 Edgbaston
02.10.89 Paul Walters L RSC 5 Hanley
13.11.89 Andre Wharton L PTS 6 Brierley Hill
05.02.90 Andre Wharton L RSC 4 Brierley Hill
04.06.90 Dave Whittle L PTS 6 Edgbaston
08.10.90 Tony Booth L RSC 3 Cleethorpes
13.11.90 Wayne Appleton L RSC 5 Edgbaston
15.04.91 Scott Newman L RSC 1 Wolverhampton
30.05.91 Darren Morris L RSC 3 Birmingham
21.05.92 Warren Stephens W PTS 6 Cradley Heath
30.10.92 Warren Stephens W PTS 6 Birmingham
04.03.93 Kevin Mabbutt L PTS 6 Peterborough
29.03.93 Andrew Jervis L PTS 6 Liverpool
19.04.93 Steve Levene L PTS 6 Northampton
26.04.93 Steve McNess L RSC 3 Lewisham
07.06.93 Gary Osborne L RSC 1 Walsall
07.09.93 Kevin Adamson L PTS 6 Stoke
20.09.93 Kevin Burton L PTS 6 Cleethorpes
13.10.93 Danny Shinkwin L PTS 6 Watford
28.10.93 Joff Pugh L PTS 6 Torquay
13.11.93 Carl van Bailey L PTS 6 Cullompton
25.11.93 Dave Whittle L PTS 6 Newcastle
06.12.93 Steve Levene L RSC 6 Birmingham
17.02.94 Steve Levene L PTS 6 Walsall
07.03.94 Kevin Burton L RSC 1 Doncaster

Career: 28 contests, won 3, lost 25.

Dennis Andries

Hackney. *Born* Guyana, 5 November, 1953
Cruiserweight. Former WBC L. Heavyweight Champion. Former Undefeated WBC Continental L. Heavyweight Champion. Former Undefeated British & Southern Area L. Heavyweight Champion. Ht. 5'11"
Manager E. Steward

16.05.78 Ray Pearce W CO 2 Newport
01.06.78 Mark Seabrook W RSC 1 Heathrow
20.06.78 Bonny McKenzie L PTS 8 Southend
18.09.78 Ken Jones W PTS 6 Mayfair
31.10.78 Neville Estaban W PTS 6 Barnsley
14.11.78 Les McAteer DREW 8 Birkenhead
22.11.78 Glen McEwan W RSC 7 Stoke
04.12.78 Tom Collins W PTS 8 Southend
22.01.79 Bunny Johnson L PTS 10 Wolverhampton
30.01.79 Tom Collins W CO 6 Southend
05.04.79 Francis Hand W RSC 8 Liverpool
06.06.79 Bonny McKenzie W PTS 8 Burslem
17.09.79 Johnny Waldron W RTD 10 Mayfair
(Southern Area L. Heavyweight Title Challenge)
27.02.80 Bunny Johnson L PTS 15 Burslem
(British L. Heavyweight Title Challenge)
17.04.80 Mustafa Wasajja L PTS 8 Copenhagen, Denmark
18.06.80 Chris Lawson W RSC 8 Burslem
23.03.81 Shaun Chalcraft W PTS 10 Mayfair
(Southern Area L. Heavyweight Title Challenge)
16.09.81 Liam Coleman W RSC 6 Burslem
12.10.81 David Pearce L RSC 7 Bloomsbury
23.11.81 Alek Penarski W PTS 10 Chesterfield
15.03.82 Tom Collins L PTS 15 Bloomsbury
(Vacant British L. Heavyweight Title)
10.08.82 Keith Bristol W PTS 10 Strand
(Southern Area L. Heavyweight Title Defence)
28.02.83 Karl Canwell W CO 4 Strand
(Southern Area L. Heavyweight Title Defence & Elim. British L. Heavyweight Title)
19.05.83 Chris Lawson W CO 4 Queensway
22.09.83 Keith Bristol W CO 4 Strand
(Southern Area L. Heavyweight Title Defence & Elim. British L. Heavyweight Title)

Dennis Andries (right), pictured against Jeff Harding, has now clocked up 58 contests in a career that began in May 1978
Peter Goldfield

26.01.84	Tom Collins W PTS 12 Strand *(British L. Heavyweight Title Challenge)*
06.04.84	Tom Collins W PTS 12 Watford *(British L. Heavyweight Title Defence)*
10.10.84	Devon Bailey W CO 12 Shoreditch *(British L. Heavyweight Title Defence)*
23.03.85	Jose Seys W RSC 3 Strand
07.05.85	Jeff Meacham W CO 4 New Orleans, USA
25.05.85	Tim Broady W RSC 5 Atlantic City, USA
06.06.85	Marcus Dorsey W CO 3 Lafayette, USA
11.12.85	Alex Blanchard DREW 12 Fulham *(European L. Heavyweight Title Challenge)*
13.02.86	Keith Bristol W RSC 6 Longford *(British L. Heavyweight Title Defence)*
30.04.86	J. B. Williamson W PTS 12 Edmonton *(WBC L. Heavyweight Title Challenge)*
10.09.86	Tony Sibson W RSC 9 Muswell Hill *(WBC & British L. Heavyweight Title Defence)*
07.03.87	Thomas Hearns L RSC 10 Detroit, USA *(WBC L. Heavyweight Title Defence)*
06.10.87	Robert Folley W PTS 10 Phoenix, USA
20.02.88	Jamie Howe W PTS 10 Detroit, USA
22.05.88	Bobby Czyz W PTS 10 Atlantic City, USA
10.09.88	Tony Harrison W RTD 7 Detroit, USA
17.10.88	Paul Maddison W RSC 4 Tucson, USA
21.02.89	Tony Willis W RSC 5 Tucson, USA *(Vacant WBC L. Heavyweight Title)*
24.06.89	Jeff Harding L RSC 12 Atlantic City, USA *(WBC L. Heavyweight Title Defence)*
26.10.89	Art Jimmerson W PTS 10 Atlantic City, USA
20.01.90	Clarismundo Silva W RSC 7 Auburn Hills, USA *(Vacant WBC Continental L. Heavyweight Title)*
28.07.90	Jeff Harding W CO 7 Melbourne, Australia *(WBC L. Heavyweight Title Challenge)*
10.10.90	Sergio Merani W RTD 4 Kensington *(WBC L. Heavyweight Title Defence)*
19.01.91	Guy Waters W PTS 12 Adelaide, Australia *(WBC L. Heavyweight Title Defence)*
11.09.91	Jeff Harding L PTS 12 Hammersmith *(WBC L. Heavyweight Title Defence)*
15.11.91	Ed Neblett W RSC 4 Tampa, USA
11.12.91	Paul Maddison W RTD 8 Duluth, USA
27.02.92	Akim Tafer L PTS 12 Beausoleil, France *(Vacant European Cruiserweight Title)*
27.02.93	David Sewell W PTS 10 Dagenham
31.03.93	Willie Jake W RTD 6 Barking
29.01.94	Crawford Ashley W RTD 4 Cardiff
26.02.94	Mike Peak W PTS 4 Earls Court
23.03.94	Chemek Saleta L PTS 12 Cardiff *(Vacant WBC International Cruiserweight Title)*

Career: 58 contests, won 45, drew 2, lost 11.

Mark Antony (Brooks)

Doncaster. *Born* Worksop, 24 January, 1968
Welterweight. Ht. 5'8"
Manager Self

16.11.87	Robbie Bowen L CO 5 Stratford on Avon
22.03.88	Paul Bowen L RSC 3 Wolverhampton
14.11.88	Phil Lashley W RSC 2 Stratford on Avon
21.11.88	Paul Chedgzoy W CO 2 Leicester
01.12.88	Andrew Robinson W PTS 6 Stafford
14.12.88	Paul Bowen L PTS 6 Evesham
02.02.89	Shaun Cooper L CO 3 Wolverhampton
20.04.89	Andrew Brightman W PTS 6 Weston super Mare
17.05.89	Mark Tibbs L PTS 6 Millwall
29.05.89	Mike Close L PTS 6 Liverpool
04.09.89	Warren Bowers L PTS 6 Grimsby
04.10.89	Karl Taylor L CO 2 Stratford
06.12.89	Peter Bowen L PTS 6 Stoke
13.02.90	Peter Bowen W RSC 1 Wolverhampton
07.03.90	Stuart Rimmer W RSC 1 Doncaster
21.03.90	Nick Hall L PTS 6 Solihull
27.03.90	Shaun Cogan L CO 1 Wolverhampton
21.05.90	Tony Feliciello L RTD 2 Grimsby
21.06.90	Andrew Robinson W PTS 6 Alfreton
31.10.90	Billy Schwer L RSC 2 Wembley
03.12.90	Nigel Senior W PTS 8 Cleethorpes
12.12.90	Richard Woolgar L RSC 5 Basildon
05.03.91	Jim Moffat L PTS 6 Glasgow
12.03.91	Wayne Windle L CO 1 Mansfield
12.11.91	Shaun Cooper L CO 1 Wolverhampton
20.01.92	Jamie Morris W RSC 5 Coventry
11.02.92	Billy Robinson L RSC 5 Wolverhampton
11.03.92	Simon Hamblett W CO 1 Stoke
11.05.92	Pat Delargy L PTS 6 Coventry
04.06.92	Darren Powell W CO 2 Burnley
23.11.92	Darren McInulty L PTS 6 Coventry
07.12.92	Spencer McCracken L CO 1 Birmingham
30.04.93	Colin Wallace L PTS 6 Glasgow
18.05.93	Steve Levene L RSC 1 Edgbaston
29.05.93	Steve Boyle L PTS 6 Paisley
17.06.93	Darren McInulty W CO 2 Bedworth
26.06.93	Ross Hale L RSC 1 Keynsham
25.10.93	Shea Neary L RSC 1 Liverpool
01.12.93	P. J. Gallagher L PTS 4 Bethnal Green
11.12.93	Tony Mock L RSC 4 Liverpool
11.01.94	Patrick Gallagher L RSC 3 Bethnal Green
09.02.94	Bobby Guynan L DIS 5 Brentwood
11.03.94	Allan Logan L PTS 6 Glasgow
28.03.94	Steve McLevy L CO 1 Musselburgh
10.06.94	Alan McDowall L PTS 8 Glasgow

Career: 45 contests, won 13, lost 32.

Nick Appiah   Les Clark

Nick Appiah

Hayes. *Born* Ghana, 29 November, 1968
L. Middleweight. Ht. 5'9"
Manager D. Gunn

29.10.92	Michael Dick W PTS 6 Hayes
24.06.93	Danny Shinkwin W PTS 6 Watford
30.09.93	Warren Stephens W PTS 6 Hayes
23.11.93	Kevin Mabbutt L PTS 6 Kettering
09.12.93	Ojay Abrahams L PTS 6 Watford
25.01.94	Nick Hall L PTS 4 Piccadilly
20.05.94	Harry Dhami L RSC 4 Acton

Career: 7 contests, won 3, lost 4.

Wayne Appleton

Pontefract. *Born* Hemsworth, 9 November, 1967
Welterweight. Ht. 5'10"
Manager T. Callighan

13.11.90	Bullit Andrews W RSC 5 Edgbaston
26.11.90	Stuart Good W CO 4 Lewisham
10.12.90	Wayne Timmins W CO 4 Birmingham
15.03.91	Andre Wharton L RSC 7 Willenhall
14.11.91	Dave Hindmarsh W RSC 8 Edinburgh
30.04.92	Kevin Adamson L RSC 2 Bayswater
01.03.93	Hughie Davey W PTS 6 Bradford
12.05.93	Richard O'Brien W RTD 2 Sheffield
25.10.93	Errol McDonald W PTS 8 Glasgow
04.12.93	Gary Murray L RTD 7 Sun City, South Africa

Career: 10 contests, won 7, lost 3.

Lee Archer

Dudley. *Born* West Bromwich, 3 January, 1971
Cruiserweight. Ht. 6'2"
Manager C. Flute

12.11.91	Paul Murray W PTS 6 Wolverhampton
24.03.92	Darryl Ritchie W PTS 6 Wolverhampton
28.04.92	Carl Smallwood L PTS 6 Wolverhampton
18.05.92	Marc Rowley W PTS 6 Bardon
05.10.92	Paul Murray W PTS 6 Bardon
13.10.92	Paul Murray W PTS 6 Wolverhampton
23.10.92	Ian Henry L RTD 1 Gateshead
24.11.92	Zak Chelli L PTS 6 Wolverhampton
09.02.93	Zak Goldman W CO 3 Wolverhampton
22.02.93	Carl Smallwood W PTS 8 Bedworth
17.03.93	Ian Henry W PTS 6 Stoke
06.05.93	Tony Behan DREW 6 Walsall
28.10.93	Nigel Rafferty W PTS 8 Walsall
04.11.93	Greg Scott-Briggs W PTS 8 Stafford
08.12.93	Greg Scott-Briggs L RTD 6 Stoke
17.02.94	Greg Scott-Briggs W PTS 8 Walsall
17.03.94	Martin Langtry L CO 4 Lincoln

Career: 17 contests, won 11, drew 1, lost 5.

Michael Armstrong (Morris)

Stoke. *Born* Moston, 18 December, 1968
Former British S. Featherweight Champion. Ht. 5'4"
Manager J. Trickett

27.01.88	John Hales W RSC 1 Stoke
02.03.88	Gypsy Johnny W RSC 2 Stoke
20.04.88	Pepe Webber W PTS 6 Stoke
16.05.88	Steve Bowles W RSC 3 Manchester
13.06.88	Tony Heath W PTS 6 Manchester
09.08.88	G. G. Corbett W DIS 6 St Helier
20.09.88	Darren Weller W PTS 8 Stoke

26.10.88	Gary King DREW 8 Stoke	
07.12.88	Mark Holt L PTS 8 Stoke	
15.02.89	Gerry McBride W RSC 5 Stoke	
19.04.89	Russell Davison W PTS 8 Stoke	
24.05.89	Anthony Barcla W PTS 8 Hanley	
04.09.89	Steve Pollard W PTS 8 Hull	
06.12.89	Russell Davison L PTS 8 Stoke	
06.03.90	Russell Davison W PTS 10 Stoke	
18.09.90	Modest Napunyi L CO 9 Stoke	

(Commonwealth Featherweight Title Challenge)

14.10.91	Barrie Kelley W CO 4 Manchester
07.12.91	Mark Holt W RSC 4 Manchester
21.01.92	Darren Elsdon W RSC 1 Stockport

(Final Elim. British S. Featherweight Title)

25.04.92	John Doherty W RSC 7 Manchester

(British S. Featherweight Title Challenge)

25.07.92	Karl Taylor W RSC 3 Manchester
13.10.92	Neil Haddock L RSC 6 Bury

(British S. Featherweight Title Defence)

10.05.94	Jonjo Irwin L PTS 12 Doncaster

(Vacant WBO Penta-Continental S. Featherweight Title)

Career: 23 contests, won 17, drew 1, lost 5.

Neil Armstrong

Paisley. *Born* Glasgow, 19 June, 1970
Flyweight. Ht. 5'5"
Manager A. Melrose

31.01.92	Mark Robertson W RSC 6 Glasgow
04.03.92	Des Gargano W PTS 6 Glasgow
12.03.92	Louis Veitch W PTS 6 Glasgow
10.04.92	Shaun Norman DREW 8 Glasgow
11.09.92	Louis Veitch W PTS 6 Glasgow
10.12.92	L. C. Wilson W PTS 6 Glasgow
29.01.93	Louis Veitch W PTS 6 Glasgow
04.03.93	Shaun Norman W RSC 8 Glasgow
26.03.93	Conn McMullen L RSC 5 Glasgow
29.05.93	Louis Veitch W PTS 10 Paisley
21.10.93	Shaun Norman W RSC 7 Glasgow
10.02.94	Rowan Williams W PTS 6 Glasgow
21.03.94	James Drummond W RSC 5 Glasgow

(Elim. British Flyweight Title. Vacant Scottish Flyweight Title)

Career: 13 contests, won 10, drew 1, lost 2.

Graham Arnold

Bury St Edmonds. *Born* Fulford, 29 June, 1968
Heavyweight. Ht. 6'3"
Manager Self

24.09.91	John Palmer W CO 2 Basildon
26.10.91	Gary Charlton L RSC 1 Brentwood
21.01.92	Steve Yorath L PTS 6 Norwich
31.03.92	Steve Yorath W PTS 6 Norwich
08.09.92	Steve Stewart L RSC 3 Norwich
23.05.93	Julius Francis L RSC 5 Brockley
08.12.93	Gary Williams W PTS 6 Hull
29.03.94	Joey Paladino L RSC 5 Wolverhampton

Career: 8 contests, won 3, lost 5.

(Gary) Crawford Ashley (Crawford)

Leeds. *Born* Leeds, 20 May, 1964
Former Undefeated British & Central Area
L. Heavyweight Champion. Ht. 6'3"
Manager F. Warren

26.03.87	Steve Ward W RSC 2 Merton
29.04.87	Lee Woolis W RSC 3 Stoke
14.09.87	Glazz Campbell L PTS 8 Bloomsbury
07.10.87	Joe Frater W RSC 5 Burnley
28.10.87	Ray Thomas W RSC 1 Stoke
03.12.87	Jonjo Greene W RSC 1 Stoke
04.05.88	Johnny Nelson L PTS 8 Solihull
15.11.88	Richard Bustin W CO 3 Norwich
22.11.88	Cordwell Hylton W CO 3 Basildon
24.01.89	John Foreman W RSC 4 Kings Heath
08.02.89	Lavell Stanley W CO 1 Kensington
28.03.89	Blaine Logsdon L RSC 2 Glasgow
10.05.89	Serg Fame W RTD 7 Solihull
31.10.89	Carl Thompson W RSC 6 Manchester

(Vacant Central Area L. Heavyweight Title)

24.01.90	Brian Schumacher W RSC 3 Preston

(Central Area L. Heavyweight Title Defence)

25.04.90	Dwain Muniz W RSC 1 Brighton
26.11.90	John Williams W RSC 1 Mayfair
12.02.91	Melvin Ricks W CO 1 Belfast
01.03.91	Graciano Rocchigiani L PTS 12 Dusseldorf, Germany

(Vacant European L. Heavyweight Title)

25.07.91	Roy Skeldon W RSC 7 Dudley

(Vacant British L. Heavyweight Title)

30.01.92	Jim Peters W RSC 1 Southampton

(British L. Heavyweight Title Defence)

25.04.92	Glazz Campbell W RSC 8 Belfast

(British L. Heavyweight Title Defence)

23.09.92	Yawe Davis DREW 12 Campione d'Italia, Italy

(Vacant European L. Heavyweight Title)

23.04.93	Michael Nunn L RSC 5 Memphis, USA

(WBA S. Middleweight Title Challenge)

29.01.94	Dennis Andries L RTD 4 Cardiff

Career: 25 contests, won 18, drew 1, lost 6.

Darren Ashton

Stoke. *Born* Stoke, 26 June, 1969
L. Heavyweight. Ht. 6'1"
Manager W. Swift

13.10.93	Tony Colclough W RSC 1 Stoke
08.12.93	Nigel Rafferty W PTS 6 Stoke
23.03.94	L. A. Williams W PTS 6 Stoke
23.05.94	Nigel Rafferty W PTS 6 Walsall

Career: 4 contests, won 4.

Dean Ashton

Stoke. *Born* Stoke, 26 November, 1967
S. Middleweight. Ht. 5'9"
Manager W. Swift

13.10.93	Phil Ball W PTS 6 Stoke
08.12.93	Mark Hale W PTS 6 Stoke
23.03.94	Shaun McCrory DREW 6 Stoke
23.05.94	Mark Smallwood L RTD 3 Walsall

Career: 4 contests, won 2, drew 1, lost 1.

Chris Aston

Leeds. *Born* Huddersfield, 7 August, 1961
L. Welterweight. Ht. 5'7"
Manager K. Tate

07.10.91	Mick Holmes W RSC 2 Bradford
28.10.91	Charles Shepherd L PTS 6 Leicester
21.11.91	Dean Hiscox W PTS 6 Stafford
09.12.91	David Thompson W PTS 6 Bradford
21.01.92	Rob Stewart L RSC 4 Stockport

28.02.92	Mark Legg L RSC 5 Irvine
29.04.92	Richard Swallow L RSC 3 Solihull
02.11.93	Jason Beard L RSC 3 Southwark
08.12.93	Kevin Toomey L PTS 6 Hull
26.01.94	Paul Hughes L PTS 6 Stoke
17.02.94	Nick Boyd L CO 3 Bury
21.03.94	Tanver Ahmed L CO 5 Glasgow
20.05.94	Keith Marner L PTS 8 Acton
06.06.94	Tanver Ahmed L CO 4 Glasgow

Career: 14 contests, won 3, lost 11.

Chris Aston   Les Clark

M. T. Atkin   Les Clark

(Mark) M. T. Atkin

Norwich. *Born* Scarborough, 13 November, 1969
L. Welterweight. Ht. 5'6"
Manager B. Hearn

15.03.94 Jason Campbell W RSC 5 Mayfair
28.06.94 Andy Davidson L RSC 1 Mayfair
Career: 2 contests, won 1, lost 1.

Mark Atkins
Cardiff. *Born* Cardiff, 3 January, 1964
Welterweight. Ht. 5'5"
Manager Self

28.09.89 Mike Morrison L PTS 6 Cardiff
17.12.91 Dave Andrews L RSC 3 Cardiff
23.10.93 Barry Thorogood L PTS 4 Cardiff
18.12.93 Joachim Gustavsson L PTS 4 Turku, Finland
14.03.94 Gilbert Jackson L PTS 6 Mayfair
Career: 5 contests, lost 5.

Richard Atkinson
Dewsbury. *Born* Dewsbury, 25 February, 1973
Cruiserweight. Ht. 6'1"
Manager K. Tate

27.04.92 Greg Scott-Briggs W PTS 6 Bradford
12.11.92 Carl Smallwood L PTS 6 Stafford
12.10.93 John Pierre L PTS 6 Wolverhampton
12.11.93 Stuart Fleet L CO 1 Hull
Career: 4 contests, won 1, lost 3.

Lee Avery
Doncaster. *Born* Doncaster, 7 November, 1969
Cruiserweight. Ht. 6'0"
Manager H. Hayes

16.09.93 Stuart Fleet L RSC 1 Hull
24.02.94 Declan Faherty L RSC 2 Hull
Career: 2 contests, lost 2.

Michael Ayers
Tooting. *Born* London, 26 January, 1965
Former Undefeated WBC International & Southern Area Lightweight Champion. Ht. 5'8"
Manager Self

16.05.89 Young Joe Rafiu W RSC 5 Wandsworth
27.06.89 Greg Egbuniwe W CO 1 Kensington
15.11.89 Mille Markovic W RSC 2 Lewisham
05.12.89 Darren Mount W RSC 2 Catford
26.04.90 Nick Hall W CO 3 Wandsworth
04.06.91 Stuart Rimmer W CO 1 Bethnal Green
22.06.91 Wayne Weekes W RSC 6 Earls Court
 (Vacant Southern Area Lightweight Title)
21.09.91 Peter Till W RSC 5 Tottenham
 (Elim. British Lightweight Title)
28.01.92 Jorge Pompey W PTS 8 Hamburg, Germany
19.02.92 Rudy Valentino W RSC 7 Muswell Hill
 (Southern Area Lightweight Title Defence. Elim. British Lightweight Title)
27.06.92 Sugar Gibiliru W RSC 6 Quinta do Lago, Portugal
13.10.92 Scott Brouwer W RSC 4 Mayfair
 (Vacant WBC International Lightweight Title)
20.02.93 Danny Myburgh W RSC 5 Earls Court
 (WBC International Lightweight Title Defence)

16.04.93 Giovanni Parisi L PTS 12 Rome, Italy
 (WBO Lightweight Title Challenge)
24.05.94 Karl Taylor DREW 8 Sunderland
Career: 15 contests, won 13, drew 1, lost 1.

Dennis Bailey
Ketering. *Born* Liverpool, 23 February, 1963
Cruiserweight. Ht. 6'0"
Manager S. Vaughan

27.11.84 Ronnie Fraser W CO 1 Wolverhampton
12.03.85 Alex Romeo W PTS 6 Birmingham
20.03.85 Alex Romeo W PTS 6 Evesham
23.05.85 Alex Romeo W PTS 6 Dudley
12.03.86 Abner Blackstock L CO 2 Stoke
20.05.86 Tony Wilson L RSC 6 Wembley
25.09.86 Tommy Taylor L CO 4 Wolverhampton
 (Vacant Midlands Area L. Heavyweight Title)
01.02.88 Johnny Nelson W PTS 8 Northampton
08.11.89 Henry Akinwande L RSC 2 Wembley
19.03.90 Steve Lewsam DREW 8 Grimsby
03.04.90 Rob Albon W RSC 4 Canvey Island
21.05.90 Steve Lewsam L PTS 8 Grimsby
23.10.90 Terry Dixon L PTS 6 Leicester
28.09.93 Albert Call DREW 6 Liverpool
11.12.93 Paul McCarthy W PTS 6 Liverpool
19.01.94 John Keeton L RTD 2 Stoke
Career: 16 contests, won 7, drew 2, lost 7.

Kevin Bailey
Sheffield. *Born* Sheffield, 24 March, 1970
L. Heavyweight. Ht. 5'10"
Manager R. Jones

12.05.93 Jimmy Tyers L PTS 6 Sheffield
15.09.93 Steve Walton L PTS 6 Newcastle
02.12.93 Robert Harper W PTS 6 Sheffield
Career: 3 contests, won 1, lost 2.

Ian Baillie
Corby. *Born* Highgate, 23 July, 1966
Flyweight. Ht. 5'2"
Manager K. Whitney

10.12.92 Tiger Singh L PTS 6 Corby
23.02.93 Graham McGrath L PTS 6 Kettering
06.12.93 Lyndon Kershaw L PTS 6 Bradford
19.12.93 Mickey Bell L CO 1 Northampton
02.02.94 Louis Veitch L RSC 1 Glasgow
04.03.94 Keith Knox L CO 3 Irvine
09.05.94 Lyndon Kershaw L PTS 6 Bradford
24.05.94 Shaun Norman L RSC 2 Leicester
Career: 8 contests, lost 8.

David Bain
Walsall. *Born* Peterborough, 2 October, 1966
L. Middleweight. Ht. 5'8"
Manager C. Flute

29.03.94 Warren Stephens W PTS 6 Wolverhampton
23.05.94 Andy Peach W RSC 6 Walsall
Career: 2 contests, won 2.

Mark Baker
Sidcup. *Born* Farnborough, 14 July, 1969
S. Middleweight. Ht. 5'9½"
Manager M. Duff

07.09.92 Jason McNeill W RSC 2 Bethnal Green
15.10.92 Graham Jenner W RTD 4 Lewisham
03.12.92 Adrian Wright W RSC 1 Lewisham
10.02.93 Paul Hanlon W RSC 2 Lewisham
26.04.93 Karl Mumford W CO 1 Lewisham
15.06.93 Alan Baptiste W PTS 6 Hemel Hempstead
14.01.94 Karl Barwise L PTS 6 Bethnal Green
11.03.94 Graham Jenner W RSC 2 Bethnal Green
26.04.94 Jerry Mortimer W PTS 6 Bethnal Green
Career: 9 contests, won 8, lost 1.

Sean Baker   Les Clark

Sean Baker
Bristol. *Born* Bristol, 21 February, 1969
Welterweight. Ht. 5'10"
Manager C. Sanigar

08.09.92 Delwyn Panayiotiou W RSC 2 Southend
05.10.92 Raziq Ali W PTS 6 Bristol
01.12.92 Wayne Panayiotiou W RSC 3 Bristol
27.01.93 Danny Harper W PTS 6 Cardiff
09.03.93 Rick North W PTS 8 Bristol
24.03.93 Steve Levene DREW 6 Belfast
27.05.93 Gavin Lane W PTS 8 Bristol
26.06.93 David Lake W PTS 4 Keynsham
13.09.93 Mark Pearce W PTS 4 Bristol
03.11.93 George Wilson W RSC 2 Bristol
13.12.93 Hughie Davey W PTS 4 Bristol
10.03.94 Paul Lynch W RTD 3 Bristol
31.03.94 Paul Lynch L RSC 3 Bristol
25.05.94 Andrew Jervis DREW 4 Bristol
Career: 14 contests, won 11, drew 2, lost 1.

Phil Ball
Doncaster. *Born* Doncaster, 23 May, 1968
S. Middleweight. Ht. 6'0½"
Manager J. Rushton

24.11.92 Martin Jolley DREW 6 Doncaster
23.02.93 Martin Jolley L RSC 5 Doncaster
01.04.93 Chris Nurse DREW 6 Evesham
29.05.93 Alan Smiles L PTS 6 Paisley
07.06.93 Justin Clements L PTS 6 Walsall

17.06.93 Mark Smallwood L RSC 1 Bedworth
13.10.93 Dean Ashton L PTS 6 Stoke
25.10.93 Peter Flint W RSC 3 Liverpool
30.11.93 Chris Nurse L PTS 6 Wolverhampton
10.02.94 Tim Robinson W PTS 6 Hull
07.03.94 Tim Robinson W PTS 6 Doncaster
10.05.94 Dave Proctor W PTS 6 Doncaster
Career: 12 contests, won 4, drew 2, lost 6.

Alan Baptiste

Luton. *Born* Luton, 17 October, 1960
S. Middleweight. Ht. 6'1"
Manager Self

29.10.84 Terry Gilbey W PTS 6 Lewisham
26.11.84 Sean O'Phoenix DREW 6 Sheffield
23.01.85 Tony Meszaros W PTS 6 Solihull
04.02.85 Oscar Angus L RSC 5 Lewisham
18.04.85 Paul Gamble W PTS 6 Mayfair
30.04.85 Karl Barwise DREW 8 Merton
16.06.85 John Graham L PTS 8 Bethnal Green
22.07.85 Dennis Boy O'Brien W PTS 6 Longford
10.10.85 Karl Barwise L PTS 8 Merton
21.10.85 Sean O'Phoenix L PTS 8 Nottingham
28.10.85 Gary Tomlinson W PTS 8 Stoke
19.11.85 Karl Barwise W PTS 6 Battersea
03.02.86 Paul Gamble W CO 8 Dulwich
17.03.86 Tony Meszaros W RSC 6 Birmingham
17.04.86 Tony Britton W PTS 8 Piccadilly
22.09.86 Tony Meszaros W RSC 7 Edgbaston
04.11.86 Michael Watson L PTS 8 Wembley
15.12.86 John Graham L PTS 8 Mayfair
23.03.87 T.P. Jenkins W RSC 3 Mayfair
07.05.87 Johnny Melfah L CO 1 Bayswater
26.10.87 John Graham L PTS 8 Piccadilly
03.11.87 Blaine Logsdon L RSC 3 Bethnal Green
29.11.88 Simon Harris L RSC 4 Battersea
07.02.89 Richard Bustin L PTS 6 Southend
16.02.89 Roland Ericsson L RSC 5 Battersea
03.10.89 Richard Bustin L PTS 6 Southend
30.04.90 Antonio Fernandez L PTS 6 Brierley Hill
14.05.90 Chris Walker L PTS 6 Leicester
08.10.90 Joe Frater DREW 6 Cleethorpes
12.11.90 Richard Bustin L RSC 1 Norwich
27.02.91 Gil Lewis L RSC 1 Wolverhampton
19.04.91 Tony Lawrence W RSC 5 Peterborough
02.05.91 Kevin Morton L RSC 2 Northampton
15.06.93 Mark Baker L PTS 6 Hemel Hempstead
06.09.93 Paul Wright L PTS 6 Liverpool
16.09.93 Gilbert Jackson L RSC 5 Southwark
Career: 36 contests, won 12, drew 3, lost 21.

Pat Barrett

Manchester. *Born* Manchester, 22 July, 1967
Welterweight. Former Undefeated British, European & Central Area L. Welterweight Champion. Ht. 5'9"
Manager M. Duff

01.05.87 Gary Barron W RSC 6 Peterborough
18.05.87 Jim Moffat W RSC 1 Glasgow
01.06.87 Paul Burke L PTS 6 Bradford
13.06.87 Eamonn Payne W RSC 3 Great Yarmouth
01.07.87 Iskender Savas W CO 1 Interlaken, Switzerland
03.08.87 Mike Russell W PTS 6 Stoke

20.10.87 Michael Howell W PTS 4 Stoke
08.02.88 Oliver Henry W RSC 2 Manchester
01.03.88 Sugar Gibiliru DREW 8 Manchester
22.03.88 Donnie Parker W PTS 6 Baltimore, USA
12.04.88 Stanley Jones W RSC 2 Cardiff
04.05.88 Lenny Gloster W PTS 8 Solihull
08.06.88 Dave McCabe W RSC 2 Glasgow
10.10.88 Dave Haggarty W RSC 7 Glasgow
01.11.88 Jeff Connors W RSC 5 Glasgow
29.11.88 Kevin Plant W PTS 10 Manchester
(*Vacant Central Area L. Welterweight Title*)
06.03.89 Dean Bramhald W RSC 7 Glasgow
28.03.89 Marc Delfosse W CO 1 Glasgow
11.04.89 Sugar Gibiliru W CO 8 Oldham
(*Central Area L. Welterweight Title Defence*)
09.05.89 Tony Willis W CO 9 St Albans
(*Vacant British L. Welterweight Title*)
07.06.89 John Rafuse W CO 6 Wembley
27.06.89 Roberto Trevino W CO 2 Glasgow
19.09.89 Dana Roston W RSC 4 Millwall
24.10.89 Robert Harkin W PTS 12 Wolverhampton
(*British L. Welterweight Title Defence*)
21.11.89 Joey Ferrell W RSC 6 Glasgow
02.06.90 Juan Nunez W RSC 1 Manchester
24.08.90 Efren Calamati W CO 4 Salerno, Italy
(*European L. Welterweight Title Challenge*)
04.10.90 Dwayne Swift W PTS 10 Bethnal Green
15.11.90 Eduardo Jacques W RSC 1 Oldham
16.01.91 Jimmy Harrison W RTD 1 Kensington
13.02.91 Salvatore Nardino W CO 6 Wembley
(*European L. Welterweight Title Defence*)
17.04.91 Mark McCreath W RSC 6 Kensington
(*European L. Welterweight Title Defence*)
09.10.91 Racheed Lawal W RSC 4 Manchester
(*European L. Welterweight Title Defence*)
19.12.91 Mike Johnson W RSC 2 Oldham
25.07.92 Manning Galloway L PTS 12 Manchester
(*WBO L. Welterweight Title Challenge*)
20.11.92 Tomas Quinones W RSC 1 Casino, Italy
19.12.92 Sam Gervins W RSC 1 San Severo, Italy
13.02.93 Juan Gonzalez W PTS 8 Manchester
22.09.93 Del Bryan L PTS 12 Bethnal Green
(*Vacant British Welterweight Title*)
01.11.93 Patrick Vungbo L PTS 12 Izegem, Belgium
(*Vacant WBF L. Middleweight Title*)
11.03.94 Donnie Parker W RSC 4 Sharon, USA
Career: 41 contests, won 36, drew 1, lost 4.

(Garrett) Gary Barron

Peterborough. *Born* Peterborough, 21 December, 1964
Welterweight. Ht. 5'10"
Manager Self

19.02.87 Tim O'Keefe W PTS 6 Peterborough
01.05.87 Pat Barrett L RSC 6 Peterborough
14.02.88 Andrew Pybus W CO 1 Peterborough
24.02.88 Kevin Plant DREW 6 Leicester
03.11.88 James Hunter W PTS 6 Leicester

14.02.89 Tony Feliciello ND 8 Wolverhampton
01.03.89 Brian Cullen L PTS 6 Stoke
17.04.89 Frankie Lake W CO 4 Birmingham
11.09.89 Darren Mount DREW 8 Manchester
04.10.89 Oliver Harrison W PTS 8 Solihull
23.10.89 Lyn Davies L CO 2 Nottingham
24.01.90 Guillermo Zuniga L CO 1 Trapani, Italy
14.12.90 Paul Charters W RSC 3 Peterborough
13.02.91 Robert McCracken L RTD 2 Wembley
19.04.91 Tony Swift DREW 8 Peterborough
14.11.91 Paul Charters L RSC 4 Gateshead
12.02.92 Carlos Chase L RSC 5 Watford
25.03.92 Donald Stokes L RSC 2 Dagenham
30.04.92 Mark McCreath L RSC 5 Mayfair
18.06.92 Marcel Herbert W PTS 6 Peterborough
09.07.92 Peter Bradley L PTS 8 Glasgow
07.12.92 Mark McCreath L RSC 5 Mayfair
26.04.93 Tony Ekubia L RSC 4 Manchester
28.07.93 Rose Hale L CO 2 Brixton
22.09.93 Derek Grainger L RTD 4 Bethnal Green
Career: 25 contests, won 7, drew 3, lost 14, no decision 1.

Karl Barwise

Tooting. *Born* London, 19 September, 1965
S. Middleweight. Ht. 5'11"
Manager Self

18.09.84 John Hargin W PTS 6 Merton
23.10.84 Tony Baker DREW 6 Battersea
20.11.84 Newton Barnett W PTS 6 Merton
30.11.84 Newton Barnett L PTS 6 Longford
19.12.84 Rocky McGran W PTS 6 Belfast
24.01.85 Paul Allen W CO 2 Streatham
11.02.85 Tony Baker W PTS 8 Dulwich
26.02.85 Mark Mills L PTS 6 Battersea
01.04.85 Dalton Jordan W PTS 8 Dulwich
30.04.85 Alan Baptiste DREW 8 Merton
10.10.85 Alan Baptiste W PTS 8 Merton
29.10.85 Christophe Tiozzo L PTS 8 Paris, France
19.11.85 Alan Baptiste L PTS 6 Battersea
30.01.86 Steve Ward W PTS 6 Merton
19.02.86 Michael Watson L RSC 3 Kensington
15.04.86 Neil Munn W PTS 6 Merton
22.04.86 Sammy Storey L PTS 6 Belfast
04.09.86 Dennis Boy O'Brien W RSC 2 Ealing
16.10.86 John Graham L PTS 6 Merton
29.10.86 Nicky Thorne DREW 6 Muswell Hill
05.09.90 Sean Heron L PTS 6 Brighton
22.09.90 Errol Christie L RTD 7 Kensington
20.03.91 Lester Jacobs L PTS 6 Wandsworth
03.04.91 Ali Forbes L RTD 4 Bethnal Green
26.04.91 Benji Good L RSC 3 Crystal Palace
30.05.91 Ray Webb L PTS 8 Mayfair
16.10.91 Andrew Flute W RSC 8 Stoke
22.10.91 Tony McCarthy W PTS 6 Wandsworth
13.11.91 Sammy Storey L PTS 6 Belfast
07.12.91 Pietro Pellizzaro L PTS 6 Rossano Calabro, Italy
12.05.92 Roland Ericsson L PTS 6 Crystal Palace
08.09.92 Richard Bustin L PTS 6 Norwich
15.09.92 Lou Gent L RSC 6 Crystal Palace
04.12.92 Neville Brown L RSC 6 Telford
04.03.93 Stefan Wright W RTD 5 Peterborough
18.03.93 James Cook L RSC 6 Lewisham
26.04.93 Eric Noi L PTS 6 Manchester
28.05.93 Eric Noi L RSC 4 Middleton
14.08.93 Fidel Castro L RSC 6 Hammersmith
28.11.93 Ray Webb L PTS 6 Southwark

14.01.94   Mark Baker W PTS 6 Bethnal Green
26.01.94   James Cook L PTS 8 Birmingham
23.02.94   Steve McCarthy L PTS 6 Watford
23.03.94   Darron Griffiths L PTS 8 Cardiff
05.04.94   Monty Wright L PTS 6 Bethnal Green
04.06.94   Joe Calzaghe L RSC 1 Cardiff
Career: 46 contests, won 14, drew 3, lost 29.

Dave Battey

Worksop. *Born* Gainsborough, 14
December, 1972
L. Heavyweight. Ht. 6'1¼"
Manager K. Richardson

24.05.94   Johnny Hooks L PTS 6 Leicester
28.06.94   Justin Clements L RSC 2 Edgbaston
Career: 2 contests, lost 2.

Jason Beard

Beckton. *Born* Whitechapel, 24 April, 1967
Welterweight. Ht. 5'8½"
Manager D. Mancini

03.12.92   Robert Whitehouse W RSC 3
             Lewisham
28.01.93   Jason Barker W RSC 3 Southwark
24.02.93   Michael Dick W RSC 5 Wembley
26.04.93   Brian Coleman W PTS 6 Lewisham
09.06.93   Phil Found W PTS 6 Lewisham
16.09.93   David Lake W PTS 6 Southwark
02.11.93   Chris Aston W RSC 3 Southwark
07.12.93   Jason Campbell W RSC 2 Bethnal
             Green
14.01.94   Steve Phillips W RTD 3 Bethnal Green
11.03.94   Dave Maj W PTS 6 Bethnal Green
Career: 10 contests, won 10.

Tony Behan

Birmingham. *Born* Birmingham, 5 March,
1967
L. Heavyweight. Ht. 6'0"
Manager Self

22.09.86   W.O. Wilson L CO 2 Mayfair
18.03.87   Paul Hanlon W PTS 4 Stoke
06.04.87   Jim Peters L PTS 4 Southampton
03.08.87   Darren Hobson L PTS 6 Stoke
19.11.87   Darren McKenna L RSC 1 Ilkeston
14.03.88   Richard Bustin L RSC 3 Norwich
25.04.88   Ted Cofie W RTD 4 Birmingham
03.05.88   Peter Elliott L PTS 6 Stoke
10.05.88   Floyd Davidson W PTS 6 Edgbaston
23.05.88   John Ellis DREW 6 Mayfair
22.09.88   Richard Carter L PTS 6
             Wolverhampton
17.10.88   Steve Kofi DREW 6 Birmingham
05.04.89   Ian Strudwick L PTS 6 Kensington
19.04.89   Peter Elliott DREW 6 Stoke
08.05.89   Ian Vokes W PTS 6 Grimsby
16.05.89   Ian Strudwick L PTS 8 Wandsworth
02.10.89   Peter Elliott L PTS 10 Hanley
             (Vacant Midlands Area S.
             Middleweight Title)
04.03.91   Paul Hanlon W PTS 6 Birmingham
13.05.91   Nigel Rafferty L DIS 7 Birmingham
23.05.91   Joey Peters L PTS 6 Southampton
02.12.91   Darryl Ritchie W RSC 1 Birmingham
20.01.92   Gil Lewis L PTS 8 Coventry
28.04.93   Trevor Small L PTS 6 Solihull
06.05.93   Lee Archer DREW 6 Walsall
23.06.93   Tony Booth L PTS 6 Gorleston
11.08.93   Graham Burton L PTS 6 Mansfield
Career: 26 contests, won 6, drew 4, lost 16.

Mickey Bell

Yarmouth. *Born* Gorleston, 17 May, 1965
Bantamweight. Ht. 5'4½"
Manager G. Holmes

11.05.93   Ricky Beard L RSC 2 Norwich
19.12.93   Ian Baillie W CO 1 Northampton
28.02.94   Gary White L PTS 6 Manchester
Career: 3 contests, won 1, lost 2.

Chris Bennett

Newcastle. *Born* Newcastle, 8 June, 1966
Lightweight. Ht. 5'9"
Manager B. Kane

22.11.88   Dean Dickinson W PTS 6 Marton
30.01.89   Geoff Ward W RSC 2 Leicester
28.02.89   Paul Charters L PTS 6 Marton
31.03.89   James Jiora W PTS 6 Scarborough
03.06.89   Michael Howell L RSC 3 Stanley
26.09.89   Billy Couzens L RSC 3 Chigwell
29.11.89   Kris McAdam W CO 3 Marton
22.03.90   Steve Pollard L PTS 4 Gateshead
21.04.90   Dominic McGuigan L PTS 6
             Sunderland
02.06.90   Juan Carlos Villareal L RSC 4 Rome,
             Italy
10.12.90   Dave Anderson L RSC 7 Glasgow
28.02.91   John Naylor L RSC 3 Sunderland
15.09.93   Colin Innes DREW 6 Newcastle
25.11.93   Alan Graham L PTS 6 Newcastle
13.05.94   Bradley Welsh L RSC 3 Kilmarnock
Career: 15 contests, won 4, drew 1, lost 10.

(Adrian) Ady Benton

Bradford. *Born* Dewsbury, 26 August, 1973
S. Bantamweight. Ht. 5'6"
Manager K. Tate

27.04.92   Mark Hargreaves W PTS 6 Bradford
29.10.92   Vince Feeney DREW 6 Bayswater
09.11.92   Stevie Woods W PTS 6 Bradford
25.01.93   Neil Parry W RSC 6 Bradford
26.02.93   James Drummond DREW 6 Irvine
08.03.93   Dave Campbell W PTS 6 Leeds
29.06.93   Michael Alldis W DIS 3 Mayfair
20.09.93   Mike Deveney L PTS 8 Glasgow
08.11.93   Chip O'Neill W RSC 5 Bradford
24.01.94   Mike Deveney W PTS 6 Glasgow
25.02.94   Paul Lloyd L RSC 5 Chester
             (Vacant Central Area S. Bantamweight
             Title)
25.04.94   Pat Clinton W RSC 1 Glasgow
Career: 12 contests, won 8, drew 2, lost 2.

Thomas Bernard

Bermondsey. *Born* Dulwich, 9 August,
1964
Featherweight. Ht. 5'10"
Manager D. Austin

07.03.88   Chris Cooper W RSC 2 Hove
15.11.88   Miguel Matthews L RSC 2 Chigwell
13.10.93   Justin Murphy L RSC 1 Bethnal Green
07.12.93   Mark Bowers L RSC 1 Bethnal Green
17.02.94   Marcus McCrae L RSC 1 Dagenham
Career: 5 contests, won 1, lost 4.

Dennis Berry

Alfreton. *Born* Birmingham, 4 April, 1967
Welterweight. Ht. 5'8"
Manager M. Shinfield

01.04.93   Lee Renshaw W RSC 3 Evesham
08.06.93   David Sumner W PTS 6 Derby
04.11.93   Andy Peach W PTS 6 Stafford
17.03.94   Rick North L PTS 6 Lincoln
16.05.94   Rick North W RSC 6 Cleethorpes
24.05.94   Norman Hutcheon W RSC 2 Leicester
28.06.94   Howard Clarke W RSC 3 Edgbaston
Career: 7 contests, won 6, lost 1.

Ensley Bingham

Manchester. *Born* Manchester, 27 May,
1963
L. Middleweight. Ht. 5'8½"
Manager Self

20.11.86   Steve Ward W CO 5 Bredbury
16.12.87   Tony Britland W CO 1 Manchester
23.02.88   Franki Moro W PTS 6 Oldham
01.03.88   Kelvin Mortimer W PTS 8 Manchester
26.04.88   Clinton McKenzie L PTS 8 Bethnal
             Green
18.10.88   Kostas Petrou L RSC 7 Oldham
22.03.89   Gary Cooper L PTS 8 Reading
26.09.89   Wally Swift Jnr W PTS 10 Oldham
             (Elim. British L. Middleweight Title)
28.03.90   Fernando Alanis L RSC 3 Manchester
06.06.90   Andy Till W DIS 3 Battersea
             (Final Elim. British L. Middleweight
             Title)
19.03.91   Wally Swift Jnr L RSC 4 Birmingham
             (Vacant British L. Middleweight Title)
29.11.91   Russell Washer W RSC 4 Manchester
29.05.92   Graham Jenner W CO 5 Manchester
18.07.92   Gordon Blair W CO 2 Manchester
02.11.92   Robert McCracken L RSC 10
             Wolverhampton
             (Elim. British L. Middleweight Title)
28.05.93   Mark Kelly W RSC 5 Middleton
14.08.93   Robert Peel W RTD 3 Hammersmith
Career: 17 contests, won 11, lost 6.

Gordon Blair

Glasgow. *Born* Glasgow, 26 February,
1969
Welterweight. Ht. 5'10"
Manager A. Melrose

21.11.89   Gavin Fitzpatrick W RSC 3 Glasgow
18.12.89   John Ritchie W PTS 4 Glasgow
19.02.90   Trevor Meikle W PTS 6 Glasgow
26.02.90   Jim Conley W RSC 3 Bradford
26.04.90   Kid Sylvester L PTS 6 Halifax
14.05.90   Trevor Ambrose W CO 5 Northampton
25.09.90   Calum Rattray W RSC 3 Glasgow
22.10.90   Shamus Casey W RSC 3 Glasgow
06.11.90   Leigh Wicks L PTS 8 Mayfair
10.12.90   Quinn Paynter W PTS 6 Glasgow
25.01.91   Danny Quigg W PTS 6 Shotts
18.02.91   Gary Logan L CO 1 Mayfair
15.04.91   Rob Pitters L PTS 6 Glasgow
31.05.91   Paul King W PTS 8 Glasgow
20.06.91   Delroy Waul W CO 2 Liverpool
24.09.91   Bozon Haule W RSC 8 Glasgow
19.11.91   Tony McKenzie L RSC 5 Norwich
31.01.92   Willie Beattie L RSC 3 Glasgow
             (Vacant Scottish Welterweight Title)
12.03.92   Mark Jay DREW 8 Glasgow
29.05.92   Ossie Maddix L PTS 6 Manchester
18.07.92   Ensley Bingham L CO 2 Manchester
27.10.92   Howard Clarke W RSC 4 Cradley
             Heath
24.11.92   Errol McDonald L RSC 5 Doncaster
29.01.93   Mark Cichocki L PTS 8 Glasgow

15.02.93 Lindon Scarlett L CO 4 Mayfair
25.06.93 Gary Logan L RSC 6 Battersea
12.03.94 Michael Smyth L RSC 4 Cardiff
13.04.94 Gilbert Jackson L RTD 1 Glasgow
Career: 28 contests, won 13, drew 1, lost 14.

Andrew Bloomer
Ynysbwl. *Born* Pontypridd, 26 September, 1964
S. Bantamweight. Ht. 5'8½"
Manager Self

30.06.91 Leigh Williams L PTS 6 Southwark
03.09.91 Alan Ley L PTS 6 Cardiff
02.10.91 Bradley Stone L PTS 6 Barking
17.10.91 Leigh Williams L PTS 6 Southwark
04.11.91 Ceri Farrell L PTS 6 Merthyr
20.11.91 Ceri Farrell L PTS 6 Cardiff
28.11.91 Chris Morris L PTS 6 Liverpool
24.02.92 Alex Docherty L PTS 6 Glasgow
08.04.92 Jacob Smith L PTS 6 Leeds
30.04.92 Tony Falcone L PTS 6 Mayfair
16.05.92 Bradley Stone L PTS 6 Muswell Hill
23.05.92 Prince Nassem Hamed L RSC 2 Birmingham
05.10.92 Tony Falcone L PTS 8 Bristol
12.11.92 Marcus Duncan L PTS 6 Burnley
29.03.93 Vince Feeney L PTS 6 Mayfair
26.04.93 Mark Bowers L PTS 6 Lewisham
04.05.93 Paul Lloyd L PTS 6 Liverpool
15.09.93 Justin Murphy L PTS 4 Bethnal Green
04.10.93 Marco Fattore L PTS 6 Mayfair
Career: 19 contests, lost 19.

Lee Blundell　　　　　Les Clark

Lee Blundell
Wigan. *Born* Wigan, 11 August, 1971
Middleweight. Ht. 6'2"
Manager J. McMillan

25.04.94 Robert Harper W RSC 2 Bury
20.05.94 Freddie Yemofio W RSC 6 Acton
Career: 2 contests, won 2.

Tony Booth
Sheffield. *Born* Hull, 30 January, 1970
L. Heavyweight. Ht. 5'11¾"
Manager B. Ingle

08.03.90 Paul Lynch L PTS 6 Watford
11.04.90 Mick Duncan W PTS 6 Dewsbury
26.04.90 Colin Manners W PTS 6 Halifax
16.05.90 Tommy Warde W PTS 6 Hull
05.06.90 Gary Dyson W PTS 6 Liverpool
05.09.90 Shaun McCrory L PTS 6 Stoke
08.10.90 Bullit Andrews W RSC 3 Cleethorpes
23.01.91 Darron Griffiths DREW 6 Stoke
06.02.91 Shaun McCrory L PTS 6 Liverpool
06.03.91 Billy Brough L PTS 6 Glasgow
18.03.91 Billy Brough W PTS 6 Glasgow
28.03.91 Neville Brown L PTS 6 Alfreton
17.05.91 Glenn Campbell L RSC 2 Bury
　　　　　(Central Area S. Middleweight Title Challenge)
25.07.91 Paul Murray W PTS 6 Dudley
01.08.91 Nick Manners DREW 8 Dewsbury
11.09.91 Jim Peters L PTS 8 Hammersmith
28.10.91 Eddie Smulders L RSC 6 Arnhem, Holland
09.12.91 Steve Lewsam L PTS 8 Cleethorpes
30.01.92 Serg Fame W PTS 6 Southampton
12.02.92 Tenko Ernie W RSC 4 Wembley
05.03.92 John Beckles W RSC 6 Battersea
26.03.92 Dave Owens W PTS 6 Hull
08.04.92 Michael Gale L PTS 8 Leeds
13.05.92 Phil Soundy W PTS 6 Kensington
02.06.92 Eddie Smulders L RSC 1 Rotterdam, Holland
18.07.92 Maurice Core L PTS 6 Manchester
07.09.92 James Cook L PTS 8 Bethnal Green
30.10.92 Roy Richie DREW 6 Istrees, France
18.11.92 Tony Wilson DREW 8 Solihull
25.12.92 Francis Wanyama L PTS 6 Izegem, Belgium
09.02.93 Tony Wilson W PTS 8 Wolverhampton
01.05.93 Ralf Rocchigiani DREW 8 Berlin, Germany
03.06.93 Victor Cordoba L PTS 8 Marseille, France
23.06.93 Tony Behan W PTS 6 Gorleston
01.07.93 Michael Gale L PTS 8 York
17.09.93 Ole Klemetsen L PTS 8 Copenhagen, Denmark
07.10.93 Denzil Browne DREW 8 York
02.11.93 James Cook L PTS 8 Southwark
12.11.93 Carlos Christie W PTS 6 Hull
28.01.94 Francis Wanyama L RSC 2 Waregem, Belgium
　　　　　(Vacant Commonwealth Cruiserweight Title)
26.03.94 Torsten May L PTS 6 Dortmund, Germany
Career: 41 contests, won 15, drew 6, lost 20.

John Bosco (Waigo)
Mitcham. *Born* Uganda, 16 July, 1967
L. Middleweight. Ht. 5'8½"
Manager M. Duff

05.12.91 Tony Kosova W CO 2 Peterborough
17.02.92 Gilbert Jackson W PTS 6 Mayfair
03.09.92 Russell Washer W RSC 2 Dunstable
19.10.92 Steve Goodwin W RSC 2 Mayfair
07.12.92 Griff Jones W RSC 1 Mayfair
28.01.93 Jerry Mortimer W RSC 4 Southwark
15.02.93 Mark Dawson W PTS 6 Mayfair
29.03.93 Winston May W RSC 3 Mayfair

10.11.93 Mark Dawson W RTD 4 Watford
26.01.94 Julian Eavis W RSC 1 Birmingham
14.03.94 Carlo Colarusso W PTS 6 Mayfair
28.04.94 Chris Peters W PTS 8 Mayfair
Career: 12 contests, won 12.

Paul Bowen
Wednesbury. *Born* West Bromwich, 27 September, 1963
L. Welterweight. Ht. 5'6"
Manager C. Flute

11.02.86 Rocky Lester L RSC 1 Wolverhampton
25.03.86 Andrew Pybus L RSC 4 Wolverhampton
06.10.86 Kevin Plant W PTS 6 Birmingham
08.12.86 Noel Rafferty W RSC 5 Birmingham
16.11.87 Tony Feliciello DREW 6 Stratford on Avon
09.02.88 Sean Hogg W CO 2 Wolverhampton
22.03.88 Mark Antony W RSC 3 Wolverhampton
13.04.88 Phil Lashley L RSC 1 Wolverhampton
14.12.88 Mark Antony W PTS 6 Evesham
18.01.89 Steve Booth W PTS 6 Stoke
20.02.89 James Jiora W PTS 6 Birmingham
21.03.89 Dave Croft W PTS 6 Wolverhampton
13.04.89 Shaun Cooper L PTS 6 Wolverhampton
08.05.89 Hugh Forde L RSC 4 Edgbaston
25.09.89 Paul Charters L PTS 8 Birmingham
11.12.89 Brendan Ryan L PTS 8 Nottingham
24.01.90 Dean Bramhald W PTS 8 Solihull
28.10.93 Mark Allen W RSC 2 Walsall
24.11.93 Hugh Collins L PTS 6 Solihull
16.12.93 Jimmy Phelan L PTS 6 Walsall
19.01.94 Carl Roberts L PTS 6 Solihull
07.04.94 Simon Hamblett W PTS 6 Walsall
18.04.94 Scott Walker L PTS 6 Manchester
Career: 23 contests, won 11, drew 1, lost 11.

Mark Bowers
Lock Heath. *Born* Fareham, 19 October, 1970
Featherweight. Ht. 5'5"
Manager M. Duff

13.05.92 Hamid Moulay W CO 1 Kensington
17.10.92 Miguel Matthews W PTS 6 Wembley
17.12.92 Chris Lyons W CO 2 Wembley
26.04.93 Andrew Bloomer W PTS 6 Lewisham
09.06.93 Kurt Griffiths W RSC 1 Lewisham
02.11.93 Chris Jickells W RSC 3 Southwark
07.12.93 Thomas Bernard W RSC 1 Bethnal Green
05.04.94 Pete Buckley W PTS 6 Bethnal Green
11.05.94 Dean Lynch W RSC 2 Stevenage
Career: 9 contests, won 9.

Warren Bowers
Grimsby. *Born* Grimsby, 14 January, 1971
Welterweight. Ht. 5'7"
Manager L. Slater

08.05.89 Andrew Brightman W CO 5 Grimsby
04.09.89 Mark Antony W PTS 6 Grimsby
14.05.90 Barry North W RSC 4 Cleethorpes
02.03.91 Andy Kent L PTS 6 Cleethorpes
25.11.91 John Baxter L RSC 3 Cleethorpes
04.06.92 Peter Reid L RSC 2 Cleethorpes
26.04.93 Colin Anderson W RSC 5 Cleethorpes
07.10.93 Ron Hopley L PTS 6 York
19.10.93 Craig Hartwell W PTS 6 Cleethorpes

08.11.93 Hughie Davey L RSC 2 Bradford
28.02.94 Ron Hopley L RSC 1 Marton
Career: 11 contests, won 5, lost 6.

Nick Boyd

Bolton. *Born* Bolton, 11 October, 1966
L. Welterweight. Ht. 5'10"
Manager Self

05.02.93 Mark O'Callaghan W PTS 6
Manchester
28.05.93 Mark Allen W CO 2 Middleton
25.07.93 Trevor Royal W PTS 6 Oldham
17.02.94 Chris Aston W CO 3 Bury

25.04.94 Brian Wright W CO 2 Bury
02.06.94 John Stovin W RSC 5 Middleton
Career: 6 contests, won 6.

Robert Braddock

Bolton on Dearne. *Born* Mexborough, 14
January 1971
Featherweight. Ht. 5'7"
Manager K. Tate

03.04.89 Ronnie Stephenson L CO 4 Manchester
13.10.89 Dave McNally L PTS 6 Preston
23.10.89 John Whitelaw W PTS 6 Hull
30.10.89 Pete Buckley L PTS 6 Birmingham

Robert Braddock

Chris Bevan

28.06.90 Pete Buckley L RSC 5 Birmingham
10.06.91 Tony Smith DREW 6 Manchester
23.09.91 Al Garrett DREW 6 Glasgow
07.10.91 Glyn Shepherd DREW 6 Bradford
13.11.91 Chris Morris L RSC 5 Liverpool
16.12.91 Carl Roberts L PTS 6 Manchester
28.04.92 Chip O'Neill L PTS 6 Houghton le
Spring
01.06.92 Alex Docherty L PTS 6 Glasgow
08.09.92 Chris Lyons W CO 5 Doncaster
05.10.92 Karl Morling L PTS 6 Northampton
09.11.92 Chip O'Neill W RSC 3 Bradford
23.11.92 Ian McLeod DREW 6 Glasgow
07.12.92 Gary White L PTS 6 Manchester
20.09.93 Hugh Collins L PTS 8 Glasgow
06.10.93 Ian McGirr L PTS 8 York
07.11.93 Wilson Docherty L RSC 3 Glasgow
07.12.93 Yifru Retta L RSC 2 Bethnal Green
Career: 21 contests, won 3, drew 4, lost 14.

Nigel Bradley

Sheffield. *Born* Sheffield, 24 February,
1968
L. Welterweight. Ht. 5'8"
Manager B. Ingle

14.12.87 Lee Amass L RSC 4 Piccadilly
29.01.88 John Townsley L PTS 6 Durham
23.03.88 Darren Darby W RSC 1 Sheffield
28.03.88 Adam Muir NC 4 Glasgow
18.04.88 Mark Kelly L PTS 6 Manchester
08.06.88 Mike Russell W PTS 6 Sheffield
09.08.88 David Bacon W RSC 5 Doncaster
26.10.88 Dean Dickinson W PTS 6 Sheffield
23.02.89 Chris Mulcahy W RSC 2 Stockport
09.03.89 Michael McDermott W RSC 5
Glasgow
04.04.89 John Mullen W RSC 6 Sheffield
08.10.90 John Townsley DREW 8 Glasgow
14.11.90 B. F. Williams W CO 2 Sheffield
29.01.91 Sugar Gibiliru L PTS 8 Stockport
11.02.92 Dean Hollington L PTS 6 Barking
18.03.92 Kris McAdam W CO 2 Glasgow
14.04.92 Dave Whittle W CO 3 Mansfield
29.09.92 Tony Swift L PTS 8 Stoke
08.02.94 Howard Clarke L RTD 6
Wolverhampton
Career: 19 contests, won 10, drew 1, lost 7, no
contest 1.

Dean Bramhald

Doncaster. *Born* Balby, 25 May, 1963
L. Welterweight. Former Central Area
Lightweight Champion. Ht. 5'7½"
Manager Self

25.01.84 Wayne Trigg L CO 3 Stoke
22.02.84 Andy Deabreu L PTS 6 Evesham
27.02.84 Billy Joe Dee W PTS 6 Nottingham
19.03.84 Billy Joe Dee L PTS 6 Bradford
27.03.84 Neville Fivey DREW 6
Wolverhampton
04.04.84 Peter Bowen L PTS 6 Evesham
12.04.84 Andy Deabreu L PTS 6 Piccadilly
09.05.84 Wayne Trigg DREW 4 Leicester
21.05.84 Doug Munro L PTS 6 Aberdeen
11.06.84 Glenn Tweedie L PTS 6 Glasgow
06.08.84 Andy Williams L PTS 6 Aintree
21.09.84 Clinton Campbell W PTS 6 Alfreton
02.10.84 John Doherty L PTS 8 Leeds
10.10.84 Rocky Lawler W RSC 5 Stoke
22.10.84 John Maloney DREW 6 Mayfair
29.10.84 Ray Newby L PTS 6 Nottingham

19.11.84	Dave Adam L PTS 6 Glasgow
27.11.84	Mickey Markie DREW 6 Wolverhampton
05.12.84	Neville Fivey W PTS 6 Stoke
17.12.84	John Maloney DREW 6 Mayfair
18.01.85	Mark Reefer L RSC 6 Bethnal Green
20.02.85	Stuart Carmichael DREW 6 Stafford
01.03.85	Craig Windsor DREW 6 Glasgow
13.03.85	Dave Adam L PTS 8 Stoke
25.03.85	Michael Marsden W PTS 8 Huddersfield
05.04.85	Bobby McDermott L PTS 8 Glasgow
18.04.85	John Doherty L PTS 8 Halifax
04.06.85	Pat Doherty L CO 6 Streatham
31.07.85	Robert Dickie L RSC 7 Porthcawl
23.09.85	Kevin Taylor L RSC 1 Bradford
21.10.85	Kevin Taylor L PTS 6 Bradford
21.11.85	Russell Jones L PTS 8 Blaenavon
30.11.85	Floyd Havard L RSC 3 Cardiff
20.01.86	Paul Downie L PTS 8 Glasgow
06.02.86	Stuart Carmichael W PTS 8 Doncaster
20.02.86	Floyd Havard L PTS 6 Halifax
10.03.86	Peter Bradley L PTS 8 Glasgow
17.03.86	Paul Downie L CO 5 Glasgow
27.04.86	Andrew Pybus W PTS 6 Doncaster
20.05.86	Eamonn McAuley L PTS 6 Wembley
02.06.86	Peter Bradley L PTS 8 Mayfair
13.06.86	Peppy Muire L RSC 7 Gloucester
30.07.86	Steve James L PTS 8 Ebbw Vale
17.11.86	Jim Moffat L PTS 6 Glasgow
25.11.86	Joey Joynson L PTS 8 Wolverhampton
03.12.86	Steve Brown L PTS 6 Stoke
15.12.86	Rocky Lester W PTS 6 Loughborough
26.01.87	Tony Swift L PTS 8 Birmingham
09.02.87	Peter Crook L PTS 8 Manchester
16.02.87	Nigel Senior L PTS 8 Stoke
04.03.87	Tony Swift L RSC 5 Dudley
06.04.87	Drew Black L PTS 8 Glasgow
27.04.87	Kevin Spratt L PTS 8 Bradford
06.05.87	Peter Bradley L RSC 4 Livingston
04.06.87	David Maw L PTS 6 Sunderland
13.06.87	Michael Betts DREW 6 Great Yarmouth
04.09.87	David Maw L PTS 6 Gateshead
14.09.87	John Bennie W PTS 6 Glasgow
07.10.87	Tony Swift L PTS 8 Stoke
19.10.87	Peter Till L PTS 8 Birmingham
11.11.87	Ron Shinkwin W PTS 8 Stafford
24.11.87	Peter Till L PTS 8 Wolverhampton
02.12.87	Tony Swift L PTS 8 Stoke
14.12.87	Ron Shinkwin L PTS 8 Bradford
20.01.88	Davy Robb L PTS 8 Stoke
29.01.88	Frankie Lake L PTS 8 Torquay
07.02.88	Damien Denny L PTS 4 Stafford
24.02.88	David Lake W PTS 6 Southend
09.03.88	Mickey Vern W CO 5 Stoke
23.03.88	Frankie Lake DREW 8 Evesham
13.04.88	Davy Robb W RSC 5 Wolverhampton
25.04.88	Nigel Senior W PTS 8 Nottingham
16.05.88	Ronnie Campbell L RSC 7 Wolverhampton
16.06.88	Mark Dinnadge W PTS 8 Croydon
26.09.88	Dave Croft DREW 4 Bradford
06.10.88	Ronnie Campbell W RSC 6 Dudley
17.10.88	Dave Griffiths L RSC 5 Mayfair
17.11.88	Tony Feliciello L PTS 8 Weston super Mare
29.11.88	Neil Foran L PTS 6 Manchester
16.12.88	Brian Sonny Nickels L PTS 6 Brentwood
26.01.89	George Baigrie W PTS 6 Newcastle
14.02.89	Steve Hogg W PTS 6 Wolverhampton
06.03.89	Pat Barrett L RSC 7 Glasgow
03.04.89	Brian Cullen W RSC 3 Manchester

19.04.89	Calum Rattray W PTS 6 Doncaster
26.04.89	Michael Driscoll L RSC 2 Southampton
29.05.89	Peter Hart L RSC 2 Liverpool
25.09.89	Ian Honeywood L RTD 4 Crystal Palace
25.10.89	Oliver Henry L PTS 6 Doncaster
28.11.89	Shaun Cooper L CO 2 Wolverhampton
17.01.90	Peter Bowen W PTS 6 Stoke
24.01.90	Paul Bowen L PTS 8 Solihull
07.03.90	Andrew Robinson L PTS 6 Doncaster
14.03.90	Shaun Cogan L PTS 6 Stoke
04.04.90	Dave Croft W PTS 6 Stafford
26.04.90	Seamus O'Sullivan L PTS 6 Wandsworth
21.05.90	Brendan Ryan DREW 6 Grimsby
05.06.90	Billy Couzens L PTS 6 Nottingham
22.06.90	Mark Dinnadge L PTS 6 Gillingham
14.11.90	Jim Lawlor DREW 8 Doncaster
13.12.90	Andrew Morgan DREW 8 Cleethorpes
10.12.90	Colin Sinnott W PTS 6 Bradford
17.12.90	Sugar Gibiliru L PTS 8 Manchester
17.01.91	Richard Burton L RTD 1 Alfreton
05.03.91	Charlie Kane L RSC 6 Glasgow
10.04.91	Ronnie Campbell W PTS 6 Wolverhampton
24.04.91	Dave Jenkins L PTS 8 Aberavon
13.05.91	Andrew Robinson L RTD 1 Birmingham
17.06.91	Malcolm Melvin L PTS 6 Edgbaston
04.07.91	Shane Sheridan L PTS 6 Alfreton
10.09.91	Mark Elliot L CO 5 Wolverhampton
08.10.91	Colin Sinnott L PTS 8 Wolverhampton
21.10.91	Colin Sinnott W PTS 6 Cleethorpes
20.11.91	Rocky Feliciello L PTS 6 Solihull
04.12.91	Ron Shinkwin W PTS 8 Stoke
22.01.92	Ray Newby L PTS 8 Solihull
30.01.92	Ron Shinkwin L PTS 6 Southampton
11.02.92	Ray Newby L RSC 7 Wolverhampton
11.03.92	Andreas Panayi W PTS 8 Stoke
24.03.92	Richard Swallow L PTS 8 Wolverhampton
06.04.92	Richard Swallow L PTS 6 Northampton
28.04.92	Darren McInulty L PTS 6 Wolverhampton
11.05.92	Darren McInulty L PTS 6 Coventry
12.06.92	Carl Wright L PTS 6 Liverpool
15.09.92	Mike Morrison W PTS 6 Crystal Palace
30.09.92	Barrie Kelley L PTS 6 Solihull
13.10.92	Bernard Paul DREW 6 Mayfair
26.11.92	Kevin Toomey W PTS 10 Hull (Central Area Lightweight Title Challenge)
12.12.92	Mark Tibbs L PTS 6 Muswell Hill
20.01.93	Dean Amory L PTS 6 Solihull
18.02.93	Kevin Toomey L PTS 10 Hull (Central Area Lightweight Title Defence)
23.03.93	Alan Peacock W PTS 6 Wolverhampton
01.04.93	Shane Sheridan W PTS 6 Evesham
30.04.93	Alan McDowall L PTS 6 Glasgow
14.05.93	Tanver Ahmed L PTS 6 Kilmarnock
07.06.93	Howard Clarke L RTD 2 Walsall
06.09.93	Joey Moffat L PTS 6 Liverpool
20.09.93	Rick North L PTS 6 Cleethorpes
28.09.93	Bernard Paul L PTS 8 Bethnal Green
28.10.93	Gary Hiscox L RSC 5 Walsall
13.12.93	Jamie Morris W RSC 3 Doncaster
Career: 141 contests, won 32, drew 14, lost 95.	

Tony Britland

Barmouth. *Born* Dolgellau, 26 November, 1960

Welterweight. Ht. 5'7"

Manager Self

12.01.87	Mark Dinnadge L RSC 3 Ealing
18.03.87	Jimmy Ward W PTS 6 Queensway
15.04.87	Kevin Hayde W PTS 6 Carmarthen
07.05.87	Simon Paul L PTS 6 Bayswater
09.06.87	Ossie Maddix L PTS 6 Manchester
17.09.87	Ian John-Lewis L PTS 6 Gravesend
24.09.87	Martin Smith DREW 6 Crystal Palace
19.10.87	Ossie Maddix L PTS 6 Manchester
30.11.87	Barry Messam L PTS 6 Nottingham
16.12.87	Ensley Bingham L CO 1 Manchester
13.04.88	Martin Smith L RSC 2 Gravesend
08.06.88	Eamonn Loughran L RSC 1 Sheffield
25.10.88	Pat Dunne W PTS 6 Pontardawe
15.11.88	Tony Gibbs DREW 8 Piccadilly
23.11.88	John Corcoran DREW 8 Solihull
07.12.88	Michael Oliver L RSC 2 Aberavon
25.01.89	John Corcoran L PTS 8 Solihull
28.02.89	Ronnie Campbell DREW 6 Dudley
16.03.89	Leigh Wicks L PTS 8 Southwark
11.04.89	Adrian Din L PTS 6 Aberavon
17.04.89	Wayne Timmins DREW 6 Birmingham
24.04.89	Adrian Din W PTS 6 Nottingham
10.05.89	Gary Logan L CO 1 Kensington
19.08.89	Jimmy Farrell L PTS 6 Cardiff
09.11.89	Jimmy Farrell L RSC 4 Cardiff
11.12.89	Alan Richards L RSC 7 Birmingham
23.04.90	Wayne Timmins L PTS 8 Birmingham
24.05.90	Wayne Timmins L PTS 8 Dudley
11.06.90	Des Robinson L PTS 8 Manchester
16.11.90	Robert Wright L RSC 3 Telford
21.02.91	Shaun Cogan L PTS 6 Walsall
06.03.91	Robert McCracken L RSC 2 Wembley
12.04.91	Darren Morris W PTS 6 Willenhall
14.05.91	Wayne Timmins L PTS 6 Dudley
03.10.91	John Corcoran W RSC 5 Burton
21.10.91	Leigh Wicks L RSC 3 Mayfair
02.12.91	Richard O'Brien L RSC 2 Birmingham
18.05.93	Spencer McCracken L CO 1 Edgbaston
29.06.93	James Campbell L PTS 6 Edgbaston
30.10.93	Tony Mock L PTS 6 Chester
Career: 40 contests, won 6, drew 5, lost 29.	

Mark Brogan

Leicester. *Born* Leicester, 24 May, 1964

L. Middleweight. Ht. 5'8"

Manager J. Griffin

03.03.86	Mike Breen DREW 4 Leicester
10.04.86	Wil Halliday L PTS 4 Leicester
15.12.86	Oliver Henry L CO 2 Loughborough
22.02.93	Dave Maj L RSC 5 Liverpool
20.09.93	Nick Ingram L RSC 4 Northampton
Career: 5 contests, drew 1, lost 4.	

Roger Brotherhood

Mansfield. *Born* Mansfield, 10 June, 1971

S. Featherweight. Ht. 5'8"

Manager J. Ashton

07.04.94	Robert Grubb W PTS 6 Walsall
Career: 1 contest, won 1.	

Matt Brown

Walworth. *Born* Camberwell, 17 February, 1971

S. Featherweight. Ht. 5'6"
Manager F. Maloney

15.06.94 Chris Lyons W CO 3 Southwark
Career: 1 contest, won 1.

Mike Anthony Brown

Brixton. *Born* Jamaica, 8 February, 1970
Lightweight. Ht. 5'8"
Manager F. Rix

23.05.93 Norman Dhalie L PTS 4 Brockley
25.06.93 G.G. Goddard W CO 2 Battersea
14.08.93 Simon Frailing W RSC 4 Hammersmith
14.04.94 Norman Dhalie W PTS 6 Battersea
22.05.94 Miguel Matthews L RSC 5 Crystal Palace

Career: 5 contests, won 3, lost 2.

Tony Brown

Liverpool. *Born* Liverpool, 10 August, 1961
Former Undefeated Central Area Welterweight & L. Welterweight Champion. Ht. 5'8"
Manager Self

29.03.82 Paul Murray W PTS 6 Liverpool
05.04.82 Glen Crump W PTS 6 Manchester
22.04.82 Mickey Williams W RSC 3 Liverpool
10.05.82 Gary Petty W RSC 5 Liverpool
17.05.82 Cecil Williams W RSC 4 Manchester
03.06.82 Errol Dennis DREW 6 Liverpool
21.06.82 Errol Dennis W CO 3 Liverpool
06.07.82 Danny Garrison W PTS 6 Leeds
23.09.82 Ian Chantler W PTS 8 Liverpool
05.10.82 Ian Chantler L PTS 8 Liverpool
18.10.82 Steve Early L PTS 6 Edgbaston
06.12.82 Steve Early L PTS 8 Edgbaston
14.03.83 Walter Clayton W PTS 10 Sheffield
(Vacant Central Area L. Welterweight Title)
20.04.83 Martin McGough W PTS 8 Solihull
03.10.83 Steve Tempro W PTS 8 Liverpool
13.10.83 Vernon Vanriel W PTS 8 Bloomsbury
30.11.83 Tony Laing L PTS 8 Piccadilly
12.03.84 Mickey Bird W RSC 6 Liverpool
04.06.84 Tony Adams L RSC 2 Mayfair
29.08.84 Joseph Lala L PTS 10 Sebokeng, South Africa
24.10.84 Kostas Petrou L PTS 8 Birmingham
31.05.85 Cliff Domville W RSC 1 Liverpool
(Vacant Central Area Welterweight Title)
22.10.85 Billy Ahearne W PTS 6 Hull
04.11.85 Phil Duckworth W RTD 5 Manchester
06.12.85 Ian Chantler W RSC 7 Liverpool
(Central Area Welterweight Title Defence)
13.03.86 Kostas Petrou W PTS 8 Alfreton
29.11.86 Rocky Kelly L RSC 11 Wandsworth
(Final Elim. British Welterweight Title)
07.04.87 Derek Wormald L RSC 6 Batley
09.05.87 George Collins L RSC 5 Wandsworth
25.04.88 Jim Kelly W PTS 8 Liverpool
10.11.89 Humphrey Harrison L PTS 6 Liverpool
13.06.94 Phil Found L RSC 4 Liverpool
Career: 32 contests, won 19, drew 1, lost 12.

Denzil Browne

Leeds. *Born* Leeds, 21 January, 1969
Cruiserweight. Ht. 6'2½"
Manager M. Duff

18.10.90 Mark Bowen W PTS 6 Dewsbury
29.11.90 R. F. McKenzie L PTS 6 Sunderland
13.12.90 Gary Railton W RSC 2 Dewsbury
21.02.91 Mark Bowen W PTS 6 Walsall
21.03.91 R. F. McKenzie W PTS 6 Dewsbury
09.05.91 Darren McKenna W PTS 6 Leeds
27.06.91 Steve Yorath W PTS 6 Leeds
01.08.91 Tony Colclough W RSC 1 Dewsbury
09.10.91 R. F. McKenzie L PTS 6 Manchester
30.10.91 Gus Mendes W RSC 6 Leeds
23.01.92 Darren McKenna W PTS 6 York
19.03.92 Ian Bulloch W PTS 8 York
23.09.92 Steve Yorath W PTS 8 Leeds
29.10.92 Sean O'Phoenix W RSC 4 Leeds
25.02.93 Cordwell Hylton W PTS 8 Bradford
22.04.93 Dave Muhammed W PTS 8 Mayfair
01.07.93 Steve Osborne W RSC 1 York
07.10.93 Tony Booth DREW 8 York
01.12.93 Lennie Howard W RSC 6 Kensington
Career: 19 contests, won 16, drew 1, lost 2.

Frank Bruno

Wandsworth. *Born* Hammersmith, 16 November, 1961
Former Undefeated European Heavyweight Champion. Ht. 6'3½"
Manager Self

17.03.82 Lupe Guerra W CO 1 Kensington
30.03.82 Harvey Steichen W RSC 2 Wembley
20.04.82 Tom Stevenson W CO 1 Kensington
04.05.82 Ron Gibbs W RSC 4 Wembley
01.06.82 Tony Moore W RSC 2 Kensington
14.09.82 George Scott W RSC 1 Wembley
23.10.82 Ali Lukasa W CO 2 Berlin, Germany
09.11.82 Rudi Gauwe W CO 2 Kensington
23.11.82 George Butzbach W RTD 1 Wembley
07.12.82 Gilberto Acuna W RSC 1 Kensington
18.01.83 Stewart Lithgo W RTD 4 Kensington
08.02.83 Peter Mulendwa W CO 3 Kensington
01.03.83 Winston Allen W RSC 2 Kensington
05.04.83 Eddie Neilson W RSC 3 Kensington
03.05.83 Scott Ledoux W RSC 3 Wembley
31.05.83 Barry Funches W RSC 5 Kensington
09.07.83 Mike Jameson W CO 2 Chicago, USA
27.09.83 Bill Sharkey W CO 1 Wembley
11.10.83 Floyd Cummings W RSC 7 Kensington
06.12.83 Walter Santemore W CO 4 Kensington
13.03.84 Juan Figueroa W CO 1 Wembley
13.05.84 James Smith L CO 10 Wembley
25.09.84 Ken Lakusta W CO 2 Wembley
(Elim. Commonwealth Heavyweight Title)
06.11.84 Jeff Jordan W RSC 3 Kensington
27.11.84 Phil Brown W PTS 10 Wembley
26.03.85 Lucien Rodriguez W RSC 1 Wembley
01.10.85 Anders Eklund W CO 4 Wembley
(European Heavyweight Title Challenge)
04.12.85 Larry Frazier W CO 2 Kensington
04.03.86 Gerrie Coetzee W CO 1 Wembley
(Final Elim. WBA Heavyweight Title)
19.07.86 Tim Witherspoon L RSC 11 Wembley
(WBA Heavyweight Title Challenge)
24.03.87 James Tillis W RSC 5 Wembley
27.06.87 Chuck Gardner W CO 1 Cannes, France
30.08.87 Reggie Gross W RSC 8 Marbella, Spain
24.10.87 Joe Bugner W RSC 8 Tottenham
25.02.89 Mike Tyson L RSC 5 Las Vegas, USA
(WBC Heavyweight Title Challenge)
20.11.91 John Emmen W CO 1 Kensington

22.04.92 Jose Ribalta W CO 2 Wembley
17.10.92 Pierre Coetzer W RSC 8 Wembley
(Elim. IBF Heavyweight Title)
24.04.93 Carl Williams W RSC 10 Birmingham
01.10.93 Lennox Lewis L RSC 7 Cardiff
(WBC Heavyweight Title Challenge)
16.03.94 Jesse Ferguson W RSC 1 Birmingham
Career: 41 contests, won 37, lost 4.

Denroy Bryan

Swindon. *Born* Birmingham, 15 November, 1959
Heavyweight. Ht. 5'11¼"
Manager Self

16.09.83 Michael Armstrong W RSC 1 Swindon
14.11.83 Michael Armstrong W RSC 4 Nantwich
22.02.84 Glenn McCrory L PTS 8 Kensington
30.04.84 Dave Garside L PTS 8 Mayfair
25.01.85 Noel Quarless L RSC 1 Liverpool
22.04.85 Ralph Irving W PTS 6 Southwark
30.05.85 Carl Gaffney L RSC 1 Halifax
12.09.85 Ian Priest W RSC 7 Swindon
01.10.85 Dave Garside L RSC 3 Wembley
14.11.85 Paul Lister L PTS 8 Newcastle
19.02.86 Gary Mason L CO 1 Kensington
01.04.87 Barry Ellis DREW 8 Southsea
12.10.87 John Emmen L PTS 8 Hertogenbosch, Holland
09.02.88 James Oyebola L RSC 6 Bethnal Green
29.03.88 Keith Ferdinand L RSC 2 Bethnal Green
16.05.88 Al Malcolm L PTS 10 Wolverhampton
(Midlands Area Heavyweight Title Challenge)
28.10.88 Jess Harding L RSC 4 Brentwood
05.12.88 David Jules DREW 6 Dudley
18.01.89 David Jules L RSC 2 Stoke
23.10.89 John Williams DREW 6 Mayfair
10.11.89 Barry Ellis W RSC 3 Battersea
05.12.89 Adam Fogerty L RSC 3 Dewsbury
03.02.90 Gary McConnell L RSC 9 Bristol
06.03.90 Manny Burgo L PTS 8 Newcastle
20.03.90 Paul Lister L PTS 8 Hartlepool
25.05.90 Cesare di Benedetto L RSC 5 Avezzano, Italy
29.11.90 Adam Fogerty L RSC 2 Sunderland
12.11.91 J. A. Bugner L PTS 4 Milton Keynes
11.12.91 Joe Egan W RSC 4 Dublin
31.01.92 Maurice Core L RSC 1 Manchester
05.10.92 Damien Caesar L RSC 5 Bristol
01.12.92 Barry Ellis W PTS 6 Bristol
22.02.93 Warren Richards L CO 4 Eltham
10.04.93 Dermot Gascoyne L PTS 6 Swansea
11.05.93 Scott Welch L RSC 4 Norwich
15.09.93 James Oyebola L RSC 5 Bethnal Green
Career: 36 contests, won 7, drew 3, lost 26.

Wayne Buck

Nottingham. *Born* Nottingham, 31 August, 1966
Heavyweight. Ht. 5'10¾"
Manager M. Shinfield

26.03.90 Tucker Richards W CO 1 Nottingham
30.04.90 Chris Hubbert L CO 4 Nottingham
04.06.92 Gary Charlton W PTS 6 Cleethorpes
08.09.92 David Jules W RSC 3 Doncaster
12.11.92 Gary Charlton W PTS 8 Stafford
02.02.93 John Harewood L RSC 3 Derby
11.03.93 Vance Idiens W PTS 8 Walsall

29.10.93 Mikael Lindblad L RTD 3 Kordoer, Denmark
28.03.94 Steve Lewsam L PTS 10 Cleethorpes
(Vacant Midlands Area Heavyweight Title)
11.05.94 J. A. Bugner DREW 6 Stevenage
Career: 10 contests, won 5, drew 1, lost 4.

Pete Buckley

Birmingham. *Born* Birmingham, 9 March, 1969
S. Bantamweight. Midlands Area S. Featherweight Champion. Ht. 5'8"
Manager Self

04.10.89 Alan Baldwin DREW 6 Stafford
10.10.89 Ronnie Stephenson L PTS 6 Wolverhampton
30.10.89 Robert Braddock W PTS 6 Birmingham
14.11.89 Neil Leitch W PTS 6 Evesham
22.11.89 Peter Judson W PTS 6 Stafford
11.12.89 Stevie Woods W PTS 6 Bradford
21.12.89 Wayne Taylor W PTS 6 Kings Heath
10.01.90 John O'Meara W PTS 6 Kensington
19.02.90 Ian McGirr L PTS 6 Birmingham
27.02.90 Miguel Matthews DREW 6 Evesham
14.03.90 Ronnie Stephenson DREW 6 Stoke
04.04.90 Ronnie Stephenson L PTS 8 Stafford
23.04.90 Ronnie Stephenson W PTS 6 Birmingham
30.04.90 Chris Clarkson L PTS 8 Mayfair
17.05.90 Johnny Bredahl L PTS 6 Aars, Denmark
04.06.90 Ronnie Stephenson W PTS 8 Birmingham
28.06.90 Robert Braddock W RSC 5 Birmingham
01.10.90 Miguel Matthews W PTS 8 Cleethorpes
09.10.90 Miguel Matthews L PTS 8 Wolverhampton
17.10.90 Tony Smith W PTS 6 Stoke
29.10.90 Miguel Matthews W PTS 8 Birmingham
21.11.90 Drew Docherty L PTS 8 Solihull
10.12.90 Neil Leitch W PTS 8 Birmingham
10.01.91 Duke McKenzie L RSC 5 Wandsworth
18.02.91 Jamie McBride L PTS 8 Glasgow
04.03.91 Brian Robb W RSC 7 Birmingham
26.03.91 Neil Leitch DREW 8 Wolverhampton
01.05.91 Mark Geraghty W PTS 8 Solihull
05.06.91 Brian Robb W PTS 10 Wolverhampton
(Vacant Midlands Area S. Featherweight Title)
09.09.91 Mike Deveney L PTS 8 Glasgow
24.09.91 Mark Bates W RTD 5 Basildon
29.10.91 John Armour L PTS 6 Kensington
14.11.91 Mike Deveney L PTS 6 Edinburgh
28.11.91 Craig Dermody L PTS 6 Liverpool
19.12.91 Craig Dermody L PTS 6 Oldham
18.01.92 Alan McKay DREW 8 Kensington
20.02.92 Brian Robb W RSC 10 Oakengates
(Midlands Area S. Featherweight Title Defence)
27.04.92 Drew Docherty L PTS 8 Glasgow
15.05.92 Ruben Condori L PTS 10 Augsburg, Germany
29.05.92 Donnie Hood L PTS 8 Glasgow
07.09.92 Duke McKenzie L RTD 3 Bethnal Green
12.11.92 Prince Nassem Hamed L PTS 6 Liverpool
19.02.93 Harald Geier L PTS 12 Vienna, Austria
(Vacant WBA Penta-Continental S. Bantamweight Title)
26.04.93 Bradley Stone L PTS 8 Lewisham
18.06.93 Eamonn McAuley L PTS 6 Belfast
01.07.93 Tony Silkstone L PTS 8 York
06.10.93 Jonjo Irwin L PTS 8 Solihull
25.10.93 Drew Docherty L PTS 8 Glasgow
06.11.93 Michael Alldis L PTS 8 Bethnal Green
30.11.93 Barry Jones L PTS 4 Cardiff
19.12.93 Shaun Anderson L PTS 6 Glasgow
22.01.94 Barry Jones L PTS 6 Cardiff
29.01.94 Prince Nassem Hamed L RSC 4 Cardiff
10.03.94 Tony Falcone L PTS 4 Bristol
29.03.94 Conn McMullen W PTS 6 Bethnal Green
05.04.94 Mark Bowers L PTS 6 Bethnal Green
13.04.94 James Murray L PTS 6 Glasgow
06.05.94 Paul Lloyd L RTD 4 Liverpool
Career: 58 contests, won 19, drew 5, lost 34.

Pete Buckley   Les Clark

(Joe) J. A. Bugner

St Ives. *Born* St Ives, 12 August, 1970
Heavyweight. Ht. 6'6"
Manager A. Smith

12.11.91 Denroy Bryan W PTS 4 Milton Keynes
06.02.92 Gary Railton W CO 3 Peterborough
05.03.92 John Harewood W PTS 4 Battersea
22.04.92 Gary McCrory W PTS 4 Wembley
07.09.92 Gary Williams W PTS 4 Bethnal Green
17.10.92 Steve Gee W PTS 6 Wembley
17.12.92 Chris Coughlan W RSC 3 Wembley
24.02.93 Steve Garber L RSC 6 Wembley
22.09.93 Gary Charlton W RSC 1 Wembley
11.05.94 Wayne Buck DREW 6 Stevenage
Career: 10 contests, won 8, drew 1, lost 1.

(Emmanuel) Manny Burgo

North Shields. *Born* North Shields, 15 June, 1961
Heavyweight. Ht. 6'1"
Manager Self

07.03.88 Tee Lewis W PTS 3 Northampton
07.03.88 Ian Nelson W PTS 6 Northampton
22.04.88 Steve Garber W PTS 6 Gateshead
18.06.88 Tony Hallett W RSC 3 Gateshead
22.11.88 Dave Garside W PTS 8 Marton
29.03.89 Chris Jacobs W PTS 8 Bethnal Green
06.03.90 Denroy Bryan W PTS 8 Newcastle
20.03.90 Neil Malpass W RSC 3 Hartlepool
15.05.90 Al Malcolm W PTS 6 South Shields
23.01.91 Steve Gee W PTS 6 Brentwood
29.04.93 Gary Charlton W PTS 6 Newcastle
15.09.93 Chris Coughlin W PTS 6 Bethnal Green
13.10.93 Carl Gaffney W PTS 6 Bethnal Green
01.12.93 Wayne Llewellyn L PTS 6 Bethnal Green
27.04.94 Julius Francis L PTS 4 Bethnal Green
Career: 15 contests, won 13, lost 2.

Manny Burgo   Les Clark

Paul Burke

Preston. *Born* Preston, 25 July, 1966
Former British & Commonwealth Lightweight Champion. Ht. 5'10"
Manager Self

21.01.87 Steve Brown W CO 4 Stoke
30.01.87 Paul Marriott L PTS 6 Kirkby
02.03.87 Brian Murphy W CO 2 Marton
06.04.87 Paul Marriott W PTS 6 Newcastle
30.04.87 Paul Gadney W PTS 6 Bethnal Green
01.06.87 Pat Barrett W PTS 6 Bradford
15.09.87 Marvin P. Gray L RSC 6 Batley
18.11.87 Rudy Valentino W PTS 6 Bethnal Green
15.12.87 James Jiora L PTS 4 Bradford
11.02.88 Paul Gadney DREW 8 Gravesend
25.01.89 Paul Charters W PTS 6 Bethnal Green
23.02.89 Mark Kelly L DIS 5 Stockport
07.03.89 Tony Connellan W RSC 5 Manchester
11.04.89 Billy Buchanan W RSC 4 Oldham
21.10.89 Aaron Kabi DREW 8 Middlesbrough
09.12.89 Angel Mona L RSC 3 Toulouse, France
23.04.90 Tony Richards L PTS 10 Glasgow
(Elim. British Lightweight Title)
25.09.90 Robert Harkin W PTS 8 Glasgow
21.01.91 Peter Bradley W PTS 10 Glasgow
(Elim. British Lightweight Title)

31.05.91	Art Blackmore W RSC 3 Manchester
20.09.91	Tony Richards W PTS 8 Manchester
09.02.92	Dave Andrews W PTS 6 Bradford
28.04.92	Paul Charters W RSC 7 Houghton le Spring
	(Final Elim. British Lightweight Title)
28.09.92	Marcel Herbert W PTS 6 Manchester
17.11.92	Jean-Baptiste Mendy L PTS 12 Paris, France
	(European Lightweight Title Challenge)
24.02.93	Billy Schwer W RSC 7 Wembley
	(British & Commonwealth Lightweight Title Challenge)
25.07.93	Lyndon Paul Walker W PTS 8 Oldham
10.11.93	Billy Schwer L PTS 12 Watford
	(British & Commonwealth Lightweight Title Defence)
22.04.94	Racheed Lawal L RSC 4 Aalborg, Denmark
	(European Lightweight Title Challenge)

Career: 29 contests, won 18, drew 2, lost 9.

Vince Burns

Battersea. *Born* Paddington, 27 July, 1970
S. Featherweight. Ht. 5'7"
Manager Self

29.04.93	Jason Hutson W RSC 1 Hayes
04.10.93	Yifru Retta L PTS 6 Mayfair

Career: 2 contests, won 1, lost 1.

Garry Burrell

Kirkcaldy. *Born* Musselburgh, 9 July, 1965
Lightweight. Ht. 5'7½"
Manager T. Gilmour

21.09.92	Alan Graham W PTS 6 Glasgow
09.11.92	Alan Graham L PTS 6 Bradford
22.02.93	Tim Hill L PTS 6 Glasgow
23.03.93	Yusuf Vorajee L PTS 6 Wolverhampton
26.04.93	Robbie Sivyer W PTS 6 Glasgow
20.09.93	Phil Found L RSC 4 Glasgow
25.11.93	Colin Innes L PTS 6 Newcastle
24.05.94	Alan Graham L PTS 6 Sunderland

Career: 8 contests, won 2, lost 6.

Graham Burton

Sheffield. *Born* Chesterfield, 16 June, 1964
S. Middleweight. Ht. 5'10"
Manager B. Ingle

10.10.88	Frank Mobbs W RSC 3 Manchester
03.11.88	Terry French W RSC 3 Manchester
16.01.89	Dave Andrews W PTS 6 Northampton
04.04.89	Spencer Alton W RSC 3 Sheffield
06.12.89	Dave Brosnan W RSC 6 Stoke
29.01.90	Darren McKenna W PTS 4 Hull
23.04.90	Stevie R. Davies W PTS 6 Bradford
05.06.90	Nick Gyaamie W PTS 6 Eltham
18.09.90	Wayne Timmins W PTS 6 Wolverhampton
17.01.91	John Ashton L PTS 10 Alfreton
12.03.91	Peter Gorny W PTS 6 Mansfield
13.06.91	Michael Gale L CO 4 Hull
12.11.91	Paul Busby L RSC 3 Wolverhampton
04.02.92	Richie Woodhall L RSC 2 Alfreton
17.03.92	Andrew Flute L PTS 8 Wolverhampton
13.10.92	Richard Carter DREW 8 Wolverhampton
24.11.92	Nigel Rafferty L PTS 8 Wolverhampton

20.01.93	Neville Brown L CO 4 Wolverhampton
24.04.93	Cornelius Carr L PTS 6 Birmingham
26.05.93	Jason McNeill W RSC 3 Mansfield
11.08.93	Tony Behan W PTS 6 Mansfield
16.03.94	Andrew Flute L PTS 6 Birmingham
18.04.94	Nigel Rafferty L PTS 8 Walsall

Career: 23 contests, won 12, drew 1, lost 10.

Kevin Burton

Doncaster. *Born* Doncaster, 20 June, 1965
L. Heavyweight. Ht. 5'10½"
Manager J. Rushton

10.05.93	Pat McNamara W RSC 2 Cleethorpes
07.06.93	Tony Colclough W PTS 6 Walsall
20.09.93	Bullit Andrews W PTS 6 Cleethorpes
30.09.93	Tony Colclough W DIS 5 Walsall
13.12.93	Tony Colclough W RSC 3 Doncaster
07.03.94	Bullit Andrews W RSC 1 Doncaster
07.04.94	Johnny Hooks L PTS 6 Walsall
10.05.94	Declan Faherty L RSC 4 Doncaster

Career: 8 contests, won 6, lost 2.

Steve Burton

Pembroke. *Born* Pembroke, 29 August, 1970
Lightweight. Ht. 5'7"
Manager D. Davies

26.04.94	Colin Dunne L CO 2 Bethnal Green
28.05.94	Everald Williams DREW 6 Queensway

Career: 2 contests, drew 1, lost 1.

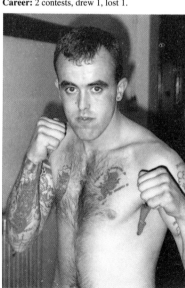

Steve Burton   Les Clark

Paul Busby

Worcester. *Born* Worcester, 20 April, 1966
Middleweight. Ht. 5'11½"
Manager B. Hearn

18.11.90	Carlos Christie W PTS 6 Birmingham
04.12.90	Marty Duke W PTS 6 Bury St Edmunds
23.01.91	Tony Wellington W RSC 2 Brentwood
27.02.91	Paul Murray W PTS 6 Wolverhampton
19.03.91	Paul Smith W PTS 6 Leicester
10.09.91	Nigel Rafferty W RSC 2 Wolverhampton

12.11.91	Graham Burton W RSC 3 Wolverhampton
17.12.91	Paul Murray W CO 3 Cardiff
01.02.92	John Kaighin W PTS 4 Birmingham
23.05.92	Stinger Mason W RSC 2 Birmingham
06.10.92	Chris Richards W PTS 6 Antwerp, Belgium
14.11.92	Paul Wesley W PTS 8 Cardiff
19.01.93	Stan King W PTS 8 Cardiff
16.03.93	Neville Brown L PTS 10 Wolverhampton
	(Elim. British Middleweight Title)
10.07.93	Wayne Ellis L RSC 5 Cardiff
03.11.93	Spencer Alton W RTD 6 Worcester
19.01.94	Colin Manners DREW 8 Solihull
15.03.94	Colin Manners W PTS 8 Mayfair
28.06.94	Wayne Ellis L TD 4 Mayfair
	(Vacant WBO Penta-Continental Middleweight Title)

Career: 19 contests, won 15, drew 1, lost 3.

Richard Bustin

Norwich. *Born* Norwich, 9 October, 1964
S. Middleweight. Ht. 5'9"
Manager Self

15.02.88	Roger Silsby L PTS 6 Copthorne
14.03.88	Tony Behan W RSC 3 Norwich
05.04.88	Steve Conway W RSC 4 Basildon
28.05.88	Winston Burnett W PTS 6 Kensington
17.10.88	Dennis Banton W RSC 5 Mayfair
15.11.88	Crawford Ashley L CO 3 Norwich
07.02.89	Alan Baptiste W PTS 6 Southend
15.05.89	Alex Romeo L RSC 2 Northampton
03.10.89	Alan Baptiste W PTS 6 Southend
17.10.89	Mick Maw W CO 2 Cardiff
14.03.90	Paul McCarthy L RSC 7 Battersea
	(Vacant Southern Area S. Middleweight Title)
12.11.90	Alan Baptiste W RSC 1 Norwich
29.01.91	Simon Harris L RSC 3 Wisbech
18.04.91	John Foreman W PTS 8 Earls Court
11.06.91	Gary Ballard L PTS 8 Leicester
19.11.91	Glazz Campbell L CO 7 Norwich
	(Vacant Southern Area L. Heavyweight Title)
31.01.92	Bobbi Joe Edwards L PTS 6 Manchester
31.03.92	Gypsy Carman L PTS 6 Norwich
27.06.92	Dariusz Michalczewski L RSC 4 Quinta do Lago, Portugal
08.07.92	Karl Barwise W PTS 6 Norwich
17.04.93	Paul Hitch W PTS 6 Washington
06.03.94	Ali Forbes L PTS 10 Southwark
	(Vacant Southern Area S. Middleweight Title)

Career: 22 contests, won 11, lost 11.

(Barrie) Blue Butterworth

Burnley. *Born* Lambeth, 5 October, 1970
L. Welterweight. Ht. 5'8½"
Manager J. Doughty

31.03.92	Brian Coleman W PTS 6 Stockport
04.06.92	Mark Allen W RSC 5 Burnley
14.09.92	Lee Soar W CO 4 Bradford
12.11.92	Dave Madden W RSC 2 Burnley
25.02.93	Ian Thomas W PTS 6 Burnley
27.05.93	Brian Coleman W PTS 6 Burnley
13.09.93	Kevin McKenzie L PTS 6 Middleton
11.11.93	Jamie Davidson W RSC 3 Burnley
25.04.94	Rob Stewart L PTS 6 Bury

Career: 9 contests, won 7, lost 2.

Craig Byrne

Birmingham. *Born* Birmingham, 12 July, 1974
S. Middleweight. Ht. 6'1"
Manager E. Cashmore

23.05.94 Richard Guy L RSC 4 Walsall
Career: 1 contest, lost 1.

Sean Byrne

Northampton. *Born* Manchester, 20 September, 1966
Middleweight. Ht. 6'0"
Manager J. Cox

06.04.92 Martin Jolley W RSC 6 Northampton
28.04.92 John McKenzie W RSC 6 Corby
05.10.92 Russell Washer W PTS 6 Northampton
20.09.93 Spencer Alton W PTS 6 Northampton
23.11.93 John Rice W PTS 6 Kettering
19.12.93 Kessem Clayton W PTS 6 Northampton
Career: 6 contests, won 6.

Damien Caesar

Stepney. *Born* Stepney, 2 October, 1965
Heavyweight. Ht. 6'5"
Manager Self

22.04.91 Larry Peart W RSC 2 Mayfair
30.05.91 Tony Colclough W RSC 1 Mayfair
17.02.92 Steve Stewart W RSC 5 Mayfair
27.04.92 Gary Williams W RSC 4 Mayfair
05.10.92 Denroy Bryan W RSC 5 Bristol
07.12.93 Joey Paladino W RSC 3 Bethnal Green
14.03.94 Vance Idiens W RSC 4 Mayfair
Career: 7 contests, won 7.

Albert Call

Grimsby. *Born* Grimsby, 17 April, 1967
Cruiserweight. Ht. 6'2"
Manager L. Billany

21.09.92 John Pierre W PTS 6 Cleethorpes
14.12.92 Art Stacey W PTS 6 Cleethorpes
22.02.93 Kenny Sandison W PTS 6 Liverpool
25.08.93 Peter Smith L PTS 6 Hammanskrall, South Africa
20.09.93 Trevor Small DREW 6 Cleethorpes
28.09.93 Dennis Bailey DREW 6 Liverpool
30.10.93 Kenley Price DREW 6 Chester
13.12.93 Trevor Small W RSC 5 Cleethorpes
17.03.94 Art Stacey W PTS 6 Lincoln
15.04.94 Cordwell Hylton L RSC 4 Hull
(Vacant Midlands Area Cruiserweight Title)
Career: 10 contests, won 5, drew 3, lost 2.

Joe Calzaghe

Newbridge. *Born* Hammersmith, 23 March, 1972
S. Middleweight. Ht. 5'11"
Manager M. Duff

01.10.93 Paul Hanlon W RSC 1 Cardiff
10.11.93 Stinger Mason W RSC 1 Watford
16.12.93 Spencer Alton W RSC 2 Newport
22.01.94 Martin Rosamond W RSC 1 Cardiff
01.03.94 Darren Littlewood W RSC 1 Dudley
04.06.94 Karl Barwise W RSC 1 Cardiff
Career: 6 contests, won 6.

Anthony Campbell   Les Clark

Anthony Campbell

Battersea. *Born* Kensington, 20 January, 1967
Lightweight. Ht. 5'6"
Manager D. Gunn

05.04.94 Andrew Reed W PTS 6 Bethnal Green
20.05.94 Malcolm Thomas W PTS 6 Acton
Career: 2 contests, won 2.

Dave Campbell

Middlesbrough. *Born* South Shields, 13 December, 1968
Bantamweight. Ht. 5'4½"
Manager A. Walker

11.09.91 Mark Hargreaves L RSC 4 Stoke
14.11.91 Dave Martin W PTS 6 Bayswater
27.11.91 Shaun Norman W PTS 6 Marton
18.05.92 Glyn Shepherd W RSC 1 Marton
23.09.92 Tony Silkstone L RSC 4 Leeds
08.03.93 Ady Benton L PTS 6 Leeds
26.03.93 Shaun Anderson L RSC 5 Glasgow
30.04.93 James Murray L PTS 6 Glasgow
11.11.93 Marcus Duncan L PTS 6 Burnley
02.06.94 Adey Lewis L RSC 1 Middleton
Career: 10 contests, won 3, lost 7.

(Glasbourne) Glazz Campbell

Brockley. *Born* Sheffield, 9 August, 1962
Former Southern Area L. Heavyweight Champion. Ht. 6'0"
Manager Self

08.10.85 Winston Burnett W PTS 6 Southend
30.10.85 Lennie Howard L PTS 8 Basildon
23.05.86 Winston Burnett W PTS 6 Newport
25.09.86 Serg Fame W PTS 8 Crystal Palace
03.11.86 Blaine Logsdon L CO 3 Manchester
29.01.87 Lou Gent L PTS 6 Merton
14.09.87 Crawford Ashley W PTS 8 Bloomsbury
03.12.87 Mike Aubrey W PTS 8 Southend
26.04.88 Agamil Yilderim DREW 8 Cologne, Germany
13.09.88 Serg Fame L PTS 10 Battersea
(Vacant Southern Area L. Heavyweight Title)
20.02.89 Pedro van Raamsdonk L PTS 8 Arnhem, Holland
25.09.89 Alek Pernarski W RSC 4 Piccadilly
23.10.89 Derek Myers L PTS 8 Mayfair
30.04.90 Mwehu Beya DREW 8 Pesara, Italy
13.06.90 Cordwell Hylton L PTS 4 Manchester
15.09.90 Noel Magee L PTS 8 Belfast
07.12.90 Henry Maske L PTS 8 Berlin, Germany
12.04.91 Maurice Core L CO 2 Manchester
29.06.91 Christophe Girard L PTS 8 Le Touquet, France
24.08.91 Mwehu Beya L PTS 6 Pesaro, Italy
02.10.91 Tony Wilson W PTS 8 Solihull
19.11.91 Richard Bustin W CO 7 Norwich
(Vacant Southern Area L. Heavyweight Title)
18.03.92 Tom Collins W PTS 10 Glasgow
(Final Elim. British L. Heavyweight Title)
25.04.92 Crawford Ashley L RSC 8 Belfast
(British L. Heavyweight Title Challenge)
28.09.93 Garry Delaney L CO 6 Bethnal Green
(Southern Area L. Heavyweight Title Defence)
13.11.93 Fabrice Tiozzo L RSC 10 Caen, France
Career: 26 contests, won 9, drew 2, lost 15.

Glenn Campbell

Bury. *Born* Bury, 22 April, 1970
Central Area S. Middleweight Champion. Ht. 5'10"
Manager J. Doughty

19.04.90 Ian Vokes W CO 1 Oldham
01.05.90 Stevie R. Davies W RSC 2 Oldham
21.05.90 Andy Marlow W RSC 6 Hanley
11.06.90 Stinger Mason W RTD 5 Manchester
26.09.90 Tony Kosova W RSC 2 Manchester
22.10.90 Simon McDougall W RSC 4 Manchester
26.11.90 Sean O'Phoenix W RSC 4 Bury
(Vacant Central Area S. Middleweight Title)
28.02.91 Simon McDougall W PTS 10 Bury
(Central Area S. Middleweight Title Defence)
17.05.91 Tony Booth W RSC 2 Bury
(Central Area S. Middleweight Title Defence)
21.01.92 Nigel Rafferty W RSC 6 Stockport
10.03.92 Carlos Christie DREW 8 Bury
05.05.92 Ian Henry W RSC 1 Preston
22.04.93 Paul Wright W RSC 4 Bury
(Elim. British S. Middleweight Title & Central Area S. Middleweight Title Defence)
17.02.94 Nigel Rafferty W RSC 7 Bury
15.03.94 Juan Carlos Scaglia L PTS 12 Mayfair
(Vacant WBO Penta-Continental S. Middleweight Title)
Career: 15 contests, won 13, drew 1, lost 1.

Jason Campbell

Brighton. *Born* Northampton, 12 November, 1970
L. Welterweight. Ht. 5'8"
Manager P. Newman

06.05.93   Adrian Chase L CO 2 Bayswater
07.12.93   Jason Beard L RSC 2 Bethnal Green
15.03.94   M. T. Atkin L RSC 5 Mayfair
Career: 3 contests, lost 3.

Jason Campbell   Les Clark

Martin Campbell

Wishaw. *Born* Wishaw, 2 December, 1966
L. Welterweight. Ht. 5'9"
Manager Self

08.06.88   Mark Jackson W RSC 4 Glasgow
22.09.88   Robert Wright L RSC 5
           Wolverhampton
14.05.93   Colin Wallace L PTS 6 Kilmarnock
09.09.93   Mick Mulcahy W PTS 6 Glasgow
21.10.93   Tanver Ahmed L PTS 6 Glasgow
Career: 5 contests, won 2, lost 3.

Mickey Cantwell

Eltham. *Born* London, 23 November, 1964
Former Undefeated Southern Area
Flyweight Champion. Ht. 5'2½"
Manager F. Maloney

21.01.91   Eduardo Vallejo W RSC 4 Crystal
           Palace
26.03.91   Mario Alberto Cruz W PTS 6 Bethnal
           Green
30.09.91   Ricky Beard W PTS 8 Kensington
23.10.91   Carlos Manrigues W RSC 5 Bethnal
           Green
14.12.91   Shaun Norman W PTS 8 Bexleyheath
16.05.92   Louis Veitch W PTS 6 Muswell Hill
10.02.93   Louis Veitch DREW 8 Lewisham
14.04.93   Darren Fifield W PTS 10 Kensington
           (Vacant Southern Area Flyweight Title)
15.09.93   Pablo Tiznado L PTS 12 Bethnal Green
           *(Vacant WBC International L.
           Flyweight Title)*
03.11.93   Anthony Hanna W PTS 8 Bristol
27.04.94   Luigi Camputaro L PTS 12 Bethnal
           Green
           (European Flyweight Title Challenge)
15.06.94   Lyndon Kershaw L PTS 8 Southwark
Career: 12 contests, won 8, drew 1, lost 3.

(George) Gypsy Carman

Ipswich. *Born* Wisbech, 23 November,
1964
Cruiserweight. Ht. 6'0"
Manager Self

30.01.84   Dave Mowbray W PTS 6 Manchester
16.02.84   Lennie Howard L RTD 1 Basildon
03.04.84   Gordon Stacey W PTS 6 Lewisham
07.06.84   Deka Williams L PTS 6 Dudley
29.10.84   Wes Taylor W PTS 6 Streatham
04.02.85   Lee White W PTS 6 Lewisham
20.02.85   Charlie Hostetter L PTS 6 Muswell
           Hill
27.03.85   Glenn McCrory L PTS 8 Gateshead
09.05.85   Barry Ellis L PTS 8 Acton
10.06.85   Chris Jacobs DREW 6 Cardiff
02.09.85   Barry Ellis L PTS 8 Coventry
31.10.85   Tee Jay L PTS 6 Wandsworth
15.03.86   Mick Cordon W PTS 8 Norwich
24.03.86   Chris Harbourne W PTS 6 Mayfair
13.09.86   Tee Jay L RSC 4 Norwich
           *(Vacant Southern Area Cruiserweight
           Title)*
20.11.86   Lou Gent L CO 1 Merton
12.01.87   Patrick Collins W PTS 8 Glasgow
19.01.87   Johnny Nelson L PTS 6 Mayfair
19.02.87   Danny Lawford L PTS 6 Peterborough
04.03.87   Tommy Taylor L PTS 8 Dudley
24.11.87   Tommy Taylor W PTS 8 Wisbech
14.03.88   Blaine Logsdon L RSC 8 Norwich
25.04.88   Gerry Storey L PTS 6 Bethnal Green
15.09.89   Carlton Headley W PTS 6 High
           Wycombe
22.02.90   Lou Gent L PTS 10 Wandsworth
           *(Southern Area Cruiserweight Title
           Challenge)*
07.05.90   Eddie Smulders L RSC 4 Arnhem,
           Holland
26.11.90   Everton Blake L PTS 6 Bethnal Green
22.10.91   Tenko Ernie W PTS 6 Wandsworth
21.01.92   Dave Lawrence W PTS 6 Norwich
31.03.92   Richard Bustin W PTS 6 Norwich
27.10.92   Everton Blake L RSC 4 Hayes
           *(Southern Area Cruiserweight Title
           Challenge)*
29.04.93   Paul McCarthy W PTS 6 Hayes
28.09.93   Scott Welch L RSC 3 Bethnal Green
Career: 33 contests, won 13, drew 1, lost 19.

Michael Carruth

Dublin. *Born* Dublin, 9 July, 1967
Welterweight. Ht. 5'8"
Manager F. Warren

26.02.94   George Wilson W PTS 6 Earls Court
21.05.94   Ricky Mabbett W CO 3 Belfast
Career: 2 contests, won 2.

Shamus Casey (West)

Alfreton. *Born* Pinxton, 13 January, 1960
Middleweight. Ht. 5'11"
Manager Self

25.01.84   Tony Burke L CO 1 Solihull
16.04.84   Ronnie Fraser L RSC 3 Nottingham
05.07.84   Craig Edwards L PTS 6 Prestatyn
21.09.84   Dave Foley W PTS 6 Alfreton
28.09.84   Dennis Boy O'Brien L PTS 6 Longford
11.10.84   Terry Gilbey L PTS 6 Barnsley
22.10.84   Dave King W PTS 6 South Shields
09.11.84   Reuben Thurley W CO 4 Alfreton
16.11.84   Tucker Watts L PTS 6 Leicester
26.11.84   Terry Gilbey L RSC 1 Liverpool

14.01.85   Mark Walker L PTS 6 Manchester
24.01.85   Tommy Campbell L PTS 8 Manchester
11.02.85   Paul Smith W PTS 6 Manchester
18.02.85   John Graham L PTS 6 Mayfair
01.03.85   Dennis Sheehan W PTS 6 Mansfield
11.03.85   Sean O'Phoenix L PTS 6 Manchester
20.03.85   Sean O'Phoenix L PTS 6 Stoke
15.04.85   Ronnie Tucker L PTS 6 Manchester
14.05.85   Dennis Sheehan L PTS 10 Mansfield
           *(Midlands Area L. Middleweight Title
           Challenge)*
05.06.85   Gary Stretch L RSC 2 Kensington
02.09.85   Newton Barnett DREW 8 Coventry
12.09.85   Cliff Curtis W RSC 7 Swindon
23.09.85   Danny Quigg L PTS 8 Glasgow
10.10.85   Davey Cox W PTS 6 Alfreton
22.10.85   Mick Mills L RSC 3 Hull
02.12.85   Newton Barnett DREW 8 Dulwich
09.12.85   Steve Ward L PTS 6 Nottingham
16.12.85   Robert Armstrong W PTS 6 Bradford
20.01.86   Billy Ahearne L PTS 8 Leicester
06.02.86   Denys Cronin L RSC 6 Doncaster
10.03.86   Neil Munn L PTS 8 Cardiff
20.03.86   Andy Wright L RSC 4 Merton
22.04.86   Franki Moro L PTS 8 Carlisle
29.04.86   John Graham L PTS 8 Piccadilly
08.05.86   Randy Henderson L PTS 8 Bayswater
19.05.86   Joe Lynch W RSC 3 Plymouth
28.05.86   Andy Wright L PTS 6 Lewisham
15.09.86   Gerry Sloof L PTS 6 Scheidam,
           Holland
23.09.86   Derek Wormald L PTS 8 Batley
06.10.86   David Scere L PTS 6 Leicester
21.10.86   David Scere W PTS 8 Hull
29.10.86   Peter Elliott W PTS 6 Stoke
25.11.86   Steve Foster L PTS 8 Manchester
15.12.86   Tucker Watts DREW 6 Loughborough
13.01.87   Robert Armstrong L PTS 6 Oldham
26.01.87   Richard Wagstaff W PTS 8 Bradford
05.02.87   Neil Patterson L PTS 6 Newcastle
20.02.87   Dennis Boy O'Brien L PTS 8
           Maidenhead
02.03.87   Roddy Maxwell L PTS 6 Glasgow
24.03.87   Ian Chantler L PTS 8 Nottingham
07.04.87   Richard Wagstaff L PTS 8 Batley
28.04.87   Sean Leighton DREW 8 Manchester
05.05.87   Dave Owens L PTS 6 Leeds
12.05.87   Jason Baxter L PTS 6 Alfreton
23.06.87   Terry Magee L CO 6 Swansea
           *(Vacant All-Ireland L. Middleweight
           Title)*
31.07.87   Cyril Jackson L RSC 5 Wrexham
22.09.87   Brian Robinson L PTS 6 Bethnal Green
28.09.87   Sean Leighton L PTS 8 Bradford
19.10.87   Sammy Storey L PTS 6 Belfast
10.11.87   Peter Brown L PTS 8 Batley
19.11.87   Kid Murray W PTS 6 Ilkeston
26.11.87   Trevor Smith L CO 4 Fulham
12.01.88   Cornelius Carr L RSC 6 Cardiff
15.02.88   Leigh Wicks L PTS 6 Copthorne
25.02.88   R. W. Smith L RSC 3 Bethnal Green
28.03.88   Tony Britton L PTS 8 Birmingham
13.06.88   Jim Kelly L PTS 6 Glasgow
25.06.88   Wayne Ellis L PTS 6 Luton
12.09.88   Shaun Cummins L CO 3 Northampton
17.10.88   Jim Kelly L PTS 6 Glasgow
01.11.88   Brian Robinson L PTS 6 Reading
17.11.88   Mark Howell L CO 1 Ilkeston
16.12.88   Conrad Oscar L PTS 6 Brentwood
25.01.89   Tony Velinor L RTD 3 Basildon
22.02.89   Mickey Murray DREW 6 Doncaster
01.03.89   Nigel Fairbairn L PTS 6 Stoke
21.03.89   Dave Thomas L PTS 6 Cottingham
29.03.89   W. O. Wilson L RSC 5 Wembley

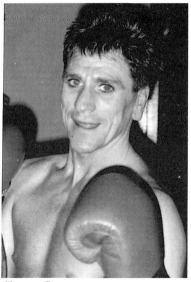

Shamus Casey   Les Clark

08.05.89	Antonio Fernandez L PTS 6 Edgbaston
31.05.89	Ossie Maddix L CO 3 Manchester
11.09.89	Terry French W PTS 6 Nottingham
18.09.89	Skip Jackson W PTS 6 Northampton
26.09.89	Theo Marius L PTS 8 Chigwell
05.10.89	Val Golding L PTS 6 Stevenage
17.10.89	Carl Harney L PTS 4 Oldham
13.11.89	Ian Vokes W RSC 5 Bradford
29.11.89	Ray Close L CO 2 Belfast
21.06.90	Skip Jackson W PTS 6 Alfreton
04.09.90	Pete Bowman W PTS 6 Southend
14.09.90	Chris Richards L PTS 6 Telford
08.10.90	Billy Brough W PTS 6 Leicester
22.10.90	Gordon Blair L RSC 3 Glasgow
22.11.90	Jimmy Thornton W PTS 6 Ilkeston
14.12.90	Stefan Wright L PTS 6 Peterborough
17.01.91	Neville Brown L RSC 4 Alfreton
21.02.91	Richie Woodhall L RSC 3 Walsall
28.03.91	Pete Bowman W PTS 6 Alfreton
12.04.91	Martin Rosamond W PTS 6 Willenhall
13.05.91	Paul King W PTS 6 Northampton
04.07.91	Dave Hall W PTS 6 Alfreton
11.09.91	Clay O'Shea L PTS 6 Hammersmith
10.10.91	Dave Johnson L PTS 6 Gateshead
17.10.91	Tyrone Eastmond L PTS 6 Mossley
14.11.91	Dave Johnson L PTS 6 Gateshead
28.11.91	Ian Vokes W PTS 6 Hull
07.12.91	Steve Foster L PTS 8 Manchester
17.03.92	Gary Osborne L RSC 5 Wolverhampton
	(Vacant Midlands Area L.
	Middleweight Title)
28.05.92	Mark Jay L PTS 8 Gosforth
25.07.92	Warren Stowe L CO 2 Manchester
16.10.92	Terry Morrill L PTS 6 Hull
23.10.92	Fran Harding L PTS 6 Liverpool
12.11.92	Gypsy Johnny Price L PTS 6 Burnley
14.12.92	Peter Wauby L PTS 6 Cleethorpes
22.02.93	Lee Ferrie L CO 3 Bedworth
07.06.93	Stephen Wilson L PTS 6 Glasgow
16.09.93	Peter Waudby L PTS 6 Hull
03.11.93	Warren Stephens W PTS 6 Worcester
13.11.93	Terry Morrill L PTS 8 Hull
30.11.93	Stuart Dunn L PTS 6 Leicester
12.12.93	Glenn Catley L PTS 4 Bristol

20.01.94	Darren Dorrington L PTS 6 Battersea
26.02.94	Adrian Dodson L CO 1 Earls Court
21.04.94	Mark Jay L PTS 6 Gateshead
16.05.94	Peter Waudby L PTS 6 Cleethorpes
02.06.94	Eric Noi L PTS 6 Middleton

Career: 125 contests, won 26, drew 5, lost 94.

Fidel Castro (Smith)

Sheffield. *Born* Nottingham, 17 April, 1963
Former British S. Middleweight Champion.
Former Undefeated Central Area
Middleweight Champion. Ht. 5'9"
Manager Self

06.04.87	Ian Bayliss W RSC 5 Newcastle
28.04.87	Nick Gyaamie W RSC 2 Manchester
29.04.87	Leigh Wicks L PTS 6 Hastings
11.05.87	Steve Foster W PTS 8 Manchester
23.09.87	Ian Jackson W PTS 6 Stoke
11.11.87	Denys Cronin W PTS 8 Usk
24.02.88	Ian Bayliss W RSC 6 Sheffield
	(Central Area Middleweight Title
	Challenge)
09.05.88	Franki Moro W RSC 2 Nottingham
18.05.88	Chris Galloway W PTS 6 Gillingham
23.05.88	Sean Heron W RSC 4 Mayfair
08.07.88	Francesco dell' Aquila L DIS 3 San Remo, Italy
19.11.88	Paul Tchoue W RSC 3 Chateau Thierry, France
23.01.89	Andre Mongalema L PTS 8 Paris, France
22.06.89	Denys Cronin W RSC 7 Stevenage
27.01.90	Thomas Covington W PTS 8 Sheffield
12.03.90	Darren McKenna W PTS 6 Hull
20.05.90	Nigel Fairbairn W RSC 7 Sheffield
20.08.90	Elvis Parks W PTS 6 Helsinki, Finland
29.10.90	Dave Owens W PTS 6 Birmingham
24.11.90	Johnny Melfah W RSC 4 Benalmadena, Spain
24.09.91	Ian Strudwick W RSC 6 Basildon
	(Vacant British S. Middleweight Title)
01.10.91	Johnny Melfah W RSC 7 Sheffield
25.02.92	Lou Gent W PTS 12 Crystal Palace
	(British S. Middleweight Title Defence)
18.07.92	Frank Eubanks W RTD 6 Manchester
23.09.92	Henry Wharton L PTS 12 Leeds
	(British S. Middleweight Title Defence.
	Commonwealth S. Middleweight Title
	Challenge)
16.12.92	Vincenzo Nardiello L PTS 12 Arricia, Italy
	(Vacant European S. Middleweight
	Title)
14.08.93	Karl Barwise W RSC 6 Hammersmith
16.09.93	James Cook L PTS 12 Southwark
	(Vacant British S. Middleweight Title)
21.05.94	Sammy Storey L PTS 6 Belfast

Career: 29 contests, won 22, lost 7.

Glenn Catley

Bristol. *Born* Sodbury, 15 March, 1972
Middleweight. Ht. 5'8"
Manager C. Sanigar

27.05.93	Rick North W PTS 4 Bristol
26.06.93	Chris Vassiliou W CO 2 Keynsham
31.08.93	Marty Duke W RSC 2 Croydon
13.09.93	Barry Thorogood W PTS 4 Bristol
03.11.93	Marty Duke W RSC 1 Bristol
13.12.93	Shamus Casey W PTS 4 Bristol
10.03.94	Mark Cichocki W PTS 6 Bristol

23.03.94	Carlo Colarusso L RSC 5 Cardiff
25.05.94	Chris Davies W RSC 1 Bristol

Career: 9 contests, won 8, lost 1.

Glenn Catley   Les Clark

Alan Ceesay

Manchester. *Born* Manchester, 3 May,
1971
Welterweight. Ht. 5'5"
Manager J. Trickett

27.09.93	Steve Scott L PTS 6 Manchester

Career: 1 contest, lost 1.

Gary Charlton (Wilkes)

Leeds. *Born* Leeds, 6 April, 1968
Heavyweight. Ht. 6'0"
Manager P. Coleman

10.10.91	John Pierre L PTS 6 Gateshead
26.10.91	Graham Arnold W RSC 1 Brentwood
11.11.91	Gary Railton L PTS 6 Bradford
23.04.92	Wayne Llewelyn L RSC 4 Eltham
04.06.92	Wayne Buck L PTS 6 Cleethorpes
07.10.92	John Harewood L PTS 6 Sunderland
12.11.92	Wayne Buck L PTS 8 Stafford
17.12.92	Kevin McBride DREW 6 Barking
23.02.93	Scott Welch W RSC 3 Doncaster
26.03.93	Mark Hulstrom L DIS 5 Copenhagen, Denmark
29.04.93	Manny Burgo L PTS 6 Newcastle
22.09.93	J. A. Bugner L RSC 1 Wembley

Career: 12 contests, won 2, drew 1, lost 9.

Adrian Chase

Watford. *Born* St Albans, 18 October, 1968
L. Welterweight. Ht. 5'9"
Manager H. Holland

06.05.93	Jason Campbell W CO 2 Bayswater
24.06.93	Delwyn Panayiotiou W CO 1 Watford
23.02.94	Dennis Griffin W PTS 6 Watford
16.05.94	Tony Gibbs W PTS 6 Heathrow

Career: 4 contests, won 4.

(Ivan) Carlos Chase

Bushey. *Born* Watford, 10 August, 1966
L. Welterweight. Ht. 5'6¾"
Manager H. Holland

28.09.89	Tony Gibbs W PTS 6 Wandsworth
12.12.89	Carl Brasier W PTS 6 Brentford
30.01.90	Barry North W RSC 1 Battersea
14.03.90	Trevor Meikle W PTS 6 Battersea
03.04.91	Seamus O'Sullivan W PTS 8 Bethnal Green
01.06.91	Marcel Herbert W PTS 6 Bethnal Green
12.11.91	Tony Swift L PTS 6 Milton Keynes
12.02.92	Gary Barron W RSC 5 Watford
30.04.92	Dave Pierre L RSC 7 Watford *(Southern Area L. Welterweight Title Challenge)*
17.09.92	Felix Kelly W RSC 2 Watford
14.04.93	Ian Honeywood W RSC 1 Kensington
01.10.93	Ross Hale L RTD 8 Cardiff *(Elim. British L. Welterweight Title)*
23.02.94	Hugh Forde L PTS 6 Watford
16.05.94	Peter Judson L PTS 4 Heathrow

Career: 14 contests, won 9, lost 5.

Zak Chelli

Leicester. *Born* Tunisia, 2 May, 1968
L. Heavyweight. Ht. 6'3"
Manager Self

24.11.92	Lee Archer W PTS 6 Wolverhampton
26.01.93	Karl Mumford W PTS 6 Leicester
22.02.93	John J. Cooke DREW 6 Bedworth
19.05.93	Nigel Rafferty W RSC 3 Leicester
18.09.93	Paul Murray L RSC 2 Leicester
06.12.93	John Foreman L RSC 4 Birmingham
20.01.94	Mark Prince L CO 1 Battersea

Career: 7 contests, won 3, drew 1, lost 3.

Marty Chesnut   Les Clark

(Martin) Marty Chestnut (Concannon)

Birmingham. *Born* Birmingham, 8 March, 1968

S. Bantamweight. Ht. 5'8"
Manager Self

29.04.93	Fred Reeve L PTS 6 Hull
07.06.93	Ian McGirr L PTS 6 Glasgow
30.10.93	Paul Lloyd L RSC 1 Chester
11.12.93	John Sillo L PTS 6 Liverpool
25.01.94	Anthony Hanna L PTS 4 Piccadilly
10.02.94	James Murray L PTS 6 Glasgow
01.03.94	Chris Lyons W PTS 6 Dudley
27.04.94	Chris Lyons L RSC 3 Bethnal Green
02.06.94	Des Gargano L PTS 6 Middleton

Career: 9 contests, won 1, lost 8.

(Peter) Carlos Christie

Birmingham. *Born* Birmingham, 17 August, 1966
Midlands Area S. Middleweight Champion. Ht. 6'0"
Manager Self

04.06.90	Roger Wilson L PTS 6 Birmingham
17.09.90	John Kaighin W PTS 6 Cardiff
27.09.90	Colin Manners W PTS 6 Birmingham
29.10.90	Paul Murray W PTS 6 Birmingham
18.11.90	Paul Busby L PTS 6 Birmingham
27.11.90	Nigel Rafferty W PTS 8 Wolverhampton
06.12.90	Nigel Rafferty W PTS 6 Wolverhampton
10.01.91	Ray Webb L PTS 6 Wandsworth
28.01.91	Gil Lewis W PTS 8 Birmingham
04.03.91	Nigel Rafferty W PTS 8 Birmingham
14.03.91	Michael Gale L PTS 8 Middleton
01.05.91	Peter Elliott W RSC 9 Solihull *(Vacant Midlands Area S. Middleweight Title)*
11.05.91	Ray Close L PTS 6 Belfast
07.09.91	Ray Close L PTS 6 Belfast
20.11.91	Nicky Piper L CO 6 Cardiff
10.03.92	Glenn Campbell DREW 8 Bury
15.09.92	Roland Ericsson W RSC 4 Crystal Palace
28.01.93	James Cook L PTS 8 Southwark
28.04.93	Sammy Storey L RSC 8 Dublin
31.08.93	Simon Harris L CO 3 Croydon
12.11.93	Tony Booth L PTS 6 Hull
28.11.93	Ali Forbes L CO 4 Southwark
22.01.94	Darron Griffiths L PTS 8 Cardiff
21.02.94	Stephen Wilson L RSC 2 Glasgow
15.06.94	William Joppy L PTS 6 Southwark

Career: 25 contests, won 9, drew 1, lost 15.

Sam Church

Bradford. *Born* Bradford, 4 March, 1959
L. Welterweight. Ht. 5'9"
Manager Self

02.07.81	Phil O'Hare W PTS 4 Pudsey
07.10.82	Peter Phillips L PTS 6 Morley
25.10.82	Dave Markey W RSC 2 Airdrie
14.02.83	Stan Atherton L PTS 6 Liverpool
25.02.83	Gary Williams L RSC 2 Doncaster
13.06.83	Dave Foley L PTS 6 Doncaster
03.03.94	Alan Graham L CO 3 Newcastle

Career: 7 contests, won 2, lost 5.

Cliff Churchward

Bournemouth. *Born* Weymouth, 7 June, 1966
L. Middleweight. Ht. 5'11"
Manager Self

04.10.89	Tony White L RSC 5 Basildon
14.11.89	Trevor Meikle L PTS 6 Evesham
22.11.89	Trevor Meikle L PTS 6 Stafford
11.12.89	Ernie Loveridge L PTS 6 Birmingham
27.02.90	Mickey Lerwill L PTS 6 Evesham
07.03.90	Eddie King L CO 6 Doncaster
28.06.90	Gary Simkiss DREW 6 Birmingham
08.12.90	Martin Rosamond L PTS 6 Bristol
23.01.91	Ernie Loveridge L PTS 6 Solihull
04.02.91	Andreas Panayi L PTS 6 Leicester
08.05.91	Kevin Sheeran L PTS 6 Millwall
20.05.91	James McGee L PTS 6 Leicester
05.06.91	Ernie Loveridge L PTS 8 Wolverhampton
17.06.91	Eddie King L PTS 6 Edgbaston
12.02.92	B. F. Williams L PTS 6 Watford
30.04.92	Danny Shinkwin W PTS 6 Watford
05.10.92	Kevin Mabbutt L PTS 6 Northampton
01.12.92	Andrew Jervis L PTS 6 Liverpool
10.12.92	Sean Metherell L PTS 6 Corby
16.03.93	Ernie Locke DREW 6 Edgbaston
07.04.93	David Larkin L RSC 4 Leeds
04.03.94	Peter Vosper L PTS 8 Weston super Mare

Career: 22 contests, won 1, drew 2, lost 19.

Mark Cichocki (Weatherill)

Hartlepool. *Born* Hartlepool, 18 October, 1967
Northern Area L. Middleweight Champion. Ht. 5'7"
Manager G. Robinson

01.12.92	Tony Trimble W PTS 6 Hartlepool
29.01.93	Gordon Blair W PTS 8 Glasgow
09.03.93	Rob Pitters W RSC 10 Hartlepool *(Vacant Northern Area L. Middleweight Title)*
06.05.93	Mick Duncan W RSC 7 Hartlepool *(Northern Area L. Middleweight Title Defence)*
12.05.93	Glyn Rhodes L PTS 6 Sheffield
02.12.93	Mark Jay W RSC 4 Hartlepool *(Northern Area L. Middleweight Title Defence)*
22.01.94	Anibal Acevedo L RTD 3 Cardiff
10.03.94	Glenn Catley L PTS 6 Bristol

Career: 8 contests, won 5, lost 3.

Howard Clarke

Warley. *Born* London, 23 September, 1967
Welterweight. Ht. 5'10"
Manager Self

15.10.91	Chris Mylan W PTS 4 Dudley
09.12.91	Claude Rossi W RSC 3 Brierley Hill
04.02.92	Julian Eavis W PTS 4 Alfreton
03.03.92	Dave Andrews W RSC 3 Cradley Heath
21.05.92	Richard O'Brien W CO 1 Cradley Heath
29.09.92	Paul King W PTS 6 Stoke
27.10.92	Gordon Blair L RSC 4 Cradley Heath
16.03.93	Paul King W PTS 6 Edgbaston
07.06.93	Dean Bramhald W RTD 2 Walsall
29.06.93	Paul King W PTS 6 Edgbaston
06.10.93	Julian Eavis L PTS 8 Solihull
30.11.93	Julian Eavis W PTS 8 Wolverhampton
08.02.94	Nigel Bradley W RTD 6 Wolverhampton
18.04.94	Andy Peach W PTS 6 Walsall
28.06.94	Dennis Berry L RSC 3 Edgbaston

Career: 15 contests, won 12, lost 3.

Chris Clarkson

Hull. *Born* Hull, 15 December, 1967
Former Undefeated Central Area
Bantamweight & Featherweight Champion.
Ht. 5'4"
Manager M. Brooks

18.03.85	Gypsy Johnny L PTS 4 Bradford
09.04.85	Terry Allen W PTS 4 South Shields
30.04.85	Terry Allen W PTS 4 Chorley
30.05.85	Gypsy Johnny L PTS 4 Blackburn
17.10.85	Tony Heath W PTS 4 Leicester
13.02.86	Glen Dainty L RSC 4 Longford
17.03.86	Jamie McBride L PTS 4 Glasgow
03.11.86	Gerry McBride DREW 6 Manchester
13.11.86	Gordon Stobie W RSC 4 Huddersfield
01.12.86	Nigel Crook L RSC 6 Nottingham
27.01.87	Donnie Hood L PTS 6 Glasgow
23.02.87	Dave Boy Mallaby W PTS 4 Bradford
02.03.87	Dave Boy Mallaby W CO 3 Nottingham
16.03.87	Pepe Webber W PTS 6 Glasgow
24.03.87	Nigel Crook W PTS 6 Hull
06.04.87	Joe Kelly L PTS 8 Glasgow
14.04.87	Jamie McBride L PTS 6 Cumbernauld
28.04.87	John Green L RSC 6 Manchester
13.06.87	Ronnie Stephenson W PTS 8 Great Yarmouth
23.09.87	Mitchell King L PTS 6 Loughborough
15.11.88	Gordon Shaw W PTS 6 Hull
29.11.88	Des Gargano L PTS 6 Manchester
14.12.88	Dave George L PTS 6 Evesham
16.02.89	Johnny Bredahl L PTS 6 Copenhagen, Denmark
09.03.89	Mark Geraghty L PTS 6 Glasgow
20.03.89	George Bailey W PTS 6 Bradford
11.07.89	Des Gargano W PTS 6 Batley
11.10.89	Gerry McBride W PTS 10 Hull
	(Vacant Central Area Bantamweight Title)
23.11.89	Drew Docherty L PTS 6 Motherwell
15.03.90	Noel Carroll W PTS 6 Manchester
19.04.90	Gerry McBride W DIS 5 Oldham
	(Vacant Central Area Featherweight Title)
30.04.90	Pete Buckley W PTS 8 Mayfair
19.11.90	James Drummond W PTS 8 Glasgow
02.03.91	Francesco Arroyo L RSC 4 Darlington
	(Vacant IBF Intercontinental Bantamweight Title)
04.04.91	Duke McKenzie L RSC 5 Watford
09.10.91	Mark Geraghty L PTS 6 Glasgow
21.10.91	Ian McGirr DREW 6 Glasgow
16.12.91	Noel Carroll L PTS 6 Manchester
03.03.92	Billy Hardy L RSC 5 Houghton le Spring
14.12.92	David Ramsden W PTS 4 Bradford
24.02.93	Bradley Stone L PTS 8 Wembley
24.09.93	Prince Nassem Hamed L CO 2 Dublin
03.03.94	Alfred Kotei L PTS 8 Ebbw Vale
15.04.94	Mike Deveney L RSC 3 Hull
13.06.94	Wayne Rigby L PTS 6 Liverpool

Career: 45 contests, won 18, drew 2, lost 25.

Dave Clavering

Bury. *Born* Bury, 21 October, 1973
S. Featherweight. Ht. 5'6"
Manager J. Doughty

16.05.94	Al Garrett W RTD 4 Morecambe

Career: 1 contest, won 1.

Kesem Clayton

Coventry. *Born* Coventry, 19 May, 1962
Middleweight. Ht. 5'9"
Manager P. Byrne

06.10.86	Rocky Reynolds W PTS 6 Birmingham
26.11.86	Kid Murray W PTS 6 Wolverhampton
21.01.87	Cecil Branch W RSC 4 Stoke
04.03.87	Ian John-Lewis W RSC 4 Dudley
30.03.87	Mark Howell L PTS 6 Birmingham
08.04.87	Kevin Hayde W PTS 6 Evesham
12.06.87	Mark Howell L PTS 6 Leamington
30.09.87	Theo Marius DREW 6 Mayfair
12.10.87	Andy Catesby W RSC 3 Mayfair
16.11.87	Rocky Feliciello W PTS 8 Stratford upon Avon
28.11.87	Mark Howell L PTS 6 Windsor
27.01.88	Cornelius Carr L PTS 6 Bethnal Green
09.03.88	Brian Robinson W PTS 6 Bethnal Green
21.03.88	Dean Barclay DREW 8 Bethnal Green
17.04.88	R. W. Smith W RSC 4 Peterborough
06.10.88	Kid Milo L RSC 4 Dudley
16.12.88	Tony Velinor W RSC 2 Brentwood
06.02.89	Michael Justin L PTS 8 Nottingham
15.03.89	Ian Chantler L CO 4 Stoke
15.07.89	Michele Mastrodonato L RSC 2 San Severo, Italy
04.10.89	Shaun Cummins W RSC 6 Solihull
22.11.89	Ian Chantler W PTS 8 Solihull
15.12.89	Benito Guida L PTS 8 Milan, Italy
24.01.90	John Ashton L PTS 10 Solihull
	(Vacant Midlands Area Middleweight Title)
12.10.90	Frederic Seillier L RSC 1 Toulon, France
22.02.91	Steve Foster L CO 6 Manchester
02.12.91	Nigel Rafferty L PTS 8 Birmingham
31.03.92	Stan King L RSC 4 Norwich
19.12.93	Sean Byrne L PTS 6 Northampton
09.04.94	Robin Reid L RSC 1 Mansfield

Career: 30 contests, won 12, drew 2, lost 16.

Justin Clements

Birmingham. *Born* Birmingham, 25 September, 1971
S. Middleweight. Ht. 5'11½"
Manager Self

02.12.91	Adrian Wright W PTS 6 Birmingham
03.03.92	Andy Manning DREW 6 Cradley Heath
16.03.93	Paul McCarthy W PTS 6 Edgbaston
18.05.93	Lee Sara W PTS 6 Edgbaston
07.06.93	Phil Ball W PTS 6 Walsall
30.09.93	Smokey Enison W PTS 6 Walsall
02.12.93	Paul Murray L PTS 6 Walsall
08.03.94	Zak Goldman W RSC 3 Edgbaston
28.06.94	Dave Battey W RSC 2 Edgbaston

Career: 9 contests, won 7, drew 1, lost 1.

Pat Clinton

Croy. *Born* Croy, 4 April, 1964
Bantamweight. Former WBO Flyweight
Champion. Former Undefeated British,
European & Scottish Flyweight Champion.
Ht. 5'3½"
Manager T. Gilmour

10.10.85	Gordon Stobie W PTS 6 Alfreton
11.11.85	Tony Rahman W PTS 6 Glasgow
24.02.86	Tony Rahman W PTS 6 Glasgow
29.04.86	Des Gargano W PTS 6 Manchester
09.06.86	George Bailey W CO 2 Glasgow
20.10.86	Ginger Staples W RSC 2 Glasgow
17.11.86	Gypsy Johnny W RSC 5 Glasgow
19.01.87	Sean Casey W CO 6 Glasgow
16.02.87	Des Gargano W PTS 6 Glasgow
14.04.87	Jose Manuel Diaz W RSC 8 Cumbernauld
19.05.87	Miguel Pequeno W CO 4 Cumbernauld
22.09.87	Joe Kelly W RSC 2 Bethnal Green
	(Final Elim. British Flyweight Title. Vacant Scottish Flyweight Title)
09.03.88	Joe Kelly W PTS 12 Bethnal Green
	(Vacant British Flyweight Title. Scottish Flyweight Title Defence)
16.02.89	Eyup Can L PTS 12 Copenhagen, Denmark
	(Vacant European Flyweight Title)
24.10.89	Danny Porter W RSC 5 Watford
	(British Flyweight Title Defence)
19.12.89	David Afan-Jones W RSC 6 Gorleston
	(British Flyweight Title Defence)
03.08.90	Salvatore Fanni W PTS 12 Cagliari, Italy
	(Vacant European Flyweight Title)
09.09.91	Armando Tapia W PTS 8 Glasgow
18.11.91	Alberto Cantu W PTS 8 Glasgow
18.03.92	Isidro Perez W PTS 12 Glasgow
	(WBO Flyweight Title Challenge)
19.09.92	Danny Porter W PTS 12 Glasgow
	(WBO Flyweight Title Defence)
15.05.93	Jacob Matlala L RSC 8 Glasgow
	(WBO Flyweight Title Defence)
25.04.94	Ady Benton L RSC 1 Glasgow

Career: 23 contests, won 20, lost 3.

Ray Close

Belfast. *Born* Belfast, 20 January, 1969
All-Ireland S. Middleweight Champion.
Former Undefeated European S.
Middleweight Champion. Ht. 5'10"
Manager B. Eastwood

19.10.88	Steve Foster W RSC 2 Belfast
14.12.88	Kevin Roper W PTS 4 Kirkby
25.01.89	B. K. Bennett W RSC 3 Belfast
08.03.89	Andy Wright W RSC 4 Belfast
12.04.89	Dennis White W RSC 2 Belfast
19.09.89	Gary Pemberton W PTS 6 Belfast
31.10.89	Rocky McGran W RSC 7 Belfast
	(Vacant All-Ireland S. Middleweight Title)
29.11.89	Shamus Casey W CO 2 Belfast
13.12.89	Denys Cronin L PTS 6 Kirkby
21.02.90	Frank Eubanks W PTS 8 Belfast
17.03.90	Denys Cronin W PTS 8 Belfast
23.05.90	Rocky McGran W RTD 1 Belfast
15.09.90	Ray Webb W PTS 8 Belfast
11.05.91	Carlos Christie W PTS 6 Belfast
07.09.91	Carlos Christie W PTS 6 Belfast
13.11.91	Simon Collins W PTS 6 Belfast
11.12.91	Terry Magee W RSC 7 Dublin
	(All-Ireland S. Middleweight Title Defence)
25.04.92	Ian Chantler W RSC 1 Belfast
03.07.92	Franck Nicotra L RSC 8 Pontault Combault, France
	(European S. Middleweight Title Challenge)
18.12.92	Jean-Roger Tsidjo W PTS 8 Clermont Ferra, France
17.03.93	Vincenzo Nardiello W PTS 12 Campione d'Italia, Italy
	(European S. Middleweight Title Challenge)

15.05.93 Chris Eubank DREW 12 Glasgow
(*WBO S. Middleweight Title
Challenge*)
16.10.93 Ray Domenge W RSC 4 Belfast
21.05.94 Chris Eubank L PTS 12 Belfast
(*WBO S. Middleweight Title
Challenge*)
Career: 24 contests, won 20, drew 1, lost 3.

Gary Cogan
Birmingham. *Born* Birmingham, 21
January, 1972
L. Welterweight. Ht. 5'9"
Manager N. Nobbs

01.03.94 Gary Hiscox L PTS 6 Dudley
29.03.94 Chris Pollock W PTS 6
Wolverhampton
28.04.94 Keith Marner L RSC 3 Mayfair
Career: 3 contests, won 1, lost 2.

Shaun Cogan   Les Clark

Shaun Cogan
Birmingham. *Born* Birmingham, 7 August,
1967
L. Welterweight. Ht. 5'8"
Manager Self

25.09.89 Peter Bowen W RSC 1 Birmingham
24.10.89 Gary Quigley W RSC 2
Wolverhampton
06.12.89 George Jones W PTS 6 Stoke
14.03.90 Dean Bramhald W PTS 6 Stoke
27.03.90 Mark Antony W CO 1 Wolverhampton
23.04.90 Mike Morrison W PTS 8 Birmingham
21.02.91 Tony Britland W PTS 6 Walsall
19.03.91 Rocky Lawlor W RSC 2 Birmingham
25.07.91 David Thompson W CO 1 Dudley
05.12.91 Steve Pollard W PTS 6 Oakengates
27.11.92 Soren Sondergaard L PTS 6 Randers,
Denmark
16.03.93 Malcolm Melvin L PTS 10 Edgbaston
(*Vacant All-Ireland L. Welterweight
Title & Midlands Area L. Welterweight
Title Challenge*)
18.05.93 Seth Jones W RSC 2 Edgbaston

15.09.93 Paul Ryan L RSC 3 Ashford
06.11.93 Bernard Paul DREW 6 Bethnal Green
02.12.93 Kane White W RSC 1 Evesham
11.01.94 Bernard Paul W PTS 6 Bethnal Green
01.03.94 Karl Taylor W PTS 6 Dudley
10.05.94 Andreas Panayi L RSC 7 Doncaster
Career: 19 contests, won 14, drew 1, lost 4.

Mark Cokely
Port Talbot. *Born* Neath, 31 July, 1970
Flyweight. Ht. 5'3"
Manager P. Boyce

27.04.94 Lyndon Kershaw L PTS 6 Solihull
20.05.94 Graham McGrath L PTS 6 Neath
Career: 2 contests, lost 2.

Carlo Colarusso
Llanelli. *Born* Swansea, 11 February, 1970
Welsh L. Middleweight Champion. Ht. 5'7"
Manager Self

14.09.89 Paul Burton W RSC 5 Basildon
11.10.89 Lindon Scarlett L PTS 8 Stoke
24.10.89 Cornelius Carr L RTD 4 Watford
22.11.89 Lindon Scarlett L PTS 8 Solihull
01.03.90 Kevin Hayde W RTD 3 Cardiff
14.03.90 Kevin Plant W PTS 8 Stoke
21.03.90 Sammy Sampson W RSC 3 Preston
06.04.90 Ray Webb W PTS 6 Telford
19.11.90 Gary Pemberton W RSC 3 Cardiff
29.11.90 Nigel Moore L PTS 6 Bayswater
24.01.91 Gary Pemberton W RSC 8 Gorseinon
(*Vacant Welsh L. Middleweight Title*)
02.03.91 Cornelius Carr L PTS 8 Darlington
11.05.92 Russell Washer W RSC 5 Llanelli
(*Welsh L. Middleweight Title Defence*)
27.06.92 Newton Barnett W RTD 5 Quinta do
Lago, Portugal
28.10.92 Lloyd Honeyghan L RSC 6 Kensington
16.03.93 Richie Woodhall L PTS 8
Wolverhampton
30.03.93 Tony Velinor W RSC 3 Cardiff
14.03.94 John Bosco L PTS 6 Mayfair
23.03.94 Glenn Catley W RSC 5 Cardiff
Career: 19 contests, won 11, lost 8.

Tony Colclough
Birmingham. *Born* Birmingham, 9 May,
1960
L. Heavyweight. Ht. 6'0"
Manager Self

15.04.91 Steve Yorath L PTS 6 Wolverhampton
30.05.91 Damien Caesar L RSC 1 Mayfair
01.08.91 Denzil Browne L RSC 1 Dewsbury
07.10.91 Karl Guest DREW 6 Birmingham
15.10.91 Jason McNeill W PTS 6 Dudley
02.12.91 Carl Guest W RSC 2 Birmingham
03.03.92 Greg Scott-Briggs L RSC 2 Cradley
Heath
21.05.92 Mark Hale DREW 6 Cradley Heath
01.06.92 Mark Hale W PTS 6 Solihull
27.11.92 Mark Hulstrom L RSC 2 Randers,
Denmark
27.02.93 Kenley Price L RSC 5 Ellesmere Port
26.04.93 Greg Scott-Briggs L RSC 4 Glasgow
07.06.93 Kevin Burton L PTS 6 Walsall
11.08.93 John Keeton L RSC 1 Mansfield
30.09.93 Kevin Burton L DIS 5 Walsall
13.10.93 Darren Ashton L RSC 1 Stoke
24.11.93 Greg Scott-Briggs L PTS 6 Solihull
01.12.93 Steve Loftus L PTS 6 Stoke
13.12.93 Kevin Burton L RSC 3 Doncaster

09.02.94 Mark Delaney L RSC 4 Brentwood
28.03.94 Dave Proctor L RSC 3 Birmingham
Career: 21 contests, won 3, drew 2, lost 16.

Tony Colclough   Les Clark

Brian Coleman
Birmingham. *Born* Birmingham, 27 July,
1969
L. Welterweight. Ht. 5'11"
Manager Self

21.11.91 Jamie Morris DREW 6 Stafford
11.12.91 Craig Hartwell DREW 6 Leicester
22.01.92 John O'Johnson L PTS 6 Stoke
20.02.92 Davy Robb L PTS 6 Oakengates
31.03.92 Blue Butterworth L PTS 6 Stockport
17.05.92 Korso Aleain L RSC 5 Harringay
17.09.92 Nicky Bardle L RSC 4 Watford
21.10.92 Jason Barker W PTS 6 Stoke
10.12.92 A. M. Milton DREW 4 Bethnal Green
31.03.93 A. M. Milton L PTS 4 Bethnal Green
26.04.93 Jason Beard L PTS 6 Lewisham
06.05.93 Mark Allen W PTS 6 Walsall
18.05.93 Sean Metherell DREW 6 Kettering
27.05.93 Blue Butterworth L PTS 6 Burnley
23.06.93 Jonathan Thaxton L PTS 8 Gorleston
11.08.93 Steve Howden L RSC 4 Mansfield
13.09.93 Mick Hoban L PTS 6 Middleton
01.12.93 A. M. Milton L PTS 4 Bethnal Green
08.12.93 Chris Pollock W PTS 6 Stoke
16.12.93 Mark Newton L PTS 6 Newport
11.01.94 Paul Knights L RSC 4 Bethnal Green
08.02.94 Andy Peach W PTS 6 Wolverhampton
18.02.94 Cam Raeside L PTS 6 Leicester
08.03.94 Chris Pollock L PTS 6 Edgbaston
29.03.94 P. J. Gallagher L PTS 6 Bethnal Green
14.04.94 Cham Joof L CO 3 Battersea
02.06.94 Scott Walker L CO 1 Middleton
Career: 27 contests, won 4, drew 4, lost 19.

Billy Collins
Stirling. *Born* Stirling, 20 May, 1968
L. Middleweight. Ht. 5'9"
Manager T. Gilmour

25.04.94 Raziq Ali W PTS 6 Glasgow
Career: 1 contest, won 1.

Hugh Collins

Stirling. *Born* Stirling, 17 August, 1969
Lightweight. Ht. 5'6"
Manager T. Gilmour

29.03.93	Tim Hill W PTS 6 Glasgow
20.09.93	Robert Braddock W PTS 8 Glasgow
24.11.93	Paul Bowen W PTS 6 Solihull
24.01.94	Colin Innes W PTS 6 Glasgow
21.02.94	Norman Dhalie W RTD 4 Glasgow
28.03.94	Trevor Royal W RSC 2 Musselburgh
25.04.94	Miguel Matthews W PTS 8 Glasgow

Career: 7 contests, won 7.

(Elton) Tom Collins

Leeds. *Born* Curacao, 1 July, 1955
Cruiserweight. Former European L.
Heavyweight Champion. Former
Undefeated British & Central Area L.
Heavyweight Champion. Ht. 5'11"
Manager Self

17.01.77	Ginger McIntyre W RSC 2 Birmingham
16.05.77	Mick Dolan W PTS 6 Manchester
01.06.77	Johnny Cox W CO 3 Dudley
23.11.77	George Gray W RSC 3 Stoke
19.01.78	Clint Jones W RSC 3 Merton
21.03.78	Joe Jackson W PTS 8 Luton
09.05.78	Harald Skog L PTS 8 Oslo, Norway
17.07.78	Karl Canwell L RSC 6 Mayfair
28.11.78	Carlton Benoit W CO 1 Sheffield
04.12.78	Dennis Andries L PTS 8 Southend
30.01.79	Dennis Andries L CO 6 Southend
22.10.79	Danny Lawford W RSC 7 Nottingham
28.11.79	Eddie Smith W PTS 8 Solihull
25.02.80	Greg Evans W RSC 1 Bradford
	(Vacant Central Area L. Heavyweight Title)
15.04.80	Chris Lawson W RSC 4 Blackpool
04.12.80	Mustafa Wasajja L PTS 8 Randers, Denmark
09.03.81	Karl Canwell W PTS 10 Bradford
	(Elim. British L. Heavyweight Title)
15.03.82	Dennis Andries W PTS 15 Bloomsbury
	(Vacant British L. Heavyweight Title)
26.05.82	Trevor Cattouse W CO 4 Leeds
	(British L. Heavyweight Title Defence)
07.10.82	John Odhiambo L RSC 5 Copenhagen, Denmark
09.03.83	Antonio Harris W RSC 6 Solihull
	(British L. Heavyweight Title Defence)
09.04.83	Alex Sua W PTS 12 Auckland, New Zealand
	(Elim. Commonwealth L. Heavyweight Title)
17.12.83	Leslie Stewart L PTS 10 Trinidad, West Indies
26.01.84	Dennis Andries L PTS 12 STRAND
	(British L. Heavyweight Title Defence)
06.04.84	Dennis Andries L PTS 12 Watford
	(British L. Heavyweight Title Challenge)
21.09.84	Alek Penarski L PTS 8 Alfreton
24.01.85	Jonjo Greene W RSC 7 Manchester
30.03.85	Chisanda Mutti L PTS 10 Dortmund, Germany
18.04.85	Andy Straughn L CO 1 Halifax
14.10.85	Harry Cowap W CO 4 Southwark
29.11.85	Ralf Rocchigiani L PTS 8 Frankfurt, Germany
20.12.85	Pierre Kabassu DREW 8 Forbach, France

01.04.86	Winston Burnett W PTS 8 Leeds
19.04.86	Yawe Davis W CO 3 San Remo, Italy
01.12.86	Alex Blanchard L PTS 10 Arnhem, Holland
11.03.87	John Moody W RSC 10 Kensington
	(Vacant British L. Heavyweight Title)
11.11.87	Alex Blanchard W CO 2 Usk
	(European L. Heavyweight Title Challenge)
11.05.88	Mark Kaylor W CO 9 Wembley
	(European L. Heavyweight Title Defence)
07.09.88	Pedro van Raamsdonk L RSC 7 Reading
	(European L. Heavyweight Title Defence)
22.03.89	Tony Wilson W RSC 2 Reading
	(British L. Heavyweight Title Challenge)
24.10.89	Jeff Harding L RTD 2 Brisbane, Australia
	(WBC L. Heavyweight Title Challenge)
11.08.90	Eric Nicoletta W CO 9 Cap d'Agde, France
	(European L. Heavyweight Title Challenge)
18.10.90	Frank Winterstein L PTS 10 Paris, France
21.12.90	Christophe Girard W CO 2 Romorantin, France
	(European L. Heavyweight Title Defence)
09.05.91	Leonzer Barber L RTD 5 Leeds
	(Vacant WBO L. Heavyweight Title)
06.12.91	Henry Maske L RSC 8 Dusseldorf, Germany
18.03.92	Glazz Campbell L PTS 10 Glasgow
	(Final Elim. British L. Heavyweight Title)
26.10.92	Steve Lewsam DREW 8 Cleethorpes
21.11.92	Joseph Chingangu L CO 2 Johannesburg, South Africa
11.08.93	Johnny Nelson L RSC 1 Mansfield
	(WBF Cruiserweight Title Challenge)

Career: 50 contests, won 26, drew 2, lost 22.

Jim Conley

Bradford. *Born* Bradford, 13 November, 1967
Welterweight. Ht. 5'10"
Manager Self

02.03.87	Johnny Hooks W RSC 2 Nottingham
16.03.87	Kevin Plant DREW 6 Manchester
27.04.87	David Bacon L PTS 6 Bradford
07.06.87	Dave Kettlewell W PTS 6 Bradford
15.09.87	Johnny Nanton L RSC 3 Kensington
02.11.87	Barry Messam L RSC 2 Bradford
15.12.87	Eddie Collins W PTS 4 Bradford
09.02.88	Dave Kettlewell W RSC 1 Bradford
28.03.88	Mike McKenzie W CO 3 Glasgow
26.04.88	Adrian Din W PTS 4 Bradford
07.11.88	Mark Holden L PTS 6 Bradford
12.12.88	Eddie Collins W RSC 2 Bradford
20.03.89	John Corcoran L RSC 5 Bradford
13.11.89	Ian Thomas L RSC 5 Bradford
26.02.90	Gordon Blair L RSC 3 Bradford
24.10.91	Allan Grainger L PTS 6 Glasgow
05.12.91	Charlie Moore L CO 2 Peterborough
21.03.94	David Sumner W PTS 6 Bradford

Career: 18 contests, won 8, drew 1, lost 9.

James Cook

Peckham. *Born* Jamaica, 17 May, 1959
Former British & European S.
Middleweight Champion. Former
Undefeated Southern Area Middleweight
Champion. Ht. 6'2"
Manager M. Duff

20.10.82	Mick Courtney W PTS 6 Strand
01.11.82	Gary Gething W RSC 2 Piccadilly
19.01.83	Paul Shell W PTS 8 Birmingham
03.02.83	Jimmy Price L PTS 6 Bloomsbury
09.03.83	Willie Wright W PTS 8 Solihull
14.04.83	Dudley McKenzie W PTS 8 Basildon
16.05.83	Eddie Smith W RSC 6 Manchester
23.11.83	Vince Gajny W RTD 6 Solihull
05.06.84	T. P. Jenkins W RSC 9 Kensington
	(Vacant Southern Area Middleweight Title & Elim. British Middleweight Title)
25.09.84	Jimmy Price L CO 2 Wembley
	(Elim. British Middleweight Title)
04.05.85	Conrad Oscar W PTS 10 Queensway
	(Southern Area Middleweight Title Defence)
02.10.85	Tony Burke L CO 2 Solihull
	(Southern Area Middleweight Title Defence)
01.03.86	Graciano Rocchigiani L PTS 8 Cologne, Germany
26.03.86	Jan Lefeber L CO 3 Amsterdam, Holland
20.05.86	Michael Watson W PTS 8 Wembley
13.02.87	Mbayo Wa Mbayo L PTS 8 Villeurbanne, France
02.10.87	Willie Wilson W CO 6 Perugia, Italy
26.10.87	Tarmo Uusivirta L PTS 10 Jyvaskyla, Finland
05.04.88	Cliff Curtis W RSC 4 Basildon
08.06.88	Herol Graham L RSC 5 Sheffield
	(Vacant British Middleweight Title)
31.01.89	Errol Christie W RSC 5 Bethnal Green
28.09.89	Brian Schumacher W RSC 5 Wandsworth
	(Final Elim. British S. Middleweight Title)
30.10.90	Sammy Storey W RSC 10 Belfast
	(British S. Middleweight Title Challenge)
10.03.91	Frank Winterstein W CO 12 Paris, France
	(Vacant European S. Middleweight Title)
01.06.91	Mark Kaylor W RTD 6 Bethnal Green
	(European S. Middleweight Title Defence)
22.10.91	Tarmo Uusiverta W RTD 7 Wandsworth
	(European S. Middleweight Title Defence)
03.04.92	Franck Nicotra L CO 1 Vitrolles, France
	(European S. Middleweight Title Defence)
07.09.92	Tony Booth W PTS 8 Bethnal Green
17.10.92	Terry Magee W RSC 5 Wembley
28.01.93	Carlos Christie W PTS 8 Southwark
18.03.93	Karl Barwise W RSC 6 Lewisham
16.09.93	Fidel Castro W PTS 12 Southwark
	(Vacant British S. Middleweight Title)
02.11.93	Tony Booth W PTS 8 Southwark
26.01.94	Karl Barwise W PTS 8 Birmingham

11.03.94 Cornelius Carr L PTS 12 Bethnal Green
(British S. Middleweight Title Defence)
Career: 35 contests, won 25, lost 10.

John J. Cooke
Coventry. *Born* Coventry, 22 January, 1966
Midlands Area L. Heavyweight Champion.
Ht. 5'10"
Manager J. Griffin

05.10.92 Paul Hanlon W RSC 1 Bardon
23.11.92 Paul Murray W CO 1 Coventry
02.12.92 Nigel Rafferty W PTS 6 Bardon
22.02.93 Zak Chelli DREW 6 Bedworth
17.06.93 Gil Lewis W RSC 9 Bedworth
(Vacant Midlands Area L. Heavyweight Title)
25.04.94 Stephen Wilson L PTS 6 Bury
21.05.94 Noel Magee L PTS 6 Belfast
Career: 7 contests, won 4. drew 1, lost 2.

Dean Cooper
Bristol. *Born* Southampton, 5 August, 1969
Middleweight. Western Area L.
Middleweight Champion. Ht. 6'0"
Manager C. Sanigar

15.09.90 Russell Washer W PTS 6 Bristol
08.10.90 Brian Keating W PTS 6 Bradford
29.10.90 Peter Reid W RSC 1 Nottingham
06.11.90 Tony Wellington W PTS 6 Southend
08.12.90 Lee Farrell W PTS 6 Bristol
04.02.91 Mike Phillips W PTS 6 Leicester
18.02.91 Andre Wharton W PTS 8 Birmingham
22.10.91 Nick Meloscia W PTS 6 Wandsworth
09.03.93 Winston May W PTS 8 Bristol
27.05.93 Robert Peel W PTS 6 Bristol
26.06.93 Julian Eavis W PTS 10 Keynsham
(Vacant Western Area L. Middleweight Title)
28.07.93 Kirkland Laing L RSC 5 Brixton
20.01.94 Jerry Mortimer W PTS 8 Battersea
10.03.94 Terry Magee W PTS 8 Bristol
31.03.94 Julian Eavis W PTS 6 Bristol
Career: 15 contests, won 14, lost 1.

Dean Cooper   Les Clark

Chris Coughlan
Swansea. *Born* Swansea, 21 May, 1963
Cruiserweight. Ht. 6'2½"
Manager C. Breen

03.10.89 Ahcene Chemali L RSC 1 Southend
03.12.89 John Foreman L RSC 2 Birmingham
10.03.90 Mark Langley W PTS 6 Bristol
28.03.90 Phil Soundy L PTS 6 Bethnal Green
05.06.90 Trevor Barry L PTS 6 Liverpool
17.09.90 Steve Yorath L PTS 6 Cardiff
06.11.90 Art Stacey L RSC 4 Southend
08.12.90 Gary McConnell L PTS 6 Bristol
16.01.91 Phil Soundy L PTS 6 Kensington
15.02.91 Neils H. Madsen L RSC 3 Randers, Denmark
04.11.91 Nick Howard W CO 3 Merthyr
11.12.91 Ray Kane L PTS 6 Dublin
18.01.92 Wayne Llewelyn L RSC 3 Kensington
17.12.92 J. A. Bugner L RSC 3 Wembley
15.09.93 Manny Burgo L PTS 6 Bethnal Green
13.10.93 Kevin McBride L PTS 4 Bethnal Green
30.11.93 Scott Welch L CO 1 Cardiff
Career: 17 contests, won 2, lost 15.

Dave Cranston
Streatham. *Born* Lambeth, 2 November, 1968
Middleweight. Ht. 5'9"
Manager G. Steene

02.06.94 Steve Thomas W PTS 6 Tooting
Career: 1 contest, won 1.

Lee Crocker   Les Clark

Lee Crocker
Swansea. *Born* Swansea, 9 May, 1969
L. Middleweight. Ht. 6'0"
Manager Self

31.01.91 Colin Manners L PTS 6 Bredbury
12.02.91 Paul Evans W RSC 2 Cardiff
04.04.91 Johnny Pinnock W RSC 5 Watford
30.06.91 Andrew Furlong DREW 6 Southwark
30.09.91 Fran Harding L RSC 3 Kensington

11.03.92 Russell Washer W PTS 6 Cardiff
30.04.92 Winston May W RSC 2 Bayswater
23.09.92 Nick Manners L CO 1 Leeds
17.12.92 Jamie Robinson L RTD 2 Barking
20.01.93 Ernie Loveridge W PTS 6 Wolverhampton
28.01.93 Clay O'Shea L RSC 1 Southwark
14.06.93 Gilbert Jackson L RSC 2 Bayswater
07.10.93 David Larkin L RSC 5 York
23.03.94 Leif Keiski L CO 2 Cardiff
04.06.94 Derek Grainger L RSC 3 Cardiff
Career: 15 contests, won 5, drew 1, lost 9.

Mario Culpeper
Manchester. *Born* Manchester, 8 December, 1970
S. Featherweight. Ht. 5'6"
Manager Self

25.09.90 Graham O'Malley W PTS 6 Glasgow
26.04.93 Mark Hargreaves W PTS 6 Manchester
28.05.93 Dougie Fox W RSC 3 Middleton
25.07.93 Kid McAuley W PTS 6 Oldham
Career: 4 contests, won 4.

Peter Culshaw
Liverpool. *Born* Liverpool, 15 May, 1973
Bantamweight. Ht. 5'6"
Manager S. Vaughan

02.07.93 Graham McGrath W PTS 6 Liverpool
28.09.93 Vince Feeney W PTS 6 Liverpool
11.12.93 Nick Tooley W RSC 1 Liverpool
25.02.94 Des Gargano W PTS 6 Chester
06.05.94 Neil Swain W PTS 6 Liverpool
Career: 5 contests, won 5.

Ryan Cummings
London. *Born* Lancaster, 17 November, 1973
L. Heavyweight. Ht. 5'11"
Manager B. Hearn

10.03.94 Terry Duffus W PTS 6 Watford
Career: 1 contest, won 1.

Shaun Cummins
Leicester. *Born* Leicester, 8 February, 1968
Middleweight. Former Undefeated WBA
Penta-Continental L. Middleweight
Champion. Ht. 6'1"
Manager F. Warren

29.09.86 Michael Justin W PTS 6 Loughborough
24.11.86 Gary Pemberton W RSC 6 Cardiff
09.02.87 Rob Thomas W PTS 8 Cardiff
23.09.87 Chris Richards W PTS 6 Loughborough
07.03.88 Antonio Fernandez W PTS 6 Northampton
12.09.88 Shamus Casey W CO 3 Northampton
24.10.88 Frank Grant L RTD 7 Northampton
01.03.89 Gary Pemberton W CO 2 Cardiff
05.04.89 Efren Olivo W RSC 1 Kensington
04.10.89 Kesem Clayton L RSC 6 Solihull
31.01.90 Tony Velinor W PTS 8 Bethnal Green
20.02.90 Brian Robinson W RSC 5 Millwall
26.04.90 Wally Swift Jnr L PTS 10 Merthyr
(Vacant Midlands Area L. Middleweight Title & Elim. British L. Middleweight Title)
18.09.90 Paul Wesley W RSC 1 Wolverhampton
31.10.90 Terry Morrill W RSC 1 Crystal Palace

23.01.91 Ian Chantler W PTS 10 Brentwood
19.03.91 Martin Smith DREW 8 Leicester
07.11.91 Jason Rowe W RSC 2 Peterborough
05.12.91 Winston May W RSC 2 Peterborough
18.06.92 Leroy Owens W RSC 2 Peterborough
26.09.92 John Kaighin W RTD 4 Earls Court
28.11.92 Steve Foster W PTS 12 Manchester
(Vacant WBA Penta-Continental L. Middleweight Title)
20.04.93 Mickey Hughes W CO 11 Brentwood
(WBA Penta-Continental L. Middleweight Title Defence)
16.02.94 John Kaighin W RSC 3 Stevenage
11.05.94 Colin Manners L RSC 6 Sheffield
Career: 25 contests, won 20, drew 1, lost 4.

Dave Curtis

Hull. Born Hull, 19 January, 1967
L. Welterweight. Ht. 5'9"
Manager L. Billany

15.04.94 Brian Hickey W PTS 6 Hull
09.05.94 Laurence Roche L PTS 6 Bradford
Career: 2 contests, won 1, lost 1.

Hughie Davey

Newcastle. Born Wallsend, 27 January, 1966
Welterweight. Ht. 5'8"
Manager T. Conroy

30.03.92 Wayne Shepherd W PTS 6 Bradford
28.04.92 Benji Joseph W RSC 4 Houghton le Spring
10.09.92 Darren McInulty W PTS 6 Southwark
21.09.92 Rick North DREW 6 Cleethorpes
23.10.92 Richard O'Brien W PTS 6 Gateshead
01.03.93 Wayne Appleton L PTS 6 Bradford
29.04.93 Paul King L PTS 6 Newcastle
11.06.93 Wayne Shepherd W PTS 6 Gateshead
04.10.93 Steve Scott W PTS 6 Bradford
08.11.93 Warren Bowers W RSC 2 Bradford
13.12.93 Sean Baker L PTS 4 Bristol
03.03.94 Paul King L PTS 10 Newcastle
(Vacant Northern Area Welterweight Title)
Career: 12 contests, won 7, drew 1, lost 4.

Andy Davidson

Salford. Born Salford, 11 March, 1972
L. Welterweight. Ht. 5'9"
Manager J. Trickett

18.04.94 Kevin McKenzie W RSC 1 Manchester
28.06.94 M. T. Atkin W RSC 1 Mayfair
Career: 2 contests, won 2.

(David) Jamie Davidson (Prescott)

Liverpool. Born Liverpool, 1 April, 1970
Welterweight. Ht. 6'0"
Manager M. Atkinson

18.11.91 Ty Zubair W PTS 6 Manchester
10.02.92 Kevin McKillan W PTS 6 Liverpool
11.03.92 Kevin McKillan DREW 6 Stoke
28.04.92 Micky Hall W PTS 6 Houghton le Spring
14.05.92 Floyd Churchill L RSC 4 Liverpool
21.06.93 George Wilson L RSC 4 Swindon
16.09.93 Delroy Leslie L PTS 6 Southwark
11.11.93 Blue Butterworth L RSC 3 Burnley
Career: 8 contests, won 3, drew 1, lost 4.

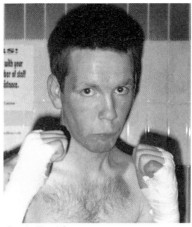

Jamie Davidson   Les Clark

Chris Davies

Rhondda. Born Pontypridd, 24 August, 1974
S. Middleweight. Ht. 5'9"
Manager D. Gardiner

27.04.94 Craig Joseph L PTS 6 Solihull
25.05.94 Glenn Catley L RSC 1 Bristol
Career: 2 contests, lost 2.

Stevie R. Davies

Newcastle. Born Consett, 27 August, 1965
L. Heavyweight. Ht. 6'3"
Manager Self

04.04.89 Sean Stringfellow L RSC 2 Manchester
22.05.89 Ian Vokes W PTS 6 Bradford
29.05.89 Trevor Barry W RSC 4 Liverpool
20.03.90 Terry French L PTS 6 Hartlepool
23.04.90 Graham Burton L PTS 6 Bradford
01.05.90 Glenn Campbell L RSC 2 Oldham
08.10.90 Sean Stringfellow W PTS 6 Leicester
22.10.90 Tony Lawrence W PTS 8 Peterborough
22.11.90 Tony Lawrence W PTS 6 Ilkeston
13.12.90 Terry French L PTS 10 Hartlepool
(Vacant Northern Area L. Heavyweight Title)
28.02.91 Kevin Morton L RSC 3 Bury
29.04.93 Martin Langtry L RSC 2 Newcastle
25.11.93 Art Stacey L PTS 6 Newcastle
08.12.93 Simon McDougall L RSC 5 Hull
Career: 14 contests, won 5, lost 9.

Kent Davis

Cwmbran. Born Stroud, 12 August, 1965
Cruiserweight. Ht. 6'2"
Manager M. Hill

27.10.93 Robert Norton L PTS 6 West Bromwich
16.12.93 L. A. Williams W RSC 2 Newport
12.03.94 Ray Kane L PTS 6 Cardiff
Career: 3 contests, won 1, lost 2.

John Davison

Newcastle. Born Newcastle, 30 September, 1958
Former Undefeated British & WBC International Featherweight Champion.

Former Undefeated WBC International S. Bantamweight Champion. Ht. 5'5"
Manager T. Conroy

22.09.88 Des Gargano W PTS 8 Newcastle
29.09.88 Des Gargano W PTS 8 Sunderland
10.10.88 Gary Maxwell W RSC 1 Nottingham
22.11.88 James Hunter W PTS 6 Marton
12.12.88 Gary Maxwell L PTS 8 Nottingham
14.02.89 Nigel Senior W RSC 8 Sunderland
11.09.89 Colin Lynch W RSC 2 Nottingham
23.10.89 Andre Seymour W PTS 8 Glasgow
06.12.89 Karl Taylor W PTS 8 Leicester
19.02.90 Bruce Flippens W RSC 6 Glasgow
20.03.90 Srikoon Narachawat W CO 5 Hartlepool
(WBC International Featherweight Title Challenge)
15.05.90 Bang Saen Yodmuaydang W RSC 5 South Shields
(WBC International Featherweight Title Defence)
13.11.90 Jae-Hyun Hwang W RSC 5 Hartlepool
(WBC International Featherweight Title Defence)
25.05.91 Fabrice Benichou L PTS 12 Brest, France
(Vacant European Featherweight Title)
09.08.91 Richard Savage W RSC 6 Juan les Pins, France
22.10.91 Sakda Sorpakdee W PTS 12 Hartlepool
(WBC International S. Bantamweight Title Challenge)
29.05.92 Fabrice Benichou L PTS 12 Amneville, France
(European Featherweight Title Challenge)
10.09.92 Tim Driscoll W CO 7 Sunderland
(Vacant British Featherweight Title)
17.04.93 Steve Robinson L PTS 12 Washington
(Vacant WBO Featherweight Title)
18.12.93 Duke McKenzie L RSC 4 Manchester
(Vacant British Featherweight Title)
Career: 20 contests, won 15, lost 5.

Russell Davison

Salford. Born Salford, 2 October, 1961
S. Featherweight. Former Central Area Featherweight Champion. Ht. 5'7"
Manager Self

22.05.86 Nigel Crook L PTS 6 Horwich
09.06.86 Gary Maxwell L PTS 6 Manchester
25.09.86 Nigel Crook L PTS 6 Preston
14.10.86 Davey Hughes W PTS 6 Manchester
25.11.86 Carl Gaynor W PTS 6 Manchester
10.12.86 Davey Hughes W PTS 6 Stoke
27.01.87 Nigel Senior DREW 8 Manchester
04.03.87 Tim Driscoll L PTS 8 Stoke
31.03.87 Stuart Carmichael W PTS 8 Oldham
26.05.87 Kevin Taylor L PTS 10 Oldham
(Central Area S. Featherweight Title Challenge)
06.10.87 Gary Maxwell L PTS 8 Manchester
16.12.87 Mike Whalley W PTS 8 Manchester
16.03.88 Gary de Roux L PTS 8 Solihull
03.05.88 Rocky Lawlor L PTS 8 Stoke
29.11.88 Mike Whalley L RSC 7 Manchester
(Vacant Central Area Featherweight Title)
25.01.89 Derek Amory W PTS 8 Solihull
19.04.89 Michael Armstrong L PTS 8 Stoke
06.12.89 Michael Armstrong W PTS 8 Stoke
23.12.89 Kevin Kelley L PTS 8 Hoogvleit, Holland

81

06.03.90	Michael Armstrong L PTS 10 Stoke
26.09.90	Steve Robinson L PTS 8 Manchester
19.11.90	Peter Judson W PTS 8 Manchester
17.12.90	Dave Buxton W PTS 8 Manchester
29.01.91	Peter Judson W PTS 10 Stockport
	(Vacant Central Area Featherweight Title)
05.03.91	Colin McMillan L PTS 6 Millwall
24.04.91	Steve Robinson L RTD 6 Preston
09.09.91	Jimmy Owens W PTS 10 Liverpool
	(Central Area Featherweight Title Defence)
29.02.92	Moussa Sangaree L RSC 5 Gravelines, France
13.10.92	Craig Dermody L PTS 10 Bury
	(Central Area Featherweight Title Defence)
24.03.93	Eamonn McAuley L PTS 6 Belfast
26.04.93	Drew Docherty L PTS 8 Glasgow
15.05.93	Alan Levene L PTS 6 Bradford
24.05.93	David Ramsden L PTS 6 Bradford
02.03.94	Ian McGirr W CO 1 Glasgow
10.04.94	Ian McGirr L PTS 6 Glasgow
06.06.94	Miguel Matthews L PTS 6 Glasgow

Career: 36 contests, won 12, drew 1, lost 23.

Mark Dawson (Lee)

Burton. *Born* Burton, 26 February, 1971
L. Middleweight. Ht. 5'8"
Manager W. Swift

03.06.92	Rick North W PTS 6 Newcastle under Lyme
09.09.92	Jimmy Vincent W PTS 6 Stoke
29.09.92	Steve Goodwin L RSC 1 Stoke
28.10.92	Steve McNess W RSC 2 Kensington
07.12.92	Steve Goodwin W PTS 6 Mayfair
27.01.93	Rick North W PTS 8 Stoke
15.02.93	John Bosco L PTS 6 Mayfair
27.02.93	Robin Reid L RSC 1 Dagenham
30.03.93	Matthew Turner L PTS 6 Cardiff
12.05.93	Steve Goodwin L PTS 10 Stoke
	(Vacant Midlands Area L. Middleweight Title)
27.05.93	Derek Wormald L RTD 5 Burnley
10.11.93	John Bosco L RTD 4 Watford
15.03.94	Stinger Mason W RSC 6 Stoke
22.03.94	Geoff McCreesh L PTS 6 Bethnal Green

Career: 14 contests, won 6, lost 8.

Roger Dean

Upminster. *Born* Singapore, 13 January, 1966
Welterweight. Ht. 5'9"
Manager M. Brennan

28.11.93	Danny Quacoe L RSC 3 Southwark
16.05.94	Nick Ingram L RSC 3 Heathrow

Career: 2 contests, lost 2.

Roy Dehara

Ashford. *Born* Lambeth, 17 September, 1963
Welterweight. Ht. 5'8"
Manager A. Urry

27.05.94	Nick Ingram L PTS 6 Ashford

Career: 1 contest, lost 1.

Garry Delaney

West Ham. *Born* Newham, 12 August, 1970

WBO Penta-Continental & Southern Area
L. Heavyweight Champion. Ht. 6'3"
Manager B. Hearn

02.10.91	Gus Mendes W RSC 1 Barking
23.10.91	Joe Frater W RSC 1 Bethnal Green
13.11.91	John Kaighin W PTS 6 Bethnal Green
11.12.91	Randy B. Powell W RSC 1 Basildon
11.02.92	Simon Harris DREW 8 Barking
12.05.92	John Williams W PTS 6 Crystal Palace
16.06.92	Nigel Rafferty W CO 5 Dagenham
15.09.92	Gil Lewis W CO 2 Crystal Palace
06.10.92	Simon McDougall W PTS 8 Antwerp, Belgium
10.11.92	John Oxenham W CO 5 Dagenham
12.12.92	Simon McDougall W PTS 8 Muswell Hill
30.01.93	Simon Collins W PTS 8 Brentwood
28.09.93	Glazz Campbell W CO 6 Bethnal Green
	(Southern Area L. Heavyweight Title Challenge)
06.11.93	John Kaighin W CO 1 Bethnal Green
21.12.93	Ray Albert W RSC 3 Mayfair
	(Vacant WBO Penta-Continental L. Heavyweight Title)
11.01.94	Jim Murray W RSC 7 Bethnal Green
	(WBO Penta-Continental L. Heavyweight Title Defence)
09.04.94	Simon Harris W CO 6 Bethnal Green
	(WBO Penta-Continental & Southern Area L. Heavyweight Title Defence)

Career: 17 contests, won 16, drew 1.

Mark Delaney   Les Clark

Mark Delaney

West Ham. *Born* London, 1 December, 1971
S. Middleweight. Ht. 5'11"
Manager B. Hearn

05.10.93	Lee Sara W RTD 5 Mayfair
11.01.94	Jason McNeill W RSC 2 Bethnal Green
22.01.94	Graham Jenner W RTD 3 Belfast
09.02.94	Tony Colclough W RSC 4 Brentwood

19.03.94	Paul Murray W CO 3 Millwall
09.04.94	Tim Robinson W RSC 2 Bethnal Green
11.06.94	Ernie Loveridge W RSC 5 Bethnal Green

Career: 7 contests, won 7.

Pat Delargy

Coventry. *Born* Hoddeston, 9 October, 1969
L. Welterweight. Ht. 5'9"
Manager P. Byrne

14.02.89	Peter Bowen W RTD 1 Wolverhampton
20.02.89	Erwin Edwards W PTS 6 Birmingham
15.03.89	Dave Croft L RSC 3 Stoke
28.06.89	Dave Pierre L RTD 2 Kenilworth
05.12.90	Dave Jenkins L RSC 4 Stafford
24.09.91	Bernard Paul L RSC 5 Basildon
11.05.92	Mark Antony W PTS 6 Coventry
28.09.93	Paul Knights L RSC 3 Bethnal Green

Career: 8 contests, won 3, lost 5.

Paul Denton (Ramsey)

Walthamstow. *Born* Birmingham, 12 April, 1970
Welterweight. Ht. 5'10"
Manager B. Ingle

18.03.93	Mark O'Callaghan W RSC 4 Lewisham
29.04.93	Dave Maj DREW 6 Mayfair
11.08.93	Billy McDougall W PTS 6 Mansfield
01.10.93	Ferid Bennecer W CO 3 Waregem, Belgium
01.12.93	Brian Hickey W CO 1 Kensington
28.01.94	Youssef Bakhouche L PTS 6 Waregem, Belgium
07.05.94	Viktor Fesechko L PTS 6 Dnepropetrousk, Ukraine

Career: 7 contests, won 4, drew 1, lost 2.

Gary de Roux

Peterborough. *Born* Manchester, 4 November, 1962
S. Featherweight. Former British Featherweight Champion. Former Undefeated Southern Area Featherweight Champion. Ht. 5'6"
Manager Self

25.09.86	Tony Carter W RSC 2 Peterborough
20.10.86	Nigel Lawrence W RSC 1 Nottingham
28.11.86	Geoff Sillitoe W RTD 1 Peterborough
15.12.86	Tim Driscoll L PTS 6 Eltham
19.02.87	Gary King W PTS 6 Peterborough
01.05.87	Nigel Senior W PTS 8 Peterborough
10.09.87	Colin Lynch W RSC 3 Peterborough
18.11.87	Steve Pollard DREW 8 Peterborough
23.02.88	Joe Duffy W RSC 2 Bedford
16.03.88	Russell Davison W PTS 8 Solihull
05.05.88	Patrick Kamy L RSC 4 Bayswater
26.11.88	Gianni di Napoli L RSC 3 Forli, Italy
20.09.89	Henry Armstrong L PTS 8 Stoke
29.11.89	James Hunter W CO 2 Marton
13.03.90	John Green W RSC 2 Bristol
19.04.90	Henry Armstrong W CO 8 Oldham
14.12.90	Alan McKay W RSC 5 Peterborough
	(Vacant Southern Area Featherweight Title)
05.03.91	Sean Murphy W CO 5 Millwall
	(British Featherweight Title Challenge)
22.05.91	Colin McMillan L RSC 7 Millwall
	(British Featherweight Title Defence)

13.11.91 Alan McKay L RSC 8 Bethnal Green
(Vacant Southern Area Featherweight Title)
06.05.93 Juan Castaneda L RSC 6 Las Vegas, USA
17.12.93 Hichem Dahmani L RSC 6 Ascona, Italy
Career: 22 contests, won 13, drew 1, lost 8.

Mike Deveney

Paisley. *Born* Elderslie, 14 December, 1965
Featherweight. Ht. 5'5"
Manager N. Sweeney

18.02.91 John George W PTS 6 Glasgow
18.03.91 Frankie Ventura W PTS 6 Piccadilly
22.04.91 Neil Leitch W PTS 6 Glasgow
09.09.91 Pete Buckley W PTS 8 Glasgow
19.09.91 Noel Carroll L PTS 6 Stockport
14.11.91 Pete Buckley W PTS 6 Edinburgh
28.01.92 Graham O'Malley L RSC 1 Piccadilly
28.02.92 Gary Hickman W PTS 6 Irvine
14.09.92 David Ramsden L PTS 6 Bradford
07.10.92 Mark Hargreaves L RSC 7 Glasgow
07.12.92 Carl Roberts W PTS 6 Manchester
27.01.93 Barry Jones L PTS 6 Cardiff
26.02.93 Alan Graham W PTS 6 Irvine
23.03.93 Colin Lynch W PTS 6 Wolverhampton
29.05.93 Dave Buxton W PTS 6 Paisley
20.09.93 Ady Benton W PTS 8 Glasgow
30.11.93 Elvis Parsley L PTS 6 Wolverhampton
24.01.94 Ady Benton W PTS 6 Glasgow
02.03.94 Yusuf Vorajee W PTS 6 Solihull
21.03.94 Chris Jickells W RSC 5 Glasgow
15.04.94 Chris Clarkson W RSC 3 Hull
06.04.94 Mark Hargreaves W PTS 6 Manchester
15.06.94 Justin Murphy L PTS 6 Southwark
Career: 23 contests, won 15, lost 8.

Norman Dhalie

Birmingham. *Born* Birmingham, 24 March, 1971
Lightweight. Ht. 5'7"
Manager Self

06.04.92 Karl Morling L PTS 6 Northampton
27.04.92 Wilson Docherty L RSC 2 Glasgow
02.07.92 John White L RSC 6 Middleton
29.09.92 Gary Marston DREW 6 Stoke
07.10.92 Jacob Smith W PTS 6 Sunderland
03.12.92 Bradley Stone L CO 4 Lewisham
26.01.93 Neil Smith L PTS 4 Leicester
13.02.93 John White L CO 2 Manchester
20.04.93 Bobby Guynan L PTS 6 Brentwood
29.04.93 Kevin Toomey L PTS 6 Hull
23.05.93 Mike Anthony Brown W PTS 4 Brockley
09.06.93 Joey Moffat L RTD 4 Liverpool
30.09.93 Simon Frailing W PTS 6 Hayes
06.10.93 Kevin McKillan L RSC 1 Solihull
06.12.93 Colin Innes W PTS 6 Bradford
16.12.93 Peter Till L PTS 8 Walsall
19.01.94 John Naylor L RSC 3 Stoke
21.02.94 Hugh Collins L RTD 4 Glasgow
14.04.94 Mike Anthony Brown L PTS 6 Battersea
28.04.94 John Stovin DREW 6 Hull
06.05.94 Sugar Gibiluru L RTD 5 Liverpool
Career: 21 contests, won 4, drew 2, lost 15.

(Hardip) Harry Dhami

Gravesend. *Born* Gravesend, 17 April, 1972

L. Midleweight. Ht. 5'10"
Manager M. Hill

29.10.92 Johnny Pinnock W PTS 6 Hayes
20.05.94 Nick Appiah W RSC 4 Acton
27.05.94 Chris Vassiliou W RSC 5 Ashford
Career: 3 contests, won 3.

Michael Dick

Aylesbury. *Born* Aylesbury, 29 October, 1964
Welterweight. Ht. 5'7"
Manager K. Sanders

29.10.92 Nick Appiah L PTS 6 Hayes
24.02.93 Jason Beard L RSC 5 Wembley
29.04.93 Steve McGovern L PTS 6 Hayes
23.05.93 Maurice Forbes L RSC 1 Brockley
24.06.93 B. F. Williams L RTD 3 Watford
13.10.93 B. F. Williams L RSC 1 Watford
Career: 6 contests, lost 6.

Robert Dickie

Swansea. *Born* Carmarthen, 23 June, 1964
Lightweight. Former Undefeated British & Scottish Featherweight Champion. Former WBC International & British S. Featherweight Champion. Ht. 5'6"
Manager Self

12.03.83 Billy Hough W PTS 6 Swindon
25.04.83 Charlie Brown W RSC 4 Aberdeen
16.05.83 George Bailey W RSC 3 Birmingham
27.05.83 Howard Williams W RSC 2 Swansea
13.06.83 Danny Flynn DREW 8 Glasgow
10.10.83 Danny Flynn L RSC 7 Glasgow
(Vacant Scottish Bantamweight Title)
14.05.84 Dave Pratt W PTS 8 Nottingham
24.10.84 Charlie Coke W RSC 3 Mayfair
24.11.84 John Sharkey W DIS 4 Solihull
(Vacant Scottish Featherweight Title)
08.12.84 Steve Enright W RSC 1 Swansea
25.02.85 John Sharkey W CO 2 Glasgow
20.03.85 John Maloney W RSC 3 Solihull
08.05.85 Mark Reefer W RSC 1 Solihull
31.07.85 Dean Bramhald W RSC 7 Porthcawl
07.10.85 Frank Khonkhobe DREW 10 Kimberley, South Africa
09.04.86 John Feeney W PTS 12 Kensington
(Vacant British Featherweight Title)
30.07.86 Steve Sims W CO 5 Ebbw Vale
(British Featherweight Title Defence)
29.10.86 John Feeney W PTS 12 Ebbw Vale
(British Featherweight Title Defence)
20.10.87 Rocky Lawlor W DIS 2 Stoke
18.01.88 Arvell Campbell W PTS 4 Cardiff
28.03.88 Hengky Gun W RSC 5 Stoke
(WBC International S. Featherweight Title Challenge)
31.08.88 Kamel Bou Ali L RSC 6 Stoke
(WBC International S. Featherweight Title Defence)
22.11.89 Gary Maxwell W RSC 8 Solihull
20.12.89 Colin Lynch W RSC 1 Swansea
22.10.90 Barrington Francis W RTD 10 Glasgow
(Elim. Commonwealth S. Featherweight Title)
05.03.91 Kevin Pritchard W RSC 8 Cardiff
(British S. Featherweight Title Challenge)
30.04.91 Sugar Gibiluru L RSC 9 Stockport
(British S. Featherweight Title Defence)

10.11.93 Phil Found L RTD 2 Ystrad
Career: 28 contests, won 22, drew 2, lost 4.

Liam Dineen

Peterlee. *Born* Horden, 17 October, 1972
Lightweight. Ht. 5'10"
Manager T. Conroy

24.05.94 Carl Roberts W PTS 6 Sunderland
Career: 1 contest, won 1.

Terry Dixon

West Ham. *Born* London, 29 July, 1966
Cruiserweight. Ht. 5'11"
Manager Self

21.09.89 Dave Mowbray W RSC 1 Southampton
30.11.89 Brendan Dempsey W RSC 8 Barking
08.03.90 Cordwell Hylton W PTS 8 Watford
06.04.90 Prince Rodney W RSC 7 Stevenage
23.10.90 Dennis Bailey W PTS 6 Leicester
07.03.91 Carl Thompson L PTS 8 Basildon
22.04.91 Everton Blake L RSC 8 Mayfair
25.03.92 Mark Bowen W RTD 1 Kensington
27.04.92 Ian Bulloch W RSC 4 Mayfair
17.10.92 Darren McKenna L RSC 3 Wembley
04.10.93 Steve Yorath W RSC 4 Mayfair
Career: 11 contests, won 8, lost 3.

Alex Docherty

Craigneuk. *Born* Motherwell, 5 June, 1972
S. Bantamweight. Ht. 5'5"
Manager T. Gilmour

24.02.92 Andrew Bloomer W PTS 6 Glasgow
01.06.92 Robert Braddock W PTS 6 Glasgow
19.09.92 Kid McAuley W PTS 6 Glasgow
26.02.93 Des Gargano L RSC 4 Irvine
07.11.93 Graham McGrath W RSC 3 Glasgow
Career: 5 contests, won 4, lost 1.

Wilson Docherty

Croy. *Born* Glasgow, 15 April, 1968
WBO Penta-Continental Featherweight Champion. Ht. 5'6"
Manager T. Gilmour

27.04.92 Norman Dhalie W RSC 2 Glasgow
09.07.92 Graham McGrath W RSC 4 Glasgow
26.04.93 Des Gargano W PTS 6 Glasgow
07.06.93 Chris Jickells W RSC 5 Glasgow
14.07.93 Anton Gilmore L PTS 8 Marula, South Africa
07.11.93 Robert Braddock W RSC 3 Glasgow
24.01.94 Paul Harvey W PTS 12 Glasgow
(Vacant WBO Penta-Continental Featherweight Title)
Career: 7 contests, won 6, lost 1.

Adrian Dodson

St Pancras. *Born* Georgetown, 20 September, 1970
L. Middleweight. Ht. 5'10"
Manager Self

31.03.93 Chris Mulcahy W RSC 1 Bethnal Green
14.04.93 Rick North W RTD 1 Kensington
06.05.93 Greg Wallace W RSC 3 Las Vegas, USA
23.06.93 Russell Washer W PTS 6 Edmonton
22.09.93 Robert Peel W CO 1 Bethnal Green

Adrian Dodson (left) made it six wins on the trot when blasting his way to a fourth round win over Julian Eavis Les Clark

23.10.93	Julian Eavis W RSC 4 Cardiff
26.02.94	Shamus Casey W CO 1 Earls Court
12.03.94	Danny Juma W PTS 6 Cardiff
09.04.94	Stuart Dunn W RSC 1 Mansfield
04.06.94	Andrew Jervis W RSC 2 Cardiff

Career: 10 contests, won 10.

Darren Dorrington Les Clark

Darren Dorrington

Bristol. *Born* Bristol, 24 July, 1968
Middleweight. Ht. 5'11"
Manager C. Sanigar

13.09.93	Justin Smart DREW 4 Bristol
03.11.93	Russell Washer W PTS 4 Bristol
20.01.94	Shamus Casey W PTS 6 Battersea
29.01.94	Barry Thorogood DREW 6 Cardiff
10.03.94	Ray Price W RSC 6 Bristol
25.05.94	Steve Thomas W PTS 4 Bristol

Career: 6 contests, won 4, drew 2.

Scott Doyle

Birmingham. *Born* Birmingham, 14 June, 1968
Welterweight. Ht. 5'8"
Manager Self

15.03.91	Chris Cooper W RSC 1 Millwall
12.04.91	Barry North W PTS 6 Willenhall
17.06.91	Tony Doyle W PTS 6 Edgbaston
07.10.91	Jason Brattley W PTS 6 Birmingham
21.11.91	Shane Sheridan W PTS 6 Ilkeston
09.12.91	Peter Till L CO 3 Brierley Hill
03.02.92	Ricky Sackfield L PTS 6 Manchester
03.03.92	Richard O'Brien W PTS 4 Cradley Heath
14.05.92	Joey Moffat L RSC 8 Liverpool
28.04.94	Andy Peach W PTS 6 Mayfair
06.05.94	Tony Mock L PTS 6 Liverpool

Career: 11 contests, won 7, lost 4.

Michael Driscoll

Portsmouth. *Born* Portsmouth, 18 May, 1969
L. Welterweight. Ht. 5'10¼"
Manager M. Fawcett

16.06.88	Dave Pierre L PTS 6 Croydon
10.07.88	David Bacon W PTS 6 Eastbourne
30.08.88	Mike Russell W CO 2 Kensington
15.09.88	Ricky Maxwell DREW 6 High Wycombe
26.10.88	Mick O'Donnell W RSC 2 Kensington
01.12.88	Neil Haddock DREW 6 Gravesend
02.02.89	Dave Croft W RSC 2 Croydon
26.04.89	Dean Bramhald W RSC 2 Southampton
31.10.89	Steve Foran DREW 6 Manchester
22.02.90	B. F. Williams W CO 2 Wandsworth
06.03.90	Billy Couzens W CO 2 Bethnal Green
26.11.90	Wayne Windle W RSC 3 Bethnal Green
02.05.91	Andrew Morgan W PTS 6 Kensington
22.06.91	Steve Foran W RSC 4 Earls Court
01.02.92	Peter Till W RSC 3 Birmingham
25.04.92	Alan Hall L PTS 6 Manchester
27.10.92	Marvin P. Gray W PTS 8 Leicester
12.12.92	Bernard Paul W RSC 2 Muswell Hill
26.01.93	Tony McKenzie L PTS 10 Leicester *(Elim. British L. Welterweight Title)*
16.03.93	Errol McDonald W PTS 10 Mayfair *(Elim. British L. Welterweight Title)*
19.05.93	Ray Newby W RTD 2 Leicester
05.10.93	Tony McKenzie W CO 5 Mayfair *(Elim. British L. Welterweight Title)*

22.01.94 Ross Hale L RSC 7 Cardiff
(Elim. British L. Welterweight Title)
Career: 23 contests, won 16, drew 3, lost 4.

James Drummond

Kilmarnock. *Born* Kilmarnock, 11 February, 1969
Scottish Flyweight Champion. Ht. 5'6"
Manager T. Gilmour

18.09.89 Tony Smith W RSC 1 Glasgow
09.10.89 Kruga Hydes W RSC 3 Glasgow
22.01.90 Kevin Jenkins L PTS 6 Glasgow
08.03.90 Kevin Jenkins W RSC 5 Glasgow
19.03.90 Neil Parry W RSC 4 Glasgow
08.10.90 Derek Amory L PTS 8 Cleethorpes
19.11.90 Chris Clarkson L PTS 8 Glasgow
18.03.91 Stewart Fishermac W RSC 8 Piccadilly
07.05.91 Des Gargano W PTS 8 Glasgow
01.06.91 Mercurio Ciaramitaro DREW 6 Ragusa, Italy
15.11.91 Salvatore Fanni L PTS 12 Omegna, Italy
(European Flyweight Title Challenge)
19.05.92 Robbie Regan L RSC 9 Cardiff
(British Flyweight Title Challenge)
22.12.92 Francis Ampofo L PTS 12 Mayfair
(Vacant British Flyweight Title)
26.02.93 Ady Benton DREW 6 Irvine
29.06.93 Ricky Beard L PTS 8 Mayfair
25.10.93 Neil Parry W RSC 2 Glasgow
22.11.93 Louis Veitch W PTS 8 Glasgow
21.03.94 Neil Armstrong W RSC 5 Glasgow
(Elim. British Flyweight Title. Vacant Scottish Flyweight Title)
Career: 18 contests, won 9, drew 2, lost 7.

John Duckworth

Burnley. *Born* Burnley, 25 May, 1971
L. Middleweight. Ht. 6'2"
Manager N. Basso

04.04.92 Warren Stephens W RSC 5 Cleethorpes
13.04.92 Steve Goodwin L PTS 6 Manchester
04.06.92 Phil Foxon W RSC 4 Burnley
05.10.92 Dave Maj DREW 6 Manchester
29.10.92 Tony Massey W RTD 4 Leeds
20.01.93 James McGee L PTS 6 Solihull
25.02.93 Tony Trimble W PTS 6 Burnley
31.03.93 Jamie Robinson L RSC 3 Barking
27.05.93 Warren Stephens W RSC 5 Burnley
15.09.93 Mark Jay W RSC 4 Newcastle
11.11.93 Darren Pilling W PTS 6 Burnley
02.03.94 Dave Johnson L PTS 8 Solihull
15.03.94 Andrew Jervis W PTS 6 Stoke
18.04.94 Craig Winter L RSC 5 Manchester
Career: 14 contests, won 9, drew 1, lost 4.

Terry Duffus

Gloucester. *Born* Gloucester, 18 September, 1960
L. Heavyweight. Ht. 5'11"
Manager Self

29.02.88 Morris Thomas W RSC 1 Bradford
21.03.88 Dave Lawrence DREW 4 Bethnal Green
05.05.88 Winston Burnett L PTS 8 Bayswater
12.05.88 Michael Madsen L PTS 4 Copenhagen, Denmark
15.11.88 David Haycock W CO 6 Chigwell
19.12.88 Dave Lawrence L PTS 6 Mayfair

17.01.89 Kevin Roper L RSC 2 Chigwell
22.03.89 Andy Balfe L PTS 6 Glasgow
26.04.89 Paul McCarthy L PTS 8 Southampton
08.05.89 Brendan Dempsey L RSC 1 Piccadilly
26.02.90 Mark Spencer W RSC 3 Crystal Palace
10.10.90 Jim Peters L RSC 2 Kensington
31.01.91 Nick Manners L RSC 1 Bredbury
07.03.91 Phil Soundy L RSC 2 Basildon
12.09.91 Keith Inglis L CO 5 Wandsworth
25.03.92 Joey Peters L RSC 1 Kensington
15.09.93 Eddie Knight L PTS 6 Ashford
10.03.94 Ryan Cummings L PTS 6 Watford
29.03.94 Paul Lawson L RSC 1 Bethnal Green
Career: 19 contests, won 4, drew 1, lost 14.

Marty Duke

Yarmouth. *Born* Yarmouth, 19 June, 1967
Welterweight. Ht. 5'9"
Manager Self

16.05.88 Wayne Timmins L PTS 6 Wolverhampton
06.09.88 Tony Cloak W PTS 6 Southend
26.09.88 Tony Cloak L RSC 2 Bedford
27.10.88 Matthew Jones L PTS 6 Birmingham
06.12.88 Peter Mundy W PTS 6 Southend
25.01.89 Tony Hodge W RSC 2 Basildon
07.02.89 Dennis White L PTS 6 Southend
04.04.89 Tony Cloak W RSC 5 Southend
27.04.89 Steve West L RSC 1 Southwark
03.10.89 Colin Ford L PTS 6 Southend
23.10.89 Andy Catesby W PTS 6 Mayfair
19.12.89 Mike Jay DREW 6 Gorleston
08.02.90 Dean Lake L RSC 4 Southwark
14.03.90 Ahmet Canbakis L RSC 6 Battersea
12.11.90 Chris Haydon W PTS 6 Norwich
04.12.90 Paul Busby L PTS 6 Bury St Edmunds
29.01.91 Paul Smith L PTS 6 Wisbech
15.04.91 James McGee W PTS 6 Leicester
08.05.91 Martin Rosamond DREW 8 Millwall
16.05.91 Danny Shinkwin L PTS 6 Battersea
30.05.91 Richie Woodhall L RSC 4 Birmingham
04.07.91 Robert McCracken L RSC 1 Alfreton
03.09.91 Eamonn Loughran L PTS 6 Cardiff
26.09.91 Adrian Riley L PTS 6 Dunstable
05.11.91 Tony McKenzie L RSC 7 Leicester
31.03.92 Ojay Abrahams L RSC 2 Norwich
08.09.92 Ricky Mabbett DREW 6 Norwich
14.11.92 Vince Rose L PTS 6 Cardiff
26.01.93 Ricky Mabbett W CO 1 Leicester
14.04.93 Kevin Lueshing L RSC 2 Kensington
23.06.93 Billy McDougall W PTS 6 Gorleston
31.08.93 Glenn Catley L RSC 2 Croydon
03.11.93 Glenn Catley L RSC 1 Bristol
28.03.94 Spencer McCracken L RSC 2 Birmingham
Career: 34 contests, won 9, drew 3, lost 22.

Marcus Duncan

Lancaster. *Born* Blackpool, 9 January, 1971
Bantamweight. Ht. 5'6"
Manager J. Doughty

12.11.92 Andrew Bloomer W PTS 6 Burnley
22.04.93 Chris Lyons W RSC 2 Bury
27.05.93 Neil Swain L PTS 6 Burnley
28.06.93 Neil Parry L RSC 2 Morecambe
13.09.93 Neil Parry W PTS 6 Middleton
11.11.93 Dave Campbell W PTS 6 Burnley
17.02.94 Jason Morris W RSC 6 Bury
21.03.94 Graham McGrath W PTS 6 Bradford
16.05.94 Daryl McKenzie W PTS 6 Morecambe
13.06.94 Matthew Harris L RSC 1 Bradford
Career: 10 contests, won 7, lost 3.

Mick Duncan

Newcastle. *Born* Newcastle, 24 August, 1969
L. Middleweight. Ht. 5'11"
Manager Self

29.09.88 Skip Jackson L RSC 3 Sunderland
13.03.89 Richard Thompson W PTS 6 Mayfair
22.03.89 B. K. Bennett L PTS 6 Sheppey
19.05.89 John Tipping W PTS 6 Gateshead
15.06.89 Paul Abercromby L RSC 2 Glasgow
12.10.89 Steve West L RSC 5 Southwark
06.03.90 Paul King L PTS 6 Newcastle
11.04.90 Tony Booth L PTS 6 Dewsbury
16.05.90 Chris Richards W PTS 6 Hull
11.06.90 Tommy Warde W PTS 6 Manchester
15.10.90 Andre Wharton L PTS 6 Brierley Hill
26.11.90 Rob Pitters DREW 6 Bury
13.12.90 Richard O'Brien W PTS 6 Hartlepool
18.02.91 Tommy Milligan L PTS 6 Glasgow
06.03.91 Danny Quigg L PTS 6 Glasgow
18.03.91 Allan Grainger W PTS 6 Glasgow
10.05.91 Rob Pitters L RSC 3 Gateshead
23.09.91 Danny Quigg DREW 6 Glasgow
07.10.91 Tyrone Eastmond L RSC 5 Bradford
18.11.91 Allan Grainger W PTS 6 Glasgow
25.11.91 Willie Yeardsley W PTS 6 Liverpool
12.12.91 Dave Johnson L PTS 6 Hartlepool
20.01.92 Mark Jay L PTS 6 Bradford
20.02.92 Leigh Wicks W PTS 8 Glasgow
06.03.92 Oleg Chalajew W PTS 8 Berlin, Germany
13.05.92 Lloyd Honeyghan L RSC 2 Kensington
27.06.92 Reiner Gies L CO 7 Halle, Germany
15.10.92 Gary Logan L PTS 8 Lewisham
06.05.93 Mark Cichocki L RSC 7 Hartlepool
(Northern Area L. Middleweight Title Challenge)
27.10.93 Kevin Adamson L RSC 3 Stoke
Career: 30 contests, won 10, drew 2, lost 18.

Brian Dunn

Hull. *Born* Cleethorpes, 16 July, 1969
L. Middleweight. Ht. 5'10"
Manager L. Billany

15.04.94 Warren Stephens W PTS 6 Hull
16.05.94 Peter Reid W RSC 4 Cleethorpes
06.06.94 Eddie Haley L PTS 6 Glasgow
Career: 3 contests, won 2, lost 1.

Stuart Dunn

Leicester. *Born* Leicester, 19 January, 1970
L. Middleweight. Ht. 5'10½"
Manager J. Baxter

15.10.91 Spencer McCracken DREW 6 Dudley
09.12.91 Wayne Panayiotiou W CO 4 Brierley Hill
23.01.92 Charlie Moore L RSC 3 York
27.10.92 Andy Peach W RSC 3 Leicester
26.01.93 Wayne Panayiotiou W RSC 2 Leicester
28.04.93 Barry Thorogood W RSC 2 Solihull
19.05.93 Matthew Turner W RSC 3 Leicester
18.09.93 Lee Ferrie L RSC 1 Leicester
10.11.93 Jamie Robinson L PTS 6 Bethnal Green
30.11.93 Shamus Casey W PTS 6 Leicester
18.02.94 Jimmy Alston W RSC 1 Leicester
09.04.94 Adrian Dodson L RSC 1 Mansfield
Career: 12 contests, won 7, drew 1, lost 4.

Colin Dunne   Les Clark

Colin Dunne

Holloway. *Born* Liverpool, 19 September, 1970

Lightweight. Ht. 5'6"

Manager T. Toole

07.12.93   Mark O'Callaghan W RSC 1 Bethnal Green
14.01.94   Wayne Jones W RSC 3 Bethnal Green
04.03.94   Malcolm Thomas W CO 1 Bethnal Green
26.04.94   Steve Burton W CO 2 Bethnal Green
17.05.94   Phil Found W PTS 6 Kettering

Career: 5 contests, won 5.

Terry Dunstan

Hackney. *Born* London, 21 October, 1968

Cruiserweight. Ht. 6'3"

Manager B. Hearn

12.11.92   Steve Osborne W PTS 6 Bayswater
25.11.92   Steve Yorath W PTS 8 Mayfair
31.03.93   Lee Prudden W PTS 6 Barking
15.09.93   Paul McCarthy W RSC 3 Ashford
02.12.93   Devon Rhooms W RSC 1 Sheffield

Career: 5 contests, won 5.

Pat Durkin

Southport. *Born* Southport, 15 February, 1969

L. Heavyweight. Ht. 6'2"

Manager N. Basso

28.10.87   Paul Jones L PTS 4 Sheffield
09.11.87   Michael Justin L PTS 4 Leicester
16.11.87   Michael McDermott L PTS 4 Glasgow
30.11.87   Mike Snagg W RSC 6 Manchester
14.12.87   Dave Kettlewell L PTS 4 Bradford
18.01.88   Frank Harrington L PTS 4 Bradford
29.01.88   Dave Kettlewell L PTS 4 Durham
08.02.88   Adrian Din L CO 2 Nottingham
11.03.88   Frank Mobbs L RSC 3 Cottingham
03.11.88   Chris Mulcahy L RSC 2 Manchester
09.10.90   Trevor Meikle L DIS 3 Liverpool
07.02.91   Phil Epton L PTS 6 Watford
25.02.91   Willie Yeardsley L PTS 6 Bradford

05.03.91   Chris Mulcahy L PTS 6 Leicester
06.06.94   Laurence Rowe L PTS 6 Manchester

Career: 15 contests, won 1, lost 14.

Darren Dyer

Islington. *Born* London, 31 July, 1966

Welterweight. Ht. 5'7½"

Manager B. Hearn

20.11.86   Trevor Grant W RSC 2 Bethnal Green
08.01.87   Del Bryan L PTS 6 Bethnal Green
26.02.87   Kid Murray W CO 3 Bethnal Green
18.04.87   Geoff Calder W RSC 2 Kensington
07.09.87   Kelvin Mortimer L RSC 1 Mayfair
25.02.88   Donald Gwynn W CO 1 Bethnal Green
13.04.88   Kent Acuff W CO 2 Bethnal Green
16.05.88   Thomas Garcia W RSC 2 Piccadilly
02.11.88   Harlein Holden W CO 2 Southwark
07.12.88   Jean-Marc Phenieux W RSC 3 Piccadilly
12.01.89   Anthony Travers W RSC 6 Southwark
29.03.89   Mario Coronado W RSC 1 Wembley
04.10.89   Efrom Brown W RSC 4 Kensington
11.01.90   Fernando Segura W CO 2 Dewsbury
14.03.90   Jorge Maysonet L RSC 2 Kensington
03.07.91   Trevor Ambrose W PTS 6 Brentwood
26.10.91   Kelvin Mortimer W RSC 2 Brentwood
26.11.91   Robert Wright W RSC 3 Bethnal Green
19.02.92   Ian John-Lewis W RSC 2 Muswell Hill
12.05.92   Del Bryan W RSC 10 Crystal Palace
10.11.92   Chris Peters W RSC 9 Dagenham
09.03.93   Marcelo Domingo di Croce L RSC 4 Hartlepool
(Vacant WBA Penta-Continental Welterweight Title)
09.04.94   Julian Eavis W PTS 8 Bethnal Green
11.06.94   Ojay Abrahams L RSC 1 Bethnal Green

Career: 24 contests, won 19, lost 5.

Paul Dyer

Portsmouth. *Born* Portsmouth, 11 July, 1970

Welterweight. Ht. 5'11½"

Manager Self

24.09.91   Mick Reid W PTS 6 Basildon
19.11.91   Dave Andrews W PTS 6 Norwich
23.02.93   Kevin Mabbutt L PTS 6 Kettering
17.06.94   Dewi Roberts W PTS 6 Plymouth

Career: 4 contests, won 3, lost 1.

Howard Eastman

Battersea. *Born* New Amsterdam, 8 December, 1970

L. Middleweight. Ht. 5'11"

Manager D. Mancini

06.03.94   John Rice W RSC 1 Southwark
14.03.94   Andy Peach W PTS 6 Mayfair
22.03.94   Steve Phillips W RSC 5 Bethnal Green

Career: 3 contests, won 3.

Julian Eavis

Yeovil. *Born* Bourton, 3 December, 1965

Welterweight. Ht. 5'7¾"

Manager Self

12.10.88   Noel Rafferty W PTS 6 Stoke
17.10.88   Steve Taggart W PTS 6 Birmingham
17.11.88   Young Gully W PTS 6 Weston super Mare
07.12.88   Adrian Din L PTS 6 Stoke

14.12.88   Young Gully L PTS 6 Evesham
30.01.89   Frank Harrington W PTS 6 Leicester
06.02.89   Young Gully L RSC 4 Nottingham
15.03.89   Steve Taggart W PTS 6 Stoke
21.03.89   Steve Hogg W PTS 6 Wolverhampton
15.04.89   Andy Tonks W PTS 6 Salisbury
09.05.89   Mark Purcell L RSC 5 Plymouth
(Western Area Welterweight Title Challenge)
25.09.89   Wayne Timmins L PTS 6 Birmingham
04.10.89   Barry Messam W PTS 8 Stafford
10.10.89   Robert Wright L PTS 8 Wolverhampton
30.10.89   Wayne Timmins L PTS 8 Birmingham
14.11.89   Bobby McGowan W PTS 6 Evesham
22.11.89   Ronnie Campbell W PTS 8 Solihull
06.12.89   Lindon Scarlett L PTS 8 Stoke
10.01.90   Gary Logan L PTS 8 Kensington
24.01.90   Kevin Plant L PTS 6 Solihull
06.02.90   Tony Connellan L PTS 8 Oldham
13.02.90   Kevin Thompson L PTS 8 Wolverhampton
27.02.90   Ernie Loveridge L PTS 6 Evesham
07.03.90   Kevin Plant L PTS 8 Doncaster
22.03.90   Wayne Timmins W PTS 8 Wolverhampton
26.04.90   Leigh Wicks DREW 8 Mayfair
24.05.90   Gary Osborne L PTS 6 Dudley
04.06.90   Paul Wesley L PTS 8 Birmingham
17.09.90   Dave Andrews L PTS 6 Cardiff
01.10.90   Kevin Plant L PTS 8 Cleethorpes
09.10.90   Ronnie Campbell DREW 6 Wolverhampton
17.10.90   Paul Wesley L PTS 6 Stoke
31.10.90   Mickey Lloyd L PTS 8 Wembley
14.11.90   Glyn Rhodes L RSC 5 Sheffield
12.12.90   Barry Messam L PTS 6 Leicester
19.12.90   Carl Wright L PTS 6 Preston
16.01.91   Gary Logan L RSC 5 Kensington
05.03.91   Eamonn Loughran L PTS 6 Cardiff
20.03.91   Kevin Plant L PTS 6 Solihull
10.04.91   Ernie Loveridge DREW 8 Wolverhampton
01.05.91   Humphrey Harrison L PTS 6 Solihull
28.05.91   Darren Liney L PTS 6 Cardiff
05.06.91   Wayne Timmins L PTS 6 Wolverhampton
11.06.91   James McGee L PTS 6 Leicester
03.07.91   Benny Collins L PTS 6 Reading
03.09.91   Michael Smyth L PTS 6 Cardiff
01.10.91   Lee Ferrie L PTS 6 Bedworth
23.10.91   Kevin Lueshing L RSC 2 Bethnal Green
26.11.91   James Campbell W PTS 8 Wolverhampton
04.12.91   Peter Reid W PTS 6 Stoke
11.12.91   James McGee DREW 6 Leicester
17.12.91   Michael Smyth L PTS 6 Cardiff
15.01.92   Robert Wright L PTS 8 Stoke
04.02.92   Howard Clarke L PTS 4 Alfreton
11.02.92   Jamie Robinson L PTS 6 Barking
24.02.92   Lee Ferrie L PTS 8 Coventry
11.03.92   Rob Pitters L PTS 6 Solihull
11.05.92   James McGee L RSC 3 Coventry
07.07.92   Ross Hale L PTS 8 Bristol
(Vacant Western Area Welterweight Title)
05.10.92   James McGee W PTS 6 Bardon
28.11.92   Warren Stowe L RSC 6 Manchester
27.01.93   Mark Kelly L PTS 8 Stoke
22.02.93   James McGee L PTS 6 Bedworth
06.03.93   Robin Reid L RSC 2 Glasgow

10.05.93	Peter Waudby L PTS 6 Cleethorpes
26.06.93	Dean Cooper L PTS 10 Keynsham
	(Vacant Western Area L. Middleweight Title)
13.09.93	Crain Fisher L PTS 6 Middleton
06.10.93	Howard Clarke W PTS 8 Solihull
23.10.93	Adrian Dodson L RSC 4 Cardiff
30.11.93	Howard Clarke L PTS 6 Wolverhampton
08.12.93	Peter Reid L PTS 6 Stoke
19.01.94	Spencer McCracken L PTS 8 Solihull
26.01.94	John Bosco L RSC 1 Birmingham
08.03.94	Malcolm Melvin L PTS 6 Edgbaston
23.03.94	Peter Reid L PTS 8 Stoke
31.03.94	Dean Cooper L PTS 6 Bristol
09.04.94	Darren Dyer L PTS 8 Bethnal Green
11.05.94	Roy Rowland L RSC 4 Stevenage

Career: 78 contests, won 14, drew 4, lost 60.

Brian Eccles

Worksop. *Born* Newcastle, 20 April, 1970
Featherweight. Ht. 5'10"
Manager K. Richardson

11.11.93	Carl Roberts L RSC 1 Burnley
08.03.94	Abdul Manna L RSC 2 Kettering

Career: 2 contests, lost 2.

(Clive) Bobbi Joe Edwards

Manchester. *Born* Jamaica, 25 December, 1957
Cruiserweight. Ht. 5'10"
Manager Self

09.10.90	Doug McKay W RSC 1 Glasgow
26.11.90	Keith Inglis W RSC 1 Mayfair
22.02.91	Cordwell Hylton L RTD 6 Manchester
29.11.91	David Brown W RSC 4 Manchester
31.01.92	Richard Bustin W PTS 6 Manchester
29.05.92	John Foreman L RSC 4 Manchester
29.10.92	Michael Gale L PTS 10 Leeds
	(Vacant Central Area L. Heavyweight Title)
30.03.93	Simon Collins W PTS 6 Cardiff
16.10.93	Ginger Tshabala L RSC 5 Belfast
25.12.93	Francis Wanyama L PTS 8 Izegem, Belgium
04.05.94	Dirk Walleyn L RSC 5 Bredene, Belgium

Career: 11 contests, won 5, lost 6.

Erwin Edwards

Clapham. *Born* Barbados, 31 October, 1966
L. Welterweight. Ht. 5'11"
Manager D. Powell

26.09.88	Mark Jackson W PTS 6 Bedford
26.10.88	Brian Cullen L PTS 6 Stoke
15.11.88	Tony Whitehouse W PTS 6 Piccadilly
29.11.88	Danny Ellis L PTS 6 Battersea
07.02.89	Muhammad Shaffique L PTS 6 Southend
20.02.89	Pat Delargy L PTS 6 Birmingham
28.02.89	Terry Collins L PTS 6 Chigwell
07.04.92	B. F. Williams L PTS 6 Southend
30.04.92	Korso Aleain L PTS 6 Bayswater
07.07.92	George Wilson W RSC 4 Bristol
08.09.92	George Wilson W RSC 3 Southend
12.11.92	Mark O'Callaghan W RSC 6 Bayswater
03.03.93	Gary Hiscox L PTS 6 Solihull
24.06.93	Dave Fallon W RSC 3 Watford
07.02.94	Mark Legg L RSC 6 Bradford

Career: 15 contests, won 6, lost 9.

Steve Edwards

Haverfordwest. *Born* Haverfordwest, 18 July, 1970
S. Featherweight. Ht. 5'4"
Manager D. Davies

02.03.92	Nigel Burder W RSC 1 Merthyr
25.02.94	George Naylor L RTD 3 Chester
28.05.94	Sugar Free Somerville W RSC 2 Queensway
25.06.94	Greg Upton DREW 6 Cullompton

Career: 4 contests, won 2, drew 1, lost 1.

Mark Elliot

Telford. *Born* Telford, 2 February, 1966
L. Welterweight. Ht. 5'9"
Manager M. Duff

10.09.91	Dean Bramhald W CO 5 Wolverhampton
12.11.91	John Smith W PTS 6 Wolverhampton
05.12.91	Mick Mulcahy W RSC 2 Cannock
17.03.92	Andrew Morgan W PTS 6 Wolverhampton
20.01.93	Wayne Windle W CO 3 Wolverhampton
16.03.93	Chris Saunders W PTS 6 Wolverhampton
27.10.93	Rob Stewart W PTS 6 West Bromwich
26.01.94	Dave Lovell W PTS 6 Birmingham
16.03.94	Phil Found W PTS 6 Birmingham

Career: 9 contests, won 9.

Wayne Ellis

Cardiff. *Born* Cardiff, 18 July, 1968
WBO Penta-Continental Middleweight Champion. Former Undefeated Welsh Middleweight Champion. Ht. 6'0"
Manager B. Hearn

25.06.88	Shamus Casey W PTS 6 Luton
07.09.88	Kevin Hayde W PTS 6 Reading
01.11.88	Dennis White W CO 2 Reading
20.12.88	Spencer Alton W RTD 4 Swansea
11.04.89	Mark Howell W PTS 6 Aberavon
09.05.89	Spencer Alton W RSC 3 St Albans
06.09.89	Ian Chantler W RSC 4 Aberavon
14.02.90	Lindon Scarlett DREW 6 Millwall
22.05.90	Paul Jones W PTS 6 St Albans
10.10.90	Frank Eubanks W PTS 6 Millwall
05.03.91	Johnny Melfah W RSC 2 Cardiff
03.09.91	Colin Manners L RSC 1 Cardiff
11.02.92	Alan Richards W PTS 10 Cardiff
	(Vacant Welsh Middleweight Title)
14.07.92	Mike Phillips W RSC 7 Mayfair
	(Welsh Middleweight Title Defence)
10.07.93	Paul Busby W RSC 5 Cardiff
30.11.93	Steve Collins L RSC 9 Cardiff
	(WBO Penta-Continental Middleweight Title Challenge)
28.06.94	Paul Busby W TD 4 Mayfair
	(Vacant WBO Penta-Continental Middleweight Title)

Career: 17 contests, won 14, drew 1, lost 2.

(Enison) Smokey Enison (Garber)

Leeds. *Born* Sierra Leone, 29 June, 1967
S. Middleweight. Ht. 6'0"
Manager P. Coleman

19.03.93	Eric Noi L RSC 5 Manchester
16.09.93	Robert Harper W RSC 1 Hull
30.09.93	Justin Clements L PTS 6 Walsall

Career: 3 contests, won 1, lost 2.

Roland Ericsson

Mayfair. *Born* Sweden, 15 February, 1962
L. Heavyweight. Ht. 5'11"
Manager G. Steene

09.10.87	Dragan Komazec W CO 1 Aosta, Finland
26.10.87	Tommy Beckett W RSC 1 Jyvaskyla, Finland
07.02.88	Derek Myers W PTS 6 Laukka, Finland
13.02.88	Russell Barker W PTS 6 Helsingor, Finland
11.09.88	Sid Conteh W PTS 6 Laukka, Finland
16.02.89	Alan Baptiste W RSC 5 Battersea
26.04.89	Abdul Amoru Sanda W RSC 5 Battersea
22.06.89	Cliff Curtis W CO 4 Stevenage
02.02.90	Simon Collins W PTS 8 Geneva, Switzerland
22.02.90	Sean Stringfellow W RSC 4 Wandsworth
06.06.90	Cliff Curtis W RSC 2 Battersea
24.11.90	Thomas Covington W RSC 6 Benalmadena, Spain
20.03.91	Mark Kaylor L RSC 4 Wandsworth
16.05.91	Johnny Melfah L RSC 4 Battersea
22.10.91	Frank Eubanks L RSC 3 Wandsworth
13.12.91	Marian Rudi W CO 3 Minden, Germany
25.02.92	Peter Vosper W RSC 6 Crystal Palace
04.04.92	Jan Franek W RSC 5 Minden, Germany
12.05.92	Karl Barwise W PTS 6 Crystal Palace
15.09.92	Carlos Christie L RSC 4 Crystal Palace
27.11.92	Terry Magee W PTS 8 Randers, Denmark
26.03.93	Simon McDougall L RSC 5 Copenhagen, Denmark
11.06.93	Rocky Reynolds W PTS 6 Randers, Denmark
18.12.93	Johnny Melfah W PTS 10 Turku, Finland

Career: 24 contests, won 19, lost 5.

Harry Escott

Sunderland. *Born* West Germany, 17 October, 1969
S. Featherweight. Ht. 5'8"
Manager P. Byrne

26.02.87	Kenny Walsh W RSC 4 Hartlepool
06.04.87	Gypsy Finch W PTS 4 Newcastle
23.04.87	Gypsy Finch W PTS 4 Newcastle
30.04.87	Craig Windsor W RSC 3 Washington
22.05.87	Ginger Staples W RSC 1 Peterlee
04.06.87	Barry Bacon W RSC 2 Sunderland
04.09.87	Kevin Plant L RSC 2 Gateshead
26.01.88	Michael Howell W RSC 4 Hartlepool
17.03.88	Ian Honeywood W RSC 4 Sunderland
25.04.88	Les Walsh W PTS 8 Bradford
23.05.88	Tony Foster L RSC 6 Bradford
22.09.88	Dave Kettlewell W PTS 6 Newcastle
14.11.88	John Townsley W PTS 8 Glasgow
30.01.89	Tony Dore DREW 8 Glasgow
14.02.89	Kevin Pritchard W RSC 3 Sunderland
13.03.89	Young Joe Rafiu W PTS 8 Glasgow
11.04.89	Muhammad Lovelock W PTS 6 Oldham
05.06.89	Gary Maxwell W PTS 8 Glasgow
11.09.89	Gary Maxwell W PTS 8 Nottingham
19.10.89	Rudy Valentino W RTD 4 Manchester
07.12.89	Joey Jacobs W PTS 6 Manchester

87

24.01.90	Tomas Arguelles W PTS 6 Sunderland
15.05.90	Kevin Pritchard L PTS 8 South Shields
13.11.90	Brian Roche L RSC 3 Hartlepool
02.03.91	Steve Walker DREW 6 Darlington
06.04.91	Darren Elsdon L RSC 2 Darlington
06.07.91	Jackie Gunguluza L CO 6 Imperia, Italy
20.09.91	Steve Walker DREW 6 Manchester
04.02.92	Neil Smith W PTS 8 Alfreton
17.03.92	Floyd Havard L RSC 7 Mayfair
27.05.92	Wilson Rodriguez L PTS 10 Cologne, Germany
07.10.92	Dominic McGuigan W RTD 5 Sunderland
30.10.92	Eugene Speed L PTS 8 Istres, France
01.12.92	Neil Haddock L PTS 10 Liverpool
18.06.93	Medhi Labdouni L PTS 8 Fontenay Sous Bois, France
21.07.93	Phil Holliday L PTS 8 Marula, South Africa
01.12.93	Floyd Havard L PTS 8 Bethnal Green
27.04.94	Kid McAuley W RTD 6 Solihull
10.05.94	Kelton McKenzie W PTS 6 Doncaster

Career: 39 contests, won 23, drew 3, lost 13.

Declan Faherty

Huddersfield. *Born* Leeds, 23 August, 1969
Cruiserweight. Ht. 6'4"
Manager P. Coleman

24.02.94	Lee Avery W RSC 2 Hull
28.02.94	Shane Meadows W CO 3 Marton
28.03.94	Jem Jackson W RTD 5 Birmingham
28.04.94	Slick Miller W RSC 2 Hull
10.05.94	Kevin Burton W RSC 4 Doncaster

Career: 5 contests, won 5.

Tony Falcone   Les Clark

(Antonio) Tony Falcone

Chippenham. *Born* Chippenham, 15 October, 1966
S. Bantamweight. Ht. 5'6"
Manager C. Sanigar

22.10.90	Karl Morling L PTS 6 Mayfair
21.11.90	Barrie Kelley L PTS 6 Chippenham

18.02.91	Barrie Kelley W PTS 6 Windsor
28.02.91	Paul Wynn W PTS 6 Sunderland
21.03.91	Tony Silkstone L PTS 6 Dewsbury
22.04.91	Alan Smith L RSC 5 Mayfair
30.05.91	Alan Smith W PTS 6 Mayfair
11.12.91	Dennis Adams W RTD 4 Basildon
30.04.92	Andrew Bloomer W PTS 6 Mayfair
07.07.92	Miguel Matthews W PTS 6 Bristol
05.10.92	Andrew Bloomer W PTS 8 Bristol
13.12.93	Des Gargano W PTS 4 Bristol
23.02.94	Conn McMullen DREW 4 Watford
10.03.94	Pete Buckley W PTS 4 Bristol
29.03.94	Justin Murphy L RSC 2 Bethnal Green

Career: 15 contests, won 9, drew 1, lost 5.

Dave Fallon

Watford. *Born* Watford, 22 June, 1967
Welterweight. Ht. 6'0"
Manager S. Holdsworth

12.09.90	Trevor Ambrose L CO 3 Battersea
14.02.91	Richard Swallow L RSC 4 Southampton
12.11.91	Tim Harmey W PTS 6 Milton Keynes
05.12.91	Sean Cave W PTS 6 Peterborough
06.05.93	Noel Henry W PTS 6 Bayswater
24.06.93	Erwin Edwards L RSC 3 Watford
10.03.94	Dave Madden L PTS 6 Watford

Career: 7 contests, won 3, lost 4.

Joe Fannin

Birmingham. *Born* Birmingham, 18 May, 1970
S. Featherweight. Ht. 5'7"
Manager Self

05.10.92	Craig Murray W RSC 1 Manchester
27.10.92	Richard Woolgar L PTS 6 Leicester
20.02.93	Patrick Gallagher L RTD 1 Earls Court
20.04.93	Alan Levene L CO 1 Brentwood
07.09.93	Gary Marston L RSC 2 Stoke

Career: 5 contests, won 1, lost 4.

Ceri Farrell

Swansea. *Born* Swansea, 27 October, 1967
Bantamweight. Ht. 5'7"
Manager Self

14.05.90	Kruga Hydes L PTS 6 Cleethorpes
06.06.90	Conn McMullen L RSC 5 Battersea
03.10.90	Tim Yeates L PTS 6 Basildon
05.12.90	Paul Dever W RSC 2 Stafford
12.12.90	Tim Yeates L PTS 6 Basildon
19.12.90	Mercurio Ciaramitaro DREW 6 Rimini, Italy
24.01.91	Kevin Jenkins L PTS 6 Gorseinon
07.02.91	Mark Tierney L PTS 6 Watford
06.03.91	Mark Tierney L PTS 6 Wembley
25.04.91	Mark Loftus L RSC 3 Basildon
04.11.91	Andrew Bloomer W PTS 6 Merthyr
20.11.91	Andrew Bloomer W PTS 6 Cardiff
29.11.91	John Green L RTD 4 Manchester
08.01.92	Miguel Matthews L PTS 6 Burton
22.01.92	Alan Ley L PTS 6 Cardiff
09.02.92	Peter Judson L PTS 6 Bradford
15.09.92	Michael Alldis L RSC 3 Crystal Palace
16.02.93	Michael Alldis L CO 1 Tooting
12.03.94	Neil Swain L CO 1 Cardiff

Career: 19 contests, won 3, drew 1, lost 15.

(Noor Alam) Wahid Fats

Manchester. *Born* Manchester, 2 September, 1971

L. Welterweight. Ht. 5'8"
Manager N. Basso

06.06.94	Ram Singh W RSC 3 Manchester

Career: 1 contest, won 1.

Marco Fattore

Watford. *Born* Italy, 17 October, 1968
Lightweight. Ht. 5'8"
Manager D. Mancini

03.09.92	Jason White W RSC 1 Dunstable
19.10.92	Carlos Domonkos W RTD 4 Mayfair
07.12.92	Steve Patton W RSC 6 Mayfair
15.02.93	Jason Hutson W PTS 6 Mayfair
29.03.93	T. J. Smith DREW 6 Mayfair
22.04.93	Jason Barker W PTS 6 Mayfair
04.10.93	Andrew Bloomer W PTS 6 Mayfair
10.11.93	Lee Fox W PTS 6 Watford
09.12.93	Jason Hutson DREW 6 Watford
10.03.94	Simon Frailing DREW 6 Watford
28.04.94	Andrew Reed DREW 6 Mayfair

Career: 11 contests, won 7, drew 4.

Darren Fearn

Carmarthen. *Born* Carmarthen, 21 February, 1969
Heavyweight. Ht. 6'2"
Manager D. Davies

25.06.94	Keith Fletcher W PTS 6 Cullompton

Career: 1 contest, won 1.

Vince Feeney

Sligo. *Born* Sligo, 12 May, 1973
Bantamweight. Ht. 5'4"
Manager J. Griffin

29.10.92	Ady Benton DREW 6 Bayswater
04.02.93	Kevin Jenkins W PTS 6 Cardiff
29.03.93	Andrew Bloomer W PTS 6 Mayfair
29.04.93	Neil Swain L PTS 6 Mayfair
28.09.93	Peter Culshaw L PTS 6 Liverpool
30.11.93	Tiger Singh W PTS 6 Leicester
18.02.94	Shaun Norman W RSC 2 Leicester
09.04.94	Neil Swain W PTS 6 Mansfield
24.05.94	Louis Veitch W PTS 6 Leicester

Career: 9 contests, won 6, drew 1, lost 2.

Vince Feeney   Les Clark

Antonio Fernandez (Golding)

Birmingham. *Born* Birmingham, 3 January, 1965
Midlands Area Middleweight Champion.
Ht. 5'11¼"
Manager B. Lynch

10.03.87	David Heath W RSC 5 Manchester
29.04.87	Darren Hobson L PTS 6 Stoke
18.11.87	Tony White W PTS 6 Solihull
19.01.88	Malcolm Melvin W RSC 4 Kings Heath
07.03.88	Shaun Cummins L PTS 6 Northampton
10.10.88	Chris Richards W PTS 6 Edgbaston
23.11.88	Chris Richards W PTS 8 Solihull
24.01.89	Paul Murray W PTS 6 Kings Heath
08.05.89	Shamus Casey W PTS 6 Edgbaston
13.11.89	Cyril Jackson W PTS 8 Brierley Hill
03.12.89	Steve Foster L PTS 8 Birmingham
06.03.90	Paul Jones L PTS 8 Stoke
30.04.90	Alan Baptiste W PTS 6 Brierley Hill
04.06.90	Chris Richards W PTS 6 Edgbaston
13.11.90	Chris Walker W PTS 6 Edgbaston
24.01.91	Franki Moro W PTS 6 Brierley Hill
07.10.91	Paul Murray W RSC 7 Birmingham
09.12.91	Paul McCarthy W PTS 8 Brierley Hill
03.03.92	Paul Wesley W PTS 10 Cradley Heath *(Vacant Midlands Area Middleweight Title)*
28.10.92	Darron Griffiths L PTS 10 Cardiff *(Elim. British Middleweight Title)*
18.05.93	Ernie Loveridge W PTS 8 Edgbaston
28.07.93	Paul Wesley W RSC 3 Brixton *(Midlands Area Middleweight Title Defence)*

Career: 22 contests, won 17, lost 5.

(Robert) Rocky Ferrari (Ewing)

Glasgow. *Born* Glasgow, 27 October, 1972
Lightweight. Ht. 5'7"
Manager A. Melrose

25.01.91	James Hunter W CO 1 Stoke
11.02.91	Sol Francis W RSC 5 Glasgow
05.03.91	Chris Saunders W PTS 4 Glasgow
11.09.92	Mick Mulcahy W PTS 6 Glasgow
28.02.94	Kevin McKenzie L PTS 6 Marton
13.05.94	Colin Innes W PTS 6 Kilmarnock

Career: 6 contests, won 5, lost 1.

Lee Ferrie

Coventry. *Born* Coventry, 10 July, 1964
L. Middleweight. Ht. 5'11"
Manager Self

01.10.91	Julian Eavis W PTS 6 Bedworth
05.11.91	Trevor Meikle W PTS 6 Leicester
11.12.91	Noel Henry W RSC 5 Leicester
20.01.92	Martin Rosamond W RSC 2 Coventry
24.02.92	Julian Eavis W PTS 8 Coventry
25.03.92	Mick Reid W RSC 3 Hinckley
22.09.93	Shamus Casey W CO 3 Bedworth
18.09.93	Stuart Dunn W RSC 1 Leicester

Career: 8 contests, won 8.

Crain Fisher

Rochdale. *Born* Littleborough, 28 February, 1966
L. Middleweight. Ht. 5'9"
Manager J. Doughty

22.10.90	Richard O'Brien W CO 3 Manchester
28.02.91	Rob Pitters L RSC 6 Bury

21.10.91	James McGee W RSC 4 Bury
13.04.92	Trevor Meikle W PTS 6 Manchester
05.05.92	Frank Harrington W RSC 4 Preston
13.10.92	Robert Riley L PTS 4 Bury
25.02.93	Jimmy Alston W RTD 2 Burnley
22.04.93	Jimmy Alston W PTS 6 Bury
13.09.93	Julian Eavis W PTS 6 Middleton
17.02.94	Dave Lovell L RSC 2 Bury

Career: 10 contests, won 7, lost 3.

Horace Fleary

Huddersfield. *Born* Huddersfield, 22 April, 1961
Middleweight. German International S. Middleweight Champion. Former Undefeated German International L. Middleweight Champion. Ht. 5'10½"
Manager O. Schroeder

04.07.87	Salvador Yanez L RSC 3 Helmstedt, Germany
17.10.87	Harald Schulte W PTS 6 Gifhorn, Germany
31.10.87	Niyazi Aytekin L PTS 6 Paderborn, Germany
23.11.87	Mourad Louati L RSC 3 The Hague, Holland
09.01.88	Yurder Demircan L RSC 4 Helmstedt, Germany
14.03.88	Henk van den Tak L PTS 6 Arnhem, Holland
12.05.88	Mike Wissenbach W PTS 6 Berlin, Germany
29.06.88	Silvio Mieckley DREW 4 Hamburg, Germany
02.07.88	Zelkjo Seslek W RSC 4 Helmstedt, Germany
16.09.88	Jose Varela L PTS 8 Berlin, Germany
28.10.88	Zelkjo Seslek W RSC 5 Braunschweig, Germany
08.11.88	Ferdinand Pachler L PTS 8 Vienna, Austria
12.11.88	Josef Kossmann W PTS 8 Oberkassel, Germany
16.11.88	Mike Wissenbach L PTS 6 Berlin, Germany
25.02.89	Paddy Pipa L PTS 8 Hamburg, Germany
16.09.89	Josef Rajic W CO 1 Wiener Neustadt, Germany
30.09.89	Owen Reece L PTS 6 Hamburg, Germany
13.10.89	Frederic Seillier L CO 1 Sete, France
10.11.89	Jean-Paul Roux L DIS 8 St Quentin, France
27.11.89	Franck Nicotra L DIS 6 Nogent, France
01.12.89	Andy Marks L PTS 8 Berlin, Germany
09.12.89	Hamedidi Maimoun L RSC 3 Grande Synthe, France
12.10.90	Joseph Kossmann W CO 8 Gelsenkirchen, Germany
04.01.91	Andreas Schweiger W CO 9 Supplingen, Germany *(Vacant German International S. Middleweight Title)*
20.03.91	Paul Wesley W RSC 5 Solihull
04.04.91	Juergen Broszeitt W CO 2 Bielfeld, Germany
22.06.91	Said Skouma L PTS 8 Paris, France
13.09.91	Nelson Alves L CO 7 Dusseldorf, Germany *(German International S. Middleweight Title Defence)*

20.11.91	Kevin Sheeran L RSC 2 Cardiff
10.01.92	Teddy Jansen W CO 2 Aachen, Germany
28.02.92	Thomas Mateoi W RSC 2 Supplingen, Germany *(Vacant German International L. Middleweight Title)*
04.04.92	Jan Mazgut W RSC 4 Minden, Germany
01.05.92	Trpmir Jandrek W RSC 2 Aachen, Germany
12.05.92	Adrian Strachan L PTS 6 Crystal Palace
19.09.92	Andy Marks W PTS 6 Kassel, Germany
01.10.92	Robert McCracken L PTS 8 Telford
02.11.92	Neville Brown L PTS 8 Wolverhampton
27.11.92	Miroslav Strbak W PTS 6 Suhl, Germany
04.12.92	Richie Woodhall L PTS 8 Telford
16.04.93	Silvio Branco L PTS 8 Rome, Italy
19.05.93	Gary Jacobs L RTD 4 Sunderland
25.07.93	Eric Noi L PTS 6 Oldham
22.09.93	Cornelius Carr L PTS 8 Wembley
11.12.93	Gary Logan L PTS 8 Dusseldorf, Germany
19.02.94	Reino van der Hoek W RTD 7 Bremen, Germany *(Vacant German International S. Middleweight Title)*

Career: 45 contests, won 17, drew 1, lost 27.

Horace Fleary   Les Clark

Stuart Fleet

Grimsby. *Born* Grimsby, 15 January, 1963
Cruiserweight. Ht. 6'0"
Manager Self

09.12.91	Rocky Shelly L RSC 1 Cleethorpes
16.09.93	Lee Avery W RSC 1 Hull
30.09.93	Robert Norton L CO 2 Walsall
12.11.93	Richard Atkinson W CO 1 Hull
10.02.94	Eddie Pyott W RSC 2 Hull

Career: 5 contests, won 3, lost 2.

Keith Fletcher

Reading. *Born* Reading, 20 July, 1967
Heavyweight. Ht. 6'0"
Manager C. Sanigar

25.06.94 Darren Fearn L PTS 6 Cullompton
Career: 1 contest, lost 1.

Peter Flint
Sheffield. *Born* Sheffield, 3 July, 1973
L. Heavyweight. Ht. 6'1"
Manager Self

02.02.93 Mark Buck L CO 2 Derby
08.06.93 Greg Scott-Briggs L RSC 1 Derby
25.10.93 Phil Ball L RSC 3 Liverpool
Career: 3 contests, lost 3.

Andrew Flute
Tipton. Born Wolverhampton, 5 March,
1970
Middleweight. Ht. 6'1"
Manager B. Hearn

24.05.89 Stinger Mason W PTS 6 Hanley
24.10.89 Paul Murray W RSC 4 Wolverhampton
22.03.90 Dave Maxwell W RSC 5 Wolverhampton
24.05.90 Spencer Alton L RSC 1 Dudley
18.09.90 Tony Hodge W CO 2 Wolverhampton
24.10.90 Nigel Rafferty W CO 6 Dudley
27.11.90 Paul Burton L PTS 6 Stoke
13.03.91 Robert Peel W PTS 6 Stoke
10.04.91 Russell Washer W PTS 6 Wolverhampton
14.05.91 Alan Richards W PTS 8 Dudley
16.10.91 Karl Barwise L RSC 8 Stoke
05.12.91 Richard Okumu DREW 8 Cannock
17.03.92 Graham Burton W PTS 8 Wolverhampton
28.04.92 Paul Smith W RSC 5 Wolverhampton
20.01.93 Glen Payton W RSC 4 Wolverhampton
16.03.93 Mark Hale W RSC 2 Wolverhampton
24.04.93 Steve Thomas W RSC 1 Birmingham
21.10.93 Terry Magee W RSC 6 Bayswater
26.01.94 Neville Brown L RTD 7 Birmingham
     (British Middleweight Title Challenge)
16.03.94 Graham Burton W PTS 6 Birmingham
Career: 20 contests, won 15, drew 1, lost 4.

Ali Forbes
Sydenham. *Born* London, 7 March, 1961
Southern Area S. Middleweight Champion.
Ht. 5'9"
Manager Self

16.02.89 David Haycock W RSC 4 Battersea
22.06.90 Andy Marlow W RTD 4 Gillingham
26.09.90 Peter Vosper W PTS 6 Mayfair
06.02.91 Adrian Wright W PTS 6 Battersea
03.04.91 Karl Barwise W RTD 4 Bethnal Green
16.05.91 Quinn Paynter DREW 6 Battersea
01.06.91 Paul McCarthy W CO 2 Bethnal Green
11.03.92 Ian Strudwick L PTS 10 Solihull
     (Southern Area S. Middleweight Title Challenge)
29.10.92 Nick Manners W RSC 3 Leeds
28.11.93 Carlos Christie W CO 4 Southwark
06.03.94 Richard Bustin W PTS 10 Southwark
     (Vacant Southern Area S. Middleweight Title)
Career: 11 contests, won 9, drew 1, lost 1.

Maurice Forbes
Brixton. *Born* Jamaica, 24 June, 1968
Welterweight. Ht. 5'10½"
Manager F. Rix

23.05.93 Michael Dick W RSC 1 Brockley
25.06.93 Kenny Scott W RSC 2 Battersea
14.08.93 Phil Found W PTS 4 Hammersmith
14.04.94 Dave Maj W RTD 2 Battersea
22.05.94 Trevor Meikle W RTD 3 Crystal Palace
Career: 5 contests, won 5.

Maurice Forbes   Les Clark

Hugh Forde
Birmingham. *Born* Birmingham, 7 May,
1964
L. Welterweight. Former British &
Commonwealth S. Featherweight
Champion. Former Undefeated Midlands
Area S. Featherweight Champion. Ht. 5'9"
Manager Self

13.05.86 Little Currie W PTS 6 Digbeth
26.06.86 Carl Cleasby W RSC 3 Edgbaston
22.09.86 Carl Gaynor W PTS 6 Edgbaston
25.10.86 Tony Graham W PTS 6 Stevenage
03.11.86 John Bennie W RSC 3 Edgbaston
08.12.86 Darren Connellan W PTS 6 Edgbaston
21.01.87 Craig Walsh W PTS 8 Solihull
07.04.87 Gary Maxwell W PTS 8 West Bromwich
24.04.87 Lambsy Kayani W PTS 8 Liverpool
14.12.87 Patrick Kamy W PTS 8 Edgbaston
19.01.88 Billy Cawley W PTS 8 Kings Heath
05.04.88 Rudy Valentino W RSC 2 Birmingham
17.06.88 Gary Maxwell W PTS 6 Edgbaston
     (Vacant Midlands Area S. Featherweight Title)
10.10.88 Wayne Weekes W RSC 7 Edgbaston
28.11.88 Brian Cullen W RTD 4 Edgbaston
08.05.89 Paul Bowen W RSC 4 Edgbaston
31.10.89 Brian Roche W RSC 2 Manchester
     (Final Elim. British S. Featherweight Title)
14.02.90 Harold Warren W PTS 8 Brentwood
25.04.90 Delfino Perez W RSC 2 Brighton
18.09.90 Joey Jacobs W RSC 11 Wolverhampton
     (British S. Featherweight Title Challenge)

24.10.90 Kevin Pritchard L CO 4 Dudley
     (British S. Featherweight Title Defence)
27.02.91 Tony Pep L RSC 9 Wolverhampton
14.05.91 Richard Joyce W RTD 5 Dudley
10.09.91 Thunder Aryeh W PTS 12 Wolverhampton
     (Commonwealth S. Featherweight Title Challenge)
12.11.91 Paul Harvey L RSC 3 Wolverhampton
     (Commonwealth S. Featherweight Title Defence)
02.11.92 Karl Taylor W PTS 6 Wolverhampton
28.09.93 Andreas Panayi L PTS 8 Liverpool
23.02.94 Carlos Chase W PTS 6 Watford
Career: 28 contests, won 24, lost 4.

Mike Fordham
Manchester. *Born* Shoreham by Sea, 6
February, 1968
L. Middleweight. Ht. 5'9"
Manager J. Doughty

29.11.93 David Sumner L RSC 4 Manchester
Career: 1 contest, lost 1.

John Foreman
Birmingham. *Born* Birmingham, 6
November, 1967
L. Heavyweight. Ht. 6'0"
Manager Self

26.10.87 Randy B. Powell W RSC 1 Birmingham
18.11.87 Dave Owens L RSC 5 Solihull
16.03.88 John Fairbairn W PTS 6 Solihull
05.04.88 David Jono W CO 1 Birmingham
11.04.88 Byron Pullen W PTS 6 Northampton
17.06.88 Gus Mendes W RSC 5 Edgbaston
28.11.88 Dave Owens W CO 1 Edgbaston
24.01.89 Crawford Ashley L RSC 4 Kings Heath
13.11.89 Everton Blake W PTS 8 Brierley Hill
03.12.89 Chris Coughlin W RSC 2 Birmingham
19.03.90 Abner Blackstock W PTS 8 Brierley Hill
04.06.90 Brian Schumacher W RSC 4 Edgbaston
03.09.90 Roy Skeldon L RTD 6 Dudley
     (Midlands Area L. Heavyweight Title Challenge & Elim. British L. Heavyweight Title)
18.04.91 Richard Bustin L PTS 8 Earls Court
22.06.91 Gil Lewis DREW 6 Earls Court
16.12.91 Steve McCarthy L PTS 8 Southampton
26.01.92 Fabrice Tiozzo L RSC 6 Saint-Ouen, France
29.05.92 Bobbi Joe Edwards W RSC 4 Manchester
06.10.92 Eddie Smulders L RSC 4 Antwerp, Belgium
20.03.93 Anthony Hembrick L RSC 6 Dusseldorf. Germany
06.12.93 Zak Chelli W RSC 4 Birmingham
08.03.94 Simon McDougall L PTS 6 Edgbaston
07.04.94 L. A. Williams W RSC 7 Walsall
14.04.94 Mark Prince L CO 3 Battersea
Career: 24 contests, won 13, drew 1, lost 10.

Frankie Foster
Newcastle. *Born* Newcastle, 25 May, 1968
Northern Area S. Featherweight Champion.
Ht. 5'6"
Manager Self

22.09.88	Mick Mulcahy W PTS 6 Newcastle
29.09.88	Paul Chedgzoy W PTS 6 Sunderland
07.11.88	Pete Roberts W PTS 4 Bradford
01.12.88	Peter English L PTS 8 Manchester
26.01.89	James Jiora W PTS 6 Newcastle
09.03.89	John Townsley W PTS 6 Glasgow
03.04.89	Jose Tuominen L PTS 4 Helsinki, Finland
24.04.89	Jim Moffat L PTS 8 Glasgow
21.06.89	Paul Gadney L PTS 6 Eltham
02.10.89	Shaun White DREW 6 Bradford
11.10.89	Lester James W PTS 6 Stoke
21.10.89	Chad Broussard L PTS 6 Middlesbrough
13.11.89	Steve Winstanley L PTS 6 Bradford
24.01.90	Kid Sumali W PTS 6 Sunderland
05.02.90	Muhammad Shaffique L PTS 6 Brierley Hill
20.03.90	Dominic McGuigan DREW 4 Hartlepool

26.04.90	Les Walsh W PTS 8 Manchester
04.06.90	Stuart Rimmer W PTS 6 Glasgow
18.10.90	Nigel Senior W CO 2 Hartlepool *(Vacant Northern Area S. Featherweight Title)*
19.11.90	Sugar Gibiliru DREW 8 Manchester
22.04.91	John Doherty L PTS 10 Glasgow *(Elim. British S. Featherweight Title)*
14.08.91	Gianni di Napoli L PTS 8 Alcamo, Italy
22.10.91	Darren Elsdon L RSC 7 Hartlepool *(Northern Area S. Featherweight Title Defence)*
31.03.92	Sugar Gibiliru L PTS 8 Stockport
10.09.92	Darren Elsdon W PTS 10 Sunderland *(Northern Area S. Featherweight Title Challenge)*
04.07.93	Stanford Ngcebeshe L PTS 10 Eldorado, South Africa
21.03.94	Dave McHale L PTS 8 Glasgow

Career: 27 contests, won 11, drew 3, lost 13.

Steve Foster

Chris Bevan

Steve Foster

Manchester. *Born* Salford, 28 December, 1960
Middleweight. Ht. 5'8½"
Manager Self

09.02.81	Pat McCarthy W RSC 3 Manchester
16.03.81	Dave Dunn L PTS 6 Manchester
26.03.81	John Lindo L RSC 1 Newcastle
28.11.85	Malcolm Melvin DREW 6 Ilkeston
06.03.86	Taffy Morris L PTS 6 Manchester
17.04.86	Martin Kielty W RSC 4 Wolverhampton
25.11.86	Shamus Casey W PTS 8 Manchester
28.04.87	Cyril Jackson W RSC 7 Manchester
11.05.87	Fidel Castro L PTS 8 Manchester
19.10.87	Cyril Jackson W RTD 3 Manchester
14.12.87	Sean Leighton L PTS 8 Bradford
27.01.88	Sammy Storey L RSC 4 Belfast
20.04.88	Tony Collins L PTS 4 Muswell Hill
19.10.88	Ray Close L RSC 2 Belfast
14.12.88	Fran Harding L PTS 6 Kirkby
01.03.89	Dario Deabreu W RSC 2 Cardiff
06.03.89	Steve Aquilina W PTS 6 Manchester
03.12.89	Antonio Fernandez W PTS 8 Birmingham
06.02.90	Sean O'Phoenix W RSC 4 Oldham
14.03.90	Andy Till L RTD 5 Battersea
02.06.90	Ian Chantler DREW 4 Manchester
22.02.91	Kesem Clayton W CO 6 Manchester
20.09.91	Colin Pitters W RTD 5 Manchester
07.12.91	Shamus Casey W PTS 8 Manchester
10.03.92	Mike Phillips W RSC 4 Bury
25.04.92	Mark Jay W RSC 7 Manchester
28.11.92	Shaun Cummins L PTS 12 Manchester *(Vacant WBA Penta-Continental L. Middleweight Title)*
25.07.93	Russell Washer W PTS 6 Oldham
18.12.93	Kevin Sheeran W RSC 4 Manchester

Career: 29 contests, won 16, drew 2, lost 11.

Tony Foster

Hull. *Born* Hull, 9 July, 1964
Central Area Lightweight Champion. Ht. 5'7"
Manager Self

04.09.87	Paul Kennedy L PTS 6 Gateshead
17.09.87	Ian Hosten L PTS 6 Gravesend
28.09.87	Steve Winstanley L PTS 6 Bradford
06.10.87	Roy Doyle L PTS 6 Manchester
03.11.87	Darren Darby L PTS 6 Cottingham
25.11.87	Kevin McCoy W RSC 4 Cottingham
02.12.87	Alan Roberts W RSC 5 Piccadilly
11.12.87	Mitchell King DREW 8 Coalville
11.01.88	Paul Chedgzoy W PTS 6 Manchester
25.01.88	Johnny Walker L PTS 6 Glasgow
01.02.88	Sean Hogg W PTS 6 Manchester
11.02.88	Lee Amass L RSC 6 Gravesend
28.03.88	Darryl Pettit W PTS 6 Bradford
22.04.88	Paul Charters L PTS 6 Gateshead
09.05.88	Gary Maxwell L PTS 6 Nottingham
17.05.88	Warren Slaney W PTS 6 Leicester
23.05.88	Harry Escott W RSC 6 Bradford
26.09.88	Peter Bradley L PTS 8 Piccadilly
17.10.88	John Townsley L PTS 8 Glasgow
15.11.88	Steve Pollard W RSC 3 Hull
12.12.88	Mark Kelly W PTS 6 Nottingham
08.02.89	Paul Gadney W PTS 6 Kensington
03.04.89	Jari Gronroos W PTS 4 Helsinki, Finland
15.04.89	Paul Moylett W PTS 6 Salisbury
27.06.89	Ian Honeywood L PTS 6 Kensington

10.10.89	Steve Pollard W RSC 3 Hull
16.11.89	Sugar Gibiliru W PTS 8 Manchester
30.11.89	Joey Jacobs L CO 4 Oldham
30.01.90	Sugar Gibiliru L PTS 10 Manchester
	(Vacant Central Area Lightweight Title)
21.04.90	Marvin P. Gray DREW 6 Sunderland
22.05.90	Marvin P. Gray L PTS 6 Stockton
15.06.90	Marcel Herbert L RSC 4 Telford
15.02.91	Jimmy Bredahl L PTS 6 Randers, Denmark
05.03.91	Floyd Havard L PTS 8 Millwall
15.04.91	Dave Anderson L PTS 8 Glasgow
12.05.91	Alain Simoes W PTS 8 Voiron, France
11.09.91	Billy Schwer L PTS 8 Hammersmith
21.11.91	Giovanni Parisi L RSC 6 Perugia, Italy
31.01.92	Angel Mona L PTS 8 Esch, Luxembourg
30.03.92	Ian Honeywood L RSC 4 Eltham
13.06.92	Pierre Lorcy L PTS 8 Levallois Perret, France
16.10.92	Tony Doyle W PTS 8 Hull
31.10.92	Dingaan Thobela L PTS 8 Earls Court
14.01.93	Alan Hall L PTS 6 Mayfair
27.02.93	Steve Foran DREW 6 Ellesmere Port
09.07.93	Giorgio Campanella L PTS 8 Barisardo, Italy
12.11.93	Micky Hall W PTS 8 Hull
10.02.94	Kid McAuley W RTD 4 Hull
18.02.94	Racheed Lawal L PTS 8 Randers, Denmark
21.04.94	Charles Shepherd W PTS 10 Hull
	(Vacant Central Area Lightweight Title)

Career: 50 contests, won 19, drew 3, lost 28.

Phil Found

Hereford. *Born* Hereford, 9 June, 1967
L. Welterweight. Ht. 5'9"
Manager D. Gardiner

30.03.93	Paul Davies W PTS 6 Cardiff
29.04.93	Delroy Leslie L PTS 6 Mayfair
09.06.93	Jason Beard L PTS 6 Lewisham
26.06.93	Paul Knights L PTS 4 Earls Court
14.08.93	Maurice Forbes L PTS 4 Hammersmith
20.09.93	Garry Burrell W RSC 4 Glasgow
16.10.93	Julien Lorcy L PTS 6 Levallois, France
10.11.93	Robert Dickie W RTD 2 Ystrad
16.12.93	Gareth Jordan L PTS 6 Newport
20.01.94	Cham Joof L RSC 1 Battersea
02.03.94	Mark Legg W RTD 4 Solihull
16.03.94	Mark Elliot L PTS 6 Birmingham
27.04.94	Micky Hall W RSC 5 Solihull
17.05.94	Colin Dunne L PTS 6 Kettering
13.06.94	Tony Brown W RSC 4 Liverpool

Career: 15 contests, won 6, lost 9.

Dougie Fox

Worksop. *Born* Worksop, 5 November, 1972
Featherweight. Ht. 5'7"
Manager K. Richardson

28.05.93	Mario Culpeper L RSC 3 Middleton
02.07.93	Gary Thornhill L CO 1 Liverpool
27.09.93	Tony Smith L RSC 5 Manchester
01.12.93	Gary Marston L RSC 1 Stoke
28.03.94	Fred Reeve L RSC 2 Cleethorpes

Career: 5 contests, lost 5.

Lee Fox

Chesterfield. *Born* Chesterfield, 20 January, 1970

S. Featherweight. Ht. 5'3¾"
Manager Self

13.11.89	Steve Armstrong W PTS 6 Manchester
06.12.89	Steve Armstrong W PTS 6 Stoke
05.02.90	Neil Leitch L PTS 6 Brierley Hill
25.04.90	Bernard McComiskey L RTD 3 Brighton
15.06.90	Chris Cooper W PTS 6 Telford
05.09.90	Nicky Lucas DREW 6 Brighton
03.10.90	Nicky Lucas L RTD 2 Basildon
26.11.90	Bobby Guynan W PTS 6 Bethnal Green
12.12.90	Mark Bates L PTS 6 Basildon
06.02.91	Bobby Guynan L PTS 6 Bethnal Green
12.03.91	Charlie Coke W PTS 6 Mansfield
26.03.91	Bobby Guynan W RTD 3 Bethnal Green
11.06.91	Neil Smith L PTS 6 Leicester
16.08.91	Felix Garcia Losada L CO 3 Marbella, Spain
21.01.92	Richard Woolgar L PTS 6 Norwich
19.02.92	Mark Bates L PTS 6 Muswell Hill
27.02.92	Wayne Rigby W PTS 6 Liverpool
14.04.92	Dean Lynch L PTS 6 Mansfield
29.04.92	Andrew Robinson W PTS 6 Stoke
29.05.92	Danny Connelly L PTS 6 Glasgow
19.10.92	Dave McHale L RSC 3 Glasgow
15.02.93	Carl Roberts L PTS 6 Manchester
16.03.93	Gareth Jordan L RSC 3 Wolverhampton
14.06.93	Yifru Retta L RTD 3 Bayswater
10.11.93	Marco Fattore L PTS 6 Watford

Career: 25 contests, won 8, drew 1, lost 16.

Simon Frailing   Les Clark

Simon Frailing

Hayes. *Born* London, 13 June, 1966
Lightweight. Ht. 5'7"
Manager D. Gunn

29.04.93	Bruce Ruegg DREW 6 Hayes
15.06.93	Bruce Ruegg L PTS 6 Hemel Hempstead
14.08.93	Mike Anthony Brown L RSC 4 Hammersmith

30.09.93	Norman Dhalie L PTS 6 Hayes
09.12.93	Andrew Reed W PTS 6 Watford
25.01.94	Craig Kelley L PTS 4 Piccadilly
10.03.94	Marco Fattore DREW 6 Watford
17.05.94	T. J. Smith L RSC 1 Kettering

Career: 8 contests, won 1, drew 2, lost 5.

Chris Francis

Stepney. *Born* London, 23 October, 1968
Lightweight. Ht. 5'6"
Manager Self

02.10.91	Rick Dimmock W PTS 6 Barking
11.02.92	Paul Donaghey L CO 2 Barking
17.02.93	Jason Lepre W RSC 2 Bethnal Green
31.03.93	Steve Patton W CO 4 Bethnal Green
13.10.93	Anthony Wanza W RSC 2 Bethnal Green
27.05.94	Andrew Reed W PTS 6 Ashford

Career: 6 contests, won 5, lost 1.

Dean Francis

Basingstoke. *Born* Basingstoke, 23 January, 1974
S. Middleweight. Ht. 5'10½"
Manager C. Sanigar

28.05.94	Darren Littlewood W PTS 4 Queensway
17.06.94	Martin Jolley W PTS 6 Plymouth

Career: 2 contests, won 2.

Dean Francis   Les Clark

Julius Francis

Woolwich. *Born* Peckham, 8 December, 1964
Heavyweight. Ht. 6'2"
Manager F. Maloney

23.05.93	Graham Arnold W RSC 5 Brockley
23.06.93	Joey Paladino W CO 4 Edmonton
24.07.93	Andre Tisdale W PTS 4 Atlantic City, USA
28.08.93	Don Sargent W RSC 2 Bismark, USA
01.12.93	John Keeton W PTS 4 Bethnal Green
27.04.94	Manny Burgo W PTS 4 Bethnal Green
25.05.94	John Ruiz L CO 4 Bristol

Career: 7 contests, won 6, lost 1.

Joe Frater

Grimsby. *Born* Jamaica, 30 April, 1961
Cruiserweight. Ht. 6'1"
Manager L. Slater

06.02.80	Nigel Savery L RSC 3 Liverpool
31.03.80	John Stone W RSC 1 Cleethorpes
14.04.80	Paul Heatley W RSC 5 Manchester
12.05.80	Chuck Hirschmann DREW 4 Manchester
16.06.80	Joe Dean W PTS 6 Manchester
09.09.80	Nigel Savery L CO 6 Mexborough
08.10.80	Steve Fox W PTS 4 Stoke
05.11.80	Willie Wright W PTS 6 Evesham
08.12.80	Steve Fenton L PTS 6 Nottingham
12.02.81	Paul Heatley L PTS 6 Bolton
30.03.81	Steve Fenton L RSC 1 Cleethorpes
21.09.81	Chris Thorne W PTS 6 Nottingham
11.11.81	Steve Babbs L PTS 6 Evesham
01.02.82	P. T. Grant W PTS 8 Newcastle
10.05.82	Devon Bailey L CO 2 Copthorne
07.06.82	Jonjo Greene L PTS 6 Manchester
21.06.82	Geoff Rymer W PTS 8 Hull
04.09.82	Andy Straughn L RSC 3 Marylebone
02.03.87	Ray Thomas L PTS 6 Birmingham
07.10.87	Crawford Ashley L RSC 5 Burnley
09.11.87	Tucker Watts L PTS 6 Leicester
22.03.88	Darren Jones L PTS 6 Wolverhampton
22.09.88	Wayne Hawkins W PTS 6 Wolverhampton
27.10.88	Dave Lawrence W PTS 6 Birmingham
10.11.88	Wayne Hawkins L RSC 3 Wolverhampton
08.05.89	Deka Williams L CO 5 Grimsby
04.09.89	Nigel Rafferty W PTS 6 Grimsby
04.12.89	Tony Lawrence W PTS 6 Grimsby
14.05.90	Dave Owens L PTS 6 Cleethorpes
08.10.90	Alan Baptiste DREW 6 Cleethorpes
11.12.90	Tony Lawrence W PTS 6 Evesham
02.03.91	Nick Vardy W RSC 1 Cleethorpes
23.04.91	Dave Owens L PTS 6 Cleethorpes
23.10.91	Garry Delaney L RSC 1 Bethnal Green
04.06.92	Greg Scott-Briggs W PTS 6 Cleethorpes
26.10.92	Dave Owens L PTS 6 Cleethorpes
26.04.93	Steve Osborne L PTS 6 Cleethorpes
28.03.94	Steve Osborne L RSC 5 Cleethorpes

Career: 38 contests, won 15, drew 2, lost 21.

Terry French

Newcastle. *Born* Newcastle, 15 January, 1967
Northern Area L. Heavyweight Champion. Ht. 5'9½"
Manager Self

10.10.88	Adrian Din L PTS 6 Nottingham
03.11.88	Graham Burton L RSC 3 Manchester
07.12.88	Anthony Lawrence W PTS 6 Stoke
13.03.89	Paul Abercromby W RSC 4 Glasgow
11.04.89	Paul Hendrick L PTS 6 Oldham
19.04.89	Mickey Murray W PTS 6 Doncaster
12.06.89	Max Wallace L PTS 6 Battersea
11.09.89	Shamus Casey L PTS 6 Nottingham
02.10.89	Hugh Fury W PTS 6 Bradford
10.10.89	Darren Pilling L PTS 6 Sunderland
23.10.89	Chris Walker W PTS 6 Nottingham
14.11.89	Dave Maxwell W PTS 6 Evesham
11.12.89	Tony Lawrence L PTS 6 Bradford
22.01.90	George Ferrie L PTS 6 Glasgow
26.02.90	Trevor Barry W RTD 4 Bradford
20.03.90	Stevie R. Davies W PTS 6 Hartlepool
09.04.90	Sean O'Phoenix DREW 8 Manchester

21.04.90	Dave Scott W RSC 3 Sunderland
15.05.90	Simon McDougall L PTS 4 South Shields
12.11.90	Eddie Collins W PTS 6 Bradford
13.12.90	Stevie R. Davies W PTS 10 Hartlepool
	(Vacant Northern Area L. Heavyweight Title)
03.04.91	Sean O'Phoenix L PTS 8 Manchester
10.05.91	Eddie Collins W PTS 6 Gateshead
10.10.91	Simon McDougall W PTS 6 Gateshead
14.11.91	Quinn Paynter L CO 6 Gateshead
03.03.92	Dave Owens L CO 1 Houghton le Spring
23.10.92	Spencer Alton W PTS 6 Gateshead
17.04.93	Simon McDougall W PTS 6 Washington
21.04.94	Ian Henry W PTS 10 Gateshead
	(Northern Area L. Heavyweight Title Defence)

Career: 29 contests, won 16, drew 1, lost 12.

Andrew Furlong

Hammersmith. *Born* Paddington, 29 July, 1967
L. Middleweight. Ht. 5'9½"
Manager Self

14.11.85	Robert Southey W PTS 6 Merton
22.11.85	Tony Richards W PTS 6 Longford
10.01.86	Bill Smith W PTS 6 Fulham
30.01.86	Marvin P. Gray W PTS 6 Merton
27.02.86	Barry Bacon W RSC 6 Merton
15.04.86	Willie Wilson W PTS 8 Merton
28.05.86	Billy Joe Dee W RSC 2 Lewisham
04.09.86	Les Remikie W PTS 8 Merton
22.10.86	Peppy Muire L RSC 2 Greenwich
20.11.86	Chubby Martin DREW 8 Merton
12.01.87	Chubby Martin W PTS 8 Ealing
22.01.87	Brian Sonny Nickels L PTS 8 Bethnal Green
25.02.87	Mark Dinnadge DREW 8 Lewisham
18.03.87	Tony Borg W PTS 8 Queensway
01.04.87	Frankie Lake W PTS 8 Southsea
30.04.87	Andrew Prescod W PTS 8 Bethnal Green
27.05.87	Wayne Weekes L RSC 1 Lewisham
25.09.87	Oliver Henry W RTD 5 Tooting
03.12.87	Eamonn McAuley W RTD 3 Belfast
18.01.88	Ian Honeywood L PTS 8 Mayfair
08.03.88	Neil Haddock W PTS 6 Holborn
19.09.88	Tony Richards L RSC 7 Mayfair
14.11.88	Joni Nyman L RSC 2 Helsinki, Finland
16.05.89	Ian John-Lewis L RSC 3 Wandsworth
12.06.89	Rocky Kelly L RSC 5 Battersea
11.10.89	Brian Robinson L PTS 6 Millwall
02.05.91	Delroy Waul L RSC 5 Tooting
30.06.91	Lee Crocker DREW 6 Southwark
12.02.92	Gary Pemberton W PTS 6 Wembley
25.03.92	Clay O'Shea DREW 6 Kensington
13.05.92	Clay O'Shea DREW 6 Kensington
16.06.92	Mickey Hughes L CO 1 Dagenham
02.10.92	Patrick Vungbo L RSC 8 Waregem, Belgium
10.04.93	Robin Reid L PTS 6 Swansea
20.05.94	Barry Thorogood W RSC 4 Acton
04.06.94	Robin Reid L RSC 2 Cardiff

Career: 36 contests, won 18, drew 5, lost 13.

Carl Gaffney

Leeds. *Born* Leeds, 15 April, 1964
Heavyweight. Ht. 6'5"
Manager T. Callighan

12.05.84	Steve Abadom W RSC 3 Hanley
02.10.84	Theo Josephs W PTS 6 Leeds
23.01.85	Alphonso Forbes L CO 1 Solihull
25.03.85	Dave Madden W RSC 1 Huddersfield
30.05.85	Denroy Bryan W RSC 1 Halifax
21.11.85	Al Malcolm W PTS 8 Huddersfield
16.01.86	Joe Threlfall L CO 3 Preston
20.02.86	Chris Devine W RSC 8 Halifax
24.10.86	Damien Marignan L PTS 8 Guadalupe, FWI
01.12.86	Michael Simwelu L RSC 7 Arnhem, Holland
14.12.88	Keith Ferdinand W PTS 8 Bethnal Green
14.06.89	Rodolfo Marin L RSC 2 Madrid, Spain
25.10.89	Andrei Oreshkin L RSC 1 Wembley
02.05.91	Sean Hunter W PTS 6 Kensington
19.09.91	Michael Murray L RSC 8 Stockport
	(Vacant Central Area Heavyweight Title)
09.02.92	Steve Garber W PTS 6 Bradford
13.02.93	Brian Nielsen L PTS 5 Randers, Denmark
26.03.93	Mikael Lindblad L RSC 2 Copenhagen, Denmark
13.10.93	Manny Burgo L PTS 6 Bethnal Green
21.12.93	Scott Welch L RSC 3 Mayfair
15.06.94	Jeff Pegues W DIS 2 Southwark

Career: 21 contests, won 10, lost 11.

Michael Gale

Leeds. *Born* Cardiff, 28 October, 1967
Central Area L. Heavyweight Champion. Ht. 5'11"
Manager M. Duff

21.09.89	Dave Lawrence W RTD 4 Harrogate
13.11.89	Coco Collins W CO 1 Manchester
05.12.89	Randy B. Powell W RSC 1 Dewsbury
11.01.90	Cliff Curtis W RSC 2 Dewsbury
24.01.90	Andy Marlow W RSC 2 Sunderland
03.03.90	Peter Vosper W RSC 2 Wembley
11.04.90	Teo Arvizu W PTS 6 Dewsbury
18.10.90	Mick Queally W RSC 5 Dewsbury
15.11.90	Steve Osborne W PTS 6 Oldham
14.03.91	Carlos Christie W PTS 8 Middleton
21.03.91	David Haycock W RSC 2 Dewsbury
09.05.91	Steve Osborne W RSC 2 Leeds
13.06.91	Graham Burton W CO 4 Hull
27.06.91	Mark Bowen W PTS 8 Leeds
30.10.91	Denys Cronin DREW 8 Leeds
23.01.92	John Kaighin W PTS 8 York
08.04.92	Tony Booth W PTS 8 Leeds
29.10.92	Bobbi Joe Edwards W PTS 10 Leeds
	(Vacant Central Area L. Heavyweight Title)
07.04.93	Brent Kosolofski L RSC 9 Leeds
	(Vacant Commonwealth L. Heavyweight Title)
01.07.93	Tony Booth W PTS 8 York
07.10.93	John Kaighin W PTS 8 York

Career: 21 contests, won 19, drew 1, lost 1.

(Patrick) P. J. Gallagher

Wood Green. *Born* Manchester, 14 February, 1973
Lightweight. Ht. 5'7"
Manager F. Maloney

15.09.93	John T. Kelly W RSC 2 Bethnal Green
13.10.93	Mike Morrison W PTS 4 Bethnal Green
01.12.93	Mark Antony W PTS 4 Bethnal Green

09.02.94 Simon Hamblett W RSC 1 Bethnal Green
29.03.94 Brian Coleman W PTS 6 Bethnal Green
15.06.94 Mark O'Callaghan W RSC 4 Southwark
Career: 6 contests, won 6.

P. J. Gallagher   Les Clark

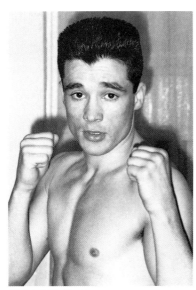

Patrick Gallagher   Les Clark

Patrick Gallagher

Islington. *Born* Manchester, 23 July, 1971
Lightweight. Ht. 5'7½"
Manager B. Hearn

22.12.92 Karl Taylor W RSC 3 Mayfair
20.02.93 Joe Fannin W RTD 1 Earls Court
21.12.93 Karl Taylor W PTS 6 Mayfair

11.01.94 Mark Antony W RSC 3 Bethnal Green
15.03.94 Karl Taylor W PTS 6 Mayfair
Career: 5 contests, won 5.

Steve Garber

Bradford. *Born* Bradford, 20 June, 1962
Heavyweight. Ht. 6'6"
Manager Self

22.04.85 Mick Cordon DREW 6 Bradford
30.05.85 Mick Cordon L PTS 6 Blackburn
02.07.85 Joe Threlfall W RSC 2 Preston
03.10.85 Dave Shelton W PTS 4 Bradford
27.11.85 Mick Cordon W PTS 6 Bradford
06.02.86 Mick Cordon L PTS 6 Doncaster
27.04.86 Mick Cordon L PTS 6 Doncaster
22.05.86 Sean Daly W PTS 6 Horwich
18.09.86 Gary McConnell L PTS 6 Weston super Mare
25.09.86 Carl Timbrell W PTS 6 Wolverhampton
22.10.86 Dave Madden W PTS 4 Bradford
01.12.86 Tony Hallett W PTS 6 Nottingham
24.02.87 Gary McConnell L CO 1 Ilford
07.10.87 Gypsy John Fury L PTS 6 Burnley
18.01.88 Mick Cordon W PTS 6 Bradford
11.02.88 John Love L CO 1 Gravesend
21.03.88 Ted Shaw W CO 1 Leicester
22.04.88 Manny Burgo L PTS 6 Gateshead
23.05.88 Ted Shaw W CO 3 Bradford
26.09.88 Gifford Shillingford W RSC 4 Bradford
25.10.88 Paul Lister L PTS 6 Hartlepool
17.11.88 Michael Murray L PTS 6 Stockport
18.01.89 Peter Nyman W PTS 6 Kensington
19.05.89 Joe Threlfall W RSC 3 Gateshead
10.10.89 Lennox Lewis L CO 1 Hull
20.03.90 Chris Hubbert W RSC 1 Hartlepool
05.05.90 Knut Blin L PTS 6 Hamburg, Germany
12.11.90 David Jules W RSC 6 Bradford
30.11.90 Steve Gee W PTS 6 Birmingham
19.03.91 Al Malcolm W RSC 5 Birmingham
30.04.91 Michael Murray L CO 1 Stockport
31.05.91 Axel Schulz L CO 5 Berlin, Germany
10.10.91 Paul Lister L PTS 8 Gateshead
09.02.92 Carl Gaffney L PTS 6 Bradford
05.04.92 David Jules W RSC 4 Bradford
08.05.92 Alexandr Miroshnichenko L RSC 1 Waregem, Belgium
18.07.92 Henry Akinwande L RTD 2 Manchester
24.02.93 J. A. Bugner W RSC 6 Wembley
15.03.94 Scott Welch L RSC 4 Mayfair
21.05.94 Clifton Mitchell L CO 1 Belfast
Career: 40 contests, won 19, drew 1, lost 20.

Des Gargano (Southern)

Manchester. *Born* Brighton, 20 December, 1960
S. Bantamweight. Ht. 5'5"
Manager J. Doughty

25.01.85 Sugar Gibiliru L PTS 4 Liverpool
18.03.85 Sugar Gibiliru L PTS 6 Liverpool
24.04.85 Glen McLaggon L PTS 6 Stoke
03.06.85 Anthony Wakefield DREW 6 Manchester
17.06.85 Anthony Wakefield W PTS 6 Manchester
03.10.85 Anthony Brown L PTS 6 Liverpool
13.10.85 Gary Maxwell L PTS 6 Sheffield
09.12.85 Robert Newbiggin W PTS 6 Nottingham
16.12.85 Gypsy Johnny W PTS 6 Bradford

24.02.86 Kevin Taylor W PTS 6 Bradford
01.04.86 Carl Cleasby L PTS 6 Leeds
07.04.86 Gerry McBride W PTS 6 Manchester
29.04.86 Pat Clinton L PTS 6 Manchester
23.09.86 David Ingram L PTS 6 Batley
24.11.86 Andrew Steadman L PTS 6 Leicester
03.12.86 Sean Murphy L PTS 6 Muswell Hill
15.12.86 Tony Heath L PTS 8 Loughborough
30.01.87 Nigel Crook L PTS 6 Kirkby
16.02.87 Pat Clinton L PTS 6 Glasgow
13.04.87 Jimmy Lee W PTS 6 Manchester
26.05.87 John Green L PTS 6 Oldham
19.10.87 John Green L PTS 6 Manchester
28.10.87 Paul Thornton W RSC 6 Stoke
09.11.87 Tony Heath L PTS 6 Leicester
26.01.88 Graham O'Malley L PTS 4 Hartlepool
23.03.88 Lambsy Kayani L PTS 6 Sheffield
29.03.88 Graham O'Malley L PTS 8 Marton
25.04.88 Ronnie Stephenson W PTS 8 Bradford
06.06.88 Darryl Pettit W PTS 6 Manchester
13.06.88 Joe Mullen L PTS 6 Glasgow
05.09.88 Wull Strike DREW 6 Glasgow
22.09.88 John Davison L PTS 8 Newcastle
29.09.88 John Davison L PTS 8 Sunderland
10.10.88 Shane Silvester L PTS 8 Edgbaston
18.10.88 Peter English L PTS 4 Oldham
28.10.88 Eyub Can L PTS 6 Copenhagen, Denmark
21.11.88 Ronnie Stephenson W PTS 6 Leicester
29.11.88 Chris Clarkson W PTS 6 Manchester
07.12.88 Renny Edwards L PTS 6 Aberavon
16.12.88 Jimmy Clark L PTS 6 Brentwood
14.02.89 Nigel Crook L PTS 10 Manchester
17.03.89 Jimmy Bredahl L PTS 6 Braedstrup, Denmark
17.04.89 Mark Priestley W PTS 8 Middleton
10.05.89 Mark Goult L PTS 8 Solihull
17.05.89 Mark Geraghty L PTS 8 Glasgow
12.06.89 Neil Parry W PTS 6 Manchester
11.07.89 Chris Clarkson L PTS 6 Batley
04.09.89 Ronnie Stephenson W PTS 6 Hull
11.09.89 Paul Dever W RSC 1 Manchester
20.09.89 Miguel Matthews W PTS 6 Stoke
05.10.89 Wayne Windle W PTS 6 Middleton
16.10.89 Wayne Windle L PTS 6 Manchester
31.10.89 Dave McNally L PTS 6 Manchester
10.11.89 Kruga Hydes L PTS 6 Liverpool
20.11.89 Dave Buxton L PTS 6 Leicester
30.11.89 Noel Carroll L PTS 6 Oldham
11.12.89 Joe Kelly L PTS 6 Bayswater
14.02.90 Danny Porter L PTS 6 Brentwood
06.03.90 Bradley Stone L PTS 6 Bethnal Green
17.03.90 John Lowey L RSC 6 Belfast
24.04.90 Jamie Morris W PTS 4 Stoke
09.05.90 Terry Collins L PTS 6 Kensington
16.05.90 Tony Doyle W PTS 6 Hull
11.06.90 Steve Armstrong W PTS 6 Manchester
05.09.90 John George L PTS 6 Stoke
01.10.90 Tony Smith W PTS 6 Cleethorpes
09.10.90 Brian Robb L PTS 6 Wolverhampton
22.10.90 John George L PTS 6 Cleethorpes
26.11.90 Tony Smith W PTS 8 Bury
03.12.90 Tony Smith W PTS 6 Cleethorpes
11.12.90 Stewart Fishermac W PTS 8 Evesham
16.01.91 Tony Smith W PTS 6 Stoke
06.02.91 Tim Driscoll L PTS 6 Bethnal Green
28.02.91 Carl Roberts W PTS 6 Bury
07.05.91 James Drummond L PTS 8 Glasgow
16.05.91 Jimmy Owens L RSC 2 Liverpool
19.08.91 Petteri Rissanen L PTS 4 Helsinki, Finland
02.10.91 Eric George L PTS 6 Solihull
24.10.91 Edward Cook L RSC 5 Glasgow
29.11.91 Harald Geier L DIS 8 Frohsdorf, Austria

31.01.92	Edward Cook L PTS 6 Glasgow	
24.02.92	Colin Lynch L PTS 6 Coventry	
04.03.92	Neil Armstrong L PTS 6 Glasgow	
11.03.92	Dennis Oakes L PTS 6 Stoke	
27.04.92	David Ramsden L PTS 6 Bradford	
01.06.92	Mark Hargreaves L PTS 6 Manchester	
08.06.92	David Ramsden L PTS 6 Bradford	
07.10.92	Prince Nassem Hamed L RSC 4 Sunderland	
20.11.92	Paul Lloyd L PTS 4 Liverpool	
26.02.93	Alex Docherty W RSC 4 Irvine	
04.04.93	Rowan Williams L PTS 4 Brockley	
26.04.93	Wilson Docherty L PTS 6 Glasgow	
01.06.93	Neil Parry W PTS 6 Manchester	
09.09.93	James Murray L PTS 6 Glasgow	
13.11.93	Richie Wenton L PTS 8 Cullompton	
13.12.93	Tony Falcone L PTS 4 Bristol	
17.02.94	Daryl McKenzie DREW 6 Bury	
25.02.94	Peter Culshaw L PTS 6 Chester	
15.03.94	Gary Marston L PTS 8 Stoke	
02.06.94	Marty Chestnut W PTS 6 Middleton	

Career: 100 contests, won 29, drew 3, lost 68.

Al Garrett (Garrity)

Glasgow. *Born* Glasgow, 21 December, 1966
Featherweight. Ht. 5'5½"
Manager T. Gilmour

23.09.91	Robert Braddock DREW 6 Glasgow
09.12.91	Chris Jickells L RSC 2 Bradford
18.11.92	Colin Innes DREW 6 Solihull
02.03.94	Daryl McKenzie L PTS 6 Glasgow
25.04.94	Daryl McKenzie W PTS 6 Glasgow
16.05.94	Dave Clavering L RTD 4 Morecambe

Career: 6 contests, won 1, drew 2, lost 3.

Dermot Gascoyne　　　　Les Clark

Dermot Gascoyne

Bexleyheath. *Born* Alfreton, 23 April, 1967
Heavyweight. Ht. 6'5"
Manager F. Warren

17.12.92	John Harewood W RSC 5 Barking
03.02.93	Steve Stewart W RSC 4 Earls Court
10.04.93	Denroy Bryan W PTS 6 Swansea

23.10.93	Vance Idiens W RSC 4 Cardiff
17.02.94	John Keeton W RSC 1 Dagenham
09.04.94	Steve Yorath W CO 3 Mansfield

Career: 6 contests, won 6.

Terry Gaskin

Doncaster. *Born* Doncaster, 20 October, 1974
Flyweight. Ht. 5'4"
Manager H. Hayes

28.03.94	Keith Knox L PTS 6 Musselburgh
09.05.94	Tiger Singh L RSC 2 Bradford

Career: 2 contests, lost 2.

Mark Geraghty

Glasgow. *Born* Paisley, 25 August, 1965
Scottish S. Featherweight Champion. Ht. 5'6"
Manager T. Gilmour

14.11.88	Mark Priestley W PTS 6 Glasgow
27.01.89	Gordon Stobie W PTS 6 Durham
14.02.89	Gary Hickman L PTS 6 Sunderland
09.03.89	Chris Clarkson W PTS 6 Glasgow
20.03.89	Ian Johnson L PTS 6 Nottingham
24.04.89	Sean Hogg W PTS 6 Glasgow
17.05.89	Des Gargano W PTS 8 Glasgow
09.06.89	Jimmy Bredahl L PTS 6 Aarhus, Denmark
02.10.89	Steve Winstanley L PTS 6 Bradford
20.11.89	Gordon Shaw W RSC 4 Glasgow
22.01.90	Neil Leitch W PTS 8 Glasgow
19.03.90	Joe Donohoe L RSC 3 Glasgow
17.09.90	Peter Judson L PTS 8 Glasgow
08.10.90	Peter Judson W PTS 8 Glasgow
19.11.90	Tony Doyle W PTS 8 Glasgow
27.11.90	Muhammad Shaffique L PTS 8 Glasgow
06.03.91	Neil Leitch W PTS 10 Glasgow *(Vacant Scottish S. Featherweight Title)*
01.05.91	Pete Buckley L PTS 8 Solihull
03.06.91	Neil Leitch L PTS 8 Glasgow
23.09.91	Neil Leitch W PTS 10 Glasgow *(Scottish S. Featherweight Title Defence)*
09.10.91	Chris Clarkson W PTS 6 Glasgow
20.11.91	Tony Feliciello L RSC 4 Solihull
24.02.92	Colin Innes W PTS 8 Glasgow
18.03.92	Barrie Kelley W PTS 8 Glasgow
19.09.92	Micky Hall W PTS 6 Glasgow
19.10.92	Kevin Lowe W PTS 8 Glasgow
28.11.92	Alan Levene L PTS 6 Manchester
02.04.93	Medhi Labdouni L PTS 8 Fontenay Sous Bois, France
07.06.93	Karl Taylor L PTS 8 Glasgow
06.10.93	Miguel Matthews W PTS 6 York
10.04.94	Miguel Matthews W PTS 8 Glasgow

Career: 31 contests, won 18, lost 13.

Tony Gibbs

Barking. *Born* London, 20 January, 1964
Welterweight. Ht. 5'6¼"
Manager R. Colson

08.10.87	Barry Messam W PTS 6 Bethnal Green
25.02.88	Mike Russell L PTS 6 Bethnal Green
08.03.88	David Lake W PTS 6 Holborn
13.04.88	David Lake W RSC 1 Gravesend
05.05.88	Mark Pearce L RSC 4 Bethnal Green
02.11.88	Gary Logan L PTS 6 Southwark
15.11.88	Tony Britland DREW 6 Piccadilly

30.11.88	Derek Grainger L CO 3 Southwark
13.03.89	Dennis Sullivan W PTS 6 Piccadilly
06.04.89	Davey Hughes L PTS 6 Cardiff
15.09.89	B. F. Williams L PTS 6 High Wycombe
28.09.89	Carlos Chase L PTS 6 Wandsworth
12.10.89	Lee Wicks L CO 2 Southwark
30.11.89	Ross Hale L PTS 6 Mayfair
03.04.90	Andy Robins W PTS 6 Southend
05.06.90	Tim Harmey L PTS 6 Eltham
18.10.90	Felix Kelly DREW 6 Wandsworth
16.11.90	Lindon Scarlett L PTS 6 Telford
08.05.91	Robert McCracken L CO 1 Kensington
20.11.91	Robert Wright L RTD 2 Solihull
02.04.92	Dean Hollington L CO 1 Basildon
16.05.94	Adrian Chase L PTS 6 Heathrow

Career: 22 contests, won 5, drew 2, lost 15.

(Dramani) Sugar Gibiliru

Liverpool. *Born* Liverpool, 13 July, 1966
Lightweight. Former British S.
Featherweight Champion. Former
Undefeated Central Area S. Featherweight
& Lightweight Champion. Ht. 5'5½"
Manager Self

30.11.84	Steve Benny L PTS 4 Liverpool
25.01.85	Des Gargano W PTS 4 Liverpool
04.02.85	Martin Power W RTD 3 Liverpool
18.03.85	Des Gargano L PTS 6 Liverpool
29.03.85	Craig Windsor L PTS 6 Liverpool
17.04.85	Carl Gaynor L PTS 6 Nantwich
29.04.85	Carl Gaynor L PTS 6 Liverpool
07.10.85	Martin Power W RSC 4 Liverpool
11.11.85	Nigel Senior W RSC 5 Liverpool
06.12.85	Anthony Brown L PTS 8 Liverpool
24.01.86	Floyd Havard L PTS 6 Muswell Hill
10.03.86	Brian Roche L PTS 8 Manchester
07.04.86	Muhammad Lovelock DREW 8 Manchester
24.05.86	Floyd Havard L PTS 8 Manchester
16.06.86	Brian Roche L PTS 8 Manchester
22.09.86	Carl Crook L PTS 6 Bradford
14.10.86	Muhammad Lovelock DREW 8 Manchester
17.11.86	Simon Eubank L PTS 8 Dulwich
20.11.86	Joey Jacobs L PTS 8 Bredbury
15.12.86	Carl Crook L PTS 8 Bradford
13.01.87	Edward Lloyd L PTS 8 Oldham
24.04.87	Dean Binch W CO 3 Liverpool
15.06.87	Muhammad Lovelock L PTS 8 Manchester
22.09.87	Ray Taylor L PTS 8 Oldham
16.11.87	Robert Harkin DREW 8 Glasgow
05.12.87	Glyn Rhodes L PTS 8 Doncaster
01.03.88	Pat Barrett DREW 8 Manchester
13.04.88	Peter Till L PTS 8 Wolverhampton
28.04.88	Mark Kelly DREW 6 Manchester
10.09.88	Jean-Charles Meuret L PTS 8 Geneva, Switzerland
28.09.88	Glyn Rhodes DREW 8 Solihull
01.12.88	Mark Kelly L PTS 6 Manchester
14.12.88	Andy Holligan L PTS 8 Kirkby
25.01.89	Ray Taylor L PTS 6 Solihull
11.04.89	Pat Barrett L CO 8 Oldham *(Central Area L. Welterweight Title Challenge)*
31.05.89	Tony Banks W CO 5 Manchester
21.06.89	Rudy Valentino L PTS 6 Eltham
19.09.89	Nigel Wenton L PTS 8 Belfast
16.11.89	Tony Foster L PTS 8 Manchester
30.01.90	Tony Foster W PTS 10 Manchester *(Vacant Central Area Lightweight Title)*

07.03.90 Peter Gabbitus W RTD 6 Doncaster
(Vacant Central Area S. Featherweight Title)
01.05.90 Mark Reefer L RSC 5 Oldham
(Commonwealth S. Featherweight Title Challenge)
07.07.90 Kris McAdam W PTS 8 Liverpool
19.11.90 Frankie Foster DREW 8 Manchester
17.12.90 Dean Bramhald W PTS 8 Manchester
29.01.91 Nigel Bradley W PTS 8 Stockport
30.04.91 Robert Dickie W RSC 9 Stockport
(British S. Featherweight Title Challenge)
19.09.91 John Doherty L PTS 12 Stockport
(British S. Featherweight Title Defence)
07.12.91 Paul Harvey L PTS 12 Manchester
(Commonwealth S. Featherweight Title Challenge)
31.03.92 Frankie Foster W PTS 8 Stockport
27.06.92 Michael Ayers L RSC 6 Quinta do Lago, Portugal
01.12.92 Ross Hale L RSC 1 Bristol
06.05.94 Norman Dhalie W RTD 5 Liverpool
Career: 53 contests, won 15, drew 7, lost 31.

(Godfrey) G. G. Goddard

Alfreton. *Born* Swaziland, 6 April, 1966
Lightweight. Ht. 5'7"
Manager Self

22.11.90 Shaun Hickey W RTD 4 Ilkeston
17.01.91 Paul Chedgzoy W RSC 3 Alfreton
13.05.91 Finn McCool L PTS 6 Northampton
20.05.91 Finn McCool W PTS 6 Bradford
23.10.91 Chubby Martin L PTS 6 Stoke
04.02.92 Kevin Toomey L PTS 6 Alfreton
11.03.92 Micky Hall DREW 6 Solihull
28.04.92 Michael Clynch L RTD 4 Corby
09.07.92 Dave McHale L RTD 4 Glasgow
18.11.92 Ian McGirr L PTS 6 Solihull
23.02.93 Jonjo Irwin L RSC 8 Doncaster
25.06.93 Mike Anthony Brown L CO 2 Battersea
13.06.94 Keith Jones W PTS 6 Liverpool
Career: 13 contests, won 4, drew 1, lost 8.

(Valentine) Val Golding

Croydon. *Born* Croydon, 9 May, 1964
S. Middleweight. Ht. 5'11"
Manager Self

17.07.89 Robbie Harron W RSC 2 Stanmore
05.10.89 Shamus Casey W PTS 6 Stevenage
12.12.89 Neil Munn W RSC 2 Brentford
14.04.90 Ian Strudwick L PTS 6 Kensington
22.09.90 Franki Moro W RSC 6 Kensington
15.10.90 Tod Nadon L RSC 6 Lewisham
04.09.91 Russell Washer W RTD 5 Bethnal Green
29.10.91 Graham Jenner W RSC 3 Kensington
18.01.92 Quinn Paynter L RSC 7 Kensington
26.09.92 Kevin Sheeran L RSC 1 Earls Court
15.09.93 John Keeton W PTS 6 Ashford
27.05.94 Jerry Mortimer W PTS 6 Ashford
Career: 12 contests, won 8, lost 4.

(Robert) Zak Goldman

Doncaster. *Born* Ainwick, 19 July, 1964
Cruiserweight. Ht. 6'2"
Manager J. Rushton

07.12.92 Paul Hanlon L PTS 6 Birmingham
15.12.92 Kenley Price L RTD 2 Liverpool

09.02.93 Lee Archer L CO 3 Wolverhampton
12.05.93 Steve Loftus L PTS 6 Stoke
08.03.94 Justin Clements L RSC 3 Edgbaston
Career: 5 contests, lost 5.

Paul Goode

Halifax. *Born* Northampton, 8 September, 1962
S. Featherweight. Ht. 5'6"
Manager T. Callighan

19.04.93 Tony Smith DREW 6 Manchester
01.06.93 Tony Smith L PTS 6 Manchester
07.02.94 Leo Turner L RSC 3 Bradford
Career: 3 contests, drew 1, lost 2.

Steve Goodwin

Sheffield. *Born* Derby, 17 February, 1966
Middleweight. Midlands Area L. Middleweight Champion. Ht. 5'11"
Manager B. Ingle

13.04.92 John Duckworth W PTS 6 Manchester
29.04.92 John Corcoran W PTS 8 Stoke
03.09.92 Steve McNess L PTS 6 Dunstable
29.09.92 Mark Dawson W RSC 1 Stoke
19.10.92 John Bosco L RSC 2 Mayfair
09.12.92 Mark Dawson L PTS 6 Mayfair
12.02.93 Said Bennajem L PTS 6 Aubervilliers, France
12.05.93 Mark Dawson W PTS 10 Stoke
(Vacant Midlands Area L. Middleweight Title)
28.07.93 Gary Stretch L PTS 6 Brixton
07.09.93 Wally Swift Jnr W RSC 7 Stoke
(Midlands Area L. Middleweight Title Defence)
02.11.93 Lloyd Honeyghan L RSC 6 Southwark
25.05.94 Wally Swift Jnr L PTS 8 Stoke
Career: 12 contests, won 5, lost 7.

Alan Graham

Newcastle. *Born* Newcastle, 7 October, 1973
Lightweight. Ht. 5'11"
Manager T. Conroy

21.09.92 Garry Burrell L PTS 6 Glasgow
09.11.92 Garry Burrell W PTS 6 Bradford
10.12.92 T. J. Smith W PTS 6 Corby
25.01.93 Leo Turner W PTS 6 Bradford
26.02.93 Mike Deveney L PTS 6 Irvine
22.04.93 Dave Buxton W PTS 6 Bury
06.05.93 John T. Kelly L PTS 6 Hartlepool
07.10.93 John Stovin L PTS 6 Hull
25.11.93 Chris Bennett W PTS 6 Newcastle
03.03.94 Sam Church W CO 3 Newcastle
21.04.94 Paul Wynn W PTS 6 Gateshead
24.05.94 Garry Burrell W PTS 6 Sunderland
06.06.94 Carl Roberts L PTS 6 Manchester
Career: 13 contests, won 8, lost 5.

Derek Grainger

Bethnal Green. *Born* London, 15 May, 1967
Welterweight. Ht. 5'7¾"
Manager Self

28.01.88 Jim Beckett W PTS 6 Bethnal Green
25.02.88 Richard Thompson W CO 3 Bethnal Green
24.03.88 Glyn Mitchell W RSC 5 Bethnal Green

05.05.88 Frank Mobbs W RSC 2 Bethnal Green
05.10.88 Gerry Beard W PTS 4 Wembley
02.11.88 Gary Dyson W RSC 4 Southwark
30.11.88 Tony Gibbs W CO 3 Southwark
16.03.89 Simon Eubank W RSC 6 Southwark
10.05.89 Ronnie Campbell W RSC 3 Kensington
12.10.89 Barry Messam W CO 1 Southwark
25.10.89 Newton Barnett W PTS 8 Wembley
06.12.89 Young Gully W RSC 3 Wembley
03.03.90 Jerry Smith W RSC 6 Wembley
14.03.90 Ray Taylor W CO 2 Kensington
09.05.90 Newton Barnett W RSC 4 Wembley
31.10.90 Kevin Plant W RSC 4 Wembley
12.12.90 Chris Peters W PTS 8 Kensington
13.02.91 Newton Barnett W RSC 3 Wembley
17.04.91 Humphrey Harrison L RSC 7 Kensington
20.11.91 Chris Blake DREW 8 Kensington
17.12.92 Bozon Haule W RSC 5 Barking
03.02.93 Trevor Meikle W RSC 6 Earls Court
31.03.93 Wayne Shepherd W RSC 4 Barking
22.09.93 Gary Barron W RTD 4 Bethnal Green
17.02.94 Del Bryan L CO 7 Dagenham
(British Welterweight Title Challenge)
04.06.94 Lee Crocker W RSC 3 Cardiff
Career: 26 contests, won 23, drew 1, lost 2.

Frank Grant   Harry Goodwin

Frank Grant

Bradford. *Born* Bradford, 22 May, 1965
Former British Middleweight Champion.
Ht. 5'11"
Manager Self

20.10.86 Lincoln Pennant L RSC 1 Bradford
01.06.87 Steve Ward W RSC 3 Bradford
10.09.87 Tony Lawrence W RSC 3 Peterborough
16.10.87 Mick Maw W PTS 6 Gateshead
29.02.88 Steve Kofi W RSC 3 Bradford
11.03.88 Gerry Richards W RSC 3 Cottingham
28.03.88 Dave Thomas W PTS 6 Bradford
24.10.88 Shaun Cummins W RTD 7 Northampton
12.12.88 Franki Moro W CO 6 Bradford
16.01.89 Mark Howell W RSC 1 Bradford
20.02.89 Franki Moro L PTS 6 Bradford
24.04.89 Peter Sorby W RSC 1 Bradford
22.05.89 Neil Munn W RSC 3 Bradford

09.11.89 Simon Collins W RTD 6 Cardiff
11.12.89 Steve Aquilina W RSC 4 Bradford
21.03.90 Kid Milo L PTS 10 Solihull
(*Elim. British S. Middleweight Title*)
12.04.91 Alan Richards W RSC 5 Manchester
31.05.91 Tim Dendy W PTS 8 Manchester
20.09.91 Conrad Oscar W CO 2 Manchester
29.11.91 Winston Wray W RSC 3 Manchester
09.02.92 Willie Ball W PTS 6 Bradford
05.04.92 Sammy Matos W CO 1 Bradford
23.09.92 Herol Graham W RSC 9 Leeds
(*British Middleweight Title Challenge*)
25.02.93 John Ashton W RTD 7 Bradford
(*British Middleweight Title Defence*)
25.07.93 Randy Smith W PTS 8 Oldham
10.11.93 Neville Brown L RSC 7 Bethnal Green
(*British Middleweight Title Defence*)
Career: 26 contests, won 22, lost 4.

Darren Greaves
Alfreton. *Born* Chesterfield, 25 May, 1971
S. Bantamweight. Ht. 5'5"
Manager J. Gaynor

06.12.93 Graham McGrath DREW 6
Birmingham
16.12.93 Graham McGrath L PTS 6 Walsall
04.03.94 Danny Ruegg W PTS 6 Weston super
Mare
25.04.94 Adey Lewis L RSC 1 Bury
Career: 4 contests, won 1, drew 1, lost 2.

John Green
Manchester. *Born* Manchester, 5 June,
1965
Former Undefeated Central Area
Bantamweight Champion. Ht. 5'5"
Manager Self

31.03.87 Albert Parr W PTS 6 Oldham
28.04.87 Chris Clarkson W RSC 6 Manchester
26.05.87 Des Gargano W PTS 6 Oldham
19.10.87 Des Gargano W PTS 6 Manchester
17.11.87 Nigel Crook W PTS 6 Manchester
16.12.87 Gerry McBride W PTS 10 Manchester
(*Central Area Bantamweight Title
Challenge*)
20.01.88 Dave George W PTS 8 Solihull
13.03.90 Gary de Roux L RSC 2 Bristol
10.10.90 Jimmy Clark L PTS 6 Millwall
22.02.91 Colin Lynch W PTS 6 Manchester
12.04.91 Sylvester Osuji W RSC 1 Manchester
31.05.91 Roland Gomez W CO 5 Manchester
20.09.91 Tony Rahman W RSC 3 Manchester
29.11.91 Ceri Farell W RTD 4 Manchester
31.01.92 Miguel Matthews DREW 6
Manchester
09.02.92 Steve Young DREW 6 Bradford
29.05.92 Ronnie Carroll W PTS 10 Manchester
(*Elim. British Bantamweight Title*)
23.10.93 Conn McMullen L PTS 6 Cardiff
Career: 18 contests, won 13, drew 2, lost 3.

Dennis Griffin
Stepney. *Born* Stepney, 9 June, 1965
L. Welterweight. Ht. 5'9"
Manager M. Brennan

31.08.93 Trevor Royal W RSC 1 Croydon
09.12.93 Keith Marner L PTS 6 Watford
19.12.93 Dave Madden W RSC 1 Northampton
23.02.94 Adrian Chase L PTS 6 Watford
Career: 4 contests, won 2, lost 2.

Dennis Griffin   Les Clark

Darron Griffiths   Les Clark

Darron Griffiths
Cardiff. *Born* Pontypridd, 11 February,
1972
Welsh S. Middleweight Champion. Ht. 6'0"
Manager F. Maloney

26.11.90 Colin Ford DREW 6 Mayfair
04.12.90 Kevin Adamson W RSC 4 Southend
23.01.91 Tony Booth DREW 6 Stoke
06.03.91 Barry Messam W PTS 6 Croydon
10.04.91 John Kaighin W PTS 6 Newport
25.04.91 Michael Graham W RSC 2 Mayfair
02.05.91 Carlton Myers W RTD 5 Kensington
21.10.91 John Ogiste W PTS 6 Mayfair
11.12.91 Adrian Wright W PTS 6 Stoke
22.01.92 Richard Okumu W PTS 8 Solihull
17.02.92 John Ogiste W RSC 5 Mayfair

29.04.92 Colin Manners DREW 8 Solihull
30.09.92 Colin Manners W PTS 10 Solihull
(*Elim. British Middleweight Title*)
28.10.92 Antonio Fernandez W PTS 10 Cardiff
(*Elim. British Middleweight Title*)
24.03.93 John Kaighin W RSC 6 Cardiff
(*Vacant Welsh S. Middleweight Title*)
22.01.94 Carlos Christie W PTS 8 Cardiff
09.02.94 Paul Hitch W PTS 6 Bethnal Green
23.03.94 Karl Barwise W PTS 8 Cardiff
27.04.94 Ray Webb W RSC 6 Bethnal Green
(*Elim. British S. Middleweight Title*)
15.06.94 Nigel Rafferty W RSC 4 Southwark
Career: 20 contests, won 17, drew 3.

Tony Griffiths
Tottenham. *Born* Tower Hamlets, 16 April,
1969
S. Middleweight. Ht. 5'9½"
Manager B. Hearn

28.06.94 Tim Robinson W RSC 6 Mayfair
Career: 1 contest, won 1.

Robert Grubb
Tipton. *Born* Stourbridge, 15 April, 1972
Lightweight. Ht. 5'4"
Manager C. Flute
17.02.94 Paul Wynn L PTS 6 Walsall
07.04.94 Roger Brotherhood L PTS 6 Walsall
Career: 2 contests, lost 2.

(George) Young Gully (Plummer)
Birmingham. *Born* Birmingham, 30 March,
1964
L. Welterweight. Ht. 5'7"
Manager Self

14.10.86 Eddie King W CO 5 Wolverhampton
23.10.86 Steve Higgins L CO 2 Birmingham
26.01.87 Johnny Hooks W RSC 2 Nottingham
30.03.87 Wil Halliday L RSC 5 Birmingham
09.02.88 Robbie Bowen W PTS 6
Wolverhampton
07.03.88 Gary Dyson W PTS 6 Piccadilly
23.03.88 Nick Meloscia L RSC 6 Evesham
18.05.88 Danny Cooper L RSC 4 Portsmouth
19.10.88 Steve Phillips DREW 6 Evesham
17.11.88 Julian Eavis L PTS 6 Weston super
Mare
14.12.88 Julian Eavis W PTS 6 Evesham
06.02.89 Julian Eavis W RSC 6 Nottingham
16.02.89 Wil Halliday W PTS 6 Stafford
20.04.89 Mike Russell W PTS 6 Weston super
Mare
22.05.89 Lenny Gloster W RSC 2 Peterborough
10.06.89 Silvio Branco L RSC 3 Milan, Italy
06.12.89 Derek Grainger L RSC 3 Wembley
13.03.90 Adrian Riley L RSC 5 Bristol
30.04.90 Trevor Meikle W PTS 6 Brierley Hill
23.05.90 Oscar Checa L RSC 2 Belfast
03.11.93 Nick Hall L RSC 2 Bristol
19.01.94 Mick Hoban L RSC 3 Solihull
Career: 22 contests, won 10, drew 1, lost 11.

Richard Guy
Cannock. *Born* Cannock, 24 September,
1969
L. Heavyweight. Ht. 6'2"
Manager C. Flute
23.05.94 Craig Byrne W RSC 4 Walsall
28.06.94 Chris Nurse L RSC 3 Edgbaston
Career: 2 contests, won 1, lost 1

Bobby Guynan

East Ham. *Born* Plaistow, 4 July, 1967
Lightweight. Ht. 5'9"
Manager Self

17.10.90	John O'Meara W RTD 2 Bethnal Green
26.11.90	Lee Fox L PTS 6 Bethnal Green
06.02.91	Lee Fox W PTS 6 Bethnal Green
26.03.91	Lee Fox L RTD 3 Bethnal Green
10.11.92	Mark Allen W RSC 2 Dagenham
30.01.93	Shaun Shinkwin W PTS 6 Brentwood
20.04.93	Norman Dhalie W PTS 6 Brentwood
26.06.93	Mike Morrison L PTS 4 Earls Court
29.11.93	Mike Morrison W DREW 6 Ingatestone
09.02.94	Mark Antony W DIS 5 Brentwood

Career: 10 contests, won 7, lost 3.

Neil Haddock　　　　　　　Les Clark

Neil Haddock

Llanelli. *Born* Newport, 22 June, 1964
Former British S. Featherweight Champion.
Former Undefeated Welsh S. Featherweight
Champion. Ht. 5'6"
Manager Self

16.02.87	Mark Purcell L PTS 6 Gloucester
19.03.87	Rudy Valentino L PTS 6 Bethnal Green
01.04.87	Gary Cass W PTS 6 Southsea
30.04.87	Carl Merrett W PTS 6 Newport
26.05.87	Joey Jacobs L PTS 8 Oldham
01.10.87	Lee Amass W RSC 4 Croydon
08.12.87	Mike Russell W PTS 8 Plymouth
17.02.88	B. F. Williams L PTS 8 Bethnal Green
24.02.88	Peter Till L PTS 8 Aberavon
08.03.88	Andrew Furlong L PTS 6 Holborn
30.03.88	Richard Adams W PTS 6 Bethnal Green
11.04.88	Mike Durvan L RSC 4 Mayfair
01.12.88	Michael Driscoll DREW 6 Gravesend
22.03.89	Lee Amass W RSC 5 Sheppey
18.09.90	Ditau Molefyane L RTD 5 Wolverhampton
18.10.90	Mark Ramsey W RSC 5 Birmingham
19.11.90	Steve Robinson L RSC 9 Cardiff
20.11.91	Barrie Kelley W PTS 6 Cardiff

Bobby Guynan　　　　　　　Les Clark

17.12.91	Andy Deabreu W RSC 3 Cardiff
11.05.92	Steve Robinson W PTS 10 Llanelli *(Vacant Welsh S. Featherweight Title)*
13.10.92	Michael Armstrong W RSC 6 Bury *(British S. Featherweight Title Challenge)*
01.12.92	Harry Escott W PTS 10 Liverpool
25.07.93	Steve Walker W RSC 7 Oldham *(British S. Featherweight Title Defence)*
01.10.93	J. T. Williams W PTS 10 Cardiff
23.03.94	Floyd Havard L RSC 10 Cardiff *(British S. Featherweight Title Defence)*
14.05.94	Jacobin Yoma L RTD 6 Cayenne, French Guyana *(European S. Featherweight Title Challenge)*

Career: 26 contests, won 14, drew 1, lost 11.

Nigel Haddock

Llanelli. *Born* Llanelli, 8 August, 1966
Featherweight. Ht. 5'5½"
Manager G. Davies

13.02.86	Paul Timmons L PTS 6 Digbeth
26.03.86	Paul Parry W PTS 6 Swansea

10.04.86	Ginger Staples W PTS 6 Weston super Mare
23.04.86	Nigel Senior W PTS 6 Stoke
19.05.86	Nigel Senior DREW 6 Nottingham
03.06.86	Albert Masih W RTD 3 Fulham
30.07.86	Tony Rahman W RSC 2 Ebbw Vale
01.10.86	Wayne Weekes L PTS 6 Lewisham
29.10.86	Nigel Senior W PTS 6 Ebbw Vale
26.11.86	Mark Reefer L RTD 3 Lewisham
15.04.87	Ginger Staples W RSC 5 Carmarthen
19.10.87	Gary Maxwell L PTS 8 Nottingham
05.11.87	John Maloney W RTD 4 Bethnal Green
18.11.87	Richie Foster W RSC 7 Bethnal Green
20.04.88	Patrick Kamy W PTS 6 Muswell Hill
02.11.88	Freddy Cruz L PTS 8 Paola, Italy
26.11.88	Maurizio Stecca L RTD 2 Forli, Italy
11.12.89	John Naylor W RSC 5 Nottingham
14.03.90	Kevin Pritchard DREW 6 Stoke
22.04.90	Ditau Molefyane L PTS 10 Spings, South Africa
30.03.93	Edward Lloyd W RTD 4 Cardiff
10.07.93	Alan Levene W RSC 5 Cardiff
30.11.93	Paul Harvey L RSC 3 Cardiff
20.05.94	Peter Harris L PTS 10 Neath *(Vacant Welsh Featherweight Title)*

Career: 24 contests, won 13, drew 2, lost 9.

Mark Hale

Nuneaton. *Born* Nuneaton, 13 October, 1969
L. Heavyweight. Ht. 5'11"
Manager Self

07.10.91 Andy Manning L PTS 6 Liverpool
07.11.91 Marc Rowley W PTS 6 Peterborough
15.01.92 Paul Murray W PTS 6 Stoke
25.03.92 Marc Rowley W PTS 6 Hinckley
11.05.92 Martin Jolley L PTS 6 Coventry
21.05.92 Tony Colclough DREW 6 Cradley Heath
01.06.92 Tony Colclough L PTS 6 Solihull
05.10.92 Martin Jolley L RSC 4 Bardon
16.03.93 Andrew Flute L RSC 2 Wolverhampton
11.05.93 Earl Ling W RSC 2 Norwich
08.12.93 Dean Ashton L RSC 1 Stoke
25.05.94 Steve Loftus L PTS 6 Stoke
Career: 12 contests, won 4, drew 1, lost 7.

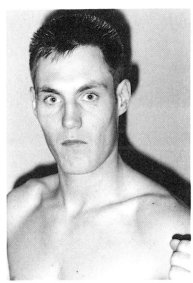

Mark Hale   Les Clark

Eddie Haley

South Shields. *Born* South Shields, 25 August, 1965
L. Middleweight. Ht. 5'9"
Manager T. Callighan

06.06.94 Brian Dunn W PTS 6 Glasgow
Career: 1 contest, won 1.

Micky Hall

Ludworth. *Born* Ludworth, 23 April, 1967
Lightweight. Ht. 5'8"
Manager T. Conroy

03.03.92 Mick Holmes W RSC 2 Houghton le Spring
11.03.92 G. G. Goddard DREW 6 Solihull
28.04.92 Jamie Davidson L PTS 6 Houghton le Spring
19.09.92 Mark Geraghty L PTS 6 Glasgow
12.10.92 Leo Turner W RSC 5 Bradford
18.11.92 Alan Ingle W RSC 3 Solihull
09.03.93 Kevin McKenzie L PTS 6 Hartlepool
17.04.93 John T. Kelly DREW 4 Washington

06.05.93 Brian Wright W PTS 6 Hartlepool
01.06.93 Kevin McKillan L PTS 6 Manchester
27.09.93 Paul Hughes W PTS 6 Manchester
04.10.93 Michael Alexander W CO 1 Bradford
12.11.93 Tony Foster L PTS 8 Hull
02.12.93 Kevin McKenzie W PTS 4 Hartlepool
10.02.94 Jimmy Phelan W PTS 6 Hull
02.03.94 Charlie Kane L RSC 2 Glasgow
27.04.94 Phil Found L RSC 5 Solihull
06.06.94 Kevin McKillan L PTS 6 Manchester
Career: 18 contests, won 8, drew 2, lost 8.

Nick Hall

Darlington. *Born* Darlington, 9 November, 1968
Welterweight. Ht. 5'9"
Manager M. Williamson

14.09.89 Paul Charters W PTS 6 Motherwell
24.10.89 Paul Day L CO 4 Watford
21.03.90 Mark Antony W PTS 6 Solihull
03.04.90 Steve Griffith W RSC 2 Canvey Island
26.04.90 Michael Ayers L CO 3 Wandsworth
03.10.90 Mike Morrison W PTS 8 Solihull
18.10.90 Peter Till L PTS 6 Birmingham
03.11.93 Young Gully W RSC 2 Bristol
25.01.94 Nick Appiah W PTS 4 Piccadilly
Career: 9 contests, won 6, lost 3

Simon Hamblett

Walsall. *Born* Walsall, 10 October, 1966
L. Welterweight. Ht. 5'8"
Manager W. Tyler

24.02.92 Jamie Morris DREW 6 Coventry
11.03.92 Mark Antony L CO 1 Stoke
09.12.92 Mark Allen DREW 6 Stoke
09.02.93 Mark Allen L PTS 6 Wolverhampton
23.02.93 Mark Allen W PTS 6 Doncaster
19.04.93 Kevin McKillan L CO 2 Manchester
07.06.93 Robbie Sivyer L PTS 6 Walsall
13.10.93 Shaun Shinkwin L PTS 6 Watford
02.12.93 Paul Robinson L RSC 2 Walsall
09.02.94 P. J. Gallagher L RSC 1 Bethnal Green
07.04.94 Paul Bowen L PTS 6 Walsall
Career: 11 contests, won 1, drew 2, lost 8.

Paul Hanlon

Birmingham. *Born* Birmingham, 25 May, 1962
S. Middleweight. Ht. 5'11"
Manager Self

18.11.86 Kevin Roper L RTD 5 Swansea
18.03.87 Tony Behan L PTS 4 Stoke
28.06.90 David Radford L RSC 2 Birmingham
18.09.90 Gary Osborne L RTD 2 Wolverhampton
17.10.90 Mike Betts L RTD 2 Stoke
04.03.91 Tony Behan L PTS 6 Birmingham
18.03.91 Willy James W CO 1 Derby
10.04.91 Lee Prudden L PTS 6 Wolverhampton
24.04.91 Dean Allen L PTS 6 Aberavon
13.05.91 Lee Prudden L PTS 6 Birmingham
23.05.91 Lee Prudden W PTS 6 Southampton
10.06.91 Jason Frieze W RSC 2 Manchester
10.09.91 Richard Carter L RSC 3 Wolverhampton
22.01.92 Lee Prudden W RSC 4 Stoke
20.02.92 Glen Payton L PTS 6 Oakengates
27.04.92 Joey Peters L CO 2 Mayfair
21.09.92 Tim Robinson W PTS 6 Cleethorpes
05.10.92 John J. Cooke L RSC 1 Bardon

24.11.92 Chris Nurse W PTS 6 Wolverhampton
07.12.92 Zak Goldman W PTS 6 Birmingham
10.02.93 Mark Baker L RSC 2 Lewisham
08.06.93 Martin Jolley L PTS 6 Derby
22.09.93 Greg Scott-Briggs L PTS 6 Chesterfield
01.10.93 Joe Calzaghe L RSC 1 Cardiff
Career: 24 contests, won 7, lost 17.

Anthony Hanna

Birmingham. *Born* Birmingham, 22 September, 1974
Flyweight. Ht. 5'6"
Manager Self

19.11.92 Nick Tooley L PTS 6 Evesham
10.12.92 Darren Fifield L RSC 6 Bethnal Green
11.05.93 Tiger Singh W PTS 6 Norwich
24.05.93 Lyndon Kershaw L PTS 6 Bradford
16.09.93 Chris Lyons W PTS 6 Southwark
06.10.93 Tiger Singh W PTS 6 Solihull
03.11.93 Mickey Cantwell L PTS 8 Bristol
25.01.94 Marty Chestnut W PTS 4 Piccadilly
10.02.94 Allan Mooney W RTD 1 Glasgow
13.04.94 Allan Mooney L PTS 6 Glasgow
22.04.94 Jesper David Jenson L PTS 6 Aalborg, Denmark
Career: 11 contests, won 5, lost 6.

Anthony Hanna   Les Clark

Japhet Hans

Leeds. *Born* Nigeria, 5 May, 1973
L. Middleweight. Ht. 5'11"
Manager P. Coleman

02.12.93 Jimmy Alston L PTS 6 Sheffield
28.02.94 Carl Smith L RSC 4 Manchester
24.05.94 Mark Jay W RSC 1 Sunderland
28.06.94 Darren Sweeney L PTS 6 Edgbaston
Career: 4 contests, won 1, lost 3.

Chris Harbourne

Birmingham. *Born* Birmingham, 24 November, 1962
Cruiserweight. Ht. 6'3¼"
Manager Self

10.10.84	Alex Romeo W PTS 6 Stoke
26.10.84	Alex Romeo W PTS 6 Wolverhampton
24.03.86	Gypsy Carman L PTS 6 Mayfair
10.04.86	Dave Shelton W CO 1 Leicester
17.04.86	Tommy Taylor L PTS 6 Wolverhampton
28.09.87	Gary McConnell W RSC 3 Dulwich
12.10.87	Jess Harding L RSC 4 Mayfair
15.02.88	Eric Cardouza L PTS 6 Mayfair
02.02.89	Deka Williams W PTS 6 Wolverhampton
01.05.93	Zelko Mavrovic L RSC 1 Berlin, Germany
08.06.93	Johnny Moth DREW 6 Derby
28.07.93	Justin Fortune L CO 3 Brixton

Career: 12 contests, won 5, drew 1, lost 6.

Fran Harding

Liverpool. *Born* Liverpool, 5 September, 1966
S. Middleweight. Ht. 6'0½"
Manager Self

27.07.87	Johnny Taupau W PTS 6 Sydney, Australia
04.05.88	B. K. Bennett W RSC 1 Wembley

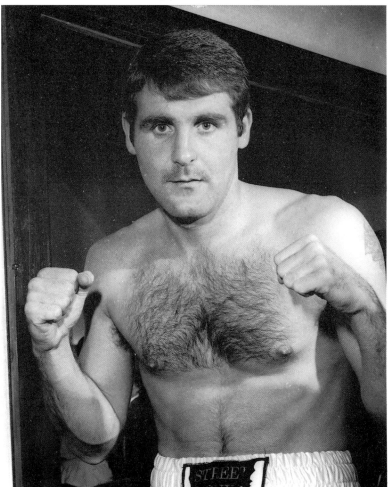

Fran Harding

Harry Goodwin

14.12.88	Steve Foster W PTS 6 Kirkby
04.05.90	Quinn Paynter W PTS 6 Liverpool
30.09.91	Lee Crocker W RSC 3 Kensington
25.09.92	Terry Magee W PTS 6 Liverpool
23.10.92	Shamus Casey W PTS 6 Liverpool
20.11.92	Marvin O'Brien W RSC 4 Liverpool
18.12.93	John Kaighin W PTS 6 Manchester

Career: 9 contests, won 9.

John Harewood

Newcastle. *Born* Ipswich, 23 February, 1964
Heavyweight. Ht. 6'3½"
Manager Self

29.11.90	Carlton Headley W RSC 5 Marton
06.04.91	Clifton Mitchell L RSC 2 Darlington
01.08.91	Clifton Mitchell L CO 1 Dewsbury
05.03.92	J. A. Bugner L PTS 4 Battersea
27.05.92	Freddy Soentgen L PTS 6 Cologne, Germany
07.10.92	Gary Charlton W PTS 6 Sunderland
30.10.92	Clement Salles W RSC 4 Istres, France
17.12.92	Dermot Gascoyne L RSC 5 Barking
02.02.93	Wayne Buck W RSC 3 Derby

20.03.93	Bernd Friedrich L RSC 4 Dusseldorf, Germany
19.05.93	Vance Idiens W CO 3 Sunderland
26.05.93	Clifton Mitchell L RSC 4 Mansfield
29.06.93	Scott Welch L RSC 5 Mayfair
17.09.93	Mikael Lindblad L RTD 3 Copenhagen, Denmark
01.12.93	Kevin McBride L RSC 3 Bethnal Green

Career: 15 contests, won 5, lost 10.

Mark Hargreaves

Burnley. *Born* Burnley, 13 September, 1970
S. Featherweight. Ht. 5'4"
Manager Self

11.09.91	Dave Campbell W RSC 4 Stoke
23.10.91	Dave Martin W PTS 6 Stoke
10.02.92	Dennis Oakes L RSC 3 Liverpool
30.03.92	Ronnie Stephenson L PTS 6 Coventry
27.04.92	Ady Benton L PTS 6 Bradford
01.06.92	Des Gargano W PTS 6 Manchester
11.09.92	Shaun Anderson L PTS 6 Glasgow
07.10.92	Mike Deveney W RSC 7 Glasgow
14.10.92	Yusuf Vorajee W RSC 4 Stoke
19.11.92	Greg Upton W RSC 3 Evesham
28.11.92	John White L PTS 4 Manchester
20.01.93	Jonjo Irwin L RSC 4 Solihull
26.04.93	Mario Culpeper L PTS 6 Manchester
01.06.93	Paul Wynn W PTS 6 Manchester
01.12.93	Justin Murphy L RSC 4 Bethnal Green
19.03.94	Wayne McCullough L RSC 3 Millwall
06.06.94	Mike Deveney L PTS 6 Manchester

Career: 17 contests, won 7, lost 10.

Robert Harper

Doncaster. *Born* Doncaster, 1 April, 1969
S. Middleweight. Ht. 5'8"
Manager H. Hayes

16.09.93	Smokey Enison L RSC 1 Hull
02.12.93	Kevin Bailey L PTS 6 Sheffield
24.02.94	Dave Proctor L PTS 6 Hull
08.03.94	Chris Nurse L PTS 6 Edgbaston
25.04.94	Lee Blundell L RSC 2 Bury

Career: 5 contests, lost 5.

Matthew Harris

Aldridge. *Born* Brownhills, 2 May, 1971
Bantamweight. Ht. 5'7"
Manager M. Shinfield

23.03.94	Yusuf Vorajee W PTS 6 Stoke
13.06.94	Marcus Duncan W RSC 1 Bradford

Career: 2 contests, won 2.

Peter Harris

Swansea. *Born* Swansea, 23 August, 1962
Welsh Featherweight Champion. Former British Featherweight Champion. Ht. 5'6½"
Manager Self

28.02.83	Dave Pratt L PTS 6 Birmingham
25.04.83	Jim Harvey DREW 6 Aberdeen
27.05.83	Brett Styles W PTS 8 Swansea
20.06.83	Danny Knaggs W PTS 6 Piccadilly
19.12.83	Kevin Howard W PTS 8 Swansea
06.02.84	Ivor Jones DREW 8 Bethnal Green
27.03.84	Johnny Dorey W RSC 6 Bethnal Green
13.06.84	Keith Wallace W PTS 10 Aberavon
28.09.84	Ray Minus L PTS 10 Nassau, Bahamas
21.11.84	John Farrell L PTS 8 Solihull

Peter Harris

20.03.85	Kid Sumali W PTS 8 Solihull
09.05.85	John Feeney L PTS 10 Warrington
09.11.85	Antoine Montero L PTS 10 Grenoble, France
26.03.86	Steve Pollard W RSC 3 Swansea
22.04.86	Roy Webb W RTD 8 Belfast
18.11.86	Kelvin Smart W PTS 10 Swansea *(Vacant Welsh Featherweight Title)*
30.04.87	Albert Parr W RSC 3 Newport
30.09.87	John Farrell W PTS 12 Solihull *(Final Elim. British Featherweight Title)*
15.12.87	Roy Williams W RSC 2 Cardiff
24.02.88	Kevin Taylor W PTS 12 Aberavon *(Vacant British Featherweight Title)*
18.05.88	Paul Hodkinson L RSC 12 Aberavon *(British Featherweight Title Defence)*
06.09.89	Paul Hodkinson L RSC 9 Aberavon *(British & European Featherweight Title Challenge)*
24.04.91	Colin Lynch W PTS 8 Aberavon
18.07.91	Steve Robinson L PTS 10 Cardiff *(Welsh Featherweight Title Defence)*
05.06.92	Stephane Haccoun L PTS 8 Marseille, France
22.12.92	Paul Harvey L PTS 8 Mayfair
21.12.93	Jonjo Irwin L PTS 6 Mayfair
20.05.94	Nigel Haddock W PTS 10 Neath *(Vacant Welsh Featherweight Title)*

Career: 28 contests, won 15, drew 2, lost 11.

Simon Harris

Hanwell. *Born* Isleworth, 26 December, 1961
L. Heavyweight. Ht. 5'11"
Manager D. Gunn

28.09.84	Douglas Isles W RSC 2 Longford
23.10.84	Ronnie Fraser W RSC 6 Battersea
20.11.84	Harry Andrews W RSC 2 Merton
30.11.84	Gordon Stacey W CO 2 Longford
05.02.85	Sean O'Phoenix W PTS 6 Battersea
23.03.85	Lou Gent W PTS 6 Strand
04.05.85	Geoff Rymer W PTS 6 Queensway
20.09.85	Dave Owens L PTS 6 Longford
10.11.86	John Williams W PTS 6 Longford
21.11.86	Lee Davis W RSC 3 Maidenhead
03.12.86	Tony Wilson L RTD 6 Muswell Hill
29.11.88	Alan Baptiste W RSC 4 Battersea
29.01.91	Richard Bustin W RSC 3 Wisbech
03.07.91	Nicky Piper L RSC 1 Reading
11.02.92	Garry Delaney DREW 8 Barking
14.04.93	Steve McCarthy W RSC 5 Kensington
31.08.93	Carlos Christie W CO 3 Croydon
30.09.93	Trevor Ambrose W PTS 6 Hayes
01.12.93	Maurice Core L RSC 11 Bethnal Green *(British L. Heavyweight Title Challenge)*
09.04.94	Garry Delaney L CO 6 Bethnal Green *(WBO Penta-Continental & Southern Area L. Heavyweight Title Challenge)*

Career: 20 contests, won 14, drew 1, lost 5.

Jason Hart

Bromley. *Born* Beckenham, 23 January, 1970
Middleweight. Ht. 5'9½"
Manager G. Steene

02.06.94	Paul Matthews L RSC 3 Tooting

Career: 1 contest, lost 1.

Jason Hart   Les Clark

Craig Hartwell

Rugby. *Born* Rugby, 24 August, 1968
Welterweight. Ht. 5'9"
Manager J. Griffin

11.12.91	Brian Coleman DREW 6 Leicester
25.03.92	Benji Joseph L PTS 6 Hinckley
18.05.92	Dean Hiscox L PTS 6 Bardon
19.10.93	Warren Bowers L PTS 6 Cleethorpes

Career: 4 contests, drew 1, lost 3.

Paul Harvey

Ilford. *Born* Islington, 10 November, 1964
Featherweight. Former Commonwealth S.
Featherweight Champion. Ht. 5'8"
Manager Self

04.10.89	Steve Walker DREW 6 Basildon
16.01.90	Darren Weller W RSC 6 Cardiff
06.03.90	James Milne W PTS 6 Bethnal Green
03.04.90	James Hunter W CO 2 Canvey Island
23.04.90	Marvin Stone W PTS 6 Crystal Palace
20.06.90	Brian Robb W PTS 6 Basildon
24.10.90	Brian Robb W RSC 2 Dudley
12.12.90	Miguel Matthews W PTS 6 Basildon
09.04.91	Alan McKay W RSC 4 Mayfair
24.04.91	Peter Gabbitus W RSC 5 Preston
26.10.91	Colin Lynch W RSC 1 Brentwood
12.11.91	Hugh Forde W RSC 3 Wolverhampton
	(Commonwealth S. Featherweight Title
	Challenge)
07.12.91	Sugar Gibiliru W PTS 12 Manchester
	(Commonwealth S. Featherweight Title
	Defence)
11.02.92	Tony Pep L PTS 12 Cardiff
	(Commonwealth S. Featherweight Title
	Defence)
02.06.92	Regilio Tuur L CO 5 Rotterdam,
	Holland
13.10.92	Brian Robb W RSC 2 Mayfair
22.12.92	Peter Harris W PTS 8 Mayfair
19.01.93	Steve Robinson L PTS 12 Cardiff
	(Vacant WBA Penta-Continental
	Featherweight Title)
19.05.93	Kelton McKenzie W RSC 7 Leicester
05.10.93	Karl Taylor L PTS 6 Mayfair
30.11.93	Nigel Haddock W RSC 3 Cardiff
24.01.94	Wilson Docherty L PTS 12 Glasgow
	(Vacant WBO Penta-Continental
	Featherweight Title)

Career: 22 contests, won 16, drew 1, lost 5.

Lee Heggs

Leicester. *Born* Leicester, 30 August, 1968
Welterweight. Ht. 5'8"
Manager M. Shinfield

20.09.93	Dave Madden L PTS 6 Northampton

Career: 1 contest, lost 1.

Chris Henry   Les Clark

Chris Henry

Tottenham. *Born* London, 21 July, 1966
Cruiserweight. Ht. 6'1"
Manager A. Urry

06.11.93	Chris Okoh L RSC 2 Bethnal Green

Career: 1 contest, lost 1.

Ian Henry

Newcastle. *Born* Gateshead, 8 May, 1967
L. Heavyweight. Ht. 6'1½"
Manager T. Conroy

26.04.90	Willy James W RSC 3 Manchester
15.05.90	Mark Whitehouse W RSC 4 South
	Shields
24.09.90	Paul Hendrick L PTS 6 Manchester
19.11.90	Shaun McCrory W PTS 6 Manchester
14.12.90	Eddie Collins W PTS 6 Peterborough
21.01.91	Shaun McCrory W PTS 6 Glasgow
28.01.91	Simon McDougall L PTS 8 Bradford
18.03.91	Ian Vokes W RSC 2 Manchester
25.03.91	Dave Lawrence W PTS 6 Bradford
10.05.91	Simon McDougall W PTS 6 Gateshead
10.10.91	Chris Walker W PTS 6 Gateshead
14.11.91	Dave Owens W PTS 8 Gateshead
27.11.91	John Oxenham W PTS 6 Marton
11.03.92	Simon McDougall W PTS 8 Solihull
05.05.92	Glenn Campbell L RSC 1 Preston
23.10.92	Lee Archer W RTD 1 Gateshead
01.03.93	Lee Prudden W PTS 6 Bradford
17.03.93	Lee Archer L PTS 6 Stoke
11.06.93	Art Stacey W PTS 6 Gateshead
22.09.93	Mohammed Isaacs L RSC 5 Eldorado
	Park, South Africa
02.12.93	Paul McCarthy W PTS 6 Hartlepool
19.03.94	Gary Ballard L RSC 4 Millwall
21.04.94	Terry French L PTS 10 Gateshead
	(Northern Area L. Heavyweight Title
	Challenge)

Career: 23 contests, won 16, lost 7.

Michael Hermon

Birmingham. *Born* Birmingham, 29 April,
1968
S. Featherweight. Ht. 5'6"
Manager E. Cashmore

04.03.94	Trevor Royal W PTS 6 Weston super
	Mare

Career: 1 contest, won 1.

Peter Hickenbottom

Great Wyrley. *Born* Walsall, 20 June, 1964
L. Welterweight. Ht. 5'8"
Manager P. Cowdell/R. Gray

23.05.94	Shane Sheridan W PTS 6 Walsall

Career: 1 contest, won 1.

Brian Hickey

Sheffield. *Born* Sheffield, 24 February,
1973
Welterweight. Ht. 5'9"
Manager B. Ingle

21.11.91	Tony Doyle L PTS 6 Ilkeston
06.02.92	Michael Clynch L DIS 5 Peterborough
21.10.92	Dean Amory L PTS 6 Stoke
12.11.92	Floyd Churchill L CO 1 Liverpool
27.02.93	Gary Thornhill L CO 4 Ellesmere Port
01.12.93	Paul Denton L CO 1 Kensington
15.04.94	Dave Curtis L PTS 6 Hull

Career: 7 contests, lost 7.

Tim Hill

North Shields. *Born* North Shields, 23
January, 1974
L. Welterweight. Ht. 5'9"
Manager T. Conroy

09.11.92	Fred Reeve W CO 4 Bradford
25.01.93	Michael Alexander L PTS 6 Bradford
22.02.93	Garry Burrell W PTS 6 Glasgow
29.03.93	Hugh Collins L PTS 6 Glasgow
08.11.93	Leo Turner W RTD 4 Bradford
17.02.94	Patrick Parton L PTS 6 Walsall
16.05.94	Robert Howard W CO 2 Morecambe

Career: 7 contests, won 4, lost 3.

Gary Hiscox

Dudley. *Born* Dudley, 25 May, 1970
L. Welterweight. Ht. 5'7¾"
Manager C. Flute

14.10.92	Alan Ingle L PTS 6 Stoke
12.11.92	Shane Sheridan W PTS 6 Stafford
27.01.93	Dave Madden W PTS 6 Stoke
03.03.93	Erwin Edwards W PTS 6 Solihull
26.06.93	Mark Tibbs L RSC 4 Earls Court
28.10.93	Dean Bramhall W RSC 5 Walsall
04.11.93	Paul Hughes W PTS 6 Stafford
25.11.93	Mark Legg L RSC 3 Tynemouth
01.03.94	Gary Cogan W PTS 6 Dudley

Career: 9 contests, won 6, lost 3.

Paul Hitch

Wingate. *Born* Hartlepool, 7 May, 1968
S. Middleweight. Ht. 5'9½"
Manager T. Conroy

10.05.91	Tony Kosova W RTD 1 Gateshead
13.05.91	Terry Johnson W PTS 6 Marton
17.06.91	Max McCracken W PTS 6 Edgbaston
22.10.91	Chris Walker W PTS 6 Hartlepool
14.11.91	Paul Burton W CO 2 Gateshead
12.12.91	Doug Calderwood W PTS 6 Hartlepool
03.03.92	Simon McDougall W PTS 6 Houghton
	le Spring
28.04.92	Chris Walker L RSC 2 Houghton le
	Spring
10.09.92	Griff Jones W RSC 2 Sunderland
23.10.92	Paul Burton W RSC 5 Gateshead
06.03.93	Bobby Mack W PTS 6 Glasgow
17.04.93	Richard Bustin L PTS 6 Washington
15.09.93	Marvin O'Brien W PTS 4 Newcastle
11.11.93	Derek Wormald L RSC 6 Burnley
09.02.94	Darron Griffiths L PTS 6 Bethnal
	Green
24.02.94	Jimmy Tyers W PTS 6 Hull
17.03.94	Martin Jolley L RSC 2 Lincoln

Career: 17 contests, won 12, lost 5.

Mick Hoban (Massie)

Glasgow. *Born* Burnley, 25 July, 1967
Welterweight. Ht. 5'9"
Manager J. Doughty

19.04.89	Steve Booth L PTS 6 Doncaster
13.10.92	Danny Kett W PTS 6 Bury
07.12.92	Lee Soar W PTS 6 Manchester
15.02.93	Brian Wright W PTS 6 Manchester
28.06.93	Michael Alexander L PTS 6
	Morecambe
13.09.93	Brian Coleman W PTS 6 Middleton
29.11.93	Pete Roberts W RSC 4 Manchester
19.01.94	Young Gully W RSC 3 Solihull

Career: 8 contests, won 6, lost 2.

Paul Hodkinson (left), shown here against Marcos Villasana, may have reached the end of the road following his defeat at the hands of WBO champion, Steve Robinson

Paul Hodkinson

Liverpool. *Born* Liverpool, 14 September, 1965
Former WBC Featherweight Champion. Former Undefeated British & European Featherweight Champion. Ht. 5'4"
Manager B. Eastwood

19.07.86	Mark Champney W CO 2 Wembley	
17.09.86	Phil Lashley W RSC 2 Kensington	
29.09.86	Les Remikie W RTD 4 Mayfair	
29.10.86	Craig Windsor W CO 2 Belfast	
17.01.87	Steve Sammy Sims W CO 5 Belfast	
26.02.87	Kamel Djadda W RSC 4 Bethnal Green	
25.04.87	Russell Jones W RSC 6 Belfast	
31.07.87	Tomas Arguelles DREW 8 Panama City, Panama	
19.10.87	Tomas Arguelles W CO 6 Belfast	
03.12.87	Marcus Smith W RSC 7 Belfast	
27.01.88	Richie Foster W RSC 3 Belfast	
18.05.88	Peter Harris W RSC 12 Aberavon	
	(British Featherweight Title Challenge)	
14.12.88	Kevin Taylor W RSC 2 Kirkby	
	(British Featherweight Title Defence)	

18.01.89	Johnny Carter W CO 1 Kensington	
12.04.89	Raymond Armand W RSC 2 Belfast	
	(Vacant European Featherweight Title)	
06.09.89	Peter Harris W RSC 9 Aberavon	
	(British & European Featherweight Title Defence)	
13.12.89	Farid Benredjeb W RSC 8 Kirkby	
	(European Featherweight Title Defence)	
28.03.90	Eduardo Montoya W RSC 3 Manchester	
	(Elim. IBF Featherweight Title)	
02.06.90	Marcos Villasana L RSC 8 Manchester	
	(Vacant WBC Featherweight Title)	
31.10.90	Guy Bellehigue W RSC 3 Wembley	
	(European Featherweight Title Defence)	
13.11.91	Marcos Villasana W PTS 12 Belfast	
	(WBC Featherweight Title Challenge)	
25.04.92	Steve Cruz W RSC 3 Belfast	
	(WBC Featherweight Title Defence)	
12.09.92	Fabrice Benichou W RSC 10 Blagnac, France	
	(WBC Featherweight Title Defence)	
03.02.93	Ricardo Cepeda W RTD 4 Earls Court	
	(WBC Featherweight Title Defence)	

28.04.93	Gregorio Vargas L RTD 7 Dublin	
	(WBC Featherweight Title Defence)	
12.03.94	Steve Robinson L CO 12 Cardiff	
	(WBO Featherweight Title Challenge)	

Career: 26 contests, won 22, drew 1, lost 3.

Andy Holligan

Liverpool. *Born* Liverpool, 6 June, 1967
Former British & Commonwealth L. Welterweight Champion. Ht. 5'5¾"
Manager F. Warren

19.10.87	Glyn Rhodes W PTS 6 Belfast	
03.12.87	Jimmy Thornton W RTD 2 Belfast	
27.01.88	Andrew Morgan W RSC 5 Belfast	
26.03.88	Tony Richards W RSC 2 Belfast	
08.06.88	David Maw W RSC 1 Sheffield	
19.10.88	Lenny Gloster W PTS 8 Belfast	
14.12.88	Sugar Gibiliru W PTS 8 Kirkby	
16.03.89	Jeff Connors W RSC 5 Southwark	
19.09.89	Billy Buchanan W RSC 5 Belfast	
25.10.89	Tony Adams W RSC 3 Wembley	
26.09.90	Mike Durvan W CO 1 Mayfair	
31.10.90	Eric Carroyez W RTD 2 Wembley	
17.04.91	Pat Ireland W RSC 2 Kensington	
16.05.91	Simon Eubank W RSC 2 Liverpool	

20.06.91	Tony Ekubia W PTS 12 Liverpool
	(British & Commonwealth L.
	Welterweight Title Challenge)
28.11.91	Steve Larrimore W RSC 8 Liverpool
	(Commonwealth L. Welterweight Title
	Defence)
27.02.92	Tony McKenzie W RSC 3 Liverpool
	(British & Commonwealth L.
	Welterweight Title Defence)
15.09.92	Tony Ekubia W CO 7 Liverpool
	(British & Commonwealth L.
	Welterweight Title Defence)
07.10.92	Dwayne Swift W PTS 10 Sunderland
12.11.92	Mark Smith W PTS 10 Liverpool
26.05.93	Lorenzo Garcia W RSC 2 Mansfield
18.12.93	Julio Cesar Chavez L RTD 5 Puebla, Mexico
	(WBC L. Welterweight Title Challenge)
26.02.94	Massimo Bertozzi W CO 5 Earls Court
25.05.94	Ross Hale L RSC 3 Bristol
	(British & Commonwealth L.
	Welterweight Title Defence)

Career: 24 contests, won 22, lost 2.

Dean Hollington

West Ham. *Born* Plaistow, 25 February, 1969
L. Welterweight. Ht. 5'9"
Manager A. Smith

20.02.90	Dave Jenkins W PTS 4 Millwall
06.04.90	Marcel Herbert W PTS 6 Stevenage
25.09.90	Andre Marcel Cleak W RSC 5 Millwall
12.02.91	Andy Robins W RSC 4 Basildon
07.03.91	Dave Jenkins W PTS 6 Basildon
17.04.91	Jim Lawlor W PTS 6 Kensington
23.10.91	John Smith W PTS 6 Bethnal Green
13.11.91	Jim Lawlor W PTS 6 Bethnal Green
11.02.92	Nigel Bradley W PTS 6 Barking
02.04.92	Tony Gibbs W CO 1 Basildon
16.05.92	Rick Bushell W RSC 2 Muswell Hill
10.02.93	John O'Johnson W PTS 6 Lewisham
26.04.93	Chris Saunders L RSC 5 Lewisham
22.09.93	Mark O'Callaghan W CO 1 Wembley
07.12.93	Jonathan Thaxton L RSC 3 Bethnal Green

Career: 15 contests, won 13, lost 2.

Donnie Hood

Glasgow. *Born* Glasgow, 3 June, 1963
Former Undefeated WBC International & Scottish Bantamweight Champion. Ht. 5'5"
Manager Self

22.09.86	Stewart Fishermac W PTS 6 Glasgow
29.09.86	Keith Ward W PTS 6 Glasgow
08.12.86	Jamie McBride DREW 8 Glasgow
22.12.86	Keith Ward L PTS 8 Glasgow
27.01.87	Chris Clarkson W PTS 6 Glasgow
09.02.87	Danny Porter W RSC 4 Glasgow
24.02.87	Danny Lee W PTS 8 Glasgow
07.09.87	Kid Sumali W PTS 8 Glasgow
15.09.87	David Ingram L PTS 8 Batley
26.10.87	Jimmy Lee W PTS 8 Glasgow
25.11.87	Brian Holmes W PTS 10 Bellahouston
	(Vacant Scottish Bantamweight Title)
28.03.88	Nigel Crook W CO 2 Glasgow
12.05.88	Eyup Can L PTS 8 Copenhagen, Denmark
17.06.88	Fransie Badenhorst L RSC 7 Durban, South Africa
05.09.88	Gerry McBride W RTD 7 Glasgow
25.10.88	Graham O'Malley W RSC 9 Hartlepool
	(Elim. British Bantamweight Title)

06.03.89	Francisco Paco Garcia W RSC 6 Glasgow
28.03.89	John Vasquez W RSC 5 Glasgow
27.06.89	Ray Minus L RSC 6 Glasgow
	(Commonwealth Bantamweight Title Challenge)
22.01.90	Dean Lynch W PTS 8 Glasgow
26.03.90	Keith Wallace W RTD 8 Glasgow
	(Elim. British Bantamweight Title)
09.10.90	Samuel Duran W PTS 12 Glasgow
	(WBC International Bantamweight Title Challenge)
10.12.90	David Moreno W RSC 4 Glasgow
25.01.91	Dave Buxton W RSC 5 Shotts
05.03.91	Virgilio Openio W PTS 12 Glasgow
	(WBC International Bantamweight Title Defence)
31.05.91	Willie Richardson W PTS 8 Glasgow
24.09.91	Rocky Commey W PTS 12 Glasgow
	(WBC International Bantamweight Title Defence)
24.10.91	Vinnie Ponzio W PTS 8 Glasgow
14.03.92	Johnny Bredahl L RSC 7 Copenhagen, Denmark
	(Vacant European Bantamweight Title)
29.05.92	Pete Buckley W PTS 8 Glasgow
25.01.93	Drew Docherty L PTS 12 Glasgow
	(British Bantamweight Title Challenge)
11.03.94	Kid McAuley W PTS 8 Glasgow

Career: 32 contests, won 24, drew 1, lost 7.

Ray Hood   Les Clark

Ray Hood

Crawley. *Born* Queensferry, 28 August, 1962
Former Undefeated Welsh Lightweight Champion. Ht. 5'8"
Manager Self

09.06.81	Alan Tombs DREW 6 Southend
29.06.81	Vince Griffin W RSC 3 Liverpool
16.09.81	Geoff Smart W RTD 4 Burslem
23.09.81	Winston Ho-Shing L PTS 6 Sheffield
06.10.81	Peter Flanagan W RSC 5 Liverpool
13.10.81	Alan Cooper DREW 6 Nantwich

28.10.81	Delroy Pearce W PTS 6 Burslem
03.11.81	Mark Crouch W CO 6 Southend
16.11.81	Winston Ho-Shing W PTS 6 Liverpool
27.01.82	Eric Wood W PTS 6 Stoke
16.02.82	Aidan Wake W CO 4 Leeds
29.03.82	Jimmy Bunclark W RSC 2 Liverpool
05.04.82	Jimmy Duncan L PTS 8 Bloomsbury
03.06.82	Delroy Pearce W PTS 8 Liverpool
30.06.82	Tommy Cook W PTS 8 Liverpool
01.11.82	Andy Thomas W PTS 8 Liverpool
04.03.83	Andy Thomas W PTS 10 Queensferry
	(Vacant Welsh Lightweight Title)
28.10.83	Jimmy Bunclark W RSC 8 Queensferry
14.11.83	Ken Foreman L PTS 8 Nantwich
22.11.83	Najib Daho L PTS 8 Manchester
15.03.84	Kevin Pritchard L PTS 8 Kirkby
06.04.84	Ian McLeod L RSC 2 Edinburgh
05.12.84	Dave Haggarty L PTS 6 Stoke
21.06.93	Anthony Wanza W PTS 6 Swindon
26.04.94	Jason Rowland L CO 1 Bethnal Green

Career: 25 contests, won 15, drew 2, lost 8.

Johnny Hooks

Nottingham. *Born* North Shields, 9 March, 1968
Cruiserweight. Ht. 6'1"
Manager J. Griffin

26.01.87	Young Gully L RSC 2 Nottingham
02.03.87	Jim Conley L RSC 2 Nottingham
18.02.94	Jim Pallatt W RSC 1 Leicester
07.04.94	Kevin Burton W PTS 6 Walsall
24.05.94	Dave Battey W PTS 6 Leicester

Career: 5 contests, won 3, lost 2.

Ron Hopley

Ripon. *Born* Ripon, 3 April, 1969
L. Middleweight. Ht. 5'8½"
Manager D. Mancini

27.11.91	William Beaton W RSC 2 Marton
23.01.92	Rick North W PTS 6 York
08.04.92	Steve Howden L PTS 6 Leeds
25.02.93	Rob Stevenson DREW 6 Bradford
07.04.93	Warren Stephens W PTS 6 Leeds
01.07.93	Rob Stevenson L PTS 6 York
07.10.93	Warren Bowers W PTS 6 York
28.02.94	Warren Bowers W RSC 1 Marton

Career: 8 contests, won 5, drew 1, lost 2.

Lennie Howard

Chelmsford. *Born* Jamaica, 5 January, 1959
Cruiserweight. Ht. 6'1"
Manager Self

28.11.83	Paul Foster W CO 2 Southwark
16.02.84	Gypsy Carman W RTD 1 Basildon
27.03.84	Alex Romeo W PTS 6 Bethnal Green
19.04.84	Robbie Turner W RSC 4 Basildon
19.11.84	Stuart Robinson L PTS 8 Eltham
31.01.85	Romal Ambrose W CO 6 Basildon
28.03.85	Jerry Golden W RSC 2 Basildon
24.04.85	Geoff Rymer W PTS 6 Shoreditch
26.06.85	Hugh Johnson L PTS 8 Basildon
30.10.85	Glazz Campbell W PTS 8 Basildon
27.02.86	John Moody L RSC 6 Bethnal Green
	(Vacant Southern Area L. Heavyweight Title)
24.04.86	T. P. Jenkins W CO 4 Bethnal Green
23.10.86	John Moody L RSC 2 Basildon
	(Southern Area L. Heavyweight Title Challenge)
20.12.86	Richard Caramanolis L RSC 1 St Ouen, France

24.02.87 Noel Magee L RSC 1 Ilford
08.10.87 Derek Angol L RSC 5 Bethnal Green
17.02.88 John Williams W RSC 5 Bethnal Green
24.03.88 Sean Daly W RSC 6 Bethnal Green
21.04.88 Winston Burnett W PTS 6 Bethnal Green
06.06.88 Johnny Nelson L CO 2 Mayfair
28.10.88 Abner Blackstock W PTS 8 Brentwood
16.02.89 Lou Gent L RSC 2 Battersea
(Vacant Southern Area Cruiserweight Title)
27.04.89 Magne Havnaa L RTD 3 Braedstrup, Denmark
06.06.89 Abner Blackstock W PTS 8 Chigwell
20.07.89 Francesco Terlizzi L PTS 6 Varese, Italy
02.10.89 Freddie Rafferty L PTS 10 Johannesburg, South Africa
16.12.89 Marcus Bott L CO 2 Pforzheim, Germany
26.09.90 Mick Queally L PTS 6 Mayfair
29.01.91 Herbie Hide L RSC 1 Wisbech
01.12.93 Denzil Browne L RSC 6 Kensington
26.01.94 Robert Norton L PTS 6 Birmingham
Career: 31 contests, won 14, lost 17.

Robert Howard

Morecambe. *Born* Morecambe, 3 August, 1967
L. Welterweight. Ht. 5'9"
Manager F. Harrington

29.11.93 Scott Smith L PTS 6 Manchester
16.05.94 Tim Hill L CO 2 Morecambe
Career: 2 contests, lost 2.

Steve Howden

Sheffield. *Born* Sheffield, 4 June, 1969
L. Welterweight. Ht. 5'8¾"
Manager B. Ingle

08.04.92 Ron Hopley W PTS 6 Leeds
01.06.92 Kevin McKillan L RSC 2 Manchester
07.07.92 Mike Morrison L CO 3 Bristol
01.10.92 Jimmy Reynolds L RTD 2 Telford
23.06.93 Shaba Edwards W RSC 1 Gorleston
11.08.93 Brian Coleman W RSC 4 Mansfield
30.11.93 Colin Anderson W PTS 6 Leicester
Career: 7 contests, won 4, lost 3.

John Hughes

Liverpool. *Born* Wrexham, 17 December, 1965
L. Middleweight. Ht. 5'7"
Manager D. Isaaman

02.06.94 Paolo Roberto L RSC 1 Tooting
Career: 1 contest, lost 1.

Paul Hughes

Manchester. *Born* Manchester, 1 December, 1966
L. Welterweight. Ht. 5'8"
Manager Self

09.10.91 Geoff Lawson W RSC 1 Marton
17.10.91 Tony Doyle W PTS 6 Mossley
13.11.91 Joey Moffat L RTD 4 Liverpool
01.06.92 Ty Zubair W PTS 6 Manchester
27.09.93 Micky Hall L PTS 6 Manchester
04.11.93 Gary Hiscox L PTS 6 Stafford
26.01.94 Chris Aston L PTS 6 Stoke

28.02.94 Michael Alexander L PTS 6 Manchester
Career: 8 contests, won 4, lost 4.

Norman Hutcheon

Leicester. *Born* Baillieston, 24 December, 1963
L. Middleweight. Ht. 5'8"
Manager J. Griffin

30.11.93 Prince Louis W PTS 6 Leicester
18.02.94 Balcar Singh W RSC 1 Leicester
24.05.94 Dennis Berry L RSC 2 Leicester
Career: 3 contests, won 2, lost 1.

Jason Hutson

Thame. *Born* London, 11 March, 1972
S. Featherweight. Ht. 5'6"
Manager W. Ball

15.02.93 Marco Fattore L PTS 6 Mayfair
29.04.93 Vince Burns L RSC 1 Hayes
31.08.93 Ian Reid L RSC 6 Croydon
09.12.93 Marco Fattore DREW 6 Watford
Career: 4 contests, drew 1, lost 3.

Cordwell Hylton

Walsall. *Born* Jamaica, 20 September, 1958
Midlands Area Cruiserweight Champion. Ht. 5'11"
Manager Self

22.09.80 Nigel Savery W PTS 6 Wolverhampton
30.10.80 Steve Fenton W CO 2 Wolverhampton
01.12.80 Liam Coleman L PTS 6 Wolverhampton
02.02.81 Steve Fenton W PTS 6 Nottingham
10.02.81 John O'Neill W RSC 6 Wolverhampton
16.03.81 Chris Lawson L RSC 5 Mayfair
13.04.81 Rupert Christie W RSC 5 Wolverhampton
11.05.81 Trevor Cattouse L PTS 8 Mayfair
05.10.81 Antonio Harris W PTS 8 Birmingham
30.11.81 Ben Lawlor W RSC 2 Birmingham
23.01.82 Chisanda Mutti L RSC 3 Berlin, Germany
16.02.82 Prince Mama Mohammed L PTS 8 Birmingham
19.03.82 Devon Bailey L RSC 2 Birmingham
24.05.82 Clive Beardsley W RSC 4 Nottingham
20.09.82 Keith Bristol NC 5 Wolverhampton
05.10.82 Alex Tompkins W PTS 8 Piccadilly
23.11.82 Winston Burnett W RSC 5 Wolverhampton
13.12.82 Steve Babbs L CO 1 Wolverhampton
15.02.83 Alek Pensarski W RSC 4 Wolverhampton
23.02.83 Devon Bailey L RSC 6 Mayfair
28.03.83 Gordon Stacey W RSC 1 Birmingham
25.04.83 Alex Tompkins W PTS 8 Southwark
19.05.83 Richard Caramanolis L CO 4 Paris, France
03.12.83 Andy Straughn L PTS 8 Marylebone
25.01.84 Romal Ambrose W RSC 3 Solihull
07.06.84 Roy Skeldon L CO 7 Dudley
01.12.84 Louis Pergaud L DIS 6 Dusseldorf, Germany
23.02.85 Chris Reid L CO 3 Belfast
25.04.85 Harry Andrews W PTS 6 Wolverhampton
05.06.85 Tony Wilson L CO 5 Kensington
12.10.87 Ivan Joseph L CO 6 Bow

24.02.88 Johnny Nelson L RSC 1 Sheffield
29.03.88 Eric Cardouza W CO 5 Wembley
05.05.88 Derek Angol L RSC 5 Wembley
19.09.88 Mike Aubrey L PTS 6 Mayfair
22.11.88 Crawford Ashley L CO 3 Basildon
02.02.89 Branko Pavlovic W RSC 2 Croydon
21.03.89 Abner Blackstock W CO 2 Wolverhampton
15.04.89 Alfredo Cacciatore L DIS 6 Vasto, Italy
21.05.89 Brendan Dempsey W PTS 8 Finsbury Park
12.08.89 Paul Muyodi L RTD 4 San Sepolcro, Italy
16.12.89 Lajos Eros L RSC 5 Milan, Italy
17.01.90 Mick Cordon W PTS 8 Stoke
08.02.90 Jim Peters W RSC 4 Southwark
08.03.90 Terry Dixon L PTS 8 Watford
25.04.90 Tee Jay L RSC 1 Millwall
13.06.90 Glazz Campbell W PTS 4 Manchester
31.10.90 Henry Maske L RSC 3 Wembley
12.02.91 Steve Lewsam W RSC 8 Wolverhampton
22.02.91 Bobbi Joe Edwards W RTD 6 Manchester
20.03.91 Roy Smith W RSC 7 Solihull
(Midland Area Cruiserweight Title Challenge)
17.05.91 Neils H. Madsen L RSC 2 Copenhagen, Denmark
22.06.91 Norbert Ekassi L CO 5 Paris, France
16.09.91 Steve Lewsam L PTS 10 Cleethorpes
(Midlands Area Cruiserweight Title Defence)
26.11.91 Tony Wilson L PTS 8 Wolverhampton
21.02.92 Markus Bott L PTS 8 Hamburg, Germany
06.03.92 Yuri Razumov DREW 6 Berlin, Germany
27.03.92 Jean-Marie Emebe W RSC 3 Creil, France
22.10.92 Chemek Saleta L RSC 4 Bethnal Green
25.02.93 Denzil Browne L PTS 8 Bradford
23.05.93 Wayne Llewelyn L RSC 3 Brockley
24.09.93 Cash McCullum DREW 8 Dublin
05.10.93 Scott Welch L RSC 1 Mayfair
03.11.93 John Ruiz L PTS 6 Bristol
29.01.94 Clifton Mitchell L RSC 1 Cardiff
03.03.94 Jacklord Jacobs L RSC 3 Ebbw Vale
15.04.94 Albert Call W RSC 4 Hull
(Vacant Midlands Area Cruiserweight Title)
22.05.94 Wayne Llewelyn L CO 2 Crystal Palace
Career: 68 contests, won 27, drew 2, lost 38, no contest 1.

Vance Idiens

Cannock. *Born* Walsall, 9 June, 1962
Heavyweight. Ht. 6'4"
Manager W. Tyler

24.10.89 Mick Cordon W PTS 6 Wolverhampton
28.11.89 Ted Shaw W CO 1 Wolverhampton
06.12.89 Mick Cordon W PTS 6 Stoke
19.02.90 David Jules W PTS 6 Birmingham
22.03.90 Mick Cordon W PTS 6 Wolverhampton
24.05.90 Tucker Richards L RSC 5 Dudley
28.06.90 Paul Neilson W PTS 8 Birmingham
27.09.90 Paul Neilson W PTS 8 Birmingham
14.11.90 Paul Neilson L RSC 2 Doncaster
05.12.91 David Jules W RSC 4 Cannock

06.03.92 Mario Scheisser L RSC 1 Berlin, Germany
09.12.92 David Jules W PTS 8 Stoke
11.03.93 Wayne Buck L PTS 8 Walsall
06.05.93 Joey Paladino W PTS 8 Walsall
19.05.93 John Harewood L CO 3 Sunderland
26.06.93 Justin Fortune L RSC 1 Keynsham
23.10.93 Dermot Gascoyne L RSC 4 Cardiff
14.03.94 Damien Caesar L RSC 4 Mayfair
14.04.94 Wayne Llewelyn L RSC 1 Battersea
Career: 19 contests, won 10, lost 9.

Vance Idiens   Les Clark

Paul Ingle
Scarborough. *Born* Scarborough, 22 June, 1972
Flyweight. Ht. 5'5"
Manager F. Maloney

23.03.94 Darren Noble W RSC 3 Cardiff
27.04.94 Graham McGrath W PTS 4 Bethnal Green
25.05.94 Neil Swain W CO 4 Bristol
Career: 3 contests, won 3.

Nick Ingram   Les Clark

Nick Ingram
Northampton. *Born* Northampton, 3 October, 1972
L. Middleweight. Ht. 5'11"
Manager J. Cox

20.09.93 Mark Brogan W RSC 4 Northampton
04.11.93 Peter Reid L RSC 5 Stafford
08.03.94 Warren Stephens W PTS 6 Kettering
16.05.94 Roger Dean W RSC 3 Heathrow
27.05.94 Roy Dehara W PTS 6 Ashford
Career: 5 contests, won 4, lost 1.

Colin Innes
Newcastle. *Born* Newcastle, 24 July, 1964
Lightweight. Ht. 5'6"
Manager N. Fawcett

10.09.90 Lee Christian W RSC 5 Northampton
24.09.90 Steve Armstrong W PTS 6 Manchester
08.10.90 Ervine Blake L PTS 6 Bradford

22.10.90 Steve Armstrong W RSC 6 Manchester
26.11.90 Carl Roberts L RSC 3 Bury
11.02.91 Steve Armstrong W PTS 6 Manchester
18.02.91 Ian McGirr L PTS 6 Glasgow
02.03.91 Tommy Smith W PTS 6 Darlington
28.03.91 Darryl Pettit W RTD 3 Alfreton
30.04.91 Noel Carroll L PTS 4 Stockport
19.09.91 Carl Roberts L PTS 4 Stockport
12.12.91 Tommy Smith L PTS 6 Hartlepool
24.02.92 Mark Geraghty L PTS 8 Glasgow
30.03.92 Chris Jickells L RSC 3 Bradford
28.05.92 Tommy Smith L PTS 6 Gosforth
05.10.92 Wayne Rigby L PTS 6 Manchester
18.11.92 Al Garrett DREW 6 Solihull
15.09.93 Chris Bennett DREW 6 Newcastle
25.11.93 Garry Burrell W PTS 6 Newcastle
06.12.93 Norman Dhalie L PTS 6 Bradford
24.01.94 Hugh Collins L PTS 6 Glasgow
03.03.94 Leo Turner DREW 6 Newcastle
21.04.94 Leo Turner W PTS 6 Gateshead
13.05.94 Rocky Ferrari L PTS 6 Kilmarnock
13.06.94 Leo Turner L PTS 6 Bradford
Career: 25 contests, won 8, drew 3, lost 14.

(John) Jonjo Irwin
Doncaster. *Born* Denaby, 31 May, 1969
WBO Penta-Continental S. Featherweight Champion. All-Ireland Featherweight Champion. Ht. 5'8"
Manager J. Rushton

08.09.92 Kid McAuley W PTS 6 Doncaster
30.09.92 Miguel Matthews W PTS 6 Solihull
24.11.92 Colin Lynch W RSC 4 Doncaster
20.01.93 Mark Hargreaves W RSC 4 Solihull
23.02.93 G. G. Goddard W RSC 8 Doncaster
16.03.93 Kid McAuley W PTS 10 Mayfair
(Vacant All-Ireland Featherweight Title)
28.04.93 Kevin Middleton L RSC 6 Solihull
06.10.93 Pete Buckley W PTS 8 Solihull
21.12.93 Peter Harris W PTS 8 Mayfair
22.01.94 Derek Amory L RSC 2 Belfast
10.05.94 Michael Armstrong W PTS 12 Doncaster
(Vacant WBO Penta-Continental S. Featherweight Title)
Career: 11 contests, won 9, lost 2.

Billy Issac
Hackney. *Born* Guildford, 14 August, 1968
Heavyweight. Ht. 6'4"
Manager Self

19.12.91 Larry Peart W RSC 3 Oldham
18.12.93 Paul McCarthy W PTS 6 Manchester
Career: 2 contests, won 2.

Gilbert Jackson (Amponsan)
Battersea. *Born* Ghana, 21 August, 1970
Middleweight. Ht. 5'10"
Manager M. Duff

17.02.92 John Bosco L PTS 6 Mayfair
05.03.92 Tony Wellington W CO 2 Battersea
22.04.92 Russell Washer W PTS 6 Wembley
08.09.92 Paul Gamble W RSC 1 Norwich
05.02.93 Carl Harney W CO 3 Manchester
14.06.93 Lee Crocker W RSC 2 Bayswater
16.09.93 Alan Baptiste W RSC 5 Southwark
02.11.93 Ernie Loveridge W RTD 3 Southwark
01.12.93 Jerry Mortimer W RSC 3 Kensington
16.02.94 Chris Richards W RSC 2 Stevenage

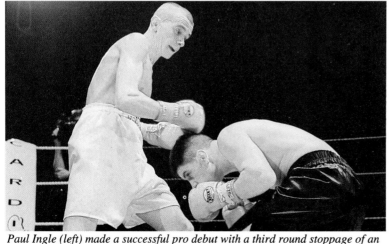

Paul Ingle (left) made a successful pro debut with a third round stoppage of an outgunned Darren Noble
                                          Les Clark

14.03.94 Mark Atkins W PTS 6 Mayfair
13.04.94 Gordon Blair W RTD 1 Glasgow
Career: 12 contests, won 11, lost 1.

(James) Jem Jackson
Birmingham. *Born* Birmingham, 22 March, 1970
Cruiserweight. Ht. 6'0"
Manager E. Cashmore

28.03.94 Declan Faherty L RTD 5 Birmingham
Career: 1 contest, lost 1.

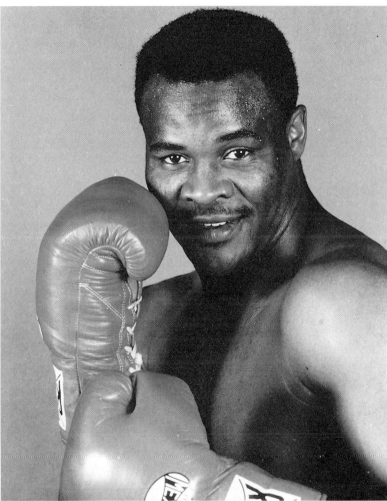

Jacklord Jacobs   John McDonald

Jacklord Jacobs
London. *Born* Nigeria, 1 January, 1970
Cruiserweight. Ht. 6'1"
Manager M. Jacobs

03.03.94 Cordwell Hylton W RSC 3 Ebbw Vale
Career: 1 contest, won 1.

Dean James (Ollah)
Birmingham. *Born* Birmingham, 23 August, 1968
Featherweight. Ht. 5'9"
Manager Self

06.12.93 Ian Richardson L RSC 4 Bradford
Career: 1 contest, lost 1.

Phil Janes
Cardiff. *Born* Carmarthen, 28 December, 1970
S. Featherweight. Ht. 5'10"
Manager D. Gardiner

23.03.94 Dean Phillips L RSC 1 Cardiff
Career: 1 contest, lost 1.

Mark Jay (Jackson)
Newcastle. *Born* Newcastle, 4 April, 1969
L. Middleweight. Ht. 5'11"
Manager Self

29.09.88 Tony Farrell W PTS 6 Sunderland
22.11.88 Dave Whittle W PTS 6 Marton
05.04.89 Lewis Welch L PTS 6 Halifax
19.05.89 Mick Mulcahy W PTS 6 Gateshead
25.09.89 Carlton Myers W PTS 6 Piccadilly
21.10.89 Ian Thomas L RSC 5 Middlesbrough
24.04.90 Ernie Loveridge L PTS 6 Stoke
30.05.90 Trevor Meikle DREW 6 Stoke
15.06.90 Trevor Meikle L RSC 5 Telford
18.10.90 Phil Epton L PTS 6 Dewsbury
19.11.90 John Mullen DREW 6 Glasgow
29.11.90 Barry Messam L RSC 5 Sunderland
09.10.91 Willie Quinn W PTS 6 Glasgow
16.12.91 Tyrone Eastmond L PTS 6 Manchester
20.01.92 Mick Duncan W PTS 6 Bradford
24.02.92 David Radford W PTS 6 Bradford
03.03.92 Dave Johnson L PTS 6 Houghton le Spring
12.03.92 Gordon Blair DREW 8 Glasgow
02.04.92 Jamie Robinson L PTS 6 Basildon
25.04.92 Steve Foster L RSC 7 Manchester
28.05.92 Shamus Casey W PTS 8 Gosforth
24.09.92 Derek Wormald L RSC 5 Stockport
01.12.92 Neil Patterson W PTS 6 Hartlepool
17.12.92 Clay O'Shea L CO 1 Wembley
09.03.93 Spencer Alton W RSC 4 Hartlepool
29.04.93 Allan Grainger W RSC 3 Newcastle
11.06.93 Tony Trimble W RSC 1 Gateshead
15.09.93 John Duckworth L RSC 4 Newcastle
02.12.93 Mark Cichocki L RSC 4 Hartlepool
(Northern Area L. Middleweight Title Challenge)
03.03.94 Dave Whittle L PTS 8 Newcastle
21.04.94 Shamus Casey W PTS 6 Gateshead
24.05.94 Japhet Hans L RSC 1 Sunderland
Career: 32 contests, won 13, drew 3, lost 16.

Graham Jenner
Hastings. *Born* Hastings, 13 May, 1962
S. Middleweight. Ht. 6'0"
Manager D. Harris

10.10.85 Gary Tomlinson L PTS 6 Merton
14.11.85 George Mac W PTS 6 Merton
05.12.85 Jason Baxter L PTS 6 Digbeth
21.01.86 Tony Stevens W PTS 6 Tunbridge Wells
25.03.86 Dave Furneaux W PTS 6 Tunbridge Wells
08.04.86 Darryl Ritchie W RSC 3 Southend
16.09.86 Tommy Becket W CO 2 Southend
25.09.86 Andy Till L PTS 6 Crystal Palace
29.10.91 Val Golding L RSC 3 Kensington
08.01.92 Paul McCarthy W PTS 6 Burton
29.02.92 Paul McCarthy W PTS 8 St Leonards
29.05.92 Ensley Bingham L CO 5 Manchester
15.10.92 Mark Baker L RTD 4 Lewisham
12.11.92 John Kaighin L RSC 5 Bayswater
03.02.93 Sammy Storey L RSC 4 Earls Court
05.05.93 Terry Magee L PTS 6 Belfast
18.12.93 Eric Noi L CO 1 Manchester
22.01.94 Mark Delaney L RTD 3 Belfast
11.03.94 Mark Baker L RSC 2 Bethnal Green
Career: 19 contests, won 7, lost 12.

Andrew Jervis
Liverpool. *Born* Liverpool, 28 June, 1969
L. Middleweight. Ht. 5'11"
Manager D. Isaaman

05.10.92 Rick North W PTS 6 Liverpool
02.11.92 Shaun Martin W CO 2 Liverpool
01.12.92 Cliff Churchward W PTS 6 Liverpool
27.01.93 Mark Ramsey L PTS 6 Stoke
22.02.93 Alan Williams W PTS 6 Liverpool
29.03.93 Bullit Andrews W PTS 6 Liverpool
09.06.93 Chris Mulcahy W PTS 6 Liverpool
15.03.94 John Duckworth L PTS 6 Stoke
25.05.94 Sean Baker DREW 4 Bristol
04.06.94 Adrian Dodson L RSC 2 Cardiff
Career: 10 contests, won 6, drew 1, lost 3.

Chris Jickells

Brigg. *Born* Scunthorpe, 26 March, 1971
S. Featherweight. Ht. 5'5"
Manager K. Tate

18.11.91	Tony Smith W RSC 4 Manchester
09.12.91	Al Garrett W RSC 2 Bradford
15.01.92	Ronnie Stephenson L PTS 6 Stoke
30.03.92	Colin Innes W RSC 3 Bradford
29.04.92	Kevin Middleton W RSC 6 Solihull
01.06.92	Dave McHale L RSC 4 Glasgow
12.10.92	Ian McGirr W RSC 3 Bradford
10.02.93	Kevin Middleton L CO 1 Lewisham
07.06.93	Wilson Docherty L RSC 5 Glasgow
02.11.93	Mark Bowers L RSC 3 Southwark
21.03.94	Mike Deveney L RSC 5 Glasgow

Career: 11 contests, won 5, lost 6.

James Jiora (Iwenjiora)

Otley. *Born* Nigeria, 6 April, 1968
L. Welterweight. Ht. 5'5"
Manager Self

07.06.87	Paul Kennedy W RSC 6 Bradford
15.09.87	Ian Murray W RSC 2 Batley
02.11.87	Michael Howell W RSC 3 Bradford
10.11.87	Marvin P. Gray L PTS 8 Batley
30.11.87	John Townsley W PTS 8 Nottingham
15.12.87	Paul Burke W PTS 4 Bradford
08.03.88	Rudy Valentino L PTS 6 Batley
26.01.89	Frankie Foster L PTS 6 Newcastle
20.02.89	Paul Bowen L PTS 6 Birmingham
20.03.89	Dean Dickinson W PTS 6 Bradford
31.03.89	Chris Bennett L PTS 5 Scarborough
11.07.89	Craig Walsh L PTS 8 Batley
05.12.89	Paul Charters L RSC 4 Dewsbury
11.01.90	Kid Sumali W PTS 4 Dewsbury
26.02.90	Brendan Ryan W PTS 6 Bradford
11.04.90	Rick Bushell L PTS 6 Dewsbury
29.11.90	Marvin P. Gray L PTS 8 Marton
13.06.91	David Thompson DREW 6 Hull
01.08.91	Chris Saunders L PTS 6 Dewsbury
09.10.91	John O'Johnson L PTS 6 Manchester
21.10.91	Charlie Kane L PTS 6 Glasgow
02.03.92	Carl Tilley L PTS 6 Marton
12.03.92	Alan McDowall L CO 2 Glasgow
13.06.94	Mark Allen W PTS 6 Bradford

Career: 24 contests, won 9, drew 1, lost 14.

Dave Johnson

Sunderland. *Born* Boldon, 10 August, 1972
Middleweight. Ht. 5'10"
Manager T. Conroy

13.05.91	Rocky Tyrell W PTS 6 Manchester
20.05.91	Griff Jones W PTS 6 Bradford
10.06.91	Tyrone Eastmond W PTS 6 Manchester
10.10.91	Shamus Casey W PTS 6 Gateshead
14.11.91	Shamus Casey W PTS 6 Gateshead
25.11.91	Mike Phillips L PTS 6 Liverpool
12.12.91	Mick Duncan W PTS 6 Hartlepool
03.03.92	Mark Jay W PTS 6 Houghton le Spring
28.04.92	Shaun McCrory DREW 6 Houghton le Spring
10.09.92	Spencer Alton W PTS 6 Sunderland
23.10.92	Griff Jones W PTS 6 Gateshead
17.04.93	Mike Phillips W PTS 6 Washington
11.06.93	Robert Riley W PTS 8 Gateshead
15.09.93	Darren Pilling W PTS 6 Newcastle
25.11.93	Dave Owens W PTS 8 Tynemouth
02.03.94	John Duckworth W PTS 8 Solihull
17.03.94	Peter Waudby L PTS 6 Lincoln
27.04.94	Barry Thorogood DREW 6 Solihull
24.05.94	Martin Jolley W PTS 6 Sunderland

Career: 19 contests, won 15, drew 2, lost 2.

Martin Jolley

Alfreton. *Born* Chesterfield, 22 November, 1967
Middleweight. Ht. 5'11½"
Manager M. Shinfield

10.03.92	Gypsy Johnny Price W RSC 3 Bury
06.04.92	Sean Byrne L RSC 6 Northampton
11.05.92	Mark Hale W PTS 6 Coventry
08.09.92	Brian McGloin W PTS 6 Doncaster
05.10.92	Mark Hale W RSC 4 Bardon
14.10.92	Carl Smallwood W PTS 6 Stoke
02.11.92	Bobby Mack L PTS 6 Wolverhampton
24.11.92	Phil Ball DREW 6 Doncaster
02.02.93	Mark McBiane W RSC 5 Derby
23.02.93	Phil Ball W RSC 5 Doncaster
12.05.93	Marvin O'Brien W PTS 6 Sheffield
08.06.93	Paul Hanlon W PTS 6 Derby
22.09.93	Nigel Rafferty L PTS 6 Chesterfield
29.10.93	Mads Larsen L CO 3 Korsoer, Denmark
02.12.93	Darren Littlewood L PTS 6 Evesham
17.03.94	Paul Hitch W RSC 2 Lincoln
25.04.94	Derek Wormald L RSC 4 Bury
24.05.94	Dave Johnson L PTS 6 Sunderland
17.06.94	Dean Francis L PTS 6 Plymouth

Career: 19 contests, won 10, drew 1, lost 8.

Barry Jones

Cardiff. *Born* Cardiff, 3 May, 1974
Featherweight. Ht. 5'7"
Manager B. Aird

28.10.92	Conn McMullen W PTS 6 Cardiff
14.12.92	Miguel Matthews W PTS 6 Cardiff
27.01.93	Mike Deveney W PTS 6 Cardiff
24.03.93	Greg Upton W RSC 2 Mayfair
28.04.93	Kid McAuley W PTS 8 Solihull
09.10.93	John White W PTS 4 Manchester
10.11.93	Neil Swain W PTS 6 Ystrad
30.11.93	Pete Buckley W PTS 4 Cardiff
16.12.93	Elvis Parsley W PTS 6 Newport
22.01.94	Pete Buckley W PTS 6 Cardiff

Career: 10 contests, won 10.

Keith Jones

Swansea. *Born* Bradwell, 4 December, 1968
L. Welterweight. Ht. 5'5¾"
Manager D. Gardiner

17.05.94	Abdul Manna L PTS 6 Kettering
13.06.94	G. G. Goddard L PTS 6 Liverpool

Career: 2 contests, lost 2.

Wayne Jones

Saltash. *Born* Halifax, 6 October, 1968
Lightweight. Ht. 5'8"
Manager N. Christian

13.11.93	Robbie Sivyer W PTS 6 Cullompton
14.01.94	Colin Dunne L RSC 3 Bethnal Green
04.03.94	Robbie Sivyer W PTS 6 Weston super Mare
17.06.94	Trevor Royal W PTS 6 Plymouth

Career: 4 contests, won 3, lost 1.

Cham Joof

Brixton. *Born* London, 19 November, 1968
Southern Area Lightweight Champion. Ht. 5'8"
Manager F. Rix

22.02.93	Chris Saunders W PTS 4 Eltham
04.04.93	Anthony Wanza W RSC 2 Brockley
14.04.93	Mike Morrison W PTS 4 Kensington
23.05.93	Charles Shepherd L PTS 4 Brockley
25.06.93	Scott Smith W RTD 2 Battersea
14.08.93	Mark Allen W RSC 3 Hammersmith
20.01.94	Phil Found W RSC 1 Battersea
14.04.94	Brian Coleman W CO 3 Battersea
22.05.94	Felix Kelly W RSC 5 Crystal Palace *(Southern Area Lightweight Title Challenge)*

Career: 9 contests, won 8, lost 1.

Cham Joof (left) scored an impressive win over Felix Kelly, to annex the latter's Southern Area lightweight title

Les Clark

Gareth Jordan

Monmouth. *Born* Usk, 19 December, 1971
Lightweight. Ht. 5'6¾"
Manager M. Duff

02.11.92	Con Cronin W RSC 2 Wolverhampton
04.12.92	Jason White W RSC 2 Telford
16.03.93	Lee Fox W RSC 3 Wolverhampton
26.05.93	Mark O'Callaghan W RSC 3 Mansfield
27.10.93	Dave Madden W RSC 5 West Bromwich
16.12.93	Phil Found W PTS 6 Newport
04.06.94	T. J. Smith W RSC 1 Cardiff

Career: 7 Contests, won 7.

Craig Joseph

Bradford. *Born* Bradford, 5 December, 1968
S. Middleweight. Ht. 6'0"
Manager T. Callighan

04.10.93 Pat McNamara W RSC 2 Bradford
07.02.94 Jimmy Tyers W PTS 6 Bradford
27.04.94 Chris Davies W PTS 6 Solihull
13.06.94 Spencer Alton W PTS 6 Bradford

Career: 4 Contests, won 4.

Peter Judson

Keighley. *Born* Keighley, 14 January, 1970
S. Featherweight. Ht. 5'7"
Manager Self

24.04.89 Darryl Pettit DREW 6 Bradford
11.07.89 Neil Leitch W PTS 6 Batley
18.09.89 Phil Lashley W PTS 6 Mayfair
02.10.89 Stevie Woods L PTS 6 Bradford
22.11.89 Pete Buckley L PTS 6 Stafford
19.02.90 Phil Lashley W CO 6 Nottingham
08.03.90 Wayne Goult L PTS 6 Peterborough
19.03.90 Andrew Robinson W PTS 6 Grimsby
26.03.90 Wayne Marston W PTS 6 Nottingham
30.04.90 Derek Amory L PTS 6 Brierley Hill
09.05.90 Brian Robb W PTS 6 Solihull
04.06.90 Jamie McBride L PTS 8 Glasgow
17.09.90 Mark Geraghty W PTS 8 Glasgow
26.09.90 Carl Roberts W PTS 6 Manchester

08.10.90 Mark Geraghty L PTS 8 Glasgow
19.11.90 Russell Davison L PTS 8 Manchester
27.11.90 Rocky Lawlor W PTS 8 Wolverhampton
29.01.91 Russell Davison L PTS 10 Stockport
(Vacant Central Area Featherweight Title)
21.02.91 Noel Carroll W PTS 8 Leeds
20.03.91 Colin Lynch W RTD 5 Solihull
01.05.91 Jimmy Owens L PTS 6 Liverpool
28.05.91 Scott Durham W PTS 6 Cardiff
24.09.91 Ian McGirr L PTS 6 Glasgow
11.11.91 Miguel Matthews W PTS 6 Stratford upon Avon
18.11.91 Jamie McBride DREW 6 Glasgow
09.02.92 Ceri Farrell W PTS 6 Bradford
05.04.92 Barrie Kelley W PTS 6 Bradford
14.11.92 J. T. Williams DREW 6 Cardiff
25.02.93 Dominic McGuigan DREW 6 Bradford
16.05.94 Carlos Chase W PTS 4 Heathrow

Career: 30 contests, won 16, drew 4, lost 10.

David Jules

Doncaster. *Born* Doncaster, 11 July, 1965
Heavyweight. Ht. 6'2"
Manager Self

12.06.87 Carl Timbrell W CO 5 Leamington
07.10.87 Carl Timbrell L RSC 3 Stoke
17.03.88 Peter Fury W RTD 2 Sunderland
21.03.88 Jess Harding L RSC 2 Bethnal Green
29.09.88 Gary McCrory L PTS 6 Sunderland
22.11.88 Gary McCrory L PTS 6 Marton
05.12.88 Denroy Bryan DREW 6 Dudley
18.01.89 Denroy Bryan W RSC 2 Stoke
22.02.89 Tony Hallett W RSC 1 Doncaster
19.04.89 Rocky Burton L RSC 3 Doncaster
11.11.89 Jimmy di Stolfo W RSC 1 Rimini, Italy
30.11.89 Biagio Chianese L RSC 2 Milan, Italy
19.02.90 Vance Idiens L PTS 6 Birmingham
07.05.90 Ramon Voorn L RSC 3 Arnhem, Holland
12.11.90 Steve Garber L RSC 6 Bradford
09.04.91 Herbie Hide L RSC 1 Mayfair
05.12.91 Vance Idiens L RSC 4 Cannock
24.02.92 Rocky Burton W CO 1 Coventry
05.04.92 Steve Garber L RSC 4 Bradford

08.09.92 Wayne Buck L RSC 3 Doncaster
09.12.92 Vance Idiens L PTS 8 Stoke
10.05.93 Steve Lewsam L CO 6 Cleethorpes
28.10.93 Joey Paladino L RSC 2 Walsall

Career: 23 contests, won 6, drew 1, lost 16.

John Kaighin

Swansea. *Born* Brecknock, 26 August, 1967
S. Middleweight. Ht. 5'11¾"
Manager M. Copp

17.09.90 Carlos Christie L PTS 6 Cardiff
24.09.90 James F. Woolley L PTS 6 Lewisham
15.10.90 Max McCracken L PTS 6 Brierley Hill
22.10.90 Stefan Wright L PTS 6 Peterborough
15.11.90 Tony Wellington W PTS 6 Oldham
13.12.90 Nick Manners L CO 3 Dewsbury
24.01.91 Robert Peel L PTS 6 Gorseinon
12.02.91 Robert Peel W PTS 6 Cardiff
15.03.91 Max McCracken DREW 6 Willenhall
10.04.91 Darron Griffiths L PTS 6 Newport
24.04.91 Paul Murray W PTS 6 Aberavon
08.05.91 Benji Good W RSC 3 Kensington
15.05.91 Robert Peel L PTS 8 Swansea
06.06.91 Peter Vosper DREW 6 Barking
30.06.91 John Ogistie L PTS 6 Southwark
29.08.91 Adrian Wright W PTS 6 Oakengates
09.09.91 Terry Johnson W RTD 2 Liverpool
11.09.91 Lester Jacobs L RSC 2 Hammersmith
22.10.91 Andy Wright DREW 6 Wandsworth
13.11.91 Gary Delaney L PTS 6 Bethnal Green
20.11.91 Keith Inglis W RSC 1 Kensington
23.01.92 Michael Gale L PTS 8 York
01.02.92 Paul Busby L PTS 4 Birmingham
25.02.92 Andy Wright L PTS 6 Crystal Palace
05.03.92 Lester Jacobs L RSC 1 Battersea
27.04.92 Bruce Scott L CO 4 Mayfair
18.07.92 Carl Harney L PTS 6 Manchester
15.09.92 Paul Wright L DIS 5 Liverpool
26.09.92 Shaun Cummins L RTD 4 Earls Court
28.10.92 Joey Peters DREW 4 Kensington
12.11.92 Graham Jenner W RSC 5 Baywater
01.12.92 Peter Vosper W RSC 4 Bristol
22.12.92 Darrit Douglas W PTS 6 Mayfair
14.01.93 Ole Klemetsen L RTD 3 Mayfair
24.03.93 Darron Griffiths L RSC 6 Cardiff
(Vacant Welsh S. Middleweight Title)
28.04.93 Ray Kane L PTS 6 Dublin
23.05.93 Mark Prince L RSC 3 Brockley
25.07.93 Maurice Core L PTS 6 Oldham
22.09.93 Sammy Storey L PTS 6 Bethnal Green
07.10.93 Michael Gale L PTS 8 York
16.10.93 Noel Magee L PTS 6 Belfast
08.11.93 Garry Delaney L CO 1 Bethnal Green
18.12.93 Fran Harding L PTS 6 Manchester
16.02.94 Shaun Cummins L RSC 3 Stevenage

Career: 44 contests, won 10, drew 4, lost 30.

Charlie Kane

Clydebank. *Born* Glasgow, 2 July, 1968
L. Welterweight. Ht. 5'10½"
Manager T. Gilmour

05.03.91 Dean Bramhald W RSC 6 Glasgow
21.10.91 James Jiora W PTS 6 Glasgow
24.02.92 Karl Taylor W PTS 8 Glasgow
10.12.92 Mick Mulcahy W RSC 2 Glasgow
07.11.93 Mick Mulcahy W RSC 2 Glasgow
25.11.93 John Smith W PTS 6 Tynemouth
02.03.94 Micky Hall W RSC 2 Glasgow
28.03.94 John Smith W PTS 6 Musselburgh

Career: 8 contests, won 8.

Peter Judson (left), out of action for over 14 months, came back to upset Carlos Chase, seen here avoiding the jab   Les Clark

Ray Kane

Belfast. *Born* Dublin, 4 June, 1968
Cruiserweight. Ht. 6'0"
Manager B. Eastwood

07.09.91	R. F. McKenzie W PTS 4 Belfast
11.12.91	Chris Coughlan W PTS 6 Dublin
28.04.93	John Kaighin W PTS 6 Dublin
05.05.93	Johnny Uphill W CO 2 Belfast
16.10.93	Jason McNeill W PTS 6 Belfast
12.03.94	Kent Davis W PTS 6 Cardiff
21.05.94	Nicky Wadman W PTS 6 Belfast

Career: 7 contests, won 7.

John Keeton

Sheffield. *Born* Sheffield, 19 May, 1972
L. Heavyweight. Ht. 6'0"
Manager B. Ingle

11.08.93	Tony Colclough W RSC 1 Mansfield
15.09.93	Val Golding L PTS 6 Ashford
27.10.93	Darren McKenna W RSC 3 Stoke
01.12.93	Julius Francis L PTS 4 Bethnal Green
19.01.94	Dennis Bailey W RTD 2 Stoke
17.02.94	Dermot Gascoyne L RSC 1 Dagenham
09.04.94	Eddie Knight W RTD 5 Mansfield
11.05.94	John Rice W RSC 5 Sheffield
02.06.94	Devon Rhooms W RSC 2 Tooting

Career: 9 contests, won 6, lost 3.

John Keeton　　　　　　Les Clark

Barrie Kelley

Llanelli. *Born* Llanelli, 14 February, 1972
Former Welsh S. Featherweight Champion.
Ht. 5'6"
Manager Self

16.10.90	Ervine Blake W PTS 6 Evesham
21.11.90	Tony Falcone W PTS 6 Chippenham
29.11.90	John O'Meara W RSC 5 Bayswater
24.01.91	Martin Evans W PTS 6 Gorseinon
18.02.91	Tony Falcone L RSC 6 Mayfair
26.03.91	Dennis Adams W PTS 6 Bethnal Green
18.07.91	Robert Smyth DREW 6 Cardiff
16.09.91	Dominic McGuigan DREW 6 Mayfair
14.10.91	Michael Armstrong L CO 4 Manchester

20.11.91	Neil Haddock L PTS 6 Cardiff
03.02.92	Noel Carroll L PTS 8 Manchester
18.03.92	Mark Geraghty L PTS 8 Glasgow
05.04.92	Peter Judson L PTS 6 Bradford
30.09.92	Dean Bramhald W PTS 6 Solihull
28.10.92	Derek Amory W PTS 6 Cardiff
19.01.93	Edward Lloyd W PTS 10 Cardiff
	(Vacant Welsh S. Featherweight Title)
10.11.93	J. T. Williams L RTD 3 Ystrad
	(Welsh S. Featherweight Title Defence)
24.02.94	Peter Till L PTS 6 Walsall

Career: 18 contests, won 8, drew 2, lost 8.

Craig Kelley

Dyfed. *Born* Swansea, 6 November, 1975
Featherweight. Ht. 5'8"
Manager B. Aird

25.01.94	Simon Frailing W PTS 4 Piccadilly
25.02.94	John Sillo L PTS 6 Chester

Career: 2 contests, won 1, lost 1.

Felix Kelly

Paddington. *Born* Sligo, 6 June, 1965
Former Southern Area Lightweight
Champion. Ht. 5'7"
Manager Self

18.10.90	Tony Gibbs DREW 6 Wandsworth
26.11.90	Steve Hearn W RSC 3 Bethnal Green
04.12.90	Frankie Ventura W PTS 6 Southend
06.02.91	Wayne Windle W PTS 6 Bethnal Green
18.02.91	Trevor Royal W RSC 4 Windsor
26.03.91	Chris Saunders W PTS 6 Bethnal Green
18.04.91	Rick Bushell W PTS 6 Earls Court
22.06.91	Rick Bushell L PTS 6 Earls Court
26.09.91	Billy Schwer L RSC 2 Dunstable
20.11.91	Tony Borg L PTS 6 Cardiff
25.03.92	Mark Tibbs DREW 8 Dagenham
17.09.92	Carlos Chase L RSC 2 Watford
07.11.92	Didier Hughes W PTS 6 Differdange, Luxembourg
02.01.93	Brian Kulen W PTS 6 Differdange, Luxembourg
13.02.93	Soren Sondergaard L CO 4 Randers, Denmark
24.03.93	Patrick Loughran L PTS 6 Belfast
03.04.93	James Osansedo L RTD 5 Vienna, Austria
14.05.93	Angel Mona L RTD 2 Dijon, France
23.06.93	A.M.Milton W CO 8 Edmonton
	(Vacant Southern Area Lightweight Title)
09.12.93	Shaun Shinkwin W PTS 10 Watford
	(Southern Area Lightweight Title Defence)
14.04.94	Edward Lloyd L RSC 6 Battersea
22.05.94	Cham Joof L RSC 5 Crystal Palace
	(Southern Area Lightweight Title Defence)

Career: 22 contests, won 10, drew 2 , lost 10.

John T. Kelly

Hartlepool. *Born* Hartlepool, 12 June, 1970
Lightweight. Ht. 5'7"
Manager G. Robinson

22.10.92	Tanver Ahmed L PTS 6 Glasgow
02.11.92	Kevin Lowe W PTS 6 Liverpool
01.12.92	Wayne Rigby W PTS 6 Hartlepool
15.02.93	Kevin McKillan L PTS 6 Manchester
09.03.93	Michael Alexander W PTS 6 Hartlepool

17.04.93	Micky Hall DREW 4 Washington
06.05.93	Alan Graham W PTS 6 Hartlepool
15.09.93	P. J. Gallagher L RSC 2 Bethnal Green
02.12.93	Brian Wright W PTS 6 Hartlepool
02.02.94	Dave McHale L CO 1 Glasgow
13.04.94	Bradley Welsh L PTS 6 Glasgow

Career: 11 contests, won 5, drew 1, lost 5.

Jesse Keough

Islington. *Born* Clapton, 7 June, 1971
L. Middleweight. Ht. 5'10"
Manager M. Williamson

27.04.94	Warren Stephens W RSC 1 Bethnal Green

Career: 1 contest, won 1.

Jessie Keough　　　　　　Les Clark

Lyndon Kershaw

Halifax. *Born* Halifax, 17 September, 1972
Flyweight. Ht. 5'6"
Manager T. Callighan

19.10.92	Stevie Woods W PTS 6 Glasgow
14.12.92	Louis Veitch DREW 6 Bradford
26.04.93	Golfraz Ahmed W PTS 6 Bradford
24.05.93	Anthony Hanna W PTS 6 Bradford
07.10.93	Louis Veitch L PTS 10 Hull
	(Vacant Central Area Flyweight Title)
06.12.93	Ian Baillie W PTS 6 Bradford
02.03.94	Tiger Singh W PTS 6 Solihull
27.04.94	Mark Cokely W PTS 6 Solihull
09.05.94	Ian Baillie W PTS 6 Bradford
15.06.94	Mickey Cantwell W PTS 8 Southwark

Career: 10 contests, won 8 , drew 1, lost 1.

Prince Kasi Kiahau

Doncaster. *Born* Doncaster, 3 October, 1967
L. Middleweight. Ht. 5'11"
Manager J. Rushton

12.10.93	Prince Louis W PTS 6 Wolverhampton
24.11.93	Steve Levene W PTS 6 Solihull

13.12.93 Rob Stevenson W RSC 5 Doncaster
07.03.94 Steve Levene W RSC 3 Doncaster
10.05.94 Billy McDougall W RTD 4 Doncaster
Career: 5 contests, won 5.

Paul King

Newcastle. *Born* Newcastle, 3 June, 1965
Northern Area Welterweight Champion.
Ht. 5'8½"
Manager Self

04.09.87 Willie MacDonald W PTS 6 Gateshead
03.11.87 Mick Mason L PTS 6 Sunderland
24.11.87 Mick Mason L PTS 6 Marton
31.01.89 Jim Larmour W RTD 4 Glasgow
27.02.90 Ian Thomas W PTS 6 Marton
06.03.90 Mick Duncan W PTS 6 Newcastle
15.11.90 Phil Epton W PTS 6 Oldham
28.02.91 Dave Kettlewell W RSC 1 Sunderland
21.03.91 Phil Epton W PTS 6 Dewsbury
13.05.91 Shamus Casey L PTS 6 Northampton
31.05.91 Gordon Blair L PTS 8 Glasgow
09.10.91 Delroy Waul L RSC 6 Manchester
29.09.92 Howard Clarke L PTS 6 Stoke
16.03.93 Howard Clarke L PTS 6 Edgbaston
29.04.93 Hughie Davey W PTS 6 Newcastle
29.06.93 Howard Clarke L PTS 6 Edgbaston
14.08.93 Gary Logan L CO 2 Hammersmith
28.11.93 Gary Logan L CO 4 Southwark
03.03.94 Hughie Davey W PTS 10 Newcastle
(Vacant Northern Area Welterweight Title)
Career: 19 contests, won 9, lost 10.

Neil Kirkwood

Barnsley. *Born* Barnsley, 30 November, 1969
Heavyweight. Ht. 6'4"
Manager S. Doyle

17.03.94 Gary Williams W RSC 1 Lincoln
16.05.94 Joey Paladino W RSC 2 Cleethorpes
Career: 2 contests, won 2.

Eddie Knight

Ashford. *Born* Ashford, 4 October, 1966
L. Heavyweight. Ht. 5'11"
Manager A. Urry

05.10.92 Shaun McCrory L PTS 6 Bristol
29.10.92 Adrian Wright L PTS 6 Bayswater
25.11.92 Julian Johnson L RSC 2 Mayfair
15.09.93 Terry Duffus W PTS 6 Ashford
09.04.94 John Keeton L RTD 5 Mansfield
27.05.94 Lee Sara W CO 2 Ashford
Career: 6 contests, won 2, lost 4.

Paul Knights

Redhill. *Born* Redhill, 5 February, 1971
L. Welterweight. Ht. 5'10"
Manager Self

26.11.91 Steve Hearn W RSC 4 Bethnal Green
19.02.92 Seth Jones W RSC 5 Muswell Hill
16.06.92 Seth Jones W PTS 6 Dagenham
10.11.92 Alex Moffatt W CO 3 Dagenham
30.01.93 Dave Lovell W PTS 6 Brentwood
20.04.93 Mark Allen W PTS 6 Brentwood
26.06.93 Phil Found W PTS 4 Earls Court
28.09.93 Pat Delargy W RSC 3 Bethnal Green
11.01.94 Brian Coleman W RSC 4 Bethnal Green
09.02.94 Mark Allen W RSC 2 Brentwood

19.03.94 Alan Peacock W PTS 6 Millwall
11.06.94 John O'Johnson L PTS 6 Bethnal Green
Career: 12 contests, won 11, lost 1.

Keith Knox

Bonnyrigg. *Born* Edinburgh, 20 June, 1967
Flyweight. Ht. 5'3"
Manager T. Gilmour

04.03.94 Ian Bailie W CO 3 Irvine
28.03.94 Terry Gaskin W PTS 6 Musselburgh
Career: 2 contests, won 2.

Kirkland Laing

Nottingham. *Born* Jamaica, 20 June, 1954
Former British & European Welterweight Champion. Ht. 5'9"
Manager Self

14.04.75 Joe Hannaford W CO 2 Nottingham
12.05.75 Liam White W PTS 8 Nottingham
29.09.75 Derek Simpson W PTS 8 Nottingham
25.11.75 Oscar Angus W PTS 6 Kensington
19.01.76 Terry Schofield W PTS 8 Nottingham
12.03.76 Charlie Cooper W PTS 8 Southend
13.04.76 Mike Manley W PTS 8 Southend
17.05.76 John Laine W RSC 3 Nottingham
22.09.76 Harry Watson W RSC 5 Mayfair
11.10.76 Jim Moore W RSC 2 Nottingham
22.11.76 Jim Montague W DIS 7 Birmingham
11.01.77 John Smith W PTS 10 Wolverhampton
08.03.77 Peter Morris DREW 10 Wolverhampton
16.11.77 Peter Morris W RSC 5 Solihull
27.09.78 Achille Mitchell W PTS 12 Solihull
(Final Elim. British Welterweight Title)
04.04.79 Henry Rhiney W RSC 10 Birmingham
(British Welterweight Title Challenge)
06.11.79 Des Morrison W PTS 8 Kensington
22.01.80 Salvo Nuciforo W RSC 6 Kensington
19.02.80 Colin Ward W RSC 5 Kensington
01.04.80 Colin Jones L RSC 9 Wembley
(British Welterweight Title Defence)
08.05.80 George Walker W PTS 8 Solihull
03.06.80 Curtis Taylor W RSC 7 Kensington
26.11.80 Joey Singleton W PTS 12 Solihull
(Final Elim. British Welterweight Title)
28.04.81 Colin Jones L RSC 9 Kensington
(British Welterweight Title Challenge)
18.11.81 Cliff Gilpin W PTS 12 Solihull
(Final Elim. British Welterweight Title)
09.02.82 Reg Ford L PTS 10 London
05.05.82 Joey Mack W CO 7 Solihull
04.09.82 Roberto Duran W PTS 10 Detroit, USA
10.09.83 Fred Hutchings L CO 10 Atlantic City, USA
27.11.84 Darwin Brewster W RSC 7 Wembley
12.02.85 Mosimo Maeleke W PTS 10 Kensington
14.03.85 Wo Lamani Wo W RSC 6 Leicester
16.06.85 Franki Moro W PTS 8 Bethnal Green
05.07.85 Brian Janssen L RTD 5 Brisbane, Australia
16.05.86 Mike Picciotti W PTS 10 Atlantic City, USA
17.09.86 Harry Theodossiadis W RSC 4 Kensington
14.03.87 Silvester Mittee W RSC 5 Southwark
(Vacant British Welterweight Title)
26.05.87 Marvin McDowell W RSC 1 Wembley

26.11.87 Rocky Kelly W RSC 5 Fulham
(British Welterweight Title Defence)
29.03.88 Sammy Floyd W PTS 8 Wembley
15.04.89 Nino la Rocca L PTS 12 Vasto, Italy
(Vacant European Welterweight Title)
15.11.89 George Collins W RSC 5 Reading
(British Welterweight Title Defence)
10.01.90 Buck Smith L RSC 7 Kensington
27.03.90 Trevor Smith W RSC 6 Mayfair
(British Welterweight Title Defence)
09.05.90 Antoine Fernandez W CO 2 Wembley
(European Welterweight Title Challenge)
10.10.90 Rocky Berg W RSC 2 Kensington
14.11.90 Patrizio Oliva L PTS 12 Campione d'Italia, Italy
(European Welterweight Title Defence)
16.01.91 Del Bryan L PTS 12 Kensington
(British Welterweight Title Defence)
16.04.91 Donovan Boucher L CO 9 Nottingham
(Commonwealth Welterweight Title Challenge)
17.02.93 Bozon Haule W RSC 3 Bethnal Green
31.03.93 Newton Barnett W PTS 8 Bethnal Green
23.06.93 Kevin Lueshing L RSC 5 Edmonton
(Vacant Southern Area L. Middleweight Title)
28.07.93 Dean Cooper W RSC 5 Brixton
15.09.93 Dave Maj W RSC 2 Ashford
Career: 54 contests, won 42, drew 1, lost 11.

David Lake   Les Clark

David Lake (Noonan)

Herne Bay. *Born* London, 31 January, 1964
Welterweight. Ht. 5'8"
Manager Self

04.11.87 Lee West L RSC 6 Gravesend
11.02.88 Mark Pellat W RSC 4 Gravesend
24.02.88 Dean Bramhald L PTS 6 Southend
08.03.88 Tony Gibbs L PTS 6 Holborn
13.04.88 Tony Gibbs L RSC 1 Gravesend
06.09.88 Shane Tonks W PTS 6 Southend
26.09.88 Steve Taggart W PTS 6 Piccadilly

04.10.88	Shane Tonks W RSC 4 Southend
24.10.88	Carl Brasier W RSC 1 Windsor
14.11.88	Jan Nyholm L PTS 4 Helsinki, Finland
06.04.89	Ian Hosten W PTS 6 Stevenage
09.05.89	Paul Day L RSC 6 St Albans
28.06.89	Steve Foran L RSC 1 Brentwood
23.10.90	Trevor Ambrose L PTS 6 Leicester
05.03.91	Benny Collins L RSC 4 Millwall
07.10.92	Michael Smyth L CO 2 Barry
26.06.93	Sean Baker L PTS 4 Keynsham
16.09.93	Jason Beard L PTS 6 Southwark
09.12.93	B. F. Williams L RSC 4 Watford
23.02.94	Steve McGovern L PTS 6 Watford

Career: 20 contests, won 6, lost 14.

Gavin Lane (Keeble)

Paignton. *Born* Rainham, 14 July, 1971
L. Middleweight. Ht. 5'11¼"
Manager J. Gaynor

28.11.91	Dewi Roberts W PTS 6 Evesham
30.03.92	Razza Campbell L PTS 6 Coventry
27.05.93	Sean Baker L PTS 8 Bristol
28.10.93	Kevin Mabbutt L PTS 6 Torquay

Career: 4 contests, won 1, lost 3.

Martin Langtry

Lincon. *Born* Hampstead, 22 May, 1964
Cruiserweight. Ht. 5'10"
Manager Self

29.04.93	Stevie R. Davies W RSC 2 Newcastle
12.05.93	Simon McDougall W PTS 6 Sheffield
20.09.93	John Pierre W PTS 6 Cleethorpes
13.12.93	Steve Osborne W PTS 6 Cleethorpes
17.03.94	Lee Archer W CO 4 Lincoln

Career: 5 contests, won 5.

David Larkin

Leeds. *Born* Pontefract, 26 April, 1972
Middleweight. Ht. 5'10½"
Manager M. Duff

29.10.92	Rick North W PTS 6 Leeds
07.04.93	Cliff Churchward W RSC 4 Leeds
19.05.93	Ray Golding W PTS 6 Sunderland
01.07.93	David Sumner W CO 5 York
07.10.93	Lee Crocker W RSC 5 York

Career: 5 contests, won 5.

Anthony Lawrence

Wolverhampton. *Born* West Bromwich, 9
October, 1963
L. Middleweight. Ht. 5'11"
Manager Self

07.12.88	Terry French L PTS 6 Stoke
18.01.89	Glyn Davies W RSC 3 Stoke
20.02.89	Martin Robinson L PTS 6 Birmingham
03.04.89	Mark Whitehouse L PTS 6 Manchester
08.05.89	Floyd Gibbs L RSC 3 Edgbaston
19.06.89	Trevor Meikle W PTS 6 Manchester
10.10.89	Reuben Thurley W PTS 6 Wolverhampton
25.10.89	Darren Parker W PTS 6 Stoke
19.02.90	Chris Walker W PTS 6 Nottingham
13.10.93	Lee Crocker L RSC 5 York
16.12.93	James McGee DREW 6 Walsall
26.01.94	Carl Smith W RSC 4 Stoke
24.02.94	Gary Osborne W RSC 3 Walsall

Career: 13 contests, won 8, drew 1, lost 4.

Danny Lawson

Plymouth. *Born* Plymouth, 27 May, 1971
Bantamweight. Ht. 5'5¾"
Manager G. Mitchell

17.06.94	Danny Ruegg W PTS 6 Plymouth

Career: 1 contest, won 1.

Paul Lawson

Bethnal Green. *Born* Dundee, 2 December,
1966
Cruiserweight. Ht. 6'3"
Manager F. Maloney

15.09.93	Bobby Mack W PTS 4 Bethnal Green
13.10.93	Art Stacey W RSC 2 Bethnal Green
01.12.93	Des Vaughan W RSC 3 Bethnal Green
09.02.94	Nicky Wadman W RSC 1 Bethnal Green
29.03.94	Terry Duffus W RSC 1 Bethnal Green
15.06.94	Art Stacey W RSC 2 Southwark

Career: 6 contests, won 6.

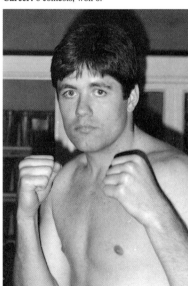

Paul Lawson   Les Clark

Mark Legg

Newcastle. *Born* South Shields, 25 March,
1970
L. Welterweight. Ht. 5'9½"
Manager T. Callighan

28.02.92	Chris Aston W RSC 5 Irvine
17.03.92	Dean Hiscox W PTS 6 Wolverhampton
18.05.92	Charles Shepherd L PTS 6 Marton
24.09.92	Ricky Sackfield W PTS 6 Stockport
25.11.93	Gary Hiscox W RSC 3 Tynemouth
07.02.94	Erwin Edwards W RSC 6 Bradford
02.03.94	Phil Found L RTD 4 Solihull
10.05.94	John O'Johnson L RSC 6 Doncaster

Career: 8 contests, won 5, lost 3.

Delroy Leslie

Wallington, *Born* Jamaica, 22 February,
1970
L. Welterweight. Ht. 5'11½"
Manager M. Duff

29.04.93	Phil Found W PTS 6 Mayfair
14.06.93	Jason Barker W RTD 3 Bayswater
16.09.93	Jamie Davidson W PTS 6 Southwark

Career: 3 contests, won 3.

Alan Levene

Liverpool. *Born* Liverpool, 26 February,
1968
Lightweight. Ht. 5'7½"
Manager Self

13.10.89	Mike Chapman W PTS 6 Preston
20.12.89	Finn McCool W RSC 2 Kirkby
24.01.90	Steve Winstanley DREW 6 Preston
17.10.90	Sugar Free Somerville DREW 6 Bethnal Green
05.05.92	Steve Winstanley W RSC 2 Preston
28.11.92	Mark Geraghty W PTS 6 Manchester
20.04.93	Joe Fannin W CO 1 Brentwood
15.05.93	Russell Davison W PTS 6 Glasgow
10.07.93	Nigel Haddock L RSC 5 Cardiff
09.02.94	Karl Taylor L RSC 2 Brentwood

Career: 10 contests, won 6, drew 2, lost 2.

Steve Levene

Birmingham. *Born* Birmingham, 23
August, 1969
L. Middleweight. Ht. 5'8½"
Manager Self

27.10.92	Steve Scott L RSC 1 Cradley Heath
07.12.92	Warren Stephens W CO 2 Birmingham
16.03.93	Alan Williams W RSC 1 Edgbaston
24.03.93	Sean Baker DREW 6 Belfast
19.04.93	Bullit Andrews W PTS 6 Northampton
18.05.93	Mark Antony L RSC 1 Edgbaston
06.09.93	Danny Peters L RSC 4 Liverpool
24.11.93	Prince Kasi Kiahau L PTS 6 Solihull
06.12.93	Bullit Andrews W RSC 6 Birmingham
17.02.94	Bullit Andrews W PTS 6 Walsall
07.03.94	Prince Kasi Kiahau L RSC 3 Doncaster

Career: 11 contests, won 5, drew 1, lost 5.

(Adrian) Adey Lewis

Bury. *Born* Bury, 31 May, 1975
Bantamweight. Ht. 5'0"
Manager J. Doughty

25.04.94	Darren Greaves W RSC 1 Bury
02.06.94	Dave Campbell W RSC 1 Middleton

Career: 2 contests, won 2.

(Gilbert) Gil Lewis

Willenhall. *Born* Coventry, 29 July, 1965
L. Heavyweight. Ht. 5'10½"
Manager Self

22.11.89	Gus Mendes W RSC 2 Solihull
17.01.90	Nigel Rafferty W PTS 6 Stoke
21.03.90	Lee Woolis W PTS 6 Solihull
24.05.90	Coco Collins W PTS 6 Dudley
21.06.90	Jimmy Ellis W PTS 6 Alfreton
06.12.90	Dave Owens W CO 2 Wolverhampton
28.01.91	Carlos Christie L PTS 8 Birmingham
27.02.91	Alan Baptiste W RSC 1 Wolverhampton
22.06.91	John Foreman DREW 6 Earls Court
01.10.91	Lee Prudden DREW 8 Bedworth
21.11.91	Art Stacey W RSC 4 Stafford
20.01.92	Tony Behan W PTS 8 Coventry
01.02.91	Ginger Tshabalala L RSC 4 Birmingham
15.09.92	Garry Delaney L CO 2 Crystal Palace

17.06.93   John J. Cooke L RSC 9 Bedworth
(Vacant Midlands Area L. Heavyweight Title)
18.04.94   Mark Smallwood L RSC 5 Walsall
Career: 16 contests, won 9, drew 2, lost 5.

Steve Lewsam
Grimsby. *Born* Cleethorpes, 8 September, 1960
Midlands Area Heavyweight Champion. Former Undefeated Midlands Area Cruiserweight Champion. Ht. 6'2"
Manager Self

22.11.82   Winston Wray W PTS 4 Liverpool
07.11.83   Wes Taylor W PTS 6 Birmingham
22.11.83   Jerry Golden L RSC 5 Manchester
27.10.88   Paul Sheldon W PTS 6 Birmingham
01.12.88   Ian Carmichael W CO 2 Stafford
07.12.88   Chris Little W RSC 1 Stoke
16.02.89   Dave Lawrence W PTS 6 Stafford
08.05.89   Abner Blackstock DREW 8 Grimsby
04.09.89   Mick Cordon W PTS 8 Grimsby
04.12.89   Abner Blackstock W PTS 8 Grimsby
09.03.90   Dennis Bailey DREW 8 Grimsby
21.05.90   Dennis Bailey W PTS 8 Grimsby
05.09.90   Herbie Hide L RSC 4 Brighton
18.11.90   Herbie Hide L RSC 1 Birmingham
12.02.91   Cordwell Hylton L RSC 8 Wolverhampton
29.04.91   Dave Muhammed L PTS 8 Cleethorpes
16.09.91   Cordwell Hylton W PTS 10 Cleethorpes
(Midlands Area Cruiserweight Title Challenge)
09.12.91   Tony Booth W PTS 8 Cleethorpes
04.06.92   Carl Thompson L RSC 8 Cleethorpes
(Vacant British Cruiserweight Title)
26.10.92   Tom Collins DREW 8 Cleethorpes
03.12.92   Eddie Smulders L CO 4 Rotterdam, Holland
10.05.93   David Jules W CO 6 Cleethorpes
28.03.94   Wayne Buck W PTS 10 Cleethorpes
(Vacant Midlands Area Heavyweight Title)
Career: 23 contests, won 13, drew 3, lost 7.

Alan Ley
Newport. *Born* Newport, 29 December, 1968
Bantamweight. Ht. 5'6"
Manager Self

03.09.91   Andrew Bloomer W PTS 6 Cardiff
22.01.92   Ceri Farrell W PTS 6 Cardiff
17.02.92   Leigh Williams W PTS 6 Mayfair
19.10.92   Shaun Norman W PTS 6 Mayfiar
24.02.93   Prince Nassem Hamed L CO 2 Wembley
28.09.93   Michael Alldis L PTS 6 Bethnal Green
29.01.94   Neil Swain L RSC 3 Cardiff
Career: 7 contests, won 4, lost 3.

Darren Littlewood
Sheffield. *Born* Sheffield, 6 November, 1974
S. Middleweight. Ht. 6'0"
Manager B. Ingle

24.11.93   Mark Smallwood L PTS 8 Solihull
02.12.93   Martin Jolley W PTS 6 Evesham
01.03.94   Joe Calzaghe L RSC 1 Dudley

28.05.94   Dean Francis L PTS 4 Queensway
Career: 4 contests, won 1, lost 3.

Wayne Llewelyn
Deptgford. *Born* Greenwich, 20 April, 1970
Heavyweight. Ht. 6'3½"
Manager Self

18.01.92   Chris Coughlan W RSC 3 Kensington
30.03.92   Steve Stewart W RSC 4 Eltham
23.04.92   Gary Charlton W RSC 4 Eltham
10.12.92   Gary McCrory W RSC 2 Glasgow
23.05.93   Cordwell Hylton W PTS 6 Brockley
01.12.93   Manny Burgo W PTS 6 Bethnal Green
14.04.94   Vance Idiens W RSC 1 Battersea
22.05.94   Cordwell Hylton W CO 2 Crystal Palace
Career: 8 contests, won 8.

Edward Lloyd
Rhyl. *Born* St Asaph, 23 April, 1963
Lightweight. Ht. 5'7½"
Manager Self

07.02.83   Stan Atherton W PTS 6 Liverpool
14.02.83   Sammy Rodgers W RSC 4 Manchester
21.02.83   Paul Cook L RSC 1 Mayfair
27.04.83   Bobby Welburn W PTS 6 Rhyl
09.05.83   Jimmy Thornton L RSC 1 Manchester
16.09.83   Jim Paton L PTS 6 Rhyl
28.11.83   John Murphy L PTS 8 Rhyl
06.02.84   Paul Keers W PTS 6 Liverpool
06.03.84   Gary Felvus L PTS 8 Stoke
12.06.84   Mickey Brooks L RSC 8 St Helens
06.08.84   Henry Arnold W RSC 6 Aintree
15.10.84   Steve Griffith L RTD 4 Liverpool
05.12.84   Jaswant Singh Ark W RSC 2 Stoke
01.02.85   Andy Williams DREW 6 Warrington
29.03.85   Billy Laidman W RSC 2 Liverpool
10.04.85   Brian Roche L RSC 7 Leeds
20.05.85   Gary Flear L PTS 8 Nottingham
19.07.85   Stanley Jones DREW 10 Colwyn Bay
(Vacant Welsh Lightweight Title)
10.02.86   Peter Bradley L PTS 8 Glasgow
06.03.86   Najib Daho L PTS 8 Manchester
24.11.86   Keith Parry L PTS 8 Cardiff
13.01.87   Sugar Gibiliru W PTS 8 Oldham
09.02.87   Craig Windsor W RSC 1 Cardiff
24.02.87   Alonzo Lopez W RTD 1 Marbella, Spain
31.10.87   Abdeselan Azowague W PTS 6 Marbella, Spain
30.11.87   Gary Maxwell L PTS 8 Nottingham
01.02.88   Colin Lynch L RTD 4 Northampton
11.02.92   Dewi Roberts W RSC 1 Cardiff
19.05.92   Mervyn Bennett W RSC 5 Cardiff
07.10.92   Steve Robinson L RTD 8 Barry
14.11.92   Carl Hook W PTS 6 Cardiff
19.01.93   Barrie Kelley L PTS 10 Cardiff
(Vacant Welsh S. Featherweight Title)
30.03.93   Nigel Haddock L RTD 4 Cardiff
05.05.93   Francisco Arroyo L RTD 3 Belfast
18.12.93   Jyrki Vierela L PTS 8 Turku, Finland
25.02.94   Gary Thornhill DREW 6 Chester
14.04.94   Felix Kelly W RSC 6 Battersea
Career: 37 contests, won 15, drew 3, lost 19.

Paul Lloyd
Ellesmere Port. *Born* Bebington, 7 December, 1968
Central Area S. Bantamweight Champion. Ht. 5'7"
Manager S. Vaughan

25.09.92   Graham McGrath W RSC 3 Liverpool

23.10.92   Kid McAuley W PTS 4 Liverpool
20.11.92   Des Gargano W PTS 4 Liverpool
15.12.92   Glyn Shepherd W RSC 1 Liverpool
27.02.93   Miguel Matthews W PTS 6 Ellesmere Port
04.05.93   Andrew Bloomer W PTS 6 Liverpool
02.07.93   Ronnie Stephenson W RTD 1 Liverpool
30.10.93   Marty Chestnut W RSC 1 Chester
11.12.93   Gerald Shelton W RSC 3 Liverpool
25.02.94   Ady Benton W RSC 5 Chester
(Vacant Central Area S. Bantamweight Title)
06.05.94   Pete Buckley W RTD 4 Liverpool
Career: 11 contests, won 11.

Ernie Locke
Cradley Heath. *Born* Warley, 1 September, 1966
Welterweight. Ht. 5'8"
Manager Self

22.02.93   Billy McDougall L PTS 6 Birmingham
16.03.93   Cliff Churchward DREW 6 Edgbaston
30.09.93   Andy Peach W PTS 6 Walsall
02.12.93   Andy Peach W RTD 3 Walsall
Career: 4 contests, won 2, drew 1, lost 1.

Steve Loftus
Stoke. *Born* Stoke, 10 October, 1971
L. Heavyweight. Ht. 6'2½"
Manager Self

29.09.92   Bobby Mack L PTS 6 Stoke
21.10.92   Paul Murray W PTS 6 Stoke
09.12.92   Lee Prudden L PTS 6 Stoke
17.03.93   Chris Nurse L PTS 6 Stoke
12.05.93   Zak Goldman W PTS 6 Stoke
07.09.93   Greg Scott-Briggs L RSC 2 Stoke
01.12.93   Tony Colclough W PTS 6 Stoke
15.03.94   Tim Robinson W PTS 6 Stoke
25.05.94   Mark Hale W PTS 6 Stoke
Career: 9 contests, won 5, lost 4.

Allan Logan
Airdrie. *Born* Bellshill, 19 October, 1971
Welterweight. Ht. 6'0"
Manager A. Melrose

19.12.93   Craig Winter L PTS 6 Glasgow
10.02.94   Ian Noble W PTS 6 Glasgow
11.03.94   Mark Antony W PTS 6 Glasgow
Career: 3 contests, won 2, lost 1.

Gary Logan
Brixton. *Born* Lambeth, 10 October, 1968
Southern Area Welterweight Champion. Ht. 5'8¾"
Manager F. Maloney

05.10.88   Peppy Muire W RTD 3 Wembley
02.11.88   Tony Gibbs W PTS 6 Southwark
07.12.88   Pat Dunne W PTS 6 Piccadilly
12.01.89   Mike Russell W CO 1 Southwark
20.02.89   Dave Griffiths W RSC 5 Mayfair
29.03.89   Ronnie Campbell W PTS 6 Wembley
10.05.89   Tony Britland W CO 1 Kensington
07.06.89   Davey Hughes W CO 1 Wembley
24.08.89   Mike English W CO 2 Tampa, USA
04.10.89   Simon Eubank W PTS 6 Kensington
12.10.89   Jimmy Thornton W PTS 6 Southwark
08.11.89   Chris Blake L PTS 8 Wembley
10.01.90   Julian Eavis W PTS 8 Kensington

Gary Logan (left) on his way to a fourth round kayo win over Paul King Les Clark

03.03.90	Anthony Joe Travis W CO 5 Wembley
09.05.90	Joseph Alexander W PTS 8 Wembley
13.09.90	Manuel Rojas W PTS 8 Watford
16.01.91	Julian Eavis W RSC 5 Kensington
18.02.91	Gordon Blair W CO 1 Mayfair
25.04.91	Trevor Ambrose W PTS 8 Mayfair
17.10.91	Des Robinson W PTS 8 Southwark
15.10.92	Mick Duncan W PTS 8 Lewisham
17.12.92	Roy Rowland W RSC 4 Wembley
	(Vacant Southern Area Welterweight Title)
23.05.93	Glyn Rhodes W CO 3 Brockley
25.06.93	Gordon Blair W RSC 6 Battersea
14.08.93	Paul King W CO 2 Hammersmith
28.11.93	Paul King W CO 4 Southwark
11.12.93	Horace Fleary W PTS 8 Dusseldorf, Germany
09.02.94	Graham Cheney L RSC 10 Bethnal Green
	(WBC International Welterweight Title Challenge)

Career: 28 contests, won 26, lost 2.

Prince Louis (Egbenoma)
Kings Lynn. *Born* Chelsea, 18 December, 1971
L. Middleweight. Ht. 5'10"
Manager G. Holmes

12.10.93	Prince Kasi Kiahau L PTS 6 Wolverhampton
30.11.93	Norman Hutcheon L PTS 6 Leicester
06.03.94	Danny Quacoe L RSC 2 Southwark

Career: 3 contests, lost 3.

Dave Lovell
Birmingham. *Born* Birmingham, 15 April, 1962
Welterweight. Ht. 5'7½"
Manager E. Cashmore

25.03.92	Billy Robinson L PTS 6 Hinckley
29.04.92	Jason Barker W PTS 6 Stoke
26.09.92	Seth Jones W RSC 4 Earls Court

27.10.92	Spencer McCracken L PTS 4 Cradley Heath
18.11.92	Alan Peacock L PTS 6 Solihull
30.01.93	Paul Knights L PTS 6 Brentwood
22.02.93	Alan Peacock L PTS 8 Glasgow
01.04.93	Richard O'Brien L PTS 6 Evesham
24.09.93	Jimmy McMahon L PTS 6 Dublin
23.11.93	Sean Metherell W RSC 3 Kettering
26.01.94	Mark Elliot L PTS 6 Birmingham
17.02.94	Craig Fisher W RSC 2 Bury
01.03.94	Mark McCreath W RSC 5 Dudley

Career: 13 contests, won 5, lost 8.

Ernie Loveridge
Wolverhampton. *Born* Bromsgrove, 7 July, 1970
S. Middleweight. Former Undefeated Midlands Area Welterweight Champion. Ht. 5'10"
Manager Self

06.02.89	Ricky Nelson L RSC 6 Nottingham
17.04.89	Martin Robinson L PTS 4 Birmingham
08.05.89	Bullit Andrews W PTS 6 Edgbaston
05.06.89	Alan Richards L PTS 6 Birmingham
19.06.89	Ian Thomas DREW 6 Manchester
28.06.89	Barry Messam L PTS 6 Kenilworth
10.10.89	Matt Sturgess W RSC 1 Wolverhampton
25.10.89	Darren Mount L PTS 6 Stoke
11.12.89	Cliff Churchward W PTS 6 Birmingham
27.02.90	Julian Eavis W PTS 6 Evesham
14.03.90	Mickey Lerwill W PTS 6 Stoke
27.03.90	Eddie King W PTS 6 Wolverhampton
24.04.90	Mark Jay W PTS 6 Stoke
24.05.90	Mickey Lerwill DREW 6 Dudley
18.09.90	Ronnie Campbell W PTS 6 Wolverhampton
24.10.90	Trevor Meikle W PTS 6 Dudley
23.01.91	Cliff Churchward W PTS 6 Solihull
27.02.91	Ronnie Campbell W PTS 8 Wolverhampton
13.03.91	John Corcoran W RSC 4 Stoke

10.04.91	Julian Eavis DREW 8 Wolverhampton
14.05.91	Paul Murray W PTS 8 Dudley
05.06.91	Cliff Churchward W PTS 8 Wolverhampton
10.09.91	Gary Osborne W RSC 1 Wolverhampton
	(Midlands Area Welterweight Title Challenge)
12.11.91	Mickey Lerwill W PTS 6 Wolverhampton
05.12.91	Jim Lawlor W PTS 8 Cannack
01.02.92	Michael Oliver W PTS 8 Birmingham
19.09.92	Paul Jones L PTS 6 Glasgow
01.10.92	Neville Brown L CO 4 Telford
20.01.93	Lee Crocker L PTS 6 Wolverhampton
17.02.93	Robert McCracken L CO 4 Bethnal Green
31.03.93	Kevin Lueshing L RSC 5 Bethnal Green
18.05.93	Antonio Fernandez L PTS 8 Edgbaston
10.07.93	Michael Smyth L RSC 6 Cardiff
09.10.93	Robin Reid L PTS 4 Manchester
02.11.93	Gilbert Jackson L RTD 3 Southwark
11.06.94	Mark Delaney L RSC 5 Bethnal Green

Career: 36 contests, won 18, drew 3, lost 15.

Kevin Lueshing
Beckenham. *Born* Beckenham, 17 April, 1968
Former Undefeated Southern Area L. Middleweight Champion. Ht. 5'11"
Manager M. Jacobs

30.09.91	John McGlynn W RSC 2 Kensington
23.10.91	Julian Eavis W RSC 2 Bethnal Green
14.12.91	Trevor Meikle W CO 3 Bexleyheath
18.01.92	Simon Eubank W CO 4 Kensington
25.03.92	Tracy Jocelyn W RSC 3 Dagenham
30.04.92	Newton Barnett W PTS 6 Kensington
03.02.93	Ian Chantler W RSC 2 Earls Court
17.02.93	Leigh Wicks W PTS 6 Bethnal Green
31.03.93	Ernie Loveridge W RSC 5 Bethnal Green
14.04.93	Marty Duke W RSC 2 Kensington
23.06.93	Kirkland Laing W RSC 5 Edmonton
	(Vacant Southern Area L. Middleweight Title)
03.03.94	Chris Saunders L RSC 4 Ebbw Vale

Career: 12 contests, won 11, lost 1.

Dean Lynch
Swansea. *Born* Swansea, 21 November, 1964
Featherweight. Ht. 5'6"
Manager Self

18.09.86	Billy Barton L PTS 6 Weston super Mare
06.10.86	Paddy Maguire W PTS 6 Birmingham
18.11.86	Phil Lashley W PTS 6 Swansea
01.03.88	Gary King L PTS 6 Southend
21.03.88	Phil Lashley W PTS 6 Bethnal Green
09.04.88	John Knight L PTS 6 Bristol
20.04.88	Henry Armstrong W PTS 6 Stoke
13.05.88	Raymond Armand L PTS 8 Hyeres, France
23.11.88	Colin Lynch L PTS 8 Solihull
12.04.89	James Hunter L RSC 4 Swansea
	(Vacant Welsh S. Featherweight Title)
12.05.89	Valerio Nati L RSC 6 Lodi, Italy
22.01.90	Donnie Hood L PTS 8 Glasgow
19.02.90	Regilio Tuur L PTS 6 Arnhem, Holland
10.03.90	Freddy Cruz L RSC 4 Lamezia Terme, Italy

14.04.92   Lee Fox W PTS 6 Mansfield
15.09.92   Henry Armstrong L RSC 5 Liverpool
14.12.92   Karl Morling W RSC 4 Northampton
07.04.93   Tony Silkstone L PTS 8 Leeds
28.04.93   Francisco Arroyo L PTS 6 Dublin
11.05.94   Mark Bowers L RSC 2 Stevenage
Career: 20 contests, won 6, lost 14.

Paul Lynch

Swansea. *Born* Swansea, 27 December, 1966
Welterweight. Ht. 5'11"
Manager Self

23.10.89   Darren Burford W PTS 6 Mayfair
16.11.89   Robbie Harron W PTS 6 Weston super Mare
20.12.89   Peter Reid W RSC 4 Swansea
08.03.90   Tony Booth W PTS 6 Watford
04.12.90   Ernie Noble W RSC 3 Southend
12.02.91   Roy Rowland W RTD 4 Basildon
01.10.91   Peter Manfredo L PTS 8 Providence, USA
12.02.92   Robert McCracken L RSC 4 Wembley
14.04.92   Paul Jones L RSC 3 Mansfield
16.02.93   Tony Velinor W PTS 8 Tooting
31.03.93   Kevin Sheeran L RSC 1 Barking
23.03.94   Robert Welin L PTS 6 Cardiff
31.03.94   Sean Baker W RSC 3 Bristol
11.05.94   Del Bryan L PTS 8 Sheffield
Career: 14 contests, won 8, lost 6.

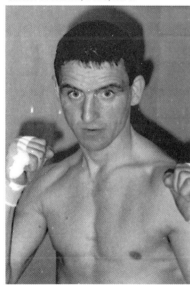

Paul Lynch   Les Clark

Chris Lyons

Birmingham. *Born* Birmingham, 2 September, 1972
Featherweight. Ht. 5'9"
Manager Self

02.12.91   Ronnie Sephenson L PTS 6 Birmingham
09.12.91   Ronnie Stephenson L PTS 6 Cleethorpes
22.01.92   Dennis Oakes L RSC 3 Stoke
17.05.92   Dave Martin DREW 6 Harringay
08.09.92   Robert Braddock L CO 5 Doncaster

13.10.92   Paul Kelly W PTS 6 Wolverhampton
30.10.92   Paul Kelly W CO 1 Birmingham
17.12.92   Mark Bowers L CO 2 Wembley
08.03.93   Chip O'Neill L PTS 6 Leeds
22.04.93   Marcus Duncan L RSC 2 Bury
26.06.93   Tim Yeates L PTS 4 Earls Court
16.09.93   Anthony Hanna L PTS 6 Southwark
30.11.93   Kid McAuley L RSC 5 Wolverhampton
01.03.94   Marty Chestnut L PTS 6 Dudley
27.04.94   Marty Chestnut W RSC 3 Bethnal Green
06.05.94   John Sillo L RSC 3 Liverpool
15.06.94   Matt Brown L CO 3 Southwark
Career: 17 contests, won 3, drew 1, lost 13.

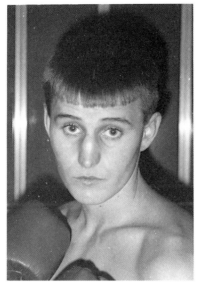

Chris Lyons   Les Clark

Ricky Mabbett

Leicester. *Born* Leicester, 27 November, 1971
Welterweight. Ht. 5'9"
Manager K. Squires

19.03.92   Phil Epton W RSC 3 York
16.06.92   Ojay Abrahams L PTS 6 Dagenham
08.09.92   Marty Duke DREW 6 Norwich
27.10.92   Steve McGovern DREW 6 Leicester
26.01.93   Marty Duke L CO 1 Leicester
16.03.93   Spencer McCracken L PTS 6 Edgbaston
26.04.93   Darren McInulty W CO 3 Cleethorpes
19.05.93   Ojay Abrahams W RSC 4 Leicester
18.09.93   Ojay Abrahams W PTS 6 Leicester
21.05.94   Michael Carruth L CO 3 Belfast
Career: 10 contests, won 4, drew 2, lost 4.

Kevin Mabbutt

Northampton. *Born* Northampton, 23 February, 1969
L. Middleweight. Ht. 5'8¼"
Manager J. Cox

06.04.92   Peter Reid L PTS 6 Northampton
28.04.92   Sean Cave W PTS 6 Corby
05.10.92   Cliff Churchward W PTS 6 Northampton

14.12.92   Billy McDougall W RTD 4 Northampton
23.02.93   Paul Dyer W PTS 6 Kettering
04.03.93   Bullit Andrews W PTS 6 Northampton
19.04.93   James Campbell W PTS 6 Northampton
20.09.93   Richard O'Brien W PTS 6 Northampton
28.10.93   Gavin Lane W PTS 6 Torquay
23.11.93   Nick Appiah W PTS 6 Kettering
19.12.93   Steve Scott W PTS 6 Northampton
08.03.94   Rick North W PTS 6 Kettering
Career: 12 contests, won 11, lost 1.

Kris McAdam

Glasgow. *Born* Glasgow, 1 January, 1964
L. Welterweight. Scottish Lightweight Champion. Ht. 5'9½"
Manager T. Gilmour

15.10.84   Bobby Welburn DREW 6 Glasgow
25.02.85   Denzil Goddard W RSC 1 Glasgow
27.03.85   Marvin P. Gray W RSC 3 Gateshead
10.05.85   Dave Smith L PTS 6 Glasgow
16.09.85   Russell Jones L PTS 6 Glasgow
09.10.89   Paul Charters L PTS 8 Glasgow
29.11.89   Chris Bennett L CO 3 Marton
19.02.90   Martin Reilly W PTS 6 Glasgow
19.03.90   Martin Reilly W RSC 8 Glasgow
26.03.90   Jim Moffat W PTS 8 Glasgow
07.09.90   Sugar Gibiliru L PTS 8 Liverpool
22.10.90   Jim Moffat W RSC 5 Glasgow
           (Scottish Lightweight Title Challenge)
22.01.91   John Smith W PTS 6 Glasgow
22.04.91   Brian Roche L RSC 2 Glasgow
           (Elim. British Lightweight Title)
18.11.91   Colin Sinnott W PTS 6 Glasgow
27.01.92   Pete Roberts W CO 2 Glasgow
18.03.92   Nigel Bradley L CO 2 Glasgow
22.02.93   Dave Madden W PTS 8 Glasgow
04.03.94   Lee Soar W CO 2 Irvine
10.04.94   John Smith L PTS 8 Glasgow
Career: 20 contests, won 11, drew 1, lost 8.

Eamonn McAuley

Belfast. *Born* Belfast, 4 January, 1966
S. Featherweight. Ht. 5'7"
Manager B. Hearn

20.05.86   Dean Bramhald W PTS 6 Wembley
29.10.86   Les Remikie W RSC 2 Belfast
17.01.87   Les Remikie W RTD 2 Belfast
26.02.87   George Jones W PTS 6 Bethnal Green
25.04.87   Tony Borg W RSC 4 Belfast
19.10.87   Nicky Lucas W RTD 3 Belfast
03.12.87   Andrew Furlong L RTD 3 Belfast
28.09.89   Greg Egbuniwe W PTS 6 Wandsworth
12.09.90   Rick Bushell W RSC 4 Battersea
24.03.93   Russell Davison W PTS 6 Belfast
18.06.93   Pete Buckley W PTS 6 Belfast
22.01.94   Kid McAuley W PTS 6 Belfast
Career: 12 contests, won 11, lost 1.

(Colin) Kid McAuley

Liverpool. *Born* Liverpool, 6 June, 1968
S. Featherweight. Ht. 5'6"
Manager J. Rushton

08.09.92   Jonjo Irwin L PTS 6 Doncaster
19.09.92   Alex Docherty L PTS 6 Glasgow
30.09.92   Yusuf Vorajee W PTS 6 Solihull
13.10.92   John White L PTS 4 Bury
23.10.92   Paul Lloyd L PTS 4 Liverpool

115

10.11.92 Michael Alldis L PTS 6 Dagenham
24.11.92 Miguel Matthews W PTS 6 Doncaster
12.12.92 Michael Alldis L CO 1 Muswell Hill
27.01.93 Yusuf Vorajee L RSC 5 Stoke
03.03.93 Kevin Middleton L PTS 8 Solihull
16.03.93 Jonjo Irwin L PTS 10 Mayfair
(Vacant All-Ireland Featherweight
Title)
28.04.93 Barry Jones L PTS 8 Solihull
14.05.93 Shaun Anderson L PTS 8 Kilmarnock
29.05.93 James Murray L PTS 6 Paisley
28.06.93 Carl Roberts W PTS 6 Morecambe
25.07.93 Mario Culpeper L PTS 6 Oldham
12.10.93 Elvis Parsley L PTS 6 Wolverhampton
30.11.93 Chris Lyons W RSC 5 Wolverhampton
22.01.94 Eamonn McAuley L PTS 6 Belfast
10.02.94 Tony Foster L RTD 4 Hull
11.03.94 Donnie Hood L PTS 8 Glasgow
27.04.94 Harry Escott L RTD 6 Solihull
02.06.94 Wayne Rigby L PTS 6 Middleton
10.06.94 Bradley Welsh L RTD 1 Glasgow
Career: 24 contests, won 4, lost 20.

Kevin McBride   Les Clark

Kevin McBride

Clones. *Born* Monaghan, 10 May, 1973
Heavyweight. Ht. 6'5"
Manager F. Maloney

17.12.92 Gary Charlton DREW 6 Barking
13.02.93 Gary Williams W PTS 4 Manchester
15.09.93 Joey Paladino W CO 2 Bethnal Green
13.10.93 Chris Coughlan W PTS 4 Bethnal
Green
01.12.93 John Harewood W RSC 3 Bethnal
Green
06.05.94 Edgar Turpin W RSC 1 Atlantic City,
USA
04.06.94 Roger Bryant W CO 1 Reno, USA
17.06.94 Stanley Wright W PTS 6 Atlantic City,
USA
Carrer: 8 contests, won 7, drew 1.

Paul McCarthy

Southampton. *Born* London, 24 March,
1961

Cruiserweight. Former Southern Area S.
Middleweight Champion. Ht. 6'0"
Manager J. Bishop

29.01.87 Eddie Brooks L PTS 6 Merton
03.03.87 Jim Beckett W CO 1 Southend
06.04.87 Gary Pemberton L RSC 4 Southampton
26.05.87 Neil Simpson W CO 1 Plymouth
25.09.87 Spencer Cummings W CO 3 Tooting
16.11.87 Newton Barnett W PTS 8 Southampton
09.12.87 Rocky Bourkriss W CO 1 Greenwich
14.12.87 Andy Wright L CO 3 Piccadilly
14.03.88 Mark Howell W RSC 2 Mayfair
21.04.88 Steve Aquilina W PTS 6 Bethnal Green
18.05.88 Joe McKenzie W RSC 3 Portsmouth
31.08.88 Denys Cronin L RSC 4 Stoke
24.11.88 Simon Collins DREW 8 Southampton
20.12.88 Simon Collins W DIS 3 Swansea
25.01.89 Brendan Dempsey W PTS 6 Bethnal
Green
02.03.89 Cliff Curtis W RTD 7 Southampton
04.04.89 Chris Galloway W RSC 4 Southend
26.04.89 Terry Duffus W PTS 8 Southampton
09.05.89 Derek Myers L PTS 6 Southend
02.10.89 Noel Magee L CO 2 Hanley
30.11.89 Dave Lawrence W PTS 6 Southwark
14.03.90 Richard Bustin W RSC 7 Battersea
(Vacant Southern Area S. Middleweight
Title)
26.05.90 Keith Halliwell W RSC 3 Reading
15.10.90 Derek Myers L PTS 8 Lewisham
23.10.90 Nicky Piper L RSC 3 Leicester
08.02.91 Fabrice Tiozzo L CO 2 Villeurbanne,
France
20.03.91 Andy Wright L CO 5 Wandsworth
(Southern Area S. Middleweight Title
Defence)
16.05.91 Lester Jacobs L PTS 6 Battersea
01.06.91 Ali Forbes L CO 2 Bethnal Green
19.11.91 Dave Lawrence DREW 6 Norwich
19.12.91 Antonio Fernandez L PTS 8 Brierley
Hill
16.12.91 Peter Vosper W PTS 6 Southampton
08.01.92 Graham Jenner L PTS 6 Burton
22.01.92 Julian Johnson DREW 6 Cardiff
29.02.92 Graham Jenner L PTS 8 St Leonards
11.03.92 Jason McNeill L PTS 6 Cardiff
30.04.92 Hussain Shah L RTD 4 Kensington
05.10.92 Barry Downes W PTS 6 Northampton
10.12.92 Stefan Wright L PTS 6 Corby
15.02.93 Bruce Scott L PTS 6 Mayfair
16.03.93 Justin Clements L PTS 6 Edgbaston
29.04.93 Gypsy Carman L PTS 6 Hayes
02.07.93 Kenley Price L PTS 6 Liverpool
28.07.93 Kenny Nevers W PTS 4 Brixton
15.09.93 Terry Dunstan L RSC 3 Ashford
02.12.93 Ian Henry L PTS 6 Hartlepool
11.12.93 Dennis Bailey L PTS 6 Liverpool
18.12.93 Billy Isaac L PTS 6 Manchester
Career: 48 contests, won 19, drew 3, lost 26.

Steve McCarthy

Southampton. *Born* East Ham, 30 July,
1962
Former Undefeated British & Southern
Area L. Heavyweight Champion. Ht. 5'11½"
Manager H. Holland

05.02.87 Russell Barnett W CO 1 Southampton
03.03.87 B. K. Bennett W CO 3 Southend
06.04.87 Winston Burnett W PTS 8
Southampton
06.10.87 Jason Baxter DREW 6 Southend
16.11.87 Paul Wesley W CO 8 Southampton

03.02.88 Andy Wright W RSC 4 Wembley
18.05.88 Mike Aubrey W RSC 4 Portsmouth
24.11.88 Serg Fame W PTS 10 Southampton
(Southern Area L. Heavyweight Title
Challenge)
02.03.89 Yves Monsieur W PTS 8 Southampton
26.04.89 Johnny Held W PTS 8 Southampton
21.09.89 Tony Wilson L RTD 3 Southampton
(Elim. British L. Heavyweight Title)
25.10.90 Serg Fame W PTS 12 Battersea
(Vacant British L. Heavyweight Title)
16.12.91 John Foreman W PTS 8 Southampton
04.04.92 Henry Maske L DIS 9 Dusseldorf,
Germany
29.09.92 Dariusz Michalczewski L DIS 3
Hamburg, Germany
14.04.93 Simon Harris L RSC 5 Kensington
23.02.94 Karl Barwise W PTS 6 Watford
Career: 17 contests, won 12, drew 1, lost 4.

Joe McCluskey

Croy. *Born* Glasgow, 13 March, 1970
L. Heavyweight. Ht. 6'0"
Manager T. Gilmour

27.04.92 John Oxenham W PTS 4 Glasgow
09.07.92 Lee Prudden W PTS 6 Glasgow
25.01.93 Andy Manning W PTS 6 Glasgow
22.11.93 Jimmy Tyers W PTS 6 Glasgow
Career: 4 contests, won 4.

Bernard McComiskey

Banbridge. *Born* Banbridge, 9 June, 1971
L. Welterweight. Ht. 5'7"
Manager Self

25.04.90 Lee Fox W RTD 3 Brighton
27.06.90 Stuart Rimmer W PTS 6 Kensington
22.09.90 Wayne Windle L PTS 6 Kensington
11.05.91 Sean Casey W RTD 3 Belfast
24.03.93 Trevor Royal W RSC 6 Belfast
18.06.93 Brian Wright W PTS 6 Belfast
22.01.94 Mike Morrison W PTS 6 Belfast
Career: 7 contests, won 6, lost 1.

Spencer McCracken

Birmingham. *Born* Birmingham, 8 August,
1969
Welterweight. Ht. 5'9"
Manager Self

15.10.91 Stuart Dunn DREW 6 Dudley
09.12.91 Seth Jones W RSC 2 Brierley Hill
27.10.92 Dave Lovell W PTS 4 Cradley Heath
07.12.92 Mark Antony W CO 1 Birmingham
22.02.93 Rick North W PTS 8 Birmingham
16.03.93 Ricky Mabbett W PTS 6 Edgbaston
18.05.93 Tony Britland W CO 1 Edgbaston
06.12.93 Jimmy Thornton W PTS 6 Birmingham
19.01.94 Julian Eavis W PTS 8 Solihull
28.03.94 Marty Duke W RSC 2 Birmingham
23.05.94 Ojay Abrahams W PTS 6 Walsall
Career: 11 contests, won 10, drew 1.

Marcus McCrae

Hackney. *Born* London, 13 November,
1969
S. Featherweight. Ht. 5'7"
Manager F. Warren

22.09.93 Miguel Matthews W PTS 6 Bethnal
Green
10.11.93 Ian Reid W PTS 6 Bethnal Green

17.02.94 Thomas Bernard W RSC 1 Dagenham
04.06.94 Andrew Reed W PTS 6 Cardiff
Career: 4 contests, won 4.

Marcus McCrae　　　　　　Les Clark

Mark McCreath

Lincoln. *Born* Bradford, 30 May, 1964
Welterweight. Former Undefeated Benelux
Welterweight Champion. Ht. 5'8½"
Manager Self

11.05.89 Tom Heiskonen W RSC 6 Tallin,
　　　　　Estonia
01.11.89 Bianto Baekelandt W CO 2 Izegem,
　　　　　Belgium
29.11.89 Abdel Lahjar W RTD 4 Paris, France
09.12.89 Pierre Conan W RSC 4 Toul, France
10.02.90 Josef Rajic W PTS 6 Roulers, France
26.03.90 Eric Capoen W RSC 1 Nogent sur
　　　　　Marne, France
19.05.90 Mohammed Berrabah W RSC 6
　　　　　Montpelier, France
11.08.90 Mohamed Oumad W RTD 5 Le cap
　　　　　d'Agde, France
05.09.90 Mehmet Demir W RSC 5 Belgrade,
　　　　　Yugoslavia
05.10.90 Patrick Vungbo L PTS 10 Waregem,
　　　　　Belgium
　　　　　(Vacant Belgium Welterweight Title)
17.04.91 Pat Barrett L RSC 6 Kensington
　　　　　*(European L. Welterweight Title
　　　　　Challenge)*
21.06.91 Freddy Demeulenaere W RSC 5
　　　　　Waregem, Belgium
　　　　　(Vacant Benelux Welterweight Title)
30.04.92 Gary Barron W RSC 5 Mayfair
01.10.92 Chris Saunders W RSC 4 Telford
07.12.92 Gary Barron W RSC 5 Mayfair
06.03.93 Valery Kayumba L RSC 11 Levallois
　　　　　Perret, France
　　　　　*(European L. Welterweight Title
　　　　　Challenge)*
26.05.93 Peter Till W PTS 8 Mansfield
27.10.93 John Smith W RSC 7 West Bromwich
01.03.94 Dave Lovell L RSC 5 Dudley
Career: 19 contests, won 15, lost 4.

Geoff McCreesh

Bracknell. *Born* Stockton, 12 June, 1970
L. Middleweight. Ht. 5'10"
Manager W. Ball

16.02.94 Tony Walton W PTS 6 Stevenage
12.03.94 Barry Thorogood W PTS 6 Cardiff
22.03.94 Mark Dawson W PTS 6 Bethnal Green
20.05.94 Robert Peel W RSC 2 Acton
Career: 4 contests, won 4.

Geoff McCreesh　　　　　　Les Clark

Glenn McCrory

Annfield Plain. *Born* Stanley, 23
September, 1964
Former IBF Cruiserweight Champion.
Former Undefeated British &
Commonwealth Cruiserweight Champion.
Ht. 6'4"
Manager D. Gregory

06.02.84 Barry Ellis W RSC 1 Mayfair
22.02.84 Denroy Bryan W PTS 6 Kensington
21.03.84 Steve Abadom W PTS 6 Mayfair
30.04.84 Frank Robinson W PTS 6 Mayfair
09.05.84 Frank Robinson W RSC 4 Mayfair
13.06.84 Andrew Gerrard W PTS 6 Aberavon
06.09.84 Andrew Gerrard W PTS 8 Gateshead
27.10.84 Tony Velasco W PTS 8 Gateshead
24.11.84 Mike Perkins W PTS 8 Gateshead
19.01.85 Nate Robinson W RSC 2 Birmingham
20.02.85 Alex Williamson W PTS 8 Muswell
　　　　　Hill
27.03.85 Gypsy Carman W PTS 8 Gateshead
28.05.85 Alphonso Forbes W CO 1 Muswell
　　　　　Hill
03.09.85 John Westgarth L CO 4 Gateshead
10.12.85 Roy Skeldon W PTS 8 Gateshead
09.04.86 Rudi Pika L PTS 8 Kensington
18.04.86 Anders Eklund L PTS 8 Randers,
　　　　　Denmark
17.06.86 Dave Garside L RSC 7 Blackpool
07.10.86 Hughroy Currie L RSC 2 Oldham
25.11.86 Joe Adams W PTS 6 Louisville, USA

08.01.87 Calvin Sherman W CO 1 Houston,
　　　　　USA
05.12.87 Danny Lawford W PTS 8 Newcastle
18.02.87 Barry Ellis W PTS 8 Fulham
31.03.87 Andy Straughn W RSC 10 Oldham
　　　　　(Elim. British Cruiserweight Title)
04.09.87 Chisanda Mutti W PTS 12 Gateshead
　　　　　*(Commonwealth Cruiserweight Title
　　　　　Challenge)*
21.01.88 Tee Jay W PTS 12 Wandsworth
　　　　　*(British Cruiserweight Title Challenge.
　　　　　Commonwealth Cruiserweight Title
　　　　　Defence)*
22.04.88 Lou Gent W RTD 8 Gateshead
　　　　　*(British & Commonwealth
　　　　　Cruiserweight Title Defence)*
01.11.88 Ron Warrior W CO 4 Oklahoma City,
　　　　　USA
15.11.88 Lorenzo Boyd W CO 2 Metairie, USA
28.02.89 Steve Mormino W PTS 10 Marton
03.06.89 Patrick Lumumba W PTS 12 Stanley
　　　　　(Vacant IBF Cruiserweight Title)
21.10.89 Siza Makhatini W CO 11
　　　　　Middlesbrough
　　　　　(IBF Cruiserweight Title Defence)
22.03.90 Jeff Lampkin L CO 3 Gateshead
　　　　　(IBF Cruiserweight Title Defence)
16.02.91 Terry Armstrong W CO 2 Thornaby
30.09.91 Lennox Lewis L CO 2 Kensington
　　　　　*(British & European Heavyweight Title
　　　　　Challenge)*
26.09.92 Mohamed Bouchiche DREW 8 Paris,
　　　　　France
20.01.93 Ric Lainhart W RSC 2 Avoriaz, France
06.05.93 Mark Young W PTS 10 Las Vegas,
　　　　　USA
16.07.93 Al Cole L PTS 12 Moscow, Russia
　　　　　(IBF Cruiserweight Title Challenge)
Career: 39 contests, won 30, drew 1, lost 8.

Shaun McCrory

Stanley, *Born* Shotley Bridge, 13 June,
1969
S. Middleweight. Ht. 6'2"
Manager Self

03.06.89 Hugh Fury W PTS 6 Stanley
10.10.89 Mick Maw L PTS 4 Sunderland
27.02.90 Ian Vokes W PTS 6 Marton
06.03.90 Benny Simmons W RSC 6 Newcastle
23.03.90 Mark Spencer W RSC 2 Chester le
　　　　　Street
21.04.90 Sean Stringfellow W PTS 6
　　　　　Sunderland
05.06.90 Alan Pennington L PTS 8 Liverpool
05.09.90 Tony Booth W PTS 6 Stoke
15.10.90 Richard Carter L PTS 8 Brierley Hill
19.11.90 Ian Henry L PTS 6 Manchester
21.01.91 Ian Henry L PTS 6 Glasgow
06.02.91 Tony Booth W PTS 6 Liverpool
13.05.91 John Oxenham W PTS 6 Marton
03.08.91 Ron Collins L PTS 8 Selvino, Italy
13.04.92 Paul Wright L PTS 6 Manchester
28.04.92 Dave Johnson DREW 6 Houghton le
　　　　　Spring
05.10.92 Eddie Knight W PTS 6 Bristol
23.03.94 Dean Ashton DREW 6 Stoke
29.03.94 Carl Smallwood L PTS 6
　　　　　Wolverhampton
16.05.94 Gypsy Johnny Price L PTS 6
　　　　　Morecambe
Career: 20 contests, won 9, drew 2, lost 9.

117

Errol McDonald

Nottingham. *Born* Nottingham, 11 March, 1964
Welterweight. Ht. 5'10"
Manager Self

21.10.85	Dave Heaver W CO 1 Mayfair	
05.11.85	Robert Armstrong W RSC 4 Wembley	
20.01.86	Lenny Gloster W PTS 8 Mayfair	
17.02.86	Kid Milo DREW 6 Mayfair	
27.02.86	Gary Flear W RSC 5 Bethnal Green	
09.04.86	Lenny Gloster W PTS 6 Kensington	
29.10.86	Gerry Beard W RSC 4 Piccadilly	
19.01.87	Mark Simpson W CO 5 Mayfair	
30.08.87	Jose Maria Castillo W RSC 3 Marbella, Spain	
30.09.87	Roy Callaghan W RSC 4 Mayfair	
18.11.87	Billy Cairns W RTD 3 Bethnal Green	
03.02.88	Mike English W RSC 2 Wembley	
29.03.88	Ramon Nunez W RSC 3 Wembley	
21.04.88	Nick Meloscia W PTS 8 Bethnal Green	
26.09.88	Jimmy Thornton W RTD 2 Piccadilly	
05.10.88	Alfredo Reyes W CO 2 Wembley	
30.11.88	Sammy Floyd W RSC 3 Southwark	
18.01.89	Nick Meloscia W RSC 1 Kensington	
19.12.89	Mick Mulcahy W RSC 3 Bethnal Green	
27.01.90	Joe Hernandez W PTS 8 Sheffield	
28.03.90	Robert Lewis W RSC 4 Bethnal Green	
25.04.90	Mario Lopez W CO 1 Brighton	
05.06.90	Steve Larrimore W RSC 9 Nottingham	
18.11.90	Ray Taylor W RTD 3 Birmingham	
23.02.91	Juan Rondon W RSC 7 Brighton	
08.06.91	Patrizio Oliva L DIS 12 La Spezia, Italy	
	(European Welterweight Title Challenge)	
10.12.91	Jose Luis Saldivia W PTS 8 Sheffield	
10.03.92	Robert Wright L CO 3 Bury	
24.11.92	Gordon Blair W RSC 5 Doncaster	
12.01.93	Otero Orlando W RSC 4 Aachen, Germany	
16.02.93	Peter Till W PTS 8 Tooting	
16.03.93	Michael Driscoll L PTS 10 Mayfair	
	(Elim. British L. Welterweight Title)	
25.10.93	Wayne Appleton L PTS 8 Glasgow	
24.01.94	Ojay Abrahams L RSC 2 Glasgow	

Career: 34 contests, won 28, drew 1, lost 5.

Billy McDougall

Birmingham. *Born* Birmingham, 11 October, 1965
Welterweight. Ht. 5'10"
Manager Self

02.11.92	Jimmy Reynolds L PTS 6 Wolverhampton	
19.11.92	Dean Carr W PTS 6 Evesham	
07.12.92	Dean Carr W PTS 6 Birmingham	
14.12.92	Kevin Mabbutt L RTD 4 Northampton	
27.01.93	Jamie Morris W PTS 6 Stoke	
22.02.93	Ernie Locke W PTS 6 Birmingham	
29.04.93	Rob Stevenson DREW 6 Hull	
06.05.93	Andy Peach W PTS 6 Walsall	
23.06.93	Marty Duke L PTS 6 Gorleston	
11.08.93	Paul Denton L PTS 6 Mansfield	
02.12.93	Cam Raeside L RSC 5 Evesham	
19.01.94	John O'Johnson W RSC 3 Stoke	
08.02.94	Richard Swallow L PTS 6 Wolverhampton	
16.02.94	Steve McNess L PTS 4 Stevenage	
10.03.94	Danny Shinkwin DREW 4 Watford	
10.05.94	Prince Kasi Kiahau L RTD 4 Doncaster	

Career: 16 contests, won 6, drew 2, lost 8.

Simon McDougall

Blackpool. *Born* Manchester, 11 July, 1968
L. Heavyweight. Ht. 5'10½"
Manager Self

14.11.88	Andrew Bravardo W CO 4 Manchester	
16.01.89	Steve Osborne L PTS 6 Bradford	
25.01.89	Steve Osborne L PTS 6 Stoke	
20.02.89	Willie Connell W RSC 4 Bradford	
04.04.89	Lee Woolis L PTS 6 Manchester	
12.10.89	George Ferrie W PTS 6 Glasgow	
30.11.89	Jimmy Cropper W PTS 6 Oldham	
07.12.89	Sean O'Phoenix L PTS 6 Manchester	
07.04.90	Eddie Smulders L PTS 6 Eindhoven, Holland	
15.05.90	Terry French W PTS 4 South Shields	
12.10.90	Ray Alberts L PTS 6 Cayenne, France	
22.10.90	Glenn Campbell L RSC 4 Manchester	
10.12.90	Morris Thomas W RSC 2 Bradford	
28.01.91	Ian Henry W PTS 8 Bradford	
28.02.91	Glenn Campbell L PTS 10 Bury	
	(Central Area S. Middleweight Title Challenge)	
23.04.91	Paul Burton L PTS 8 Evesham	
10.05.91	Ian Henry L PTS 6 Gateshead	
30.09.91	Doug Calderwood W RSC 4 Liverpool	
10.10.91	Terry French L PTS 6 Gateshead	
19.10.91	Andrea Magi L RSC 5 Terni, Italy	
03.03.92	Paul Hitch L PTS 6 Houghton le Spring	
11.03.92	Ian Henry L PTS 8 Solihull	
30.03.92	Nigel Rafferty L PTS 8 Coventry	
08.06.92	Mark McBiane L PTS 6 Bradford	
06.10.92	Garry Delaney L PTS 8 Antwerp, Belgium	
12.12.92	Garry Delaney L PTS 8 Muswell Hill	
04.03.93	Alan Smiles L PTS 6 Glasgow	
26.03.93	Roland Ericsson W RSC 5 Copenhagen, Denmark	
17.04.93	Terry French L PTS 6 Washington	
12.05.93	Martin Langtry L PTS 6 Sheffield	
14.08.93	Mark Prince L PTS 6 Hammersmith	
04.10.93	Bruce Scott L PTS 6 Mayfair	
15.10.93	Christophe Girard L PTS 8 Romorantin, France	
08.12.93	Stevie R. Davies L RSC 5 Hull	
29.01.94	Ole Klemetsen L RTD 5 Cardiff	
08.03.94	John Foreman W PTS 6 Edgbaston	
11.05.94	Monty Wright W PTS 6 Stevenage	

Career: 37 contests, won 13, lost 24.

Alan McDowall

Renfrew. *Born* Renfrew, 29 September, 1967
Lightweight. Ht. 5'10"
Manager Self

24.09.91	Johnny Patterson W PTS 4 Glasgow	
28.11.91	Johnny Patterson W PTS 6 Glasgow	
31.01.92	Charles Shepherd W RSC 3 Glasgow	
20.02.92	Mark O'Callaghan W PTS 6 Glasgow	
12.03.92	James Jiora W CO 2 Glasgow	
29.05.92	Karl Taylor W PTS 6 Glasgow	
22.10.92	Robert Lloyd W RTD 4 Glasgow	
30.04.93	Dean Bramhald W PTS 6 Glasgow	
29.05.93	Rob Stewart DREW 6 Paisley	
19.12.93	Dean Amory W PTS 8 Glasgow	
10.06.94	Mark Antony W PTS 8 Glasgow	

Career: 11 contests, won 10, drew 1.

James McGee

Bedworth. *Born* Nuneaton, 9 May, 1968
L. Middleweight. Ht. 6'1"
Manager J. Griffin

19.03.91	Adrian Din W PTS 6 Leicester	
15.04.91	Marty Duke L PTS 6 Leicester	
20.05.91	Cliff Churchward W PTS 6 Leicester	
11.06.91	Julian Eavis W PTS 6 Leicester	
01.10.91	Trevor Meikle L PTS 6 Bedworth	
21.10.91	Crain Fisher L RSC 4 Bury	
11.12.91	Julian Eavis DREW 6 Leicester	
11.02.92	Chris Mulcahy W PTS 6 Wolverhampton	
25.03.92	Darren Morris DREW 6 Hinckley	
11.05.92	Julian Eavis W RSC 3 Coventry	
05.10.92	Julian Eavis L PTS 6 Bardon	
23.11.92	James Campbell DREW 6 Coventry	
20.01.93	John Duckworth L PTS 6 Solihull	
22.02.93	Julian Eavis W PTS 6 Bedworth	
24.03.93	Damien Denny L CO 2 Belfast	
	(Final Elim. All-Ireland L. Middleweight Title)	
16.12.93	Anthony Lawrence DREW 6 Walsall	
26.01.94	Wayne Shepherd L PTS 6 Stoke	

Career: 17 contests, won 6, drew 4, lost 7.

Ian McGirr

Clydebank. *Born* Clydebank, 14 April, 1968
S. Featherweight. Ht. 5'6¼"
Manager T. Gilmour

23.11.89	Edward Cook W PTS 6 Motherwell	
18.12.89	James Milne W PTS 6 Glasgow	
19.02.90	Pete Buckley W PTS 6 Birmingham	
26.03.90	Edward Cook L PTS 6 Glasgow	
09.10.90	Steve Walker L RSC 4 Glasgow	
19.11.90	Edward Cook L PTS 6 Glasgow	
18.02.91	Colin Innes W PTS 6 Glasgow	
18.03.91	Noel Carroll L PTS 6 Manchester	
22.03.91	Edward Cook L PTS 6 Irvine	
24.09.91	Peter Judson W PTS 6 Glasgow	
08.10.91	Tony Feliciello L PTS 8 Wolverhampton	
21.10.91	Chris Clarkson DREW 6 Glasgow	
12.12.91	Darren Elsdon L CO 4 Hartlepool	
21.09.92	Chip O' Neill W PTS 6 Glasgow	
12.10.92	Chris Jickells L RSC 3 Bradford	
18.11.92	G.G.Goddard W PTS 6 Solihull	
13.02.93	Jyrki Vierela L PTS 6 Randers, Denmark	
25.02.93	Carl Roberts W PTS 6 Burnley	
07.06.93	Marty Chestnut W PTS 6 Glasgow	
06.10.93	Robert Braddock W PTS 8 York	
22.11.93	Miguel Matthews W PTS 6 Glasgow	
02.03.94	Russell Davison L CO 1 Glasgow	
10.04.94	Russell Davison W PTS 6 Glasgow	
14.06.94	Medhi Labdouni L RSC 1 Epernay, France	

Career: 24 contests, won 12, drew 1, lost 11.

Steve McGovern

Bembridge. *Born* Newport, IOW, 17 April, 1969
Welterweight. Ht. 5'9"
Manager Self

21.09.89	Mike Morrison W PTS 6 Southampton	
17.04.90	Justin Graham W PTS 6 Millwall	
21.01.91	Mark Dinnadge W PTS 6 Crystal Palace	
23.02.91	Tim Harmey W PTS 6 Brighton	
23.04.91	Frank Harrington W PTS 6 Evesham	
08.05.91	A.M.Milton W PTS 6 Millwall	
16.12.91	Chris Mylan W PTS 8 Southampton	
03.03.92	Tony Swift L RSC 4 Cradley Heath	
27.10.92	Ricky Mabbett DREW 6 Leicester	

29.04.93 Michael Dick W PTS 6 Hayes
23.06.93 Joel Ani W PTS 6 Edmonton
23.02.94 David Lake W PTS 6 Watford
Career: 12 contests, won 10, drew 1, lost 1.

Graham McGrath

Warley. *Born* West Bromwich, 31 July, 1962
Bantamweight. Ht. 5'4"
Manager Self

21.05.92 Paul Kelly W RSC 2 Cradley Heath
01.06.92 Greg Upton L PTS 6 Solihull
09.07.92 Wilson Docherty L RSC 4 Glasgow
25.09.92 Paul Lloyd L RSC 3 Liverpool
02.11.92 Dennis Oakes L PTS 4 Liverpool
01.12.92 Leo Beirne W PTS 6 Liverpool
10.12.92 Shaun Anderson L PTS 6 Glasgow
14.01.93 Darren Fifield L PTS 4 Mayfair
21.01.93 Shaun Anderson L PTS 6 Glasgow
23.02.93 Ian Baillie W PTS 6 Kettering
29.03.93 Ian McLeod L PTS 6 Glasgow
19.04.93 Karl Morling L RSC 6 Northampton
23.06.93 Rowan Williams L PTS 4 Edmonton
02.07.93 Peter Culshaw L PTS 6 Liverpool
09.09.93 Shaun Anderson L PTS 6 Glasgow
28.09.93 John Sillo L PTS 6 Liverpool
06.10.93 Neil Parry DREW 6 York
21.10.93 James Murray L PTS 6 Glasgow
28.10.93 Greg Upton L PTS 8 Torquay
07.11.93 Alex Docherty L RSC 3 Glasgow
06.12.93 Darren Greaves DREW 6 Birmingham
16.12.93 Darren Greaves W PTS 6 Walsall
19.01.94 Gary White L PTS 6 Solihull
21.02.94 Ian McLeod L CO 6 Glasgow
21.03.94 Marcus Duncan L PTS 6 Bradford
28.03.94 Jason Morris W PTS 6 Birmingham
27.04.94 Paul Ingle L PTS 4 Bethnal Green
20.05.94 Mark Cokely W PTS 6 Neath
10.06.94 James Murray L PTS 8 Glasgow
Career: 29 contests, won 6, drew 2, lost 21.

Dominic McGuigan

Newcastle. *Born* Hexham, 13 June, 1963
S. Featherweight. Ht. 5'6"
Manager Self

10.10.89 Dave Buxton W PTS 6 Sunderland
24.01.90 John Milne DREW 6 Sunderland
20.03.90 Frankie Foster DREW 4 Hartlepool
21.04.90 Chris Bennett W PTS 6 Sunderland
22.05.90 Lester James L PTS 6 Stockton
16.09.91 Barrie Kelley DREW 6 Mayfair
28.11.91 John Milne W RTD 3 Glasgow
30.04.92 Kevin Lowe W RSC 6 Mayfair
15.05.92 Rene Walker L PTS 8 Augsburg, Germany
07.10.92 Harry Escott L RTD 5 Sunderland
12.11.92 Kevin Lowe W RSC 2 Liverpool
25.02.93 Peter Judson DREW 6 Bradford
27.03.93 Giorgio Campanella L RSC 3 Evian, France
19.05.93 J.T.Williams W PTS 6 Sunderland
03.06.93 Eugene Speed L CO 1 Marseille, France
21.10.93 John Stovin L PTS 6 Bayswater
02.12.93 Peter Till L RSC 2 Walsall
Career: 17 contests, won 6, drew 4, lost 7.

Dave McHale

Glasgow. *Born* Glasgow, 29 April, 1967
S. Featherweight. Ht. 5'7"
Manager T. Gilmour

08.10.90 Sol Francis W RSC 2 Glasgow
25.11.91 Eddie Garbutt W RSC 1 Liverpool
30.03.92 Kevin Lowe W RSC 5 Glasgow
01.06.92 Chris Jickells W RSC 4 Glasgow
09.07.92 G. G. Goddard W RTD 4 Glasgow
19.10.92 Lee Fox W RSC 3 Glasgow
23.11.92 Karl Taylor W PTS 8 Glasgow
15.05.93 Miguel Matthews W RSC 4 Glasgow
02.02.94 John T. Kelly W CO 1 Glasgow
21.03.94 Frankie Foster W PTS 8 Glasgow
Career: 10 contests, won 10.

Bobby Mack (McKenzie)

Birmingham. *Born* Birmingham, 12 April, 1968
L. Heavyweight. Ht. 5'11"
Manager Self

29.09.92 Steve Loftus W PTS 6 Stoke
02.11.92 Martin Jolley W PTS 6 Wolverhampton
03.12.92 Joey Peters L PTS 6 Lewisham
06.03.93 Paul Hitch L PTS 6 Glasgow
04.04.93 Mark Prince L RSC 2 Brockley
15.09.93 Paul Lawson L PTS 4 Bethnal Green
24.09.93 Montell Griffin L PTS 6 Dublin
21.10.93 Nicky Wadman W PTS 6 Bayswater
16.12.93 Bruce Scott L RSC 4 Newport
16.02.94 Monty Wright L RSC 3 Stevenage
Career: 10 contests, won 3, lost 7.

Bobby Mack   Les Clark

Alan McKay

Willesden. *Born* Watford, 1 June, 1967
Former Southern Area Featherweight Champion. Ht. 5'6"
Manager Self

19.09.88 Mike Chapman W PTS 6 Mayfair
15.11.88 Mark Holt W PTS 6 Piccadilly
12.01.89 Jamie Hind W RSC 3 Southwark
31.01.89 Colin McMillan W RSC 3 Bethnal Green
01.03.89 Jeff Dobson W PTS 6 Bethnal Green
27.04.89 Tony Dore W PTS 6 Southwark
26.05.89 Nicky Lucas W PTS 6 Bethnal Green

04.09.89 Jari Gronroos DREW 6 Helsinki, Finland
24.10.89 Tim Driscoll L PTS 6 Bethnal Green
28.11.89 Steve Walker DREW 6 Battersea
03.05.90 Gary Hickman W PTS 8 Kensington
22.10.90 Steve Robinson W PTS 6 Mayfair
14.12.90 Gary de Roux L RSC 5 Peterborough
(Vacant Southern Area Featherweight Title)
09.04.91 Paul Harvey L RSC 4 Mayfair
13.11.91 Gary de Roux W RSC 8 Bethnal Green
(Vacant Southern Area Featherweight Title)
18.01.92 Pete Buckley DREW 8 Kensington
27.10.92 Kelton McKenzie W PTS 10 Cradley Heath
(Elim. British Featherweight Title)
27.06.93 Sean Murphy L RSC 9 Dagenham
(Vacant British Featherweight Title)
24.05.94 Billy Hardy L RSC 8 Sunderland
(Vacant British Featherweight Title)•
Career: 19 contests, won 11, drew 3, lost 5.

Darren McKenna

Alfreton. *Born* Sheffield, 21 December, 1962
L. Heavyweight. Ht. 5'11"
Manager B. Ingle

19.11.87 Tony Behan W RSC 1 Ilkeston
24.11.87 Calvin Hart L PTS 4 Wisbech
02.12.87 Darren Jones L RSC 3 Stoke
20.01.88 Darren Jones L PTS 6 Stoke
27.01.88 Sean Stringfellow L CO 3 Stoke
07.03.88 David Jono W DIS 3 Manchester
08.03.88 Peter Brown L PTS 6 Batley
29.03.88 Russell Barker L RSC 4 Marton
17.05.88 Tucker Watts W RSC 2 Leicester
06.06.88 Carl Thompson L RSC 2 Manchester
05.09.88 Russell Barker L RSC 3 Manchester
07.11.88 Morris Thomas L CO 4 Bradford
24.05.89 Peter Elliott L PTS 8 Hanley
05.10.89 Jimmy Cropper L PTS 4 Middleton
23.10.89 Sean Stringfellow W RSC 8 Hull
29.01.90 Graham Burton L PTS 4 Hull
06.03.90 Peter Elliott L PTS 8 Stoke
12.03.90 Fidel Castro L PTS 6 Hull
05.04.90 Allan Millett W RSC 2 Liverpool
17.04.90 Nicky Piper L RTD 4 Millwall
12.09.90 Steve Aquilina DREW 8 Stafford
08.10.90 Dave Owens L PTS 6 Leicester
09.05.91 Denzil Browne L PTS 6 Leeds
24.06.91 Johnny Held L PTS 8 Rotterdam, Holland
23.01.92 Denzil Browne L PTS 6 York
03.06.92 Morris Thomas W RSC 2 Newcastle under Lyme
17.10.92 Terry Dixon W RSC 3 Wembley
27.01.93 Steve Osborne W PTS 6 Stoke
27.10.93 John Keeton L RSC 3 Stoke
21.04.94 Art Stacey L PTS 6 Hull
Career: 30 contests, won 8, drew 1, lost 21.

(Anthony) Daryl McKenzie

Paisley. *Born* Johnstone, 20 August, 1965
S. Bantamweight. Ht. 5'4"
Manager N. Sweeney

17.02.94 Des Gargano DREW 6 Bury
02.03.94 Al Garrett W PTS 6 Glasgow
25.04.94 Al Garrett L PTS 6 Glasgow
16.05.94 Marcus Duncan L PTS 6 Morecambe
Career: 4 contests, won 1, drew 1, lost 2.

119

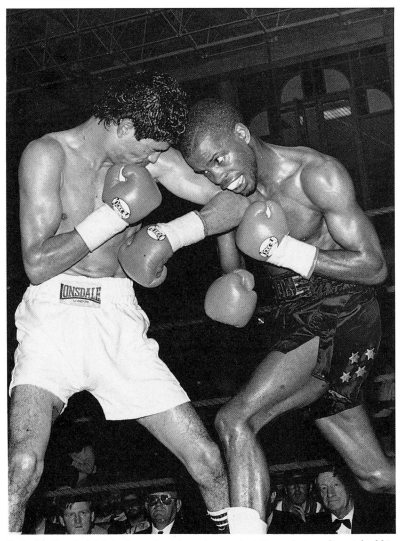

Duke McKenzie (right), shown here in action against Cesar Soto, relinquished his British featherweight title to challenge WBO champion, Steve Robinson   Tony Fitch

Duke McKenzie

Croydon. *Born* Croydon, 5 May, 1963
Former Undefeated British Featherweight
Champion. Former WBO S. Bantamweight
& Bantamweight Champion. Former IBF
Flyweight Champion. Former Undefeated
British & European Flyweight Champion.
Ht. 5'7"
Manager Self

23.11.82	Charlie Brown W RSC 1 Wembley	
24.01.83	Andy King W RSC 2 Mayfair	
27.02.83	Dave Pierson W RSC 1 Las Vegas, USA	
03.03.83	Gregorio Hernandez W RSC 3 Los Angeles, USA	
19.03.83	Lupe Sanchez W CO 2 Reno, USA	
18.10.83	Jerry Davis W RSC 2 Atlantic City, USA	
22.11.83	Alain Limarola W PTS 6 Wembley	
15.01.84	David Capo W PTS 4 Atlantic City, USA	
23.05.84	Gary Roberts W CO 1 Mayfair	
06.03.85	Julio Guerrero W PTS 8 Kensington	
05.06.85	Danny Flynn W RSC 4 Kensington *(Vacant British Flyweight Title)*	
16.10.85	Orlando Maestre W PTS 8 Kensington	
19.02.86	Sonny Long W PTS 10 Kensington	
20.05.86	Charlie Magri W RTD 5 Wembley *(British Flyweight Title Defence & European Flyweight Title Challenge)*	
19.11.86	Lee Cargle W PTS 10 Atlantic City, USA	
17.12.86	Piero Pinna W PTS 12 Acqui Terme, Italy *(European Flyweight Title Defence)*	
24.03.87	Jose Manuel Diaz W PTS 8 Wembley	
02.12.87	Juan Herrera W PTS 10 Wembley	
09.03.88	Agapito Gomez W CO 2 Wembley *(European Flyweight Title Defence)*	
04.05.88	Jose Gallegos W PTS 10 Wembley	

05.10.88	Rolando Bohol W CO 11 Wembley *(IBF Flyweight Title Challenge)*	
30.11.88	Artemio Ruiz W PTS 10 Southwark	
08.03.89	Tony de Luca W RSC 4 Kensington *(IBF Flyweight Title Defence)*	
07.06.89	Dave Boy McAuley L PTS 12 Wembley *(IBF Flyweight Title Defence)*	
12.10.89	Dave Moreno W PTS 10 Southwark	
08.11.89	Memo Flores W PTS 8 Wembley	
30.09.90	Thierry Jacob L PTS 12 Calais, France *(Vacant European Bantamweight Title)*	
10.01.91	Pete Buckley W RSC 5 Wandsworth	
07.02.91	Julio Blanco W RSC 7 Watford	
04.04.91	Chris Clarkson W RSC 5 Watford	
30.06.91	Gaby Canizales W PTS 12 Southwark *(WBO Bantamweight Title Challenge)*	
12.09.91	Cesar Soto W PTS 12 Wandsworth *(WBO Bantamweight Title Defence)*	
25.03.92	Wilfredo Vargas W RSC 8 Kensington *(WBO Bantamweight Title Defence)*	
13.05.92	Rafael del Valle L CO 1 Kensington *(WBO Bantamweight Title Defence)*	
07.09.92	Pete Buckley W RTD 3 Bethnal Green	
15.10.92	Jesse Benavides W PTS 12 Lewisham *(WBO S. Bantamweight Title Challenge)*	
09.06.93	Daniel Jimenez L PTS 12 Lewisham *(WBO S. Bantamweight Title Defence)*	
18.12.93	John Davison W RSC 4 Manchester *(Vacant British Featherweight Title)*	
29.01.94	Marcelo Rodriguez W PTS 8 Cardiff	

Career: 39 contests, won 35, lost 4.

Kelton McKenzie

Nottingham. *Born* Leicester, 18 September, 1968
S. Featherweight. Midlands Area
Featherweight Champion. Ht. 5'7"
Manager J. Griffin

18.10.90	Tony Silkstone L PTS 6 Dewsbury	
29.11.90	Neil Leitch DREW 6 Marton	
11.12.90	Sylvester Osuji W PTS 6 Evesham	
21.01.91	J. T. Williams DREW 6 Crystal Palace	
14.03.91	Craig Dermody L RSC 3 Middleton	
01.05.91	Tim Yeates W PTS 6 Bethnal Green	
17.06.91	Derek Amory W RSC 6 Edgbaston	
05.11.91	Richard Woolgar W RSC 5 Leicester	
22.01.92	Colin Lynch W RSC 5 Solihull	
26.03.92	Brian Robb W RSC 4 Telford	
29.04.92	Elvis Parsley W RSC 5 Solihull *(Vacant Midlands Area Featherweight Title)*	
18.07.92	Steve Walker W CO 2 Manchester	
27.10.92	Alan McKay L PTS 10 Cradley Heath *(Elim. British Featherweight Title)*	
28.04.93	Richie Wenton L PTS 8 Dublin	
19.05.93	Paul Harvey L RSC 7 Leicester	
04.10.93	Mehdi Labdouni L PTS 8 Paris, France	
10.05.94	Harry Escott L PTS 6 Doncaster	

Career: 17 contests, won 8, drew 2, lost 7.

Kevin McKenzie

Hartlepool. *Born* Hartlepool, 18 October, 1968
L. Welterweight. Ht. 5'7½"
Manager G. Robinson

08.06.92	Jason Brattley W RTD 3 Bradford	
21.09.92	Alan Ingle W PTS 6 Glasgow	
22.10.92	Dave Anderson L RSC 3 Glasgow	
01.12.92	Seth Jones L RSC 3 Hartlepool	

09.03.93 Micky Hall W PTS 6 Hartlepool
17.04.93 Paul Charters L RSC 4 Washington
(Vacant Northern Area L.Welterweight Title)
13.09.93 Blue Butterworth W PTS 6 Middleton
02.12.93 Micky Hall L PTS 6 Hartlepool
02.02.94 Steve McLevy L PTS 6 Glasgow
28.02.94 Rocky Ferrari W PTS 6 Marton
18.04.94 Andy Davidson L RSC 1 Manchester
Career: 11 contests, won 5, lost 6.

(Roger) R. F. McKenzie

Croydon. *Born* Croydon, 3 October, 1965
Former Southern Area Heavyweight Champion. Ht. 6'2"
Manager Self

31.01.89 Gerry Storey W PTS 6 Bethnal Green
24.09.90 Mark Bowen L RSC 1 Mayfair
29.11.90 Denzil Browne W PTS 6 Sunderland
12.02.91 Noel Magee L PTS 6 Belfast
21.03.91 Denzil Browne L PTS 6 Dewsbury
28.05.91 Steve Yorath L PTS 6 Cardiff
07.09.91 Ray Kane L PTS 4 Belfast
09.10.91 Denzil Browne W PTS 6 Manchester
28.10.91 Pedro van Raamsdonk W CO 7 Arnhem, Holland
12.12.91 Norbert Ekassi L RSC 3 Massy, France
14.03.92 Neils H. Madsen L PTS 6 Copenhagen, Denmark
25.04.92 Noel Magee L PTS 8 Belfast
31.10.92 Warren Richards DREW 6 Earls Court
13.02.93 Magne Havnaa W RTD 5 Randers, Denmark
31.03.93 Warren Richards W RSC 8 Bethnal Green
(Vacant Southern Area Heavyweight Title)
17.09.93 Brian Neilsen L PTS 6 Copenhagen, Denmark
13.10.93 James Oyebola L RSC 1 Bethnal Green
(Southern Area Heavyweight Title Defence)
11.12.93 Bernd Friedrich W RSC 2 Dusseldorf, Germany
25.03.94 Mark Hulstrom L PTS 6 Bernholme, Denmark
Career: 19 contests, won 7, drew 1, lost 11.

Tony McKenzie

Leicester. *Born* Leicester, 4 March, 1963
Former British L. Welterweight Champion. Ht. 5'9"
Manager B. Hearn

22.11.83 Albert Buchanan W CO 3 Wolverhampton
07.12.83 Peter Flanagan W PTS 6 Stoke
30.01.84 Vince Bailey W RSC 1 Birmingham
27.02.84 David Irving W RSC 3 Birmingham
15.03.84 Johnny Grant W RSC 4 Leicester
16.04.84 Danny Shinkwin L RSC 1 Birmingham
09.05.84 Ray Price W PTS 8 Leicester
03.10.84 Michael Harris L PTS 8 Solihull
10.10.84 Manny Romain W CO 5 Stoke
29.10.84 Peter Flanagan W RSC 8 Nottingham
16.11.84 Lenny Gloster W PTS 8 Leicester
14.03.85 Tony Laing L RSC 8 Leicester
(Vacant Midlands Area L. Welterweight Title)
07.09.85 Tony Adams W PTS 8 Isle of Man
20.11.85 Rocky Feliciello W RSC 6 Solihull
19.03.86 Simon Eubank W RSC 4 Solihull

07.05.86 Michael Harris W PTS 10 Solihull
(Elim. British L. Welterweight Title)
20.09.86 Clinton McKenzie W RSC 3 Hemel Hempstead
(Vacant British L. Welterweight Title)
25.10.86 Michael Harris W CO 10 Stevenage
(British L. Welterweight Title Defence)
29.11.86 Ford Jennings W RSC 5 Wandsworth
28.01.87 Lloyd Christie L RSC 3 Croydon
(British L. Welterweight Title Defence)
12.05.87 Dave Griffiths W RSC 3 Alfreton
03.11.87 Kelvin Mortimer W RSC 3 Bethnal Green
24.02.88 Jeff Connors W RSC 2 Leicester
03.11.88 Abdelatif Lofti Ben Sayel L RSC 2 Leicester
27.01.90 Benji Marquez DREW 8 Sheffield
20.03.90 Benji Marquez W PTS 8 Norwich
05.06.90 Art Blackmore W RSC 4 Nottingham
19.03.91 King Zaka W RSC 1 Leicester
(Elim. Commonwealth L. Welterweight Title)
11.06.91 Alberto Machong W CO 3 Leicester
(Elim. Commonwealth L. Welterweight Title)
05.11.91 Marty Duke W RSC 7 Leicester
19.11.91 Gordon Blair W RSC 5 Norwich
27.02.92 Andy Holligan L RSC 3 Liverpool
(British & Commonwealth L. Welterweight Title Challenge)
26.01.93 Michael Driscoll W PTS 10 Leicester
(Elim. British L. Welterweight Title)
05.10.93 Michael Driscoll L CO 5 Mayfair
(Elim. British L. Welterweight Title)
Career: 34 contests, won 26, drew 1, lost 7.

Kevin McKillan

Manchester. *Born* Belfast, 1 March, 1969
L. Welterweight. Ht. 5'8"
Manager N. Basso

28.10.91 Michael Byrne W PTS 6 Leicester
13.11.91 Barry Glanister W PTS 6 Liverpool
22.01.92 Sugar Boy Wright W PTS 6 Solihull
10.02.92 Jamie Davidson L PTS 6 Liverpool
11.03.92 Jamie Davidson DREW 6 Stoke
01.06.92 Steve Howden W RSC 2 Manchester
12.06.92 Floyd Churchill W PTS 6 Liverpool
25.09.92 John Smith W PTS 6 Liverpool
07.10.92 J. T. Williams L PTS 6 Barry
20.11.92 Steve Foran L PTS 6 Liverpool
15.02.93 John T. Kelly W PTS 6 Manchester
19.04.93 Simon Hamblett W CO 2 Manchester
26.04.93 Steve Walker DREW 8 Manchester
01.06.93 Micky Hall W PTS 6 Manchester
06.10.93 Norman Dhalie W RSC 1 Solihull
29.10.93 Soren Sondergaard L CO 2 Korsoer, Denmark
26.01.94 Dean Amory W PTS 8 Stoke
06.06.94 Micky Hall W PTS 6 Manchester
Career: 18 contests, won 12, drew 2, lost 4.

Ian McLeod

Kilmarnock. *Born* Edinburgh, 11 June, 1969
S. Featherweight. Ht. 5'9"
Manager T. Gilmour

23.11.92 Robert Braddock DREW 6 Glasgow
29.03.93 Graham McGrath W PTS 6 Glasgow
21.02.94 Graham McGrath W CO 6 Glasgow
04.03.94 Chip O'Neill W RSC 2 Irvine
Career: 4 contests, won 3, drew 1.

Steve McLevy

Glasgow. *Born* Glasgow, 23 September, 1972
L. Welterweight. Ht. 5'8"
Manager R. Watt

22.11.93 Dewi Roberts W RSC 1 Glasgow
02.02.94 Kevin McKenzie W PTS 6 Glasgow
28.03.94 Mark Antony W CO 1 Musselburgh
Career: 3 contests, won 3.

Colin McMillan

Barking. *Born* London, 12 February, 1966
Former WBO Featherweight Champion.
Former Undefeated British & Commonwealth Featherweight Champion.
Ht. 5'5¼"
Manager Self

29.11.88 Mike Chapman W PTS 6 Battersea
10.12.88 Aldrich Johnson W PTS 6 Crystal Palace
31.01.89 Alan McKay L RSC 3 Bethnal Green
12.06.89 Miguel Matthews W RSC 3 Battersea
19.09.89 Graham O'Malley W PTS 8 Millwall
11.10.89 Marcel Herbert W PTS 6 Millwall
30.11.89 Sylvester Osuji W RSC 4 Barking
14.02.90 Vidal Tellez W RSC 2 Millwall
17.04.90 Jesus Muniz W PTS 8 Millwall
03.05.90 Steve Walker W PTS 6 Kensington
05.07.90 Tyrone Miller W CO 2 Greensville, USA
17.07.90 Malcolm Rougeaux W CO 1 Lake Charles, USA
25.09.90 Darren Weller W RSC 2 Millwall
10.10.90 Graham O'Malley W PTS 6 Millwall
12.11.90 Mark Holt W PTS 6 Norwich
05.03.91 Russell Davison W PTS 6 Millwall
26.04.91 Willie Richardson W PTS 8 Crystal Palace
22.05.91 Gary de Roux W RSC 7 Millwall
(British Featherweight Title Challenge)
03.07.91 Herbie Bivalacqua W RSC 3 Reading
04.09.91 Kevin Pritchard W RSC 7 Bethnal Green
(British Featherweight Title Defence)
29.10.91 Sean Murphy W PTS 12 Kensington
(British Featherweight Title Defence)
18.01.92 Percy Commey W PTS 12 Kensington
(Vacant Commonwealth Featherweight Title)
25.03.92 Tommy Valdez W CO 6 Dagenham
16.05.92 Maurizio Stecca W PTS 12 Muswell Hill
(WBO Featherweight Title Challenge)
26.09.92 Ruben Palacio L RSC 8 Earls Court
(WBO Featherweight Title Defence)
23.10.93 Steve Robinson L PTS 12 Cardiff
(WBO Featherweight Title Challenge)
Career: 26 contests, won 23, lost 3.

Conn McMullen

Acton. *Born* Larne, 21 June, 1967
Bantamweight. Ht. 5'6"
Manager F. Maloney

06.06.90 Ceri Farrell W RSC 5 Battersea
04.12.90 Neil Parry W RSC 2 Southend
12.11.91 Mark Loftus W PTS 6 Milton Keynes
28.10.92 Barry Jones L PTS 6 Cardiff
26.03.93 Neil Armstrong W RSC 5 Glasgow
05.05.93 Miguel Matthews DREW 6 Belfast

18.06.93	Wayne McCullough L RSC 3 Belfast
25.08.93	Anton Gilmore L PTS 8 Hammanskrall, South Africa
23.10.93	John Green W PTS 6 Cardiff
23.02.94	Tony Falcone DREW 4 Watford
29.03.94	Pete Buckley L PTS 6 Bethnal Green
11.06.94	Michael Alldis L PTS 8 Bethnal Green

Career: 12 contests, won 5, drew 2, lost 5.

Pat McNamara

Leeds. *Born* Bradford, 2 June, 1967
L. Heavyweight. Ht. 6'2"
Manager P. Coleman

10.05.93	Kevin Burton L RSC 2 Cleethorpes
04.10.93	Craig Joseph L RSC 2 Bradford

Career: 2 contests, lost 2.

Jason McNeill

Swansea. *Born* Bristol, 12 August, 1971
S. Middleweight. Ht. 6'1"
Manager D. Davies

03.10.91	Mark Pain L PTS 6 Burton
15.10.91	Tony Colclough L PTS 6 Dudley
28.11.91	Mark McBiane W PTS 6 Evesham
21.01.92	Gypsy Johnny Price L PTS 4 Stockport
11.03.92	Paul McCarthy W PTS 6 Cardiff
23.04.92	Abel Asinamali L CO 3 Eltham
07.09.92	Mark Baker L RSC 2 Glasgow
23.10.92	Paul Wright L RSC 1 Liverpool
06.02.93	Karl Mumford L PTS 6 Cardiff
22.02.93	Kenny Nevers L RSC 1 Eltham
10.04.93	Julian Johnson L PTS 6 Swansea
26.05.93	Graham Burton L RSC 3 Mansfield
16.10.93	Ray Kane L PTS 6 Belfast
03.11.93	Dale Nixon L RSC 1 Bristol
11.01.94	Mark Delaney L RSC 2 Bethnal Green

Career: 15 contests, won 2, lost 13.

Jason McNeill   Les Clark

Steve McNess

Bethnal Green. *Born* Bow, 17 November, 1969
L. Middleweight. Ht. 5'10½"
Manager M. Duff

22.04.92	Rick North W PTS 6 Wembley
13.05.92	Mark Verikios L RSC 5 Kensington
03.09.92	Steve Goodwin W PTS 6 Dunstable
28.10.92	Mark Dawson L RSC 2 Kensington
28.01.93	Steve Scott W PTS 6 Southwark
26.04.93	Bullit Andrews W RSC 3 Lewisham
15.06.93	Martin Rosamond L RSC 5 Hempstead
07.12.93	Robert Whitehouse W RSC 3 Bethnal Green
16.02.94	Billy McDougall W PTS 4 Stevenage
11.03.94	Tony Walton W PTS 4 Bethnal Green

Career: 10 contests, won 7, lost 3.

Dave Madden

Birmingham. *Born* Birmingham, 18 June, 1967
Welterweight. Ht. 5'10"
Manager Self

12.11.92	Blue Butterworth L RSC 2 Burnley
27.01.93	Gary Hiscox L PTS 6 Stoke
22.02.93	Kris McAdam L PTS 8 Glasgow
20.09.93	Lee Heggs W PTS 6 Northampton
27.10.93	Gareth Jordan L RSC 5 West Bromwich
19.12.93	Dennis Griffin L RSC 1 Northampton
10.03.94	Dave Fallon W PTS 6 Watford
16.05.94	Danny Quacoe L RSC 4 Heathrow

Career: 8 contests, won 2, lost 6.

Dave Madden   Les Clark

Noel Magee

Belfast. *Born* Belfast, 16 December, 1965
L. Heavyweight. Ht. 6'1"
Manager Self

22.05.85	Nigel Prickett W CO 1 Stoke
12.09.85	Dave Furneaux W RSC 3 Swindon
28.10.85	Eddie Chatterton W RSC 1 Stoke
06.11.85	Winston Burnett W PTS 8 Nantwich
11.12.85	Winston Burnett W PTS 8 Stoke
22.01.86	Blaine Logsdon W PTS 8 Stoke
20.02.86	Barry Ahmed W PTS 8 Newcastle
05.03.86	Winston Burnett W PTS 8 Stoke
23.04.86	Barry Ahmed W RSC 7 Stoke

30.05.86	Geoff Rymer W CO 1 Stoke
13.10.86	Jimmy Ellis W PTS 8 Dulwich
17.11.86	Serg Fame W PTS 8 Dulwich
24.02.87	Lennie Howard W RSC 1 Ilford
03.08.87	Jimmy Ellis W RSC 6 Stoke
20.10.87	Johnny Held L PTS 8 Stoke
13.02.88	Rufino Angulo DREW 8 Paris, France
03.05.88	Mike Brothers W CO 6 Stoke
15.11.88	Ian Bulloch DREW 10 Hull
15.02.89	Yves Monsieur L RSC 5 Stoke
02.10.89	Paul McCarthy W CO 2 Hanley
29.11.89	Sammy Storey L RSC 9 Belfast (*British S. Middleweight Title Challenge*)
15.09.90	Glazz Campbell W PTS 8 Belfast
30.10.90	Johnny Melfah W PTS 6 Belfast
12.02.91	R. F. McKenzie W PTS 6 Belfast
11.05.91	Simon Collins W PTS 8 Belfast
13.11.91	Frankie Minton W RSC 3 Belfast
11.12.91	Tony Wilson W RSC 3 Dublin
25.04.92	R. F. McKenzie W PTS 8 Belfast
28.09.92	Maurice Core L RSC 9 Manchester (*Vacant British L. Heavyweight Title*)
22.05.93	Dariusz Michalczewski L RSC 8 Aachen, Germany
16.10.93	John Kaighin W PTS 6 Belfast
21.05.94	John J. Cooke W PTS 6 Belfast

Career: 32 contests, won 25, drew 2, lost 5.

Terry Magee

Ammanford. *Born* Belfast, 1 November, 1964
Middleweight. Former Undefeated All-Ireland L. Middleweight Champion. Ht. 5'10½"
Manager Self

29.11.82	Robbie Turner W PTS 6 Brighton
08.12.82	Tony Baker W PTS 6 Piccadilly
07.02.83	Alex Romeo L PTS 6 Piccadilly
21.02.83	Tony Burke L PTS 6 Piccadilly
16.09.83	David Scere W PTS 6 Rhyl
28.11.83	Winston Wray W PTS 6 Rhyl
06.02.84	Craig Edwards W RSC 3 Liverpool
03.03.84	Lou Johnson W RSC 2 Stoke
12.05.84	Cornelius Chisholm W RTD 3 Hanley
12.09.84	Phil O'Hare W PTS 8 Stoke
24.10.84	Nick Riozzi W RSC 5 Stoke
05.12.84	Harry Watson W RSC 3 Stoke
20.03.85	Gary Tomlinson DREW 8 Stoke
17.04.85	Gary Pearce W PTS 8 Nantwich
25.09.85	Franki Moro W PTS 10 Stoke
11.12.85	Gerry Sloof W RSC 6 Stoke
07.05.86	Gary Stretch L RSC 7 Kensington
23.06.87	Shamus Casey W CO 6 Swansea (*Vacant All-Ireland L. Middleweight Title*)
01.11.87	Charles Oosthuizen L RSC 8 Johannesburg, South Africa
26.03.88	Chris Richards W PTS 8 Belfast
14.06.88	Tony Britton W PTS 6 Birmingham
28.09.88	Wally Swift Jnr W PTS 8 Solihull
07.12.88	Kevin Hayde W PTS 8 Aberavon
12.04.89	Tony Britton W PTS 8 Swansea
16.11.89	Jimmy Gourad W PTS 8 Weston super Mare
26.03.90	Gilbert Dele L RTD 3 Paris, France (*European L. Middleweight Title Challenge*)
01.06.91	Andy Till L RSC 4 Bethnal Green
11.12.91	Ray Close L RSC 7 Dublin (*All-Ireland S. Middleweight Title Challenge*)

25.09.92 Fran Harding L PTS 6 Liverpool
17.10.92 James Cook L RSC 5 Wembley
27.11.92 Roland Ericsson L PTS 8 Randers, Denmark
05.05.93 Graham Jenner W PTS 6 Belfast
21.10.93 Andrew Flute L RSC 6 Bayswater
10.03.94 Dean Cooper L PTS 8 Bristol
Career: 34 contests, won 21, drew 1, lost 12.

Dave Maj   Les Clark

Dave Maj (Majekodunmi)

Liverpool. *Born* Liverpool, 21 November, 1964
Welterweight. Ht. 5'10¼"
Manager Self

24.06.91 Benji Joseph W RSC 4 Liverpool
09.09.91 Mark Verikios L PTS 6 Liverpool
14.10.91 David Maw L PTS 6 Manchester
16.12.91 Wayne Shepherd DREW 6 Manchester
03.02.92 Wayne Shepherd W PTS 6 Manchester
09.03.92 Willie Yeardsley W RSC 1 Manchester
13.04.92 Peter Reid W CO 1 Manchester
14.05.92 Andreas Panayi L CO 6 Liverpool
05.10.92 John Duckworth DREW 6 Manchester
12.11.92 Mark Verikios L PTS 6 Liverpool
22.02.93 Mark Brogan W RSC 5 Liverpool
29.04.93 Paul Denton DREW 6 Mayfair
21.06.93 Chris Peters L RSC 4 Swindon
15.09.93 Kirkland Laing L RSC 2 Ashford
01.12.93 Kevin Adamson L RSC 2 Stoke
11.03.94 Jason Beard L RSC 6 Bethnal Green
14.04.94 Maurice Forbes L RTD 2 Battersea
Career: 17 contests, won 5, drew 3, lost 9.

Abdul Manna

Battersea. *Born* Bangladesh, 5 April, 1972
Featherweight. Ht. 5'3"
Manager T. Toole

08.03.94 Brian Eccles W RSC 2 Kettering
17.05.94 Keith Jones W PTS 6 Kettering
Career: 2 contests, won 2.

Colin Manners

Leeds. *Born* Leeds, 4 July, 1962
Middleweight. Ht. 5'10"
Manager Self

26.04.90 Tony Booth L PTS 6 Halifax
27.09.90 Carlos Christie L PTS 6 Birmingham
18.10.90 Carlton Myers W CO 2 Dewsbury
25.10.90 Colin Ford L PTS 6 Bayswater
12.12.90 Tony Kosova W PTS 6 Leicester
31.01.91 Lee Crocker W PTS 6 Bredbury
18.02.91 John Ogiste L PTS 6 Mayfair
14.03.91 John Ogiste L PTS 8 Middleton
01.05.91 Darren Parker W CO 2 Solihull
05.06.91 Richard Carter W CO 1 Wolverhampton
03.09.91 Wayne Ellis W RSC 1 Cardiff
29.04.92 Darron Griffiths DREW 8 Solihull
14.07.92 Stan King W PTS 8 Mayfair
30.09.92 Darron Griffiths L PTS 10 Solihull *(Elim. British Middleweight Title)*
23.02.93 Chris Pyatt L CO 3 Doncaster
15.07.93 Juan Medina Padilla L PTS 8 La Linea, Gibralter
19.01.94 Paul Busby DREW 8 Solihull
15.03.94 Paul Busby L PTS 8 Mayfair
11.05.94 Shaun Cummins W RSC 6 Sheffield
Career: 19 contests, won 8, drew 2, lost 9.

Keith Marner   Les Clark

Keith Marner

Bracknell. *Born* Wokingham, 11 April, 1961
L. Welterweight. Ht. 5'8"
Manager W. Ball

30.09.93 Ron Shinkwin W PTS 6 Hayes
09.12.93 Dennis Griffin W PTS 6 Watford
10.03.94 John O'Johnson W RSC 5 Watford
28.04.94 Gary Cogan W RSC 3 Mayfair
20.05.94 Chris Aston W PTS 8 Acton
Career: 5 contests, won 5.

Gary Marston

Stoke. *Born* Taunton, 11 December, 1966
Featherweight. Ht. 5'4"
Manager Self

29.09.92 Norman Dhalie DREW 6 Stoke
17.03.93 Jason Morris W PTS 6 Stoke
12.05.93 Phil Lashley W RSC 2 Stoke
07.09.93 Joe Fannin W RSC 2 Stoke
27.10.93 Jobie Tyers W PTS 6 Stoke
01.12.93 Dougie Fox W RSC 1 Stoke
15.03.94 Des Gargano W PTS 8 Stoke
Career: 7 contests, won 6, drew 1.

(Paul) Stinger Mason

Sheffield. *Born* Sheffield, 27 February, 1964
L. Heavyweight. Ht. 5'8"
Manager Self

19.04.89 Sean Stringfellow W PTS 6 Stoke
24.05.89 Andrew Flute L PTS 6 Hanley
16.11.89 Tony Lawrence DREW 6 Ilkeston
27.01.90 Ian Vokes W PTS 6 Sheffield
28.03.90 Cliff Curtis W PTS 6 Bethnal Green
20.05.90 Tony Hodge W CO 2 Sheffield
11.06.90 Glenn Campbell L RTD 5 Manchester
12.11.90 Adrian Wright L RSC 4 Stratford upon Avon
13.03.91 Mike Phillips DREW 6 Stoke
13.05.91 Doug Calderwood L CO 3 Manchester
23.10.91 Roger Wilson DREW 6 Stoke
11.11.91 Russell Washer W PTS 4 Stratford upon Avon
23.05.92 Paul Busby L RSC 2 Birmingham
28.09.92 Quinn Paynter L CO 1 Manchester
20.09.93 Stephen Wilson L RSC 6 Glasgow
10.11.93 Joe Calzaghe L RSC 1 Watford
15.03.94 Mark Dawson L RSC 6 Stoke
02.06.94 Luan Morena L PTS 6 Tooting
Career: 18 contests, won 5, drew 3, lost 10.

(Nicholas) Miguel Matthews

Ystalfera. *Born* Glanamman, 22 December, 1965
S. Featherweight. Ht. 5'7"
Manager Self

21.09.88 Terry Collins L PTS 6 Basildon
28.09.88 Eugene Maloney DREW 6 Edmonton
25.10.88 Hugh Ruse L PTS 6 Pontadawe
15.11.88 Tommy Bernard W RSC 2 Chigwell
14.12.88 Richie Wenton L CO 2 Kirkby
14.02.89 Brian Robb W RSC 2 Wolverhampton
06.03.89 Mickey Markie L PTS 8 Northampton
21.03.89 Ronnie Stephenson DREW 6 Wolverhampton
11.04.89 Hugh Ruse W PTS 6 Aberavon
05.06.89 Lester James DREW 6 Birmingham
12.06.89 Colin McMillan L RSC 3 Battersea
06.09.89 Marcel Herbert L PTS 6 Aberavon
20.09.89 Des Gargano L PTS 6 Stoke
28.09.89 Steve Walker L PTS 6 Cardiff
17.10.89 Alan Roberts W PTS 6 Cardiff
24.10.89 Jimmy Clark L PTS 6 Watford
06.11.89 Mickey Markie DREW 8 Northampton
03.12.89 Johnny Bredahl L PTS 6 Copenhagen, Denmark
19.02.90 Mickey Markie L PTS 8 Kettering
27.02.90 Pete Buckley DREW 6 Evesham
21.03.90 Rocky Lawlor L PTS 8 Solihull
03.09.90 Derek Amory L PTS 6 Dudley
01.10.90 Pete Buckley L PTS 8 Cleethorpes

09.10.90	Pete Buckley W PTS 8 Wolverhampton
29.10.90	Pete Buckley L PTS 8 Birmingham
21.11.90	Jason Primera L PTS 8 Solihull
12.12.90	Paul Harvey L PTS 6 Basildon
19.12.90	Paul Forrest L PTS 6 Preston
07.03.91	Bradley Stone L RSC 4 Basildon
04.04.91	Mark Tierney L PTS 6 Watford
16.04.91	Craig Dermody L PTS 6 Nottingham
25.04.91	Bradley Stone L PTS 6 Basildon
23.05.91	Jason Lepre L PTS 6 Southampton
31.05.91	Danny Connelly L PTS 8 Glasgow
13.06.91	Tony Silkstone L PTS 6 Hull
24.06.91	Jimmy Owens L PTS 6 Liverpool
09.09.91	Moussa Sangare L RSC 5 Forges les Eux, France
09.10.91	Mark Loftus DREW 6 Manchester
24.10.91	Kevin Middleton L PTS 6 Dunstable
31.10.91	Brian Robb DREW 6 Oakengates
11.11.91	Peter Judson L PTS 6 Stratford on Avon
21.11.91	Craig Dermody L PTS 6 Burton
28.11.91	Dave Hardie L PTS 6 Glasgow
11.12.91	Jimmy Clark L PTS 6 Basildon
08.01.92	Ceri Farrell W PTS 6 Burton
31.01.92	John Green DREW 6 Manchester
20.02.92	Edward Cook L PTS 6 Glasgow
27.02.92	Craig Dermody L PTS 6 Liverpool
25.03.92	John Armour L PTS 6 Dagenham
01.06.92	Danny Porter L PTS 6 Glasgow
07.07.92	Tony Falcone L PTS 6 Bristol
14.07.92	Prince Nassem Hamed L RSC 3 Mayfair
30.09.92	Jonjo Irwin L PTS 6 Solihull
17.10.92	Mark Bowers L PTS 6 Wembley
24.11.92	Kid McAuley L PTS 6 Doncaster
14.12.92	Barry Jones L PTS 6 Cardiff
30.01.93	Tim Yeates L PTS 6 Brentwood
27.02.93	Paul Lloyd L PTS 6 Ellesmere Port
18.03.93	Kevin Middleton L PTS 6 Lewisham
17.04.93	Fabian Zavattini L PTS 6 Lausanne, Switzerland
05.05.93	Conn McMullen DREW 6 Belfast
15.05.93	Dave McHale L RSC 4 Glasgow
10.07.93	Russell Rees L PTS 6 Cardiff
22.09.93	Marcus McCrae L PTS 6 Bethnal Green
06.10.93	Mark Geraghty L PTS 6 York
30.10.93	Gary Thornhill L PTS 6 Chester
22.11.93	Ian McGirr L PTS 6 Glasgow
29.11.93	Tim Yeates DREW 6 Ingatestone
18.12.93	John White L PTS 6 Manchester
14.01.94	Kevin Middleton L PTS 6 Bethnal Green
28.01.94	Frederic Perez L PTS 8 Sete, France
10.04.94	Mark Geraghty L PTS 8 Glasgow
25.04.94	Hugh Collins L PTS 8 Glasgow
22.05.94	Mike Anthony Brown W RSC 5 Crystal Palace
06.06.94	Russell Davison W PTS 6 Glasgow

Career: 75 contests, won 8, drew 10, lost 57.

Paul Matthews

Llanelli. *Born* Gorseinon, 26 September, 1968
Middleweight. Ht. 5'8"
Manager G. Davies

23.03.94	Steve Thomas W PTS 6 Cardiff
02.06.94	Jason Hart W RSC 3 Tooting

Career: 2 contests, won 2.

Shane Meadows

Wingate. *Born* Durham, 25 May, 1967
Cruiserweight. Ht. 5'10"
Manager G. Robinson

28.02.94	Declan Faherty L CO 3 Marton

Career: 1 contest, lost 1.

Trevor Meikle

Scunthorpe. *Born* Scunthorpe, 29 January, 1967
Welterweight. Ht. 5'9"
Manager K. Tate

16.05.89	Lewis Welch DREW 6 Halifax
12.06.89	Chris Mulcahy L PTS 6 Manchester
19.06.89	Anthony Lawrence L PTS 6 Manchester
11.07.89	Chris Mulcahy L PTS 6 Batley
10.10.89	Steve Hardman DREW 6 Manchester
23.10.89	Mick Mulcahy W PTS 6 Cleethorpes
06.11.89	Ian Thomas W PTS 6 Northampton
14.11.89	Cliff Churchward W PTS 6 Evesham
22.11.89	Cliff Churchward W PTS 6 Stafford
11.12.89	Barry Messam L CO 5 Nottingham
05.02.90	Malcolm Melvin L PTS 6 Brierley Hill
19.02.90	Gordon Blair L PTS 6 Glasgow
27.02.90	Dave Whittle DREW 8 Marton
14.03.90	Carlos Chase L PTS 6 Battersea
27.03.90	Barry Messam W PTS 6 Leicester
30.04.90	Young Gully L PTS 6 Brierley Hill
21.05.90	Frank Harrington W RSC 5 Hanley
30.05.90	Mark Jay DREW 6 Stoke
15.06.90	Mark Jay W RSC 5 Telford
14.09.90	Mickey Lerwill DREW 8 Telford
03.10.90	Jim Lawlor L PTS 6 Solihull
09.10.90	Pat Durkin W DIS 3 Liverpool
24.10.90	Ernie Loveridge L PTS 6 Dudley
06.11.90	Stuart Good L PTS 6 Southend
21.11.90	Jim Lawlor L PTS 6 Solihull
29.11.90	Dave Whittle L PTS 6 Marton
10.12.90	Kevin Spratt L PTS 6 Bradford
11.02.91	Steve Hardman L PTS 6 Manchester
21.02.91	Colin Sinnott W PTS 6 Leeds
27.02.91	Andreas Panayi W PTS 6 Wolverhampton
03.04.91	Mick Mulcahy W PTS 6 Manchester
10.04.91	Wayne Timmins L PTS 6 Wolverhampton
22.04.91	Nick Cope W RSC 2 Glasgow
01.05.91	Tommy Milligan L PTS 6 Liverpool
09.05.91	Tod Riggs L PTS 6 Leeds
03.06.91	Tommy Milligan L PTS 6 Glasgow
10.06.91	Chris Mulcahy DREW 6 Manchester
14.08.91	Efren Calamati L RSC 4 Alcamo, Italy
23.09.91	Alan Peacock W PTS 6 Glasgow
01.10.91	James McGee L PTS 6 Bedworth
05.11.91	Lee Ferrie L PTS 6 Leicester
25.11.91	Mark Kelly W PTS 8 Cleethorpes
05.12.91	Mickey Lerwill L PTS 6 Oakengates
14.12.91	Kevin Lueshing L CO 3 Bexleyheath
28.01.92	Alan Peacock L PTS 8 Piccadilly
29.02.92	Andre Kimbu L RTD 5 Gravelines, France
13.04.92	Crain Fisher L PTS 6 Manchester
30.04.92	B. F. Williams L PTS 6 Watford
14.09.92	Kevin Spratt W RSC 4 Bradford
23.10.92	Andreas Panayi L PTS 6 Liverpool
26.11.92	Willie Yeardsley W PTS 6 Hull
03.02.93	Derek Grainger L RSC 6 Earls Court
13.12.93	Rick North L PTS 6 Cleethorpes
22.05.94	Maurice Forbes L RTD 3 Crystal Palace

Career: 54 contests, won 17, drew 6, lost 31.

Johnny Melfah

Gloucester. *Born* Gloucester, 14 December, 1960
S. Middleweight. Ht. 5'9½"
Manager Self

08.09.86	Winston Wray L RSC 3 Dulwich
13.10.86	Andy Sumner W CO 3 Dulwich
17.11.86	Graeme Ahmed W PTS 6 Dulwich
15.12.86	Mark Mills W CO 5 Eltham
07.05.87	Alan Baptiste W CO 1 Bayswater
30.09.87	Cliff Gilpin W PTS 8 Solihull
12.10.87	Tony Burke W RSC 2 Bow
21.01.88	Carl Penn W CO 1 Wandsworth
18.03.88	Reggie Miller W RTD 5 Wandsworth
23.11.88	Herol Graham L RSC 5 Bethnal Green
	(British Middleweight Title Challenge)
08.02.89	Mustapha Cole W RTD 5 Kensington
22.03.89	Winston Wray W RSC 6 Gloucester
27.06.89	Kid Milo L CO 7 Kensington
05.11.89	Chris Eubank L CO 4 Kensington
30.10.90	Noel Magee L PTS 6 Belfast
24.11.90	Fidel Castro L RSC 4 Benalmadena, Spain
23.02.91	Sean Heron W PTS 8 Brighton
05.03.91	Wayne Ellis L RSC 2 Cardiff
16.05.91	Roland Ericsson W RSC 4 Battersea
07.09.91	Sammy Storey L PTS 8 Belfast
01.10.91	Fidel Castro L RSC 7 Sheffield
12.05.92	Lou Gent W RSC 3 Crystal Palace
25.07.92	Nicky Piper L RSC 5 Manchester
	(Elim. British S. Middleweight Title)
06.02.93	Steve Collins L RSC 3 Cardiff
18.12.93	Roland Ericsson L PTS 10 Turku, Finland
22.01.94	Steve Collins L RSC 4 Belfast

Career: 26 contests, won 13, lost 13.

Malcolm Melvin

Birmingham. *Born* Birmingham, 5 February, 1967
All-Ireland & Midlands Area L. Welterweight Champion. Ht. 5'7"
Manager Self

29.11.85	Steve Foster DREW 6 Ilkeston
04.12.85	Simon Collins L PTS 6 Stoke
24.03.86	Rocky McGran L PTS 6 Mayfair
10.04.86	Lincoln Pennant W PTS 6 Leicester
21.04.86	Malcolm Davies W PTS 6 Birmingham
07.05.86	Julian Monville W PTS 6 Solihull
19.01.88	Antonio Fernandez L RSC 4 Kings Heath
07.03.88	John Ellis L PTS 6 Piccadilly
03.12.89	Dave Jenkins W PTS 6 Birmingham
05.02.90	Trevor Meikle W PTS 6 Brierley Hill
22.02.90	Chris Saunders L PTS 4 Hull
19.03.90	Barry North W PTS 6 Brierley Hill
30.04.90	Andy Kent W RSC 5 Brierley Hill
04.06.90	Brendan Ryan L RSC 7 Edgbaston
03.09.90	Dave Jenkins W PTS 8 Dudley
13.11.90	Brendan Ryan W PTS 10 Edgbaston
	(Vacant Midlands Area L. Welterweight Title)
18.03.91	Carl Brasier W PTS 6 Piccadilly
17.06.91	Dean Bramhall W PTS 6 Edgbaston
21.05.92	Mark Kelly W PTS 8 Cradley Heath
05.10.92	Ross Hale L PTS 10 Bristol
	(Elim. British L. Welterweight Title)
17.11.92	Tusikoleta Nkalankete DREW 8 Paris, France
16.03.93	Shaun Cogan W PTS 10 Edgbaston
	(Vacant All-Ireland L. Welterweight

Title & Midlands Area L. Welterweight Title Defence)

29.06.93	Mark Kelly W PTS 6 Edgbaston
24.11.93	Alan Peacock W PTS 8 Solihull
08.03.94	Julian Eavis W PTS 6 Edgbaston
28.06.94	John Smith W PTS 6 Edgbaston

Career: 26 contests, won 17, drew 2, lost 7.

Sean Metherell

Kettering. *Born* Kettering, 29 March, 1966
Welterweight. Ht. 5'9"
Manager C. Hogben

10.12.92	Cliff Churchward W PTS 6 Corby
23.02.93	George Wilson L PTS 6 Kettering
04.03.93	Simon Fisher W RSC 1 Peterborough
18.05.93	Brian Coleman DREW 6 Kettering
23.11.93	Dave Lovell L RSC 3 Kettering

Career: 5 contests, won 2, drew 1, lost 2.

Kevin Middleton

Downham. *Born* Deptford, 5 July, 1968
Featherweight. Ht. 5'7"
Manager M. Duff

24.10.91	Miguel Matthews W PTS 6 Dunstable
07.04.92	Pat Maher W CO 4 Southend
29.04.92	Chris Jickells L RSC 6 Solihull
15.10.92	Bradley Stone L PTS 6 Lewisham
04.12.92	Brian Robb W RSC 1 Telford
10.02.93	Chris Jickells W CO 1 Lewisham
03.03.93	Kid McAuley W PTS 8 Solihull
18.03.93	Miguel Matthews W PTS 6 Lewisham
28.04.93	Jonjo Irwin W RSC 6 Solihull
14.01.94	Miguel Matthews W PTS 6 Bethnal Green
05.04.94	Elvis Parsley L RSC 4 Bethnal Green

Career: 11 contests, won 8, lost 3.

(Alvin) Slick Miller

Doncaster. *Born* Doncaster, 12 May, 1968
Cruiserweight. Ht. 6'2"
Manager T. Petersen

28.04.94	Declan Faherty L RSC 2 Hull

Career: 1 contest, lost 1.

(Alkis) A. M. Milton (Alkiviadov)

Streatham. *Born* London, 5 May, 1965
L. Welterweight. Ht. 5'3¾"
Manager Self

24.10.84	Kenny Watson L PTS 6 Mayfair
24.01.85	John Wilder W RTD 3 Streatham
04.02.85	John Faulkner L PTS 6 Lewisham
30.04.85	Kenny Watson W PTS 6 Merton
28.11.85	Brian Sonny Nickels L CO 4 Bethnal Green
04.09.86	Kevin Spratt DREW 6 Merton
19.11.87	Lee West L PTS 6 Wandsworth
10.05.88	Peter Hart L RSC 1 Tottenham
06.12.88	Shane Tonks W PTS 6 Southend
03.04.90	Dave Jenkins L PTS 6 Southend
25.09.90	Ray Newby W PTS 6 Millwall
12.11.90	Darren Morris W PTS 6 Norwich
08.05.91	Steve McGovern L PTS 6 Millwall
08.01.92	Darren Morris L PTS 6 Burton
31.10.92	Rick Bushell DREW 4 Earls Court
10.12.92	Brian Coleman DREW 4 Bethnal Green
17.02.93	Rick Bushell W RSC 1 Bethnal Green
31.03.93	Brian Coleman W PTS 4 Bethnal Green

23.06.93	Felix Kelly L CO 8 Edmonton *(Vacant Southern Area Lightweight Title)*
01.12.93	Brian Coleman W PTS 4 Bethnal Green

Career: 20 contests, won 8, drew 3, lost 9.

Clifton Mitchell

Sheffield. *Born* Derby, 29 October, 1965
Heavyweight. Ht. 6'2½"
Manager Self

06.04.91	John Harewood W RSC 2 Darlington
01.08.91	John Harewood W CO 1 Dewsbury
03.10.91	Tucker Richards W PTS 6 Burton
21.11.91	Tucker Richards W RSC 6 Burton
14.04.91	Michael Murray W RSC 8 Mansfield
16.03.93	Vivian Schwalger W CO 1 Wolverhampton
26.05.93	John Harewood W RSC 4 Mansfield
18.12.93	Jim Huffman W RSC 8 Cardiff
29.01.94	Cordwell Hylton W RSC 1 Cardiff
26.02.94	Jean Chanet W RSC 2 Earls Court
11.05.94	Emanuel Brites Camargo W RSC 1 Sheffield
21.05.94	Steve Garber W CO 1 Belfast

Career: 12 contests, won 12.

Clifton Mitchell   Les Clark

Norman Mitchell

Alfreton. *Born* Rotherham, 7 November, 1965
L. Middleweight. Ht. 5'11"
Manager M. Shinfield

22.09.93	Warren Stephens W PTS 6 Chesterfield

Career: 1 contest, won 1.

Tony Mock

Liverpool. *Born* Liverpool, 3 May, 1969
Welterweight. Ht. 5'8"
Manager Self

30.10.93	Tony Britland W PTS 6 Chester
11.12.93	Mark Antony W RSC 4 Liverpool

25.02.94	Mike Morrison W PTS 6 Chester
06.05.94	Scott Doyle W PTS 6 Liverpool

Career: 4 contests, won 4.

Joey Moffat

Liverpool. *Born* Liverpool, 14 February, 1964
Welterweight. Ht. 5'8"
Manager C.Moorcroft

10.03.90	Dave Jenkins L PTS 6 Bristol
13.11.91	Paul Hughes W RTD 4 Liverpool
28.11.91	Kevin Lowe W PTS 6 Liverpool
10.02.92	Tony Doyle W RSC 3 Liverpool
27.01.92	Kevin Lowe W PTS 6 Liverpool
29.04.92	Pete Roberts W RSC 3 Liverpool
14.05.92	Scott Doyle W RSC 8 Liverpool
15.09.92	Carl Tilley W PTS 6 Liverpool
09.06.93	Norman Dhalie W RTD 4 Liverpool
06.09.93	Dean Bramhald W PTS 6 Liverpool

Career: 10 contests, won 9, lost 1.

Allan Mooney

Glasgow. *Born* Glasgow, 6 July, 1972
Flyweight. Ht. 5'4"
Manager A. Melrose

21.10.93	Darren Noble L PTS 6 Glasgow
10.02.94	Anthony Hanna L RTD 1 Glasgow
13.04.94	Anthony Hanna W PTS 6 Glasgow

Career: 3 contests, won 1, lost 2.

Andrew Morgan

Merthyr. *Born* Neath, 20 February, 1963
Welterweight. Ht. 5'6"
Manager Self

22.06.87	Young John Dicken W CO 1 Stafford
05.10.87	Gerry Courtney W PTS 6 Piccadilly
24.11.87	Davy Robb W PTS 6 Wolverhampton
27.01.88	Andy Holligan L RSC 5 Belfast
28.09.88	David Postane L PTS 6 Edmonton
25.10.88	Mark Purcell L RTD 4 Portardawe
05.12.88	Tony Whitehouse W RSC 2 Dudley
06.02.89	Michael Howell W PTS 8 Swansea
29.03.89	Seamus O'Sullivan L PTS 6 Bethnal Green
09.05.89	Oliver Henry W RSC 5 Southend
27.09.90	Stuart Rimmer L PTS 6 Birmingham
03.12.90	Dean Bramhald DREW 8 Cleethorpes
12.02.91	Stuart Rimmer W PTS 8 Wolverhampton
26.03.91	John Smith W RSC 4 Wolverhampton
24.04.91	John Smith W PTS 6 Aberavon
02.05.91	Michael Driscoll L PTS 6 Kensington
17.03.92	Mark Elliot L PTS 6 Wolverhampton
30.04.93	Jean Chiarelli L RSC 4 Charrat, France
20.05.94	Michael Alexander L PTS 6 Neath

Career: 19 contests, won 9, drew 1, lost 9.

Karl Morling

Northampton. *Born* Douglas, IOM, 26 December, 1970
Featherweight. Ht. 5'4"
Manager J. Cox

15.10.90	Lee Christian W RSC 2 Kettering
22.10.90	Tony Falcone W PTS 6 Mayfair
31.01.91	Craig Dermody L RSC 5 Bredbury
02.05.91	Sol Francis W RSC 3 Northampton
13.05.91	Paul Wynn W RSC 2 Northampton
06.04.92	Norman Dhalie W PTS 6 Northampton
05.10.92	Robert Braddock W PTS 6 Northampton

125

14.12.92 Dean Lynch L RSC 4 Northampton
19.04.93 Graham McGrath W RSC 6 Northampton
01.12.93 John Armour L CO 3 Kensington
Career: 10 contests, won 7, lost 3.

Terry Morrill

Hull. *Born* Hull, 2 February, 1965
L. Middleweight. Former Central Area L. Middleweight Champion. Ht. 5'10¼"
Manager Self

10.12.88 Chris Richards W PTS 6 Crystal Palace
08.02.89 Newton Barnett W PTS 6 Kensington
28.03.89 Skip Jackson L RSC 5 Glasgow
27.06.89 Mark Howell W PTS 6 Kensington
10.10.89 Spencer Alton W PTS 6 Hull
15.11.89 Davey Hughes DREW 4 Lewisham
08.12.89 Tony Baker W PTS 6 Doncaster
22.02.90 Mark Holden W RSC 7 Hull
(Central Area L. Middleweight Title Challenge)
10.04.90 Ernie Noble W RSC 7 Doncaster
20.05.90 Jason Rowe L CO 6 Sheffield
(Central Area L. Middleweight Title Defence)
31.10.90 Shaun Cummins L RSC 1 Crystal Palace
14.03.91 Delroy Waul DREW 8 Middleton
28.05.91 Eamonn Loughran L CO 1 Cardiff
16.10.92 Shamus Casey W PTS 6 Hull
16.09.93 Des Robinson W PTS 8 Hull
12.11.93 Shamus Casey W PTS 8 Hull
Career: 16 contests, won 10, drew 2, lost 4.

Terry Morrill

Jamie Morris

Nuneaton. *Born* Nuneaton, 15 February, 1970
L. Welterweight. Ht. 5'9"
Manager P. Byrne

28.06.89 Phil Lashley W RSC 1 Kenilworth
05.09.89 Carl Brasier L RSC 3 Southend
10.10.89 Andrew Robinson L PTS 6 Wolverhampton

06.12.89 Wayne Taylor L RSC 5 Leicester
17.01.90 Lee Ahmed L PTS 6 Stoke
05.02.90 Lee Ahmed W PTS 6 Leicester
27.02.90 Lee Ahmed W PTS 6 Evesham
06.03.90 George Bailey W PTS 6 Bradford
06.04.90 Rick Dimmock L PTS 6 Stevenage
24.04.90 Des Gargano L PTS 4 Stoke
30.04.90 Neil Leitch L PTS 6 Nottingham
14.05.90 Tony Heath L PTS 6 Leicester
01.10.91 Michael Byrne DREW 4 Bedworth
16.10.91 Michael Byrne W PTS 6 Stoke
11.11.91 Mitchell Barney DREW 6 Stratford upon Avon
21.11.91 Brian Coleman DREW 6 Stafford
04.12.91 Sugar Boy Wright L PTS 6 Stoke
20.01.92 Mark Antony L RSC 5 Coventry
24.02.92 Simon Hamblett DREW 6 Coventry
11.03.92 Razza Campbell L PTS 6 Stoke
24.03.92 Mark Allen W PTS 6 Wolverhampton
27.01.93 Billy McDougall L PTS 6 Stoke
11.03.93 Mark Allen DREW 6 Walsall
17.06.93 Chris Pollock L RSC 1 Bedworth
13.12.93 Dean Bramhald L RSC 3 Doncaster
Career: 25 contests, won 6, drew 5, lost 14.

Jason Morris

Birmingham. *Born* Birmingham, 28 May, 1972
Bantamweight. Ht. 5'2"
Manager Self

08.09.92 Jacob Smith L PTS 6 Manchester
22.02.93 Stevie Woods W CO 4 Glasgow
17.03.93 Gary Marston L PTS 6 Stoke
17.02.94 Marcus Duncan L RSC 6 Bury
28.03.94 Graham McGrath L PTS 6 Birmingham
Career: 5 contests, won 1, lost 4.

Mike Morrison

Pembroke. *Born* Prestatyn, 24 February, 1963
L. Welterweight. Ht. 5'7"
Manager Self

14.09.89 Paul Day L PTS 6 Basildon
21.09.89 Steve McGovern L PTS 6 Southampton
28.09.89 Mark Atkins W PTS 6 Cardiff
11.10.89 Richard Burton L PTS 6 Stoke
15.11.89 Jason Rowland L PTS 6 Reading
30.11.89 Mo Hussein L PTS 8 Barking
20.12.89 Nigel Dobson L PTS 6 Kirkby
16.01.90 B. F. Williams L PTS 6 Cardiff
24.01.90 Carl Wright L PTS 6 Preston
01.03.90 Russell Jones L PTS 6 Cardiff
13.03.90 Nick Meloscia L PTS 6 Bristol
21.03.90 Steve Foran L PTS 6 Preston
10.04.90 Chris Saunders L PTS 6 Doncaster
23.04.90 Shaun Cogan L PTS 8 Birmingham
30.04.90 Shaun Cooper L PTS 6 Brierley Hill
22.05.90 Jason Rowland L PTS 6 St Albans
05.09.90 Tim Harmey L PTS 6 Brighton
12.09.90 Jimmy Harrison L PTS 6 Battersea
25.09.90 Mark Tibbs L PTS 6 Millwall
03.10.90 Nick Hall L PTS 8 Solihull
10.10.90 Benny Collins L PTS 6 Millwall
12.12.90 Eamonn Loughran L PTS 6 Basildon
10.01.91 Rick Bushell L PTS 6 Wandsworth
24.01.91 Andy Williams L PTS 8 Gorseinon
31.01.91 Richard Burton L PTS 6 Bredbury
06.03.91 Mark Tibbs L RSC 4 Wembley
02.05.91 Richard Swallow L PTS 6 Northampton
23.05.91 Martin Rosamond L PTS 6 Southampton

18.07.91 Michael Smyth L RSC 2 Cardiff
07.07.92 Steve Howden W CO 3 Bristol
15.09.92 Dean Bramhald L PTS 6 Crystal Palace
28.10.92 Mervyn Bennett L PTS 6 Cardiff
14.12.92 Mervyn Bennett L PTS 6 Cardiff
27.02.93 Paul Ryan L PTS 6 Dagenham
09.03.93 Trevor Royal W PTS 6 Bristol
14.04.93 Cham Joof L PTS 4 Kensington
23.04.93 Djamel Lifa L PTS 6 St Brieuc, France
26.06.93 Bobby Guynan W PTS 4 Earls Court
13.10.93 P. J. Gallagher L PTS 4 Bethnal Green
10.11.93 Sean Knight L PTS 6 Ystrad
29.11.93 Bobby Guynan L PTS 6 Ingatestone
22.01.94 Bernard McComiskey L PTS 6 Belfast
25.02.94 Tony Mock L PTS 6 Chester
06.03.94 Everald Williams L PTS 4 Southwark
Career: 44 contests, won 4, lost 40.

Jerry Mortimer

Clapham. *Born* Mauritius, 22 June, 1962
S. Middleweight. Ht. 5'9"
Manager B. Aird

21.10.91 Steve Thomas L PTS 6 Mayfair
12.02.92 Darren Murphy W PTS 6 Watford
02.03.92 Lee Farrell W PTS 6 Merthyr
28.04.92 Stefan Wright L RSC 4 Corby
08.09.92 Robert Whitehouse W RSC 3 Southend
15.10.92 Russell Washer W RSC 5 Lewisham
14.12.92 Gareth Boddy W PTS 6 Cardiff
28.01.93 John Bosco L RSC 4 Southwark
09.03.93 Paul Smith W PTS 6 Bristol
01.12.93 Gilbert Jackson L RSC 3 Kensington
20.01.94 Dean Cooper L PTS 8 Battersea
24.02.94 Mark Smallwood L PTS 6 Walsall
10.03.94 Dale Nixon DREW 4 Bristol
26.04.94 Mark Baker L PTS 6 Bethnal Green
27.05.94 Val Golding L PTS 6 Ashford
Career: 15 contests, won 6, drew 1, lost 8.

Jerry Mortimer   Les Clark

Chris Mulcahy

Manchester. *Born* Rochdale, 18 June, 1963
L. Middleweight. Ht. 6'0"
Manager Self

11.10.88	Robbie Bowen W PTS 6 Wolverhampton
25.10.88	Dave Croft W PTS 6 Cottingham
03.11.88	Pat Durkin W RSC 2 Manchester
21.11.88	Ian Midwood-Tate L CO 1 Leicester
23.02.89	Nigel Bradley L RSC 2 Stockport
17.04.89	Dave Kettlewell W PTS 6 Middleton
24.04.89	Kevin Toomey W PTS 6 Bradford
19.05.89	Dave Whittle W PTS 6 Gateshead
25.05.89	Martin Ogilvie L PTS 6 Dundee
12.06.89	Trevor Meikle W PTS 6 Manchester
11.07.89	Trevor Meikle W PTS 6 Batley
03.10.89	Banco Bell W RSC 1 Cottingham
23.10.89	Karl Ince L CO 5 Cleethorpes
20.11.89	Ian Thomas W PTS 6 Leicester
14.05.90	Mark Kelly L PTS 8 Cleethorpes
11.06.90	Alan Peacock L RSC 3 Manchester
05.03.91	Pat Durkin W PTS 6 Leicester
03.04.91	Willie Yeardsley L PTS 6 Manchester
10.06.91	Trevor Meikle DREW 6 Manchester
02.10.91	Robert Wright L RSC 1 Solihull
21.11.91	Richard O'Brien L RSC 2 Ilkeston
20.01.92	Darren McInulty L PTS 6 Coventry
11.02.92	James McGee L PTS 6 Wolverhampton
04.04.92	Rob Stevenson W PTS 8 Cleethorpes
01.06.92	Rob Stevenson W PTS 6 Manchester
03.09.92	John Smith DREW 6 Liverpool
16.10.92	Peter Waudby L RSC 4 Hull
24.11.92	Richard Swallow L PTS 6 Wolverhampton
02.12.92	Colin Anderson W PTS 6 Bardon
02.02.93	Spencer Alton L RSC 3 Derby
08.03.93	Danny Harper L PTS 8 Leeds
31.03.93	Adrian Dodson L RSC 1 Bethnal Green
01.06.93	Tony Trimble L PTS 6 Manchester
09.06.93	Andrew Jervis L PTS 6 Liverpool
27.09.93	David Sumner W PTS 6 Manchester
19.10.93	Rick North DREW 6 Cleethorpes
27.10.93	Rick North L PTS 6 Stoke
29.11.93	Carl Smith L CO 1 Manchester

Career: 38 contests, won 15, drew 3, lost 20.

Mick Mulcahy

Manchester. *Born* Rochdale, 9 May, 1966
L. Welterweight. Ht. 5'8"
Manager Self

06.06.88	Nick Langley W RSC 5 Manchester
05.09.88	Johnny Walker W PTS 4 Glasgow
22.09.88	Frankie Foster L PTS 6 Newcastle
02.10.88	Niel Leggett DREW 6 Peterborough
25.10.88	Wayne Windle W PTS 6 Cottingham
03.11.88	Peter English L RSC 4 Manchester
12.12.88	Steve Taggart L PTS 6 Birmingham
25.01.89	Mark Tibbs L CO 1 Bethnal Green
23.02.89	Sean Conn W CO 1 Stockport
13.03.89	Dean Dickinson W PTS 6 Leicester
17.04.89	Neil Leitch W RSC 2 Middleton
19.05.89	Mark Jay L PTS 6 Gateshead
29.05.89	George Kerr L PTS 6 Dundee
12.06.89	Muhammad Shaffique L RSC 2 Manchester
11.09.89	Dave Croft W PTS 4 Manchester
19.09.89	Billy Couzens L PTS 6 Bethnal Green
03.10.89	Kevin Toomey W CO 5 Cottingham
13.10.89	Carl Wright L PTS 6 Preston
23.10.89	Trevor Meikle L PTS 6 Cleethorpes
31.10.89	Carl Wright L PTS 6 Manchester
10.11.89	Chris McReedy L PTS 6 Liverpool
20.11.89	Brendan Ryan L PTS 6 Leicester
04.12.89	Brian Cullen L PTS 8 Manchester

19.12.89	Errol McDonald L RSC 3 Bethnal Green
24.04.90	Brian Cullen L PTS 8 Stoke
22.10.90	Wayne Windle L PTS 4 Cleethorpes
12.11.90	Richard Joyce L RSC 6 Stratford upon Avon
12.12.90	Neil Porter DREW 6 Stoke
24.01.91	Robert McCracken L RSC 1 Brierley Hill
05.03.91	Darren Morris L PTS 6 Leicester
03.04.91	Trevor Meikle L PTS 6 Manchester
15.04.91	Andreas Panayi L RSC 2 Leicester
10.06.91	Mike Calderwood L PTS 6 Manchester
18.11.91	Benji Joseph L PTS 6 Manchester
28.11.91	B. K. Bennett L PTS 6 Evesham
05.12.91	Mark Elliot L RSC 2 Cannock
17.03.92	Bernard Paul L PTS 6 Mayfair
04.04.92	Michael Byrne L RSC 4 Cleethorpes
01.06.92	Jason Brattley L PTS 6 Manchester
11.09.92	Rocky Ferrari L PTS 6 Glasgow
25.09.92	Carl Wright L PTS 8 Liverpool
10.12.92	Charlie Kane L RSC 2 Glasgow
02.02.93	Shane Sheridan L PTS 6 Derby
19.03.93	Steve Walker L RSC 6 Manchester
01.06.93	Wayne Windle W PTS 6 Manchester
09.09.93	Martin Campbell L PTS 6 Glasgow
07.11.93	Charlie Kane L RSC 2 Glasgow

Career: 47 contests, won 10, drew 2, lost 35.

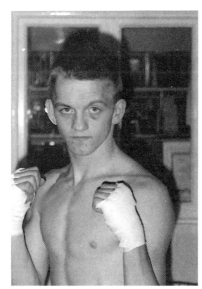

Justin Murphy Les Clark

Justin Murphy

Brighton. *Born* Brighton, 21 February, 1974
Featherweight. Ht. 5'7"
Manager F. Maloney

15.09.93	Andrew Bloomer W PTS 4 Bethnal Green
13.10.93	Thomas Bernard W RSC 1 Bethnal Green
01.12.93	Mark Hargreaves W PTS 4 Bethnal Green
25.01.94	Jobie Tyers W RSC 3 Piccadilly
29.03.94	Tony Falcone W RSC 2 Bethnal Green
15.06.94	Mike Deveney W PTS 6 Southwark

Career: 6 contests, won 6.

Sean Murphy

St Albans, *Born* St Albans, 1 December, 1964
Lightweight. Former British Featherweight Champion. Ht. 5'6"
Manager F. Warren

20.09.86	Albert Parr W PTS 6 Hemel Hempstead
09.10.86	Gordon Stobie W CO 5 Croydon
25.10.86	Simon Turner W PTS 6 Stevenage
03.12.86	Des Gargano W PTS 6 Muswell Hill
28.01.87	Keith Ward W RTD 4 Croydon
22.04.87	Kelvin Smart W CO 3 Kensington
09.05.87	Derek Amory W RSC 2 Wandsworth
01.07.87	Ray Minus L RSC 5 Kensington *(Commonwealth Bantamweight Title Challenge)*
09.08.87	Ronnie Stephenson W RSC 1 Windsor
16.09.87	David Williams W CO 1 Kensington
15.11.88	Craig Windsor W RSC 1 Norwich
01.12.88	Rocky Lawlor W RSC 2 Edmonton
31.01.89	Kid Sumali W RTD 2 Reading
07.03.89	Mike Whalley W PTS 6 Wisbech *(Elim. British Featherweight Title)*
08.05.89	Jesus Muniz W PTS 8 St Albans
19.09.89	Les Fabri W PTS 8 Millwall
24.10.89	Gerardo Castillo W RSC 1 Watford
08.03.90	Mario Lozano W PTS 8 Watford
22.05.90	John Doherty W CO 3 St Albans *(Vacant British Featherweight Title)*
25.09.90	Johnny B. Good W CO 2 Millwall *(British Featherweight Title Defence)*
05.03.91	Gary de Roux L CO 5 Millwall *(British Featherweight Title Defence)*
22.05.91	Ines Alvarado W PTS 8 Millwall
29.10.91	Colin McMillan L PTS 12 Kensington *(British Featherweight Title Challenge)*
30.04.92	Ian Honeywood W RSC 1 Kensington
27.02.93	Alan McKay W RSC 9 Dagenham *(Vacant British Featherweight Title)*
10.07.93	Steve Robinson L CO 9 Cardiff *(WBO Featherweight Title Challenge)*
16.02.94	Billy Schwer L RSC 3 Stevenage *(British & Commonwealth Lightweight Title Challenge)*

Career: 27 contests, won 22, lost 5.

James Murray

Newmains. *Born* Lanark, 7 December, 1969
Bantamweight. Ht. 5'4"
Manager Self

26.03.93	L. C. Wilson W RSC 4 Glasgow
30.04.93	Dave Campbell W PTS 6 Glasgow
29.05.93	Kid McAuley W PTS 6 Paisley
09.09.93	Des Gargano W PTS 6 Glasgow
21.10.93	Graham McGrath W PTS 6 Glasgow
10.11.93	Paul Webster L PTS 4 Bethnal Green
10.02.94	Marty Chestnut W PTS 6 Glasgow
11.03.94	Paul Wynn W PTS 6 Glasgow
13.04.94	Pete Buckley W PTS 6 Glasgow
10.06.94	Graham McGrath W PTS 8 Glasgow

Career: 10 contests, won 9, lost 1.

Paul Murray

Birmingham. *Born* Birmingham, 8 January, 1961
Middleweight. Ht. 5'9"
Manager P. Byrne

04.09.80　Gerry White W PTS 6 Morecambe
11.09.80　Graeme Ahmed L PTS 6 Hartlepool
29.09.80　Richard Wilson L PTS 6 Bedworth
08.10.80　Carl North W CO 2 Stoke
14.10.80　Steve McLeod W PTS 6 Wolverhampton
20.10.80　Steve Davies DREW 6 Birmingham
30.10.80　John Wiggins W PTS 6 Wolverhampton
07.11.80　Archie Salman L PTS 6 Cambuslang
18.11.80　John Wiggins L PTS 6 Shrewsbury
26.11.80　Mike Clemow L PTS 8 Stoke
08.12.80　John Wiggins L PTS 6 Nottingham
26.01.81　Errol Dennis W PTS 6 Edgbaston
16.03.81　Dennis Sheehan DREW 6 Nottingham
15.04.81　Nigel Thomas DREW 8 Evesham
28.05.81　Martin McGough L PTS 6 Edgbaston
09.07.81　Roger Guest L CO 8 Dudley
21.09.81　Gary Buckle DREW 6 Wolverhampton
07.10.81　Kostas Petrou W RSC 5 Solihull
13.10.81　Gary Buckle L PTS 6 Wolverhampton
24.11.81　Nick Riozzi W PTS 6 Wolverhampton
25.01.82　Martin McGough L RSC 4 Wolverhampton
22.02.82　Gary Buckle W PTS 8 Nottingham
10.03.82　Ron Pearce L PTS 8 Solihull
23.03.82　Errol Dennis L PTS 6 Wolverhampton
29.03.82　Tony Brown L PTS 6 Liverpool
07.04.82　Dennis Sheehan W PTS 6 Evesham
28.04.82　Lee Roy W CO 3 Burslem
17.05.82　Paul Costigan L PTS 8 Manchester
24.05.82　Dennis Sheehan DREW 6 Nottingham
07.06.82　Kostas Petrou L PTS 6 Edgbaston
13.09.82　Paul Costigan W PTS 6 Manchester
18.10.82　Kostas Petrou L RSC 5 Edgbaston
15.02.83　Bert Myrie L PTS 6 Wolverhampton
21.02.83　Steve Tempro L DIS 3 Edgbaston
01.03.83　Chris Pyatt L RTD 2 Kensington
17.05.83　T. P. Jenkins L PTS 6 Bethnal Green
23.06.83　Wayne Hawkins L PTS 6 Wolverhampton
19.09.83　Bert Myrie W PTS 8 Nottingham
26.10.83　Steve Henty L PTS 6 Stoke
14.11.83　Kid Sadler L PTS 8 Manchester
14.12.83　John Andrews L PTS 6 Stoke
19.03.84　Wayne Barker L PTS 8 Manchester
27.03.84　Rocky Kelly L RTD 5 Battersea
08.10.84　Gavin Stirrup L PTS 6 Manchester
26.01.87　Chris Walker L PTS 4 Bethnal Green
10.02.87　Chris Walker W PTS 4 Wolverhampton
16.02.87　Chris Galloway W PTS 6 Mayfair
24.02.87　Nicky Thorne L PTS 6 Wandsworth
03.08.87　Peter Elliott L PTS 6 Stoke
07.09.87　Dusty Miller L RTD 4 Mayfair
25.01.88　Paul Wesley L PTS 8 Birmingham
29.02.88　Paul Wesley DREW 8 Birmingham
14.03.88　Mickey Hughes L RSC 4 Mayfair
19.10.88　Geoff Calder NC 5 Evesham
26.10.88　Franki Moro L PTS 6 Stoke
05.12.88　Richard Carter L PTS 6 Dudley
24.01.89　Antonio Fernandez L PTS 6 Kings Heath
24.10.89　Andrew Flute L RSC 4 Wolverhampton
21.06.90　Spencer Alton L PTS 6 Alfreton
13.09.90　Nigel Rafferty L PTS 6 Watford
27.09.90　Nigel Rafferty DREW 6 Birmingham
09.10.90　Nigel Rafferty L PTS 6 Wolverhampton
18.10.90　Nick Manners L PTS 6 Dewsbury
29.10.90　Carlos Christie L PTS 6 Birmingham
16.12.90　Wayne Hawkins L PTS 6 Wolverhampton

28.01.91　Lee Prudden L PTS 6 Birmingham
06.02.91　Paul Walters DREW 6 Liverpool
27.02.91　Paul Busby L PTS 6 Wolverhampton
13.03.91　Lee Prudden DREW 6 Stoke
24.04.91　John Kaighin L PTS 6 Aberavon
14.05.91　Ernie Loveridge L PTS 8 Dudley
30.05.91　Robert McCracken L RSC 2 Birmingham
25.07.91　Tony Booth L PTS 6 Dudley
07.10.91　Antonio Fernandez L RSC 7 Birmingham
12.11.91　Lee Archer L PTS 6 Wolverhampton
05.12.91　Richard Carter L PTS 8 Cannock
17.12.91　Paul Busby L CO 3 Cardiff
15.01.92　Mark Hale L PTS 6 Stoke
06.02.92　John McKenzie L PTS 6 Peterborough
19.02.92　James F. Woolley W CO 4 Muswell Hill
26.03.92　Neville Brown L CO 3 Telford
05.10.92　Lee Archer L PTS 6 Bardon
13.10.92　Lee Archer L PTS 6 Wolverhampton
21.10.92　Steve Loftus L PTS 6 Stoke
23.11.92　John J. Cooke L CO 1 Coventry
17.06.93　Carl Smallwood L PTS 6 Bedworth
18.09.93　Zak Chelli W RSC 2 Leicester
02.12.93　Justin Clements W PTS 6 Walsall
19.03.94　Mark Delaney L CO 3 Millwall
17.06.94　Peter Vosper L PTS 8 Plymouth
Career: 90 contests, won 17, drew 9, lost 63, no contest 1.

George Naylor

Liverpool. *Born* Liverpool, 4 September, 1968
Lightweight. Ht. 5'7"
Manager S. Vaughan

25.09.92　Charles Shepherd L RSC 4 Liverpool
30.10.92　Dean Martin W PTS 6 Birmingham
20.11.92　Emlyn Rees W PTS 6 Liverpool
15.12.92　Renny Edwards L RSC 5 Liverpool
02.07.93　Bruce Ruegg W PTS 6 Liverpool
30.10.93　Paul Wynn W RSC 3 Chester
25.02.94　Steve Edwards W RTD 3 Chester
Career: 7 contests, won 5, lost 2.

John Naylor

Liverpool. *Born* Liverpool, 25 June, 1967
Lightweight. Ht. 5'8"
Manager S. Vaughan

10.03.88　Paul Charters W PTS 6 Croydon
18.03.88　Alan Roberts W RSC 1 Wandsworth
26.09.88　Kid Sumali W PTS 8 Bedford
31.10.88　Gerry McBride W PTS 8 Bedford
25.01.89　Colin Lynch L CO 1 Solihull
11.12.89　Nigel Haddock L RSC 5 Nottingham
28.02.91　Chris Bennett W RSC 3 Sunderland
14.03.91　Neil Smith L RSC 6 Middleton
19.01.94　Norman Dhalie W RSC 3 Stoke
Career: 9 contests, won 6, lost 3.

(Jimmy) Shea Neary

Liverpool. *Born* Liverpool, 18 May, 1968
L. Welterweight. Ht. 5'7½"
Manager B. Devine

03.09.92　Simon Ford W RSC 1 Liverpool
05.10.92　Shaun Armstrong W RSC 6 Liverpool
02.11.92　Jason Barker W RSC 3 Liverpool
01.12.92　Chris Saunders W PTS 6 Liverpool
22.02.93　Vaughan Carnegie W RSC 1 Liverpool
29.03.93　John Smith W PTS 6 Liverpool

06.09.93　Wayne Shepherd W RTD 2 Liverpool
25.10.93　Mark Antony W RSC 1 Liverpool
13.06.94　Mark Pearce W RSC 4 Liverpool
Career: 9 contests, won 9.

Johnny Nelson

Sheffield. *Born* Sheffield, 4 January, 1967
WBF Heavyweight Champion. Former
WBF Cruiserweight Champion. Former
Undefeated British, European & Central
Area Cruiserweight Champion. Ht. 6'2"
Manager G. Steene

18.03.86　Peter Brown L PTS 6 Hull
15.05.86　Tommy Taylor L PTS 6 Dudley
03.10.86　Magne Havnaa L PTS 4 Copenhagen, Denmark
20.11.86　Chris Little W PTS 6 Bredbury
19.01.87　Gypsy Carman W PTS 6 Mayfair
02.03.87　Doug Young W PTS 6 Huddersfield
10.03.87　Sean Daly W RSC 1 Manchester
28.04.87　Brian Schumacher L PTS 8 Halifax
03.06.87　Byron Pullen W RSC 3 Southwark
14.12.87　Jon McBean W RSC 6 Edgbaston
01.02.88　Dennis Bailey L PTS 8 Northampton
24.02.88　Cordwell Hylton W RSC 1 Sheffield
25.04.88　Kenny Jones W CO 1 Liverpool
04.05.88　Crawford Ashley W PTS 8 Solihull
06.06.88　Lennie Howard W CO 2 Mayfair
31.08.88　Andrew Gerrard W PTS 8 Stoke
26.10.88　Danny Lawford W RSC 2 Sheffield
　　　　　(Vacant Central Area Cruiserweight Title)
04.04.89　Steve Mormino W RSC 2 Sheffield
21.05.89　Andy Straughn W CO 8 Finsbury Park
　　　　　(British Cruiserweight Title Challenge)
02.10.89　Ian Bulloch W CO 2 Hanley
　　　　　(British Cruiserweight Title Defence)
27.01.90　Carlos de Leon DREW 12 Sheffield
　　　　　(WBC Cruiserweight Title Challenge)
14.02.90　Dino Homsey W RSC 7 Brentwood
28.03.90　Lou Gent W CO 4 Bethnal Green
　　　　　(British Cruiserweight Title Defence)
27.06.90　Arthur Weathers W RSC 2 Kensington
05.09.90　Andre Smith W PTS 8 Brighton
14.12.90　Markus Bott W RSC 12 Karlsruhe, Germany
　　　　　(Vacant European Cruiserweight Title)
12.03.91　Yves Monsieur W RTD 8 Mansfield
　　　　　(European Cruiserweight Title Defence)
16.05.92　James Warring L PTS 12 Fredericksburg, USA
　　　　　(IBF Cruiserweight Title Challenge)
15.08.92　Norbert Ekassi L RSC 3 Ajaccio, France
29.10.92　Corrie Sanders L PTS 10 Morula, South Africa
30.04.93　Dave Russell W RSC 11 Melbourne, Australia
　　　　　(WBF Cruiserweight Title Challenge)
11.08.93　Tom Collins W RSC 1 Mansfield
　　　　　(WBF Cruiserweight Title Defence)
01.10.93　Francis Wanyama L DIS 10 Waregem, Belgium
　　　　　(WBF Cruiserweight Title Defence)
20.11.93　Jimmy Thunder W PTS 12 Auckland, New Zealand
　　　　　(WBF Heavyweight Title Challenge)
05.04.94　Henry Akinwande L PTS 10 Bethnal Green
Career: 35 contests, won 24, drew 1, lost 10.

Kenny Nevers

Hackney. *Born* Hackney, 10 August, 1967
L. Heavyweight. Ht. 5'11"
Manager B. Lynch

10.12.92	Hussain Shah L PTS 4 Bethnal Green	
22.02.93	Jason McNeill W RSC 1 Eltham	
04.04.93	Hussain Shah W RSC 4 Brockley	
28.07.93	Paul McCarthy L PTS 4 Brixton	

Career: 4 contests, won 2, lost 2.

Scott Newman

Sheffield. *Born* Heanor, 15 May, 1970
L. Middleweight. Ht. 5'9"
Manager M. Shinfield

23.01.91	Paul Walters L PTS 6 Stoke	
15.04.91	Bullit Andrews W RSC 1 Wolverhampton	
13.10.93	Anthony Lawrence L PTS 6 Stoke	
02.12.93	Warren Stephens W DIS 4 Evesham	

Career: 4 contests, won 2, lost 2.

Mark Newton

Cwmbran. *Born* Newport, 20 May, 1970
Lightweight. Ht. 5'7"
Manager M. Duff

16.12.93	Brian Coleman W PTS 6 Newport	

Career: 1 contest, won 1.

Dale Nixon

Taunton. *Born* Exeter, 11 May, 1970
S. Middleweight. Ht. 6'2"
Manager C. Sanigar

09.03.93	Ian Vokes W RSC 2 Bristol	
27.05.93	Chris Nurse W RSC 2 Bristol	
26.06.93	Tim Robinson W RSC 2 Keynsham	
03.11.93	Jason McNeill W RSC 1 Bristol	
10.03.94	Jerry Mortimer DREW 4 Bristol	
31.03.94	Steve Thomas DREW 4 Bristol	
25.06.94	Robert Peel W PTS 6 Cullompton	

Career: 7 contests, won 5, drew 2.

Scott Newman   Chris Bevan

Darren Noble

Newcastle. *Born* Newcastle, 2 October, 1969
Flyweight. Ht. 5'3"
Manager A. Walker

21.10.93	Allan Mooney W PTS 6 Glasgow	
23.03.94	Paul Ingle L RSC 3 Cardiff	

Career: 2 contests, won 1, lost 1.

Darren Noble   Les Clark

Ian Noble

Blackhall. *Born* Easington, 24 August, 1971
L. Middleweight. Ht. 5'7"
Manager G. Robinson

06.05.93	Michael Alexander L PTS 6 Hartlepool	
02.12.93	Rob Stevenson L PTS 6 Hartlepool	
10.02.94	Allan Logan L PTS 6 Glasgow	

Career: 3 contests, lost 3.

Eric Noi

Manchester. *Born* Manchester, 12 May, 1967
S. Middleweight. Ht. 5'11"
Manager F. Warren

05.02.93	Tim Robinson W RSC 4 Manchester	
19.03.93	Smokey Enison W RSC 5 Manchester	
26.04.93	Karl Barwise W PTS 6 Manchester	
28.05.93	Karl Barwise W RSC 4 Middleton	
25.07.93	Horace Fleary W PTS 6 Oldham	
18.12.93	Graham Jenner W CO 1 Manchester	
02.06.94	Shamus Casey W PTS 6 Middleton	

Career: 7 contests, won 7.

Shaun Norman

Leicester. *Born* Leicester, 1 April, 1970
Flyweight. Ht. 5'3"
Manager W. Swift

11.11.91	Louis Veitch W RSC 5 Bradford	
27.11.91	Dave Campbell L PTS 6 Marton	

14.12.91	Mickey Cantwell L PTS 8 Bexley Heath
20.02.92	Dave Hardie L PTS 6 Glasgow
10.04.92	Neil Armstrong DREW 8 Glasgow
25.04.92	Prince Nassem Hamed L RSC 2 Manchester
16.06.92	Francis Ampofo L RSC 4 Dagenham
19.10.92	Alan Ley L PTS 6 Mayfair
23.11.92	Paul Weir L PTS 8 Glasgow
04.03.93	Neil Armstrong L RSC 8 Glasgow
21.10.93	Neil Armstrong L RSC 7 Glasgow
18.02.94	Vince Feeney L RSC 2 Leicester
24.05.94	Ian Baillie W RSC 2 Leicester

Career: 13 contests, won 2, drew 1, lost 10.

Rick North

Grimsby. *Born* Grimsby, 2 February, 1968
Welterweight. Ht. 5'8½"
Manager B. Ingle

28.05.91	Michael Smyth L RSC 1 Cardiff
16.09.91	Eddie King W RSC 5 Cleethorpes
21.01.91	Steve Bricknell W PTS 6 Cleethorpes
11.11.91	Darren McInulty L PTS 6 Stratford upon Avon
09.12.91	Michael Byrne W RSC 2 Cleethorpes
23.01.92	Ron Hopley L PTS 6 York
19.02.92	Bernard Paul L PTS 6 Muswell Hill
11.03.92	Patrick Loughran L PTS 6 Stoke
22.04.92	Steve McNess L PTS 6 Wembley
03.06.92	Mark Dawson L PTS 6 Newcastle under Lyme
03.09.92	Andreas Panayi DREW 6 Liverpool
21.09.92	Hughie Davey DREW 6 Cleethorpes
05.10.92	Andrew Jervis L PTS 6 Liverpool
21.10.92	Jim Lawlor W PTS 6 Stoke
29.10.92	David Larkin L PTS 6 Leeds
20.11.92	Andreas Panayi L PTS 6 Liverpool
14.12.92	Lee Soar W PTS 6 Cleethorpes
27.01.93	Mark Dawson L PTS 8 Stoke
22.02.93	Spencer McCracken L PTS 8 Birmingham
09.03.93	Sean Baker L PTS 8 Bristol
14.04.93	Adrian Dodson L RTD 1 Kensington
27.05.93	Glenn Catley L PTS 4 Brisol
20.09.93	Dean Bramhald W PTS 6 Cleethorpes
30.09.93	Gary Osborne L PTS 6 Walsall
19.10.93	Chris Mulcahy DREW 6 Cleethorpes
27.10.93	Chris Mulcahy W PTS 6 Stoke
13.12.93	Trevor Meikle W PTS 6 Cleethorpes
26.01.94	Lindon Scarlett L RSC 6 Birmingham *(Vacant Midlands Area Welterweight Title)*
08.03.94	Kevin Mabbutt L PTS 6 Kettering
17.03.94	Dennis Berry W PTS 6 Lincoln
21.04.94	Dave Whittle L PTS 6 Gateshead
16.05.94	Dennis Berry L RSC 6 Cleethorpes

Career: 32 contests, won 9, drew 3, lost 20.

Robert Norton

Stourbridge. *Born* Dudley, 20 January, 1972
Cruiserweight. Ht. 6'2"
Manager G. Hayward

30.09.93	Stuart Fleet W CO 2 Walsall
27.10.93	Kent Davis W PTS 6 West Bromwich
02.12.93	Eddie Pyatt W RSC 2 Walsall
26.01.94	Lennie Howard W PTS 6 Birmingham
17.05.94	Steve Osborne W PTS 6 Kettering

Career: 5 contests, won 5.

Chris Nurse

Birmingham. *Born* Birmingham, 17 May, 1968
S. Middleweight. Ht. 6'1"
Manager E. Cashmore

24.11.92	Paul Hanlon L PTS 6 Wolverhampton
17.03.93	Steve Loftus W PTS 6 Stoke
01.04.93	Phil Ball DREW 6 Evesham
27.05.93	Dale Nixon L RSC 2 Bristol
30.11.93	Phil Ball W PTS 6 Wolverhampton
08.03.94	Robert Harper W PTS 6 Edgbaston
28.06.94	Richard Guy W RSC 3 Edgbaston

Career: 7 contests, won 4, drew 1, lost 2.

(David) Marvin O'Brien (Powell)

Leeds. *Born* Leeds, 3 September, 1966
S. Middleweight. Ht. 5'11"
Manager T. Callighan

31.01.90	Tony Hodge L RSC 3 Bethnal Green
04.04.90	Gary Osborne L CO 2 Stafford
07.09.90	Mike Phillips L RSC 1 Liverpool
12.11.90	Mike Phillips W PTS 6 Liverpool
17.01.91	Barry Messam L PTS 6 Alfreton
21.02.91	Russell Washer DREW 6 Walsall
02.03.91	Quinn Paynter DREW 6 Irvine
21.03.91	Nick Manners L CO 2 Dewsbury
31.05.91	Carl Harney W RSC 5 Manchester
24.06.91	Frank Eubanks L PTS 6 Liverpool
06.09.91	Cornelius Carr L RSC 7 Salemi, Italy
02.03.92	John Oxenham L PTS 6 Marton
26.03.92	John Ashton L PTS 8 Telford
05.04.92	Quinn Paynter L PTS 6 Bradford
17.05.92	Lester Jacobs L PTS 6 Harringay
20.11.92	Fran Harding L RSC 4 Liverpool
16.02.93	Andy Wright L PTS 6 Tooting
12.05.93	Martin Jolley L PTS 6 Sheffield
15.09.93	Paul Hitch L PTS 4 Newcastle
15.10.93	Bruno Girard L PTS 6 Romorantin, France
03.12.93	Mads Larsen L PTS 6 Randers, Denmark
02.02.94	Willie Quinn L PTS 6 Glasgow
06.06.94	Willie Quinn L RSC 4 Glasgow

Career: 23 contests, won 2, drew 2, lost 19.

Marvin O'Brien   Les Clark

Richard O'Brien

Alfreton. *Born* Chesterfield, 29 October, 1971
L. Middleweight. Ht. 5'10"
Manager M. Shinfield

14.05.90	Finn McCool W RSC 3 Northampton
21.05.90	Andy Rowbotham W RSC 5 Bradford
21.06.90	Jim Lawlor DREW 6 Alfreton
15.10.90	Richard Swallow W RTD 1 Kettering
22.10.90	Crain Fisher L CO 3 Manchester
13.12.90	Mick Duncan L PTS 6 Hartlepool
17.01.91	Steve Hardman L PTS 6 Alfreton
11.02.91	Neil Porter W RSC 4 Manchester
21.02.91	Darren Morris W PTS 6 Walsall
28.03.91	Trevor Ambrose L RSC 1 Alfreton
21.10.91	Tony Connellan L PTS 8 Bury
21.11.91	Chris Mulcahy W RSC 2 Ilkeston
02.12.91	Tony Britland W RSC 2 Birmingham
04.02.92	Darren McInulty W PTS 4 Alfreton
03.03.92	Scott Doyle L PTS 4 Cradley Heath
21.05.92	Howard Clarke L CO 1 Cradley Heath
23.10.92	Hughie Davey L PTS 6 Gateshead
11.03.93	Andy Peach W PTS 6 Walsall
01.04.93	Dave Lovell W PTS 6 Evesham
12.05.93	Wayne Appleton L RTD 2 Sheffield
20.09.93	Kevin Mabbutt L PTS 6 Northampton

Career: 21 contests, won 10, drew 1, lost 10.

Mark O'Callaghan

Tunbridge Wells. *Born* Tunbridge Wells, 17 January, 1969
Lightweight. Ht. 5'7"
Manager Self

03.10.91	Chris Mylan DREW 6 Burton
24.10.91	Nicky Lucas W PTS 6 Dunstable
11.12.91	Richard Joyce L RSC 3 Stoke
20.02.92	Alan McDowall L PTS 6 Glasgow
12.11.92	Erwin Edwards L RSC 6 Bayswater
20.01.93	Sugar Boy Wright W CO 1 Wolverhampton
05.02.93	Nick Boyd L PTS 6 Manchester
18.03.93	Paul Denton L RSC 4 Lewisham
22.04.93	Trevor Royal W PTS 6 Mayfair
26.05.93	Gareth Jordan L RSC 3 Mansfield
22.09.93	Dean Hollington L CO 1 Wembley
07.12.93	Colin Dunne L RSC 1 Bethnal Green
15.06.94	P. J. Gallagher L RSC 4 Southwark

Career: 13 contests, won 3, drew 1, lost 9.

(Paul) John O'Johnson (Johnson)

Nottingham. *Born* Nottingham, 2 November, 1969
L. Welterweight. Ht. 5'5"
Manager Self

29.08.91	Seth Jones W DIS 1 Oakengates
09.10.91	James Jiora W PTS 6 Manchester
24.10.91	Carl Hook L PTS 6 Dunstable
31.10.91	Darren Morris W PTS 6 Oakengates
26.11.91	Bernard Paul L PTS 6 Bethnal Green
22.01.92	Brian Coleman W PTS 6 Stoke
30.01.92	Chris Saunders W PTS 6 Southampton
20.02.92	Alan Peacock W PTS 6 Glasgow
09.03.92	Ricky Sackfield W PTS 6 Manchester
26.03.92	Davy Robb L PTS 6 Telford
03.06.92	Jason Barker W PTS 6 Newcastle under Lyme
09.09.92	Chris Saunders DREW 6 Stoke
05.10.92	Andreas Panayi L RTD 1 Liverpool
09.12.92	Jason Barker W PTS 8 Stoke
10.02.93	Dean Hollington L PTS 6 Lewisham
17.03.93	Jonathan Thaxton L PTS 6 Stoke

19.01.94   Billy McDougall L RSC 3 Stoke
10.03.94   Keith Marner L RSC 5 Watford
10.05.94   Mark Legg W RSC 6 Doncaster
11.06.94   Paul Knights W PTS 6 Bethnal Green
28.06.94   Andreas Panayi L RSC 5 Mayfair
Career: 21 contests, won 11, drew 1, lost 9.

Chris Okoh

Camberwell. *Born* Carshalton, 18 April, 1969
Cruiserweight. Ht. 6'2"
Manager B. Hearn

16.03.93   Lee Prudden W PTS 6 Mayfair
10.07.93   Steve Yorath W PTS 6 Cardiff
28.09.93   Steve Osborne W RSC 5 Bethnal Green
06.11.93   Chris Henry W RSC 2 Bethnal Green
09.04.94   Art Stacey W PTS 6 Bethnal Green
Career: 5 contests, won 5.

Chris Okoh   Les Clark

(Mike) Chip O'Neill

Sunderland. *Born* Sunderland, 10 December, 1963
Featherweight. Ht. 5'6½"
Manager T. Conroy

28.06.82   Charlie Brown L PTS 6 Bradford
20.09.82   Danny Flynn L RSC 2 Glasgow
07.03.83   Charlie Brown L RSC 3 Glasgow
28.04.92   Robert Braddock W PTS 6 Houghton le Spring
10.09.92   Vince Wilson W RSC 1 Sunderland
21.09.92   Ian McGirr L PTS 6 Glasgow
05.10.92   Phil Lashley W PTS 6 Manchester
09.11.92   Robert Braddock L RSC 3 Bradford
19.01.93   Russell Rees L RSC 1 Cardiff
08.03.93   Chris Lyons W PTS 6 Leeds
29.04.93   Paul Wynn L PTS 6 Newcastle
07.10.93   Fred Reeve W RSC 2 Hull
08.11.93   Ady Benton L RSC 5 Bradford
13.12.93   Paul Richards L PTS 6 Bristol
04.03.94   Ian McLeod L RSC 2 Irvine
24.05.94   Paul Wynn W PTS 6 Sunderland
Career: 16 contests, won 6, lost 10.

Gary Osborne

Walsall. *Born* Bloxwich, 24 August, 1963
Former Undefeated Midlands Area L. Middleweight Champion. Former Midlands Area Welterweight Champion. Ht. 5'10"
Manager Self

08.05.89   Peter Reid W CO 5 Edgbaston
22.03.90   Peter Reid W CO 1 Wolverhampton
04.04.90   Marvin O'Brien W CO 2 Stafford
24.05.90   Julian Eavis W PTS 6 Dudley
18.09.90   Paul Hanlon W RTD 2 Wolverhampton
17.10.90   Chris Richards W PTS 8 Stoke
06.12.90   Darren Morris W PTS 8 Wolverhampton
10.04.91   Mickey Lerwill W PTS 10 Wolverhampton
     (Vacant Midlands Area Welterweight Title)
10.09.91   Ernie Loveridge L RSC 1 Wolverhampton
     (Midlands Area Welterweight Title Defence)
17.03.92   Shamus Casey W RSC 5 Wolverhampton
     (Vacant Midlands Area L. Middleweight Title)
28.04.92   Gary Pemberton W CO 3 Wolverhampton
07.06.93   Bullit Andrews W RSC 1 Walsall
30.09.93   Rick North W PTS 6 Walsall
24.02.94   Anthony Lawrence L RSC 3 Walsall
Career: 14 contests, won 12, lost 2.

Steve Osborne

Nottingham. *Born* Nottingham, 27 June, 1965
Cruiserweight. Ht. 5'9"
Manager Self

28.05.87   Gary Railton L PTS 6 Jarrow
09.06.87   Ian Bulloch L PTS 6 Manchester
24.09.87   Bobby Frankham L PTS 6 Glasgow
05.10.87   Ray Thomas L RSC 8 Piccadilly
14.12.87   Branko Pavlovic L RSC 3 Bedford
16.01.89   Simon McDougall W PTS 6 Bradford
25.01.89   Simon McDougall W PTS 6 Stoke
02.02.89   Dave Furneaux W CO 4 Southwark
13.02.89   Carl Thompson L PTS 6 Manchester
06.03.89   Jimmy Cropper W PTS 6 Manchester
05.04.89   Jimmy Cropper L PTS 6 Halifax
16.05.89   Henry Brewer W PTS 6 Halifax
12.06.89   Carl Thompson L PTS 8 Manchester
16.11.89   Dave Lawrence W PTS 6 Ilkeston
19.12.89   Herbie Hide L RSC 6 Bethnal Green
05.02.90   Dave Lawrence W PTS 8 Piccadilly
20.02.90   Rob Albon L PTS 6 Brentwood
03.03.90   Darren Westover L RSC 6 Wembley
15.11.90   Michael Gale L PTS 6 Oldham
08.12.90   Neils H. Madsen L RSC 6 Aalborg, Denmark
16.04.91   Art Stacey DREW 6 Nottingham
09.05.91   Michael Gale L RSC 2 Leeds
11.11.91   Art Stacey L PTS 6 Bradford
21.11.91   Bruce Scott L PTS 6 Burton
29.11.91   Maurice Core L PTS 6 Manchester
12.02.92   Phil Soundy L PTS 6 Wembley
12.11.92   Terry Dunstan L PTS 6 Bayswater
10.12.92   Ole Klemetsen L RSC 1 Bethnal Green
27.01.93   Darren McKenna L PTS 6 Stoke
22.02.93   Nicky Wadman L PTS 6 Eltham
26.04.93   Joe Frater W PTS 6 Cleethorpes
01.07.93   Denzil Browne L RSC 1 York

28.09.93   Chris Okoh L RSC 5 Bethnal Green
10.11.93   Monty Wright L RSC 3 Watford
13.12.93   Martin Langtry L PTS 6 Cleethorpes
28.03.94   Joe Frater W RSC 5 Cleethorpes
05.04.94   Bruce Scott L RSC 5 Bethnal Green
17.05.94   Robert Norton L PTS 6 Kettering
Career: 38 contests, won 9, drew 1, lost 28.

Clay O'Shea

Islington. *Born* London, 3 November,1966
L. Middleweight. Ht. 6'0"
Manager D. Mancini

20.02.90   Carlton Myers W RSC 1 Brentford
14.03.90   Tony Grizzle W RSC 1 Kensington
04.10.90   Benji Good W CO 2 Bethnal Green
31.10.90   Remy Duverger W PTS 6 Wembley
04.04.91   Robert Peel W PTS 6 Watford
11.09.91   Shamus Casey W PTS 6 Hammersmith
26.09.91   Tony Wellington W CO 1 Dunstable
25.03.92   Andrew Furlong DREW 6 Kensington
13.05.92   Andrew Furlong DREW 6 Kensington
15.10.92   Steve Thomas W PTS 6 Lewisham
17.12.92   Mark Jay W CO 1 Wembley
28.01.93   Lee Crocker W RSC 1 Southwark
26.04.94   Steve Thomas W PTS 6 Bethnal Green
Career: 13 contests, won 11, drew 2.

Dave Owens

Castleford. *Born* Castleford, 11 December, 1954
S. Middleweight. L. Heavyweight. Former Undefeated Central Area Middleweight Champion. Ht. 6'1"
Manager Self

12.05.76   Steve Heavisides W RSC 2 Bradford
08.06.76   Joe Jackson W PTS 4 Bradford
10.09.76   Carl McCarthy W CO 2 Digbeth
21.09.76   Steve Fenton W RSC 3 Bethnal Green
27.09.76   Neville Estaban DREW 6 Piccadilly
30.11.76   Owen Robinson W PTS 6 Leeds
20.04.77   Billy Hill W RSC 2 Manchester
27.04.77   Jim Moore W PTS 8 Bradford
15.05.77   Howard Mills W RSC 8 Manchester
10.07.77   Pat Brogan W RSC 9 Birmingham
     (Vacant Central Area Middleweight Title)
13.03.78   Paul Shutt W RSC 2 Nottingham
08.05.78   Howard Mills L RTD 4 Nottingham
04.09.78   Glen McEwan L CO 1 Wakefield
07.12.78   Torben Anderson L PTS 6 Copenhagen, Denmark
12.03.79   Romal Ambrose L PTS 8 Manchester
20.09.79   Dave Davies W CO 3 Liverpool
17.10.79   Jimmy Pickard W RSC 4 Piccadilly
     (Central Area Middleweight Title Defence)
29.04.80   Eddie Smith L CO 1 Stockport
12.08.80   Doug James L PTS 8 Gowerton
13.10.80   Earl Edwards L RSC 3 Windsor
03.09.85   Barry Ahmed DREW 6 Gateshead
20.09.85   Simon Harris W PTS 6 Longford
25.10.85   Nye Williams W PTS 8 Fulham
20.01.86   Tony Wilson L RSC 2 Mayfair
01.12.86   Pedro van Raamsdonk L CO 1 Arnhem, Holland
02.03.87   Peter Brown L PTS 8 Huddersfield
05.05.87   Shamus Casey W PTS 6 Leeds
18.11.87   John Foreman W RSC 5 Solihull
05.12.87   Darryl Ritchie L DIS 7 Doncaster
07.02.88   Brian Schumacher L CO 1 Stafford
28.11.88   John Foreman L CO 1 Edgbaston

31.01.89   Adam Cook DREW 6 Reading
13.03.89   James Wray L PTS 6 Glasgow
01.05.89   Jose Seys L RSC 6 Waregem, Belgium
20.11.89   Steve Williams DREW 6 Glasgow
19.12.89   Nicky Piper L CO 1 Gorleston
06.04.90   Everton Blake L RSC 6 Stevenage
14.05.90   Joe Frater W PTS 6 Cleethorpes
24.09.90   Sean O'Phoenix L PTS 8 Manchester
08.10.90   Darren McKenna W PTS 6 Leicester
29.10.90   Fidel Castro L PTS 6 Birmingham
18.11.90   Sean Heron L PTS 8 Birmingham
06.12.90   Gil Lewis L CO 2 Wolverhampton
17.02.91   Anton Josipovic L PTS 8 Prijedor, Yugoslavia
24.03.91   Christophe Girard L RSC 7 Vichy, France
23.04.91   Joe Frater W PTS 6 Evesham
27.05.91   Eddie Smulders L RSC 1 Rotterdam, Holland
14.11.91   Ian Henry L PTS 8 Gateshead
03.03.92   Terry French W CO 1 Houghton le Spring
26.03.92   Tony Booth L PTS 6 Hull
14.04.92   Martin Smith L PTS 6 Mansfield
26.10.92   Joe Frater W PTS 6 Cleethorpes
04.12.92   Bernard Bonzon L RSC 5 Geneva, Switzerland
06.03.93   Stephen Wilson L RSC 2 Glasgow
15.05.93   Willie Quinn L PTS 6 Glasgow
25.11.93   Dave Johnson L PTS 8 Tynemouth
28.03.94   Stephen Wilson L CO 2 Musselburgh

Career: 57 contests, won 21, drew 4, lost 32.

James Oyebola

Paddington. *Born* Nigeria, 10 June, 1961
WBC International & Southern Area
Heavyweight Champion. Ht. 6'9"
Manager Self

01.07.87   Andrew Gerrard W PTS 6 Kensington
16.09.87   Ian Priest W RSC 2 Kensington
03.11.87   Carl Timbrell W CO 2 Bethnal Green
24.11.87   Mike Jones L RSC 2 Wisbech
09.02.88   Denroy Bryan W RSC 6 Bethnal Green
10.05.88   Andrew Gerrard DREW 6 Tottenham
07.09.88   Tee Lewis W CO 1 Reading
01.11.88   Dorcey Gayman W RSC 1 Reading
23.11.88   Everton Christian W CO 1 Bethnal Green
31.01.89   John Westgarth W CO 3 Reading
15.02.89   Art Terry W CO 5 Bethnal Green
07.03.89   John Westgarth L RSC 5 Wisbech
12.04.91   Stan Campbell W CO 1 Greenville, USA
18.05.91   Bonyongo Destroyer W CO 1 Harare, Zimbabwe
      (Final Elim. African Heavyweight Title)
15.09.93   Denroy Bryan W RSC 5 Bethnal Green
13.10.93   R. F. McKenzie W RSC 1 Bethnal Green
      (Southern Area Heavyweight Title Challenge)
01.12.93   Jimmy Bills W PTS 8 Bethnal Green
09.02.94   Ladislao Mijangos W RSC 2 Bethnal Green
06.05.94   Scott Welch W CO 5 Atlantic City, USA
      (Vacant WBC International Heavyweight Title)

Career: 19 contests, won 16, drew 1, lost 2.

Joey Paladino

St Helens. *Born* Whiston, 29 August, 1965
Heavyweight. Ht. 6'6"
Manager R. Gray

06.05.93   Vance Idiens L PTS 8 Walsall
23.06.93   Julius Francis L CO 4 Edmonton
15.09.93   Kevin McBride L CO 2 Bethnal Green
28.10.93   David Jules W RSC 2 Walsall
06.11.93   Scott Welch L RSC 3 Bethnal Green
07.12.93   Damien Caesar L RSC 3 Bethnal Green
29.03.94   Graham Arnold W RSC 5 Wolverhampton
16.05.94   Neil Kirkwood L RSC 2 Cleethorpes

Career: 8 contests, won 2, lost 6.

Joey Paladino   Les Clark

Jim Pallatt

Leicester. *Born* Leicester, 8 September, 1969
Cruiserweight. Ht. 6'0"
Manager J. Griffin

18.02.94   Johnny Hooks L RSC 1 Leicester

Career: 1 contest, lost 1.

Andreas Panayi

St Helens. *Born* Cyprus, 14 July, 1969
L. Welterweight. Ht. 5'6"
Manager B. Hearn

21.11.90   Trevor Ambrose L RSC 5 Solihull
04.02.91   Cliff Churchward W PTS 6 Leicester
12.02.91   Eddie King W CO 2 Wolverhampton
27.02.91   Trevor Meikle L PTS 6 Wolverhampton
15.04.91   Mick Mulcahy W RSC 2 Leicester
24.04.91   Darren Morris DREW 6 Stoke
11.09.91   Robert Riley W PTS 6 Stoke
30.09.91   Steve Hardman W RSC 5 Liverpool
23.10.91   Darren Morris W PTS 6 Stoke
25.11.91   Marvin P. Gray W PTS 8 Liverpool
11.12.91   Mark Kelly DREW 8 Stoke
11.03.92   Dean Bramhald L PTS 8 Stoke
14.05.92   Dave Maj W CO 6 Liverpool
03.09.92   Rick North DREW 6 Liverpool
05.10.92   John O'Johnson W RTD 1 Liverpool
23.10.92   Trevor Meikle W PTS 6 Liverpool
20.11.92   Rick North W PTS 6 Liverpool
15.12.92   Mark Kelly W PTS 6 Liverpool
27.01.93   Ross Hale W RSC 3 Cardiff
27.02.93   Darren McInulty W PTS 6 Ellesmere Port
04.05.93   Jimmy Thornton W CO 2 Liverpool
02.07.93   Mark Ramsey DREW 6 Liverpool
28.09.93   Hugh Forde W PTS 8 Liverpool
11.12.93   Bobby Butters W CO 3 Liverpool
09.04.94   Tony Swift L PTS 8 Bethnal Green
10.05.94   Shaun Cogan W RSC 7 Doncaster
11.06.94   Tony Swift W PTS 8 Bethnal Green
28.06.94   John O'Johnson W RSC 5 Mayfair

Career: 28 contests, won 20, drew 4, lost 4.

Andreas Panayi   Les Clark

Delwyn Panayiotiou

Llanelli. *Born* Morriston, 26 September, 1967
Welterweight. Ht. 5'8"
Manager M. Copp

08.09.92   Sean Baker L RSC 2 Southend
09.06.93   Charlie Paine L PTS 6 Liverpool
24.06.93   Adrian Chase L CO 1 Watford
14.01.94   Nicky Thurbin L RTD 3 Bethnal Green

Career: 4 contests, lost 4.

Neil Parry

Middlesbrough. *Born* Middlesbrough, 21 June, 1969
Bantamweight. Ht. 5'5"
Manager T. Callighan

12.06.89   Des Gargano L PTS 6 Manchester
21.12.89   Kevin Jenkins L PTS 6 Kings Heath
31.01.90   Francis Ampofo L PTS 6 Bethnal Green
12.03.90   Paul Dever W PTS 6 Hull
19.03.90   James Drummond L RSC 4 Glasgow
27.11.90   Stevie Woods W PTS 6 Glasgow
04.12.90   Conn McMullen L RSC 2 Southend
21.01.91   Stevie Woods L PTS 8 Glasgow

06.02.91 Paul Dever W PTS 6 Liverpool
05.03.91 Tony Smith DREW 6 Leicester
24.04.91 Paul Dever DREW 6 Stoke
17.05.91 Gary White L PTS 6 Bury
03.06.91 Stevie Woods W RSC 2 Glasgow
20.06.91 Tony Smith W PTS 6 Liverpool
12.09.91 Mark Tierney L PTS 6 Wandsworth
21.10.91 Neil Johnston L PTS 8 Glasgow
27.01.92 Drew Docherty L RSC 4 Glasgow
28.02.92 Stevie Woods W PTS 6 Irvine
11.05.92 Tim Yeates L PTS 6 Piccadilly
21.09.92 Paul Weir L RSC 4 Glasgow
27.11.92 Eyup Can L PTS 6 Randers, Denmark
25.01.93 Ady Benton L RSC 6 Bradford
29.03.93 Louis Veitch L PTS 6 Glasgow
01.06.93 Des Gargano L PTS 6 Manchester
28.06.93 Marcus Duncan W RSC 2 Morecambe
13.09.93 Marcus Duncan L PTS 6 Middleton
06.10.93 Graham McGrath DREW 6 York
25.10.93 James Drummond L RSC 2 Glasgow
19.02.94 Harald Geier L CO 3 Hamburg, Germany
Career: 29 contests, won 7, drew 3, lost 19.

Elvis Parsley

Bloxwich. *Born* Walsall, 6 December, 1962
S. Featherweight. Ht. 5'7½"
Manager Self

04.06.90 Phil Lashley W RSC 3 Birmingham
20.06.90 Mark Bates L CO 1 Basildon
27.09.90 Andrew Robinson W RTD 3 Birmingham
10.12.90 Karl Taylor W PTS 6 Birmingham
18.02.91 Peter Campbell W RSC 3 Derby
01.05.91 Neil Leitch W CO 2 Solihull
20.05.91 Neil Smith L RSC 2 Leicester
02.10.91 Muhammad Shaffique W CO 1 Solihull
29.04.92 Kelton McKenzie L RSC 5 Solihull
(Vacant Midlands Area Featherweight Title)
28.04.93 Dean Amory L PTS 6 Solihull
12.10.93 Kid McAuley W PTS 6 Wolverhampton
30.11.93 Mike Deveney W PTS 6 Wolverhampton
16.12.93 Barry Jones L PTS 6 Newport
05.04.94 Kevin Middleton W RSC 4 Bethnal Green
Career: 14 contests, won 9, lost 5.

Patrick Parton

Telford. *Born* Shifnal, 5 September, 1965
Lightweight. Ht. 5'11"
Manager D. Nelson

23.02.93 T. J. Smith L PTS 6 Kettering
24.06.93 Shaun Shinkwin DREW 6 Watford
17.02.94 Tim Hill W PTS 6 Walsall
24.02.94 Malcolm Thomas W PTS 6 Walsall
18.04.94 Mark Allen W PTS 6 Walsall
23.05.94 Mark Allen W PTS 6 Walsall
Career: 6 contests, won 4, drew 1, lost 1.

Bernard Paul

Tottenham. *Born* Mauritius, 22 October, 1965
L. Welterweight. Ht. 5'7½"
Manager Self

01.05.91 Trevor Royal W CO 1 Bethnal Green
04.06.91 Dave Jenkins W RSC 1 Bethnal Green
24.09.91 Pat Delargy W RSC 5 Basildon
26.10.91 Gordon Webster W RSC 4 Brentwood

26.11.91 John O'Johnson W PTS 6 Bethnal Green
19.02.92 Rick North W PTS 6 Muswell Hill
17.03.92 Mick Mulcahy W PTS 6 Mayfair
16.06.92 Brendan Ryan W CO 6 Dagenham
13.10.92 Dean Bramhald DREW 6 Mayfair
10.11.92 Ray Newby DREW 6 Dagenham
12.12.92 Michael Driscoll L RSC 2 Muswell Hill
20.04.93 Ray Newby DREW 6 Brentwood
28.09.93 Dean Bramhald W PTS 8 Bethnal Green
08.11.93 Shaun Cogan DREW 6 Bethnal Green
11.01.94 Shaun Cogan L PTS 6 Bethnal Green
Career: 15 contests, won 9, drew 4, lost 2.

Quinn Paynter

Manchester. *Born* Bermuda, 19 August, 1965
S. Middleweight. Ht. 5'9"
Manager Self

12.10.89 Willie Beattie L PTS 8 Glasgow
19.10.89 Paul Hendrick W RSC 5 Manchester
11.01.90 Tommy McCallum W RSC 2 Dewsbury
15.01.90 Benji Good W PTS 6 Mayfair
23.02.90 Mike Paul W RTD 4 Irvine
08.03.90 Graeme Watson W PTS 6 Glasgow
26.03.90 George Ferrie W RSC 6 Glasgow
04.05.90 Fran Harding L PTS 6 Liverpool
17.08.90 Hector Rosario L PTS 8 Hamilton, Bermuda
10.12.90 Gordon Blair L PTS 6 Glasgow
21.01.91 W. O. Wilson W PTS 8 Crystal Palace
02.03.91 Marvin O'Brien DREW 6 Irvine
16.05.91 Ali Forbes DREW 6 Battersea
14.11.91 Terry French W CO 6 Gateshead
18.01.92 Val Golding W RSC 7 Kensington
05.04.92 Marvin O'Brien W PTS 6 Bradford
18.07.92 Chris Richards W RSC 4 Manchester
15.09.92 John Ogiste W PTS 6 Liverpool
28.09.92 Stinger Mason W CO 1 Manchester
14.08.93 Russell Washer W RSC 4 Hammersmith
15.09.93 Hussain Shah W PTS 8 Bethnal Green
03.12.93 Abdul Amidou L RSC 7 Randers, Denmark
Career: 22 contests, won 15, drew 2, lost 5.

Andy Peach   Les Clark

Andy Peach

Bloxwich. *Born* Bloxwich, 1 August, 1971
L. Middleweight. Ht. 5'8"
Manager W. Tyler

27.10.92 Stuart Dunn L RSC 3 Leicester
09.12.92 Jason Fores W PTS 6 Stoke
09.02.93 Ray Golding L PTS 6 Wolverhampton
11.03.93 Richard O'Brien L PTS 6 Walsall
06.05.93 Billy McDougall L PTS 6 Walsall
30.09.93 Ernie Locke L PTS 6 Walsall
04.11.93 Dennis Berry L PTS 6 Stafford
02.12.93 Ernie Locke L RTD 3 Walsall
08.02.94 Brian Coleman L PTS 6 Wolverhampton
04.03.94 Nicky Thurbin L PTS 6 Bethnal Green
14.03.94 Howard Eastman L PTS 6 Mayfair
18.04.94 Howard Clarke L PTS 6 Walsall
28.04.94 Scott Doyle L PTS 6 Mayfair
23.05.94 David Bain L RSC 6 Walsall
Career: 14 contests, won 1, lost 13.

Alan Peacock

Cumbernauld. *Born* Glasgow, 17 February, 1969
L. Welterweight. Ht. 5'7"
Manager T. Gilmour

23.02.90 Gary Quigley W PTS 6 Irvine
08.03.90 Gary Quigley W PTS 6 Glasgow
29.05.90 John Ritchie W PTS 6 Glasgow
11.06.90 Chris Mulcahy W RSC 3 Manchester
17.09.90 John Ritchie W PTS 6 Glasgow
09.10.90 Dave Anderson L RSC 3 Glasgow
27.11.90 Stuart Rimmer W RSC 4 Glasgow
11.02.91 Oliver Harrison L RSC 6 Glasgow
18.03.91 Darren Mount L PTS 8 Glasgow
27.03.91 Giovanni Parisi L PTS 6 Mestre, Italy
06.04.91 Alan Hall L PTS 6 Darlington
25.05.91 Giorgio Campanella L CO 1 Trezzano, Italy
23.09.91 Trevor Meikle L PTS 6 Glasgow
27.11.91 Dave Whittle L PTS 6 Marton
28.01.92 Trevor Meikle L PTS 8 Piccadilly
20.02.92 John O'Johnson L PTS 6 Glasgow
04.03.92 Rob Stewart DREW 8 Glasgow
12.03.92 Dave Whittle DREW 8 Glasgow
30.03.92 Peter Bradley L PTS 8 Glasgow
07.10.92 John Smith DREW 6 Glasgow
18.11.92 Dave Lovell W PTS 6 Solihull
22.02.93 Dave Lovell W PTS 8 Glasgow
23.03.93 Dean Bramhald L PTS 6 Wolverhampton
24.11.93 Malcolm Melvin L PTS 8 Solihull
21.02.94 John Smith W RSC 4 Glasgow
19.03.94 Paul Knights L PTS 6 Millwall
Career: 26 contests, won 11, drew 3, lost 12.

Mark Pearce

Cardiff. *Born* Cardiff, 29 June, 1963
L. Welterweight. Ht. 5'7"
Manager Self

16.05.83 Young Yousuf W PTS 6 Birmingham
23.05.83 Dave Pratt W PTS 6 Mayfair
22.09.83 Dave Pratt DREW 6 Cardiff
01.12.83 Mark Reefer L PTS 6 Basildon
10.12.83 Mike Wilkes W PTS 6 Swansea
30.01.84 Dave Pratt L PTS 8 Birmingham
31.03.84 Steve Topliss L PTS 8 Derby
15.06.84 Joey Joynson L PTS 8 Liverpool
10.10.84 Alec Irvine DREW 8 Evesham
06.11.84 Pat Doherty L RSC 4 Kensington

133

18.01.85 Steve Griffith L PTS 8 Bethnal Green
12.02.85 Kenny Walsh W PTS 8 Wolverhampton
06.03.85 Alex Dickson L PTS 6 Kensington
21.03.85 Muhammad Lovelock L PTS 8 Manchester
21.10.85 Paul Downie L PTS 8 Glasgow
21.11.85 Andy Williams L PTS 8 Blaenavon
05.03.86 Ray Newby DREW 6 Stoke
28.04.86 Andy Williams L PTS 10 Cardiff
(Vacant Welsh Lightweight Title)
29.10.86 Russell Jones L PTS 10 Ebbw Vale
(Vacant Welsh S. Featherweight Title)
24.11.86 Tony Borg W PTS 8 Cardiff
18.03.87 Marvin P. Gray L PTS 8 Solihull
07.04.87 Ray Newby W PTS 8 West Bromwich
12.05.87 Najib Daho L RSC 2 Alfreton
28.10.87 Mike Russell DREW 8 Swansea
02.12.87 Rudy Valentino L PTS 6 Piccadilly
18.01.88 Dave Griffiths L PTS 10 Cardiff
(Vacant Welsh L. Welterweight Title)
05.05.88 Tony Gibbs W RSC 4 Bethnal Green
25.01.89 Nigel Wenton L PTS 6 Belfast
12.05.89 Stefano Cassi L RTD 4 Lodi, Italy
19.08.89 Dave Griffiths L PTS 10 Cardiff
(Welsh L. Welterweight Title Challenge)
31.10.89 Eamonn Loughran L PTS 6 Belfast
05.03.91 Jim Lawlor L PTS 6 Cardiff
29.10.91 Mick Meloscia W RTD 2 Cardiff
20.02.93 Mark Tibbs L PTS 6 Earls Court
13.09.93 Sean Baker L PTS 4 Bristol
13.06.94 Shea Neary L RSC 4 Liverpool
Career: 36 contests, won 8, drew 4, lost 24.

Robert Peel

Llandovery. *Born* Birmingham, 11 January, 1969
Middleweight. Ht. 5'10"
Manager Self

24.01.91 John Kaighin W PTS 6 Gorseinon
12.02.91 John Kaighin W PTS 6 Cardiff
13.03.91 Andrew Flute L PTS 6 Stoke
04.04.91 Clay O'Shea L PTS 6 Watford
12.04.91 Adrian Wright L RSC 6 Willenhall
15.05.91 John Kaighin L PTS 8 Swansea
29.10.91 Jason Matthews L RSC 6 Cardiff
03.02.92 Warren Stowe L PTS 6 Manchester
02.03.92 Steve Thomas DREW 6 Merthyr
11.05.92 Steve Thomas L PTS 6 Llanelli
04.06.92 Darren Pilling L PTS 6 Burnley
28.10.92 Barry Thorogood L PTS 6 Cardiff
24.03.93 Russell Washer W PTS 6 Cardiff
27.05.93 Dean Cooper L PTS 6 Bristol
14.08.93 Ensley Bingham L RTD 3 Hammersmith
22.09.93 Adrian Dodson L CO 1 Bethnal Green
10.11.93 Barry Thorogood L PTS 6 Ystrad
20.05.94 Geoff McCreesh L RSC 2 Acton
25.06.94 Dale Nixon L PTS 6 Cullompton
Career: 19 contests, won 3, drew 1, lost 15.

Gary Pemberton

Cardiff. *Born* Cardiff, 15 May, 1960
L. Middleweight. Ht. 5'10"
Manager Self

10.09.86 Johnny Nanton W RSC 4 Muswell Hill
20.10.86 Alex Mullen L RSC 4 Glasgow
24.11.86 Shaun Cummins L RSC 6 Cardiff
28.01.87 Tommy Shiels L CO 1 Croydon
06.04.87 Paul McCarthy W RSC 4 Southampton
23.06.87 Shaun West L RSC 2 Swansea

28.09.87 Simon Paul W RSC 1 Dulwich
06.10.87 Danny Shinkwin W RSC 2 Southend
28.10.87 Mark Howell W PTS 6 Swansea
19.11.87 Steve Huxtable W RSC 4 Weston super Mare
01.03.88 Alex Romeo L RSC 3 Southend
14.04.88 Tony Britton DREW 8 Piccadilly
07.06.88 Winston Wray L PTS 6 Southend
04.10.88 Tony Cloak W RSC 1 Southend
25.10.88 Kevin Hayde L CO 4 Pontardawe
14.12.88 Crisanto Espana L RTD 1 Kirkby
01.03.89 Shaun Cummins L CO 2 Cardiff
19.08.89 Alan Richards W PTS 6 Cardiff
19.09.89 Ray Close L PTS 6 Belfast
25.09.89 Steve Craggs W CO 1 Leicester
11.10.89 Tony Collins L CO 1 Millwall
06.12.89 Jimmy McDonagh L RSC 2 Wembley
16.01.90 Jimmy Farrell L RSC 2 Cardiff
15.06.90 Chris Richards L RTD 1 Telford
13.09.90 B. K. Bennett W RSC 4 Watford
04.10.90 Brian Robinson L PTS 6 Bethnal Green
29.10.90 Tony Kosova W RSC 1 Nottingham
19.11.90 Carlo Colarusso L RSC 3 Cardiff
24.01.91 Carlo Colarusso L RSC 8 Gorseinon
(Vacant Welsh L Middleweight Title)
10.04.91 Colin Pitters L RSC 3 Newport
01.10.91 Adrian Strachan L RSC 2 Sheffield
12.02.92 Andrew Furlong L PTS 6 Wembley
28.04.92 Gary Osborne L CO 3 Wolverhampton
22.10.92 Jamie Robinson L RSC 3 Bethnal Green
11.05.93 Vince Rose L PTS 6 Norwich
25.06.93 Miodrag Perunovic L RSC 4 Belgrade, Yugoslavia
30.11.93 Matthew Turner L RTD 3 Cardiff
Career: 37 contests, won 11, drew 1, lost 25.

Chris Peters

Swindon. *Born* Johannesburg, South Africa, 11 April, 1963
Former Undefeated Transvaal Welterweight Champion. Ht. 5'7¾"
Manager Self

21.09.85 Johannes Dladla L PTS 4 Johannesburg, South Africa
05.11.85 Barry Zeka W PTS 4 Crown Mines, South Africa
19.02.86 Lemuel Naude W CO 2 Johannesburg, South Africa
28.06.86 David Lekoma W PTS 4 Mmbatho, South Africa
27.04.87 Gift Sithole DREW 6 Johannesburg, South Africa
23.06.87 Aaron Kabi L PTS 6 Johannesburg, South Africa
27.07.87 Gift Sithole L PTS 6 Johannesburg, South Africa
28.09.87 Obed Masango DREW 6 Johannesburg, South Africa
06.11.87 Goodman Mlotsha W PTS 6 Kagiso, South Africa
27.02.88 Mbulelo Ndlazi L PTS 6 Johannesburg, South Africa
09.05.88 Frans Mthimunye W PTS 6 Potshefstroom, South Africa
09.07.88 Obed Masango W PTS 6 Secunda, South Africa
07.09.88 Lloyd Mamfe W PTS 6 Johannesburg, South Africa
26.11.88 Gift Sithole W PTS 6 Thaba Nehu, South Africa
11.02.89 Alessandro Duran L PTS 8 Capo d'Orlando, Italy

17.04.89 Patrick Mthimkulu W PTS 8 Springs, South Africa
27.06.89 Mbulelo Mdlazi W PTS 10 Eldorado Park, South Africa
(Transvaal Welterweight Title)
08.04.90 Linda Nondzaba DREW 8 Port Elizabeth, South Africa
22.06.90 Frederick Siswana L PTS 10 Johannesburg, South Africa
(Transvaal Welterweight Title)
04.08.90 Wally Myburgh W PTS 10 Sun City, South Africa
12.12.90 Derek Grainger L PTS 8 Albert Hall
18.02.91 Trevor Smith W PTS 8 Windsor
14.09.91 Henry Johnson DREW 8 Johannesburg, South Africa
14.12.91 Louis Howard L PTS 8 Cape Town, South Africa
16.02.92 Abram Gumede L PTS 8 Johannesburg, South Africa
23.05.92 Lindon Scarlett DREW 8 Birmingham
29.09.92 Del Bryan L PTS 10 Stoke
10.11.92 Darren Dyer L RSC 9 Dagenham
21.06.93 Dave Maj W RSC 4 Swindon
27.10.93 Lindon Scarlett L PTS 8 West Bromwich
01.12.93 Robert McCracken L PTS 8 Albert Hall
28.04.94 John Bosco L PTS 8 Mayfair
Career: 32 contests, won 13, drew 5, lost 14.

Chris Peters   Les Clark

Danny Peters

Liverpool. *Born* Liverpool, 19 July, 1973
L. Middleweight. Ht. 5'10"
Manager B. Devine

06.09.93 Steve Levene W RSC 4 Liverpool
25.10.93 Russell Washer W PTS 6 Liverpool
Career: 2 contests, won 2.

Jimmy Phelan

Hull. *Born* London, 18 June, 1971
Lightweight. Ht. 5'9"
Manager M. Brooks

23.11.93 T. J. Smith L PTS 6 Kettering

16.12.93   Paul Bowen W PTS 6 Walsall
10.02.94   Micky Hall L PTS 6 Hull
Career: 3 contests, won 1, lost 2.

Dean Phillips

Swansea. *Born* Swansea, 1 February, 1976
Featherweight. Ht. 5'6"
Manager C. Breen

10.03.94   Paul Richards L PTS 6 Bristol
23.03.94   Phil Janes W RSC 1 Cardiff
Career: 2 contests, won 1, lost 1.

Dean Phillips   Les Clark

Steve Phillips

Doncaster. *Born* Denaby Main, 21 October, 1968
L. Middleweight. Ht. 5'10"
Manager K. Richardson

07.10.87   Robbie Bowen W PTS 6 Stoke
13.10.87   Steve Taggart W CO 5 Wolverhampton
19.10.87   Andrew Pybus W PTS 4 Birmingham
09.11.87   Davy Robb L PTS 6 Birmingham
16.11.87   Peter Bowen DREW 6 Stratford on Avon
24.11.87   Robbie Bowen W PTS 6 Wolverhampton
02.12.87   Andrew Pybus W PTS 6 Stoke
15.12.87   Dave Croft W PTS 6 Bradford
18.01.88   David Binns L PTS 6 Bradford
08.02.88   Oliver Harrison L PTS 6 Manchester
01.03.88   Mike Calderwood W PTS 6 Manchester
09.03.88   Joff Pugh W PTS 6 Stoke
20.04.88   Frankie Lake DREW 8 Torquay
06.10.88   Davy Robb L PTS 8 Dudley
19.10.88   Young Gully DREW 6 Evesham
10.11.88   Shaun Cooper L PTS 6 Wolverhampton
17.11.88   Peter Hart L PTS 6 Weston super Mare
24.11.88   Danny Cooper L PTS 6 Southampton
01.12.88   Steve Taggart W PTS 6 Stafford
26.01.89   Dave Hindmarsh L PTS 6 Newcastle

10.11.93   Paul Ryan L RSC 3 Bethnal Green
14.01.94   Jason Beard L RTD 3 Bethnal Green
22.03.94   Howard Eastman L RSC 5 Bethnal Green
Career: 23 contests, won 9, drew 3, lost 11.

Steve Phillips   Les Clark

(Warren) John Pierre

Newcastle. *Born* Newcastle, 22 April, 1966
Cruiserweight. Ht. 6'0"
Manager A. Walker

10.10.91   Gary Charlton W PTS 6 Gateshead
20.01.92   Art Stacey L PTS 6 Bradford
21.09.92   Albert Call L PTS 6 Cleethorpes
20.09.93   Martin Langtry L PTS 6 Cleethorpes
12.10.93   Richard Atkinson W PTS 6 Wolverhampton
21.10.93   Alan Smiles L PTS 6 Glasgow
08.12.93   Art Stacey L PTS 6 Hull
19.12.93   Alan Smith DREW 6 Glasgow
Career: 8 contests, won 2, drew 1, lost 5.

Darren Pilling

Burnley. *Born* Burnley, 18 January, 1967
L. Middleweight. Ht. 5'8½"
Manager J. Doughty

03.09.88   Malcolm Davies W RSC 5 Bristol
06.10.88   Paul Hendrick L PTS 6 Manchester
26.10.88   Mark Holden L PTS 6 Sheffield
14.11.88   Paul Burton L RSC 2 Manchester
10.10.89   Terry French W PTS 6 Sunderland
16.11.89   Carl Watson W PTS 6 Ilkeston
30.01.90   Spencer Alton W PTS 6 Manchester
05.03.90   Alan Richards W PTS 8 Northampton
22.03.90   Paul Jones L RTD 7 Gateshead
04.06.92   Robert Peel W PTS 6 Burnley
24.09.92   Geoff Calder W RSC 5 Stockport
12.11.92   Robert Riley L PTS 6 Burnley
15.09.93   Dave Johnson L PTS 6 Newcastle
11.11.93   John Duckworth L PTS 6 Burnley
02.03.94   Barry Thorogood L PTS 6 Solihull
Career: 15 contests, won 7, lost 8.

Nicky Piper

Cardiff. *Born* Cardiff, 5 May, 1966
L. Heavyweight. Former Undefeated WBA
Penta-Continental S. Middleweight
Champion. Ht. 6'3"
Manager Self

06.09.89   Kevin Roper W CO 2 Aberavon
17.10.89   Gus Mendes W RSC 3 Cardiff
19.12.89   Dave Owens W CO 1 Gorleston
17.04.90   Darren McKenna W RTD 4 Millwall
22.05.90   Maurice Core DREW 6 St Albans
23.10.90   Paul McCarthy W RSC 3 Leicester
12.11.90   John Ellis W CO 1 Norwich
05.03.91   Johnny Held W RSC 3 Millwall
08.05.91   Serge Bolivard W RSC 1 Millwall
22.05.91   Martin Lopez W CO 1 Millwall
03.07.91   Simon Harris W RSC 1 Reading
04.09.91   Carl Thompson L RSC 3 Bethnal Green
29.10.91   Franki Moro W RSC 4 Kensington
20.11.91   Carlos Christie W CO 6 Cardiff
22.01.92   Frank Eubanks W PTS 10 Cardiff
           (Elim. British S. Middleweight Title)
11.03.92   Ron Amundsen W PTS 10 Cardiff
16.05.92   Larry Prather W PTS 8 Muswell Hill
25.07.92   Johnny Melfah W RSC 5 Manchester
           (Elim. British S. Middleweight Title)
12.12.92   Nigel Benn L RSC 11 Muswell Hill
           (WBC S. Middleweight Title Challenge)
13.02.93   Miguel Maldonado W PTS 12 Manchester
           (Vacant WBA Penta-Continental S. Middleweight Title)
10.04.93   Chris Sande W RSC 9 Swansea
           (WBA Penta-Continental S. Middleweight Title Defence)
10.07.93   Trevor Ambrose W RSC 5 Cardiff
23.10.93   Frank Rhodes DREW 8 Cardiff
29.01.94   Leonzer Barber L RSC 9 Cardiff
           (WBO L. Heavyweight Title Challenge)
Career: 24 contests, won 19, drew 2, lost 3.

Colin Pitters

Birmingham. *Born* Birmingham, 1 October, 1956
L. Middleweight. Ht. 6'3"
Manager Self

03.04.89   Des Robinson L PTS 6 Birmingham
21.12.89   Alan Richards W PTS 6 Kings Heath
13.02.90   Spencer Alton L PTS 6 Wolverhampton
27.03.90   Alan Richards L PTS 8 Wolverhampton
06.04.90   Trevor Ambrose L PTS 6 Telford
28.01.91   Lee Farrell W PTS 6 Birmingham
04.02.91   Barry Messam W PTS 6 Leicester
18.02.91   Richard Okumu W PTS 6 Birmingham
10.04.91   Gary Pemberton W RSC 3 Newport
24.04.91   Chris Richards W RSC 6 Stoke
20.09.91   Steve Foster L RTD 5 Manchester
31.10.91   Richie Woodhall L PTS 8 Oakengates
21.11.91   Neville Brown L RSC 3 Burton
15.04.94   Peter Waudby L PTS 8 Hull
Career: 14 contests, won 6, lost 8.

Rob Pitters

Gateshead. *Born* Birmingham, 28 May, 1960
L. Middleweight. Ht. 6'1"
Manager T. Conroy

26.09.90   Neil Porter DREW 6 Manchester

135

08.10.90	Colin Sinnott W PTS 6 Bradford
15.10.90	Mickey Costello W RSC 4 Kettering
26.11.90	Mick Duncan DREW 6 Bury
13.12.90	Karl Ince W RSC 5 Hartlepool
21.02.91	Martin Rosamond W RSC 2 Walsall
28.02.91	Crain Fisher W RSC 6 Bury
15.04.91	Gordon Blair W PTS 6 Glasgow
10.05.91	Mick Duncan W RSC 3 Gateshead
17.05.91	Mike Phillips L PTS 8 Bury
22.10.91	Mike Phillips W PTS 4 Hartlepool
11.03.92	Julian Eavis W PTS 6 Solihull
04.06.92	Warren Stowe L PTS 8 Burnley
09.03.93	Mark Cichocki L RSC 10 Hartlepool
	(Vacant Northern Area L.
	Middleweight Title)
18.06.93	Damien Denny L RSC 3 Belfast
17.02.94	Warren Stowe L RSC 1 Bury

Career: 16 contests, won 9, drew 2, lost 5.

Steve Pollard

Hull. *Born* Hull, 18 December, 1957
L. Welterweight. Former Central Area
Featherweight Champion. Ht. 5'7"
Manager Self

28.04.80	Bryn Jones W PTS 6 Piccadilly
27.05.80	Pat Mallon W PTS 6 Glasgow
02.06.80	Andy Thomas W PTS 6 Piccadilly
02.10.80	Eddie Glass W PTS 6 Hull
03.11.80	Rocky Bantleman W CO 2 Piccadilly
01.12.80	Chris McCallum W PTS 6 Hull
17.02.81	Billy Laidman W PTS 6 Leeds
02.03.81	Bryn Jones W RSC 5 Piccadilly
30.03.81	John Sharkey L RSC 6 Glasgow
27.04.81	Ian McLeod L PTS 8 Piccadilly
01.06.81	Gary Lucas L PTS 8 Piccadilly
11.06.81	John Sharkey W PTS 8 Hull
08.03.82	Brian Hyslop DREW 8 Hamilton
22.04.82	Rocky Bantleman W RSC 8 Piccadilly
10.05.82	Lee Graham DREW 8 Piccadilly
26.05.82	Alan Tombs DREW 8 Piccadilly
23.09.82	Pat Doherty L PTS 8 Merton
26.10.82	Lee Halford L PTS 8 Hull
25.11.82	Kevin Howard L PTS 6 Sunderland
10.02.83	Keith Foreman L PTS 8 Sunderland
29.03.83	Steve Farnsworth W RSC 2 Hull
	(Central Area Featherweight Title
	Challenge)
18.06.83	Andre Blanco W PTS 8 Izegem,
	Belgium
04.10.83	Jim McDonnell L RSC 5 Bethnal
	Green
22.11.83	Joey Joynson L PTS 8 Wembley
22.01.84	Jean-Marc Renard L PTS 8 Izegem,
	Belgium
13.11.84	Jim McDonnell L RSC 6 Bethnal
	Green
17.12.84	John Doherty L PTS 10 Bradford
	(Central Area Featherweight Title
	Defence)
12.03.85	Mike Whalley L RSC 8 Manchester
20.01.86	Alex Dickson L RSC 7 Glasgow
10.03.86	Dave Savage L PTS 8 Glasgow
26.03.86	Peter Harris L PTS 8 Swansea
13.11.86	Dean Marsden L CO 7 Huddersfield
07.04.87	Darren Connellan W PTS 8 Batley
15.04.87	Paul Gadney L PTS 8 Lewisham
30.04.87	Gary Nickels L RSC 1 Wandsworth
22.09.87	Kevin Taylor L PTS 8 Oldham
18.11.87	Gary de Roux DREW 8 Peterborough
11.12.87	Gary Maxwell L PTS 8 Coalville
28.01.88	John Bennie L PTS 6 Bethnal Green
24.02.88	Craig Windsor L PTS 8 Glasgow
09.03.88	Peter Bradley L PTS 8 Bethnal Green

30.03.88	Scott Durham W PTS 8 Bethnal Green
25.04.88	Colin Lynch W PTS 8 Birmingham
18.05.88	John Bennie W PTS 8 Lewisham
30.08.88	Mike Chapman W PTS 8 Kensington
15.11.88	Tony Foster L RSC 3 Hull
17.01.89	Peter Bradley L PTS 8 Chigwell
31.05.89	Carl Crook L RSC 4 Manchester
04.09.89	Michael Armstrong L PTS 8 Hull
10.10.89	Tony Foster L RSC 3 Hull
22.03.90	Chris Bennett W PTS 4 Gateshead
07.04.90	Frankie Dewinter L PTS 6 St Elois
	Vyve, Belgium
20.05.90	Mark Ramsey L PTS 6 Sheffield
30.11.90	Shaun Cooper L PTS 6 Birmingham
11.02.91	Dave Anderson L PTS 6 Glasgow
02.03.91	Alan Hall L PTS 6 Darlington
05.12.91	Shaun Cogan L PTS 6 Oakengates
18.01.92	Ian Honeywood L PTS 6 Kensington
30.03.92	J. T. Williams W PTS 6 Eltham
30.04.92	Jason Rowland L RSC 2 Kensington
10.09.92	Paul Charters L RTD 5 Sunderland
16.10.92	Kevin Toomey L RSC 7 Hull
12.11.93	Kevin Toomey W PTS 8 Hull

Career: 63 contests, won 20, drew 4, lost 39.

Chris Pollock

Bedworth. *Born* Coventry, 2 October, 1972
Welterweight. Ht. 5'10½"
Manager P. Byrne

17.06.93	Jamie Morris W RSC 1 Bedworth
03.11.93	Kenny Scott W PTS 6 Worcester
08.12.93	Brian Coleman L PTS 6 Stoke
08.03.94	Brian Coleman W PTS 6 Edgbaston
29.03.94	Gary Cogan L PTS 6 Wolverhampton

Career: 5 contests, won 3, lost 2.

Danny Porter

Hitchin. *Born* Biggleswade, 27 April, 1964
Flyweight. Ht. 5'3"
Manager Self

09.11.86	Antti Juntumaa L PTS 4 Vasa, Finland
09.02.87	Donnie Hood L RSC 4 Glasgow
08.04.87	Pepe Webber W CO 5 Evesham
07.03.88	David Afan-Jones W RSC 4 Piccadilly
10.05.88	Phil Dicks W RSC 4 Southend
30.09.88	Gordon Shaw W RSC 1 Gillingham
15.11.88	Mark Goult L PTS 6 Norwich
07.12.88	Paul Dever W CO 1 Stoke
06.04.89	Francisco Paco Garcia W PTS 8
	Stevenage
22.06.89	Amon Neequaye W RSC 7 Stevenage
24.10.89	Pat Clinton L RSC 5 Watford
	(British Flyweight Title Challenge)
14.02.90	Des Gargano W PTS 6 Brentwood
20.03.90	Mark Goult L PTS 10 Norwich
	(Vacant Southern Area Bantamweight
	Title)
06.07.90	Alfred Kotei L PTS 12 Brentwood
	(Commonwealth Flyweight Title
	Challenge)
31.10.90	Pablo Salazar W RSC 7 Crystal Palace
19.03.91	Kevin Jenkins W PTS 6 Leicester
12.06.91	Salvatore Fanni L RSC 9 Sassari, Italy
	(European Flyweight Title Challenge)
19.11.91	Kevin Jenkins W RSC 2 Norwich
12.02.92	Salvatore Fanni DREW 12 Sarno, Italy
	(European Flyweight Title Challenge)
01.06.92	Miguel Matthews W PTS 6 Glasgow
19.09.92	Pat Clinton L PTS 12 Glasgow
	(WBO Flyweight Title Challenge)
30.03.93	Robbie Regan L RSC 3 Cardiff
	(European Flyweight Title Challenge)

13.10.93	Darren Fifield L RSC 9 Bethnal Green
	(Vacant Commonwealth Flyweight
	Title)
09.02.94	Darren Fifield L RSC 6 Bethnal Green
	(Commonwealth Flyweight Title
	Challenge)

Career: 24 contests, won 12, drew 1, lost 11.

Gypsy Johnny Price

Bolton. *Born* Wigan, 10 April, 1973
S. Middleweight. Ht. 5'10"
Manager J. Doughty

21.10.91	Graham Wassell W RSC 5 Bury
21.01.92	Jason McNeill W PTS 4 Stockport
10.03.92	Martin Jolley L RSC 3 Bury
12.11.92	Shamus Casey W PTS 6 Burnley
09.03.93	Cliff Taylor W RSC 6 Hartlepool
19.04.93	Graham Wassell W RSC 1 Manchester
16.05.94	Shaun McCrory W PTS 6 Morecambe

Career: 7 contests, won 6, lost 1.

Kenley Price

Liverpool. *Born* Liverpool, 30 December,
1965
Cruiserweight. Ht. 6'1½"
Manager Self

15.12.92	Zak Goldman W RTD 2 Liverpool
27.02.93	Tony Colclough W RSC 5 Ellesmere
	Port
02.07.93	Paul McCarthy W PTS 6 Liverpool
30.10.93	Albert Call DREW 6 Chester

Career: 4 contests, won 3, drew 1.

Ray Price

Swansea. *Born* Swansea, 16 July, 1961
S. Middleweight. Former Welsh L.
Welterweight Champion. Ht. 5'10"
Manager C. Breen

30.04.79	Gerry Howland DREW 4 Barnsley
17.09.79	Tim Moloney L PTS 4 Mayfair
24.09.79	Bonnet Bryan W PTS 4 Mayfair
16.10.79	Kid Curtis W CO 2 West Bromwich
22.10.79	Bill Smith DREW 6 Mayfair
30.10.79	Phillip Morris DREW 6 Caerphilly
06.11.79	Neil Brown W PTS 6 Stafford
21.11.79	Neil Brown W PTS 6 Evesham
28.11.79	Shaun Durkin DREW 6 Doncaster
03.12.79	Tim Moloney L PTS 6 Marylebone
11.12.79	Young John Daly L PTS 6 Milton
	Keynes
17.03.80	Terry Parkinson W PTS 6 Mayfair
19.05.80	Colin Wake L PTS 6 Piccadilly
26.03.81	Billy Vivian L PTS 8 Ebbw Vale
07.04.81	Tyrell Wilson W PTS 6 Newport
11.05.81	Barry Price W PTS 6 Copthorne
08.06.81	John Lindo W RSC 2 Bradford
13.10.81	Robbie Robinson L CO 1 Blackpool
22.03.82	Geoff Pegler W PTS 10 Swansea
	(Vacant Welsh L. Welterweight Title)
25.10.82	Willie Booth L PTS 8 Airdrie
09.11.82	Tony Adams L RSC 1 Kensington
02.03.83	Lee Halford W PTS 6 Evesham
21.03.83	Gunther Roomes L RSC 1 Mayfair
27.05.83	Geoff Pegler NC 1 Swansea
	(Welsh L. Welterweight Title Defence)
04.10.83	Mo Hussein L PTS 8 Bethnal Green
19.12.83	Geoff Pegler L RTD 8 Swansea
	(Welsh L. Welterweight Title Defence)
30.01.84	Steve Tempro W PTS 8 Birmingham
14.03.84	Ken Foreman L PTS 6 Mayfair

09.05.84	Tony McKenzie L PTS 8 Leicester
13.06.84	Michael Harris L PTS 10 Aberavon *(Vacant Welsh L. Welterweight Title)*
30.06.84	David Irving L RSC 4 Belfast
08.12.84	Franki Moro L PTS 8 Swansea
04.02.85	Claude Rossi W RSC 6 Nottingham
18.09.85	George Collins L PTS 4 Muswell Hill
02.12.85	Steve Ellwood L RSC 5 Dulwich
07.10.92	Steve Thomas W PTS 6 Barry
10.04.93	Russell Washer L RSC 4 Swansea
10.03.94	Darren Dorrington L RSC 6 Bristol

Career: 38 contests, won 13, drew 4, lost 20, no contest 1.

Mark Prince

Tottenham. *Born* London, 10 March, 1969
L. Heavyweight. Ht. 6'1"
Manager Self

04.04.93	Bobby Mack W RSC 2 Brockley
23.05.93	John Kaighin W RSC 3 Brockley
25.06.93	Art Stacey W CO 2 Battersea
14.08.93	Simon McDougall W PTS 6 Hammersmith
20.01.94	Zak Chelli W CO 1 Battersea
14.04.94	John Foreman W CO 3 Battersea

Career: 6 contests, won 6.

Mark Prince   Les Clark

(Paul) Dave Proctor

Leeds. *Born* Leeds, 25 August, 1972
S. Middleweight. Ht. 5'11"
Manager P. Coleman

24.02.94	Robert Harper W PTS 6 Hull
28.03.94	Tony Colclough W RSC 3 Birmingham
10.05.94	Phil Ball L PTS 6 Doncaster

Career: 3 contests, won 2, lost 1.

(Joffree) Joff Pugh

Torquay. *Born* Torquay, 7 October, 1965
L. Middleweight. Ht. 5'9"
Manager J. Gaynor

09.12.87	Cecil Branch W PTS 6 Evesham
29.01.88	Kevin Plant L RSC 1 Torquay
09.03.88	Steve Phillips L PTS 6 Stoke
23.03.88	Cecil Branch W PTS 6 Evesham
20.04.88	Andrew Pybus L PTS 8 Torquay
14.06.88	Robert Wright L RSC 5 Dudley
20.04.89	Dave Croft W PTS 6 Weston super Mare
08.05.89	Steve Taggart W PTS 6 Grimsby
24.10.89	Shaun Cooper L RSC 1 Wolverhampton
28.10.93	Bullit Andrews W PTS 6 Torquay

Career: 10 contests, won 5, lost 5.

Chris Pyatt

Leicester. *Born* Islington, 3 July, 1963
Former WBO Middleweight Champion.
Former Undefeated WBC International
Middleweight Champion. Former European
L. Middleweight Champion. Former
Undefeated British & Commonwealth L.
Middleweight Champion. Ht. 5'8½"
Manager Self

01.03.83	Paul Murray W RTD 2 Kensington
05.04.83	Billy Waith W RSC 8 Kensington

Chris Pyatt

137

28.04.83 Lee Hartshorn W RSC 3 Leicester
27.09.83 Darwin Brewster W PTS 8 Wembley
08.10.83 Tyrone Demby W RSC 2 Atlantic City, USA
22.11.83 Tony Britton W RSC 4 Wembley
22.02.84 Judas Clottey W PTS 8 Kensington
15.03.84 Pat Thomas W PTS 10 Leicester
09.05.84 Franki Moro W CO 4 Leicester
23.05.84 Alfonso Redondo W RSC 3 Mayfair
16.10.84 John Ridgman W RSC 1 Kensington
16.11.84 Brian Anderson W PTS 12 Leicester
(Final Elim. British L. Middleweight Title)
12.02.85 Helier Custos W RSC 5 Kensington
05.06.85 Graeme Ahmed W RSC 3 Kensington
01.07.85 Mosimo Maeleke W RSC 6 Mayfair
23.09.85 Sabiyala Diavilia L RSC 4 Mayfair
19.02.86 Prince Rodney W CO 9 Kensington
(British L. Middleweight Title Challenge)
20.05.86 Thomas Smith W RSC 1 Wembley
17.09.86 John van Elteren W RSC 1 Kensington
(Vacant European L. Middleweight Title)
25.10.86 Renaldo Hernandez W RSC 3 Paris, France
28.01.87 Gianfranco Rosi L PTS 12 Perugia, Italy
(European L. Middleweight Title Defence)
18.04.87 Dennis Johnson W CO 2 Kensington
26.05.87 Sammy Floyd W RSC 2 Wembley
28.10.87 Gilbert Josamu W PTS 8 Wembley
28.05.88 Jose Duarte W RSC 4 Kensington
23.11.88 Eddie Hall W RSC 2 Bethnal Green
01.12.88 Knox Brown W RSC 2 Edmonton
14.12.88 Tyrone Moore W CO 1 Bethnal Green
15.02.89 Russell Mitchell W RSC 4 Bethnal Green
17.05.89 Daniel Dominguez W RSC 10 Millwall
11.10.89 Wayne Harris W RSC 3 Millwall
25.04.90 Daniel Sclarandi W RSC 2 Millwall
23.10.90 John David Jackson L PTS 12 Leicester
(WBO L. Middleweight Title Challenge)
05.11.91 Craig Trotter W PTS 12 Leicester
(Vacant Commonwealth L. Middleweight Title)
01.02.92 Ambrose Mlilo W RSC 3 Birmingham
(Commonwealth L. Middleweight Title Defence)
31.03.92 Melvyn Wynn W CO 3 Norwich
28.04.92 James Tapisha W RSC 1 Wolverhampton
(Commonwealth L. Middleweight Title Defence)
23.05.92 Ian Strudwick W PTS 10 Birmingham
27.10.92 Adolfo Caballero W CO 5 Leicester
(Vacant WBC International Middleweight Title)
26.01.93 Danny Garcia W PTS 12 Leicester
(WBC International Middleweight Title Defence)
23.02.93 Colin Manners W CO 3 Doncaster
16.03.93 Paul Wesley W PTS 10 Mayfair
10.05.93 Sumbu Kalambay W PTS 12 Leicester
(Vacant WBO Middleweight Title)
18.09.93 Hugo Corti W CO 6 Leicester
(WBO Middleweight Title Defence)
09.02.94 Mark Cameron W CO 1 Brentwood
(WBO Middleweight Title Defence)
11.05.94 Steve Collins L RSC 5 Sheffield
(WBO Middleweight Title Defence)
Career: 46 contests, won 42, lost 4.

Eddie Pyott

Coventry. Born New Zealand, 28 December, 1971
Cruiserweight. Ht. 6'3"
Manager P. Byrne

02.12.93 Robert Norton L RSC 2 Walsall
10.02.94 Stuart Fleet L RSC 2 Hull
Career: 2 contests, lost 2.

Danny Quacoe

Horsham. Born Hammersmith, 30 December, 1965
Welterweight. Ht. 5'10"
Manager H. Holland

22.10.92 Joel Ani L CO 1 Bethnal Green
28.11.93 Roger Dean W RSC 3 Southwark
06.03.94 Prince Louis W RSC 2 Southwark
16.05.94 Dave Madden W RSC 4 Heathrow
Career: 4 contests, won 3, lost 1.

Danny Quacoe   Les Clark

Paul Quarrie

Tottenham. Born London, 14 June, 1964
L. Middleweight. Ht. 5'9"
Manager F. Rix

10.03.94 Sean Baker L RTD 3 Bristol
Career: 1 contest, lost 1.

Willie Quinn

Haddington. Born Edinburgh, 17 February, 1972
Middleweight. Ht. 5'11½"
Manager T. Gilmour

09.10.91 Mark Jay L PTS 6 Glasgow
27.01.92 Hugh Fury W RSC 3 Glasgow
18.03.92 Andy Manning W PTS 6 Glasgow
30.03.92 John McKenzie W RSC 4 Glasgow
19.09.92 Martin Rosamond W RSC 4 Glasgow
25.01.93 Mike Phillips W PTS 6 Glasgow
06.03.93 Steve Thomas W RSC 4 Glasgow
15.05.93 Dave Owens W PTS 6 Glasgow
30.11.93 Russell Washer W PTS 6 Cardiff

02.02.94 Marvin O'Brien W PTS 6 Glasgow
28.03.94 Spencer Alton W RTD 3 Musselburgh
06.06.94 Marvin O'Brien W RSC 4 Glasgow
Career: 12 contests, won 11, lost 1.

Cam Raeside

Ilkeston. Born Canada, 7 May, 1968
Welterweight. Ht. 5'8"
Manager M. Shinfield

02.12.93 Billy McDougall W RSC 5 Evesham
18.02.94 Brian Coleman W PTS 6 Leicester
Career: 2 contests, won 2.

Nigel Rafferty

Wolverhampton. Born Wolverhampton, 29 December, 1967
L. Heavyweight. Ht. 5'11"
Manager Self

05.06.89 Carl Watson L PTS 6 Birmingham
28.06.89 Tony Hodge L PTS 6 Brentwood
06.07.89 Tony Hodge W PTS 6 Chigwell
04.09.89 Joe Frater L PTS 6 Grimsby
24.10.89 Paul Wesley W PTS 6 Wolverhampton
22.11.89 Paul Wesley W PTS 8 Stafford
28.11.89 Paul Wesley W PTS 6 Wolverhampton
04.12.89 Dean Murray W PTS 6 Grimsby
20.12.89 Paul Wright DREW 6 Kirkby
17.01.90 Gil Lewis L PTS 6 Stoke
31.01.90 Antoine Tarver L PTS 4 Bethnal Green
19.02.90 Paul Wesley W PTS 8 Birmingham
19.03.90 Terry Gilbey W PTS 6 Grimsby
01.05.90 Sean Heron L RSC 2 Oldham
13.09.90 Paul Murray W PTS 6 Watford
27.09.90 Paul Murray DREW 6 Wolverhampton
09.10.90 Paul Murray W PTS 6 Wolverhampton
24.10.90 Andrew Flute L CO 6 Dudley
27.11.90 Carlos Christie L PTS 6 Wolverhampton
06.12.90 Carlos Christie L PTS 6 Wolverhampton
28.01.91 Alan Richards DREW 8 Birmingham
04.03.91 Carlos Christie L PTS 8 Birmingham
26.03.91 Lee Prudden W PTS 6 Wolverhampton
13.05.91 Tony Behan W DIS 7 Birmingham
05.06.91 Lee Prudden W PTS 6 Wolverhampton
10.09.91 Paul Busby L RSC 2 Wolverhampton
20.11.91 Julian Johnson DREW 6 Cardiff
02.12.91 Kesem Clayton W PTS 8 Birmingham
21.01.92 Glenn Campbell L RSC 6 Stockport
30.03.92 Simon McDougall W PTS 8 Coventry
25.04.92 Sammy Storey L RSC 3 Belfast
16.06.92 Garry Delaney L CO 5 Dagenham
24.11.92 Graham Burton W PTS 8 Wolverhampton
02.12.92 John J. Cooke L PTS 6 Bardon
23.03.93 Stephen Wilson W RSC 3 Wolverhampton
14.04.93 Ole Klemetsen L RSC 2 Kensington
19.05.93 Zak Chelli L RSC 3 Leicester
22.09.93 Martin Jolley W PTS 6 Chesterfield
12.10.93 Carl Smallwood DREW 8 Wolverhampton
28.10.93 Lee Archer L PTS 8 Walsall
08.12.93 Darren Ashton L PTS 6 Stoke
26.01.94 Monty Wright L PTS 6 Birmingham
08.02.94 Greg Scott-Briggs W PTS 6 Wolverhampton
17.02.94 Glenn Campbell L RSC 7 Bury
18.04.94 Graham Burton W PTS 8 Walsall
23.05.94 Darren Ashton L PTS 6 Walsall
15.06.94 Darron Griffiths W RSC 4 Southwark
Career: 47 contests, won 19, drew 5, lost 23.

Mark Ramsey

Small Heath. *Born* Birmingham, 24 January, 1968
L. Welterweight. Ht. 5'7½"
Manager Self

15.11.89	Mick O'Donnell W RSC 1 Lewisham
08.12.89	Dave Pierre L RSC 2 Doncaster
22.02.90	Karl Taylor W RSC 4 Hull
10.04.90	George Jones W RSC 6 Doncaster
20.05.90	Steve Pollard W PTS 6 Sheffield
18.10.90	Neil Haddock L RSC 5 Birmingham
30.05.91	Colin Sinnott W PTS 6 Birmingham
05.12.91	Carl Hook W RSC 5 Oakengates
27.01.93	Andrew Jervis W PTS 6 Stoke
12.02.93	Reymond Deva W PTS 6 Aubervilliers, France
04.03.93	Dave Pierre L PTS 8 Peterborough
01.05.93	Vyacheslav Ianowski L PTS 8 Berlin, Germany
02.07.93	Andreas Panayi DREW 6 Liverpool
05.08.93	Jean Chiarelli W RSC 4 Ascona, Italy
01.10.93	Freddy Demeulenaere W RSC 3 Waregem, Belgium
26.03.94	James Osunsedo W RSC 4 Dortmund, Germany
07.05.94	Andrei Sinepupov L PTS 12 Dnepropetrousk, Ukraine *(Vacant WBO Penta-Continental Lightweight Title)*

Career: 17 contests, won 11, drew 1, lost 5.

Andrew Reed   Les Clark

(Peter) Andrew Reed

Potters Bar. *Born* Egham, 22 November, 1962
Lightweight. Ht. 5'7"
Manager Self

09.12.93	Simon Frailing L PTS 6 Watford
29.01.94	Russell Rees L PTS 6 Cardiff
08.03.94	T. J. Smith L PTS 6 Kettering
05.04.94	Anthony Campbell L PTS 6 Bethnal Green
28.04.94	Marco Fattore DREW 6 Mayfair

27.05.94	Chris Francis L PTS 6 Ashford
04.06.94	Marcus McCrae L PTS 6 Cardiff

Career: 7 contests, drew 1, lost 6.

Russell Rees

Gilfach Goch. *Born* Pontypridd, 4 October, 1974
S. Featherweight. Ht. 5'7"
Manager D. Gardiner

19.01.93	Chip O'Neill W RSC 1 Cardiff
06.02.93	Eunan Devenney W RSC 3 Cardiff
30.03.93	Ian Reid W PTS 6 Cardiff
10.07.93	Miguel Matthews W PTS 6 Cardiff
29.01.94	Andrew Reed W PTS 6 Cardiff

Career: 5 contests, won 5.

Russell Rees   Les Clark

Fred Reeve

Hull. *Born* Hull, 14 April, 1969
S. Featherweight. Ht. 5'5½"
Manager M. Toomey

09.11.92	Tim Hill L CO 4 Bradford
14.12.92	Leo Turner L RSC 2 Bradford
19.03.93	Kevin Haidarah W RSC 2 Manchester
29.04.93	Marty Chestnut W PTS 6 Hull
07.10.93	Chip O'Neill L RSC 2 Hull
03.03.94	Ian Richardson L PTS 6 Newcastle
28.03.94	Dougie Fox W RSC 2 Cleethorpes
28.04.94	Ian Richardson L RSC 2 Hull

Career: 8 contests, won 3, lost 5.

Robbie Regan

Cefn Forest. *Born* Caerphilly, 30 August, 1968
Former Undefeated British, European & Welsh Flyweight Champion. Ht. 5'4"
Manager D. Gardiner

19.08.89	Eric George DREW 6 Cardiff
06.03.90	Francis Ampofo W RSC 6 Bethnal Green
26.04.90	Kevin Downer W RSC 4 Merthyr
20.06.90	Dave McNally DREW 6 Basildon

19.11.90	Ricky Beard W RSC 6 Cardiff
21.12.90	Michele Poddighe DREW 6 Sassari, Italy
12.02.91	Kevin Jenkins W PTS 10 Cardiff *(Vacant Welsh Flyweight Title)*
28.05.91	Joe Kelly W PTS 12 Cardiff *(Vacant British Flyweight Title)*
03.09.91	Francis Ampofo L RSC 11 Cardiff *(British Flyweight Title Defence)*
17.12.91	Francis Ampofo W PTS 12 Cardiff *(British Flyweight Title Challenge)*
11.02.92	Juan Bautista W CO 1 Cardiff
19.05.92	James Drummond W RSC 9 Cardiff *(British Flyweight Title Defence)*
14.11.92	Salvatore Fanni W PTS 12 Cardiff *(European Flyweight Title Challenge)*
30.03.93	Danny Porter W RSC 3 Cardiff *(European Flyweight Title Defence)*
26.06.93	Adrian Ochoa W PTS 10 Earls Court
29.01.94	Michele Poddighe W PTS 10 Cardiff
12.03.94	Mauricio Bernal W PTS 8 Cardiff

Career: 17 contests, won 13, drew 3, lost 1.

Ian Reid

Balham. *Born* Lambeth, 30 August, 1972
S. Featherweight. Ht. 5'2"
Manager Self

30.03.93	Russell Rees L PTS 6 Cardiff
31.08.93	Jason Hutson W RSC 6 Croydon
10.11.93	Marcus McCrae L PTS 6 Bethnal Green

Career: 3 contests, won 1, lost 2.

Ian Reid   Les Clark

Peter Reid

Alfreton. *Born* Derby, 19 February, 1966
L. Middleweight. Ht. 5'10½"
Manager M. Shinfield

01.09.86	Andy Till L RSC 6 Ealing
10.10.86	John Davies L RSC 2 Gloucester
12.12.88	Mark Holden L RSC 4 Manchester
16.01.89	Steve Kiernan W PTS 6 Bradford
27.01.89	Frank Mobbs W PTS 4 Durham
22.02.89	Frank Mobbs W PTS 4 Bradford

01.03.89	Bullit Andrews W RSC 2 Stoke
08.05.89	Gary Osborne L CO 5 Edgbaston
26.09.89	Jim Beckett L PTS 8 Chigwell
13.11.89	Martin Robinson L PTS 6 Brierley Hill
20.12.89	Paul Lynch L RSC 4 Swansea
10.03.90	Martin Rosamond W RSC 6 Bristol
22.03.90	Gary Osborne L CO 1 Wolverhampton
18.10.90	Andrew Tucker L PTS 6 Hartlepool
29.10.90	Dean Cooper L RSC 1 Nottingham
21.11.91	Robert Riley W PTS 6 Ilkeston
04.12.91	Julian Eavis L PTS 6 Stoke
20.02.92	James Campbell L PTS 6 Oakengates
06.04.92	Kevin Mabbutt W PTS 6 Northampton
13.04.92	Dave Maj L CO 1 Manchester
04.06.92	Warren Bowers W RSC 2 Cleethorpes
12.11.92	Dean Hiscox W PTS 6 Stafford
19.10.93	Adey Allen W PTS 6 Cleethorpes
04.11.93	Nick Ingram W RSC 5 Stafford
08.12.93	Julian Eavis W PTS 6 Stoke
23.03.94	Julian Eavis W PTS 8 Stoke
16.05.94	Brian Dunn L RSC 4 Cleethorpes

Career: 27 contests, won 13, lost 14.

Robin Reid

Warrington. Liverpool, 19 February, 1972
L. Middleweight. Ht. 5'9"
Manager F. Warren

27.02.93	Mark Dawson W RSC 1 Dagenham
06.03.93	Julian Eavis W RSC 2 Glasgow
10.04.93	Andrew Furlong W PTS 6 Swansea
10.09.93	Juan Garcia W PTS 6 San Antonio, USA
09.10.93	Ernie Loveridge W PTS 4 Manchester
18.12.93	Danny Juma DREW 6 Manchester
09.04.94	Kesem Clayton W RSC 1 Mansfield
04.06.94	Andrew Furlong W RSC 2 Cardiff

Career: 8 contests, won 7, drew 1.

Yifru Retta   Les Clark

Yifru Retta

Canning Town. *Born* Ethiopia, 24
September, 1971
S. Featherweight. Ht. 5'8½"
Manager T. Lawless

14.06.93	Lee Fox W RTD 3 Bayswater
04.10.93	Vince Burns W PTS 6 Mayfair
07.12.93	Robert Braddock W RSC 2 Bethnal Green
04.03.94	Derek Amory W RSC 1 Bethnal Green
22.03.94	John Stovin W RSC 3 Bethnal Green
11.05.94	Guilluame Dibateza W PTS 6 Stevenage

Career: 6 contests, won 6.

Devon Rhooms

Sydenham. *Born* London, 24 July, 1965
Cruiserweight. Ht. 6'1"
Manager G. Steene

31.08.93	Steve Yorath W PTS 6 Croydon
02.12.93	Terry Dunstan L RSC 1 Sheffield
22.03.94	Phil Soundy L CO 2 Bethnal Green
02.06.94	John Keeton L RSC 2 Tooting

Career: 4 contests, won 1, lost 3.

Devon Rhooms   Les Clark

John Rice

Brighton. *Born* Johnstone, 25 June, 1965
S. Middleweight. Ht. 5'9"
Manager P. Newman

23.11.93	Sean Byrne L PTS 6 Kettering
07.12.93	Nicky Thurbin L PTS 6 Bethnal Green
06.03.94	Howard Eastman L RSC 1 Southwark
11.05.94	John Keeton L RSC 5 Sheffield

Career: 4 contests, lost 4.

Chris Richards

Nottingham. *Born* Nottingham, 4 April,
1964
Middleweight. Ht. 5'5¼"
Manager W. Swift

07.09.87	Darren Bowen W RSC 1 Mayfair
23.09.87	Shaun Cummins L PTS 6 Loughborough
13.10.87	Damien Denny L PTS 6 Windsor
03.11.87	Brian Robinson L PTS 6 Bethnal Green
18.01.88	Stan King W CO 5 Mayfair
29.01.88	Lou Ayres W RSC 3 Holborn

26.03.88	Terry Magee L PTS 8 Belfast
28.05.88	Tony Collins L RSC 3 Kensington
10.10.88	Antonio Fernandez L PTS 6 Edgbaston
23.11.88	Antonio Fernandez L PTS 8 Solihull
10.12.88	Terry Morrill L PTS 6 Crystal Palace
16.01.89	Mark Holden L DIS 3 Northampton
24.01.89	Ian Strudwick L PTS 6 Wandsworth
13.02.89	G. L. Booth W RSC 8 Manchester
10.03.89	Theo Marius L RSC 2 Brentwood
08.05.89	G. L. Booth W RSC 2 Manchester
22.05.89	B. K. Bennett L PTS 8 Mayfair
16.05.90	Mick Duncan L PTS 6 Hull
04.06.90	Antonio Fernandez L PTS 8 Edgbaston
15.06.90	Gary Pemberton W RTD 1 Telford
14.09.90	Shamus Casey W PTS 6 Telford
17.10.90	Gary Osborne L PTS 8 Stoke
13.11.90	Andrew Tucker W RSC 2 Hartlepool
13.12.90	Neville Brown L RSC 2 Dewsbury
13.02.91	Delroy Waul L PTS 6 Wembley
16.04.91	Paul Smith DREW 6 Nottingham
24.04.91	Colin Pitters L RSC 6 Stoke
26.11.91	Adrian Strachan L PTS 6 Bethnal Green
26.03.92	Glen Payton W PTS 6 Telford
18.06.92	Stefan Wright L PTS 6 Peterborough
18.07.92	Quinn Paynter L RSC 6 Manchester
06.10.92	Paul Busby L PTS 6 Antwerp, Belgium
13.12.93	Peter Waudby L PTS 6 Cleethorpes
16.02.94	Gilbert Jackson L RSC 2 Stevenage
25.04.94	Warren Stowe L PTS 6 Bury
25.05.94	Kevin Adamson L RSC 2 Stoke

Career: 36 contests, won 9, drew 1, lost 26.

Paul Richards

Bristol. *Born* Bristol, 14 January, 1973
Featherweight. Ht. 5'8"
Manager G. Sanigar

13.12.93	Chip O'Neill W PTS 6 Bristol
10.03.94	Dean Phillips W PTS 6 Bristol

Career: 2 contests, won 2.

Ian Richardson

Newcastle. *Born* Newcastle, 26 March,
1971
S. Featherweight. Ht. 5'6"
Manager N. Fawcett

06.12.93	Dean James W RSC 4 Bradford
03.03.94	Fred Reeve W PTS 6 Newcastle
28.04.94	Fred Reeve W RSC 2 Hull
09.05.94	Leo Turner DREW 6 Bradford

Career: 4 contests, won 3, drew 1.

Wayne Rigby

Manchester. *Born* Manchester, 19 July,
1973
S. Featherweight. Ht. 5'6"
Manager J. Doughty

27.02.92	Lee Fox L PTS 6 Liverpool
08.06.92	Leo Turner W PTS 6 Bradford
02.07.92	Leo Turner W CO 5 Middleton
05.10.92	Colin Innes L PTS 6 Manchester
01.12.92	John T. Kelly L PTS 6 Hartlepool
02.06.94	Kid McAuley W PTS 6 Middleton
13.06.94	Chris Clarkson W PTS 6 Liverpool

Career: 7 contests, won 5, lost 2.

Carl Roberts

Blackburn. *Born* Blackburn, 19 March,
1970
Lightweight. Ht. 5'7"
Manager J. Trickett

26.09.90	Peter Judson L PTS 6 Manchester
22.10.90	Shaun Hickey W CO 4 Manchester
26.11.90	Colin Innes W RSC 3 Bury
17.12.90	Trevor Royal W PTS 6 Manchester
29.01.91	Derek Amory L PTS 4 Stockport
28.02.91	Des Gargano L PTS 6 Bury
03.04.91	Neil Leitch L RSC 6 Manchester
19.09.91	Colin Innes W PTS 4 Stockport
14.10.91	Kevin Lowe W PTS 6 Manchester
16.12.91	Robert Braddock W PTS 6 Manchester
10.03.92	Graham O'Malley L PTS 6 Bury
07.12.92	Mike Deveney L PTS 6 Manchester
15.02.93	Lee Fox W PTS 6 Manchester
25.02.93	Ian McGirr L PTS 6 Burnley
28.06.93	Kid McAuley L PTS 6 Morecambe
11.11.93	Brian Eccles W RSC 1 Burnley
19.01.94	Paul Bowen W PTS 6 Solihull
24.05.94	Liam Dineen L PTS 6 Sunderland
06.06.94	Alan Graham W PTS 6 Manchester

Career: 19 contests, won 10, lost 9.

Dewi Roberts

Dolgellau. *Born* Bangor, 11 September, 1968
L. Welterweight. Ht. 5'10"
Manager Self

28.11.91	Gavin Lane L PTS 6 Evesham
11.02.92	Edward Lloyd L RSC 1 Cardiff
11.05.92	Nigel Burder W CO 3 Llanelli
22.11.93	Steve McLevy L RSC 1 Glasgow
24.02.94	Paul Robinson W RSC 6 Walsall
04.03.94	Jason Rowland L RSC 1 Bethnal Green
17.06.94	Paul Dyer L PTS 6 Plymouth
25.06.94	Carl van Bailey W RSC 2 Cullompton

Career: 8 contests, won 3, lost 5.

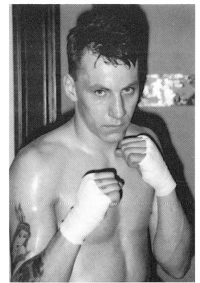

Dewi Roberts　　　　　　Les Clark

Pete Roberts

Hull. *Born* Liverpool, 15 July, 1967
L. Welterweight. Ht. 5'4"
Manager M. Toomey

25.10.88	Mark Jackson W CO 2 Hartlepool
07.11.88	Frankie Foster L PTS 4 Bradford
17.11.88	Tony Banks L PTS 6 Stockport

20.03.89	Brendan Ryan L PTS 6 Nottingham
05.04.90	Mike Close W CO 1 Liverpool
23.04.90	Brendan Ryan L PTS 6 Bradford
04.05.90	John Smith W PTS 6 Liverpool
09.10.90	John Smith L PTS 8 Liverpool
25.02.91	Peter Crook W RSC 6 Bradford
13.06.91	Wayne Windle L RSC 7 Hull
	(Vacant Central Area Lightweight Title)
07.10.91	John Smith W PTS 8 Liverpool
28.11.91	Dave Anderson L RSC 3 Glasgow
27.01.92	Kris McAdam L CO 2 Glasgow
29.04.92	Joey Moffat L PTS 8 Liverpool
29.04.93	Michael Alexander L RSC 2 Hull
29.11.93	Mick Hoban L RSC 4 Manchester

Career: 16 contests, won 5, lost 11.

Des Robinson

Manchester. *Born* Manchester, 5 January, 1969
L. Welterweight. Ht. 5'9"
Manager Self

26.09.89	Carl Watson W RTD 2 Oldham
05.10.89	Tommy Warde W RSC 2 Middleton
19.10.89	Martin Smith L PTS 4 Manchester
10.11.89	Richard Adams DREW 6 Battersea
16.11.89	David Heath W RSC 3 Manchester
03.12.89	Colin Pitters W PTS 6 Birmingham
27.02.90	Ricky Nelson W RSC 6 Manchester
15.03.90	Jim Talbot W PTS 8 Manchester
26.03.90	Tony Baker W PTS 8 Bradford
26.04.90	Rocky Bryan W PTS 6 Wandsworth
22.05.90	Jimmy Harrison W PTS 6 St Albans
11.06.90	Tony Britland W PTS 6 Manchester
25.10.90	Razor Addo L PTS 8 Bayswater
11.02.91	Willie Beattie L PTS 8 Glasgow
19.03.91	Lindon Scarlett L RSC 4 Birmingham
17.10.91	Gary Logan L PTS 8 Southwark
28.09.92	Darren Morris W PTS 6 Manchester
14.11.92	Michael Smyth L PTS 6 Cardiff
16.09.93	Terry Morrill L PTS 8 Hull
21.05.94	Danny Juma L PTS 6 Belfast

Career: 20 contests, won 11, drew 1, lost 8.

Jamie Robinson

West Ham. *Born* London, 12 September, 1968
L. Middleweight. Ht. 5'9"
Manager F. Warren

17.08.90	Duke de Palma W PTS 4 Las Vegas, USA
04.10.90	Rodney Knox L RSC 1 Atlantic City, USA
23.10.91	Dave Whittle W RSC 4 Bethnal Green
13.11.91	Michael Oliver W PTS 6 Bethnal Green
11.02.92	Julian Eavis W PTS 6 Barking
02.04.92	Mark Jay W PTS 6 Basildon
22.10.92	Gary Pemberton W RSC 3 Bethnal Green
17.12.92	Lee Crocker W RTD 2 Barking
27.02.93	Russell Washer W PTS 6 Dagenham
31.03.93	John Duckworth W RSC 3 Barking
10.11.93	Stuart Dunn W PTS 6 Bethnal Green
17.02.94	Steve Scott W CO 2 Dagenham

Career: 12 contests, won 11, lost 1.

Paul Robinson

Tipton. *Born* West Bromwich, 18 August, 1972
L. Welterweight. Ht. 5'10"
Manager D. Powell

02.12.93	Simon Hamblett W RSC 2 Walsall
24.02.94	Dewi Roberts L RSC 6 Walsall

Career: 2 contests, won 1, lost 1.

Tim Robinson

Grimsby. *Born* Cleethorpes, 28 June, 1968
S. Middleweight. Ht. 5'10"
Manager Self

21.09.92	Paul Hanlon L PTS 6 Cleethorpes
16.10.92	Griff Jones L RSC 3 Hull
14.12.92	Mohammed Malik W RSC 3 Cleethorpes
14.01.93	Hussain Shah L PTS 4 Mayfair
05.02.93	Eric Noi L RSC 4 Manchester
10.05.93	Mark Smallwood L RSC 4 Cleethorpes
26.06.93	Dale Nixon L RSC 2 Keynsham
10.02.94	Phil Ball L PTS 6 Hull
07.03.94	Phil Ball L PTS 6 Doncaster
15.03.94	Steve Loftus L PTS 6 Stoke
09.04.94	Mark Delaney L RSC 2 Bethnal Green
28.06.94	Tony Griffiths L RSC 6 Mayfair

Career: 12 contests, won 1, lost 11.

Tim Robinson　　　　　　Les Clark

Laurence Roche

Bradford. *Born* Manchester, 28 April, 1972
Welterweight. Ht. 5'7"
Manager J. Celebanski

06.12.93	Scott Smith W RSC 3 Bradford
28.03.94	Michael Alexander L PTS 6 Cleethorpes
09.05.94	Dave Curtis W PTS 6 Bradford
13.06.94	Michael Alexander W PTS 6 Bradford

Career: 4 contests, won 3, lost 1.

Martin Rosamond

Southampton. *Born* Cyprus, 10 March, 1969
S. Middleweight. Ht. 5'10"
Manager Self

02.03.89	Andy Tonks W RSC 2 Southampton
04.04.89	B. K. Bennett L PTS 6 Southend
26.04.89	Johnny Stone L RSC 3 Southampton

141

21.09.89 Tony Grizzle W RSC 5 Southampton
28.09.89 Max Wallace L RSC 1 Wandsworth
08.02.90 Darren Burford L RSC 5 Southwark
10.03.90 Peter Reid L RSC 6 Bristol
21.05.90 Tony Grizzle W RSC 2 Mayfair
22.06.90 Jimmy McDonagh W RSC 6 Gillingham
18.10.90 Matthew Jones W PTS 6 Birmingham
06.11.90 Kid Sylvester L RSC 3 Mayfair
08.12.90 Cliff Churchward W PTS 6 Bristol
21.02.91 Rob Pitters L RSC 2 Walsall
12.04.91 Shamus Casey L PTS 6 Willenhall
23.04.91 Barry Messam L PTS 6 Evesham
08.05.91 Marty Duke DREW 8 Millwall
23.05.91 Mike Morrison W PTS 6 Southampton
04.06.91 Adrian Strachan L PTS 6 Bethnal Green
03.07.91 Kevin Sheeran L CO 1 Reading
24.09.91 Adrian Strachan L PTS 6 Basildon
20.01.92 Lee Ferrie L RSC 2 Coventry
19.09.92 Willie Quinn L RSC 4 Glasgow
18.05.93 Eddie Collins W PTS 6 Kettering
15.06.93 Steve McNess W RSC 5 Hemel Hempstead
30.09.93 Freddie Yemofio W PTS 6 Hayes
13.11.93 Peter Vosper L PTS 6 Cullompton
22.01.94 Joe Calzaghe L RSC 1 Cardiff
Career: 27 contests, won 10, drew 1, lost 16.

Vince Rose

Tottenham. *Born* London, 9 July, 1968
L. Middleweight. Ht. 5'8"
Manager B. Hearn

13.10.92 Ojay Abrahams W RSC 3 Mayfair
14.11.92 Marty Duke W PTS 6 Cardiff
30.01.93 Ojay Abrahams DREW 6 Brentwood
11.05.93 Gary Pemberton W PTS 6 Norwich
11.01.94 Warren Stephens W PTS 6 Bethnal Green
09.02.94 Ojay Abrahams L PTS 6 Brentwood
28.06.94 Said Bennajem L PTS 6 Mayfair
Career: 7 contests, won 4, drew 1, lost 2.

(Paul) Laurence Rowe (Page)

Manchester. *Born* Manchester, 26 March, 1972
L. Heavyweight. Ht. 5'11"
Manager N. Basso

06.06.94 Pat Durkin W PTS 6 Manchester
Career: 1 contest, won 1.

Jason Rowland

West Ham. *Born* London, 6 August, 1970
L. Welterweight. Ht. 5'9¾"
Manager Self

19.09.89 Terry Smith W RSC 1 Millwall
15.11.89 Mike Morrison W PTS 6 Reading
14.02.90 Eamonn Payne W PTS 6 Millwall
17.04.90 Dave Jenkins W CO 1 Millwall
22.05.90 Mike Morrison W PTS 6 St Albans
12.02.91 Vaughan Carnegie W PTS 6 Basildon
07.03.91 Vaughan Carnegie W CO 2 Basildon
11.12.91 Brian Cullen W RSC 4 Basildon
30.04.92 Steve Pollard W RSC 2 Kensington
17.12.92 Jimmy Vincent W PTS 6 Wembley
10.02.93 Seth Jones W RSC 2 Lewisham
18.03.93 John Smith W PTS 6 Lewisham
04.03.94 Dewi Roberts W RSC 1 Bethnal Green
26.04.94 Ray Hood W CO 1 Bethnal Green
Career: 14 contests, won 14.

Roy Rowland

West Ham. *Born* London, 19 May, 1967
Welterweight. Ht. 5'10"
Manager Self

29.10.86 Nick Lucas W PTS 6 Muswell Hill
03.12.86 Nick Meloscia W PTS 6 Muswell Hill
13.01.87 Ray Golding W PTS 6 Oldham
04.03.87 Andy Cox W RSC 3 Basildon
22.09.87 Brian Wareing W CO 1 Bethnal Green
03.11.87 Wil Halliday W RSC 1 Bethnal Green
02.12.87 Roy Callaghan W PTS 6 Kensington
09.03.88 Dave Haggarty W RSC 1 Bethnal Green
29.03.88 Nick Meloscia L RSC 1 Bethnal Green
07.09.88 Kelvin Mortimer W PTS 6 Reading
01.11.88 Kevin Hayde W PTS 6 Reading
25.01.89 Andy Tonks W RTD 1 Bethnal Green
15.02.89 Mike Russell W RSC 2 Bethnal Green
28.03.89 Paul Seddon W RSC 3 Bethnal Green
14.09.89 John Smith W RSC 3 Basildon
15.11.89 Lloyd Lee W PTS 8 Reading
25.04.90 Peter Eubank W RSC 8 Millwall
12.02.91 Paul Lynch L RTD 4 Basildon
06.06.91 Mark Kelly W RSC 4 Barking
02.10.91 Peter Eubank W PTS 8 Barking
25.03.92 Humphrey Harrison W CO 7 Dagenham
28.10.92 Darren Morris W RSC 2 Kensington
17.12.92 Gary Logan L RSC 4 Wembley
(*Vacant Southern Area Welterweight Title*)
10.11.93 Peter Waudby L RSC 5 Watford
11.05.94 Julian Eavis W RSC 4 Stevenage
Career: 25 contests, won 21, lost 4.

Trevor Royal

Bristol. *Born* Bristol, 8 May, 1962
Lightweight. Ht. 5'7"
Manager P. Dwyer

15.09.90 Dave Jenkins L RSC 4 Bristol
29.10.90 Peter Campbell L PTS 6 Nottingham
21.11.90 Gavin Fitzpatrick W PTS 6 Chippenham
08.12.90 Gavin Fitzpatrick W RSC 1 Bristol
17.12.90 Carl Roberts L PTS 6 Manchester
06.02.91 Steve Hearn DREW 6 Battersea
18.02.91 Felix Kelly L RSC 4 Windsor
03.04.91 Terry Riley W RTD 4 Bethnal Green
10.04.91 Robert Smyth L PTS 6 Newport
22.04.91 Kevin Toomey L PTS 6 Bradford
01.05.91 Bernard Paul L CO 1 Bethnal Green
10.06.91 Bobby Beckles L PTS 6 Manchester
09.03.93 Mike Morrison L PTS 6 Bristol
24.03.93 Bernard McComiskey L RSC 6 Belfast
22.04.93 Mark O'Callaghan L PTS 6 Mayfair
27.05.93 Greg Upton L CO 2 Bristol
(*Vacant Western Area S. Featherweight Title*)
25.07.93 Nick Boyd L PTS 6 Oldham
31.08.93 Dennis Griffin L RSC 1 Croydon
04.03.94 Michael Hermon L PTS 6 Weston super Mare
28.03.94 Hugh Collins L RSC 2 Musselburgh
17.06.94 Wayne Jones L PTS 6 Plymouth
Career: 21 contests, won 3, drew 1, lost 17.

Bruce Ruegg

Bournemouth. *Born* Wimborne, 31 July, 1970
S. Featherweight. Ht. 5'5"
Manager J. Bishop

29.04.93 Simon Frailing DREW 6 Hayes
18.05.93 Nicky Towns L PTS 6 Kettering

15.06.93 Simon Frailing W PTS 6 Hemel Hempstead
02.07.93 George Naylor W PTS 6 Liverpool
Career: 4 contests, won 1, drew 1, lost 2.

Danny Rueg   Les Clark

Danny Ruegg

Bournemouth. *Born* Poole, 28 November, 1974
S. Bantamweight. Ht. 5'5"
Manager J. Bishop

30.09.93 Johnny Simpson L PTS 6 Hayes
17.02.94 Paul Webster L PTS 4 Dagenham
04.03.94 Darren Greaves L PTS 6 Weston super Mare
17.06.94 Danny Lawson L PTS 6 Plymouth
Career: 4 contests, lost 4.

Paul Ryan

Hackney. *Born* South Ockenham, 2 February, 1965
L. Welterweight. Ht. 5'8"
Manager Self

26.09.91 Chris Mylan W PTS 6 Dunstable
18.01.92 Alex Sterling W RSC 4 Kensington
25.03.92 Michael Clynch W RSC 4 Dagenham
16.05.92 Greg Egbuniwe W RSC 4 Muswell Hill
26.09.92 Korso Aleain W CO 4 Earls Court
17.12.92 Rick Bushell W RSC 1 Barking
03.02.93 Neil Smith W RSC 1 Earls Court
27.02.93 Mike Morrison W PTS 6 Dagenham
15.09.93 Shaun Cogan W RSC 3 Ashford
10.11.93 Steve Phillips W RSC 3 Bethnal Green
17.02.94 Rob Stewart W RSC 4 Dagenham
09.04.94 Carl Wright W RSC 6 Mansfield
Career: 12 contests, won 12.

Lee Sara (Thomas)

Carmarthen. *Born* Carmarthen, 30 January, 1970
Middleweight. Ht. 5'11"
Manager D. Davies

18.05.93 Justin Clements L PTS 6 Edgbaston

31.08.93 Freddie Yemofio W PTS 6 Croydon
05.10.93 Mark Delaney L RTD 5 Mayfair
27.05.94 Eddie Knight L CO 2 Ashford
Career: 4 contests, won 1, lost 3.

Chris Saunders

Barnsley. *Born* Barnsley, 15 August, 1969
Welterweight. Ht. 5'8"
Manager B. Ingle

22.02.90 Malcolm Melvin W PTS 4 Hull
10.04.90 Mike Morrison W PTS 6 Doncaster
20.05.90 Justin Graham W RSC 3 Sheffield
29.11.90 Ross Hale L PTS 6 Bayswater
05.03.91 Rocky Ferrari W PTS 4 Glasgow
19.03.91 Richard Woolgar W RSC 3 Leicester
26.03.91 Felix Kelly L PTS 6 Bethnal Green
17.04.91 Billy Schwer L RSC 1 Kensington
16.05.91 Richard Burton L PTS 6 Liverpool
06.06.91 Mark Tibbs W RSC 6 Barking
30.06.91 Billy Schwer L RSC 3 Southwark
01.08.91 James Jiora W PTS 6 Dewsbury
03.10.91 Gary Flear L PTS 6 Burton
24.10.91 Ron Shinkwin W PTS 6 Dunstable
21.11.91 Jason Matthews L RSC 4 Burton
30.01.92 John O'Johnson L PTS 6 Southampton
11.02.92 Eddie King W RSC 4 Wolverhampton
27.02.92 Richard Burton L PTS 10 Liverpool
(Vacant Central Area L. Welterweight Title)
09.09.92 John O'Johnson DREW 6 Stoke
01.10.92 Mark McCreath L RSC 4 Telford
01.12.92 Shea Neary L PTS 6 Liverpool
22.02.93 Cham Joof L PTS 4 Eltham
16.03.93 Mark Elliot L PTS 6 Wolverhampton
26.04.93 Dean Hollington W RSC 5 Lewisham
23.10.93 Michael Smyth L PTS 6 Cardiff
02.12.93 Rob Stewart L PTS 4 Sheffield
03.03.94 Kevin Lueshing W RSC 4 Ebbw Vale
04.06.94 Jose Varela W CO 2 Dortmund, Germany
Career: 28 contests, won 11, drew 1, lost 16.

Lindon Scarlett

Dudley. *Born* Dudley, 11 January, 1967
Midlands Area Welterweight Champion.
Ht. 5'10"
Manager M. Duff

22.04.87 Tommy Shiels L PTS 6 Kensington
07.05.87 Dusty Miller W PTS 6 Bayswater
09.11.87 Sean Heron L PTS 6 Glasgow
20.01.88 Simon Paul W PTS 6 Solihull
12.04.88 Ted Kershaw L RSC 7 Oldham
11.10.89 Carlo Colarusso L PTS 8 Stoke
22.11.89 Carlo Colarusso W PTS 8 Solihull
06.12.89 Julian Eavis W PTS 8 Stoke
14.02.90 Wayne Ellis DREW 6 Millwall
13.03.90 Romolo Casamonica L PTS 8 Milan, Italy
08.05.90 Mickey Lloyd L RSC 2 Brentford
18.10.90 Kevin Spratt W RSC 2 Birmingham
16.11.90 Tony Gibbs W PTS 6 Telford
19.03.91 Des Robinson W RSC 4 Birmingham
24.10.91 Razor Addo W PTS 8 Bayswater
22.01.92 Kelvin Mortimer W RSC 1 Solihull
08.02.92 Javier Castillejos L PTS 8 Madrid, Spain
23.05.92 Chris Peters DREW 8 Birmingham
15.02.93 Gordon Blair W CO 4 Mayfair
27.10.93 Chris Peters W PTS 8 West Bromwich
26.01.94 Rick North W RSC 6 Birmingham
(Vacant Midlands Area Welterweight Title)
Career: 21 contests, won 13, drew 2, lost 6.

Bruce Scott   Les Clark

Bruce Scott

Hackney. *Born* Jamaica, 16 August, 1969
L. Heavyweight. Ht. 5'9½"
Manager M. Duff

25.04.91 Mark Bowen L PTS 6 Mayfair
16.09.91 Randy B. Powell W RSC 5 Mayfair
21.11.91 Steve Osborne W PTS 6 Burton
27.04.92 John Kaighin W CO 4 Mayfair
07.09.92 Lee Prudden W PTS 6 Bethnal Green
03.12.92 Mark Pain W RSC 5 Lewisham
15.02.93 Paul McCarthy W PTS 6 Mayfair
22.04.93 Sean O'Phoenix W RSC 3 Mayfair
14.06.93 John Oxenham W RSC 1 Bayswater
04.10.93 Simon McDougall W PTS 6 Mayfair
16.12.93 Bobby Mack W RSC 4 Newport
05.04.94 Steve Osborne W RSC 5 Bethnal Green
Career: 12 contests, won 11, lost 1.

Kenny Scott

Chesterfield. *Born* Chesterfield, 23 April, 1967
Welterweight. Ht. 6'1"
Manager M. Shinfield

25.06.93 Maurice Forbes L RSC 2 Battersea
22.09.93 Colin Anderson L PTS 6 Chesterfield
03.11.93 Chris Pollock L PTS 6 Worcester
30.11.93 Adey Allen L PTS 6 Leicester
Career: 4 contests, lost 4.

Steve Scott

Chorley. *Born* Fulwood, 20 January, 1966
L. Middleweight. Ht. 5'11"
Manager J. McMillan

04.03.92 Allan Grainger L PTS 6 Glasgow
26.03.92 Rob Stevenson L PTS 6 Hull
14.09.92 Danny Harper DREW 6 Bradford
27.10.92 Steve Levene W RSC 1 Cradley Heath
30.10.92 James Campbell L PTS 6 Birmingham

26.11.92 Rob Stevenson W PTS 6 Hull
14.12.92 Kevin Spratt L PTS 6 Bradford
28.01.93 Steve McNess L PTS 6 Southwark
22.02.93 James Campbell L PTS 6 Birmingham
04.03.93 Eddie Collins W RSC 1 Peterborough
26.03.93 Colin Wallace L PTS 6 Glasgow
26.04.93 John Stronach L PTS 6 Bradford
29.05.93 Colin Wallace L PTS 6 Paisley
11.06.93 Dave Whittle L PTS 6 Gateshead
27.09.93 Alan Ceesay W PTS 6 Manchester
04.10.93 Hughie Davey L PTS 6 Bradford
03.11.93 Andre Wharton L PTS 6 Worcester
19.12.93 Kevin Mabbutt L PTS 6 Northampton
17.02.94 Jamie Robinson L CO 2 Dagenham
Career: 19 contests, won 4, drew 1, lost 14.

Greg Scott-Briggs

Chesterfield. *Born* Swaziland, 6 February, 1966
L. Heavyweight. Ht. 6'1"
Manager M. Shinfield

04.02.92 Mark McBiane W PTS 6 Alfreton
03.03.92 Tony Colclough W RSC 2 Cradley Heath
30.03.92 Carl Smallwood L PTS 6 Coventry
27.04.92 Richard Atkinson L PTS 6 Bradford
28.05.92 Steve Walton W PTS 6 Gosforth
04.06.92 Joe Frater L PTS 6 Cleethorpes
30.09.92 Carl Smallwood L PTS 6 Solihull
17.03.93 Carl Smallwood L PTS 8 Stoke
26.04.93 Tony Colclough W RSC 4 Glasgow
08.06.93 Peter Flint W RSC 1 Derby
07.09.93 Steve Loftus W RSC 2 Stoke
22.09.93 Paul Hanlon W PTS 6 Chesterfield
04.11.93 Lee Archer L PTS 8 Stafford
24.11.93 Tony Colclough W PTS 6 Solihull
08.12.93 Lee Archer W RTD 6 Stoke
08.02.94 Nigel Rafferty L PTS 6 Wolverhampton
17.02.94 Lee Archer L PTS 8 Walsall
11.03.94 Monty Wright L CO 1 Bethnal Green
Career: 18 contests, won 9, lost 9.

Hussain Shah

Crayford. *Born* Pakistan, 1 June, 1964
S. Middleweight. Ht. 6'0"
Manager Self

30.04.92 Paul McCarthy W RTD 4 Kensington
26.09.92 Nicky Wadman W RSC 4 Earls Court
10.12.92 Kenny Nevers W PTS 4 Bethnal Green
14.01.93 Tim Robinson W PTS 4 Mayfair
28.02.93 George Allison W PTS 6 Georgetown, Guyana
04.04.93 Kenny Nevers L RSC 4 Brockley
15.09.93 Quinn Paynter L PTS 8 Bethnal Green
Career: 7 contests, won 5, lost 2.

Kevin Sheeran

Crawley. *Born* Redhill, 10 August, 1971
Middleweight. Ht. 6'0"
Manager Self

05.03.91 Richard Okumu L RSC 2 Millwall
08.05.91 Cliff Churchward W PTS 6 Millwall
22.05.91 Stuart Good W PTS 6 Millwall
03.07.91 Martin Rosamond W CO 1 Reading
04.09.91 Clive Dixon W RSC 4 Bethnal Green
29.10.91 Dave Hall W RSC 1 Kensington
20.11.91 Horace Fleary W RSC 2 Cardiff
02.04.92 Mike Russell W RSC 2 Basildon
30.04.92 Tracy Jocelyn W RSC 3 Kensington

143

26.09.92 Val Golding W RSC 1 Earls Court
03.02.93 Russell Washer W PTS 6 Earls Court
27.02.93 Gareth Boddy W RSC 1 Dagenham
31.03.93 Paul Lynch W RSC 1 Barking
28.04.93 Danny Juma W RSC 8 Dublin
10.11.93 Russell Washer W PTS 6 Bethnal Green
18.12.93 Steve Foster L RSC 4 Manchester
Career: 16 contests, won 14, lost 2.

Charles Shepherd

Carlisle. *Born* Burnley, 28 June, 1970
Lightweight. Ht. 5'4"
Manager J. Doughty

28.10.91 Chris Aston W PTS 6 Leicester
31.01.92 Alan McDowall L RSC 3 Glasgow
18.05.92 Mark Legg W PTS 6 Marton
25.09.92 George Naylor W RSC 4 Liverpool
22.10.92 Didier Hughes L PTS 4 Bethnal Green
13.02.93 Nigel Wenton W PTS 8 Manchester
23.05.93 Cham Joof W PTS 4 Brockley
21.10.93 Karl Taylor W RTD 5 Bayswater
09.02.94 Justin Juuko L RSC 5 Bethnal Green
21.04.94 Tony Foster L PTS 10 Hull
(Vacant Central Area Lightweight Title)
Career: 10 contests, won 6, lost 4.

Charles Shepherd   Les Clark

Wayne Shepherd

Carlisle. *Born* Whiston, 3 June, 1959
Welterweight. Ht. 5'6"
Manager N. Basso

07.10.91 Benji Joseph W PTS 6 Bradford
28.10.91 Noel Henry W PTS 6 Leicester
16.12.91 Dave Maj DREW 6 Manchester
03.02.92 Dave Maj L PTS 6 Manchester
30.03.92 Hughie Davey L PTS 6 Bradford
18.05.92 Dave Whittle W PTS 6 Marton
14.10.92 Richard Swallow L PTS 6 Stoke
31.10.92 George Scott L RSC 6 Earls Court
13.02.93 Delroy Waul L RSC 5 Manchester
31.03.93 Derek Grainger L RSC 4 Barking
11.06.93 Hughie Davey L PTS 6 Gateshead
06.09.93 Shea Neary L RTD 2 Liverpool

26.01.94 James McGee W PTS 6 Stoke
28.02.94 Craig Winter L PTS 6 Manchester
Career: 14 contests, won 4, drew 1, lost 9.

Shane Sheridan

Derby. *Born* Reading, 5 November, 1968
L. Welterweight. Ht. 5'9"
Manager J. Ashton

28.03.91 David Thompson W CO 5 Alfreton
04.07.91 Dean Bramhald W PTS 6 Alfreton
21.11.91 Scott Doyle L PTS 6 Ilkeston
12.11.92 Gary Hiscox L PTS 6 Stafford
09.12.92 Alex Moffatt W PTS 6 Stoke
02.03.93 Mick Mulcahy W PTS 6 Derby
01.04.93 Dean Bramhald L PTS 6 Evesham
23.05.94 Peter Hickenbottom L PTS 6 Walsall
Career: 8 contests, won 4, lost 4.

Danny Shinkwin

Boreham Wood. *Born* Watford, 25 November, 1961
Welterweight. Ht. 5'9¼"
Manager J. Barclay

01.04.82 Mark Crouch W PTS 6 Walthamstow
19.04.82 Gary Petty W PTS 6 Bristol
27.04.82 Eric Purkis L PTS 6 Southend
04.09.82 Dan Myers W PTS 6 Piccadilly
06.04.84 Elvis Morton L PTS 6 Watford
16.04.84 Tony McKenzie W RSC 1 Birmingham
19.05.84 Colin Neagle L PTS 6 Bristol
05.06.84 David Irving L CO 2 Kensington
25.09.87 Eddie Brooks L PTS 6 Tooting
06.10.87 Gary Pemberton L RSC 2 Southend
11.11.87 Kevin Thompson L CO 4 Stafford
20.01.88 Martin Smith L PTS 6 Hornsey
16.05.91 Marty Duke W PTS 6 Battersea
12.11.91 Kevin Adamson L RSC 4 Milton Keynes
12.02.92 Mike Russell W PTS 6 Watford
30.04.92 Cliff Churchward L PTS 6 Watford
17.09.92 Bozon Haule DREW 6 Watford
29.04.93 Johnny Pinnock L RSC 3 Hayes
24.06.93 Nick Appiah L PTS 6 Watford
13.10.93 Bullit Andrews W PTS 6 Watford
10.03.94 Billy McDougall DREW 4 Watford
Career: 21 contests, won 7, drew 2, lost 12.

Ron Shinkwin

Boreham Wood. *Born* Watford, 27 November, 1964
L. Welterweight. Ht. 5'11"
Manager J. Barclay

06.05.82 Vince Vahey L PTS 4 Mayfair
13.09.82 Shaun Robinson L PTS 4 Brighton
11.10.82 Glyn Mitchell L PTS 4 Bristol
26.11.82 Jim Paton L PTS 4 Glasgow
14.02.83 Michael Betts W PTS 4 Lewisham
16.03.83 Michael Betts W PTS 6 Cheltenham
21.03.83 Willie Wilson DREW 4 Nottingham
16.04.83 Graeme Griffin W PTS 4 Bristol
25.04.83 Chris Harvey L PTS 4 Southwark
10.05.83 Abdul Kareem L PTS 6 Southend
05.09.83 Ricky Andrews W PTS 6 Mayfair
06.10.83 T-Roy Smith DREW 6 Basildon
23.11.83 Carl Green W PTS 6 Solihull
16.02.84 John Faulkner W PTS 6 Basildon
07.03.84 Steve Friel L PTS 6 Brighton
06.04.84 Mike Durvan L PTS 6 Watford
31.05.84 Gary Champion W CO 6 Basildon
25.10.84 Wayne Poultney W PTS 6 Birmingham
26.11.84 Jimmy Thornton L RSC 2 Sheffield

31.01.85 Teddy Anderson L PTS 8 Basildon
11.02.85 Willie Wilson W RSC 5 Dulwich
01.03.85 Tommy Cook L PTS 8 Glasgow
04.05.85 Abdul Kareem L RSC 5 Queensway
12.10.87 Paul Seddon DREW 6 Mayfair
11.11.87 Dean Bramhald L PTS 8 Stafford
18.11.87 Dave Kettlewell W PTS 6 Peterborough
14.12.87 Dean Bramhald W PTS 8 Bedford
06.02.88 Mike Russell W PTS 8 Newbury
16.03.88 Tony Swift L PTS 8 Solihull
26.09.91 Carl Hook W PTS 8 Dunstable
24.10.91 Chris Saunders L PTS 6 Dunstable
04.12.91 Dean Bramhald L PTS 8 Stoke
16.12.91 Danny Cooper L PTS 6 Southampton
30.01.92 Dean Bramhald W PTS 6 Southampton
24.03.92 Ray Newby L PTS 8 Wolverhampton
30.04.92 Jess Rundan W RSC 1 Watford
18.05.92 Ray Newby L RSC 5 Bardon
30.09.93 Keith Marner L PTS 6 Hayes
Career: 38 contests, won 15, drew 3, lost 20.

Ron Shinkwin   Les Clark

Shaun Shinkwin

Boreham Wood. *Born* Watford, 30 November, 1962
Lightweight. Ht. 5'9½"
Manager J. Barclay

01.04.82 Billy Ruzgar L PTS 4 Walthamstow
19.04.82 Vince Vahey L PTS 4 Bristol
10.05.82 Kevin Hay W PTS 6 Copthorne
08.06.82 Eugene Maloney W PTS 4 Southend
14.06.82 Eddie Morgan L PTS 6 Mayfair
13.10.82 Joe Donohoe L PTS 6 Walthamstow
22.11.82 Allen Terry W PTS 4 Lewisham
29.11.82 Carl Gaynor W PTS 6 Southwark
06.12.82 Eddie Morgan DREW 6 Bristol
24.01.83 Steve King W RSC 5 Mayfair
31.01.83 Carl Gaynor L PTS 6 Southwark
21.02.83 Dave Pratt W PTS 6 Mayfair
09.03.83 Eddie Morgan W PTS 6 Solihull
17.03.83 Chris Harvey W PTS 6 Marylebone
16.04.83 Michael Harris L PTS 6 Bristol
12.02.92 Greg Egbuniwe L DIS 1 Watford
29.10.92 Steve Hearn W PTS 6 Hayes

30.01.93 Boby Guynan L PTS 6 Brentwood
29.04.93 Noel Henry W PTS 6 Hayes
24.06.93 Patrick Parton DREW 6 Watford
13.10.93 Simon Hamblett W PTS 6 Watford
09.12.93 Felix Kelly L PTS 10 Watford
(Southern Area Lightweight Title Challenge)
Career: 22 contests, won 11, drew 2, lost 9.

Tony Silkstone
Leeds. *Born* Leeds, 2 March, 1968
Bantamweight. Ht. 5'5"
Manager M. Duff

11.04.90 Andrew Robinson W PTS 6 Dewsbury
26.04.90 Andrew Robinson W PTS 6 Halifax
18.10.90 Kelton McKenzie W PTS 6 Dewsbury
15.11.90 Sean Casey W PTS 6 Oldham
13.12.90 Neil Smith W PTS 6 Dewsbury
21.03.91 Tony Falcone W PTS 6 Dewsbury
09.05.91 Alan Smith W PTS 6 Leeds
13.06.91 Miguel Matthews W PTS 6 Hull
01.08.91 Dave Buxton W PTS 6 Dewsbury
30.10.91 Renny Edwards W PTS 6 Leeds
08.04.92 Edward Cook W PTS 8 Leeds
23.09.92 Dave Campbell W RSC 4 Leeds
07.04.93 Dean Lynch W PTS 8 Leeds
01.07.93 Pete Buckley W PTS 8 York
22.09.93 Bradley Stone L RSC 3 Wembley
(Final Elim. British S. Bantamweight Title)
Career: 15 contests, won 14, lost 1.

John Sillo (Sillitoe)
Liverpool. *Born* Oxford, 10 February, 1965
Featherweight. Ht. 5'5"
Manager Self

28.09.93 Graham McGrath W PTS 6 Liverpool
11.12.93 Marty Chestnut W PTS 6 Liverpool
25.02.94 Craig Kelley W PTS 6 Chester
06.05.94 Chris Lyons W RSC 3 Liverpool
Career: 4 contests, won 4.

Kevin Simons
Swansea. *Born* Swansea, 8 November, 1968
S. Featherweight. Ht. 5'6"
Manager C. Breen

22.01.92 Jason Lepre L PTS 6 Cardiff
22.09.93 Paul Webster L RSC 2 Bethnal Green
Career: 2 contests, lost 2.

Johnny Simpson
Hayes. *Born* Hammersmith, 14 April, 1968
Bantamweight. Ht. 5'4"
Manager D. Gunn

30.09.93 Danny Ruegg W PTS 6 Hayes
Career: 1 contest, won 1.

Balcar Singh
Bradford. *Born* India, 15 November, 1969
Welterweight. Ht. 5'10"
Manager K. Tate

18.02.94 Norman Hutcheon L RSC 1 Leicester
Career: 1 contest, lost 1.

(Raminderbir) Ram Singh
Wisbech. *Born* Crewe, 13 August, 1969
Lightweight. Ht. 5'11"
Manager B. Lee

06.06.94 Wahid Fats L RSC 3 Manchester
Career: 1 contest, lost 1.

(Sukhdarshan) Tiger Singh (Mahal)
Peterborough. *Born* India, 28 October, 1970
Flyweight. Ht. 5'8"
Manager Self

10.12.92 Ian Baillie W PTS 6 Corby
11.05.93 Anthony Hanna L PTS 6 Norwich
06.10.93 Anthony Hanna L PTS 6 Solihull
28.10.93 Nick Tooley L PTS 6 Torquay
30.11.93 Vince Feeney L PTS 6 Leicester
02.03.94 Lyndon Kershaw L PTS 6 Solihull
09.05.94 Terry Gaskin W RSC 2 Bradford
Career: 7 contests, won 2, lost 5.

Robbie Sivyer
Alfreton. *Born* Chesterfield, 22 September, 1973
Lightweight. Ht. 5'9"
Manager J. Gaynor

26.04.93 Garry Burrell L PTS 6 Glasgow
07.06.93 Simon Hamblett W PTS 6 Walsall
29.06.93 Mark Allen L PTS 6 Edgbaston
22.09.93 John Stovin L PTS 6 Chesterfield
13.11.93 Wayne Jones L PTS 6 Cullompton
04.03.94 Wayne Jones L PTS 6 Weston super Mare
Career: 6 contests, won 1, lost 5.

Trevor Small
Birmingham. *Born* Solihull, 26 February, 1968
Cruiserweight. Ht. 6'0"
Manager W. Swift

09.12.92 Sean O'Phoenix W PTS 6 Stoke
20.01.93 Art Stacey W PTS 6 Solihull
28.04.93 Tony Behan W PTS 6 Solihull
20.09.93 Albert Call DREW 6 Cleethorpes
06.10.93 Art Stacey W PTS 6 Solihull
02.11.93 Phil Soundy W RSC 6 Southwark
13.12.93 Albert Call L RSC 5 Cleethorpes
Career: 7 contests, won 5, drew 1, lost 1.

Carl Smallwood
Atherstone. *Born* Nuneaton, 15 April, 1973
L. Heavyweight. Ht. 6'1¼"
Manager Self

30.03.92 Greg Scott-Briggs W PTS 6 Coventry
28.04.92 Lee Archer W PTS 6 Wolverhampton
30.09.92 Greg Scott-Briggs W PTS 6 Solihull
14.10.92 Martin Jolley L PTS 6 Stoke
12.11.92 Richard Atkinson W PTS 6 Stafford
22.02.93 Lee Archer L PTS 8 Bedford
17.03.93 Greg Scott-Briggs W PTS 8 Stoke
17.06.93 Paul Murray W PTS 6 Bedworth
12.10.93 Nigel Rafferty DREW 8 Wolverhampton
29.03.94 Shaun McCrory W PTS 6 Wolverhampton
Career: 10 contests, won 7, drew 1, lost 2.

Mark Smallwood
Atherstone. *Born* Nuneaton, 30 January, 1975
S. Middleweight. Ht. 6'2"
Manager R. Gray

22.02.93 John Dempsey W CO 1 Bedworth

17.03.93 Sean Smith W RSC 1 Stoke
10.05.93 Tim Robinson W RSC 4 Cleethorpes
17.06.93 Phil Ball W RSC 1 Bedworth
24.11.93 Darren Littlewood W PTS 8 Solihull
24.02.94 Jerry Mortimer W PTS 6 Walsall
18.04.94 Gil Lewis W RSC 5 Walsall
23.05.94 Dean Ashton W RTD 3 Walsall
Career: 8 contests, won 8.

Justin Smart
Tonyrefail. *Born* Pontypridd, 24 April, 1973
L. Middleweight. Ht. 6'0"
Manager D. Gardiner

13.09.93 Darren Dorrington DREW 6 Bristol
Career: 1 contest, drew 1.

Alan Smiles
Edinburgh. *Born* Leith, 9 March, 1965
L. Heavyweight. Ht. 6'0"
Manager A. Melrose

29.01.93 Nicky Wadman W PTS 6 Glasgow
04.03.93 Simon McDougall W PTS 6 Glasgow
29.05.93 Phil Ball W PTS 6 Paisley
21.10.93 John Pierre W PTS 6 Glasgow
19.12.93 John Pierre DREW 6 Glasgow
Career: 5 contests, won 4, drew 1.

Andrew Smith
Bedworth. *Born* Nuneaton, 15 February, 1975
Lightweight. Ht. 5'5"
Manager C. Gunns

20.05.94 Marc Smith DREW 6 Neath
Career: 1 contest, drew 1.

Carl Smith
Manchester. *Born* Hereford, 31 March, 1968
L. Middleweight. Ht. 5'9"
Manager N. Basso

29.11.93 Chris Mulcahy W CO 1 Manchester
26.01.94 Anthony Lawrence L RSC 4 Stoke
28.02.94 Japhet Hans W RSC 4 Manchester
18.04.94 Jimmy Alston L PTS 6 Manchester
06.06.94 Jimmy Alston DREW 6 Manchester
Career: 5 contests, won 2, drew 1, lost 2.

John Smith
Liverpool. *Born* Liverpool, 13 October, 1959
Welterweight. Ht. 5'9"
Manager Self

26.06.86 Ray Golding W PTS 6 Edgbaston
22.09.86 John Townsley W PTS 6 Edgbaston
06.11.86 Robert Harkin L PTS 8 Glasgow
20.11.86 John Best L PTS 6 Bredbury
08.12.86 Gary Sommerville DREW 8 Edgbaston
18.03.87 John Best L RSC 2 Solihull
24.04.87 Brian Wareing L PTS 8 Liverpool
24.09.87 John Dickson L PTS 6 Glasgow
01.02.88 Peter Crook L PTS 6 Manchester
17.03.88 Mick Mason DREW 8 Sunderland
29.03.88 Paul Seddon W RSC 4 Marton
17.06.88 Gary Sommerville W RSC 5 Edgbaston
28.11.88 Gary Sommerville L PTS 8 Edgbaston
24.01.89 Mark Kelly L PTS 8 Kings Heath

145

22.03.89 John Davies L PTS 8 Solihull
17.07.89 Richard Adams W RSC 3 Stanmore
08.09.89 Muhammad Lovelock W PTS 6 Liverpool
14.09.89 Roy Rowland L RSC 3 Basildon
17.10.89 Jim Talbot L PTS 6 Oldham
25.10.89 Kevin Plant L PTS 6 Doncaster
10.11.89 Seamus O'Sullivan L PTS 6 Battersea
30.11.89 Dave Pierre L PTS 6 Mayfair
08.12.89 Alan Hall L RSC 2 Doncaster
29.01.90 Darren Mount L PTS 8 Liverpool
08.03.90 Dave Pierre L PTS 6 Peterborough
19.03.90 Brendan Ryan L PTS 6 Leicester
05.04.90 Darren Mount L PTS 8 Liverpool
04.05.90 Pete Roberts L PTS 6 Liverpool
24.09.90 Mark Dinnadge W RTD 2 Lewisham
09.10.90 Pete Roberts W PTS 8 Liverpool
13.11.90 Paul Charters L RSC 4 Hartlepool
21.01.91 Kris McAdam L PTS 6 Glasgow
07.02.91 Billy Schwer L RSC 2 Watford
26.03.91 Andrew Morgan L RSC 4 Wolverhampton
24.04.91 Andrew Morgan L PTS 6 Aberavon
16.05.91 Kevin Toomey L PTS 6 Liverpool
13.06.91 Kevin Toomey L PTS 6 Hull
25.07.91 Robert McCracken L RTD 1 Dudley
07.10.91 Pete Roberts L PTS 8 Liverpool
23.10.91 Dean Hollington L PTS 6 Bethnal Green
12.11.91 Mark Elliot L PTS 6 Wolverhampton
21.11.91 Richard Burton L PTS 6 Burton
02.12.91 Mike Calderwood DREW 8 Liverpool
19.12.91 Richard Burton L PTS 6 Oldham
01.02.92 George Scott L RSC 3 Birmingham
03.03.92 Paul Charters L PTS 8 Houghton le Spring
12.05.92 Ross Hale L CO 1 Crystal Palace
03.09.92 Chris Mulcahy DREW 6 Liverpool
25.09.92 Kevin McKillan L PTS 6 Liverpool
07.10.92 Alan Peacock DREW 6 Glasgow
12.11.92 Mark Tibbs L RSC 6 Bayswater
18.03.93 Jason Rowland L PTS 6 Lewisham
29.03.93 Shea Neary L PTS 6 Liverpool
13.09.93 Rob Stewart DREW 6 Middleton
22.09.93 Jonathan Thaxton L PTS 6 Wembley
27.10.93 Mark McCreath L RSC 7 West Bromwich
25.11.93 Charlie Kane L PTS 6 Tynemouth
21.02.94 Alan Peacock L RSC 4 Glasgow
28.03.94 Charlie Kane L PTS 6 Musselburgh
10.04.94 Kris McAdam W PTS 8 Glasgow
28.06.94 Malcolm Melvin L PTS 6 Edgbaston
Career: 61 contests, won 9, drew 6, lost 46.

Marc Smith
Swansea. *Born* Kingston, 31 August, 1974
Lightweight. Ht. 5'9"
Manager P. Boyce

20.05.94 Andrew Smith DREW 6 Neath
Career: 1 contest, drew 1.

Scott Smith
Birmingham. *Born* Birmingham, 11 July, 1969
L. Welterweight. Ht. 5'8"
Manager Self

09.12.92 Jonathan Thaxton L PTS 6 Stoke
11.03.93 Lee Ryan W PTS 6 Walsall
25.06.93 Cham Joof L RTD 2 Battersea
29.11.93 Robert Howard W PTS 6 Manchester
06.12.93 Laurence Roche L RSC 3 Bradford
Career: 5 contests, won 2, lost 3.

(Terry) T. J. Smith
Kettering. *Born* Kettering 17 October, 1967
Lightweight. Ht. 5'7½"
Manager C. Hogben

29.04.92 Floyd Churchill L RSC 2 Liverpool
10.12.92 Alan Graham L PTS 6 Corby
23.02.93 Patrick Parton W PTS 6 Kettering
29.03.93 Marco Fattore DREW 6 Mayfair
19.04.93 Lee Ryan W RSC 2 Northampton
18.05.93 Dean Martin W RSC 3 Kettering
23.11.93 Jimmy Phelan W PTS 6 Kettering
08.03.94 Andrew Reed W PTS 6 Kettering
17.05.94 Simon Frailing W RSC 1 Kettering
04.06.94 Gareth Jordan L RSC 1 Cardiff
Career: 10 contests, won 6, drew 1, lost 3.

Tony Smith
Burnley. *Born* Burnley, 4 May, 1969
Featherweight. Ht. 5'5"
Manager N. Basso

18.05.87 Gordon Shaw L PTS 6 Glasgow
07.09.87 Gordon Shaw W PTS 6 Glasgow
14.09.87 Gordon Shaw L PTS 6 Glasgow
07.10.87 John Hales W RSC 4 Burnley
26.10.87 Wull Strike L RSC 5 Glasgow
07.12.87 Joe Mullen L RSC 6 Glasgow
25.01.88 Mark Robertson L RSC 1 Glasgow
25.04.88 John Hales W RSC 5 Nottingham
08.06.88 Gordon Shaw L PTS 6 Glasgow
18.06.88 Mark Priestley W RSC 6 Gateshead
05.09.88 Paul Dever W PTS 6 Manchester
12.09.88 Mickey Markie DREW 6 Northampton
06.10.88 Gordon Stobie W PTS 6 Manchester
29.10.88 Salvatore Fanni L RSC 1 Milan, Italy
16.01.89 Mickey Markie L RSC 2 Northampton
05.04.89 George Bailey W PTS 6 Halifax
17.04.89 Seamus Tuohy DREW 6 Middleton
18.09.89 James Drummond L RSC 1 Glasgow
30.11.89 Seamus Tuohy L PTS 6 Oldham
29.01.90 Billy Proud W PTS 6 Bradford
27.02.90 Billy Proud L RSC 2 Marton
14.05.90 Stewart Fishermac L PTS 6 Leicester
21.05.90 Stevie Woods L RSC 6 Bradford
17.10.90 Pete Buckley L PTS 6 Stoke
24.10.90 Paul Dever W PTS 8 Stoke
26.11.90 Des Gargano L PTS 8 Bury
03.12.90 Des Gargano L PTS 6 Cleethorpes
16.01.91 Des Gargano L PTS 6 Stoke
05.03.91 Neil Parry DREW 6 Leicester
18.03.91 Gary White L PTS 6 Manchester
07.05.91 Stevie Woods L RTD 2 Glasgow
10.06.91 Robert Braddock DREW 6 Manchester
20.06.91 Neil Parry L PTS 6 Liverpool
01.10.91 Des Gargano L PTS 6 Cleethorpes
28.10.91 Glyn Shepherd L PTS 6 Leicester
18.11.91 Chris Jickells L RSC 4 Manchester
01.06.92 Craig Murray L RSC 2 Manchester
19.04.93 Paul Goode DREW 6 Manchester
01.06.93 Paul Goode W PTS 6 Manchester
27.09.93 Dougie Fox W RSC 5 Manchester
Career: 40 contests, won 11, drew 5, lost 24.

Michael Smyth
Barry. *Born* Caerphilly, 22 February, 1970
Welterweight. Ht. 5'9¾"
Manager D. Gardiner

02.05.91 Carl Brasier W RSC 2 Kensington
28.05.91 Rick North W RSC 1 Cardiff
18.07.91 Mike Morrison W RSC 2 Cardiff
03.09.91 Julian Eavis W PTS 6 Cardiff
20.11.91 Mike Russell W RSC 3 Cardiff

17.12.91 Julian Eavis W PTS 6 Cardiff
19.05.92 Ojay Abrahams W PTS 6 Cardiff
07.10.92 David Lake W CO 2 Barry
14.11.92 Des Robinson W PTS 6 Cardiff
10.07.93 Ernie Loveridge W RSC 6 Cardiff
23.10.93 Chris Saunders W PTS 6 Cardiff
12.03.94 Gordon Blair W RSC 4 Cardiff
Career: 12 contests, won 12.

Lee Soar
Barnsley. *Born* Barnsley, 12 October, 1970
L. Welterweight. Ht. 5'10"
Manager K. Tate

25.11.91 Mark Broome W PTS 6 Cleethorpes
28.01.92 Steve Bricknell W PTS 6 Piccadilly
14.09.92 Blue Butterworth L CO 4 Bradford
07.12.92 Mick Hoban L PTS 6 Manchester
14.12.92 Rick North L PTS 6 Cleethorpes
04.03.94 Kris McAdam L CO 2 Irvine
Career: 6 contests, won 2, lost 4.

Lee Soar   Chris Bevan

(Simon) Sugar Free Somerville
Tottenham. *Born* London, 1 December, 1967
Lightweight. Ht. 5'8½"
Manager F. Rix

29.05.90 Gary Cody W PTS 6 Bethnal Green
17.10.90 Alan Levene DREW 6 Bethnal Green
26.11.90 Andrew Robinson L PTS 6 Bethnal Green
28.05.94 Steve Edwards L RSC 2 Queensway
Career: 4 contests, won 1, drew 1, lost 2.

Phil Soundy
Benfleet. *Born* Benfleet, 24 October, 1966
Cruiserweight. Ht. 5'11½"
Manager Self

04.10.89	Coco Collins W RSC 2 Basildon
24.10.89	Trevor Barry W RSC 1 Bethnal Green
14.02.90	Andy Balfe W RSC 3 Brentwood
28.03.90	Chris Coughlan W PTS 6 Bethnal Green
22.05.90	Cliff Curtis W PTS 6 Canvey Island
06.07.90	Steve Yorath W CO 3 Brentwood
12.09.90	Rob Albon W RSC 1 Bethnal Green
03.10.90	Steve Yorath W PTS 6 Basildon
12.12.90	David Haycock W RSC 3 Kensington
16.01.91	Chris Coughlan W PTS 6 Kensington
12.02.91	Gus Mendes W RSC 3 Basildon
07.03.91	Terry Duffus W RSC 2 Basildon
24.04.91	Steve Yorath L PTS 6 Basildon
11.09.91	Gus Mendes L RSC 3 Hammersmith
12.02.92	Steve Osborne W PTS 6 Wembley
22.04.92	Lee Prudden W RSC 5 Wembley
13.05.92	Tony Booth L PTS 6 Kensington
07.09.92	Dean Allen W RTD 4 Bethnal Green
28.10.92	Des Vaughan W RTD 4 Kensington
22.09.93	Art Stacey W PTS 6 Wembley
02.11.93	Trevor Small L RSC 6 Southwark
22.03.94	Devon Rhooms W CO 2 Bethnal Green

Career: 22 contests, won 18, lost 4.

(Mick) Art Stacey

Leeds. *Born* Leeds, 26 September, 1964
Cruiserweight. Ht. 6'0½"
Manager K. Tate

09.10.90	Trevor Barry DREW 6 Liverpool
06.11.90	Chris Coughlan W RSC 4 Southend
27.11.90	Allan Millett W PTS 6 Liverpool
21.02.91	Tony Lawrence W PTS 6 Leeds
18.03.91	Paul Gearon W RSC 1 Derby
16.04.91	Steve Osborne DREW 6 Nottingham
03.06.91	Dennis Afflick W PTS 6 Glasgow
11.11.91	Steve Osborne W PTS 6 Bradford
21.11.91	Gil Lewis L RSC 4 Stafford
20.01.92	John Pierre W PTS 8 Bradford
26.10.92	Ian Bulloch L PTS 6 Cleethorpes
27.11.92	Neils H. Madsen L PTS 8 Randers, Denmark
14.12.92	Albert Call L PTS 6 Cleethorpes
20.01.93	Trevor Small L PTS 6 Solihull

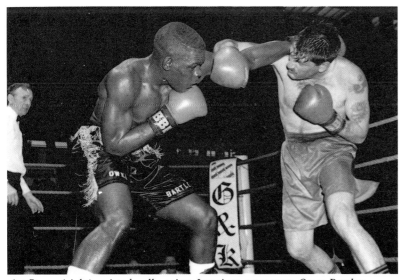

Art Stacey (right) resisted well against Jamaican newcomer, Owen Bartley, before going down to a six-round points defeat   Les Clark

08.03.93	Lee Prudden DREW 6 Leeds
11.06.93	Ian Henry L PTS 6 Gateshead
25.06.93	Mark Prince L CO 2 Battersea
22.09.93	Phil Soundy L PTS 6 Wembley
06.10.93	Trevor Small L PTS 6 Solihull
13.10.93	Paul Lawson L RSC 2 Bethnal Green
25.11.93	Stevie R. Davies W PTS 6 Newcastle
08.12.93	John Pierre W PTS 6 Hull
17.03.94	Albert Call L PTS 6 Lincoln
09.04.94	Chris Okoh L PTS 6 Bethnal Green
21.04.94	Darren McKenna W PTS 6 Hull
11.05.94	Darren Westover L PTS 6 Stevenage
22.05.94	Owen Bartley L PTS 6 Crystal Palace
15.06.94	Paul Lawson L RSC 2 Southwark

Career: 28 contests, won 10, drew 3, lost 15.

Warren Stephens

Birmingham. *Born* Birmingham, 18 May, 1970
L. Middleweight. Ht. 6'0"
Manager Self

04.04.92	John Duckworth L RSC 5 Cleethorpes
21.05.92	Bullit Andrews L RSC 6 Cradley Heath
30.10.92	Bullit Andrews L PTS 6 Birmingham
23.11.92	Simon Fisher W PTS 6 Coventry
07.12.92	Steve Levene L CO 2 Birmingham
18.02.93	Rob Stevenson L PTS 6 Hull
07.04.93	Ron Hopley L PTS 6 Leeds
27.05.93	John Duckworth L RSC 5 Burnley
22.09.93	Norman Mitchell L PTS 6 Chesterfield
30.09.93	Nick Appiah L PTS 6 Hayes
03.11.93	Shamus Casey L PTS 6 Worcester
02.12.93	Scott Newman L DIS 4 Evesham
11.01.94	Vince Rose L PTS 6 Bethnal Green
16.02.94	Nicky Thurbin L PTS 6 Stevenage
08.03.94	Nick Ingram L PTS 6 Kettering
16.03.94	Carl van Bailey W PTS 6 Birmingham
29.03.94	David Bain L PTS 6 Wolverhampton
15.04.94	Brian Dunn L PTS 6 Hull
27.04.94	Jesse Keough L RSC 1 Bethnal Green

Career: 19 contests, won 2, lost 17.

Ronnie Stephenson

Doncaster. *Born* Doncaster, 18 November, 1960
Featherweight. Ht. 5'8"
Manager Self

22.01.86	Paddy Maguire W PTS 4 Stoke
10.03.86	Jamie McBride L PTS 4 Glasgow
27.04.86	Phil Lashley W PTS 4 Doncaster
03.06.86	Billy Cawley L PTS 6 Wolverhampton
15.09.86	Gerry McBride W PTS 6 Manchester
22.09.86	Bobby McDermott DREW 6 Manchester
24.11.86	Gerry McBride L PTS 8 Leicester
10.03.87	Gerry McBride L RSC 7 Manchester *(Vacant Central Area Bantamweight Title)*
06.05.87	Joe Kelly L PTS 8 Livingston
13.06.87	Chris Clarkson L PTS 8 Great Yarmouth
09.08.87	Sean Murphy L RSC 1 Windsor
14.09.87	Bobby McDermott L RSC 2 Glasgow
09.11.87	Phil Lashley DREW 4 Birmingham
24.11.87	Chris Cooper W RSC 4 Wolverhampton
14.12.87	Nigel Crook L PTS 6 Bradford
29.01.88	Chris Cooper W PTS 6 Torquay
24.02.88	Chris Cooper W PTS 6 Southend
14.03.88	Mark Goult L RSC 4 Norwich
11.04.88	Joe Mullen L PTS 8 Glasgow
25.04.88	Des Gargano L PTS 8 Bradford
14.05.88	Andre Hoeffler L PTS 6 Anderlecht, Belgium
26.05.88	Glen Dainty L RSC 6 Bethnal Green
09.06.88	Phil Lashley L PTS 6 Manchester
19.10.88	Chris Cooper W PTS 6 Evesham
14.11.88	Mike Close L PTS 4 Stratford upon Avon
21.11.88	Des Gargano L PTS 6 Leicester
07.12.88	Mark Walker W RSC 6 Stoke
14.02.89	Alan Roberts W PTS 6 Wolverhampton
06.03.89	Mark Walker W RTD 5 Leicester
21.03.89	Miguel Matthews DREW 6 Wolverhampton
03.04.89	Robert Braddock W CO 4 Manchester
04.09.89	Des Gargano L PTS 6 Hull
10.10.89	Pete Buckley W PTS 6 Wolverhampton
13.11.89	Dave Buxton L RTD 2 Bradford
14.03.90	Pete Buckley DREW 6 Stoke
27.03.90	Phil Lashley L PTS 6 Wolverhampton
04.04.90	Pete Buckley W PTS 8 Stafford
23.04.90	Pete Buckley L PTS 6 Birmingham
21.05.90	Phil Lashley W PTS 6 Grimsby
04.06.90	Pete Buckley L PTS 8 Birmingham
03.12.90	Dave Annis L PTS 6 Cleethorpes
21.10.91	Phil Lashley W PTS 6 Cleethorpes
21.11.91	Phil Lashley W PTS 6 Stafford
02.12.91	Chris Lyons W PTS 6 Birmingham
09.12.91	Chris Lyons W PTS 6 Cleethorpes
15.01.92	Chris Jickells W PTS 6 Stoke
30.03.92	Mark Hargreaves W PTS 6 Coventry
25.07.92	John White L PTS 6 Manchester
29.05.93	Shaun Anderson L PTS 6 Paisley
02.07.93	Paul Lloyd L RTD 1 Liverpool

Career: 50 contests, won 20, drew 4, lost 26.

Rob Stevenson

Hull. *Born* Hull, 16 March, 1971
L. Middleweight. Ht. 5'9"
Manager M. Toomey

28.11.91	Matt Mowatt L PTS 6 Hull

26.03.92 Steve Scott W PTS 6 Hull
04.04.92 Chris Mulcahy L PTS 8 Cleethorpes
29.04.92 Alan Williams W PTS 6 Liverpool
01.06.92 Chris Mulcahy L PTS 6 Manchester
13.10.92 Dean Hiscox L PTS 6 Wolverhampton
26.11.92 Steve Scott L PTS 6 Hull
18.02.93 Warren Stephens W PTS 6 Hull
25.02.93 Ron Hopley DREW 6 Bradford
29.04.93 Billy McDougall DREW 6 Hull
01.07.93 Ron Hopley W PTS 6 York
02.12.93 Ian Noble W PTS 6 Hartlepool
13.12.93 Prince Kasi Kiahau L RSC 5 Doncaster
24.02.94 David Sumner W PTS 6 Hull
Career: 14 contests, won 6, drew 2, lost 6.

Clayon Stewart
Paddington. *Born* London, 8 March, 1963
Middleweight. Ht. 5'10"
Manager I. Akay

22.01.86 G. L. Booth L PTS 6 Stoke
17.04.86 Danny Garrison W CO 3
Wolverhampton
26.06.86 Victor Carvalho L CO 3 Hsboa,
Portugal
01.10.86 Roy Horn W PTS 6 Bournemouth
11.11.86 Russell Burnett L PTS 6 Southampton
06.04.87 Russell Burnett L PTS 6 Southampton
26.11.90 Tony Wellington L PTS 6 Mayfair
08.12.90 Tony Wellington L RSC 1 Bristol
06.02.91 Gary Booker L PTS 6 Battersea
18.02.91 Darren Murphy L PTS 6 Windsor
10.11.93 Kevin Adamson L RSC 1 Bethnal
Green
Career: 11 contests, won 2, lost 9.

Clayon Stewart   Les Clark

Rob Stewart
Darwen. *Born* Blackburn, 17 January, 1965
L. Welterweight. Ht. 5'8¼"
Manager Self

14.10.91 Gary Pagden W PTS 6 Manchester
21.10.91 Ricky Sackfield W PTS 6 Bury
04.12.91 Dean Carr W RTD 5 Stoke
21.01.92 Chris Aston W RSC 4 Stockport

24.02.92 Tony Banks DREW 6 Bradford
04.03.92 Alan Peacock DREW 8 Glasgow
31.03.92 Mike Calderwood W PTS 4 Stockport
24.09.92 Richard Burton L PTS 10 Stockport
*(Central Area L. Welterweight Title
Challenge)*
25.02.93 Alan Ingle W PTS 6 Burnley
29.03.93 Peter Bradley L RSC 5 Glasgow
29.05.93 Alan McDowall DREW 6 Paisley
13.09.93 John Smith DREW 6 Middleton
27.10.93 Mark Elliot L PTS 6 West Bromwich
02.12.93 Chris Saunders W PTS 4 Sheffield
17.02.94 Paul Ryan L RSC 4 Dagenham
25.04.94 Blue Butterworth W PTS 6 Bury
Career: 16 contests, won 8, drew 4, lost 4.

Rob Stewart   Les Clark

Bradley Stone
Canning Town. *Born* Mile End, 27 May,
1970
S. Bantamweight. Ht. 5'5¾"
Manager J. Tibbs

06.03.90 Des Gargano W PTS 6 Bethnal Green
28.03.90 Stevie Woods W RSC 2 Bethnal Green
14.04.90 Kruga Hydes W PTS 6 Kensington
29.05.90 Gary Hickman DREW 6 Bethnal Green
10.07.90 Andrew Robinson W PTS 6 Canvey
Island
10.10.90 Gary Jones W RSC 3 Millwall
12.02.91 Stewart Fishermac W PTS 6 Basildon
07.03.91 Miguel Matthews W RSC 4 Basildon
25.04.91 Miguel Matthews W PTS 6 Basildon
02.10.91 Andrew Bloomer W PTS 6 Barking
02.04.92 Colin Lynch W RSC 3 Basildon
16.05.92 Andrew Bloomer W PTS 6 Muswell
Hill
15.10.92 Kevin Middleton W PTS 6 Lewisham
03.12.92 Norman Dhalie W CO 4 Lewisham
24.02.93 Chris Clarkson W PTS 8 Wembley
26.04.93 Pete Buckley W PTS 8 Lewisham
09.06.93 Colin Lynch W RTD 1 Lewisham
22.09.93 Tony Silkstone W RSC 3 Wembley
*(Final Elim. British S. Bantamweight
Title)*
04.03.94 Boualem Belkif L RSC 5 Bethnal
Green

26.04.94 Richie Wenton L RSC 10 Bethnal
Green
(Vacant British S. Bantamweight Title)
Career: 20 contests, won 17, drew 1, lost 2.

Sammy Storey
Belfast. *Born* Belfast, 9 August, 1963
Former British S. Middleweight Champion.
Former All-Ireland Middleweight
Champion. Ht. 6'0"
Manager Self

03.12.85 Nigel Shingles W RSC 6 Belfast
05.02.86 Sean O'Phoenix W PTS 6 Sheffield
22.04.86 Karl Barwise W PTS 6 Belfast
29.10.86 Jimmy Ellis W RSC 5 Belfast
25.04.87 Rocky McGran W PTS 10 Belfast
*(Vacant All-Ireland Middleweight
Title)*
19.10.87 Shamus Casey W PTS 6 Belfast
05.12.87 Paul Mitchell W PTS 6 Doncaster
27.01.88 Steve Foster W RSC 4 Belfast
18.03.88 Steve Collins L PTS 10 Boston, USA
*(All-Ireland Middleweight Title
Defence)*
19.10.88 Tony Lawrence W RSC 3 Belfast
07.12.88 Darren Hobson W RSC 6 Belfast
25.01.89 Abdul Amoru Sanda W RSC 8 Belfast
08.03.89 Kevin Roper W RSC 3 Belfast
19.09.89 Tony Burke W PTS 12 Belfast
(Vacant British S. Middleweight Title)
29.11.89 Noel Magee W RSC 9 Belfast
(British S. Middleweight Title Defence)
17.03.90 Simon Collins W CO 7 Belfast
30.10.90 James Cook L RSC 10 Belfast
(British S. Middleweight Title Defence)
31.05.91 Saldi Ali L PTS 8 Berlin, Germany
07.09.91 Johnny Melfah W PTS 8 Belfast
13.11.91 Karl Barwise W PTS 6 Belfast
25.04.92 Nigel Rafferty W RSC 3 Belfast
03.02.93 Graham Jenner W RSC 4 Earls Court
28.04.93 Carlos Christie W RSC 8 Dublin
22.09.93 John Kaighin W PTS 6 Bethnal Green
21.05.94 Fidel Castro W PTS 6 Belfast
Career: 25 contests, won 22, lost 3.

John Stovin
Hull. *Born* Hull, 20 April, 1972
Lightweight. Ht. 6'0"
Manager M. Toomey

22.09.93 Robbie Sivyer W PTS 6 Chesterfield
07.10.93 Alan Graham W PTS 6 Hull
21.10.93 Dominic McGuigan W PTS 6
Bayswater
22.03.94 Yifru Retta L RSC 3 Bethnal Green
28.04.94 Norman Dhalie DREW 6 Hull
02.06.94 Nick Boyd L RSC 5 Middleton
Career: 6 contests, won 3, drew 1, lost 2.

Warren Stowe
Burnley. *Born* Burnley, 30 January, 1965
Central Area L. Middleweight Champion.
Ht. 5'8"
Manager J. Doughty

21.10.91 Matt Mowatt W RSC 3 Bury
07.12.91 Griff Jones W RSC 6 Manchester
03.02.92 Robert Peel W PTS 6 Manchester
10.03.92 B. K. Bennett W PTS 6 Bury
25.04.92 David Radford W RSC 3 Manchester
04.06.92 Rob Pitters W PTS 8 Burnley
25.07.92 Shamus Casey W CO 2 Manchester

24.09.92 Mike Phillips W RSC 1 Stockport
12.11.92 Steve Thomas W RSC 1 Burnley
28.11.92 Julian Eavis W RSC 6 Manchester
25.02.93 Robert Riley W DIS 4 Burnley
(Vacant Central Area L. Middleweight Title)
22.04.93 Leigh Wicks W PTS 6 Bury
27.05.93 Peter Waudby W PTS 6 Burnley
09.10.93 Paul Wesley L PTS 10 Manchester
(Elim. British L. Middleweight Title)
17.02.94 Rob Pitters W RSC 1 Bury
25.04.94 Chris Richards W PTS 6 Bury
Career: 16 contests, won 15, lost 1.

Gary Stretch

St Helens. *Born* St Helens, 4 November, 1965
Middleweight. Former Undefeated British, WBC International & Central Area L. Middleweight Champion. Ht. 6'0"
Manager Self

14.04.85 Steve Tempro W RSC 6 Bethnal Green
09.05.85 Bobby Welburn W RSC 3 Warrington
05.06.85 Shamus Casey W RSC 2 Kensington
13.06.85 Lenny Gloster W RSC 3 Hartlepool
01.10.85 Jim Kelly W PTS 6 Wembley
04.12.85 Julian Monville L RSC 2 Kensington
05.02.86 Manny Romain W CO 2 Sheffield
04.03.86 Ian Martin W CO 1 Wembley
24.03.86 Franki Moro W PTS 8 Mayfair
09.04.86 Graeme Ahmed W PTS 8 Kensington
07.05.86 Terry Magee W RSC 7 Kensington
17.09.86 Darwin Brewster W PTS 8 Kensington
15.12.86 Steve Davies W RSC 4 Mayfair
08.01.87 Winston Wray W RSC 2 Bethnal Green
19.02.87 Sammy Sampson W RSC 2 St Helens
(Central Area L. Middleweight Title Challenge)
02.12.87 Denys Cronin W PTS 8 Kensington
09.02.88 Tommy McCallum W CO 1 Bethnal Green
26.04.88 Robin Smith W RSC 4 Bethnal Green
07.09.88 Gary Cooper W PTS 12 Reading
(British L. Middleweight Title Challenge)
17.05.89 Rafael Sena W PTS 10 Millwall
11.10.89 Derek Wormald W RSC 1 Millwall
(British L. Middleweight Title Defence)
14.02.90 Ramon Alegre W RSC 6 Millwall
(Vacant WBC International L. Middleweight Title)
26.05.90 Eduardo Contrerras W PTS 10 Reading
18.04.91 Chris Eubank L RSC 6 Earls Court
(WBO Middleweight Title Challenge)
28.07.93 Steve Goodwin W PTS 6 Brixton
Career: 25 contests, won 23, lost 2.

David Sumner

Preston. *Born* Preston, 24 August, 1964
L. Middleweight. Ht. 5'8¾"
Manager M. Chapman

24.05.93 Raziq Ali L PTS 6 Bradford
08.06.93 Dennis Berry L PTS 6 Derby
01.07.93 David Larkin L CO 5 York
27.09.93 Chris Mulcahy L PTS 6 Manchester
29.11.93 Mike Fordham W RSC 4 Manchester
24.02.94 Rob Stevenson L PTS 6 Hull
21.03.94 Jim Conley L PTS 6 Bradford
Career: 7 contests, won 1, lost 6.

Neil Swain

Gilfach Goch. *Born* Pontypridd, 4 September, 1971
Flyweight. Ht. 5'5"
Manager D. Gardiner

29.04.93 Vince Feeney W PTS 6 Mayfair
27.05.93 Marcus Duncan W PTS 6 Burnley
01.10.93 Rowan Williams W PTS 6 Cardiff
16.10.93 Philippe Desavoye W PTS 6 Levallois, France
10.11.93 Barry Jones L PTS 6 Ystrad
29.01.94 Alan Ley W RSC 3 Cardiff
12.03.94 Ceri Farrell W CO 1 Cardiff
09.04.94 Vince Feeney L PTS 6 Mansfield
06.05.94 Peter Culshaw L PTS 6 Liverpool
25.05.94 Paul Ingle L CO 4 Bristol
Career: 10 contests, won 6, lost 4.

Richard Swallow

Northampton. *Born* Northampton, 10 February, 1970
Welterweight. Ht. 5'8"
Manager Self

15.10.90 Richard O'Brien L RTD 1 Kettering
14.02.91 Dave Fallon W RSC 4 Southampton
06.03.91 Carl Brasier W PTS 6 Croydon
02.05.91 Mike Morrison W PTS 6 Northampton
24.03.92 Dean Bramhald W PTS 8 Wolverhampton
06.04.92 Dean Bramhald W PTS 6 Northampton
29.04.92 Chris Aston W RSC 3 Solihull
14.10.92 Wayne Shepherd W PTS 8 Stoke
24.11.92 Chris Mulcahy W PTS 6 Wolverhampton
20.01.93 Ray Newby W PTS 8 Solihull
03.03.93 Ray Newby L PTS 8 Solihull
11.06.93 Soren Sondergaard L RTD 3 Randers, Denmark
08.02.94 Billy McDougall W PTS 6 Wolverhampton
Career: 13 contests, won 10, lost 3.

Darren Sweeney

Birmingham. *Born* London, 3 March, 1971
Middleweight. Ht. 5'11"
Manager R. Gray/P. Cowdell

28.06.94 Japhet Hans W PTS 6 Edgbaston
Career: 1 contest, won 1.

Tony Swift

Birmingham. *Born* Solihull, 29 June, 1968
L. Welterweight. Ht. 5'10"
Manager W. Swift

25.09.86 Barry Bacon W PTS 6 Wolverhampton
06.10.86 Wil Halliday W PTS 6 Birmingham
23.10.86 Patrick Loftus W PTS 6 Birmingham
26.11.86 Adam Muir W PTS 6 Wolverhampton
08.12.86 George Baigrie W PTS 6 Birmingham
26.01.87 Dean Bramhald W PTS 8 Birmingham
04.03.87 Dean Bramhald W RSC 5 Dudley
25.03.87 Peter Bowen W PTS 8 Stafford
22.06.87 Peter Bowen W PTS 8 Stafford
07.10.87 Dean Bramhald W PTS 8 Stoke
19.10.87 Kevin Plant W PTS 8 Birmingham
02.12.87 Dean Bramhald W PTS 8 Stoke
16.03.88 Ron Shinkwin W PTS 8 Solihull
04.05.88 Kevin Plant DREW 8 Solihull
28.09.88 Kevin Plant DREW 8 Solihull
23.11.88 Lenny Gloster L PTS 8 Solihull

12.06.89 Humphrey Harrison W PTS 8 Manchester
28.11.89 Seamus O'Sullivan W RSC 1 Battersea
16.02.90 Ramses Evilio W PTS 6 Bilbao, Spain
30.05.90 Darren Mount W PTS 8 Stoke
05.09.90 Glyn Rhodes L RSC 7 Stoke
25.10.90 Jimmy Harrison L PTS 6 Battersea
19.04.91 Gary Barron DREW 8 Peterborough
12.11.91 Carlos Chase W PTS 6 Milton Keynes
03.03.92 Steve McGovern W RSC 4 Cradley Heath
10.04.92 Willie Beattie W PTS 10 Glasgow
(Elim. British Welterweight Title)
29.09.92 Nigel Bradley W PTS 8 Stoke
05.10.93 Andrew Murray L RSC 6 Mayfair
(Vacant Commonwealth Welterweight Title)
09.04.94 Andreas Panayi W PTS 8 Bethnal Green
11.06.94 Andreas Panayi L PTS 8 Bethnal Green
Career: 30 contests, won 22, drew 3, lost 5.

Tony Swift   Les Clark

Wally Swift Jnr

Birmingham. *Born* Nottingham, 17 February, 1966
Middleweight. Former British L. Middleweight Champion. Former Undefeated Midlands Area L. Middleweight Champion. Ht. 5'7"
Manager W. Swift

25.09.85 John Conlan W RTD 3 Stoke
11.11.85 Steve Craggs W RTD 4 Birmingham
09.12.85 Steve Tempro W RSC 4 Birmingham
22.01.86 Teddy Anderson W RSC 6 Solihull
03.02.86 Frankie Lake W PTS 8 Birmingham
24.03.86 Paul Cook W PTS 8 Mayfair
02.06.86 Gerry Beard W PTS 8 Mayfair
08.09.86 Steve Ellwood W PTS 8 Dulwich
13.10.86 Dean Barclay DREW 8 Dulwich
19.11.86 Franki Moro W PTS 8 Solihull
03.12.86 Ian Chantler W PTS 8 Stoke
22.01.87 Dave Dent L PTS 8 Bethnal Green
10.02.87 Granville Allen W RSC 4 Wolverhampton

24.02.87	Dave McCabe L PTS 8 Glasgow
30.03.87	John Ashton W PTS 8 Birmingham
20.10.87	John Ashton L PTS 8 Stoke
20.01.88	Tommy McCallum W PTS 8 Solihull
28.03.88	Ossie Maddix L PTS 8 Stoke
04.05.88	Chris Blake W PTS 8 Solihull
28.09.88	Terry Magee L PTS 8 Solihull
25.01.89	Kevin Hayde W PTS 8 Solihull
01.03.89	Andy Till L PTS 8 Bethnal Green
13.03.89	Tony Britton W PTS 8 Mayfair
08.04.89	Alfonso Redondo W PTS 8 Madrid, Spain
19.08.89	Suzuki Miranda W PTS 6 Benidorm, Spain
26.09.89	Ensley Bingham L PTS 10 Oldham *(Elim. British L. Middleweight Title)*
26.04.90	Shaun Cummins W PTS 10 Merthyr *(Vacant Midlands Area L. Middleweight Title & Elim. British L. Middleweight Title)*
18.09.90	Mark Holden W RSC 3 Stoke
21.11.90	Alan Richards W PTS 8 Solihull
23.01.91	Paul Wesley W PTS 10 Solihull *(Midlands Area L. Middleweight Title Defence)*
19.03.91	Ensley Bingham W RSC 4 Birmingham *(Vacant British L. Middlweight Title)*
03.07.91	Tony Collins W PTS 12 Reading *(British L. Middleweight Title Defence)*
08.01.92	Randy Williams W PTS 10 Burton
18.04.92	Jean-Claude Fontana L PTS 12 Hyeres, France *(European L. Middleweight Title Challenge)*
17.09.92	Andy Till L PTS 12 Watford *(British L. Middleweight Title Defence)*
14.04.93	Andy Till L RSC 4 Kensington *(British L. Middleweight Title Challenge)*
07.09.93	Steve Goodwin L RSC 7 Stoke *(Midlands Area L. Middleweight Title Challenge)*
25.05.94	Steve Goodwin W PTS 8 Stoke

Career: 38 contests, won 26, drew 1, lost 11.

Karl Taylor

Birmingham. *Born* Birmingham, 5 January, 1966
Midlands Area Lightweight Champion. Ht. 5'5"
Manager Self

18.03.87	Steve Brown W PTS 6 Stoke
06.04.87	Paul Taylor L PTS 6 Southampton
12.06.87	Mark Begley W RSC 1 Leamington
18.11.87	Colin Lynch W RSC 4 Solihull
29.02.88	Peter Bradley L PTS 8 Birmingham
04.10.89	Mark Antony W CO 2 Stafford
30.10.89	Tony Feliciello L PTS 8 Birmingham
06.12.89	John Davison L PTS 8 Leicester
23.12.89	Regilio Tuur L RSC 2 Hoogvliet, Holland
22.02.90	Mark Ramsey L RSC 4 Hull
29.10.90	Steve Walker DREW 6 Birmingham
10.12.90	Elvis Parsley L PTS 6 Birmingham
16.01.91	Wayne Windle W PTS 8 Stoke
02.05.91	Billy Schwer L RSC 2 Northampton
25.07.91	Peter Till L RSC 4 Dudley *(Midlands Area Lightweight Title Challenge)*
24.02.92	Charlie Kane L PTS 8 Glasgow
28.04.92	Richard Woolgar W PTS 6 Wolverhampton

29.05.92	Alan McDowall L PTS 6 Glasgow
25.07.92	Michael Armstrong L RSC 3 Manchester
02.11.92	Hugh Forde L PTS 6 Wolverhampton
23.11.92	Dave McHale L PTS 8 Glasgow
22.12.92	Patrick Gallagher L RSC 3 Mayfair
13.02.93	Craig Dermody L RSC 5 Manchester
31.03.93	Craig Dermody W PTS 6 Barking
07.06.93	Mark Geraghty W PTS 8 Glasgow
13.08.93	Giorgio Campanella L CO 6 Arezzo, Italy
05.10.93	Paul Harvey W PTS 6 Mayfair
21.10.93	Charles Shepherd L RTD 5 Bayswater
21.12.93	Patrick Gallagher L PTS 6 Mayfair
09.02.94	Alan Levene W RSC 2 Brentwood
01.03.94	Shaun Cogan L PTS 6 Dudley
15.03.94	Patrick Gallagher L PTS 6 Mayfair
18.04.94	Peter Till W PTS 10 Walsall *(Midlands Area Lightweight Title Challenge)*
24.05.94	Michael Ayers DREW 8 Sunderland

Career: 34 contests, won 11, drew 2, lost 21.

Jonathan Thaxton

Norwich. *Born* Norwich, 10 September, 1974
Southern Area L. Welterweight Champion. Ht. 5'6"
Manager B. Ingle

09.12.92	Scott Smith W PTS 6 Stoke
03.03.93	Dean Hiscox W PTS 6 Solihull
17.03.93	John O'Johnson W PTS 6 Stoke
23.06.93	Brian Coleman W PTS 8 Gorleston
22.09.93	John Smith W PTS 6 Wembley
07.12.93	Dean Hollington W RSC 3 Bethnal Green
10.03.94	B. F. Williams W RSC 4 Watford *(Vacant Southern Area L. Welterweight Title)*

Career: 7 contests, won 7.

(Lee) Malcolm Thomas

Llanelli. *Born* Swansea, 2 January, 1972
L. Welterweight. Ht. 5'6"
Manager D. Davies

24.02.94	Patrick Parton L PTS 6 Walsall
04.03.94	Colin Dunne L CO 1 Bethnal Green
20.05.94	Anthony Campbell L PTS 6 Acton

Career: 3 contests, lost 3.

Steve Thomas

Merthyr. *Born* Merthyr, 13 June, 1970
Middleweight. Ht. 6'0"
Manager D. Gardiner

21.10.91	Jerry Mortimer W PTS 6 Mayfair
04.11.91	Andy Manning W PTS 6 Merthyr
02.03.92	Robert Peel DREW 6 Merthyr
08.04.92	Charlie Moore L RSC 3 Leeds
11.05.92	Robert Peel W PTS 6 Llanelli
07.10.92	Ray Price L PTS 6 Barry
15.10.92	Clay O'Shea L PTS 6 Lewisham
12.11.92	Warren Stowe L RSC 1 Burnley
19.01.93	Matthew Turner L PTS 6 Cardiff
06.02.93	Mike Phillips DREW 6 Cardiff
06.03.93	Willie Quinn L RSC 4 Glasgow
10.04.93	Darren Pullman DREW 6 Swansea
24.04.93	Andrew Flute L RSC 1 Birmingham
23.03.94	Paul Matthews L PTS 6 Cardiff
31.03.94	Dale Nixon DREW 4 Bristol
26.04.94	Clay O'Shea L PTS 6 Bethnal Green

25.05.94	Darren Dorrington L PTS 4 Bristol
02.06.94	Dave Cranston L PTS 6 Tooting

Career: 18 contests, won 3, drew 4, lost 11.

Steve Thomas   Les Clark

Gary Thornhill

Liverpool. *Born* Liverpool, 11 February, 1968
S. Featherweight. Ht. 5'6½"
Manager S. Vaughan

27.02.93	Brian Hickey W CO 4 Ellesmere Port
02.07.93	Dougie Fox W CO 1 Liverpool
30.10.93	Miguel Matthews W PTS 6 Chester
01.12.93	Wayne Windle W PTS 6 Stoke
25.02.94	Edward Lloyd DREW 6 Chester
06.05.94	Derek Amory W RSC 1 Liverpool

Career: 6 contests, won 5, drew 1.

Jimmy Thornton

Sheffield. *Born* Sheffield, 22 September, 1964
L. Middleweight. Ht. 5'8"
Manager Self

25.11.82	Stuart Carmichael W PTS 6 Morley
14.12.82	Seamus McGuinness L PTS 6 Belfast
09.05.83	Edward Lloyd W RSC 1 Manchester
12.05.83	Colin Roscoe W RSC 2 Morley
23.05.83	Peter Flanagan W RSC 3 Sheffield
13.06.83	Gary Williams W RTD 5 Doncaster
12.09.83	Lee Halford L PTS 8 Leicester
29.02.84	Ray Murray W PTS 6 Sheffield
12.03.84	Lenny Gloster L PTS 6 Manchester
09.04.84	Dave Haggarty L PTS 8 Glasgow
06.06.84	Peter Bowen W PTS 6 Sheffield
22.07.84	Peter Bowen W RSC 2 Sheffield
25.10.84	Dan Myers W PTS 6 Birmingham
26.11.84	Ron Shinkwin W RSC 2 Sheffield
10.12.84	Ray Murray W RSC 4 Nottingham
04.02.85	Steve Tempro W RSC 4 Birmingham
20.03.85	Mickey Bird W PTS 6 Stoke
10.04.85	Ricky Richards L PTS 6 Leeds
31.05.85	Rocky Feliciello L PTS 8 Liverpool
24.03.87	Kelvin Mortimer W PTS 6 Nottingham

13.04.87　Peter Ashcroft L PTS 6 Manchester
12.05.87　Tony Ekubia L PTS 6 Alfreton
09.08.87　George Collins L RSC 1 Windsor
03.12.87　Andy Holligan L RTD 2 Belfast
09.03.88　Damien Denny L PTS 8 Bethnal Green
12.04.88　Tony Ekubia L RSC 5 Oldham
09.08.88　Del Bryan L PTS 6 St Helier
26.09.88　Errol McDonald L RTD 2 Piccadilly
07.12.88　Paul Jones L PTS 6 Stoke
06.03.89　Dave Andrews L PTS 6 Northampton
21.04.89　Roy Callaghan W RSC 3 Bethnal Green
19.05.89　Ray Taylor L PTS 8 Gateshead
06.07.89　Jim Beckett L PTS 8 Chigwell
12.10.89　Gary Logan L PTS 6 Southwark
29.01.90　Tony Baker L PTS 8 Bradford
22.11.90　Shamus Casey L PTS 6 Ilkeston
13.02.91　Neville Brown L RSC 1 Wembley
02.03.92　Dave Whittle W PTS 6 Marton
02.07.92　Delroy Waul L RSC 6 Middleton
04.05.93　Andreas Panayi L CO 2 Liverpool
06.12.93　Spencer McCracken L PTS 6 Birmingham

Career: 41 contests, won 17, lost 24.

Barry Thorogood

Cardiff. *Born* Cardiff, 1 December, 1972
L. Middleweight. Ht. 6'0"
Manager D. Gardiner

28.10.92　Robert Peel W PTS 6 Cardiff
14.12.92　James Campbell W RSC 4 Cardiff
27.01.93　Russell Washer W PTS 6 Cardiff
24.03.93　Darren McInulty W PTS 6 Cardiff
28.04.93　Stuart Dunn L RSC 2 Solihull
13.09.93　Glenn Catley L PTS 4 Bristol
23.10.93　Mark Atkins W PTS 4 Cardiff
10.11.93　Robert Peel W PTS 6 Ystrad
29.01.94　Darren Dorrington DREW 6 Cardiff
02.03.94　Darren Pilling W PTS 6 Solihull
12.03.94　Geoff McCreesh L PTS 6 Cardiff
27.04.94　Dave Johnson DREW 8 Solihull
20.05.94　Andrew Furlong L RSC 4 Acton

Career: 13 contests, won 7, drew 2, lost 4.

Barry Thorogood　　　　Les Clark

Nicky Thurbin

Ilford. *Born* Ilford, 26 October, 1971
L. Middleweight. Ht. 5'10"
Manager M. Duff

07.12.93　John Rice W PTS 6 Bethnal Green
14.01.94　Delwyn Panayiotiou W RTD 3 Bethnal Green
16.02.94　Warren Stephens W PTS 6 Stevenage
04.03.94　Andy Peach W PTS 6 Bethnal Green
22.03.94　Carl Winstone W PTS 6 Bethnal Green

Career: 5 contests, won 5.

Nicky Thurbin　　　　Les Clark

Mark Tibbs

West Ham. *Born* London, 7 May, 1969
L. Welterweight. Ht. 5'10"
Manager D. Powell

15.11.88　Mike Chapman W PTS 6 Norwich
23.11.88　Shane Tonks W PTS 6 Bethnal Green
14.12.88　G. G. Corbett W PTS 6 Bethnal Green
25.01.89　Mick Mulcahy W CO 1 Bethnal Green
15.02.89　Jamie Hind W RSC 1 Bethnal Green
05.04.89　Steve Taggart W CO 1 Kensington
17.05.89　Mark Antony W PTS 6 Millwall
19.09.89　Hugh Ruse W RSC 3 Millwall
11.10.89　Dave Croft W RSC 5 Millwall
20.02.90　Mark Fairman W CO 2 Millwall
25.04.90　Eddie King W CO 1 Millwall
25.09.90　Mike Morrison W PTS 6 Millwall
06.03.91　Mike Morrison W RSC 4 Wembley
06.06.91　Chris Saunders L RSC 6 Barking
23.10.91　Rick Bushell W RSC 4 Bethnal Green
13.11.91　David Thompson W PTS 6 Bethnal Green
11.12.91　Rick Bushell W RSC 2 Basildon
25.03.92　Felix Kelly DREW 8 Dagenham
12.11.92　John Smith W RSC 6 Bayswater
12.12.92　Dean Bramhald W PTS 6 Muswell Hill
20.02.93　Mark Pearce W PTS 6 Earls Court
06.03.93　Jimmy Vincent L PTS 6 Glasgow
26.06.93　Gary Hiscox W RSC 4 Earls Court
09.02.94　Kevin Toomey W RSC 4 Bethnal Green

29.03.94　George Wilson W RSC 6 Bethnal Green

Career: 25 contests, won 22, drew 1, lost 2.

Andy Till

Northolt. *Born* Perivale, 22 August, 1963
Former British L. Middleweight Champion.
Former Undefeated WBC International &
Southern Area L. Middleweight Champion.
Ht. 5'9"
Manager H. Holland

01.09.86　Peter Reid W RSC 6 Ealing
25.09.86　Graham Jenner W PTS 6 Crystal Palace
10.11.86　Randy Henderson W PTS 6 Longford
12.01.87　Tony Lawrence W RSC 4 Ealing
18.02.87　Ian Bayliss W PTS 6 Fulham
30.04.87　Dean Scarfe L PTS 8 Wandsworth
24.09.87　Andy Wright W RSC 2 Crystal Palace
19.02.88　Geoff Sharp W RSC 5 Longford
29.11.88　W. O. Wilson W PTS 10 Battersea
01.03.89　Wally Swift Jnr W PTS 8 Bethnal Green
12.06.89　Tony Britton W RTD 8 Battersea
　　　　　(Vacant Southern Area L. Middleweight Title)
10.11.89　Nigel Fairbairn W RSC 8 Battersea
14.03.90　Steve Foster W RTD 5 Battersea
06.06.90　Ensley Bingham L DIS 3 Battersea
　　　　　(Final Elim. British L. Middleweight Title)
12.09.90　Alan Richards W PTS 8 Battersea
06.02.91　Alan Richards W PTS 8 Battersea
01.06.91　Terry Magee W RSC 4 Bethnal Green
15.10.91　John Davies W PTS 12 Dudley
　　　　　(Vacant WBC International L. Middleweight Title)
17.09.92　Wally Swift Jnr W PTS 12 Watford
　　　　　(British L. Middleweight Title Challenge)
10.12.92　Tony Collins W RSC 3 Bethnal Green
　　　　　(British L. Middleweight Title Defence)
14.04.93　Wally Swift Jnr W RSC 4 Kensington
　　　　　(British L. Middleweight Title Defence)
23.06.93　Laurent Boudouani L RTD 4 Edmonton
　　　　　(European L. Middleweight Title Challenge)
23.02.94　Robert McCracken L PTS 12 Watford
　　　　　(British L. Middleweight Title Defence)

Career: 23 contests, won 19, lost 4.

Peter Till

Walsall. *Born* Walsall, 19 August, 1963
Former Midlands Area Lightweight
Champion. Ht. 5'6"
Manager R. Gray/P. Cowdell

25.04.85　Clinton Campbell W CO 1 Wolverhampton
23.05.85　J. J. Mudd W PTS 6 Dudley
17.10.85　Patrick Loftus W PTS 6 Leicester
14.11.85　Paul Wetter W RSC 3 Dudley
27.01.86　George Jones W PTS 8 Dudley
17.04.86　Tyrell Wilson W CO 5 Wolverhampton
15.05.86　Les Remikie W PTS 6 Dudley
03.06.86　Ray Newby L PTS 10 Wolverhampton
　　　　　(Vacant Midlands Area Lightweight Title)
25.09.86　Gerry Beard DREW 8 Wolverhampton

Peter Till   Les Clark

26.11.86	Gerry Beard W CO 4 Wolverhampton
28.01.87	George Baigrie W PTS 8 Dudley
04.03.87	Carl Merrett W PTS 8 Dudley
30.03.87	Tony Richards L PTS 8 Birmingham
19.07.87	Aladin Stevens L CO 4 Johannesburg, South Africa
19.10.87	Dean Bramhald W PTS 8 Birmingham
24.11.87	Dean Bramhald W PTS 8 Wolverhampton
07.02.88	Michael Marsden W CO 1 Stafford
24.02.88	Neil Haddock W PTS 8 Aberavon
13.04.88	Sugar Gibiliru W PTS 8 Wolverhampton
14.06.88	Ray Newby W PTS 10 Dudley *(Midlands Area Lightweight Title Challenge)*
22.09.88	Jim Moffat W RSC 4 Wolverhampton
10.11.88	George Jones W RSC 8 Wolverhampton *(Midlands Area Lightweight Title Defence)*
02.02.89	Camel Touati W RSC 3 Wolverhampton
13.04.89	Phillipe Binante W RSC 3 Wolverhampton
21.12.89	Tony Richards L CO 8 Kings Heath
18.10.90	Nick Hall W PTS 6 Birmingham
30.11.90	Ray Newby W PTS 8 Birmingham
21.02.91	Paul Charters L RSC 6 Walsall *(Elim. British Lightweight Title)*
31.05.91	Valery Kayumba L RSC 3 Grenoble, France
25.07.91	Karl Taylor W RSC 4 Dudley *(Midlands Area Lightweight Title Defence)*
21.09.91	Michael Ayers L RSC 5 Tottenham *(Elim. British Lightweight Title)*
09.12.91	Scott Doyle W CO 3 Brierley Hill
01.02.92	Michael Driscoll L RSC 3 Birmingham
17.03.92	Mark Reefer W RSC 3 Mayfair
04.06.92	Racheed Lawal L RSC 1 Randers, Denmark
15.08.92	Dingaan Thobela L RSC 9 Springs, South Africa
16.02.93	Errol McDonald L PTS 8 Tooting
26.05.93	Mark McCreath L PTS 8 Mansfield

02.12.93	Dominic McGuigan W RSC 2 Walsall
16.12.93	Norman Dhalie W PTS 8 Walsall
24.02.94	Barrie Kelley W PTS 6 Walsall
18.04.94	Karl Taylor L PTS 10 Walsall *(Midlands Area Lightweight Title Defence)*
10.06.94	Dave Anderson L PTS 6 Glasgow

Career: 43 contests, won 28, drew 1, lost 14.

Nick Tooley

Teignmouth. *Born* Exeter, 19 December, 1970
Flyweight. Ht. 5'2"
Manager Self

26.10.92	Louis Veitch W PTS 6 Cleethorpes
19.11.92	Anthony Hanna W PTS 6 Evesham
17.02.93	Rowan Williams L PTS 4 Bethnal Green
28.10.93	Tiger Singh W PTS 6 Torquay
11.12.93	Peter Culshaw L RSC 1 Liverpool

Career: 5 contests, won 3, lost 2.

Kevin Toomey

Hull. *Born* Hull, 19 September, 1967
Former Undefeated Central Area
Lightweight Champion. Ht. 5'9"
Manager M. Toomey

24.04.89	Chris Mulcahy L PTS 6 Bradford
04.09.89	Andy Rowbotham W RSC 1 Grimsby
03.10.89	Mick Mulcahy L CO 5 Cottingham
01.11.90	Joel Forbes W PTS 6 Hull
12.12.90	Andy Kent DREW 6 Leicester
24.01.91	Barry North W PTS 6 Brierley Hill
18.02.91	Andy Kent L RSC 5 Derby
22.04.91	Trevor Royal W PTS 6 Bradford
16.05.91	John Smith W PTS 6 Liverpool
13.06.91	John Smith W PTS 6 Hull
30.09.91	Mike Calderwood L RSC 2 Liverpool
28.11.91	David Thompson W PTS 6 Hull
10.12.91	Wayne Windle L PTS 6 Sheffield
04.02.92	G. G. Goddard W PTS 6 Alfreton
26.03.92	Wayne Windle W DIS 8 Hull *(Central Area Lightweight Title Challenge)*
11.09.92	Dave Anderson L PTS 8 Glasgow
16.10.92	Steve Pollard W RSC 7 Hull
26.11.92	Dean Bramhald L PTS 10 Hull *(Central Area Lightweight Title Defence)*
18.02.93	Dean Bramhald W PTS 10 Hull *(Central Area Lightweight Title Challenge)*
29.04.93	Norman Dhalie W PTS 6 Hull
28.05.93	Phil Holliday L RSC 2 Johannesburg, South Africa
12.11.93	Steve Pollard L PTS 8 Hull
08.12.93	Chris Aston W PTS 6 Hull
09.02.94	Mark Tibbs L RSC 4 Bethnal Green

Career: 24 contests, won 13, drew 1, lost 10.

Leo Turner

Bradford. *Born* Bradford, 17 September, 1970
Lightweight. Ht. 5'9"
Manager J. Celebanski

08.06.92	Wayne Rigby L PTS 6 Bradford
02.07.92	Wayne Rigby L CO 5 Middleton
12.10.92	Micky Hall L RSC 5 Bradford
14.12.92	Fred Reeve W RSC 2 Bradford
25.01.93	Alan Graham L PTS 6 Bradford

08.11.93	Tim Hill L RTD 4 Bradford
07.02.94	Paul Goode W RSC 3 Bradford
03.03.94	Colin Innes DREW 6 Newcastle
21.04.94	Colin Innes L PTS 6 Gateshead
09.05.94	Ian Richardson DREW 6 Bradford
13.06.94	Colin Innes W PTS 6 Bradford

Career: 11 contests, won 3, drew 2, lost 6.

Matthew Turner

Rhoose. *Born* Cardiff, 20 September, 1968
L. Middleweight. Ht. 5'9"
Manager B. Hearn

19.01.93	Steve Thomas W PTS 6 Cardiff
30.03.93	Mark Dawson W PTS 6 Cardiff
19.05.93	Stuart Dunn L RSC 3 Leicester
30.11.93	Gary Pemberton W RTD 4 Cardiff

Career: 4 contests, won 3, lost 1.

Jimmy Tyers

Spennymoor. *Born* Bishop Auckland, 23 March, 1967
L. Heavyweight. Ht. 6'0"
Manager T. Callighan

19.04.93	Mark Buck W RSC 4 Manchester
12.05.93	Kevin Bailey W PTS 6 Sheffield
22.11.93	Joe McCluskey L PTS 6 Glasgow
07.02.94	Craig Joseph L PTS 6 Bradford
24.02.94	Paul Hitch L PTS 6 Hull

Career: 5 contests, won 2, lost 3.

Jobie Tyers

Newcastle. *Born* Cleveland, 8 August, 1975
S. Bantamweight. Ht. 5'4"
Manager D. Gregory

27.10.93	Gary Marston L PTS 6 Stoke
25.01.94	Justin Murphy L RSC 3 Piccadilly

Career: 2 contests, lost 2.

Greg Upton   Les Clark

Greg Upton

Teignmouth. *Born* Canada, 11 June, 1971
Lightweight. Western Area S.
Featherweight Champion. Ht. 5'5½"
Manager G. Bousted

28.11.91	Eunan Devenney W PTS 6 Evesham
29.04.92	Chris Morris W RSC 2 Liverpool
01.06.92	Graham McGrath W PTS 6 Solihull
19.11.92	Mark Hargreaves L RSC 3 Evesham
24.03.93	Barry Jones L RSC 2 Cardiff
27.05.93	Trevor Royal W CO 2 Bristol
	(Vacant Western Area S.
	Featherweight Title)
28.10.93	Graham McGrath W PTS 8 Torquay
03.03.94	Sean Knight L RSC 6 Ebbw Vale
25.06.94	Steve Edwards DREW 6 Cullompton

Career: 9 contests, won 5, drew 1, lost 3.

Rudy Valentino (Isaacs)

Plumstead. *Born* London, 6 July, 1964
L. Welterweight. Ht. 5'6"
Manager Self

22.10.86	Mike Russell W PTS 6 Greenwich
26.11.86	Tim O'Keefe W PTS 6 Lewisham
19.03.87	Neil Haddock W PTS 6 Bethnal Green
30.04.87	Marvin P. Gray W PTS 6 Washington
15.09.87	Peter Crook L PTS 6 Kensington
18.11.87	Paul Burke L PTS 6 Bethnal Green
02.12.87	Mark Pearce W PTS 6 Piccadilly
18.01.88	John Dickson W PTS 6 Mayfair
08.03.88	James Jiora W PTS 6 Batley
05.04.88	Hugh Forde L RSC 2 Birmingham
18.05.88	Chubby Martin L RSC 5 Lewisham
08.02.89	Paul Moylett W RSC 2 Kensington
15.02.89	Richard Joyce L PTS 6 Stoke
24.04.89	Steve Topliss W PTS 6 Nottingham
21.06.89	Sugar Gibiliru W PTS 6 Eltham
04.09.89	Jose Tuominen L RSC 2 Helsinki, Finland
19.10.89	Harry Escott L RTD 4 Manchester

27.03.90	Peter Bradley L PTS 8 Mayfair
23.04.90	Lee Amass W RSC 6 Crystal Palace
28.05.90	Pierre Lorcy L PTS 8 Paris, France
20.10.90	Gianni di Napoli DREW 8 Leon, France
15.12.90	Angel Mona L PTS 8 Vichy, France
10.04.91	Marcel Herbert W RSC 3 Newport
	((Elim. British Lightweight Title)
17.07.91	Giovanni Parisi L PTS 8 Abbiategrasso, Italy
13.09.91	Giorgio Campanella L PTS 8 Gaggiano, Italy
19.02.92	Michael Ayers L RSC 7 Muswell Hill
	(Southern Area Lightweight Title Challenge & Elim. British Lightweight Title)
17.09.93	Soren Sondergaard L PTS 6 Copenhagen, Denmark
29.10.93	Racheed Lawal L CO 1 Korsoer, Denmark

Career: 28 contests, won 12, drew 1, lost 15.

Carl van Bailey

Cullompton. *Born* St. Albans, 5 October, 1963
L. Middleweight. Ht. 5'8"
Manager D. Brownson

13.11.93	Bullit Andrews W PTS 6 Cullompton
16.03.94	Warren Stephens L PTS 6 Birmingham
25.06.94	Dewi Roberts L RSC 2 Cullompton

Career: 3 contests, won 1, lost 2.

Chris Vassiliou

Margate. *Born* Hitchin, 18 June, 1963
L. Middleweight. Ht. 5'11"
Manager P. Byrne

22.02.93	Darren Blackford L RSC 1 Eltham
26.06.93	Glenn Catley L CO 2 Keynsham
27.05.94	Harry Dhamie L RSC 5 Ashford

Career: 3 contests, lost 3.

Des Vaughan

Sydenham. *Born* Lewisham, 3 January, 1965
Cruiserweight. Ht. 6'4"
Manager Self

25.10.90	Coco Collins W CO 1 Battersea
18.02.91	Rob Albon L PTS 6 Windsor
05.03.92	Rocky Shelly W RSC 5 Battersea
28.10.92	Phil Soundy L RTD 4 Kensington
18.09.93	Scott Welch L RSC 2 Leicester
01.12.93	Paul Lawson L RSC 3 Bethnal Green

Career: 6 contests, won 2, lost 4.

Louis Veitch

Glasgow. *Born* Glasgow, 9 March, 1963
Central Area Flyweight Champion. Ht. 5'2"
Manager J. McMillan

09.10.91	Tucker Thomas W RSC 4 Marton
11.11.91	Shaun Norman L RSC 5 Bradford
12.03.92	Neil Armstrong L PTS 6 Glasgow
10.04.92	Mark Robertson L PTS 6 Glasgow
16.05.92	Mickey Cantwell L PTS 6 Muswell Hill
09.07.92	Paul Weir L PTS 6 Glasgow
11.09.92	Neil Armstrong L PTS 6 Glasgow
26.10.92	Nick Tooley L PTS 6 Cleethorpes
14.12.92	Lyndon Kershaw DREW 6 Bradford

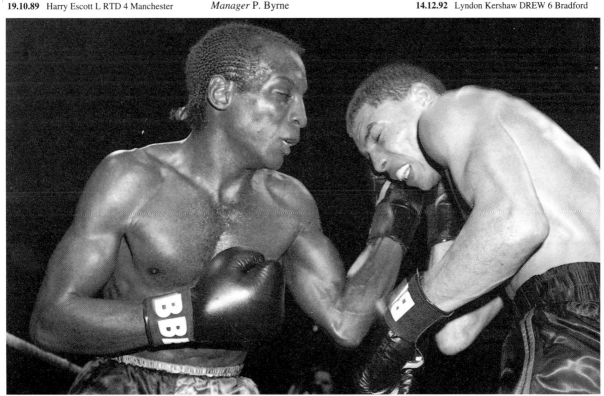

Rudy Valentino (left) in action against Michael Ayers

Les Clark

29.01.93 Neil Armstrong L PTS 6 Glasgow
10.02.93 Mickey Cantwell DREW 8 Lewisham
29.03.93 Neil Parry W PTS 6 Glasgow
29.05.93 Neil Armstrong L PTS 10 Paisley
07.10.93 Lyndon Kershaw W PTS 10 Hull
(Vacant Central Area Flyweight Title)
22.11.93 James Drummond L PTS 8 Glasgow
02.02.94 Ian Baillie W RSC 1 Glasgow
25.03.94 Jesper David Jensen L PTS 6
Bornholme, Denmark
24.05.94 Vince Feeney L PTS 6 Leicester
Career: 18 contests, won 4, drew 2, lost 12.

Yusuf Vorajee

Coventry. *Born* Bradford, 21 August, 1969
Featherweight. Ht. 5'5½"
Manager R. Gray

30.09.92 Kid McAuley L PTS 6 Solihull
14.10.92 Mark Hargreaves L RSC 4 Stoke
27.01.93 Kid McAuley W RSC 5 Stoke
03.03.93 Stewart Fishermac W RSC 2 Solihull
23.03.93 Garry Burrell W PTS 6
Wolverhampton
05.05.93 John White L PTS 6 Belfast
02.03.94 Mike Deveney L PTS 6 Solihull
23.03.94 Matthew Harris L PTS 6 Stoke
Career: 8 contests, won 3, lost 5.

Peter Vosper

Plymouth. *Born* Plymouth, 6 October, 1966
S. Middleweight. Ht. 5'10"
Manager N. Christian

15.02.89 Mark White W PTS 6 Bethnal Green
01.03.89 Lester Jacobs L PTS 6 Bethnal Green
29.03.89 George Moody L PTS 6 Bethnal Green
09.05.89 Tony Cloak W RSC 2 Plymouth
20.06.89 Spencer Alton W PTS 6 Plymouth
17.10.89 Spencer Alton DREW 8 Plymouth
30.11.89 Ray Webb L PTS 6 Southwark
03.03.90 Michael Gale L RSC 2 Wembley
26.04.90 Michael Clarke L PTS 6 Wandsworth
21.05.90 Chris Walker W RSC 2 Mayfair
26.09.90 Ali Forbes L PTS 6 Mayfair
12.04.91 Frank Eubanks L RSC 1 Manchester
30.05.91 Russell Washer W PTS 6 Mayfair
06.06.91 John Kaighin DREW 6 Barking
27.06.91 Nick Manners L RSC 1 Leeds
16.12.91 Paul McCarthy L PTS 6 Southampton
25.02.92 Roland Ericsson L RSC 6 Crystal
Palace
01.12.92 John Kaighin L RSC 4 Bristol
13.11.93 Martin Rosamond W PTS 6
Cullompton
04.03.94 Cliff Churchward W PTS 8 Weston
super Mare
17.06.94 Paul Murray W PTS 8 Plymouth
Career: 21 contests, won 8, drew 2, lost 11.

Nicky Wadman

Brighton. *Born* Brighton, 8 August, 1965
Cruiserweight. Ht. 6'1"
Manager Self

11.03.92 Julian Johnson W PTS 6 Cardiff
23.04.92 Mark McBiane W RSC 1 Eltham
26.09.92 Hussain Shah L RSC 4 Earls Court
29.01.93 Alan Smiles L PTS 6 Glasgow
22.02.93 Steve Osborne W PTS 6 Eltham
21.10.93 Bobby Mack L PTS 6 Bayswater
09.02.94 Paul Lawson L RSC 1 Bethnal Green
21.05.94 Ray Kane L PTS 6 Belfast
Career: 8 contests, won 3, lost 5.

Scott Walker

Shaw. *Born* Oldham, 5 December, 1970
L. Welterweight. Ht. 5'5"
Manager J. Doughty

18.04.94 Paul Bowen W PTS 6 Manchester
02.06.94 Brian Coleman W CO 1 Middleton
Career: 2 contests, won 2.

Steve Walker

Manchester. *Born* Manchester, 25 June,
1963
S. Featherweight. Ht. 5'7"
Manager Self

14.09.89 Edward Cook L PTS 6 Motherwell
28.09.89 Miguel Matthews W PTS 6 Cardiff
04.10.89 Paul Harvey DREW 6 Basildon
30.10.89 Jason Lepre W CO 2 Piccadilly
04.11.89 Edward Cook W PTS 4 Eastbourne
28.11.89 Alan McKay DREW 6 Battersea
18.12.89 John Milne DREW 6 Glasgow
23.02.90 Tommy Graham W RSC 4 Irvine
08.03.90 John Milne DREW 8 Glasgow
28.03.90 Francisco Arroyo W PTS 6 Manchester
03.05.90 Colin McMillan L PTS 6 Wembley
04.06.90 Gary Peynado W PTS 6 Edgbaston
09.10.90 Ian McGirr W RSC 4 Glasgow
29.10.90 Karl Taylor DREW 6 Birmingham
12.11.90 Muhammad Shaffique W PTS 6
Stratford upon Avon
24.01.91 Richie Foster W PTS 8 Brierley Hill
02.03.91 Harry Escott DREW 6 Darlington
19.03.91 Mark Holt W PTS 8 Birmingham
20.09.91 Harry Escott DREW 6 Manchester
13.11.91 Ian Honeywood L PTS 6 Bethnal
Green
18.07.92 Kelton McKenzie L CO 2 Manchester
19.03.93 Mick Mulcahy W RSC 6 Manchester
26.04.93 Kevin McKillan DREW 8 Manchester
25.07.93 Neil Haddock L RSC 7 Oldham
(British S. Featherweight Title
Challenge)
Career: 24 contests, won 11, drew 8, lost 5.

Steve Walton

Whitley Bay. *Born* Wallsend, 3 December,
1972
L. Heavyweight. Ht. 6'2"
Manager N. Fawcett

28.05.92 Greg Scott-Briggs L PTS 6 Gosforth
15.09.93 Kevin Bailey W PTS 6 Newcastle
Career: 2 contests, won 1, lost 1.

Tony Walton

Liverpool. *Born* Liverpool, 28 September,
1972
L. Middleweight. Ht. 5'10"
Manager C. Moorcroft

16.02.94 Geoff McCreesh L PTS 6 Stevenage
11.03.94 Steve McNess L PTS 4 Bethnal Green
Career: 2 contests, lost 2.

Anthony Wanza

Croydon. *Born* Trinidad, 15 December,
1961
Lightweight. Ht. 5'7"
Manager G. Steene

29.05.81 Martin Julius DREW 4 Port of Spain,
Trinidad

29.01.82 Walt Bishop L PTS 6 Port of Spain,
Trinidad
19.08.83 Waldron Brooks W PTS 8 Port of
Spain, Trinidad
02.12.83 Samuel Brutus L PTS 8 Port of Spain,
Trinidad
01.12.88 Muhammad Aleen L RSC 3 Port of
Spain, Trinidad
03.11.89 Harvey Huggins DREW 8 Port of
Spain, Trinidad
04.04.93 Cham Joof L RSC 2 Brockley
21.06.93 Ray Hood L PTS 6 Swindon
13.10.93 Chris Francis L RSC 2 Bethnal Green
Career: 9 contests, won 1, drew 2, lost 6.

Russell Washer

Swansea. *Born* Swansea, 21 January, 1962
Middleweight. Ht. 5'10"
Manager Self

15.09.90 Dean Cooper L PTS 6 Bristol
02.10.90 Nick Gyaamie W RSC 4 Eltham
16.10.90 Wayne Panayiotiou W RSC 2 Evesham
29.10.90 Chris Walker L RSC 2 Nottingham
11.12.90 Matt Mowatt W RSC 6 Evesham
24.01.91 Wayne Panayiotiou W RSC 4
Gorseinon
21.02.91 Marvin O'Brien DREW 6 Walsall
19.03.91 Tony Meszaros L PTS 6 Birmingham
10.04.91 Andrew Flute L PTS 6 Wolverhampton
30.05.91 Peter Vosper L PTS 6 Mayfair
04.09.91 Val Golding L RTD 5 Bethnal Green
11.11.91 Stinger Mason L PTS 4 Stratford on
Avon
20.11.91 Alan Richards L PTS 6 Cardiff
29.11.91 Ensley Bingham L RSC 4 Manchester
11.03.92 Lee Crocker L PTS 6 Cardiff
22.04.92 Gilbert Jackson L PTS 6 Wembley
11.05.92 Carlo Colarusso L RSC 5 Llanelli
(Welsh L. Middleweight Title
Challenge)
18.06.92 Tony Collins L RSC 2 Peterborough
03.09.92 John Bosco L RSC 2 Dunstable
05.10.92 Sean Byrne L PTS 6 Northampton
15.10.92 Jerry Mortimer L RSC 5 Lewisham
28.11.92 Paul Wright L PTS 8 Manchester
10.12.92 Abel Asinamali W PTS 6 Bethnal
Green
27.01.93 Barry Thorogood L PTS 6 Cardiff
03.02.93 Kevin Sheeran L PTS 6 Earls Court
27.02.93 Jamie Robinson L PTS 6 Dagenham
24.03.93 Robert Peel L PTS 6 Cardiff
31.03.93 Kevin Adamson L PTS 6 Barking
10.04.93 Ray Price W RSC 4 Swansea
23.05.93 Darren Blackford W PTS 6 Brockley
23.06.93 Adrian Dodson L PTS 6 Edmonton
25.07.93 Steve Foster L PTS 6 Oldham
14.08.93 Quinn Paynter L RSC 4 Hammersmith
22.09.93 Kevin Adamson L PTS 6 Bethnal
Green
25.10.93 Danny Peters L PTS 6 Liverpool
03.11.93 Darren Dorrington L PTS 4 Bristol
10.11.93 Kevin Sheeran L PTS 6 Bethnal Green
30.11.93 Willie Quinn L PTS 6 Cardiff
23.02.94 Robert Allen L RSC 4 Watford
Career: 39 contests, won 7, drew 1, lost 31.

Peter Waudby

Hull. *Born* Hull, 18 November, 1970
Middleweight. Ht. 5'10½"
Manager L. Billany

21.09.92 Simon Fisher W RSC 2 Cleethorpes
16.10.92 Chris Mulcahy W RSC 4 Hull
14.12.92 Shamus Casey W PTS 6 Cleethorpes

10.05.93	Julian Eavis W PTS 6 Cleethorpes
27.05.93	Warren Stowe L PTS 6 Burnley
16.09.93	Shamus Casey W PTS 6 Hull
10.11.93	Roy Rowland W RSC 5 Watford
13.12.93	Chris Richards W PTS 6 Cleethorpes
17.03.94	Dave Johnson W PTS 6 Lincoln
15.04.94	Colin Pitters W PTS 8 Hull
16.05.94	Shamus Casey W PTS 6 Cleethorpes

Career: 11 contests, won 10, lost 1.

Delroy Waul

Manchester. *Born* Manchester, 3 May, 1970
Welterweight. Ht. 6'1"
Manager F. Warren

29.05.89	Calum Rattray W PTS 6 Dundee
12.06.89	Calum Rattray W PTS 6 Glasgow
25.09.89	Jimmy Reynolds W RSC 4 Birmingham
10.10.89	David Maw W PTS 4 Sunderland
05.12.89	Richard Adams W RSC 4 Dewsbury
11.01.90	Richard Adams W RSC 3 Dewsbury
22.10.90	Jim Talbot W RTD 3 Mayfair
15.11.90	Mike Russell W CO 1 Oldham
13.12.90	Kid Sylvester W RSC 6 Dewsbury
31.01.91	Kevin Hayde W RSC 6 Bredbury
13.02.91	Chris Richards W PTS 6 Wembley
14.03.91	Terry Morrill DREW 8 Middleton
02.05.91	Andrew Furlong W RSC 5 Northampton
16.05.91	Paul Wesley W RSC 7 Liverpool
20.06.91	Gordon Blair L CO 2 Liverpool
09.10.91	Paul King W RSC 6 Manchester
19.12.91	Jason Rowe W RSC 4 Oldham
31.01.92	Patrick Vungbo L DIS 8 Waregem, Belgium
02.07.92	Jimmy Thornton W RSC 6 Middleton
13.02.93	Wayne Shepherd W RSC 5 Manchester
25.06.93	Bruno Wuestenberg L PTS 8 Brussels, Belgium
01.11.93	Lansana Diallo DREW 6 Izegem, Belgium

Career: 22 contests, won 17, drew 2, lost 3.

Ray Webb

Stepney. *Born* Hackney, 10 March, 1966
S. Middleweight. Ht. 5'11"
Manager Self

02.11.88	Doug Calderwood W RSC 6 Southwark
12.01.89	Robert Gomez W RSC 1 Southwark
30.11.89	Peter Vosper W PTS 6 Southwark
06.04.90	Carlo Colarusso L PTS 6 Telford
15.09.90	Ray Close L PTS 8 Belfast
06.11.90	Ahmet Canbakis W PTS 6 Mayfair
08.12.90	Franck Nicotra L PTS 8 Ferrara, Italy
10.01.91	Carlos Christie W PTS 6 Wandsworth
27.03.91	Silvio Branco L PTS 8 Mestre, Italy
30.05.91	Karl Barwise W PTS 8 Mayfair
11.12.91	Ian Strudwick L CO 8 Basildon (Vacant Southern Area S. Middleweight Title)
06.03.92	Oleg Volkov L PTS 8 Berlin, Germany
28.11.93	Karl Barwise W PTS 6 Southwark
06.03.94	Trevor Ambrose W RSC 6 Southwark
27.04.94	Darron Griffiths L RSC 6 Bethnal Green (Elim. British S. Middleweight Title)

Career: 15 contests, won 8, lost 7.

Paul Webster   Les Clark

Paul Webster

Barking. *Born* Doncaster, 26 December, 1974
S. Bantamweight. Ht. 5'6"
Manager B. Lynch

22.09.93	Kevin Simons W RSC 2 Bethnal Green
10.11.93	James Murray W PTS 4 Bethnal Green
17.02.94	Danny Ruegg W PTS 4 Dagenham

Career: 3 contests, won 3.

Paul Weir

Irvine. *Born* Glasgow, 16 September, 1967
Flyweight. Former Undefeated WBO M. Flyweight Champion. Ht. 5'3"
Manager T. Gilmour

27.04.92	Eduardo Vallejo W CO 2 Glasgow
09.07.92	Louis Veitch W PTS 6 Glasgow
21.09.92	Neil Parry W RSC 4 Glasgow
23.11.92	Shaun Norman W PTS 8 Glasgow
06.03.93	Kevin Jenkins W PTS 8 Glasgow
15.05.93	Fernando Martinez W RSC 7 Glasgow (Vacant WBO M. Flyweight Title)
25.10.93	Lindi Memani W PTS 12 Glasgow (WBO M. Flyweight Title Defence)
02.02.94	Josue Camacho L PTS 12 Glasgow (WBO L. Flyweight Title Challenge)

Career: 8 contests, won 7, lost 1.

Paul Weir   George Ashton

Scott Welch

Brighton. *Born* Yarmouth, 21 April, 1968
Heavyweight. Ht. 6'2"
Manager B. Hearn

08.09.92	John Williams W RSC 5 Norwich	
06.10.92	Gary Williams W PTS 4 Antwerp, Belgium	
23.02.93	Gary Charlton L RSC 3 Doncaster	
11.05.93	Denroy Bryan W RSC 4 Norwich	
29.06.93	John Harewood W RSC 5 Mayfair	
18.09.93	Des Vaughan W RSC 2 Leicester	
28.09.93	Gypsy Carman W RSC 3 Bethnal Green	
05.10.93	Cordwell Hylton W RSC 1 Mayfair	
06.11.93	Joey Paladino W RSC 3 Bethnal Green	
30.11.93	Chris Coughlan W CO 1 Cardiff	
21.12.93	Carl Gaffney W RSC 3 Mayfair	
15.03.94	Steve Garber W RSC 4 Mayfair	
06.05.94	James Oyebola L CO 5 Atlantic City, USA	

(Vacant WBC International Heavyweight Title)

Career: 13 contests, won 11, lost 2.

Bradley Welsh

Edinburgh. *Born* Edinburgh, 4 November, 1970
Lightweight. Ht. 5'10"
Manager A. Melrose

11.03.94	Brian Wright W PTS 6 Glasgow	
13.04.94	John T. Kelly W PTS 6 Glasgow	
13.05.94	Chris Bennett W RSC 3 Kilmarnock	
10.06.94	Kid McAuley W RTD 1 Glasgow	

Career: 4 contests, won 4.

Paul Wesley

Birmingham. *Born* Birmingham, 2 May, 1962
Middleweight. Ht. 5'9"
Manager N. Nobbs

20.02.87	B. K. Bennett L PTS 6 Maidenhead	
18.03.87	Darryl Ritchie DREW 4 Stoke	
08.04.87	Dean Murray W PTS 6 Evesham	
29.04.87	John Wright W PTS 4 Loughborough	
12.06.87	Leon Thomas W RSC 2 Leamington	
16.11.87	Steve McCarthy L CO 8 Southampton	
25.01.88	Paul Murray W PTS 8 Birmingham	
29.02.88	Paul Murray DREW 8 Birmingham	
15.03.88	Johnny Williamson W CO 2 Bournemouth	
09.04.88	Joe McKenzie W RSC 6 Bristol	
10.05.88	Tony Meszaros W PTS 8 Edgbaston	
21.03.89	Carlton Warren L CO 2 Wandsworth	
10.05.89	Rod Douglas L CO 1 Kensington	
24.10.89	Nigel Rafferty L PTS 6 Wolverhampton	
22.11.89	Nigel Rafferty L PTS 8 Stafford	
28.11.89	Nigel Rafferty L PTS 6 Wolverhampton	
05.12.89	Ian Strudwick L PTS 6 Catford	
24.01.90	Rocky Feliciello W PTS 6 Solihull	
19.02.90	Nigel Rafferty L PTS 8 Birmingham	
22.03.90	John Ashton L PTS 10 Wolverhampton	

(Midlands Area Middleweight Title Challenge)

17.04.90	Winston May DREW 8 Millwall	
09.05.90	Alan Richards W PTS 8 Solihull	
04.06.90	Julian Eavis W PTS 8 Birmingham	
18.09.90	Shaun Cummins L RSC 1 Wolverhampton	
17.10.90	Julian Eavis W PTS 6 Stoke	
23.01.91	Wally Swift Jnr L PTS 10 Solihull	

(Midlands Area L. Middleweight Title Challenge)

20.03.91	Horace Fleary L RSC 5 Solihull	
16.05.91	Delroy Waul L RSC 7 Liverpool	
04.07.91	Neville Brown W RSC 1 Alfreton	
31.07.91	Francesco dell'Aquila L PTS 8 Casella, Italy	
03.10.91	Neville Brown L PTS 8 Burton	
29.10.91	Tony Collins DREW 8 Kensington	
03.03.92	Antonio Fernandez L PTS 10 Cradley Heath	

(Vacant Midlands Area Middleweight Title)

10.04.92	Jean-Charles Meuret L PTS 8 Geneva, Switzerland	
03.06.92	Sumbu Kalambay L PTS 10 Salice Terme, Italy	
29.10.92	Ian Strudwick W RSC 1 Bayswater	
14.11.92	Paul Busby L PTS 8 Cardiff	
24.11.92	Paul Jones W RSC 2 Doncaster	
16.03.93	Chris Pyatt L PTS 10 Mayfair	
04.06.93	Jacques le Blanc L PTS 10 Moncton, Canada	
28.07.93	Antonio Fernandez L RSC 3 Brixton	

(Midlands Area Middleweight Title Challenge)

09.10.93	Warren Stowe W PTS 10 Manchester	

(Elim. British L. Middleweight Title)

09.02.94	Steve Collins L PTS 8 Brentwood	

Career: 43 contests, won 15, drew 4, lost 24.

Paul Wesley   Les Clark

Darren Westover

Ilford. *Born* Plaistow, 3 September, 1963
Cruiserweight. Ht. 6'3"
Manager M. Duff

04.10.89	Dave Furneaux W RSC 1 Kensington	
25.10.89	David Haycock W RSC 2 Wembley	
06.12.89	Kevin Roper W RSC 1 Wembley	
03.03.90	Steve Osborne W RSC 6 Wembley	
26.04.94	Newbirth Mukosi W RSC 5 Bethnal Green	
11.05.94	Art Stacey W PTS 6 Stevenage	

Career: 6 contests, won 6.

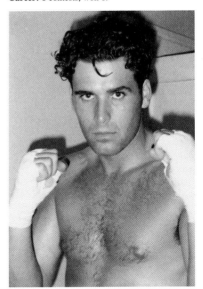

Darren Westover   Les Clark

Andre Wharton

Brierley Hill. *Born* Wordsley, 16 June, 1969
L. Middleweight. Ht. 5'8"
Manager M. Shinfield

13.11.89	Bullit Andrews W PTS 6 Brierley Hill	
05.02.90	Bullit Andrews W RSC 4 Brierley Hill	
19.03.90	Gary Dyson DREW 6 Brierley Hill	
03.09.90	David Radford W RSC 5 Dudley	
15.10.90	Mick Duncan W PTS 6 Brierley Hill	
24.01.91	Stefan Wright W RSC 5 Brierley Hill	
18.02.91	Dean Cooper L PTS 8 Birmingham	
15.03.91	Wayne Appleton W RSC 7 Willenhall	
27.10.92	Geoff Calder W PTS 4 Cradley Heath	
03.11.93	Steve Scott W PTS 6 Worcester	

Career: 10 contests, won 8, drew 1, lost 1.

Gary White

Rochdale. *Born* Littleborough, 13 April, 1971
Bantamweight. Ht. 5'7"
Manager J. Doughty

28.02.91	Stevie Woods W PTS 6 Bury	
18.03.91	Tony Smith W PTS 6 Manchester	
17.05.91	Neil Parry W PTS 6 Bury	
07.12.92	Robert Braddock W PTS 6 Manchester	
19.01.94	Graham McGrath W PTS 6 Solihull	
28.02.94	Mickey Bell W PTS 6 Manchester	

Career: 6 contests, won 6.

John White

Salford. *Born* Manchester, 6 November, 1970
Featherweight. Ht. 5'6"
Manager F. Warren

27.02.92	Alan Smith W RSC 1 Liverpool	
02.07.92	Norman Dhalie W RSC 6 Middleton	

25.07.92	Ronnie Stephenson W PTS 6 Manchester	
13.10.92	Kid McAuley W PTS 4 Bury	
28.11.92	Mark Hargreaves W PTS 4 Manchester	
13.02.93	Norman Dhalie W CO 2 Manchester	
05.05.93	Yusuf Vorajee W PTS 6 Belfast	
09.10.93	Barry Jones L PTS 4 Manchester	
18.12.93	Miguel Matthews W PTS 6 Manchester	

Career: 9 contests, won 8, lost 1.

(Anthony) Kane White
Chesterfield. *Born* Chesterfield, 7 June, 1969
Welterweight. Ht. 5'10"
Manager M. Shinfield

02.12.93 Shaun Cogan L RSC 1 Evesham
Career: 1 contest, lost 1.

Robert Whitehouse
Swansea. *Born* Oxford, 9 October, 1965
Welterweight. Ht. 5'9"
Manager M. Copp

08.09.92 Jerry Mortimer L RSC 3 Southend
23.10.92 Steve Foran L RSC 2 Liverpool
03.12.92 Jason Beard L RSC 3 Lewisham
27.02.93 Kevin Adamson L RSC 1 Dagenham
07.12.93 Steve McNess L RSC 3 Bethnal Green
Career: 5 contests, lost 5.

Dave Whittle
Newcastle. *Born* North Shields, 19 May, 1966
L. Middleweight. Ht. 5'9"
Manager T. Conroy

22.11.88 Mark Jay L PTS 6 Marton
28.02.89 Tony Farrell W PTS 6 Marton
31.03.89 Seamus Sheridan W RSC 2 Scarborough
19.05.89 Chris Mulcahy L PTS 6 Gateshead
03.06.89 Ian Thomas W PTS 6 Stanley
13.12.89 Ian Thomas W PTS 6 Kirkby
27.02.90 Trevor Meikle DREW 8 Marton
04.06.90 Bullit Andrews W PTS 6 Edgbaston
29.11.90 Trevor Meikle W PTS 6 Marton
13.05.91 Barry Messam L PTS 6 Marton
23.10.91 Jamie Robinson L RSC 4 Bethnal Green
27.11.91 Alan Peacock W PTS 6 Marton
02.03.92 Jimmy Thornton L PTS 6 Marton
12.03.92 Alan Peacock DREW 8 Glasgow
14.04.92 Nigel Bradley L CO 3 Mansfield
18.05.92 Wayne Shepherd L PTS 6 Marton
17.03.93 Dean Hiscox W PTS 6 Stoke
11.06.93 Steve Scott W PTS 6 Gateshead
25.11.93 Bullit Andrews W PTS 6 Newcastle
03.03.94 Mark Jay W PTS 8 Newcastle
21.04.94 Rick North W PTS 6 Gateshead
Career: 21 contests, won 12, drew 2, lost 7.

(Robert) B. F. Williams
Watford. *Born* Park Royal, 14 December, 1965
L. Welterweight. Ht. 5'11"
Manager R. Colson

28.05.86 Kenny Watson W RSC 5 Lewisham
01.10.86 Andrew Prescod L RSC 4 Lewisham
27.01.87 Jess Rundan L PTS 6 Plymouth

18.02.87	Dave Nash W RSC 3 Fulham	
19.03.87	Les Remikie W PTS 6 Bethnal Green	
15.04.87	John Mullen L PTS 6 Lewisham	
30.04.87	Paul Kennedy W PTS 6 Washington	
18.09.87	Mike Russell W PTS 8 Swindon	
19.11.87	Ian Hosten W PTS 6 Wandsworth	
09.12.87	Chubby Martin DREW 8 Greenwich	
17.02.88	Neil Haddock W PTS 8 Bethnal Green	
28.09.88	Tony Borg L RSC 7 Edmonton	
28.11.88	Jim Lawlor L PTS 6 Edgbaston	
31.01.89	Danny Ellis W RSC 6 Bethnal Green	
29.03.89	Paul Charters W PTS 6 Bethnal Green	
26.04.89	Seamus O'Sullivan L RSC 6 Battersea	
15.09.89	Tony Gibbs W PTS 6 High Wycombe	
25.10.89	Richard Joyce W RSC 4 Stoke	
12.12.89	Steve Taggart W RSC 2 Brentford	
16.01.90	Mike Morrison W PTS 6 Cardiff	
22.02.90	Michael Driscoll L CO 2 Wandsworth	
25.10.90	Danny Cooper L PTS 6 Battersea	
14.11.90	Nigel Bradley L CO 2 Sheffield	
07.02.91	Rick Bushell L RTD 2 Watford	
12.02.92	Cliff Churchward W PTS 6 Watford	
07.04.92	Erwin Edwards W PTS 6 Southend	
30.04.92	Trevor Meikle W PTS 6 Watford	
17.09.92	James Campbell W PTS 6 Watford	
17.04.93	Jean Chiarelli L PTS 8 Gaillard, France	
24.06.93	Michael Dick W RTD 3 Watford	
13.10.93	Michael Dick W RSC 1 Watford	
09.12.93	David Lake W RSC 4 Watford	
10.03.94	Jonathan Thaxton L RSC 4 Watford	
	(Vacant Southern Area L. Welterweight Title)	

Career: 33 contests, won 20, drew 1, lost 12.

Derek Williams
Battersea. *Born* Stockwell, 11 March, 1965
Former European & Commonwealth Heavyweight Champion. Ht. 6'5"
Manager Self

24.10.84 Tony Tricker W RSC 6 Mayfair
24.01.85 Mike Creasey W RSC 3 Streatham
11.02.85 Barry Ellis W RSC 2 Dulwich
25.03.85 Alphonso Forbes W RSC 2 Merton
20.09.85 Ron Ellis L PTS 8 Longford
30.01.86 Steve Gee W PTS 6 Merton

Derek Williams   Peter Shaw

22.02.87	Steve Gee W PTS 6 Wembley	
24.03.87	Andrew Gerrard W PTS 6 Wembley	
25.06.87	Jess Harding W PTS 6 Bethnal Green	
08.10.87	John Westgarth W RSC 7 Bethnal Green	
28.01.88	Dave Garside W PTS 10 Bethnal Green	
18.05.88	Mark Young W CO 4 Portsmouth	
26.10.88	John Westgarth W RSC 2 Kensington	
29.11.88	Young Haumona W CO 4 Kensington	
	(Vacant Commonwealth Heavyweight Title)	
14.02.89	Noel Quarless W CO 1 Wandsworth	
05.04.89	Al Evans W RSC 2 Kensington	
24.08.89	Mark Wills L PTS 8 New York, USA	
05.12.89	Hughroy Currie W RSC 1 Catford	
	(Vacant European Heavyweight Title. Commonwealth Heavyweight Title Defence)	
03.02.90	Jean Chanet L PTS 12 St Didier, France	
	(European Heavyweight Title Defence)	
28.05.90	Jean Chanet L PTS 12 Paris, France	
	(European Heavyweight Title Challenge)	
01.05.91	Jimmy Thunder W RSC 2 Bethnal Green	
	(Commonwealth Heavyweight Title Defence)	
30.09.91	David Bey W RTD 6 Kensington	
18.01.92	Tim Anderson W RSC 1 Kensington	
30.04.92	Lennox Lewis L RSC 3 Kensington	
	(Commonwealth Heavyweight Title Defence. British & European Heavyweight Title Challenge)	
25.03.93	Bert Cooper L PTS 10 Atlantic City, USA	
03.12.93	Jose Ribalta DREW 3 St Louis, USA	

Career: 26 contests, won 19, drew 1, lost 6.

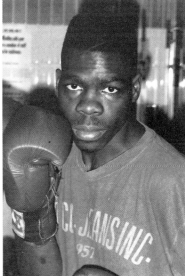

Everald Williams   Les Clark

Everald Williams
Hornsey. *Born* Jamaica, 10 June, 1969
L. Welterweight. Ht. 5'9"
Manager J. Ryan

05.03.92 Korso Aleain W CO 6 Battersea

28.11.93 Michael Alexander W PTS 6 Southwark
06.03.94 Mike Morrison W PTS 4 Southwark
28.05.94 Steve Burton DREW 6 Queensway
Career: 4 contests, won 3, drew 1.

Gary Williams

Nottingham. *Born* Nottingham, 25 September, 1965
Heavyweight, Ht. 5'11½"
Manager W. Swift

27.04.92 Damien Caesar L RSC 4 Mayfair
07.09.92 J. A. Bugner L PTS 4 Bethnal Green
06.10.92 Scott Welch L PTS 4 Antwerp, Belgium
01.12.92 Kenny Sandison W PTS 6 Liverpool
27.01.93 Kenny Sandison DREW 6 Stoke
13.02.93 Kevin McBride L PTS 4 Manchester
01.03.93 Ashley Naylor DREW 6 Bradford
29.03.93 Kevin Cullinane W RSC 2 Liverpool
26.04.93 Ashley Naylor W PTS 6 Bradford
21.07.93 Peter Smith L RSC 4 Marula, South Africa
08.12.93 Graham Arnold L PTS 6 Hull

02.02.94 Vincenzo Cantatore L CO 2 Ferrara, Italy
17.03.94 Neil Kirkwood L RSC 1 Lincoln
Career: 13 contests, won 3, drew 2, lost 8.

(John) J. T. Williams

Cwmbran. *Born* Pontylottyn, 22 May, 1970
Welsh S. Featherweight Champion. Ht. 5'6¾"
Manager M. Jacobs

21.01.91 Kelton McKenzie DREW 6 Crystal Palace
10.04.91 Dave Buxton W PTS 8 Newport
28.05.91 Frankie Ventura W PTS 6 Cardiff
18.07.91 Billy Barton W PTS 6 Cardiff
22.01.92 Derek Amory W PTS 6 Cardiff
30.03.92 Steve Pollard L PTS 6 Eltham
07.10.92 Kevin McKillan W PTS 6 Barry
14.11.92 Peter Judson DREW 6 Cardiff
19.05.93 Dominic McGuigan L PTS 6 Sunderland
01.10.93 Neil Haddock L PTS 10 Cardiff

10.11.93 Barrie Kelley W RTD 3 Ystrad
(Welsh S. Featherweight Title Challenge)
03.03.94 Wayne Windle W RSC 3 Ebbw Vale
Career: 12 contests, won 7, drew 2, lost 3.

(Lee) L. A. Williams

Blackwell. *Born* Caerphilly, 16 March, 1968
Cruiserweight. Ht. 5'10"
Manager D. Gardiner

17.11.88 Ted Cofie L RSC 4 Ilkeston
15.09.89 Rob Albon DREW 6 High Wycombe
24.10.89 Herbie Hide L CO 2 Bethnal Green
16.12.93 Kent Davis L RSC 2 Newport
23.03.94 Darren Ashton L PTS 6 Stoke
07.04.94 John Foreman L RSC 7 Walsall
Career: 6 contests, drew 1, lost 5.

Rowan Williams

Birmingham. *Born* Birmingham, 18 March, 1968
Flyweight. Ht. 5'5½"
Manager Self

17.02.93 Nick Tooley W PTS 4 Bethnal Green
04.04.93 Des Gargano W PTS 4 Brockley
23.06.93 Graham McGrath W PTS 4 Edmonton
01.10.93 Neil Swain L PTS 6 Cardiff
10.02.94 Neil Armstrong L PTS 6 Glasgow
Career: 5 contests, won 3, lost 2.

George Wilson   Les Clark

George Wilson

Camberwell. *Born* London, 7 April, 1966
Welterweight. Ht. 5'10"
Manager F. Rix

18.06.92 Sean Cave L PTS 6 Peterborough
07.07.92 Erwin Edwards L RSC 4 Bristol
08.09.92 Erwin Edwards L RSC 3 Southend
16.02.93 Derrick Daniel W PTS 6 Tooting
23.02.93 Sean Metherell W PTS 6 Kettering
29.03.93 Joel Ani L PTS 6 Mayfair

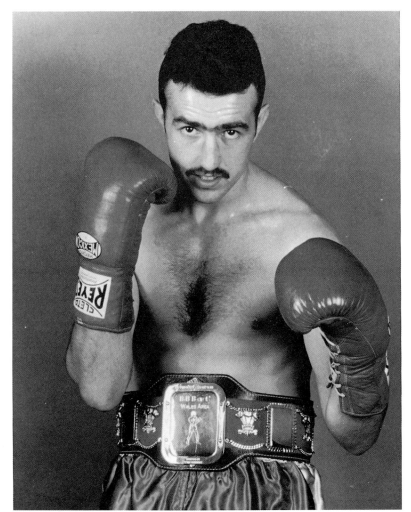

J. T. Williams   John McDonald

21.06.93 Jamie Davidson W RSC 4 Swindon
03.11.93 Sean Baker L RSC 2 Bristol
26.02.94 Michael Carruth L PTS 6 Earls Court
29.03.94 Mark Tibbs L RSC 6 Bethnal Green
Career: 10 contests, won 3, lost 7.

Stephen Wilson

Wallyford. *Born* Edinburgh, 30 March, 1971
S. Middleweight. Ht. 6'0"
Manager T. Gilmour

23.11.92 Lee Prudden W PTS 6 Glasgow
25.01.93 Paul Smith W RSC 1 Glasgow
06.03.93 Dave Owens W RSC 2 Glasgow
23.03.93 Nigel Rafferty L RSC 3 Wolverhampton
07.06.93 Shamus Casey W PTS 6 Glasgow
20.09.93 Stinger Mason W RSC 6 Glasgow
21.02.94 Carlos Christie W RSC 2 Glasgow
28.03.94 Dave Owens W CO 2 Musselburgh
25.04.94 John J. Cooke W PTS 6 Bury
Career: 9 contests, won 8, lost 1.

(Winston) W. O. Wilson

Wandsworth. *Born* Coventry, 9 March, 1965
Southern Area Middleweight Champion. Former Undefeated Southern Area L. Middleweight Champion. Ht. 6'3"
Manager H. Holland

25.03.86 Floyd Davidson W RSC 3 Wandsworth
19.05.86 Steve Ward L DIS 4 Nottingham
08.09.86 Freddie James W PTS 6 Dulwich
22.09.86 Tony Behan W CO 2 Mayfair
25.09.86 Gerald McCarthy W RSC 1 Crystal Palace
23.10.86 Simon Collins W PTS 8 Birmingham
02.03.87 Alex Mullen L PTS 8 Glasgow
01.10.87 Joao Cabreiro W PTS 6 Croydon
28.01.88 Jimmy Cable W CO 2 Bethnal Green
29.11.88 Andy Till L PTS 10 Battersea
29.03.89 Shamus Casey W RSC 5 Wembley
07.06.89 Franki Moro W RTD 4 Wembley
04.10.89 Kevin Hayde W PTS 8 Kensington
14.03.90 Newton Barnett W RSC 1 Kensington
21.01.91 Quinn Paynter L PTS 8 Crystal Palace
07.11.91 Nigel Fairbairn W RSC 8 Peterborough
          (Vacant Southern Area L. Middleweight Title)
06.05.93 John Ogiste W RSC 8 Bayswater
          (Vacant Southern Area Middleweight Title)
23.06.93 Ian Strudwick W RSC 8 Edmonton
          (Southern Area Middleweight Title Defence)
23.02.94 Trevor Ambrose L RSC 5 Watford
Career: 19 contests, won 14, lost 5.

Wayne Windle

Sheffield. *Born* Sheffield, 18 October, 1968
Former Central Area Lightweight Champion. Ht. 5'8"
Manager Self

25.10.88 Mick Mulcahy L PTS 6 Cottingham
17.11.88 Dave Pratt L PTS 6 Ilkeston
02.02.89 Jeff Dobson L RSC 6 Croydon
04.04.89 John Ritchie DREW 4 Sheffield
05.10.89 Des Gargano L PTS 6 Middleton
16.10.89 Des Gargano W PTS 6 Manchester
16.11.89 Noel Carroll L PTS 6 Manchester

04.12.89 Brendan Ryan DREW 6 Manchester
29.01.90 Mike Close W PTS 6 Liverpool
05.02.90 Mike Close W PTS 6 Brierley Hill
22.02.90 Bernard McComiskey W PTS 6 Kensington
12.03.90 Barry North W PTS 6 Hull
21.03.90 Neil Foran L PTS 6 Preston
29.05.90 Terry Collins L PTS 6 Bethnal Green
11.06.90 Muhammad Lovelock W PTS 6 Manchester
12.09.90 Brian Cullen W RSC 1 Stafford
08.10.90 Johnny Walker DREW 6 Leicester
22.10.90 Mick Mulcahy W PTS 4 Cleethorpes
14.11.90 Andy Robins W PTS 6 Sheffield
26.11.90 Michael Driscoll L RSC 3 Bethnal Green
16.01.91 Karl Taylor L PTS 8 Stoke
06.02.91 Felix Kelly L PTS 6 Bethnal Green
12.03.91 Mark Antony W CO 1 Mansfield
24.04.91 Steve Foran L CO 3 Preston
13.06.91 Pete Roberts W RSC 7 Hull
          (Vacant Central Area Lightweight Title)
16.08.91 Aukunun L PTS 6 Marbella, Spain
21.09.91 George Scott L CO 2 Tottenham
10.12.91 Kevin Toomey W PTS 6 Sheffield
26.03.92 Kevin Toomey L DIS 8 Hull
          (Central Area Lightweight Title Defence)
03.09.92 Billy Schwer L CO 1 Dunstable
20.01.93 Mark Elliot L CO 3 Wolverhampton
01.06.93 Mick Mulcahy L PTS 6 Manchester
01.12.93 Gary Thornhill L PTS 6 Stoke
03.03.94 J. T. Williams L RSC 3 Ebbw Vale
Career: 34 contests, won 12, drew 3, lost 19.

Carl Winstone

Newport. *Born* Pontypool, 21 December, 1967
L. Middleweight. Ht. 6'0"
Manager A. Blackstock

22.03.94 Nicky Thurbin L PTS 6 Bethnal Green
Career: 1 contest, lost 1.

Carl Winstone   Les Clark

Craig Winter

Warrington. *Born* Aylesbury, 10 September, 1971
L. Middleweight. Ht. 5'10"
Manager R. Jones

19.12.93 Allan Logan W PTS 6 Glasgow
28.02.94 Wayne Shepherd W PTS 6 Manchester
18.04.94 John Duckworth W RSC 5 Manchester
Career: 3 contests, won 3.

Derek Wormald

Rochdale. *Born* Rochdale, 24 May, 1965
Middleweight. Ht. 5'10"
Manager J. Doughty

28.04.86 Dave Binsteed W RSC 2 Liverpool
20.05.86 Taffy Morris W PTS 6 Huddersfield
16.06.86 Claude Rossi W PTS 6 Manchester
23.09.86 Shamus Casey W PTS 8 Batley
16.10.86 Nigel Moore DREW 6 Merton
11.11.86 David Scere W RSC 3 Batley
25.11.86 Cliff Domville W RSC 4 Manchester
08.12.86 Martin McGough W RTD 4 Edgbaston
10.02.87 Manny Romain W CO 3 Batley
07.04.87 Tony Brown W RSC 6 Batley
28.04.87 Johnny Stone W RSC 1 Manchester
15.09.87 Sammy Sampson W PTS 10 Batley
09.02.88 Richard Wagstaff W RSC 6 Bradford
23.02.88 Judas Clottey W PTS 10 Oldham
12.04.88 John Ashton W RSC 4 Oldham
          (Elim. British L. Middleweight Title)
11.10.89 Gary Stretch L RSC 1 Millwall
          (British L. Middleweight Title Challenge)
24.09.92 Mark Jay W RSC 5 Stockport
27.05.93 Mark Dawson W RTD 5 Burnley
11.11.93 Paul Hitch W RSC 6 Burnley
25.04.94 Martin Jolley W RSC 4 Bury
Career: 20 contests, won 18, drew 1, lost 1.

Andy Wright

Tooting. *Born* Aldershot, 20 December, 1963
Former Undefeated Southern Area S. Middleweight Champion. Ht. 5'11½"
Manager Self

20.03.86 Shamus Casey W RSC 4 Merton
15.04.86 J. J. Smith L PTS 6 Merton
28.05.86 Shamus Casey W PTS 6 Lewisham
04.09.86 Kevin Roper W CO 2 Merton
20.11.86 Winston Burnett W PTS 8 Merton
24.02.87 Nick Vardy W CO 1 Wandsworth
03.06.87 Simon Collins DREW 6 Southwark
24.09.87 Andy Till L RSC 2 Crystal Palace
01.12.87 Alex Romeo W RSC 2 Southend
14.12.87 Paul McCarthy W CO 3 Piccadilly
03.02.88 Steve McCarthy L RSC 4 Wembley
30.03.88 Errol Christie L CO 2 Bethnal Green
15.11.88 Darren Hobson L RSC 3 Hull
08.03.89 Ray Close L RSC 4 Belfast
20.03.91 Paul McCarthy W CO 5 Wandsworth
          (Southern Area S. Middleweight Title Challenge)
22.10.91 John Kaighin DREW 6 Wandsworth
25.02.92 John Kaighin W PTS 6 Crystal Palace
16.02.93 Marvin O'Brien W PTS 6 Tooting
02.06.94 Hunter Clay L RSC 7 Tooting
Career: 19 contests, won 10, drew 2, lost 7.

Brian Wright

Shildon. *Born* Northallerton, 12 December, 1969
L. Welterweight. Ht. 5'8½"
Manager G. Robinson

15.02.93 Mick Hoban L PTS 6 Manchester
06.05.93 Micky Hall L PTS 6 Hartlepool
18.06.93 Bernard McComiskey L PTS 6 Belfast
09.09.93 Tanver Ahmed L RTD 5 Glasgow
02.12.93 John T. Kelly L PTS 6 Hartlepool
11.03.94 Bradley Welsh L PTS 6 Glasgow
25.04.94 Nick Boyd L CO 2 Bury
Career: 7 contests, lost 7.

Carl Wright

Liverpool. *Born* Liverpoool, 19 February, 1969
L. Welterweight. Ht. 5'7"
Manager Self

13.10.89 Mick Mulcahy W PTS 6 Preston
31.10.89 Mick Mulcahy W PTS 6 Manchester
24.01.90 Mike Morrison W PTS 6 Preston
19.12.90 Julian Eavis W PTS 6 Preston
31.03.92 Ricky Sackfield W RSC 1 Stockport
14.05.92 Brendan Ryan W PTS 4 Liverpool
12.06.92 Dean Bramhald W PTS 6 Liverpool
15.09.92 Wayne Panayiotiou W RSC 2 Liverpool
25.09.92 Mick Mulcahy W PTS 8 Liverpool
12.11.92 Jim Lawlor W RSC 3 Liverpool
29.04.93 Marcel Herbert W PTS 8 Mayfair
09.04.94 Paul Ryan L RSC 6 Mansfield
Career: 12 contests, won 11, lost 1.

Monty Wright   Les Clark

Monty Wright

Biggleswade. *Born* Bedford, 1 November, 1969
L. Heavyweight. Ht. 5'9"
Manager M. Duff

10.11.93 Steve Osborne W RSC 3 Watford

26.01.94 Nigel Rafferty W PTS 6 Birmingham
16.02.94 Bobby Mack W RSC 3 Stevenage
11.03.94 Greg Scott-Briggs W CO 1 Bethnal Green
05.04.94 Karl Barwise W PTS 6 Bethnal Green
11.05.94 Simon McDougall L PTS 6 Stevenage
Career: 6 contests, won 5, lost 1.

Paul Wright

Liverpool. *Born* Liverpool, 24 February, 1966
S. Middleweight. Ht. 5'9¾"
Manager Self

13.10.89 Andy Balfe W RSC 1 Preston
31.10.89 John Tipping W RSC 1 Manchester
20.12.89 Nigel Rafferty DREW 6 Kirkby
13.04.92 Shaun McCrory W PTS 6 Manchester
14.05.92 Chris Walker W PTS 6 Liverpool
15.09.92 John Kaighin W DIS 5 Liverpool
23.10.92 Jason McNeill W RSC 1 Liverpool
28.11.92 Russell Washer W PTS 8 Manchester
05.02.93 Sean Smith W RSC 2 Manchester
22.04.93 Glenn Campbell L RSC 4 Bury
(Elim. British S. Middleweight Title & Central Area S. Middleweight Title Challenge)
06.09.93 Alan Baptiste W PTS 6 Liverpool
Career: 11 contests, won 9, drew 1, lost 1.

Paul Wynn

Newcastle. *Born* Newcastle, 23 March, 1972
Featherweight. Ht. 5'6"
Manager N. Fawcett

28.02.91 Tony Falcone L PTS 6 Sunderland
06.04.91 Tommy Smith L PTS 6 Darlington
13.05.91 Karl Morling L RSC 2 Northampton
29.04.93 Chip O'Neill W PTS 6 Newcastle
06.05.93 Tommy Smith W PTS 6 Hartlepool
01.06.93 Mark Hargreaves L PTS 6 Manchester
30.10.93 George Naylor L RSC 3 Chester
17.02.94 Robert Grubb W PTS 6 Walsall
11.03.94 James Murray L PTS 6 Glasgow
13.04.94 Shaun Anderson DREW 6 Glasgow
21.04.94 Alan Graham L PTS 6 Gateshead
13.05.94 Shaun Anderson W PTS 8 Kilmarnock
24.05.94 Chip O'Neill L PTS 6 Sunderland
10.06.94 Dennis Holbaek Pedersen L PTS 6 Kolding, Denmark
Career: 14 contests, won 4, drew 1, lost 9.

Tim Yeates

Stanford le Hope. *Born* Worcester, 19 August, 1966
S. Bantamweight. Ht. 5'7"
Manager Self

03.10.90 Ceri Farrell W PTS 6 Basildon
17.10.90 Kevin Jenkins W PTS 6 Bethnal Green
12.12.90 Ceri Farrell W PTS 6 Basildon
23.01.91 Eric George W RSC 6 Brentwood
01.05.91 Kelton McKenzie L PTS 6 Bethnal Green
11.05.92 Neil Parry W PTS 6 Piccadilly
30.01.93 Miguel Matthews W PTS 6 Brentwood
20.04.93 Ricky Beard W PTS 6 Brentwood
26.06.93 Chris Lyons W PTS 4 Earls Court
29.11.93 Miguel Matthews DREW 6 Ingatestone
Career: 10 contests, won 8, drew 1, lost 1.

Freddie Yemofio

Hayes. *Born* London, 15 July, 1969
Middleweight. Ht. 5'10"
Manager D. Gunn

31.08.93 Lee Sara L PTS 6 Croydon
30.09.93 Martin Rosamond L PTS 6 Hayes
20.05.94 Lee Blundell L RSC 6 Acton
Career: 3 contests, lost 3.

Freddie Yemofio   Les Clark

Steve Yorath

Cardiff. *Born* Cardiff, 8 August, 1965
Cruiserweight. Ht. 6'2"
Manager Self

21.11.85 Dai Davies L RSC 5 Blaenavon
13.03.86 John Ashton L CO 3 Alfreton
08.05.90 Rob Albon L PTS 6 Brentford
06.07.90 Phil Soundy L CO 3 Brentwood
17.09.90 Chris Coughlan W PTS 6 Cardiff
24.09.90 John Williams L PTS 6 Mayfair
03.10.90 Phil Soundy L PTS 6 Basildon
19.10.90 Neils H. Madsen L PTS 6 Skive, Denmark
15.04.91 Tony Colclough W PTS 6 Wolverhampton
24.04.91 Phil Soundy W PTS 6 Basildon
28.05.91 R. F. McKenzie W PTS 6 Cardiff
27.06.91 Denzil Browne L PTS 6 Leeds
21.01.92 Graham Arnold W PTS 6 Norwich
31.03.92 Graham Arnold L PTS 6 Norwich
18.05.92 Maro van Spaendonck L PTS 4 Valkenswaard, Holland
23.09.92 Denzil Browne L PTS 8 Leeds
25.11.92 Terry Dunstan L PTS 8 Mayfair
24.02.93 Derek Angol L RSC 5 Wembley
03.04.93 Biko Botowamungu L RSC 5 Vienna, Austria
10.07.93 Chris Okoh L PTS 6 Cardiff
31.08.93 Devon Rhooms L PTS 6 Croydon
04.10.93 Terry Dixon L RSC 4 Mayfair
09.04.94 Dermot Gascoyne L CO 3 Mansfield
Career: 23 contests, won 5, lost 18.

British Title Bouts during 1993-94

26 July, 1993   Neil Haddock (Wales) W RSC 7 Steve Walker (England), Sports Centre, Oldham (S. Featherweight Title). Referee: Larry O'Connell. Surviving a two inch cut beneath the right eye, inflicted in the second round, Haddock dumped Walker for counts of six and eight in rounds six and seven, respectively, to force the referee's intervention at 2.46 of the seventh. Haddock thus became the first man to retain his title in the weight class' last 14 championship fights.

16 September, 1993   James Cook 11.12½ (England) W PTS 12 Fidel Castro 11.13¾ (England), Elephant & Castle Leisure Centre, London (Vacant S. Middleweight Title). Referee: John Coyle. With Henry Wharton vacating the title to concentrate on a shot at Nigel Benn, a disappointing fight with very little action to find his successor, saw Castro on the wrong end of 118½-117 disputed verdict.

22 September, 1993   Del Bryan 10.7 (England) W PTS 12 Pat Barrett 10.6½ (England), York Hall, London (Vacant Welterweight Title). Referee: Larry O'Connell. Fully deserving the 117½-116 verdict, Bryan outworked the inconsistent Barrett almost throughout to win the title vacated by Gary Jacobs on becoming European champion. By his victory, former champion, Bryan, also won a Lonsdale Belt outright.

10 November, 1993   Paul Burke 9.8 (England) L PTS 12 Billy Schwer 9.8¾ (England), Town Hall, Watford (Lightweight Title). Referee: John Coyle. Although Burke fought back well after suffering three knockdowns, Schwer was good value for his 118½-116 points win. With his victory, Schwer regained the title he had lost to Burke almost nine months earlier.

Maurice Core (right) maintained his hold on the British light-heavyweight crown with a solid win over game challenger,
Simon Harris

Les Clark

10 November, 1993   Frank Grant 11.5½ (England) L RSC 7 Neville Brown 11.6 (England), York Hall, London (Middleweight Title). Referee: Roy Francis. By the sixth round, with Brown decidedly on top, Grant sustained a badly cut right-eye and with the damage worsening the champion was pulled out by the referee at 1.12 of the following session.

1 December, 1993   Maurice Core 12.7 (England) W RSC 11 Simon Harris 12.4 (England), York Hall, London (L. Heavyweight Title). Referee: Mickey Vann. Despite being floored in the fourth, Harris fought back well until running out of gas in the 11th and being rescued by the referee at 1.41 of the round.

18 December, 1993   Duke McKenzie 8.13 (England) W RSC 4 John Davison 8.13 (England), Wythenshawe Forum, Manchester (Vacant Featherweight Title). Referee: Paul Thomas. The title had been declared vacant after Sean Murphy's loss at the hands of Steve Robinson and McKenzie lost no time in proving he was well suited to the 126 lbs division. Floored and outclassed, Davison was saved from taking further punishment at 2.59 of the fourth.

26 January, 1994   Neville Brown 11.6 (England) W RTD 7 Andrew Flute (England), Aston Villa Leisure Centre, Birmingham (Middleweight Title). Referee: John Coyle. Flute was retired by his corner at the end of the seventh round, suffering a mass of cuts and bruises, but not before he had shown up Brown's would be limitations at the highest level.

16 February, 1994   Billy Schwer 9.7¾ (England) W RSC 3 Sean Murphy 9.8¼ (England), Ice Bowl, Stevenage (Lightweight Title). Referee: Larry O'Connell. A relatively easy victory for Schwer, and one that bought him a Lonsdale Belt outright, saw the challenger floored four times and given a thorough going-over before being humanely rescued by the referee at 1.32 of the third round.

17 February, 1994   Del Bryan 10.5 (England) W CO 7 Derek Grainger 10.5 (England), Goresbrook Leisure Centre, Dagenham (Welterweight Title). Referee: Billy Rafferty. Counted out at 0.55 of the seventh, Grainger had put up sterling resistance without ever looking likely to win and there were those who felt he should have been saved the indignity of a kayo.

23 February, 1994   Andy Till 10.13 (England) L PTS 12 Robert McCracken 10.12½ (England), Town Hall, Watford (L. Middleweight Title). Referee: Mickey Vann. Defiant to the end, Till had oppressed from the opening bell only to go down to a 118½-116½ points defeat. Both men suffered cut eyes, McCracken in the second and Till at the end of the tenth, but in a tough, mauling brawl of a fight, it was the challenger's reach and more correct hitting that ultimately took the eye. On the result, Till announced that he would be retiring from the ring.

11 March, 1994   James Cook 11.13¼ (England) L PTS 12 Cornelius Carr 11.11 (England), York Hall, London (S. Middleweight Title). Referee: Paul Thomas. Although the challenger made a negative start, he put his boxing together in the latter stages as Cook ran out of ideas. Picking up the fight in the ninth, Carr floored the champion for a count of six in round ten and was well worth his 118-116½ points victory.

23 March, 1994   Neil Haddock 9.4 (Wales) L RSC 10 Floyd Havard 9.4 (Wales), Star Leisure Centre, Cardiff (S. Featherweight Title). Referee: Roy Francis. In a battle of southpaws, Havard's hand speed gave him superiority and had he had the power an even earlier victory would have been on the cards. As it was, Haddock was cut on the right eye in the opening round, but lasted until 0.35 of the tenth before the referee decided that the damage was too bad for him to continue.

26 April, 1994   Richie Wenton 8.8½ (England) W RSC 10 Bradley Stone 8.8¾ (England), York Hall, London (Vacant S. Bantamweight Title). Referee: John Keane. This fight will be remembered for its tragic aftermath rather than as the inaugural title bout for the weight class. In short, it will be remembered as Bradley Stone's last contest in the ring. Having been stopped on his feet at 1.15 of the tenth, after flooring Wenton two rounds earlier in what had been a fairly even contest, Stone left the arena under his own steam, only to lapse into a coma several hours later. Following an operation to remove a blood clot, the boxing world was already in a state of shock when Bradley died two days later.

24 May, 1994   Billy Hardy 8.12½ (England) W RSC 8 Alan McKay 8.12½ (England), Crowtree Leisure Centre, Sunderland (Vacant Featherweight Title). Referee: Paul Thomas. Following Duke McKenzie's decision to vacate the crown to concentrate on a crack at the WBO title, the former bantam champion and current Commonwealth titleholder, Hardy, was matched against the tough southpaw, McKay, to decide his successor. After four rounds, it seemed clear that Hardy's right would be the match-winner and that proved to be the case, leaving a battered McKay to be rescued by the referee at 0.26 of the eighth.

25 May, 1994   Andy Holligan 9.13¾ (England) L RSC 3 Ross Hale 9.13¼ (England), Colston Hall, Bristol (L. Welterweight Title). Referee: Dave Parris. A brand new champion was crowned as Hale showed maturity and sound judgement, coupled with solid punching power, to floor Holligan in the first and then send the champion tottering along the ropes to force a stoppage win at 1.59 of the third round.

British Area Title Bouts during 1993-94

Central Area

Titleholders at 30 June 1994
Fly: Louis Veitch. **Bantam:** *vacant.* **S. Bantam:** Paul Lloyd.
Feather: *vacant.* **S. Feather:** Floyd Churchill. **Light:** Tony
Foster. **L. Welter:** Richard Burton. **Welter:** *vacant.* **L. Middle:**
Warren Stowe. **Middle:** *vacant.* **S. Middle:** Glenn Campbell. **L.
Heavy:** Michael Gale. **Cruiser:** *vacant.* **Heavy:** *vacant.*

7 October 1993	Louis Veitch W PTS 10 Lyndon Kershaw, Hull (Vacant Fly)
25 February 1994	Paul Lloyd W RSC 5 Ady Benton, Chester (Vacant S. Bantam)
21 April 1994	Tony Foster W PTS 10 Charles Shepherd, Hull (Vacant Light)

During the above period, Chris Clarkson (Bantam), Craig
Dermody (Feather), Kevin Toomey (Light), Ossie Maddix
(Welter) and Michael Murray (Heavy) relinquished their titles.

Midlands Area

Titleholders at 30 June 1994
Fly: *vacant.* **Bantam:** *vacant.* **S. Bantam:** *vacant.* **Feather:**
Kelton McKenzie. **S. Feather:** Pete Buckley. **Light:** Karl Taylor.
L. Welter: Malcolm Melvin. **Welter:** Lindon Scarlett. **L. Middle:**
Steve Goodwin. **Middle:** Antonio Fernandez. **S. Middle:** Carlos
Christie. **L. Heavy:** John J. Cooke. **Cruiser:** Cordwell Hylton.
Heavy: Steve Lewsam.

28 July 1993	Antonio Fernandez W RSC 3 Paul Wesley, London (Middle)
7 September 1993	Steve Goodwin W RSC 7 Wally Swift Jnr, Stoke (L. Middle)
26 January 1994	Lindon Scarlett W RSC 6 Rick North, Birmingham (Vacant Welter)
28 March 1994	Steve Lewsam W PTS 10 Wayne Buck, Cleethorpes (Vacant Heavy)
15 April 1994	Cordwell Hylton W RSC 4 Albert Call, Hull (Vacant Cruiser)
18 April 1994	Peter Till L PTS 10 Karl Taylor, Walsall (Light)

During the above period, Steve Lewsam (Cruiser) relinquished his
title.

Northern Area

Titleholders at 30 June 1994
Fly: *vacant.* **Bantam:** *vacant.* **S. Bantam:** *vacant.* **Feather:**
vacant. **S. Feather:** Frankie Foster. **Light:** *vacant.* **L. Welter:**
Paul Charters. **Welter:** Paul King. **L. Middle:** Mark Cichocki.
Middle: *vacant.* **S. Middle:** *vacant.* **L. Heavy:** Terry French.
Cruiser: *vacant.* **Heavy:** Paul Lister.

2 November 1993	Mark Cichocki W RSC 4 Mark Jay, Hartlepool (L. Middle)
3 March 1994	Paul King W PTS 10 Hughie Davey, Newcastle (Vacant Welter)
21 April 1994	Terry French W PTS 10 Ian Henry, Gateshead (L. Heavy)

Ali Forbes (left) outpoints Richard Bustin to win the vacant Southern Area super-middleweight title   Les Clark

In one the contenders for "Fight of the Year", Felix Kelly (left), the Southern Area Lightweight champion, successfully defended his title against Shaun Shinkwin

Les Clark

Northern Ireland Area
Titleholders at 30 June 1994 - None.

Scottish Area
Titleholders at 30 June 1994
Fly: James Drummond. **Bantam:** *vacant.* **S. Bantam:** *vacant.* **Feather:** *vacant.* **S. Feather:** Mark Geraghty. **Light:** Kris McAdam. **L. Welter:** *vacant.* **Welter:** Willie Beattie. **L. Middle:** *vacant.* **Middle:** *vacant.* **S. Middle:** *vacant.* **L. Heavy:** *vacant.* **Cruiser:** *vacant.* **Heavy:** *vacant.*

21 March 1994   James Drummond W RSC 5 Neil Armstrong, Glasgow (Vacant Fly)
During the above period, Jamie McBride (Feather) relinquished his title.

Southern Area
Titleholders at 30 June 1994
Fly: *vacant.* **Bantam:** *vacant.* **S. Bantam:** *vacant.* **Feather:** *vacant.* **S. Feather:** *vacant.* **Light:** Cham Joof. **L. Welter:** Jonathan Thaxton. **Welter:** Gary Logan. **L. Middle:** *vacant.* **Middle:** W. O. Wilson. **S. Middle:** Ali Forbes. **L. Heavy:** Garry Delaney. **Cruiser:** John Graham. **Heavy:** James Oyebola.

28 September 1993   Glazz Campbell L CO 6 Garry Delaney, London (L. Heavy)
13 October 1993   R. F. McKenzie L RSC 1 James Oyebola, London (Heavy)
9 December 1993   Felix Kelly W PTS 10 Shaun Shinkwin, Watford (Light)
6 March 1994   Ali Forbes W PTS 10 Richard Bustin, London (Vacant S. Middle)
10 March 1994   Jonathan Thaxton W RSC 4 B. F. Williams, Watford (Vacant L. Welter)

9 April 1994   Garry Delaney W CO 6 Simon Harris, London (L. Heavy)
22 May 1994   Felix Kelly L RSC 5 Cham Joof, Crystal Palace (Light)
During the above period, Dave Pierre (L. Welter) retired, while Mickey Cantwell (Fly) and Kevin Lueshing (L. Middle) relinquished their titles.

Welsh Area
Titleholders at 30 June 1994
Fly: *vacant.* **Bantam:** *vacant.* **S. Bantam:** *vacant.* **Feather:** Peter Harris. **S. Feather:** J. T. Williams. **Light:** Mervyn Bennett. **L. Welter:** *vacant.* **Welter:** *vacant.* **L. Middle:** Carlo Colarusso. **Middle:** *vacant.* **S. Middle:** Darron Griffiths. **L. Heavy:** *vacant.* **Cruiser:** *vacant.* **Heavy:** Chris Jacobs.

10 November 1993   Barrie Kelley L RTD 3 J. T. Williams, Ystrad (S. Feather)
20 May 1994   Peter Harris W PTS 10 Nigel Haddock, Neath (Vacant Feather)
During the above period, Wayne Ellis (Middle) relinquished his title, while John Davies (Welter) retired.

Western Area
Titleholders at 30 June 1994
Fly: *vacant.* **Bantam:** *vacant.* **S. Bantam:** *vacant.* **Feather:** *vacant.* **S. Feather:** Greg Upton. **Light:** *vacant.* **L. Welter:** *vacant.* **Welter:** *vacant.* **L. Middle:** Dean Cooper. **Middle:** *vacant.* **S. Middle:** *vacant.* **L. Heavy:** *vacant.* **Cruiser:** *vacant.* **Heavy:** *vacant.*

During the above period, Ross Hale relinquished the welterweight title on winning the British and Commonwealth light-welter crowns.

Lord Lonsdale Challenge Belts: Outright Winners

The original belts were donated to the National Sporting Club by Lord Lonsdale and did not bear his name, the inscription reading "The National Sporting Club's Challenge Belt." It was not until the British Boxing Board of Control was formed that the emblems were reintroduced and the belts became known as the Lord Lonsdale Challenge Belts. The first contest involving the BBBoC belt was Benny Lynch versus Pat Palmer for the flyweight title on 16 September 1936. To win a belt outright a champion must score three title match victories at the same weight, not necessarily consecutively.

Outright Winners of the National Sporting Club's Challenge Belt, 1909-1935 (20)

FLYWEIGHT	Jimmy Wilde; Jackie Brown
BANTAMWEIGHT	Digger Stanley; Joe Fox; Jim Higgins; Johnny Brown; Johnny King
FEATHERWEIGHT	Jim Driscoll; Tancy Lee; Johnny Cuthbert; Nel Tarleton
LIGHTWEIGHT	Freddie Welsh
WELTERWEIGHT	Johnny Basham; Jack Hood
MIDDLEWEIGHT	Pat O'Keefe; Len Harvey; Jock McAvoy
L. HEAVYWEIGHT	Dick Smith
HEAVYWEIGHT	Bombardier Billy Wells; Jack Petersen

Outright Winners of the BBBoC Lord Lonsdale Challenge Belts, 1936-1994 (83)

FLYWEIGHT	Jackie Paterson; Terry Allen; Walter McGowan; John McCluskey; Hugh Russell; Charlie Magri; Pat Clinton; Robbie Regan
BANTAMWEIGHT	Johnny King; Peter Keenan (2); Freddie Gilroy; Alan Rudkin; Johnny Owen; Billy Hardy
FEATHERWEIGHT	Nel Tarleton; Ronnie Clayton (2); Charlie Hill; Howard Winstone (2); Evan Armstrong; Pat Cowdell; Robert Dickie; Paul Hodkinson; Colin McMillan; Sean Murphy
S. FEATHERWEIGHT	Jimmy Anderson; John Doherty
LIGHTWEIGHT	Eric Boon; Billy Thompson; Joe Lucy; Dave Charnley; Maurice Cullen; Ken Buchanan; Jim Watt; George Feeney; Tony Willis; Carl Crook; Billy Schwer
L. WELTERWEIGHT	Joey Singleton; Colin Power; Clinton McKenzie (2); Lloyd Christie; Andy Holligan
WELTERWEIGHT	Ernie Roderick; Wally Thom; Brian Curvis (2); Ralph Charles; Colin Jones; Lloyd Honeyghan; Kirkland Laing; Del Bryan
L. MIDDLEWEIGHT	Maurice Hope; Jimmy Batten; Pat Thomas; Prince Rodney; Andy Till
MIDDLEWEIGHT	Pat McAteer; Terry Downes; Johnny Pritchett; Bunny Sterling; Alan Minter; Kevin Finnegan; Roy Gumbs; Tony Sibson; Herol Graham
L. HEAVYWEIGHT	Randy Turpin; Chic Calderwood; Chris Finnegan; Bunny Johnson; Tom Collins; Dennis Andries; Tony Wilson; Crawford Ashley
CRUISERWEIGHT	Johnny Nelson
HEAVYWEIGHT	Henry Cooper (3); Horace Notice; Lennox Lewis

NOTES: Jim Driscoll was the first champion to win an NSC belt outright, whilst Eric Boon later became the first champion to put three notches on a BBBoC belt.

Nel Tarleton and Johnny King are the only champions to have won both belts outright.

Freddie Welsh and Johnny King, each with just two notches on an NSC Lonsdale belt, were allowed to keep their spoils after winning British Empire titles, while Walter McGowan and Charlie Magri, with one notch on a BBBoC belt, kept their awards under the three years/no available challengers ruling.

Henry Cooper holds the record number of belts won by a single fighter, three in all.

Chris and Kevin Finnegan are the only brothers to have won belts outright.

Jim Higgins holds the record for winning an NSC belt outright in the shortest time, 279 days, whilst Colin McMillan won a BBBoC belt in just 160 days.

THE LONSDALE INTERNATIONAL SPORTING CLUB

President: The Earl Grey
Vice-President: Lord Addington
Patrons: Reg Gutteridge (UK); Tom Pendry, MP (UK); Angelo Dundee (USA);
                    Thomas Hauser (USA); Chris Greyvenstein (SA); Kepler Wessels (SA);
                    Joe Koizumi (Japan)

A club for sportsmen and sportswomen genuinely seeking the furtherance and well being of amateur and professional boxing, holding regular banquets to honour great sporting personalities. Those honoured since the Club's formation in 1992, to celebrate 100 years of gloved boxing, include Ingemar Johansson, Floyd Patterson, Willie Pep, Brian London, Duke McKenzie, Reg Gutteridge, Jack Powell, Billy Walker, Kepler Wessels

Applications for membership should be addressed to:
                    Geraldine Davies, Lonsdale International Sporting Club,
                    21 Beak Street, London W1R 3LB.
                    Tel: 071 434 1741   Fax: 071 734 2094

                    Directors: Bernard Hart; Frank Tyner

WINNING COMBINATION

Tel: (091) 567 6871
Fax: (091) 565 2581

Tommy Conroy - Manager and Trainer
Annette Conroy - First North-East Lady Promoter
Matchmaker: Graham Lockwood (0805) 434457
Trainers: Micky Hitch, Charlie Armstrong and Malcolm Gates

144 High Street East, East End
Sunderland, Tyne & Wear,
SR1 2BL

Tommy Conroy's Sunderland Based Stable

Frankie Foster (Newcastle) Super-Featherweight
Ian Henry (Gateshead) Light -Heavyweight
Rob Pitters (Gateshead) Light-Middleweight
Paul Hitch (Wingate) Middleweight
Dave Johnson (Boldon) Middleweight
Micky Hall (Ludworth) Lightweight
Chip O'Neill (Sunderland) Featherweight
Hughie Davey (Wallsend) Welterweight
Alan Graham (Newcastle) Lightweight
Tim Hill (Whitley Bay) Lightweight
Dave Whittle (North Shields) Welterweight
Liam Dineen (Peterlee) Lightweight
Paul Quarmby (Hetton-le-Hole) Super-Bantamweight
Paul Scott (Newbiggin) Light-Welterweight
Shaun O'Neill (Sunderland) Light-Welterweight

British Champions, 1891-1994

Shows the tenure of each British champion at each weight from 1891, when the National Sporting Club was founded and championship bouts were contested under Marquess of Queensberry Rules, using gloves.

Between 1891 and 1929, the year that the BBBoC was formed, men who held general recognition are shown **in bold,** as champions, while the others are seen purely as claimants.

Champions born outside Britain, who won open titles in this country, are not shown at the risk of confusing the issue further.

Also, it must be stated that many of the champions and claimants listed below, prior to 1909, were no more than English titleholders, having fought for the "Championship of England", but for our purposes they carry the "British" label.

Prior to 1909, the year that the Lord Lonsdale Challenge Belt was introduced and weight classes subsequently standardised, poundages within divisions could vary quite substantially, thus enabling men fighting at different weights to claim the same "title" at the same time. A brief history of the weight fluctuations between 1891 and 1909, shows:

Bantamweight   Billy Plimmer was recognised as the British titleholder in 1891 at 110 lbs and became accepted as world champion when George Dixon, the number one in America's eyes, gradually increased his weight. In 1895 Pedlar Palmer took the British title at 112 lbs, but by 1900 he had developed into a 114 pounder. Between 1902 and 1904, Joe Bowker defended regularly at 116 lbs and in 1909 the NSC standardised the weight at 118 lbs, even though the USA continued for a short while to accept only 116 lbs.

Featherweight   Between 1891 and 1895, one of the most prestigious championship belts in this country was fought for at 126 lbs and although George Dixon was recognised in the USA as world featherweight champion, gradually moving from 114 to 122 lbs, no major contests took place in Britain during the above period at his weight. It was only in 1895, when Fred Johnson took the British title at 120 lbs, losing it to Ben Jordan two years later, that we came into line with the USA. Ben Jordan became an outstanding champion, who, between 1898 and 1899, was seen by the NSC as world champion at 120 lbs. However, first Harry Greenfield, then Jabez White and Wil Curley, continued to claim the 126 lbs version of the British title and it was only in 1900 when Jack Roberts beat Curley, that the weight limit was finally standardised at nine stone.

Lightweight   Outstanding champions often carried their weights as they grew in size. A perfect example of this was Dick Burge, the British lightweight champion from 1891-1901, who gradually increased from 134 to 144 lbs, while still maintaining his right to the title. It was not until 1902 that Jabez White brought the division into line with the USA. Later, both White and then Goldswain, carried their weight up to 140 lbs and it was left to Johnny Summers to set the current limit of 135 lbs.

Welterweight   The presence of Dick Burge fighting from 134 to 144 lbs plus up until 1900, explains quite adequately why the welterweight division, although very popular in the USA, did not take off in this country until 1902. The championship was contested between 142 and 146 lbs in those days and was not really supported by the NSC, but by 1909 with their backing it finally became established at 147 lbs.

Note that the Lonsdale Belt notches (title bout wins) relate to NSC, 1909-1935, and BBBoC, 1936-1994.

Champions in **bold** are accorded national recognition.

*Undefeated champions (Includes men who may have forfeited their titles).

Title Holder	Lonsdale Belt Notches	Tenure	Title Holder	Lonsdale Belt Notches	Tenure	Title Holder	Lonsdale Belt Notches	Tenure
Flyweight (112 lbs)			Teddy Gardner*	1	1952	**Francis Ampofo**	1	1992-
Sid Smith		1911	Terry Allen*	2	1952-1954			
Sid Smith	1	1911-1913	Dai Dower*	1	1955-1957	**Bantamweight (118 lbs)**		
Bill Ladbury		1913-1914	Frankie Jones	2	1957-1960	**Billy Plimmer**		1891-1895
Percy Jones*	1	1914	Johnny Caldwell*	1	1960-1961	Tom Gardner		1892
Tancy Lee	1	1915	Jackie Brown	1	1962-1963	Willie Smith		1892-1896
Joe Symonds	1	1915-1916	Walter McGowan*	1	1963-1966	Nunc Wallace		1893-1895
Jimmy Wilde*	3	1916-1923	John McCluskey*	3	1967-1977	George Corfield		1893-1895
Elky Clark*	2	1924-1927	Charlie Magri*	1	1977-1981	**Pedlar Palmer**		1895-1900
Johnny Hill*	1	1927-1929	Kelvin Smart*	1	1982-1984	George Corfield		1895-1896
Jackie Brown		1929-1930	Hugh Russell*	3	1984-1985	Billy Plimmer		1896-1898
Bert Kirby	1	1930-1931	Duke McKenzie*	2	1985-1986	Harry Ware		1899-1900
Jackie Brown	3	1931-1935	Dave Boy McAuley*	1	1986-1988	**Harry Ware**		1900-1902
Benny Lynch*	2	1935-1938	Pat Clinton*	3	1988-1991	Andrew Tokell		1901-1902
Jackie Paterson	4	1939-1948	Robbie Regan	1	1991	Jim Williams		1902
Rinty Monaghan*	1	1948-1950	Francis Ampofo	1	1991	**Andrew Tokell**		1902
Terry Allen	1	1951-1952	Robbie Regan*	2	1991-1992	**Harry Ware**		1902

Title Holder	Lonsdale Belt Notches	Tenure
Joe Bowker		1902-1910
Owen Moran		1905-1907
Digger Stanley		1906-1910
Digger Stanley	2	1910-1913
Bill Beynon	1	1913
Digger Stanley	1	1913-1914
Curley Walker*	1	1914-1915
Joe Fox*	3	1915-1917
Tommy Noble	1	1918-1919
Walter Ross*	1	1919-1920
Jim Higgins	3	1920-1922
Tommy Harrison		1922-1923
Bugler Harry Lake	1	1923
Johnny Brown*	3	1923-1928
Alf Pattenden	2	1928-1929
Johnny Brown		1928
Teddy Baldock		1928-1929
Teddy Baldock*	1	1929-1931
Dick Corbett	1	1931-1932
Johnny King	1	1932-1934
Dick Corbett*	1	1934
Johnny King	1+2	1935-1947
Jackie Paterson	2	1947-1949
Stan Rowan*	1	1949
Danny O'Sullivan	1	1949-1951
Peter Keenan	3	1951-1953
John Kelly	1	1953-1954
Peter Keenan	3	1954-1959
Freddie Gilroy*	4	1959-1963
Johnny Caldwell	1	1964-1965
Alan Rudkin	1	1965-1966
Walter McGowan	1	1966-1968
Alan Rudkin*	4	1968-1972
Johnny Clark*	1	1973-1974
Dave Needham	1	1974-1975
Paddy Maguire	1	1975-1977
Johnny Owen*	4	1977-1980
John Feeney	1	1981-1983
Hugh Russell	1	1983
Davy Larmour	1	1983
John Feeney	1	1983-1985
Ray Gilbody	2	1985-1987
Billy Hardy*	5	1987-1991
Joe Kelly	1	1992
Drew Docherty	2	1992-

S. Bantamweight (130 lbs)

Title Holder	Lonsdale Belt Notches	Tenure
Richie Wenton	1	1994-

Featherweight (126 lbs)

Title Holder	Lonsdale Belt Notches	Tenure
Fred Johnson		1890-1895
Billy Reader		1891
Billy Reader		1891-1892
Harry Spurden		1892-1895
Fred Johnson		1895-1897
Harry Greenfield		1896-1899
Ben Jordan*		1897-1900
Jabez White		1899-1900
Wil Curley		1900-1901
Jack Roberts		1901-1902
Wil Curley		1902-1903
Ben Jordan*		1902-1905
Joe Bowker*		1905
Johnny Summers		1906
Joe Bowker		1905-1906
Jim Driscoll		1906-1907
Spike Robson*		1906-1907
Jim Driscoll*	3	1907-1913
Spike Robson		1907-1910

Title Holder	Lonsdale Belt Notches	Tenure
Ted Kid Lewis*	1	1913-1914
Llew Edwards*	1	1915-1917
Charlie Hardcastle	1	1917
Tancy Lee*	3	1917-1919
Mike Honeyman	2	1920-1921
Joe Fox*	1	1921-1922
George McKenzie	2	1924-1925
Johnny Curley	2	1925-1927
Johnny Cuthbert	1	1927-1928
Harry Corbett	1	1928-1929
Johnny Cuthbert	2	1929-1931
Nel Tarleton	1	1931-1932
Seaman Tommy Watson	2	1932-1934
Nel Tarleton	2	1934-1936
Johnny McGrory*	1	1936-1938
Jim Spider Kelly	1	1938-1939
Johnny Cusick	1	1939-1940
Nel Tarleton*	3	1940-1947
Ronnie Clayton	6	1947-1954
Sammy McCarthy	1	1954-1955
Billy Spider Kelly	1	1955-1956
Charlie Hill	3	1956-1959
Bobby Neill	1	1959-1960
Terry Spinks	2	1960-1961
Howard Winstone*	7	1961-1969
Jimmy Revie	2	1969-1971
Evan Armstrong	2	1971-1972
Tommy Glencross	1	1972-1973
Evan Armstrong*	2	1973-1975
Vernon Sollas	1	1975-1977
Alan Richardson	2	1977-1978
Dave Needham	2	1978-1979
Pat Cowdell*	3	1979-1982
Steve Sims*	1	1982-1983
Barry McGuigan*	2	1983-1986
Robert Dickie*	3	1986-1988
Peter Harris	1	1988
Paul Hodkinson*	3	1988-1990
Sean Murphy	2	1990-1991
Gary de Roux	1	1991
Colin McMillan*	3	1991-1992
John Davison*	1	1992-1993
Sean Murphy*	1	1993
Duke McKenzie*	1	1993-1994
Billy Hardy	1	1994-

S. Featherweight (130 lbs)

Title Holder	Lonsdale Belt Notches	Tenure
Jimmy Anderson*	3	1968-1970
John Doherty	1	1986
Pat Cowdell	1	1986
Najib Daho	1	1986-1987
Pat Cowdell	1	1987-1988
Floyd Havard	1	1988-1989
John Doherty	1	1989-1990
Joey Jacobs	1	1990
Hugh Forde	1	1990
Kevin Pritchard	1	1990-1991
Robert Dickie	1	1991
Sugar Gibiliru	1	1991
John Doherty	1	1991-1992
Michael Armstrong	1	1992
Neil Haddock	2	1992-1994
Floyd Havard	1	1994-

Lightweight (135 lbs)

Title Holder	Lonsdale Belt Notches	Tenure
Dick Burge		1891-1897
Harry Nickless		1891-1894
Tom Causer		1894-1897
Tom Causer		1897

Title Holder	Lonsdale Belt Notches	Tenure
Dick Burge*		1897-1901
Jabez White		1902-1906
Jack Goldswain		1906-1908
Johnny Summers		1908-1909
Freddie Welsh	1	1909-1911
Matt Wells	1	1911-1912
Freddie Welsh*	1	1912-1919
Bob Marriott*	1	1919-1920
Ernie Rice	1	1921-1922
Seaman Nobby Hall		1922-1923
Harry Mason		1923-1924
Ernie Izzard	2	1924-1925
Harry Mason		1924-1925
Harry Mason*	1	1925-1928
Sam Steward		1928-1929
Fred Webster		1929-1930
Al Foreman*	1	1930-1932
Johnny Cuthbert		1932-1934
Harry Mizler		1934
Jackie Kid Berg		1934-1936
Jimmy Walsh	1	1936-1938
Dave Crowley	1	1938
Eric Boon	3	1938-1944
Ronnie James*	1	1944-1947
Billy Thompson	3	1947-1951
Tommy McGovern	1	1951-1952
Frank Johnson*	1	1952-1953
Joe Lucy	1	1953-1955
Frank Johnson	1	1955-1956
Joe Lucy	2	1956-1957
Dave Charnley*	3	1957-1965
Maurice Cullen*	4	1965-1968
Ken Buchanan*	2	1968-1971
Willie Reilly*	1	1972
Jim Watt	1	1972-1973
Ken Buchanan*	1	1973-1974
Jim Watt*	2	1975-1977
Charlie Nash*	1	1978-1979
Ray Cattouse	2	1980-1982
George Feeney*	3	1982-1985
Tony Willis	3	1985-1987
Alex Dickson	1	1987-1988
Steve Boyle*	2	1988-1990
Carl Crook	5	1990-1992
Billy Schwer	1	1992-1993
Paul Burke	1	1993
Billy Schwer	2	1993-

L. Welterweight (140 lbs)

Title Holder	Lonsdale Belt Notches	Tenure
Des Rea	1	1968-1969
Vic Andreetti*	2	1969-1970
Des Morrison	1	1973-1974
Pat McCormack	1	1974
Joey Singleton	3	1974-1976
Dave Boy Green*	1	1976-1977
Colin Power*	2	1977-1978
Clinton McKenzie	1	1978-1979
Colin Power	1	1979
Clinton McKenzie	5	1979-1984
Terry Marsh*	1	1984-1986
Tony Laing*	1	1986
Tony McKenzie	2	1986-1987
Lloyd Christie	3	1987-1989
Clinton McKenzie*	1	1989
Pat Barrett*	2	1989-1990
Tony Ekubia	1	1990-1991
Andy Holligan	3	1991-1994
Ross Hale	1	1994-

Welterweight (147 lbs)

Title Holder	Lonsdale Belt Notches	Tenure
Charlie Allum		1903-1904
Charlie Knock		1904-1906
Curly Watson*		1906-1910
Young Joseph		1908-1910
Young Joseph	1	1910-1911
Arthur Evernden		1911-1912
Johnny Summers		1912
Johnny Summers	2	1912-1914
Tom McCormick		1914
Matt Wells*		1914
Johnny Basham	3	1914-1920
Matt Wells		1914-1919
Ted Kid Lewis		1920-1924
Tommy Milligan*		1924-1925
Hamilton Johnny Brown		1925
Harry Mason		1925-1926
Jack Hood*	3	1926-1934
Harry Mason		1934
Pat Butler*		1934-1936
Dave McCleave		1936
Jake Kilrain	1	1936-1939
Ernie Roderick	5	1939-1948
Henry Hall	1	1948-1949
Eddie Thomas	2	1949-1951
Wally Thom	1	1951-1952
Cliff Curvis*	1	1952-1953
Wally Thom	2	1953-1956
Peter Waterman*	2	1956-1958
Tommy Molloy	2	1958-1960
Wally Swift	1	1960
Brian Curvis*	7	1960-1966
Johnny Cooke	2	1967-1968
Ralph Charles*	3	1968-1972
Bobby Arthur	1	1972-1973
John H. Stracey*	1	1973-1975
Pat Thomas	2	1975-1976
Henry Rhiney	2	1976-1979
Kirkland Laing	1	1979-1980
Colin Jones*	3	1980-1982
Lloyd Honeyghan*	2	1983-1985
Kostas Petrou	1	1985
Sylvester Mittee	1	1985
Lloyd Honeyghan*	1	1985-1986
Kirkland Laing	4	1987-1991
Del Bryan	2	1991-1992
Gary Jacobs*	2	1992-1993
Del Bryan	2	1993-

L. Middleweight (154 lbs)

Title Holder	Lonsdale Belt Notches	Tenure
Larry Paul	2	1973-1974
Maurice Hope⁺	3	1974-1977
Jimmy Batten	3	1977-1979
Pat Thomas	3	1979-1981
Herol Graham*	2	1981-1983
Prince Rodney*	1	1983-1984
Jimmy Cable	2	1984-1985
Prince Rodney	2	1985-1986
Chris Pyatt*	1	1986
Lloyd Hibbert*	1	1987
Gary Cooper	1	1988
Gary Stretch*	2	1988-1990
Wally Swift Jnr	2	1991-1992
Andy Till	3	1992-1994
Robert McCracken	1	1994-

Middleweight (160 lbs)

Title Holder	Lonsdale Belt Notches	Tenure
Ted Pritchard*		1891-1892
Ted White		1893-1896
Ted Pritchard		1894
Anthony Diamond		1898
Dido Plumb		1900
Jack Palmer		1902-1903
Charlie Allum		1905-1906
Pat O'Keefe		1906
Pat O'Keefe*		1906
Tom Thomas	1	1906-1910
Jim Sullivan*	1	1910-1912
Jack Harrison*	1	1912-1913
Pat O'Keefe	2	1914-1916
Bandsman Jack Blake	1	1916-1918
Pat O'Keefe*	1	1918-1919
Ted Kid Lewis		1920-1921
Tom Gummer	1	1920-1921
Gus Platts		1921
Johnny Basham*		1921
Ted Kid Lewis	2	1921-1923
Johnny Basham		1921
Roland Todd*		1923-1925
Roland Todd		1925-1927
Tommy Milligan	1	1926-1928
Frank Moody		1927-1928
Alex Ireland		1928-1929
Len Harvey	5	1929-1933
Jock McAvoy*	3+2	1933-1944
Ernie Roderick	1	1945-1946
Vince Hawkins	1	1946-1948
Dick Turpin	2	1948-1950
Albert Finch	1	1950
Randy Turpin*	1	1950-1954
Johnny Sullivan	1	1954-1955
Pat McAteer*	3	1955-1958
Terry Downes	1	1958-1959
John Cowboy McCormack	1	1959
Terry Downes*	2	1959-1962
George Aldridge	1	1962-1963
Mick Leahy	1	1963-1964
Wally Swift	1	1964-1965
Johnny Pritchett*	4	1965-1969
Les McAteer	1	1969-1970
Mark Rowe	1	1970
Bunny Sterling	4	1970-1974
Kevin Finnegan*	1	1974
Bunny Sterling*	1	1975
Alan Minter*	3	1975-1977
Kevin Finnegan	1	1977
Alan Minter*	1	1977-1978
Tony Sibson	1	1979
Kevin Finnegan*	1	1979-1980
Roy Gumbs	3	1981-1983
Mark Kaylor	1	1983-1984
Tony Sibson	1	1984
Herol Graham*	1	1985-1986
Brian Anderson	1	1986-1987
Tony Sibson*	1	1987-1988
Herol Graham	4	1988-1992
Frank Grant	2	1992-1993
Neville Brown	2	1993-

S. Middleweight (168 lbs)

Title Holder	Lonsdale Belt Notches	Tenure
Sammy Storey	2	1989-1990
James Cook*	1	1990-1991
Fidel Castro	2	1991-1992
Henry Wharton*	1	1992-1993
James Cook	1	1993-1994
Cornelius Carr	1	1994-

L. Heavyweight (175lbs)

Title Holder	Lonsdale Belt Notches	Tenure
Dennis Haugh		1913-1914
Dick Smith	2	1914-1916
Harry Reeve*	1	1916-1917
Dick Smith*	1	1918-1919
Boy McCormick*	1	1919-1921
Jack Bloomfield*	1	1922-1924
Tom Berry	1	1925-1927
Gipsy Daniels*	1	1927
Frank Moody	1	1927-1929
Harry Crossley	1	1929-1932
Jack Petersen*	1	1932
Len Harvey*	1	1933-1934
Eddie Phillips		1935-1937
Jock McAvoy	1	1937-1938
Len Harvey	2	1938-1942
Freddie Mills*	1	1942-1950
Don Cockell	2	1950-1952
Randy Turpin*	1	1952
Dennis Powell	1	1953
Alex Buxton	2	1953-1955
Randy Turpin*	1	1955
Ron Barton*	1	1956
Randy Turpin*	2	1956-1958
Chic Calderwood*	4	1960-1966
Young John McCormack	2	1967-1969
Eddie Avoth	1	1969-1971
Chris Finnegan*	1	1971-1973
John Conteh*	2	1973-1974
Johnny Frankham	1	1975
Chris Finnegan*	1	1975-1976
Tim Wood	1	1976-1977
Bunny Johnson*	3	1977-1981
Tom Collins	3	1982-1984
Dennis Andries	5	1984-1986
Tom Collins*	1	1987
Tony Wilson	3	1987-1989
Tom Collins*	1	1989-1990
Steve McCarthy*	1	1990-1991
Crawford Ashley*	3	1991-1992
Maurice Core	2	1992-

Cruiserweight (190 lbs)

Title Holder	Lonsdale Belt Notches	Tenure
Sam Reeson*	1	1985-1986
Andy Straughn	1	1986-1987
Roy Smith	1	1987
Tee Jay	1	1987-1988
Glenn McCrory*	2	1988
Andy Straughn	1	1988-1989
Johnny Nelson*	3	1989-1991
Derek Angol*	2	1991-1992
Carl Thompson⁺	1	1992-1994

Heavyweight (190 lbs +)

Title Holder	Lonsdale Belt Notches	Tenure
Charlie Mitchell*		1882-1894
Ted Pritchard		1891-1895
Jem Smith*		1895-1896
George Chrisp		1901
Jack Scales		1901-1902
Jack Palmer		1903-1906
Gunner Moir		1906-1909
Iron Hague		1909-1910
P.O. Curran		1910-1911
Iron Hague		1910-1911
Bombardier Billy Wells	3	1911-1919
Joe Beckett*		1919
Frank Goddard	1	1919
Joe Beckett		1919
Joe Beckett*	1	1919-1923

169

Title Holder	Lonsdale Belt Notches	Tenure	Title Holder	Lonsdale Belt Notches	Tenure	Title Holder	Lonsdale Belt Notches	Tenure
Frank Goddard		1923-1926	Johnny Williams	1	1952-1953	Joe Bugner*	1	1976-1977
Phil Scott*		1926-1931	Don Cockell*	1	1953-1956	John L. Gardner*	2	1978-1980
Reggie Meen		1931-1932	Joe Erskine	2	1956-1958	Gordon Ferris	1	1981
Jack Petersen	3	1932-1933	Brian London	1	1958-1959	Neville Meade	1	1981-1983
Len Harvey		1933-1934	Henry Cooper*	9	1959-1969	David Pearce*	1	1983-1985
Jack Petersen		1934-1936	Jack Bodell	1	1969-1970	Hughroy Currie	1	1985-1986
Ben Foord		1936-1937	Henry Cooper	1	1970-1971	Horace Notice*	4	1986-1988
Tommy Farr*	1	1937-1938	Joe Bugner	1	1971	Gary Mason	2	1989-1991
Len Harvey*	1	1938-1942	Jack Bodell	1	1971-1972	Lennox Lewis*	3	1991-1993
Jack London	1	1944-1945	Danny McAlinden	1	1972-1975	Herbie Hide*	1	1993-1994
Bruce Woodcock	2	1945-1950	Bunny Johnson	1	1975			
Jack Gardner	1	1950-1952	Richard Dunn	2	1975-1976			

Randy Turpin (right), the former undefeated British middleweight (1950-1954) and light-heavyweight (1952, 1955 and 1956-1958) champion, pictured here defeating the legendary Sugar Ray Robinson to become world middleweight champion in 1951

Commonwealth Title Bouts during 1993-94

5 October, 1993   Andrew Murray 10.6 (Guyana) W RSC 6 Tony Swift 10.1¾ (England), Grosvenor House, London (Vacant Welterweight Title). Referee: Larry O'Connell. Fighting for the title vacated by Eamonn Loughran (on becoming WBO champion), Swift was up against it right from the opening bell against the classy southpaw, Murray, and was rescued at 1.53 of the sixth suffering a badly cut left eye.

13 October, 1993   Darren Fifield 7.13½ (England) W RSC 9 Danny Porter 8.0 (England), York Hall, London (Vacant Flyweight Title). Referee: Billy Rafferty. In a hastily made match, Fifield, having only his seventh contest, survived a sixth round knockdown to cut Porter over both eyes and force a stoppage at 1.16 of the ninth. The title had earlier been vacated by Francis Ampofo.

27 October, 1993   Richie Woodhall 11.6 (England) W PTS 12 Gary Meekison 11.6 (Canada), Gala Baths, West Bromwich (Middleweight Title). Referee: Dave Parris. Woodhall easily retained his title with a 119½-114½ points win, but was forced to travel the full route, almost single-handedly, after banging up his suspect right-hand.

10 November, 1993   Paul Burke 9.8 (England) L PTS 12 Billy Schwer 9.8¼ (England), Town Hall, Watford (Lightweight Title). Referee: John Coyle. For a report, see under British Title Bouts, 1993-94.

2 December, 1993   Tony Pep 9.2¾ (Canada) W PTS 12 Glen Forde 9.3¼ (Guyana), Edmonton, Canada (S. Featherweight Title). Scorecard: 118-110, 116-111, 116-111.

14 January, 1994   John Armour 8.6 (England) W RSC 7 Rufus Adebayo 8.4¼ (Nigeria), York Hall, London (Bantamweight Title). Referee: Mickey Vann. Having taken his man apart gradually with the southpaw jab, Armour finally went to work in the seventh and dropped Adebayo with a crisp right-left. Although the Nigerian was up at three, the referee had seen enough and waved it off with 0.71 of the round remaining.

British and Commonwealth lightweight champion, Billy Schwer, stands over Sean Murphy moments before the referee stepped in to rescue the badly beaten challenger

Les Clark

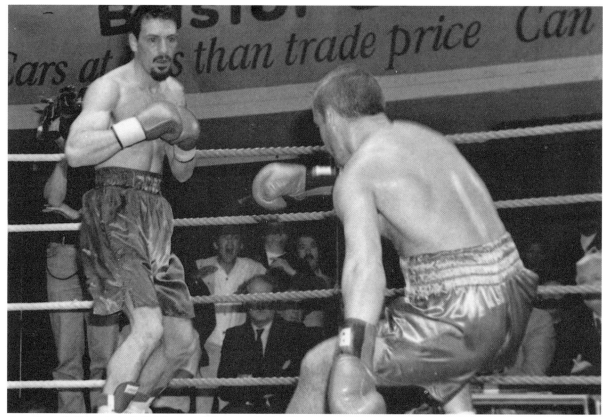

Ross Hale (left) sends Andy Holligan crashing to a third round stoppage defeat. With his victory, Hale won the British and Commonwealth light-welterweight titles

Les Clark

28 January, 1994   Francis Wanyama 13.0 (Uganda) W RSC 2 Tony Booth 13.2 (England), Waregem, Belgium (Vacant Cruiserweight Title). Referee: Mickey Vann. Taking part in the first Commonwealth title bout ever held in Belgium and fighting for the championship belt vacated by Derek Angol, Booth was just not up to the task. The referee gave the Englishman every chance, but stopped the action at 2.55 of the second round with Booth taking heavy punishment on the ropes without return.

9 February, 1994   Darren Fifield 7.13¼ (England) W RSC 6 Danny Porter 8.0 (England), York Hall, London (Flyweight Title). Referee: Roy Francis. After making an excellent start, Porter was gradually pegged back by a confident champion and yet again fell victim to eye damage when he was pulled out by Roy Francis at 2.08 of round six.

16 February, 1994   Billy Schwer 9.7¾ (England) W RSC 3 Sean Murphy 9.8¼ (England), Ice Bowl, Stevenage (Lightweight Title). Referee: Larry O'Connell. For a report, see under British Title Bouts, 1993-94.

26 February, 1994   Lloyd Honeyghan 10.12½ (England) W RSC 6 Kevin Adamson 10.13½ (England), Earls Court Arena, London (L. Middleweight Title). Referee: Dave Parris. The inexperienced Adamson, having survived a bad spell in the first and lasting another five sessions without ever establishing himself, eventually succumbed to a barrage of punches which sent him crashing to a stoppage defeat at 2.99 of round six.

11 May, 1994   Billy Schwer 9.8¼ (England) W RSC 9 Howard Grant 9.7½ (Canada), Ice Bowl, Stevenage (Lightweight Title). Referee: Mickey Vann. Schwer overcame cuts over both eyes and severe physical disadvantages, to blast his way to a ninth round stoppage win and a worthy world rating. Grant had been badly hurt in the eighth, but somehow survived until 2.57 of the ninth before the referee came to his aid.

24 May, 1994   Billy Hardy 8.12½ (England) W RSC 8 Alan McKay 8.12½ (England), Crowtree Leisure Centre, Sunderland (Featherweight Title). Referee: Paul Thomas. For a report, see under British Title Bouts, 1993-94.

25 May, 1994   Andy Holligan 9.13¾ (England) L RSC 3 Ross Hale 9.13¼ (England), Colston Hall, Bristol (L. Welterweight Title). Referee: Dave Parris. For a report, see under British Title Bouts, 1993-94.

Commonwealth Champions, 1908-1994

Prior to 1970, the championship was contested as for the British Empire title.

COMMONWEALTH COUNTRY CODE
A = Australia; BAH = Bahamas; BAR = Barbados; BER = Bermuda; C = Canada; E = England; F = Fiji; GH = Ghana; GU = Guyana; I = Ireland; J = Jamaica; K = Kenya; N = Nigeria; NZ = New Zealand; NI = Northern Ireland; PNG = Papua New Guinea; SA = South Africa; SAM = Samoa; S = Scotland; T = Tonga; TR = Trinidad; U = Uganda; W = Wales; ZA = Zambia; ZI = Zimbabwe.

*Undefeated champions (Includes men who may have forfeited their titles)

Alfred Kotey (Ghana), who held the Commonwealth flyweight title between 1989 and 1993, pictured with his newly won WBO bantamweight belt   John McDonald

Title Holder	Country	Tenure
Flyweight (112 lbs)		
Elky Clark*	S	1924-1927
Jackie Paterson	S	1940-1948
Rinty Monaghan*	NI	1948-1950
Teddy Gardner	E	1952
Jake Tuli	SA	1952-1954
Dai Dower*	W	1954-1957
Frankie Jones	S	1957
Dennis Adams*	SA	1957-1962
Jackie Brown	S	1962-1963
Walter McGowan*	S	1963-1969
John McCluskey	S	1970-1971
Henry Nissen	A	1971-1974
Big Jim West*	A	1974-1975
Patrick Mambwe	ZA	1976-1979
Ray Amoo	N	1980
Steve Muchoki	K	1980-1983
Keith Wallace*	E	1983-1984
Richard Clarke*	J	1986-1987
Nana Yaw Konadu*	GH	1987-1989
Alfred Kotey*	GH	1989-1993
Francis Ampofo*	E	1993
Darren Fifield	E	1993-
Bantamweight (118 lbs)		
Jim Higgins	S	1920-1922
Tommy Harrison	E	1922-1923
Bugler Harry Lake	E	1923
Johnny Brown	E	1923-1928
Teddy Baldock*	E	1928-1930
Dick Corbett	E	1930-1932
Johnny King	E	1932-1934
Dick Corbett*	E	1934
Jim Brady	S	1941-1945
Jackie Paterson	S	1945-1949
Stan Rowan	E	1949
Vic Toweel	SA	1949-1952
Jimmy Carruthers*	A	1952-1954
Peter Keenan	S	1955-1959
Freddie Gilroy*	NI	1959-1963
Johnny Caldwell	NI	1964-1965
Alan Rudkin	E	1965-1966
Walter McGowan	S	1966-1968
Alan Rudkin	E	1968-1969
Lionel Rose*	A	1969
Alan Rudkin*	E	1970-1972
Paul Ferreri	A	1972-1977
Sulley Shittu*	GH	1977-1978
Johnny Owen*	W	1978-1980
Paul Ferreri	A	1981-1986
Ray Minus*	BAH	1986-1991
John Armour	E	1992-
Featherweight (126 lbs)		
Jim Driscoll*	W	1908-1913
Llew Edwards*	W	1915-1917
Johnny McGrory*	S	1936-1938
Jim Spider Kelly	NI	1938-1939
Johnny Cusick	E	1939-1940
Nel Tarleton*	E	1940-1947
Tiger Al Phillips	E	1947

Title Holder	Country	Tenure
Ronnie Clayton	E	1947-1951
Roy Ankrah	GH	1951-1954
Billy Spider Kelly	NI	1954-1955
Hogan Kid Bassey*	N	1955-1957
Percy Lewis	TR	1957-1960
Floyd Robertson	GH	1960-1967
John O'Brien	S	1967
Johnny Famechon*	A	1967-1969
Toro George	NZ	1970-1972
Bobby Dunne	A	1972-1974
Evan Armstrong	S	1974
David Kotey*	GH	1974-1975
Eddie Ndukwu	N	1977-1980
Pat Ford*	GU	1980-1981
Azumah Nelson*	GH	1981-1985
Tyrone Downes*	BAR	1986-1988
Thunder Aryeh	GH	1988-1989
Oblitey Commey	GH	1989-1990
Modest Napunyi	K	1990-1991
Barrington Francis*	C	1991
Colin McMillan*	E	1992
Billy Hardy	E	1992-

S. Featherweight (130 lbs)

Title Holder	Country	Tenure
Billy Moeller	A	1975-1977
Johnny Aba*	PNG	1977-1982
Langton Tinago	ZI	1983-1984
John Sichula	ZA	1984
Lester Ellis*	A	1984-1985
John Sichula	ZA	1985-1986
Sam Akromah	GH	1986-1987
John Sichula	ZA	1987-1989
Mark Reefer*	E	1989-1990
Thunder Aryeh	GH	1990-1991
Hugh Forde	E	1991
Paul Harvey	E	1991-1992
Tony Pep	C	1992-

Lightweight (135 lbs)

Title Holder	Country	Tenure
Freddie Welsh*	W	1912-1914
Al Foreman	E	1930-1933
Jimmy Kelso	A	1933
Al Foreman*	E	1933-1934
Laurie Stevens	SA	1936
Arthur King	C	1948-1951
Frank Johnson	E	1953
Pat Ford	A	1953-1954
Ivor Germain	BAR	1954
Pat Ford*	A	1954-1955
Johnny van Rensburg	SA	1955-1956
Willie Toweel	SA	1956-1959
Dave Charnley	E	1959-1962
Bunny Grant	J	1962-1967
Manny Santos*	NZ	1967
Love Allotey	GH	1967-1968
Percy Hayles*	J	1968-1975
Jonathan Dele	N	1975-1977
Lennox Blackmore	GU	1977-1978
Hogan Jimoh	N	1978-1980
Langton Tinago	ZI	1980-1981
Barry Michael	A	1981-1982
Claude Noel	T	1982-1984
Graeme Brooke	A	1984-1985
Barry Michael	A	1985-1986
Langton Tinago	ZI	1986-1987
Mo Hussein	E	1987-1989
Pat Doherty	E	1989
Najib Daho	E	1989-1990
Carl Crook	E	1990-1992
Billy Schwer	E	1992-1993
Paul Burke	E	1993
Billy Schwer	E	1993-

L. Welterweight (140 lbs)

Title Holder	Country	Tenure
Joe Tetteh	GH	1972-1973
Hector Thompson	A	1973-1977
Baby Cassius Austin	A	1977-1978
Jeff Malcolm	A	1978-1979
Obisia Nwankpa	N	1979-1983
Billy Famous*	N	1983-1986
Tony Laing	E	1987-1988

Title Holder	Country	Tenure
Lester Ellis	A	1988-1989
Steve Larrimore	BAH	1989
Tony Ekubia	E	1989-1991
Andy Holligan	E	1991-1994
Ross Hale	E	1994-

Welterweight (147 lbs)

Title Holder	Country	Tenure
Johnny Summers	E	1912-1914
Tom McCormick	I	1914
Matt Wells	E	1914-1919
Johnny Basham	W	1919-1920
Ted Kid Lewis	E	1920-1924
Tommy Milligan*	S	1924-1925
Eddie Thomas	W	1951
Wally Thom	E	1951-1952
Cliff Curvis	W	1952
Gerald Dreyer	SA	1952-1954
Barry Brown	NZ	1954
George Barnes	A	1954-1956
Darby Brown	A	1956
George Barnes	A	1956-1958
Johnny van Rensburg	SA	1958
George Barnes	A	1958-1960
Brian Curvis*	W	1960-1966
Johnny Cooke	E	1967-1968
Ralph Charles*	E	1968-1972
Clyde Gray	C	1973-1979
Chris Clarke	C	1979
Clyde Gray*	C	1979-1980
Colin Jones*	W	1981-1984
Sylvester Mittee	E	1984-1985
Lloyd Honeyghan*	E	1985-1986
Brian Janssen	A	1987
Wilf Gentzen	A	1987-1988
Gary Jacobs	S	1988-1989
Donovan Boucher	C	1989-1992
Eamonn Loughran*	NI	1992-1993
Andrew Murray	GU	1993-

L. Middleweight (154 lbs)

Title Holder	Country	Tenure
Charkey Ramon*	A	1972-1975
Maurice Hope*	E	1976-1979
Kenny Bristol	GU	1979-1981
Herol Graham*	E	1981-1984
Ken Salisbury	A	1984-1985
Nick Wilshire	E	1985-1987
Lloyd Hibbert	E	1987
Troy Waters*	A	1987-1991
Chris Pyatt*	E	1991-1992
Mickey Hughes	E	1992-1993
Lloyd Honeyghan	E	1993-

Middleweight (160 lbs)

Title Holder	Country	Tenure
Ted Kid Lewis	E	1922-1923
Roland Todd*	E	1923-1925
Len Johnson*	E	1926
Tommy Milligan	S	1926-1928
Alex Ireland	S	1928-1929
Len Harvey	E	1929-1933
Jock McAvoy*	E	1933-1939
Ron Richards*	A	1940-1941
Bos Murphy	NZ	1948
Dick Turpin	E	1948-1949
Dave Sands*	A	1949-1952
Randy Turpin*	E	1952-1954
Johnny Sullivan	E	1954-1955
Pat McAteer	E	1955-1958
Dick Tiger	N	1958-1960
Wilf Greaves	C	1960
Dick Tiger*	N	1960-1962
Gomeo Brennan	BAH	1963-1964
Tuna Scanlon	NZ	1964
Gomeo Brennan	BAH	1964-1966
Blair Richardson*	C	1966-1967
Milo Calhoun	J	1967
Johnny Pritchett*	E	1967-1969
Les McAteer	E	1969-1970
Mark Rowe	E	1970
Bunny Sterling	E	1970-1972
Tony Mundine*	A	1972-1975
Monty Betham	NZ	1975-1978

Title Holder	Country	Tenure
Al Korovou	A	1978
Ayub Kalule*	U	1978-1980
Tony Sibson*	E	1980-1983
Roy Gumbs	E	1983
Mark Kaylor	E	1983-1984
Tony Sibson*	E	1984-1988
Nigel Benn	E	1988-1989
Michael Watson*	E	1989-1991
Richie Woodhall	E	1992-

S. Middleweight (168 lbs)

Title Holder	Country	Tenure
Rod Carr	A	1989-1990
Lou Cafaro*	A	1990-1991
Henry Wharton	E	1991-

L. Heavyweight (175 lbs)

Title Holder	Country	Tenure
Jack Bloomfield*	E	1923-1924
Tom Berry	E	1927
Gipsy Daniels*	W	1927
Len Harvey	E	1939-1942
Freddie Mills*	E	1942-1950
Randy Turpin*	E	1952-1955
Gordon Wallace	C	1956-1957
Yvon Durelle*	C	1957-1959
Chic Calderwood*	S	1960-1966
Bob Dunlop*	A	1968-1970
Eddie Avoth	W	1970-1971
Chris Finnegan	E	1971-1973
John Conteh*	E	1973-1974
Steve Aczel	A	1975
Tony Mundine	A	1975-1978
Gary Summerhays	C	1978-1979
Lottie Mwale	ZA	1979-1985
Leslie Stewart*	TR	1985-1987
Willie Featherstone	C	1987-1989
Guy Waters*	A	1989-1993
Brent Kosolofski	C	1993-

Cruiserweight (190 lbs)

Title Holder	Country	Tenure
Stewart Lithgo	E	1984
Chisanda Mutti	ZA	1984-1987
Glenn McCrory*	E	1987-1989
Apollo Sweet	A	1989
Derek Angol*	E	1989-1993
Francis Wanyama	U	1994-

Heavyweight (190 lbs +)

Title Holder	Country	Tenure
Tommy Burns	C	1910
P.O. Curran	I	1911
Dan Flynn	I	1911
Bombardier Billy Wells	E	1911-1919
Joe Beckett*	E	1919-1923
Phil Scott	E	1926-1931
Larry Gains	C	1931-1934
Len Harvey	E	1934
Jack Petersen	W	1934-1936
Ben Foord	SA	1936-1937
Tommy Farr*	W	1937-1938
Len Harvey*	E	1939-1942
Jack London	E	1944-1945
Bruce Woodcock	E	1945-1950
Jack Gardner	E	1950-1952
Johnny Williams	W	1952-1953
Don Cockell*	E	1953-1956
Joe Bygraves	J	1956-1957
Joe Erskine	W	1957-1958
Brian London	E	1958-1959
Henry Cooper	E	1959-1971
Joe Bugner	E	1971
Jack Bodell	E	1971-1972
Danny McAlinden	NI	1972-1975
Bunny Johnson	E	1975
Richard Dunn	E	1975-1976
Joe Bugner*	E	1976-1977
John L. Gardner*	E	1978-1981
Trevor Berbick*	C	1981-1986
Horace Notice*	E	1986-1988
Derek Williams	E	1988-1992
Lennox Lewis*	E	1992-1993
Henry Akinwande	E	1993-

European Title Bouts during 1993-94

All of last season's title bouts are shown in date order and give the boxers' respective weights, along with the scorecard, if going to a decision. There is also a short summary of any bout that involved a British contestant and British officials, where applicable, are listed.

25 August, 1993 Vincenzo Belcastro 8.5½ (Italy) W PTS 12 Antonio Picardi 8.5¾ (Italy), Urbino, Italy (Bantamweight Title). Scorecards: 118-111, 118-111, 117-112.

22 September, 1993 Gary Jacobs 10.6¾ (Scotland) W RSC 5 Daniel Bicchieray 10.6½ (France), Grand Hall, Wembley (Welterweight Title). Cut over both eyes and without the technique to duly worry Jacobs, Bicchieray was pulled out of the fight by the referee at 1.08 of the fifth round.

22 September, 1993 Luigi Camputaro 7.12½ (Italy) W PTS 12 Salvatore Fanni 7.8¾ (Italy), Oristano, Italy (Vacant Flyweight Title). Scorecard: 116-114, 116-113, 115-113. Robbie Regan had relinquished title in July 1993 to concentrate his efforts on a clash with the WBO champion, Jacob Matlala.

24 September, 1993 Maurizio Stecca 8.13¼ (Italy) L RTD 8 Stephane Haccoun 8.13¼ (France), Marseilles, France (Featherweight Title).

2 October, 1993 Jacobin Yoma 9.4 (France) W RSC 8 Areski Bakir 9.3¾ (France), Cayenne, French Guyana (S. Featherweight Title).

5 October, 1993 Laurent Boudouani 10.13¾ (France) L RTD 9 Bernard Razzano 10.12 (France), Dijon, France (L. Middleweight Title).

5 October, 1993 Jean-Baptiste Mendy 9.7¼ (France) W RTD 10 Angel Mona 9.8½ (France), Dijon, France (Lightweight Title). The title was declared vacant on Mendy taking on Miguel Gonzalez for the latter's WBC crown on 29 March 1994.

13 November, 1993 Eddy Smulders 12.4 (Holland) W PTS 12 Eric Nicoletta 12.5¾ (France), Castelnau le Naz, France (L. Heavyweight Title). Scorecard: 118-114, 117-113, 115-114.

26 November, 1993 Vincenzo Nardiello 11.13¼ (Italy) W PTS 12 Mauro Galvano 11.10¾ (Italy), Marino, Italy (Vacant S. Middleweight Title). Scorecard: 118-113, 117-112, 117-113. Ray Close had vacated title in September 1993 to concentrate on a return against WBO world champion, Chris Eubank.

1 December, 1993 Henry Akinwande 16.3½ (England) W RSC 4 Biagio Chianese 18.12 (Italy), Albert Hall, London (Heavyweight Title). After dominating the exchanges throughout, Akinwande ended the giant Italian's feeble challenge at 2.16 of the fourth round when a right-uppercut gashed him so badly that the referee was forced to intervene immediately.

4 December, 1993 Valery Kayumba 9.13¾ (France) L CO 2 Christian Merle 9.13 (France), Levallois, France (L. Welterweight Title).

11 December, 1993 Agostino Cardamone 11.4¾ (Italy) W PTS 12 Frederic Seillier 11.4 (France), Berck sur Mer, France (Middleweight Title). Scorecard: 117-114, 117-114, 115-113. Refereed by Roy Francis.

11 January, 1994 Bernard Razzano 11.0 (France) L RTD 6 Javier Castillejos 11.0 (Spain), Dijon, France (L. Middleweight Title). Referred by John Coyle.

28 January, 1994 Jacobin Yoma 9.3 (France) W RSC 8 Rimvidas Bilius 9.3¾ (Lithuania), Cayenne, French Guyana (S. Featherweight Title).

1 February, 1994 Gary Jacobs 10.7 (Scotland) W PTS 12 Tek Nkalankete 10.5 (France), Paris, France (Welterweight Title). Scorecard: 116-112, 118-114, 117-114. Smashed to the floor in the opening seconds, Nkalankete survived the shock to battle back and to give Jacobs a bit of a scrap. Jacobs finished with cuts to both eyes, but had the whiphand throughout.

2 February, 1994 Massimiliano Duran 13.7½ (Italy) L CO 8 Carl Thompson 13.6¾ (England), Ferrara, Italy (Cruiserweight Title). Away from home, Thompson pulled off a tremendous win when he put Duran down for the full count at 2.20 of round eight. The Italian had survived an earlier assault in round two, but this time Thompson made sure.

2 February, 1994 Vincenzo Belcastro 8.6 (Italy) W PTS 12 Drew Docherty 8.5½ (Scotland), Kelvin Hall, Glasgow (Bantamweight Title). Scorecard: 116-113, 118-112, 117-115. Having scored an early knockdown success, Docherty could not have been blamed for thinking it was going to be a good night's work. However, Belcastro had other ideas and proceeded to hustle the Scot all over the ring to finish a worthy points winner.

19 February, 1994 Javier Castillejos 10.13¾ (Spain) W RSC 3 Santo Colombo 10.12¼ (Italy), Madrid, Spain (L. Middleweight Title).

175

5 March, 1994   Eddy Smulders 12.5½ (Holland) L RSC 7 Fabrice Tiozzo 12.6 (France), Lyon, France (L. Heavyweight Title). One of the judges was Dave Parris.

22 March, 1994   Stephane Haccoun 8.13¼ (France) L RTD 9 Stefano Zoff 9.0 (Italy), Charleroi, Belgium (Featherweight Title).

25 March, 1994   Javier Castillejos 10.13¾ (Spain) W RTD 4 Valentino Manca 10.13½ (Italy), Cordoba, Spain (L. Middleweight) Title).

13 April, 1994   Gary Jacobs 10.6¼ (Scotland) W CO 8 Alessandro Duran 10.6⅛ (Italy), Scottish Exhibition Centre, Glasgow (Welterweight Title). With the fight evenly balanced, Jacobs produced a cracking right-hook to send the challenger down and out at 3.05 of the eighth round. Prior to that, Jacobs had dropped Duran twice in the third, only for the tough, rangy Italian to come right back into the fight to give the champion all the trouble he could handle.

14 April, 1994   Agostino Cardamone 11.5½ (Italy) W PTS 12 Gino Lelong 11.5¾ (France), Vitoria, Spain (Middleweight Title). Scorecard: 120-111, 120-112, 119-116.

17 April, 1994   Christian Merle 9.13 (France) L RSC 3 Valery Kayumba 9.13½ (France), Clermont Ferrand, France (L. Welterweight Title).

22 April, 1994   Racheed Lawal 9.8¼ (Denmark) W RSC 4 Paul Burke 9.8 (England), Aalborg, Denmark (Vacant Lightweight Title). Having knocked Lawal down in the second, one could have been forgiven for thinking that it was only a matter of time before Burke applied the finishing blow. However, the naturalised Dane had other ideas. While staggering around from the effects of another heavy punch in the fourth, and with Burke looking to end it there and then, the Englishman amazingly walked on to a "sucker" punch to be counted out himself.

27 April, 1994   Luigi Camputaro 7.12¾ (Italy) W PTS 12 Mickey Cantwell 7.13½ (England), York Hall, London (Flyweight Title). Scorecard: 115-114, 115-114, 116-113. Although Camputaro was cut in the opening round, he never let it worry him unduly and just about deserved the nod in an evenly contested little battle. Cantwell probably lost his opportunity when fading in the middle rounds, but put up a fine performance overall.

11 May, 1994   Vincenzo Belcastro 8.4¾ (Italy) L PTS 12 Prince Nassem Hamed 8.6 (England), Ponds Forge Arena, Sheffield (Bantamweight Title). Scorecard: 110-119, 109-120, 107-12 0. Getting up from a first round knockdown merely prolonged the agony for Belcastro as he was comprehensively outboxed and outclassed throughout the remainder of the contest. However, Hamed marred an almost flawless performance with his continuous taunting of a brave opponent and will need to keep that unnecessary element of his make-up in check if he is to carry the flag.

14 May, 1994   Jacobin Yoma 9.2 (France) W RTD 6 Neil Haddock 9.3¾ (Wales), Cayenne, French Guyana (S. Featherweight Title). Retiring on his stool at the end of the sixth round, Haddock had been on the receiving end throughout after suffering a broken nose early into the contest. It had been a brave display, but one that appeared doomed from the beginning.

20 May, 1994   Javier Castillejos 11.0 (Spain) W PTS 12 Patrick Vungbo 10.13¾ (Belgium), Madrid, Spain (L. Middleweight Title). Scorecard: 116-115, 115-113, 119-111. Mickey Vann acted as one of the judges.

4 June, 1994   Valery Kayumba 9.13¾ (France) L PTS 12 Khalid Rahilou 9.13¼ (France), Levallois Perret, France (L. Welterweight Title). Scorecard: 112-118, 115-117, 113-115.

11 June, 1994   Vincenzo Nardiello 12.0 (Italy) L RTD 5 Frederic Seillier 11.13½ (France), Toulon, France (S. Middleweight Title). Larry O'Connell refereed.

14 June, 1994   Carl Thompson 13.6¾ (England) W RSC 6 Akim Tafer 13.8 (France), Epernay, France (Cruiserweight Title). Technically limited and easy to hit, Thompson, having bounced back from two knockdowns himself, again proved his power when stopping Tafer in the sixth round. The end came when Tafer was sent crashing to the floor, the recipient of a powerful left-right combination and, although he somehow got to his feet, the referee continued to count him out.

Luigi Camputaro (Italy) lifts the EBU flyweight belt aloft following a successful defence against England's Mickey Cantwell   Les Clark

European Champions, 1909-1994

Prior to 1946, the championship was contested under the auspices of the International Boxing Union, re-named that year as the European Boxing Union (EBU).

EUROPEAN COUNTRY CODE
AU = Austria; BEL = Belgium; CZ = Czechoslovakia; DEN = Denmark; E = England; FIN = Finland; FR = France; GER = Germany; GRE = Greece; HOL = Holland; HUN = Hungary; ITA = Italy; LUX = Luxembourg; NI = Northern Ireland; NOR = Norway; POR = Portugal; ROM = Romania; S = Scotland; SP = Spain; SWE = Sweden; SWI = Switzerland; TU = Turkey; W = Wales; YUG = Yugoslavia.

*Undefeated champions (Includes men who may have forfeited their titles)

Title Holder	Country	Tenure	Title Holder	Country	Tenure	Title Holder	Country	Tenure
Flyweight (112 lbs)			Terry Allen	E	1950	Salvatore Fanni	ITA	1991-1992
Sid Smith	E	1913	Jean Sneyers*	BEL	1950-1951	Robbie Regan*	W	1992-1993
Bill Ladbury	E	1913-1914	Teddy Gardner*	E	1952	Luigi Camputaro	ITA	1993-
Percy Jones*	W	1914	Louis Skena*	FR	1953-1954			
Tancy Lee	S	1915-1916	Nazzareno Giannelli	ITA	1954-1955	**Bantamweight (118 lbs)**		
Jimmy Wilde*	W	1916-1923	Dai Dower	W	1955	Joe Bowker	E	1910
Michel Montreuil	BEL	1923-1925	Young Martin	SP	1955-1959	Digger Stanley	E	1910-1912
Elky Clark	S	1925-1927	Risto Luukkonen	FIN	1959-1961	Charles Ledoux	FR	1912-1921
Emile Pladner	FR	1928	Salvatore Burruni*	ITA	1961-1965	Tommy Harrison	E	1921-1922
Johnny Hill	S	1928-1929	Rene Libeer*	FR	1965-1966	Charles Ledoux	FR	1922-1923
Emile Pladner	FR	1929	Fernando Atzori	ITA	1967-1972	Bugler Harry Lake	E	1923
Eugene Huat*	FR	1929	Fritz Chervet*	SWI	1972-1973	Johnny Brown*	E	1923-1924
Kid Oliva	FR	1930	Fernando Atzori	ITA	1973	Henry Scillie*	BEL	1925-1928
Lucien Popescu	ROM	1930-1931	Fritz Chervet*	SWI	1973-1974	Domenico Bernasconi	ITA	1929
Jackie Brown*	E	1931-1932	Franco Udella	ITA	1974-1979	Carlos Flix	SP	1929-1931
Praxile Gyde	FR	1932-1935	Charlie Magri*	E	1979-1983	Lucien Popescu	ROM	1931-1932
Kid David*	BEL	1935-1936	Antoine Montero*	FR	1983-1984	Domenico Bernasconi*	ITA	1932
Ernst Weiss	AU	1936	Charlie Magri*	E	1984-1985	Nicholas Biquet	BEL	1932-1935
Valentin Angelmann*	FR	1936-1938	Franco Cherchi	ITA	1985	Maurice Dubois	SWI	1935-1936
Enrico Urbinati*	ITA	1938-1943	Charlie Magri	E	1985-1986	Joseph Decico	FR	1936
Raoul Degryse	BEL	1946-1947	Duke McKenzie*	E	1986-1988	Aurel Toma*	ROM	1936-1937
Maurice Sandeyron	FR	1947-1949	Eyup Can*	TU	1989-1990	Nicholas Biquet*	BEL	1937-1938
Rinty Monaghan*	NI	1949-1950	Pat Clinton*	S	1990-1991	Aurel Toma	ROM	1938-1939
						Ernst Weiss	AU	1939
						Gino Cattaneo	ITA	1939-1941
						Gino Bondavilli*	ITA	1941-1943
						Jackie Paterson	S	1946
						Theo Medina	FR	1946-1947
						Peter Kane	E	1947-1948
						Guido Ferracin	ITA	1948-1949
						Luis Romero	SP	1949-1951
						Peter Keenan	S	1951-1952
						Jean Sneyers*	BEL	1952-1953
						Peter Keenan	S	1953
						John Kelly	NI	1953-1954
						Robert Cohen*	FR	1954-1955
						Mario D'Agata	ITA	1955-1958
						Piero Rollo	ITA	1958-1959
						Freddie Gilroy	NI	1959-1960
						Pierre Cossemyns	BEL	1961-1962
						Piero Rollo	ITA	1962
						Alphonse Halimi	FR	1962
						Piero Rollo	ITA	1962-1963
						Mimoun Ben Ali	SP	1963
						Risto Luukkonen*	FIN	1963-1964
						Mimoun Ben Ali	SP	1965
						Tommaso Galli	ITA	1965-1966
						Mimoun Ben Ali	SP	1966-1968
						Salvatore Burruni*	ITA	1968-1969
						Franco Zurlo	ITA	1969-1971
						Alan Rudkin	E	1971
						Agustin Senin*	SP	1971-1973
						Johnny Clark*	E	1973-1974
						Bob Allotey	SP	1974-1975

England's Mickey Cantwell (left) gave it his best shot, but lacked the neccesary power to upset the 112lbs champion, Luigi Camputaro   Les Clark

Prince Nassem Hamed (right) boxed his way to a comprehensive points win over the European bantamweight champion, Vincenzo Belcastro, and promises to go all the way   Les Clark

Title Holder	Country	Tenure	Title Holder	Country	Tenure	Title Holder	Country	Tenure
Daniel Trioulaire	FR	1975-1976	Henri Hebrans	BEL	1924-1925	Manuel Masso	SP	1977
Salvatore Fabrizio	ITA	1976-1977	Antonio Ruiz	SP	1925-1928	Roberto Castanon*	SP	1977-1981
Franco Zurlo	ITA	1977-1978	Luigi Quadrini	ITA	1928-1929	Salvatore Melluzzo	ITA	1981-1982
Juan Francisco			Knud Larsen	DEN	1929	Pat Cowdell*	E	1982-1983
Rodriguez	SP	1978-1980	Jose Girones*	SP	1929-1934	Loris Stecca*	ITA	1983
Johnny Owen*	W	1980	Maurice Holtzer*	FR	1935-1938	Barry McGuigan*	NI	1983-1985
Valerio Nati	ITA	1980-1982	Phil Dolhem	BEL	1938-1939	Jim McDonnell*	E	1985-1987
Giuseppe Fossati	ITA	1982-1983	Lucien Popescu	ROM	1939-1941	Valerio Nati*	ITA	1987
Walter Giorgetti*	ITA	1983-1984	Ernst Weiss	AU	1941	Jean-Marc Renard*	BEL	1988-1989
Ciro de Leva*	ITA	1984-1986	Gino Bondavilli	ITA	1941-1945	Paul Hodkinson*	E	1989-1991
Antoine Montero	FR	1986-1987	Ermanno Bonetti*	ITA	1945-1946	Fabrice Benichou	FR	1991-1992
Louis Gomis*	FR	1987-1988	Tiger Al Phillips	E	1947	Maurizio Stecca	ITA	1992-1993
Fabrice Benichou	FR	1988	Ronnie Clayton	E	1947-1948	Herve Jacob	FR	1993
Vincenzo Belcastro*	ITA	1988-1990	Ray Famechon	FR	1948-1953	Maurizio Stecca	ITA	1993
Thierry Jacob*	FR	1990-1992	Jean Sneyers	BEL	1953-1954	Stephane Haccoun	FR	1993-1994
Johnny Bredahl*	DEN	1992	Ray Famechon	FR	1954-1955	Stefano Zoff	ITA	1994-
Vincenzo Belcastro	ITA	1993-1994	Fred Galiana*	SP	1955-1956			
Prince Nassem Hamed	E	1994-	Cherif Hamia*	FR	1957-1958	**S. Featherweight (130 lbs)**		
			Sergio Caprari	ITA	1958-1959	Tommaso Galli	ITA	1971-1972
Featherweight (126 lbs)			Gracieux Lamperti	FR	1959-1962	Domenico Chiloiro	ITA	1972
Young Joey Smith	E	1911	Alberto Serti	ITA	1962-1963	Lothar Abend	GER	1972-1974
Jean Poesy	FR	1911-1912	Howard Winstone*	W	1963-1967	Sven-Erik Paulsen*	NOR	1974-1976
Jim Driscoll*	W	1912-1913	Jose Legra*	SP	1967-1968	Roland Cazeaux	FR	1976
Ted Kid Lewis*	E	1913-1914	Manuel Calvo	SP	1968-1969	Natale Vezzoli	ITA	1976-1979
Louis de Ponthieu*	FR	1919-1920	Tommaso Galli	ITA	1969-1970	Carlos Hernandez	SP	1979
Arthur Wyns	BEL	1920-1922	Jose Legra*	SP	1970-1972	Rodolfo Sanchez	SP	1979
Eugene Criqui*	FR	1922-1923	Gitano Jiminez	SP	1973-1975	Carlos Hernandez	SP	1979-1982
Edouard Mascart	FR	1923-1924	Elio Cotena	ITA	1975-1976	Cornelius		
Charles Ledoux	FR	1924	Nino Jimenez	SP	1976-1977	Boza-Edwards*	E	1982

Title Holder	Country	Tenure
Roberto Castanon	SP	1982-1983
Alfredo Raininger	ITA	1983-1984
Jean-Marc Renard	BEL	1984
Pat Cowdell*	E	1984-1985
Jean-Marc Renard*	BEL	1986-1987
Salvatore Curcetti	ITA	1987-1988
Piero Morello	ITA	1988
Lars Lund Jensen	DEN	1988
Racheed Lawal	DEN	1988-1989
Daniel Londas*	FR	1989-1991
Jimmy Bredahl*	DEN	1992
Regilio Tuur	HOL	1992-1993
Jacobin Yoma	FR	1993-

Lightweight (135 lbs)

Title Holder	Country	Tenure
Freddie Welsh	W	1909-1911
Matt Wells	E	1911-1912
Freddie Welsh*	W	1912-1914
Bob Marriott	E	1919-1920
Georges Papin	FR	1920-1921
Ernie Rice	E	1921-1922
Seaman Nobby Hall	E	1922-1923
Harry Mason*	E	1923
Fred Bretonnel	FR	1924
Lucien Vinez	FR	1924-1927
Luis Rayo*	SP	1927-1928
Aime Raphael	FR	1928-1929
Francois Sybille	BEL	1929-1930
Alf Howard	E	1930
Francois Sybille	BEL	1930-1931
Bep van Klaveren	HOL	1931-1932
Cleto Locatelli	ITA	1932
Francois Sybille	BEL	1932-1933
Cleto Locatelli*	ITA	1933
Francois Sybille	BEL	1934
Carlo Orlandi*	ITA	1934-1935
Enrico Venturi*	ITA	1935-1936
Vittorio Tamagnini	I.	1936-1937
Maurice Arnault	FR	1937
Gustave Humery*	FR	1937-1938
Aldo Spoldi*	ITA	1938-1939
Karl Blaho	AU	1940-1941
Bruno Bisterzo	ITA	1941
Ascenzo Botta	ITA	1941
Bruno Bisterzo	ITA	1941-1942
Ascenzo Botta	ITA	1942
Roberto Proietti	ITA	1942-1943
Bruno Bisterzo	ITA	1943-1946
Roberto Proietti*	ITA	1946
Emile Dicristo	FR	1946-1947
Kid Dussart	BEL	1947
Roberto Proietti	ITA	1947-1948
Billy Thompson	E	1948-1949
Kid Dussart	BEL	1949
Roberto Proietti*	ITA	1949-1950
Pierre Montane	FR	1951
Elis Ask	FIN	1951-1952
Jorgen Johansen	DEN	1952-1954
Duilio Loi*	ITA	1954-1959
Mario Vecchiatto	ITA	1959-1960
Dave Charnley*	E	1960-1963
Conny Rudhof*	GER	1963-1964
Willi Quatuor	GER	1964-1965
Franco Brondi	ITA	1965
Maurice Tavant	FR	1965-1966
Borge Krogh	DEN	1966-1967
Pedro Carrasco*	SP	1967-1969
Miguel Velazquez	SP	1970-1971
Antonio Puddu	ITA	1971-1974
Ken Buchanan*	S	1974-1975

Title Holder	Country	Tenure
Fernand Roelandts	BEL	1976
Perico Fernandez*	SP	1976-1977
Jim Watt*	S	1977-1979
Charlie Nash*	NI	1979-1980
Francisco Leon	SP	1980
Charlie Nash	NI	1980-1981
Joey Gibilisco	ITA	1981-1983
Lucio Cusma	ITA	1983-1984
Rene Weller	GER	1984-1986
Gert Bo Jacobsen*	DEN	1986-1988
Rene Weller*	GER	1988
Policarpo Diaz*	SP	1988-1990
Antonio Renzo	ITA	1991-1992
Jean-Baptiste Mendy*	FR	1992-1994
Racheed Lawal	DEN	1994-

L. Welterweight (140 lbs)

Title Holder	Country	Tenure
Olli Maki*	FIN	1964-1965
Juan Sombrita-Albornoz	SP	1965
Willi Quatuor*	GER	1965-1966
Conny Rudhof	GER	1967
Johann Orsolics	AU	1967-1968
Bruno Arcari*	ITA	1968-1970
Rene Roque	FR	1970-1971
Pedro Carrasco*	SP	1971-1972
Roger Zami	FR	1972
Cemal Kamaci	TU	1972-1973
Toni Ortiz	SP	1973-1974
Perico Fernandez*	SP	1974
Jose Ramon Gomez-Fouz	SP	1975
Cemal Kamaci	TU	1975-1976
Dave Boy Green*	E	1976-1977
Primo Bandini	ITA	1977
Jean-Baptiste Piedvache	FR	1977-1978
Colin Power	E	1978
Fernando Sanchez	SP	1978-1979
Jose Luis Heredia	SP	1979
Jo Kimpuani*	FR	1979-1980
Giuseppe Martinese	ITA	1980
Antonio Guinaldo	SP	1980-1981
Clinton McKenzie	E	1981-1982
Robert Gambini	FR	1982-1983
Patrizio Oliva*	ITA	1983-1985
Terry Marsh*	E	1985-1986
Tusikoleta Nkalankete	FR	1987-1989
Efren Calamati	ITA	1989-1990
Pat Barrett*	E	1990-1992
Valery Kayumba	ITA	1992-1993
Christian Merle	FR	1993-1994
Valery Kayumba	FR	1994
Khalid Rahilou	FR	1994-

Welterweight (147 lbs)

Title Holder	Country	Tenure
Young Joseph	E	1910-1911
Georges Carpentier*	FR	1911-1912
Albert Badoud*	SWI	1915-1919
Johnny Basham	W	1919-1920
Ted Kid Lewis*	E	1920
Piet Hobin*	BEL	1921-1925
Mario Bosisio*	ITA	1925-1928
Alf Genon	BEL	1928-1929
Gustave Roth	BEL	1929-1932
Adrien Aneet	BEL	1932-1933
Jack Hood*	E	1933
Gustav Eder*	GER	1934-1936
Felix Wouters	BEL	1936-1938
Saverio Turiello	ITA	1938-1939
Marcel Cerdan*	FR	1939-1942
Ernie Roderick	E	1946-1947
Robert Villemain*	FR	1947-1948

Title Holder	Country	Tenure
Livio Minelli	ITA	1949-1950
Michele Palermo	ITA	1950 1951
Eddie Thomas	W	1951
Charles Humez*	FR	1951-1952
Gilbert Lavoine	FR	1953-1954
Wally Thom	E	1954-1955
Idrissa Dione	FR	1955-1956
Emilio Marconi	ITA	1956-1958
Peter Waterman*	E	1958
Emilio Marconi	ITA	1958-1959
Duilio Loi*	ITA	1959-1963
Fortunato Manca*	ITA	1964-1965
Jean Josselin	FR	1966-1967
Carmelo Bossi	ITA	1967-1968
Fighting Mack	HOL	1968-1969
Silvano Bertini	ITA	1969
Jean Josselin	FR	1969
Johann Orsolics	AU	1969-1970
Ralph Charles	E	1970-1971
Roger Menetrey	FR	1971-1974
John H. Stracey*	E	1974-1975
Marco Scano	ITA	1976-1977
Jorgen Hansen	DEN	1977
Jorg Eipel	GER	1977
Alain Marion	FR	1977-1978
Jorgen Hansen	DEN	1978
Josef Pachler	AU	1978
Henry Rhiney	E	1978-1979
Dave Boy Green	E	1979
Jorgen Hansen*	DEN	1979-1981
Hans-Henrik Palm	DEN	1982
Colin Jones*	W	1982-1983
Gilles Elbilia*	FR	1983-1984
Gianfranco Rosi	ITA	1984-1985
Lloyd Honeyghan*	E	1985-1986
Jose Varela	GER	1986-1987
Alfonso Redondo	SP	1987
Mauro Martelli*	SWI	1987-1988
Nino la Rocca	ITA	1989
Antoine Fernandez	FR	1989-1990
Kirkland Laing	E	1990
Patrizio Oliva*	ITA	1990-1992
Ludovic Proto	FR	1992-1993
Gary Jacobs	S	1993-

L. Middleweight (154 lbs)

Title Holder	Country	Tenure
Bruno Visintin	ITA	1964-1966
Bo Hogberg	SWE	1966
Yolande Leveque	FR	1966
Sandro Mazzinghi*	ITA	1966-1968
Remo Golfarini	ITA	1968-1969
Gerhard Piaskowy	GER	1969-1970
Jose Hernandez	SP	1970-1972
Juan Carlos Duran	ITA	1972-1973
Jacques Kechichian	FR	1973-1974
Jose Duran	SP	1974-1975
Eckhard Dagge	GER	1975-1976
Vito Antuofermo	ITA	1976
Maurice Hope*	E	1976-1978
Gilbert Cohen	FR	1978-1979
Marijan Benes	YUG	1979-1981
Louis Acaries	FR	1981
Luigi Minchillo*	ITA	1981-1983
Herol Graham*	E	1983-1984
Jimmy Cable	E	1984
Georg Steinherr*	GER	1984-1985
Said Skouma*	FR	1985-1986
Chris Pyatt	E	1986-1987
Gianfranco Rosi*	ITA	1987
Rene Jacquot*	FR	1988-1989

Title Holder	Country	Tenure
Edip Secovic	AU	1989
Giuseppe Leto	ITA	1989
Gilbert Dele*	FR	1989-1990
Said Skouma	FR	1991
Mourad Louati	HOL	1991
Jean-Claude Fontana	FR	1991-1992
Laurent Boudouani	FR	1992-1993
Bernard Razzano	FR	1993-1994
Javier Castillejos	SP	1994-

Middleweight (160 lbs)

Title Holder	Country	Tenure
Georges Carpentier*	FR	1912-1918
Ercole Balzac	FR	1920-1921
Gus Platts	E	1921
Johnny Basham	W	1921
Ted Kid Lewis	E	1921-1923
Roland Todd	E	1923-1924
Bruno Frattini	ITA	1924-1925
Tommy Milligan*	S	1925
Rene Devos*	BEL	1926-1927
Mario Bosisio	ITA	1928
Leone Jacovacci	ITA	1928-1929
Marcel Thil	FR	1929-1930
Mario Bosisio	ITA	1930-1931
Poldi Steinbach	AU	1931
Hein Domgoergen*	GER	1931-1932
Ignacio Ara*	SP	1932-1933
Gustave Roth	BEL	1933-1934
Marcel Thil	FR	1934-1938
Edouard Tenet	FR	1938
Bep van Klaveren	HOL	1938
Anton Christoforidis	GRE	1938-1939
Edouard Tenet*	FR	1939
Josef Besselmann*	GER	1942-1943
Marcel Cerdan	FR	1947-1948
Cyrille Delannoit	BEL	1948
Marcel Cerdan*	FR	1948
Cyrille Delannoit	BEL	1948-1949
Tiberio Mitri*	ITA	1949-1950
Randy Turpin	E	1951-1954
Tiberio Mitri	ITA	1954
Charles Humez	FR	1954-1958
Gustav Scholz*	GER	1958-1961
John Cowboy McCormack	S	1961-1962
Chris Christensen	DEN	1962
Laszlo Papp*	HUN	1962-1965
Nino Benvenuti*	ITA	1965-1967
Juan Carlos Duran	ITA	1967-1969
Tom Bogs	DEN	1969-1970
Juan Carlos Duran	ITA	1970-1971
Jean-Claude Bouttier*	FR	1971-1972
Tom Bogs*	DEN	1973
Elio Calcabrini	ITA	1973-1974
Jean-Claude Bouttier	FR	1974
Kevin Finnegan	E	1974-1975
Gratien Tonna*	FR	1975
Bunny Sterling	E	1976
Angelo Jacopucci	ITA	1976
Germano Valsecchi	ITA	1976-1977
Alan Minter	E	1977
Gratien Tonna*	FR	1977-1978
Alan Minter*	E	1978-1979
Kevin Finnegan	E	1980
Matteo Salvemini	ITA	1980
Tony Sibson*	E	1980-1982
Louis Acaries	FR	1982-1984
Tony Sibson*	E	1984-1985
Ayub Kalule	DEN	1985-1986
Herol Graham	E	1986-1987

Title Holder	Country	Tenure
Sumbu Kalambay*	ITA	1987
Pierre Joly	FR	1987-1988
Christophe Tiozzo*	FR	1988-1989
Francesco dell' Aquila	ITA	1989-1990
Sumbu Kalambay*	ITA	1990-1993
Agostino Cardamone	ITA	1993-

S. Middleweight (168 lbs)

Title Holder	Country	Tenure
Mauro Galvano	ITA	1990-1991
James Cook	E	1991-1992
Franck Nicotra*	FR	1992
Vincenzo Nardiello	ITA	1992-1993
Ray Close*	NI	1993
Vinzenzo Nardiello	ITA	1993-1994
Frederic Seillier	FR	1994-

L. Heavyweight (175 lbs)

Title Holder	Country	Tenure
Georges Carpentier	FR	1913-1922
Battling Siki	FR	1922-1923
Emile Morelle	FR	1923
Raymond Bonnel	FR	1923-1924
Louis Clement	SWI	1924-1926
Herman van T'Hof	HOL	1926
Fernand Delarge	BEL	1926-1927
Max Schmeling*	GER	1927-1928
Michele Bonaglia*	ITA	1929-1930
Ernst Pistulla*	GER	1931-1932
Adolf Heuser*	GER	1932
John Andersson*	SWE	1933
Martinez de Alfara	SP	1934
Marcel Thil*	FR	1934-1935
Merlo Preciso	ITA	1935
Hein Lazek	AU	1935-1936
Gustave Roth	BEL	1936-1938
Adolf Heuser*	GER	1938-1939
Luigi Musina*	ITA	1942-1943
Freddie Mills*	E	1947-1950
Albert Yvel	FR	1950-1951
Don Cockell*	E	1951-1952
Conny Rux*	GER	1952
Jacques Hairabedian	FR	1953-1954
Gerhard Hecht	GER	1954-1955
Willi Hoepner	GER	1955
Gerhard Hecht	GER	1955-1957
Artemio Calzavara	ITA	1957-1958
Willi Hoepner	GER	1958
Erich Schoeppner*	GER	1958-1962
Giulio Rinaldi	ITA	1962-1964
Gustav Scholz*	GER	1964-1965
Giulio Rinaldi	ITA	1965-1966
Piero del Papa	ITA	1966-1967
Lothar Stengel	GER	1967-1968
Tom Bogs	DEN	1968-1969
Yvan Prebeg	YUG	1969-1970
Piero del Papa	ITA	1970-1971
Conny Velensek	GER	1971-1972
Chris Finnegan	E	1972
Rudiger Schmidtke	GER	1972-1973
John Conteh*	E	1973-1974
Domenico Adinolfi	ITA	1974-1976
Mate Parlov*	YUG	1976-1977
Aldo Traversaro	ITA	1977-1979
Rudi Koopmans	HOL	1979-1984
Richard Caramonolis	FR	1984
Alex Blanchard	HOL	1984-1987
Tom Collins	E	1987-1988
Pedro van Raamsdonk	HOL	1988
Jan Lefeber	HOL	1988-1989
Eric Nicoletta	FR	1989-1990
Tom Collins*	E	1990-1991

Title Holder	Country	Tenure
Graciano Rocchigiani*	GER	1991-1992
Eddie Smulders	HOL	1993-1994
Fabrice Tiozzo	FR	1994-

Cruiserweight (190 lbs)

Title Holder	Country	Tenure
Sam Reeson*	E	1987-1988
Angelo Rottoli	ITA	1989
Anaclet Wamba*	FR	1989-1990
Johnny Nelson*	E	1990-1992
Akim Tafer*	FR	1992-1993
Massimiliano Duran	ITA	1993-1994
Carl Thompson	E	1994-

Heavyweight (190 lbs +)

Title Holder	Country	Tenure
Georges Carpentier	FR	1913-1922
Battling Siki*	FR	1922-1923
Erminio Spalla	ITA	1923-1926
Paolino Uzcudun*	SP	1926-1928
Pierre Charles	BEL	1929-1931
Hein Muller	GER	1931-1932
Pierre Charles	BEL	1932-1933
Paolino Uzcudun	SP	1933
Primo Carnera*	ITA	1933-1935
Pierre Charles	BEL	1935-1937
Arno Kolblin	GER	1937-1938
Hein Lazek	AU	1938-1939
Adolf Heuser	GER	1939
Max Schmeling*	GER	1939-1941
Olle Tandberg	SWE	1943
Karel Sys*	BEL	1943-1946
Bruce Woodcock*	E	1946-1949
Joe Weidin	AU	1950-1951
Jack Gardner	E	1951
Hein Ten Hoff	GER	1951-1952
Karel Sys	BEL	1952
Heinz Neuhaus	GER	1952-1955
Franco Cavicchi	ITA	1955-1956
Ingemar Johansson*	SWE	1956-1959
Dick Richardson	W	1960-1962
Ingemar Johansson*	SWE	1962-1963
Henry Cooper*	E	1964
Karl Mildenberger	GER	1964-1968
Henry Cooper*	E	1968-1969
Peter Weiland	GER	1969-1970
Jose Urtain	SP	1970
Henry Cooper	E	1970-1971
Joe Bugner	E	1971
Jack Bodell	E	1971
Jose Urtain	SP	1971-1972
Jurgen Blin	GER	1972
Joe Bugner*	E	1972-1975
Richard Dunn	E	1976
Joe Bugner*	E	1976-1977
Jean-Pierre Coopman	BEL	1977
Lucien Rodriguez	FR	1977
Alfredo Evangelista	SP	1977-1979
Lorenzo Zanon*	SP	1979-1980
John L. Gardner*	E	1980-1981
Lucien Rodriguez	FR	1981-1984
Steffen Tangstad	NOR	1984-1985
Anders Eklund	SWE	1985
Frank Bruno*	E	1985-1986
Steffen Tangstad*	NOR	1986
Alfredo Evangelista	SP	1987
Anders Eklund	SWE	1987
Francesco Damiani*	ITA	1987-1989
Derek Williams	E	1989-1990
Jean Chanet	FR	1990
Lennox Lewis*	E	1990-1992
Henry Akinwande	E	1993-

A-Z of Current World Champions

by Eric Armit

Shows the record since 1 July 1993, plus career summary, for all men holding IBF/WBA/WBC/WBO titles as at 30 June 1994. The author has also produced a pen portrait of the men who first won titles between 1 July 1993 and 30 June 1994. Incidentally, the place name given is the respective boxer's domicile and may not necessarily be his birthplace, while all nicknames are shown where applicable. Not included are fighters such as Michael Bentt (WBO-Heavy), Simon Brown (WBC-L. Middle), Jose Luis Bueno (WBC-S. Fly), Evander Holyfield (WBA/IBF-Heavy), Junior Jones (WBA-Bantam) and Frankie Randall (WBC-L. Welter), who won and lost titles during the period in question.

Yuri (Ebihara) Arbachakov

Kemerova, Armenia. *Born* 22 October, 1966
WBC Flyweight Champion. Former Undefeated Japanese Flyweight Champion

16.07.93	Ysaias Zamudio W PTS 12 Kobe *(WBC Flyweight Title Defence)*
13.12.93	Nam-Hoon Cha W PTS 12 Kyoto *(WBC Flyweight Title Defence)*
16.05.94	Hiroshi Kobayashi W RSC 9 Tokyo
Career: 18 contests, won 18.	

Leonzer Barber

Detroit, USA. *Born* 18 February, 1966
WBO L. Heavyweight Champion. Former Undefeated WBC Con Am L. Heavyweight Champion

29.09.93	Andrea Magi W PTS 12 Pesaro *(WBO L. Heavyweight Title Defence)*
29.01.94	Nicky Piper W RSC 9 Cardiff *(WBO L. Heavyweight Title Defence)*
Career: 20 contests, won 19, lost 1.	

A battered Leonzer Barber gives a victory salute after belting out Britain's Nicky Piper   Les Clark

Nigel (Dark Destroyer) Benn

Ilford, England. *Born* 22 January, 1964
WBC S. Middleweight Champion. Former WBO & Commonwealth Middleweight Champion

Note: Full record will be found in the Current British-Based Champions: Career Records' section.

Nigel Benn kisses his dad after another successful defence   Les Clark

Julio Cesar (Navajo) Borboa

Guaymas, Mexico. *Born* 12 August, 1969
IBF S. Flyweight Champion

21.08.93	Carlos Mercado W CO 3 Kalispel *(IBF S. Flyweight Title Defence)*
26.11.93	Rolando Pascua W RSC 5 Hermosillo *(IBF S. Flyweight Title Defence)*
25.04.94	Jorge Roman W RSC 4 Los Angeles *(IBF S. Flyweight Title Defence)*
21.05.94	Jaji Sibali W RSC 9 Temba *(IBF S. Flyweight Title Defence)*
Career: 27 contests, won 23, lost 4.	

Johnny Bredahl

Copenhagen, Denmark. *Born* 27 August, 1968
WBO S. Flyweight Champion. Former Undefeated European Bantamweight Champion

17.09.93	Antonio Morales W RSC 3 Copenhagen
29.10.93	Eduardo Nazario W DIS 4 Korsor *(WBO S. Flyweight Title Defence)*
25.03.94	Eduardo Nazario W PTS 12 Aakirkeby *(WBO S. Flyweight Title Defence)*
Career: 20 contests, won 20.	

Josue (Dickie) Camacho

Guaynabo, Puerto Rico. *Born* 31 January, 1969
WBO L. Flyweight Champion. Former Undefeated Puerto Rican Flyweight Champion

25.09.93	Julio Acevedo W RSC 8 Guaynabo
02.02.94	Paul Weir W PTS 12 Glasgow *(WBO Flyweight Title Defence)*
Career: 17 contests, won 15, lost 2.	

Orlando Canizales

Laredo, USA. *Born* 25 November, 1965
IBF Bantamweight Champion. Former Undefeated USBA S. Flyweight Champion. Former Undefeated NABF Flyweight Champion

20.11.93	Juvenal Berrio W PTS 12 Temba *(IBF Bantamweight Title Defence)*
26.02.94	Gerardo Martinez W RSC 4 San Jose *(IBF Bantamweight Title Defence)*
07.06.94	Rolando Bohol W RSC 5 South Padre Island *(IBF Bantamweight Title Defence)*
Career: 40 contests, won 37, drew 1, lost 1, no decision 1.	

Julio Cesar (Super Star) Chavez

Ciudad Obregon, Mexico. *Born* 12 July, 1962
WBC L. Welterweight Champion. Former Undefeated IBF
L. Welterweight Champion. Former Undefeated WBC & WBA
Lightweight Champion. Former Undefeated WBC S. Featherweight Champion

10.09.93	Pernell Whitaker DREW 12 San Antonio *(WBC Welterweight Title Challenge)*
30.10.93	Mike Powell W RSC 5 Juarez
18.12.93	Andy Holligan W RSC 5 Puebla *(WBC L. Welterweight Title Defence)*
29.01.94	Frankie Randall L PTS 12 Las Vegas *(WBC L. Welterweight Title Defence)*
07.05.94	Frankie Randall W TD 8 Las Vegas *(WBC L. Welterweight Title Challenge)*

Career: 92 contests, won 90, drew 1, lost 1.

Juan M. (Latigo) Coggi

Santa Fe, Argentine. *Born* 19 December, 1961
WBA L. Welterweight Champion. Former Undefeated Argentinian
L. Welterweight Champion

13.08.93	Jose Barbosa W PTS 12 Buenos Aires *(WBA L. Welterweight Title Defence)*
24.09.93	Guillermo Cruz W RSC 10 Tucuman *(WBA L. Welterweight Title Defence)*
17.12.93	Eder Gonzalez W RSC 7 Tucuman *(WBA L. Welterweight Title Defence)*
18.03.94	Eder Gonzalez W RSC 3 Las Vegas *(WBA L. Welterweight Title Defence)*

Career: 70 contests, won 66, drew 2, lost 2.

Juan M. Coggi

Al (Ice) Cole

Suffern, USA. *Born* 21 April, 1964
IBF Cruiserweight Champion. Former Unbeaten USBA Cruiserweight Champion

16.07.93	Glenn McCrory W PTS 12 Moscow *(IBF Cruiserweight Title Defence)*
17.11.93	Vince Boulware W RSC 5 Atlantic City *(IBF Cruiserweight Title Defence)*

Career: 25 contests, won 24, lost 1.

Steve Collins

Dublin, Ireland. *Born* 21 July, 1964
WBO Middleweight Champion. Former Undefeated All-Ireland, USBA and WBO Penta-Continental Middleweight Champion

A leading Irish amateur, and having won the national middleweight title in 1986, he turned professional later that year under the watchful eyes of the famous Petronelli brothers in the USA (Boston). Tall for the weight at 5'11", with a sound defence and strong right-hand punching power and the ability to take a good shot, even at the beginning of his pro career the tough southpaw was expected to go a considerable way in the game. He did not disappoint. After victories over seven run of the mill opponents, Steve was matched against fellow Irishman, Sammy Storey, in a fight that also carried the vacant all-Ireland middleweight title. It was the first time that an Irish title had been contested in America and Steve boxed his way to a sound ten round points decision in front of his exiled fans. His next real test came against the up-and-coming Paul McPeak. Having put McPeak out of contention, following a ninth round stoppage win, the Irishman next outpointed the highly rated Kevin Watts. That was no easy task and he had to survive an 11th round knockdown to ultimately outpunch the champion and win the USBA title, before successfully defending against the dangerous Tony Thornton. Those sterling victories gave him the credentials to step up in class against WBA champion, Mike McCallum, as a late replacement for the injured Michael Watson. Although the experienced champion retained his crown, it was not before the Irishman

had given him a good run for his money. It was then back to domestic business, but after two wins over Fermin Chirino and Eddie Hall in Boston, and with his contract with the Petronelli's expiring on 17 March 1991, he went home to Ireland and signed up with Barney Eastwood. While Steve's new campaign got underway with good victories over Kenny Snow, Jean-Noel Camara and Danny Morgan, they were followed by losing title attempts against Reggie Johnson and Sumbu Kalambay. The match against Johnson carried the vacant WBA title tag and although Steve boxed well in a close fight he was hampered by cuts, while his attempt to lift the European championship from the veteran Kalambay's head in Italy also narrowly failed. Next came the move that would finally change his fortune. After five fights under the Eastwood umbrella he became self managed and signed a promotional agreement with Barry Hearn, sealing his Matchroom debut with a three round stoppage win over Johnny Melfah. This result was followed by further inside the distance victories over Ian Strudwick, Gerhard Botes (vacant WBO Penta-Continental title), Wayne Ellis (WBO Penta-Continental title defence) and Melfah again, before he settled for an eight round points win over hardman, Paul Wesley, in the run-up to a crack at WBO champion, Chris Pyatt. The fight with Pyatt proved third time lucky as Steve lifted the WBO title with a stunning fifth round stoppage win and now looks set to cash in on his new crown this coming season.

Note: Full record will be found in the Current British-Based Champions: Career Records' section.

Oscar de la Hoya

Montebello, USA. *Born* 4 February, 1973
WBO S. Featherweight Champion

Born in the tough section of east Los Angeles, his grandfather, father and brother Juan all boxed as professionals and subsequently Oscar was taken to the gym for the first time when he was only six. While his father trained him, his mother gave him great encouragement until she died of cancer in 1990. Currently being hailed as the new "Golden Boy" of American boxing, Oscar won National Golden Gloves titles and was twice the United States champion, but lost in the 1991 World Championships to Marco Rudolph from Germany, his first defeat in over five years. However, he gained revenge against Rudolph at the Olympic Games in Barcelona in 1992 and won the gold medal at 132 lbs, the only American to win a boxing gold at the Games. Despite receiving considerable financial backing from top manager Shelly Finkel during his time as an amateur, while winning 223 of 228 fights, Oscar shocked the game by signing up with unknown Robert Mittleman and Steve Nelson when he turned professional, being paid a $500,000 cash bonus, a $250.000 house loan and a new car to sign up. Earned $200,000 for his first professional fight in November 1992, stopping Lamar Williams in one round. Next, Oscar halted Clifford Hicks, Paris Alexander, Curtis Strong and Jeff Mayweather, until Mike Grable climbed off the floor twice to last the distance, before losing on points in April 1993. His career continued to progress, with useful Frankie Avelar halted in four rounds in May, veteran Troy Dorsey stopped on a cut in one round in June, Renaldo Carter battered to defeat and Angelo Nunez stopped on a cut. Then, in October, Oscar suffered a shock when he had to climb off the floor to knock out the Mexican veteran, Narciso Valenzuela, in one round. Won the WBO title by halting Jimmy Bredahl in ten rounds, having Bredahl down in the first and second rounds in a one sided fight, but was on the floor in his defence against Giorgio Campanella. Fortunately, he recovered quickly and outclassed the previously unbeaten Italian. 5'11" tall and a classy boxer who hits hard with both hands, Oscar is in the same mould as his heroes Julio Cesar Chavez and Alexis Arguello. Had to pay a forfeit when failing to make the weight against Dorsey and was his lightest ever as a professional when beating Bredahl, so it will be no surprise if he quickly outgrows the super-featherweights. Although he broke with his managers in controversial circumstances, which tarnished his image somewhat, outside the ring Oscar is studying architecture and plans to be out of the sport within the next three to four years.

14.08.93	Renaldo Carter W RSC 6 Bay St Louis
27.08.93	Angelo Nunez W RTD 5 Los Angeles
30.10.93	Narciso Valenzuela W CO 1 Phoenix
05.03.94	Jimmy Bredahl W RTD 10 Los Angeles *(WBO S. Featherweight Title Challenge)*
27.05.94	Giorgio Campanella W RSC 3 Las Vegas *(WBO S. Featherweight Title Defence)*

Career: 13 contests, won 13.

Rafael del Valle

Santurce, Puerto Rico. *Born* 16 October, 1967
WBO Bantamweight Champion

Inactive during 1993-94.

Career: 15 contests, won 15.

Chris Eubank

Brighton, England. *Born* 8 August, 1966
WBO S. Middleweight Champion.
Former Undefeated WBO Middleweight Champion. Former Undefeated WBC International Middleweight Champion.

Note: Full records will be found in the Current British-Based Champions: Career Records' section.

Silvio (Leo) Gamez

Parmana, Venezuela. *Born* 8 August, 1963
WBA L. Flyweight Champion. Former Undefeated Venezuelan L. Flyweight Champion

One of 12 children, Silvio started boxing at the age of 14 and lost only 7 of 76 amateur fights. Turned professional in 1985 and won the Venezuelan light-flyweight title in April 1987 with a second round kayo of Pedro Nieves. Became the first WBA champion in the mini-flyweight division in January 1988 when he won a disputed decision over local fighter, Bong-Jun Kim, in Pusan and his only defence came in April of the same year when halting Kenji Yokozawa on a cut in three rounds in Tokyo. Weight troubles forced him to relinquish the WBA title in March 1989, and he again moved up to light-flyweight. In April 1989 he lost a split decision to Myung-Woo Yuh in a challenge for the WBA title, having hurt the champion in the eighth round. Faced Yuh again for the title in November, but this time he lost clearly on points. Silvio was then inactive for 11 months before challenging Yong-Kang Kim for the WBA flyweight crown and losing on a close, but unanimous decision. Stayed busy with good wins in Venezuela over top rated fighters such as Carlos Rodriguez and Benedicto Murillo, before being matched with Shiro Yahiro in Tokyo for the vacant WBA title in October 1993. Little "Leo" gave away 7" in height to the Japanese fighter, but picked up his second championship by flooring Yahiro twice and stopping him in round nine. In his first defence he halted his number one contender, Juan Antonio Torres, in *seven rounds,* in the challenger's hometown. Travelled again for his second defence and had to overcome some attempted shenanigans with the scales and a trip to the canvas to escape with a draw against the Thai, Kaj Ratchabandit. Only a shade over 5'0" tall, "Leo" is a muscular, flat-footed fighter with good punching power and a hard right upper-cut, with 19 quick wins on his record.

10.07.93	Oswaldo Osorio W CO 2 Caracas
21.10.93	Shiro Yahiro W RSC 9 Tokyo *(Vacant WBA L. Flyweight Title)*
05.02.94	Juan Antonio Torres W RSC 7 Panama City *(WBA L. Flyweight Title Defence)*
27.06.94	Kaj Ratchabandit DREW 12 Bangkok *(WBA L. Flyweight Title Defence)*

Career: 30 contests, won 26, drew 1, lost 3.

Nestor (Tito) Giovannini

Rafaela, Argentine. *Born* 7 February, 1961
WBO Cruiserweight Champion.

Former Undefeated WBC International L. Heavyweight Champion. Former Argentinian L. Heavyweight Champion

20.11.93	Markus Bott W PTS 12 Hamburg *(WBO Cruiserweight Title Defence)*
07.04.94	Jose Eduardo dos Santos W CO 5 Sunchales
06.05.94	Antonio Aguirre W PTS 10 Rafaela
Career: 44 contests, won 34, drew 3, lost 7.	

Humberto Gonzalez

Humberto (Chiquita) Gonzalez

Mexico City, Mexico. *Born* 25 March, 1966
WBC & IBF L. Flyweight Champion. Former Undefeated Mexican L. Flyweight Champion

A tough little battler who is only 5'1" tall, but possesses a heavy punch, Humberto is referred to by his countrymen as the Pipino Cuevas of the lower divisions. Turned professional in September 1984, as a stable-mate of Cuevas, and showed his power immediately by stopping 18 of his first 19 opponents, including world rated Ruben Padilla and Santiago Mendez. Won the Mexican light-flyweight title in September 1987 with a points verdict over Jorge Cano and successfully defended his crown in 1988 when knocking out Jose Luis Zepeda and halting Javier Varguez. Travelled to Korea in June 1989, securing the WBC title with a points victory over Yul-Woo Lee, and returned to Korea again in December to decision the great Jung-Koo Chang in his first defence. Really looked unbeatable in 1990 as he knocked out Francisco Tejedor and halted Luis Monzote, Jung-Keun Lim and Jorge Rivera in title bouts, before being brought down to earth with a bang in December when he was knocked out in six rounds by the unsung Filipino, Rolando Pascua. Humberto was cut early and seemed to lose heart. He regained the title in June 1991 with a points decision over Melchor Cob Castro, but was unimpressive when beating Domingo Sosa on points in a defence in January 1992. Then came a desperate battle with Kwang-Son Kim, before he stopped the Korean in the last round in June 1992. Had an easy kayo win over Napa Kiatwanchai in a title defence in September, but struggled to outpoint Castro in a return in December. That victory set-up a unification match with the IBF champion, Michael Carbajal, in March 1993. Humberto looked to be on the way to an upset when he floored Carbajal twice, but Michael produced the punches in the seventh round to score a dramatic kayo in the fight of the year. After a couple of wins over Pablo Tiznado and Armando Diaz, Humberto faced Carbajal again in February and this time, with the help of top trainer, Nacho Beristan, he fooled everyone by choosing to box. Overcoming a bad cut, which almost led to the fight being stopped in the fourth round, he won a split decision to regain his old crown, while also lifting the IBF title and ending Carbajal's unbeaten run. The hard punching switch hitter showed he has brains to go with his power and a third fight with Carbajal should make them both rich. Humberto has stopped or knocked out 26 opponents.

28.08.93	Pablo Tiznado W PTS 10 Los Angeles
17.11.93	Armando Diaz W PTS 10 Atlantic City
19.02.94	Michael Carbajal W PTS 12 Los Angeles *(WBC & IBF L. Flyweight Title Challenge)*
Career: 39 contests, won 37, lost 2.	

Miguel (Angel) Gonzalez

Ensenada, Mexico. *Born* 15 November, 1970
WBC Lightweight Champion. Former Undefeated WBC International Lightweight Champion

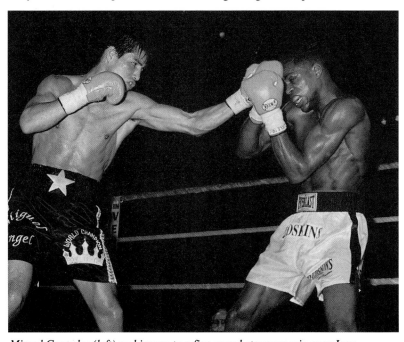

Miguel Gonzalez (left) on his way to a five round stoppage win over Jean-Baptiste Mendy

13.08.93	David Sample W PTS 12 Guadalajara *(WBC Lightweight Title Defence)*
27.11.93	Wilfredo Rocha W RSC 11 Mexico City *(WBC Lightweight Title Defence)*
29.03.94	Jean-Baptiste Mendy W RSC 5 Levallois *(WBC Lightweight Title Defence)*
15.06.94	Kenny Baysmore W RSC 6 Juarez

Career: 33 contests, won 33.

Jeff (Hit Man) Harding

Sydney, Australia. *Born* 5 February, 1965
WBC L. Heavyweight Champion.
Former Undefeated OPBF &
Australian L. Heavyweight Champion

Inactive during 1993-94

Career: 15 contests, won 15.

Genaro (Chicanito) Hernandez

Los Angeles, USA. *Born* 10 May, 1966
WBA S. Featherweight Champion

11.10.93	Harold Warren W PTS 12 Los Angeles *(WBA S. Featherweight Title Defence)*
31.01.94	Jorge Ramirez W RSC 8 Los Angeles *(WBA S. Featherweight Title Defence)*

Career: 31 contests, won 30, drew 1.

Herbie (The Dancing Destroyer) Hide

Norwich. *Born* 27 August, 1971
WBO Heavyweight Champion.
Former Undefeated British, WBC
International and WBO Penta-
Continental Heavyweight Champion.

Still maturing, Herbie is young as heavyweights go, but has already shown that he can effectively combine power with speed. Even as a young amateur novice the signs were there for all to see. In his first senior season as a very inexperienced amateur the Nigerian born, 17-year-old, Herbie, reached the ABA finals, where it was no disgrace to be outpointed by the then reigning champion and current European and Commonwealth titleholder, Henry Akinwande. His

Jeff Harding (right) in action against Dennis Andries   Peter Goldfield

potential was such that a professional career beckoned him. Joining Barry Hearn's Matchroom stable, he made his paid debut with a second round kayo of L. A. Williams on 24 October 1989 and quickly ran up 13 further inside the distance victories before being matched against Canadian, Conroy Nelson, for the vacant WBC International heavyweight title in January 1992. The furthest he had travelled prior to that was six rounds and, although he had done everything asked of him, some were already beginning to question his stamina. Anyway, this was not a night where questions would be answered on whether Herbie had a stamina problem, or not, and ended with Nelson stretched out at 35 seconds of the second round. Next time out, a fight against blubbery Percell Davis, saw the American being counted out inside 70 seconds of an appaling mismatch and, after taking six months out of the ring, Herbie came back with a seventh round stoppage of brave Jean Chanet. The former European champion posed few problems, other than the ability to soak up punishment incessantly, while Herbie was unable to find a finishing blow and appeared to tire dramatically before the Frenchman was pulled out. However,

a tougher fight was just around the corner. Defending the WBC International title in Antwerp against Craig Petersen, Herbie was floored in the first and cut in the second, before getting the range and taking the Australian out in the seventh round. Following that, in 1993, James Pritchard was stopped inside two rounds, Juan Antonio Diaz (three), Michael Murray (five) and Jerry Halstead (four). Incidentally, Herbie collected the vacant Penta-Continental title in beating Diaz, which he defended against Halstead, and won the vacant British crown when defeating Murray. Still, there continued to be the doubters, even though all 22 opponents had been despatched inside the distance. Their views were reinforced in September 1993 when Everett Martin forced Herbie to travel the full ten rounds for the first time. Although flooring the American a couple of times, and weighing-in at a career heaviest 15 stone 5 lbs, Herbie was unable to put away the two stone heavier Martin and had to be satisfied with an overwhelming points win. Before the year was out, he had stopped Americans, Mike Dixon (WBA Penta-Continental title defence) and Jeff Lampkin (WBC International title defence) and earned a March 1994

185

crack at the new WBO champion, Michael Bentt. Bentt, an exiled Englishman, had destroyed the much fancied Tommy Morrison to win the WBO title and was expected to have too much of everything for Herbie. However, Herbie surpassed himself. Brought to a peak by the excellent Freddie King, and showing real skills allied to fast hands and punching power, he blasted out the hapless Bentt in round seven, following an earlier knockdown in the third. And, while the American visited hospital and was advised never to box again, the new champion could look forward to some lucrative defences and a possible say in any unification plans. Still only 24, if he continues to improve and add natural weight to his 6'2" frame, Herbie could ultimately dominate the heavyweight division.

Note: Full record will be found in the Current British-Based Champions: Career Records' section.

Virgil (Sugar) Hill

Williston, USA. *Born* 18 January, 1964
WBA L. Heavyweight Champion. Former Undefeated WBC International & Con Am L. Heavyweight Champion

28.08.93	Sergio Merani W PTS 12 Bismark *(WBA L. Heavyweight Title Defence)*
09.11.93	Saul Montana W RSC 10 Fargo *(WBA L. Heavyweight Title Defence)*
17.12.93	Guy Waters W PTS 12 Minot *(WBA L. Heavyweight Title Defence)*
Career: 39 contests, won 38, lost 1.	

Daniel Jimenez

Camuy, Puerto Rico. *Born* 21 November, 1969
WBO S. Bantamweight Champion

30.10.93	Felix Garcia Losada W RSC 5 Zaragoza *(WBO S. Bantamweight Title Defence)*
01.10.93	Manuel Santiago W RSC 2 Camuy
07.01.94	Felix Garcia Losada W PTS 12 Palma de Mallorca *(WBO S. Bantamweight Title Defence)*
25.06.94	Cristobal Pasqual W PTS 12 Utrera *(WBO S. Bantamweight Title Defence)*
Career: 21 contests, won 16, drew 1, lost 3, no contest 1.	

John Michael Johnson

John Michael Johnson

San Antonio, USA. *Born* 23 June, 1968
WBA Bantamweight Champion. Former Undefeated WBC Con Am and USBA S. Flyweight Champion

In a year of upsets, John Michael Johnson sprang one of the biggest when he battered previously unbeaten Junior Jones to defeat to lift the WBA bantamweight title. 5'7" tall, he claimed 78 wins in 93 amateur fights, before turning professional in July 1986. Lost in only his second fight to local rival, John Vasquez, but halted Vasquez in one round in a return bout. His management then threw him into a few tough matches on the road that saw him lose points verdicts to prospects, Renaldo Carter, Jones and Johnny Tapia, mostly in the other guys' backyard. He returned to action in San Antonio and, in August 1990, won the vacant WBC Continental Americas super-flyweight title on a technical decision over Javier Diaz. John Michael had only two bouts in 1991, but registered good wins over Armando Diaz and Roland Gomez and, in his only fight in 1992, he overcame a broken nose and rib injury to win the vacant USBA title with a points decision against Abner Barajas. Although he was fairly busy in 1993, with five wins, he was not making any progress and changed manager and trainer. His lucky break followed quickly when his stablemate Robert Quiroga was unable to fight Junior

Jones and his manager convinced the champion to accept John Michael as a substitute. He was outboxed by Jones for long periods, but floored the New Yorker twice and finally wore him down for an 11th round stoppage. A quick learner and a hard puncher, he has improved greatly under the training of Tony Ayala Snr., but has still to prove he was not just the right man in the right place against Jones. Has 14 wins inside the distance.

26.08.93	Rodolfo Robles W RSC 6 San Antonio
22.12.93	Arturo Estrada W RSC 8 San Antonio
22.04.94	Junior Jones W RSC 11 Las Vegas *(WBA Bantamweight Title Challenge)*
Career: 22 contests, won 18, lost 4.	

Tom (Boom Boom) Johnson

Evansville, USA. *Born* 15 July, 1964
IBF Featherweight Champion. Former Undefeated WBA Americas Featherweight Champion

24.08.93	Jose Garcia W PTS 10 Atlantic City
11.09.93	Sugar Baby Rojas W PTS 12 Miami *(IBF Featherweight Title Defence)*
30.11.93	Stephane Haccoun W RSC 9 Marseilles *(IBF Featherweight Title Defence)*
12.02.94	Orlando Soto W PTS 12 St Louis *(IBF Featherweight Title Defence)*
11.06.94	Benny Amparo W RSC 12 Atlantic City *(IBF Featherweight Title Defence)*
Career: 39 contests, won 36, drew 1, lost 2.	

Roy Jones

Pensacola, USA. *Born* 16 January, 1969
IBF Middleweight Champion

14.08.93	Sugar Boy Malinga W CO 6 Bay St Louis
30.11.93	Fermin Chirino W PTS 10 Pensacola
22.03.94	Danny Garcia W RSC 6 Pensacola
27.05.94	Thomas Tate W RSC 2 Las Vegas *(IBF Middleweight Title Defence)*
Career: 26 contests, won 26.	

Hiroshi (Untouchable) Kawashima

Tokushima, Japan. *Born* 27 March, 1970
WBC S. Flyweight Champion. Former Undefeated Japanese S. Flyweight Champion

His father, an avid boxing fan who fought as an amateur, started to teach Hiroshi to fight when he was still only three years old, while his brother, Shinobu, challenged for the IBF flyweight title in 1985, only to lose on a kayo to Soon-Chon Kwon. Hiroshi was an outstanding amateur, winning the All-Japan High School championship and beating current WBA champion, Katsuya Onizuka, and top flyweight contender, Puma Toguchi. Turned professional in August 1988 and,as a stablemate to former world champion, Hideyuki Ohashi, he was expected to rise quickly to the top, but instead, literally fell on his face when he was knocked out in six rounds by previous victim Toguchi in a preliminary round of the 1988 Japanese annual tournament for novices. His recklessness led to a second kayo loss in April 1989, when mediocre Mitsu Kawashima put him out in the first round. The disappointment continued in his next bout when he was held to a split draw by Korean, Chong-Pil Kim. It looked like another bad night in October 1990 after he was floored in one round by Sung-Kyu Kim, but Hiroshi saved his career by blazing back to kayo Kim in round three. He received a further setback during a win over Alan Escalante in January 1991, when he fractured a hand and was out of the ring for 13 months. Finally, in July 1992, Hiroshi began to fulfil his promise as he floored and outpointed defending champion, Hideki Kioke, to win the Japanese super-flyweight title. Made successful defences when knocking out Tatsuya Sugi in October 1992 and halting Tatsuya Matsuo and Kenichi Matsumura in 1993, before relinquishing the title. His big chance came when he challenged Jose Luis Bueno for the WBC crown in May. Hiroshi proved too fast and slick, dropping the champion in the 11th round, with only the bell saving the Mexican from a kayo, and the unanimous decision in his favour was a formality as he fulfilled his father's long time dreams. Once a wild slugger, he altered his style after his early losses and is now much more of a boxer, although a question mark still remains over his chin. A southpaw, Hiroshi has 12 quick wins to his credit.

05.10.93	Kap-Chul Choi W CO 5 Tokyo
04.05.94	Jose Luis Bueno W PTS 12 Yokohama
	(WBC S. Flyweight Title Challenge)

Career: 17 contests, won 14, drew 1, lost 2.

Kevin Kelley

New York, USA. *Born* 29 June, 1967
WBC Featherweight Champion.
Former Undefeated WBC Con Am Featherweight Champion

Twice New York Golden Gloves champion at 119 lbs, he started boxing only because he liked the boxing jacket he saw another youth wearing. The peak of his amateur career came in 1988 when, close to a berth on the US Olympic team, he lost at 125lb to Carl Daniels. The classy southpaw turned professional in September 1988 and fought regularly until the end of 1989, until a broken hand put him out of action for nine months. Along with his then stablemate, Regilio Tuur, he also fought in Holland and Belgium. Scored his first big win in March 1991 when he won a decision over tough little Harold Warren and then, in July, knocked out world rated James Pipps in four rounds. That victory was soured after he was fined for taunting Pipps when he was on the canvas. His first championship attempt saw him win the WBC Continental Americas title in November 1991, when he halted the Colombian Rafael Zuniga in

Kevin Kelley

four rounds. That was followed by a tough defence in February 1992 against the former IBF champion, Troy Dorsey. The fight was a real war which could have gone either way, but, in the end, the officials gave it to Kevin. He then marked time with a series of wins against mediocre opposition, whilst politics and circumstances delayed his shot at the world title. Finally, he received his chance in December when he faced Goyo Vargas, who had taken the WBC title from Paul Hodkinson. Although Kevin confused the champion with his southpaw jab, he had to survive being floored in the ninth round, ultimately being declared the winner on a unanimous decision. Also had to climb off the floor to retain his title against Jesse Benavides, but swept the late rounds to take a unanimous decision, before stopping game Georgie Navarro in six rounds of a non title fight. A colourful self-publicist, Kevin is 5'7" tall, very fast, with an excellent jab, and has 26 wins inside the distance.

08.07.93	Adolpho Castillo W RSC 2 New York	
11.09.93	Pat Simeon W PTS 10 Miami	
04.12.93	Gregorio Vargas W PTS 12 Reno *(WBC Featherweight Title Challenge)*	
06.05.94	Jesse Benavides W PTS 12 Atlantic City *(WBC Featherweight Title Defence)*	
26.06.94	Georgie Navarro W RSC 6 Atlantic City	
Career: 39 contests, won 39.		

(Jesse) James Leija

San Antonio, USA. *Born* 8 July, 1966
WBC S. Featherweight Champion.
Former Undefeated NABF Featherweight Champion

A High School graduate, James is managed by Lester Bradford and trained by his father Jesse Snr., who was a good amateur fighter. 5'5" tall, he did not start fighting as an amateur until he was 19 and lost in the US Olympic trials in 1988 to Kelcie Banks. Turned professional in October 1988 and kept busy with undemanding learning fights in and around San Antonio for a couple of years. Had a scare against Roy Muniz in March 1990 when badly cut, but eventually put the latter away in the third round.

Was held to a controversial draw by experienced Ed Parker in October 1990, but, in February 1991, decisioned Mark Fernandez, the man who beat Steve Boyle over here. In May 1992, James beat Filipino, Miguel Arrozal, who was thrown out in the eighth round for low blows and, five months later, took a unanimous verdict over Steve McCrory. Won the NABF featherweight title in March 1992 after suffering a bad cut in his bout with Jose Martinez and being declared the winner on a technical decision. He then busted up tough Troy Dorsey in five rounds in a title defence, in October 1992, with Troy unable to come out for round six. Next came a very hard battle with former world champion, Louie Espinoza, in a title defence in March 1993, where he had to hold off a late rally to take a very close verdict. Finally, he got a world title opportunity when challenging Azumah Nelson for the WBC super-featherweight title in front of his own fans in September. However, the champion used all of his experience to hold off the young challenger and a close fight was ruled a controversial draw. Two outings later, James made no mistake in the return as he floored the great African in the second and was just too busy for the aging champion. A sharp, compact battler, he has stopped or knocked out 13 opponents.

10.09.93	Azumah Nelson DREW 12 San Antonio *(WBC S. Featherweight Title Challenge)*	
23.03.94	Tomas Valdez W RSC 3 San Antonio	
07.05.94	Azumah Nelson W PTS 12 Las Vegas *(WBC S. Featherweight Title Challenge)*	
Career: 30 contests, won 28, drew 2.		

Lennox Lewis

Crayford, England. *Born* 2 September, 1965
WBC Heavyweight Champion. Former Undefeated British, Commonwealth & European Heavyweight Champion

Note: Full record will be found in the Current British-Based Champions: Career Records' section.

Steve (Lightning) Little

Reading, USA. *Born* 9 June, 1965
WBA S. Middleweight Champion.

May have been lucky to catch Michael Nunn on a bad night, but Steve went from inactive journeyman to world champion. Learned his boxing in Philadelphia, with his talented cousins Meldrick and Myron Taylor, and claimed 42 wins in 45 amateur fights, without ever scaling the heights in the national tournaments. Turned professional as a welterweight in December 1983 and proved to be a popular club fighter in the New Jersey area, scoring some useful wins, but also losing decisions to Tony Montgomery, Joe Summers and Mark Breland. Won and lost against prospect Glenn Wolfe, when running out of gas and retiring after eight rounds in their second fight in September 1985. Scored a big win in March 1986, proving too young and fast for former WBA welterweight champion, Pipino Cuevas, and easily outpointed the Mexican, but then lost decisions to Tyrone Trice and Dave Gutierrez. Steve blew a big chance when he moved up to light-middleweight in April 1988, giving a poor display against Robert Hines and losing a tame decision for the USBA crown. His fall continued as he suffered a brutal kayo at the hands of Terry Norris in December for the NABF title and was beaten on points by Canadian, Dave Hilton, in March 1989. Despite these losses, he was given a shot at John David Jackson for the WBO title in April 1989 and was well behind on points when stopped on a bad cut. Returning to the ring in 1991, Steve jumped straight from light-middleweight to super-middleweight and had mixed success, winning and losing against Tyrone Frazier, being defeated by Adam Garland, and fighting a tough draw, with Merqui Sosa in January 1992. After scoring wins over modest opposition in September and December 1992, he was then inactive until called upon to fight Nunn 14 months later. Despite ring rust and giving away 4" in height, Steve took his chance, flooring Nunn with a sweeping left within 30 seconds of the start and winning a split verdict. A stocky, busy fighter, with a good left-hook, it is unlikely that Steve has suddenly become a talented craftsman and the Nunn result may flatter him, although that remains to be seen. Has only five wins inside the distance on his record.

26.02.94	Michael Nunn W PTS 12 London *(WBA S. Middleweight Title Challenge)*
Career: 37 contests, won 22, drew 2, lost 13.	

Ricardo (Finito) Lopez

Cuernavaca, Mexico. *Born* 25 July, 1967
WBC M. Flyweight Champion.
Former Undefeated WBC Con Am
M. Flyweight Champion

03.07.93	Saman Sorjaturong W RSC 2 Nuevo Laredo *(WBC M. Flyweight Title Defence)*
17.09.93	Toto Powpongsawang W RSC 11 Bangkok *(WBC M. Flyweight Title Defence)*
18.12.93	Manny Melchor W CO 11 Lake Tahoe *(WBC M. Flyweight Title Defence)*
07.05.94	Kermin Guardia W PTS 12 Las Vegas *(WBC M. Flyweight Title Defence)*
Career: 36 contests, won 36.	

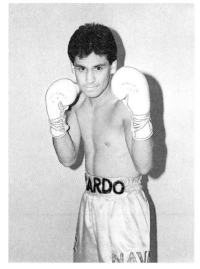

Ricardo Lopez

Eamonn Loughran

Ballymena. *Born* 5 June, 1970
WBO Welterweight Champion.
Former Undefeated Commonwealth
Welterweight Champion

As an amateur star of the Young Ireland side, and just a few days past his 17th birthday, Eamonn won a silver medal in the World Junior Championships of 1987, before deciding to discard the singlet and punch for pay later that year. After turning professional with Barney Eastwood, he kicked off with a disqualification win over one Adam Muir on 3 December 1987 and followed that up with victories over Tony Britland, Stan King, Ricky Nelson, Mark Pearce and Ronnie Campbell, interspersed with a four round draw in Panama City against Antonio Campbell, before deciding to call it a day with the Belfast stable at the end of 1989. He returned, having had a year away from the ring, to be managed by Barry Hearn under the Matchroom banner and made a winning start with a two round stoppage over the American, Parrish Johnson. The year 1991 saw him defeat a succession of English fighters, before he stepped up a gear with an eight round points victory over Juan Carlos Ortiz in Hamburg (October 1991). Next time out, in March 1992, Eamonn let a perfectly good opportunity slip by when he was disqualified in the fifth round of a British welterweight title eliminator against Tony Ekubia. Losing his unbeaten record was one thing, but headbutting his opponent was another, especially after he had been floored in the previous round. Came back with good wins over Kelvin Mortimer and Judas Clottey to be matched against Commonwealth champion, Donovan Boucher, that November. Although thought to be in over his head by many, Eamonn gave a stunning display of box-fighting – with solid body shots eventually taking their toll – to demolish a very good fighter inside three rounds and win himself a title. Following a good win over Desbon Seaton, Eamonn again impressed when putting his Commonwealth title on the line in February 1993 against tough Guyanan, Michael Benjamin, outpunching his foe throughout to serve a warning to other welters. Again it was the body shots that paved the way for victory and Benjamin was rescued by the referee in round six,

having been chopped down unceremoniously by a cracking right-hander. Eamonn then took a long break from the ring before being matched to challenge Gert Bo Jacobsen for his WBO welterweight title in October 1993. Unfortunately, Jacobsen contracted flu a few days prior to the fight taking place and then decided to relinquish the title, leaving Eamonn without an opponent. However, at the 11th hour, the American, Lorenzo Smith, was drafted in to face the Irishman in what would become a fight for the vacant title. Although Smith's good boxing skills kept him in contention throughout, it was Eamonn's more solid and cleaner punching that eventually won the day. He was less than impressive in his first defence, where Alessandro Duran was the opponent and Belfast again the venue. The Italian certainly knew how to spoil and although Eamonn won a wide decision in a mauling, brawling affair, he would be best suited in the short term to making further defences in order to gain further experience rather than trying to unify the title. At 5'9", he is an excellent body puncher who can generally be expected to wear the opposition down, but would probably struggle against the likes of Pernell Whitaker, with his vast range of boxing skills, and Ike Quartey, the biggest single hitter in the division today. However, Eamonn has time on his side and with proper matching should enjoy a lucrative career.

Note: Full record will be found in the Current British-Based Champions: Career Records' section.

Gerald McClellan

Freeport, USA. *Born* 23 October, 1967
WBC Middleweight Champion.
Former Undefeated WBO
Middleweight Champion

06.08.93	Jay Bell W CO 1 Bayamon *(WBC Middleweight Title Defence)*
04.03.94	Gilbert Baptist W RSC 1 Las Vegas *(WBC Middleweight Title Defence)*
07.05.94	Julian Jackson W RSC 1 Las Vegas *(WBC Middleweight Title Defence)*
Career: 33 contests, won 31, lost 2.	

Kennedy McKinney

Memphis, USA. *Born* 10 January, 1966
IBF S. Bantamweight Champion. Former Undefeated USBA
S. Bantamweight Champion

17.07.93	Rudy Zavala W RSC 3 Memphis *(IBF S. Bantamweight Title Defence)*
16.10.93	Jesus Salud W PTS 12 Lake Tahoe *(IBF S. Bantamweight Title Defence)*
19.02.94	Jose Rincones W CO 5 Temba *(IBF S. Bantamweight Title Defence)*
18.04.94	Welcome Ncita W PTS 12 South Padre Island *(IBF S. Bantamweight Title Defence)*
Career: 28 contests, won 27, drew 1.	

Henry Maske

Trevenbrietzen, Germany. *Born* 6 January, 1964
IBF L. Heavyweight Champion

18.09.93	Anthony Hembrick W PTS 12 Dusseldorf *(IBF L. Heavyweight Title Defence)*
11.12.93	David Vedder W PTS 12 Dusseldorf *(IBF L. Heavyweight Title Defence)*
26.03.94	Ernie Magdaleno W RSC 9 Dortmund *(IBF L. Heavyweight Title Defence)*
04.06.94	Andrea Magi W PTS 12 Dortmund *(IBF L. Heavyweight Title Defence)*
Career: 24 contests, won 24.	

Jacob (Baby Jake) Matlala

Johannesburg, South Africa. *Born* 8 January, 1962
WBO Flyweight Champion. Former Undefeated South African
L. Flyweight Champion

24.07.93	Pablo Tiznado W PTS 10 Johannesburg
04.12.93	Luigi Camputaro W RTD 7 Sun City *(WBO Flyweight Title Defence)*
11.06.94	Francis Ampofo W RTD 9 London *(WBO Flyweight Title Defence)*
Career: 50 contests, won 40, drew 1, lost 9.	

Juan (John John) Molina

Fajardo, Puerto Rico. *Born* 17 March, 1965
IBF S. Featherweight Champion. Former Undefeated WBO
S. Featherweight Champion

09.10.93	Bernard Taylor W RSC 8 San Juan *(IBF S. Featherweight Title Defence)*
22.01.94	Floyd Harvard W RTD 6 Cardiff *(IBF S. Featherweight Title Defence)*
22.04.94	Gregorio Vargas W PTS 12 Las Vegas *(IBF S. Featherweight Title Defence)*
Career: 38 contests, won 35, lost 3.	

Michael Moorer

Monessen, USA. *Born* 12 November, 1967
IBF & WBA Heavyweight Champion. Former Unbeaten WBO Heavyweight and L. Heavyweight Champion

Although hailed as the first ever southpaw heavyweight champion after beating Evander Holyfield, he arguably achieved claim to fame that when winning the WBO title in 1992. Born in Brooklyn, he started boxing when he was 12 years old, going on to win the 1986 National Golden Gloves championship and represent the US in a number of international matches. After turning professional with Manny Steward's Kronk team in 1988, he stopped his first 25 opponents and, in December 1988, collected the vacant WBO light-heavyweight title with a fifth round stoppage of Ramzi Hassan. An active champion, the 6'1" tall, Michael, defended his title nine times with none of his challengers managing to last to the final bell. On leaving Kronk, he relinquished the WBO title in 1991 and moved straight up to heavyweight. Was shaken by Alex Stewart in their July 1991 clash, but came back to floor the Jamaican three times and halt him in round four. He was finally taken the distance and even floored, for the first time as a professional, when outpointing Everett Martin in March 1992. And, two months later, had to come off the canvas twice in a wild fight with Bert Cooper before halting Cooper in the fifth round to win the vacant WBO crown. Once again, Michael relinquished his WBO title, this time without even making a defence. Following a series of dull, unimpressive performances against moderate opposition and accepting stand aside money to allow the Riddick Bowe-Evander Holyfield return, he finally insisted on his title shot and, for the first time, impressed as a heavyweight in climbing off the floor to outpoint Holyfield. Subsequent revelations over Holyfield's health have not reduced Michael's achievement, but he still has things to prove as a champion. His relationships with his managers and trainers have often been stormy and his behaviour out of the ring has created a poor image. Michael has not looked a damaging puncher at heavyweight, but has a good southpaw jab and should become more motivated as a champion. Now trained by Teddy Atlas, he has 30 quick wins under his belt.

04.12.93	Mike Evans W PTS 10 Reno
22.04.94	Evander Holyfield W PTS 12 Las Vegas *(IBF & WBA Heavyweight Title Challenge)*
Career: 35 contests, won 35.	

Orzubek (Gussie) Nazarov

Kant, Russia. *Born* 30 August, 1966
WBA Lightweight Champion. Former Undefeated OPBF & Japanese Lightweight Champion

Based in Japan, "Gussie" is a strong relentless body puncher, with a stiff southpaw jab, although he is often seen as being too mechanical. His name is sometimes spelt Olzubek, but he was always Orzubek when fighting as a "Simon Pure". As an amateur, he was the Russian titleholder in 1985, 1987 and 1988, won the European championship in 1987, after eliminating Michael Carruth from the competition, and finished with 153 wins from 165 bouts. Turning professional in February 1990, he quickly blew aside the local opposition, stopping his first eight opponents and winning the Japanese title in his sixth fight, following a kayo of Kenji Yagi in four rounds (April 1991). He later proved his stamina when taken the distance for the first time in December 1991, outpointing the Thai, Downmai Sithkodom. In May 1992, Orzubek won the OPBF title with a unanimous decision over the veteran, Iwao Otomo, and defended same three times that year, with inside the distance wins over Francis Velasquez, Nopratanoi

Vorvorapol and Ernie Alesna. After two more successful defences in 1993, a kayo of Kwang-Sik Song and points win over Boy Ligas, the Russian relinquished the OPBF title in order to go for the WBA crown held by South African, Dingaan Thobela. Fighting at altitude in Johannesburg posed no problems for Orzubek and, overcoming a brief knockdown and a closed right eye, he easily outpointed Thobela to lift the title. Returned to South Africa again for his first defence in March 1994 and won a unanimous verdict after putting the former champion down in the seventh and weakening him throughout with vicious body punching. His current record includes 14 inside the distance victories, which he looks set to add to.

19.07.93	Boy Ligas W PTS 12 Tokyo *(OPBF Lightweight Title Defence)*
30.10.93	Dingaan Thobela W PTS 12 Johannesburg *(WBA Lightweight Title Challenge)*
19.03.94	Dingaan Thobela W PTS 12 Temba *(WBA Lightweight Title Defence)*
Career: 19 contests, won 19.	

Orlin Norris

Orlin (Boscoe Bear) Norris

Lubbock, USA. *Born* 4 October, 1965 WBA Cruiserweight Champion. Former Undefeated NABF Cruiserweight Champion. Former NABF Heavyweight Champion

Elder brother of Terry Norris. Only 5'11" tall with a 70" reach, he started boxing at 11 years of age. Won the 1986 Golden Gloves title at heavyweight and claimed only ten losses in over 300 fights as an amateur. Turned professional in June 1986 as a cruiserweight and was outpointed in only his third fight by Olian Alexander, before moving up to heavyweight and winning the NABF title with a majority verdict in November 1987 over Larry Alexander. Registered a good win in March 1988, when outpointing Renaldo Snipes in his first title defence, and scored decisions over Dwain Bonds and Jesse Ferguson in title fights later that year. Further title victories over Greg Page and Dee Collier in 1989 put him close to a world title shot, but, in November 1989, he dropped a hairline decision to Tony Tubbs. Orlin lost his title, but Tubbs had failed a drugs test and the bout was declared a no decision. Although he attempted to regain the title in February 1990, he was forced to retire after eight rounds against Bert Cooper. Later that year, in November, he decisioned Oliver McCall and continued to campaign at heavyweight. He did regain the NABF crown briefly, after knocking out Lionel Washington in one round in April 1991, but gave away too much height and weight to the 6'5", Tony Tucker, in June and lost the title on a unanimous verdict. After that defeat he gave up the heavyweight division and moved down to cruiserweight. In winning the vacant NABF title on a technical decision over Jesse Shelby in August 1991, Orlin looked a new fighter at the weight and retained the championship with wins over Anthony Hembrick, David Sewell and Richard Mason to put himself in line for a big money match with the WBA champion, Bobby Czyz. Unfortunately, Czyz was stripped of the title when he could not fight due to injury and Orlin faced the hard punching Argentinian, Marcelo Figueroa, for the vacant title in November, instead. He had Figueroa on the canvas after just 25 seconds and gave him a steady

beating until the referee halted the fight in round six. Following a non-title fight against Art Jimmerson, Orlin had a tough first defence against Arthur Williams when, despite flooring the challenger in the first, he had to overcome a bad cut to win an unpopular decision. He may still be having trouble getting down to cruiserweight, but due to his lack of inches will always struggle at heavyweight against the big boys. Has a good chin, but is not a big puncher, despite his 21 stoppage victories, and is prone to cuts.

19.08.93	Jack Basting W RSC 4 Sedalia
06.11.93	Marcelo Figueroa W RSC 6 Paris *(Vacant WBA Cruiserweight Title)*
09.01.94	Art Jimmerson W RSC 3 Del Mar
04.03.94	Arthur Williams W PTS 12 Las Vegas *(WBA Cruiserweight Title Defence)*
Career: 44 contests, won 40, lost 3, no decision 1.	

Terry Norris

Lubbock, USA. *Born* 17 June, 1967 WBC L. Middleweight Champion. Former Undefeated NABF L. Middleweight Champion

10.09.93	Joe Gatti W RSC 1 San Antonio *(WBC L. Middleweight Title Defence)*
18.12.93	Simon Brown L CO 4 Puebla *(WBC L. Middleweight Title Defence)*
18.03.94	Armando Campas W CO 4 Las Vegas
07.05.94	Simon Brown W PTS 12 Las Vegas *(WBC L. Middleweight Title Challenge)*
Career: 42 contests, won 38, lost 4.	

Katsuya Onizuka

Fukuoka, Japan. *Born* 12 March, 1970 WBA S. Flyweight Champion. Former Undefeated Japanese S. Flyweight Champion

05.11.93	Khaoyai Mahasarakam W PTS 12 Tokyo *(WBA S. Flyweight Title Defence)*
03.04.94	Seung-Koo Lee W PTS 12 Tokyo *(WBA S. Flyweight Title Defence)*
Career: 24 contests, won 24.	

Zack Padilla

Azusa, USA. *Born* 15 March, 1963 WBO L. Welterweight Champion

19.11.93	Efrem Calamati W RTD 7 Arezzo *(WBO Welterweight Title Defence)*
16.12.93	Ray Oliveira W PTS 12 Ledyard *(WBO Welterweight Title Defence)*
12.03.94	Dwayne Swift W RSC 4 Los Angeles
18.04.94	Harold Miller W RTD 6 Rotterdam *(WBO Welterweight Title Defence)*
Career: 23 contests, won 21, drew 1, lost 1.	

Tracy Harris Patterson

New Paltz, USA. *Born* 26 December, 1964
WBC S. Bantamweight Champion.
Former Undefeated NABF
S. Bantamweight Champion

25.09.93	Daniel Zaragoza W RSC 7 Poughkeepsie *(WBC S. Bantamweight Title Defence)*
08.01.94	Steve Young W CO 5 Catskill
09.04.94	Richard Duran W PTS 12 Reno *(WBC S. Bantamweight Title Defence)*
Career: 53 contests, won 50, drew 1, lost 2.	

Tracy Harris Patterson

Verno Phillips

Troy, USA. *Born* 29 November, 1969
WBO L. Middleweight Champion

Turned professional as a welterweight in January 1988, after an undistinguished time as an amateur when he claimed 52 wins in 64 bouts, but never reached a final in any major competition. Did not make an auspicious start as a professional either, being stopped and outpointed by Carl Sullivan in a

couple of bouts at the end of 1988. Moved up in class in January 1990, but suffered two standing counts against Larry Barnes on the way to a clear points defeat. Turned in his best performance when he outpointed useful Curtis Summitt in February, but then lost a decision to former amateur star, Kenny Gould, in April. After a couple of wins he took the unusual step of moving his base to Argentina. He was an immediate hit there as he knocked out the former South American champion, Hector Hugo Vilte, in four rounds in November 1990 and closed the year by forcing tough Marcelo di Crocce to retire in the ninth round of a fight just one week later. He returned to Argentina again in 1991, but was unlucky to be held to a draw by Ramon Jara in May. In his next bout in June, he faced the unbeaten Julio Cesar, Vasquez, the current WBA light-middleweight champion, in a real war. Verno had Vasquez badly hurt in the sixth round and defenceless at the bell, but Vasquez's handlers invaded the ring claiming that Verno had landed a punch after the bell. Vasquez was saved from a kayo, but, after changing their mind four times, the Argentinian Federation finally disqualified Vasquez due to the actions of his cornermen. Verno stayed in Argentina until the end of 1992 and had six more fights, winning them all. He returned to New York in December 1992 and outpointed Mickey Ward in an erratic performance, having Ward on the floor three times, but failing to stop him. He picked up his first professional title in May 1993, halting Panamanian Rafael Williams in five exciting rounds for the New York State light-middleweight title, and then faced former world champion, Lupe Aquino, for the vacant WBO crown in October. Verno was on the canvas in the first round but hit too hard for the Mexican veteran and forced the referee to rescue Aquino in the seventh round. His curious climb to fame in Argentina makes him still largely unkown in his own land, but he is unbeaten in his last 15 bouts and seems to have found power that was lacking in his early fights. Has 12 inside the distance wins on his record, with ten coming in his last 14 bouts.

30.10.93	Lupe Aquino W RSC 7 Phoenix *(Vacant WBO L. Middleweight Title)*
Career: 27 contests, won 22, drew 1, lost 4.	

Chana Porpaoin

Petchaboon, Thailand. *Born* 25 March, 1966
WBA M. Flyweight Champion.
Former Undefeated Thai M. Flyweight Champion

22.08.93	Ronnie Magramo W PTS 12 Bangkok *(WBA M. Flyweight Title Defence)*
28.11.93	Rafael Torres W CO 4 Pichit *(WBA M. Flyweight Title Defence)*
26.03.94	Carlos Murillo W PTS 12 Chonburi *(WBA M. Flyweight Title Defence)*
Career: 31 contests, won 31.	

Ike (Bazooka) Quartey

Accra, Ghana. *Born* 27 November, 1969
WBA Welterweight Champion.
Former Undefeated Ghanaian, African Boxing Council and WBC International L. Welterweight Champion

Known as Ike, although his real christian name is Issifu, he is a thunderous punching fighter who ranks alongside John Mugabi as the hardest single hitter to come out of Africa. As an amateur he competed in the 1987 World Junior championships in Cuba at featherweight, but lost a 3-2 decision to Hungarian, Laszlo Szugs, in the semi-finals. A year later, he represented Ghana in the 1988 Olympics, this time as a light-welterweight, but lost in the second series to Australian, Grahame Cheney, on a unanimous decision. After that, Ike turned professional at home in November 1988, knocking out Jaffar Balogoun in his third fight and winning the vacant Ghanaian light-welterweight title in his sixth outing. Collected the African title in December 1990 with a first round kayo of Mohammad Muritala and quickly ran out of opposition. He then appeared briefly, in California, in November 1991, where he gave notice of his class by flooring former Olympian, Kelcie Banks, twice and halting him in round seven. Following that, he moved to Europe, where he came under the management of the Acaries brothers. Had a tough fight with unbeaten Juan Carlos Villarreal for the WBC International title in April 1992, but a badly swollen face forced the Argentinian out of the fight in round five, and defended with a crushing first round kayo of Alfredo Juarena in June 1992, before moving up to welterweight. He seemed to lose some of his zip at the heavier poundage and was taken the distance for the first time in March 1993 by Mario Morales. Although Ike beat former WBC light-welterweight champion, Lonnie Smith, in October 1993, he was forced to wait through eight months of delays for a shot at the WBA title held by unbeaten Venuzuelan, Cristano Espana. The African finally arrived at the highest level when battering Espana to defeat in round 11. Ike is a good boxer, but it is the sheer power of his heavy hooks which make him so dangerous and he has stopped or knocked out 23 opponents.

23.09.93	Rocky Mory W RSC 1 Accra	
16.10.93	Lonnie Smith W PTS 10 Levallois	
04.06.94	Crisanto Espana W RSC 11 Levallois	
	(WBA Welterweight Title Challenge)	

Career: 27 contests, won 27.

Steve Robinson

Cardiff, Wales. *Born* 13 December, 1968
WBO Featherweight Champion.
Former Undefeated Welsh & WBA Penta-Continental Featherweight Champion

Note: Full record will be found in the Current British-Based Champions: Career Records' section.

Jake (The Snake) Rodriguez

New York, USA. *Born* 2 October, 1965
IBF L. Welterweight Champion

Christened Evaristo, Jake is a 5'8" tall southpaw with a 72" reach. Born Arroyo, Puerto Rico, and one of 13 children, he started boxing in Puerto Rico at the age of 12 and continued with the sport when the family moved to New York. After turning professional in September 1988, with a tough four round draw against Ron Hammonds, his all-action style made him a popular and busy fighter on cards in New York and Atlantic City as he put together a winning run. Lost his unbeaten record in unusual circumstances, when he was knocked out by Mike Brown in September 1989, only for the referee to disqualify Brown for hitting on the break. Brown's management protested against the decision and the New Jersey Commission changed the result to a kayo win for Brown. Jake drew in May 1990 with Canadian prospect, Howard Grant, then came through some tough matches when battering John Rafuse to a points defeat and winning split decisions over Carl Griffiths and Oscar Ponce. Suffered his second loss to future world champion, Felix Trinidad, in December 1991, but scored four wins in 1992. Two highly impressive performances saw him climb off the floor twice to outpoint Julio Flores and also beat the Russian southpaw, Sergei Stepanov. Registered three more wins in 1993, but was disappointed when negotiations for a fight with Julio Cesar Chavez fell through. Jake then got a big break when Charles Murray agreed to defend his IBF title against him in February. Despite being a heavy outsider in the betting, Jake controlled the fight from the start, dictating the pace and giving Murray no punching room. At the end he looked a clear winner, but was only given a majority decision. Defended his title in April in a fast paced fight with clever Ray Oliveira, flooring his man in the fifth round and winning a unanimous decision. A pressure fighter, although not a big puncher, with only six quick wins on his record, he has a good chin and plenty of stamina. Interestingly enough, he still works as a mechanic at a motor cycle shop.

13.02.94	Charles Murray W PTS 12 Atlantic City	
	(IBF L. Welterweight Title Challenge)	
21.04.94	Ray Oliveira W PTS 12 Ledyard	
	(IBF L. Welterweight Title Defence)	

Career: 29 contests, won 25, drew 2, lost 2.

Eloy Rojas

Caracas, Venezuela. *Born* 25 March, 1967
WBA Featherweight Champion.
Former Undefeated Venezuelan and Latin American Featherweight Champion

Turned professional in December 1986, after an impressive campaign as an amateur and decisioned Miguel Nieyes in his first fight. It was to be four and a half years before anyone lasted the distance with Eloy again as he compiled a Venezuelan record of 21 stoppages or knockouts in a row, with only seven opponents surviving beyond the third round. Won the Venezuelan featherweight title in August 1988, halting Luis Rodriguez in two rounds and the Latin American crown in July 1989, following a sixth round kayo of Ernesto Quintana. Eloy then retained his Venezuelan title with a first round blowout of Gustavo Inciarte in August 1989. At the end of the year his manager did a deal with the Japanese promoter, Akihiko Honda, to get Eloy some fights in Nippon. Facing the former Thai champion, Jimmy Sithfaidang, in Tokyo, in February 1990, he blasted him out in four rounds and since no Japanese fighter would then face him he had to be content with inside the distance wins over another Thai, Eak Donjadee, and Korean, Bong-Jun Lee, before returning to Venezuela at the end of 1990. Travelling to South Korea in September 1991 to challenge Kyun-Yung Park for the WBA title, and a heavy favourite due to his impressive showings in Japan, he was floored in the first round and later suffered a cut and loss of confidence as Park out-hustled him to take an easy decision. His stock fell again in December 1992 when he could only manage a draw in Santiago with Carlos Uribe for the Latin American crown. After that, Eloy needed some good wins to earn a second shot at Park. A reversal of form duly arrived in 1993 as he outpointed highly rated fellow countryman, Giovanni Nieves, and then halted Uribe in six rounds. The second fight with Park in

Kwangmyong in December was a rough, foul-filled brawl, but Eloy provided the better boxing and won the WBA title on a split decision. His first defence saw him return to Japan to knock out Seiji Asakawa in five rounds. Eloy is a tall stylish boxer, with real power in both hands, and only four of his 27 wins have been on points.

07.08.93	Carlos Uribe W RSC 6 Turmero *(Latin American Featherweight Title Defence)*
04.12.93	Kyun-Yung Park W PTS 12 Kwangmyong *(WBA Featherweight Title Challenge)*
19.03.94	Seiji Asakawa W RSC 5 Kobe *(WBA Featherweight Title Defence)*
Career: 29 contests, won 27, drew 1, lost 1.	

Gianfranco Rosi

Assisi, Italy. *Born* 5 August, 1957
IBF L. Middleweight Champion.
Former WBC L. Middleweight Champion. Former Undefeated European L. Middleweight Champion. Former Undefeated Italian Welterweight Champion

04.03.94	Vince Pettway T. Draw 6 Las Vegas *(IBF L. Middleweight Title Defence)*
Career: 61 contests, won 57, drew 1, lost 3.	

Rafael Ruelas

Sylmar, USA. *Born* 26 April, 1971
IBF Lightweight Champion. Former Undefeated NABF Featherweight & Lightweight Champion

One of 13 children, he was born in Yerba Bueno, Mexico, but moved to the United States in 1979. Followed his brothers Juan and Gabriel into professional boxing when joining the Ten Goose team in January 1989 and won his first 27 fights. His first big victory came in March 1991 when he floored former WBA champion, Steve Cruz, four times and knocked him out in round three to lift the vacant NABF featherweight title. Unfortunately, weight problems forced him to move up to super-featherweight and then lightweight in quick succession. Challenged Mauro Gutierrez for the

WBA Continental Americas lightweight title in July 1991, but was floored and counted out in the second round. Rafael took the count on one knee and claimed he misjudged the count and could easily have risen. Scored a unanimous decision over former world champion, Rocky Lockridge, in January 1992 and gained revenge over Gutierrez with a clear points victory in July. The officials had him six, seven and eight points ahead, respectively. Won the vacant NABF lightweight crown in November 1992 by halting the former IBF featherweight champion, Jorge Paez. Rafael had Paez down twice in the first round and, although the colourful Mexican rallied, he was a bloody mess when the referee stopped the fight after the bell at the end of round ten. In March 1993, he retained his title with a third round stoppage of Robert Rivera and in July put himself in line for a world title shot when he came in as a late substitute and won a unanimous decision over Darryl Tyson. Two fights later, Rafael challenged Fred Pendleton for the IBF crown in February, but was almost blown away in the first round after being floored twice. Surviving with difficulty, being on the canvas twice more, he then slowly wore the veteran champion down and won a clear decision with a strong finish. In his first defence he had too much power for Mike Evgen and gave him a methodical beating until the referee intervened in round three. 5'11" tall, with a 74" reach, Rafael is a rangy, fast puncher and has halted 32 victims. On the other side of the spectrum, his defence has been shown to be leaky, but he is strong and gutsy and most of all, a great competitor.

17.07.93	Darryl Tyson W PTS 10 Las Vegas
19.08.93	Conrad Lopez W RSC 1 Irvine
22.10.93	Manuel Hernandez W RSC 1 Boise
19.02.94	Fred Pendleton W PTS 12 Los Angeles *(IBF Lightweight Title Challenge)*
27.05.94	Mike Evgen W RSC 3 Las Vegas *(IBF Lightweight Title Defence)*
Career: 42 contests, won 41, lost 1.	

Alex (El Nene) Sanchez

Playa Ponce, Puerto Rico. *Born* 6 May, 1973
WBO M. Flyweight Champion

A brilliant hard-punching youngster, who turned professional at 19 years of age in October 1992, Alex scored seven easy wins before moving up to the eight round class in July 1983 with a points win over experienced Manuel Santos. Destroyed former Mexican WBO flyweight title challenger, Eduardo Vallejo, in one round in October and knocked out the Spanish bantamweight champion, Jose Juarez, in four rounds in Zaragoza. When Paul Weir vacated the WBO title, Alex faced Orlando Malone for the crown and stopped him in the first round to become champion just 14 months after turning professional. In January, he made a farcical defence of his title with another first round victory, this time over unknown Mexican, Arturo Garcia. Sanchez has tremendous potential, but has not yet faced a real test. Although he has stopped ten opponents, seven in the first round, he may not realise his full potential until he goes for one of the other versions of the title.

03.07.93	Jose Bartolomei W CO 1 Hato Rey
17.07.93	Miguel Santos W PTS 8 San Juan
01.10.93	Eduardo Vallejo W RSC 1 Camuy
15.10.93	Francisco Carrasco W RSC 1 Yabucoa
29.10.93	Jose Juarez W RSC 4 Zaragoza
22.12.93	Orlando Malone W RSC 1 San Juan *(Vacant WBO M. Flyweight Title)*
07.01.94	Arturo Garcia W RSC 1 Palma de Mallorca *(WBO M. Flyweight Title Defence)*
11.06.94	Jose Rodriguez W CO 3 Zaragoza
Career: 14 contests, won 14.	

Pichit Sitbangprachan

Nakhon Chaiaphun, Thailand. *Born* 15 January, 1966
IBF Flyweight Champion

11.07.93	Kyung-Yun Lee W RSC 1 Bangkok *(IBF Flyweight Title Defence)*
08.08.93	Juan Salazar W RSC 5 Bangkok
03.10.93	Miguel Martinez W RSC 9 Chaiyaphum *(IBF Flyweight Title Defence)*
23.01.94	Arthur Johnson W PTS 12 Surat Thani *(IBF Flyweight Title Defence)*
08.05.94	Jose Luis Zepeda W PTS 12 Rajburi *(IBF Flyweight Title Defence)*
Career: 20 contests, won 20.	

Saen Sorploenchit

Phatumthani, Thailand. *Born* 15 May, 1972

WBA Flyweight Champion

Called the "second Pone Kingpetch" in Thailand, due to his stylish boxing, he turned professional in September 1991 and was already rated number two in the national flyweight ratings after only three fights. Beat Filipino prospect, Melvin Magramo, in November 1992 and then cleaned up the rest of the Philippines' flyweights by outpointing Jesse Maca and Dan Nietes and knocking out the then national champion, Little Gun Pumar, in the space of six months during 1993. Closed the year by decisioning the former IBF title challenger, Mexican, Antonio Perez. Thanks to a millionaire backer with no expense spared, he landed a shot at the WBA champion, David Griman, in February, with the Venezuelan receiving double the normal purse for a title bout in the division. Griman picked up the money, but left his title behind as he was out-jabbed by the young Thai to lose a unanimous decision. The new titleholder made his first defence only two months later against the former champion, Jesus Rojas. After a slow start, Saen dominated all the way until the Venezuelan turned his back in apparent surrender in the tenth round. However, the referee realised that the challenger had changed his mind within a split second and allowed him to restart the action. The decision for Saen was a formality and he beat his third Venezuelan in a row when he took a majority decision over another ex-champion, Aquiles Guzman, winning clearly, despite dubious scoring by one official. Saen's backer has provided him with a delux gym for his training and he has responded with some brilliant performances. A good boxer with fast hands, he is not a noted puncher, but one who relies more on accuracy. Has an imported Cuban trainer and also has a good voice, even singing the National Anthem before his fights.

11.07.93	Little Gun Pumar W CO 10 Nakonsawan	
03.10.93	Antonio Perez W PTS 10 Chaiyaphoom	
13.02.94	David Griman W PTS 12 Chachoengsao *(WBA Flyweight Title Challenge)*	
10.04.94	Jesus Rojas W PTS 12 Samut Prakan *(WBA Flyweight Title Defence)*	
12.06.94	Aquiles Guzman W PTS 12 Bangkok *(WBA Flyweight Title Defence)*	

Career: 19 contests, won 19.

Ratanapol Sowvoraphin

Dankoonthod, Thailand. *Born* 6 June, 1973

IBF M. Flyweight Champion. Former Undefeated IBF Intercontinental M. Flyweight Champion

26.09.93	Domingus Siwalete W RSC 4 Bangkok *(IBF M. Flyweight Title Defence)*
10.12.93	Felix Naranjo W RSC 2 Supan Buri *(IBF M. Flyweight Title Defence)*
27.02.94	Ronnie Magramo W PTS 12 Bangmulnak *(IBF M. Flyweight Title Defence)*
14.05.94	Roger Espanol W RSC 6 Saraburi *(IBF M. Flyweight Title Defence)*

Career: 21 contests, won 18, drew 1, lost 2.

James (Lights Out) Toney

Grand Rapids, USA. *Born* 24 August, 1968

IBF S. Middleweight Champion. Former Undefeated IBF Middleweight Champion

29.07.93	Danny Garcia W RTD 6 Bushkill
24.08.93	Larry Prather W PTS 10 Detroit
29.10.93	Tony Thornton W PTS 12 Tulsa *(IBF S. Middleweight Title Defence)*
16.01.94	Anthony Hembrick W RSC 7 Bushkill
05.03.94	Tim Littles W RSC 4 Los Angeles *(IBF S. Middleweight Title Defence)*
18.05.94	Vince Durham W PTS 10 Rosemont

Career: 45 contests, won 43, drew 2.

Felix Trinidad

Cupoy Alto, Puerto Rico. *Born* 10 January, 1973

IBF Welterweight Champion

06.08.93	Luis Garcia W RSC 1 Bayamon *(IBF Welterweight Title Defence)*
23.10.93	Anthony Stephens W CO 10 Fort Lauderdale *(IBF Welterweight Title Defence)*
29.01.94	Hector Camacho W PTS 12 Las Vegas *(IBF Welterweight Title Defence)*

Career: 23 contests, won 23.

Julio Cesar Vasquez

Santa Fe, Argentine. *Born* 13 July, 1966

WBA L. Middleweight Champion

11.07.93	Alejandro Ugueto W PTS 12 Tucuman *(WBA L. Middleweight Title Defence)*
21.08.93	Aaron Davis W PTS 12 Monte Carlo *(WBA L. Middleweight Title Defence)*
01.10.93	Han Kim W RSC 3 Buenos Aires
22.01.94	Juan Padilla W PTS 12 Alma Ata *(WBA L. Middleweight Title Defence)*
04.03.94	Arman Picar W RSC 2 Las Vegas *(WBA L. Middleweight Title Defence)*
08.04.94	Ricardo Nunez W PTS 12 Tucuman *(WBA L. Middleweight Title Defence)*
21.05.94	Ahmet Dottuev W RSC 10 Belfast *(WBA L. Middleweight Title Defence)*

Career: 51 contests, won 50, lost 1.

Wilfredo Vasquez

Rio Piedras, Puerto Rico. *Born* 2 August, 1960

WBA S. Bantamweight Champion. Former WBA Bantamweight Champion. Former Undefeated Puerto Rican and IBF Intercontinental Bantamweight Champion

18.11.93	Hiroki Yokota W PTS 12 Tokyo *(WBA S. Bantamweight Title Defence)*
02.03.94	Yuichi Kasai W RSC 1 Tokyo *(WBA S. Bantamweight Title Defence)*

Career: 48 contests, won 39, drew 3, lost 6.

Anaclet Wamba

Saint Brieuc, France. *Born* 6 January, 1960

WBC Cruiserweight Champion. Former Undefeated European Cruiserweight Champion

16.10.93	Akim Tafer W RTD 7 Levallois
	(WBC Cruiserweight Title Defence)
24.04.94	Mike de Vito W RSC 4 Limoges
Career: 45 contests, won 43, lost 2.	

Pernell (Sweet Pea) Whitaker

Norfolk, USA. *Born* 2 January, 1964
WBC Welterweight Champion.
Former Undefeated IBF
L. Welterweight Champion. Former
Undefeated IBF, WBA & WBC
Lightweight Champion. Former
Undefeated NABF & USBA
Lightweight Champion

10.09.93	Julio Cesar Chavez DREW 12 San Antonio
	(WBC Welterweight Title Defence)
09.04.94	Santos Cardona W PTS 12 Norfolk
	(WBC Welterweight Title Defence)
Career: 35 contests, won 33, drew 1, lost 1.	

Pernell Whitaker

Yasuei Yakushiji

Tsukumi, Japan. *Born* 22 July, 1968
WBC Bantamweight Champion.
Former Undefeated Japanese
Bantamweight Champion

5'8" tall, stable-mate of former
WBC super-bantamweight champion,
Kiyoshi Hatanaka, Yasuei is based in
Nagoya and trained by Californian,

Mack Kurihara. Won 21 of 26 amateur
fights, with nine stoppages, before
turning professional in July 1987.
Made an indifferent start, winning only
three of his first six fights, but then put
together nine consecutive stoppages as
he somehow found extra punching
power. Yasuei floored Keiichi Ozaki
three times and forced him to retire in
nine rounds in June 1991, to collect the
Japanese bantamweight crown and
then earned a world rating with a close
decision over top Filipino, Rey
Paciones, in September. Following
that, he retained his national title with
a first round win over Yukio Nakatani
in December, but then relinquished
and battled at super-bantamweight in
1992. Scored wins over Filipinos,
Ricarte Cainiela and Ruben de la Cruz,
and Korean, Jing-Min Suh. Continued
in the same division in 1993 until
offered the chance as a controversial
substitute to challenge southpaw, Jung-
Il Byun, for the WBC title. The fight
was not spectacular, but the judges
preferred Yasuei's harder punches to
the greater volume thrown by Byun,
and a strong finish earned him a split
decision and the title. In his first
defence he withstood the body punches
of Josefino Suarez and a cut to win.
The challenger had Yasuei badly hurt
in the tenth, but stormed back to
register a count out with wicked body
shots of his own. A methodical
puncher, he has yet to prove he is a
real force, as the win over Byun was
controversial and only five of his
fights have been outside Nagoya. Has
15 stoppages or knock outs on his
record.

Yasuei Yakushiji

World Title Bouts during 1993-94

All of last season's title bouts are shown by weight class in date order and give the boxers' respective weights, along with the scorecard, if going to a decision. There is also a short summary of any bout that involved a British contestant, and British officials, where applicable, are listed.

MINI-FLYWEIGHT (7st.7lbs)

Titleholders as at 1 July, 1994
IBF   – Ratanapol Sowvoraphin (Thailand)
WBA – Chana Porpaoin (Thailand)
WBC – Ricardo Lopez (Mexico)
WBO – Alex Sanchez (Mexico)

3 July, 1993   Ricardo Lopez 7.6 (Mexico) W RSC 2 Saman Sorjaturong 7.7 (Thailand), Nuevo Laredo, Mexico (WBC).

22 August, 1993   Chana Porpaoin 7.7 (Thailand) W PTS 12 Ronnie Magramo 7.7 (Philippines), Bankok, Thailand (WBA). Scorecard: 119-109, 119-111, 117-114.

19 September, 1993   Ricardo Lopez 7.5½ (Mexico) W RSC 11 Toto Porpongsawang 7.4 (Thailand), Bangkok, Thailand (WBC).

26 September, 1993   Ratanapol Sowvoraphin 7.6 (Thailand) W RSC 4 Domingus Siwalete 7.5½ (Indonesia), Bangkok, Thailand (IBF).

26 October, 1993   Paul Weir 7.6½ (Scotland) W PTS 12 Lindi Memani 7.7 (South Africa), Forte Crest Hotel, Glasgow (WBO). Scorecard: 116-111, 116-113, 117-112. Although hampered by a cut right-eye from the third round, the little Scot was good value with his better boxing. In January 1994, Weir relinquished title in order to challenge for the light-flyweight crown.

28 November, 1993   Chana Porpaoin 7.7 (Thailand) W CO 4 Rafael Torres 7.7 (Dominican Republic), Pichit, Thailand (WBA).

10 December, 1993   Ratanapol Sowvoraphin 7.6½ (Thailand) W RSC 2 Felix Naranjo 7.5½ (Colombia), Supan Buri, Thailand (IBF).

18 December, 1993   Ricardo Lopez 7.6¼ (Mexico) W CO 11 Manny Melchor 7.7 (Philippines), Lake Tahoe, USA (WBC).

22 December, 1993   Alex Sanchez 7.4 (Mexico) W RSC 1 Orlando Malone 7.6 (USA), San Juan, Puerto Rico (WBO).

7 January, 1994   Alex Sanchez 7.7 (Mexico) W RSC 1 Arturo Garcia Mayen 7.7 (Mexico), Palma de Mallorca, Spain (WBO).

27 February, 1994   Ratanapol Sowvoraphin 7.7 (Thailand) W PTS 12 Ronnie Magramo 7.5½ (Philippines), Bangmulnak, Thailand (IBF). Scorecard: 118-110, 118-111, 115-113.

26 March, 1994   Chana Porpaoin 7.7 (Thailand) W PTS 12 Carlos Murillo 7.7 (Panama), Chonburi, Thailand (WBA). Scorecard: 117-114, 118-113, 114-114. John Coyle refereed.

7 May, 1994   Ricardo Lopez 7.7 (Mexico) W PTS 12 Kermin Guardia 7.6 (Colombia), Las Vegas, USA (WBC). Scorecard: 119-109, 117-110, 117-110.

14 May, 1994   Ratanapol Sowvoraphin 7.7 (Thailand) W RSC 6 Roger Espanol (Philippines), Saraburi, Thailand (IBF).

LIGHT-FLYWEIGHT (7st.10lbs)

Titleholders as at 1 July, 1994
IBF   – Humberto Gonzalez (Mexico)
WBA – Silvio Gamez (Venezuela)
WBC – Humberto Gonzalez (Mexico)
WBO – Josue Camacho (Puerto Rico)

17 July, 1993   Michael Carbajal 7.10 (USA) W RSC 7 Kwang-Sun Kim 7.10 (South Korea), Las Vegas, USA (WBC/IBF).

25 July, 1993   Myung-Woo Yuh 7.10 (South Korea) W PTS 12 Yuichi Hosono 7.9¾ (Japan), Kyongju, South Korea (WBA). Scorecard: 119-110, 118-110, 120-111. Yuh relinquished title when he retired in September 1993.

21 October, 1993   Silvio Gamez 7.10 (Venezuela) W RSC 9 Shiro Yahiro 7.10 (Japan), Tokyo, Japan (WBA).

30 October, 1993   Michael Carbajal 7.10 (USA) W RSC 5 Domingo Sosa 7.10 (Dominican Republic), Phoenix, USA (WBC/IBF).

2 February, 1994   Josue Camacho 7.10 (Puerto Rico) W PTS 12 Paul Weir 7.9½ (Scotland), Kelvin Hall, Glasgow (WBO). Scorecard: 115-114, 118-111, 116-112. A negative bout of poor quality saw the little Scot not doing enough good work to capture the title. However, if nothing else, Weir would have learned from the fight and will improve with further experience.

5 February, 1994   Silvio Gamez 7.10 (Venezuela) W RSC 7 Juan Antonio Torres 7.10 (Panama), Panama City, Panama (WBA).

19 February, 1994   Michael Carbajal 7.10 (USA) L PTS 12 Humberto Gonzalez 7.10 (Mexico), Los Angeles, USA (WBC/IBF). Scorecard: 112-117, 116-114, 113-115.

27 June, 1994   Silvio Gamez 7.10 (Venezuela) DREW 12 Kaj Ratchabandit 7.10 (Thailand), Bangkok, Thailand (WBA). Scorecard: 114-114, 115-114, 114-115.

FLYWEIGHT (8st)

Titleholders as at 1 July, 1994

IBF   –   Pichit Sitbangprachan (Thailand)
WBA   –   Saen Sowploenchit (Thailand)
WBC   –   Yuri Arbachakov (Russia)
WBO   –   Jacob Matlala (South Africa)

11 July, 1993   Pichit Sitbangprachan 8.0 (Thailand) W RSC 1 Kyung-Yun Lee 7.13¾ (South Korea), Bangkok, Thailand (IBF).

16 July, 1993   Yuri Arbachakov 7.13¾ (Russia) W PTS 12 Ysaias Zamudio 7.13½ (USA), Kobe City, Japan (WBC). Scorecards: 117-115, 116-113, 116-112.

3 October, 1993   Pichit Sitbangprachan 8.0 (Thailand) W RSC 9 Miguel Martinez 8.0 (Mexico), Chaiyaphum, Thailand (IBF).

4 October, 1993   David Griman 8.0 (Venezuela) W PTS 12 Alvaro Mercado 7.13¼ (Colombia), Puerto la Cruz, Venezuela (WBA). Scorecard: 116-112, 17-113, 116-113.

4 December, 1993   Jacob Matlala 7.12¾ (South Africa) W RTD 7 Luigi Camputaro 7.13¾ (Italy), Sun City, Bophuthatswana (WBO).

13 December, 1993   Yuri Arbachakov 7.13¼ (Russia) W PTS 12 Nam-Hoon Cha 8.0 (South Korea), Kyoto, Japan (WBC). Scorecards: 117-113, 116-112, 118-111.

23 January, 1994   Pichit Sitbangprachan 8.0 (Thailand) W PTS 12 Arthur Johnson 8.0 (USA), Surat Thani, Thailand (IBF). Scorecard: 118-110, 115-113, 115-113.

13 February, 1994   David Griman 8.0 (Venezuela) L PTS 12 Saen Sowploenchit 8.0 (Thailand), Chachoengsao, Thailand (WBA). Scorecard: 114-115, 112-117, 111-120.

10 April, 1994   Saen Sowploenchit 8.0 (Thailand) W PTS 12 Jesus Rojas 8.0 (Venezuela), Samut Prakan, Thailand (WBA). Scorecard: 117-111, 118-110, 118-109.

8 May 1994   Pichit Sitbangprachan 8.0 (Thailand) W PTS 12 Jose Luis Zepeda 7.12 (Mexico), Rajburi, Thailand (IBF). Scorecard: 115-113, 115-113, 112-115.

11 June, 1994   Jacob Matlala 7.12 (South Africa) W RTD 9 Francis Ampofo 7.13¾ (England), York Hall, London (WBO). Out of the ring for nearly a year was no way to prepare for a world title fight. And that proved to be the case as Ampofo was unable to keep the little Zulu at bay. Floored by a body punch in the ninth and almost exhausted, having run out of ideas, Ampofo was retired by his corner at the end of the round.

12 June, 1994   Saen Sowploenchit 8.0 (Thailand) W PTS 12 Aquiles Guzman 8.0 (Venezuela), Bangkok, Thailand (WBA). Scorecard: 117-112, 115-115, 117-113.

SUPER-FLYWEIGHT (8st.3lbs)

Titleholders as at 1 July, 1994

IBF   –   Julio Cesar Borboa (Mexico)
WBA   –   Katsuya Onizuka (Japan)
WBC   –   Hiroshi Kawashima (Japan)
WBO   –   Johnny Bredahl (Denmark)

3 July, 1993   Sung-Il Moon 8.3 (South Korea) W PTS 12 Carlos Salazar 8.2½ (Argentine), Seoul, South Korea (WBC). Scorecard: 114-115, 116-112, 116-111.

21 August, 1993   Julio Cesar Borboa 8.3 (Mexico) W CO 3 Carlos Mercado 8.2½ (Colombia), Kalispel, Mexico (IBF).

29 October, 1993   Johnny Bredahl 8.2¾ (Denmark) W DIS 4 Eduardo Nazario 8.2½ (Puerto Rico), Korsor, Denmark (WBO).

5 November, 1993   Katsuya Onizuka 8.3 (Japan) W PTS 12 Khaoyai Mahasarakam 8.3 (Thailand), Tokyo, Japan (WBA). Scorecard: 116-111, 116-114, 115-113.

13 November, 1993   Sung-Il Moon 8.3 (South Korea) L PTS 12 Jose Luis Bueno 8.3 (Mexico), Pohang, South Korea (WBC). Scorecard: 112-117, 115-114, 110-118.

26 November, 1993   Julio Cesar Borboa 8.3 (Mexico) W RSC 5 Rolando Pascua 8.3 (Philippines), Hermosillo, Mexico (IBF).

25 March, 1994   Johnny Bredahl 8.2¾ (Denmark) W PTS 12 Eduardo Nazario 8.2¾ (Puerto Rico), Aakirkeby, Denmark (WBO). Scorecard: 118-111, 118-109, 119-110.

3 April, 1994   Katsuya Onizuka 8.3 (Japan) W PTS 12 Seung-Koo Lee 8.3 (South Korea), Tokyo, Japan (WBA). Scorecard: 115-112, 115-114, 115-114.

25 April, 1994   Julio Cesar Borboa 8.1 (Mexico) W RSC 4 Jorge Roman 8.2 (Mexico), Los Angeles, USA (IBF).

4 May, 1994   Jose Luis Bueno 8.2¾ (Mexico) L PTS 12 Hiroshi Kawashima 8.3 (Japan), Yokohama, Japan (WBC). Scorecard: 113-114, 112-114, 110-116.

21 May, 1994   Julio Cesar Borboa 8.2 (Mexico) W RSC 9 Jaji Sibali 8.3 (South Africa), Temba, Bophuthatswana (IBF).

BANTAMWEIGHT (8st.6lbs)

Titleholders as at 1 July, 1994
IBF   – Orlando Canizales (USA)
WBA   – John Michael Johnson (USA)
WBC   – Yasuei Yakushiji (Japan)
WBO   – Rafael del Valle (Puerto Rico)

8 July, 1993   Jorge Elicier Julio 8.6 (Colombia) W PTS 12 Ricardo Vargas 8.4½ (Mexico), Tijuana, Mexico (WBA). Scorecard: 114-114, 117-110, 117-111.

22 July, 1993   Joichiro Tatsuyoshi 8.5 (Japan) W PTS 12 Victor Rabanales 8.5 (Mexico), Osaka, Japan (WBC). Scorecard: 115-114, 116-114, 114-115. With the champion, Il-Jung Byun, sidelined with an injured hand, this was an interim title fight. However, when Byun was fit again, it was another Jap, Yasuei Yakushiji, who challenged him.

23 October, 1993   Jorge Elicier Julio 8.6 (Colombia) L PTS 12 Junior Jones 8.6 (USA), Atlantic City, USA (WBA). Scorecard: 109-117, 111-116, 111-116.

20 November, 1993   Orlando Canizales 8.6 (USA) W PTS 12 Juvenal Berrio 8.6 (Colombia), Temba, Bophuthatswana (IBF). Scorecard: 116-112, 115-112, 116-110.

23 December, 1993   Jung-Il Byun 8.6 (South Korea) L PTS 12 Yasuei Yakushiji 8.5½ (Japan), Nagoya, Japan (WBC). Scorecard: 113-115, 115-113, 115-116.

8 January, 1994   Junior Jones 8.6 (USA) W PTS 12 Elvis Alvarez 8.6 (Colombia), Catskill, USA (WBA). Scorecard: 119-109, 120-108, 120-108.

26 February, 1994   Orlando Canizales 8.6 (USA) W RSC 4 Gerardo Martinez 8.6 (USA), San Jose, USA (IBF).

16 April, 1994   Yasuei Yakushiji 8.5¾ (Japan) W CO 10 Josefino Suarez 8.4¾ (Mexico), Nagoya, Japan (WBC).

22 April, 1994   Junior Jones 8.6 (USA) L RSC 11 John Michael Johnson 8.6 (USA), Las Vegas, USA (WBA).

7 June, 1994   Orlando Canizales 8.6 (USA) W RSC 5 Rolando Bohol 8.5½ (Philippines), South Padre Island, USA (IBF).

SUPER-BANTAMWEIGHT (8st.10lbs)

Titleholders as at 1 July, 1994
IBF   – Kennedy McKinney (USA)
WBA   – Wilfredo Vasquez (Puerto Rico)
WBC   – Tracy Harris Patterson (USA)
WBO   – Daniel Jimenez (Puerto Rico)

17 July, 1993   Kennedy McKinney 8.9 (USA) W RSC 3 Rudy Zavala 8.10 (USA), Memphis, USA (IBF).

25 September, 1993   Tracy Harris Patterson 8.10 (USA) W RSC 7 Daniel Zaragoza 8.10 (Mexico), Poughkeepsie, USA (WBC).

16 October, 1993   Kennedy McKinney 8.10 (USA) W PTS 12 Jesus Salud 8.10 (USA), Lake Tahoe, USA (IBF). Scorecard: 118-110, 119-109, 119-109.

30 October, 1993   Daniel Jimenez 8.10 (Puerto Rico) W RSC 5 Felix Garcia Losada 8.10 (Spain), Zaragoza, Spain (WBO).

18 November, 1993   Wilfredo Vasquez 8.10 W PTS 12 Hiroki Yokota 8.9 (Japan), Tokyo, Japan (WBA). Scorecard: 116-112, 116-112, 115-113.

7 January, 1994   Daniel Jimenez 8.10 (Puerto Rico) W PTS 12 Felix Garcia Losada 8.10 (Spain), Palma de Mallorca, Spain (WBO). Scorecard: 117-112, 117-115, 118-115.

19 February, 1994   Kennedy McKinney 8.9¾ (USA) W CO 5 Jose Rincones 8.9 (Venezuela), Temba, Bophuthatswana (IBF).

2 March, 1994   Wilfredo Vasquez 8.10 (Puerto Rico) W RSC 1 Yuichi Kasai 8.10 (Japan), Tokyo, Japan (WBA).

9 April, 1994   Tracy Harris Patterson 8.10 (USA) W PTS 12 Richard Duran 8.9 (USA), Reno, USA (WBC). Scorecard: 116-112, 117-112, 118-110.

16 April, 1994   Kennedy McKinney 8.10 (USA) W PTS 12 Welcome Ncita 8.10 (South Africa), South Padre Island, USA (IBF). Scorecard: 114-114, 117-110, 117-111.

25 June, 1994   Daniel Jimenez 8.10 (Puerto Rico) W PTS 12 Cristobal Pasqual 8.10 (Spain), Utrera, Spain (WBO). No scorecard available at time of going to press.

FEATHERWEIGHT (9st.)

Titleholders as at 1 July, 1994
IBF   – Tom Johnson (USA)
WBA   – Eloy Rojas (Venezuela)
WBC   – Kevin Kelley (USA)
WBO   – Steve Robinson (Wales)

10 July, 1993   Steve Robinson 9.0 (Wales) W CO 9 Sean Murphy 8.13¾ (England), National Ice Rink, Cardiff (WBO). A hard fight saw Murphy come apart at the seams in the ninth when a sustained attack of non-stop punching forced him to the deck where he was counted out by Roy Francis in the act of rising at 0.40. Mickey Vann, Paul Thomas and Dave Parris acted as judges.

4 September, 1993   Kyun-Yung Park 8.13 (Japan) W PTS 12 Tae-Shik Chun 8.13¾ (South Korea), Damyong, South Korea (WBA). Scorecard: 118-112, 117-111, 118-110.

11 September, 1993   Tom Johnson 8.13½ (USA) W PTS 12 Sugar Baby Rojas 9.3¾ (Colombia), Miami, USA (IBF). Scorecard: 119-109, 119-109, 119-109. Rojas failed to make the weight, therefore the title was not at risk.

23 October, 1993   Steve Robinson 8.13½ (Wales) W PTS 12 Colin McMillan 8.13¼ (England), National Ice Rink, Cardiff (WBO). Scorecard: Roy Francis 117-113, 116-113, 117-111. Constant aggression won the fight for Robinson as the challenger failed to keep his man at bay. To be fair to McMillan, he had fought with a badly swollen right hand from the fifth round on, and without the use of a stopping blow, the task was beyond him. Paul Thomas refereed.

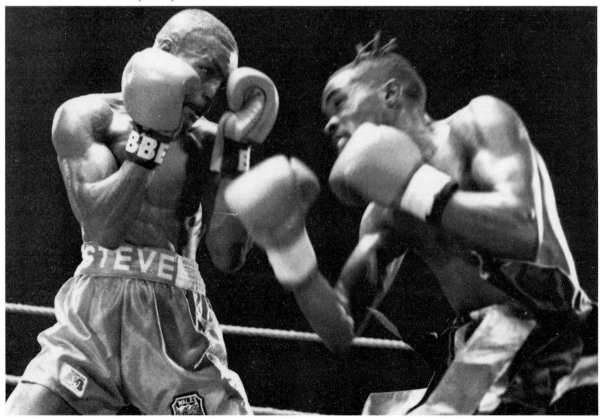

Steve Robinson (left) covers up against Colin McMillan during his successful WBO featherweight title defence last October

Les Clark

30 November, 1993   Tom Johnson 8.13¾ (USA) W RSC 9 Stephane Haccoun 8.13 (France), Marseilles, France (IBF).

4 December, 1993   Gregorio Vargas 9.0 (Mexico) L PTS 12 Kevin Kelley 8.13 (USA), Reno, USA (WBC). Scorecard: 112-115, 112-115, 111-116.

4 December, 1993   Kyun-Yung Park 8.13¼ (South Korea) L PTS 12 Eloy Rojas 8.13¾ (Venezuela), Kwangmyung, South Korea (WBA). Scorecard: 111-115, 112-113, 114-111.

12 February, 1994   Tom Johnson 9.0 (USA) W PTS 12 Orlando Soto 9.0 (Panama), St Louis, USA (IBF). Scorecard: 115-111, 117-109, 116-110.

12 March, 1994   Steve Robinson 8.13 (Wales) W RSC 12 Paul Hodkinson 9.0 (England), National Ice Rink, Cardiff (WBO). In an extremely hard-fought battle, Robinson came on strong in the latter rounds to grind the former champion down to a frazzle. Hodkinson finally ran out of steam in the 12th round and, after struggling off the floor following a battery of head blows, he was immediately floored again. This time, however, Dave Parris had seen enough and called a halt to the proceedings with just 1.60 of the contest remaining. Paul Thomas was one of the judges.

19 March, 1994   Eloy Rojas 8.12¾ (Venezuela) W RSC 5 Seiji Asakawa 9.0 (Japan), Kobe, Japan (WBA).

6 May, 1994   Kevin Kelley 9.0 (USA) W PTS 12 Jesse Benavides 9.0 (USA), Atlantic City, USA (WBC). Scorecard: 116-112, 117-111, 116-111.

4 June, 1994   Steve Robinson 8.13¾ (Wales) W PTS 12 Freddy Cruz 8.13¼ (Dominican Republic), National Ice Rink, Cardiff (WBO). Scorecard: 116-112, 117-110, 118-109. Although unable to force his clever rival out of the contest summarily, Robinson's workrate was just too much for Cruz to handle. The challenger simply lacked the power to halt the ever-pressing Robinson in his tracks and went down to a wide points defeat.

11 June, 1994   Tom Johnson 9.0 (USA) W RSC 12 Bennie Amparo 9.0 (USA), Atlantic City, USA (IBF).

SUPER-FEATHERWEIGHT (9st.4lbs)

Titleholders as at 1 July, 1994
IBF   – Juan Molina (Puerto Rico)
WBA   – Genaro Hernandez (USA)
WBC   – James Leija (USA)
WBO   – Oscar de la Hoya (USA)

10 September, 1993   Azumah Nelson 9.2½ (Ghana) DREW 12 James Leija 9.3 (USA), San Antonio, USA (WBC). Scorecard: 113-115, 115-115, 118-112.

17 September, 1993   Jimmy Bredahl 9.3 (Denmark) W PTS 12 Renato Cornett 9.3 (Australia), Copenhagen, Denmark (WBO). Scorecard: 117-112, 118-111, 118-111.

9 October, 1993   Juan Molina 9.4 (Puerto Rico) W RSC 8 Bernard Taylor 9.3½ (USA), San Juan, Puerto Rico (IBF).

11 October, 1993   Genaro Hernandez 9.4 (USA) W PTS 12 Harold Warren 9.4 (USA), Los Angeles, USA (WBA). Scorecard: 119-109, 118-115, 118-110.

22 January, 1994   Juan Molina 9.2 (Puerto Rico) W RTD 6 Floyd Havard 9.4 (Wales), Welsh Institute of Sport, Cardiff (IBF). Knocked down twice, unfortunately for the British fans, Havard lacked the power at the highest level to go with his excellent technique. Molina proved to be from the top drawer and it came as no surprise when Havard was retired by his corner after the second knockdown, suffering a broken nose. Roy Francis was one of the judges.

31 January, 1994   Genaro Hernandez 9.4 (USA) W RSC 8 Jorge Ramirez 9.4 (Mexico), Los Angeles, USA (WBA).

5 March, 1994   Jimmy Bredahl 9.4 (Denmark) L RTD 10 Oscar de la Hoya 9.2¾ (USA), Los Angeles, USA (WBO).

22 April, 1994   Juan Molina 9.3½ (Puerto Rico) W PTS 12 Gregorio Vargas 9.4 (Mexico), Las Vegas, USA (IBF). Scorecard: 118-110, 117-112, 118-110.

7 May, 1994   Azumah Nelson 9.3½ (Ghana) L PTS 12 James Leija 9.4 (USA), Las Vegas, USA (WBC). Scorecard: 113-114, 110-117, 109-117.

27 May, 1994   Oscar de la Hoya 9.4 (USA) W RSC 3 Giorgio Campanella 9.4 (Italy), Las Vegas, USA (WBO). Paul Thomas was one of the judges.

LIGHTWEIGHT (9st.9lbs)

Titleholders as at 1 July, 1994
IBF   – Rafael Ruelas (USA)
WBA   – Orzubek Nazarov (Russia)
WBC   – Miguel Gonzalez (Mexico)
WBO   – Vacant

17 July, 1993   Fred Pendleton 9.9 (USA) W PTS 12 Jorge Paez 9.9 (Mexico), Las Vegas, USA (IBF). Scorecard: 116-111, 116-111, 116-110.

13 August, 1993   Miguel Gonzalez 9.9 (Mexico) W PTS 12 David Sample 9.8¾ (USA), Guadalajara, Mexico (WBC). Scorecard: 120-110, 116-111, 116-112.

24 September, 1993   Giovanni Parisi 9.8½ (Italy) W PTS 12 Antonio Rivera 9.8¼ (Puerto Rico), Rome, Italy (WBO). Scorecard: 116-112, 116-113, 115-113. Having difficulty in making the weight, Parisi relinquished title in May 1994.

30 October, 1993   Dingaan Thobela 9.8¼ (South Africa) L PTS 12 Orzubek Nazarov 9.8 (Russia), Johannesburg, South Africa (WBA). Scorecard: 108-118, 111-117, 114-115.

27 November, 1993   Miguel Gonzales 9.9 (Mexico) W RSC 11 Wilfredo Rocha 9.8¾ (Colombia), Mexico City, Mexico (WBC).

19 February, 1994   Fed Pendleton 9.9 (USA) L PTS 12 Rafael Ruelas 9.9 (USA), Los Angeles, USA (IBF). Scorecard: 112-114, 111-116, 110-115.

19 March, 1994   Orzubek Nazarov 9.8¼ (Russia) W PTS 12 Dingaan Thobela 9.8¾ (South Africa), Temba, Bophuthatswana (WBA). Scorecard: 118-108, 118-111, 118-110.

29 March, 1994   Miguel Gonzalez 9.9 (Mexico) W RSC 5 Jean-Baptiste Mendy 9.7¼ (France), Levallois Perret, France (WBC).

27 May, 1994   Rafael Ruelas 9.9 (USA) W RSC 3 Mike Evgen 9.9 (USA), Las Vegas, USA (IBF).

LIGHT-WELTERWEIGHT (10st.)

Titleholders as at 1 July, 1994
IBF   – Jake Rodriguez (USA)
WBA   – Juan M. Coggi (Argentine)
WBC   – Julio Cesar Chavez (Mexico)
WBO   – Zack Padilla (USA)

24 July, 1993   Charles Murray 10.0 (USA) W PTS 12 Juan Laporte 10.0 (Puerto Rico), Atlantic City, USA (IBF). Scorecard: 118-110, 120-107, 118-110.

13 August, 1993   Juan M. Coggi 9.13¾ (Argentine) W PTS 12 Jose Barbosa 9.13¼ (Venezuela). Buenos Aires, Argentine (WBA). Scorecard: 119-114, 118-112, 117-111.

24 September, 1993   Juan M. Coggi 10.0 (Argentine) W RSC 10 Guillermo Cruz 9.13¼ (Mexico), Tucuman, Argentine (WBA).

19 November, 1993   Charles Murray 10.0 (USA) W RTD 5 Courtney Hooper 9.13 (USA), Atlantic City, USA (IBF).

19 November, 1993   Zack Padilla 9.13 (USA) W RTD 7 Efrem Calamati 9.13½ (Italy), Arezzo, Italy (WBO). Roy Francis and Dave Parris were among the three judges.

16 December, 1993   Zack Padilla 9.12½ (USA) W PTS 12 Ray Oliveira 9.13 (USA), Ledyard, USA (WBO). Scorecard: 118-110, 117-112, 116-113.

17 December, 1993   Juan M. Coggi 9.13¾ (Argentine) W RSC 7 Eder Gonzalez 9.13¾ (Colombia), Tucuman, Argentine (WBA).

18 December, 1993   Julio Cesar Chavez 9.13¼ (Mexico) W RTD 5 Andy Holligan 10.0 (England), Puebla, Mexico (WBC). After grimly soldiering on when others would have taken an easier option, Holligan was pulled out by his cornermen at the end of the fifth. Although he had taken a beating and was badly cut, he had not been floored and was stoic to the end.

29 January, 1994   Julio Cesar Chavez 10.0 (Mexico) L PTS 12 Frankie Randall 10.0 (USA), Las Vegas, USA (WBC). Scorecard: 114-113, 113-114, 111-116.

13 February, 1994   Charles Murray 10.0 (USA) L PTS 12 Jake Rodriguez 10.0 (USA), Atlantic City, USA (IBF). Scorecard: 113-115, 114-114, 112-116.

18 March, 1994   Juan M. Coggi 10.0 (Argentine) W RSC 3 Eder Gonzalez 10.0 (Colombia), Las Vegas, USA (WBA).

18 April, 1994   Zack Padilla 9.11¾ (USA) W RTD 6 Harold Miller 9.10¾ (USA), Rotterdam, USA (WBO).

21 April, 1994   Jake Rodriguez 10.0 (USA) W PTS 12 Ray Oliveira 10.0 (USA), Ledyard, USA (IBF). Scorecard: 115-112, 116-111, 119-108.

7 May, 1994   Frankie Randall 10.0 (USA) L TD 8 Julio Cesar Chavez 10.0 (USA), Las Vegas, USA (WBC). Scorecard: 74-77, 76-75, 75-76.

WELTERWEIGHT (10st. 7lbs)

Titleholders as at 1 July, 1994
IBF   –   Felix Trinidad (Puerto Rico)
WBA   –   Ike Quartey (Ghana)
WBC   –   Pernell Whitaker(USA)
WBO   –   Eamonn Loughran (Ireland)

6 August, 1993   Felix Trinidad 10.6½ (Puerto Rico) W RSC 1 Luis Garcia 10.6 (Venezuela), Bayamon, Puerto Rico (IBF).

10 September, 1993   Pernell Whitaker 11.5 (USA) DREW 12 Julio Cesar Chavez 10.2 (Mexico), San Antonio, USA (WBC). Scorecard: Mickey Vann 115-115, 115-115, 115-113.

9 October, 1993   Cristanto Espana 10.7 (Venezuela) W RSC 10 Donovan Boucher 10.7 (Canada), Old Trafford, Manchester (WBA). The bout was refereed by John Coyle.

16 October, 1993   Eamonn Loughran 10.6 (Ireland) W PTS 12 Lorenzo Smith 10.6½ (USA), King's Hall, Belfast (WBO). Scorecard: 118-110, 116-112, 117-112. Initially, Loughran was to have challenged then champion, Gert Bo Jacobsen. However, the Dane relinquished his title a week earlier and a match against Smith was hastily arranged for the vacant crown. Smith, although cut over the right-eye in the first, proved a worthy substitute with his fast stepping style, but lacked the punch to keep the more powerful Loughran at bay and ultimately went down on points.

23 October, 1993   Felix Trinidad 10.7 (Puerto Rico) W CO 10 Anthony Stephens 10.5 (USA), Fort Lauderdale, USA (IBF).

22 January, 1994   Eamonn Loughran 10.6¾ (Ireland) W PTS 12 Alessandro Duran 10.6¾ (Italy), King's Hall, Belfast (WBO). Scorecard: 117-111, 117-112, 117-112. Faced with a crafty opponent, Loughran looked only half the fighter the crowd had expected. But championships are won on aggression and although Duran made things tough for Loughran, and at times exposed his limitations, it was the Irishman's better workrate that saw him home.

29 January, 1994   Felix Trinidad 10.7 (Puerto Rico) W PTS 12 Hector Camacho 10.7 (Puerto Rico), Las Vegas, USA (IBF). Scorecard: 117-109, 118-110, 119-106.

9 April, 1994   Pernell Whitaker 10.7 (USA)W PTS 12 Santos Cardona 10.6½ (Puerto Rico), Norfolk, USA (WBC). Scorecard: 119-109, Larry O'Connell 119-111, 119-109.

4 June, 1994   Crisanto Espana 10.7 (Venezuela) L RSC 11 Ike Quartey 10.7 (Ghana), Levallois Perret, France (WBA).

LIGHT-MIDDLEWEIGHT (11st.)

Titleholders as at 1 July, 1994
IBF   –   Gianfranco Rosi (Italy)
WBA   –   Julio Cesar Vasquez (Argentine)
WBC   –   Terry Norris (USA)
WBO   –   Verno Phillips (USA)

10 July, 1993   Julio Cesar Vasquez 10.13¼ (Argentine) W PTS 12 Alejandro Ugueto 11.0 (Venezuela), Tucuman, Argentine (WBA). Scorecard: 118-111, 119-111, 119-114.

21 August, 1993   Julio Cesar Vasquez 10.13 (Argentine) W PTS 12 Aaron Davis 11.0 (USA), Monte Carlo, Monaco (WBA). Scorecard: 116-115, 115-115, 115-114.

10 September, 1993   Terry Norris 10.13½ (USA) W RSC 1 Joe Gatti 10.13¾ (USA), San Antonio, USA (WBC).

30 October, 1993   Verno Phillips 10.11½ (USA) W RSC 7 Lupe Aquino 11.0 (Mexico), Phoenix, USA (WBO). Among the judges was Paul Thomas. John David Jackson had vacated the title in July 1993 after experiencing difficulty making the weight.

18 December, 1993   Terry Norris 10.11¼ (USA) L CO 4 Simon Brown 10.13½ (USA), Puebla, Mexico (WBC).

22 January, 1994   Julio Cesar Vasquez 10.13¾ (Argentine) W PTS 12 Juan Padilla 10.12½ (Spain), Alma Ata, Kazakhstan (WBA). Scorecard: 119-102, 117-107, 120-105.

29 January, 1994   Simon Brown 10.13 (USA) W PTS 12 Troy Waters 10.13 (Australia), Las Vegas, USA (WBC). Scorecard: 118-111, 116-112, 114-114.

4 March, 1994   Julio Cesar Chavez 11.0 (Argentine) W RSC 2 Arman Picar 10.13½ (Philippines), Las Vegas, USA (WBA).

4 March, 1994   Gianfranco Rosi 11.0 (Italy) T DRAW 6 Vince Pettway 10.10 (USA), Las Vegas, USA (IBF). Scorecard: 49-45, 49-45, 48-46.

8 April, 1994   Julio Cesar Vasquez 10.12¾ (Argentine) W PTS 12 Ricardo Nunez 10.12¼ (Argentine), Tucuman, Argentine (WBA). Scorecard: 118-114, 118-112, 118-113.

7 May, 1994   Simon Brown 11.0 (USA) L PTS 12 Terry Norris 10.13 (USA), Las Vegas, USA (WBC). Scorecard: 109-119, 111-117, 112-116.

21 May, 1994   Julio Cesar Vasquez 10.13¾ (Argentine) W RSC 10 Ahmet Dottuev 10.13 (Russia), King's Hall, Belfast (WBA). The fight was refereed by John Coyle.

MIDDLEWEIGHT (11st.6lbs)

Titleholders as at 1 July, 1994
IBF   –   Roy Jones (USA)
WBA –   Vacant
WBC –   Gerald McClellan (USA)
WBO –   Steve Collins (Ireland)

6 August, 1993   Gerald McClellan 11.5½ (USA) W CO 1 Jay Bell 11.3½ (USA), Bayamon, Puerto Rico (WBC).

18 September, 1993   Chris Pyatt 11.4 (England) W CO 6 Hugo Corti 11.5 (Argentine), Granby Halls, Leicester (WBO). Although Corti appeared to be on the brink of a shock first round win, Pyatt stayed calm and controlled to take hold of the fight and then to knock the resistance out of the tough Argentinian. The expected finish came in the sixth, when Corti was bowled over by a heavy left-right combination and was counted out at 1.58, with his resilience broken and nothing left in the tank.

1 October, 1993   Reggie Johnson 11.6 (USA) L PTS 12 John David Jackson 11.5½ (USA), Buenos Aires, Argentine (WBA). Scorecard: 114-115, 113-115, 114-115. Jackson was stripped by the WBA in May 1994 for taking a non-title fight without having their authorisation.

9 February, 1994   Chris Pyatt 11.5¼ (England) W RSC 1 Mark Cameron 11.4½ (South Africa), International Centre, Brentwood (WBO). The South African provided a futile challenge for the hard-hitting Pyatt and ultimately succumbed to two heavy right hands that saw him counted out at 3.07 of the opening round.

4 March, 1994   Gerald McClellan 11.5 (USA) W RSC 1 Gilbert Baptist 11.4 (USA), Las Vegas, USA (WBC).

7 May, 1994   Gerald McClellan 11.6 (USA) W RSC 1 Julian Jackson 11.6 (USA), Las Vegas, USA (WBC).

11 May, 1994   Chris Pyatt 11.5 (England) L RSC 5 Steve Collins 11.5 (Ireland), Ponds Forge Arena, Sheffield (WBO). It did not take us long to realise that Pyatt was susceptible to the right hand counters of Collins and it was the effects of such a punch that brought the contest to a sudden end at 2.27 of round six. At that point, Pyatt, having survived a mandatory eight count, was rescued by Paul Thomas when apparently unable to fight back.

27 May, 1994   Roy Jones 11.5 (USA) W RSC 2 Thomas Tate 11.5½ (USA), Las Vegas, USA (IBF).

SUPER-MIDDLEWEIGHT (12st.)

Titleholders as at 1 July, 1994
IBF   –   James Toney (USA)
WBA –   Steve Little (USA)
WBC –   Nigel Benn (England)
WBO –   Chris Eubank (England)

9 October, 1993   Nigel Benn 11.13 (England) DREW 12 Chris Eubank 12.0 (England), Old Trafford, Manchester (WBC/WBO). Scorecard: Harry Gibbs 113-115, 114-114, 115-113. As in their first fight this was another thriller. However, this time round, Benn was distinctly unlucky to get no more than a share of the spoils and had he not had a point deducted by referee, Larry O'Connell, in round six for a low blow, he would have won. Although the contest lacked comparison with their earlier war of attrition, it was still great value, with the quantity supplied by Benn and the quality by Eubank.

29 October, 1993   James Toney 12.0 (USA) W PTS 12 Tony Thornton 11.13 (USA), Tulsa, USA (IBF). Scorecard: 118-110, 118-110, 116-112.

18 December, 1993   Michael Nunn 12.0 (USA) W PTS 12 Merqui Sosa (Dominican Republic), Puebla, Mexico (WBA). Scorecard: 116-113, 116-112, 116-112.

5 February, 1994   Chris Eubank 12.0 (England) W PTS 12 Graciano Rocchigiani 11.8¾ (Germany), Berlin, Germany (WBO). Scorecard: 115-113, 118-109, 114-113. Another safety-first display by Eubank saw him again come perilously close to losing his "much cherished" title. While many saw the fight closer than the judges, had Rocchigiani, who was cut by the side of the right eye during the eighth, been capable of upping his workrate just slightly, the title could have easily changed hands, especially after Eubank was deducted a point for holding in the 11th.

26 February, 1994   Nigel Benn 12.0 (England) W PTS 12 Henry Wharton 11.13½ (England), Earls Court Arena, London (WBC). Scorecards: Adrian Morgan 115-113, Sid Nathan 118-114, 117-112. In a fight he always seemed likely to lose, Wharton's only moment of glory came in the fifth when Benn was floored after taking a left-hook. Apart from that, he appeared to be chasing shadows as Benn, dispensing with his normal helter-skelter style, cagily boxed his way to a comprehensive points win.

26 February, 1994   Michael Nunn 11.13 (USA) L PTS 12 Steve Little 12.0 (USA), Earls Court Arena, London (WBA). Scorecard: 115-113, 114-116, 112-115.

5 March, 1994   James Toney 11.13¾ (USA) W RSC 4 Tim Littles 11.12½ (USA), Los Angeles, USA (IBF).

21 May, 1994   Chris Eubank 11.13¾ (England) W PTS 12 Ray Close 12.0 (Ireland), King's Hall, Belfast (WBO). Scorecard: 118-112, Roy Francis 114-117, 115-114. Installment two of Eubank v Close, saw the latter improve upon their first fight to score a debatable points win. However, controversy raged on after the announcement that Eubank had again retained his title when one of the judges' scorecards went missing. While the calls to force Eubank into a mandatory defence against Close went unanswered, it seems almost inconceivable that the pair will not meet again in 1994-95. The fight was refereed by Paul Thomas.

LIGHT-HEAVYWEIGHT (12st.7lbs)

Titleholders as at 1 July, 1994
IBF   –   Henry Maske (Germany)
WBA   –   Virgil Hill (USA)
WBC   –   Jeff Harding (Australia)
WBO   –   Leonzer Barber (USA)

28 August, 1993   Virgil Hill 12.6¾ (USA) W PTS 12 Sergio Merani 12.6½ (Argentine), Bismark, USA (WBA). Scorecard: 119-100, 119-112, 119-112.

18 September, 1993   Henry Maske 12.4½ (Germany) W PTS 12 Anthony Hembrick 12.3½ (USA), Dusseldorf, Germany (IBF). Scorecard: 119-109, 119-108, 119-108.

29 September, 1993   Leonzer Barber 12.6½ (USA) W PTS 12 Andrea Magi 12.6¼ (Italy), Pesaro, Italy (WBO). Scorecard: 116-113, 115-114, 115-113.

9 November, 1993   Virgil Hill 12.7 (USA) W RSC 10 Saul Montana 12.7 (USA), Fargo, USA (WBA).

11 December, 1993   Henry Maske 12.6¾ (Germany) W PTS 12 David Vedder 12.4½ (USA), Dusseldorf, Germany (IBF). Scorecard: 118-110, 120-107, 120-108.

17 December, 1993   Virgil Hill 12.7 (USA) W PTS 12 Guy Waters 12.5½ (Australia), Minot, USA (WBA). Scorecard: 120-108, 119-110, 120-108.

29 January, 1994   Leonzer Barber 12.7 (USA) W RSC 9 Nicky Piper 12.6¾ (Wales), National Ice Rink, Cardiff (WBO). With Piper apparently well on his way to a points victory and with Barber suffering a terribly swollen right eye that would have necessitated retirement in the not too distant future, he left his jaw exposed to a crunching left-hook and paid the ultimate price. Somehow, Piper managed to rise at seven, but was sent crashing again and his marvellous challenge came to an end at 1.40 of round nine when the referee came to his rescue.

After making a cracking start to his WBO light-heavyweight title challenge against Leonzer Barber, and appearing to be an odds on winner, Nicky Piper (left) was rescued by the referee in round nine   Les Clark

4 March, 1994   Mike McCallum 12.7 (Jamaica) W RSC 5 Randall Yonker 12.6 (USA), Las Vegas, USA (WBC). Ruled out with a cut eye just a week before defending his WBC crown against McCallum, Jeff Harding had to sit it out as the latter won the interim title.

26 March, 1994   Henry Maske 12.6¾ (Germany) W RSC 9 Ernie Magdaleno 12.6¾ (USA), Dortmund, Germany (IBF).

4 June, 1994   Henry Maske 12.5¾ (Germany) W PTS 12 Andrea Magi 12.6½ (Italy), Dortmund, Germany (IBF). Scorecard: 117-114, 117-112, 119-110.

CRUISERWEIGHT (13st.8lbs)

Titleholders as at 1 July, 1994

IBF – Al Cole (USA)

WBA – Orlin Norris (USA)

WBC – Anaclet Wamba (France)

WBO – Nestor Giovannini (Argentine)

16 July, 1993   Al Cole 13.8 (USA) W PTS 12 Glenn McCrory 13.8 (England), Moscow, Russia (IBF). Scorecard: 118-109, 118-109, 117-110. Although he bravely fought back well to go the distance, after being twice floored in the sixth, McCrory had no effective answer to the powerful and speedy champion and while the Englishman answered his many critics, it was Cole's accurate hitting that won the day.

16 October, 1993   Anaclet Wamba 13.8 (France) W RTD 7 Akim Tafer 13.7½ (France), Levallois Perret, France (WBC). Larry O'Connell was one of the judges.

6 November, 1993   Orlin Norris 13.6¼ (USA) W RSC 6 Marcelo Figueroa 13.6¼ (Argentine), Paris, France (WBA). Bobby Czyz had forfeited title in September 1993 due to inactivity.

17 Novmber, 1993   Al Cole 13.8 (USA) W RSC 5 Vincent Boulware 13.8 (USA), Atlantic City, USA (IBF).

20 November, 1993   Nestor Giovannini 13.7 (Argentine) W PTS 12 Markus Bott 13.7 (Germany), Hamburg, Germany (WBO). Scorecard: 118-109, 117-110, 117-110.

4 March, 1994   Orlin Norris 13.5 (USA) W PTS 12 Arthur Williams 13.7 (USA), Las Vegas, USA (WBA). Scorecard: 112-114, 114-112, 118-110.

HEAVYWEIGHT (13st.8lbs +)

Titleholders as at 1 July, 1994

IBF – Michael Moorer (USA)

WBA – Michael Moorer (USA)

WBC – Lennox Lewis (England)

WBO – Herbie Hide (USA)

30 August, 1993   Tommy Morrison 16.2 (USA) W RTD 4 Tim Tomashek 14.9 (USA), Kansas City, USA (WBO). Following the fight, the WBO withdrew title status after overruling their supervisor and deciding that Tomashek was not of championship class.

1 October, 1993   Lennox Lewis 16.5 (England) W RSC 7 Frank Bruno 17.0 (England), Arms Park, Cardiff (WBC). Lethargic for six rounds and seemingly unable to work himself into the fight, Lewis suddenly exploded a big left-hook on Bruno in the seventh. As Bruno tottered along the ropes under an avalanche of leather the referee jumped between the two men and most of us thought that was that. Amazingly, however, Mickey Vann waved them on, but as more heavy rights crashed in on the defenceless Bruno, he quickly called a halt with 1.50 of the round still remaining. While Bruno covered himself in glory, Lewis left many questions unanswered. Adrian Morgan acted as one of the judges.

29 October, 1993   Tommy Morrison 16.3 (USA) L RSC 1 Michael Bentt 16.2 (USA), Tulsa, USA (WBO).

6 November, 1993   Riddick Bowe 17.8 (USA) L PTS 12 Evander Holyfield 15.7 (USA), Las Vegas, USA (WBA/IBF). Scorecard: 113-115, 114-114, 114-115.

19 March, 1994   Michael Bentt 16.6 (USA) L CO 7 Herbie Hide 15.6 (England), The New Den, London (WBO). Following their ungentlemanly street scuffle, which brought nothing but shame to boxing, Hide made Bentt appear almost pedestrian at times in a one-sided victory. Somehow, Bentt recovered from a peach of a right-uppercut that floored him in the third round, but he became more and more demoralised as Hide patiently boxed from distance. However, the seventh round saw the finish. After boxing well in the early stages of the round, Bentt was smashed to the canvas where Paul Thomas counted him out with just 0.10 of the round remaining.

22 April, 1994   Evander Holyfield 15.4 (USA) L PTS 12 Michael Moorer 15.4 (USA), Las Vegas, USA (WBA/IBF). Scorecard: 114-115, 112-116, 114-114.

6 May, 1994   Lennox Lewis 16.11 (England) W RSC 8 Phil Jackson 15.8 (USA), Atlantic City, USA (WBC). Having put Jackson on the floor with just 20 seconds on the clock and twice again in the fifth, Lewis was perfectly content to stick out the jab and bide his time, before finding the finishing blows, a right-uppercut followed by left and right-hooks. With no hope of Jackson rising, the referee rescued him at 1.35 of round eight. John Keane acted as one of the judges.

World Title Bouts (M. Flyweight to Lightweight), 1891-1993

I have attempted to set out by weight division, in two instalments (Light-Welterweight to Heavyweight will be in the 1996 edition), every championship bout contested under Queensberry Rules that has been reported as such since the beginning of gloves. There is also a synopsis for each weight class, giving its brief history prior to the first recognised gloved title fight. Obviously, to those who understand the problems involved in this "minefield" of an exercise, I could not have done this single-handedly.Without the massive aid of Professor Luckett Davis and Harold Alderman, who are properly thanked within the acknowledgements, Bob Soderman and Hy Rosenberg, on the other side of the Atlantic, and Bill Matthews and Derek O'Dell, here in Britain, this work could not have been pieced together.

Boxing grew up in Great Britain and quickly spread to the USA, but it was not until the champions of these two countries came together in the latter part of the last century that it developed on an international scale. Organisations then came into existence solely for the purpose of controlling professional boxing. The National Sporting Club of Great Britain was formed in 1891, later to be amalgamated into the British Boxing Board of Control in 1929, and by the early part of the century the sport had also begun to boom among the French, who, in 1911, were instrumental in setting up the International Boxing Union to look after the interests of boxing in Europe. Following the Second World War, the body became known as the European Boxing Union.

Prior to the 1920s, and the advent of boxing commissions in America, there was much confusion in a sport that has always cried out for firm controls. While the Americans recognised the champion as a man who could only lose his title in the ring, championships travelled badly, with European fighters being frozen out unless they made their base in the USA. Exacerbating the problems were over 20 years of boxing in many States where the law demanded contests should only go ahead as exhibitions and that decisions could not be rendered. Thus a champion could only lose his title if he was knocked out or rescued by the referee. Although Georges Carpentier, George Chip, Al McCoy, Mike O'Dowd, Jack Britton and Benny Leonard, won their titles in this fashion, it was a ludicrous situation and one that allowed Johnny Kilbane to keep his featherweight crown from 1912 to 1923, without making more than one "proper" defence for close on ten years. Also, newspaper decisions given the day after the fight almost put the press in control of boxing, especially when they got behind a certain fighter to a man. This led to a lot of top class Americans moving their base first to Europe and then, with the advent of World War One, to Australia. However, with the coming of the Walker Law in 1920, the New York State Athletic Commission was legally constituted to govern the sport and with it came the abolition of no-decision fights in New York. At the same time, several of the independent States of America became affiliated to form the National Boxing Association and by the end of the 1920s, no-decision fights were almost a thing of the past.

While America enjoyed the fruits of their "golden age" of boxing, things began to change for the better elsewhere. Boxing took off in many countries such as Africa, South America and the Far-East, notably in Japan and Thailand, who produced world flyweight champions in Yoshio Shirai (1952) and Pone Kingpetch (1960), respectively. By 1962, the NBA had been re-named the World Boxing Association, having trebled its original State membership and, in 1963, in an effort to increase its balance of power, Britain supported the setting up of the World Boxing Council, which brought together the NYSAC and its satellite States with the BBBoC, the Commonwealth and the EBU. More recently, the International Boxing Federation, an offshoot of the WBA, and the World Boxing Organisation, have also sprung to prominence on the world boxing stage.

Unfortunately, many records from a bygone age suffered greatly from inaccuracies and it is because of that I have attempted to record all "reported" world title fights in order to try, once and for all, to analyse the true state of world championship boxing as it travelled down the years. One thing you are sure to notice is that many of the so-called world title contests were fought above the recognised weight limit of the day, even allowing for the fact that a champion could carry his weight within reason. Another point worth noting is the number of contests given championship status by promoters for no other reason than putting money on the gate. When reading the title related captions, you have to bear in mind, as already mentioned, there were no governing bodies in America before 1920, even though the NYSAC was partially set-up in 1911, and only champions who were generally recognised throughout the boxing world (not claimants) are shown in **bold** from 1891 to 1993. Certain no-decision fights are listed because they were either billed as being for the championship or involved a champion risking his title and I have prefixed the result with ND regardless of whether it went the full course or not. Many historians do not recognise no-decision affairs even if they were billed as title fights because they were not fought under full championship conditions, but that would mean ignoring Dempsey v Carpentier, for example. Also, prior to the bantam (1915), feather (1920) and light (1913) weights being standardised throughout the world of boxing, individual weights are recorded where known. And where weights are shown in brackets following the result, it denotes the contracted poundage within the Articles of Agreement and that both men were inside.

The Ring Record Book (1942-1987) and the Boxing News Annual (1944-1985), who both capitalised on existing information in earlier record books such as Everlast (1922-1937), Annuaire du Ring (1909-1939), Andrews (1903-1937) and the Police Gazette Annual (1896-1918) and countless newspapers and magazines, have been fully researched, along with much other material, to ascertain reported world title fights for the period in question. One of the great problems of researching the Ring Record Book through the Ring Magazine, was editor Nat Fleischer's insistence over many years that there should be just one champion.

Of course, it would be nice to go back to the days of one champion per weight division, although there were less than you might think, but, to be fair, many of the top men would be frozen out. Also, would you like to go back to the 1920s when just eight, including two no-decision, heavyweight title fights were held! The best solution is to accept what we have today as progress, but somehow find a way to force the IBF, WBA, WBC and WBO champions to box-off at least every two years in order to find a universally accepted champion in each division.

Country Code (Codes relate to place of domicile, not necessarily birthplace)
A-Australia; ARG-Argentina; ARM-Armenia; AU-Austria; BAH-Bahamas; BAR-Barbados; BEL-Belgium; BR-Brazil; C-Canada; CH-Chile; COL-Colombia; CR-Costa Rica; CUB-Cuba; CZ-Czechoslovakia; DEN-Denmark; DOM-Dominican Republic; EC-Ecuador; FIN-Finland; FR-France; GB-Great Britain; GER-Germany; GH-Ghana; GRE-Greece; GU-Guyana; HA-Hawaii; HOL-Holland; I-Ireland; IC-Ivory Coast; INDON-Indonesia; ITA-Italy; J-Jamaica; JAP-Japan; K-Kenya; MEX-Mexico; MOR-Morocco; N-Nigeria; NIC-Nicaragua; NOR-Norway; NZ-New Zealand; PAN-Panama; PAR-Paraguay; PE-Peru; PH-Philippines; PNG-Papua New Guinea; PR-Puerto Rico; SA-South Africa; SK-South Korea; SP-Spain; SWE-Sweden; SWI-Switzerland; TH-Thailand; TO-Togo; TR-Trinidad; TUN-Tunisia; U-Uganda; UR-Uruguay; USA-United States of America; VEN-Venezuela; YUG-Yugoslavia; ZA-Zambia.

Mini-Flyweight (105 lbs)

The minimum flyweight (otherwise known as the straw-weight) division, was instigated by the International Boxing Federation in 1987 with a view to giving better opportunities to their members in the Far-East. It soon caught on and, within six months, the World Boxing Council, followed by the World Boxing Association, had organised title fights of their own.

14.06.87 Kyung-Yung Lee (SK) W CO 2 Masaharu Kawakami (JAP), Bujok - IBF. *Kyung-Yung Lee relinquished IBF version of title in December 1987 in order to challenge for the WBC crown.*

18.10.87 Hiroki Ioka (JAP) W PTS 12 Mai Thornburifarm (TH), Oaska - WBC

10.01.88 Luis Gamez (VEN) W PTS 12 Bong-Jun Kim (SK), Pusan - WBA

31.01.88 Hiroki Ioka (JAP) W RSC 12 Kyung-Yung Lee (SK), Osaka - WBC

24.03.88 Samuth Sithnaruepol (TH) W RSC 11 Domingo Lucas (PH), Bangkok - IBF

24.04.88 Silvio Gamez (VEN) W RSC 3 Kenji Yokozawa (JAP), Tokyo - WBA. *Luis Gamez relinquished WBA version of title in February 1989 to campaign at light-flyweight.*

05.06.88 Hiroki Ioka (JAP) DREW 12 Napa Kiatwanchai (TH), Osaka - WBC

29.08.88 Samuth Sithnaruepol (TH) W PTS 15 In-Kyu Hwang (SK), Bangkok - IBF

13.11.88 Napa Kiatwanchai (TH) W PTS 12 Hiroki Ioka (JAP), Osaka - WBC

11.02.89 Napa Kiatwanchai (TH) W PTS 12 John Arief (INDON), Bangkok - WBC

23.03.89 Samuth Sithnaruepol (TH) DREW 12 Nico Thomas (INDON), Jakarta - IBF

16.04.89 Bong-Jun Kim (SK) W RSC 7 Agustin Garcia (COL), Seoul - WBA

10.06.89 Napa Kiatwanchai (TH) W RSC 11 Hiroki Ioka (JAP), Osaka - WBC

17.06.89 Nico Thomas (INDON) W PTS 12 Samuth Sithnaruepol (TH), Jakarta - IBF

06.08.89 Bong-Jun Kim (SK) W PTS 12 Sam-Jung Lee (SK), Seoul - WBA

31.08.89 Rafael Torres (DOM) W PTS 12 Yamil Caraballo (COL), Santa Domingo - WBO

21.09.89 Eric Chavez (PH) W CO 5 Nico Thomas (INDON), Jakarta - IBF

22.10.89 Bong-Jun Kim (SK) W RSC 9 John Arief (INDON), Pohang - WBA

12.11.89 Jum-Hwan Choi (SK) W RSC 12 Napa Kiatwanchai (TH), Seoul - WBC

07.02.90 Hideyuki Ohashi (JAP) W CO 9 Jum-Hwan Choi (SK), Tokyo - WBC

10.02.90 Bong-Jun Kim (SK) W RSC 3 Petchai Chuwatana (TH), Seoul - WBA

22.02.90 Fahlan Lukmingkwan (TH) W RSC 7 Eric Chavez (PH), Bangkok - IBF

13.05.90 Bong-Jun Kim (SK) W TD 5 Silverio Barcenas (PAN), Seoul - WBA. *Ahead on two of the judges' scorecards at the time, Kim retained his title by decision after he was accidentally cut and pulled out of the fight by the doctor.*

08.06.90 Hideyuki Ohashi (JAP) W PTS 12 Napa Kiatwanchai (TH), Tokyo - WBC

14.06.90 Fahlan Lukmingkwan (TH) W PTS 12 Joe Constantino (PH), Bangkok - IBF

31.07.90 Rafael Torres (DOM) W PTS 12 Husni Ray (INDON), Jakarta - WBO. *Rafael Torres forfeited WBO version of title in May 1992 due to inactivity.*

15.08.90 Fahlan Lukmingkwan (TH) W PTS 12 Eric Chavez (PH), Bangkok - IBF

25.10.90 Ricardo Lopez (MEX) W RSC 5 Hideyuki Ohashi (JAP), Tokyo - WBC

03.11.90 Bong-Jun Kim (SK) W PTS 12 Silverio Barcenas (PAN), Seoul - WBA

20.12.90 Fahlan Lukmingkwan (TH) DREW 12 Domingo Lucas (PH), Bangkok - IBF

02.02.91 Hi-Yon Choi (SK) W PTS 12 Bong-Jun Kim (SK), Pujan - WBA

19.05.91 Ricardo Lopez (MEX) W RSC 8 Kimio Hirano (JAP), Shizoka - WBC

15.06.91 Hi-Yon Choi (SK) W PTS 12 Sugar Ray Mike (PH), Seoul - WBA

02.07.91 Fahlan Lukmingkwan (TH) W PTS 12 Abdy Pohan (INDON), Bangkok - IBF

21.10.91 Fahlan Lukmingkwan (TH) W PTS 12 Andy Tabanas (PH), Bangkok - IBF

26.10.91 Hi-Yon Choi (SK) W PTS 12 Bong-Jun Kim (SK), Seoul - WBA

22.12.91 Ricardo Lopez (MEX) W PTS 12 Kyung-Yun Lee (SK), Inchon - WBC

22.02.92 Hi-Yon Choi (SK) W RSC 10 Ryuichi Hosono (JAP), Seoul - WBA

23.02.92 Fahlan Lukmingkwan (TH) W CO 2 Felix Naranjo (COL), Bangkok - IBF

16.03.92 Ricardo Lopez (MEX) W PTS 12 Domingo Lucas (PH), Mexico City - WBC

13.06.92 Hi-Yon Choi (SK) W CO 3 Rommel Lawas (PH), Inchon - WBA

14.06.92 Fahlan Lukmingkwan (TH) W RSC 8 Said Iskander (INDON), Bangkok - IBF

22.08.92 Ricardo Lopez (MEX) W CO 5 Singprasert Kitikasem (TH), Ciudad - WBC

06.09.92 Manny Melchor (PH) W PTS 12 Fahlan Lukmingkwan (TH), Bangkok - IBF

11.10.92 Ricardo Lopez (MEX) W CO 2 Rocky Lim (JAP), Tokyo - WBC

14.10.92 Hideyuki Ohashi (JAP) W PTS 12 Hi-Yon Choi (SK), Tokyo - WBA

10.12.92 Ratanapol Sowvoraphin (TH) W PTS 12 Manny Melchor (PH), Bangkok - IBF

31.01.93 Ricardo Lopez (MEX) W RSC 9 Kwang-Soo Oh (SK), Seoul - WBC

10.02.93 Chana Porpaoin (TH) W PTS 12 Hideyuki Ohashi (JAP), Tokyo - WBA

14.03.93 Ratanapol Sowvoraphin (TH) W RSC 7 Nico Thomas (INDON), Nakon - IBF

09.05.93 Chana Porpaoin (TH) W PTS 12 Carlos Murillo (PAN), Bangkok - WBA

15.05.93 Paul Weir (GB) W RSC 7 Fernando Martinez (MEX), Scottish Exhibition Centre, Glasgow - WBO

27.06.93 Ratanapol Sowvoraphin (TH) W RTD 7 Ala Villamor (PH), Bangkok - IBF

Light-Flyweight (108 lbs)

Known also as the junior-flyweight division, it was introduced in 1975 by the World Boxing Council, who finally recognised that some fighters, especially in the Far-East and Mexico, were just too light to take on fully-fledged flyweights. Within a matter of months, the World Boxing Association had also accepted the need for the weight class and followed suite.

04.04.75 Franco Udella (ITA) W DIS 12 Valentin Martinez (MEX), Milan - WBC. *Franco Udella forfeited WBC recognition in August 1975 for failing to defend against Rafael Lovera.*

23.08.75 Jaime Rios (PAN) W PTS 15 Rigoberto Marcano (VEN), Panama City - WBA

13.09.75 Luis Estaba (VEN) W CO 4 Rafael Lovera (PAR), Caracas - WBC. *It was later learnt that Lovera had never boxed as a professional and that his record had been "invented".*

17.12.75 Luis Estaba (VEN) W RSC 10 Takenobu Shimabakuro (JAP), Okinawa - WBC

03.01.76 Jaime Rios (PAN) W PTS 15 Kazunori Tenryu (JAP), Kagoshima - WBA

14.02.76 Luis Estaba (VEN) W PTS 15 Leo Palacios (MEX), Caracas - WBC

02.05.76 Luis Estaba (VEN) W PTS 15 Juan Alvarez (MEX), Caracas - WBC

02.07.76 Juan Guzman (DOM) W PTS 15 Jaime Rios (PAN), St Domingo - WBA

17.07.76 Luis Estaba (VEN) W CO 3 Franco Udella (ITA), Maracay - WBC

26.09.76 Luis Estaba (VEN) W RTD 10 Rodolfo Rodriguez (ARG), Caracas - WBC

10.10.76 Yoko Gushiken (JAP) W CO 7 Juan Guzman (DOM), Kofu - WBA

21.11.76 Luis Estaba (VEN) W RSC 10 Valentin Martinez (MEX), Caracas - WBC

30.01.77 Yoko Gushiken (JAP) W PTS 15 Jaime Rios (PAN), Tokyo - WBA

15.05.77 Luis Estaba (VEN) W PTS 15 Rafael Pedroza (PAN), Caracas - WBC

22.05.77 Yoko Gushiken (JAP) W PTS 15 Rigoberto Marcano (VEN), Sapporo - WBA

17.07.77 Luis Estaba (VEN) W PTS 15 Ricardo Estupinan (COL), Cruz - WBC

21.08.77 Luis Estaba (VEN) W RSC 11 Juan Alvarez (MEX), Cruz - WBC

18.09.77 Luis Estaba (VEN) W CO 15 Orlando Hernandez (CR), Caracas - WBC

09.10.77 Yoko Gushiken (JAP) W RSC 4 Montsayarm Mahachai (TH), Oita - WBA

30.10.77 Luis Estaba (VEN) W PTS 15 Sor Vorasingh (TH), Caracas - WBC

29.01.78 Yoko Gushiken (JAP) W RSC 14 Aniceto Vargas (PH), Nagoya - WBA

19.02.78 Freddie Castillo (MEX) W RSC 14 Luis Estaba (VEN), Caracas - WBC

06.05.78 Sor Vorasingh (TH) W PTS 15 Freddie Castillo (MEX), Bangkok - WBC

07.05.78 Yoko Gushiken (JAP) W RSC 13 Jaime Rios (PAN), Hiroshima - WBA

29.07.78 Sor Vorasingh (TH) W RTD 5 Luis Estaba (VEN), Caracas - WBC

30.09.78 Sung-Jun Kim (SK) W CO 3 Sor Vorasingh (TH), Seoul - WBC

15.10.78 Yoko Gushiken (JAP) W CO 4 Sang-Il Chung (SK), Tokyo - WBA

07.01.79 Yoko Gushiken (JAP) W CO 7 Rigoberto Marcano (VEN), Kawasaki - WBA

31.03.79 Sung-Jun Kim (SK) DREW 15 Hector Melendez (DOM), Seoul - WBC

08.04.79 Yoko Gushiken (JAP) W RSC 7 Alfonso Lopez (PAN), Tokyo - WBA

28.07.79 Sung-Jun Kim (SK) W PTS 15 Stony Carupo (PH), Seoul - WBC

29.07.79 Yoko Gushiken (JAP) W PTS 15 Rafael Pedroza (PAN), Kitakyushi - WBA

21.10.79 Sung-Jun Kim (SK) W PTS 15 Hector Melendez (DOM), Seoul - WBC

28.10.79 Yoko Gushiken (JAP) W RSC 7 Tito Abella (PH), Tokyo - WBA

03.01.80 Shigeo Nakajima (JAP) W PTS 15 Sung-Jun Kim (SK), Tokyo - WBC

27.01.80 Yoko Gushiken (JAP) W PTS 15 Yong-Hyun Kim (SK), Osaka - WBA

24.03.80 Hilario Zapata (PAN) W PTS 15 Shigeo Nakajima (JAP), Tokyo - WBC

01.06.80 Yoko Gushiken (JAP) W RSC 8 Martin Vargas (CH), Kochi City - WBA

07.06.80 Hilario Zapata (PAN) W PTS 15 Chi-Bok Kim (SK), Seoul - WBC

04.08.80 Hilario Zapata (PAN) W PTS 15 Hector Melendez (DOM), Caracas - WBC

17.09.80 Hilario Zapata (PAN) W RSC 11 Shigeo Nakajima (JAP), Gifu - WBC

12.10.80 Yoko Gushiken (JAP) W PTS 15 Pedro Flores (MEX), Kanazawa - WBA

01.12.80 Hilario Zapata (PAN) W PTS 15 Reynaldo Becerra (VEN), Caracas - WBC

08.02.81 Hilario Zapata (PAN) W RSC 13 Joey Olivo (USA), Panama City - WBC

08.03.81 Pedro Flores (MEX) W RTD 12 Yoko Gushiken (JAP), Gushikawa - WBA

24.04.81 Hilario Zapata (PAN) W PTS 15 Rudy Crawford (USA), San Francisco - WBC

19.07.81 Hwan-Jin Kim (SK) W RSC 13 Pedro Flores (MEX), Taegu - WBA

15.08.81 Hilario Zapata (PAN) W PTS 15 German Torres (MEX), Panama City - WBC

11.10.81 Hwan-Jin Kim (SK) W PTS 15 Alfonso Lopez (PAN), Daejon - WBA

06.11.81 Hilario Zapata (PAN) W RSC 10 Sor Vorasingh (TH), Korat - WBC

16.12.81 Katsuo Tokashiki (JAP) W PTS 15 Hwan-Jin Kim (SK), Sendai - WBA

06.02.82 Amado Ursua (MEX) W CO 2 Hilario Zapata (PAN), Panama City - WBC

04.04.82 Katsuo Tokashiki (JAP) W PTS 15 Lupe Madera (MEX), Sendai - WBA

13.04.82 Tadashi Tomori (JAP) W PTS 15 Amado Ursua (MEX), Tokyo - WBC

07.07.82 Katsuo Tokashiki (JAP) W CO 8 Masahara Inami (JAP), Tokyo - WBA

20.07.82 Hilario Zapata (PAN) W PTS 15 Tadashi Tomori (JAP), Kanazawa - WBC

18.09.82 Hilario Zapata (PAN) W PTS 15 Jung-Koo Chang (SK), Chonju - WBC

10.10.82 Katsuo Tokashiki (JAP) W PTS 15 Sung-Nam Kim (SK), Tokyo - WBA

30.11.82 Hilario Zapata (PAN) W RSC 8 Tadashi Tomori (JAP), Tokyo - WBC

09.01.83 Katsuo Tokashiki (JAP) W PTS 15 Hwan-Jin Kim (SK), Kyoto - WBA

26.03.83 Jung-Koo Chang (SK) W RSC 3 Hilario Zapata (PAN), Daejon - WBC

10.04.83 Katsuo Tokashiki (JAP) DREW 15 Lupe Madera (MEX), Tokyo - WBA

11.06.83 Jung-Koo Chang (SK) W RSC 2 Masaharu Iha (JAP), Taegu - WBC

10.07.83 Lupe Madera (MEX) W TD 4 Katsuo Tokashiki (JAP), Tokyo - WBA. *Madera, who received a severe cut following a clash of heads, remained champion under an WBA ruling stipulating that if either boxer was accidentally injured after the completion of the third round and could not carry on, the decision would be awarded to the man ahead at the time.*

10.09.83 Jung-Koo Chang (SK) W PTS 12 German Torres (MEX), Daejon - WBC

23.10.83 Lupe Madera (MEX) W PTS 12 Katsuo Tokashiki (JAP), Sapporo - WBA

10.12.83 Dodie Penalosa (PH) W RSC 11 Satoshi Shingaki (JAP), Osaka - IBF

31.03.84 Jung-Koo Chang (SK) W PTS 12 Sot Chitalada (TH), Pusan - WBC

13.05.84 Dodie Penalosa (PH) W RSC 9 Jae-Hong Kim (SK), Seoul - IBF

19.05.84 Francisco Quiroz (DOM) W CO 9 Lupe Madera (MEX), Maracaibo - WBA

18.08.84 Jung-Koo Chang (SK) W RSC 9 Katsuo Tokashiki (JAP), Pohang - WBC

18.08.84 Francisco Quiroz (DOM) W CO 2 Victor Sierra (PAN), Panama City - WBA

16.11.84 Dodie Penalosa (PH) W PTS 15 Jum-Hwan Choi (SK), Manila - IBF

15.12.84 Jung-Koo Chang (SK) W PTS 12 Tadashi Kuramochi (JAP), Pusan - WBC

29.03.85 Joey Olivo (USA) W PTS 15 Francisco Quiroz (DOM), Miami - WBA

27.04.85 Jung-Koo Chang (SK) W PTS 12 German Torres (MEX), Ulsan - WBC

28.07.85 Joey Olivo (USA) W PTS 15 Moon-Jin Choi (SK), Seoul - WBA

03.08.85 Jung-Koo Chang (SK) W PTS 15 Francisco Montiel (MEX), Seoul - WBC

12.10.85 Dodie Penalosa (PH) W CO 3 Yani Hagler (INDON), Jakarta - IBF. *Dodie Penalosa forfeited IBF recognition immediately after he had challenged Hilario Zapata for the WBA flyweight title on 5 July 1986.*

10.11.85 Jung-Koo Chang (SK) W PTS 12 Jorge Cano (MEX), Daejon - WBC

08.12.85 Myung-Woo Yuh (SK) W PTS 15 Joey Olivo (USA), Seoul - WBA

09.03.86 Myung-Woo Yuh (SK) W PTS 15 Jose de Jesus (PR), Suwon - WBA

13.04.86 Jung-Koo Chang (SK) W PTS 12 German Torres (MEX), Kwangju - WBC

14.06.86 Myung-Woo Yuh (SK) W RSC 12 Tomohiro Kiyuna (JAP), Inchon - WBA

13.09.86 Jung-Koo Chang (SK) W PTS 12 Francisco Montiel (MEX), Seoul - WBC

30.11.86 Myung-Woo Yuh (SK) W PTS 15 Mario de Marco (ARG), Seoul - WBA

07.12.86 Jum-Hwan Choi (SK) W PTS 15 Cho-Woon Park (SK), Pusan - IBF

14.12.86 Jung-Koo Chang (SK) W RSC 5 Hideyuki Ohashi (JAP), Inchon - WBC

01.03.87 Myung-Woo Yuh (SK) W RSC 1 Eduardo Tunon (PAN), Seoul - WBA

29.03.87 Jum-Hwan Choi (SK) W PTS 15 Tacy Macalos (PH), Seoul - IBF

19.04.87 Jung-Koo Chang (SK) W RSC 6 Efren Pinto (MEX), Seoul - WBC

07.06.87 Myung-Woo Yuh (SK) W RSC 15 Benedicto Murillo (PAN), Pusan - WBA

28.06.87 Jung-Koo Chang (SK) W RSC 10 Agustin Garcia (COL), Seoul - WBC

05.07.87 Jum-Hwan Choi (SK) W RSC 4 Toshihiko Matsuta (JAP), Seoul - IBF

09.08.87 Jum-Hwan Choi (SK) W RSC 3 Azadin Anhar (INDON), Jakarta - IBF

20.09.87 Myung-Woo Yuh (SK) W CO 8 Rodolfo Blanco (COL), Inchon - WBA

13.12.87 Jung-Koo Chang (SK) W PTS 12 Isidro Perez (MEX), Seoul - WBC

07.02.88 Myung-Woo Yuh (SK) W PTS 12 Wilibaldo Salazar (MEX), Seoul - WBA

12.06.88 Myung-Woo Yuh (SK) W PTS 12 Jose de Jesus (PR), Seoul - WBA

27.06.88 Jung-Koo Chang (SK) W RSC 8 Hideyuki Ohashi (JAP), Tokyo - WBC. *Jung-Koo Chang relinquished WBC version of title in October 1988 due to illness.*

28.08.88 Myung-Woo Yuh (SK) W CO 6 Putt Ohyuthanakorn (TH), Pusan - WBA

05.11.88 Tacy Macalos (PH) W PTS 12 Jum-Hwan Choi (SK), Manila - IBF

06.11.88 Myung-Woo Yuh (SK) W CO 7 Bahar Udin (INDON), Seoul - WBA

11.12.88 German Torres (MEX) W PTS 12 Soon-Jung Kang (SK), Seoul - WBC

12.02.89 Myung-Woo Yuh (SK) W RSC 10 Katsumi Komiyama (JAP), Chungju - WBA

19.03.89 Yul-Woo Lee (SK) W CO 9 German Torres (MEX), Taejon - WBC

02.05.89 Muangchai Kitikasem (TH) W PTS 12 Tacy Macalos (PH), Bangkok - IBF

19.05.89 Jose de Jesus (PR) W RSC 9 Fernando Martinez (MEX), San Juan - WBO

11.06.89 Myung-Woo Yuh (SK) W PTS 12 Mario de Marco (ARG), Seoul - WBA

25.06.89 Humberto Gonzalez (MEX) W PTS 12 Yul-Woo Lee (SK), Seoul - WBC

24.09.89 Myung-Woo Yuh (SK) W CO 11 Kenbun Taiho (JAP), Suanbo - WBA

06.10.89 Muangchai Kitikasem (TH) W RSC 7 Tacy Macalos (PH), Bangkok - IBF

21.10.89 Jose de Jesus (PR) W PTS 12 Isidro Perez (MEX), San Juan - WBO

09.12.89 Humberto Gonzalez (MEX) W PTS 12 Jung-Koo Chang (SK), Seoul - WBC

14.01.90 Myung-Woo Yuh (SK) W RSC 7 Hitashi Takashima (JAP), Seoul - WBA

19.01.90 Muangchai Kitikasem (TH) W RSC 3 Chung-Jae Lee (SK), Bangkok - IBF

24.03.90 Humberto Gonzalez (MEX) W CO 3 Francisco Tejedor (COL), Mexico City - WBC

10.04.90 Muangchai Kitikasem (TH) W PTS 12 Abdy Pohan (INDON), Bangkok - IBF

29.04.90 Myung-Woo Yuh (SK) W PTS 12 Silvio Gamez (VEN), Seoul - WBA

06.05.90 Jose de Jesus (PR) W CO 5 Alli Galvez (CH), Talcahuano - WBO

04.06.90 Humberto Gonzalez (MEX) W RSC 3 Luis Monzote (CUB), Los Angeles - WBC

24.07.90 Humberto Gonzalez (MEX) W RSC 5 Jung-Keun Lim (SK), Los Angeles - WBC

29.07.90 Michael Carbajal (USA) W RSC 7 Muangchai Kitikasem (TH), Phoenix - IBF

26.08.90 Humberto Gonzalez (MEX) W CO 8 Jorge Rivera (MEX), Cancun - WBC

10.11.90 Jose de Jesus (PR) W RSC 7 Abdy Pohan (INDON), Medan - WBO. *Jose de Jesus forfeited WBO version of title in May 1992 due to inactivity.*

10.11.90 Myung-Woo Yuh (SK) W PTS 12 Silvio Gamez (VEN), Seoul - WBA

08.12.90 Michael Carbajal (USA) W CO 4 Leon Salazar (PAN), Scottsdale - IBF

19.12.90 Rolando Pascua (PH) W CO 6 Humberto Gonzalez (MEX), Los Angeles - WBC

17.02.91 Michael Carbajal (USA) W CO 2 Macario Santos (MEX), Las Vegas - IBF

17.03.91 Michael Carbajal (USA) W PTS 12 Javier Varquez (MEX), Las Vegas - IBF

25.03.91 Melchor Cob Castro (MEX) W RTD 10 Rolando Pascua (PH), Los Angeles - WBC

28.04.91 Myung-Woo Yuh (SK) W RSC 10 Kajkong Danphoothai (TH), Masan - WBA

10.05.91 Michael Carbajal (USA) W PTS 12 Hector Patri (ARG), Davenport - IBF

03.06.91 Humberto Gonzalez (MEX) W PTS 12 Melchor Cob Castro (MEX), Las Vegas - WBC

17.12.91 Hiroki Ioka (JAP) W PTS 12 Myung-Woo Yuh (SK), Osaka - WBA

27.01.92 Humberto Gonzalez (MEX) W PTS 12 Domingo Sosa (DOM), Los Angeles - WBC

15.02.92 Michael Carbajal (USA) W PTS 12 Marcos Pancheco (MEX), Phoenix - IBF

31.03.92 Hiroki Ioka (JAP) W PTS 12 Noel Tunacao (PH), Osaka - WBA

07.06.92 Humberto Gonzalez (MEX) W RSC 12 Kwang-Sun Kim (SK), Seoul - WBC

15.06.92 Hiroki Ioka (JAP) W PTS 12 Bong-Jun Kim (SK), Osaka - WBA

31.07.92 Josue Camacho (PR) W CO 6 Eduardo Vallejo (MEX), San Juan - WBO

14.09.92 Humberto Gonzalez (MEX) W RSC 2 Napa Kiatwanchai (TH), Los Angeles - WBC

18.11.92 Myung-Woo Yuh (SK) W PTS 12 Hiroki Ioka (JAP), Osaka - WBA

07.12.92 Humberto Gonzalez (MEX) W PTS 12 Melchor Cob Castro (MEX), Los Angeles - WBC

12.12.92 Michael Carbajal (USA) W RSC 8 Robinson Cuestas (PAN), Phoenix - IBF

13.03.93 Michael Carbajal (USA) W CO 7 Humberto Gonzalez (MEX), Las Vegas - IBF/WBC

Flyweight (112 lbs)

Established by the National Sporting Club in Britain in 1910, it was introduced in order to protect men who were just too small to be fighting at the ever increasing bantamweight limit. Prior to this time, everything below feather fell into the bantam, and later, paperweight categories. Finally, on 4 December 1911, the NSC got round to organising a championship fight at the weight between Sid Smith, who was already recognised as the British champion in some quarters, and Joe Wilson. Billed as a British title fight, Smith won on points over 20 rounds at the club and was recognised as world champion on this side of the Atlantic. Earlier, in America, Johnny Coulon, the USA's 112 lb bantamweight champion, had claimed the new title, but, by March 1910, he had moved up to 116 lbs. Smith next outpointed fellow Englishmen, Curley Walker (19 September 1912) and Sam Kellar (24 February 1913), over 20 rounds at The Ring in Blackfriars, London, before going forward to challenge the Frenchman, Eugene Criqui, for the International Boxing Union version of the title.

11.04.13 Sid Smith (GB) W PTS 20 Eugene Criqui (FR), Paris - GB/IBU

02.06.13 Bill Ladbury (GB) W RSC 11 Sid Smith (GB), The Ring, London - GB/IBU

26.01.14 Percy Jones (GB) W PTS 20 Bill Ladbury (GB), NSC, London - GB/IBU

26.03.14 Percy Jones (GB) W PTS 20 Eugene Criqui (FR), The Stadium, Liverpool - GB/IBU

15.05.14 Joe Symonds (GB) W RSC 18 Percy Jones (GB), Old Cosmo Rink, Plymouth. *Jones should have forfeited his GB/IBU version of the title on the scales when weighing-in two and a half pounds overweight, but the NSC refused to recognise the winner and matched Jones against Jimmy Berry at the Club. That fight fizzled out after Jones successfully weighed-in, only for Berry not to turn up. Berry later stated that he had informed officials earlier that he was unable to make 112 lbs.*

19.10.14 Tancy Lee (GB) W RSC 14 Percy Jones (GB), NSC, London. *Although the fight went ahead at catchweights, Jones had already forfeited his GB/IBU version of the title when coming in overweight.*

16.11.14 Jimmy Wilde (GB) W PTS 15 Joe Symonds (GB), The Ring, London. *With the NSC still not recognising Symonds' claim, he was matched by the promoters at the Blackfriars' Ring against the sensational Jimmy Wilde for their version of the title.*

03.12.14 Jimmy Wilde (GB) W CO 9 Sid Smith (GB), The Stadium, Liverpool. *Wilde successfully defended his claim to the title in this fight, before going to the NSC to meet Tancy Lee in a decider where the winner would be generally recognised on this side of the Atlantic as champion.*

25.01.15 Tancy Lee (GB) W RSC 17 Jimmy Wilde (GB), NSC, London - GB/IBU

18.10.15 Joe Symonds (GB) W RSC 16 Tancy Lee (GB), NSC, London - GB/IBU

14.02.16 Jimmy Wilde (GB) W RSC 12 Joe Symonds (GB), NSC, London - GB/IBU

24.04.16 Jimmy Wilde (GB) W RTD 11 Johnny Rosner (USA), The Stadium, Liverpool - GB/IBU

26.06.16 Jimmy Wilde (GB) W RSC 11 Tancy Lee (GB), NSC, London - GB/IBU

31.07.16 Jimmy Wilde (GB) W CO 10 Johnny Hughes (GB), Kensal Rise Athletic Ground, London - GB/IBU

18.12.16 **Jimmy Wilde** (GB) W CO 11 Young Zulu Kid (USA), Holborn Stadium, London

12.03.17 **Jimmy Wilde** (GB) W RTD 4 George Clark (GB), NSC, London

29.04.18 **Jimmy Wilde** (GB) W RSC 2 Dick Heasman (GB), NSC, London. *Not billed as a world title bout, but with Wilde defending his British and European crowns and both men inside the weight limit, the world championship was also automatically at stake. Come 1919, with Jimmy Wilde fighting mainly in the bantamweight division, there was great interest in America to find a worthy challenger for this title. Earlier, Johnny Rosner had won the vacant American title when knocking out the Young Zulu Kid in seven rounds, on 28 September 1917 in Brooklyn, but Wilde had already defeated both men. However, things stirred when Young Montreal outpointed Rosner over 12 rounds in Providence on 10 April 1919 to become American champion, but shortly afterwards he relinquished the belt to campaign as a bantam. To find a successor, two semi-final legs were held in New York City on 11 February 1921 and Johnny Buff outpointed Frankie Mason over 15 rounds, while Abe Goldstein knocked out Patsy Wallace inside seven rounds. The final of the competition saw Buff kayo Goldstein in the second round on 31 March 1921, but he himself was knocked out in the 11th by Pancho Villa on 14 September 1922. Villa twice successfully defended the title on points over 15 rounds, beating Goldstein (17 November 1922) and Terry Martin (29 December 1922), before being outscored over the same distance by Frankie Genaro on 1 March 1923. With all the aforementioned bouts having taken place in New York, the promoter, Tex Rickard, lulled Jimmy Wilde out of semi-retirement to defend his title in the "big apple". To the surprise of many, it was not Genaro who was selected to face the Welshman, but Villa, on the grounds that the little Filipino was bigger box-office.*

18.06.23 **Pancho Villa** (PH) W CO 7 Jimmy Wilde (GB), New York City

13.10.23 **Pancho Villa** (PH) W PTS 15 Benny Schwartz (USA), Baltimore

08.02.24 **Pancho Villa** (PH) W PTS 15 Georgie Rivers (USA), New York City. *While billed as a title bout, the championship was not at stake after Rivers weighed in at 116½ lbs.*

30.05.24 **Pancho Villa** (PH) W PTS 15 Frankie Ash (GB), Brooklyn

01.05.25 **Pancho Villa** (PH) W PTS 15 Clever Sencio (PH), Manila.

Pancho Villa died from a poisoned tooth infection on 14 July 1925 and the title became vacant. As the reigning American champion, Frankie Genaro claimed the title on the strength of his 1923 victory over Villa, but before outright acceptance was forthcoming, he was asked to defend his American title against Fidel la Barba.

22.08.25 Fidel la Barba (USA) W PTS 10 Frankie Genaro (USA), Los Angeles - USA. *La Barba won the American title and claimed the American version of the world championship on the result.*

08.07.26 Fidel la Barba (USA) W PTS 10 Georgie Rivers (USA), Los Angeles - USA. *Billed as an American title fight, the American version of the world championship was automatically on the line. Following these two victories, la Barba was matched against the European champion, Elky Clark, in order to once again unify the title.*

21.01.27 **Fidel la Barba** (USA) W PTS 12 Elky Clark (GB), New York City. *Fidel la Barba relinquished the title on announcing his retirement in August 1927 and the NBA, then California and New York, and later, Britain and the IBU, all instigated their own tournaments to find a successor.*

22.10.27 Pinky Silverburg (USA) W DIS 7 Ruby Bradley (USA), Bridgeport - NBA. *Pinky Silverburg forfeited NBA version of the title in November 1927 for failing to meet Ernie Jarvis within the agreed period.*

28.10.27 Johnny McCoy (USA) W PTS 10 Tommy Hughes (USA), Los Angeles - CALIFORNIA

28.11.27 Frenchy Belanger (C) W PTS 10 Frankie Genaro (USA), Toronto. *Although shown in the Ring Record Book as being for the vacant NBA title, according to the Toronto Daily Mail (newspaper) report, it was merely billed as a final eliminator.*

16.12.27 Izzy Schwartz (USA) W PTS 15 Newsboy Brown (USA), New York City - NY

19.12.27 Frenchy Belanger (C) W PTS 12 Ernie Jarvis (GB), Toronto - NBA

03.01.28 Newsboy Brown (USA) W PTS 10 Johnny McCoy (USA), Los Angeles - CALIFORNIA

06.02.28 Frankie Genaro (USA) W PTS 10 Frenchy Belanger (C), Toronto - NBA

09.04.28 Izzy Schwartz (USA) W PTS 15 Routier Parra (CH), New York City - NY

20.07.28 Izzy Schwartz (USA) W DIS 4 Frisco Grande (PH), Rockaway - NY

03.08.28 Izzy Schwartz (USA) W CO 4 Little Jeff Smith (USA), Rockaway - NY

29.08.28 Johnny Hill (GB) W PTS 15 Newsboy Brown (USA), Clapton Stadium, London - GB/CALIFORNIA

15.10.28 Frankie Genaro (USA) W PTS 10 Frenchy Belanger (C), Toronto - NBA

03.12.28 Frenchy Belanger (C) W PTS 10 Willie Davies (USA), Toronto. *According to the Ring Record Book title listings this was a championship bout. However, the Toronto Daily Mail (newspaper) report, in recognising Frankie Genaro as the NBA champion, stated that this fight should only be considered an eliminator.*

07.02.29 Emile Pladner (FR) W CO 6 Johnny Hill (GB), Paris. *Occasionally, incorrectly quoted as being a world title fight, as in the last Ring Record Book, the match was made at 115 lbs in order to protect Hill's European championship belt. There is no doubt that following it, however, he was no longer recognised in California as champion.*

02.03.29 Emile Pladner (FR) W CO 1 Frankie Genaro (USA), Paris - NBA/IBU

12.03.29 Izzy Schwartz (USA) W PTS 12 Frenchy Belanger (C), Toronto - NY. *Contested on NBA territory, the NYSAC gave Schwartz permission to defend their title against Belanger as long as the winner promised to meet the number one contender, Emile Pladner, within a designated period.*

21.03.29 Johnny Hill (GB) W PTS 15 Ernie Jarvis (GB), Albert Hall, London. *Advertised as a British and European title fight, Hill's British version of the world championship was also at stake.*

18.04.29 Frankie Genaro (USA) W DIS 5 Emile Pladner (FR), Paris - NBA/IBU

29.06.29 Johnny Hill (GB) W DIS 10 Ernie Jarvis (GB), Cartyne Greyhound Track, Glasgow. *Billed for the British title, Hill's British version of the world championship was yet again automatically at stake. The title was left vacant on 27 September 1929, the day of Hill's untimely death.*

22.08.29 Willie la Morte (USA) W PTS 15 Izzy Schwartz (USA), Newark. *Although being a member of the NBA, who recognised Frankie Genaro as champion, the New Jersey Boxing Commission permitted the promoter to advertise the contest as a championship fight, while insisting that both men make the limit, before* *announcing immediately prior to the battle that no title was at stake. Following the fight, the NYSAC withdrew its support of Schwartz and, in refusing to recognise la Morte, set up an elimination tournament at Madison Square Gardens to find a new champion. A four-legged affair on 4 November 1929, saw Black Bill, Eugene Huat, Ruby Bradley and Midget Wolgast outscore Willie Davies, Schwartz, Ernie Peters and Johnny McCoy, respectively, before the Cuban eliminated Huat, also on points over ten rounds, to book himself a place in the final against Wolgast, who drew a bye after Bradley pulled out.*

17.10.29 Frankie Genaro (USA) W PTS 15 Ernie Jarvis (GB), Albert Hall, London - NBA/IBU

21.11.29 Willie la Morte (USA) W RSC 7 Frisco Grande (PH), Paterson. *Listed as a title fight by the Ring Record Book and billed as one over 15 rounds, it was not recognised as such by the NYSAC, or in New Jersey, who, as a member of the NBA still viewed Frankie Genaro as champion. Naturally, la Morte, a New Yorker by birth, continued to claim the championship with good cause until being defeated by Midget Wolgast on the New York title. Also, at the end of 1929, Pablo Dano, a Filipino who had beaten la Morte and drawn with Izzy Schwartz, laid claim to the title to further confuse the issue. However, although a good fighter, Dana's claim fell on deaf ears and he received no official backing.*

18.01.30 Frankie Genaro (USA) W RTD 12 Yvon Trevidic (FR), Paris - NBA/IBU

21.03.30 Midget Wolgast (USA) W PTS 15 Black Bill (CUB), New York City - NY

16.05.30 Midget Wolgast (USA) W CO 6 Willie la Morte (USA), New York City - NY

10.06.30 Frankie Genaro (USA) W PTS 10 Frenchy Belanger (C), Toronto - NBA/IBU

06.08.30 Frankie Genaro (USA) W PTS 10 Willie la Morte (USA), Newark. *Although recorded in the Boxing News Annual as an NBA championship bout, it was, in fact, a non-title contest, with Genaro weighing in at 115 lbs and la Morte 117, respectively.*

26.12.30 Frankie Genaro (USA) DREW 15 Midget Wolgast (USA), New York City

25.03.31 Frankie Genaro (USA) DREW 15 Victor Ferrand (SP), Madrid - NBA/IBU. *At the finish, Ferrand was four points ahead on the referee's scorecard, but, under IBU rules, the challenger had to have a lead of at least five points for the title to change hands.*

13.07.31 Midget Wolgast (USA) W PTS 15 Ruby Bradley (USA), Brooklyn - NY

16.07.31 Frankie Genaro (USA) W CO 4 Routier Parra (CH), North Adams. *Shown in the Ring Record Book as an NBA/IBU title fight, according to the New York Herald & Tribune (newspaper) report it was a non-title bout at catchweights.*

30.07.31 Frankie Genaro (USA) W CO 6 Jackie Harmon (USA), Waterbury - NBA/IBU

03.10.31 Frankie Genaro (USA) W PTS 15 Valentin Angelmann (FR), Paris - NBA/IBU

27.10.31 Young Perez (FR) W CO 2 Frankie Genaro (USA), Paris - NBA/IBU

31.10.32 Jackie Brown (GB) W RSC 13 Young Perez (FR), Belle Vue, Manchester - NBA/IBU

12.06.33 Jackie Brown (GB) W PTS 15 Valentin Angelmann (FR), Olympia, London - NBA/IBU

11.09.33 Jackie Brown (GB) W PTS 15 Valentin Angelmann (FR), Belle Vue, Manchester - NBA/IBU

11.12.33 Jackie Brown (GB) W PTS 15 Ginger Foran (GB), Belle Vue, Manchester - NBA/IBU

18.06.34 Jackie Brown (GB) DREW 15 Valentin Angelmann (FR), Belle Vue, Manchester - NBA/IBU. *Jackie Brown forfeited IBU recognition in September 1936 for failing to meet Valentin Angelmann.*

09.09.35 Benny Lynch (GB) W RTD 2 Jackie Brown (GB), Belle Vue, Manchester - NBA

16.09.35 Small Montana (PH) W PTS 10 Midget Wolgast (USA), Oakland - NY/CALIFORNIA

16.12.35 Small Montana (PH) W PTS 10 Tuffy Pierpont (USA), Oakland - NY/CALIFORNIA

06.01.36 Valentin Angelmann (FR) W RTD 5 Kid David (BEL), Paris - IBU

16.09.36 Benny Lynch (GB) W CO 8 Pat Palmer (GB), Shawfield Park, Glasgow - NBA

12.12.36 Valentin Angelmann (FR) W PTS 15 Ernst Weiss (AU), Paris - IBU. *Valentin Angelmann forfeited IBU recognition following a 12 round points defeat at the hands of Peter Kane in Paris on 18 January 1937.*

19.01.37 Benny Lynch (GB) W PTS 15 Small Montana (PH), The Arena, Wembley

13.10.37 Benny Lynch (GB) W CO 13 Peter Kane (GB), Shawfield Park, Glasgow.

24.03.38 Benny Lynch (GB) DREW 12 Peter Kane (GB), The Stadium, Liverpool. *Originally billed as a title fight, Lynch failed to make the weight and was fortunate not to forfeit the championship.*

29.06.38 Benny Lynch (GB) W CO 11 Jackie Jurich (USA), Shawfield Park, Glasgow. *Billed as a championship fight, Lynch finally forfeited the title on the scales when weighing in six and a half pounds overweight. Although the fight went ahead, the little Scot's career was effectively over and Peter Kane was matched against Jurich for the vacant title, while the claims of the Filipino eight stoners, Little Dado and Small Montana, were strongly supported in California.*

22.09.38 Peter Kane (GB) W PTS 15 Jackie Jurich (USA), Anfield Football Ground, Liverpool - NY/IBU/NBA. *Having won the title, Peter Kane also found that he was having a struggle to make the weight and in May 1939 he announced that he was relinquishing the title to campaign as a bantamweight.*

30.11.38 Little Dado (PH) W PTS 10 Small Montana (PH), Oakland - CALIFORNIA. *Although Little Dado was recognised in California as world champion, it did not stop a promotion going ahead in the same town, matching the loser, Montana, with Jackie Jurich on 3 March 1939 for the vacant American title, the latter winning via a seventh round kayo. Then, on 1 September 1939, the newly formed World Championship Committee agreed to recognise the winner of Dado v Enrico Urbinati (European champion) as world champion, but, unfortunately, due to the war, that fight fell through. Meanwhile, in defence of his American title, Jurich outpointed Montana after ten rounds on 4 October 1939, before suffering a tenth round kayo defeat at the hands of Little Pancho in Los Angeles on 11 December 1939. Both men were inside 112 lbs and, three days later, Little Dado was proclaimed World flyweight champion. Prior to that, around the end of October, Little Pancho had asked the NBA to consider him as their champion, but ultimately lost out to his compatriot.*

17.06.40 Little Dado (PH) DREW 10 Little Pancho (PH), San Francisco - CALIFORNIA. *With Dado still recognised by the NBA, this contest was authorised by the Californian Boxing Commission for their version of the title.*

21.02.41 Little Dado (PH) W PTS 10 Jackie Jurich (USA), Honolulu - NBA. *Inactive for almost all of 1942, Dado came back towards the end of that year as a fully-fledged bantam and with Peter Kane still able to make eight stone, the Englishman was allowed to defend his old title against Jackie Paterson in June 1943.*

19.06.43 Jackie Paterson (GB) W CO 1 Peter Kane (GB), Hampden Park, Glasgow

10.07.46 Jackie Paterson (GB) W PTS 15 Joe Curran (GB), Hampden Park, Glasgow. *Jackie Paterson forfeited NBA recognition in July 1947, having thrice pulled out of title defences against Dado Marino and a match between the latter and Rinty Monaghan was announced to decide the championship. Initially, Paterson had also been stripped by the BBBoC, but following an injunction in the High Court he was later reinstated.*

20.10.47 Rinty Monaghan (GB) W PTS 15 Dado Marino (HA), Harringay Arena, London - NBA

23.03.48 Rinty Monaghan (GB) W CO 7 Jackie Paterson (GB), King's Hall, Belfast

05.04.49 Rinty Monaghan (GB) W PTS 15 Maurice Sandeyron (FR), King's Hall, Belfast

30.09.49 Rinty Monaghan (GB) DREW 15 Terry Allen (GB), King's Hall, Belfast. *Rinty Monaghan retired as undefeated champion in April 1950 and the two leading contenders, Terry Allen and the French champion, Honore Pratesi, were matched for the vacant title.*

25.04.50 Terry Allen (GB) W PTS 15 Honore Pratesi (FR), Harringay Arena, London

01.08.50 Dado Marino (HA) W PTS 15 Terry Allen (GB), Honolulu

01.11.51 Dado Marino (HA) W PTS 15 Terry Allen (GB), Honolulu

19.05.52 Yoshio Shirai (JAP) W PTS 15 Dado Marino (HA), Tokyo

15.11.52 Yoshio Shirai (JAP) W PTS 15 Dado Marino (HA), Tokyo

18.05.53 Yoshio Shirai (JAP) W PTS 15 Tanny Campo (PH), Tokyo

27.10.53 Yoshio Shirai (JAP) W PTS 15 Terry Allen (GB), Tokyo

23.05.54 Yoshio Shirai (JAP) W PTS 15 Leo Espinosa (PH), Tokyo

26.11.54 Pascual Perez (ARG) W PTS 15 Yoshio Shirai (JAP), Tokyo

13.04.55 Pascual Perez (ARG) W CO 3 Albert Barenghi (ARG), Buenos Aires. *Not billed as a championship fight, the title was at stake, however, with both men making the weight.*

30.05.55 Pascual Perez (ARG) W CO 5 Yoshio Shirai (JAP), Tokyo

22.10.55 Pascual Perez (ARG) W PTS 10 Danny Kid (PH), Buenos Aires. *Yet again Perez unnecessarily risked his crown in a non-title fight, with both men inside the limit.*

11.01.56 **Pascual Perez** (ARG) W PTS 15 Leo Espinosa (PH), Buenos Aires

10.02.56 **Pascual Perez** (ARG) W PTS 10 Antonio Gomez (ARG), Mar del Plata. *This was the third time that Perez stood to lose his crown in a non-title bout when his opponent was allowed to make the weight.*

31.03.56 **Pascual Perez** (ARG) W PTS 10 Marcelo Quiroga (ARG), Buenos Aires. *Another non-title fight where the champion risked his crown against an opponent who was inside the weight.*

30.06.56 **Pascual Perez** (ARG) W RTD 11 Oscar Suarez (CUB), Montevideo

03.08.56 **Pascual Perez** (ARG) W RSC 5 Ricardo Valdez (ARG), Tandil. *Not billed as a title fight, but another case of Perez not caring that his rival was inside eight stone.*

25.08.56 **Pascual Perez** (ARG) W CO 3 Hector Almaraz (ARG), Rosario. *With Almaraz making the weight, Perez's crown was once again at risk in a non-title bout.*

30.03.57 **Pascual Perez** (ARG) W CO 1 Dai Dower (GB), Buenos Aires

12.07.57 **Pascual Perez** (ARG) W CO 3 Luis Angel Jiminez (ARG), Buenos Aires. *Continuing to put his crown at risk against his compatriots in non-title matches, Perez allowed Jiminez to weigh-in below the eight stone mark.*

16.08.57 **Pascual Perez** (ARG) W CO 3 Pablo Sosa (ARG), Tandil. *Not a title bout, but simply one where Perez' crown was yet again at risk with Sosa inside the limit.*

07.12.57 **Pascual Perez** (ARG) W CO 3 Young Martin (SP), Buenos Aires

19.04.58 **Pascual Perez** (ARG) W PTS 15 Ramon Arias (VEN), Caracas

15.12.58 **Pascual Perez** (ARG) W PTS 15 Dommy Ursua (PH), Manila

10.08.59 **Pascual Perez** (ARG) W PTS 15 Kenji Yonekura (JAP), Tokyo

05.11.59 **Pascual Perez** (ARG) W CO 13 Sadao Yaoita (JAP), Osaka

16.04.60 **Pone Kingpetch** (TH) W PTS 15 Pascual Perez (ARG), Bangkok

22.09.60 **Pone Kingpetch** (TH) W RSC 8 Pascual Perez (ARG), Los Angeles

27.06.61 **Pone Kingpetch** (TH) W PTS 15 Mitsunori Seki (JAP), Tokyo

30.05.62 **Pone Kingpetch** (TH) W PTS 15 Kyo Noguchi (JAP), Tokyo

10.10.62 **Fighting Harada** (JAP) W CO 11 Pone Kingpetch (TH), Tokyo

12.01.63 **Pone Kingpetch** (TH) W PTS 15 Fighting Harada (JAP), Tokyo

18.09.63 **Hiroyuki Ebihara** (JAP) W CO 1 Pone Kingpetch (TH), Tokyo

23.01.64 **Pone Kingpetch** (TH) W PTS 15 Hiroyuki Ebihara (JAP), Bangkok

23.04.65 **Salvatore Burruni** (ITA) W PTS 15 Pone Kingpetch (TH), Rome. *Salvatore Burruni forfeited WBA recognition in November 1965 after failing to defend against the number one challenger, Hiroyuki Ebihara, within the given deadline. Following the announcement, the latter was matched for the vacant WBA title against Horacio Accavallo, who had outpointed Burruni three months earlier, but had to be replaced by Katsuyoshi Takayama when injured in training.*

02.12.65 Salvatore Burruni (ITA) W CO 13 Rocky Gattellari (A), Sydney - WBC

01.03.66 Horacio Accavallo (ARG) W PTS 15 Katsuyoshi Takayama (JAP), Tokyo - WBA

14.06.66 Walter McGowan (GB) W PTS 15 Salvatore Burruni (ITA), The Arena, Wembley - WBC

15.07.66 Horacio Accavallo (ARG) W PTS 15 Hiroyuki Ebihara (JAP), Buenos Aires - WBA

10.12.66 Horacio Accavallo (ARG) W PTS 15 Efren Torres (MEX), Buenos Aires - WBA

30.12.66 Chartchai Chionoi (TH) W RSC 9 Walter McGowan (GB), Bangkok - WBC

26.07.67 Chartchai Chionoi (TH) W CO 3 Puntip Keosuriya (TH), Bangkok - WBC

13.08.67 Horacio Accavallo (ARG) W PTS 15 Hiroyuki Ebihara (JAP), Buenos Aires - WBA. *Horacio Accavallo retired as undefeated WBA champion in October 1968.*

19.09.67 Chartchai Chionoi (TH) W RSC 7 Walter McGowan (GB), The Arena, Wembley - WBC

28.01.68 Chartchai Chionoi (TH) W RSC 13 Efren Torres (MEX), Mexico City - WBC

10.11.68 Chartchai Chionoi (TH) W PTS 15 Bernabe Villacampo (PH), Bangkok - WBC

23.02.69 Efren Torres (MEX) W RSC 8 Chartchai Chionoi (TH), Mexico City - WBC

30.03.69 Hiroyuki Ebihara (JAP) W PTS 15 Jose Severino (BR), Sapporo - WBA

19.10.69 Bernabe Villacampo (PH) W PTS 15 Hiroyuki Ebihara (JAP), Tokyo - WBA

28.11.69 Efren Torres (MEX) W PTS 15 Susumu Hanagata (JAP), Guadalajara - WBC

20.03.70 Chartchai Chionoi (TH) W PTS 15 Efren Torres (MEX), Bangkok - WBC

06.04.70 Berkrerk Chartvanchai (TH) W PTS 15 Bernabe Villacampo (PH), Bangkok - WBA

21.10.70 Masao Ohba (JAP) W RSC 13 Berkrerk Chartvanchai (TH), Tokyo - WBA

07.12.70 Erbito Salavarria (PH) W RSC 2 Chartchai Chionoi (TH), Bangkok - WBC

01.04.71 Masao Ohba (JAP) W PTS 15 Betulio Gonzalez (VEN), Tokyo - WBA

30.04.71 Erbito Salavarria (PH) W PTS 15 Susumu Hanagata (JAP), Manila - WBC

23.10.71 Masao Ohba (JAP) W PTS 15 Fernando Cabanela (PH), Tokyo - WBA

20.11.71 Erbito Salavarria (PH) DREW 15 Betulio Gonzalez (VEN), Caracas - WBC. *Erbito Salavarria forfeited WBC recognition immediately after the fight for allegedly using an illegal stimulant and Betulio Gonzalez was proclaimed their champion.*

04.03.72 Masao Ohba (JAP) W PTS 15 Susumu Hanagata (JAP), Tokyo - WBA

03.06.72 Betulio Gonzalez (VEN) W CO 4 Socrates Batoto (PH), Caracas - WBC

20.06.72 Masao Ohba (JAP) W CO 5 Orlando Amores (PAN), Tokyo - WBA

29.09.72 Venice Borkorsor (TH) W RTD 10 Betulio Gonzales (VEN), Bangkok - WBC

02.01.73 Masao Ohba (JAP) W RSC 12 Chartchai Chionoi (TH), Tokyo - WBA. *Masao Ohba left WBA version of title vacant in January 1973 when he died in a road accident.*

09.02.73 Venice Borkorsor (TH) W PTS 15 Erbito Salavarria (PH), Bangkok - WBC. *Venice Borkorsor relinquished WBC version of title in August 1973 to campaign as a bantamweight.*

17.05.73 Chartchai Chionoi (TH) W RSC 4 Fritz Chervet (SWI), Bangkok - WBA

04.08.73 Betulio Gonzalez (VEN) W PTS 15 Miguel Canto (MEX), Caracas - WBC

27.10.73 Chartchai Chionoi (TH) W PTS 15 Susumu Hanagata (JAP), Bangkok - WBA

17.11.73 Betulio Gonzalez (VEN) W RSC 11 Alberto Morales (MEX), Caracas - WBC

27.04.74 Chartchai Chionoi (TH) W PTS 15 Fritz Chervet (SWI), Zurich - WBA

20.07.74 Betulio Gonzalez (VEN) W RSC 10 Franco Udella (ITA), Sabbiadoro - WBC

01.10.74 Shoji Oguma (JAP) W PTS 15 Betulio Gonzalez (VEN), Tokyo - WBC

18.10.74 Susumu Hanagata (JAP) W RSC 6 Chartchai Chionoi (TH), Yokohama - WBA. *Chartchai Chionoi forfeited the WBA version of the title before the fight when he weighed in at 115¾ lbs. However, the contest went ahead and following the decision, Susumu Hanagata was proclaimed champion.*

08.01.75 Miguel Canto (MEX) W PTS 15 Shoji Oguma (JAP), Sendai - WBC

01.04.75 Erbito Salavarria (PH) W PTS 15 Susumu Hanagata (JAP), Toyama - WBA

24.05.75 Miguel Canto (MEX) W PTS 15 Betulio Gonzalez (VEN), Monterrey - WBC

23.08.75 Miguel Canto (MEX) W RSC 11 Jiro Takada (JAP), Merida - WBC

07.10.75 Erbito Salavarria (PH) W PTS 15 Susumu Hanagata (JAP), Yokohama - WBA

13.12.75 Miguel Canto (MEX) W PTS 15 Ignacio Espinal (DOM), Merida - WBC

27.02.76 Alfonso Lopez (PAN) W RSC 15 Erbito Salavarria (PH), Manila - WBA

21.04.76 Alfonso Lopez (PAN) W PTS 15 Shoji Oguma (JAP), Tokyo - WBA

15.05.76 Miguel Canto (MEX) W PTS 15 Susumu Hanagata (JAP), Merida - WBC

02.10.76 Guty Espadas (MEX) W RSC 13 Alfonso Lopez (PAN), Los Angeles - WBA

03.10.76 Miguel Canto (MEX) W PTS 15 Betulio Gonzalez (VEN), Caracas - WBC

19.11.76 Miguel Canto (MEX) W PTS 15 Orlando Javierta (PH), Los Angeles - WBC

01.01.77 Guty Espadas (MEX) W RTD 7 Jiro Takada (JAP), Tokyo - WBA

24.04.77 Miguel Canto (MEX) W PTS 15 Reyes Arnal (VEN), Caracas - WBC

30.04.77 Guty Espadas (MEX) W RSC 13 Alfonso Lopez (PAN), Merida - WBA

15.06.77 Miguel Canto (MEX) W PTS 15 Kimio Furesawa (JAP), Tokyo - WBC

17.09.77 Miguel Canto (MEX) W PTS 15 Martin Vargas (CH), Merida - WBC

19.11.77 Guty Espadas (MEX) W CO 8 Alex Santana (NIC), Los Angeles - WBA

30.11.77 Miguel Canto (MEX) W PTS 15 Martin Vargas (CH), Santiago - WBC

02.01.78 Guty Espadas (MEX) W RSC 7 Kimio Furesawa (JAP), Tokyo - WBA

04.01.78 Miguel Canto (MEX) W PTS 15 Shoji Oguma (JAP), Tokyo - WBC

18.04.78 Miguel Canto (MEX) W PTS 15 Shoji Oguma (JAP), Tokyo - WBC

13.08.78 Betulio Gonzalez (VEN) W PTS 15 Guty Espadas (MEX), Maracay - WBA

04.11.78 Betulio Gonzalez (VEN) W RSC 12 Martin Vargas (CH), Maracay - WBA

20.11.78 Miguel Canto (MEX) W PTS 15 Tacomron Vibonchai (TH), Houston - WBC

29.01.79 Betulio Gonzalez (VEN) DREW 15 Shoji Oguma (JAP), Hamamatsu - WBA

10.02.79 Miguel Canto (MEX) W PTS15 Antonio Avelar (MEX), Merida - WBC

18.03.79 Chan-He Park (SK) W PTS 15 Miguel Canto (MEX), Pusan - WBC

19.05.79 Chan-He Park (SK) W PTS 15 Tsutomo Igarashi (JAP), Seoul - WBC

06.07.79 Betulio Gonzalez (VEN) W CO 12 Shoji Oguma (JAP), Utsunomiya - WBA

09.09.79 Chan-He Park (SK) DREW 15 Miguel Canto (MEX), Seoul - WBC

16.11.79 Luis Ibarra (PAN) W PTS 15 Betulio Gonzalez (VEN), Maracay - WBA

16.12.79 Chan-He Park (SK) W CO 2 Guty Espadas (MEX), Pusan - WBC

09.02.80 Chan-He Park (SK) W PTS 15 Arnel Arrozal (PH), Seoul - WBC

16.02.80 Tae-Shik Kim (SK) W CO 2 Luis Ibarra, (PAN) Seoul - WBA

13.04.80 Chan-He Park (SK) W PTS 15 Alberto Morales (MEX), Taegu - WBC

18.05.80 Shoji Oguma (JAP) W CO 9 Chan-He Park (SK), Seoul - WBC

29.06.80 Tae-Shik Kim (SK) W PTS 15 Arnel Arrozal (PH), Seoul - WBA

28.07.80 Shoji Oguma (JAP) W PTS 15 Sung-Jun Kim (SK), Tokyo - WBC

18.10.80 Shoji Oguma (JAP) W PTS 15 Chan-He Park (SK), Sendai - WBC

13.12.80 Peter Mathebula (SA) W PTS 15 Tae-Shik Kim (SK), Los Angeles - WBA

03.02.81 Shoji Oguma (JAP) W PTS 15 Chan-He Park (SK), Tokyo - WBC

28.03.81 Santos Laciar (ARG) W RSC 7 Peter Mathebula (SA), Soweto - WBA

12.05.81 Antonio Avelar (MEX) W CO 7 Shoji Oguma (JAP), Mito City - WBC

06.06.81 Luis Ibarra (PAN) W PTS 15 Santos Laciar (ARG), Buenos Aires - WBA

30.08.81 Antonio Avelar (MEX) W CO 2 Tae-Shik Kim (SK), Seoul - WBC

26.09.81 Juan Herrera (MEX) W CO 11 Luis Ibarra (PAN), Merida - WBA

26.12.81 Juan Herrera (MEX) W RSC 7 Betulio Gonzalaz (VEN), Merida - WBA

20.03.82 Prudencio Cardona (COL) W CO 1 Antonio Avelar (MEX), Tampico - WBC

01.05.82 Santos Laciar (ARG) W RSC 13 Juan Herrera (MEX), Merida - WBA

24.07.82 Freddie Castillo (MEX) W PTS 15 Prudencio Cardona (COL), Merida - WBC

14.08.82 Santos Laciar (ARG) W PTS 15 Betulio Gonzalez (VEN), Maracaibo - WBA

05.11.82 Santos Laciar (ARG) W RSC 13 Steve Muchoki (K), Copenhagen - WBA

06.11.82 Eleoncio Mercedes (DOM) W PTS 15 Freddie Castillo (MEX), Los Angeles - WBC

04.03.83 Santos Laciar (ARG) W CO 9 Ramon Neri (DOM) Cordoba - WBA

15.03.83 Charlie Magri (GB) W RSC 7 Eleoncio Mercedes (DOM), The Arena, Wembley - WBC

05.05.83 Santos Laciar (ARG) W RSC 2 Suichi Hozumi (JAP), Shizuoka - WBA

17.07.83 Santos Laciar (ARG) W CO 1 Hi-Sup Shin (SK), Cheju - WBA

27.09.83 Frank Cedeno (PH) W RSC 6 Charlie Magri (GB), The Arena, Wembley - WBC

24.12.83 Soon-Chun Kwon (SK) W CO 5 Rene Busayong (PH), Seoul - IBF

18.01.84 Koji Kobayashi (JAP) W RSC 2 Frank Cedeno (PH), Tokyo - WBC

28.01.84 Santos Laciar (ARG) W PTS 15 Juan Herrera (MEX), Marsala - WBA

25.02.84 Soon-Chun Kwon (SK) W TD 12 Roger Castillo (PH), Seoul - IBF. *Ahead on the judges' scorecards at the time, Kwon retained his title by decision after he was accidentally cut and pulled out of the fight by the doctor.*

09.04.84 Gabriel Bernal (MEX) W CO 2 Koji Kobayashi (JAP), Tokyo - WBC

19.05.84 Soon-Chun Kwon (SK) W PTS 15 Ian Clyde (C), Daejon - IBF

01.06.84 Gabriel Bernal (MEX) W RSC 11 Antoine Montero (FR), Nimes - WBC

07.09.84 Soon-Chun Kwon (SK) W RSC 12 Joaquin Caraballo (PH), Chungju - IBF

15.09.84 Santos Laciar (ARG) W CO 10 Prudencio Cardona (COL), Cordoba - WBA

08.10.84 Sot Chitalada (TH) W PTS 12 Gabriel Bernal (MEX), Bangkok - WBC

08.12.84 Santos Laciar (ARG) W PTS 15 Hilario Zapata (PAN), Buenos Aires - WBA

25.01.85 Soon-Chun Kwon (SK) DREW 15 Chong-Kwang Chung (SK), Daejon - IBF

20.02.85 Sot Chitalada (TH) W RTD 4 Charlie Magri (GB), Alexandra Pavilion, London - WBC

14.04.85 Soon-Chun Kwon (SK) W CO 3 Shinobu Kawashima (JAP), Pohang - IBF

06.05.85 Santos Laciar (ARG) W PTS 15 Antoine Montero (FR), Grenoble - WBA. *Santos Laciar relinquished WBA version of title in July 1985 due to increasing weight problems.*

22.06.85 Sot Chitalada (TH) DREW 12 Gabriel Bernal (MEX), Bangkok - WBC

17.07.85 Soon-Chun Kwon (SK) DREW 15 Chong-Kwan Chung (SK), Masan - IBF

05.10.85 Hilario Zapata (PAN) W PTS 15 Alonzo Gonzales (USA), Panama City - WBA

20.12.85 Chong-Kwan Chung (SK) W RSC 4 Soon-Chun Kwon (SK), Taegu - IBF

31.01.86 Hilario Zapata (PAN) W PTS 15 Javier Lucas (MEX), Panama City - WBA

22.02.86 Sot Chitalada (TH) W PTS 15 Freddie Castillo (MEX), Kuwait City - WBC

07.04.86 Hilario Zapata (PAN) W PTS 15 Suichi Hozumi (JAP), Nirasaki - WBA

27.04.86 Bi-Won Chung (SK) W PTS 15 Chong-Kwan Chung (SK), Pusan - IBF

05.07.86 Hilario Zapata (PAN) W PTS 15 Dodie Penalosa (PH), Manila - WBA

02.08.86 Hi-Sup Shin (SK) W RSC 15 Bi-Won Chung (SK), Inchon - IBF

13.09.86 Hilario Zapata (PAN) W PTS 15 Alberto Castro (COL), Panama City - WBA

22.11.86 Hi-Sup Shin (SK) W RSC 13 Henry Brent (USA), Chunchon - IBF

06.12.86 Hilario Zapata (PAN) W PTS 15 Claudemir Dias (BR), Salvador - WBA

10.12.86 Sot Chitalada (TH) W PTS 12 Gabriel Bernal (MEX), Bangkok - WBC

13.02.87 Fidel Bassa (COL) W PTS 15 Hilario Zapata (PAN), Barranquilla - WBA

22.02.87 Dodie Penalosa (PH) W CO 5 Hi-Sup Shin (SK), Inchon - IBF

25.04.87 Fidel Bassa (COL) W CO 13 Dave McAuley (GB), King's Hall, Belfast - WBA

15.08.87 Fidel Bassa (COL) DREW 15 Hilario Zapata (PAN), Panama City - WBA

05.09.87 Chang-Ho Choi (SK) W CO 11 Dodie Penalosa (PH), Manila - IBF

05.09.87 Sot Chitalada (TH) W CO 4 Rae-Ki Ahn (SK), Bangkok - WBC

18.12.87 Fidel Bassa (COL) W PTS 12 Felix Marty (DOM), Cartagena - WBA

16.01.88 Rolando Bohol (PH) W PTS 15 Chang-Ho Choi (SK), Manila - IBF

31.01.88 Sot Chitalada (TH) W RSC 7 Hideaki Kamishiro (JAP), Osaka - WBC

26.03.88 Fidel Bassa (COL) W PTS 12 Dave McAuley (GB), King's Hall, Belfast - WBA

06.05.88 Rolando Bohol (PH) W PTS 15 Cho-Woon Park (SK), Manila - IBF

23.07.88 Yong-Kang Kim (SK) W PTS 12 Sot Chitalada (TH), Pohang - WBC

02.10.88 Fidel Bassa (COL) W PTS 12 Raymond Medel (USA), San Antonio - WBA

05.10.88 Duke McKenzie (GB) W CO 11 Rolando Bohol (PH), Grand Hall, Wembley - IBF

13.11.88 Yong-Kang Kim (SK) W PTS 12 Emil Romano (PH), Chungju - WBC

03.03.89 Elvis Alvarez (COL) W PTS 12 Miguel Mercedes (DOM), Medellin - WBO. *Elvis Alvarez relinquished WBO version of title in October 1989 in order to try for a crack at one of the other organisation's crowns.*

05.03.89 Yong-Kang Kim (SK) W PTS 12 Yukhito Tamakuma (JAP), Aomori- WBC

08.03.89 Duke McKenzie (GB) W RSC 4 Tony de Luca (USA), Albert Hall, London - IBF

15.04.89 Fidel Bassa (COL) W RSC 6 Julio Gudino (PAN), Barranquilla - WBA

03.06.89 Sot Chitalada (TH) W PTS 12 Yong-Kang Kim (SK), Trang - WBC

07.06.89 Dave McAuley (GB) W PTS 12 Duke McKenzie (GB), The Arena, Wembley - IBF

30.09.89 Jesus Rojas (VEN) W PTS 12 Fidel Bassa (COL), Barranquilla - WBA

08.11.89 Dave McAuley (GB) W PTS 12 Dodie Penalosa (PH), Grand Hall, Wembley - IBF

30.01.90 Sot Chitalada (TH) W PTS 12 Ric Siodoro (PH), Bangkok - WBC

10.03.90 Yul-Woo Lee (SK) W PTS 12 Jesus Rojas (VEN), Taejon - WBA

17.03.90 Dave McAuley (GB) W PTS 12 Louis Curtis (USA), King's Hall, Belfast - IBF

01.05.90 Sot Chitalada (TH) W PTS 12 Carlos Salazar (ARG), Bangkok - WBC

28.07.90 Yukihito Tamakuma (JAP) W RSC 10 Yul-Woo Lee (SK), Mito - WBA

18.08.90 Isidro Perez (MEX) W RSC 12 Angel Rosario (PRO, Ponce - WBO

09.09.90 Sot Chitalada (TH) W CO 1 Richard Clark (J), Kingston - WBC

15.09.90 Dave McAuley (GB) W PTS 12 Rodolfo Blanco (COL), King's Hall, Belfast - IBF

03.11.90 Isidro Perez (MEX) W PTS 12 Alli Galvez (CH), Acapulco - WBO

24.11.90 Sot Chitalada (TH) W PTS 12 Jung-Koo Chang (SK), Seoul - WBC

06.12.90 Yukihito Tamakuma (JAP) DREW 12 Jesus Rojas (VEN), Aomori - WBA

15.02.91 Muangchai Kitikasem (TH) W RSC 6 Sot Chitalada (TH), Ayuthaya - WBC

14.03.91 Elvis Alvarez (COL) W PTS 12 Yukihito Tamakuma (JAP), Tokyo - WBA

11.05.91 Dave McAuley (GB) W PTS 12 Pedro Feliciano (PR), Maysfield Leisure Centre, Belfast - IBF

18.05.91 Muangchai Kitikasem (TH) W RSC 12 Jung-Koo Chang (SK), Seoul - WBC

01.06.91 Yong-Kang Kim (SK) W PTS 12 Elvis Alvarez (COL), Seoul - WBA

10.08.91 Isidro Perez (MEX) W PTS 12 Alli Galvez (CH), Santiago - WBO

07.09.91 Dave McAuley (GB) W CO 10 Jacob Matlala (SA), Maysfield Leisure Centre, Belfast - IBF

05.10.91 Yong-Kang Kim (SK) W PTS 12 Silvio Gamez (VEN), Inchon - WBA

25.10.91 Muangchai Kitikasem (TH) W PTS 12 Alberto Jimenez (MEX), Bangkok - WBC

28.02.92 Muangchai Kitikasem (TH) W RSC 9 Sot Chitalada (TH), Samut Prakan - WBC

18.03.92 Pat Clinton (GB) W PTS 12 Isidro Perez (MEX), Kelvin Hall, Glasgow - WBO

24.03.92 Yong-Kang Kim (SK) W CO 6 Jon Penalosa (PH), Inchon - WBA

11.06.92 Rodolfo Blanco (COL) W PTS 12 Dave McAuley (GB), Bilbao - IBF

23.06.92 Yuri Arbachakov (ARM) W CO 8 Muangchai Kitikasem (TH), Tokyo - WBC

19.09.92 Pat Clinton (GB) W PTS 12 Danny Porter (GB), Scottish Exhibition Centre, Glasgow - WBO

26.09.92 Aquiles Guzman (VEN) W PTS 12 Yong-Kang Kim (SK), Pohang - WBA

20.10.92 Yuri Arbachakov (ARM) W PTS 12 Yun-Un Chin (SK), Tokyo - WBC

29.11.92 Pichit Sitbangprachan (TH) W CO 3 Rodolfo Blanco (COL), Bangkok - IBF

15.12.92 David Griman (VEN) W PTS 12 Aquiles Guzman (VEN), Caracas - WBA

06.03.93 Pichit Sitbangprachan (TH) W RSC 4 Antonio Perez (MEX), Uttaradit - IBF

20.03.93 Yuri Arbachakov (ARM) W RSC 9 Muangchai Kitikasem (TH), Lopburi - WBC

15.05.93 Jacob Matlala (SA) W RSC 8 Pat Clinton (GB), Scottish Exhibition Centre, Glasgow - WBO

21.06.93 David Griman (VEN) W RSC 8 Hiroki Ioka (JAP), Osaka - WBA

Super-Flyweight (115 lbs)

Under pressure from their membership to increase the prospects of the smaller men, the World Boxing Council introduced the division in 1979. However, it took the World Boxing Association a further two years before they recognised the new weight class, naming it junior-bantam.

02.02.80 Rafael Orono (VEN) W PTS 15 Seung-Hoon Lee (SK), Caracas - WBC

14.04.80 Rafael Orono (VEN) W PTS 15 Ramon Soria (ARG), Caracas - WBC

28.07.80 Rafael Orono (VEN) DREW 15 Willie Jensen (USA), Caracas - WBC

15.09.80 Rafael Orono (VEN) W RSC 3 Jovito Rengifo (VEN), Barquisimeto - WBC

24.01.81 Chul-Ho Kim (SK) W CO 9 Rafael Orono (VEN), San Christobal - WBC

22.04.81 Chul-Ho Kim (SK) W PTS 15 Jiro Watanabe (JAP), Seoul - WBC

29.07.81 Chul-Ho Kim (SK) W CO 12 Willie Jensen (USA), Pusan - WBC

12.09.81 Gustavo Ballas (ARG) W RSC 8 Sok-Chul Baek (SK), Buenos Aires - WBA

18.11.81 Chul-Ho Kim (SK) W RSC 9 Jackal Maruyama (JAP), Pusan - WBC

05.12.81 Rafael Pedroza (PAN) W PTS 15 Gustavo Ballas (ARG), Panama City - WBA

10.02.82 Chul-Ho Kim (SK) W CO 8 Koki Ishii (JAP), Taegu - WBC

08.04.82 Jiro Watanabe (JAP) W PTS 15 Rafael Pedroza (PAN), Osaka - WBA

04.07.82 Chul-Ho Kim (SK) DREW 15 Raul Valdez (MEX), Daejon - WBC

29.07.82 Jiro Watanabe (JAP) W RSC 9 Gustavo Ballas (ARG), Osaka - WBA

11.11.82 Jiro Watanabe (JAP) W RTD 12 Shoji Oguma (JAP), Hamamatsu - WBA

28.11.82 Rafael Orono (VEN) W CO 6 Chul-Ho Kim (SK), Seoul - WBC

31.01.83 Rafael Orono (VEN) W CO 4 Pedro Romero (PAN), Caracas - WBC

24.02.83 Jiro Watanabe (JAP) W CO 8 Luis Ibanez (PE), Tsu City - WBA

09.05.83 Rafael Orono (VEN) W PTS 12 Raul Valdez (MEX), Caracas - WBC

23.06.83 Jiro Watanabe (JAP) W PTS 15 Roberto Ramirez (MEX), Sendai - WBA

06.10.83 Jiro Watanabe (JAP) W TD 11 Soon-Chun Kwon (SK), Osaka - WBA. *Under WBA rules, Watanabe, deemed by the judges to be ahead on points at the time, was awarded the decision after an accidental clash of heads had forced him out of the fight.*

29.10.83 Rafael Orono (VEN) W RSC 5 Orlando Maldonado (PR), Caracas - WBC

27.11.83 Payao Poontarat (TH) W PTS 12 Rafael Orono (VEN), Pattaya - WBC

10.12.83 Joo-Do Chun (SK) W CO 5 Ken Kasugai (JAP), Osaka - IBF

28.01.84 Joo-Do Chun (SK) W CO 12 Prayoonsak Muangsurin (TH), Seoul - IBF

15.03.84 Jiro Watanabe (JAP) W RSC 15 Celso Chavez (PAN), Osaka - WBA. *Jiro Watanabe forfeited WBA recognition immediately after winning the WBC version of the title on 5 July 1984.*

17.03.84 Joo-Do Chun (SK) W CO 1 Diego de Villa (PH), Kwangju - IBF

28.03.84 Payao Poontarat (TH) W RSC 10 Guty Espadas (MEX), Bangkok - WBC

26.05.84 Joo-Do Chun (SK) W RSC 6 Felix Marques (PR), Wonju - IBF

05.07.84 Jiro Watanabe (JAP) W PTS 12 Payao Poontarat (TH), Osada - WBC

20.07.84 Joo-Do Chun (SK) W CO 7 William Develos (PH), Pusan - IBF

21.11.84 Kaosai Galaxy (TH) W CO 6 Euscbio Espinal (DOM), Bangkok - WBA

29.11.84 Jiro Watanabe (JAP) W RSC 11 Payao Poontarat (TH), Kumamoto - WBC

06.01.85 Joo-Do Chun (SK) W CO 15 Kwang-Gu Park (SK), Ulsan - IBF

06.03.85 Kaosai Galaxy (TH) W CO 7 Dong-Chun Lee (SK), Bangkok - WBA

03.05.85 Elly Pical (INDON) W RSC 8 Joo-Do Chun (SK), Jakarta - IBF

09.05.85 Jiro Watanabe (JAP) W PTS 12 Julio Solano (DOM), Tokyo - WBC

17.07.85 Kaosai Galaxy (TH) W RSC 5 Rafael Orono (VEN), Bangkok - WBA

25.08.85 Elly Pical (INDON) W RSC 3 Wayne Mulholland (A), Jakarta - IBF

17.09.85 Jiro Watanabe (JAP) W RSC 7 Katsuo Katsuma (JAP), Osaka - WBC

13.12.85 Jiro Watanabe (JAP) W CO 5 Yun-Sok Hwang (SK), Taegu - WBC

23.12.85 Kaosai Galaxy (TH) W RSC 2 Edgar Monserrat (PAN), Bangkok - WBA

15.02.86 Cesar Polanco (DOM) W PTS 15 Elly Pical (INDON), Jakarta - IBF

30.03.86 Gilberto Roman (MEX) W PTS 12 Jiro Watanabe (JAP), Osaka - WBC

15.05.86 Gilberto Roman (MEX) W PTS 12 Edgar Monserrat (PAN), Paris - WBC

05.07.86 Elly Pical (INDON) W CO 3 Cesar Polanco (DOM), Jakarta - IBF

18.07.86 Gilberto Roman (MEX) W PTS 12 Ruben Condori (ARG), Salta - WBC

30.08.86 Gilberto Roman (MEX) DREW 12 Santos Laciar (ARG), Cordoba - WBC

01.11.86 Kaosai Galaxy (TH) W CO 5 Israel Contrerras (VEN), Curacao - WBA

03.12.86 Elly Pical (INDON) W CO 10 Dong-Chun Lee (SK), Jakarta - IBF. *Elly Pical forfeited IBF recognition in March 1987, after he challenged for the WBA S. flyweight title.*

15.12.86 Gilberto Roman (MEX) W PTS 12 Kongtoranee Payakarun (TH), Bangkok - WBC

31.01.87 Gilberto Roman (MEX) W RSC 9 Antoine Montero (FR), Montpelier - WBC

28.02.87 Kaosai Galaxy (TH) W CO 13 Elly Pical (INDON), Jakarta - WBA

19.03.87 Gilberto Roman (MEX) W PTS 12 Frank Cedeno (PH), Mexicali - WBC

16.05.87 Santos Laciar (ARG) W RSC 11 Gilberto Roman (MEX), Reims - WBC

17.05.87 Tae-Il Chang (SK) W PTS 15 Soon-Chun Kwon (SK), Pusan - IBF

08.08.87 Jesus Rojas (COL) W PTS 12 Santos Laciar (ARG), Miami - WBC

12.10.87 Kaosai Galaxy (TH) W RSC 3 Byong-Kwan Chung (SK), Bangkok - WBA

17.10.87 Elly Pical (INDON) W PTS 15 Tae-Il Chang (SK), Jakarta - IBF

24.10.87 Jesus Rojas (COL) W RSC 4 Gustavo Ballas (ARG), Miami - WBC

26.01.88 Kaosai Galaxy (TH) W PTS 12 Kongtoranee Payakarun (TH), Bangkok - WBA

20.02.88 Elly Pical (INDON) W PTS 15 Raul Diaz (COL), Pontianak - IBF

08.04.88 Gilberto Roman (MEX) W PTS 12 Jesus Rojas (COL), Miami - WBC

09.07.88 Gilberto Roman (MEX) W RSC 5 Yoshiyuki Uchida (JAP), Kawagoe - WBC

03.09.88 Elly Pical (INDON) W PTS 12 Chang-Ki Kim (SK), Surabaya - IBF

03.09.88 Gilberto Roman (MEX) W PTS 12 Kiyoshi Hatanaka (JAP), Nagoya - WBC

09.10.88 Kaosai Galaxy (TH) W CO 8 Chang-Ho Choi (SK), Seoul - WBA

07.11.88 Gilberto Roman (MEX) W PTS 12 Jesus Rojas (COL), Las Vegas - WBC

15.01.89 Kaosai Galaxy (TH) W CO 2 Tae-Il Chang (SK), Bangkok - WBA

25.02.89 Elly Pical (INDON) W PTS 12 Mike Phelps (USA), Singapore - IBF

08.04.89 Kaosai Galaxy (TH) W PTS 12 Kenji Matsumura (JAP), Yokohama - WBA

29.04.89 Jose Ruiz (PR) W PTS 12 Jesus Rojas (COL), San Juan - WBO

05.06.89 Gilberto Roman (MEX) W PTS 12 Juan Carazo (PR), Los Angeles - WBC

29.07.89 Kaosai Galaxy (TH) W RSC 10 Alberto Castro (COL), Surin - WBA

09.09.89 Jose Ruiz (PR) W RSC 1 Juan Carazo (PR), San Juan - WBO

12.09.89 Gilberto Roman (MEX) W PTS 12 Santos Laciar (ARG), Los Angeles - WBC

14.10.89 Juan Polo Perez (COL) W PTS 12 Elly Pical (INDON), Roanoke - IBF

21.10.89 Jose Ruiz (PR) W RSC 12 Angel Rosario (PR), San Juan - WBO

31.10.89 Kaosai Galaxy (TH) W CO 12 Kenji Matsumara (JAP), Kobe - WBA

07.11.89 Nana Yaw Konadu (GH) W PTS 12 Gilberto Roman (MEX), Mexico City - WBC

20.01.90 Sung-Il Moon (SK) W PTS 12 Nana Yaw Konadu (GH), Seoul - WBC

29.03.90 Kaosai Galaxy (TH) W CO 5 Ari Blanca (PH), Bangkok - WBA

21.04.90 Robert Quiroga (USA) W PTS 12 Juan Polo Perez (COL), The Crowtree Leisure Centre, Sunderland - IBF

09.06.90 Sung-Il Moon (SK) W RTD 8 Gilberto Roman (MEX), Seoul - WBC

30.06.90 Kaosai Galaxy (TH) W RSC 8 Schunichi Nakajima (JAP), Chiang Mai - WBA

18.08.90 Jose Ruiz (PR) W RSC 8 Wilfredo Vargas (PR), Ponce - WBO

29.09.90 Kaosai Galaxy (TH) W CO 6 Yong-Kang Kim (SK), Suphan Buri - WBA

03.11.90 Jose Ruiz (PR) W PTS 12 Armando Velasco (MEX), Acapulco - WBO

06.10.90 Robert Quiroga (USA) W RTD 3 Vuyani Nene (SA), Benevento - IBF

20.10.90 Sung-Il Moon (SK) W TD 5 Kenji Matsumura (JAP), Seoul - WBC. *Ahead on all three judges' scorecards at the time of the stoppage, Moon had sustained cuts through clumsy headwork by the challenger as early as the third round. However, during the interval between the fifth and sixth rounds, the doctor deemed the damage too serious for him to continue and he was returned the winner.*

09.12.90 Kaosai Galaxy (TH) W CO 6 Ernesto Ford (PAN), Petchabun - WBA

26.01.91 Robert Quiroga (USA) W PTS 12 Vincenzo Belcastro (ITA), Capo d'Orlando - IBF

16.03.91 Sung-Il Moon (SK) W RSC 4 Nana Yaw Konadu (GH), Zaragoza - WBC

06.04.91 Kaosai Galaxy (TH) W RSC 5 Jae-Suk Park (SK), Samut Songkram - WBA

15.06.91 Robert Quiroga (USA) W PTS 12 Akeem Anifowashe (N), San Antonio - IBF

20.07.91 Kaosai Galaxy (TH) W RSC 5 David Griman (VEN), Bangkok - WBA

20.07.91 Sung-Il Moon (SK) W CO 5 Ernesto Ford (PAN), Seoul - WBC

22.12.91 Kaosai Galaxy (TH) W PTS 12 Armando Castro (MEX), Bangkok - WBA. *Kaosai Galaxy retired in January 1992.*

22.12.91 Sung-Il Moon (SK) W RSC 6 Torsak Pongsupa (TH), Inchon - WBC

15.02.92 Robert Quiroga (USA) W PTS 12 Carlos Mercardo (COL), Salerno - IBF

22.02.92 Jose Quirino (MEX) W PTS 12 Jose Ruiz (PR), Las Vegas - WBO

10.04.92 Katsuya Onizuka (JAP) W PTS 12 Thalerngsak Sitbobay (TH), Tokyo - WBA

04.07.92 Sung-Il Moon (SK) W RSC 8 Armando Salazar (MEX), Inchon - WBC

11.07.92 Robert Quiroga (USA) W PTS 12 Jose Ruiz (PR), Las Vegas - IBF

04.09.92 Johnny Bredahl (DEN) W PTS 12 Jose Quirino (MEX), Copenhagen - WBO

11.09.92 Katsuya Onizuka (JAP) W RSC 5 Kenichi Matsumura (JAP), Tokyo - WBA

31.10.92 Sung-Il Moon (SK) W PTS 12 Greg Richardson (USA), Seoul - WBC

11.12.92 Katsuya Onizuka (JAP) W PTS 12 Armando Castro (MEX), Tokyo - WBA

16.01.93 Julio Cesar Borboa (MEX) W RSC 12 Robert Quiroga (USA), San Antonio - IBF

27.02.93 Sung-Il Moon (SK) W RSC 1 Hilario Zapata (PAN), Seoul - WBC

26.03.93 Johnny Bredahl (DEN) W PTS 12 Rafael Caban (PR), Copenhagen - WBO

21.05.93 Katsuya Onizuka (JAP) W PTS 12 Jae-Shin Lim (SK), Tokyo - WBA

22.05.93 Julio Cesar Borboa (MEX) W PTS 12 Joel Luna Zarate (MEX), Mexico City - IBF

Bantamweight (118 lbs)

Named after the bantam cock, a ferocious bird from the illegal sport of cock-fighting, the weight class goes right back to the days of the London Prize Ring. However, the earliest recorded information only dates back to 1856, when an American bare-fist fighter, Charles Lynch, weighing around 112 lbs, came to England to fight Simon Finighty. After 95 rounds, Finighty was declared the winner, but then lost the title after 43 rounds of a return engagement in November 1859. Interest in the division then lapsed, until another American, Tommy Kelly, who scaled around 105 lbs, claimed the title in 1887. Although he was knocked out in eight rounds by Hughey Boyle on 24 December 1887 (New York City), the victor disappeared from the scene and Kelly reclaimed the title. At that time his claim was disputed by a young Canadian, George Dixon, but after the pair had fought a nine round draw in Boston on 10 May 1888, and with the position still unresolved, they went their separate ways. Kelly lost his share of the title to Chappie Moran (GB), after a ten round points decision went against him on 5 June 1889 in Brooklyn, but won it back by knocking his rival out in the tenth on 31 January 1890 in New York City. He then successfully defended at the same venue against Benny Murphy (USA), following a three round knockout on 5 March 1890. Meanwhile, Dixon, by now scaling around 115 lbs, was fighting among the featherweights, leaving the way clear for Kelly to consolidate his position and when the newly crowned British champion, Billy Plimmer, arrived in America throwing out challenges, the pair were matched to contest the bantamweight title at 110 lbs.

09.05.92 **Billy Plimmer** (GB) W CO 10 Tommy Kelly (USA), Coney Island. *Weights (lbs): Plimmer (108), Kelly (108½).*

28.12.92 **Billy Plimmer** (GB) W RSC 8 Joe McGrath (USA), Coney Island *(110 lbs).*

15.09.94 Jimmy Barry (USA) W CO 28 Casper Leon (USA), Lamont. *Recorded in early record books as a title fight, it was, effectively, for the American version of the world 106 lbs championship.*

24.09.94 **Billy Plimmer** (GB) DREW 25 Johnny Murphy (USA), New Orleans. *Although shown as a world title fight in the Ring Record Book, a statement backed up by the New Orleans Daily Picayune (newspaper), who reported on it as such, with Plimmer's title winning weight standing at 110 lbs, it was contested at 115 lbs. Weights (lbs): Plimmer (114½), Murphy (114¾).*

26.11.94 **Billy Plimmer** (GB) W CO 3 Charley Kelly (USA), Coney Island. *According to the Philadelphia Item (newspaper) report of the day, the championship was at stake in a match made at 114lbs. However, with the recognised weight limit standing at 110 lbs, it would not have been generally considered a title fight.*

30.03.95 Jimmy Barry (USA) NC 14 Casper Leon (USA), Chicago. *Barry was defending the American version of the 106 lbs title.*

28.05.95 **Billy Plimmer** (GB) W CO 7 George Corfield (GB), NSC, London *(110 lbs).*

21.10.95 Jimmy Barry (USA) W CO 4 Jack Madden (USA), Maspeth. *Although Barry successfully defended the American version of the 106 lbs title in this fight, it would soon be recognised that he was, by now, just too light to make a challenge for the "popular" championship.*

25.11.95 **Pedlar Palmer** (GB) W DIS 14 Billy Plimmer (GB), London. *Under the auspices of the NSC, the match was made and accepted at 112 lbs, an increase of two pounds on Plimmer's last defence.*

12.10.96 **Pedlar Palmer** (GB) W PTS 20 Johnny Murphy (USA), NSC, London. *With Palmer growing fast, the NSC set the weight for this match at 116 lbs.*

25.01.97 **Pedlar Palmer** (GB) W RSC 14 Ernie Stanton (USA), NSC, London. *Weights (lbs): Palmer (115½), Stanton (116).*

30.01.97 Jimmy Barry (USA) DREW 20 Sammy Kelly (USA), New York City. *Another successful defence of the American version of the world 106/108 lbs title for Barry.*

09.03.97 Sammy Kelly (USA) W CO 20 Billy Plimmer (GB), The Olympic Club, Birmingham. *With Palmer recognised as the lineal champion, this fight was advertised as being for the world 115 lbs title. However, while not recognised anywhere else in Britain, Kelly used his victory as a springboard into the next weight class.*

18.10.97 **Pedlar Palmer** (GB) W PTS 20 Dave Sullivan (USA), NSC, London. *Although recorded as a title fight by the Ring Record Book and billed as one, in a match made at 116 lbs, Palmer scaled 115½, while Sullivan came in over the weight at 118.*

06.12.97 Jimmy Barry (USA) W CO 20 Walter Croot (GB), NSC, London. *With Palmer defending the "popular" title at 116 lbs, Barry won*

the vacant 108 lbs bantamweight crown in this fight. Unfortunately, though, there was a tragic aftermath when Croot failed to regain consciousness and died.

30.05.98 Jimmy Barry (USA) DREW 20 Casper Leon (USA), New York City. *A defence of the world 108 lbs title.*

12.12.98 **Pedlar Palmer** (GB) W RSC 17 Billy Plimmer (GB), NSC, London. *Weights (lbs): Palmer (116), Plimmer (115).*

29.12.98 Jimmy Barry (USA) DREW 20 Casper Leon (USA), Davenport. *This successful defence of his 108 lbs title proved to be Barry's penultimate fight and he retired in September 1899.*

17.04.99 **Pedlar Palmer** (GB) W RSC 3 Billy Rotchford (USA), NSC, London. *Weights (lbs): Palmer (115½), Rotchford (115).*

12.09.99 **Terry McGovern** (USA) W CO 1 Pedlar Palmer (GB), Tuckahoe. *Weights (lbs) McGovern (115½), Palmer (113½).*

09.10.99 **Terry McGovern** (USA) W CO 1 Billy Rotchford (USA), Chicago. *Another fight occasionally shown as a title bout, was, in fact, just a six rounder. Paul Zabala (boxing historian), who researched the Chicago Tribune (newspaper) for this period, gave no indication that the championship was involved, although it is more than possible that Rotchford made the weight.*

22.12.99 **Terry McGovern** (USA) W CO 2 Harry Forbes (USA), New York City. *Although recorded in the Boxing News Annual as a title fight, it was contested at 118 lbs, way above the weight limit at that time. By now, McGovern was growing fast and in January 1900 he became world featherweight champion.*

12.03.00 Dan Dougherty (USA) W CO 10 Steve Flanagan (USA), Brooklyn. *Following his victory in a match made at 105 lbs, Dougherty claimed the world bantamweight title at that weight.*

26.05.00 Dan Dougherty (USA) W PTS 20 Tommy Feltz (USA), Brooklyn. *Although shown in the Ring Record Book as a championship fight, with Dougherty weighing 110 lbs and Feltz 106, the Philadelphia Item (newspaper) report does not indicate that a title was involved.*

04.08.00 Dan Dougherty (USA) W PTS 25 Tommy Feltz (USA), Brooklyn. *Billed as a title fight at 108 lbs, with other men around with equally good claims, this would have been viewed as an eliminating contest.*

06.09.00 Harry Forbes (USA) DREW 20 Casper Leon (USA), St Joseph. *While recorded in the Boxing News Annual as a title bout, the Philadelphia Item (newspaper) report does not indicate that it was. However, with Forbes recognised as a leading claimant, the fight should be given some credence.*

18.03.01 Harry Harris (USA) W PTS 15 Pedlar Palmer (GB), NSC, London. *Unable to agree terms with Harry Ware, instead, Harris took on Palmer in a match made at 115 lbs. Although shown in the Ring Record Book as a title bout, prior to the 1986 edition, it was not announced from the ring as such. As it was, Harris had great difficulty making the weight and declared afterwards that he would not enter into any future engagement under 118 lbs.*

02.04.01 Harry Forbes (USA) W RSC 15 Casper Leon (USA), Memphis. *Yet another fight for Forbes, recorded in the Boxing News Annual as a title bout, that was not indicated as being one in the Philadelphia Item (newspaper) report of the day. Eventually, however, while not recognised in Britain, Forbes would meet Dan Dougherty for the American version of the vacant 115 lbs title.*

29.05.01 Dan Dougherty (USA) W PTS 10 Kid McFadden (USA), San Francisco. *Prior to the fight, Terry McGovern, the featherweight champion, proclaimed his sparring partner, Dougherty, as his successor and stipulated that the title weight should be set at 115 lbs at ringside. Surprisingly, not scheduled for 20 rounds, Dougherty v McFadden, although advertised for the world 115 lbs title, was merely a supporting contest to McGovern v Aurelio Herrera.*

11.11.01 Harry Forbes (USA) W CO 2 Dan Dougherty (USA), St Louis - USA *(115 lbs).*

23.01.02 Harry Forbes (USA) W CO 4 Dan Dougherty (USA), St Louis - USA *(115 lbs).*

27.02.02 Harry Forbes (USA) W PTS 15 Tommy Feltz (USA), St Louis - USA. *Although Forbes had already defeated Dan Dougherty to become the American 115 lbs champion, the Mirror of Life indicated that following his victory over Feltz, full recognition was forthcoming.*

01.05.02 Harry Forbes (USA) DREW 20 Johnny Reagan (USA), St Louis - USA. *The Chicago Daily Tribune (newspaper) report stated that both men weighed in safely under the 115 lbs demanded by the Articles of Agreement. The Tribune also went on to say that Forbes held the American version of the title. Bearing all that in mind, one must assume that Forbes' 115 lbs title was on the line for this one.*

23.12.02 Harry Forbes (USA) W RSC 7 Frankie Neil (USA), Oakland - USA. *According to the San Francisco Chronicle (newspaper) report on the title fight, Forbes struggled to make the required 115 lbs, while Neil was well inside.*

27.02.03 Harry Forbes (USA) W PTS 10 Andrew Tokell (GB), Detroit - USA. *Early Ring Record Books tell us that this fight, made at 115 lbs with both men on the weight, finally unified the title. However, Tokell was not even the recognised British champion, an honour which was in the possession of Harry Ware, a man who had been claiming the world 114 lbs title after his repeated challenges to all the leading Americans had gone unheeded.*

24.03.03 Harry Forbes (USA) W CO 9 Johnny Kelly (USA), New Orleans. *Having his first contest since defeating Andrew Tokell, Forbes met Kelly over ten rounds at 118 lbs (three pounds above the class limit), but with the latter coming in below 115 lbs and announced as the challenger, according to the New Orleans Daily Picayune (newspaper) report, had he lost, the champion may well have forfeited his title.*

13.08.03 Frankie Neil (USA) W CO 2 Harry Forbes (USA), San Francisco - USA. *Following the guidelines covered by the Articles of Agreement, both men were inside the requisite 116 lbs.*

04.09.03 Frankie Neil (USA) W CO 15 Billy de Coursey (USA), Los Angeles - USA. *Recorded in the Ring Record Book as a defence of Neil's 115 lbs title, according to the Los Angeles Daily Times (newspaper) report, both were inside 115 lbs ringside for what turned out to be a great championship contest.*

16.10.03 Frankie Neil (USA) DREW 20 Johnny Reagan (USA), Los Angeles - USA. *Although no weights were given in the Los Angeles Daily Times (newspaper) report of the (billed) title fight, the previous day the paper had quoted Reagan as saying that he had got down to 112 lbs and expected to be inside 115 lbs on the night. Meanwhile, on the other side of the Atlantic, Joe Bowker, who had cleared up the British title confusion by beating Harry Ware (114 lbs) and Andrew Tokell (116 lbs) and after successfully defending against Bill King (116 lbs), was matched for the world 116 lbs title against Al Fellows, a man described as the unbeaten American 112 lbs champion.*

09.11.03 Joe Bowker (GB) W RTD 9 Al Fellows (USA), NSC, London - GB *(116 lbs).*

18.04.04 Digger Stanley (GB) W PTS 15 Jimmy Walsh (USA), NSC, London. *Not recognised as being for the "popular" title, with the fight contested at 112 lbs.*

27.05.04 Frankie Neil (USA) W CO 1 Tommy Moore (USA), Chicago - USA. *Although shown in early record books as being a title defence, it was not, with Chicago unable to stage anything more than six rounders. But, with Moore purportedly making the weight, Neil's title was undoubtedly at risk.*

30.05.04 Joe Bowker (GB) W PTS 20 Owen Moran (GB), NSC, London. *Advertised as an English bantamweight title defence at 116 lbs, Bowker also held the British version of the world championship at that weight and that would have been at stake as well.*

06.06.04 Digger Stanley (GB) DREW 15 Jimmy Walsh (USA), NSC, London. *A return match for the British version of the 112 lbs title.*

17.06.04 Frankie Neil (USA) W CO 3 Harry Forbes (USA), Chicago - USA. *As in Neil v Moore, the same conditions applied.*

17.10.04 **Joe Bowker** (GB) W PTS 20 Frankie Neil (USA), NSC, London. *Although weighing 116½ lbs to Bowker's 116, on arriving back in America, Neil continued to claim the title at 115 lbs (ringside), even though he was, by now, campaigning as a featherweight. However, Bowker was generally recognised, even in America.*

23.01.05 Owen Moran (GB) W PTS 20 Digger Stanley (GB), NSC, London. *With Joe Bowker recognised as the bantamweight champion at 116 lbs, this fight was billed as being for the 114 lbs title.*

29.03.05 Jimmy Walsh (USA) ND-W RSC 6 Monte Attell (USA), Philadelphia. *Although recorded in the Boxing News Annual as a title fight, it was merely a no-decision affair. Bearing in mind that Joe Bowker was recognised on both sides of the Atlantic as the lineal champion, but had recently fought at featherweight, Walsh laid claim to the American version of the title.*

23.05.05 Jimmy Walsh (USA) W PTS 15 Willie Gibbs (USA), Chelsea, Mass. *Another bout recorded as title fight by the Boxing News Annual, yet according to the Boston Herald and Post (newspaper) reports, there was no mention that any championship was involved.*

29.05.05 **Joe Bowker** (GB) W PTS 20 Pinky Evans (USA), NSC, London. *Immediately after his victory over Evans (115 lbs), Bowker (116 lbs) followed up his British featherweight championship success against Pedlar Palmer by moving into the nine stone division on a more permanent basis and the title was claimed by Jimmy Walsh, Digger Stanley and Owen Moran.*

20.10.05 Jimmy Walsh (USA) W PTS 15 Digger Stanley (GB), Chelsea. *Recorded as a title fight in the Ring Record Book, with both men inside 116 lbs, according to the Boston Post (newspaper) report, the bantamweight crown was not at stake as Frankie Neil was still recognised as the American champion. However, that did not stop*

Walsh continuing to claim the title before moving up to challenge for the featherweight crown in October 1906.

02.11.05 Owen Moran (GB) W CO Al Fellows (USA), The Gymnastic Club, Liverpool. *Although billed as a title bout at 116 lbs by the promoter, the contest was of 20 x two minute rounds duration, only, and was not generally recognised.*

20.01.06 Digger Stanley (GB) W PTS 20 Ike Bradley (GB), Ginnett's Circus, Newcastle. *In yet another fight billed as a championship contest in Britain, this time at 112 lbs, Stanley emerged the winner.*

13.12.06 Digger Stanley (GB) W PTS 20 Ike Bradley (GB), The Gymnastic Club, Liverpool. *For the second time in a year, Stanley met Bradley in a fight advertised as being for the world title at 114 lbs, but still recognition was not forthcoming. Even though Stanley had a victory over Walsh, his claim was overruled by the NSC, who were forced to remind him that he had earlier lost to Owen Moran and that the Birmingham man would be their representative in an international title match against Al Delmont.*

01.03.07 Kid Murphy (USA) W PTS 10 Johnny Coulon (C), Milwaukee. *With the "popular" bantamweight title being contested at 116 lbs, Murphy, following in the footsteps of Jimmy Barry, claimed the 105 lbs championship following his victory.*

22.04.07 Owen Moran (GB) W PTS 20 Al Delmont (USA), NSC, London - GB. *That was the last time Moran made 116 lbs and next time out he had moved up to 120 lbs, prior to challenging Abe Attell for the featherweight title.*

06.06.07 Al Delmont (USA) W DIS 17 Digger Stanley (GB), The Gymnastic Club, Liverpool. *Billed as title fight at 116 lbs, maybe, but not recognised as one, it was simply seen as a defence of Stanley's already weakened claim.*

08.01.08 Johnny Coulon (C) W PTS 10 Kid Murphy (USA), Peoria. *Billed for the 105 lbs title.*

29.01.08 Johnny Coulon (C) W PTS 10 Kid Murphy (USA), Peoria. *Billed for the 105 lbs title.*

20.02.08 Johnny Coulon (C) W CO 9 Cooney Kelly (USA), Peoria. *Billed for the 105 lbs title.*

13.03.08 Johnny Coulon (C) W PTS 10 Young Terry McGovern (USA), Peoria. *According to the Los Angeles Times (newspaper) report, this was a defence of Coulon's paperweight (light-bantamweight) title. Made at 105 lbs, Coulon weighed 103½ to McGovern's 104.*

26.06.08 Jimmy Walsh (USA) W CO 11 Jimmy Carroll (USA), San Francisco. *Although the Boxing News Annual stated that Walsh reclaimed the title at 116 lbs after this result, there was nothing in the Philadelphia Item or San Francisco Chronicle (newspaper) reports to suggest that was the case.*

09.10.08 Jimmy Walsh (USA) W PTS 15 Young Britt (USA), Baltimore. *As in Walsh v Carroll, it was logged in the Boxing News Annual as a title fight, but there was nothing in the Philadelphia Item (newspaper) report to indicate that the championship was involved.*

21.12.08 Jimmy Walsh (USA) DREW 15 Monte Attell (USA), San Francisco. *Again recorded in the Boxing News Annual as a title fight, with nothing in the Philadelphia Item or San Francisco Chronicle (newspaper) reports to suggest that it was.*

11.02.09 Johnny Coulon (C) ND-W RTD 5 Kid Murphy (USA), New York City. *Although a no-decision contest, Coulon's 105 lbs title was at stake, with Murphy making the weight.*

22.02.09 Monte Attell (USA) W PTS 20 Jimmy Reagan (USA), San Francisco. *Reported in the San Francisco Chronicle (newspaper) as an eliminating contest for the championship held by Johnny Coulon, with both men announced as being inside 115 lbs, it was the heavy bantamweight crown that Attell was claiming, not the latter's 105 lbs crown.*

24.05.09 Jimmy Walsh (USA) DREW 15 Digger Stanley (GB), NSC, London. *After failing to further consolidate his title aspirations, Walsh once more moved up to the featherweight division. Following that decision, Monte Attell upped his claim to the title, while Britain supported Digger Stanley and Joe Bowker.*

19.06.09 Monte Attell (USA) W RSC 18 Frankie Neil (USA), San Francisco - USA *(116 lbs).*

12.10.09 Monte Attell (USA) ND-L PTS 10 Danny Webster (USA), Los Angeles - USA. *Following the fight, Webster was presented with a championship belt after being awarded the "press" decision.*

23.11.09 Monte Attell (USA) ND-DREW 10 Danny Webster (USA), Los Angeles - USA. *Attell's claim to the USA 116 lbs "popular" bantamweight title was again at stake.*

17.12.09 Monte Attell (USA) DREW 20 Danny Webster (USA), San Francisco - USA *(116 lbs).*

29.01.10 Johnny Coulon (C) W CO 9 Earl Denning (USA), New Orleans. *Again billed as a defence of his bantamweight title, although Coulon had by now raised the weight limit to 112 lbs.*

14.02.10 Digger Stanley (GB) DREW 20 Young Pierce (USA), NSC, London. *Following this contest, which ended in stalemate, Joe Bowker knocked out Frenchman, Jean Audony, inside eight rounds at the club on 7 March 1910, and went forward to meet Stanley to decide Britain's version of the world championship at 118 lbs.*

19.02.10 Johnny Coulon (C) W PTS 10 Jim Kenrick (GB), New Orleans. *Another successful defence of Coulon's title at 112 lbs and at this stage of his career he claimed the newly formed flyweight championship. However, he changed his mind and made the decision to eventually challenge for the "popular" title, then standing at 116 lbs.*

22.02.10 Frankie Conley (USA) W RTD 42 Monte Attell (USA), Los Angeles - USA. *Scheduled for 42 rounds, both men scaled inside the required 116 lbs at 10.0 a.m. on the day of the fight.*

06.03.10 Johnny Coulon (C) W CO 19 Jim Kenrick (GB), New Orleans. *Billed as a title fight over 20 rounds, just two weeks after the pair met at 112 lbs, both men were inside the contracted 115 lbs ringside.*

17.10.10 Digger Stanley (GB) W CO 8 Joe Bowker (GB), NSC, London - GB. *Under the auspices of the NSC, the weights for this contest were set at 118 lbs. However, with the fight not recognised in America, it would not be until 1915 that the weight limit on both sides of the Atlantic would stand at 118 lbs, where it has remained until this day.*

05.12.10 Digger Stanley (GB) W PTS 20 Johnny Condon (GB), The Ring, London - GB *(118 lbs).*

19.12.10 Johnny Coulon (C) NC 5 Earl Denning (USA), Memphis. *Following this successful defence at 115 lbs, Coulon moved up to challenge Conley for the 116 lbs version of the title.*

26.02.11 Johnny Coulon (C) W PTS 20 Frankie Conley (USA), New Orleans - USA. *(116 lbs).*

28.03.11 Johnny Coulon (C) ND-W PTS 10 Harry Forbes (USA), Kenosha - USA

14.09.11 Digger Stanley (GB) W PTS 20 Ike Bradley (GB), The Stadium, Liverpool - GB. *Weights (lbs): Stanley (115½), Bradley (116½).*

22.01.12 Johnny Coulon (C) ND-W CO 3 Harry Forbes (USA), Kenosha - USA. *Forbes weighed 115 lbs.*

03.02.12 Johnny Coulon (C) W PTS 20 Frankie Conley (USA), Los Angeles - USA. *Weights (lbs): Coulon (112), Conley (116).*

18.02.12 Johnny Coulon (C) W PTS 20 Frankie Burns (USA), New Orleans - USA. *Weights (lbs): Coulon (111), Burns (116).*

22.04.12 Digger Stanley (GB) W PTS 20 Charles Ledoux (FR), London - GB/IBU. *Weights (lbs): Stanley (115½), Ledoux (116½).*

23.06.12 Charles Ledoux (FR) W CO 7 Digger Stanley (GB), Dieppe - GB/IBU *(118 lbs).*

02.07.12 Johnny Coulon (C) ND-W PTS 10 Young Wagner (USA), New York City - USA

16.10.12 Charles Ledoux (FR) W DIS 7 Georges Gaillard (FR), Paris. *Recorded in the Boxing News Annual as a GB/IBU title defence for Ledoux, it was not fought under championship conditions, with first Ledoux, then Gaillard, refusing to weigh-in.*

18.10.12 Johnny Coulon (C) ND-L PTS 10 Kid Williams (USA), New York City - USA

23.06.13 Johnny Coulon (C) ND-W PTS 10 Frankie Burns (USA), Kenosha - USA

24.06.13 Eddie Campi (USA) W PTS 20 Charles Ledoux (FR), Los Angeles. *Billed as a championship fight at 116 lbs, Campi claimed the IBU version of the title on the result.*

15.07.13 Kid Williams (USA) W RSC 16 Charles Ledoux (FR), Los Angeles. *With Ledoux still smarting over his defeat at the hands of Eddie Campi less than three weeks earlier, he met Williams in yet another billed title fight at 116 lbs. Although the title tag was almost meaningless, it was a further step up the ladder for Williams.*

10.10.13 Eddie Campi (USA) DREW 15 Frankie Burns (USA), Denver. *There was nothing in the San Francisco Chronicle (newspaper) to suggest that the above was a championship fight, but with Campi holding the European version of the 116 lbs title and Burns being a natural bantam, it is probably safe to assume that both men were inside 116 lbs and had the latter won he would have claimed same. However, Campi's next contest, a 20 round points win over Benny Chavez on 4 November 1913 (Los Angeles), was made at 118 lbs and did not involve the title.*

31.01.14 Kid Williams (USA) W CO 12 Eddie Campi (USA), Los Angeles. *By his victory, Williams won the IBU version of the title at 116 lbs and was booked to fight Coulon in a unifying contest.*

09.06.14 **Kid Williams** (USA) W CO 3 Johnny Coulon (C), Los Angeles. *Both men weighed 116 lbs.*

30.06.14 **Kid Williams** (USA) ND-W PTS 10 Pete Herman (USA), New Orleans. *Having his first contest since beating Johnny Coulon,*

Williams, at 116 lbs, risked his newly won title against Pete Herman who weighed in at 114 lbs.

28.09.14 **Kid Williams** (USA) ND-W CO 4 Kid Herman (USA), Philadelphia

25.12.14 **Kid Williams** (USA) ND-W PTS 10 Johnny Daly (USA), New York City

24.07.15 **Kid Williams** (USA) ND-W PTS 10 Jimmy Taylor (USA), Baltimore

10.09.15 **Kid Williams** (USA) ND-L DIS 5 Johnny Ertle (USA), St Paul. *Following a no-decision contest, Williams' right to the title was disputed by Ertle after the champion had been disqualified for persistently landing low blows. Although Ertle (112 lbs) had made the weight, his claim was not taken too seriously as Williams successfully argued that because the contest had taken place in a State where decisions were prohibitied, he could not legally be disqualified.*

28.10.15 **Kid Williams** (USA) ND-L PTS 8 Pal Moore (USA), Memphis

06.12.15 **Kid Williams** (USA) DREW 20 Frankie Burns (USA), New Orleans. *With this fight, the weight class in America fell into line with the British at 118 lbs. For the record, Williams scaled 117¼ to Burns' 118.*

07.02.16 **Kid Williams** (USA) DREW 20 Pete Herman (USA), New Orleans

09.01.17 **Pete Herman** (USA) W PTS 20 Kid Williams (USA), New Orleans

13.06.17 **Pete Herman** (USA) ND-L PTS 6 Kid Williams (USA), Philadelphia

05.11.17 **Pete Herman** (USA) W PTS 20 Frankie Burns (USA), New Orleans

10.04.18 Pal Moore (USA) W PTS 15 Johnny Ertle (USA), Baltimore. *Although Pete Herman was generally recognised, it did not stop Moore self-styling himself as champion following his victory over Ertle. However, his claim to the title evaporated on 4 June 1919 when he was beaten on points over 15 rounds at the NSC (London) by the world flyweight champion, Jimmy Wilde.*

03.07.18 Pete Herman (USA) ND-L PTS 10 Frankie Burns (USA), Jersey City

24.03.19 Pete Herman (USA) ND-L PTS 8 Pal Moore (USA), Memphis

04.07.19 Joe Burman (USA) ND-W CO 7 Pete Herman (USA), Benton Harbor. *Certain early record books record this fight as having taken place, but, according to the Ring Record Book, Herman received a ten round "press" draw against Dick Griffin at Fort Wayne on the same day and the above contest is not even acknowledged.*

01.03.20 Pete Herman (USA) ND-DREW 8 Earl Puryear (USA), Trenton

22.12.20 Joe Lynch (USA) W PTS 15 Pete Herman (USA), New York City

21.06.21 Joe Lynch (USA) W CO 1 Sammy Sandow (USA), New York City. *Occasionally shown as being a championship defence, in fact it was a non-title fight, with Lynch weighing 118½ lbs and Sandow 122¾.*

25.07.21 Pete Herman (USA) W PTS 15 Joe Lynch (USA), Brooklyn

23.09.21 **Johnny Buff** (USA) W PTS 15 Pete Herman (USA), New York City

10.11.21 **Johnny Buff** (USA) W PTS 15 Jackie Sharkey (USA), New York City

10.07.22 Joe Lynch (USA) W RTD 14 Johnny Buff (USA), New York City

22.12.22 Joe Lynch (USA) W PTS 15 Midget Smith (USA), New York City

04.04.23 Joe Lynch (USA) ND-W PTS 10 Midget Smith (USA), Chicago

19.10.23 Abe Goldstein (USA) W PTS 12 Joe Burman (USA), New York City. *Booked to defend his title against Burman, Lynch withdrew after being injured in an accident just two days before the contest was due to take place. Goldstein substituted and the NYSAC stated that Lynch would remain suspended in New York until he met the winner under full championship conditions. Early editions of the Ring Record Book confused the above fight as being for the New York version of the title.*

21.03.24 **Abe Goldstein** (USA) W PTS 15 Joe Lynch (USA), New York City

16.07.24 **Abe Goldstein** (USA) W PTS 15 Charles Ledoux (FR), New York City

08.09.24 **Abe Goldstein** (USA) W PTS 15 Tommy Ryan (USA), Long Island City

19.12.24 **Eddie Martin** (USA) W PTS 15 Abe Goldstein (USA), New York City

24.02.25 **Eddie Martin** (USA) ND-L PTS 12 Carl Tremaine (USA), Cleveland

20.03.25 **Charlie Rosenberg** (USA) W PTS 15 Eddie Martin (USA), New York City. *Amazingly, Rosenberg took off 39 lbs before coming into the ring weighing 116 lbs.*

23.07.25 **Charlie Rosenberg** (USA) W CO 4 Eddie Shea (USA), New York City. *After what appeared to most onlookers as having been a savage affair while it lasted, the NYSAC suspended Rosenberg indefinitely and Shea for life. It was rumoured that Shea's life had been threatened unless he "threw" the fight and with an armed gangster sitting at ringside, understandably, he did just that. Evidently, just to show who was boss, Shea went after Rosenberg for three rounds, giving him a real licking, and following a blistering exchange in the fourth, he made it "look good" when taking the full count. However, the Commissioner was not fooled, especially after a suspicious fluctuation in the odds just before the fight. Controversy was never far away when Rosenberg was around and during the preceeding weeks, he had once more been forced to drastically reduce in weight, this time by 23 lbs.*

02.03.26 **Charlie Rosenberg** (USA) ND-W PTS 10 George Butch (USA), St Louis. *Ring Record Books prior to 1986 had recognised the above as a title fight, but as a no-decision affair and at catchweights, it could not have been.*

04.02.27 **Charlie Rosenberg** (USA) W PTS 15 Bushy Graham (USA), New York City. *Somewhat surprisingly, Rosenberg had his suspension lifted for this fight, but then forfeited his title on the scales when weighing in at 122½ lbs. The fight went ahead as planned and had Graham won he would have been proclaimed champion. However, not only did Graham not win, but both men were suspended in New York for a year, following the discovery of a secret agreement regarding purse money. In the meantime, the Illinois Boxing Commission sanctioned a bout between Bud Taylor and Eddie Shea as being for their version of the title.*

24.02.27 Bud Taylor (USA) W PTS 10 Eddie Shea (USA), Chicago - ILLINOIS. *Following his victory, Taylor was matched against Tony Canzoneri for the NBA version of the title.*

26.03.27 Bud Taylor (USA) DREW 10 Tony Canzoneri (USA), Chicago - NBA

05.05.27 Teddy Baldock (GB) W PTS 15 Archie Bell (USA), Albert Hall, London - GB

24.06.27 Bud Taylor (USA) W PTS 10 Tony Canzoneri (USA), Chicago - NBA. *Bud Taylor never made a defence and, following a ten round non-title points defeat at the hands of Santiago Zorrilla on 27 July 1928 in San Francisco, he relinquished the NBA version of the title 26 days later due to increasing weight problems. He was then absent from the ring until January 1929.*

06.10.27 Willie Smith (SA) W PTS 15 Teddy Baldock (GB), Albert Hall, London - GB. *Teddy Baldock forfeited the British version on the scales when two pounds overweight. The contest went ahead and Smith claimed the title, following his victory. However, he gave up the opportunity of entering an elimination series when deciding to move into the featherweight division in January 1928. Shortly after this, Bushy Graham, who had finally served the 12 month suspension, was matched against Izzy Schwartz for New York's version of the title.*

23.05.28 Bushy Graham (USA) W PTS 15 Izzy Schwartz (USA), Brooklyn - NY. *In January 1929, Bushy Graham announced that he was relinquishing the New York version of the title in order to campaign as a featherweight, having earlier been outpointed over ten rounds by Fidel la Barba in a catchweight contest on 11 September 1928 (Los Angeles). La Barba himself then became yet another casualty of the weight making process and after Al Brown had eliminated two of the front runners, Kid Francis (on points over 12 rounds on 13 September 1928 in New York City) and the IBU champion, Domenico Bernasconi (on points over ten rounds on 24 March 1929 in Madrid), most organisations recognised the forthcoming New York championship match between Al Brown and Gregorio Vidal, who had kayoed Joey Scalfaro inside two rounds on 17 May 1929 (New York City), as being for the vacant title.*

18.06.29 **Al Brown** (PAN) W PTS 15 Gregorio Vidal (SP), Long Island City

28.08.29 **Al Brown** (PAN) W PTS 10 Knud Larsen (DEN), Copenhagen. *Shown in early record books as a title fight, the 1979 Boxing News Special stated that it could not have been, with the match made at 128 lbs in order to protect Larsen's European featherweight title.*

08.02.30 **Al Brown** (PAN) W DIS 4 Johnny Erickson (USA), New York City

04.10.30 **Al Brown** (PAN) W PTS 15 Eugene Huat (FR), Paris

11.02.31 **Al Brown** (PAN) W PTS 10 Nick Bensa (FR), Paris. *Although recorded in the Boxing News Annual as a title fight, it was not. Bensa was the current French featherweight champion and took Brown on at catchweights. In April 1931, with Brown remaining*

in Europe, he forfeited recognition in Canada when the Montreal Boxing Commission threw their weight behind Norwegian, Pete Sanstol, following his win over the country's leading bantam, Bobby Leitham.

20.05.31 Pete Sanstol (NOR) W PTS 10 Archie Bell (USA), Montreal - CANADA

17.06.31 Pete Sanstol (NOR) W PTS 15 Art Giroux (C), Montreal - CANADA

25.08.31 **Al Brown** (PAN) W PTS 15 Pete Sanstol (NOR), Montreal

27.10.31 **Al Brown** (PAN) W PTS 15 Eugene Huat (FR), Montreal

10.07.32 **Al Brown** (PAN) W PTS 15 Kid Francis (ITA), Marseilles. *Declared a no-contest after certain members of the audience took away the judges' scorecards, both of whom had voted for Brown, justice was finally served when the IBU awarded the contest to Brown the following day.*

19.09.32 **Al Brown** (PAN) W CO 1 Emile Pladner (FR), Toronto

12.10.32 Speedy Dado (PH) W PTS 10 Young Tommy (PH), Oakland - CALIFORNIA. *Initially billed as a State title fight, after defeating Tommy (116 lbs), Dado, who weighed the same, was pronounced world champion by the Californian Boxing Commission. A couple of months later, in February 1933, Dado was offered terms to meet Al Brown in Paris, but somehow agreement could not be reached and differences could not be resolved.*

18.03.33 Al Brown (PAN) W PTS 12 Dom Bernasconi (ITA), Milan - NBA/NY/IBU

19.05.33 Young Tommy (PH) W PTS 10 Speedy Dado (PH), San Francisco - CALIFORNIA

03.07.33 Al Brown (PAN) W PTS 15 Johnny King (GB), Belle Vue, Manchester - NBA/NY/IBU

24.10.33 Speedy Dado (PH) W PTS 10 Young Tommy (PH), Los Angeles - CALIFORNIA

05.12.33 Baby Casanova (MEX) W PTS 10 Speedy Dado (PH), Los Angeles - CALIFORNIA

19.02.34 Al Brown (PAN) W PTS 15 Young Perez (FR), Paris - NBA/NY/IBU

16.04.34 Al Brown (PAN) W PTS 10 Kid Francis (ITA), Paris. *Another contest recorded in certain annuals as a title fight for Brown that on inspection did not involve the championship and, as such, should be removed from the listings. A month later, Brown forfeited NBA recognition when failing to defend against the leading contender, Baby Casanova.*

07.05.34 Sixto Escobar (PR) W CO 8 Bobby Leitham (C), Holyoke. *Recorded in early Boxing News Annuals as a title fight that was not generally recognised, in fact, it was not even billed as such.*

05.06.34 Sixto Escobar (PR) W PTS 15 Joey Archibald (USA), Holyoke. *As in the fight above, it was recorded as a title fight in early Boxing News Annuals, but was not recognised as such.*

05.06.34 Sixto Escobar (PR) W RSC 5 Bobby Leitham (C), Montreal - CANADA. *Anxious to promote the claims of Leitham, the Montreal Boxing Commission threw their weight behind him and sanctioned a match between him and Escobar as being for their version of the title.*

24.06.34 Sixto Escobar (PR) W CO 9 Baby Casanova (MEX), Montreal - NBA

08.08.34 Sixto Escobar (PR) W PTS 15 Eugene Huat (FR), Montreal - NBA

01.11.34 Al Brown (PAN) W CO 10 Young Perez (FR), Tunis - NY/IBU. *On walking to his corner during the tenth round, claiming he had been fouled and that Brown should be disqualified, the referee ignored Perez' protestations and, after he refused to continue, counted him out.*

03.05.35 Lou Salica (USA) W PTS 10 Midget Wolgast (USA), Los Angeles - CALIFORNIA

01.06.35 Baltazar Sangchilli (SP) W PTS 15 Al Brown (PAN), Valencia - NY/IBU

11.06.35 Lou Salica (USA) W PTS 10 Pablo Dano (PH), Los Angeles - CALIFORNIA. *With the new titleholder, Sangchilli, campaigning in Europe, NY joined hands with the NBA in deciding to recognise the winner of the forthcoming American title fight between Lou Salica and Sixto Escobar as world champion.*

26.08.35 Lou Salica (USA) W PTS 15 Sixto Escobar (PR), New York City - NBA/NY

15.11.35 Sixto Escobar (PR) W PTS 15 Lou Salica (USA), New York City - NBA/NY

29.06.36 Tony Marino (USA) W CO 14 Baltazar Sangchilli (SP), New York City. *Sangchilli, who held the IBU version of the title, finally came to America to press his claim after the NYSAC persisted in not recognising him as champion. Although the Ring Magazine saw the Spaniard as the lineal champion, by dint of his victory over Al Brown, the fight could not be given title billing as New York already supported Sixto Escobar as their titleholder.*

31.08.36 **Sixto Escobar** (PR) W RSC 13 Tony Marino (USA), New York City

13.10.36 **Sixto Escobar** (PR) W CO 1 Carlos Quintana (PAN), New York City

21.02.37 **Sixto Escobar** (PR) W PTS 15 Lou Salica (USA), San Juan

23.09.37 **Harry Jeffra** (USA) W PTS 15 Sixto Escobar (PR), New York City

20.02.38 **Sixto Escobar** (PR) W PTS 15 Harry Jeffra (USA), San Juan. *Sixto Escobar forfeited IBU recognition in February 1938 when the authority decided to match Al Brown against Baltazar Sangchilli for their version of the title.*

04.03.38 Al Brown (PAN) W PTS 15 Baltazar Sangchilli (SP), Paris - IBU. *During an international boxing convention held in Rome in May 1938, the IBU agreed to refuse to recognise all individually-made world champions, including their own Al Brown, in an effort to stand by one universally recognised champion.*

27.08.38 Star Frisco (PH) W DIS 6 Mickey Miller (A), Newcastle - AUSTRALIA. *Outside of Australia, Frisco (116 lbs) was accorded no recognition whatsoever and his claim quickly disintegrated. In a match made over 15 rounds, Miller weighed 117½ lbs.*

02.04.39 **Sixto Escobar** (PR) W PTS 15 Kayo Morgan (USA), San Juan. *Sixto Escobar relinquished the title due to weight making difficulties, following a ten round points defeat at the hands of Tony Olivera (120 lbs) in Oakland on 4 October 1939. The NBA then proclaimed George Pace as their champion on 2 November 1939, having earlier ordered Escobar to meet the winner of the Henry Hook v Pace contest held in Cleveland on 1 March 1939, which had been won by the latter on points over ten rounds. While the NBA supported Pace, California matched Olivera against Salica for their version of the title.*

17.11.39 Lou Salica (USA) W PTS 10 Tony Olivera (USA), Los Angeles - CALIFORNIA

14.12.39 Tony Olivera (USA) W PTS 10 Lou Salica (USA), Los Angeles. *Although billed for the Californian version of the title, it could not be recognised as such with Olivera weighing 118¾ lbs.*

04.03.40 Lou Salica (USA) DREW 15 George Pace (USA), Toronto - NBA. *Having retained his title under the auspices of the NBA, Pace agreed to give Salica a rematch later in the year, this time in New York.*

24.04.40 Little Dado (PH) W PTS 10 Tony Olivera (USA), Oakland. *Often mistaken as a version of the world championship, it was for the Californian State and North American titles, only. However, at the same time, it was also recognised as a world title eliminator.*

24.09.40 **Lou Salica** (USA) W PTS 15 George Pace (USA), New York City

02.12.40 **Lou Salica** (USA) W RSC 3 Small Montana (PH), Toronto. *Not recorded in the Ring Record Book as a title fight, although shown as such in early post-war Boxing News Annuals, with Salica weighing 118 lbs and Montana scaling 114, it was a successful first defence for the champion according to the New York Times (newspaper) report.*

13.01.41 Lou Salica (USA) W PTS 15 Tommy Forte (USA), Philadelphia

24.01.41 Little Dado (PH) W PTS 10 Tony Olivera (USA), Honolulu. *Occasionally shown as being for the Hawaiian version of the world title, with Dado weighing 115 lbs to Olivera's 117½, the bout was advertised and recognised as an Hawaiian championship fight only.*

15.04.41 Kenny Lindsay (C) W PTS 10 Tony Olivera (USA), Vancouver - CANADA. *Advertised as a title fight in Canada, elsewhere it was seen as a travesty, with neither man considered to be the outstanding challenger at that given time.*

25.04.41 Lou Salica (USA) W PTS 15 Lou Transparenti (USA), Baltimore - NY/NBA

16.06.41 Lou Salica (USA) W PTS 15 Tommy Forte (USA), Philadelphia - NY/NBA.

02.01.42 Manuel Ortiz (USA) W PTS 10 Tony Olivera (USA), Los Angeles. *Recorded in some annuals as being for the Californian version of the title, is incorrect. Ortiz won the State title only, with California, at that point in time a member of the NBA, having joined on 7 September 1940, not empowered to create champions of their own volition.*

07.08.42 Manuel Ortiz (USA) W PTS 12 Lou Salica (USA), Los Angeles - NBA. *Because it was not contested over 15 rounds, the NYSAC refused to accept it as a title fight and continued to recognise Salica as champion.*

01.01.43 Manuel Ortiz (USA) W PTS 10 Kenny Lindsay (C), Portland - NBA

27.01.43 Manuel Ortiz (USA) W RSC 10 George Freitas (USA), Oakland - NBA

28.02.43 Kui Kong Young (HA) DREW 15 Rush Dalma (PH), Honolulu -

TBC. As the first 15 rounder on Hawaiian soil, it was recognised by the Territorial Boxing Commission as being for their version of the world title. Following the fight, although Young had been lucky to get a draw, the TBC supported him as champion on the grounds that Manuel Ortiz had refused to come to Hawaii to defend the NYSAC/NBA title against him.

10.03.43 Manuel Ortiz (USA) W RSC 11 Lou Salica (USA), Oakland - NY/NBA

28.04.43 Manuel Ortiz (USA) W CO 6 Lupe Cordoza (USA), Fort Worth - NY/NBA

02.05.43 Kui Kong Young (HA) W CO 8 Dado Marino (HA), Honolulu - TBC. *An Hawaiian title bout that was also recognised by the Territorial Boxing Commission as involving the world title, saw Young weighing 116¾ lbs to Marino's 116.*

26.05.43 Manuel Ortiz (USA) W PTS 15 Joe Robleto (USA), Los Angeles - NY/NBA

04.07.43 Kui Kong Young (HA) W RSC 8 Little Dado (PH), Honolulu - TBC. *Another successful defence of the Territorial Boxing Commission's version of the world title for Young who scaled 118 lbs to Dado's 117½.*

12.07.43 Manuel Ortiz (USA) W CO 7 Joe Robleto (USA), Seattle - NY/NBA

01.10.43 Manuel Ortiz (USA) W CO 4 Leonardo Lopez (USA), Los Angeles - NY/NBA

10.10.43 Rush Dalma (PH) W PTS 15 Kui Kong Young (HA), Honolulu - TBC. *The victim of several debatable decisions at the hands of Young (118), Dalma (116½) was finally rewarded for his perseverance.*

23.11.43 Manuel Ortiz (USA) W PTS 15 Benny Goldberg (USA), Los Angeles - NY/NBA

14.03.44 Manuel Ortiz (USA) W PTS 15 Ernesto Aguilar (MEX), Los Angeles - NY/NBA

04.04.44 Manuel Ortiz (USA) W PTS 15 Tony Olivera (USA), Los Angeles - NY/NBA

11.06.44 Rush Dalma (PH) W PTS 12 Kui Kong Young (HA), Honolulu - TBC. *Following a defeat at the hands of Willie James in Honolulu on 5 August 1945, Dalma retired.*

12.09.44 Manuel Ortiz (USA) W CO 4 Luis Castillo (MEX), Los Angeles - NY/NBA

14.11.44 Manuel Ortiz (USA) W RSC 9 Luis Castillo (MEX), Los Angeles - NY/NBA

25.02.46 **Manuel Ortiz** (USA) W CO 13 Luis Castillo (MEX), San Francisco

26.05.46 **Manuel Ortiz** (USA) W CO 5 Kenny Lindsay (C), Los Angeles

10.06.46 **Manuel Ortiz** (USA) W CO 11 Jackie Jurich (USA), San Francisco

06.01.47 **Harold Dade** (USA) W PTS 15 Manuel Ortiz (USA), San Francisco

11.03.47 **Manuel Ortiz** (USA) W PTS 15 Harold Dade (USA), Los Angeles

30.05.47 **Manuel Ortiz** (USA) W PTS 15 Kui Kong Young (HA), Honolulu

20.12.47 **Manuel Ortiz** (USA) W PTS 15 Tirso del Rosario (PH), Manila

04.07.48 **Manuel Ortiz** (USA) W RSC 8 Memo Valero (MEX), Mexicali

01.03.49 **Manuel Ortiz** (USA) W PTS 15 Dado Marino (HA), Honolulu

31.05.50 **Vic Toweel** (SA) W PTS 15 Manuel Ortiz (USA), Johannesburg

02.12.50 **Vic Toweel** (SA) W RTD 10 Danny O'Sullivan (GB), Johannesburg. *O'Sullivan was down 20 times in all before being forced to retire, a record for any weight class in a world title fight.*

17.11.51 **Vic Toweel** (SA) W PTS 15 Luis Romero (SP), Johannesburg

26.01.52 **Vic Toweel** (SA) W PTS 15 Peter Keenan (GB), Johannesburg

15.11.52 **Jimmy Carruthers** (A) W CO 1 Vic Toweel (SA), Johannesburg

21.03.53 **Jimmy Carruthers** (A) W CO 10 Vic Toweel (SA), Johannesburg

13.11.53 **Jimmy Carruthers** (A) W PTS 15 Pappy Gault (USA), Sydney

02.05.54 **Jimmy Carruthers** (A) W PTS 12 Chamrern Songkitrat (TH), Bangkok. *Come the announcement by Jimmy Carruthers in May 1954 that he was retiring, the World Championship Committee eventually selected Robert Cohen and Chamrern Songkitrat to contest the vacant title.*

19.09.54 **Robert Cohen** (FR) W PTS 15 Chamrern Songkitrat (TH), Bangkok. *The following day, Pierre Cossemyns of Belgium outpointed the Australian, Bobby Sinn, in Sydney. The fight had initially been billed for the Australian version of the world title and of 15 rounds duration. However, Cossemyns, who had already been informed by the World Boxing Commission that he would be meeting the winner of Cohen v Songkitrat, would not comply with the billing and successfully demanded that the distance be reduced to 12 rounds. Robert Cohen later forfeited*

NBA recognition when he failed to engage Raton Macias within 90 days of his victory over Songkitrat. Following that decision, Macias was matched with the Thai for the NBA version of the title.

09.03.55 Raton Macias (MEX) W RSC 11 Chamrern Songkitrat (TH), San Francisco - NBA

03.09.55 Robert Cohen (FR) DREW 15 Willie Toweel (SA), Johannesburg - NY/EBU

25.03.56 Raton Macias (MEX) W CO 10 Leo Espinosa (PH), Mexico City - NBA

29.06.56 Mario D'Agata (ITA) W RTD 6 Robert Cohen (FR), Rome - NY/EBU

01.04.57 Alphonse Halimi (FR) W PTS 15 Mario D'Agata (ITA), Paris - NY/EBU. *During the third round the lighting apparatus above the ring burst into flames and the deaf-mute, D'Agata, intimated with great difficulty that he had suffered burns, while Halimi kept fighting. Following a delay of 15 minutes, the fight went ahead and although the champion's manager protested with great vigour that a no-contest be declared, he was overruled by the officials in charge.*

15.06.57 Raton Macias (MEX) W RSC 11 Dommy Ursua (PH), San Francisco - NBA

06.11.57 **Alphonse Halimi** (FR) W PTS 15 Raton Macias (MEX), Los Angeles

08.07.59 **Joe Becerra** (MEX) W CO 8 Alphonse Halimi (FR), Los Angeles

04.02.60 **Joe Becerra** (MEX) W CO 9 Alphonse Halimi (FR), Los Angeles

23.05.60 **Joe Becerra** (MEX) W PTS 15 Kenji Yonekura (JAP), Tokyo. *Joe Becerra announced his retirement immediately after being knocked out in eight rounds by his compatriot, Eloy Sanchez, in Juarez on 30 August 1960. Shortly afterwards, Sanchez was matched against Eder Jofre, the South American champion, for the NBA version of the title, on the proviso that the winner would fight either Alphonse Halimi or Freddie Gilroy within 90 days. That was totally unacceptable in Europe and Halimi v Gilroy was given the blessing of the EBU as a world title bout in its own right.*

25.10.60 Alphonse Halimi (FR) W PTS 15 Freddie Gilroy (GB), The Arena, Wembley - EBU

18.11.60 Eder Jofre (BR) W CO 6 Eloy Sanchez (MEX), Los Angeles - NBA

25.03.61 Eder Jofre (BR) W RTD 9 Piero Rollo (ITA), Rio de Janeiro - NBA

30.05.61 Johnny Caldwell (GB) W PTS 15 Alphonse Halimi (FR), The Arena, Wembley - EBU

19.08.61 Eder Jofre (BR) W RSC 7 Ramon Arias (VEN), Caracas - NBA

31.10.61 Johnny Caldwell (GB) W PTS 15 Alphonse Halimi (FR), The Arena, Wembley - EBU

18.01.62 **Eder Jofre** (BR) W RTD 10 Johnny Caldwell (GB), Sao Paulo

04.05.62 **Eder Jofre** (BR) W RSC 10 Herman Marquez (USA), San Francisco

11.09.62 **Eder Jofre** (BR) W CO 6 Joe Medel (MEX), Sao Paulo

04.04.63 **Eder Jofre** (BR) W CO 3 Katsutoshi Aoki (JAP), Tokyo

18.05.63 **Eder Jofre** (BR) W RTD 11 Johnny Jamito (PH), Quezon City

27.11.64 **Eder Jofre** (BR) W CO 7 Bernardo Caraballo (COL), Bogota

17.05.65 **Fighting Harada** (JAP) W PTS 15 Eder Jofre (BR), Nagoya

30.11.65 **Fighting Harada** (JAP) W PTS 15 Alan Rudkin (GB), Tokyo

01.06.66 **Fighting Harada** (JAP) W PTS 15 Eder Jofre (BR), Tokyo

03.01.67 **Fighting Harada** (JAP) W PTS 15 Joe Medel (MEX), Nagoya

04.07.67 **Fighting Harada** (JAP) W PTS 15 Bernardo Caraballo (COL), Tokyo

26.02.68 **Lionel Rose** (A) W PTS 15 Fighting Harada (JAP), Tokyo

02.07.68 **Lionel Rose** (A) W PTS 15 Takao Sakurai (JAP), Tokyo

06.12.68 **Lionel Rose** (A) W PTS 15 Chuchu Castillo (MEX), Los Angeles

08.03.69 **Lionel Rose** (A) W PTS 15 Alan Rudkin (GB), Melbourne

22.08.69 **Ruben Olivares** (MEX) W CO 5 Lionel Rose (A), Los Angeles

12.12.69 **Ruben Olivares** (MEX) W RSC 2 Alan Rudkin (GB), Los Angeles

18.04.70 **Ruben Olivares** (MEX) W PTS 15 Chuchu Castillo (MEX), Los Angeles

16.10.70 **Chuchu Castillo** (MEX) W RSC 14 Ruben Olivares (MEX), Los Angeles

03.04.71 **Ruben Olivares** (MEX) W PTS 15 Chuchu Castillo (MEX), Los Angeles

25.10.71 **Ruben Olivares** (MEX) W RSC 14 Katsutoshi Kanazawa (JAP), Nagoya

14.12.71 **Ruben Olivares** (MEX) W RSC 11 Jesus Pimental (MEX), Los Angeles

19.03.72 **Rafael Herrera** (MEX) W CO 8 Ruben Olivares (MEX), Mexico City

30.07.72 **Enrique Pinder** (PAN) W PTS 15 Rafael Herrera (MEX),

Panama City. *Enrique Pinder forfeited WBC recognition in December 1972 after failing to defend against the leading challenger, Rodolfo Martinez, within the stipulated period. Following that announcement, the WBC matched Martinez against the man Pinder beat for the title, former champion, Rafael Herrera.*

20.01.73 Romeo Anaya (MEX) W CO 3 Enrique Pinder (PAN), Panama City - WBA

15.04.73 Rafael Herrera (MEX) W RSC 12 Rodolfo Martinez (MEX), Monterrey - WBC

28.04.73 Romeo Anaya (MEX) W PTS 15 Rogelio Lara (MEX), Los Angeles - WBA

18.08.73 Romeo Anaya (MEX) W CO 3 Enrique Pinder (PAN), Los Angeles - WBA

13.10.73 Rafael Herrera (MEX) W PTS 15 Venice Borkorsor (TH), Los Angeles - WBC

03.11.73 Arnold Taylor (SA) W CO 14 Romeo Anaya (MEX), Johannesburg - WBA

25.05.74 Rafael Herrera (MEX) W CO 6 Romeo Anaya (MEX), Mexico City - WBC

03.07.74 Soo-Hwan Hong (SK) W PTS 15 Arnold Taylor (SA), Durban - WBA

07.12.74 Rodolfo Martinez (MEX) W RSC 4 Rafael Herrera (MEX), Merida - WBC

28.12.74 Soo-Hwan Hong (SK) W PTS 15 Fernando Canabela (PH), Seoul - WBA

14.03.75 Alfonso Zamora (MEX) W CO 4 Soo-Hwan Hong (SK), Los Angeles - WBA

31.05.75 Rodolfo Martinez (MEX) W RSC 7 Nestor Jiminez (COL), Bogota - WBC

30.08.75 Alfonso Zamora (MEX) W CO 4 Thanomjit Sukhothai (TH), Los Angeles - WBA

08.10.75 Rodolfo Martinez (MEX) W PTS 15 Hisami Numata (JAP), Sendai - WBC

06.12.75 Alfonso Zamora (MEX) W CO 1 Socrates Batoto (PH), Mexico City - WBA

30.01.76 Rodolfo Martinez (MEX) W PTS 15 Venice Borkorsor (TH), Bangkok - WBC

03.04.76 Alfonso Zamora (MEX) W CO 2 Eusebio Pedroza (PAN), Mexicali - WBA

08.05.76 Carlos Zarate (MEX) W CO 9 Rodolfo Martinez (MEX), Los Angeles - WBC

10.07.76 Alfonso Zamora (MEX) W CO 3 Gilberto Illueca (PAN), Juarez - WBA

28.08.76 Carlos Zarate (MEX) W RSC 12 Paul Ferreri (A), Los Angeles - WBC

16.10.76 Alfonso Zamora (MEX) W RSC 12 Soo-Hwan Hong (SK), Inchon - WBA

13.11.76 Carlos Zarate (MEX) W CO 4 Waruinge Nakayama (K), Culiacan - WBC

05.02.77 Carlos Zarate (MEX) W RSC 3 Fernando Cabanela (PH), Mexico City - WBC

29.01.77 Carlos Zarate (MEX) W RSC 6 Danilio Batista (BR), Los Angeles - WBC

19.11.77 Jorge Lujan (PAN) W CO 10 Alfonso Zamora (MEX), Los Angeles - WBA

02.12.77 Carlos Zarate (MEX) W RSC 5 Juan Francisco Rodriguez (SP), Madrid - WBC

25.02.78 Carlos Zarate (MEX) W RSC 8 Albert Davila (USA), Los Angeles - WBC

18.03.78 Jorge Lujan (PAN) W RTD 11 Roberto Rubaldino (MEX), San Antonio - WBA

22.04.78 Carlos Zarate (MEX) W RSC 13 Andres Hernandez (PR), San Juan - WBC

09.06.78 Carlos Zarate (MEX) W CO 4 Emilio Hernandez (VEN), Las Vegas - WBC

15.09.78 Jorge Lujan (PAN) W PTS 15 Albert Davila (USA), New Orleans - WBA

10.03.79 Carlos Zarate (MEX) W CO 3 Mensah Kpalongo (TO), Los Angeles - WBC

08.04.79 Jorge Lujan (PAN) W RSC 15 Cleo Garcia (NIC), Las Vegas - WBA

02.06.79 Lupe Pintor (MEX) W PTS 15 Carlos Zarate (MEX), Las Vegas - WBC

06.10.79 Jorge Lujan (PAN) W CO 15 Roberto Rubaldino (MEX), McAllen - WBA

09.02.80 Lupe Pintor (MEX) W RSC 12 Alberto Sandoval (USA), Los Angeles - WBC

02.04.80 Jorge Lujan (PAN) W RSC 9 Shuichi Isogami (JAP), Tokyo - WBA

11.06.80 Lupe Pintor (MEX) DREW 15 Eijiro Murata (JAP), Tokyo - WBC

29.08.80 Julian Solis (PR) W PTS 15 Jorge Lujan (PAN), Miami - WBA

19.09.80 Lupe Pintor (MEX) W CO 12 Johnny Owen (GB), Los Angeles - WBC. *After being knocked out, Johnny Owen failed to regain consciousness and died in hospital 46 days later.*

14.11.80 Jeff Chandler (USA) W RSC 14 Julian Solis (PR), Miami - WBA

19.12.80 Lupe Pintor (MEX) W PTS 15 Albert Davila (USA), Las Vegas - WBC

31.01.81 Jeff Chandler (USA) W PTS 15 Jorge Lujan (PAN), Philadelphia - WBA

22.02.81 Lupe Pintor (MEX) W PTS 15 Jose Uziga (ARG), Houston - WBC

05.04.81 Jeff Chandler (USA) DREW 15 Eijiro Murata (JAP), Tokyo - WBA

25.07.81 Jeff Chandler (USA) W CO 7 Julian Solis (PR), Atlantic City - WBA

26.07.81 Lupe Pintor (MEX) W RSC 8 Jovito Rengifo (VEN), Las Vegas - WBC

22.09.81 Lupe Pintor (MEX) W CO 15 Hurricane Teru (JAP), Nagoya - WBC

10.12.81 Jeff Chandler (USA) W RSC 13 Eijiro Murata (JAP), Atlantic City - WBA

27.03.82 Jeff Chandler (USA) W RSC 6 Johnny Carter (USA), Philadelphia - WBA

03.06.82 Lupe Pintor (MEX) W RSC 11 Seung-Hoon Lee (SK), Los Angeles - WBC. *Lupe Pintor relinquished WBC title in July 1983 following a motor cycle accident.*

27.10.82 Jeff Chandler (USA) W RSC 9 Miguel Iriarle (PAN), Atlantic City - WBA

13.03.83 Jeff Chandler (USA) W PTS 15 Gaby Canizales (USA), Atlantic City - WBA

01.09.83 Albert Davila (USA) W CO 12 Kiko Bejines (MEX), Los Angeles - WBC. *Kiko Bejines was taken unconscious from the ring on a stretcher and, following an operation to remove a blood clot from his brain, died in hospital three days later.*

11.09.83 Jeff Chandler (USA) W RSC 10 Eijiro Murata (JAP), Tokyo - WBA

17.12.83 Jeff Chandler (USA) W RSC 7 Oscar Muniz (USA), Atlantic City - WBA

07.04.84 Richard Sandoval (USA) W RSC 15 Jeff Chandler (USA), Atlantic City - WBA

16.04.84 Satoshi Shingaki (JAP) W RSC 8 Elmer Magallano (PH), Kashiwara - IBF

26.05.84 Albert Davila (USA) W RSC 11 Enrique Sanchez (DOM), Miami - WBC. *Albert Davila forfeited WBC version of title in February 1985 due to inactivity.*

04.08.84 Satoshi Shingaki (JAP) W PTS 15 Joves de la Puz (PH), Naha City - IBF

22.09.84 Richard Sandoval (USA) W PTS 15 Edgar Roman (VEN), Monaco - WBA

15.12.84 Richard Sandoval (USA) W RSC 8 Cardenio Ulloa (CH), Miami - WBA

26.04.85 Jeff Fenech (A) W RSC 9 Satoshi Shingaki (JAP), Sydney - IBF

04.05.85 Daniel Zaragoza (MEX) W DIS 7 Fred Jackson (USA), Aruba - WBC

09.08.85 Miguel Lora (COL) W PTS 12 Daniel Zaragoza (MEX), Miami - WBC

23.08.85 Jeff Fenech (A) W CO 3 Satoshi Shingaki (JAP), Sydney - IBF

02.12.85 Jeff Fenech (A) W PTS 15 Jerome Coffee (USA), Sydney - IBF

08.02.86 Miguel Lora (COL) W PTS 12 Wilfredo Vasquez (PR), Miami - WBC

10.03.86 Gaby Canizales (USA) W RSC 7 Richard Sandoval (USA), Las Vegas - WBA

04.06.86 Bernardo Pinango (VEN) W PTS 15 Gaby Canizales (USA), East Rutherford - WBA

18.07.86 Jeff Fenech (A) W RSC 14 Steve McCrory (USA), Sydney - IBF. *Jeff Fenech relinquished IBF version of title in February 1987 in order to challenge Samart Payakarun for the WBC super-bantamweight crown.*

23.08.86 Miguel Lora (COL) W RSC 6 Enrique Sanchez (DOM), Miami - WBC

04.10.86 Bernardo Pinango (VEN) W RSC 10 Ciro de Leva (ITA), Turin - WBA

15.11.86 Miguel Lora (COL) W PTS 12 Albert Davila (USA), Barranquilla - WBC

22.11.86 Bernardo Pinango (VEN) W RSC 15 Simon Skosana (SA), Johannesburg - WBA

03.02.87 Bernardo Pinango (VEN) W PTS 15 Frankie Duarte (USA), Los Angeles - WBA. *Bernardo Pinango relinquished WBA version of the title immediately after the fight, having struggled to make the weight.*

29.03.87 Takuya Muguruma (JAP) W CO 5 Azael Moran (PAN), Moriguchi - WBA

15.05.87 Kelvin Seabrooks (USA) W CO 5 Miguel Maturana (COL), Cartagena - IBF

24.05.87 Chang-Yung Park (SK) W RSC 11 Takuya Muguruma (JAP), Moriguchi - WBA

04.07.87 Kelvin Seabrooks (USA) NC 9 Thierry Jacob (FR), Calais - IBF. *Jacob retired in his corner at the end of the ninth round due to a badly cut eye after his manager refused to let him continue. Unfortunately, for Jacob, his manager had misinterpreted the IBF ruling on accidental head clashes occuring after six rounds and the referee awarded the contest to Seabrooks. However, an hour later, the IBF officials in charge, amended the result to that of no-contest.*

25.07.87 Miguel Lora (COL) W RSC 4 Antonio Avelar (MEX), Miami - WBC

04.10.87 Wilfredo Vasquez (PR) W RSC 10 Chan-Yung Park (SK), Seoul - WBA

18.11.87 Kelvin Seabrooks (USA) W RSC 4 Ernie Cataluna (PH), San Cataldo - IBF

27.11.87 Miguel Lora (COL) W PTS 12 Ray Minus (BAH), Miami - WBC

17.01.88 Wilfredo Vasquez (PR) DREW 12 Takuya Muguruma (JAP), Osaka - WBA

06.02.88 Kelvin Seabrooks (USA) W RSC 2 Fernando Beltran (MEX), Paris - IBF

30.04.88 Miguel Lora (COL) W PTS 12 Lucio Lopez (ARG), Cartagena - WBC

09.05.88 Kaokor Galaxy (TH) W PTS 12 Wilfredo Vasquez (PR), Bangkok - WBA

09.07.88 Orlando Canizales (USA) W RSC 15 Kelvin Seabrooks (USA), Atlantic City - IBF

01.08.88 Miguel Lora (COL) W PTS 12 Albert Davila (USA), Los Angeles - WBC

14.08.88 Sung-Il Moon (SK) W TD 6 Kaokor Galaxy (TH), Pusan - WBA. *Moon, ahead on all three judges' scorecards, sustained a badly damaged right-eye after an accidental clash of heads in the sixth round and, unable to continue, he was returned the winner and new champion in only his seventh fight.*

29.10.88 Raul Perez (MEX) W PTS 12 Miguel Lora (COL), Las Vegas - WBC

27.11.88 Sung-Il Moon (SK) W CO 7 Edgar Monserrat (PAN), Seoul - WBA

29.11.88 Orlando Canizales (USA) W CO 1 Jimmy Navarro (USA), San Antonio - IBF

03.02.89 Israel Contrerras (VEN) W CO 1 Maurizio Lupino (ITA), Caracas - WBO

19.02.89 Sung-Il Moon (SK) W RSC 5 Chaiki Kobayashi (JAP), Taejon - WBA

09.03.89 Raul Perez (MEX) W PTS 12 Lucio Lopez (ARG), Los Angeles - WBC

24.06.89 Orlando Canizales (USA) W RSC 11 Kelvin Seabrooks (USA), Atlantic City - IBF

08.07.89 Kaokor Galaxy (TH) W PTS 12 Sung-Il Moon (SK), Bangkok - WBA

26.08.89 Raul Perez (MEX) W RTD 7 Cardenio Ulloa (CH), Santiago - WBC

18.10.89 Luisito Espinosa (PH) W RSC 1 Kaokor Galaxy (TH), Bangkok - WBA

23.10.89 Raul Perez (MEX) W PTS 12 Diego Avila (MEX), Los Angeles - WBC

22.01.90 Raul Perez (MEX) W PTS 12 Gaby Canizales (USA), Los Angeles - WBC

24.01.90 Orlando Canizales (USA) W PTS 12 Billy Hardy (GB), Crowtree Leisure Centre, Sunderland - IBF

07.05.90 Raul Perez (MEX) W RSC 9 Gerardo Martinez (USA), Los Angeles - WBC

30.05.90 Luisito Espinosa (PH) W RTD 8 Hurley Snead (USA), Bangkok - WBA

10.06.90 Orlando Canizales (USA) W RSC 2 Paul Gonzales (USA), El Paso - IBF

14.08.90 Orlando Canizales (USA) W RSC 5 Eddie Rangel (USA), Saratogo Springs - IBF

02.09.90 Israel Contrerras (VEN) W RSC 9 Ray Minus (BAH), Nassau - WBO. *Israel Contrerras relinquished WBO version of title in January 1991 in order to challenge for the WBA crown.*

14.09.90 Raul Perez (MEX) DREW 12 Jose Valdez (MEX), Culican - WBC

12.10.90 Luisito Espinosa (PH) W CO 1 Yong-Man Chung (SK), Manila - WBA

29.11.90 Luisito Espinosa (PH) W PTS 12 Thalerngsak Sitbobay (TH), Bangkok - WBA

17.12.90 Raul Perez (MEX) W CO 8 Chanquito Carmona (MEX), Tijuana - WBC

25.02.91 Greg Richardson (USA) W PTS 12 Raul Perez (MEX), Los Angeles - WBC

12.03.91 Gaby Canizales (USA) W CO 2 Miguel Lora (COL), Detroit - WBO

04.05.91 Orlando Canizales (USA) W RSC 8 Billy Hardy (GB), Laredo - IBF

20.05.91 Greg Richardson (USA) W PTS 12 Victor Rabanales (MEX), Los Angeles - WBC

30.06.91 Duke McKenzie (GB) W PTS 12 Gaby Canizales (USA), Elephant and Castle Leisure Centre, London - WBO

12.09.91 Duke McKenzie (GB) W PTS 12 Cesar Soto (MEX), Latchmere Leisure Centre, London - WBO

19.09.91 Joichiro Tatsuyshi (JAP) W RTD 10 Greg Richardson (USA), Tokyo - WBC. *Joichiro Tatsuyshi relinquished the WBC version of the title in March 1992 after suffering a serious eye injury, on the proviso that he would get first crack at the title when fit again. On that basis, a match between Victor Rabanales and Yong-Hoon Lee, which had initially been made for the "interim title", became a contest to decide the vacant WBC championship.*

22.09.91 Orlando Canizales (USA) W PTS 12 Fernie Morales (USA), Indio - IBF

19.10.91 Israel Contrerras (VEN) W CO 5 Luisito Espinosa (PH), Manila - WBA

21.12.91 Orlando Canizales (USA) W RSC 11 Ray Minus (BAH), Laredo - IBF

15.03.92 Eddie Cook (USA) W CO 5 Israel Contrerras (VEN), Las Vegas - WBA

25.03.92 Duke McKenzie (GB) W RSC 8 Wilfredo Vargas (PR), Albert Hall, London - WBO

30.03.92 Victor Rabanales (MEX) W TD 9 Yong-Hoon Lee (SK), Los Angeles - WBC. *Both men were careless with their headwork at times and it was a butt from Lee which ended the fight early. Rabanales, ahead on two judges' scorecards at the time, was declared the winner, the margin of victory being a second round knockdown.*

23.04.92 Orlando Canizales (USA) W PTS 12 Francisco Alvarez (COL), Paris - IBF

13.05.92 Rafael del Valle (PR) W CO 1 Duke McKenzie (GB), Albert Hall, London - WBO

16.05.92 Victor Rabanales (MEX) W RSC 4 Luis Ocampo (ARG), Tuxtla - WBC

27.07.92 Victor Rabanales (MEX) W PTS 12 Chang-Kyun Oh (SK), Los Angeles - WBC

17.09.92 Victor Rabanales (MEX) W RSC 9 Joichiro Tatsuyoshi (JAP), Osaka - WBC

18.09.92 Orlando Canizales (USA) W PTS 12 Samuel Duran (PH), Bozeman - IBF

09.10.92 Jorge Elicier Julio (COL) W PTS 12 Eddie Cook (USA), Cartagena - WBA

25.01.93 Victor Rabanales (MEX) W PTS 12 Dio Andujar (PH), Los Angeles - WBC

24.03.93 Rafael del Valle (PR) W RSC 5 Wilfredo Vargas (PR), Conado - WBO

27.03.93 Orlando Canizales (USA) W RTD 11 Clarence Adams (USA), Evian les Bains - IBF

28.03.93 Il-Jung Byun (SK) W PTS 12 Victor Rabanales (MEX), Kyungju - WBC

03.04.93 Jorge Elicier Julio (COL) W RTD 8 Francisco Alvarez (COL), Cartagena - WBA

28.05.93 Il-Jung Byun (SK) W PTS 12 Josefino Suarez (MEX), Seoul - WBC. *With Il-Jung Byun unable to defend his WBC title due to an injured hand, Joichiro Tatsuyshi outpointed Victor Rabanales over 12 rounds on 22 July 1993, in a battle to decide the "interim title". However, on Byun's return to the ring, it was another Japanese fighter, Yasuei Yakushiji, who challenged him.*

19.06.93 Rafael del Valle (PR) W PTS 12 Miguel Lora (COL), Hato Rey - WBO

19.06.93 Orlando Canizales (USA) NC 3 Derrick Whiteboy (SA), Houston - IBF. *The fight was declared a no-contest when a clash of heads left Canizales, who sustained a badly cut left-eye, unable to continue.*

Super-Bantamweight (122 lbs)

On 21 September 1922, in a fight billed by the promoter as being for the vacant 122 lbs title, Jack Kid Wolfe outpointed Joe Lynch over 15 rounds in New York City. The contest was not given official backing in New York, however, as Charley Beecher had earlier claimed the same title after outscoring Freddie Jacks over 12 rounds on 28 February 1921, also in New York City, and had successfully defended over the same distance at the same venue against Tibby Watson on 16 September 1922. Next time out, on 26 December 1922, in Toronto, Wolfe was outpointed over ten rounds by Benny Gould, who then knocked out Charley Beecher in the fifth round on 6 March 1923 (New York City), before being kayoed himself in the eighth by Mike Dundee on 10 April 1923 (New York City). Meanwhile, Wolfe still considered himself the 122 lbs champion and "defended" against Carl Duane on 29 August 1923 at Long Island. Although Wolfe came to the scales almost two pounds overweight, Duane won the 12 rounder on points, but neither he nor Dundee showed any inclination to come together and the "title" rapidly fell into disuse. It re-appeared briefly in Philadelphia on 27 June 1928 when Harry Blitman outpointed Tony Canzoneri over ten rounds, but disappeared just as quickly. The 122 lbs championship next turned up in the Philippines in 1935, when Lew Farber outpointed Cris Pineda over 12 rounds in Manila, but Farber quickly lost the "title" to Star Frisco. A further six years went by before a little known body calling themselves the American Federation of Boxing started the ball rolling again with a series of eight rounders in New York City. After appointing Lou Barbetta as their recognised champion, he was outpointed by Davey Crawford (22 July 1941), before Crawford befell a similar fate himself at the hands of Aaron Seltzer (2 September 1941). His successor was Joey Iannotti, who after outscoring Seltzer (6 October 1941), held on to his laurels next time out with a draw against Johnny Compo (29 January 1942), before going down on points to Seltzer (17 February 1942), in a rematch that turned out to be the last contest held under the auspices of the ABF. Resurrected as the super-bantamweight division by the World Boxing Council in 1976, the weight class is recognised as the junior-featherweight division by both the World Boxing Association and the International Boxing Federation.

03.04.76 Rigoberto Riasco (PAN) W RTD 8 Waruinge Nakayama (K), Panama City - WBC

12.06.76 Rigoberto Riasco (PAN) W CO 10 Livio Nolasco (DOM), Panama City - WBC

01.08.76 Rigoberto Riasco (PAN) W PTS 15 Dong-Kyun Yum (SK), Pusan - WBC. *Initially announced as a split decision win for Riasco, 25 minutes later the referee came back to explain that he had found a mistake in his tally and that Yum was the winner and new champion. The WBC confirmed Yum as champion, but following a statement from the referee that he had been forced at gunpoint to change the decision, Riasco was eventually reinstated.*

10.10.76 Royal Kobayashi (JAP) W RSC 8 Rigoberto Riasco (PAN), Tokyo - WBC

24.11.76 Dong-Kyun Yum (SK) W PTS 15 Royal Kobayashi (JAP), Seoul - WBC

13.02.77 Dong-Kyun Yum (SK) W PTS 15 Jose Cervantes (COL), Seoul - WBC

21.05.77 Wilfredo Gomez (PR) W CO 12 Dong-Kyun Yum (SK), San Juan - WBC

11.07.77 Wilfredo Gomez (PR) W CO 5 Raul Tirado (MEX), San Juan - WBC

26.11.77 Soo-Hwan Hong (SK) W CO 3 Hector Carrasquilla (PAN), Panama City - WBA

19.01.78 Wilfredo Gomez (PR) W CO 3 Royal Kobayashi (JAP), Kitakyushu - WBC

01.02.78 Soo-Hwan Hong (SK) W PTS 15 Yu Kasahara (JAP), Tokyo - WBA

08.04.78 Wilfredo Gomez (PR) W RSC 7 Juan Antonio Lopez (MEX), Bayamon - WBC

06.05.78 Ricardo Cardona (COL) W RSC 12 Soo-Hwan Hong (SK), Seoul - WBA

02.06.78 Wilfredo Gomez (PR) W RSC 3 Sakad Petchyindee (TH), Korat - WBC

02.09.78 Ricardo Cardona (COL) W PTS 15 Ruben Valdez (COL), Cartagena - WBA

09.09.78 Wilfredo Gomez (PR) W RSC 13 Leonardo Cruz (DOM), San Juan - WBC

28.10.78 Wilfredo Gomez (PR) W RSC 5 Carlos Zarate (MEX), San Juan - WBC

12.11.78 Ricardo Cardona (COL) W PTS 15 Soon-Hyun Chung (SK), Seoul - WBA

09.03.79 Wilfredo Gomez (PR) W RSC 5 Nestor Jimenez (COL), New York City - WBC

16.06.79 Wilfredo Gomez (PR) W RSC 5 Jesus Hernandez (NIC) San Juan - WBC

23.06.79 Ricardo Cardona (COL) W PTS 15 Soon-Hyun Chung (SK), Seoul - WBA

06.09.79 Ricardo Cardona (COL) W PTS 15 Yukio Segawa (JAP), Hachinohe - WBA

28.09.79 Wilfredo Gomez (PR) W RSC 10 Carlos Mendoza (PAN), Las Vegas - WBC

26.10.79 Wilfredo Gomez (PR) W RSC 5 Nicky Perez (USA), New York City - WBC

15.12.79 Ricardo Cardona (COL) W PTS 15 Sergio Palma (ARG), Barranquilla - WBA

03.02.80 Wilfredo Gomez (PR) W RTD 6 Ruben Valdez (COL), Las Vegas - WBC

04.05.80 Leo Randolph (USA) W RSC 15 Ricardo Cardona (COL), Seattle - WBA

09.08.80 Sergio Palma (ARG) W CO 6 Leo Randolph (USA), Washington - WBA

22.08.80 Wilfredo Gomez (PR) W RSC 5 Derrick Holmes (USA), Las Vegas - WBC

08.11.80 Sergio Palma (ARG) W RSC 9 Ulisses Morales (PAN), Buenos Aires - WBA

13.12.80 Wilfredo Gomez (PR) W CO 3 Jose Cervantes (COL), Miami - WBC

04.04.81 Sergio Palma (ARG) W PTS 15 Leonardo Cruz (DOM), Buenos Aires - WBA

15.08.81 Sergio Palma (ARG) W RSC 12 Ricardo Cardona (COL), Buenos Aires - WBA

03.10.81 Sergio Palma (ARG) W PTS 15 Vichit Muangroi-et (TH), Buenos Aires - WBA

15.01.82 Sergio Palma (ARG) W PTS 15 Jorge Lujan (PAN), Cordoba - WBA

27.03.82 Wilfredo Gomez (PR) W RSC 6 Juan Meza (MEX), Atlantic City - WBC

11.06.82 Wilfredo Gomez (PR) W CO 10 Juan Antonio Lopez (MEX), Las Vegas - WBC

12.06.82 Leonardo Cruz (DOM) W PTS 15 Sergio Palma (ARG), Miami - WBA

18.08.82 Wilfredo Gomez (PR) W RTD 7 Roberto Rubaldino (MEX), San Juan - WBC

13.11.82 Leonardo Cruz (DOM) W CO 8 Benito Badilla (CH), San Juan - WBA

03.12.82 Wilfredo Gomez (PR) W RSC 14 Lupe Pintor (MEX), New Orleans - WBC. *Wilfredo Gomez relinquished WBC version of the title in April 1983 due to weight making difficulties.*

16.03.83 Leonardo Cruz (DOM) W PTS 15 Soon-Hyun Chung (SK), San Juan - WBA

15.06.83 Jaime Garza (USA) W RSC 2 Bobby Berna (PH), Los Angeles - WBC

26.08.83 Leonardo Cruz (DOM) W PTS 15 Cleo Garcia (NIC), St Domingo - WBA

04.12.83 Bobby Berna (PH) W RTD 11 Seung-In Suh (SK), Seoul - IBF

22.02.84 Loris Stecca (ITA) W RSC 12 Leonardo Cruz (DOM), Milan - WBA

15.04.84 Seung-In Suh (SK) W CO 10 Bobby Berna (PH), Seoul - IBF

26.05.84 Jaime Garza (USA) W CO 3 Felipe Orozco (COL), Miami - WBC

26.05.84 Victor Callejas (PR) W RSC 8 Loris Stecca (ITA), Guaynabo - WBA

08.07.84 Seung-In Suh (SK) W CO 4 Cleo Garcia (NIC), Seoul - IBF

03.11.84 Juan Meza (MEX) W CO 1 Jaime Garza (USA), Kingston, NY - WBC

03.01.85 Ji-Won Kim (SK) W CO 10 Seung-In Suh (SK), Seoul - IBF

02.02.85 Victor Callejas (PR) W PTS 15 Seung-Hoon Lee (SK), San Juan - WBA

30.03.85 Ji-Won Kim (SK) W PTS 15 Ruben Palacio (COL), Suwon - IBF

19.04.85 Juan Meza (MEX) W RSC 6 Mike Ayala (USA), Los Angeles - WBC

28.06.85 Ji-Won Kim (SK) W CO 4 Bobby Berna (PH), Pusan - IBF

18.08.85 Lupe Pintor (MEX) W PTS 12 Juan Meza (MEX), Mexico City - WBC

09.10.85 Ji-Won Kim (SK) W CO 1 Seung-In Suh (SK), Seoul - IBF

08.11.85 Victor Callejas (PR) W RTD 6 Loris Stecca (ITA), Rimini - WBA. *Victor Callejas forfeited WBA recognition in December 1986 for failing to defend against Louie Espinosa.*

18.01.86 Samart Payakarun (TH) W CO 5 Lupe Pintor (MEX), Bangkok - WBC. *Although Pintor forfeited the WBC version of the title on the scales when he came in three pounds overweight, the fight went ahead on the basis that if Payakarun won he would be proclaimed champion.*

01.06.86 Ji-Won Kim (SK) W CO 2 Rudy Casicas (PH), Inchon - IBF. *Ji-Won Kim retired as undefeated IBF champion in November 1986.*

10.12.86 Samart Payakarun (TH) W CO 12 Juan Meza (MEX), Bangkok - WBC

16.01.87 Louie Espinosa (USA) W RSC 4 Tommy Valoy (DOM), Phoenix - WBA

18.01.87 Seung-Hoon Lee (SK) W CO 9 Prayoonsak Muangsurin (TH), Pohang - IBF

05.04.87 Seung-Hoon Lee (SK) W CO 10 Jorge Urbina Diaz (MEX), Seoul - IBF

08.05.87 Jeff Fenech (A) W RSC 4 Samart Payakarun (TH), Sydney - WBC

10.07.87 Jeff Fenech (A) W RTD 5 Greg Richardson (USA), Sydney - WBC

15.07.87 Louie Espinosa (USA) W RSC 15 Manuel Vilchez (VEN), Phoenix - WBA

19.07.87 Seung-Hoon Lee (SK) W CO 5 Lion Collins (PH), Seoul - IBF

15.08.87 Louie Espinosa (USA) W CO 9 Mike Ayala (USA), San Antonio - WBA

16.10.87 Jeff Fenech (A) W TD 4 Carlos Zarate (MEX), Sydney - WBC. *After Fenech suffered a cut-eye, following an accidental clash of heads, under the WBC ruling, the referee ordered the score-cards to be added up and declared him the winner by 40-34 on all cards. Jeff Fenech relinquished WBC version of title in January 1988 to challenge for the WBC featherweight crown.*

28.11.87 Julio Gervacio (DOM) W PTS 12 Louie Espinosa (USA), San Juan - WBA

27.12.87 Seung-Hoon Lee (SK) W PTS 15 Jose Sanabria (VEN), Pohang - IBF. *Seung-Hoon Lee relinquished IBF version of title in March 1988 in order to challenge for the WBC crown.*

27.02.88 Bernardo Pinango (VEN) W PTS 12 Julio Gervacio (DOM), San Juan - WBA

29.02.88 Daniel Zaragoza (MEX) W RSC 10 Carlos Zarate (MEX), Los Angeles - WBC

21.05.88 Jose Sanabria (VEN) W CO 5 Moises Fuentes (COL), Bucaramanga - IBF

28.05.88 Juan J. Estrada (MEX) W PTS 12 Bernardo Pinango (VEN), Tijuana - WBA

29.05.88 Daniel Zaragoza (MEX) DREW 12 Seung-Hoon Lee (SK), Youchan - WBC

21.08.88 Jose Sanabria (VEN) W PTS 12 Vincenzo Belcastro (ITA), Capo d'Orlando - IBF

26.09.88 Jose Sanabria (VEN) W RSC 10 Fabrice Benichou (FR), Noget sur Marne - IBF

15.10.88 Juan J. Estrada (MEX) W RSC 11 Takuya Muguruma (JAP), Moriguchi - WBA

11.11.88 Jose Sanabria (VEN) W RSC 6 Thierry Jacob (FR), Gravelines - IBF

21.11.88 Daniel Zaragoza (MEX) W CO 5 Valerio Nati (ITA), Forli - WBC

10.03.89 Fabrice Benichou (FR) W PTS 12 Jose Sanabria (VEN), Limoges - IBF

04.04.89 Juan J. Estrada (MEX) W RSC 10 Jesus Poll (VEN), Los Angeles - WBA

29.04.89 Kenny Mitchell (USA) W PTS 12 Julio Gervacio (DOM), San Juan - WBO

11.06.89 Fabrice Benichou (FR) W CO 5 Franie Badenhorst (SA), Frasnone - IBF

22.06.89 Daniel Zaragoza (MEX) W PTS 12 Paul Banke (USA), Los Angeles - WBC

10.07.89 Juan J. Estrada (MEX) W PTS 12 Luis Mendoza (MEX), Tijuana - WBA

01.09.89 Daniel Zaragoza (MEX) W RSC 10 Frankie Duarte (USA), Los Angeles - WBC

09.09.89 Kenny Mitchell (USA) W PTS 12 Simon Skosana (SA), San Juan - WBO

07.10.89 Fabrice Benichou (FR) W PTS 12 Ramon Cruz (DOM), Bordeaux - IBF

03.12.89 Daniel Zaragoza (MEX) W PTS 12 Chan-Yung Park (SK), Seoul - WBC

09.12.89 Valerio Nati (ITA) W DIS 4 Kenny Mitchell (USA), Teramo - WBO

11.12.89 Jesus Salud (USA) W DIS 9 Juan J. Estrada (MEX), Los Angeles - WBA. *Jesus Salud forfeited WBA version of title in April 1990 for failing to defend against Luis Mendoza.*

10.03.90 Welcome Ncita (SA) W PTS 12 Fabrice Benichou (FR), Tel Aviv - IBF

23.04.90 Paul Banke (USA) W RSC 9 Daniel Zaragoza (MEX), Los Angeles - WBC

12.05.90 Orlando Fernandez (PR) W RSC 10 Valerio Nati (ITA), Sassari - WBO

25.05.90 Luis Mendoza (COL) DREW 12 Reuben Palacio (COL), Cartagena - WBA

02.06.90 Welcome Ncita (SA) W RSC 7 Ramon Cruz (DOM), Rome - IBF

17.08.90 Paul Banke (USA) W RSC 12 Ki-Jun Lee (SK), Seoul - WBC

11.09.90 Luis Mendoza (COL) W RSC 3 Reuben Palacio (COL), Miami - WBA

29.09.90 Welcome Ncita (SA) W RSC 8 Gerardo Lopez (PAN), Aosta - IBF

18.10.90 Luis Mendoza (COL) W PTS 12 Fabrice Benichou (FR), Paris - WBA

05.11.90 Pedro Decima (ARG) W RSC 4 Paul Banke (USA), Los Angeles - WBC

19.01.91 Luis Mendoza (COL) W RSC 8 Noree Jockygym (TH), Bangkok - WBA

03.02.91 Kiyoshi Hatanaka (JAP) W RSC 8 Pedro Decima (ARG), Nagoya - WBC

27.02.91 Welcome Ncita (SA) W PTS 12 Jesus Rojas (COL), St Vincent - IBF

21.04.91 Luis Mendoza (COL) W PTS 12 Carlos Uribe (CH), Cartagena - WBA

24.05.91 Jesse Benavides (USA) W PTS 12 Orlando Fernandez (PR), Corpus Christi - WBO

30.05.91 Luis Mendoza (COL) W CO 7 Joao Cardosa de Oliveira (BR), Madrid - WBA

14.06.91 Daniel Zaragoza (MEX) W PTS 12 Kiyoshi Hatanaka (JAP), Tokyo - WBC

15.06.91 Welcome Ncita (SA) W PTS 12 Hurley Snead (USA), San Antonio - IBF

24.08.91 Daniel Zaragoza (MEX) W PTS 12 Huh Chun (SK), Seoul - WBC

31.08.91 Jesse Benavides (USA) W RSC 5 Fernando Ramos (MEX), Corpus Christi - WBO

28.09.91 Welcome Ncita (SA) W PTS 12 Jesus Rojas (COL), Sun City - IBF

07.10.91 Raul Perez (MEX) W PTS 12 Luis Mendoza (COL), Los Angeles - WBA

09.12.91 Daniel Zaragoza (MEX) W PTS 12 Paul Banke (USA), Los Angeles - WBC

20.03.92 Thierry Jacob (FR) W PTS 12 Daniel Zaragoza (MEX), Calais - WBC

27.03.92 Wilfredo Vasquez (PR) W RSC 3 Raul Perez (MEX), Mexico City - WBA

18.04.92 Welcome Ncita (SA) W PTS 12 Jesus Salud (USA), Treviola - IBF

23.06.92 Tracy Harris Patterson (USA) W RSC 2 Thierry Jacob (FR), Albany - WBC

27.06.92 Wilfredo Vasquez (PR) W PTS 12 Freddy Cruz (DOM), Gorle - WBA

15.10.92 Duke McKenzie (GB) W PTS 12 Jesse Benavides (USA), Lewisham Theatre, London - WBO

02.12.92 Kennedy McKinney (USA) W CO 11 Welcome Ncita (SA), Tortoli - IBF

05.12.92 Tracy Harris Patterson (USA) DREW 12 Daniel Zarragoza (MEX), Berck sur Mer - WBC

05.12.92 Wilfredo Vasquez (PR) W RSC 8 Thierry Jacob (FR), Berck sur Mer - WBA

06.03.93 Wilfredo Vasquez (PR) W PTS 12 Luis Mendoza (COL), Levallois Perret - WBA

13.03.93 Tracy Harris Patterson (USA) W PTS 12 Jesse Benavides (USA), Poughkeepsie - WBC

17.04.93 Kennedy McKinney (USA) W PTS 12 Richard Duran (USA), Sacramento - IBF

09.06.93 Daniel Jimenez (PR) W PTS 12 Duke McKenzie (GB), Lewisham Theatre, London - WBO

24.06.93 Wilfredo Vasquez (PR) W CO 10 Thierry Jacob (FR), Bordeaux - WBA

Featherweight (126 lbs)

The division started life in the early 1860s and, although the first man to claim the championship appears to have been Dick Hollywood, the initial sign of positive action came when England's George Seddons beat Tommy Kelly for the title in Portsmouth, New Hampshire, on 7 October 1868. Shortly afterwards, Kelly laid claim to the title when Seddons found he could no longer make the weight and by the late 1870s, Long Tom Ryan also found recognition as champion. He was quickly followed by Jack Keenan, but when the latter was defeated by Young Mitchell on 22 June 1885, another American, Harry Gilmore, also claimed the title. It was around this time that the division was finally popularised. On 31 March 1889, in Kouts, Indiana, Ike Weir (Irish-born, but based in Boston) drew over 80 rounds with Frank Murphy (GB) and, with the result indecisive, other men joined in the activity. In San Francisco, on 3 June 1889, Americans, Dal Hawkins and Freddie Bogan, fought for 75 rounds until darkness halted the action and, on resuming the following day, the former knocked his rival out in the 90th round. Hawkins seems to have temporarily outgrown the weight class at this stage, leaving Torpedo Billy Murphy (NZ) to become champion as far as the Antipodes were concerned, when he knocked out Ike Weir (124½ lbs) in 14 rounds on 13 January 1890 (San Francisco). At this juncture, the featherweight limit in America was recognised to be 112 to 114 lbs, while in Britain it stood between 122 and 126 lbs, and it is for that reason we have placed the Canadian, George Dixon, in this category. Dixon came to the force when he drew over 70 rounds with Cal McCarthy in Boston on 7 February 1890 and followed that up with an 18th round stoppage over Nunc Wallace at the Pelican Club (London) on 27 June 1890, while McCarthy beat Mike McGoff in July 1890 (New York City). Before Dixon and McCarthy could settle their dispute in the States, Young Griffo stopped Murphy in the 15th round on 2 September 1890 (Sydney) and then successfully defended his title in the same city against Paddy Moran (13th round kayo on 14 November 1890) and George Powell (20th round disqualification on 12 March 1891). In America, during the same period, Dixon had stopped Johnny Murphy inside 40 rounds on 23 October 1890 (Providence), before going on to halt McCarthy in 22 rounds on 31 March 1891 (Troy). By now, Dixon weighed 115 lbs and it was at that weight that he kayoed the Australian, Abe Willis, in the fifth round of their San Francisco contest on 28 July 1891. A day earlier, in Sydney, Young Griffo had knocked out Billy Murphy inside 22 rounds and at the same venue he later kayoed Mick McCarthy in the fourth on 22 March 1892. By this time, however, Griffo had carried his weight from 126 to 130 lbs and had ceased to be recognised outside of Australia, while Dixon, still a growing lad, went forward to fight the British champion, Fred Johnson, for the international title at 117 lbs.

27.06.92 **George Dixon** (C) W CO 14 Fred Johnson (GB), Coney Island

06.09.92 **George Dixon** (C) W CO 8 Jack Skelly (USA), New Orleans. *A gallant failure, Skelly (116 lbs) will remain in the record books as the first man to challenge for a world title on his professional debut.*

09.11.92 Young Griffo (A) DREW 25 Martin Denny (USA), Sydney. *Too heavy to contest the "popular" title, Griffo, still recognised as champion in the Antipodes, continued to defend at 130 lbs.*

20.12.92 Young Griffo (A) W PTS 12 Jerry Marshall (USA), Sydney. *130 lbs title.*

28.02.93 Young Griffo (A) W DIS 4 Jerry Marshall (USA), Sydney. *130 lbs title.*

07.08.93 **George Dixon** (C) W CO 3 Eddie Pierce (USA), Coney Island. *Although Dixon weighed 116 lbs to Pierce's 120 lbs, the champion effectively moved the class limit to the latter poundage for this defence.*

25.09.93 **George Dixon** (C) W CO 7 Solly Smith (USA), Coney Island *(120 lbs).*

29.06.94 **George Dixon** (C) DREW 20 Young Griffo (A), Boston. *Recorded in the 1979 Boxing News Special as a title fight, it was quite possibly billed as one, but Dixon's championship belt was not at stake with Griffo not far short of 130 lbs.*

31.07.95 **George Dixon** (C) W RTD 4 Tommy Connelly (USA), Boston. *Although Connelly was seen as the challenger in some quarters, it was not a world title defence for Dixon, with both men agreeing to weigh 126 lbs on the night.*

27.08.95 **George Dixon** (C) W PTS 25 Johnny Griffin (USA), Boston. *Fought at 128 lbs, the title could not have been involved as stated in the Ring Record Book.*

05.12.95 **George Dixon** (C) DREW 10 Frank Erne (USA), New York City. *Shown in the pre-1986 Ring Record Book as a title fight, it was*

not, according to the Philadelphia Item (newspaper) report, with both men weighing 126 lbs.

17.03.96 **George Dixon** (C) W CO 8 Jerry Marshall (USA), Boston. *In a match made at 123 lbs, Dixon weighed 123 lbs and Marshall 126. Needless to say, the title was not involved, even though the Ring Record Book showed it to be.*

16.09.96 **George Dixon** (C) DREW 20 Martin Flaherty (USA), Boston. *Although the championship was dependent on the result, according to the Philadelphia Item (newspaper) report and shown as such in the Ring Record Book, with Flaherty weighing 124½ lbs, Dixon's title was ultimately not at risk.*

25.09.96 **George Dixon** (C) DREW 20 Tommy White (USA), New York City. *According to the Philadelphia Item (newspaper) report and the Ring Record Book, it was a title defence, but as the match was made at 125 lbs, had White won, it is doubtful whether his claim would have been accepted.*

09.11.96 **Solly Smith** (USA) W CO 8 Willie Smith (GB), NSC, London. *Advertised as being for the world 118 lbs title, with Dixon recognised as the lineal champion, Smith's victory cut no ice on the other side of the Atlantic.*

27.11.96 **Frank Erne** (USA) W PTS 20 George Dixon (C), New York City. *Following his win in an advertised title fight at 122 lbs, Erne was recognised as champion.*

22.01.97 **George Dixon** (C) W CO 6 Billy Murphy (NZ), New York City. *Although recorded in the Ring Record Book as a title fight, Dixon (118 lbs) had already lost his championship to Frank Erne. Murphy weighed 120 lbs.*

15.02.97 **George Dixon** (C) DREW 20 Jack Downey (USA), New York City. *With Frank Erne recognised as the featherweight champion at 122 lbs, Dixon continued to bill himself as the 118 lbs titleholder and defend his old title at that weight.*

24.03.97 **George Dixon** (C) W PTS 25 Frank Erne (USA), New York City. *In an advertised title match made at 122 lbs, Dixon regained the championship.*

26.04.97 **George Dixon** (C) W PTS 20 Johnny Griffin (USA), New York City. *Listed in the Ring Record Book as a title fight, Dixon's title was not considered at risk with the match made at 128lbs.*

03.05.97 **Harry Greenfield** (GB) W RSC 8 Larry Barnes (USA), Olympic Club, Birmingham. *Advertised for the 126 lbs featherweight title, but the winner was not generally recognised as such, even in Britain.*

23.07.97 **George Dixon** (C) DREW 20 Dal Hawkins (USA), San Francisco. *Although the Philadelphia Item (newspaper) report gave it as a battle for championship honours, a statement supported down the years by the Ring Record Book, a day earlier the San Francisco Chronicle (newspaper) saw it as a catchweight contest with Hawkins due to come to the ring at 128 lbs to Dixon's 124.*

04.10.97 **Solly Smith** (USA) W PTS 20 George Dixon (C), San Francisco. *In the aftermath of defeat, Dixon's manager, O'Rourke, declared that as the match had been made at 118 lbs and Smith had come in at 120, the title had not been at stake. However, that excuse did not wear with the pressmen, who accepted Smith as the new champion, while Dixon continued to bill himself likewise.*

08.11.97 **Wil Curley** (GB) W PTS 20 Patsy Haley (USA), Standard Theatre, Gateshead. *Although winning a bout advertised for the 117 lbs featherweight title, Curley was only recognised in the north-east of England.*

29.11.97 **Ben Jordan** (GB) W DIS 18 Tommy White (USA), NSC, London. *After Dave Wallace was taken ill, with White graciously declining to take the forfeit, Jordan took his place. Billed for the British version of the 124 lbs title, the Englishman weighed 122½ lbs to White's 124.*

23.02.98 **Spike Sullivan** (USA) W CO 15 Harry Greenfield (GB), NSC, London. *Advertised for the 126 lbs title, Greenfield lost his claim, while Sullivan was hardly recognised on either side of the Atlantic.*

31.03.98 George Dixon (C) DREW 20 Tommy White (USA), Syracuse. *Making his comeback after losing to Solly Smith, Dixon failed to acknowledge Smith and continued to bill himself as champion. Early Boxing News Annuals listed this one as a title fight, an entry that was eventually remedied, but in fairness to them it was probably advertised as such. However, neither the New York Herald or the Boston Post (newspapers) indicated that this was a title bout and, made no mention of weights.*

04.04.98 **Ben Jordan** (GB) W RTD 17 Eddie Curry (USA), NSC, London - GB. *Billed for the British version of the world 122 lbs title.*

06.06.98 George Dixon (C) W PTS 20 Eddie Santry (USA), New York City. *Once listed in the Ring Record Book as an advertised title fight, there was no mention in the New York Herald (newspaper) report of it involving the title, merely stating that it was a match made at 125 lbs.*

01.07.98 **Ben Jordan** (GB) W PTS 25 George Dixon (C), New York City. *Not a billed title fight as suggested in the Ring Record Book, but one where Jordan's claim to the championship was at stake. For the record, Jordan came in at 122 lbs, while Dixon scaled 115½ lbs.*

07.07.98 **Solly Smith** (USA) W DIS 7 Billy O'Donnell (USA), Buffalo - USA. *Recorded in the Ring Record Book as a title fight, albeit without weights, neither the New York Herald or Buffalo Courier (newspaper) reports indicate that the championship was involved.*

01.08.98 Solly Smith (USA) DREW 25 Tommy White (USA), Coney Island - USA *(122 lbs).*

26.09.98 **Dave Sullivan** (USA) W RTD 5 Solly Smith (USA), Coney Island - USA *(122 lbs).*

27.10.98 **Jabez White** (GB) W RTD 12 Mike Sears (USA), Olympic Club, Birmingham. *Advertised for the world championship at 123 lbs, needless to say, White's claim was hardly recognised on either side of the Atlantic.*

11.11.98 George Dixon (C) W DIS 10 Dave Sullivan (USA), New York City - USA. *Weights (lbs): Dixon (119), Sullivan (122).*

29.11.98 George Dixon (C) W PTS 25 Oscar Gardner (USA), New York City - USA. *Both men scaled 122 lbs.*

17.01.99 George Dixon (C) W CO 10 Young Pluto (A), New York City - USA. *Weights (lbs): Dixon (113½), Pluto (122).*

15.05.99 George Dixon (C) W PTS 20 Kid Broad (USA), Buffalo - USA. *Recorded as a title fight in the Ring Record Book, this writer and prof. L. V. Davis could find no evidence to suggest it was billed as such after perusing newspaper reports in the Buffalo Courier, Boston Post, New York Herald, New York Times and Chicago Tribune. Both men were accustomed to fighting over 20 rounds and no weights were given.*

29.05.99 **Ben Jordan** (GB) W CO 9 Harry Greenfield (GB), NSC, London - GB. *Billed for the British version of the 124 lbs title.*

02.06.99 George Dixon (C) W PTS 25 Joe Bernstein (USA), New York City - USA. *This is yet another fight listed in the Ring Record Book as a title bout that should be treated with caution. The New York Herald (newspaper) report made no mention of the championship being at stake and made it clear that although the recognised weight limit of the day stood at 122 lbs, the above match had been articled for 124 lbs.*

11.07.99 George Dixon (C) W PTS 20 Tommy White (USA), Denver - USA. *Advertised as a title fight it should not be considered as such with Dixon weighing 125½ lbs to White's 120, although, had the latter won, the championship would almost certainly have changed hands.*

11.08.99 George Dixon (C) DREW 20 Eddie Santry (USA), New York City - USA. *The New York Herald made no mention of this as a title fight, although it is listed as such in the Ring Record Book, merely drawing attention to the fact that the Articles of Agreement called for both men to weigh inside 127 lbs.*

10.10.99 **Eddie Santry** (USA) W CO 10 Ben Jordan (GB), New York City. *Again, not an advertised title fight as implied in the Ring Record Book, Santry, by his victory, merely took over Jordan's claim to the championship.*

02.11.99 George Dixon (C) W PTS 25 Wil Curley (GB), New York City - USA *(122 lbs).*

21.11.99 George Dixon (C) W PTS 25 Eddie Lenny (USA), New York City - USA *(122 lbs).*

09.01.00 **Terry McGovern** (USA) W RSC 8 George Dixon (C), New York City - USA. *In a title match at 118 lbs, with both men supposedly scaling 116½, the championship changed hands.*

01.02.00 **Terry McGovern** (USA) W CO 5 Eddie Santry (USA), Chicago. *Although recorded in the Ring Record Book as a championship defence, it could not have been, with Chicago only able to stage contests of six rounds duration at the time. By his defeat, however, Santry lost any claim he had to the title*

09.03.00 **Terry McGovern** (USA) W CO 3 Oscar Gardner (USA), New York City *(122 lbs).*

28.05.00 **Ben Jordan** (GB) W CO 4 Tommy Hogan (USA), NSC, London. *Billed as the British version of the world 124 lbs championship, it had no effect on the "popular" title.*

12.06.00 **Terry McGovern** (USA) W CO 3 Tommy White (USA), Coney Island. *Recorded as a title defence in the Ring Record Book, with the match made at 122 lbs according to the Philadelphia Item (newspaper), it was probably acceptable for McGovern at 124 lbs to increase the weight class limit by two pounds, but with White tipping the beam at 128½ lbs, the championship would surely not have been on the line.*

02.11.00 **Terry McGovern** (USA) W CO 7 Joe Bernstein (USA), Louisville. *The New Orleans Daily Picayune (newspaper) reported it as a title fight made at 126 lbs, with both men announced as being inside the weight and Bernstein claiming to be 125 lbs.*

30.04.01 **Terry McGovern** (USA) W CO 4 Oscar Gardner (USA), San Francisco. *Yet another billed championship battle for McGovern over and above the recognised weight class limit of the day (122 lbs), saw the champion scaling 123 to Gardner's 123½ lbs.*

29.05.01 **Terry McGovern** (USA) W CO 5 Aurelio Herrera (USA), San Francisco. *Illustrated as a title bout in the Ring Record Book, there was no mention of the championship being at stake in the San Francisco Chronicle (newspaper) report. In a match made at 126 lbs and scheduled for 20 rounds, the paper claimed that McGovern, who carried Herrera for five rounds, would have great difficulty getting down to 122 lbs again.*

20.10.01 George Dixon (C) DREW 20 Abe Attell (USA), Cripple Creek. *Knowing that Terry McGovern was having difficulty making the weight, Dixon once again claimed the crown at 122 lbs, but found little support.*

28.10.01 Abe Attell (USA) W PTS 15 George Dixon (C), St Louis. *With McGovern still recognised as the lineal champion, Attell at the age of 17, got little or no support at the time following his victory, while Dixon faded into obscurity. Today, neither of the above two fights are seen as having involved the championship, even though they were advertised as such.*

28.11.01 **Young Corbett II** (USA) W CO 2 Terry McGovern (USA), Hartford. *Taking into account that both men on the heavy side, the match was made at 126 lbs and accepted as a championship contest.*

23.05.02 **Young Corbett** II (USA) W PTS 10 Kid Broad (USA), Denver. *Shown as a title fight in early Boxing News Annuals, there was no indication in the Philadelphia Item (newspaper) report that the championship was involved.*

23.06.02 Ben Jordan (GB) W CO 15 Kid McFadden (USA), NSC, London. *Billed for the British version of the 120 lbs title, for the winner, Jordan, it was the last time he would be seen on the world stage and six fights later he had retired.*

16.10.02 **Young Corbett** II (USA) W RTD 7 Joe Bernstein (USA), Baltimore. *Although Bernstein came in at 124½ lbs and stood to win the title if he got lucky, Corbett was now around the 130 lbs mark, but continued to "defend" at that weight, although not generally recognised.*

14.01.03 Young Corbett II (USA) W RSC 18 Austin Rice (USA), Hot Springs. *130 lbs title*

26.02.03 Young Corbett II (USA) DREW 20 Eddie Hanlon (USA), San Francisco. *130 lbs title.*

31.03.03 Young Corbett II (USA) W CO 11 Terry McGovern (USA), San Francisco. *130 lbs title.*

03.09.03 Abe Attell (USA) W PTS 20 Johnny Reagan (USA), St Louis. *In a match made at 122 lbs, this fight was generally acknowledged as being for the vacant title.*

27.10.03 Young Corbett II (USA) W CO 11 Hugh Murphy (USA), Boston. *130 lbs title.*

19.11.03 George Dixon (C) W PTS 20 Pedlar Palmer (GB), New Goodwin Club, Newcastle. *Billed for the world 120 lbs title over 20 x two minute rounds, Palmer came in at 122 lbs, while Dixon, who made the weight, gained no recognition from the result whatsoever.*

29.12.03 Young Corbett II (USA) W CO 16 Eddie Hanlon (USA), San Francisco. *130 lbs title.*

01.02.04 Abe Attell (USA) W CO 5 Harry Forbes (USA), St Louis. *(122 lbs).*

29.02.04 Young Corbett II (USA) W CO 11 Dave Sullivan (USA), San Francisco. *130 lbs title.*

25.03.04 Jimmy Britt (USA) W PTS 20 Young Corbett 11 (USA), San Francisco. *Britt was already recognised in some quarters as the "white" lightweight champion and the 130 lbs title merely moved up a division with him.*

23.06.04 Abe Attell (USA) W PTS 15 Johnny Reagan (USA), St Louis. *Regarded as a title fight by the Ring Record Book, and mistakenly shown as a 20 rounder at that, the contest was reported briefly upon in the Philadelphia Item, San Francisco (the town where Attell was both born and domiciled) Chronicle and Los Angeles Times (newspapers) without ever indicating either the weights or that the championship was involved.*

13.10.04 Tommy Sullivan (USA) W CO 5 Abe Attell (USA), St Louis. *Recent Ring Record Books have shown this to be a title defence for Attell in which he lost his title. Although Attell certainly lost, according to the Philadelphia Item (newspaper) report the fight was made at 124 lbs and did not involve the 122 lbs "popular" title. Afterwards, Attell continued to be supported as champion by the press of the day, while Sullivan remained inactive for close on two years.*

22.02.05 Abe Attell (USA) DREW 15 Kid Goodman (USA), Chelsea. *Although shown in the Boxing News Annual as a title fight, that, it was not, with neither man weighing in and both fighters agreeing beforehand on a drawn decision.*

22.02.06 **Abe Attell** (USA) W PTS 15 Jimmy Walsh (USA), Chelsea. *In a fight that was generally recognised as a championship match, Attell (120 lbs) met the current world bantamweight champion, Jimmy Walsh (120 lbs), who had eliminated Johnny Reagan from the title chase via a fifth round kayo on 12 February 1906 (Chelsea, Massachusetts).*

15.03.06 **Abe Attell** (USA) W DIS 3 Tony Moran (USA), Baltimore. *Not even reported in the Philadelphia Item, an excellent paper for boxing coverage at the time, with Attell fighting on 13 and 19 March, I think it is safe to assume that his title would not have been at stake for this go. No weights were recorded in the Ring Record Book.*

11.05.06 **Abe Attell** (USA) DREW 20 Kid Herman (USA), Los Angeles. *Although no weights were given and the Los Angeles Daily Times made no mention of it being a title bout, the same newspaper was quick to point out that, on top of his purse, Attell was fighting for a championship belt.*

04.07.06 **Abe Attell** (USA) W PTS 20 Frankie Neil (USA), Los Angeles. *Weights (lbs): Attell (120), Neil (118).*

30.10.06 **Abe Attell** (USA) W PTS 20 Harry Baker (USA), Los Angeles. *Billed as a title defence for Attell, according to the Los Angeles Daily Times (newspaper) report, the Articles of Agreement had explicitly stated that Baker should make 122 lbs in ring gear. The fight went ahead under championship conditions even though Baker was unable to improve on 122½ lbs in ring attire, whereas Attell scaled a comfortable 120½.*

16.11.06 **Abe Attell** (USA) W PTS 15 Billy de Coursey (USA), San Diego. *Although weights were not given, the San Francisco Chronicle (newspaper) report of the fight confirmed that Attell retained his 122 lbs title on his victory. On that basis one can only assume that both men were inside the weight.*

07.12.06 **Abe Attell** (USA) W CO 8 Jimmy Walsh (USA), Los Angeles. *Although the Los Angeles Daily Times (newspaper) report did not give the fighters' (ringside) weights, a day earlier, it was announced that Walsh would come into the ring at no more than 119½ lbs.*

18.01.07 **Abe Attell** (USA) W CO 8 Harry Baker (USA), Los Angeles. *Weighing in at ringside, Attell was comfortable at 121¼ lbs, while Baker had great difficulty, only making the required 122 lbs after several attempts.*

24.05.07 **Abe Attell** (USA) W PTS 20 Kid Solomon (USA), Los Angeles. *Solomon was forced to make 122 lbs just 30 minutes before the fight, a concession that considerably weakened him. In another twist, having kept the audience waiting and threatening to depart, Attell only stepped into the ring when $1500 had been advanced.*

22.08.07 Owen Moran (GB) W CO 18 Young Pierce (USA), The Gynmnastic Club, Liverpool. *Billed for the world 120 lbs, Moran used his victory as a stepping stone for a challenge on the "popular" version held by Abe Attell.*

29.10.07 **Abe Attell** (USA) W CO 4 Freddie Weeks (USA), Los Angeles. *Scheduled for 20 rounds, Attell failed to tip the beam at 122 lbs, while Weeks, after several attempts, only made it at the expense of everything, bar his trunks.*

01.01.08 **Abe Attell** (USA) DREW 25 Owen Moran (GB), San Francisco. *Moran weighed 120¼ lbs, with Attell also inside the 122 lbs mark.*

31.01.08 **Abe Attell** (USA) W RTD 13 Frankie Neil (USA), San Francisco. *With the weights not shown in the Ring Record Book, research has recently been carried out to determine whether it was a title fight or not. While the San Francisco Chronicle (newspaper) mentioned nothing specific, other than Neil being comfortably inside the 122 lbs marker, Prof. Luckett Davis was able to confirm that the Philadelphia Item (newspaper) report categorically stated that the title was on the line.*

28.02.08 **Abe Attell** (USA) W RSC 7 Eddie Kelly (USA), San Francisco. *According to the San Francisco Chronicle (newspaper) report it was a championship bout, with both men thought to be inside 122 lbs (no weights were announced). The fight came to an end when the police called a halt after the third knockdown.*

30.04.08 **Abe Attell** (USA) W RSC 4 Tommy Sullivan (USA), San Francisco. *Original articles were signed for a match at 123 lbs, but when Sullivan found that he could not make the weight a few days before the fight was due to take place, it was agreed that he could come in at 126 lbs. Although billed as a championship fight it could not be considered as such and following his defeat, Sullivan lost any remaining claim he may have had to the title.*

07.09.08 **Abe Attell** (USA) DREW 23 Owen Moran (GB), San Francisco *(122 lbs).*

29.12.08 **Abe Attell** (USA) W CO 8 Biz Mackey (USA), New Orleans. *Not included in post-war record books as a title fight, according to the New Orleans Daily Picayune (newspaper) report, Attell defended his championship, with both men announced as being inside 122 lbs.*

14.01.09 Abe Attell (USA) W CO 10 Freddie Weeks (USA), Goldfield *(122 lbs)*.

04.02.09 Abe Attell (USA) W RTD 7 Eddie Kelly (USA), New Orleans. *While not openly called a title defence in the New Orleans Daily Picayune (newspaper) pre-fight report, Attell was quoted as saying that he anticipated scoring a comprehensive victory over his challenger. No weights were announced.*

19.02.09 Abe Attell (USA) ND-L PTS 10 Jim Driscoll (GB), New York City. *Following this no-decision fight, during which he had been comprehensively outboxed, according to all attendant pressmen, Attell tried desperately to force a title shot, to no avail, and, on arriving home, he was supported by the NSC and declared champion.*

26.03.09 Abe Attell (USA) W CO 8 Frankie White (USA), Dayton - USA. *Although removed from the last Ring Record Book as a title bout, Prof. Luckett Davis remembered seeing it reported as such in the Milwaukee Free Press (newspaper), which would imply that both men scaled inside 122 lbs. However, while the San Francisco (Attell's birthplace) Chronicle (newspaper) report mentioned it as a 20 rounder, there was no reference to the fighters' weights or that the title was involved.*

28.02.10 Abe Attell (USA) ND-W CO 7 Harry Forbes (USA), Troy - USA

22.08.10 Abe Attell (USA) W CO 3 Eddie Merino (C), Calgary. *Recorded in the Ring Record Book as a title defence for Attell, that statement should be discarded as the match was actually made at the lightweight limit, as was his next contest against Billy Lauder.*

05.09.10 Abe Attell (USA) W CO 17 Billy Lauder (C), Winnipeg. *After beating Lauder in a match made at 133 lbs, with both men inside, Attell actually laid claim to his opponent's Canadian lightweight title. Whether the fight took place in Calgary or Winnipeg is still in doubt, but a title bout it was not.*

24.10.10 Abe Attell (USA) W PTS 10 Johnny Kilbane (USA), Kansas City - USA. *According to the Philadelphia Item (newspaper) report, the title was at stake even though no weights were made available. In summing up, although unlikely to have been advertised as a championship bout, it would be a racing certainty to accept that Kilbane made 122 lbs.*

13.11.10 Abe Attell (USA) DREW 15 Frankie Conley (USA), New Orleans - USA. *Recorded as a championship battle in the Ring Record Book, the fight had been originally scheduled for 20 rounds, but was reduced to 15 when Attell, having difficulty making the weight, decided to go ahead only at catchweights. Although Attell's weight was announced as 124 lbs, with the bantamweight champion, Conley, scaling 121, the New Orleans Daily Picayune (newspaper) merely confirmed that it was not a "tiff".*

28.05.11 Joe Coster (USA) W PTS 20 Frankie Conley (USA), New Orleans. *Unable to get a rematch with Attell, Conley was signed up to fight Coster at 122 lbs in a contest given title billing by the promoter. However, Attell was still recognised as the lineal champion and Conley's claim to the title evaporated when he was beaten by Coster. The winner, Coster, then lost his chance of a crack at the title when disqualified in the eighth round of a no-decision contest against Jimmy Walsh in New York City on 10 April 1912.*

22.02.12 Johnny Kilbane (USA) W PTS 20 Abe Attell (USA), Los Angeles - USA *(122 lbs)*.

21.05.12 Johnny Kilbane (USA) DREW 12 Jimmy Walsh (USA), Boston - USA. *Shown in the Ring Record Book as a title fight, the Boston Post (newspaper) claimed it to be the first championship contest in the "Hub" for years, but in the next breath called it a contest at catchweights, with Kilbane due to come to the ring at 125 lbs against Walsh's 122. According to the paper, Walsh would have claimed the title had he won.*

03.06.12 Jim Driscoll (GB) W CO 12 Jean Poesy (FR), NSC, London - GB/IBU *(126 lbs)*.

04.07.12 Johnny Kilbane (USA) ND-W PTS 12 Tommy Dixon (USA), Cleveland - USA

19.09.12 Johnny Kilbane (USA) ND-W PTS 10 Eddie O'Keefe (USA), New York City - USA

14.10.12 Johnny Kilbane (USA) ND-W PTS 12 Eddie O'Keefe (USA), Cleveland - USA

03.12.12 Johnny Kilbane (USA) ND-W RSC 9 Monte Attell (USA), Cleveland - USA

27.01.13 Jim Driscoll (GB) DREW 20 Owen Moran (GB), NSC, London - GB/IBU. *Jim Driscoll relinquished GB/IBU 126 lbs version of the title on announcing his retirement in February 1913.*

29.04.13 Johnny Kilbane (USA) DREW 20 Johnny Dundee (USA), Los Angeles *(122 lbs)*.

10.06.13 Johnny Kilbane (USA) W RSC 6 Jimmy Fox (USA), Oakland. *Recorded in the Ring Record Book as a title fight, it is difficult to understand how it got listed as such. According to the San Francisco Chronicle (newspaper) report it was a catchweight*

contest scheduled for ten rounds, with Kilbane looking to come in at around 130 lbs. After two no-decision affairs in New York City against Benny Leonard, a fourth round kayo win on 3 May 1912 and a ten round "press" victory on 18 August 1913, and following repeated challenges to Kilbane to no avail, Canadian, Frankie Fleming, laid claim to the title. Other men to do likewise around this time were Willie Jackson, K.O. Chaney and Johnny Dundee. Although Dundee was unable to entice Kilbane into the ring again, the other three men would be dismissed by the champion in no-decision bouts.

16.09.13 Johnny Kilbane (USA) W PTS 12 Jimmy Walsh (USA), Boston. *There was nothing in the Boston Daily Globe or Post (newspaper) reports, including weights, to suggest that the title was on the line, even though the Ring Record Book tells us it was.*

10.11.13 Johnny Kilbane (USA) ND-W CO 1 Eddie O'Keefe (USA), Philadelphia

06.09.15 Johnny Kilbane (USA) ND-W PTS 12 Alvie Miller (USA), Cedar Point

11.10.15 Johnny Kilbane (USA) ND-W PTS 12 Cal Delaney (USA), Akron

04.09.16 Johnny Kilbane (USA) W CO 3 K.O. Chaney (USA), Cedar Point. *Although taking place in Ohio, a State that in the main only allowed no-decision contests, this pairing was given special dispensation to be settled by the referee if both men were still standing after 15 rounds of boxing. Incidentally, both Kilbane and Chaney were announced as being within the required 122 lbs marker.*

26.03.17 Johnny Kilbane (USA) DREW 12 Eddie Wallace (USA), Bridgeport. *Again, recorded in the Ring Record Book as a title bout, there was nothing in the Boston Daily Globe (newspaper) report to indicate that it was.*

21.04.20 Johnny Kilbane (USA) ND-W CO 7 Alvie Miller (USA), Lorain. *In a match made at 126 lbs, the American version of the weight class previously recognised as being 122 lbs, finally fell into line with the rest of the world.*

07.10.20 Tommy Noble (GB) W PTS 15 Johnny Murray (USA), New York City. *With promoter, Tex Rickard, rapidly losing patience due to Johnny Kilbane's refusal to defend the title on a "proper" basis, he lined up Noble and Murray to fight for the State's "unofficial" version. Although Noble won a diamond studded championship belt, his "title" was never taken seriously and he returned to England without being asked to make a defence.*

25.05.21 Johnny Kilbane (USA) ND-W PTS 10 Freddie Jacks (GB), Cleveland

17.09.21 Johnny Kilbane (USA) ND-W CO 7 Danny Frush (GB), Cleveland. *Following this, Kilbane was inactive for almost one and a half years and had all but retired. It therefore came as no surprise when the NYSAC "officially" stripped him of the title for his inability to defend against the number one challenger, Johnny Dundee.*

15.08.22 Johnny Dundee (USA) W CO 9 Danny Frush (GB), Brooklyn - NY. *In May 1923, with Johnny Kilbane finally booked to defend his remaining portion of the championship, Johnny Dundee was temporarily unavailable. However, as not to stand in the way of unifying the title, the European champion was brought in as the challenger, with Dundee to be given first crack at the winner within 60 days.*

02.06.23 Eugene Criqui (FR) W CO 6 Johnny Kilbane (USA), New York City

26.07.23 Johnny Dundee (USA) W PTS 15 Eugene Criqui (FR), New York City. *When Dundee relinquished the title in August 1924, due to difficulty in making the weight, the NYSAC organised an elimination tournament to be held exclusively in New York City. Six men were invited to take part, namely Lou Paluso, Kid Kaplan, Bobby Garcia, Mike Dundee, Jose Lombardo and Danny Kramer. Unfortunately, protests from Babe Herman and Billy Defoe, which eventually found support, were filed too late and the first round had already been completed on 24 November 1924. Ten round decisions were secured by Kaplan over Garcia, Kramer over Dundee and Lombardo over Paluso, before the semi-final leg saw Kaplan kayo Lombardo in four rounds on 12 December 1924, while Kramer received a bye.*

02.01.25 Kid Kaplan (USA) W RTD 9 Danny Kramer (USA), New York City. *On the same bill, Babe Herman forced Billy Defoe to retire in the eighth round and in doing so would be Kaplan's first challenger.*

27.08.25 Kid Kaplan (USA) DREW 15 Babe Herman (USA), Waterbury

18.12.25 Kid Kaplan (USA) W PTS 15 Babe Herman (USA), New York City

28.06.26 Kid Kaplan (USA) W PTS 10 Bobby Garcia (USA), Hartford. *Often recorded in early Boxing News Annuals as a title bout, Kaplan was having great difficulty making the weight and this one*

was fought at catchweights, before he relinquished his belt the following month. In the moves to find a new champion, Massachusetts, who had a vested interest, pipped both New York and the NBA when matching Honeyboy Finnegan against Chic Suggs for their version of the title. The match was made after Suggs had earlier outpointed Babe Herman over ten rounds in Boston on 9 June 1926 and Finnegan had achieved a similar result against Red Chapman at the same venue on 16 September 1926.

15.11.26 Honeyboy Finnegan (USA) W PTS 10 Chic Suggs (USA), Boston - MASSACHUSETTS. *Finnegan forfeited Massachusetts' recognition in June 1927 when unable to make the weight.*

12.09.27 Benny Bass (USA) W PTS 10 Red Chapman (USA), Philadelphia - NBA

24.10.27 Tony Canzoneri (USA) W PTS 15 Johnny Dundee (USA), New York City - NY

10.02.28 **Tony Canzoneri** (USA) W PTS 15 Benny Bass (USA), New York City

28.09.28 **Andre Routis** (USA) W PTS 15 Tony Canzoneri (USA), New York City

27.05.29 **Andre Routis** (FR) W RSC 3 Buster Brown (USA), Baltimore

23.09.29 **Bat Battalino** (USA) W PTS 15 Andre Routis (FR), Hartford

15.07.30 **Bat Battalino** (USA) W CO 5 Ignacio Fernandez (PH), Hartford

12.12.30 **Bat Battalino** (USA) W PTS 15 Kid Chocolate (CUB), New York City

22.05.31 **Bat Battalino** (USA) W PTS 15 Fidel la Barba (USA), New York City

01.07.31 **Bat Battalino** (USA) W PTS 10 Bobby Brady (USA), Jersey City. *Although contested at catchweights, certain Annuals persisted in recording it as a title fight. The one thing we can be certain of, however, was that from then on, Battalino would always be struggling to make the weight.*

23.07.31 **Bat Battalino** (USA) W PTS 10 Freddie Miller (USA), Cincinnati

04.11.31 **Bat Battalino** (USA) W PTS 10 Earl Mastro (USA), Chicago

27.01.32 **Bat Battalino** (USA) NC 3 Freddie Miller (USA), Cincinnati. *Battalino forfeited the NBA version of the title on the scales after coming in three pounds overweight for a defence against stablemate, Miller. The fight went ahead, but following the announcement that Miller had been declared the winner after Battalino visited the canvas without a punch being thrown, the result was retrospectively declared a no-contest. Earlier, the NYSAC had already vacated the title after Battalino had come into a prospective defence against Lew Feldman, weighing in at 135½ lbs. For these actions, Battalino was suspended $5,000. Meanwhile, the NBA set up two semi-final legs in Detroit on 29 April 1932 to find a new champion. After Tommy Paul outpointed Frankie Wallace over ten rounds, a feat emulated by Johnny Pena against Fidel la Barba, the pair went forward to contest the final.*

26.05.32 Tommy Paul (USA) W PTS 10 Johnny Pena (PR), Detroit - NBA

25.08.32 Lew Feldman (USA) W PTS 10 Tommy Paul (USA), Coney Island. *Recorded in early Boxing News Annuals as a title fight, although not generally recognised as such, the NBA championship was not involved. However, following his victory, Feldman was matched against Kid Chocolate for the New York version of the title.*

16.09.32 Baby Arizmendi (MEX) W PTS 10 Tommy Paul (USA), Mexico City. *This was yet another fight shown in early Boxing News Annuals as involving the title, although, to be fair, it could have been recognised in Mexico as such, but, in any case, Paul continued to be recognised by the NBA. In December 1932, following wins over Newsboy Brown and Archie Bell, sandwiching a draw against Varias Milling, Arizmendi was proclaimed as the world featherweight champion by the Californian Boxing Commission.*

13.10.32 Kid Chocolate (CUB) W RSC 12 Lew Feldman (USA), New York City - NY

09.12.32 Kid Chocolate (CUB) W PTS 15 Fidel la Barba (USA), New York City - NY

13.01.33 Freddie Miller (USA) W PTS 10 Tommy Paul (USA), Chicago - NBA

28.02.33 Freddie Miller (USA) W PTS 10 Baby Arizmendi (MEX), Los Angeles - NBA

09.03.33 Freddie Miller (USA) W PTS 10 Little Dempsey (PH), Sacramento. *Occasionally shown as having involved the NBA championship, in fact, it was a non-title fight with Miller scaling 128 lbs to Dempsey's 129.*

21.03.33 Freddie Miller (USA) W PTS 10 Speedy Dado (PH), Los Angeles - NBA

19.05.33 Kid Chocolate (CUB) W PTS 15 Seaman Tommy Watson (GB), New York City - NY. *Unable to make the weight any longer, Chocolate relinquished the New York version of the title in February 1934.*

11.07.33 Freddie Miller (USA) W CO 4 Abie Israel (USA), Seattle - NBA

01.01.34 Freddie Miller (USA) W PTS 10 Jackie Sharkey (USA), Cincinnati - NBA

13.07.34 Freddie Miller (USA) W CO 8 Gene Espinosa (USA), Watsonville - NBA. *Although not recorded in the Ring Record Book as a title fight, the above was advertised as such and both men were inside 126 lbs.*

30.08.34 Baby Arizmendi (MEX) W PTS 15 Mike Belloise (USA), New York City. *With the NYSAC still not recognising Miller as champion, they had planned to set up an extensive elimination tournament in order to produce a successor, but, unfortunately, too many good men were unavailable. After much debate, a fight between Arizmendi and Belloise went ahead to decide the New York State title, not the NYSAC version of the title, as recorded in certain boxing annuals. In the semi-final legs, held on 11 May, Arizmendi and Belloise had outpointed Al Roth and Petey Hayes, each over ten rounds, respectively.*

20.09.34 Freddie Miller (USA) W PTS 15 Nel Tarleton (GB), Anfield Football Ground, Liverpool - NBA

01.01.35 Baby Arizmendi (MEX) W PTS 12 Henry Armstrong (USA), Mexico City - MEXICO/CALIFORNIA

17.02.35 Freddie Miller (USA) W CO 1 Jose Girones (SP), Barcelona - NBA

12.06.35 Freddie Miller (USA) W PTS 15 Nel Tarleton (GB), Stanley Racetrack, Liverpool - NBA

22.10.35 Freddie Miller (USA) W PTS 15 Vernon Cormier (USA), Boston - NBA

08.01.36 Mike Belloise (USA) W RSC 14 Claude Varner (USA), New York City. *Shown at one time in the Boxing News Annual as a NYSAC title fight, but later corrected, with the New York, Illinois and Californian Boxing Commissions not recognising Freddie Miller as champion, Belloise (New York) v Varner (California) was billed as a world championship eliminator, only.*

18.02.36 Freddie Miller (USA) W PTS 12 Johnny Pena (PR), Seattle - NBA

02.03.36 Freddie Miller (USA) W PTS 15 Petey Sarron (USA), Miami - NBA

03.04.36 Mike Belloise (USA) W CO 14 Everette Rightmire (USA), Chicago. *Another Belloise fight recorded in the Boxing News Annual as a championship battle, although later corrected, this was a final eliminator, with the winner to take on Baby Arizmendi for the New York, Illinois and Californian versions of the title. That was the general idea, but somehow the match was not made and Belloise was proclaimed NYSAC champion later that month.*

11.05.36 Petey Sarron (USA) W PTS 15 Freddie Miller (USA), Washington - NBA

22.07.36 Petey Sarron (USA) W PTS 15 Baby Manuel (USA), Dallas - NBA

04.08.36 Henry Armstrong (USA) W PTS 10 Baby Arizmendi (MEX), Los Angeles - MEXICO/CALIFORNIA

03.09.36 Mike Belloise (USA) W CO 9 Dave Crowley (GB), New York City - NY.

27.10.36 Henry Armstrong (USA) W PTS 10 Mike Belloise (USA), Los Angeles - MEXICO/CALIFORNIA. *Although advertised as a Californian world title defence by Armstrong, and with both men inside 126 lbs, it was not recognised as such by the NYSAC, who continued to support Belloise as their world champion even though he lost. However, less than a year later, on 10 August 1937, Belloise, due to defend against Armstrong, was forced to abdicate the New York version of the title on suffering a serious illness. He did so on the premise that he would be given the opportunity of winning it back if and when he returned to the ring. Meanwhile, Armstrong was matched against Petey Sarron in a unification fight.*

04.09.37 Petey Sarron (USA) W PTS 12 Freddie Miller (USA), Johannesburg - NBA

05.10.37 Maurice Holtzer (FR) W PTS 15 Phil Dolhem (BEL), Algiers - IBU

29.10.37 Henry Armstrong (USA) W CO 6 Petey Sarron (USA), New York City - NY/NBA. *Henry Armstrong relinquished New York/NBA version of the title in November 1938 on becoming world champion at lightweight and welterweight.*

19.02.38 Maurice Holtzer (FR) DREW 15 Maurice Dubois (SWI), Geneva - IBU. *During an international boxing convention held in Rome in May 1938, which was attended by many leading authorities within the sport, the IBU agreed to refuse to recognise all individually-made world champions, including their own Maurice Holtzer, in an effort to stand by one universally acknowledged champion.*

17.06.38 Leo Rodak (USA) W PTS 15 Jackie Wilson (USA), Baltimore - MARYLAND

17.10.38 Joey Archibald (USA) W PTS 15 Mike Belloise (USA), New York City - NY

24.10.38 Leo Rodak (USA) W PTS 15 Freddie Miller (USA), Washington - MARYLAND

04.11.38 Claude Varner (USA) W CO 9 Mickey Miller (A), Melbourne. *Following his win, Varner was accorded no recognition outside of Melbourne, let alone the rest of Australia and any claim he may have had quickly disintegrated. Billed as the first title bout in Australia since Burns v Johnson and conveniently forgetting Frisco v Miller on 27 August 1938, it was contested over 15 rounds, with Miller coming in at 123½ lbs to Varner's 126.*

05.12.38 Petey Scalzo (USA) W CO 2 Joey Archibald (USA), New York City. *Recorded in early Boxing News Annuals as a championship contest, it was, in fact, a non-title fight at catchweights and Archibald remained NYSAC champion.*

29.12.38 Leo Rodak (USA) W PTS 10 Leone Efrati (USA), Chicago. *Shown in early Boxing News Annuals as a title fight, it was only afterwards that the NBA proclaimed Rodak as their champion. The contest itself was decided at catchweights, with Rodak weighing 129 lbs and Efrati 130½ and, although Rodak was later surprisingly defeated by Everette Rightmire, he still went forward as the NBA representative in a unification clash with Joey Archibald.*

18.04.39 **Joey Archibald** (USA) W PTS 15 Leo Rodak (USA), Providence

28.09.39 **Joey Archibald** (USA) W PTS 15 Harry Jeffra (USA), Washington. *Joey Archibald forfeited NBA recognition in April 1940 for failing to meet the leading challenger, Petey Scalzo and Scalzo was proclaimed as their champion on 1 May 1940.*

08.05.40 Jimmy Perrin (USA) W PTS 15 Bobby Ruffin (USA), New Orleans - LOUISIANA

15.05.40 Petey Scalzo (USA) W RSC 6 Frankie Covelli (USA), Washington. *Shown as an NBA title fight in some record books, although billed as a championship match, it was not supported by the Maryland Boxing Commission, who, along with the NYSAC, recognised Joey Archibald as champion.*

20.05.40 Harry Jeffra (USA) W PTS 15 Joey Archibald (USA), Baltimore - NY/MARYLAND

10.07.40 Petey Scalzo (USA) W RSC 15 Bobby Poison Ivy (USA), Hartford - NBA

29.07.40 Harry Jeffra (USA) W PTS 15 Spider Armstrong (C), Baltimore - NY/MARYLAND

26.08.40 Petey Scalzo (USA) W PTS 10 Jimmy Perrin (USA), New Orleans. *Following this defeat at the hands of the NBA champion, Scalzo, Perrin, forfeited Louisianan recognition. A non-title fight at catchweights, it was shown in the Boxing News Annual at one time as a championship fight.*

12.05.41 Joey Archibald (USA) W PTS 15 Harry Jeffra (USA), Washington - NY/MARYLAND

19.05.41 Petey Scalzo (USA) W PTS 15 Phil Zwick (USA), Milwaukee - NBA

01.07.41 Richie Lemos (USA) W CO 5 Petey Scalzo (USA), Los Angeles - NBA

11.09.41 Chalky Wright (MEX) W CO 11 Joey Archibald (USA), Washington - NY/MARYLAND

15.09.41 Harry Jeffra (USA) W PTS 12 Lou Transparenti (USA), Baltimore. *Another State title fight that was earlier recorded as being for the Maryland version of the championship, but corrected in the 1979 Boxing News Special, it merely helped Jeffra to get a crack at Chalky Wright for the NYSAC version.*

18.11.41 Jackie Wilson (USA) W PTS 12 Richie Lemos (USA), Los Angeles - NBA

16.12.41 Jackie Wilson (USA) W PTS 12 Richie Lemos (USA), Los Angeles - NBA

19.06.42 Chalky Wright (MEX) W RSC 10 Harry Jeffra (USA), Baltimore - NY/MARYLAND

25.09.42 Chalky Wright (MEX) W PTS 15 Lulu Constantino (USA), New York City - NY

20.11.42 Willie Pep (USA) W PTS 15 Chalky Wright (MEX), New York City - NY

18.01.43 Jackie Callura (C) W PTS 15 Jackie Wilson (USA), Providence - NBA

18.03.43 Jackie Callura (C) W PTS 15 Jackie Wilson (USA), Boston - NBA

08.06.43 Willie Pep (USA) W PTS 15 Sal Bartolo (USA), Boston - NY/MASSACHUSETTS

16.08.43 Phil Terranova (USA) W CO 8 Jackie Callura (C), New Orleans - NBA

27.12.43 Phil Terranova (USA) W RSC 6 Jackie Callura (C), New Orleans - NBA

10.03.44 Sal Bartolo (USA) W PTS 15 Phil Terranova (USA), Boston - NBA

05.05.44 Sal Bartolo (USA) W PTS 15 Phil Terranova (USA), Boston - NBA

29.09.44 Willie Pep (USA) W PTS 15 Chalky Wright (MEX), New York City - NY

15.12.44 Sal Bartolo (USA) W PTS 15 Willie Roache (USA), Boston - NBA

19.02.45 Willie Pep (USA) W PTS 15 Phil Terranova (USA), New York City - NY

03.05.46 Sal Bartolo (USA) W CO 6 Spider Armstrong (C), Boston - NBA

07.06.46 **Willie Pep** (USA) W CO 12 Sal Bartolo (USA), New York City

22.08.47 **Willie Pep** (USA) W CO 12 Jock Leslie (USA), Flint

24.02.48 **Willie Pep** (USA) W RSC 10 Humberto Sierra (CUB), Miami

29.10.48 Sandy Saddler (USA) W CO 4 Willie Pep (USA), New York City

11.02.49 Willie Pep (USA) W PTS 15 Sandy Saddler (USA), New York City

20.09.49 Willie Pep (USA) W RSC 7 Eddie Compo (USA), Waterbury

16.01.50 Willie Pep (USA) W CO 5 Charley Riley (USA), St Louis

17.03.50 Willie Pep (USA) W PTS 15 Ray Famechon (FR), New York City

08.09.50 Sandy Saddler (USA) W RTD 8 Willie Pep (USA), New York City

26.09.51 Sandy Saddler (USA) W RTD 9 Willie Pep (USA), New York City. *In May 1952, Sandy Saddler was inducted into the Army and the NBA and EBU decided to appoint an "interim champion" in his absence, with the winner of Ray Famechon (France) v Roy Ankrah (Ghana) fighting American, Percy Bassett, in the final. Bassett was duly crowned on 9 February 1953 in Paris when he retired Famechon in the third, but, after also forcing Lulu Perez (USA) to retire in the 11th on 25 June 1954, he lost the "interim title" to Teddy Davis (USA) on 26 November 1954, when going down on points over 12 rounds. The last two fights took place in New York City.*

25.02.55 Sandy Saddler (USA) W PTS 15 Teddy Davis (USA), New York City

18.01.56 Sandy Saddler (USA) W RSC 13 Flash Elorde (PH), San Francisco. *Sandy Saddler relinquished title and retired as the undefeated champion in January 1957, having suffered serious eye damage. For the first time in boxing history, a World Championship Committee was set up to organise a series of eliminators. It was agreed that the number one challenger, the European champion, Cherif Hamia, would fight the winner of Hogan Kid Bassey v Miguel Berios. Berios had already eliminated Carmelo Costa from the tournament, but was unable to advance any further, being outpointed over 12 rounds by the Nigerian on 27 April 1957 in Washington.*

24.06.57 Hogan Kid Bassey (N) W RSC 10 Cherif Hamia (FR), Paris

01.04.58 Hogan Kid Bassey (N) W CO 3 Ricardo Moreno (MEX), Los Angeles

18.03.59 Davey Moore (USA) W RTD 13 Hogan Kid Bassey (N), Los Angeles

19.08.59 Davey Moore (USA) W RTD 10 Hogan Kid Bassey (N), Los Angeles

29.08.60 Davey Moore (USA) W PTS 15 Kazuo Takayama (JAP), Tokyo

08.04.61 Davey Moore (USA) W CO 1 Danny Valdez (USA), Los Angeles

13.11.61 Davey Moore (USA) W PTS 15 Kazuo Takayama (JAP), Tokyo

17.08.62 Davey Moore (USA) W RSC 2 Olli Maki (FIN), Helsinki

21.03.63 Sugar Ramos (CUB) W RTD 10 Davey Moore (USA), Los Angeles. *After collapsing in the dressing room following the fight, Davey Moore failed to regain consciousness and died in hospital two days later.*

13.07.63 Sugar Ramos (CUB) W PTS 15 Rafiu King (N), Mexico City

28.02.64 Sugar Ramos (CUB) W RTD 6 Mitsunori Seki (JAP), Tokyo

09.05.64 Sugar Ramos (CUB) W PTS 15 Floyd Robertson (GH), Accra. *Following the fight, the Ghanaian Boxing Commission altered the result to that of a no-contest and later changed the decision in Robertson's favour. However, the rest of the world continued to recognise Ramos as the champion.*

26.09.64 **Vicente Saldivar** (MEX) W RTD 11 Sugar Ramos (CUB), Mexico City

06.12.64 **Vicente Saldivar** (MEX) W RSC 11 Delfino Rosales (MEX), Guanajuanato. *This Mexican title fight occasionally turns up in record books as a world championship match, although not billed as one. The reason being that as both men were obviously inside the weight, Saldivar's world title would have been at risk had he lost. Shortly afterwards, Saldivar relinquished his Mexican title.*

07.05.65 **Vicente Saldivar** (MEX) W RSC 15 Raul Rojas (USA), Los Angeles

07.09.65 **Vicente Saldivar** (MEX) W PTS 15 Howard Winstone (GB), Earls Court, London

12.02.66 **Vicente Saldivar** (MEX) W CO 2 Floyd Robertson (GH), Mexico City

07.08.66 **Vicente Saldivar** (MEX) W PTS 15 Mitsunori Seki (JAP), Mexico City

29.01.67 **Vicente Saldivar** (MEX) W RSC 7 Mitsunori Seki (JAP), Mexico City

15.06.67 **Vicente Saldivar** (MEX) W PTS 15 Howard Winstone (GB), Ninian Park, Cardiff

14.10.67 **Vicente Saldivar** (MEX) W RTD 12 Howard Winstone (GB), Mexico City. *Following Saldivar's announcement at the end of the fight that he was retiring, the WBC immediately matched Winstone against Mitsunori Seki for the vacant crown and, with the WBA slow to make a statement, the Californian Boxing Commission set up a fight between Raul Rojas and Antonio Herrera for their version of the title.*

14.12.67 Raul Rojas (USA) W PTS 15 Antonio Herrera (COL), Los Angeles - CALIFORNIA

23.01.68 Howard Winstone (GB) W RSC 9 Mitsunori Seki (JAP),Albert Hall, London - WBC

28.03.68 Raul Rojas (USA) W PTS 15 Enrique Higgins (COL), Los Angeles - WBA

20.05.68 Johnny Famechon (A) W DIS 13 Bobby Valdez (USA), Sydney - AUSTRALIA

24.07.68 Jose Legra (CUB) W RSC 5 Howard Winstone (GB), Coney Beach Arena, Porthcawl - WBC

28.09.68 Shozo Saijyo (JAP) W PTS 15 Raul Rojas (USA), Los Angeles - WBA

21.01.69 Johnny Famechon (A) W PTS 15 Jose Legra (CUB), Albert Hall, London - WBC

09.02.69 Shozo Saijyo (JAP) W PTS 15 Pedro Gomez (VEN), Tokyo - WBA

28.07.69 Johnny Famechon (A) W PTS 15 Fighting Harada (JAP), Sydney - WBC

07.09.69 Shozo Saijyo (JAP) W CO 2 Jose Luis Pimental (MEX), Sapporo - WBA

06.01.70 Johnny Famechon (A) W CO 14 Fighting Harada (JAP), Tokyo - WBC

08.02.70 Shozo Saijyo (JAP) W PTS 15 Godfrey Stevens (CH), Tokyo - WBA

09.05.70 Vicente Saldivar (MEX) W PTS 15 Johnny Famechon (A), Rome - WBC

05.07.70 Shozo Saijyo (JAP) W PTS 15 Frankie Crawford (USA), Sendai - WBA

11.12.70 Kuniaki Shibata (JAP) W RSC 12 Vicente Saldivar (MEX), Tijuana - WBC

28.02.71 Shozo Saijyo (JAP) W PTS 15 Frankie Crawford (USA), Utsonomuja - WBA

03.06.71 Kuniaki Shibata (JAP) W CO 1 Raul Cruz (MEX), Tokyo - WBC

02.09.71 Antonio Gomez (VEN) W RSC 5 Shozo Saijyo (JAP), Tokyo - WBA

11.11.71 Kuniaki Shibata (JAP) DREW 15 Ernesto Marcel (PAN), Matsuyama - WBC

06.02.72 Antonio Gomez (VEN) W CO 7 Raul Martinez (MEX), Maracay - WBA

19.05.72 Clemente Sanchez (MEX) W CO 3 Kuniaki Shibata (JAP), Tokyo - WBC

19.08.72 Ernesto Marcel (PAN) W PTS 15 Antonio Gomez (VEN), Maracay - WBA

03.12.72 Ernesto Marcel (PAN) W RSC 6 Enrique Garcia (MEX), Panama City - WBA

16.12.72 Jose Legra (CUB) W RSC 10 Clemente Sanchez (MEX), Monterrey - WBC. *Sanchez forfeited his title on the scales before the fight began when weighing in three pounds overweight. As not to spoil the promotion, the fight went ahead and Legra was proclaimed champion on the result.*

05.05.73 Eder Jofre (BR) W PTS 15 Jose Legra (CUB), Brasilia - WBC

14.07.73 Ernesto Marcel (PAN) W RTD 11 Antonio Gomez (VEN), Panama City - WBA

08.09.73 Ernesto Marcel (PAN) W CO 9 Spider Nemoto (JAP), Panama City - WBA

21.10.73 Eder Jofre (BR) W CO 4 Vicente Saldivar (MEX), Salvador - WBC. *Eder Jofre forfeited WBC recognition in June 1974 for failing to defend against Alfredo Marcano.*

16.02.74 Ernesto Marcel (PAN) W PTS 15 Alexis Arguello (NIC), Panama City - WBA. *Ernesto Marcel retired as undefeated WBA champion in May 1974.*

09.07.74 Ruben Olivares (MEX) W RSC 7 Zensuke Utagawa (JAP), Los Angeles - WBA

07.09.74 Bobby Chacon (USA) W RSC 9 Alfredo Marcano (VEN), Los Angeles - WBC

23.11.74 Alexis Arguello (NIC) W CO 13 Ruben Olivares (MEX), Los Angeles - WBA

01.03.75 Bobby Chacon (USA) W CO 2 Jesus Estrada (MEX), Los Angeles - WBC

15.03.75 Alexis Arguello (NIC) W RSC 8 Leonel Hernandez (VEN), Caracas - WBA

31.05.75 Alexis Arguello (NIC) W RSC 2 Rigoberto Riasco (PAN), Managua - WBA

20.06.75 Ruben Olivares (MEX) W RSC 2 Bobby Chacon (USA), Los Angeles - WBC

20.09.75 David Kotey (GH) W PTS 15 Ruben Olivares (MEX), Los Angeles - WBC

12.10.75 Alexis Arguello (NIC) W CO 5 Royal Kobayashi (JAP), Tokyo - WBA

06.03.76 David Kotey (GH) W RSC 12 Flipper Uehara (JAP), Accra - WBC

19.06.76 Alexis Arguello (NIC) W CO 3 Salvatore Torres (MEX), Los Angeles - WBA. *Alexis Arguello relinquished WBA version of title in June 1977 due to weight making difficulties.*

16.07.76 David Kotey (GH) W RSC 3 Shigeo Fukuyama (JAP), Tokyo - WBC

05.11.76 Danny Lopez (USA) W PTS 15 David Kotey (GH), Accra - WBC

15.01.77 Rafael Ortega (PAN) W PTS 15 Francisco Coronado (NIC), Panama City - WBA

29.05.77 Rafael Ortega (PAN) W PTS 15 Flipper Uehara (JAP), Okinawa - WBA

13.09.77 Danny Lopez (USA) W RSC 7 Jose Torres (MEX), Los Angeles - WBC

17.12.77 Cecilio Lastra (SP) W PTS 15 Rafael Ortega (PAN), Torrelavega - WBA

15.02.78 Danny Lopez (USA) W RSC 6 David Kotey (GH), Las Vegas - WBC

15.04.78 Eusebio Pedroza (PAN) W CO 13 Cecilio Lastra (SP), Panama City - WBA

23.04.78 Danny Lopez (USA) W RSC 6 Jose de Paula (BR), Los Angeles - WBC

02.07.78 Eusebio Pedroza (PAN) W RSC 12 Ernesto Herrera (MEX), Panama City - WBA

15.09.78 Danny Lopez (USA) W CO 2 Juan Malvarez (ARG), New Orleans - WBC

21.10.78 Danny Lopez (USA) W DIS 4 Fel Clemente (PH), Pesaro - WBC

27.11.78 Eusebio Pedroza (PAN) W PTS 15 Enrique Solis (PR), San Juan - WBA

09.01.79 Eusebio Pedroza (PAN) W RTD 13 Royal Kobayashi (JAP), Tokyo - WBA

10.03.79 Danny Lopez (USA) W CO 2 Roberto Castanon (SP), Salt Lake City - WBC

08.04.79 Eusebio Pedroza (PAN) W RSC 11 Hector Carrasquilla (PAN), Panama City - WBA

17.06.79 Danny Lopez (USA) W CO 15 Mike Ayala (USA), San Antonio - WBC. *Ayala was actually counted out earlier, in the 11th round, but after protests from his camp that the referee had taken up the count too early were supported by the timekeeper, he was allowed to continue.*

21.07.79 Eusebio Pedroza (PAN) W RSC 12 Ruben Olivares (MEX), Houston - WBA

25.09.79 Danny Lopez (USA) W RSC 3 Jose Caba (DOM), Los Angeles - WBC

17.11.79 Eusebio Pedroza (PAN) W RSC 11 Johnny Aba (PNG), Port Moresby - WBA

22.01.80 Eusebio Pedroza (PAN) W PTS 15 Spider Nemoto (JAP), Tokyo - WBA

02.02.80 Salvador Sanchez (MEX) W RSC 13 Danny Lopez (USA), Phoenix - WBC

29.03.80 Eusebio Pedroza (PAN) W CO 9 Juan Malvarez (ARG), Panama City - WBA

12.04.80 Salvador Sanchez (MEX) W PTS 15 Ruben Castillo (USA), Tucson - WBC

21.06.80 Salvador Sanchez (MEX) W RSC 14 Danny Lopez (USA), Las Vegas - WBC

20.07.80 Eusebio Pedroza (PAN) W CO 9 Sa-Wang Kim (SK), Seoul - WBA

13.09.80 Salvador Sanchez (MEX) W PTS 15 Pat Ford (GU), San Antonio - WBC

04.10.80 Eusebio Pedroza (PAN) W PTS 15 Rocky Lockridge (USA), McAfee - WBA

13.12.80 Salvador Sanchez (MEX) W PTS 15 Juan Laporte (PR), El Paso - WBC

14.02.81 Eusebio Pedroza (PAN) W CO 13 Pat Ford (GU), Panama City - WBA

22.03.81 Salvador Sanchez (MEX) W RSC 10 Roberto Castanon (SP), Las Vegas - WBC

01.08.81 Eusebio Pedroza (PAN) W CO 7 Carlos Pinango (VEN), Caracas - WBA

21.08.81 Salvador Sanchez (MEX) W RSC 8 Wilfredo Gomez (PR), Las Vegas - WBC

05.12.81 Eusebio Pedroza (PAN) W CO 5 Bashew Sibaca (SA), Panama City - WBA

12.12.81 Salvador Sanchez (MEX) W PTS 15 Pat Cowdell (GB), Houston - WBC

24.01.82 Eusebio Pedroza (PAN) W PTS 15 Juan Laporte (PR), Atlantic City - WBA

08.05.82 Salvador Sanchez (MEX) W PTS 15 Rocky Garcia (USA), Dallas - WBC

21.07.82 Salvador Sanchez (MEX) W RSC 15 Azumah Nelson (GH), New York City - WBC. *Salvador Sanchez left WBC version of title vacant when he died in a road crash in August 1982.*

15.09.82 Juan Laporte (PR) W RTD 10 Mario Miranda (COL), New York City - WBC

16.10.82 Eusebio Pedroza (PAN) DREW 15 Bernard Taylor (USA), Charlotte - WBA

20.02.83 Juan Laporte (PR) W PTS 12 Ruben Castillo (USA), San Juan - WBC

24.04.83 Eusebio Pedroza (PAN) W PTS 15 Rocky Lockridge (USA), Liguma - WBA

25.06.83 Juan Laporte (PR) W PTS 12 Johnny de la Rosa (DOM), San Juan - WBC

22.10.83 Eusebio Pedroza (PAN) W PTS 15 Jose Caba (DOM), San Remo - WBA

04.03.84 Min-Keun Oh (SK) W CO 2 Joko Arter (PH), Seoul - IBF

31.03.84 Wilfredo Gomez (PR) W PTS 12 Juan Laporte (PR), San Juan - WBC

27.05.84 Eusebio Pedroza (PAN) W PTS 15 Angel Mayor (VEN), Maracaibo - WBA

10.06.84 Min-Keun Oh (SK) W PTS 15 Kelvin Lampkin (USA), Seoul - IBF

08.12.84 Azumah Nelson (GH) W RSC 11 Wilfredo Gomez (PR), San Juan - WBC

02.02.85 Eusebio Pedroza (PAN) W PTS 15 Jorge Lujan (PAN), Panama City - WBA

07.04.85 Min-Keun Oh (SK) W PTS 15 Irving Mitchell (USA), Pusan - IBF

08.06.85 Barry McGuigan (GB) W PTS 15 Eusebio Pedroza (PAN), Loftus Road, London - WBA

06.09.85 Azumah Nelson (GH) W CO 5 Juvenal Ordenes (CH), Miami - WBC

28.09.85 Barry McGuigan (GB) W RTD 8 Bernard Taylor (USA), King's Hall, Belfast - WBA

12.10.85 Azumah Nelson (GH) W CO 1 Pat Cowdell (GB), National Exhibition Centre, Birmingham - WBC

29.11.85 Ki-Yung Chung (SK) W RSC 15 Min-Keun Oh (SK), Chonju - IBF

15.02.86 Barry McGuigan (GB) W RSC 14 Danilo Cabrera (DOM), Dublin - WBA

16.02.86 Ki-Yung Chung (SK) W RTD 6 Tyrone Jackson (USA), Ulsan - IBF

25.02.86 Azumah Nelson (GH) W PTS 12 Marcos Villasana (MEX), Los Angeles - WBC

18.05.86 Ki-Yung Chung (SK) W PTS 15 Richard Savage (USA), Taegu - IBF

22.06.86 Azumah Nelson (GH) W RSC 10 Danilo Cabrera (DOM), San Juan - WBC

23.06.86 Steve Cruz (USA) W PTS 15 Barry McGuigan (GB), Las Vegas - WBA

30.08.86 Antonio Rivera (PR) W RTD 10 Ki-Yung Chung (SK), Osan - IBF

06.03.87 Antonio Esparragoza (VEN) W RSC 12 Steve Cruz (USA), Fort Worth - WBA

07.03.87 Azumah Nelson (GH) W CO 6 Mauro Gutierrez (MEX), Las Vegas - WBC

26.07.87 Antonio Esparragoza (VEN) W CO 10 Pascual Aranda (MEX), Houston - WBA

29.08.87 Azumah Nelson (GH) W PTS 12 Marcos Villasana (MEX), Los Angeles - WBC. *Azumah Nelson relinquished WBC version of title in January 1988 in order to contest the vacant super-featherweight crown.*

23.01.88 Calvin Grove (USA) W RSC 4 Antonio Rivera (PR), Gamaches, France - IBF

07.03.88 Jeff Fenech (A) W RSC 10 Victor Callejas (PR), Sydney - WBC

17.05.88 Calvin Grove (USA) W PTS 15 Myron Taylor (USA), Atlantic City - IBF

23.06.88 Antonio Esparragoza (VEN) DREW 12 Marcos Villasana (MEX), Los Angeles - WBA

04.08.88 Jorge Paez (MEX) W PTS 15 Calvin Grove (USA), Mexicali - IBF

12.08.88 Jeff Fenech (A) W RSC 5 Tyrone Downes (BAR), Melbourne - WBC

05.11.88 Antonio Esparragoza (VEN) W CO 8 Jose Marmolejo (PAN), Marsala - WBA

30.11.88 Jeff Fenech (A) W RSC 5 George Navarro (USA), Melbourne - WBC

28.01.89 Maurizio Stecca (ITA) W RSC 6 Pedro Nolasco (DOM), Milan - WBO

25.03.89 Antonio Esparragoza (VEN) W CO 10 Mitsuru Sugiya (JAP), Kawasaki - WBA

30.03.89 Jorge Paez (MEX) W CO 11 Calvin Grove (USA), Mexicali - IBF

08.04.89 Jeff Fenech (A) W PTS 12 Marcos Villasana (MEX), Melbourne - WBC. *Jeff Fenech relinquished WBC version of title immediately after the fight due to difficulty making the weight.*

21.05.89 Jorge Paez (MEX) DREW 12 Louie Espinosa (USA), Phoenix - IBF

02.06.89 Antonio Esparragoza (VEN) W CO 6 Jean-Marc Renard (BEL), Namur - WBA

16.06.89 Maurizio Stecca (ITA) W RSC 9 Angel Mayor (VEN), Milan - WBO

06.08.89 Jorge Paez (MEX) W PTS 12 Steve Cruz (USA), El Paso - IBF

16.09.89 Jorge Paez (MEX) W CO 2 Jose Mario Lopez (ARG), Mexico City - IBF

22.09.89 Antonio Esparragoza (VEN) W CO 5 Eduardo Montoya (MEX), Mexicali - WBA

11.11.89 Louie Espinosa (USA) W RSC 7 Maurizio Stecca (ITA), Rimini - WBO

09.12.89 Jorge Paez (MEX) W RSC 6 Lupe Gutierrez (USA), Reno - IBF

04.02.90 Jorge Paez (MEX) W PTS 12 Troy Dorsey (USA), Las Vegas - IBF

07.04.90 Jorge Paez (MEX) W PTS 12 Louie Espinosa (USA), Las Vegas - IBF/WBO

12.05.90 Antonio Esparragoza (VEN) W PTS 12 Chan-Mok Park (SK), Seoul - WBA

02.06.90 Marcos Villasana (MEX) W RSC 8 Paul Hodkinson (GB), G-Mex Centre, Manchester - WBC

08.07.90 Jorge Paez (MEX) DREW 12 Troy Dorsey (USA), Las Vegas - IBF/WBO. *Jorge Paez relinquished IBF/WBO versions of title in April 1991 to campaign at super-featherweight.*

30.09.90 Marcos Villasana (MEX) W RSC 8 Javier Marquez (MEX), Mexico City - WBC

26.01.91 Maurizio Stecca (ITA) W RSC 5 Armando Reyes (DOM), Sassari - WBO

30.03.91 Kyun-Yung Park (SK) W PTS 12 Antonio Esparragoza (VEN), Kwangju - WBA

11.04.91 Marcos Villasana (MEX) W RSC 6 Rafael Zuniga (COL), Mexico City - WBC

03.06.91 Troy Dorsey (USA W CO 1 Alfred Rangel (USA), Las Vegas - IBF

15.06.91 Maurizio Stecca (ITA) W PTS 12 Fernando Ramos (MEX), Mantichiari - WBO

15.06.91 Kyun-Yung Park (SK) W RSC 6 Masuaki Takeda (JAP), Seoul - WBA

12.08.91 Manuel Medina (MEX) W PTS 12 Troy Dorsey (USA), Los Angeles - IBF

16.08.91 Marcos Villasana (MEX) W PTS 12 Ricardo Cepeda (PR), Marbella - WBC

14.09.91 Kyun-Yung Park (SK) W PTS 12 Eloy Rojas (VEN), Mokpo - WBA

09.11.91 Maurizio Stecca (ITA) W RTD 9 Tim Driscoll (GB), Campione d'Italia - WBO

13.11.91 Paul Hodkinson (GB) W PTS 12 Marcos Villasana (MEX), Maysfield Leisure Centre, Belfast - WBC

18.11.91 Manuel Medina (MEX) W TD 9 Tom Johnson (USA), Los Angeles - IBF. *Under IBF rules if an accidental clash of heads after six rounds causes the proceedings to be halted, the fight goes to the scorecards and it was on that basis that Medina retained his title.*

25.01.92 Kyun-Yung Park (SK) W CO 9 Seiji Asakawa (JAP) Seoul - WBA

14.03.92 Manuel Medina (MEX) W PTS 12 Fabrice Benichou (FR), Antibes - IBF

25.04.92 Paul Hodkinson (GB) W RSC 3 Steve Cruz (USA), Maysfield Leisure Centre, Belfast - WBC

25.04.92 Kyun-Yung Park (SK) W RSC 11 Koji Matsumoto (JAP), Ansan - WBA

16.05.92 Colin McMillan (GB) W PTS 12 Maurizio Stecca (ITA), Alexandra Palace, London - WBO

22.07.92 Manuel Medina (MEX) W RTD 10 Fabrizio Cappai (ITA), Capo d'Orlando - IBF

29.08.92 Kyun-Yung Park (SK) W PTS 12 Giovanni Neves (VEN), Taeju - WBA

12.09.92 Paul Hodkinson (GB) W RSC 10 Fabrice Benichou (FR), Blagnac - WBC

26.09.92 Ruben Palacio (COL) W RTD 8 Colin McMillan (GB), Olympia National Hall, London - WBO. *Ruben Palacio forfeited WBO version of title when he was pronounced HIV positive in April 1993.*

23.10.92 Manuel Medina (MEX) W PTS 12 Moussa Sangare (FR), Gravelines - IBF

19.12.92 Kyun-Yung Park (SK) W PTS 12 Ever Beleno (COL), Changwon - WBA

03.02.93 Paul Hodkinson (GB) W RTD 4 Ricardo Cepeda (PR), Olympia National Hall, London - WBC

26.02.93 Tom Johnson (USA) W PTS 12 Manuel Medina (MEX), Melun - IBF

20.03.93 Kyun-Yung Park (SK) W RSC 4 Thanomchit Kiatkriengkrai (TH), Chejudo - WBA

17.04.93 Steve Robinson (GB) W PTS 12 John Davison (GB), Northumbria Leisure Centre, Washington - WBO

28.04.93 Gregorio Vargas (MEX) W RTD 7 Paul Hodkinson (GB), Dublin - WBC

Super-Featherweight (130 lbs)

Also known as the junior-lightweight division, the weight class was the earliest of the "junior" divisions, if you disregard the light-heavyweights. Prior to being accepted by the New York State Athletic Commission, after promoter Tex Rickard put up a belt valued at $2,500 in 1921, there had already been some activity at 130 lbs. Although Johnny Dundee is generally recognised as being the first champion, back in 1914 Battling Kid Nelson (USA) claimed the unofficial title tag in fights against Fritz Schmidt (won on points over ten rounds in Germany) and Gerry Anderson (won by a knockout in the second round in London), before being outpointed over 15 rounds by Benny Kid Berger in Liverpool. Two years later, in Providence, on 15 March 1917, Artie O'Leary outpointed fellow American, Jimmy Kane, over 15 rounds, to re-introduce the weight class, but he appears not to have defended same.

18.11.21 Johnny Dundee (USA) W DIS 5 K.O. Chaney (USA), New York City - NY

06.07.22 Johnny Dundee (USA) W PTS 15 Jackie Sharkey (USA), New York City - NY

28.08.22 Johnny Dundee (USA) W PTS 15 Pepper Martin (USA), New York City - NY

02.02.23 Johnny Dundee (USA) W PTS 15 Elino Flores (PH), New York City - NY

30.05.23 Jack Bernstein (USA) W PTS 15 Johnny Dundee (USA), New York City - NY

25.06.23 Jack Bernstein (USA) ND-W CO 5 Freddie Jacks (GB), Philadelphia - NY/NBA. *Jacks weighed 130 lbs.*

17.12.23 Johnny Dundee (USA) W PTS 15 Jack Bernstein (USA), New York City - NY-NBA

20.06.24 Kid Sullivan (USA) W PTS 10 Johnny Dundee (USA), Brooklyn - NY/NBA

18.08.24 Kid Sullivan (USA) W PTS 15 Pepper Martin (USA), New York City - NY/NBA

15.10.24 Kid Sullivan (USA) W CO 5 Mike Ballerino (USA), New York City - NY/NBA

01.04.25 Mike Ballerino (USA) W PTS 10 Kid Sullivan (USA), Philadelphia - NY/NBA

06.07.25 Mike Ballerino (USA) W PTS 15 Pepper Martin (USA), Long Island - NY/NBA

02.12.25 Tod Morgan (USA) W RTD 10 Mike Ballerino (USA), Los Angeles - NY/NBA

03.06.26 Tod Morgan (USA) W RTD 6 Kid Sullivan (USA), Brooklyn - NY/NBA

30.09.26 Tod Morgan (USA) W PTS 15 Joe Glick (USA), New York City - NY/NBA

19.10.26 Tod Morgan (USA) W PTS 10 Johnny Dundee (USA), San Francisco - NY/NBA

19.11.26 Tod Morgan (USA) W PTS 15 Carl Duane (USA), New York City - NY/NBA

28.05.27 Tod Morgan (USA) W PTS 12 Vic Foley (C), Vancouver - NY/NBA

16.12.27 Tod Morgan (USA) W DIS 14 Joe Glick (USA), New York City - NY/NBA

24.05.28 Tod Morgan (USA) W PTS 15 Eddie Martin (USA), New York City - NY/NBA

18.07.28 Tod Morgan (USA) W PTS 15 Eddie Martin (USA), Brooklyn - NY/NBA

03.12.28 Tod Morgan (USA) DREW 10 Santiago Zorilla (PAN), San Francisco - NY/NBA

01.01.29 Tod Morgan (USA) ND-L PTS 10 Joey Sangor (USA), Milwauke - NY/NBA. *Sangor weighed 128 lbs.*

05.04.29 Tod Morgan (USA) W PTS 10 Santiago Zorilla (PAN), Los Angeles - NY/NBA

20.05.29 Tod Morgan (USA) W PTS 10 Baby Sal Sorio (USA), Los Angeles - NY/NBA

20.12.29 Benny Bass (USA) W CO 2 Tod Morgan (USA), New York City NY/NBA. *After the bout, both fighters' purses were suspended while the New York State Athletic Commission conducted an investigation into a possible betting coup, but, with no conclusive evidence forthcoming, both men were eventually cleared of any misconduct. A short while later, on 1 January 1930, in an unrelated announcement, the NYSAC decided not to acknowledge "junior" titles in future, leaving Bass recognised by the NBA, only.*

03.02.30 Benny Bass (USA) ND-W RSC 4 Davey Abad (PAN), St Louis - NBA

28.03.30 Benny Bass (USA) ND-L PTS 10 Eddie Shea (USA), St Louis - NBA. *Shea weighed 126½ lbs.*

05.01.31 Benny Bass (USA) W PTS 10 Lew Massey (USA), Philadelphia - NBA

15.07.31 Kid Chocolate (CUB) W RSC 7 Benny Bass (USA), Philadelphia - NBA

10.04.32 Kid Chocolate (CUB) W PTS 15 Davey Abad (PAN), Havana - NBA

04.08.32 Kid Chocolate (CUB) W PTS 10 Eddie Shea (USA), Chicago - NBA. *On 20 September 1932, the National Boxing Association also decided not to recognise "junior" titles in future, although independent States such as Pennsylvania and Ohio were happy to support their own champions or contests taking place on their territory.*

13.10.32 Kid Chocolate (CUB) W RSC 12 Lew Feldman (USA), New York City. *Although billed for the NYSAC version of the world featherweight title, with both men inside 126 lbs, technically, Chocolate's 130 lbs crown was also at stake.*

09.12.32 Kid Chocolate (CUB) W PTS 15 Fidel la Barba (USA), New York City. *The same circumstances applied as in Chocolate v Feldman above.*

01.05.33 Kid Chocolate (CUB) W PTS 10 Johnny Farr (USA), Philadelphia - PENNSYLVANIA

19.05.33 Kid Chocolate (CUB) W PTS 15 Seaman Tommy Watson (GB), New York City. *Billed for the NYSAC version of the world featherweight title only, as in his contests against Feldman and la Barba, Chocolate's 130 lbs crown was also at stake.*

04.12.33 Kid Chocolate (CUB) W PTS 10 Frankie Wallace (USA), Cleveland - PENNSYLVANIA/OHIO

25.12.33 Frankie Klick (USA) W RSC 7 Kid Chocolate (CUB), Philadelphia - PENNSYLVANIA. *Two fights later, and two and a half months after winning the title, Frankie Klick was challenging Barney Ross for the Illinois/Californian version of the light-welterweight crown. He never fought at 130 lbs again and the weight division fell into disuse. However, in 1949, Sandy Saddler, who had recently lost his world featherweight title to Willie Pep, re-established it in Ohio while waiting for a further crack at Pep.*

06.12.49 Sandy Saddler (USA) W PTS 10 Orlando Zulueta (CUB), Cleveland - OHIO

18.04.50 Sandy Saddler (USA) W RSC 9 Lauro Salas (MEX), Cleveland - OHIO

28.02.51 Sandy Saddler (USA) W CO 2 Diego Sosa (CUB), Havana - OHIO/CUBA. *Following the fight against Sosa, Saddler showed no further interest in the super-featherweight division, concentrating instead on defending his world featherweight crown. Once again, the title faded into obscurity and it would be another eight years before the weight class was popularised, this time indefinitely.*

20.07.59 Harold Gomes (USA) W PTS 15 Paul Jorgensen (USA), Providence - NBA

16.03.60 Flash Elorde (PH) W CO 7 Harold Gomes (USA), Quezon City - NBA

17.08.60 Flash Elorde (PH) W CO 1 Harold Gomes (USA), San Francisco - NBA

19.03.61 Flash Elorde (PH) W PTS 15 Joey Lopes (USA), Manila - NBA

16.12.61 Flash Elorde (PH) W RSC 1 Sergio Caprari (ITA), Manila - NBA

23.06.62 Flash Elorde (PH) W PTS 15 Auburn Copeland (USA), Manila - NBA

16.02.63 Flash Elorde (PH) W PTS 15 Johnny Bizzarro (USA), Manila - WBA

03.08.63 Flash Elorde (PH) W PTS 10 Love Allotey (GH), Manila. *Shown in the 1964 Boxing News Annual as a 15 round WBA championship fight, in reality it was a ten round non-title affair at catchweights.*

16.11.63 Flash Elorde (PII) W DIS 11 Love Allotey (GH), Quezon City - WBA

27.07.64 Flash Elorde (PH) W RSC 12 Teruo Kosaka (JAP), Tokyo - WBA

05.06.65 Flash Elorde (PH) W CO 15 Teruo Kosaka (JAP), Quezon City - WBA

04.12.65 Flash Elorde (PH) W PTS 15 Kang-Il Suh (SK), Quezon City - WBA

22.10.66 Flash Elorde (PH) W PTS 15 Vicente Derado (ARG), Quezon City - WBA

25.05.67 Raul Rojas (USA) W PTS 15 Vicente Derado (ARG), Los Angeles - CALIFORNIA

15.06.67 Yoshiaki Numata (JAP) W PTS 15 Flash Elorde (PH), Tokyo - WBA

14.09.67 Raul Rojas (USA) W PTS 15 Kang-Il Suh (SK), Los Angeles - CALIFORNIA. *Raul Rojas relinquished the Californian version of the title on becoming world featherweight champion in December 1967.*

14.12.67 Hiroshi Kobayashi (JAP) W CO 12 Yoshiaki Numata (JAP), Tokyo - WBA

30.03.68 Hiroshi Kobayashi (JAP) DREW 15 Rene Barrientos (PH), Tokyo - WBA

06.10.68 Hiroshi Kobayashi (JAP) W PTS 15 Jaime Valladeres (EC), Tokyo - WBA

15.02.69 Rene Barrientos (PH) W PTS 15 Ruben Navarro (USA), Quezon City - WBC

06.04.69 Hiroshi Kobayashi (JAP) W PTS 15 Antonio Amaya (PAN), Tokyo - WBA

09.11.69 Hiroshi Kobayashi (JAP) W PTS 15 Carlos Canete (ARG), Tokyo - WBA

05.04.70 Yoshiaki Numata (JAP) W PTS 15 Rene Barrientos (PH), Tokyo - WBC

23.08.70 Hiroshi Kobayashi (JAP) W PTS 15 Antonio Amaya (PAN), Tokyo - WBA

27.09.70 Yoshiaki Numata (JAP) W CO 5 Raul Rojas (USA), Tokyo - WBC

03.01.71 Yoshiaki Numata (JAP) W PTS 15 Rene Barrientos (PH), Shizuaka - WBC

03.03.71 Hiroshi Kobayashi (JAP) W PTS 15 Ricardo Arredondo (MEX), Tokyo - WBA

30.05.71 Yoshiaki Numata (JAP) W PTS 15 Lionel Rose (A), Hiroshima - WBC

29.07.71 Alfredo Marcano (VEN) W RTD 10 Hiroshi Kobayashi (JAP), Aomori - WBA

10.10.71 Ricardo Arredondo (MEX) W CO 10 Yoshiaki Numata (JAP), Sendai - WBC

07.11.71 Alfredo Marcano (VEN) W RSC 4 Kenji Iwata (JAP), Caracas - WBA

29.01.72 Ricardo Arredondo (MEX) W PTS 15 Jose Marin (CR), San Jose - WBC

22.04.72 Ricardo Arredondo (MEX) W CO 5 William Martinez (NIC), Mexico City - WBC

25.04.72 Ben Villaflor (PH) W PTS 15 Alfredo Marcano (VEN), Honolulu - WBA

05.09.72 Ben Villaflor (PH) DREW 15 Victor Echegaray (ARG), Honolulu - WBA

15.09.72 Ricardo Arredondo (MEX) W CO 12 Susumu Okabe (JAP), Tokyo - WBC

06.03.73 Ricardo Arredondo (MEX) W PTS 15 Apollo Yoshio (JAP), Fukuoka City - WBC

12.03.73 Kuniaki Shibata (JAP) W PTS 15 Ben Villaflor (PH), Honolulu - WBA

19.06.73 Kuniaki Shibata (JAP) W PTS 15 Victor Echegaray (ARG), Tokyo - WBA

01.09.73 Ricardo Arredondo (MEX) W RSC 6 Morito Kashiwaba (JAP), Tokyo - WBC

18.10.73 Ben Villaflor (PH) W CO 1 Kuniaki Shibata (JAP), Honolulu - WBA

28.02.74 Kuniaki Shibata (JAP) W PTS 15 Ricardo Arredondo (MEX), Tokyo - WBC

14.03.74 Ben Villaflor (PH) DREW 15 Apollo Yoshio (JAP), Toyama - WBA

27.06.74 Kuniaki Shibata (JAP) W PTS 15 Antonio Amaya (PAN), Tokyo - WBC

03.08.74 Kuniaki Shibata (JAP) W RSC 15 Ramiro Bolanos (EC), Tokyo - WBC

24.08.74 Ben Villaflor (PH) W RSC 2 Yasutsune Uehara (JAP), Honolulu - WBA

13.03.75 Ben Villaflor (PH) W PTS 15 Hyun-Chi Kim (SK), Quezon City - WBA

27.03.75 Kuniaki Shibata (JAP) W PTS 15 Ould Makloufi (FR), Fukuoka City - WBC

05.07.75 Alfredo Escalera (PR) W CO 2 Kuniaki Shibata (JAP), Kasamatsu - WBC

20.09.75 Alfredo Escalera (PR) DREW 15 Leonel Hernandez (VEN), Caracas - WBC

12.12.75 Alfredo Escalera (PR) W RSC 9 Sven-Erik Paulsen (NOR), Oslo - WBC

12.01.76 Ben Villaflor (PH) W RSC 13 Morito Kashiwaba (JAP), Tokyo - WBA

20.02.76 Alfredo Escalera (PR) W RSC 13 Jose Fernandez (DOM), San Juan - WBC

01.04.76 Alfredo Escalera (PR) W RSC 6 Buzzsaw Yamabe (JAP), Nara - WBC. *Although the fight was stopped by the referee, following a riot, the Japanese Boxing Commission announced that the result had been changed to that of no-decision on the grounds that there had been no count administered or any consultation with the ringside doctor. That statement was later overruled by the WBC, who allowed the result to stand.*

13.04.76 Ben Villaflor (PH) DREW 15 Sam Serrano (PR), Honolulu - WBA

01.07.76 Alfredo Escalera (PR) W PTS 15 Buzzsaw Yamabe (JAP), Nara - WBC

18.09.76 Alfredo Escalera (PR) W RTD 12 Ray Lunny (USA), San Juan - WBC

16.10.76 Sam Serrano (PR) W PTS 15 Ben Villaflor (PH), San Juan - WBA

30.11.76 Alfredo Escalera (PR) W PTS 15 Tyrone Everett (USA), Philadelphia - WBC

15.01.77 Sam Serrano (PR) W RSC 11 Alberto Herrera (EC), Guayaquil - WBA

17.03.77 Alfredo Escalera (PR) W RSC 6 Ronnie McGarvey (USA), San Juan - WBC

16.05.77 Alfredo Escalera (PR) W CO 8 Carlos Becerril (MEX), Landover - WBC

26.06.77 Sam Serrano (PR) W PTS 15 Leonel Hernandez (VEN), Cruz - WBA

27.08.77 Sam Serrano (PR) W PTS 15 Apollo Yoshio (JAP), San Juan - WBA

10.09.77 Alfredo Escalera (PR) W PTS 15 Sigfredo Rodriguez (MEX), San Juan - WBC

19.11.77 Sam Serrano (PR) W RSC 10 Tae-Ho Kim (SK), San Juan - WBA

28.01.78 Alexis Arguello (NIC) W RSC 13 Alfredo Escalera (PR), Bayamon - WBC

18.02.78 Sam Serrano (PR) W PTS 15 Mario Martinez (NIC), San Juan - WBA

29.04.78 Alexis Arguello (NIC) W RSC 5 Rey Tam (PH), Los Angeles - WBC

03.06.78 Alexis Arguello (NIC) W CO 1 Diego Alcala (PAN), San Juan - WBC

08.07.78 Sam Serrano (PR) W RSC 9 Yong-Ho Oh (SK), San Juan - WBA

10.11.78 Alexis Arguello (NIC) W PTS 15 Arturo Leon (MEX), Las Vegas - WBC

29.11.78 Sam Serrano (PR) W PTS 15 Takas Maruki (JAP), Nagoya - WBA

04.02.79 Alexis Arguello (NIC) W CO 13 Alfredo Escalera (PR), Rimini - WBC

18.02.79 Sam Serrano (PR) W PTS 15 Julio Valdez (DOM), San Juan - WBA

14.04.79 Sam Serrano (PR) W RSC 8 Nkosana Mgxaji (SA), Capetown - WBA

08.07.79 Alexis Arguello (NIC) W RSC 11 Rafael Limon (MEX), New York City - WBC

16.11.79 Alexis Arguello (NIC) W RTD 7 Bobby Chacon (USA), Los Angeles - WBC

20.01.80 Alexis Arguello (NIC) W RSC 11 Ruben Castillo (USA), Tucson - WBC

03.04.80 Sam Serrano (PR) W RSC 13 Battle Hawk Kazama (JAP), Nara - WBA

27.04.80 Alexis Arguello (NIC) W RSC 4 Rolando Navarrete (PH), San Juan - WBC. *Alexis Arguello relinquished WBC version of the title in October 1980 to campaign as a lightweight.*

02.08.80 Yasutsune Uehara (JAP) W CO 6 Sam Serrano (PR), Detroit - WBA

20.11.80 Yasutsune Uehara (JAP) W PTS 15 Leonel Hernandez (VEN), Tokyo - WBA

11.12.80 Rafael Limon (MEX) W RSC 15 Ildefonso Bethelmy (VEN), Los Angeles - WBC

08.03.81 Cornelius Boza-Edwards (U) W PTS 15 Rafael Limon (MEX), Stockton - WBC

09.04.81 Sam Serrano (PR) W PTS 15 Yasutsune Uehara (JAP), Wakayama - WBA

30.05.81 Cornelius Boza-Edwards (U) W RTD 13 Bobby Chacon (USA), Las Vegas - WBC

29.06.81 Sam Serrano (PR) W PTS 15 Leonel Hernandez (VEN), Caracas - WBA

29.08.81 Rolando Navarrete (PH) W CO 5 Cornelius Boza-Edwards (U), Reggio - WBC

10.12.81 Sam Serrano (PR) W RSC 12 Hikaru Tomonari (JAP), San Juan - WBA

16.01.82 Rolando Navarrete (PH) W CO 11 Chung-Il Choi (SK), Manila - WBC

29.05.82 Rafael Limon (MEX) W CO 12 Rolando Navarrete (PH), Las Vegas - WBC

05.06.82 Sam Serrano (PR) NC 11 Benedicto Villablanca (CH), Santiago - WBA. *Initially, Villablanca was announced as the winner after Serrano collected a badly cut-eye and the fight was stopped on the ringside doctor's orders. However, following an enquiry, the WBA stated that there had been irregularities and that the fight should now be classified as a no-contest.*

18.09.82 Rafael Limon (MEX) W RSC 7 Chung-Il Choi (SK), Los Angeles - WBC

11.12.82 Bobby Chacon (USA) W PTS 15 Rafael Limon (MEX), Sacramento - WBC

19.01.83 Roger Mayweather (USA) W CO 8 Sam Serrano (PR), San Juan - WBA

20.04.83 Roger Mayweather (USA) W RSC 8 Jorge Alvarado (PAN), San Jose - WBA

15.05.83 Bobby Chacon (USA) W PTS 12 Cornelius Boza-Edwards (U), Las Vegas - WBC. *Bobby Chacon forfeited WBC recognition in June 1983 following a contractual dispute.*

07.08.83 Hector Camacho (PR) W RSC 5 Rafael Limon (MEX), San Juan - WBC

17.08.83 Roger Mayweather (USA) W CO 1 Benedicto Villablanca (CH), Las Vegas - WBA

18.11.83 Hector Camacho (PR) W CO 5 Rafael Solis (PR), San Juan - WBC. *Hector Camacho relinquished WBC version of title in June 1984 to campaign as a lightweight.*

26.02.84 Rocky Lockridge (USA) W CO 1 Roger Mayweather (USA), Beaumont - WBA

22.04.84 Hwan-Kil Yuh (SK) W PTS 15 Rod Sequenan (PH), Seoul - IBF

12.06.84 Rocky Lockridge (USA) W RSC 11 Taej-In Moon (SK), Anchorage - WBA

13.09.84 Julio Cesar Chavez (MEX) W RSC 8 Mario Martinez (MEX), Los Angeles - WBC

16.09.84 Hwan-Kil Yuh (SK) W CO 6 Sak Galexi (TH), Pohang - IBF

27.01.85 Rocky Lockridge (USA) W RSC 6 Kamel Bou Ali (TUN), Riva del Garda - WBA

15.02.85 Lester Ellis (A) W PTS 15 Hwan-Kil Yuh (SK), Melbourne - IBF

19.04.85 Julio Cesar Chavez (MEX) W RSC 6 Ruben Castillo (USA), Los Angeles - WBC

26.04.85 Lester Ellis (A) W CO 13 Rod Sequenan (PH), Melbourne - IBF

19.05.85 Wilfredo Gomez (PR) W PTS 15 Rocky Lockridge (USA), San Juan - WBA

07.07.85 Julio Cesar Chavez (MEX) W RSC 2 Roger Mayweather (USA), Las Vegas - WBC

12.07.85 Barry Michael (A) W PTS 15 Lester Ellis (A), Melbourne - IBF

22.09.85 Julio Cesar Chavez (MEX) W PTS 12 Dwight Pratchett (USA), Las Vegas - WBC

18.10.85 Barry Michael (A) W RSC 4 Jin-Shik Choi (SK), Darwin - IBF

15.05.86 Julio Cesar Chavez (MEX) W RSC 5 Faustino Barrios (ARG), Paris - WBC

23.05.86 Barry Michael (A) W RSC 4 Mark Fernandez (USA), Melbourne - IBF

24.05.86 Alfredo Layne (PAN) W RSC 9 Wilfredo Gomez (PR), San Juan - WBA

13.06.86 Julio Cesar Chavez (MEX) W RSC 7 Refugio Rojas (USA), New York City - WBC

03.08.86 Julio Cesar Chavez (MEX) W PTS 12 Rocky Lockridge (USA), Monaco - WBC

23.08.86 Barry Michael (A) W PTS 12 Najib Daho (GB), Granada Studio, Manchester - IBF

27.09.86 Brian Mitchell (SA) W RSC 10 Alfredo Layne (PAN), Sun City - WBA

12.12.86 Julio Cesar Chavez (MEX) W PTS 12 Juan Laporte (PR), New York City - WBC

27.03.87 Brian Mitchell (SA) DREW 15 Jose Rivera (PR), San Juan - WBA

18.04.87 Julio Cesar Chavez (MEX) W RSC 3 Francisco Tomas Cruz (BR), Nimes - WBC

31.07.87 Brian Mitchell (SA) W RSC 14 Francisco Fernandez (PAN), Panama City - WBA

09.08.87 Rocky Lockridge (USA) W RTD 8 Barry Mitchell (A), Blazer's Night Club, Windsor - IBF

21.08.87 Julio Cesar Chavez (MEX) W PTS 12 Danilo Cabrera (DOM), Tijuana - WBC. *Julio Cesar Chavez relinquished WBC version of the title after becoming WBA lightweight champion on 21 November 1987.*

03.10.87 Brian Mitchell (SA) W PTS 15 Daniel Londas (FR), Gravelines - WBA

25.10.87 Rocky Lockridge (USA) W RSC 10 Johnny de la Rosa (DOM), Tucson - IBF

19.12.87 Brian Mitchell (SA) W RTD 8 Salvatore Curcetti (ITA), Capo d'Orlando - WBA

29.02.88 Azumah Nelson (GH) W PTS 12 Mario Martinez (MEX), Los Angeles - WBC

02.04.88 Rocky Lockridge (USA) W PTS 15 Harold Knight (USA), Atlantic City - IBF

26.04.88 Brian Mitchell (SA) W PTS 12 Jose Rivera (PR), Madrid - WBA

25.06.88 Azumah Nelson (GH) W RSC 9 Lupe Suarez (USA), Atlantic City - WBC

27.07.88 Tony Lopez (USA) W PTS 12 Rocky Lockridge (USA), Sacramento - IBF

27.10.88 Tony Lopez (USA) W PTS 12 Juan Molina (PR), Sacramento - IBF

02.11.88 Brian Mitchell (SA) W PTS 12 Jim McDonnell (GB), Elephant & Castle Recreation Centre, London - WBA

10.12.88 Azumah Nelson (GH) W CO 3 Sydnei dal Rovere (BR), Accra - WBC

10.02.89 Brian Mitchell (SA) W RSC 8 Salvatore Bottiglieri (ITA), Capo d'Orlando - WBA

25.02.89 Azumah Nelson (GH) W RSC 12 Mario Martinez (MEX), Las Vegas - WBC

05.03.89 Tony Lopez (USA) W PTS 12 Rocky Lockridge (USA), Sacramento - IBF

29.04.89 Juan Molina (PR) W PTS 12 Juan Laporte (PR), San Juan - WBO. *Juan Molina relinquished WBO version of the title in September 1989 prior to becoming IBF champion.*

18.06.89 Tony Lopez (USA) W CO 8 Tyrone Jackson (USA), Stateline - IBF

01.07.89 Brian Mitchell (SA) W TD 9 Jackie Beard (USA) Crotone - WBA. *Ahead on the judges' scorecards, Mitchell sustained a bad (accidental) cut and, unable to continue, was awarded the technical decision.*

28.09.89 Brian Mitchell (SA) W RSC 7 Irving Mitchell (USA), Lewiston - WBA

07.10.89 Juan Molina (PR) W RSC 10 Tony Lopez (USA), Sacramento - IBF

05.11.89 Azumah Nelson (GH) W CO 12 Jim McDonnell (GB), Albert Hall, London - WBC

09.12.89 Kamel Bou Ali (TUN) W CO 8 Antonio Rivera (PR), Terano - WBO

28.01.90 Juan Molina (PR) W RSC 6 Lupe Suarez (USA), Atlantic City - IBF

14.03.90 Brian Mitchell (SA) W PTS 12 Jackie Beard (USA), Grossetto - WBA

20.05.90 Tony Lopez (USA) W PTS 12 Juan Molina (PR), Reno - IBF

22.09.90 Tony Lopez (USA) W PTS 12 Jorge Paez (MEX), Sacramento - IBF

29.09.90 Brian Mitchell (SA) W PTS 12 Frankie Mitchell (USA), Aosta - WBA

13.10.90 Azumah Nelson (GH) W PTS 12 Juan Laporte (PR), Sydney - WBC

20.10.90 Kamel Bou Ali (TUN) NC 2 Pedro Villegas (ARG), Cesena - WBO. *Although Villegas complained of being butted repeatedly*

after the doctor ruled him out at the end of the second round, the referee decided that the head clashes were six of one and half a dozen of the other and ruled a no-contest.

15.03.91 Brian Mitchell (SA) DREW 12 Tony Lopez (USA), Sacramento - WBA/IBF. *Brian Mitchell relinquished WBA version of the title in April 1991 to avoid a mandatory challenger in order to go in search of the IBF crown and a rematch with Tony Lopez.*

01.06.91 Kamel Bou Ali (TUN) W CO 3 Joey Jacobs (GB), Ragusa - WBO

28.06.91 Azumah Nelson (GH) DREW 12 Jeff Fenech (A), Las Vegas - WBC

28.06.91 Joey Gamache (USA) W RSC 10 Jerry N'Gobeni (SA), Lewiston - WBA. *Joey Gamache relinquished the WBA version of the title in October 1991 due to difficulty in making the weight.*

12.07.91 Tony Lopez (USA) W RSC 6 Lupe Guttierez (USA), Lake Tahoe - IBF

13.09.91 Brian Mitchell (SA) W PTS 12 Tony Lopez (USA), Sacramento - IBF. *Brian Mitchell retired as undefeated IBF champion in January 1992.*

22.11.91 Genaro Hernandez (USA) W RTD 9 Daniel Londas (FR), Epernay - WBA

22.02.92 Juan Molina (PR) W RSC 4 Jackie Gunguluza (SA), Sun City - IBF

24.02.92 Genaro Hernandez (USA) W PTS 12 Omar Catari (VEN) Los Angeles - WBA

01.03.92 Azumah Nelson (GH) W RSC 8 Jeff Fenech (A), Melbourne - WBC

21.03.92 Daniel Londas (FR) W PTS 12 Kamel Bou Ali (TUN), San Rufo - WBO

15.07.92 Genaro Hernandez (USA) W PTS 12 Masuaki Takeda (JAP), Fukuoka - WBA

22.08.92 Juan Molina (PR) W RSC 4 Fernando Caicedo (COL), Bayamon - IBF

04.09.92 Jimmy Bredahl (DEN) W PTS 12 Daniel Londas (FR), Copenhagen - WBO

07.11.92 Azumah Nelson (GH) W PTS 12 Calvin Grove (USA), Lake Tahoe - WBC

20.11.92 Genaro Hernandez (USA) W RSC 6 Yuji Watanabe (JAP), Tokyo - WBA

13.02.93 Juan Molina (PR) W RSC 8 Francisco Segura (MEX), Bayamon - IBF

20.02.93 Azumah Nelson (GH) W PTS 12 Gabriel Ruelas (MEX), Mexico City - WBC

26.04.93 Genaro Hernandez (USA) T DRAW 1 Raul Perez (MEX), Los Angeles - WBA. *A terrible clash of heads after just 28 seconds, left Perez in no position to continue and the referee no alternative than to record a technical draw under the WBA ruling.*

26.06.93 Juan Molina (PR) W PTS 12 Manuel Medina (MEX), Atlantic City - IBF

28.06.93 Genaro Hernandez (USA) W CO 8 Raul Perez (MEX), Los Angeles - WBA

Lightweight (135 lbs)

The lightweight division can be traced back to Caleb Baldwin at the end of the 18th century and involved many memorable contests, none more so than one on 6 October 1872, when two Englishmen fought for the American title and a purse of $2000. The champion, Arthur Chambers, beat his great rival, Billy Edwards, on a 35th round disqualification at Squirrel Island, but after he retired in 1879, there was no recognised champion until 1883. It was then that Jack "The Nonpareil" Dempsey forged to the top, but he quickly outgrew the weight class and another Irish-American, Jack McAuliffe, was next to claim the title. McAuliffe had won the American crown when beating Billy Frazier in 1886, prior to landing the Queensberry Rules' title by knocking out the Canadian, Harry Gilmore, inside 28 rounds on 14 January 1887 in Lawrence. His successful defences, before temporarily retiring in December 1894, were against Jem Carney (drew over 74 rounds in Revere on 16 November 1887), Billy Myer (drew over 64 rounds in Judson on 23 February 1889), Jimmy Carroll (won by a 47th round kayo in San Francisco on 21 March 1890), Austin Gibbons (won by a sixth round stoppage in Hoboken on 11 September 1891), Billy Myer (won by a 15th round kayo in New Orleans on 5 September 1892) and Young Griffo (won on points over ten rounds at Coney Island on 27 August 1894). Earlier, one of McAuliffe's old opponents, Jem Carney, who was considered by

many as world champion on the other side of the Atlantic, had lost his title claim to Dick Burge on an 11th round disqualification at the London Hop and Malt Exchange on 25 May 1891. Even prior to McAuliffe's retirement, Burge was claiming the world title as British champion and knocked out Harry Nickless in the 28th round of a billed world title bout, albeit at 140 lbs, in London on 4 May 1894. Meanwhile, in America, George Lavigne quickly took over the mantle from McAuliffe, beating Andy Bowen, who died following an 18th round knockout defeat in New Orleans on 14 December 1894. As the new American champion, Lavigne successfully defended his title against Jimmy Handler (won by a fifth round kayo in Maspeth on 26 August 1895), Young Griffo (drew over 20 rounds in Maspeth on 12 October 1895) and Joe Walcott (won on points over 15 rounds in Maspeth on 2 December 1895). The stage was now set for the first truly international fight at the weight with gloves.

01.06.96 George Lavigne (USA) W CO 17 Dick Burge (GB), NSC, London. *With Lavigne weighing 134 lbs and Burge 136, the NSC still considered it to be a worthy championship contest, even though the class limit stood at 133 lbs in America.*

27.10.96 George Lavigne (USA) W CO 24 Jack Everhardt (USA), New York City. *Although recorded in the Ring Record Book as a title fight, it could not have been with the match made at 137 lbs.*

24.11.96 Eddie Connolly (C) W CO 5 Tom Causer (GB), Olympic Club, Birmingham. *Billed by the promoter for the vacant 132 lbs championship, a pound below the "popular" weight, the winner was only recognised as a worthy opponent for Lavigne, and not as a world champion.*

08.02.97 George Lavigne (USA) W PTS 25 Kid McPartland (USA), New York City. *Weights (lbs): Lavigne (131), McPartland (132¼).*

30.04.97 George Lavigne (USA) W RSC 11 Eddie Connolly (C), New York City. *Weights (lbs): Lavigne (132), Connolly (132).*

29.10.97 George Lavigne (USA) W RTD 12 Joe Walcott (USA), San Francisco. *While shown in the Ring Record Book as a title fight, it was not advertised as one and was made at 135 lbs, two pounds over the recognised limit.*

17.03.98 George Lavigne (USA) DREW 20 Jack Daly (USA), Cleveland. *Again, not advertised as a title bout, but recorded in the Ring Record Book as being for the championship, even though it was contested at 137 lbs.*

28.09.98 George Lavigne (USA) DREW 20 Frank Erne (USA), Coney Island *(133 lbs).*

17.10.98 Jack Daly (USA) W PTS 20 Jim Curran (GB), Syracuse. *Reported in "Famous Fights, Past and Present" as a title fight, it was fought way above the weight class limit of the day, with Daly ten pounds heavier than his rival. Regardless of that, Lavigne was the recognised lineal champion and any further progress for Daly was stunted when he was outpointed over 25 rounds by future champion, Joe Gans, on 27 December 1898 (New York City).*

25.11.98 George Lavigne (USA) W PTS 20 Tom Tracy (A), San Francisco. *Recorded as a title fight in the Ring Record Book, there was no mention of that in the San Francisco Chronicle (newspaper) report which stated that Lavigne conceeded Tracy the privilege of weighing in at 142 lbs.*

03.07.99 Frank Erne (USA) W PTS 20 George Lavigne (USA), Buffalo. *No weights were announced, but all concerned, apart from the champion's brother (Billy Lavigne claimed that Erne weighed in at 135 lbs), were happy that both men were inside the agreed 133 lbs and the title changed hands.*

04.12.99 Frank Erne (USA) DREW 25 Jack O'Brien (USA), Coney Island *(133 lbs).*

26.02.00 Tommy Hogan (USA) W CO 8 Bill Chester (GB), NSC, London. *Billed for the British version of the world 128 lbs championship, Hogan lost any weak claim to the "popular" title he may have had when kayoed by Ben Jordan on 28 May 1900 (see under featherweights).*

23.03.00 Frank Erne (USA) W RTD 12 Joe Gans (USA), New York City. *Weights (lbs): Erne (131), Gans (133).*

16.07.00 Terry McGovern (USA) W RTD 3 Frank Erne (USA), New York City. *Although a battle between two champions, it did not involve the championship as a special deal had been struck before the fight. Erne agreed that he would come into the ring weighing 128 lbs (five pounds under the accepted limit) and would win by a kayo inside ten rounds or forfeit his purse.*

12.05.02 Joe Gans (USA) W CO 1 Frank Erne (USA), Fort Erie. *Weights (lbs): Gans (133¼), Erne (132½).*

21.06.02 Jabez White (GB) W PTS 15 Spike Sullivan (USA), NSC, London. *White was the British champion at 134 lbs and it was at that weight the fight was billed as being for the world title. At the* *time, the American lightweight limit stood at 133 lbs and with Joe Gans recognised as champion, White's victory cut no ice on the other side of the Atlantic.*

24.06.02 Frank Erne (USA) W CO 7 Jim Maloney (GB), NSC, London. *Following his defeat at the hands of Joe Gans, Erne laid claim to the "white" lightweight title. Although weighing 136½ lbs to Maloney's 138, the above fight was billed for the world lightweight title at 138 lbs.*

27.06.02 Joe Gans (USA) W RTD 3 George McFadden (USA), San Francisco. *Prior to the fight, recorded in the Ring Record Book as involving the championship, McFadden demanded that the 133 lbs limit be adhered to. However, no weights were announced and the same newspaper reported that although a title fight, McFadden looked completely out of condition. If that was true, it is unlikely that the challenger made the requisite weight and even at the time, the fight was viewed with much suspicion.*

24.07.02 Joe Gans (USA) W CO 15 Rufe Turner (USA), Oakland. *Shown in the Ring Record Book as a successful defence for the champion, with the two men weighing 135 and 135½ lbs, respectively, the title was not at stake.*

17.09.02 Joe Gans (USA) W CO 5 Gus Gardner (USA), Baltimore. *Another fight that has been recorded down the years by ensuing Ring Record Books without verification of weights, according to the Philadelphia (Gardner's hometown) Item (newspaper) report, the bout was scheduled for 20 rounds with Gans' lightweight title at stake.*

13.10.02 Joe Gans (USA) W CO 5 Kid McPartland (USA), Fort Erie. *Reported in the Ring Record Book as a defence for Gans, with both men weighing 135 lbs, the title was not involved.*

14.11.02 Joe Gans (USA) W CO 14 Charley Seiger (USA), Baltimore. *Occasionally mentioned as being a title fight, but with both men asked to make 138 lbs, the championship was not at stake.*

26.11.02 Jimmy Britt (USA) W CO 7 Frank Erne (USA), San Francisco. *Billed for the "white" title.*

01.01.03 Joe Gans (USA) W DIS 11 Gus Gardner (USA), New Brittain. *According to the Philadelphia Item (newspaper) it was a world title fight, but no weights were listed even though the contest was reported in detail. Although the Ring Record Book supports that view, the writer feels that since Gans had fought Charley Seiger over ten rounds in Boston the previous evening, it is highly unlikely that he would have risked his title in this fashion.*

09.03.03 Jack O'Keefe (USA) W DIS 6 Jimmy Britt (USA), Portland. *With both men inside 133 lbs, this was a "white" lightweight title fight according to the San Francisco Chronicle (newspaper). Although Britt was disqualified for persistent low blows, O'Keefe, who was clearly beaten and knocked out, received no support, whatsoever, and Britt continued to claim the "white" title.*

11.03.03 Joe Gans (USA) W CO 11 Steve Crosby (USA), Hot Springs. *Historically recorded in the Ring Record Book championship listings, according to the Philadelphia Item (newspaper) report, the fight was scheduled for 20 rounds at 134 lbs with Gans' title on the line. However, with the weight class limit set at 133 lbs, this should not be considered as a defence of the "popular" title.*

28.04.03 Jimmy Britt (USA) W PTS 20 Willie Fitzgerald (USA), San Francisco. *Billed for the "white" title.*

29.05.03 Joe Gans (USA) W CO 10 Willie Fitzgerald (USA), San Francisco. *Shown in the Ring Record Book as a championship fight, according to the San Francisco Chronicle, Gans continued his hold on the title after a successful defence at 135 lbs. Nevertheless, with the championship weight set at 133 lbs, this should not be judged a title defence.*

13.06.03 Jimmy Britt (USA) DREW 20 Jack O'Keefe (USA), Butte. *Billed for the "white" title.*

04.07.03 Joe Gans (USA) W CO 5 Buddy King (USA), Butte. *Although the New Orleans Daily Picayune (newspaper) report at the time stated that "Gans successfully defended his 'coloured' title on his victory", there was nothing in the report apertaining to weights and as a prospective championship fight it should be viewed with suspicion until more facts surface.*

10.11.03 Jimmy Britt (USA) W PTS 20 Charley Seiger (USA), San Francisco. *Billed for the "white" title.*

20.11.03 Jimmy Britt (USA) W PTS 25 Martin Canole (USA), Colma. *Billed for the "white" title.*

12.01.04 Joe Gans (USA) W PTS 10 Willie Fitzgerald (USA), Detroit. *With the recognised weight of the day standing at 133 lbs, this contest, made at 135 lbs, was still recorded as a title fight in the last Ring Record Book, although not shown within Gans' record as such.*

25.03.04 Joe Gans (USA) W PTS 15 Jack Blackburn (USA), Baltimore. *The Philadelphia Item (newspaper) carried the curious statement that this was "understood" to be a championship battle and that*

both men weighed in at 140 lbs. This was paradoxical, as the limit was 133 lbs at the time. Presumably, the Item meant to say that this was not a title fight.

28.03.04 Joe Gans (USA) W PTS 10 Gus Gardner (USA), Saginaw. *Recorded in the 1979 Boxing News Special as a title fight, with the match made at 138 lbs, it should not be regarded as one.*

21.04.04 Joe Gans (USA) W PTS 15 Sam Bolen (USA), Baltimore. *Occasionally described as a title fight, the author of that statement was possibly confused by the fact that main events in Baltimore at the time were more often than not of 15 rounds duration. With no weights available, it was not considered a championship bout by the Philadelphia Item (newspaper).*

31.10.04 Joe Gans (USA) W DIS 5 Jimmy Britt (USA), San Francisco. *Following the verdict, Britt, who had been disqualified for twice hitting Gans when he was down, claimed the title, stating that the referee's decision had been unwarranted as the champion was already badly beaten. With Gans not willing to make the weight in a return, Britt, already holder of the "white" title, went forward to meet Battling Nelson for what was generally considered to be a match worthy of the vacant crown. Nelson was an automatic choice, having beaten Martin Canole (18th round kayo on 20 May 1904 in San Francisco), Eddie Hanlon (19th round kayo on 29 July 1904 in San Francisco), Aurelio Herrera (points over 20 rounds on 5 September 1904 in Butte) and Young Corbett (tenth round kayo on 29 November 1904 in San Francisco), in his most recent fights.*

20.12.04 **Jimmy Britt** (USA) W PTS 20 Battling Nelson (USA), San Francisco *(133 lbs).*

05.05.05 **Jimmy Britt** (USA) W PTS 20 Jabez White (GB), San Francisco *(133 lbs).*

21.07.05 **Jimmy Britt** (USA) W PTS 20 Kid Sullivan (USA), San Francisco *(133 lbs).*

09.09.05 **Battling Nelson** (USA) W CO 18 Jimmy Britt (USA), San Francisco *(133 lbs).*

03.09.06 Joe Gans (USA) W DIS 42 Battling Nelson (USA), Goldfield *(133 lbs).*

01.01.07 Joe Gans (USA) W CO 8 Kid Herman (USA), Tonopah *(133 lbs).*

31.07.07 Jimmy Britt (USA) W PTS 20 Battling Nelson (USA), San Francisco. *Britt regained the "white" lightweight title on his victory. Both men were inside 133 lbs.*

09.09.07 Joe Gans (USA) W RTD 6 Jimmy Britt (USA), San Francisco. *Both men weighed 132 lbs.*

27.09.07 Joe Gans (USA) W PTS 20 George Memsic (USA), Los Angeles. *In a championship match made at 135 (not 133) lbs, both men made the weight according to the Los Angeles Daily Times (newspaper) report on the fight.*

01.04.08 Joe Gans (USA) ND-W CO 3 Spike Robson (USA), Philadelphia

14.05.08 Joe Gans (USA) W RSC 11 Rudy Unholz (USA), San Francisco. *Weights (lbs): Gans (133), Unholz (132¾).*

04.07.08 **Battling Nelson** (USA) W CO 17 Joe Gans (USA), San Francisco *(133 lbs).*

09.09.08 **Battling Nelson** (USA) W CO 21 Joe Gans (USA), San Francisco. *Weights (lbs): Nelson (131¾), Gans (133).*

22.02.09 Johnny Summers (GB) W PTS 20 Jimmy Britt (USA), NSC, London. *Advertised as a title fight, Summers won nothing more than Britt's contentious "white" championship claim, if that, and, before the year was over, had been superseded as British champion by Freddie Welsh.*

29.05.09 **Battling Nelson** (USA) W CO 23 Dick Hyland (USA), San Francisco *(133 lbs).*

22.06.09 Battling Nelson (USA) W CO 5 Jack Clifford (USA), Oklahoma City. *Although this fight has been regarded by the Ring Record Book down the ages as involving the title, this writer found nothing in the Chicago (Nelson's home-base) Tribune, San Francisco Chronicle or Los Angeles Times (newspapers) to suggest it was. Reported in some detail, but with no weights made available, it was a scheduled 15 rounder, with Clifford, a former victim and sparring partner of Nelson, not considered a worthy opponent for the champion. Add to that the knowledge that Nelson "officially" defended over much longer distances and this just does not stand up as a title fight.*

21.01.10 Battling Nelson (USA) W CO 8 Eddie Lang (USA), Memphis. *Recorded in the Ring Record Book as a title bout, albeit without mention of the weight, the Chicago Tribune (newspaper) merely reported the fight as an eight round (the maximum distance allowed by Tennessee law at the time) warm-up for Nelson to prepare him for his forthcoming championship battle against Ad Wolgast.*

22.02.10 **Ad Wolgast** (USA) W RSC 40 Battling Nelson (USA), Richmond. *Scheduled for 45 rounds, Wolgast tipped the beam at*

an official 132¼ lbs, boosting his actual weight by over eight pounds, while Nelson came in spot on the 133 mark.

30.05.10 Freddie Welsh (GB) DREW 20 Packey McFarland (USA), NSC, London - GB. *Following his British championship win over Johnny Summers, the NSC matched Welsh against McFarland for the British version of the world title.*

08.02.11 **Ad Wolgast** (USA) ND-L PTS 6 Knockout Brown (USA), Philadelphia

17.03.11 **Ad Wolgast** (USA) W RSC 9 George Memsic (USA), Los Angeles. *Left out of the Guinness Boxing Who's Who as a championship fight, the Los Angeles Daily Times (newspaper) gave it as a title defence at 133 lbs, with Wolgast making 129½ to Memsic's 132½ on the day before the fight.*

31.03.11 **Ad Wolgast** (USA) W RTD 5 Antonio la Grave (USA), San Francisco. *Knowing that la Grave was walking about at around 140 lbs, two weeks prior to their championship contest, Wolgast insisted on a ringside weigh-in. While Wolgast was obviously comfortable at 131 lbs, la Grave, who barely made the required 133 lbs, was drained at the weight and slumped to a quick defeat.*

26.04.11 **Ad Wolgast** (USA) ND-W RSC 2 One Round Hogan (USA), New York City. *Hogan weighed 132½ lbs.*

27.05.11 **Ad Wolgast** (USA) W RTD 16 Frankie Burns (USA), San Francisco *(133 lbs).*

04.07.11 **Ad Wolgast** (USA) W CO 13 Owen Moran (GB), San Francisco. *Both men were announced as being inside 133 lbs, with Moran scaling 130 the day before the fight.*

04.07.12 **Ad Wolgast** (USA) W CO 13 Joe Rivers (USA), Los Angeles. *An amazing fight shrouded in controversy, saw both men knocked down simultaneously, before the referee lifted Wolgast (130 lbs) up and supported him, while counting Rivers (133 lbs) out.*

28.11.12 **Willie Ritchie** (USA) W DIS 16 Ad Wolgast (USA), San Francisco *(133 lbs).*

16.12.12 Freddie Welsh (GB) W PTS 20 Hughie Mehegan (A), NSC, London - GB. *Having recently won back his British and European titles from Matt Wells, and bearing in mind his successful American campaign, the National Sporting Club matched Welsh against the Australian, Hughie Mehegan, in a fight advertised as being for the vacant British Empire and world (British version) lightweight championships at 135 lbs. Welsh had originally signed to fight Ad Wolgast for the title, but the champion had pulled out with apendicitis and when fit again, with the Welshman back in Britain, Willie Ritchie had grasped the opportunity instead.*

04.07.13 Willie Ritchie (USA) W CO 11 Joe Rivers (USA), San Francisco - USA. *Ritchie, who was already struggling to make the recognised American lightweight limit, arbitrarily raised the poundage to 134 lbs for this one, with both men inside.*

10.11.13 Willie Ritchie (USA) ND-W PTS 10 Leach Cross (USA), New York City - USA. *Again, in quick succession, Ritchie raised the American version of the weight class by one pound to 135 lbs, which then fell into line with Britain, where it has remained to this day.*

12.03.14 Willie Ritchie (USA) ND-W PTS 10 Ad Wolgast (USA), Milwaukee - USA

17.04.14 Willie Ritchie (USA) W PTS 20 Tommy Murphy (USA), San Francisco - USA. *Weights (lbs): Ritchie (135), Murphy (134½).*

26.05.14 Willie Ritchie (USA) ND-L PTS 10 Charley White (USA), Milwaukee - USA

07.07.14 **Freddie Welsh** (GB) W PTS 20 Willie Ritchie (USA), Olympia, London.

02.11.14 **Freddie Welsh** (GB) ND-W RSC 8 Ad Wolgast (USA), New York City

02.12.14 **Freddie Welsh** (GB) ND-L PTS 10 Joe Shugrue (USA), New York City

11.03.15 **Freddie Welsh** (GB) ND-L PTS 10 Willie Ritchie (USA), New York City

17.03.15 **Freddie Welsh** (GB) ND-W PTS 10 Hal Stewart (USA), Fort Wayne

31.03.16 **Freddie Welsh** (GB) ND-L PTS 10 Benny Leonard (USA), New York City

04.07.16 **Freddie Welsh** (GB) ND-W DIS 11 Ad Wolgast (USA), Denver

28.07.16 **Freddie Welsh** (GB) ND-W PTS 10 Benny Leonard (USA), Brooklyn. *Leonard weighed 132½ lbs.*

04.09.16 **Freddie Welsh** (GB) W PTS 20 Charley White (USA), Colorado Springs. *White was a dangerous, but often wild puncher, and, following a low blow delivered during the third round, a 30 minute interval had to be authorised in order to give Welsh sufficient time to recover.*

16.01.17 **Freddie Welsh** (GB) ND-L PTS 10 Richie Mitchell (USA), Milwaukee

28.05.17 **Benny Leonard** (USA) ND-W RSC 9 Freddie Welsh (GB), New York City. *When a champion fought in a no-decision contest – as regulated under the Frawley Law in New York between 1911 and 1920 – the only way he could lose his title, unless he stipulated a poundage above the limit for the weight class, was if he failed to last the distance. Although Welsh scaled 136¾ lbs, Leonard weighed 133 lbs and it was on that basis that the American received recognition as champion.*

04.06.17 **Benny Leonard** (USA) ND-W PTS 6 Joe Welsh (USA), Philadelphia

25.07.17 **Benny Leonard** (USA) ND-W CO 3 Johnny Kilbane (USA), Philadelphia

21.09.17 **Benny Leonard** (USA) ND-W RSC 1 Leo Johnson (USA), New York City

28.04.19 **Benny Leonard** (USA) ND-W RSC 8 Willie Ritchie (USA), Newark

11.08.19 **Benny Leonard** (USA) ND-W PTS 6 Patsy Cline (USA), Philadelphia

09.02.20 **Benny Leonard** (USA) ND-W PTS 8 Johnny Dundee (USA), Jersey City. *Dundee weighed 132½ lbs.*

05.07.20 **Benny Leonard** (USA) ND-W CO 9 Charley White (USA), Benton Harbor. *Actually billed as a fight that would decide the championship, it was merely a ten round no-decision affair that achieved notoriety for the fact that Leonard recovered from a terrible knockdown scare to save his title. The Chicago Tribune (newspaper) reported that while Leonard weighed in at 136½ lbs, White, a pound inside the championship weight, looked fit at 134 and would have been crowned champion had he won inside the distance.*

25.09.20 **Benny Leonard** (USA) ND-W PTS 10 Pal Moran (USA), Chicago. *Moran weighed 130 lbs.*

26.11.20 **Benny Leonard** (USA) W RSC 14 Joe Welling (USA), New York City

14.01.21 **Benny Leonard** (USA) W RSC 6 Richie Mitchell (USA), New York City

06.06.21 **Benny Leonard** (USA) ND-W PTS 12 Rocky Kansas (USA), Harrison. *Kansas weighed 134 lbs.*

10.02.22 **Benny Leonard** (USA) W PTS 15 Rocky Kansas (USA), New York City

25.02.22 **Benny Leonard** (USA) ND-W PTS 10 Pal Moran (USA), New Orleans

04.07.22 **Benny Leonard** (USA) ND-W RSC 8 Rocky Kansas (USA), Michigan City

27.07.22 **Benny Leonard** (USA) ND-W PTS 12 Lew Tendler (USA), Jersey City. *Tendler weighed 134¾ lbs.*

05.08.22 **Benny Leonard** (USA) ND-W PTS 10 Ever Hammer (USA), Michigan City

29.05.23 **Benny Leonard** (USA) ND-W RSC 10 Pinkey Mitchell (USA), Chicago

09.07.23 **Benny Leonard** (USA) ND-W PTS 8 Alex Hart (USA), Philadelphia

23.07.23 **Benny Leonard** (USA) W PTS 15 Lew Tendler (USA), New York City. *Although the announced weights were given as Leonard (134) and Tendler (133), the weigh-in was a private affair, with newspapermen excluded, and it was several years later before it transpired that the two men had weighed 137½ lbs and 138, respectively. However, with both men accepting the situation, it is still regarded as a title fight, merely proving that Leonard was having difficulty making the weight in what was ultimately to be his final defence.*

07.09.23 **Benny Leonard** (USA) ND-W PTS 8 Johnny Mendelsohn (USA), Philadelphia

01.08.24 **Benny Leonard** (USA) ND-W PTS 10 Pal Moran (USA), Cleveland. *In January 1925, Leonard relinquished his title on announcing his retirement and, with the division thrown into disarray, the NYSAC sponsored an elimination tournament to determine his successor. With over 50 men involved, it took more than six months to reach a conclusion, but after beating Eddie Wagner, Clyde Jeakle, Sammy Mandell and Benny Valger, the surprise package, Jimmy Goodrich, fought his way through to the final to face Stanislaus Loayza, a man who had defeated Cirilin Orlano, Tommy White, Lou Paluso, Pete Hartley, Aramis del Pino and Alf Simmons, on his way to a title shot. The pre-tournament favourites had been Sammy Mandell and Sid Terris, who dropped out following a points defeat at the hands of the former.*

13.07.25 Jimmy Goodrich (USA) W RSC 2 Stanislaus Loayza (CH), Long Island - NY

07.12.25 **Rocky Kansas** (USA) W PTS 15 Jimmy Goodrich (USA), Buffalo

03.07.26 **Sammy Mandell** (USA) W PTS 10 Rocky Kansas (USA), Chicago

21.05.28 Sammy Mandell (USA) W PTS 15 Jimmy McLarnin (USA), New York City

02.08.29 Sammy Mandell (USA) W PTS 10 Tony Canzoneri (USA), Chicago

17.07.30 Al Singer (USA) W CO 1 Sammy Mandell (USA), New York City

14.11.30 Tony Canzoneri (USA) W CO 1 Al Singer (USA), New York City

24.04.31 Tony Canzoneri (USA) W CO 3 Jackie Kid Berg (GB), Chicago. *With the result, Canzoneri also won Berg's NBA light-welterweight title, which had also been up for grabs.*

10.09.31 Tony Canzoneri (USA) W PTS 15 Jackie Kid Berg (GB), New York City

20.11.31 Tony Canzoneri (USA) W PTS 15 Kid Chocolate (CUB), New York City

04.11.32 Tony Canzoneri (USA) W PTS 15 Billy Petrolle (USA), New York City

23.06.33 Barney Ross (USA) W PTS 10 Tony Canzoneri (USA), Chicago. *With the result, and recognised by Illinois, Ross also won Canzoneri's light-welterweight title, which had also been up for grabs.*

12.09.33 Barney Ross (USA) W PTS 15 Tony Canzoneri (USA), New York City. *When Barney Ross relinquished the title in April 1935, after being suspended for failing to defend against the number one challenger, Lou Ambers, the New York State Athletic Commission immediately stepped in and matched Ambers, who had outpointed Sammy Fuller in a 15 round eliminator on 1 March 1935 (New York City), with former champion, Tony Canzoneri.*

10.05.35 Tony Canzoneri (USA) W PTS 15 Lou Ambers (USA), New York City

04.10.35 Tony Canzoneri (USA) W PTS 15 Al Roth (USA), New York City

03.09.36 Lou Ambers (USA) W PTS 15 Tony Canzoneri (USA), New York City

07.05.37 Lou Ambers (USA) W PTS 15 Tony Canzoneri (USA), New York City

23.09.37 Lou Ambers (USA) W PTS 15 Pedro Montanez (PR), New York City

17.08.38 Henry Armstrong (USA) W PTS 15 Lou Ambers (USA), New York City. *Armstrong's win gave him the proud record of becoming the only man in ring history to hold three world titles simultaneously.*

16.03.39 Henry Armstrong (USA) W CO 1 Lew Feldman (USA), St Louis. *The Ring Record Book has always shown this contest as being for the welterweight title, but, in truth, it was also in defence of Armstrong's lightweight crown, with Feldman, who was competing in that division at the time, scaling 134 lbs to the champion's 135.*

22.08.39 Lou Ambers (USA) W PTS 15 Henry Armstrong (USA), New York City. *Lou Ambers forfeited NBA recognition in April 1940 after he failed to sign for a defence against Davey Day. Day had outscored Sammy Angott over 12 rounds of an eliminator in Chicago on 8 December 1939 and, to find a new champion, the NBA matched the pair in a return.*

03.05.40 Sammy Angott (USA) W PTS 15 Davey Day (USA), Louisville - NBA

10.05.40 Lew Jenkins (USA) W RSC 3 Lou Ambers (USA), New York City - NY

22.11.40 Lew Jenkins (USA) W RSC 2 Pete Lello (USA), New York City - NY

02.05.41 Sammy Angott (USA) W PTS 12 Dave Castilloux (C), Louisville - NBA. *For many years this fight was inadvertently recorded as an NBA championship fight by the Boxing News Annual, when in fact it was a non-title affair, with Angott weighing 136 lbs and Castilloux 137, respectively.*

19.12.41 Sammy Angott (USA) W PTS 15 Lew Jenkins (USA), New York City

15.05.42 Sammy Angott (USA) W PTS 15 Allie Stolz (USA), New York City. *Sammy Angott relinquished title in November 1942, when retiring due to an injured hand, and Beau Jack, having eliminated Allie Stolz on a seventh round stoppage in New York City on 13 November 1942, was matched against Tippy Larkin to decide New York's version of the vacant title.*

18.12.42 Beau Jack (USA) W CO 3 Tippy Larkin (USA), New York City - NY

04.01.43 Slugger White (USA) W PTS 15 Willie Joyce (USA), Baltimore - MARYLAND. *Following White's win for the Maryland version of the title, Sammy Angott announced that he was returning to the ring and was looking to regain his old crown. With the NY title already under challenge from Bob Montgomery, who had just*

stopped Chester Rico in the eighth round of a NY eliminator on 8 January 1943, the NBA eventually matched the former champion against White for their vacant title.

21.05.43 Bob Montgomery (USA) W PTS 15 Beau Jack (USA), New York City - NY

27.10.43 Sammy Angott (USA) W PTS 15 Slugger White (USA), Los Angeles - NBA

19.11.43 Beau Jack (USA) W PTS 15 Bob Montgomery (USA), New York City - NY

03.03.44 Bob Montgomery (USA) W PTS 15 Beau Jack (USA), New York City - NY

08.03.44 Juan Zurita (MEX) W PTS 15 Sammy Angott (USA), Los Angeles - NBA

18.04.45 Ike Williams (USA) W CO 2 Juan Zurita (MEX), Mexico - NBA

30.04.46 Ike Williams (USA) W RSC 8 Enrique Bolanos (USA), Los Angeles - NBA

28.06.46 Bob Montgomery (USA) W CO 13 Allie Stolz (USA), New York City - NY

04.09.46 Ike Williams (USA) W CO 9 Ronnie James (GB), Ninian Park, Cardiff - NBA

26.11.46 Bob Montgomery (USA) W CO 8 Wesley Mouzon (USA), Philadelphia - NY/PENNSYLVANIA

04.08.47 Ike Williams (USA) W CO 6 Bob Montgomery (USA), Philadelphia

25.05.48 Ike Williams (USA) W PTS 15 Enrique Bolanos (USA), Los Angeles

12.07.48 Ike Williams (USA) W RSC 6 Beau Jack (USA), Philadelphia

23.09.48 Ike Williams (USA) W CO 10 Jesse Flores (USA), New York City

21.07.49 Ike Williams (USA) W RSC 4 Enrique Bolanos (USA), Los Angeles

05.12.49 Ike Williams (USA) W PTS 15 Freddie Dawson (USA), Philadelphia

25.05.51 Jimmy Carter (USA) W RSC 14 Ike Williams (USA), New York City

14.11.51 Jimmy Carter (USA) W PTS 15 Art Aragon (USA), Los Angeles

01.04.52 Jimmy Carter (USA) W PTS 15 Lauro Salas (MEX), Los Angeles

14.05.52 Lauro Salas (MEX) W PTS 15 Jimmy Carter (USA), Los Angeles

23.09.52 Lauro Salas (MEX) W CO 5 Ramon Young (USA), Phoenix. *Although billed as a non-title fight, with both men inside the class limit, Salas' championship belt was put at risk.*

15.10.52 Jimmy Carter (USA) W PTS 15 Lauro Salas (MEX), Chicago

24.04.53 Jimmy Carter (USA) W RSC 4 Tommy Collins (USA), Boston

12.06.53 Jimmy Carter (USA) W RSC 13 George Araujo (USA), New York City

11.11.53 Jimmy Carter (USA) W CO 5 Armand Savoie (C), Montreal

05.03.54 Paddy de Marco (USA) W PTS 15 Jimmy Carter (USA), New York City

17.11.54 Jimmy Carter (USA) W RSC 15 Paddy de Marco (USA), San Francisco

29.06.55 Wallace Bud Smith (USA) W PTS 15 Jimmy Carter (USA), Boston

19.10.55 Wallace Bud Smith (USA) W PTS 15 Jimmy Carter (USA), Cincinnati

24.08.56 Joe Brown (USA) W PTS 15 Wallace Bud Smith (USA), New Orleans

13.02.57 Joe Brown (USA) W RSC 10 Wallace Bud Smith (USA), Miami

19.06.57 Joe Brown (USA) W RSC 15 Orlando Zulueta (CUB), Denver

04.12.57 Joe Brown (USA) W RSC 11 Joey Lopes (USA), Chicago

07.05.58 Joe Brown (USA) W RSC 8 Ralph Dupas (USA), Houston

23.07.58 Joe Brown (USA) W PTS 15 Kenny Lane (USA), Houston

11.02.59 Joe Brown (USA) W PTS 15 Johnny Busso (USA), Houston

03.06.59 Joe Brown (USA) W RTD 8 Paolo Rossi (ITA), Washington

02.12.59 Joe Brown (USA) W RTD 5 Dave Charnley (GB), Houston

28.10.60 Joe Brown (USA) W PTS 15 Cisco Andrade (USA), Los Angeles

18.04.61 Joe Brown (USA) W PTS 15 Dave Charnley (GB), Earls Court, London

28.10.61 Joe Brown (USA) W PTS 15 Bert Somodio (PH), Quezon City

21.04.62 Carlos Ortiz (PR) W PTS 15 Joe Brown (USA), Las Vegas

03.12.62 Carlos Ortiz (PR) W CO 5 Teruo Kosaka (JAP), Tokyo

07.04.63 Carlos Ortiz (PR) W RSC 13 Doug Vaillant (CUB), San Juan. *Carlos Ortiz forfeited recognition in Michigan in July 1963 for failing to defend against number one contender, Kenny Lane.*

19.08.63 Kenny Lane (USA) W PTS 15 Paul Armstead (USA), Saginaw - MICHIGAN

15.02.64 Carlos Ortiz (PR) W RSC 14 Flash Elorde (PH), Manila - WBA/WBC

11.04.64 Carlos Ortiz (PR) W PTS 15 Kenny Lane (USA), San Juan

10.04.65 Ismael Laguna (PAN) W PTS 15 Carlos Ortiz (PR), Panama City

13.11.65 Carlos Ortiz (PR) W PTS 15 Ismael Laguna (PAN), San Juan

20.06.66 Carlos Ortiz (PR) W RSC 12 Johnny Bizzarro (USA), Pittsburg

22.10.66 Carlos Ortiz (PR) W RSC 5 Sugar Ramos (CUB), Mexico City. *When the fight was stopped, due to Ramos sustaining a cut eye, a riot broke out among the crowd and the WBC executive, in overruling the referee, ordered Ortiz to return to the ring immediately. Ortiz refused and two days later the WBC vacated the title and ordered a rematch.*

28.11.66 Carlos Ortiz (PR) W CO 14 Flash Elorde (PH), New York City - WBA

01.07.67 Carlos Ortiz (PR) W RSC 4 Sugar Ramos (CUB), San Juan

16.08.67 Carlos Ortiz (PR) W PTS 15 Ismael Laguna (PAN), New York City

29.06.68 Carlos Teo Cruz (DOM) W PTS 15 Carlos Ortiz (PR), St Domingo

28.09.68 Carlos Teo Cruz (DOM) W PTS 15 Mando Ramos (USA), Los Angeles

18.02.69 Mando Ramos (USA) W RSC 11 Carlos Teo Cruz (DOM), Los Angeles

04.10.69 Mando Ramos (USA) W RSC 6 Yoshiaki Numata (JAP), Los Angeles

03.03.70 Ismael Laguna (PAN) W RTD 9 Mando Ramos (USA), Los Angeles

07.06.70 Ismael Laguna (PAN) W RSC 13 Guts Ishimatsu (JAP), Panama City. *Ismael Laguna forfeited the WBC version of the title in May 1970 when he failed to give Mando Ramos a return, signing to meet Ken Buchanan, instead.*

26.09.70 Ken Buchanan (GB) W PTS 15 Ismael Laguna (PAN), San Juan - WBA

12.02.71 Ken Buchanan (GB) W PTS 15 Ruben Navarro (USA), Los Angeles. *With Buchanan due to defend against Mando Ramos, the above fight was still recognised by the WBC even though the challenger pulled out a couple of days prior to the off and had to be replaced. In June 1971, however, Buchanan forfeited the WBC version of the title during a contractual dispute. Having been told that he must defend against their stipulated challenger, he signed for a return against Laguna, an action which was followed by the WBC matching Pedro Carrasco and Ramos for their version of the title.*

13.09.71 Ken Buchanan (GB) W PTS 15 Ismael Laguna (PAN), New York City - WBA

05.11.71 Pedro Carrasco (SP) W DIS 11 Mando Ramos (USA), Madrid - WBC

18.02.72 Mando Ramos (USA) W PTS 15 Pedro Carrasco (SP), Los Angeles - WBC. *Following the fight, the WBC withdrew championship status after deciding that the decision had been "influenced locally".*

26.06.72 Roberto Duran (PAN) W RSC 13 Ken Buchanan (GB), New York City - WBA

28.06.72 Mando Ramos (USA) W PTS 15 Pedro Carrasco (SP), Madrid - WBC. *The WBC continued to recognise Ramos as champion despite protests by the Spanish Boxing Federation that the verdict be annulled after post-fight dope tests on the champion proved positive.*

15.09.72 Chango Carmona (MEX) W RSC 8 Mando Ramos (USA), Los Angeles - WBC

10.11.72 Rodolfo Gonzales (MEX) W RTD 12 Chango Carmona (MEX), Los Angeles - WBC

20.01.73 Roberto Duran (PAN) W CO 5 Jimmy Robertson (USA), Panama City - WBA

17.03.73 Rodolfo Gonzales (MEX) W RSC 9 Ruben Navarro (USA), Los Angeles - WBC

02.06.73 Roberto Duran (PAN) W RSC 8 Hector Thompson (A), Panama City - WBA

08.09.73 Roberto Duran (PAN) W RSC 10 Guts Ishimatsu (JAP), Panama City - WBA

27.10.73 Rodolfo Gonzalez (MEX) W RTD 10 Antonio Puddu (ITA), Los Angeles - WBC

16.03.74 Roberto Duran (PAN) W RSC 11 Esteban de Jesus (PR), Panama City - WBA

11.04.74 Guts Ishimatsu (JAP) W CO 8 Rodolfo Gonzalez (MEX), Tokyo - WBC

13.09.74 Guts Ishimatsu (JAP) DREW 15 Tury Pineda (MEX), Nagoya - WBC

28.11.74 Guts Ishimatsu (JAP) W CO 12 Rodolfo Gonzalez (MEX), Osaka - WBC

21.12.74 Roberto Duran (PAN) W RSC 1 Masataka Takayama (JAP), San Jose - WBA

27.02.75 Guts Ishimatsu (JAP) W PTS 15 Ken Buchanan (GB), Tokyo - WBC

02.03.75 Roberto Duran (PAN) W CO 14 Ray Lampkin (USA), Panama City - WBA

05.06.75 Guts Ishimatsu (JAP) W PTS 15 Tury Pineda (MEX), Osaka - WBC

04.12.75 Guts Ishimatsu (JAP) W CO 14 Alvaro Rojas (CR), Tokyo - WBC

14.12.75 Roberto Duran (PAN) W CO 15 Leoncio Ortiz (MEX), San Juan - WBA

08.05.76 Esteban de Jesus (PR) W PTS 15 Guts Ishimatsu (JAP), Bayamon - WBC

22.05.76 Roberto Duran (PAN) W CO 14 Lou Bizzaro (USA), Fort Erie - WBA

10.09.76 Esteban de Jesus (PR) W CO 7 Hector Medina (DOM), Bayamon - WBC

15.10.76 Roberto Duran (PAN) W CO 1 Alvaro Rojas (CR), Los Angeles - WBA

29.01.77 Roberto Duran (PAN) W CO 13 Vilomar Fernandez (DOM), Miami - WBA

12.02.77 Esteban de Jesus (PR) W RSC 6 Buzzsaw Yamabe (JAP), Bayamon - WBC

25.06.77 Esteban de Jesus (PR) W CO 11 Vicente Mijares (MEX), Bayamon - WBC

17.09.77 Roberto Duran (PAN) W PTS 15 Edwin Viruet (PR), Philadelphia - WBA

21.01.78 **Roberto Duran** (PAN) W CO 12 Esteban de Jesus (PR), Las Vegas. *Roberto Duran relinquished the title in January 1979, due to increasing weight problems, having been told by the WBC that he had to defend against Jim Watt. Following the announcement, the latter was immediately matched against Alfredo Pitalua to contest the WBC version of the title. Meanwhile, the WBA set up two final eliminators between Johnny Lira v Vilomar Fernandez and Ernesto Espana v Claude Noel, but after Fernandez and Lira failed to agree terms, the latter contest went ahead for the WBA's vacant title.*

17.04.79 Jim Watt (GB) W RSC 12 Alfredo Pitalua (COL), Kelvin Hall, Glasgow - WBC

16.06.79 Ernesto Espana (VEN) W CO 13 Claude Noel (TR), San Juan - WBA

04.08.79 Ernesto Espana (VEN) W RSC 9 Johnny Lira (USA), Chicago - WBA

03.11.79 Jim Watt (GB) W RSC 9 Roberto Vasquez (USA), Kelvin Hall, Glasgow - WBC

02.03.80 Hilmer Kenty (USA) W RSC 9 Ernesto Espana (VEN), Detroit - WBA

14.03.80 Jim Watt (GB) W RSC 4 Charlie Nash (GB), Kelvin Hall, Glasgow - WBC

07.06.80 Jim Watt (GB) W PTS 15 Howard Davis (USA), Ibrox Park, Glasgow - WBC

02.08.80 Hilmer Kenty (USA) W RSC 9 Yong-Ho Oh (SK), Detroit - WBA

20.09.80 Hilmer Kenty (USA) W RSC 4 Ernesto Espana (VEN), San Juan - WBA

01.11.80 Jim Watt (GB) W RSC 12 Sean O'Grady (USA), Kelvin Hall, Glasgow - WBC

08.11.80 Hilmer Kenty (USA) W PTS 15 Vilomar Fernandez (DOM), Detroit - WBA

12.04.81 Sean O'Grady (USA) W PTS 15 Hilmer Kenty (USA), Atlantic City - WBA. *Sean O'Grady forfeited WBA recognition in August 1981, following a contractual dispute.*

20.06.81 Alexis Arguello (NIC) W PTS 15 Jim Watt (GB), The Arena, Wembley - WBC

12.09.81 Claude Noel (TR) W PTS 15 Gato Gonzalez (MEX), Atlantic City - WBA

03.10.81 Alexis Arguello (NIC) W RSC 14 Ray Mancini (USA), Atlantic City - WBC

31.10.81 Andy Ganigan (USA) W CO 2 Sean O'Grady (USA), Little Rock. *Not generally recognised as a title fight, the match was both made and promoted by a body calling themselves the World Athletic Association, who came together in order to support O'Grady's claim to the title.*

21.11.81 Alexis Arguello (NIC) W CO 7 Robert Elizondo (USA), Las Vegas - WBC

05.12.81 Arturo Frias (USA) W CO 8 Claude Noel (TR), Las Vegas - WBA

30.01.82 Arturo Frias (USA) W TD 9 Ernesto Espana (VEN), Atlantic City - WBA. *A controversial ending saw Frias save his title after the fight was stopped on the orders of the doctor. The referee ruled that Frias' eye damage had been caused accidentally and, under WBA rules it went to the judges, with the champion leading on all three cards.*

13.02.82 Alexis Arguello (NIC) W RSC 6 Bubba Busceme (USA), Beaumont - WBC

08.05.82 Ray Mancini (USA) W RSC 1 Arturo Frias (USA), Las Vegas - WBA

22.05.82 Alexis Arguello (NIC) W CO 5 Andy Ganigan (USA), Las Vegas - WBC. *Alexis Arguello relinquished WBC version of title in February 1983 after becoming WBA light-welterweight champion.*

24.07.82 Ray Mancini (USA) W RSC 6 Ernesto Espana (VEN), Warren - WBA

13.11.82 Ray Mancini (USA) W RSC 14 Deuk-Koo Kim (SK), Las Vegas - WBA. *Taken unconscious from the ring on a stretcher, Deuk-Koo Kim failed to survive an operation to remove a blod clot from the brain and died in hospital several days later.*

01.05.83 Edwin Rosario (PR) W PTS 12 Jose Luis Ramirez (MEX), San Juan - WBC

15.09.83 Ray Mancini (USA) W CO 9 Orlando Romero (PE), New York City - WBA

14.01.84 Ray Mancini (USA) W RSC 3 Bobby Chacon (USA), Reno - WBA

30.01.84 Charlie Choo Choo Brown (USA) W PTS 15 Melvin Paul (USA), Atlantic City - IBF

17.03.84 Edwin Rosario (PR) W RSC 1 Robert Elizondo (USA), San Juan - WBC

15.04.84 Harry Arroyo (USA) W RSC 14 Charlie Choo Choo Brown (USA), Atlantic City - IBF

01.06.84 Livingstone Bramble (USA) W RSC 14 Ray Mancini (USA), Buffalo - WBA

23.06.84 Edwin Rosario (PR) W PTS 12 Howard Davis (USA), San Juan - WBC

01.09.84 Harry Arroyo (USA) W RSC 8 Charlie White Lightning Brown (USA), Youngstown - IBF

03.11.84 Jose Luis Ramirez (MEX) W RSC 4 Edwin Rosario (PR), San Juan - WBC

12.01.85 Harry Arroyo (USA) W RSC 11 Terrence Alli (GU), Atlantic City - IBF

16.02.85 Livingstone Bramble (USA) W PTS 15 Ray Mancini (USA), Reno - WBA

06.04.85 Jimmy Paul (USA) W PTS 15 Harry Arroyo (USA), Atlantic City - IBF

30.06.85 Jimmy Paul (USA) W RSC 14 Robin Blake (USA), Las Vegas - IBF

10.08.85 Hector Camacho (PR) W PTS 12 Jose Luis Ramirez (MEX), Las Vegas - WBC

16.02.86 Livingstone Bramble (USA) W RSC 13 Tyrone Crawley (USA), Reno - WBA

04.06.86 Jimmy Paul (USA) W PTS 15 Irleis Perez (CUB), East Rutherford - IBF

13.06.86 Hector Camacho (PR) W PTS 12 Edwin Rosario (PR), New York City - WBC

15.08.86 Jimmy Paul (USA) W PTS 15 Darryl Tyson (USA), Detroit - IBF

26.09.86 Hector Camacho (PR) W PTS 12 Cornelius Boza-Edwards (U), Miami - WBC. *Hector Camacho relinquished WBC version of title in May 1987 due to weight making difficulties.*

26.09.86 Edwin Rosario (PR) W CO 2 Livingstone Bramble (USA), Miami - WBA

05.12.86 Greg Haugen (USA) W PTS 15 Jimmy Paul (USA), Las Vegas - IBF

07.06.87 Vinny Pazienza (USA) W PTS 15 Greg Haugen (USA), Providence - IBF

19.07.87 Jose Luis Ramirez (MEX) W PTS 12 Terrence Alli (GU), St Tropez - WBC

11.08.87 Edwin Rosario (PR) W CO 8 Juan Nazario (PR), Chicago - WBA

10.10.87 Jose Luis Ramirez (MEX) W CO 5 Cornelius Boza-Edwards (U), Paris - WBC

21.11.87 Julio Cesar Chavez (MEX) W RSC 11 Edwin Rosario (PR), Las Vegas - WBA

06.02.88 Greg Haugen (USA) W PTS 15 Vinny Pazienza (USA), Atlantic City - IBF

12.03.88 Jose Luis Ramirez (MEX) W PTS 12 Pernell Whitaker (USA), Paris - WBC

11.04.88 Greg Haugen (USA) W TD 11 Miguel Santana (PR), Tacoma - IBF. *When Haugen suffered a terrible cut right-eye late in the 11th round and the doctor decided it was too bad for him to continue, the fight went to the scorecards under IBF regulations. Initially, the result was announced as a win for Santana, but shortly afterwards it transpired that Haugen had won on two judges' scorecards and Santana's joy was short lived.*

16.04.88 Julio Cesar Chavez (MEX) W RSC 6 Rodolfo Aguilar (PAN), Las Vegas - WBA

28.10.88 Greg Haugen (USA) W RTD 10 Gert Bo Jacobsen (DEN), Copenhagen - IBF

29.10.88 Julio Cesar Chavez (MEX) W TD 11 Jose Luis Ramirez (MEX), Las Vegas - WBA/WBC. *Stopped under doctor's orders after an accidental crack of heads left Ramirez unable to continue, Chavez, ahead on all three judges' scorecards at the time, picked up the technical decision. Julio Cesar Chavez relinquished WBA/WBC versions of title on becoming WBC light-welterweight champion in May 1989.*

21.01.89 Mauricio Aceves (MEX) DREW 12 Amancio Castro (COL), Monteria - WBO

18.02.89 Pernell Whitaker (USA) W PTS 12 Greg Haugen (USA), Hampton - IBF

30.04.89 Pernell Whitaker (USA) W RSC 3 Louie Lomeli (USA), Norfolk - IBF

08.05.89 Mauricio Aceves (MEX) W PTS 12 Amancio Castro (COL), Santa Ana - WBO

09.07.89 Edwin Rosario (PR) W RSC 6 Anthony Jones (USA), Atlantic City - WBA

20.08.89 Pernell Whitaker (USA) W PTS 12 Jose Luis Ramirez (MEX), Norfolk - IBF/WBC

30.08.89 Mauricio Aceves (MEX) W RSC 10 Oscar Bejines (MEX), Los Angeles - WBO

03.02.90 Pernell Whitaker (USA) W PTS 12 Fred Pendleton (USA), Atlantic City - IBF/WBC

04.04.90 Juan Nazario (PR) W RSC 8 Edwin Rosario (PR), New York City - WBA

19.05.90 Pernell Whitaker (USA) W PTS 12 Azumah Nelson (GH), Las Vegas - IBF/WBC

11.08.90 Pernell Whitaker (USA) W CO 1 Juan Nazario (PR), Stateline - IBF/WBA/WBC

22.09.90 Dingaan Thobela (SA) W PTS 12 Maurico Aceves (MEX), Brownsville - WBO

02.02.91 Dingaan Thobela (SA) W PTS 12 Mario Martinez (MEX), San Jose - WBO

23.02.91 Pernell Whitaker (USA) W PTS 12 Anthony Jones (USA), Las Vegas - IBF/WBA/WBC

27.07.91 Pernell Whitaker (USA) W PTS 12 Policarpo Diaz (SP), Norfolk - IBF/WBA/WBC

14.09.91 Dingaan Thobela (SA) W PTS 12 Antonio Rivera (PR), Johannesburg - WBO. *Dingaan Thobela relinquished WBO version of the title in July 1992 in order to challenge for the WBA crown.*

05.10.91 Pernell Whitaker (USA) W PTS 12 Jorge Paez (MEX), Reno - IBF/WBA/WBC. *Pernell Whitaker relinquished IBF/WBA/WBC versions of the title in February 1992 to challenge for the IBF light-welterweight crown.*

12.06.92 Joey Gamache (USA) W RTD 8 Chil-Sung Chun (SK), Portland - WBA

24.08.92 Miguel Gonzalez (MEX) W RTD 9 Wilfredo Rocha (COL), Mexico City - WBC

29.08.92 Fred Pendleton (USA) T DRAW 2 Tracy Spann (USA), Reno - IBF. *Dropped and cut and unable to continue after an accidental clash of heads, Pendleton's situation gave the referee no alternative under IBF rules than to call a technical draw.*

25.09.92 Giovanni Parisi (ITA) W RSC 10 Javier Altamirano (MEX), Voghera - WBO

24.10.92 Tony Lopez (USA) W RSC 11 Joey Gamache (USA), Portland - WBA

05.12.92 Miguel Gonzalez (MEX) W PTS 12 Darryl Tyson (USA), Mexico City - WBC

10.01.93 Fred Pendleton (USA) W PTS 12 Tracy Spann (USA), Atlantic City - IBF

12.02.93 Tony Lopez (USA) W PTS 12 Dingaan Thobela (SA), Sacramento - WBA

16.04.93 Giovanni Parisi (ITA) W PTS 12 Michael Ayers (GB), Rome - WBO

26.04.93 Miguel Gonzalez (MEX) W PTS 12 Hector Lopez (MEX), Aguascalientes - WBC

26.06.93 Dingaan Thobela (SA) W PTS 12 Tony Lopez (USA), Sun City - WBA

World Champions (L. Welterweight to Heavyweight), 1891-1993

Since last year's listings were published, much research on world championship boxing has taken place as you can see from the section, World Title Bouts (M. Flyweight to Lightweight), 1891-1993. The corrections have been built into the listings where possible, but the full extent of the changes will not be known until the exercise is fully completed in time for the 1996 Yearbook. However, even at this point in time, the writer is happy to accept the fact that the Dixie Kid was never fully recognised in America as the welterweight champion after beating Joe Walcott and that men such as Mike Glover and Jack Britton were only shown as champions in 1915 after historians over the years tidied up the descent of the welterweight title without sufficient evidence to back them up. Also, what has become much clearer is the fact that as there were no governing bodies operating in America before 1920, men like Mike Twin Sullivan, Frank Mantell, Harry Lewis and Jimmy Gardner did not have sufficient backing throughout their own country as to justify world championship recognition in the 147 lbs division. Another man to benefit at the hands of boxing historians down the years was Jack O'Brien. He has now been removed from the light-heavyweight listings since it was discovered that his fight with Bob Fitzsimmons was a heavyweight title eliminator. Because both men were inside 175 lbs, Fitzsimmons technically forfeited his title, but there is simply no evidence available to suggest that O'Brien ever claimed the crown. There seems to be no doubt that O'Brien clearly saw himself as a heavyweight, a fact supported when one assesses his record and sees no sign of activity in light-heavyweight division. All that aside, the following is an attempt to list every champion under Queensberry Rules since the beginning of gloves at 140 lbs and above.

Championship Status Code:

AU=Austria; AUST = Australia; CALIF = California; CAN=Canada; EBU = European Boxing Union; FR = France; GB = Great Britain; IBF = International Boxing Federation; IBU = International Boxing Union; ILL=Illinois; LOUIS = Louisiana; MARY = Maryland; MASS = Massachusetts; NBA = National Boxing Association; NY = New York; PEN = Pennsylvania; SA=South Africa; USA = United States; WBA = World Boxing Association; WBC = World Boxing Council; WBO = World Boxing Organisation.

Champions in **bold** are accorded universal recognition.

* Undefeated champions (Does not include men who forfeited titles).

Title Holder	Birthplace	Tenure	Status	Title Holder	Birthplace	Tenure	Status
L. Welterweight (140 lbs)				Aaron Pryor*	USA	1980-1983	WBA
Mushy Callahan	USA	1926-1929	NBA/NY	Leroy Haley	USA	1982-1983	WBC
Mushy Callahan	USA	1929-1930	NBA	Bruce Curry	USA	1983-1984	WBC
Jackie Kid Berg	England	1930-1931	NBA	Johnny Bumphus	USA	1984	WBA
Tony Canzoneri	USA	1931-1932	NBA	Bill Costello	USA	1984-1985	WBC
Johnny Jadick	USA	1932	NBA	Gene Hatcher	USA	1984-1985	IBF
Johnny Jadick	USA	1932-1933	PEN	Aaron Pryor	USA	1984-1985	IBF
Battling Shaw	Mexico	1933	LOUIS	Ubaldo Sacco	Argentine	1985-1986	WBA
Tony Canzoneri	USA	1933	LOUIS	Lonnie Smith	USA	1985-1986	WBC
Barney Ross*	USA	1933-1935	ILL	Patrizio Oliva	Italy	1986-1987	WBA
Maxie Berger	Canada	1939	CAN	Gary Hinton	USA	1986	IBF
Harry Weekly	USA	1940-1942	LOUIS	Rene Arredondo	Mexico	1986	WBC
Tippy Larkin*	USA	1946-1947	MASS/NY	Tsuyoshi Hamada	Japan	1986-1987	WBC
Carlos Oritz	Puerto Rico	1959-1960	NBA	Joe Manley	USA	1986-1987	IBF
Duilio Loi	Italy	1960-1962	NBA	Terry Marsh*	England	1987	IBF
Eddie Perkins	USA	1962	NBA	Juan M. Coggi	Argentine	1987-1990	WBA
Duilio Loi*	Italy	1962-1963	NBA	Rene Arredondo	Mexico	1987	WBC
Roberto Cruz	Philippines	1963	WBA	Roger Mayweather	USA	1987-1989	WBC
Eddie Perkins	USA	1963-1965	WBA	James McGirt	USA	1988	IBF
Carlos Hernandez	Venezuela	1965-1966	WBA	Meldrick Taylor	USA	1988-1990	IBF
Sandro Lopopolo	Italy	1966-1967	WBA	Hector Camacho	Puerto Rico	1989-1991	WBO
Paul Fujii	Hawaii	1967-1968	WBA	Julio Cesar Chavez	Mexico	1989-1990	WBC
Nicolino Loche	Argentine	1968-1972	WBA	Julio Cesar Chavez	Mexico	1990-1991	IBF/WBC
Pedro Adigue	Philippines	1968-1970	WBC	Loreto Garza	USA	1990-1991	WBA
Bruno Arcari*	Italy	1970-1974	WBC	Greg Haugen	USA	1991	WBO
Alfonso Frazer	Panama	1972	WBA	Hector Camacho*	Puerto Rico	1991-1992	WBO
Antonio Cervantes	Colombia	1972-1976	WBA	Edwin Rosario	Puerto Rico	1991-1992	WBA
Perico Fernandez	Spain	1974-1975	WBC	Julio Cesar Chavez	Mexico	1991-	WBC
Saensak Muangsurin	Thailand	1975-1976	WBC	Rafael Pineda	Colombia	1991-1992	IBF
Wilfred Benitez	USA	1976	WBA	Akinobu Hiranaka	Japan	1992	WBA
Miguel Velasquez	Spain	1976	WBC	Carlos Gonzalez	Mexico	1992-1993	WBO
Saensak Muangsurin	Thailand	1976-1978	WBC	Pernell Whitaker*	USA	1992-1993	IBF
Antonio Cervantes	Colombia	1977-1980	WBA	Morris East	Philippines	1992-1993	WBA
Wilfred Benitez*	USA	1977	NY	Juan M. Coggi	Argentine	1993-	WBA
Sang-Hyun Kim	S Korea	1978-1980	WBC	Charles Murray	USA	1993-	IBF
Saoul Mamby	USA	1980-1982	WBC	Zack Padilla	USA	1993-	WBO

Title Holder	Birthplace	Tenure	Status	Title Holder	Birthplace	Tenure	Status
Welterweight (147 lbs)				Tommy Freeman	USA	1930-1931	
Mysterious Billy Smith	USA	1892-1894		**Young Jack Thompson**	USA	1931	
Tommy Ryan*	USA	1894-1898		**Lou Brouillard**	Canada	1931-1932	
Mysterious Billy Smith	USA	1898-1900		**Jackie Fields**	USA	1932-1933	
Matty Matthews	USA	1900-1901		**Young Corbett III**	Italy	1933	
Eddie Connolly	USA	1900		**Jimmy McLarnin**	Ireland	1933-1934	
Rube Ferns	USA	1900		**Barney Ross**	USA	1934	
Matty Matthews	USA	1900-1901		**Jimmy McLarnin**	Ireland	1934-1935	
Joe Walcott	Barbados	1901-1906		**Barney Ross**	USA	1935-1938	
Honey Mellody	USA	1906-1907		Barney Ross	USA	1938	NY/NBA
Harry Lewis	USA	1910-1912	GB/FR	Felix Wouters	Belgium	1938	IBU
Jimmy Clabby	USA	1910-1912	AUSTR	**Henry Armstrong**	USA	1938-1940	
Matt Wells	England	1914-1915	AUSTR	**Fritzie Zivic**	USA	1940-1941	
Ted Kid Lewis	England	1915-1916		Fritzie Zivic	USA	1940-1941	NY/NBA
Jack Britton	USA	1916-1917		Izzy Jannazzo	USA	1940-1941	MARY
Ted Kid Lewis	England	1917-1919		Red Cochrane	USA	1941	NY/NBA
Jack Britton	USA	1919-1922		**Red Cochrane**	USA	1941-1946	
Mickey Walker	USA	1922-1923		**Marty Servo**	USA	1946	
Mickey Walker	USA	1923-1925	NBA	**Sugar Ray Robinson***	USA	1946-1951	
Dave Shade	USA	1923	NY	Johnny Bratton	USA	1951	NBA
Jimmy Jones	USA	1923	NY/MASS	Kid Gavilan	Cuba	1951-1952	NBA/NY
Mickey Walker	USA	1925-1926		**Kid Gavilan**	Cuba	1952-1954	
Pete Latzo	USA	1926-1927		**Johnny Saxton**	USA	1954-1955	
Joe Dundee	Italy	1927-1929		**Tony de Marco**	USA	1955	
Joe Dundee	Italy	1929	NY	**Carmen Basilio**	USA	1955-1956	
Jackie Fields	USA	1929	NBA	**Johnny Saxton**	USA	1956	
Jackie Fields	USA	1929-1930		**Carmen Basilio***	USA	1956-1957	
Young Jack Thompson	USA	1930		Virgil Akins	USA	1957-1958	MASS

Two great former champions, Roberto Duran (left) and Sugar Ray Leonard, spar for an opening. The pair met twice for the welterweight title in 1980 with one win apiece

Chris Farina

Title Holder	Birthplace	Tenure	Status
Virgil Akins	USA	1958	
Don Jordan	Dom Republic	1958-1960	
Benny Kid Paret	Cuba	1960-1961	
Emile Griffith	Virgin Islands	1961	
Benny Kid Paret	Cuba	1961-1962	
Emile Griffith	Virgin Islands	1962-1963	
Luis Rodriguez	Cuba	1963	
Emile Griffith*	Virgin Islands	1963-1966	
Willie Ludick	S Africa	1966-1968	SA
Curtis Cokes	USA	1966-1968	WBA/WBC
Curtis Cokes	USA	1966-1967	WBA
Charley Shipes	USA	1966-1967	CALIF
Curtis Cokes	USA	1968-1969	
Jose Napoles	Cuba	1969-1970	
Billy Backus	USA	1970-1971	
Jose Napoles	Cuba	1971-1975	
Jose Napoles	Cuba	1972-1974	WBA/WBC
Hedgemon Lewis	USA	1972-1974	NY
Jose Napoles	Cuba	1974-1975	
Jose Napoles	Cuba	1975	WBC
Angel Espada	Puerto Rico	1975-1976	WBA
John H. Stracey	England	1975-1976	WBC
Carlos Palomino	Mexico	1976-1979	WBC
Pipino Cuevas	Mexico	1976-1980	WBA
Wilfred Benitez	USA	1979	WBC
Sugar Ray Leonard	USA	1979-1980	WBC
Roberto Duran	Panama	1980	WBC
Thomas Hearns	USA	1980-1981	WBA
Sugar Ray Leonard	USA	1980-1981	WBC
Sugar Ray Leonard*	USA	1981-1982	
Don Curry	USA	1983-1984	WBA
Milton McCrory	USA	1983-1985	WBC
Don Curry	USA	1984-1985	WBA/IBF
Don Curry	USA	1985-1986	
Lloyd Honeyghan	Jamaica	1986	
Lloyd Honeyghan	Jamaica	1986-1987	WBC/IBF
Mark Breland	USA	1987	WBA
Marlon Starling	USA	1987-1988	WBA
Jorge Vaca	Mexico	1987-1988	WBC
Lloyd Honeyghan	Jamaica	1988-1989	WBC
Simon Brown	Jamaica	1988-1991	IBF
Tomas Molinares	Colombia	1988	WBA
Mark Breland	USA	1989-1990	WBA
Marlon Starling	USA	1989-1990	WBC
Genaro Leon*	Mexico	1989	WBO
Manning Galloway	USA	1989-1993	WBO
Aaron Davis	USA	1990-1991	WBA
Maurice Blocker	USA	1990	WBC
Meldrick Taylor	USA	1991-1992	WBA
Simon Brown	Jamaica	1991	WBC/IBF
Simon Brown	Jamaica	1991	WBC
Maurice Blocker	USA	1991-1993	IBF
James McGirt	USA	1991-1993	WBC
Crisanto Espana	Venezuela	1992-	WBA
Gert Bo Jacobsen	Denmark	1993-	WBO
Pernell Whitaker	USA	1993-	WBC
Felix Trinidad	Puerto Rico	1993-	IBF

L. Middleweight (154 lbs)

Title Holder	Birthplace	Tenure	Status
Emile Griffith*	USA	1962-1963	AU
Denny Moyer	USA	1962-1963	WBA
Ralph Dupas	USA	1963	WBA
Sandro Mazzinghi	Italy	1963-1965	WBA
Nino Benvenuti	Italy	1965-1966	WBA
Ki-Soo Kim	S Korea	1966-1968	WBA
Sandro Mazzinghi	Italy	1968-1969	WBA
Freddie Little	USA	1969-1970	WBA
Carmelo Bossi	Italy	1970-1971	WBA
Koichi Wajima	Japan	1971-1974	WBA
Oscar Albarado	USA	1974-1975	WBA

Title Holder	Birthplace	Tenure	Status
Koichi Wajima	Japan	1975	WBA
Miguel de Oliveira	Brazil	1975	WBC
Jae-Do Yuh	S Korea	1975-1976	WBA
Elisha Obed	Bahamas	1975-1976	WBC
Koichi Wajima	Japan	1976	WBA
Jose Duran	Spain	1976	WBA
Eckhard Dagge	Germany	1976-1977	WBC
Miguel Castellini	Argentine	1976-1977	WBA
Eddie Gazo	Nicaragua	1977-1978	WBA
Rocky Mattioli	Italy	1977-1979	WBC
Masashi Kudo	Japan	1978-1979	WBA
Maurice Hope	Antigua	1979-1981	WBC
Ayub Kalule	Uganda	1979-1981	WBA
Wilfred Benitez	USA	1981-1982	WBC
Sugar Ray Leonard*	USA	1981	WBA
Tadashi Mihara	Japan	1981-1982	WBA
Davey Moore	USA	1982-1983	WBA
Thomas Hearns*	USA	1982-1986	WBC
Roberto Duran*	Panama	1983-1984	WBA
Mark Medal	USA	1984	IBF
Mike McCallum*	Jamaica	1984-1987	WBA
Carlos Santos	Puerto Rico	1984-1986	IBF
Buster Drayton	USA	1986-1987	IBF
Duane Thomas	USA	1986-1987	WBC
Matthew Hilton	Canada	1987-1988	IBF
Lupe Aquino	Mexico	1987	WBC
Gianfranco Rosi	Italy	1987-1988	WBC
Julian Jackson*	Virgin Islands	1987-1990	WBA
Don Curry	USA	1988-1989	WBC
Robert Hines	USA	1988-1989	IBF
John David Jackson	USA	1988-	WBO
Darrin van Horn	USA	1989	IBF
Rene Jacqot	France	1989	WBC
John Mugabi	Uganda	1989-1990	WBC
Gianfranco Rosi	Italy	1989-	IBF
Terry Norris	USA	1990-	WBC
Gilbert Dele	France	1991	WBA
Vinnie Pazienza*	USA	1991-1992	WBA
Julio Cesar Vasquez	Argentine	1992-	WBA

Middleweight (160 lbs)

Title Holder	Birthplace	Tenure	Status
Nonpareil Jack Dempsey	Ireland	1891	
Bob Fitzsimmons*	England	1891-1897	
Kid McCoy*	USA	1897-1898	
Tommy Ryan*	USA	1898-1907	
Stanley Ketchel	USA	1908	
Billy Papke	USA	1908	
Stanley Ketchel*	USA	1908-1910	
Billy Papke	USA	1911-1912	GB
Georges Carpentier	France	1912	IBU
Billy Papke	USA	1912-1913	IBU
Frank Klaus	USA	1913	IBU
George Chip	USA	1913-1914	USA
Eddie McGoorty	USA	1914	AUSTR
Jeff Smith	USA	1914	AUSTR
Al McCoy	USA	1914-1917	USA
Mick King	Australia	1914	AUSTR
Jeff Smith	USA	1914-1915	AUSTR
Les Darcy*	Australia	1915-1917	AUSTR
Mike O'Dowd	USA	1917-1920	
Johnny Wilson	USA	1920-1922	
Johnny Wilson	USA	1922-1923	NBA
Bryan Downey	USA	1922	OHIO
Dave Rosenberg	USA	1922	NY
Jock Malone	USA	1922-1923	OHIO
Mike O'Dowd	USA	1922-1923	NY
Harry Greb	USA	1923-1926	
Tiger Flowers	USA	1926	
Mickey Walker*	USA	1926-1931	
Gorilla Jones	USA	1931-1932	NBA

Title Holder	Birthplace	Tenure	Status	Title Holder	Birthplace	Tenure	Status
Marcel Thil	France	1932-1937	IBU	Julian Jackson	Virgin Islands	1990-1993	WBC
Ben Jeby	USA	1933	NY	James Toney*	USA	1991-1993	IBF
Lou Brouillard	Canada	1933	NY/NBA	Gerald McClellan*	USA	1991-1993	WBO
Teddy Yarosz	USA	1933-1934	PENN	Reggie Johnson	USA	1992-	WBA
Vince Dundee	USA	1933-1934	NY/NBA	Gerald McClellan	USA	1993-	WBC
Teddy Yarosz	USA	1934-1935	NY/NBA	Chris Pyatt	England	1993-	WBO
Babe Risko	USA	1935-1936	NY/NBA	Roy Jones	USA	1993-	IBF
Freddie Steele	USA	1936-1938	NY/NBA				
Freddie Steele	USA	1938	NBA	**S. Middleweight (168 lbs)**			
Fred Apostoli	USA	1937-1938	IBU	Murray Sutherland	Scotland	1984	IBF
Fred Apostoli	USA	1937-1939	NY	Chong-Pal Park*	S Korea	1984-1987	IBF
Edouard Tenet	France	1938	IBU	Chong-Pal Park	S Korea	1987-1988	WBA
Al Hostak	USA	1938	NBA	Graciano Rocchigiani*	Germany	1988-1989	IBF
Solly Krieger	USA	1938-1939	NBA	Fully Obelmejias	Venezuela	1988-1989	WBA
Al Hostak	USA	1939-1940	NBA	Sugar Ray Leonard*	USA	1988-1990	WBC
Ceferino Garcia	Philippines	1939-1940	NY	Thomas Hearns*	USA	1988-1991	WBO
Ken Overlin	USA	1940-1941	NY	In-Chul Baek	S Korea	1989-1990	WBA
Tony Zale	USA	1940-1941	NBA	Lindell Holmes	USA	1990-1991	IBF
Billy Soose	USA	1941	NY	Christophe Tiozzo	France	1990-1991	WBA
Tony Zale	USA	1941-1947		Mauro Galvano	Italy	1990-1992	WBC
Rocky Graziano	USA	1947-1948		Victor Cordoba	Panama	1991-1992	WBA
Tony Zale	USA	1948		Darrin van Horn	USA	1991-1992	IBF
Marcel Cerdan	Algeria	1948-1949		Chris Eubank	England	1991-	WBO
Jake la Motta	USA	1949-1950		Iran Barkley	USA	1992-1993	IBF
Jake la Motta	USA	1950-1951	NY/NBA	Michael Nunn	USA	1992-	WBA
Sugar Ray Robinson	USA	1950-1951	PEN	Nigel Benn	England	1992-	WBC
Sugar Ray Robinson	USA	1951		James Toney	USA	1993-	IBF
Randy Turpin	England	1951					
Sugar Ray Robinson*	USA	1951-1952		**L. Heavyweight (175 lbs)**			
Randy Turpin	England	1953	EBU	Jack Root	Austria	1903	USA
Carl Bobo Olson	Hawaii	1953-1955		George Gardner	Ireland	1903	USA
Sugar Ray Robinson	USA	1955-1957		Bob Fitzsimmons	England	1903-1905	USA
Gene Fullmer	USA	1957		Jack Dillon	USA	1912-1916	USA
Sugar Ray Robinson	USA	1957		Battling Levinsky	USA	1916-1920	USA
Carmen Basilio	USA	1957-1958		**Georges Carpentier**	France	1920-1922	
Sugar Ray Robinson	USA	1958-1959		**Battling Siki**	Senegal	1922-1923	
Sugar Ray Robinson	USA	1959-1960	NY/EBU	**Mike McTigue**	Ireland	1923-1925	
Gene Fullmer	USA	1959-1962	NBA	**Paul Berlenbach**	USA	1925-1926	
Paul Pender	USA	1960-1961	NY/EBU	**Jack Delaney***	Canada	1926-1927	
Terry Downes	England	1961-1962	NY/EBU	Jimmy Slattery	USA	1927	NBA
Paul Pender	USA	1962-1963	NY/EBU	Tommy Loughran	USA	1927	NY
Dick Tiger	Nigeria	1962-1963	NBA	**Tommy Loughran***	USA	1927-1929	
Dick Tiger	Nigeria	1963		Jimmy Slattery	USA	1930	NY
Joey Giardello	USA	1963-1965		**Maxie Rosenbloom**	USA	1930-1931	
Dick Tiger	Nigeria	1965-1966		Maxie Rosenbloom	USA	1931-1933	NY
Emile Griffith	Virgin Islands	1966-1967		George Nichols	USA	1932	NBA
Nino Benvenuti	Italy	1967		Bob Godwin	USA	1933	NBA
Emile Griffith	Virgin Islands	1967-1968		**Maxie Rosenbloom**	USA	1933-1934	
Nino Benvenuti	Italy	1968-1970		**Bob Olin**	USA	1934-1935	
Carlos Monzon	Argentine	1970-1974		Al McCoy	Canada	1935	CAN
Carlos Monzon	Argentine	1974-1976	WBA	Bob Olin	USA	1935	NY/NBA
Rodrigo Valdez	Colombia	1974-1976	WBC	John Henry Lewis	USA	1935-1938	NY/NBA
Carlos Monzon	Argentine	1976-1977		Hein Lazek	Austria	1935-1936	IBU
Carlos Monzon*	Argentine	1977	WBA	Gustav Roth	Belgium	1936-1938	IBU
Rodrigo Valdez	Colombia	1977-1978		Ad Heuser	Germany	1938	IBU
Hugo Corro	Argentine	1978-1979		**John Henry Lewis***	USA	1938	
Vito Antuofermo	Italy	1979-1980		Melio Bettina	USA	1939	NY
Alan Minter	England	1980		Len Harvey	England	1939-1942	GB
Marvin Hagler	USA	1980-1987		Billy Conn	USA	1939-1940	NY/NBA
Marvin Hagler	USA	1987	WBC/IBF	Anton Christoforidis	Greece	1941	NBA
Sugar Ray Leonard	USA	1987	WBC	Gus Lesnevich	USA	1941-1946	NY/NBA
Frank Tate	USA	1987-1988	IBF	Freddie Mills	England	1942-1946	GB
Sumbu Kalambay	Zaire	1987-1988	WBA	**Gus Lesnevich**	USA	1946-1948	
Thomas Hearns	USA	1987-1988	WBC	**Freddie Mills**	England	1948-1950	
Iran Barkley	USA	1988-1989	WBC	**Joey Maxim**	USA	1950-1952	
Michael Nunn	USA	1988-1991	IBF	**Archie Moore**	USA	1952-1960	
Roberto Duran	Panama	1989-1990	WBC	Archie Moore	USA	1960-1962	NY/EBU
Doug de Witt	USA	1989-1990	WBO	Harold Johnson	USA	1961-1962	NBA
Mike McCallum	Jamaica	1989-1991	WBA	**Harold Johnson**	USA	1962-1963	
Nigel Benn	England	1990	WBO	**Willie Pastrano**	USA	1963-1965	
Chris Eubank*	England	1990-1991	WBO	**Jose Torres**	Puerto Rico	1965-1966	

Thomas Hearns, a world champion at every weight between welter and light-heavy

Peter Goldfield

Title Holder	Birthplace	Tenure	Status
Dick Tiger	Nigeria	1966-1968	
Bob Foster	USA	1968-1971	
Bob Foster	USA	1971-1972	WBC
Vicente Rondon	Venezuela	1971-1972	WBA
Bob Foster*	USA	1972-1974	
John Conteh	England	1974-1977	WBC
Victor Galindez	Argentine	1974-1978	WBA
Miguel Cuello	Argentine	1977-1978	WBC
Mate Parlov	Yugoslavia	1978	WBC
Mike Rossman	USA	1978-1979	WBA
Marvin Johnson	USA	1978-1979	WBC
Victor Galindez	Argentine	1979	WBA
Matt Saad Muhammad	USA	1979-1981	WBC
Marvin Johnson	USA	1979-1980	WBA
Mustafa Muhammad	USA	1980-1981	WBA
Michael Spinks	USA	1981-1983	WBA
Dwight Muhammad Qawi	USA	1981-1983	WBC
Michael Spinks*	USA	1983-1985	
J. B. Williamson	USA	1985-1986	WBC
Slobodan Kacar	Yugoslavia	1985-1986	IBF
Marvin Johnson	USA	1986-1987	WBA
Dennis Andries	Guyana	1986-1987	WBC
Bobby Czyz	USA	1986-1987	IBF
Thomas Hearns*	USA	1987	WBC
Leslie Stewart	Trinidad	1987	WBA
Virgil Hill	USA	1987-1991	WBA
Charles Williams	USA	1987-1993	IBF
Don Lalonde	Canada	1987-1988	WBC
Sugar Ray Leonard*	USA	1988	WBC
Michael Moorer*	USA	1988-1991	WBO
Dennis Andries	Guyana	1989	WBC
Jeff Harding	Australia	1989-1990	WBC
Dennis Andries	England	1990-1991	WBC
Thomas Hearns	USA	1991-1992	WBA
Leonzer Barber	USA	1991-	WBO
Jeff Harding	Australia	1991-	WBC
Iran Barkley*	USA	1992	WBA
Virgil Hill	USA	1992-	WBA
Henry Maske	Germany	1993-	IBF

Cruiserweight (190 lbs)

Title Holder	Birthplace	Tenure	Status
Marvin Camel	USA	1979-1980	WBC
Carlos de Leon	Puerto Rico	1980-1982	WBC
Ossie Ocasio	Puerto Rico	1982-1984	WBA
S. T. Gordon	USA	1982-1983	WBC
Marvin Camel	USA	1983-1984	IBF
Carlos de Leon	Puerto Rico	1983-1985	WBC
Lee Roy Murphy	USA	1984-1986	IBF
Piet Crous	S Africa	1984-1985	WBA
Alfonso Ratliff	USA	1985	WBC
Dwight Muhammad Qawi	USA	1985-1986	WBA
Bernard Benton	USA	1985-1986	WBC
Carlos de Leon	Puerto Rico	1986-1988	WBC
Rickey Parkey	USA	1986-1987	IBF
Evander Holyfield	USA	1986-1987	WBA
Evander Holyfield	USA	1987-1988	WBA/IBF
Evander Holyfield*	USA	1988	
Taoufik Belbouli*	France	1989	WBA
Carlos de Leon	Puerto Rico	1989-1990	WBC
Glenn McCrory	England	1989-1990	IBF
Robert Daniels	USA	1989-1991	WBA
Boone Pultz	USA	1989-1990	WBO
Jeff Lampkin*	USA	1990-1991	IBF
Magne Havnaa*	Norway	1990-1992	WBO
Masimilliano Duran	Italy	1990-1991	WBC
Bobby Czyz	USA	1991-	WBA
Anaclet Wamba	France	1991-	WBC
James Warring	USA	1991-1992	IBF
Tyrone Booze	USA	1992-1993	WBO
Al Cole	USA	1992-	IBF

Title Holder	Birthplace	Tenure	Status
Markus Bott	Germany	1993	WBO
Nestor Giovannini	Argentine	1993-	WBO

Heavyweight (190 lbs +)

Title Holder	Birthplace	Tenure	Status
James J. Corbett	USA	1892-1897	
Bob Fitzsimmons	England	1897-1899	
James J. Jeffries*	USA	1899-1905	
Marvin Hart	USA	1905-1906	
Tommy Burns	Canada	1906-1908	
Jack Johnson	USA	1908-1915	
Jess Willard	USA	1915-1919	
Jack Dempsey	USA	1919-1926	
Gene Tunney*	USA	1926-1928	
Max Schmeling	Germany	1930-1932	
Jack Sharkey	USA	1932-1933	
Primo Carnera	Italy	1933-1934	
Max Baer	USA	1934-1935	
James J. Braddock	USA	1935	
James J. Braddock	USA	1935-1936	NY/NBA
George Godfrey	USA	1935-1936	IBU
James J. Braddock	USA	1936-1937	
Joe Louis*	USA	1937-1949	
Ezzard Charles	USA	1949-1951	NBA
Lee Savold	USA	1950-1951	GB/EBU
Ezzard Charles	USA	1951	
Jersey Joe Walcott	USA	1951-1952	
Rocky Marciano*	USA	1952-1956	
Floyd Patterson	USA	1956-1959	
Ingemar Johansson	Sweden	1959-1960	
Floyd Patterson	USA	1960-1962	
Sonny Liston	USA	1962-1964	
Muhammad Ali	USA	1964-1965	
Muhammad Ali	USA	1965-1967	WBC
Ernie Terrell	USA	1965-1967	WBA
Muhammad Ali	USA	1967	
Joe Frazier	USA	1968-1970	WBC
Jimmy Ellis	USA	1968-1970	WBA
Joe Frazier	USA	1970-1973	
George Foreman	USA	1973-1974	
Muhammad Ali	USA	1974-1978	
Leon Spinks	USA	1978	
Leon Spinks	USA	1978	WBA
Larry Holmes*	USA	1978-1983	WBC
Muhammad Ali*	USA	1978-1979	WBA
John Tate	USA	1979-1980	WBA
Mike Weaver	USA	1980-1982	WBA
Michael Dokes	USA	1982-1983	WBA
Gerrie Coetzee	S Africa	1983-1984	WBA
Tim Witherspoon	USA	1984	WBC
Pinklon Thomas	USA	1984-1986	WBC
Larry Holmes	USA	1984-1985	IBF
Greg Page	USA	1984-1985	WBA
Tony Tubbs	USA	1985-1986	WBA
Michael Spinks	USA	1985-1987	IBF
Tim Witherspoon	USA	1986	WBA
Trevor Berbick	Jamaica	1986	WBC
Mike Tyson	USA	1986-1987	WBC
James Smith	USA	1986-1987	WBA
Mike Tyson	USA	1987	WBA/WBC
Tony Tucker	USA	1987	IBF
Mike Tyson	USA	1987-1989	
Mike Tyson	USA	1989-1990	IBF/WBA/WBC
Francesco Damiani	Italy	1989-1991	WBO
James Douglas	USA	1990	IBF/WBA/WBC
Evander Holyfield	USA	1990-1992	IBF/WBA/WBC
Ray Mercer	USA	1991-1992	WBO
Michael Moorer*	USA	1992-1993	WBO
Riddick Bowe	USA	1992	IBF/WBA/WBC
Riddick Bowe	USA	1992-	IBF/WBA
Lennox Lewis	England	1992-	WBC
Tommy Morrison	USA	1993-	WBO

Highlights from the 1993-94 Amateur Season

by David Prior

The revolution in amateur boxing, which had started at the ABA annual general meeting in September 1992, finally culminated in the dissolution of the Amateur Boxing Association, which included the Council and National Committee. In its place, the Amateur Boxing Association of England Limited was formed under the Companies Act 1985.

The six directors of the company were all members of an Emergency Steering Committee, which had been set up to formulate plans for the future of the sport. Rod Robertson (CSBA) was elected Chairman and the other directors were Mick Ryan (North East), Owen Cookson (Midlands), Jim McCarthy (Southern), Bill Webster (North West) and Ken Short (London), with former ABA official Colin Brown as Secretary. Later came the establishment of an Executive Council, comprising the directors and representatives from the various associations.

A number of cost cutting measures were introduced, including an office move from Francis House to temporary accommodation at Crystal Palace and, for the first time, there were registration fees for coaches, officials and boxers. The financial constraints also meant a limited international programme, including a decision not to take part in multi-national tournaments for the time being.

Happily, the season finished on an upbeat note, with a marvellous multi-national event in Liverpool and with a team boxing in the U19 tournament in Sardinia. The Sports Council grant, which had been withdrawn for a while, was restored, albeit at a lower figure for the financial year ended March 1994, but increased for the forthcoming 1994-95 season. But, it was, perhaps, inevitable that so many changes in such a short space of time would be the subject of much debate and controversy within the sport. Greeted by some with enthusiasm, less keenly by others, and the usual quota of "don't knows", the next crucial stage of the new look governing body is the annual general meeting scheduled for 24 September 1994.

The gender reforms which had started some time ago, continued with 20-year-old Sharon Ellis, from the Liverpool-based Rotunda club, obtaining her assistant coaching certificate, the establishment of an all-female club in Dunfermline and, across the Atlantic, the very first

In winning the 1994 ABA light-heavyweight title, Kelly Oliver (left) emulated Billy Knight (1972-1974) and Andy Straughn (1980-1981), who were also victorious three years running

Les Clark

female exhibition contest in the USA amateur championships. Not long, I wonder, before we hear an MC announcement that the winner by a unanimous decision is Jane Smith in the red corner!

Although the immediate post-Olympic period tends to be a bit of an anti-climax, first in 1993 came the World Senior championships in Tampere (reported on last year). That was followed by a double European helping with the seniors in Bursa, Turkey (6-12 September) and the under-19s in Salonica, Greece, from 27 September to 2 October.

In Bursa, there were merited bronze medals for Danny Williams (England), Paul Griffin (Ireland) and Kevin McCormack from Wales, with only Scotland coming home medal-less. Heavyweight Williams had decisive stoppage wins over Edin Barjic (Bosnia Herzgovina) and Dimitri Karpekov (Ukraine), before being halted by the hard punching Poeder Dondiago from Holland. Ireland's defending featherweight titleholder from 1991, Paul Griffin, first outpointed Laszlo Bognar from Hungary, then Germany's Frank Sygmund and Ivan Chornie (Mongolia), prior to withdrawing from the semi-finals because of injury. Triple ABA champion, and now eight-times Welsh ABA titleholder, Kevin McCormack, was the third bronze medallist, at super-heavyweight, with wins over Slavisa Jankovic, an unusual independent entry, and Oleg Belikov (Ukraine), before losing to the eventual gold medallist, Svilen Rusinov, from Bulgaria. Bulgaria, whose Serefim Todorov won Euro title number three, headed up the gold medal list, with three, and, although the "Iron Curtain" no longer exists, it was a total eclipse by the east Europeans, who had 11 champions. They also won more than a fair share of the silver and bronze. Only the now combined Germany, with one gold, two silver and three bronze, from this side of Europe, were in contention.

The four home countries also sent boxers to the U19 championships in Greece, but it was just England's Danny Costello, then 18-years old, who reached the medal stages. With less than 20 bouts on his record card, flyweight Costello won twice for his bronze medal, against Engin Karokoc (Turkey) and Assen Bonev (Bulgaria), but lost in the semi-finals to Rovcan Husseinov from Azerbaijan. Husseinov created his own niche in European boxing history by winning the Senior and Under-19 titles in the same year. Russia had things very much their own way, with seven gold medals, followed by Ukraine (three) and Germany and Azerbaijan with one each.

It was a successful Acropolis Cup in Greece (June 1993) for Wales, with top honours for Mark Hughes (light-fly), Jason Cook (featherweight) and Gareth Lawrence (lightweight). There were also bronze medals for Richard Vowles (bantamweight) and Kevin McCormack (super-heavy). There were to be no medals for anyone in 1994 when the event was cancelled.

In August 1993, the pre-Commonwealth Games was held in Victoria, British Columbia.

The AIBA Challenge match was staged in Dublin over two days (11/12 March 1994), with an excellent win by the host country's Damaen Kelly over double world champion, Waldemar Font (Cuba). Featherweight Paul Griffin came

within the proverbial "inch" of beating the talented Serafim Todorov from Bulgaria, but, after an 11-11 draw, Todorov got the decision on a 51-41 punch countback. The third Irishman in action, light-welterweight Mark Winters, had the misfortune to meet Olympic and World titleholder, Hector Vinent, another Cuban, and, after taking a body punch, was counted out on his feet in the opening round.

The Liverpool International Festival of Amateur Boxing (23-28 May) was a fantastic success. It was the first multi-national tournament to be held in this country since the ABA centenary event in 1980 and attracted 97 boxers from 15 countries, producing 85 contests in the imposing St George's Hall. Fittingly, England topped the medals, including gold for David Burke (bantamweight), Peter Richardson (light-welterweight) and Danny Williams at super-heavyweight, while Irish welterweight, Neil Gough, came out on top in his weight division.

A five-man U19 team signalled England's successful return to the continental multi-national trail in May 1994. Lightweight Danny Happe won silver and Sunderland's Billy Tyrrell got a bronze in the 13th Italia tournament in Sardinia.

It was just Scotland (four boxers) and Ireland (two) who travelled from this part of the world to Bangkok for the World Cup (3-10 June) when 12 weights were contested over the distance of five x two minute rounds. There was to be no success for the home countries. Germany came top (three gold medals), with the Cubans, unusually, in second position (two), with one gold each for Kazhakstan, Uzbekistan, Romania, Bulgaria, Azerbaijan, Ukraine and Armenia.

There were just 11 team matches in the season, mostly domestic affairs, with the only foreign opposition from Holland, Hungary and the USA (versus Ireland) and Norway against England).

At the beginning of the season, in October 1993, England lost 6-3 to Ireland in Dublin. A fortnight later, England renewed fistic acquaintances with Norway after a break of nearly 40 years at senior level and won 4-3 in Oslo. The fixture marked the elevation of U19 star Danny Costello to the seniors in the same season. Flyweight Costello outpointed Arne Marius Stolan by a wide margin. Later in November it was the turn of the England U19 boxers, who scored a comfortable 5-3 win over their Scottish counterparts in London. A scheduled January (1994) senior meeting between the two countries was cancelled because of lack of interest in staging the fixture this side of the border. This left the England U19s to finish off the season, but not on a winning note. Ireland came over to London to register a comfortable 6-2 victory.

It was a good season for Ireland, with just the one setback in Budapest in December when a combined senior/under-19 team crashed to a 9-2 loss to Hungary. Otherwise it was all plusses for boxers from the Emerald Isle. In addition to the two wins over England, Wales were thrashed 9-1 in Ballina in November. Lightweight Gareth Lawrence was the only visitor to win, with a points decision over Eddie Bolger. The season was completed, successfully, with a 7-4 win over America in Dublin

Kevin Short shocked the 1992 ABA welterweight winner, Mark Santini, in scoring three knockdowns on his way to becoming the 1994 champion at the weight   Les Clark

(April) and a 4-3 victory over Holland in Rotterham (in May). It was the first meeting between Ireland and Holland for quite some time. Following their loss to Ireland earlier in the season, Wales failed to get back on the winning trail in January 1994 when in a first-time international in North Wales, in Holywell, Scotland won 6-3. Two months later, in April, Wales drew 5-5 with Scotland in Aberdeen and in the second match of the tour, won 7-5 in Dundee.

Not in any sense an "international", there was an incredibly talented Russian Armed Forces team who came to Portsmouth and London in December 1993 and beat the Combined Services 5-2 and then 3-0. Only eight of the 16 visiting boxers could be matched (their pedigree would

have made them more than a match in a full scale international) and even with Channel Islander Eddie Stuart drafted in for the second meeting, there was nothing to stop them. Stuart lost to world ranked Alexander Lebsiak.

The ABA championship finals left (London) town again and for the second year running were staged at the National Indoor Arena in Birmingham. It was a new look all-England affair following the withdrawal of Scotland and Wales after a disagreement on how the event should be organised – solely the prerogative of the ABAE – and the decision not to pay expenses of the boxers. It was reminiscent of 1972 when the selfsame argument threatened a Celt withdrawal, but was avoided at the last minute. Subsequent agreement between the three countries, which led to the introduction of the Great Britain semi-final stage, came too late for the Scots and Welsh to enter for 1973. With a new format to be introduced in 1995 – there has been a draw for the quarter-finals between eight divisions which will operate for two years and there will then be a further draw – it seems likely that future ABA championships will be all-England events.

In the end, the finals provided a quality night of boxing, with sponsorship coming, by way of the Wolverhampton Sporting Club, licensed promoters of professional boxing by the British Boxing Board of Control. Shades of John Douglas, Val Barker and Eugene Cox, three of the "old time" officials from the very early days of the sport, probably still turning at great speed in their graves! There were nine brand new champions at Birmingham, not only a sign of emerging new talent but also the result of a noticeable number of the top stars turning to the paid ranks. Kelly Oliver was the only defending champion in the true sense, winning his third title at light-heavyweight. David Starie moved up from light-middle to take the middleweight honours and Alan Temple, the 1992 featherweight titleholder, won at light-welterweight.

With the 1993 light-flyweight champion, Mark Hughes, not taking part because of the Welsh withdrawal, the new titleholder was Gary Jones from Sefton, who outpointed Darren Fox from the Royal Air Force. Fox failed to break the 20 year absence of an RAF boxer winning a national title; Neville Meade had won the heavyweight division in 1974. Once again, the shortage of boxers in this weight meant that there had been just one preliminary contest, in one of the quarter-finals. Fox (CSBA) outpointed Duncan Barriball (Launceston, Western Counties) and that was a disputed majority decision. In the final, the higher workrate of Jones earned him the majority decision and title, with Fox not able to capitalise on his reach and height advantages.

At flyweight, Danny Costello (Hollington) took over from recent pro signing, Paul Ingle, with a unanimous decision over Owen Spensley (Royal Air Force), with Spensley emulating Fox earlier when unable to rectify the RAF's poor record in recent championships. Another young Londoner, Spencer Oliver from Finchley, took the bantamweight crown with a second round stoppage of former Scottish international, John McLean, now turning out for Basingstoke. After two previous losing appearances in the finals to record breaking eight-times champion, John Lyon, it was not to be third time lucky for McLean against a supremely fit and confident Oliver. The 1993 champion Richard Evatt did not enter.

With Jason Cook, Wales, featherweight champion from last year not taking part in the 1994 event, Dean Pithie hustled, bustled and maintained constant pressure against Stephen Smith (Repton Cedar Street), on his way to a unanimous points win, to give the Midlands based Willenahll club their first-ever ABA champion. In fact, the preceding wins by Gary Jones, Danny Costello and Spencer Oliver had marked the debut of their respective clubs on to the ABA championship roll of honour.

At lightweight, Andy Green (Phil Thomas School of Boxing) squeezed home on a majority over Ian Smith from St Pancras and that win, plus a bronze medal in the Liverpool multi-national, earned Green a place in the England team for the Commonwealth Games in Canada. Scotland's Bradley Welsh, who won the title in 1993, is now boxing with his vest off.

With last season's titleholder Peter Richardson not entering the championships because of an out-of-the ring injury, an intriguing pairing with fellow north-easterner, Alan Temple (Hartlepool Boys Welfare), was not to be. Temple won his second national title with a decisive win in the third against fellow southpaw Richie Edwards (St Patricks) and, in a surprise move, turned pro just before the Liverpool multi-national. Both Temple and Richardson, now with Repton Cedar Street, had been named for the Liverpool tournament, but the extremely successful (gold medal) comeback for the latter earned him a place in the Commonwealth Games team.

There was an unexpected and shock win for Army welterweight and Welsh born Kevin Short, who dropped former champion Mark Santini three times before taking the unanimious decision. Last year's winner, Chris Bessey, had moved up to light-middleweight, but had lost in the semi-finals to eventual champion, Wayne Alexander (Lynn).

The light-middleweight final was all over in just two minutes, but it was exciting and explosive stuff. Alexander, the winner, who took over from David Starie, won against Steven Bendall from the Triumph outfit. The hard punching Londoner found himself on the deck in the opening seconds from a Bendall straight left, but roared back with his heavy artillery to force two counts on Bendall before it was stopped.

Moving up to middleweight, David Starie made it two championship victories in a row with a unanimous win over Eddie Stuart from the Leonis club in the Channel Islands. There were only brief glimpses of Starie's best endeavours, as the experienced Stuart worked in close preventing his opponent space to move and deliver his stock-in-trade, fast combinations. Joe Calzaghe, the 1993 titleholder, is now plying his undoubted talent in the paid ranks.

In 1992, Kelly Oliver (Bracebridge) won his first ABA title at light-heavyweight with a humdinger of a win over Paul Rogers. Oliver retained the title the following year (against Anthony Todd) and won for the third time with a repeat win over Rogers (Penhill RBL). It was practically a replica of their previous contest – nine minutes of courage, skill, fitness and all the ingredients of the best in amateur boxing. Oliver's win equalled the post-war record of Billy Knight and Andy Straughn, who both won three consecutive titles at the weight.

The second visit to the National Indoor Arena by Army heavyweight Steve Burford proved successful this time (in 1993 he had lost to Paul Lawson), when he clearly outpointed Israel Ajose (All Stars).

In the final bout of the evening (at super-heavyweight),

Danny Watts won a third title for the Army with a deserved decision over Mohammed Khamkhoer, from Russia, but now boxing for Fitzroy Lodge. Khamkhoer appeared "unbeatable" in the early stages of his title bid, but looked vulnerable against the big right-hand punches of Keith Fletcher before winning in the semi-finals, while Watts had taken full advantage of a second chance at the title. He had been beaten by Kevin McCormack in the CSBA final, but McCormack opted to go for Welsh ABA title number eight, which he won. Flu prevented the 1993 champion, Mike McKenzie, from competing.

In Dublin it was a parade of champions past and present in the Irish senior championships in February, when six of the seven defending titleholders successfully retained their titles, including featherweight Paul Griffin from Mount Tallant, who won for the fourth consecutive year. Martin McQuillan (Holy Family, Drogheda), Damaen Kelly (Holy Trinity), Neil Gough (St Paul's), Jim Webb (Holy Trinity) and Paul Douglas (Holy Family) were the other 1993 titleholders to win again. New boys on the block, so to speak, were Tommy Waite (Cairn Lodge), Glen Stephens (Crumlin), Billy Walsh (St Colman's) and George Douglas (South Meath), although, strictly speaking, only Stephens and Walsh won for the first time, while Denis Galvin (St Saviour's) won again, for the fifth time. It was title number four for comebacking Gordon Joyce (Sunnyside) at light-heavyweight and some few years after he had won three light-welterweight titles in a row between 1986 and 1988.

Brian Carr (Auchengeich) kept a firm grip on the featherweight division in the Scottish championships at Grangemouth in March, with his fifth consecutive win and this title event would not be the same without Jim Pender (St Francis). He won the light-welterweight category for the seventh time. Lee Munro (Dennistoun), Paul Shepherd (Sparta), Ronnie McPhee (Glenboig), Jamie Coyle (Bannockburn), Alan Wolecki (St Francis), Joe Townsley (Cleland), Mike Sangster (Bonnyrigg), John Wilson (Edinburgh University), Alex Kelly (Meadowbank) and Colin Brown (Gartcosh) completed the 1994 list of champions.

It was a McCormack family affair in the Welsh championships at Cardiff (in April) when super-heavyweight Kevin (Coed Eva and Royal Navy) won his eighth title (two at heavyweight and the rest in the top weight) to equal the record set by Rhys Howells some 60 odd years ago. Brother, Brendan, from Coed Eva, won the heavyweight division. There was a tremendous upset in the lightweights when Vince Powell (Army) knocked out Gareth Lawrence from Highfields in the second round, but it was Lawrence who was selected for the Commonwealth Games after Powell was unable, and unwilling, to take part in a trial bout. Mark Hughes (Gwent, Swansea) weighed in at light-flyweight for the fifth time and without an opponent in sight became champion again. Jason Cook (Maesteg), Karl Thomas (Pentywyn) and Tim Brown (Idris) won for the second time, while it was championship debuts for Jason Thomas (Merthyr), Henry Jones (Pembroke Dock), Andrew Robinson (Pennar), Byron Hayward

(Newbridge) and Grant Briggs (Pontypridd).

In the first of the U17 championships at York Hall in December 1993 – the Junior ABAs – there was a shock win for Steven Burke (Sefton), an impressive one for Albert Coates (Medway Golden Gloves) and a north-east double for Michael Hunter (Hartlepool Boys Welfare) and Stephen Hodgson (Shildon), all in Class "A". In Class "B" there was a popular victory for Charlie Rumble (St Mary's) and a Wednesbury twosome for Jason Nightingale and James Gould. Excellent wins were registered by Martin McDonagh (Lynn) and Michael Jennings (Chorley), while Henry Smith (Avalon) took a title back to the west country.

In the U17 team events, England and Ireland tied for first place in the four nation Daily Star Golden Gloves tournament in Glasgow in June 1993. Each country won five gold medals, which left just one each for Wales and Scotland. In the sixth tournament – in June 1994 – back in London for the third time after a tour of Cardiff, Dublin and Glasgow – England came top of the medals league with five gold, followed by Ireland (three). Wales and Scotland got two apiece.

In the 1993 Gaelic Games in Coatbridge, Scotland (June 1993), Ireland (six gold), Scotland (five), and Wales (four), was the final tally, with a brotherly double for Gerald and Lawrence Murphy contributing to the host country's tally. In the May 1994 fixture, Gerald Murphy won again, but it was Scotland's only success. Wales got three but Ireland, with a massive 11 gold medals, won the President's Trophy for the 11th successive year.

In the schoolboy boxing world, there was a rare Sunday tournament in one of the preliminary rounds of the annual championships. The finals, in March 1994, were staged at a new venue – the Aston Villa Leisure Centre – after many

Andy Green (left) squeezes home on points against Ian Smith in the ABA lightweight final to earn himself selection for the Commonwealth Games　　Les Clark

253

years at the Assembly Rooms in Derby. It was the usual marathon – 42 bouts and one walkover! In the pick of the Junior "A" division, Gareth Metcalfe (Stockton Boys), Steven Matthews (Waterloo) and Stephen Rushton (Penhill RBL) all won and there was success for Levi Coates (Medway Golden Gloves), Tony Dodson (Gemini), Levi Tute (Moss Side) and Martin Power (St Pancras) in Junior "B". Moving up the age scale, Barney Doherty (Dale Youth), Bobby Beck (Repton Cedar Street), Richard Hatton (Sale West), Danny Mahoney (Highfield), Andrew Larkins (Bracknell Boys) and Damien Short (Berry Boys), won titles in the Intermediate division. At Senior level there were championship wins for Michael Jennings (Chorley), Neil Linford (Belgrave), Scott Rees (Gilfach Goch), Chris Williams (Merthyr), James Rooney (Hartlepool Catholic Boys) and Stuart Elwell (Wednesbury). Although not quite the championship treble for the Pryce brothers from Newbridge, Bradley, Delroy and Byron (Bradley and Delroy won, but Byron lost to Stuart Green (Islington)), there was, however, a club treble for the Hull based St Paul's when Wayne Curwood, Paul Croll and Jim Betts all became schoolboy titleholders.

Also among the schoolboys, there was a full programme of internationals for England. From April 1993 to June 1994 there were 12 – against Russia, Scotland, Ulster and Wales, with England winning three, drawing three and losing six.

The three NABC-CYP finals ended the 1993-94 championship season in May with Class "A" at Newcastle. Richard Hatton (Sale West) was selected as the "best winner" and his opponent, Bobby Beck (Repton Cedar Street), "best runner-up". Stylist of the night was Paul Croll (St Paul's). In Class "B" (in Bristol), Jason Booth (Radford Boys) and Neil Linford (Begrave) completed a trio of championship wins – Junior ABA, Schoolboy and Boys' Clubs. Kevin Lear (West Ham) and his opponent Jim Betts (St Paul's) were selected as "best winner" and "best runner-up", respectively, while James Rooney (Hartlepool Catholic Boys) picked up the "best stylist" trophy. Patience and persistence finally paid off for Wayne Nuurah (Devonport), when he won his first national title after losing in three previous finals. It was a similar story in the Class "C" finals at the London Hilton when Mehrdud Takalo-Bighashi (Margate) won his first championship in his fifth finals appearance and was also selected "best winner". Jamie Perkins (Highfields) was chosen as the "best stylist", Mark Payne (Bell Green) "best runner-up" and Alistair Coward (All Stars) the "most courageous".

Sadly, the 1993-94 season saw the deaths of Bill Cox, former ABA Chairman and Secretary, long serving officials from London, Harry Hadden and Fred Perry, Doug Cobb from the Eastern Counties and Bill Cowan, a former top official in many capacities, from Scotland. From the Irish boxing world of the past, five-times national champion, Dick Hearn, also passed away. In July, there was the sudden death, following a motoring accident, of top Cuban boxer, Roberto Balado. Since winning a gold medal in the World U19 championships in 1987, Roberto was unbeatable in major competitions, having taken three

consecutive golds in the World Senior championships, and in the 1992 Olympics. In June he had confirmed his top world status by winning the super-heavyweight division in the World Cup in Bangkok.

Former double ABA champion, Keith Howlett, was awarded the MBE in the 1993 Queen's Birthday Honours.

Computer scoring finally made its debut in England in 1994, first at the Liverpool multi-national event and then in the Daily Star Golden Gloves tournament. It would appear that the new technological system of scoring is here to stay, but while solving some of the problems that bedevilled the sport in the past, the requirement that at least three of the judges must register a scoring punch within a one-second time span can produce an unrealistic result of boxer "A" beating boxer "B" by three punches to nil over nine minutes of boxing! Much more authentic is the punch countback procedure.

And when they do go wrong! In the bantamweight final of the Irish Intermediate championships in Dublin, late in 1993, William Downey (Blarney) was declared the winner over Paul Whelan of Neilstown by a 6-3 tally. It was clear to everyone that Whelan had won, but it then emerged that one computer had malfunctioned. A second contest was ordered and Whelan won on points.

It is one of these strange quirks of journalism that any review of what has happened in the past invariably finishes with a look at what is going to happen in the future!

Just before this Yearbook appears the XV Commonwealth Games will have been held in Victoria, British Columbia. Although coming too late for this article, the list of gold medallists and results of bouts featuring boxers from England, Northern Ireland, Scotland and Wales appear in the sections "International Amateur Champions, 1904-1994" and "British and Irish International Matches, 1993-94."

The selection of some of the boxers for England and Wales generated protest and alternatives, but, in both cases, the selectors stood firm and no changes were made. Scotland and Ireland were relatively trouble free and everyone was happy when light-heavyweight, John Wilson, originally first reserve, went to Canada after athlete Liz McColgan pulled out because of injury.

Next came the World U19 championships in Istanbul, Turkey (8-18 September) and then in just under two years it is the Olympic Games in Atlanta, USA. Yet again, amateur boxing is under threat for exclusion from the Games, along with some other sports, following a recommendation of the IOC Programme Commission. The final decision, one way or the other, will have been taken by the IOC in September, but at least boxing is guaranteed in Atlanta.

Another threat, if that is the right word to use, is the tremendous loss of so many of the top amateur stars to the paid ranks. The move to box for pay is inevitable and understandable, but the build up to the Olympics is a four-year programme which started immediately after the 1992 event in Barcelona ended. The process is both time consuming and expensive and we must try and find a way to keep our leading boxers in the amateur ranks a little longer.

ABA National Championships, 1993-94

Combined Services v Western Counties

Combined Services

Combined Services Championships   The Military Boxing Centre - 3 March
L. Fly: *final:* D. Fox (RAF) wo. **Fly:** *final:* O. Spensley (RAF) wo. **Bantam:** *final:* D. Duncan (Army) w pts P. Brolly (RAF). **Feather:** *final:* T. Rajcoomar (Army) w pts C. Baird (RN). **Light:** *final:* K. Brown (RN) wo. **L. Welter:** *semi-finals:* J. Gardner (Army) wo, K. Crumplin (RN) w pts B. Horner (RN; *final:* J. Gardner w pts K. Crumplin. **Welter:** *semi-finals:* A. Henderson (RAF) wo, K. Short (Army) w pts T. French (RN); *final:* K. Short w pts A. Henderson. **L. Middle:** *final:* C. Bessey (Army) w pts S. Pepperall (RAF). **Middle:** *final:* S. Hamer (Army) w rsc 3 P. Treslove (Army). **L. Heavy:** *final:* J. Gosling (RAF) w rsc 3 M. Quirey (Army). **Heavy:** *final:* S. Burford (Army) wo. **S. Heavy:** *final:* K. McCormack (RN) w pts D. Watts (Army)

Western Counties

Western Counties Northern Division Championships   The Olympiad Sports Centre, Chippenham - 5 February
L. Fly: no entries. **Fly:** no entries. **Bantam:** *final:* M. Braden (Walcot) wo. **Feather:** *final:* S. Lucas (Walcot) wo. **Light:** *final:* M. Trowell (Alderney) wo. **L. Welter:** *final:* T. Knowles (Malmesbury) w pts A. Clarke (National Smelting). **Welter:** *semi-finals:* I. McDonald (Kingswood) wo, J. Wrona (Penhill) w dis 2 D. Kelly (Bronx); *final:* J. Wrona w rsc 3 I. McDonald. **L. Middle:** *final:* J. Turley (Penhill) w pts A. Derrick (Taunton). **Middle:** *final:* C. Powell (National Smelting) w pts M. Bailey (Avalon). **L. Heavy:** *final:* P. Rogers (Penhill) w pts C. Kerr (Bronx). **Heavy:** *semi-finals:* P. Day (Walcot) wo, D. Poulson (Taunton) w co 2 D. Beatty (Frome); *final:* P. Day w rsc 1 D. Poulson. **S. Heavy:** *final:* K. Oputu (St George) wo.

Western Counties Southern Division Championships   The Guildhall, Devonport - 5 February
L. Fly: *final:* D. Barriball (Launceston) wo. **Fly:** no entries. **Bantam:** *final:* G. Nicette (Torbay) w pts D. Lawson (Devonport). **Feather:** *semi-finals:* P. Dytham (Weymouth) wo, M. Stuckey (Apollo) w pts K. Hodkinson (Leonis); *final:* P. Dytham w pts M. Stuckey. **Light:** *quarter-finals:* L. Willock (Paignton) wo, J. Phillips (Otter Vale) wo, M. Pickard (Weymouth) w pts C. McBurnie (Pisces), T. Peacock (Leonis) w pts P. Hardcastle (Devonport); *semi-finals:* L. Willock w pts J. Phillips, T. Peacock w pts M. Pickard; *final:* T. Peacock w pts L. Willock. **L. Welter:** *semi-finals:* I. Lewis (Paignton) wo, J. Hudson (Lympstone) w rsc 2 P. Kamara (Bridport); *final:* I. Lewis w pts J. Hudson. **Welter:** *semi-finals:* J. Glasser (Paignton) w rtd 2 J. Simmons (Saxon), S. Daniel (Camborne) w pts M. Marshall (Devonport); *final:* J. Glasser w rtd 2 S. Daniel. **L. Middle:** *quarter-finals:* P. Reynolds (Torbay) wo, S. Charlton (Otter Vale) wo, K. Owen (Bideford) w pts D. Plumb (Launceston), S. Hennessey (Leonis) w pts P. Lepage (Weymouth); *semi-finals:* P. Reynolds w pts S. Charlton, K. Owen w rtd 3 S. Hennessey; *final:* K. Owen w pts P. Reynolds. **Middle:** *semi-finals:* E. Stuart (Leonis) w rsc 1 D. White (Axe Vale), D. Norris (Paignton) w pts E. Miles (Camborne); *final:* E. Stuart w rsc 1 D. Norris. **L. Heavy:** *semi-finals:* A. Stables (Devonport) wo, L. Rousseau (Pisces) w pts I. Tennant (Truro); *final:* L. Rousseau w rsc 3 A. Stables. **Heavy:** *final:* N. Kendall

(Apollo) w rtd 2 S. Cockayne (Exmouth). **S. Heavy:** *final:* G. Mentor (Bournemouth) wo.

Western Counties Finals   The Barnstaple Hotel, Barnstaple - 26 February
L. Fly: D. Barriball (Launceston) wo. **Fly:** no entries. **Bantam:** G. Nicette (Torbay) w rtd 2 M. Braden (Walcot). **Feather:** P. Dytham (Weymouth) w pts S. Lucas (Walcot). **Light:** T. Peacock (Leonis) w rsc 3 M. Trowell (Alderney). **L. Welter:** T. Knowles (Malmesbury) w pts I. Lewis (Paignton). **Welter:** J. Glasser (Paignton) w pts J. Wrona (Penhill). **L. Middle:** J. Turley (Penhill) w pts K. Owen (Bideford). **Middle:** E. Stuart (Leonis) w pts C. Powell (National Smelting). **L. Heavy:** P. Rogers (Penhill) w pts L. Rousseau (Pisces). **Heavy:** P. Day (Walcott) w co 1 N. Kendall (Appolo). **S. Heavy:** K. Oputu (St George) w co 2 G. Mentor (Bournemouth)

Combined Services v Western Counties

The Military Boxing Centre, Aldershot - 17 March
L. Fly: D. Fox (RAF) w pts D. Barriball (Launceston). **Fly:** O. Spensley (RAF) wo. **Bantam:** G. Nicette (Torbay) w rsc 3 D. Duncan (Army). **Feather:** P. Dytham (Weymouth) w pts C. Baird (RN) - replaced T. Rajcoomer (Army). **Light:** T. Peacock (Leonis) w rsc 3 K. Brown (RN). **L. Welter:** J. Gardner (Army) w pts T. Knowles (Malmesbury). **Welter:** K. Short (Army) w pts J. Glasser (Paignton). **L. Middle:** C. Bessey (Army) w rsc 3 J. Turley (Penhill). **Middle:** E. Stuart (Leonis) w pts S. Hamer (Army). **L. Heavy:** P. Rogers (Penhill) w pts J. Gosling (RAF). **Heavy:** S. Burford (Army) w pts P. Day (Walcot). **S. Heavy:** D. Watts (Army) w pts K. Oputu (St George). Watts replaced K. McCormack (RN).

Eastern Counties v Home Counties v Midland Counties v Southern Counties

Eastern Counties

Essex Division   The Civic Hall, Grays - 21 January
L. Fly: no entries. **Fly:** no entries. **Bantam:** *final:* M. Reynolds (Colchester) wo. **Feather:** *final:* D. Dainty (Canvey) wo. **Light:** no entries. **L. Welter:** *semi-finals:* G. Smith (Canvey) wo, M. Saliu (Colchester) w pts J. Deadman (Rayleigh); *final:* G. Smith w dis 3 M. Saliu. **Welter:** *final:* L. Catling (Rayleigh) w pts D. Downer (Colchester). **L. Middle:** *final:* P. Reynolds (Belhus Park) w pts D. Sharp (Halstead). **Middle:** *semi-finals:* M. Woodcraft (Canvey) w rsc 2 P. Turner (Halstead), L. Taylor (Mersea) w pts R. Hadley (Chelmsford); *final:* M. Woodcraft w pts L. Taylor. **L. Heavy:** *final:* L. Woolcock (Canvey) w co 3 K. Manders (Halstead). **Heavy:** *final:* G. Cox (Canvey) wo. **S. Heavy:** *final:* A. Herron (Chalvedon) wo.

Mid-Anglia Division   The Guildhall, Cambridge - 27 January
L. Fly: no entries. **Fly:** no entries. **Bantam:** no entries. **Feather:** no entries. **Light:** no entries. **L. Welter:** no entries. **Welter:** *final:* J. Mahoney (Aldermans) w rtd 1 S. Hay (St Neotts). **L. Middle:** *final:* L. Baxter (Chatteris) wo. **Middle:** no entries. **L. Heavy:** *final:* M. Redhead (Cambridge & Soham) wo. **Heavy:** no entries. **S. Heavy:** no entries.

Norfolk Division   The Leisure Centre, Watton - 22 January
L. Fly: no entries. **Fly:** no entries. **Bantam:** no entries. **Feather:** *final:* L. Cozens (Norwich) wo. **Light:** *final:* T. Stimson (Kings Lynn) wo. **L. Welter:** *final:* S. Garner (Dereham) w dis 3 J. Spurling (Kings Lynn). **Welter:** *final:* K. Elliott (Norwich) wo. **L. Middle:** *final:* G. Hewitt (Kings Lynn) wo. **Middle:** *semi-finals:* J. Bevis (Norwich) wo, A. Gray (Kingfisher) w pts S. Wilton (Aylesham); *final:* A. Gray w pts J. Bevis. **L. Heavy:** *final:* M. O'Brien (North Lynn) wo. **Heavy:** *final:* C. Elden (Norwich) wo. **S. Heavy:** *final:* M. Hooks (North Lynn) wo.

Suffolk Division   The Corn Exchange, Bury St Edmunds - 20 January
L. Fly: no entries. **Fly:** no entries. **Bantam:** no entries. **Feather:** no entries. **Light:** *final:* M. Hawthorne (Lowestoft) wo. **L. Welter:** no entries. **Welter:** no entries. **L. Middle:** *final:* A. Ewen (Arcade) w pts A. Cook (Triple A). **Middle:** *final:* D. Starie (Hurstlea & Kerridge) wo. **L. Heavy:** no entries. **Heavy:** no entries. **S. Heavy:** no entries.

Lee Woolcock (Canvey Island), the Essex light-heavyweight champion for 1993-94

Eastern Counties Semi-Finals & Finals   The Leisure Centre, Swaffham - 5 February
L. Fly: no entries. **Fly:** no entries. **Bantam:** *final:* M. Reynolds (Colchester) wo. **Feather:** *final:* D. Dainty (Canvey) w rtd 2 L.

Cozens (Norwich). **Light:** *final:* M. Hawthorne (Lowestoft) w pts T. Stimson (Kings Lynn). **L. Welter:** *final:* G. Smith (Canvey) w pts S. Garner (Dereham). **Welter:** *semi-finals:* J. Mahoney (Aldermans) wo, K. Elliott (Norwich) w pts L. Catling (Rayleigh); *final:* J. Mahoney w rsc 1 K. Elliott. **L. Middle:** *semi-finals:* A. Ewen (Arcade) w pts G. Hewitt (Kings Lynn), P. Reynolds (Belhus Park) w pts L. Baxter (Chatteris); *final:* A. Ewen w rsc 2 P. Reynolds. **Middle:** *semi-finals:* A. Gray (Kingfisher) wo, D. Starie (Hurstleigh & Kerridge) w rtd 2 M. Woodcraft (Canvey); *final:* D. Starie w co 1 A. Gray. **L. Heavy:** *semi-finals:* L. Woolcock (Canvey) wo, M. Redhead (Cambridge & Soham) w rtd 1 M. O'Brien (North Lynn); *final:* M. Redhead w rsc 2 L. Woolcock. **Heavy:** *final:* C. Elden (Norwich) w pts G. Cox (Canvey). **S. Heavy:** *final:* A. Herron (Chalvedon) w rtd 1 M. Hooks (North Lynn).

Home Counties

Home Counties Championships   The Leisure Centre, Bletchley - 26 February & The Town Hall, Oxford - 2 March
L. Fly: *final:* J. Lock (Henley) wo. **Fly:** no entries. **Bantam:** no entries. **Feather:** *final:* J. Gynn (Stevenage) wo. **Light:** *semi-finals:* J. O'Sullivan (Bushey) wo, A. McBeal (Hitchin) w co 3 W. Holloway (Mo's); *final:* A. McBeal w co 2 J. O'Sullivan. **L. Welter:** *quarter-finals:* M. Calvert (Stevenage) wo, A. Tomlin (Bedford) wo, M. Leonard (South Oxhey) w pts P. Malcolm (Lewsey), T. Turner (Pinewood Starr) w pts T. Gonsalves (Henley); *semi-finals:* M. Leonard w pts M. Calvert, T. Turner w pts A. Tomlin; *final:* T. Turner w pts M. Leonard. **Welter:** *final:* K. McCarthy (Bedford) w pts A. Smith (St Albans). **L. Middle:** *final:* J. Loosley (Mo's) w pts E. Randall (Bushey). **Middle:** *final:* M. Hilding (Pinewood Starr) wo. **L. Heavy:** *semi-finals:* S. Lawlor (Luton Irish) wo, P. Watts (Henley) w pts R. Baptiste (Lewsey); *final:* S. Lawlor w pts P. Watts. **Heavy:** *final:* M. Sprott (Bulmershe) w pts A. Barnes (Oxford YMCA). **S. Heavy:** *final:* K. Fletcher (Reading) wo.

Midland Counties

Derbyshire Division   The Friary Hotel, Derby - 18 January
L. Fly: no entries. **Fly:** no entries. **Bantam:** no entries. **Feather:** no entries. **Light:** *final:* V. Broomhead (Buxton) w pts D. Ashley (Merlin). **L. Welter:** *final:* L. Dunn (Chesterfield) w pts S. Williamson (Merlin). **Welter:** *final:* G. Beardsley (Belper) w rsc 1 M. Radford (Merlin). **L. Middle:** *final:* K. Gibbons (Derby) w co 1 R. Watkinson (Belper). **Middle:** *final:* T. Watson (Royal Oak) w pts A. Palmer (Trinity). **L. Heavy:** no entries. **Heavy:** *final:* A. Aziz (Derby) w pts J. Oakes (Draycott). **S. Heavy:** no entries.

Leicester, Rutland & Northamptonshire Division   Friendlies WMC, Northampton - 20 January
L. Fly: no entries. **Fly:** *final:* A. Pope (Wellingborough) wo. **Bantam:** *final:* P. Neale (Alexton) wo. **Feather:** no entries. **Light:** *final:* A. Thomas (Wellingborough) wo. **L. Welter:** no entries. **Welter:** *final:* S. Mabbutt (Belgrave) wo. **L. Middle:** *final:* I. Moore (Earl Shilton) wo. **Middle:** *semi-finals:* S. Beasley (Northampton) w pts A. Foster (Henry Street), C. Williams (Belgrave) w pts M. Thompson (Henry Street); *final:* S. Beasley w rtd 3 C. Williams. **L. Heavy:** no entries. **Heavy:** no entries. **S. Heavy:** No entries.

Nottinghamshire & Lincolnshire Division   The Miners Welfare Club, Harworth - 8 January
L. Fly: no entries. **Fly:** no entries. **Bantam:** no entries. **Feather:**

final: J. Yarnell (Phoenix) w pts K. Gerowski (Cotgrave). **Light:** *final:* R. Brotherhood (Huthwaite) w pts J. Dullingham (Ashfield). **L. Welter:** *final:* M. Watson (Phoenix) w pts G. Jenkinson (St Giles). **Welter:** *final:* D. Kirk (Huthwaite) w pts J. Dean (Lincoln). **L. Middle:** *semi-finals:* J. Khaliq (Ruddington) wo, D. Tring (Eastwood) w pts R. Watson (Grantham); *final:* J. Khaliq w rsc 1 D. Tring. **Middle:** *final:* A. Lovelace (Boston) w pts R. Sail (Bulwell). **L. Heavy:** *final:* K. Oliver (Bracebridge) wo. **Heavy:** *final:* N. Williamson (Bulwell) wo. **S. Heavy:** *final:* R. Slater (Phoenix) wo.

Warwickshire Division   Alfred Herbert Social Club, Coventry - 21 January
L. Fly: no entries. **Fly:** *final:* G. Payne (Bell Green) wo. **Bantam:** no entries. **Feather:** *final:* D. Pithie (Willenhall) w pts L. Arthur (Triumph). **Light:** *final:* D. Kehoe (Triumph) wo. **L. Welter:** *final:* I. Carroll (Triumph) wo. **L. Middle:** *final:* S. Bendall (Triumph) wo. **Middle:** *final:* J. Twite (Triumph) wo. **L. Heavy:** *final:* D. Bendall (Triumph) wo. **Heavy:** *final:* N. Simpson (Willenhall) wo. **S. Heavy:** no entries.

Midland Counties (North Zone) Semi-Finals& Finals   The Harpur Social Club, Buxton - 27 January, The Colliery Club, Coventry - 28 January & The Grove Sports Centre, Newark - 4 February
L. Fly: no entries. **Fly:** *final:* G. Payne (Bell Green) w rsc 2 A. Pope (Wellingborough). **Bantam:** *final:* P. Neale (Alexton) wo. **Feather:** *final:* D. Pithie (Willenhall) w pts J. Yarnell (Phoenix). **Light:** *semi-finals:* D. Kehoe (Triumph) w rsc 2 A. Thomas (Wellingborough), V. Broomhead (Buxton) w pts R. Brotherhood (Huthwaite); *final:* D. Kehoe w pts V. Broomhead. **L. Welter:** *semi-finals:* I. Carroll (Triumph) wo, L. Dunn (Chesterfield) w pts M. Watson (Phoenix); *final:* L. Dunn w pts I. Carroll. **Welter:** *semi-finals:* S. Mabbutt (Belgrave) wo, G. Beardsley (Belper) w pts D. Kirk (Huthwaite); *final:* S. Mabbutt w pts G. Beardsley. **L. Middle:** *semi-finals:* S. Bendall (Triumph) w rsc 2 I. Moore (Earl Shilton), K. Gibbons (Derby) w co 2 J. Khaliq (Ruddington); *final:* S. Bendall w pts K. Gibbons. **Middle:** *semi-finals:* J. Twite (Triumph) w pts S. Beasley (Northampton), A. Lovelace (Boston) w pts T. Watson (Royal Oak); *final:* A. Lovelace w pts J. Twite. **L. Heavy:** *final:* K. Oliver (Bracebridge) w pts D. Bendall (Triumph). **Heavy:** *semi-finals:* N. Simpson (Willenhall) wo, A. Aziz (Derby) w rsc 2 N. Williamson (Bulwell); *final:* N. Simpson w pts A. Aziz. **S. Heavy:** *final:* R. Slater (Phoenix) wo.

Birmingham Division   The Irish Community Centre, Digbeth - 16 January
L. Fly: no entries. **Fly:** no entries. **Bantam:** no entries. **Feather:** no entries. **Light:** no entries. **L. Welter:** *final:* A. Maynard (Small Heath) w pts S. Sherrington (Birmingham). **Welter:** *final:* M. Santini (Birmingham) w pts J. Scanlon (Birmingham). **L. Middle:** *final:* P. Elcott (Coleshill) wo. **Middle:** *final:* D. Sweeney (Small Heath) w rtd 2 J. Gavin (Rover). **L. Heavy:** *final:* A. McVeigh (Small Heath) w pts L. Page (Birmingham). **Heavy:** no entries. **S. Heavy:** *final:* K. Norville (Birmingham) wo.

North Staffordshire Division   Kay's Club, Stoke on Trent - 11 January
L. Fly: no entries. **Fly:** no entries. **Bantam:** no entries. **Feather:** no entries. **Light:** no entries. **L. Welter:** *final:* S. Wooliscroft (Queensberry) wo. **Welter:** no entries. **L. Middle:** *final:* M. Galor (Burton) wo. **Middle:** no entries. **L. Heavy:** *final:* P. Donnelly (Brownhills) wo. **Heavy:** *final:* R. Francis (The Orme) wo. **S. Heavy:** no entries.

South Staffordshire Division   The Labour Club, Brierley Hill - 13 January & The Gala Baths, West Bromwich - 21 January
L. Fly: no entries. **Fly:** *final:* D. Spencer (Pleck) wo. **Bantam:** no entries. **Feather:** no entries. **Light:** *final:* G. Reid (Wolverhampton) w pts C. Allen (Scotlands). **L. Welter:** *final:* M. Richards (Wednesbury) w pts S. Cockayne (Pleck). **Welter:** *final:* P. Nightingale (Wednesbury) w pts M. Bamford (Silver Street). **L. Middle:** *final:* A. Houldey (Wednesbury) w rsc 2 I. Lainchbury (Rugeley Police). **Middle:** *semi-finals:* S. Martin (Wolverhampton) wo, A. Gardner (Wolverhampton) w pts U. Williams (Wolverhampton); *final:* S. Martin w pts A. Gardner. **L. Heavy:** *final:* M. Pugh (Silver Street) wo. **Heavy:** *final:* D. Webb (Wednesbury) w pts P. Simms (Red Lion). **S. Heavy:** *final:* B. Summers (Wednesbury) wo.

West Mercia Division   The Heath Hotel, Bewdley - 21 January
L. Fly: no entries. **Fly:** no entries. **Bantam:** no entries. **Feather:** no entries. **Light:** *final:* J. Gonzales (Warley) wo. **L. Welter:** *final:* S. Handley (Warley) wo. **Welter:** *final:* W. Clayton (Worcester) wo. **L. Middle:** *final:* J. Adams (Warley) w pts G. Richards (Windmill). **Middle:** *final:* R. Doran (Shrewsbury & Severnside) wo. **L. Heavy:** no entries. **Heavy:** no entries. **S. Heavy:** no entries.

Midland Counties (South Zone) Semi-Finals & Finals   The Saddlers Club, Walsall - 27 January, The Hardy Spicer Social Club, Birmingham - 29 January & The Castle Vale Social Club, Birmingham - 5 February
L. Fly: no entries. **Fly:** *final:* D. Spencer (Pleck) wo. **Bantam:** no entries. **Feather:** no entries. **Light:** *final:* J. Gonzales (Warley) w pts G. Reid (Wolverhampton). **L. Welter:** *semi-finals:* A. Maynard (Small Heath) w pts S. Handley (Warley), M. Richards (Wednesbury) w pts S. Wooliscroft (Queensberry); *final:* A. Maynard wo M. Richards. **Welter:** *semi-finals:* P. Nightingale (Wednesbury) wo, M. Santini (Birmingham) w rsc 3 W. Clayton (Worcester); *final:* M. Santini w pts P. Nightingale. **L. Middle:** *semi-finals:* A. Houldey (Wednesbury) w pts M. Galor (Burton), J. Adams (Warley) w rsc 2 P. Elcott (Coleshill); *final:* A. Houldey w pts J. Adams. **Middle:** *semi-finals:* S. Martin (Wolverhampton) wo, D. Sweeney (Small Heath) w pts R. Doran (Shrewsbury & Severnside); *final:* D. Sweeney w dis 2 S. Martin. **L. Heavy:** *semi-finals:* A. McVeigh (Small Heath) wo, P. Donnelly (Brownhills) w pts M. Pugh (Silver Street); *final:* A. McVeigh w pts P. Donnelly. **Heavy:** *final:* R. Francis (The Orme) w pts D. Webb (Wednesbury). **S. Heavy:** *final:* B. Summers (Wednesbury) w rsc 3 K. Norville (Birmingham).

Midland Counties Finals   The Longbridge Exhibition Hall, Birmingham - 19 February
L. Fly: no entries. **Fly:** G. Payne (Bell Green) w pts D. Spencer (Pleck). **Bantam:** P. Neale (Alexton) wo. **Feather:** D. Pithie (Willenhall) wo. **Light:** J. Gonzalez (Warley) w pts D. Kehoe (Triumph). **L. Welter:** A. Maynard (Small Heath) w pts L. Dunn (Chesterfield). **Welter:** M. Santini (Birmingham) w rsc 2 S., Mabbutt (Belgrave). **L. Middle:** S. Bendall (Triumph) w pts A. Houldey (Wednesbury). **Middle:** D. Sweeney (Small Heath) w pts A. Lovelace (Boston). **L. Heavy:** K. Oliver (Bracebridge) w rsc 2 A. McVeigh (Small Heath). **Heavy:** N. Simpson (Willenhall) w pts R. Francis (The Orme). **S. Heavy:** B. Summers (Wednesbury) w co 2 R. Slater (Phoenix).

Southern Counties

Southern Counties Championships   The Leisure Centre, Woking - 12 & 18 February
L. Fly: no entries. **Fly:** *final:* C. Ramsey (Leigh Park) w pts T.

Craig (Basingstoke). **Bantam:** *final:* J. McLean (Basingstoke) wo. **Feather:** *semi-finals:* G. White (St Leonard's) wo, M. Wright (St Mary's) w pts S. Michael (Titchfield); *final:* M. Wright w rsc 2 G. White. **Light:** *quarter-finals:* D. Tatton (St Mary's) wo, M. Bloomfield (St Leonard's) w pts R. Cox (Brighton), P. Bedford (Basingstoke) w dis 3 M. Mann (Fareham), D. Lavender (Foley) w pts B. Urquhart (Westree); *semi-finals:* D. Tatton w pts M. Bloomfield, D. Lavender w rsc 1 P. Bedford; *final:* D. Tatton w rsc 1 D. Lavender. **L. Welter:** *quarter-finals:* W. Rothwell (Westree) wo, R. Harrison (Faversham) w pts G. Murphy (Hove), S. Fenton (Camberley) w rsc 2 J. Carter (Ashford), T. Bayrack (Crawley) w pts J. Newton (Seaford); *semi-finals:* R. Harrison w pts W. Rothwell, T. Bayrack w pts S. Fenton; *final:* R. Harrison w rsc 2 T. Bayrack. **Welter:** *quarter-finals:* S. Cullen (Faversham) wo, P. Miles (Foley) w rsc 2 D. Beech (Onslow), J. Moore (Fareham) w co 2 G. Moriano (Camberley), K. Rayment (St Mary's) w rtd 3 R. Head (Westree); *semi-finals:* P. Miles w co 1 S. Cullen, K. Rayment w rsc 1 J. Moore; *final:* P. Miles w pts K. Rayment. **L. Middle:** *prelims:* B. Brooks (Westree) wo, A. Gilbert (Crawley) wo, J. Cole (Cowes) wo, D. Brazil (Aldershot) wo, Y. Bello (Parade) wo, J. Bloomfield (St Leonard's) w pts S. Sheeran (Crawley), S. Laight (Southampton) w rsc 3 M. Voisey (Cowes), P. D'Santos (Woking) w pts G. Neil (Camberley); *quarter-finals:* B. Brooks w pts A. Gilbert, J. Cole w rsc 1 D. Brazil, J. Bloomfield w pts Y. Bello, P. D'Santos w pts S. Laight; *semi-finals:* B. Brooks w pts J. Cole, J. Bloomfield w rsc 2 P.D'Santos; *final:* J. Bloomfield w pts B. Brooks. **Middle:** *semi-finals:* A. Wilford (Faversham) wo, D. Francis (Basingstoke) w co 1 G. McCann (Woking); *final:* D. Francis w rsc 2 A. Wilford. **L. Heavy:** *semi-finals:* M. Snipe (Brighton) w rsc 2 M. Barney (Fareham), J. Fletcher (Woking) w pts J. Diggins (Foley); *final:* M. Snipe w pts J. Fletcher. **Heavy:** *semi-finals:* G. Russell (Lydd) wo, J. McCormack (Ramsgate) w pts G., Scraggs (Seaford); *final:* J. McCormack w co 2 G. Russell. **S. Heavy:** *semi-finals:* D. Chilman (Orpington) wo, C. Eastwood (Foley) w dis 1 C. Parsons (Seaford); *final:* D. Chilman wo C. Eastwood.

Regional Semi-Finals & Finals

The Leisure Centre, Woking - 5 March, Molin's Recreation Club, Saunderton - 5 March & Fox Hollies Leisure Centre, Birmingham - 2 April
L. Fly: *final:* J. Locke (Henley) wo. **Fly:** *final:* G. Payne (Bell Green) w pts C. Ramsey (Leigh Park). **Bantam:** *semi-finals:* M. Reynolds (Colchester) wo, J. McLean (Basingstoke) w pts P. Neale (Alexton); *final:* J. McLean w pts M. Reynolds. **Feather:** *semi-finals:* D. Dainty (Canvey) w pts J. Gynn (Stevenage), D. Pithie (Willenhall) w pts M. Wright (St Mary's); *final:* D. Pithie w pts D. Dainty. **Light:** *semi-finals:* M. Hawthorne (Lowestoft) w rtd 3 A. McBeal (Hitchin), J. Gonzales (Warley) wo D. Tatton (St Mary's); *final:* M. Hawthorne w pts J. Gonzalez. **L. Welter:** *semi-finals:* G. Smith (Canvey) w pts T. Turner (Pinewood Starr), A. Maynard (Small Heath) w rsc 3 R. Harrison (Faversham); *final:* G. Smith w pts A. Maynard. **Welter:** *semi-finals:* K. McCarthy (Bedford) w rsc 3 J. Mahoney (Aldermans), M. Santini (Birmingham) w pts P. Miles (Foley); *final:* M. Santini w rsc 3 K. McCarthy. **L. Middle:** *semi-finals:* A. Ewen (Arcade) w pts E. Randall (Bushey) - replaced J. Loosley (Mo's), S. Bendall (Triumph) w pts J. Bloomfield (St Leonard's); *final:* S. Bendall w co 2 A. Ewen. **Middle:** *semi-finals:* D. Starie (Hurstleigh & Kerridge) w co 2 M. Hilding (Pinewood Starr), D. Francis (Basingstoke) w pts D. Sweeney (Small Heath); *final:* D. Starie w pts D. Francis. **L. Heavy:** *semi-finals:* S. Lawlor (Luton Irish) w pts M. Redhead (Cambridge & Soham), K. Oliver (Bracebridge) w pts M. Snipe (Brighton); *final:* K. Oliver w pts S. Lawlor. **Heavy:**

semi-finals: M. Sprott (Bulmershe) w pts C. Elden (Norwich), N. Simpson (Willenhall) w rsc 3 J. McCormack (Ramsgate); *final:* N. Simpson w pts M. Sprott. **S. Heavy:** B. Summers (Wednesbury) wo D. Chilman (Orpington), K. Fletcher (Reading) wo A. Herron (Chalvedon); *final:* K. Fletcher w co 2 B. Summers.

London

North East Division   York Hall, Bethnal Green - 18 February
L. Fly no entries. **Fly:** no entries. **Bantam:** *final:* M. Jones (Repton) wo. **Feather:** *semi-finals:* S. Murray (West Ham) wo, S. Smith (Repton) w rsc 2 D. Lutaaya (St Monica's); *final:* S. Smith w pts S. Murray. **Light:** *final:* K. Wing (Repton) wo. **L. Welter:** *quarter-finals:* M. Riviere (West Ham) wo, T. Cesay (Repton) wo, M. Holgate (St Monica's) wo, K. Asare (Lion) w pts G. Turner (Hornchurch); *semi-finals:* M. Riviere w pts T. Cesay, M. Holgate w rsc 3 K. Asare; *final:* M. Holgate wo M. Riviere. **Welter:** *semi-finals:* P. Wright (Repton) wo L. Omar (Repton) w rsc 1 S. Roberts (West Ham); *final:* P. Wright wo L. Omar. **L. Middle:** *quarter-finals:* D. Thompson (St Monica's) wo, S. Wright (Repton) wo, H. Lawrence (West Ham) wo, T. Taylor (Repton) w dis 2 C. Houliston (Alma); *semi-finals:* D. Thompson w pts S. Wright, T. Taylor w pts H. Lawrence; *final:* T. Taylor w dis 3 D. Thompson. **Middle:** *semi-finals:* J. Branch (Repton) wo, J. Matthews (Crown & Manor) w rsc 1 B. Allen (St Monica's); *final:* J. Matthews w rsc 1 J. Branch. **L. Heavy:** *quarter-finals:* M. Kalombo (West Ham) wo, M. Oshungburt (St Monica's) wo, M. Thomas (West Ham) wo, N. Mirza (Repton) w pts E. Antoine (County); *semi-finals:* N. Mirza w co 3 M. Thomas, M. Kalombo w pts M. Oshungburt; *final:* N. Mirza w co 1 M. Kalombo. **Heavy:** *final:* D. Negus (Five Star) w pts S. Lukacs. **S. Heavy:** *final:* J. Beecroft (Gator) wo.

North-West Division   The Town Hall, Wembley - 7 February & The Irish Centre, Camden - 14 February
L. Fly: no entries. **Fly:** *final:* M. Alexander (Islington) w dis 3 R. Ramzan (St Patrick's). **Bantam:** *final:* S. Oliver (Finchley) wo. **Feather:** *final:* P. Mullings (St Patrick's) w pts M. Brown (St Pancras). **Light:** *semi-finals:* I. Smith (St Pancras) wo, N. King (St Patrick's) w pts D. Brown (Hayes); *final:* I. Smith w pts N. King. **L. Welter:** *final:* R. Edwards (St Patrick's) wo. **Welter:** *semi-finals:* S. Bardoville (All Stars) w pts A. Lazarus (St Patrick's), S. Vaughan (Northolt) w pts A. Mushandu (Islington); *final:* S. Vaughan w pts S. Bardoville. **L. Middle:** *semi-finals:* D. Magee (Angel) w pts B. McDonagh (All Stars), M. Scott (Islington) w pts E. Giordano (Islington); *final:* D. Magee w co 3 M. Scott. **Middle:** *final:* G. Reyniers (St Patrick's) w pts W. Jackson (Islington). **L. Heavy:** *quarter-finals:* M. Witter (Hayes) wo, P. Wiltshire (Northolt) wo, A. Griffiths (New Enterprise) wo, B. Leslie (Islington) w rtd 1 S. Miller (Angel); *semi-finals:* M. Witter w 1 P. Wiltshire, B. Leslie w pts A. Griffiths; *final:* B. Leslie w rsc 2 M. Witter. **Heavy:** *final:* I. Ajose (All Stars) w rsc 2 L. Polimis (All Stars). **S. Heavy:** *final:* A. Harrison (Northolt) w rsc 2 W. Ferguson (All Stars).

South-East Division   The Crook Log Leisure Centre, Bexleyheath - 19 February & The Town Hall, Battersea - 22 February
L.Fly: no entries. **Fly:** *final:* D. Costello (Hollington) wo. **Bantam:** *final:* D. Easton (New Addington) wo. **Feather:** *final:* E. Lam (Fitzroy Lodge) wo. **Light:** *semi-finals:* L. Reynolds (Fitzroy Lodge) w pts C. Williams (Eltham), J. Alldis (Lynn) w pts C. Stanley (Fitzroy Lodge); *final:* J. Alldis w rsc 3 L. Reynolds. **L. Welter:** *semi-finals:* G. Burdon (Fitzroy Lodge) wo, D. McGovern (Lynn) w rsc 2 S. Rowlands (South Reach); *final:* D. McGovern w

pts G. Burdon. **Welter:** *final:* S. Fearon (Lynn) w dis 3 L. Linguard (BK Movers). **L. Middle:** *semi-finals:* W. Alexander (Lynn) wo, P. Carr (Fisher) w co 2 A. Howell (Fitzroy Lodge); *final:* W. Alexander w co 1 P. Carr. **Middle:** *quarter-finals:* T. Owoh (Lynn) wo, A. Talwo (Fisher) wo, S. Johnson (Lynn) w rsc 3 L. Arscott (Honour Oak), S. Mitchell (St Peter's) w pts J. Hart (Bromley & Downham); *semi-finals:* T. Owoh w rtd 2 A. Talwo, S. Johnson w rsc 2 S. Mitchell; *final:* S. Johnson w rsc 2 T. Owoh. **L. Heavy:** *quarter-finals:* D. Archibald (Lynn) wo, T. Callum (Lynn) wo, J. Sawicki (Eltham) w pts K. Mitchell (Lynn), S. Hewitt (Fitzroy Lodge) w rtd 2 G. Oliver (South Reach); *semi-finals:* D. Archibald w pts T. Callum, S. Hewitt w pts J. Sawicki; *final:* D. Archibald w pts S. Hewitt. **Heavy:** *semi-finals:* V. Clark (BK Movers) wo, W. Gibson (St Peter's) w pts D. Williams (Lynn); *final:* V. Clark w rsc 1 W. Gibson. **S. Heavy:** *quarter-finals:* M. Khamkhoer (Fitzroy Lodge) wo, E. Gandi (Lynn) wo, K. Long (BK Movers) wo, H. Senior (Lynn) w rsc 2 D. Williams (New Addington); *semi-finals:* M. Khamkhoer w pts H. Senior, E. Gandi w dis 1 K. Long; *final:* M. Khamkhoer w rsc 2 E. Gandi.

South-West Division   The Town Hall, Battersea - 22 February
L. Fly: no entries. **Fly:** no entries. **Bantam:** no entries. **Feather:** no entries. **Light:** *final:* F. Wilson (Battersea) wo. **L. Welter:** no entries. **Welter:** *final:* A. Gray (Battersea) w pts E. White-Overton (Tolworth). **L. Middle:** *semi-finals:* R. Williams (Earlsfield) wo, B. Ellis (Tolworth) w rsc 2 S. Bodigi (Met Police); *final:* R. Williams w pts B. Ellis. **Middle:** *final:* C. Campbell (Earlsfield) w co 2 D. Kyel (Battersea). **L. Heavy:** *semi-finals:* N. Eastwood (Tolworth) wo, F. Annan (Battersea) w rsc 1 R. Scott (Earlsfield); *final:* N. Eastwood w pts F. Annan. **Heavy:** *final:* A. Ayres (Battersea) w rsc 2 D. Davies (Earlsfield). **S. Heavy:** *final:* P. Thompson (Balham) wo.

London Semi-Finals & Finals   The National Sports Centre, Crystal Palace - 3 & 17 March
L. Fly: no entries. **Fly:** *final:* D. Costello (Hollington) w pts M. Alexander (Islington). **Bantam:** *semi-finals:* D. Easton (New Addington) wo, S. Oliver (Finchley) w pts M. Jones (Repton); *final:* S. Oliver w pts D. Easton. **Feather:** *semi-finals:* E. Lam (Fitzroy Lodge) wo, S. Smith (Repton) w pts P. Mullings (St Patrick's); *final:* S. Smith w pts E. Lam. **Light:** *semi-finals:* I. Smith (St Pancras) w pts F. Wilson (Battersea), J. Alldis (Lynn) wo K. Wing (Repton); *final:* I. Smith w pts J. Alldis. **L. Welter:** *semi-finals:* M. Holgate (St Monica's) wo, R. Edwards (St Patrick's) w co 3 D. McGovern (Lynn); *final:* R. Edwards w rsc 2 M. Holgate. **Welter:** *semi-finals:* P. Wright (Repton) w pts S. Fearon (Lynn), A. Gray (Battersea) w pts S. Vaughan (Northolt); *final:* P. Wright w dis 2 A. Gray. **L. Middle:** *semi-finals:* T. Taylor (Repton) w pts R. Williams (Earlsfield), W. Alexander (Lynn) w co 1 D. Magee (Angel); *final:* W. Alexander w rsc 2 T. Taylor. **Middle:** *semi-finals:* J. Matthews (Crown & Manor) w rsc 3 G. Reyniers (St Patrick's), S. Johnson (Lynn) wo C. Campbell (Earlsfield); *final:* J. Matthews w pts S. Johnson. **L. Heavy:** *semi-finals:* D. Archibald (Lynn) w pts N. Eastwood (Tolworth), N. Mirza (Repton) w pts B. Leslie (Islington); *final:* N. Mirza w pts D. Archibald. **Heavy:** *semi-finals:* V. Clark (BK Movers) w pts D. Negus (Five Star), I. Ajose (All Stars) w pts A. Ayres (Battersea); *final:* I. Ajose w rsc 1 V. Clark. **S. Heavy:** *semi-finals:* M. Khamkhoer (Fitzroy Lodge) w rsc 2 P. Thompson (Balham), A. Harrison (Northolt) w rsc 1 J. Beecroft (Gator); *final:* M. Khamkhoer w rsc 2 A. Harrison.

Northern Counties
North-East Counties

North-East Division   The Leisure Centre, Gateshead - 4 & 11 February
L. Fly: no entries. **Fly:** *final:* S. Parry (Lambton Street) wo. **Bantam:** no entries. **Feather:** *final:* S. Grant (Aycliffe) w pts P. Quarmby (Elemore). **Light:** *final:* A. Green (Phil Thomas SOB) w pts A. McLean (Hylton Castle). **L. Welter:** *quarter-finals:* W. Tyrell (Sunderland) wo, J. Tytler (Phil Thomas SOB) w rsc 2 M. Finneran (Grainger Park), S. Hall (Darlington) w pts M. McLean ((Hylton Castle), A. Temple (Hartlepool BW) w rsc 2 G. Douglas (Hartlepool Catholic); *semi-finals:* S. Hall w pts J. Tytler, A. Temple w rtd 1 W. Tyrell; *final:* A. Temple w pts S. Hall. **Welter:** *semi-finals:* M. Hall (Darlington) w pts J. Bell (Washington), J. Green (Phil Thomas SOB) w dis 3 J. Spencer (Wellington); *final:* M. Hall w pts J. Green. **L. Middle:** *semi-finals:* M. Johnson (Grainger Park) w rtd 2 C Beddison (Birtley), M. Lumley (Lambton Street) w pts J. Mett (Phil Thomas SOB); *final:* M. Johnson w pts M. Lumley. **Middle:** *semi-finals:* M. Smith (Hartlepool Catholic) w pts G. Grounds (Phil Thomas SOB), A. Rowbotham (Hartlepool BW) w pts D. Toward (Birtley); *final:* A. Rowbotham w pts M. Smith. **L. Heavy:** *semi-finals:* A. Todd (Darlington) wo, E. Haley (Simonside) w pts D. McFarlane (Birtley); *final:* A. Todd wo E. Haley. **Heavy:** *final:* K. Duke (Sunderland) w rsc 2 M. McGuiness (Darlington). **S. Heavy:** *final:* G. McGhin (Sunderland) w co 1 J. Hall (Ryton).

Yorkshire & Humberside Divisions   The Irish Centre, Leeds - 4 February & The Dome, Barnsley - 11 February
L. Fly: no entries. **Fly:** no entries. **Bantam:** *final:* N. Wilders (Five Towns) wo. **Feather:** *final:* J. Whittaker (Halifax) wo. **Light:** *semi-finals:* R. Latibeaudiere (Meanwood) wo, L. Crosby (St Paul's) w pts M. McIvor (Batley & Dewsbury); *final:* L. Crosby w pts R. Latibeaudiere. **L. Welter:** *quarter-finals:* T. Whittaker (PDC) wo, C. Yates (Tom Hill) wo, R. Vanzie (Karmand Centre) w pts R. Sampson (Fullflow), M. Johnson (Manor) w rsc 1 T. O'Brien (Meanwood); *semi-finals:* M. Johnson w pts T. Whittaker, R. Vanzie w rsc 2 C. Yates; *final:* R. Vanzie w co 2 M. Johnson. **Welter:** *quarter-finals:* C. Winstanley (PDC) wo, R. Burton (Barnsley) w pts A. Ellis (Hull Fish Trades), J. Witter (Bradford Police) w rsc 1 W. Christian (Manor), G. Matsell (Hull Fish Trades) w rtd 1 C. Appleton (Five Towns); *semi-finals:* J. Witter w rsc 1 C. Winstanley, G. Matsell w pts R. Burton; *final:* G. Matsell w pts J. Witter. **L. Middle:** *quarter-finals:* D. Galloway (Parsons Cross) wo, S. Smith (Burmantofts) w pts M. Hickinbottom (Wombwell), L. Murtagh (Hunslet) w pts D. Roche (Burmantofts), M. Barker (St Paul's) w pts S. Stokes (Parsons Cross); *semi-finals:* M. Barker w rtd 1 S. Smith, L. Murtagh w pts D. Galloway; *final:* M. Barker w pts L. Murtagh. **Middle:** *semi-finals:* S. Hendry (Burmantofts) w pts K. Robertshaw (Hunslet), R. Rhodes (Unity) w rsc 2 J. Sharpe (White Rose); *final:* R. Rhodes w rsc 1 S. Hendry. **L. Heavy:** *final:* J. Warters (St Patrick's) w rsc 3 G. Dunbar (St Paul's). **Heavy:** *final:* A. Carr (Scarborough) wo. **S. Heavy:** *final:* G. Fitzgerald (Plant Works) wo.

North-East Counties Finals   The Light Waves Leisure Centre, Wakefield - 24 February
L. Fly: no entries. **Fly:** S. Parry (Lambton Street) wo. **Bantam:** N. Wilders (Five Towns) wo. **Feather:** J. Whittaker (Halifax) w pts S. Grant (Aycliffe). **Light:** A. Green (Phil Thomas SOB) w pts L. Crosby (St Paul's). **L. Welter:** A. Temple (Hartlepool BW) wo R. Vanzie (Karmand Centre). **Welter:** M. Hall (Darlington) w pts J. Witter (Bradford Police) - replaced G. Matsell (Hull Fish Trades). **L. Middle:** M. Barker (St Paul's) w pts M. Lumley (Lambton Street) - replaced M. Johnson (Grainger Park). **Middle:** R. Rhodes (Unity) w pts A. Rowbotham (Hartlepool BW). **L. Heavy:** A. Todd (Darlington) w pts J. Warters (St Patrick's). **Heavy:** K. Duke

(Sunderland) w co 1 A. Carr (Scarborough). **S. Heavy:** G. McGhinn (Sunderland) w co 1 G. Fitzgerald (Plant Works).

North-West Counties

East Lancashire & Cheshire Division   The Pembroke Halls, Walkden - 4 & 18 February & The Civic Hall, Middleton - 11 February

L. Fly: no entries. **Fly:** *final:* G. Lewis (Arrow) wo. **Bantam:** *semi-finals:* S. Bell (Stockport & Bredbury) wo, A. Lewis (Bury) w co 1 K. Noteman (Currock House); *final:* S. Bell w pts A. Lewis. **Feather:** *final:* M. Brodie (Ancoats) w rsc 1 R. King (Our Lady & St John). **Light:** *semi-finals:* G. Hibbert (Gallagher Boys) w pts R. Duckworth (Fox), D. Clavering (Bury) w pts J. Knight (Preston & Fulwood); *final:* D. Clavering w pts G. Hibbert. **L. Welter:** *final:* A. Davidson (Fox) w rsc 2 S. Walker (Boarshaw). **Welter:** *final:* B. Gonzalez (Preston Red Rose) w pts J. Barrow (Preston & Fulwood). **L. Middle:** *quarter-finals:* J. Aikenhead (Sale West) w rsc 1 D. Bateman (Moss Side), J. Whiteside (Preston Red Rose) w rsc 1 A. Feno (Stockport & Bredbury), J. Hammant (Ardwick) w pts G. Thorpe (Sandygate), D. Richards (Barrow) w pts P. Street (West Gorton); *semi-finals:* J. Whiteside w pts J. Aikenhead, J. Hammant w pts D. Richards; *final:* J. Whiteside wo J. Hammant. **Middle:** *semi-finals:* L. Blundell (Preston Red Rose) w rsc 1 R. Traynor (Arrow), P. Heneghan (Moss Side) w rsc 2 L. Hogan (Arrow); *final:* P. Heneghan w rsc 1 L. Blundell. **L. Heavy:** *semi-finals:* M. Hickson (Blackpool) w co 2 P. Hazelwood (Fox), G. Williams (Collyhurst & Moston) w rsc 3 D. Myer (Droylsden); *final:* G. Williams w pts M. Hickson. **Heavy:** *semi-finals:* M. Levi (Collyhurst & Moston) w pts G. Wilson (Bury), M. Ellis (Blackpool) w pts J. Quayson (Moss Side); *final:* M. Ellis w pts M. Levi. **S. Heavy:** *final:* R. Allen (Preston & Fulwood) w rsc 1 M. Holden (Droylsden).

West Lancashire & Cheshire Division   Lambeth Road Gym, Liverpool - 4 February & Everton Park Sports Centre, Liverpool - 11 & 18 February

L. Fly: *final:* G. Jones (Sefton) wo. **Fly:** *final:* D. Vlasman (Gemini) wo. **Bantam:** *semi-finals:* D. Burke (Salidbury) wo, A. Mulholland (Transport) w pts K. Roberts (Gemini); *final:* D. Burke w pts A. Mulholland. **Feather:** *semi-finals:* C. Pennington (St Helens) wo, A. Moon (Kirkby) w pts J. Heyes (Gemini); *final:* A. Moon w rsc 3 C. Pennington. **Light:** *final:* J. Mellor (Transport) w pts D. Swift (Gemini). **L. Welter:** *semi-finals:* L. Rimmer (Salisbury) wo, J. Vlasman (Gemini) w pts M. Thompson (St Helens); *final:* J. Vlasman w pts L. Rimmer. **Welter:** *final:* P. Burns (Gemini) w pts J. Jones (Sefton). **L. Middle:** *final:* R. Murray (Golden Gloves) w pts L. Burns (Gemini). **Middle:** *quarter-finals:* R. Hill (Knowsley Vale) wo, M. Donoghue (Salisbury) wo, A. Roberts (Lowe House) wo, J. Naylor (Rotunda) w pts R. Burns (Gemini); *semi-finals:* J. Naylor w pts R. Hill, M. Donoghue w pts A. Roberts; *final:* J. Naylor w pts M. Donoghue. **L. Heavy:** *final:* G. Drew (Long Lane) wo. **Heavy:** *semi-finals:* G. Sandland (Rotunda) wo, D. Chubbs (Kirkby) w pts P. Swift (Lowe House); *final:* D. Chubbs w rsc 2 G. Sandland. **S. Heavy:** *semi-finals:* P. Dickinson (Tuebrook) w dis 3 D. Thomas (Litherland), S. Bristow (Rotunda) w pts A. Dodd (Coach House); *final:* S. Bristow w pts P. Dickinson.

North-West Counties Finals   Everton Park Sports Centre, Liverpool - 4 March

L. Fly: G. Jones (Sefton) wo. **Fly:** G. Lewis (Arrow) w pts D. Vlasman (Gemini). **Bantam:** D. Burke (Salisbury) w pts S. Bell (Stockport & Bredbury). **Feather:** A. Moon (Kirkby) w pts M.

Brodie (Ancoats). **Light:** J. Mellor (Transport) w rsc 3 D. Clavering (Bury). **L. Welter:** J. Vlasman (Gemini) wo A. Davidson (Fox). **Welter:** P. Burns (Gemini) w pts B. Gonzalez (Preston Red Rose). **L. Middle:** R. Murray (Golden Gloves) w pts J. Whiteside (Preston Red Rose). **Middle:** P. Heneghan (Moss Side) w pts J. Naylor (Rotunda). **L. Heavy:** G. Williams (Collyhurst) & Moston) w pts G. Drew (Long Lane). **Heavy:** M. Ellis (Blackpool) w co 2 D. Chubbs (Kirkby). **S. Heavy:** R. Allen (Preston & Fulwood) w pts S. Bristow (Rotunda).

Northern Counties Finals

The Pavilion, Thornaby - 11 March

L. Fly: G. Jones (Sefton) wo. **Fly:** S. Parry (Lambton Street) w rsc 2 G. Lewis (Arrow). **Bantam:** D. Burke (Salisbury) w pts N. Wilders (Five Towns). **Feather:** A. Moon (Kirkby) w rsc 3 J. Whittaker (Halifax). **Light:** A. Green (Phil Thomas SOB) w pts J. Mellor (Transport). **L. Welter:** A. Temple (Hartlepool BW) w rsc 2 J. Vlasman (Gemini). **Welter:** M. Hall (Darlington) w pts P. Burns (Gemini). **L. Middle:** R. Murray (Golden Gloves) w rsc 2 M. Barker (St Paul's). **Middle:** R. Rhodes (Unity) w pts P. Heneghan (Moss Side). **L. Heavy:** G. Williams (Collyhurst & Moston) w rsc 3 J. Warters (St Patrick's) - replaced A. Todd (Darlington). **Heavy:** M. Ellis (Blackpool) w rtd 3 K. Duke (Sunderland). **S. Heavy:** R. Allen (Preston & Fulwood) w pts G. McGhin (Sunderland).

English ABA Semi-Final & Finals

The Leisure Centre, Gateshead - 12 April & The National Indoor Arena, Birmingham - 4 May

L. Fly: *semi-finals:* D. Fox (RAF) wo, G. Jones (Sefton) wo J. Locke (Henley); *final:* G. Jones w pts D. Fox. **Fly:** *semi-finals:* D. Costello (Hollington) w rsc 3 G. Payne (Bell Green), O. Spensley (RAF) w pts S. Parry (Lambton Street); *final:* D. Costello w pts O. Spensley. **Bantam:** *semi-finals:* S. Oliver (Finchley) w pts D. Burke (Salisbury), J. McLean (Basingstoke) w rsc 3 G. Nicette (Torbay); *final:* S. Oliver w rsc 2 J. McLean. **Feather:** *semi-finals:* S. Smith (Repton) w pts A. Moon (Kirkby), D. Pithie (Willenhall) w rsc 1 P. Dytham (Weymouth); *final:* D. Pithie w pts S. Smith. **Light:** *semi-finals:* I. Smith (St Pancras) w pts T. Peacock (Leonis), A. Green (Phil Thomas SOB) w pts M. Hawthorne (Lowestoft); *final:* A. Green w pts I. Smith. **L. Welter:** *semi-finals:* R. Edwards (St Patrick's) w pts J. Gardner (Army), A. Temple (Hartlepool BW) w pts G. Smith (Canvey); *final:* A. Temple w rsc 3 R. Edwards. **Welter:** *semi-finals:* K. Short (Army) w pts P. Wright (Repton), M. Santini (Birmingham) w pts M. Hall (Darlington); *final:* K. Short w pts M. Santini. **L. Middle:** *semi-finals:* W. Alexander (Lynn) w rsc 2 C. Bessey (Army), S. Bendall (Triumph) w pts R. Murray (Golden Gloves); *final:* W. Alexander w rsc 1 S. Bendall. **Middle:** *semi-finals:* D. Starie (Hurstleigh & Kerridge) w rsc 2 J. Matthews (Crown & Manor), E. Stuart (Leonis) w rsc 2 R. Rhodes (Unity); *final:* D. Starie w pts E. Stuart. **L. Heavy:** *semi-finals:* K. Oliver (Bracebridge) w rsc 2 G. Williams (Collyhurst & Moston), P. Rogers (Penhill) w co 3 N. Mirza (Repton); *final:* K. Oliver w pts P. Rogers. **Heavy:** *semi-finals:* I. Ajose (All Stars) w pts M. Ellis (Blackpool), S. Burford (Army) w rsc 3 N. Simpson (Willenhall); *final:* S. Burford w pts I. Ajose. **S. Heavy:** *semi-finals:* D. Watts (Army) w pts R. Allen (Preston & Fulwood), M. Khamkhoer (Fitzroy Lodge) w pts K. Fletcher (Reading); *final:* D. Watts w pts M. Khamkhoer.

Irish Championships, 1993-94

Senior Tournament

The National Stadium, Dublin - 11, 12 & 18 February
L. Fly: *semi-finals:* M. McQuillan (Holy Family, Drogheda) wo, J. Prior (Darndale, Dublin) w pts C. Moffat (Holy Family, Belfast); *final:* M. McQuillan w pts J. Prior. **Fly:** *final:* D. Kelly (Holy Trinity, Belfast) w pts D. Hosford (Greenmount, Cork). **Bantam:** *semi-finals:* T. Waite (Cairn Lodge, Belfast) wo, D. McAree (Immaculata, Belfast) w pts P. Murphy (St Paul's, Waterford); *final:* T. Waite w pts D. McAree. **Feather:** *quarter-finals:* P. Griffin (Mount Tallant, Dublin) wo. A. Patterson (St Patrick's, Newry) w pts J. Conlon (Holy Trinity, Belfast), T. Carlyle (Sacred Heart, Dublin) w pts S. Redmond (Kilmount, Dublin), P. Ireland (St George's & St Malachy's, Belfast) w pts S. Spence (Holy Family & Golden Gloves, Belfast); *semi-finals:* P. Griffin w pts A. Patterson, P. Ireland w rtd 2 T. Carlyle; *final:* P. Griffin w pts P. Ireland. **Light:** *quarter-finals:* G. Stephens (Crumlin, Dublin) wo, J. McEvoy (Edenmore, Dublin) w pts M. Dillon (Golden Cobra, Dublin), E. Bolger (Wexford CBS) w pts S. Cowman (St Paul's, Waterford), M. Reneghan (Keady, Armagh) w pts G. Ormonde (Donore, Dublin); *semi-finals:* G. Stephens w pts J. McEvoy, E. Bolger w pts M. Reneghan; *final:* G. Stephens w pts E. Bolger. **L. Welter:** *quarter-finals:* W. Walsh (St Coleman's, Cork) wo, S. McCann (Holy Family, Belfast) wo, S. Barrett (Rylane, Cork) wo, F. Carruth (Drimnagh, Dublin) w pts G. Ward (Darndale, Dublin); *semi-finals:* W. Walsh w pts S. McCann, S. Barrett w pts F. Carruth; *final:* W. Walsh w pts S. Barrett. **Welter:** *prelims:* N. Gough (St Paul's, Waterford) wo, R. O'Connor (St Canice's, Dublin) wo, E. Fisher (Holy Trinity, Belfast) wo, S. Gibson (Immaculata, Belfast) wo, N. Sinclair (Holy Family, Belfast) wo, W. McLoughlin (Glin, Dublin) wo, T. Lawler (Kilcullen, Kildare) wo, M. McBride (St Bridget's, Edenderry, Offaly) w rsc 2 J. McCormack (St Saviour's, Dublin); *quarter-finals:* N. Gough w pts R. O'Connor, E. Fisher w pts S. Gibson, N. Sinclair w pts W. McLoughlin, T. Lawlor w pts M. McBride; *semi-finals:* N. Gough w pts E. Fisher, N. Sinclair w pts T. Lawlor; *final:* N. Gough w pts N. Sinclair. **L. Middle:** *prelims:* J. Webb (Holy Trinity, Belfast) wo, M. McBride (St Bridget's, Edenderry, Offaly) wo, M. Roche (Sunnyside, Cork) wo, K. Walsh (St Coleman's, Cork) wo, B. Magee (Holy Trinity, Belfast) wo, S. McCluskey (Dockers, Belfast) wo, R. Fox (Phibsboro, Dublin) wo, A. McFadden (Dunfanaghy, Donegal) w pts P. Collins (Ashbourne, Meath); *quarter-finals:* J. Webb w pts J. McBride, M. Roche w pts K. Walsh, B. Magee w pts S. McCluskey, A. McFadden w pts R. Fox; *semi-finals:* J. Webb w pts M. Roche, A. McFadden w pts B. Magee; *final:* J. Webb w pts A. McFadden. **Middle:** *semi-finals:* D. Ryan (Raphoe, Donegal) wo, D. Galvin (St Saviour's, Dublin) w co 2 R. Dooris (Enniskillen, Fermanagh); *final:* D. Galvin w pts D. Ryan. **L. Heavy:** *prelims:* G. Joyce (Sunnyside, Cork) wo, S. Kirk (Cairn Lodge, Belfast) wo, S. Lawlor (Grangecon, Kildare) wo, S. Stoute (Edenmore, Dublin) wo, A. Sheerin (Swinford, Mayo) wo, M. Brennan (St Anne's, Westport, Mayo) wo, A. Crampton (St Broughan's, Offaly) w rtd 2 A. Brady (Galway), D. Curran (CIE, Dublin) w pts P. Deane (Ballina, Mayo); *quarter-finals:* G. Joyce w pts S. Kirk, S. Lawlor w pts S. Stoute, A. Sheerin w pts M. Brennan, D. Curran w pts A. Crampton; *semi-finals:* G. Joyce w pts S. Lawlor, A. Sheerin w pts D. Curran; *final:* G. Joyce w pts A. Sheerin. **Heavyweight:** *quarter-finals:* P. Douglas (Holy Family, Belfast) wo, D. Griffin (Drimnagh, Dublin) wo, P. Doran (Phibsboro, Dublin) wo, D. Cowley (St Michan's, Dublin) w pts T. Clifford (Castleisland, Kerry); *semi-finals:* P. Douglas w rsc 2 D. Griffin, P. Doran w pts D. Cowley; *final:* P. Douglas w pts P. Doran. **S. Heavy:** *final:* G. Douglas (South Meath, Meath) wo.

Intermediate Finals

The National Stadium, Dublin - 3 December
L. Fly: P. Phelan (St Michael's, Athy, Kildare) w pts S. Donaghue (Brosnia, Meath). **Fly:** W. Valentine (St Saviour's, Dublin) w pts K. Moore (St Francis, Limerick). **Bantam:** P. Whelan (Neilstown, Dublin) w pts W. Downey (Blarney, Cork). **Feather:** T. Carlyle (Sacred Heart, Dublin) w rsc 2 E. Nolan (Rylane, Cork). **Light:** J. Morrissey (Sunnyside, Cork) w pts M. Dillon (Golden Cobra, Dublin). **L. Welter:** L. Murphy (St Matthew's, Dublin) w pts J. Drumm (CIE, Dublin). **Welter:** W. Egan (Neilstown, Dublin) w pts J. Fox (Carrickmore, Tyrone). **L. Middle:** T. Fitzgerald (Ballyvolane, Cork) w pts J. Kelly (Sean McDermott's, Tyrone). **Middle:** K. Walsh (St Coleman's, Cork) w pts P. Collins (Ashbourne, Meath). **L. Heavy:** S. Collier (Loughgorman, Wexford) w pts M. Crampton (St Broughan's, Offaly). **Heavy:** J. Clancy (Kilfenora, Clare) w pts B. Devine (Dockers, Belfast). **S. Heavy:** D. Redmond (Small Heath, Birmingham) w pts D. Walsh (Knockagoshel, Kerry).

Junior Finals

The National Stadium, Dublin - 13 May
L. Fly: P. Phelan (St Michael's, Athy, Kildare) w pts J. Stacey (Crumlin, Dublin). **Fly:** B. Walsh (Darndale, Dublin) w pts T. Benn (Cavan). **Bantam:** G. Middleton (Sacred Heart, Dublin) w rsc 1 B. McMullan (Scorpion, Belfast). **Feather:** P. O'Donnell (Carrickmore, Tyrone) w pts I. Hackett (Holy Family, Drogheda). **Light:** F. Barrett (Olympic, Galway) w rsc 1 M. O'Mainin (Rosmuc Camus, Galway). **L. Welter:** A. Dunne (St Saviour's, Dublin) w co 3 M. Blaney (Holy Trinity, Belfast). **Welter:** D. Devers (Ballina, Mayo) w rsc 3 S. Egan (Cloghan, Offaly). **L. Middle:** J. Kelly (Sean McDermott's, Tyrone) w pts A. O'Neill (Castlecomer, Kilkenny). **Middle:** B. Crowley (Ennis, Clare) w pts R. Breathnach (Rosmuc Camus, Galway). **L. Heavy:** H. McNally (Antrim) w rtd 3 M. Duffy (Glin, Dublin). **Heavy:** C. O'Grady (St Patrick's, Meath) w rsc 1 M. Clancy (Kilfenora, Clare). **S. Heavy:** B. McGinley (St Patrick's, Keady, Armagh) wo.

Irish Senior Titles: Record Championship Wins

10: Jim O'Sullivan, 1980-1990. **9:** Gerry O'Colmain, 1943-1952; Harry Perry, 1952-1962. **8:** Nick Dowling, 1968-1975; E. Smyth, 1932-1940. **7:** J. J. Chase, 1926-1932; Jim McCourt, 1963-1972. **6:** Brian Byrne, 1975-1983; Ollie Byrne, 1954-1967; M. Flanagan, 1925-1931; P. Hughes, 1929-1935; Kieran Joyce, 1983-1988; F. Kerr, 1932-1938; Mick McKeon, 1945-1951; Tommy Milligan, 1950-1955; W. J. Murphy, 1924-1932; J. O'Driscoll, 1924-1934; Ando Reddy, 1951-1961; Billy Walsh, 1983-1991. **5:** Willie Byrne, 1959-1963; Paul Fitzgerald, 1982-1988; Dennis Galvin, 1989-1994; R. Hearns, 1933-1938; Brendan McCarthy, 1967-1971; Charlie Nash, 1970-1975. **4:** Ken Beattie, 1977-1982; Paul Buttimer, 1987-1983; Michael Carruth, 1987-1992; Dave Connell, 1946-1951; Peter Crotty, 1949-1952; Paul Douglas, 1989-1994; Gordon Ferris, 1973-1977; Paul Griffin, 1991-1994; Gordon Joyce, 1986-1994; Joe Lawlor, 1986-1991; Eamonn McCusker, 1965-1969; Jack O'Rourke, 1963-1971; Danno Power, 1958-1962; Phil Sutcliffe, 1977-1985; Eddie Treacy, 1961-1969; T. J. Tubridy, 1912-1923.

Scottish Championships, 1993-94

Meadowbank Stadium, Edinburgh - 26 February, The Fairfield Social Club, Glasgow - 14 March, The Hydro Hotel, Dunblane - 18 March & The Sports Centre, Grangemouth - 24 March

L. Fly: *final:* L. Munro (Dennistoun) w pts T. Walker (Dennistoun). **Fly:** *quarter-finals:* P. Shepherd (Sparta) wo, S. Sheridan (Osprey) wo, M. Crossan (Dennistoun) w pts P. Dignam (Bellahouston), S. Dickson (Hasties) w pts J. O'Mellon (Croy); *semi-finals:* P. Shepherd wo S. Sheridan, S. Dickson w pts M. Crossan; *final:* P. Shepherd w pts S. Dixon. **Bantam:** *semi-finals:* R. McPhee (Glenboig) w pts R. Hanley (Bellahouston), A. Brennan (Barn) w co 2 G. McWhirter (Larkhall); *final:* R. McPhee w pts R. Brennan. **Feather:** *quarter-finals:* R. Hay (Barn) w pts L. Sharp (Portobello), P. Watson (Barn) w rsc 2 T. McDonald (Perth), R. Kennedy (Springhill) w pts M. Simpson (Astoria), B. Carr (Auchengeich) w rsc 1 M. Gaunt (Dunfermline); *semi-finals:* R. Hay w pts P. Watson, B. Carr w rsc 1 R. Kennedy; *final:* B. Carr w pts R. Hay. **Light:** *quarter-finals:* M. Gowans (Selkirk) wo, A. McDonald (Bannockburn) w rsc 2 K. Stuart (Elgin), G. Fernie (Bonnyrigg) w pts J. Keating (Cambuskenneth), J. Coyle (Bannockburn) w pts J. Miller (Bannockburn); *semi-finals:* M. Gowans w dis 3 A. McDonald, J. Coyle w pts G. Fernie; *final:* J. Coyle w pts M. Gowans. **L. Welter:** *prelims:* G. Hughes (Drumchapel) wo, J. Docherty (Portobello) wo, D. Gordon (Springside) w pts W. Mason (Springhill), D. Evans (Barn) w pts E. Kelly (Cambusnethan), G. McLevy (Clydeview) w pts M. Breslin (Croy), W. Leckie (Haddington) w pts M. McConnachie (Astoria), J. Pender (St Francis) w pts S. Taylor (Kingdom), J. Howett (Lochee) w rsc 1 G. Summel (Bellahouston); *quarter-finals:* J. Docherty w pts G. Hughes, D. Gordon w pts D. Evans, G. McLevy w pts W. Leckie, J. Pender w pts J. Howett; *semi-finals:* J. Docherty wo D. Gordon, J. Pender w pts G. McLevy; *final:* J. Pender w pts J. Docherty. **Welter:** *prelims:* N. Thompson (Osprey) wo, A. McDonald (Camelon) wo, L. McBride (Elgin) wo, A. Craig (Aberdeen) wo, J. Gilheaney (Cleland) wo, C. McNeill (Springhill) w pts I. Sturrock (Linwood), A. Wolecki (St Francis) w pts M. Henderson (Springhill), C. Lynch (Leith) w pts J. Kane (Lanark); *quarter-finals:* A. McDonald w pts L. McBride, A. Craig w pts J. Gilheaney, C. McNeill w pts N. Thompson, A. Wolecki w pts C. Lynch; *semi-finals:* A. McDonald w pts A. Craig, A. Wolecki w pts C. McNeill; *final:* A. Wolecki w pts A. McDonald. **L. Middle:** *prelims:* Joe Townsley (Springhill) wo, C. Millard (Meadowbank) wo, M. Flynn (Blantyre) wo, W. McPhee (Huntley) wo, R. Mackie (Hayton) w pts A. Howitt (Dundee), B. Laidlaw (Cardenden) w pts T. Quinn (Haddington), L. Murphy (Forgewood) w pts M. Fleming (Kingdom), C. Edmonds (St Francis) w pts S. Allan (Tayport); *quarter-finals:* Joe Townsley w pts C. Millard, W. McPhee w pts M. Flynn, B. Laidlaw w pts R. Mackie, L. Murphy w pts C. Edmonds; *semi-finals:* Joe Townsley w rsc 2 W. McPhee, L. Murphy w rsc 3 B. Laidlaw; *final:* Joe Townsley w pts L. Murphy. **Middle:** *prelims:* D. Flintoff (Aberdeen) wo, M. Sangster (Bonnyrigg) wo, J. Day (Springside) wo, D. Hamilton (Croy) wo, D. Stewart (Dunfermline) wo, A. Walker (Arbroath) w pts B. Falcone (Zetland), Jackie Townsley (Cleland) w pts S. Crichton (Blantyre), T. Jenner (Meadowbank) w pts P. Murphy (Springhill); *quarter-finals:* D. Flintoff w pts A. Walker, Jackie Townsley w pts T. Jenner, M. Sangster w pts J. Day, D. Hamilton w pts D. Stewart; *semi-finals:* M. Sangster w pts D. Hamilton, Jackie Townsley w pts D. Flintoff; *final:* M. Sangster w pts Jackie Townsley. **L. Heavy:** *prelims:* J. Wilson (Edinburgh University) wo, a. Fleming (Kingdom) wo, S. McFarlane (Cleland) wo, D. Sharkey (Cambuskenneth) w pts J. Morrison (Caley), S.

Kerr (Lanark) w rsc 2 A. Caulfield (St Francis), L. Powles (Arbroath) w pts M. Todd (Wellmeadow), R. Campbell (Port Glasgow) w pts A. Young (Denbeath), W. Cane (Four Isles) w pts S. Topen (Lochee); *quarter-finals:* J. Wilson w pts A. Fleming, S. McFarlane w pts D. Sharkey, S. Kerr w pts L. Powles, R. Campbell; *semi-finals:* J. Wilson w rsc 2 S. McFarlane, W. Cane w pts S. Kerr; *final:* J. Wilson w pts W. Cane. **Heavy:** *prelims:* I. Longstaff (St Mary's) wo, N. Robertson (Bannockburn) wo, N. Siggs (Perth) wo, J. Reilly (Lochee) wo, A. Kelly (Meadowbank) wo, J. Steele (Blantyre) wo, M. Neil (Osprey) wo, J. Cowie (Bannockburn) w rsc 2 F. McLaughlin (Stirling); *quarter-finals:* I. Longstaff w pts N. Robertson, N. Siggs w pts J. Reilly, A. Kelly w pts J. Steele, M. Neil w pts J. Cowie; *semi-finals:* N. Siggs w pts I. Longstaff, A. Kelly w pts M. Neil; *final:* A. Kelly w pts N. Siggs. **S. Heavy:** *quarter-finals:* C. Brown (Gartcosh) wo, A. McGuire (Perth) wo, G. Evans (Leith) wo, G. Seal (Barn) w co 1 J. Akinlami (Larkhall); *semi-finals:* G. Evans wo G. Seal, C. Brown w co 1 S. McGuire; *final:* C. Brown w pts G. Evans.

Michael Crossan, the 1993 light-flyweight champion from Dennistoun, disappointed at flyweight last season

Les Clark

Welsh Championships, 1993-94

The Afan Lido Sports Centre, Port Talbot - 26 February, The Leisure Centre, Llantwit Major - 12 March, The Tynewydd Labour Club, Treorchy - 16 March & Sophia Gardens, Cardiff - 1 April

L. Fly: *final:* M. Hughes (Gwent) wo. **Fly:** *final:* J. Thomas (Merthyr) w rsc 1 R. Said (St Joseph's). **Bantam:** *semi-finals:* R. Vowles (Llanharan) w rsc 1 D. Davies (Welshpool), H. Jones (Pembroke Dock) w rsc 2 A. Greenaway (Gelligaer); *final:* H. Jones w pts R. Vowles. **Feather:** *final:* J. Cook (Maesteg) w co 2 A. Fletcher (Newtown). **Light:** *semi-finals:* G. Lawrence (Highfields) wo, V. Powell (Army) w rsc 1 G. Howells (Vale); *final:* V. Powell w co 2 G. Lawrence. **L. Welter:** *prelims:* R. Jones (Prince of Wales) wo, L. Winney (Llandudoch) w pts J. Cheal (Preseli), J. Morgan (Cardiff YMCA) w rsc 1 S. John (Garw Valley), M. Smith (Swansea Docks) w dis 3 D. Hartland (Vale), P. Samuels (Crindau) w pts J. Davies (Cwmgorse), P. Feal (Prince of Wales) w dis 2 L. Butler (Llanharan), A. Robinson (Pennar) w rsc 2 P. Chappell (Porthcawl & Pyle), K. Jones (Fleur de Lys) w rsc 2 J. Shahid (Prince of Wales); *quarter-finals:* L. Winney w rsc 2 R. Jones, J. Morgan w rsc 1 M. Smith, P. Samuels w rsc 1 P. Feal, A. Robinson w rsc 1 K. Jones; *semi-finals:* J. Morgan w pts L. Winney, A. Robinson w pts P. Samuels; *final:* A. Robinson w pts J. Morgan. **Welter:** *quarter-finals:* J. Janes (Highfields) wo, P. Killian (Cwmcarn) w rsc 2 J. Williams (Gwent), K. Thomas (Pentwyn) w rsc 2 G. Powell (St Joseph's), R. Padfield (Rhondda) w rsc 3 C. Rees (Garw Valley); *semi-finals:* J. Janes wo R. Padfield, K. Thomas w pts P. Killian; *final:* K. Thomas w rsc 2 J. Janes. **L. Middle:** *prelims:* S. Pepperall (Vale) wo, G. Lovell (Pontypool & Panteg) wo, A. Williams (Abercynon) wo, N. Davies (Merthyr) w co 3 J. Lewis (Welshpool), C. Thomas (Llansamlet) w pts P. Wynne (Prince of Wales), C. Smith (Splott) w co 1 W. Jones (Clywd), D. Williams (Gwent) w pts R. Jones (Hawarden), B. Hayward (Newbridge) w rsc 2 G. Harvey (St Joseph's); *quarter-finals:* S. Pepperall w pts G. Lovell, C. Smith w pts A. Williams, N. Davies w pts D. Williams, B. Hayward w rsc 1 C. Thomas; *semi-finals:* C. Smith w pts S. Pepperall, B. Hayward w dis 3 N. Davies; *final:* B. Hayward w co 3 C. Smith. **Middle:** *prelims:* W. Mpuku (Hawarden) wo, J. Small (Prince of Wales) wo, G. Briggs (Pontypridd) wo, P. Heal (Chepstow) wo, N. Pearce (Splott) w pts J. Robinson (Vale), B. Pritchard (Llangefni) w pts S. Stradling (Rhoose), J. James (Pennar) w co 1 P. Wilkes (Welshpool), M. Trinder (Coed Eva) w pts M. Vowles (Llanharan); *quarter-finals:* G. Briggs w rsc 1 P. Heal, N. Pearce wo B. Pritchard, J. James w pts M. Trinder, W. Mpuku w pts J. Small; *semi-finals:* G. Briggs w co 1 N. Pearce, J. James w pts W. Mpuku; *final:* G. Briggs w co 1 J. James. **L. Heavy:** *prelims:* T. Brown (Idris) wo, H. Price (Roath) wo, M. Durrani (St Joseph's) wo, C. Gibbs (Coed Eva) wo, S. Onyenu (RAOB) wo, M. Tolton (Swansea Docks) wo, L. Hogan (Mold) w pts S. Pritchard (Fleur de Lys), S. Thomas (Shotton) w pts M. Jones (Porthcawl & Pyle); *quarter-finals:* T. Brown w dis 1 H. Price, M. Durrani w pts C. Gibbs, S. Onyenu w dis 3 M. Tolton, S. Thomas w pts L. Hogan; *semi-finals:* T. Brown w pts M. Durrani, S. Onyenu w pts S. Thomas; *final:* T. Brown w dis 3 S. Onyenu. **Heavy:** *quarter-finals:* B. Ludlow (Llanbradach) wo, H. Hartt (Preseli) wo, G. Paders (Crindau) w pts M. Quinn (Premier), B. McCormack (Coed Eva) w pts D. Pippin (Newport); *semi-finals:* B. Ludlow w dis 2 H. Hartt, B. McCormack w rsc 2 G. Paders; *final:* B. McCormack w pts B. Ludlow. **S. Heavy:** *quarter-finals:* H. Jokarzadeh (Roath) wo, K. McCormack (Coed Eva) wo, R. Fenton (Victoria Park) w co 1 S. Weaver (Torfaen), P. Lewis (Mold) w dis 2 A. Griffiths (Trelewis); *semi-finals:* R. Fenton w rsc 1 P. Lewis, K. McCormack w pts H. Jokarzadeh; *final:* K. McCormack w pts R. Fenton.

Welsh lightweight champion for 1994, Vince Powell (right), shown in action against recent professional recruit, Bradley Welsh
Les Clark

British and Irish International Matches and Championships, 1993-94

Internationals

Ireland (6) v England (3)   **National Stadium, Dublin - 29 October**
(Irish names first): **Fly:** D. McKenna l pts S. Parry. **Bantam:** T. Waite w pts G. Nicette. **Light:** P. Ferris l pts A. Temple. **Welter:** N. Gough w pts M. Santini. **Middle:** D. Ryan w pts J. Matthews; D. Galvin w pts D. Starie. **L. Heavy:** P. Deane w pts P. Watts. **Heavy:** P. Douglas l pts S. Burford. **S. Heavy:** D. Corbett w co 1 M. McKenzie.

Norway (3) v England (4)   Oslo, Norway - 13 November
(English names first): **Fly:** D. Costello w pts A. Marius. **L. Welter:** R. Wileman l pts A. Styve; J. Vlasman w pts G. Vestik. **Welter:** C. Bessey w pts T. Vestik. **Middle:** D. Francis l pts T. Hansvold. **L. Heavy:** P. Rogers w pts R. Petajamaa. **Heavy:** M. Ellis l pts P. M. Tronvold.

Ireland (9) v Wales (1)   Downhill Hotel, Ballina - 20 November
(Irish names first): **L. Fly:** J. Prior w pts H. Woods. **Fly:** D. Hosford w pts J. Price. **Bantam:** T. Waite w pts R. Vowles. **Light:** E. Bolger l pts G. Lawrence. **L. Welter:** E. Magee w rsc 2 L. Winney; W. Walsh w pts J. Davies. **Welter:** J. McCormack w pts D. Winney; W. Egan w pts J. Jaynes. **L. Middle:** J. Webb w pts P. Wynn. **L. Heavy:** P. Deane w pts T. Brown.

Young England (4) v Young Scotland (3)   Hilton Hotel, London - 22 November
(English names first): **L. Fly:** R. Sheehan w pts S. Dickson. **Bantam:** S. Oliver w pts R. McPhee. **Feather:** T. Feechan l pts P. Watson. **Light:** A. McLean w rsc 2 G. Fernie; D. Happe w co 1 D. Stewart. **L. Welter:** G. Hopkins l pts J. Docherty. **Welter:** G. Wild l pts A. Wolecki.

Hungary (6) v Ireland (1)   Debrecen, Hungary - 11 December
(Irish names first): **Fly:** D. Hosford l rsc 2 G. Farkis. **Bantam:** T. Waite l pts J. Kovacs. **Feather:** P. Griffin w pts L. Bognor. **Welter:** N. Gough l rsc 3 L. Szabo. **L. Middle:** J. Webb l pts G. Mizsei. **L. Heavy:** S. Kirk l rsc 1 G. Lakata. **S. Heavy:** D. Corbett l pts P. Hart.

Young Hungary (3) v Young Ireland (1)   Debrecen, Hungary - 11 December
(Irish names first): **Feather:** T. Carlyle w pts Z. Pinter. **Light:** J. Morrissey l pts V. Balogh. **Welter:** W. Egan l pts K. Gregerik. **Middle:** T. Donnelly l pts Z. Chelbik.

Wales (3) v Scotland (6)   Springfield Hotel, Holywell - 14 January
(Welsh names first): **L. Fly:** H. Woods w pts L. Munro. **Bantam:** R. Vowles l pts R. McPhee. **Feather:** H. Jones l rsc 2 P. Watson. **Light:** G. Lawrence w co 2 G. Hughes. **L. Welter:** J. Davies l pts J. Pender. **Welter:** K. Thomas l pts A. Wolecki. **L. Middle:** D. Williams l pts J. Townsley. **L. Heavy:** T. Brown l pts W. Cane. **Heavy:** H. Hartt w dis 1 I. Longstaff.

Young England (2) v Young Ireland (6)   Royal Lancaster Hotel, London - 7 February
(English names first): **L. Fly:** C. Rumble l pts L. Cunningham; R. Sheehan l rsc 3 P. Phelan. **Feather:** L. Eedle l pts C. Meredith. **Light:** D. Happe w rsc 1 M. Blaney. **L. Welter:** J. Hare w pts A.

Dunne. **Welter:** P. Larner l pts D. Devers. **Middle:** B. Stevens l pts B. Crowley. **L. Heavy:** D. Coates l rtd 2 C. O'Grady.

Scotland (5) v Wales (5)   Beach Ballroom, Aberdeen - 12 April
(Scottish names first): **Fly:** S. Dickson w pts J. Thomas. **Bantam:** R. McPhee w pts R. Vowles. **Feather:** M. Simpson l rsc 1 J. Price. **Light:** M. Gowans l rsc 3 V. Powell. **L. Welter:** G. McLevy l pts A Robinson. **Welter:** A. McDonald w pts K. Thomas. **L. Middle:** A. Craig w pts B. Hayward; B. Laidlaw l pts S. Pepperall. **Middle:** D. Flintoff l rsc 1 G. Briggs. **L. Heavy:** J. Wilson w pts T. Brown.

Scotland (5) v Wales (7)   Angus Hotel, Dundee - 14 April
(Scottish names first): **L. Fly:** L. Munro l rsc 1 M. Hughes. **Fly:** P. Shepherd w pts J. Thomas. **Bantam:** A. Brennan w pts R. Vowles. **Feather:** R. Hay l pts J. Cook; P. Watson l pts J. Price. **Light:** J. Coyle l pts V. Powell. **L. Welter:** J. Pender w pts P. Sammuels. **Welter:** A Wolecki w pts K. Thomas. **L. Middle:** J. Townsley w pts B. Hayward; C. Edmonds l pts S. Pepperall. **Middle:** M. Sangster l pts G. Briggs. **L. Heavy:** S. Kerr l pts T. Brown.

Ireland (7) v USA (4)   National Stadium, Dublin - 29 April
(Irish names first): **L. Fly:** J. Prior w pts D. Carey. **Fly:** D. McKenna l pts M. O'Malley. **Bantam:** T. Waite l pts S. Hernandez. **Feather:** P. Ireland w pts F. Sepulveda. **Light:** G. Stephens l pts T. Cauthen. **L. Welter:** W. Walsh w pts F. Samad. **Welter:** N. Gough w pts J. Corn. **L. Middle:** J. Webb w pts J. Archuleta. **Middle:** D. Galvin w pts S. Swartz. **L. Heavy:** G. Joyce l pts A Stewart. **Heavy:** P. Douglas w pts M. Simpkins.

Holland (3) v Ireland (4)   Rotterdam, Holland - 15 May
(Irish names first): **Light:** E. Bolger l pts A. Santana. **L. Welter:** W. Walsh l pts N. Amine. **Welter:** N. Gough l pts H. Janssen; N. Sinclair l pts H. Doorenbosch. **L. Heavy:** P. Deane l pts E. van der Heuvel; A. Sheerin w pts W. Sterkenberg. **Heavy:** P. Douglas w rsc 2 R. Weigerse.

Championships

European Games   Bursa, Turkey - 7 to 12 September
L. Fly: M. Hughes (Wales) l pts H. Mamedov (Azerbaijan). **Fly:** K. Knox (Scotland) l pts V. Nyman (Israel); D. Kelly (Ireland) l pts A. Pakey (Russia); P. Ingle (England) w pts M. Ishankulov (Belarus), l rsc 3 V. Nyman (Israel). **Bantam:** P. Shepherd (Scotland) l pts A. Kazandjan (Armenia). **Feather:** B. Carr (Scotland) l pts V. Goncharov (Ukraine); P. Griffin (Ireland) w pts L. Bognar (Hungary), w pts F. Sygmund (Germany), w pts I. Chornei (Moldova), withdrew injured. **Light:** M. Winters (Ireland) l pts V. Issever (Turkey); B. Welsh (Scotland) l dis 3 S. Orest (Ukraine); A. Temple (England) l pts S. Scriabin (Moldova). **L. Welter:** J. Williams (Wales) l pts N. Suleymanogiu (Turkey); E. Magee (Ireland) l rsc 3 K. Tchikvinitse (Georgia); P. Richardson (England) w rtd 2 M Gowans (Scotland), l pts N. Suleymanogiu (Turkey). **L. Middle:** D. Starie (England) l pts R. Sarganessian (Armenia). **L. Heavy:** K. Oliver (England) l rsc 1 S. Samilsan (Turkey). **Heavy:** D. Williams (England) w rtd 1 E. Barjic (Bosnia), w rsc 2 D. Karpekov (Ukraine), l co 1 P. Dondiago (Holland). **S. Heavy:** K. McCormack (Wales) w pts S. Jankovic (Yugoslavia), w rsc 1 O. Belikov (Ukraine), l pts S. Rusinov (Bulgaria).

European Junior Games   Salonika, Greece - 27 September to 2 October

L. Fly: M. Crossan (Scotland) l dis 2 J. Zajaczkowski (Poland). **Fly:** O. Duddy (Ireland) w pts M. Samarin (Russia), l rsc 2 J. Nagy (Hungary); D. Costello (England) w pts E. Karakoc (Turkey), w rsc 2 A. Bonev (Bulgaria), l pts R. Husseinov (Azerbaijan). **Bantam:** L. Sharpe (Scotland) l co 1 A. Korneev (Russia); A Patterson (IRL) w pts S. Nieva (Sweden), l co 1 V. Gavriliouk (Moldova). **Feather:** G. Hibbert (England) l pts B. Sogomonian (Armenia); P. Watson (Scotland) l pts P. Podlas (Poland); J. Cook (Wales) w pts S. Ostroshapkin (Belarus), l pts V. Kvasiouk (Moldova). **Light:** G. Lawrence (Wales) w pts V. Borov (Moldova); J. Morrissey (Ireland) w pts M. Masar (Yugoslavia), w pts G. Lawrence (Wales), l pts M. Yikealo (Sweden); J. Coyle (Scotland) w pts I. Khadarovitch (Latvia), w pts J. Stastny (Czechoslovakia), l rsc 1 O. Sergeev (Russia). **Welter:** A. Wolecki (Scotland) l pts M. Sokol (Poland); W. Egan (Ireland) w pts G. Wild (England), l pts C. Bladt (Denmark). **L. Middle:** L. Murphy (Scotland) l pts S. Bozic (Croatia); B. Magee (Ireland) w pts J. Guest (England), l pts E. Makarenko (Russia). **Middle:** B. Crowley (Ireland) w pts M. Smith (England), l pts D. Droukovski (Russia). **L. Heavy:** A. Dowling (England) w rsc 2 S. Nebrigic (Yugoslavia), l pts C. Tischler (Germany).

Commonwealth Games   Victoria, Canada - 19 to 27 August

L. Fly: C. Moffett (N. Ireland) l pts B. Sah (India); L. Munro (Scotland) l rsc 2 A. Kassim (Uganda). **Fly:** D. Kelly (N. Ireland) w pts C. Scott (Canada); D. Costello (England) w pts H. Gereo-Darelson (Papua New Guinea), w pts D. Kelly (N. Ireland); P. Shepherd (Scotland) w pts M. Mbwana (Tanzania), w pts E. Osiobe (Nigeria), w pts D. Costello (England), w pts D. Karanja (Kenya). **Bantam:** R. McPhee (Scotland) l pts A. Chongo (Zambia); T. Waite (N. Ireland) w pts C. Lambert (Canada), l pts O. Odutayo (Nigeria); R. Vowles (Wales) w rsc 2 C. Towo (Zimbabwe); S. Oliver (England) w rsc 2 G. Taniveke (Solomon Islands), w pts R. Vowles (Wales), l pts R. Peden (Australia). **Feather:** B. Carr (Scotland) l pts A. Katiti (Namibia); D. Pithie (England) l rsc 2 M. Hassan (Tanzania); A. Patterson (N. Ireland) l rsc 2 C. Patton (Canada); J. Cook (Wales) w pts F. Passingan (Papua New Guinea), w pts A. Daniel (Nigeria), w pts M. Hassan (Tanzania), l pts C. Patton (Canada). **Light:** J. Coyle (Scotland) l pts J. Zabackly (Australia); A. Green (England) l rsc 1 K. Fiaui (New Zealand); G. Lawrence (Wales) w pts B. Carnagie (Jamaica); M. Reneghan (N. Ireland) w pts H. Kungsi (Papua New Guinea), w pts G. Lawrence (Wales), w pts A. Hussain (Pakistan), l pts M. Strange (Canada). **L. Welter:** A. Robinson (Wales) w pts J. Ditlhabang (Botswana), l pts D. Fulanse (Zambia); J. Pender (Scotland) w pts F. Muwonge (Uganda), w pts D. Bernard (Jamaica), l rsc 1 T. Moro (Ghana); M. Winters (N. Ireland) w pts I. Kamukuju (Namibia), w pts S. Carr (S. Africa), w pts T. Shailer (New Zealand); P. Richardson (England) w pts J. Pagendam (Canada), w pts D. Fulanse (Zambia), w pts T. Moro (Ghana), w pts M. Winters (N. Ireland). **Welter:** K. Thomas (Wales) w rsc 3 R. Njie (Gambia); P. Burns (England) w pts J. Mestre (S. Africa), l pts W. Fleming (Canada); N. Sinclair (N. Ireland) w rsc 2 A. Wolecki (Scotland), w rsc 1 K. Thomas (Wales), w rsc 2 R. Rowles (Australia), w pts E. Albert (Nigeria). **L. Middle:** J. Townsley (Scotland) w rsc 2 E. Barnes (Cayman Islands), w pts A. Ishmael (Ghana), l pts R. Gasio (W. Samoa); J. Webb (N. Ireland) w pts S. Connell (Australia), wo R. Cadeau (Seychelles), w pts R. Gasio (W. Samoa). **Middle:** G. Briggs (Wales) l pts R. Donaldson (Canada); D. Ryan (N. Ireland) l pts P. Wanyoike (Kenya). **L. Heavy:** S. Kirk (N. Ireland) w pts D. Lungu (Zimbabwe), l pts F. Mabiletsa (Botswana); K. Oliver (England) w pts J. Crawford (Australia); J. Wilson (Scotland) w pts J. Ayiro (Uganda), w pts K. Oliver (England), w pts F. Mabiletsa (Botswana), l rsc 1 D. Brown (Canada). **Heavy:** P. Douglas (N. Ireland) l pts O. Ahmed (Kenya). **S. Heavy:** K. McCormack (Wales) l co 1 D. Dokiwari (Nigeria); D. Williams (England) w pts S. Hinton (Canada), l pts D. Dokiwari (Nigeria).

A regular England international, until turning pro in 1994, Alan Temple (right) is shown here winning last season's ABA light-welterweight title

Les Clark

British Junior Championship Finals, 1993-94

National Association of Boy's Clubs

Mayfair Suite, Newcastle - 13 May
Class A: 42 kg: C. Johanneson (Burmantofts) w pts J. Evans (Chichester). 45 kg: P. Croll (St Paul's) w pts T. Brocklebank (Canvey). 48 kg: J. Harvey (Wednesbury w pts G. Algar. 51 kg: K. Fox (Bracebridge) w pts B. Doherty (Dale). 54 kg: J. Biggerstaff (Dale) w pts C. Skelton (Hartlepool Catholic). 57 kg: N. Lee (Repton) w pts G. Earl (Luton High Town). 60 kg: R. Hatton (Sale West) w rsc 3 R. Beck (Repton). 63.5 kg: D. Mahoney (Highfield) w rsc 2 Y. Idris (Birmingham). 67 kg: G. Hutchon (Battersea) w dis 3 J. Lee (Desborough). 71 kg: J. Smith (Foley) w co 1 J. Gharu (Repton).

Marriott Hotel, Bristol - 6 May
Class B: 45 kg: J. Booth (Radford) w pts J. Martin (Canvey). 48 kg: P. Jones (Nottingham GG) w pts C. Rumble (St Mary's). 51 kg:J. Rooney (Hartlepool Catholic) w rsc 3 G. Wood (Brighton). 54 kg: K. Lear (West Ham) w pts J. Betts (St Paul's). 57 kg: W. Nuurah (Devonport) w pts S. Elwell (Wednesbury). 60 kg: R. Bangher (Bedford) w pts S. Bowes (Battersea). 63.5 kg: R. Dakin-Weston (Highfields) w pts M. Clark (Grangetown). 67 kg: F. Doherty (Islington & Finsbury) w pts M. Jennings (Litherland). 71 kg: N. Linford (Belgrave) w rsc 3 T. Doherty (Islington & Finsbury). 74 kg: G. Diggins (Foley) w pts D. Toas (Shildon). 77 kg: D. Coats (Highfield) w pts M. Lacey (Manby).

Hilton Hotel, Mayfair - 9 May
Class C: 48 kg: R. Sheehan (Lion) wo. 51 kg: J. Perkins (Highfields) w pts I. Hussain (Birmingham). 54 kg: E. Pickering (RHP) w pts M. Bush (West Ham). 57 kg: N. Coe (Hornchurch & Elm Park) w pts M. Payne (Bell Green). 60 kg: D. Walker (Fisher) w rsc 1 C. Wall (Gemini). 63.5 kg: J. Hare (Batley & Dewsbury) w pts D. James (Phoenix). 67 kg: H. Sheeraz (Pinewood Starr) w pts P. Larner (Bognor). 71 kg: M. Takalo-Bighashi (Margate) w rsc 2 D. Rhodes (Hunslet). 75 kg: C. Wake (Shildon) w pts A. Coward (All Stars). 81 kg: M. Krence (St Michael's) w pts S. Ashford (Exeter). 91 kg: S. Honeywell (Rayleigh Mill) w pts D. Clark (Grangetown).

Schools

Aston Villa Leisure Centre, Birmingham - 26 March
Junior A: 32 kg: B. Pryce (Newbridge) w pts D. Cook (Hornchurch & Elm Park). 34 kg: S. Matthews (Waterloo) w pts B. Tokeley (Clacton). 36 kg: M. Burke (Newham) w pts S. Truscott (South Bank). 39 kg: H. Lee (Canterbury) w pts D. Power (South Bank). 42 kg: C. Johnson (Chesterfield) w pts C. Brown (Bracknell). 45 kg: D. Thomas (Harlepool Catholic) w pts M. McLaughlin (Luton High Town). 48 kg: R. Wood (Pleck) w pts W. Bayliss (Phoenix). 51 kg: D. Smith (Partington) w pts G. Smith (Foley). 54 kg: S. Rushton (Penhill) w pts A. Khan (Sedbergh). 57 kg: G. Metcalf (Stockton) w co 2 R. Welsh (Cambridge & Soham).

Junior B: 36 kg: N. Cook (Hornchurch & Elm Park) w pts R. Nelson (Batley & Dewsbury). 39 kg: J. Cronin (Old Vic) w pts S. Symes (West Hill). 42 kg: D. Mulholland (Transport) w pts D. Fearon (St George's). 45 kg: D. Carter (Hartlepool BW) w dis 3 J. McKay (Newham). 48 kg: M. Power (St Pancras) w pts G. Monaghan (Lanbradach). 51 kg: N. Smith (Birmingham) w pts A. Johnstone (Bracknell). 54 kg: L. Tute

(Moss Side) w pts M. Hickman (Titchfield). 57 kg: L. Coates (Medway GG) w co 2 C. Lamb (Roath). 60 kg: W. Curwood (St Paul's) w pts J. Gunn (Canvey). 63 kg: A. Dodson (Gemini) w rsc 2 D. Wood (Dereham). 66 kg: G. Simpson (Old Vic) w pts P. Pierson (Trojan Police).

Intermediate: 39 kg: D. Pryce (Newbridge) w pts J. O'Sullivan (Medway GG). 42 kg: M. Woodward (Highfields) wo G. Steadman (West Ham). 45 kg: P. Croll (St Paul's) w pts J. McDonagh (Dale). 48 kg: V. Lynes (Hornchurch & Elm Park) w pts T. Rowley (Hartlepool BW). 51 kg: B. Doherty (Dale) w pts C. Adams (Gilfach Goch). 54 kg: M. Lomax (West Ham) w pts J. Fletcher (Batley & Dewsbury). 57 kg: R. Beck (Repton) w pts K. Kavanagh (Austin Rover). 60 kg: R. Hatton (Sale West) w co 1 S. Purdie (Canterbury). 63 kg: D. Mahoney (Highfield) w pts J. Marsden (Teams). 66 kg: A. Larkins (Bracknell) w pts R. Rooney (Croxteth). 69 kg: D. Short (Barry) w rsc 2 S. Akers (Dinnington).

Senior: 42 kg: J. Booth (Radford) w pts D. Craft (Ruislip). 45 kg: S. Green (Islington & Finsbury) w pts B. Pryce (Newbridge). 48 kg: C. Williams (Merthyr) w pts C. Rumble (St Mary's). 51 kg: J. Rooney (Hartlepool Catholic) w rsc 1 M. O'Callaghan (West Ham). 54 kg: J. Betts (St Paul's) w pts M. McDonagh (Lynn). 57 kg: S. Elwell (Wednesbury) w pts N. Lee (Repton). 60 kg: S. Rees (Gilfach Goch) w co 2 J. Read (Foley). 63.5 kg: M. Jennings (Chorley) w pts A. Coates (Medway GG). 67 kg: D. Real (Henry Street) w dis 3 G. Hutchon (Battersea). 71 kg: N. Linford (Belgrave) w co 1 D. Frost (Leigh Park). 75 kg: G. Diggins (Foley) w pts D. Wright (Dewsbury & Batley).

ABA Youth

York Hall, Bethnal Green, London - 4 December
Class A: 42 kg: M. Hunter (Hartlepool BW) w rsc 1 N. Fagan (Leigh Park). 45 kg: A. Woods (Tower Hill) w pts T. Brocklebank (Canvey). 48 kg: S. Hodgson (Shildon) w rsc 1 A. Farrow (Colchester). 51 kg: B. Doherty (Dale) w pts J. Rooney (Hartlepool Catholic). 54 kg: A. Kelly (Darlington) w pts D. Brown (March). 57 kg: R. Beck (Repton) wo R. Hatton (Sale West). 60 kg: J. Read (Foley) w pts D. Reynolds (Market District). 63.5 kg: A. Coates (Medway GG) w rsc 1 A. Stones (Langley Spartan). 67 kg: S. Burke (Sefton) w rsc 2 J. Cole (Repton). 71 kg: H. Smith (Avalon) w rsc 2 D. Robinson (Willy Freund).

Class B: 42 kg: J. Booth (Radford) w pts S. Conway (Batley & Dewsbury). 45 kg: M. Thompson (Phil Thomas SOB) w pts S. Green (Islington & Finsbury). 48 kg: C. Rumble (St Mary's) w pts M. O'Gara (Old Vic). 51 kg: J. Nightingale (Wednesbury) w pts K. Cawley (St Pancras). 54 kg: M. McDonagh (Lynn) w pts M. Armstrong (Moston & Collyhurst). 57 kg: J. Gould (Wednesbury) w pts R. Bangher (Bedford). 63.5 kg: M. Jennings (Chorley) w pts J. Harrison (Saxon). 67 kg: M. Barr (Kingston) w rsc 1 R. Smith (Wednesbury). 71 kg: N. Linford (Belgrave) w pts D. Doyle (Belhus Park). 74 kg: L. Shepherd (Didcott) w rsc 1 R. Chandler (Leigh Park). 77 kg: D. Coates (Highfield, Kent) and M. Jones (Barking) both dis 2.

ABA Champions, 1881-1994

Sefton's Gary Jones leaps for joy on being announced as the 1994 ABA champion at light-flyweight   Les Clark

L. Flyweight
1971 M. Abrams
1972 M. Abrams
1973 M. Abrams
1974 C. Magri
1975 M. Lawless
1976 P. Fletcher
1977 P. Fletcher
1978 J. Dawson
1979 J. Dawson
1980 T. Barker
1981 J. Lyon
1982 J. Lyon
1983 J. Lyon
1984 J. Lyon
1985 M. Epton
1986 M. Epton
1987 M. Epton
1988 M. Cantwell
1989 M. Cantwell
1990 N. Tooley
1991 P. Culshaw
1992 D. Fifield
1993 M. Hughes
1994 G. Jones

Flyweight
1920 H. Groves
1921 W. Cuthbertson
1922 E. Warwick
1923 L. Tarrant
1924 E. Warwick
1925 E. Warwick
1926 J. Hill
1927 J. Roland
1928 C. Taylor
1929 T. Pardoe
1930 T. Pardoe
1931 T. Pardoe
1932 T. Pardoe
1933 T. Pardoe
1934 P. Palmer
1935 G. Fayaud
1936 G. Fayaud
1937 P. O'Donaghue
1938 A. Russell
1939 D. McKay
1944 A. Avent
1945 J. Bryce
1946 R. Gallacher
1947 J. Clinton
1948 H. Carpenter
1949 H. Riley
1950 A. Jones

1951 G. John
1952 D. Dower
1953 R. Currie
1954 R. Currie
1955 D. Lloyd
1956 T. Spinks
1957 R. Davies
1958 J. Brown
1959 M. Gushlow
1960 D. Lee
1961 W. McGowan
1962 M. Pye
1963 M. Laud
1964 J. McCluskey
1965 J. McCluskey
1966 P. Maguire
1967 S. Curtis
1968 J. McGonigle
1969 D. Needham
1970 D. Needham
1971 P. Wakefield
1972 M. O'Sullivan
1973 R. Hilton
1974 M. O'Sullivan
1975 C. Magri
1976 C. Magri
1977 C. Magri
1978 G. Nickels
1979 R. Gilbody
1980 K. Wallace
1981 K. Wallace
1982 J. Kelly
1983 S. Nolan
1984 P. Clinton
1985 P. Clinton
1986 J. Lyon
1987 J. Lyon
1988 J. Lyon
1989 J. Lyon
1990 J. Armour
1991 P. Ingle
1992 K. Knox
1993 P. Ingle
1994 D. Costello

Bantamweight
1884 A. Woodward
1885 A. Woodward
1886 T. Isley
1887 T. Isley
1888 H. Oakman
1889 H. Brown
1890 J. Rowe
1891 E. Moore
1892 F. Godbold
1893 E. Watson
1894 P. Jones
1895 P. Jones
1896 P. Jones
1897 C. Lamb
1898 F. Herring
1899 A. Avent
1900 J. Freeman
1901 W. Morgan
1902 A. Miner
1903 H. Perry
1904 H. Perry
1905 W. Webb

1906 T. Ringer
1907 E. Adams
1908 H. Thomas
1909 J. Condon
1910 W. Webb
1911 W. Allen
1912 W. Allen
1913 A. Wye
1914 W. Allen
1919 W. Allen
1920 G. McKenzie
1921 L. Tarrant
1922 W. Boulding
1923 A. Smith
1924 L. Tarrant
1925 A. Goom
1926 F. Webster
1927 E. Warwick
1928 J. Garland
1929 F. Bennett
1930 H. Mizler
1931 F. Bennett
1932 J. Treadaway
1933 G. Johnston
1934 A. Barnes
1935 L. Case
1936 A. Barnes
1937 A. Barnes
1938 J. Pottinger
1939 R. Watson
1944 R. Bissell
1945 P. Brander
1946 C. Squire
1947 D. O'Sullivan
1948 T. Profitt
1949 T. Miller
1950 K. Lawrence
1951 T. Nicholls
1952 T. Nicholls
1953 J. Smillie
1954 J. Smillie
1955 G. Dormer
1956 O. Reilly
1957 J. Morrissey
1958 H. Winstone
1959 D. Weller
1960 F. Taylor
1961 P. Benneyworth
1962 P. Benneyworth
1963 B. Packer
1964 B. Packer
1965 R. Mallon
1966 J. Clark
1967 M. Carter
1968 M. Carter
1969 M. Piner
1970 A. Oxley
1971 G. Turpin
1972 G. Turpin
1973 P. Cowdell
1974 S. Ogilvie
1975 S. Ogilvie
1976 J. Bambrick
1977 J. Turner
1978 J. Turner
1979 R. Ashton
1980 R. Gilbody
1981 P. Jones

1982 R. Gilbody	
1983 J. Hyland	
1984 J. Hyland	
1985 S. Murphy	
1986 S. Murphy	
1987 J. Sillitoe	
1988 K. Howlett	
1989 K. Howlett	
1990 P. Lloyd	
1991 D. Hardie	
1992 P. Mullings	
1993 R. Evatt	
1994 S. Oliver	

Featherweight

1881 T. Hill
1882 T. Hill
1883 T. Hill
1884 E. Hutchings
1885 J. Pennell
1886 T. McNeil
1887 J. Pennell
1888 J. Taylor
1889 G. Belsey
1890 G. Belsey
1891 F. Curtis
1892 F. Curtis
1893 T. Davidson
1894 R. Gunn
1895 R. Gunn
1896 R. Gunn
1897 N. Smith
1898 P. Lunn
1899 J. Scholes
1900 R. Lee
1901 C. Clarke
1902 C. Clarke
1903 J. Godfrey
1904 C. Morris
1905 H. Holmes
1906 A. Miner
1907 C. Morris
1908 T. Ringer
1909 A. Lambert
1910 C. Houghton
1911 H. Bowers
1912 G. Baker
1913 G. Baker
1914 G. Baker
1919 G. Baker
1920 J. Fleming
1921 G. Baker
1922 E. Swash
1923 E. Swash
1924 A. Beavis
1925 A. Beavis
1926 R. Minshull
1927 F. Webster
1928 F. Meachem
1929 F. Meachem
1930 J. Duffield
1931 B. Caplan
1932 H. Mizler
1933 J. Walters
1934 J. Treadaway
1935 E. Ryan
1936 J. Treadaway
1937 A. Harper
1938 C. Gallie
1939 C. Gallie
1944 D. Sullivan
1945 J. Carter

1946 P. Brander
1947 S. Evans
1948 P. Brander
1949 H. Gilliland
1950 P. Brander
1951 J. Travers
1952 P. Lewis
1953 P. Lewis
1954 D. Charnley
1955 T. Nicholls
1956 T. Nicholls
1957 M. Collins
1958 M. Collins
1959 G. Judge
1960 P. Lundgren
1961 P. Cheevers
1962 B. Wilson
1963 A. Riley
1964 R. Smith
1965 K. Buchanan
1966 H. Baxter
1967 K. Cooper
1968 J. Cheshire
1969 A. Richardson
1970 D. Polak
1971 T. Wright
1972 K. Laing
1973 J. Lynch
1974 G. Gilbody
1975 R. Beaumont
1976 P. Cowdell
1977 P. Cowdell
1978 M. O'Brien
1979 P. Hanlon
1980 M. Hanif
1981 P. Hanlon
1982 H. Henry
1983 P. Bradley
1984 K. Taylor
1985 F. Havard
1986 P. Hodkinson
1987 P. English
1988 D. Anderson
1989 P. Richardson
1990 B. Carr
1991 J. Irwin
1992 A. Temple
1993 J. Cook
1994 D. Pithie

Lightweight

1881 F. Hobday
1882 A. Bettinson
1883 A. Diamond
1884 A. Diamond
1885 A. Diamond
1886 G. Roberts
1887 J. Hair
1888 A. Newton
1889 W. Neale
1890 A. Newton
1891 E. Dettmer
1892 E. Dettmer
1893 W. Campbell
1894 W. Campbell
1895 A. Randall
1896 A. Vanderhout
1897 A. Vanderhout
1898 H. Marks
1899 H. Brewer
1900 G. Humphries
1901 A. Warner
1902 A. Warner

1903 H. Fergus
1904 M. Wells
1905 M. Wells
1906 M. Wells
1907 M. Wells
1908 H. Holmes
1909 F. Grace
1910 T. Tees
1911 A. Spenceley
1912 R. Marriott
1913 R. Grace
1914 R. Marriott
1919 F. Grace
1920 F. Grace
1921 G. Shorter
1922 G. Renouf
1923 G. Shorter
1924 W. White
1925 E. Viney
1926 T. Slater
1927 W. Hunt
1928 F. Webster
1929 W. Hunt
1930 J. Waples
1931 D. McCleave
1932 F. Meachem
1933 H. Mizler
1934 J. Rolland
1935 F. Frost
1936 F. Simpson
1937 A. Danahar
1938 T. McGrath
1939 H. Groves
1944 W. Thompson
1945 J. Williamson
1946 E. Thomas
1947 C. Morrissey
1948 R. Cooper
1949 A. Smith
1950 R. Latham
1951 R. Hinson
1952 F. Reardon
1953 D. Hinson
1954 G. Whelan
1955 S. Coffey
1956 R. McTaggart
1957 J. Kidd
1958 R. McTaggart
1959 P. Warwick
1960 R. McTaggart
1961 P. Warwick
1962 B. Whelan
1963 B. O'Sullivan
1964 J. Dunne
1965 A. White
1966 J. Head
1967 T. Waller
1968 J. Watt
1969 H. Hayes
1970 N. Cole
1971 J. Singleton
1972 N. Cole
1973 T. Dunn
1974 J. Lynch
1975 P. Cowdell
1976 S. Mittee
1977 G. Gilbody
1978 T. Marsh
1979 G. Gilbody
1980 G. Gilbody
1981 G. Gilbody
1982 J. McDonnell
1983 K. Willis

1984 A. Dickson
1985 E. McAuley
1986 J. Jacobs
1987 M. Ayers
1988 C. Kane
1989 M. Ramsey
1990 P. Gallagher
1991 P. Ramsey
1992 D. Amory
1993 B. Welsh

L. Welterweight

1951 W. Connor
1952 P. Waterman
1953 D. Hughes
1954 G. Martin
1955 F. McQuillan
1956 D. Stone
1957 D. Stone
1958 R. Kane
1959 R. Kane
1960 R. Day
1961 B. Brazier
1962 B. Brazier
1963 R. McTaggart
1964 R. Taylor
1965 R. McTaggart
1966 W. Hiatt
1967 B. Hudspeth
1968 E. Cole
1969 J. Stracey
1970 D. Davies
1971 M. Kingwell
1972 T. Waller
1973 N. Cole
1974 P. Kelly
1975 J. Zeraschi
1976 C. McKenzie
1977 J. Douglas
1978 D. Williams
1979 E. Copeland
1980 A. Willis
1981 A. Willis
1982 A. Adams
1983 D. Dent
1984 D. Griffiths
1985 I. Mustafa
1986 J. Alsop
1987 A. Holligan
1988 A. Hall
1989 A. Hall
1990 J. Pender
1991 J. Matthews
1992 D. McCarrick
1993 P. Richardson
1994 A. Temple

Welterweight

1920 F. Whitbread
1921 A. Ireland
1922 E. White
1923 P. Green
1924 P. O'Hanrahan
1925 P. O'Hanrahan
1926 B. Marshall
1927 H. Dunn
1928 H. Bone
1929 T. Wigmore
1930 F. Brooman
1931 J. Barry
1932 D. McCleave
1933 P. Peters

1934 D. McCleave
1935 D. Lynch
1936 W. Pack
1937 D. Lynch
1938 C. Webster
1939 R. Thomas
1944 H. Hall
1945 R. Turpin
1946 J. Ryan
1947 J. Ryan
1948 M. Shacklady
1949 A. Buxton
1950 T. Ratcliffe
1951 J. Maloney
1952 J. Maloney
1953 L. Morgan
1954 N. Gargano
1955 N. Gargano
1956 N. Gargano
1957 R. Warnes
1958 B. Nancurvis
1959 J. McGrail
1960 C. Humphries
1961 A. Lewis
1962 J. Pritchett
1963 J. Pritchett
1964 M. Varley
1965 P. Henderson
1966 P. Cragg
1967 D. Cranswick
1968 A. Tottoh
1969 T. Henderson
1970 T. Waller
1971 D. Davies
1972 T. Francis
1973 T. Waller
1974 T. Waller
1975 W. Bennett
1976 C. Jones
1977 C. Jones
1978 E. Byrne
1979 J. Frost
1980 T. Marsh
1981 T. Marsh
1982 C. Pyatt
1983 R. McKenley
1984 M. Hughes
1985 E. McDonald
1986 D. Dyer
1987 M. Elliot
1988 M. McCreath
1989 M. Elliot
1990 A. Carew
1991 J. Calzaghe
1992 M. Santini
1993 C. Bessey
1994 K. Short

L. Middleweight

1951 A. Lay
1952 B. Foster
1953 B. Wells
1954 B. Wells
1955 B. Foster
1956 J. McCormack
1957 J. Cunningham
1958 S. Pearson
1959 S. Pearson
1960 W. Fisher
1961 J. Gamble
1962 J. Lloyd

1963 A. Wyper	**Middleweight**	1912 E. Chandler	1952 T. Gooding	1984 B. Schumacher
1964 W. Robinson	1881 T. Bellhouse	1913 W. Bradley	1953 R. Barton	1985 D. Cronin
1965 P. Dwyer	1882 A. H. Curnick	1914 H. Brown	1954 K. Phillips	1986 N. Benn
1966 T. Imrie	1883 A. J. Curnick	1919 H. Mallin	1955 F. Hope	1987 R. Douglas
1967 A. Edwards	1884 W. Brown	1920 H. Mallin	1956 R. Redrup	1988 M. Edwards
1968 E. Blake	1885 M. Salmon	1921 H. Mallin	1957 P. Burke	1989 S. Johnson
1969 T. Imrie	1886 W. King	1922 H. Mallin	1958 P. Hill	1990 S. Wilson
1970 D. Simmonds	1887 R. Hair	1923 H. Mallin	1959 F. Elderfield	1991 M. Edwards
1971 A. Edwards	1888 R. Hair	1924 J. Elliot	1960 R. Addison	1992 L. Woolcock
1972 L. Paul	1889 G. Sykes	1925 J. Elliot	1961 J. Caiger	1993 J. Calzaghe
1973 R. Maxwell	1890 J. Hoare	1926 F. P. Crawley	1962 A. Matthews	1994 D. Starie
1974 R. Maxwell	1891 J. Steers	1927 F. P. Crawley	1963 A. Matthews	
1975 A. Harrison	1892 J. Steers	1928 F. Mallin	1964 W. Stack	**L. Heavyweight**
1976 W. Lauder	1893 J. Steers	1929 F. Mallin	1965 W. Robinson	1920 H. Franks
1977 C. Malarkey	1894 W. Sykes	1930 F. Mallin	1966 C. Finnegan	1921 L. Collett
1978 E. Henderson	1895 G. Townsend	1931 F. Mallin	1967 A. Ball	1922 H. Mitchell
1979 D. Brewster	1896 W. Ross	1932 F. Mallin	1968 P. McCann	1923 H. Mitchell
1980 J. Price	1897 W. Dees	1933 A. Shawyer	1969 D. Wallington	1924 H. Mitchell
1981 E. Christie	1898 G. Townsend	1934 J. Magill	1970 J. Conteh	1925 H. Mitchell
1982 D. Milligan	1899 R. Warnes	1935 J. Magill	1971 A. Minter	1926 D. McCorkindale
1983 R. Douglas	1900 E. Mann	1936 A. Harrington	1972 F. Lucas	1927 A. Jackson
1984 R. Douglas	1901 R. Warnes	1937 M. Dennis	1973 F. Lucas	1928 A. Jackson
1985 R. Douglas	1902 E. Mann	1938 H. Tiller	1974 D. Odwell	1929 J. Goyder
1986 T. Velinor	1903 R. Warnes	1939 H. Davies	1975 D. Odwell	1930 J. Murphy
1987 N. Brown	1904 E. Mann	1944 J. Hockley	1976 E. Burke	1931 J. Petersen
1988 W. Ellis	1905 J. Douglas	1945 R. Parker	1977 R. Davies	1932 J. Goyder
1989 N. Brown	1906 A. Murdock	1946 R. Turpin	1978 H. Graham	1933 G. Brennan
1990 T. Taylor	1907 R. Warnes	1947 R. Agland	1979 N. Wilshire	1934 G. Brennan
1991 T. Taylor	1908 W. Child	1948 J. Wright	1980 M. Kaylor	1935 R. Hearns
1992 J. Calzaghe	1909 W. Child	1949 S. Lewis	1981 B. Schumacher	1936 J. Magill
1993 D. Starie	1910 R. Warnes	1950 P. Longo	1982 J. Price	1937 J. Wilby
1994 W. Alexander	1911 W. Child	1951 E. Ludlam	1983 T. Forbes	1938 A. S. Brown

Steve Burford (right) shown on his way to a clear points victory over Israel Ajose in the 1994 ABA heavyweight final   Les Clark

1939 B. Woodcock	1978 V. Smith	1897 G. Townsend	1936 V. Stuart	1975 G. McEwan
1944 E. Shackleton	1979 A. Straughn	1898 G. Townsend	1937 V. Stuart	1976 J. Rafferty
1945 A. Watson	1980 A. Straughn	1899 F. Parks	1938 G. Preston	1977 G. Adair
1946 J. Taylor	1981 A. Straughn	1900 W. Dees	1939 A. Porter	1978 J. Awome
1947 A. Watson	1982 G. Crawford	1901 F. Parks	1944 M. Hart	1979 A. Palmer
1948 D. Scott	1983 A. Wilson	1902 F. Parks	1945 D. Scott	1980 F. Bruno
1949 *Declared no contest*	1984 A. Wilson	1903 F. Dickson	1946 P. Floyd	1981 A. Elliott
1950 P. Messervy	1985 J. Beckles	1904 A. Horner	1947 G. Scriven	1982 H. Hylton
1951 G. Walker	1986 J. Moran	1905 F. Parks	1948 J. Gardner	1983 H. Notice
1952 H. Cooper	1987 J. Beckles	1906 F. Parks	1949 A. Worrall	1984 D. Young
1953 H. Cooper	1988 H. Lawson	1907 H. Brewer	1950 P. Toch	1985 H. Hylton
1954 A. Madigan	1989 N. Piper	1908 S. Evans	1951 A. Halsey	1986 E. Cardouza
1955 D. Rent	1990 J. McCluskey	1909 C. Brown	1952 E. Hearn	1987 J. Moran
1956 D. Mooney	1991 A. Todd	1910 F. Storbeck	1953 J. Erskine	1988 H. Akinwande
1957 T. Green	1992 K. Oliver	1911 W. Hazell	1954 B. Harper	1989 H. Akinwande
1958 J. Leeming	1993 K. Oliver	1912 R. Smith	1955 D. Rowe	1990 K. Inglis
1959 J. Ould	1994 K. Oliver	1913 R. Smith	1956 D. Rent	1991 P. Lawson
1960 J. Ould		1914 E. Chandler	1957 D. Thomas	1992 S. Welch
1961 J. Bodell	**Heavyweight**	1919 H. Brown	1958 D. Thomas	1993 P. Lawson
1962 J. Hendrickson	1881 R. Frost-Smith	1920 R. Rawson	1959 D. Thomas	1994 S. Burford
1963 P. Murphy	1882 H. Dearsley	1921 R. Rawson	1960 L. Hobbs	
1964 J. Fisher	1883 H. Dearsley	1922 T. Evans	1961 W. Walker	**S. Heavyweight**
1965 E. Whistler	1884 H. Dearsley	1923 E. Eagan	1962 R. Dryden	1982 A. Elliott
1966 R. Tighe	1885 W. West	1924 A. Clifton	1963 R. Sanders	1983 K. Ferdinand
1967 M. Smith	1886 A. Diamond	1925 D. Lister	1964 C. Woodhouse	1984 R. Wells
1968 R. Brittle	1887 E. White	1926 T. Petersen	1965 W. Wells	1985 G. Williamson
1969 J. Frankham	1888 W. King	1927 C. Capper	1966 A. Brogan	1986 J. Oyebola
1970 J. Rafferty	1889 A. Bowman	1928 J. L. Driscoll	1967 P. Boddington	1987 J. Oyebola
1971 J. Conteh	1890 J. Steers	1929 P. Floyd	1968 W. Wells	1988 K. McCormack
1972 W. Knight	1891 V. Barker	1930 V. Stuart	1969 A. Burton	1989 P. Passley
1973 W. Knight	1892 J. Steers	1931 M. Flanagan	1970 J. Gilmour	1990 K. McCormack
1974 W. Knight	1893 J. Steers	1932 V. Stuart	1971 L. Stevens	1991 K. McCormack
1975 M. Heath	1894 H. King	1933 C. O'Grady	1972 T. Wood	1992 M. Hopper
1976 G. Evans	1895 W. E. Johnstone	1934 P. Floyd	1973 G. McEwan	1993 M. McKenzie
1977 C. Lawson	1896 W. E. Johnstone	1935 P. Floyd	1974 N. Meade	1994 D. Watts

As the first Russian to compete in the ABA championships, Mohammed Khamkhoer (right) was surprisingly outpointed in the super-heavyweight final by the unsung Danny Watts

Les Clark

International Amateur Champions, 1904-1994

Shows all Olympic, World, European & Commonwealth champions since 1904. British silver and bronze medal winners are shown throughout, where applicable.

Country Code

ARG = Argentine; ARM = Armenia; AUS = Australia; AUT = Austria; AZE = Azerbaijan; BEL = Belgium; BUL = Bulgaria; CAN = Canada; CEY = Ceylon (now Sri Lanka); CUB = Cuba; DEN = Denmark; DOM = Dominican Republic; ENG = England; ESP = Spain; EST = Estonia; FIJ = Fiji Islands; FIN = Finland; FRA = France; GBR = United Kingdom; GDR = German Democratic Republic; GEO = Georgia; GER = Germany (but West Germany only from 1968-1990); GHA = Ghana; GUY = Guyana; HOL = Netherlands; HUN = Hungary; IRL = Ireland; ITA = Italy; JAM = Jamaica; JPN = Japan; KEN = Kenya; LIT = Lithuania; MEX = Mexico; NKO = North Korea; NIG = Nigeria; NIR = Northern Ireland; NOR = Norway; NZL = New Zealand; POL = Poland; PUR = Puerto Rico; ROM = Romania; RUS = Russia; SAF = South Africa; SCO = Scotland; SKO = South Korea; SR = Southern Rhodesia; STV = St Vincent; SWE = Sweden; TCH = Czechoslovakia; TUR = Turkey; UGA = Uganda; UKR = Ukraine; URS = USSR; USA = United States of America; VEN = Venezuela; WAL = Wales; YUG = Yugoslavia; ZAM = Zambia.

Olympic Champions, 1904-1992

St Louis, USA - 1904
Fly: G. Finnegan (USA). **Bantam:** O. Kirk (USA). **Feather:** O. Kirk (USA). **Light:** H. Spangler (USA). **Welter:** A. Young (USA). **Middle:** C. May (USA). **Heavy:** S. Berger (USA).

London, England - 1908
Bantam: H. Thomas (GBR). **Feather:** R. Gunn (GBR). **Light:** F. Grace (GBR). **Middle:** J.W.H.T. Douglas (GBR). **Heavy:** A. Oldham (GBR).
Silver medals: J. Condon (GBR), C. Morris (GBR), F. Spiller (GBR), S. Evans (GBR).
Bronze medals: W. Webb (GBR), H. Rodding (GBR), T. Ringer (GBR), H. Johnson (GBR), R. Warnes (GBR), W. Philo (GBR), F. Parks (GBR).

Antwerp, Belgium - 1920
Fly: F. Genaro (USA). **Bantam:** C. Walker (SAF). **Feather:** R. Fritsch (FRA). **Light:** S. Mossberg (USA). **Welter:** T. Schneider (CAN). **Middle:** H. Mallin (GBR). **L. Heavy:** E. Eagan (USA). **Heavy:** R. Rawson (GBR).
Silver medal: A. Ireland (GBR).
Bronze medals: W. Cuthbertson (GBR), G. McKenzie (GBR), H. Franks (GBR).

Paris, France - 1924
Fly: F. la Barba (USA). **Bantam:** W. Smith (SAF). **Feather:** J. Fields (USA). **Light:** H. Nielson (DEN). **Welter:** J. Delarge (BEL). **Middle:** H. Mallin (GBR). **L. Heavy:** H. Mitchell (GBR). **Heavy:** O. von Porat (NOR).
Silver medals: J. McKenzie (GBR), J. Elliot (GBR).

Amsterdam, Holland - 1928
Fly: A. Kocsis (HUN). **Bantam:** V. Tamagnini (ITA). **Feather:** B. van Klaveren (HOL). **Light:** C. Orlando (ITA). **Welter:** E. Morgan (NZL). **Middle:** P. Toscani (ITA). **L. Heavy:** V. Avendano (ARG). **Heavy:** A. Rodriguez Jurado (ARG).

Los Angeles, USA - 1932
Fly: I. Enekes (HUN). **Bantam:** H. Gwynne (CAN). **Feather:** C. Robledo (ARG). **Light:** L. Stevens (SAF). **Welter:** E. Flynn (USA). **Middle:** C. Barth (USA). **L. Heavy:** D. Carstens (SAF). **Heavy:** A. Lovell (ARG).

Berlin, West Germany - 1936
Fly: W. Kaiser (GER). **Bantam:** U. Sergo (ITA). **Feather:** O. Casanova (ARG). **Light:** I. Harangi (HUN). **Welter:** S. Suvio (FIN). **Middle:** J. Despeaux (FRA). **L. Heavy:** R. Michelot (FRA). **Heavy:** H. Runge (GER).

London, England - 1948
Fly: P. Perez (ARG). **Bantam:** T. Csik (HUN). **Feather:** E. Formenti (ITA). **Light:** G. Dreyer (SAF). **Welter:** J. Torma (TCH). **Middle:** L. Papp (HUN). **L. Heavy:** G. Hunter (SAF). **Heavy:** R. Iglesas (ARG).
Silver medals: J. Wright (GBR), D. Scott (GBR).

Helsinki, Finland - 1952
Fly: N. Brooks (USA). **Bantam:** P. Hamalainen (FIN). **Feather:** J. Zachara (TCH). **Light:** A. Bolognesi (ITA). **L. Welter:** C. Adkins (USA). **Welter:** Z. Chychla (POL). **L. Middle:** L. Papp (HUN). **Middle:** F. Patterson (USA). **L. Heavy:** N. Lee (USA). **Heavy:** E. Sanders (USA).
Silver medal: J. McNally (IRL).

Melbourne, Australia - 1956
Fly: T. Spinks (GBR). **Bantam:** W. Behrendt (GER). **Feather:** V. Safronov (URS). **Light:** R. McTaggart (GBR). **L. Welter:** V. Jengibarian (URS). **Welter:** N. Linca (ROM). **L. Middle:** L. Papp (HUN). **Middle:** G. Schatkov (URS). **L. Heavy:** J. Boyd (USA). **Heavy:** P. Rademacher (USA).
Silver medals: T. Nicholls (GBR), F. Tiedt (IRL).
Bronze medals: J. Caldwell (IRL), F. Gilroy (IRL), A. Bryne (IRL), N. Gargano (GBR), J. McCormack (GBR).

Rome, Italy - 1960
Fly: G. Torok (HUN). **Bantam:** O. Grigoryev (URS). **Feather:** F. Musso (ITA). **Light:** K. Pazdzior (POL). **L. Welter:** B. Nemecek (TCH). **Welter:** N. Benvenuti (ITA). **L. Middle:** W. McClure (USA). **Middle:** E. Crook (USA). **L. Heavy:** C. Clay (USA). **Heavy:** F. de Piccoli (ITA).
Bronze medals: R. McTaggart (GBR), J. Lloyd (GBR), W. Fisher (GBR).

Tokyo, Japan - 1964
Fly: F. Atzori (ITA). **Bantam:** T. Sakurai (JPN). **Feather:** S. Stepashkin (URS). **Light:** J. Grudzien (POL). **L. Welter:** J. Kulej (POL). **Welter:** M. Kasprzyk (POL). **L. Middle:** B. Lagutin (URS). **Middle:** V. Popenchenko (URS). **L. Heavy:** C. Pinto (ITA). **Heavy:** J. Frazier (USA).
Bronze medal: J. McCourt (IRL).

Mexico City, Mexico - 1968
L. Fly: F. Rodriguez (VEN). **Fly:** R. Delgado (MEX). **Bantam:** V. Sokolov (URS). **Feather:** A. Roldan (MEX). **Light:** R. Harris (USA). **L. Welter:** J. Kulej (POL). **Welter:** M. Wolke (GDR). **L. Middle:** B. Lagutin (URS). **Middle:** C. Finnegan (GBR). **L. Heavy:** D. Poznyak (URS). **Heavy:** G. Foreman (USA).

Munich, West Germany - 1972
L. Fly: G. Gedo (HUN). **Fly:** G. Kostadinov (BUL). **Bantam:** O. Martinez (CUB). **Feather:** B. Kusnetsov (BUL). **Light:** J. Szczepanski (POL). **L. Welter:** R. Seales (USA). **Welter:** E. Correa (CUB). **L. Middle:** D. Kottysch (GER). **Middle:** V. Lemeschev (URS). **L. Heavy:** M. Parlov (YUG). **Heavy:** T. Stevenson (CUB).
Bronze medals: R. Evans (GBR), G. Turpin (GBR), A. Minter (GBR).

Montreal, Canada - 1976
L. Fly: J. Hernandez (CUB). **Fly:** L. Randolph (USA). **Bantam:** Y-J. Gu (NKO). **Feather:** A. Herrera (CUB). **Light:** H. Davis (USA). **L. Welter:** R. Leonard (USA). **Welter:** J. Bachfield (GDR). **L. Middle:** J. Rybicki (POL). **Middle:** M. Spinks (USA). **L. Heavy:** L. Spinks (USA). **Heavy:** T. Stevenson (CUB).
Bronze medal: P. Cowdell (GBR).

Moscow, USSR - 1980
L. Fly: S. Sabirov (URS). **Fly:** P. Lessov (BUL). **Bantam:** J. Hernandez (CUB). **Feather:** R. Fink (GDR). **Light:** A. Herrera (CUB). **L. Welter:** P. Oliva (ITA). **Welter:** A. Aldama (CUB). **L. Middle:** A. Martinez (CUB). **Middle:** J. Gomez (CUB). **L. Heavy:** S. Kacar (YUG). **Heavy:** T. Stevenson (CUB).
Bronze medals: H. Russell (IRL), A. Willis (GBR).

Los Angeles, USA - 1984
L. Fly: P. Gonzalez (USA). **Fly:** S. McCrory (USA). **Bantam:** M. Stecca (ITA). **Feather:** M. Taylor (USA). **Light:** P. Whitaker (USA). **L. Welter:** J. Page (USA). **Welter:** M. Breland (USA). **L. Middle:** F. Tate (USA). **Middle:** J-S. Shin (SKO). **L. Heavy:** A. Josipovic (YUG). **Heavy:** H. Tillman (USA). **S. Heavy:** T. Biggs (USA).
Bronze medal: B. Wells (GBR).

Seoul, South Korea - 1988
L. Fly: I. Mustafov (BUL). **Fly:** H-S. Kim (SKO). **Bantam:** K. McKinney (USA). **Feather:** G. Parisi (ITA). **Light:** A. Zuelow (GDR). **L. Welter:** V. Yanovsky (URS). **Welter:** R. Wangila (KEN). **L. Middle:** S-H. Park (SKO). **Middle:** H. Maske (GDR). **L. Heavy:** A. Maynard (USA). **Heavy:** R. Mercer (USA). **S. Heavy:** L. Lewis (CAN).
Bronze medal: R. Woodhall (GBR).

Barcelona, Spain - 1992
L. Fly: R. Marcelo (CUB). **Fly:** C-C. Su (NKO). **Bantam:** J. Casamayor (CUB). **Feather:** A. Tews (GER). **Light:** O. de la Hoya (USA). **L. Welter:** H. Vinent (CUB). **Welter:** M. Carruth (IRL). **L. Middle:** J. Lemus (CUB). **Middle:** A. Hernandez (CUB). **L. Heavy:** T. May (GER). **Heavy:** F. Savon (CUB). **S. Heavy:** R. Balado (CUB).
Silver medal: W. McCullough (IRL).
Bronze medal: R. Reid (GBR).

World Champions, 1974-1993

Havana, Cuba - 1974
L. Fly: J. Hernandez (CUB). **Fly:** D. Rodriguez (CUB). **Bantam:** W. Gomez (PUR). **Feather:** H. Davis (USA). **Light:** V. Solomin (URS). **L. Welter:** A. Kalule (UGA). **Welter:** E. Correa (CUB). **L. Middle:** R. Garbey (CUB). **Middle:** R. Riskiev (URS). **L. Heavy:** M. Parlov (YUG). **Heavy:** T. Stevenson (CUB).

Belgrade, Yugoslavia - 1978
L. Fly: S. Muchoki (KEN). **Fly:** H. Strednicki (POL). **Bantam:** A. Horta (CUB). **Feather:** A. Herrera (CUB). **Light:** D. Andeh (NIG). **L. Welter:** V. Lvov (URS). **Welter:** V. Rachkov (URS). **L. Middle:** V. Savchenko (URS). **Middle:** J. Gomez (CUB). **L. Heavy:** S. Soria (CUB). **Heavy:** T. Stevenson (CUB).

Munich, West Germany - 1982
L. Fly: I. Mustafov (BUL). **Fly:** Y. Alexandrov (URS). **Bantam:** F. Favors (USA). **Feather:** A. Horta (CUB). **Light:** A. Herrera (CUB). **L. Welter:** C. Garcia (CUB). **Welter:** M. Breland (USA). **L. Middle:** A. Koshkin (URS). **Middle:** B. Comas (CUB). **L. Heavy:** P. Romero (CUB). **Heavy:** A. Jagubkin (URS). **S. Heavy:** T. Biggs (USA).
Bronze medal: T. Corr (IRL).

Reno, USA - 1986
L. Fly: J. Odelin (CUB). **Fly:** P. Reyes (CUB). **Bantam:** S-I. Moon (SKO). **Feather:** K. Banks (USA). **Light:** A. Horta (CUB). **L. Welter:** V. Shishov (URS). **Welter:** K. Gould (USA). **L. Middle:** A. Espinosa (CUB). **Middle:** D. Allen (USA). **L. Heavy:** P. Romero (CUB). **Heavy:** F. Savon (CUB). **S. Heavy:** T. Stevenson (CUB).

Moscow, USSR - 1989
L. Fly: E. Griffin (USA). **Fly:** Y. Arbachakov (URS). **Bantam:** E. Carrion (CUB). **Feather:** A. Khamatov (URS). **Light:** J. Gonzalez (CUB). **L. Welter:** I. Ruzinkov (URS). **Welter:** F. Vastag. **L. Middle:** I. Akopokhian (URS). **Middle:** A. Kurniavka (URS). **L. Heavy:** H. Maske (GDR). **Heavy:** F. Savon (CUB). **S. Heavy:** R. Balado (CUB).
Bronze medal: M. Carruth (IRL).

Sydney, Australia - 1991
L. Fly: E. Griffin (USA). **Fly:** I. Kovacs (HUN). **Bantam:** S. Todorov (BUL). **Feather:** K. Kirkorov (BUL). **Light:** M. Rudolph (GER). **L. Welter:** K. Tsziu (URS). **Welter:** J. Hernandez (CUB). **L. Middle:** J. Lemus (CUB). **Middle:** T. Russo (ITA). **L. Heavy:** T. May (GER). **Heavy:** F. Savon (CUB). **S. Heavy:** R. Balado (CUB).

Tampere, Finland - 1993
L. Fly: N. Munchian (ARM). **Fly:** W. Font (CUB). **Bantam:** A. Christov (BUL). **Feather:** S. Todorov (BUL). **Light:** D. Austin (CUB). **L. Welter:** H. Vinent (CUB). **Welter:** J. Hernandez (CUB). **L. Middle:** F. Vastag (ROM). **Middle:** A. Hernandez (CUB). **L. Heavy:** R. Garbey (CUB). **Heavy:** F. Savon (CUB). **S. Heavy:** R. Balado (CUB).
Bronze medal: D. Kelly (NIR).

World Junior Champions, 1979-1992

Yokohama, Japan - 1979
L. Fly: R. Shannon (USA). **Fly:** P. Lessov (BUL). **Bantam:** P-K. Choi (SKO). **Feather:** Y. Gladychev (URS). **Light:** R. Blake (USA). **L. Welter:** I. Akopokhian (URS). **Welter:** M. McCrory (USA). **L. Middle:** A. Mayes (USA). **Middle:** A. Milov (URS). **L. Heavy:** A. Lebedev (URS). **Heavy:** M. Frazier (USA).
Silver medals: N. Wilshire (ENG), D. Cross (ENG).
Bronze medal: I. Scott (SCO).

Santa Domingo, Dominican Republic - 1983
L. Fly: M. Herrera (DOM). **Fly:** J. Gonzalez (CUB). **Bantam:** J. Molina (PUR). **Feather:** A. Miesses (DOM). **Light:** A. Beltre (DOM). **L. Welter:** A. Espinoza (CUB). **Welter:** M. Watkins (USA). **L. Middle:** U. Castillo (CUB). **Middle:** R. Batista (CUB). **L. Heavy:** O. Pought (USA). **Heavy:** A. Williams (USA). **S. Heavy:** L. Lewis (CAN).

Bucharest, Romania - 1985
L. Fly: R-S. Hwang (SKO). **Fly:** T. Marcelica (ROM). **Bantam:** R. Diaz (CUB). **Feather:** D. Maeran (ROM). **Light:** J. Teiche (GDR). **L. Welter:** W. Saeger (GDR). **Welter:** A. Stoianov (BUL). **L. Middle:** M. Franek (TCH). **Middle:** O. Zahalotskih (URS). **L. Heavy:** B. Riddick (USA). **Heavy:** F. Savon (CUB). **S. Heavy:** A. Prianichnikov (URS).

Havana, Cuba - 1987
L. Fly: E. Paisan (CUB). **Fly:** C. Daniels (USA). **Bantam:** A. Moya (CUB). **Feather:** G. Iliyasov (URS). **Light:** J. Hernandez (CUB). **L. Welter:** L. Mihai (ROM). **Welter:** F. Vastag (ROM). **L. Middle:** A. Lobsyak (URS). **Middle:** W. Martinez (CUB). **L. Heavy:** D. Yeliseyev (URS). **Heavy:** R. Balado (CUB). **S. Heavy:** L. Martinez (CUB).
Silver medal: E. Loughran (IRL).
Bronze medal: D. Galvin (IRL).

San Juan, Puerto Rico - 1989
L. Fly: D. Petrov (BUL). **Fly:** N. Monchai (FRA). **Bantam:** J. Casamayor (CUB). **Feather:** C. Febres (PUR). **Light:** A. Acevedo (PUR). **L. Welter:** E. Berger (GDR). **Welter:** A. Hernandez (CUB). **L. Middle:** L. Bedey (CUB). **Middle:** R. Garbey (CUB). **L. Heavy:** R. Alvarez (CUB). **Heavy:** K. Johnson (CAN). **S. Heavy:** A. Burdiantz (URS).
Silver medals: E. Magee (IRL), R. Reid (ENG), S. Wilson (SCO).

Lima, Peru - 1990
L. Fly: D. Alicea (PUR). **Fly:** K. Pielert (GDR). **Bantam:** K. Baravi (URS). **Feather:** A. Vaughan (ENG). **Light:** J. Mendez (CUB). **L. Welter:** H. Vinent (CUB). **Welter:** A. Hernandez (CUB). **L. Middle:** A. Kakauridze (URS). **Middle:** J. Gomez (CUB). **L. Heavy:** B. Torsten (GDR). **Heavy:** I. Andreev (URS). **S. Heavy:** J. Quesada (CUB).
Bronze medal: P. Ingle (ENG).

Montreal, Canada - 1992
L. Fly: W. Font (CUB). **Fly:** J. Oragon (CUB). **Bantam:** N. Machado (CUB). **Feather:** M. Stewart (CAN). **Light:** D. Austin (CUB). **L. Welter:** O. Saitov (RUS). **Welter:** L. Brors (GER). **L. Middle:** J. Acosta (CUB). **Middle:** I. Arsangaliev (RUS). **L. Heavy:** S. Samilsan (TUR). **Heavy:** G. Kandeliaki (GEO). **S. Heavy:** M. Porchnev (RUS).
Bronze medal: N. Sinclair (IRL).

European Champions, 1924-1993

Paris, France - 1924
Fly: J. McKenzie (GBR). **Bantam:** J. Ces (FRA). **Feather:** R. de Vergnie (BEL). **Light:** N. Nielsen (DEN). **Welter:** J. Delarge (BEL). **Middle:** H. Mallin (GBR). **L. Heavy:** H. Mitchell (GBR). **Heavy:** O. von Porat (NOR).

Stockholm, Sweden - 1925
Fly: E. Pladner (FRA). **Bantam:** A. Rule (GBR). **Feather:** P. Andren (SWE). **Light:** S. Johanssen (SWE). **Welter:** H. Nielsen (DEN). **Middle:** F. Crawley (GBR). **L. Heavy:** T. Petersen (DEN). **Heavy:** B. Persson (SWE).
Silver medals: J. James (GBR), E. Viney (GBR), D. Lister (GBR).

Berlin, Germany - 1927
Fly: L. Boman (SWE). **Bantam:** K. Dalchow (GER). **Feather:** F. Dubbers (GER). **Light:** H. Domgoergen (GER). **Welter:** R. Caneva (ITA). **Middle:** J. Christensen (NOR). **L. Heavy:** H. Muller (GER). **Heavy:** N. Ramm (SWE).

Amsterdam, Holland - 1928

Fly: A. Kocsis (HUN). **Bantam:** V. Tamagnini (ITA). **Feather:** B. van Klaveren (HOL). **Light:** C. Orlandi (ITA). **Welter:** R. Galataud (FRA). **Middle:** P. Toscani (ITA). **L. Heavy:** E. Pistulla (GER). **Heavy:** N. Ramm (SWE).

Budapest, Hungary - 1930

Fly: I. Enekes (HUN). **Bantam:** J. Szeles (HUN). **Feather:** G. Szabo (HUN). **Light:** M. Bianchini (ITA). **Welter:** J. Besselmann (GER). **Middle:** C. Meroni (ITA). **L. Heavy:** T. Petersen (DEN). **Heavy:** J. Michaelson (DEN).

Los Angeles, USA - 1932

Fly: I. Enekes (HUN). **Bantam:** H. Ziglarski (GER). **Feather:** J. Schleinkofer (GER). **Light:** T. Ahlqvist (SWE). **Welter:** E. Campe (GER). **Middle:** R. Michelot (FRA). **L. Heavy:** G. Rossi (ITA). **Heavy:** L. Rovati (ITA).

Budapest, Hungary - 1934

Fly: P. Palmer (GBR). **Bantam:** I. Enekes (HUN). **Feather:** O. Kaestner GER). **Light:** E. Facchini (ITA). **Welter:** D. McCleave (GBR). **Middle:** S. Szigetti (HUN). **L. Heavy:** P. Zehetmayer (AUT). **Heavy:** G. Baerlund (FIN).
Bronze medal: P. Floyd (GBR).

Milan, Italy - 1937

Fly: I. Enekes (HUN). **Bantam:** U. Sergo (ITA). **Feather:** A. Polus (POL). **Light:** H. Nuremberg (GER). **Welter:** M. Murach (GER). **Middle:** H. Chmielewski (POL). **L. Heavy:** S. Szigetti (HUN). **Heavy:** O. Tandberg (SWE).

Dublin, Eire - 1939

Fly: J. Ingle (IRL). **Bantam:** U. Sergo (ITA). **Feather:** P. Dowdall (IRL). **Light:** H. Nuremberg (GER). **Welter:** A. Kolczyski (POL). **Middle:** A. Raedek (EST). **L. Heavy:** L. Musina (ITA). **Heavy:** O. Tandberg (SWE).
Bronze medal: C. Evenden (IRL).

Dublin, Eire - 1947

Fly: L. Martinez (ESP). **Bantam:** L. Bogacs (HUN). **Feather:** K. Kreuger (SWE). **Light:** J. Vissers (BEL). **Welter:** J. Ryan (ENG). **Middle:** A. Escudie (FRA). **L. Heavy:** H. Quentemeyer (HOL). **Heavy:** G. O'Colmain (IRL).
Silver medals: J. Clinton (SCO), P. Maguire (IRL), W. Thom (ENG), G. Scriven (ENG).
Bronze medals: J. Dwyer (SCO), A. Sanderson (ENG), W. Frith (SCO), E. Cantwell (IRL), K. Wyatt (ENG).

Oslo, Norway - 1949

Fly: J. Kasperczak (POL). **Bantam:** G. Zuddas (ITA). **Feather:** J. Bataille (FRA). **Light:** M. McCullagh (IRL). **Welter:** J. Torma (TCH). **Middle:** L. Papp (HUN). **L. Heavy:** L. di Segni (ITA). **Heavy:** L. Bene (HUN).
Bronze medal: D. Connell (IRL).

Milan, Italy - 1951

Fly: A. Pozzali (ITA). **Bantam:** V. Dall'Osso (ITA). **Feather:** J. Ventaja (FRA). **Light:** B. Visintin (ITA). **L. Welter:** H. Schelling (GER). **Welter:** Z. Chychla (POL). **L. Middle:** L. Papp (HUN). **Middle:** S. Sjolin (SWE). **L. Heavy:** M. Limage (BEL). **Heavy:** G. di Segni (ITA).
Silver medal: J. Kelly (IRL).
Bronze medals: D. Connell (IRL), T. Milligan (IRL), A. Lay (ENG).

Warsaw, Poland - 1953

Fly: H. Kukier (POL). **Bantam:** Z. Stefaniuk (POL). **Feather:** J. Kruza (POL). **Light:** V. Jengibarian (URS). **L. Welter:** L. Drogosz (POL). **Welter:** Z. Chychla (POL). **L. Middle:** B. Wells (ENG). **Middle:** D. Wemhoner (GER). **L. Heavy:** U. Nietchke (GER). **Heavy:** A. Schotzikas (URS).
Silver medal: T. Milligan (IRL).
Bronze medals: J. McNally (IRL), R. Barton (ENG).

Berlin, West Germany - 1955

Fly: E. Basel (GER). **Bantam:** Z. Stefaniuk (POL). **Feather:** T. Nicholls (ENG). **Light:** H. Kurschat (GER). **L. Welter:** L. Drogosz (POL). **Welter:** N. Gargano (ENG). **L. Middle:** Z. Pietrzykowski (POL). **Middle:** G. Schatkov (URS). **L. Heavy:** E. Schoeppner (GER). **Heavy:** A. Schotzikas (URS).

Prague, Czechoslovakia - 1957

Fly: M. Homberg (GER). **Bantam:** O. Grigoryev (URS). **Feather:** D. Venilov (BUL). **Light:** K. Pazdzior (POL). **L. Welter:** V. Jengibarian (URS). **Welter:** M. Graus (GER). **L. Middle:** N. Benvenuti (ITA) **Middle:** Z. Pietrzykowski (POL). **L. Heavy:** G. Negrea (ROM). **Heavy:** A. Abramov (URS).
Bronze medals: R. Davies (WAL), J. Morrissey (SCO), J. Kidd (SCO), F. Teidt (IRL).

Lucerne, Switzerland - 1959

Fly: M. Homberg (GER). **Bantam:** H. Rascher (GER). **Feather:** J. Adamski (POL). **Light:** O. Maki (FIN). **L. Welter:** V. Jengibarian (URS). **Welter:** L. Drogosz (POL). **L. Middle:** N. Benvenuti (ITA). **Middle:** G. Schatkov (URS). **L. Heavy:** Z. Pietrzykowski (POL). **Heavy:** A. Abramov (URS).
Silver medal: D. Thomas (ENG).
Bronze medals: A. McClean (IRL), H. Perry (IRL), C. McCoy (IRL), H. Scott (ENG).

Belgrade, Yugoslavia - 1961

Fly: P. Vacca (ITA). **Bantam:** S. Sivko (URS). **Feather:** F. Taylor (ENG). **Light:** R. McTaggart (SCO). **L. Welter:** A. Tamulis (URS). **Welter:** R. Tamulis (URS). **L. Middle:** B. Lagutin (URS). **Middle:** T. Walasek (POL). **L. Heavy:** G. Saraudi (ITA). **Heavy:** A. Abramov (URS).
Bronze medals: P. Warwick (ENG), I. McKenzie (SCO), J. Bodell (ENG).

Moscow, USSR - 1963

Fly: V. Bystrov (URS). **Bantam:** O. Grigoryev (URS). **Feather:** S. Stepashkin (URS). **Light:** J. Kajdi (HUN). **L. Welter:** J. Kulej (POL). **Welter:** R. Tamulis (URS). **L. Middle:** B. Lagutin (URS). **Middle:** V. Popenchenko (URS). **L. Heavy:** Z. Pietrzykowski (POL). **Heavy:** J. Nemec (TCH).
Silver medal: A. Wyper (SCO).

Berlin, East Germany - 1965

Fly: H. Freisdadt (GER). **Bantam:** O. Grigoryev (URS). **Feather:** S. Stepashkin (URS). **Light:** V. Barranikov (URS). **L. Welter:** J. Kulej (POL). **Welter:** R. Tamulis (URS). **L. Middle:** V. Ageyev (URS). **Middle:** V. Popenchenko (URS). **L. Heavy:** D. Poznyak (URS). **Heavy:** A. Isosimov (URS).
Silver medal: B. Robinson (ENG).
Bronze medals: J. McCluskey (SCO), K. Buchanan (SCO), J. McCourt (IRL).

Rome, Italy - 1967

Fly: H. Skrzyczak (POL). **Bantam:** N. Giju (ROM). **Feather:** R. Petek (POL). **Light:** J. Grudzien (POL). **L. Welter:** V. Frolov (URS). **Welter:** B. Nemecek (TCH). **L. Middle:** V. Ageyev (URS). **Middle:** M. Casati (ITA). **L. Heavy:** D. Poznyak (URS). **Heavy:** M. Baruzzi (ITA).
Silver medal: P. Boddington (ENG).

Bucharest, Romania - 1969

L. Fly: G. Gedo (HUN). **Fly:** C. Ciuca (ROM). **Bantam:** A. Dumitrescu (ROM). **Feather:** L. Orban (HUN). **Light:** S. Cutov (ROM). **L. Welter:** V. Frolov (URS). **Welter:** G. Meier (GER). **L. Middle:** V. Tregubov (URS). **Middle:** V. Tarasenkov (URS). **L. Heavy:** D. Poznyak (URS). **Heavy:** I. Alexe (ROM).
Bronze medals: M. Dowling (IRL), M. Piner (ENG), A. Richardson (ENG), T. Imrie (SCO).

Madrid, Spain - 1971

L. Fly: G. Gedo (HUN). **Fly:** J. Rodriguez (ESP). **Bantam:** T. Badar (HUN). **Feather:** R. Tomczyk (POL). **Light:** J. Szczepanski (POL). **L. Welter:** U. Beyer (GDR). **Welter:** J. Kajdi (HUN). **L. Middle:** V. Tregubov (URS). **Middle:** J. Juotsiavitchus (URS). **L. Heavy:** M. Parlov (BUL). **Heavy:** V. Tchernishev (URS).
Bronze medals: N. McLaughlin (IRL), M. Dowling (IRL), B. McCarthy (IRL), M. Kingwell (ENG), L. Stevens (ENG).

Belgrade, Yugoslavia - 1973

L. Fly: V. Zasypko (URS). **Fly:** C. Gruescu (ROM). **Bantam:** A. Cosentino (FRA). **Feather:** S. Forster (GDR). **Light:** S. Cutov (ROM). **L. Welter:** M. Benes (YUG). **Welter:** S. Csjef (HUN). **L. Middle:** A. Klimanov (URS). **Middle:** V. Lemechev (URS). **L. Heavy:** M. Parlov (YUG). **Heavy:** V. Ulyanich (URS).
Bronze medal: J. Bambrick (SCO).

Katowice, Poland - 1975

L. Fly: A. Tkachenko (URS). **Fly:** V. Zasypko (URS). **Bantam:** V. Rybakov (URS). **Feather:** T. Badari (HUN). **Light:** S. Cutov (ROM). **L. Welter:** V. Limasov (URS). **Welter:** K. Marjaama (FIN). **L. Middle:** W. Rudnowski (POL). **Middle:** V. Lemechev (URS). **L. Heavy:** A. Klimanov (URS). **Heavy:** A. Biegalski (POL).
Bronze medals: C. Magri (ENG), P. Cowdell (ENG), G. McEwan (ENG).

Halle, East Germany - 1977

L. Fly: H. Srednicki (POL). **Fly:** L. Blazynski (POL). **Bantam:** S. Forster (GDR). **Feather:** R. Nowakowski (GDR). **Light:** A. Rusevski (YUG). **L. Welter:** B. Gajda (POL). **Welter:** V. Limasov (URS). **L. Middle:** V. Saychenko (URS). **Middle:** I. Shaposhnikov (URS). **L. Heavy:** D. Kvachadze (URS). **Heavy:** E. Gorstkov (URS).
Bronze medal: P. Sutcliffe (IRL).

Cologne, West Germany - 1979

L. Fly: S. Sabirov (URS). **Fly:** H. Strednicki (POL). **Bantam:** N. Khrapzov (URS). **Feather:** V. Rybakov (URS). **Light.** V. Demianenko (URS). **L. Welter:** S. Konakbaev (URS). **Welter:** E. Muller (GER). **L. Middle:** M. Perunovic (YUG). **Middle:** T. Uusiverta (FIN). **L. Heavy:** A. Nikolyan (URS). **Heavy:** E. Gorstkov (URS). **S. Heavy:** P. Hussing (GER).
Bronze medal: P. Sutcliffe (IRL).

Tampere, Finland - 1981

L. Fly: I. Mustafov (BUL). **Fly:** P. Lessov (BUL). **Bantam:** V. Miroschnichenko (URS). **Feather:** R. Nowakowski (GDR). **Light:** V. Rybakov (URS). **L. Welter:** V. Shisov (URS). **Welter:** S. Konakvbaev (URS). **L. Middle:** A. Koshkin (URS). **Middle:** J. Torbek (URS). **L. Heavy:** A Krupin (URS). **Heavy:** A. Jagupkin (URS). **S. Heavy:** F. Damiani (ITA).
Bronze medal: G. Hawkins (IRL).

Varna, Bulgaria - 1983

L. Fly: I. Mustafov (BUL). **Fly:** P. Lessov (BUL). **Bantam:** Y. Alexandrov (URS). **Feather:** S. Nurkazov (URS). **Light:** E. Chuprenski (BUL). **L. Welter:** V. Shishov (URS). **Welter:** P. Galkin (URS). **L. Middle:** V. Laptev (URS). **Middle:** V. Melnik (URS). **L. Heavy:** V. Kokhanovski (URS). **Heavy:** A. Jagubkin (URS). **S. Heavy:** F. Damiani (ITA).
Bronze medal: K. Joyce (IRL).

Budapest, Hungary - 1985

L. Fly: R. Breitbarth (GDR). **Fly:** D. Berg (GDR). **Bantam:** L. Simic (YUG). **Feather:** S. Khachatrian (URS). **Light:** E. Chuprenski (BUL) **L. Welter:** S. Mehnert (GDR). **Welter:** I. Akopokhian (URS). **L. Middle:** M. Timm (GDR). **Middle:** H. Maske (GDR). **L. Heavy:** N. Shanavasov (URS). **Heavy:** A. Jagubkin (URS). **S. Heavy:** F. Somodi (HUN).
Bronze medals: S. Casey (IRL), J. Beckles (ENG).

Turin, Italy - 1987

L. Fly: N. Munchyan (URS). **Fly:** A. Tews (GDR). **Bantam:** A. Hristov (BUL). **Feather:** M. Kazaryan (URS). **Light:** O. Nazarov (URS). **L. Welter:** B. Abadjier (BUL). **Welter:** V. Shishov (URS). **L. Middle:** E. Richter (GDR). **Middle:** H. Maske (GDR). **L. Heavy:** Y. Vaulin (URS). **Heavy:** A. Vanderlijde (HOL). **S. Heavy:** U. Kaden (GDR).
Bronze medal: N. Brown (ENG).

Athens, Greece - 1989

L. Fly: I.Mustafov (BUL). **Fly:** Y. Arbachakov (URS). **Bantam:** S. Todorov (BUL). **Feather:** K. Kirkorov (BUL). **Light:** K. Tsziu (URS). **L. Welter:** I. Ruznikov (URS). **Welter:** S. Mehnert (GDR). **L. Middle:** I. Akopokhian (URS). **Middle:** H. Maske (GDR). **L. Heavy:** S. Lange (GDR). **Heavy:** A. Vanderlijde (HOL). **S. Heavy:** U. Kaden (GDR).
Bronze Medal: D. Anderson (SCO).

Gothenburg, Sweden - 1991

L. Fly: I. Marinov (BUL). **Fly:** I. Kovacs (HUN). **Bantam:** S. Todorov (BUL). **Feather:** P. Griffin (IRL). **Light:** V. Nistor (ROM). **L. Welter:** K. Tsziu (URS). **Welter:** R. Welin (SWE). **L. Middle:** I. Akopokhian (URS). **Middle:** S. Otke (GER). **L. Heavy:** D. Michalczewski (GER). **Heavy:** A. Vanderlijde (HOL). **S. Heavy:** E. Beloussov (URS).
Bronze medals: P. Weir (SCO), A. Vaughan (ENG).

Bursa, Turkey - 1993

L. Fly: D. Petrov (BUL). **Fly:** R. Husseinov (AZE). **Bantam:** R. Malakhbetov (RUS). **Feather:** S. Todorov (BUL). **Light:** J. Bielski (POL). **L. Welter:** N. Suleymanogiu (TUR). **Welter:** V. Karpaclauskas (LIT). **L. Middle:** F. Vastag (ROM). **Middle:** D. Eigenbrodt (GER). **L. Heavy:** I. Kshinin (RUS). **Heavy:** G. Kandelaki (GEO). **S. Heavy:** S. Rusinov (BUL).
Bronze medals: P. Griffin (IRL), D. Williams (ENG), K. McCormack (WAL).

Note: Gold medals were awarded to the Europeans who went the furthest in the Olympic Games of 1924, 1928 & 1932.

European Junior Champions, 1970-1993

Miskolc, Hungary - 1970

L. Fly: Gluck (HUN). **Fly:** Z. Kismeneth (HUN). **Bantam:** A. Levitschev (URS). **Feather:** Andrianov (URS). **Light:** L. Juhasz (HUN). **L. Welter:** K. Nemec (HUN). **Welter:** Davidov (URS). **L. Middle:** A. Lemeschev (URS). **Middle:** N. Anfimov (URS). **L. Heavy:** O. Sasche (GDR). **Heavy:** J. Reder (HUN).
Bronze medals: D. Needham (ENG), R. Barlow (ENG), L. Stevens (ENG).

Bucharest, Romania - 1972

L. Fly: A. Turei (ROM). **Fly:** Condurat (ROM). **Bantam:** V. Solomin (URS). **Feather:** V. Lvov (URS). **Light:** S. Cutov (ROM). **L. Welter:** R. Pierwieniecki (POL). **Welter:** Zorov (URS). **L. Middle:** Babescu (ROM). **Middle:** V. Lemeschev (URS). **L. Heavy:** Mirounik (URS). **Heavy:** Subutin (URS).
Bronze medals: J. Gale (ENG), R. Maxwell (ENG), D. Odwell (ENG).

Kiev, Russia - 1974

L. Fly: A. Tkachenko (URS). **Fly:** V. Rybakov (URS). **Bantam:** C. Andreikovski (BUL). **Feather:** V. Sorokin (URS). **Light:** V. Limasov (URS). **L. Welter:** N. Sigov (URS). **Welter:** M. Bychkov (URS). **L. Middle:** V. Danshin (URS). **Middle:** D. Jende (GDR). **L. Heavy:** K. Dafinoiu (ROM). **Heavy:** K. Mashev (BUL).
Silver medal: C. Magri (ENG).
Bronze medals: G. Gilbody (ENG), K. Laing (ENG).

Izmir, Turkey - 1976

L. Fly: C. Seican (ROM). **Fly:** G. Khratsov (URS). **Bantam:** M. Navros (URS). **Feather:** V. Demoianeko (URS). **Light:** M. Puzovic (YUG). **L. Welter:** V. Zverev (URS). **Welter:** K. Ozoglouz (TUR). **L. Middle:** W. Lauder (SCO). **Middle:** H. Lenhart (GER). **L. Heavy:** I. Yantchauskas (URS). **Heavy:** B. Enjenyan (URS).
Silver medal: J. Decker (ENG).
Bronze medals: I. McLeod (SCO), N. Croombes (ENG).

Dublin, Ireland - 1978

L. Fly: R. Marx (GDR). **Fly:** D. Radu (ROM). **Bantam:** S. Khatchatrian (URS). **Feather:** H. Loukmanov (URS). **Light:** P. Oliva (ITA). **L. Welter:** V. Laptiev (URS). **Welter:** R. Filimanov (URS). **L. Middle:** A. Beliave (URS). **Middle:** G. Zinkovitch (URS). **L. Heavy:** I. Jolta (ROM). **Heavy:** P. Stoimenov (BUL).
Silver medals: M. Holmes (IRL), P. Hanlon (ENG), M. Courtney (ENG).
Bronze medals: T. Thompson (IRL), J. Turner (ENG), M. Bennett (WAL), J. McAllister (SCO), C. Devine (ENG).

Rimini, Italy - 1980

L. Fly: A. Mikoulin (URS). **Fly:** J. Varadi (HUN). **Bantam:** F. Rauschning (GDR). **Feather:** J. Gladychev (URS). **Light:** V. Shishov (URS). **L. Welter:** R. Lomski (BUL). **Welter:** T. Holonics (GDR). **L. Middle:** N. Wilshire (ENG). **Middle:** S. Laptiev (URS). **L. Heavy:** V. Dolgoun (URS). **Heavy:** V. Tioumentsev (URS). **S. Heavy:** S. Kormihtsine (URS).
Bronze medals: N. Potter (ENG), B. McGuigan (IRL), M. Brereton (IRL), D. Cross (ENG).

Schwerin, East Germany - 1982

L. Fly: R. Kabirov (URS). **Fly:** I. Filchev (BUL). **Bantam:** M. Stecca (ITA). **Feather:** B. Blagoev (BUL). **Light:** E. Chakimov (URS). **L. Welter:** S. Mehnert (GDR). **Welter:** T. Schmitz (GDR). **L. Middle:** B. Shararov (URS). **Middle:** E. Christie (ENG). **L. Heavy:** Y. Waulin (URS). **Heavy:** A. Popov (URS). **S. Heavy:** V. Aldoshin (URS).
Silver medal: D. Kenny (ENG).
Bronze medal: O. Jones (ENG).

Tampere, Finland - 1984

L. Fly: R. Breitbart (GDR). **Fly:** D. Berg (GDR). **Bantam:** K. Khdrian (URS). **Feather:** O. Nazarov (URS). **Light:** C. Furnikov (BUL). **L. Welter:** W. Schmidt (GDR). **Welter:** K. Doinov (BUL). **L. Middle:** O. Volkov (URS). **Middle:** R. Ryll (GDR). **L. Heavy:** G. Peskov (URS). **Heavy:** R. Draskovic (YUG). **S. Heavy:** L. Kamenov (BUL).
Bronze medals: J. Lowey (IRL), F. Harding (ENG), N. Moore (ENG).

Brondy, Denmark - 1986

L. Fly: S. Todorov (BUL). **Fly:** S. Galotian (URS). **Bantam:** D. Drumm (GDR). **Feather:** K. Tsziu (URS). **Light:** G. Akopkhian (URS). **L. Welter:** F. Vastag (ROM). **Welter:** S. Karavaev (URS). **L. Middle:** E. Elibaev (URS). **Middle:** A. Kurnabka (URS). **L. Heavy:** A. Schultz (GDR). **Heavy:** A. Golota (POL). **S. Heavy:** A. Prianichnikov (URS).

Gdansk, Poland - 1988

L. Fly: I. Kovacs (HUN). **Fly:** M. Beyer (GDR). **Bantam:** M. Aitzanov (URS). **Feather:** M. Rudolph (GDR). **Light:** M. Shaburov (URS). **L. Welter:** G. Campanella (ITA). **Welter:** D. Konsun (URS). **L. Middle:** K. Kiselev (URS). **Middle:** A. Rudenko (URS). **L. Heavy:** O. Velikanov (URS). **Heavy:** A. Ter-Okopian (URS). **S. Heavy:** E. Belusov (URS).
Bronze medals: P. Ramsey (ENG), M. Smyth (WAL).

Usti Nad Labem, Czechoslovakia - 1990

L. Fly: Z. Paliani (URS). **Fly:** K. Pielert (GDR). **Bantam:** K. Baravi (URS). **Feather:** P. Gvasalia (URS). **Light:** J. Hildenbrandt (GDR). **L. Welter:** N. Smanov (URS). **Welter:** A. Preda (ROM). **L. Middle:** A. Kakauridze (URS). **Middle:** J. Schwank (GDR). **L. Heavy:** Iljin (URS). **Heavy:** I. Andrejev (URS). **S. Heavy:** W. Fischer (GDR).
Silver medals: A. Todd (ENG).
Bronze medal: P. Craig (ENG).

Edinburgh, Scotland - 1992

L. Fly: M. Ismailov (URS). **Fly:** F. Brennfuhrer (GER). **Bantam:** S. Kuchler (GER). **Feather:** M. Silantiev (URS). **Light:** S. Shcherbakov (URS). **L. Welter:** O. Saitov (URS). **Welter:** H. Kurlumaz (TUR). **L. Middle:** Z. Erdie (HUN). **Middle:** V. Zhirov (URS). **L. Heavy:** D. Gorbachev (URS). **Heavy:** L. Achkasov (URS). **S. Heavy:** A. Mamedov (URS).
Silver medals: M. Hall (ENG), B. Jones (WAL).
Bronze medals: F. Slane (IRL), G. Stephens (IRL), C. Davies (WAL).

Salonika, Greece - 1993

L. Fly: O. Kiroukhine (UKR). **Fly:** R. Husseinov (AZE). **Bantam:** M. Kulbe (GER). **Feather:** E. Zakharov (RUS). **Light:** O. Sergeev (RUS). **L. Welter:** A. Selihanov (RUS). **Welter:** O. Kudinov (UKR). **L. Middle:** E. Makarenko (RUS). **Middle:** D. Droukovski (RUS). **L. Heavy:** A. Voida (RUS). **Heavy:** V. Klitchko (UKR). **S. Heavy:** A. Moiseev (RUS).
Bronze medal: D. Costello (ENG).

Note: The age limit for the championships were reduced from 21 to 19 in 1976.

Commonwealth Champions, 1930-1994

Hamilton, Canada - 1930

Fly: W. Smith (SAF). **Bantam:** H. Mizler (ENG). **Feather:** F. Meacham (ENG). **Light:** J. Rolland (SCO). **Welter:** L. Hall (SAF). **Middle:** F. Mallin (ENG). **L. Heavy:** J. Goyder (ENG). **Heavy:** V. Stuart (ENG).
Silver medals: T. Pardoe (ENG), T. Holt (SCO).
Bronze medals: A. Lyons (SCO), A. Love (ENG), F. Breeman (ENG).

Wembley, England - 1934

Fly: P. Palmer (ENG). **Bantam:** F. Ryan (ENG). **Feather:** C. Cattarall (SAF). **Light:** L. Cook (AUS). **Welter:** D. McCleave (ENG). **Middle:** A. Shawyer (ENG). **L. Heavy:** G. Brennan (ENG). **Heavy:** P. Floyd (ENG).
Silver medals: A. Barnes (WAL), J. Jones (WAL), F. Taylor (WAL), J. Holton (SCO).
Bronze medals: J. Pottinger (WAL), T. Wells (SCO), H. Moy (ENG), W. Duncan (NIR), J. Magill (NIR), Lord D. Douglas-Hamilton (SCO).

Melbourne, Australia - 1938

Fly: J. Joubert (SAF). **Bantam:** W. Butler (ENG). **Feather:** A. Henricus (CEY). **Light:** H. Groves (ENG). **Welter:** W. Smith (AUS). **Middle:** D. Reardon (WAL). **L. Heavy:** N. Wolmarans (SAF). **Heavy:** T. Osborne (CAN).
Silver medals: J. Watson (SCO), M. Dennis (ENG).
Bronze medals: H. Cameron (SCO), J. Wilby (ENG).

Auckland, New Zealand - 1950

Fly: H. Riley (SCO). **Bantam:** J. van Rensburg (SAF). **Feather:** H. Gilliland (SCO). **Light:** R. Latham (ENG). **Welter:** T. Ratcliffe (ENG). **Middle:** T. van Schalkwyk (SAF). **L. Heavy:** D. Scott (ENG). **Heavy:** F. Creagh (NZL).
Bronze medals: P. Brander (ENG).

Vancouver, Canada - 1954

Fly: R. Currie (SCO). **Bantam:** J. Smillie (SCO). **Feather:** L. Leisching (SAF). **Light:** P. van Staden (SR). **L. Welter:** M. Bergin (CAN). **Welter:** N. Gargano (ENG). **L. Middle:** W. Greaves (CAN). **Middle:** J. van de Kolff (SAF). **L. Heavy:** P. van Vuuren (SAF). **Heavy:** B. Harper (ENG).
Silver medals: M. Collins (WAL), F. McQuillan (SCO).
Bronze medals: D. Charnley (ENG), B. Wells (ENG).

Cardiff, Wales - 1958

Fly: J. Brown (SCO). **Bantam:** H. Winstone (WAL). **Feather:** W. Taylor (AUS). **Light:** R. McTaggart (SCO). **L. Welter:** H. Loubscher (SAF). **Welter:** J. Greyling (SAF). **L. Middle:** G. Webster (SAF). **Middle:** T. Milligan (NIR). **L. Heavy:** A. Madigan (AUS). **Heavy:** D. Bekker (SAF).
Silver medals: T. Bache (ENG), M. Collins (WAL), J. Jordan (NIR), R. Kane (SCO), S. Pearson (ENG), A. Higgins (WAL), D. Thomas (ENG).
Bronze medals: P. Lavery (NIR), D. Braithwaite (WAL), R. Hanna (NIR), A. Owen (SCO), J. McClory (NIR), J. Cooke (ENG), J. Jacobs (ENG), B. Nancurvis (ENG), R. Scott (SCO), W. Brown (WAL), J. Caiger (ENG), W. Bannon (SCO), R. Pleace (WAL).

Perth, Australia - 1962

Fly: R. Mallon (SCO). **Bantam:** J. Dynevor (AUS). **Feather:** J. McDermott (SCO). **Light:** E. Blay (GHA). **L. Welter:** C. Quartey (GHA). **Welter:** W. Coe (NZL). **L. Middle:** H. Mann (CAN). **Middle:** M. Calhoun (JAM). **L. Heavy:** A. Madigan (AUS). **Heavy:** G. Oywello (UGA).
Silver medals: R. McTaggart (SCO), J. Pritchett (ENG).
Bronze medals: M. Pye (ENG), P. Benneyworth (ENG), B. Whelan (ENG), B. Brazier (ENG), C. Rice (NIR), T. Menzies (SCO), H. Christie (NIR).

Kingston, Jamaica - 1966

Fly: S. Shittu (GHA). **Bantam:** E. Ndukwu (NIG). **Feather:** P. Waruinge (KEN). **Light:** A. Andeh (NIG). **L. Welter:** J. McCourt (NIR). **Welter:** E. Blay (GHA). **L. Middle:** M. Rowe (ENG). **Middle:** J. Darkey (GHA). **L. Heavy:** R. Tighe (ENG). **Heavy:** W. Kini (NZL).
Silver medals: P. Maguire (NIR), R. Thurston (ENG), R. Arthur (ENG), T. Imrie (SCO).
Bronze medals: S. Lockhart (NIR), A. Peace (SCO), F. Young (NIR), J. Turpin (ENG), D. McAlinden (NIR).

Edinburgh, Scotland - 1970

L. Fly: J. Odwori (UGA). **Fly:** D. Needham (ENG). **Bantam:** S. Shittu (GHA). **Feather:** P. Waruinge (KEN). **Light:** A. Adeyemi (NIG). **L. Welter:** M. Muruli (UGA). **Welter:** E. Ankudcy (GHA). **L. Middle:** T. Imrie (ENG). **Middle:** J. Conteh (ENG). **L. Heavy:** F. Ayinla (NIG). **Heavy:** B. Masanda (UGA).
Silver medals: T. Davies (WAL), J. Gillan (SCO), D. Davies (WAL), J. McKinty (NIR).
Bronze medals: M. Abrams (ENG), A. McHugh (SCO), D. Larmour (NIR), S. Oglivie (SCO), A. Richardson (ENG), T. Joyce (SCO), P. Doherty (NIR), J. Rafferty (SCO), L. Stevens (ENG).

Christchurch, New Zealand - 1974

L. Fly: S. Muchoki (KEN). **Fly:** D. Larmour (NIR). **Bantam:** P. Cowdell (ENG). **Feather:** E. Ndukwu (NIG). **Light:** A. Kalule (UGA). **L. Welter:** O. Nwankpa (NIG). **Welter:** M. Muruli (UGA). **L. Middle:** L. Mwale (ZAM). **Middle:** F. Lucas (STV). **L. Heavy:** W. Knight (ENG). **Heavy:** N. Meade (ENG).
Silver medals: E. McKenzie (WAL), A. Harrison (SCO).
Bronze medals: J. Bambrick (SCO), J. Douglas (SCO), J. Rodgers (NIR), S. Cooney (SCO), R. Davies (ENG), C. Speare (ENG), G. Ferris (NIR).

Edmonton, Canada - 1978

L. Fly: S. Muchoki (KEN). **Fly:** M. Irungu (KEN). **Bantam:** B. McGuigan (NIR). **Feather:** A. Nelson (GHA). **Light:** G. Hamill (NIR). **L. Welter:** W. Braithwaite (GUY). **Welter:** M. McCallum (JAM). **L. Middle:** K. Perlette (CAN). **Middle:** P. McElwaine (AUS). **L. Heavy:** R. Fortin (CAN). **Heavy:** J. Awome (ENG).

Silver medals: J. Douglas (SCO), K. Beattie (NIR), D. Parkes (ENG), V. Smith (ENG).

Bronze medals: H. Russell (NIR), M. O'Brien (ENG), J. McAllister (SCO), T. Feal (WAL).

Brisbane, Australia - 1982

L. Fly: A. Wachire (KEN). **Fly:** M. Mutua (KEN). **Bantam:** J. Orewa (NIG). **Feather:** P. Konyegwachie (NIG). **Light:** H. Khalili (KEN). **L. Welter:** C. Ossai (NIG). **Welter:** C. Pyatt (ENG). **L. Middle:** S. O'Sullivan (CAN). **Middle:** J. Price (ENG). **L. Heavy:** F. Sani (FIJ). **Heavy:** W. de Wit (CAN).

Silver medals: J. Lyon (ENG), J. Kelly (SCO), R. Webb (NIR), P. Hanlon (ENG), J. McDonnell (ENG), N. Croombes (ENG), H. Hylton (ENG).

Bronze medals: R. Gilbody (ENG), C. McIntosh (ENG), R. Corr (NIR).

Edinburgh, Scotland - 1986

L. Fly: S. Olson (CAN). **Fly:** J. Lyon (ENG). **Bantam:** S. Murphy (ENG). **Feather:** B. Downey (CAN). **Light:** A. Dar (CAN). **L. Welter:** H. Grant (CAN). **Welter:** D. Dyer (ENG). **L. Middle:** D. Sherry (CAN). **Middle:** R. Douglas (ENG). **L. Heavy:** J. Moran (ENG). **Heavy:** J. Peau (NZL). **S. Heavy:** L. Lewis (CAN).

Silver medals: M. Epton (ENG), R. Nash (NIR), P. English (ENG), N. Haddock (WAL), J. McAlister (SCO), H. Lawson (SCO), D. Young (SCO), A. Evans (WAL).

Bronze medals: W. Docherty (SCO), J. Todd (NIR), K. Webber (WAL), G. Brooks (SCO), J. Wallace (SCO), C. Carleton (NIR), J. Jacobs (ENG), B. Lowe (NIR), D. Denny (NIR), G. Thomas (WAL), A. Mullen (SCO), G. Ferrie (SCO), P. Tinney (NIR), B. Pullen (WAL), E. Cardouza (ENG), J. Oyebola (ENG).

Auckland, New Zealand - 1990

L. Fly: J. Juko (UGA). **Fly:** W. McCullough (NIR). **Bantam:** S. Mohammed (NIG). **Feather:** J. Irwin (ENG). **Light:** G. Nyakana (UGA). **L. Welter:** C. Kane (SCO). **Welter:** D. Defiagbon (NIG). **L. Middle:** R. Woodhall (ENG). **Middle:** C. Johnson (CAN). **L. Heavy:** J. Akhasamba (KEN). **Heavy:** G. Onyango (KEN). **S. Heavy:** M. Kenny (NZL).

Bronze medals: D. Anderson (SCO), M. Edwards (ENG), P. Douglas (NIR).

Victoria, Canada - 1994

L. Fly: H. Ramadhani (KEN). **Fly:** P. Shepherd (SCO). **Bantam:** R. Peden (AUS). **Feather:** C. Patton (CAN). **Light:** M. Strange (CAN). **L. Welter:** P. Richardson (ENG). **Welter:** N. Sinclair (NIR). **L. Middle:** J. Webb (NIR). **Middle:** R. Donaldson (CAN). **L. Heavy:** D. Brown (CAN). **Heavy:** O. Ahmed (KEN). **S. Heavy:** D. Dokiwari (NIG).

Silver medals: S. Oliver (ENG), J. Cook (WAL), M. Reneghan (NIR), M. Winters (NIR), J. Wilson (SCO).

Bronze medals: D. Costello (ENG), J. Townsley (SCO), D. Williams (ENG).

Spencer Oliver (left), shown here beating John McLean in the 1994 ABA bantamweight final, won silver for England in the recent Commonwealth Games

Les Clark

Directory of Ex-Boxers' Associations

by Ron Olver

BOURNEMOUTH Founded 1980. HQ: Mallard Road Bus Services Social Club, Bournemouth. Dai Dower (P); Peter Fay (C & S), 44 Avenue Road, Christchurch, Dorset; Ken Wells (VC); Percy Singer (T).

CORK Founded 1973. HQ: Acra House, Maylor Street, Cork. Johnny Fitzgerald (P & C); John Cronin (VC); Eamer Coughlan (T); Tim O'Sullivan (S & PRO), Acra House, Maylor Street, Dublin.

CORNWALL Founded 1989. HQ: St Austell British Legion and Redruth British Legion in alternate months. Roy Coote (P); Stan Cullis (C); Len Magee (VC); Jimmy Miller (T); John Soloman (S), 115 Albany Road, Redruth.

CROYDON Founded 1982. HQ: The Prince Of Wales, Thornton Heath. Tom Powell, BEM (P); Bill Goddard (C); Bill Curd (VC); Morton Lewis (T); Gilbert Allnutt (S), 25 Melrose Avenue, Norbury, London SW16 4RX.

EASTERN AREA Founded 1973. HQ: Norfolk Dumpling, Cattle Market, Hall Road, Norwich. Brian Fitzmaurice (P); Alfred Smith (C); Clive Campling (VC); Eric Middleton (T & S), 48 City Road, Norwich NR1 3AU.

IPSWICH Founded 1970. HQ: Flying Horse, Waterford Road, Ipswich. Alby Kingham (P); Frank Webb (C); Vic Thurlow (T); Nigel Wheeler (PRO & S); 20 Stratford Road, Ipswich 1PL 6OF.

IRISH Founded 1973. HQ: National Boxing Stadium, South Circular Road, Dublin. Maxie McCullagh (P); Gerry O' Colmain (C); Willie Duggan (VC); Tommy Butler (T); Denis Morrison (S), 55 Philipsburgh Terrace, Marino, Dublin.

KENT Founded 1967. HQ: Chatham WMC, New Road, Chatham. Teddy Bryant (P); Alf Tingley (C); Mick Smith (VC); Fred Atkins (T); Ray Lambert (PRO); Paul Nihill MBE, (S), 59 Balfour Road, Rochester, Kent.

LEEDS Founded 1952. HQ: North Leeds WMC, Burmantofts, Lincoln Green, Leeds 9. Johnny Durkin (P); Harry Hare (C); Frankie Brown (VC); Alan Alster (T); Steve Butler (PRO); Paul Seymour (S), 16 Brander Grove, Leeds 9.

LEFT-HOOK CLUB Betty Faux (S), 144 Longmoor Lane, Aintree, Liverpool. No regular meetings. Formed specifically with the aim of holding functions to raise money in order to help former boxers in need.

LEICESTER Founded 1972. HQ: Belgrave WMC, Checketts Road, Leicester. Pat Butler (P); Mick Greaves (C); Mrs Rita Jones (T); Norman Jones (S), 60 Dumbleton Avenue, Leicester LE3 2EG.

LONDON Founded 1971. HQ; St Pancras Conservative Club, Argyle Street, London. Jack Powell (P); Micky O'Sullivan (C); Andy Williamson (VC); Ron Olver (PRO); Ray Caulfield (T); Mrs Mary Powell (S), 36 St Peters Street, Islington, London N1 8JT.

MANCHESTER Founded 1968. HQ: British Rail Social Club, Store Street, Manchester. Jackie Braddock (P); Tommy Proffit (C); Jack Edwards (VC); Eddie Lillis (T); Jackie Moran (S), 4 Cooper House, Boundry Lane, Hulme, Manchester.

MERSEYSIDE (Liverpool) Founded 1973. HQ: Queens Hotel, Derby Square, Liverpool. Johnny Cooke (P); Terry Riley (C); Jim Boyd (VC); Jim Jenkinson (T); Billy Davies (S), 7 Rockford Walk, Southdene, Kirkby, Liverpool.

NORTHAMPTONSHIRE Founded 1981. HQ: Exclusive Club, Gold Street, Northampton. Tony Perrett (P); John Cullen (C); Winston Hughes (T); Keith Hall (S), 29 Sydney Street, Kettering, Northants NN16 0HZ.

NORTHERN FEDERATION Founded 1974. Several member EBAs. Annual Gala. Eddie Monahan (S), 16 Braemar Avenue, Marshside, Southport.

NORTHERN IRELAND Founded 1970. HQ: Ulster Sports Club, Belfast. J. Bradbury (P); Gerry Smyth (C); J. Hill (VC); J. Garrett (T); Al Gibson (S), 900 Crumlin Road, Belfast.

NORTH STAFFS & SOUTH CHESHIRE Founded 1969. HQ: The Saggar Makers Bottom Knocker, Market Place, Burslem, Stoke on Trent. Tut Whalley (P); Roy Simms (VC); Les Dean (S); John Greatbach (T); Billy Tudor (C & PRO), 133 Sprinkbank Road, Chell Heath, Stoke on Trent, Staffs ST6 6HW.

NORWICH HQ: West End Retreat, Brown Street, Norwich. Les King (P); John Pipe (C); Jack Wakefield (T); Dick Sadd (S), 76 Orchard Street, Norwich.

NOTTINGHAM Founded 1979. HQ: The Lion Hotel, Clumber Street, Nottingham. Frank Parkes (P); Frank Hayes (C); John Kinsella (T); Jim Shrewsbury (S), 219 Rosecroft Drive, Nottingham NG5 6EL.

NOTTS & DERBY Founded 1973. Billy Strange (C); Dick Johnson (S & PRO), 15 Church Street, Pinxton, Nottingham.

PLYMOUTH Founded 1982. HQ: Exmouth Road Social Club, Stoke, Plymouth. George Borg (P); Tom Pryce-Davies (C); Doug Halliday (VC); Arthur Willis (T); Buck Taylor (S), 15 Greenbank Avenue, St Judes, Plymouth PL4 9BT.

PRESTON Founded 1973. HQ: County Arms Hotel, Deepdale Road, Preston. Albert Bradley (P); Brian Petherwick (C); Frank Brown (T); Ted Sumner (S), 7 Kew Gardens, Penwortham, Preston PR1 0DR.

READING Founded 1977. HQ: Salisbury Club, Kings Road, Reading. Roland Dakin (P); Bob Pitman (C); Arnold Whatmore (T); Bob Sturgess (S).

ST HELENS Founded 1983. HQ: Travellers Rest Hotel, Crab Street, St Helens. George Thomas (C); Jimmy O'Keefe (VC); Tommy McNamara (T); Paul Britch (S), 40 Ashtons Green Drive, Parr, St Helens.

SEFTON Founded 1975. HQ: St Benet's Parochial Club, Netherton, Bootle. Alf Lunt (T); Johnny Holmes (S); 41 Higher End Park, Sefton, Bootle.

SLOUGH Founded 1973. HQ: Faraday Hall Ex-Servicemen's Club, Faraday Road, Slough. Max Quartermain (P); Jack Bridge (C); Charlie Knight (T); Ernie Watkins (S), 5 Sunbury Road, Eton, Windsor.

SQUARE RING Founded 1978. HQ: Torquay Social Club. George Pook (P); Maxie Beech (VC); Billy Burke (S); Johnny Mudge (T); Paul King (C), 10 Pine Court Apartments, Middle Warberry Road, Torquay.

SUNDERLAND Founded 1959. HQ: Hendon Gardens, Sunderland. Bert Ingram (P); Terry Lynn (C); Joe Riley (PRO); Les Simm (S), 21 Orchard Street, Pallion, Sunderland SR4 6QL.

SUSSEX Founded 1974. HQ: Brighton & Hove Sports & Social Club, Conway Street, Hove. Bill Pullum (P); Bert Hollows (C); Harry Parkinson (T); John Ford (S), 69 Moyne Close, Hove, Sussex.

SWANSEA & SOUTH WEST WALES Founded 1983. HQ: Villiers Arms, Neath Road, Hafod, Swansea. Cliff Curvis (P); Gordon Pape (C); Ernie Wallis (T); Len Smith (S), Cockett Inn, Cockett, Swansea SA2 0GB.

TRAMORE Founded 1981. HQ: Robinson Bar, Main Street, Tramore, Co Waterford. T. Flynn (P); J. Dunne (C); C. O'Reilly (VC); W. Hutchinson (T); N. Graham (PRO); Pete Graham (S), 3 Riverstown, Tramore.

TYNESIDE Founded 1970. HQ: The Swan Public House, Heworth. Billy Charlton (P); Maxie Walsh (C); Gordon Smith (VC); Malcolm Dinning (T); Dave McCormick (S); Bill Wilkie (PRO), 60 Calderdale Avenue, Walker, Newcastle NE6 4HN.

WELSH Founded 1976. HQ: Rhydyfelin Rugby Club, Pontypridd, Mid Glamorgan. Syd Worgan (P & S); Vernon Ball (C); Howard Winstone (VC); Llew Miles (T & PRO), 7 Edward Street, Miskin, Mountain Ash, Mid Glamorgan.

The above information is set at the time of going to press and no responsibility can be taken for any changes in officers or addresses of HQs that may happen between then and publication.

ABBREVIATIONS
P - President. C - Chairman. VC - Vice Chairman. T - Treasurer. S - Secretary. PRO - Public Relations Officer.

Henry Cooper, one of Britain's most popular former boxers, and now a member of LEBA (London Ex-Boxers' Association)

Obituaries

by Ron Olver

It is impossible to list everyone, but I have again done my level best to include final tributes for as many of the well-known boxers and other well-known names within the sport, who have passed away since the 1994 Yearbook was published. We honour them and will remember them.

ANGELL Steve *Born* Hemel Hempstead, 25 April, 1951. *Died* May, 1994. *Pro* 1973-1978. After 14 straight wins, Steve was beaten by Des Morrison for the Southern Area welterweight title (1974). Was also beaten by Billy Waith in a final eliminator for the British welterweight title (1977) and by Peter Neal for the Southern Area welterweight title (1978). A member of the well-known Cricklewood boxing family, comprising Mick (middle) and Fred (bantam), Steve beat Ray Fallone, Tommy Joyce, Herbie McLean, Derek Simpson, Henry Rhiney, Achille Mitchell and Johnny Pincham.

ARCEL Ray *Born* Terre Haute, Indiana, USA, 30 August 1899 *Died* March, 1994. One of the all-time greats as trainer, second and mentor. Learned his trade in Grupps Gym, New York City, under the guidance of Frank "Doc" Bagley and Dai Dollings. Among the champions with whom Ray was associated were Benny Leonard, Jack "Kid" Berg, Charley "Phil" Rosenberg, Lou Brouillard, Barney Ross, Freddie Steele, Tony Zale, Ezzard Charles and Jimmy Braddock. He first "retired" in 1954 to build up a steel handling firm in New York, but made a "comeback" in 1971 to assist Alfonso "Peppermint" Frazer win the WBA light-welterweight title. He then helped the Legendary Roberto Duran and retired again after being in Larry Holmes' corner against Gerry Cooney. Although himself not well, Jack "Kid" Berg insisted on going to America to celebrate Ray's birthday a few years before Jack himself passed on.

ASHUN Gordon *Born* Bootle. *Died* October, 1993, aged 72. *Pro* 1939-1950. Joined the Gordon Institute at age of 15, Where trainer Laddy Walker steered him to victory in the Dom Volante Cup, a competition for lightweights open to all Merseywide amateurs. Just before World War II, Gordon won the Territorial Army Championships for the Liverpool-Scottish. After around 40 amateur bouts, he turned pro in 1939, losing his first three contests all inside the distance, and all under the name of "Kid Ash." Went back to the drawing board and, under the management of Harold Higginson, kayoed Peter Herron in one round. Joined the Army in 1942 and served with 7th Armoured Division in North Africa, then on to the Salerno landings in Italy, and finally was in the thick of things on D-Day. During that time he beat Billy Hardacre, Mick Howard and Billy Barnes and drew with Al Phillips (1941). Left the Army in 1946 and resumed his boxing career, beating Ginger Ward, Johnny Ingle, Dennis Chadwick, Dick Shields, all under manager Jimmy Duffy. Also defeated Jim Watson, Teddy Lee, but was twice beaten by Johnny Sullivan. Was a fitter/welder with English Electric Company and founder of Merseyside EBA and of Mayfair BTC. Once turned down the chance of playing for Liverpool FC, preferring to box instead.

BANASKO Peter *From* Liverpool. *Died* 22 November, 1993 aged 77. Started boxing at the age of nine at St Malachy's Gym and by the time he was 14 had competed in over 100 bouts, under trainer, Ted Denvir. After twice winning British schoolboys' titles, he turned pro in 1933 as a flyweight, retiring in the early 1940s as a lightweight. Although handicapped by brittle hands, he had 50 bouts, beating Billy Warnock, Fred Bebbington, Joe Horridge, Benny Thackray, Ivor Drew and Con Flynn. After serving in the Army as a Sergeant PTI, he turned to managing, and looked after future world featherweight champion, Hogan Bassey, when the latter first came to Britain. They parted company after Bassey won the Empire title (1955) and Peter retired from the sport. He also managed other Nigerian boxers such as Sandy Manuel, Bola Lawal, Jimmy Zale and Israel Boyle. Did charity work for the Catholic Church and helped with "Meals on Wheels", but was virtually housebound after a heart attack in 1988.

BARTLETT Johnny *Born* Kings Cross, London. *Died* March, 1994. Changed his name from Fred Wilson and boxed as a pro between 1932 and 1946. Averaged a fight a month for most of his career, beating Fred Bloomfield, Harry Fox, Bill Godfrey, Tommy Luscombe, Dave Smith, Bill Knight, Jim Trainor, Jack Stone and Charlie Scott. Had three bouts with Jack Powell, winning the first and losing the next two. Also drew with Billy Barr, Red Pullen and Harry Lister.

BASSETT Percy *Born* Philadelphia, USA, 1928. *Died* July, 1993. Fighting as a pro featherweight between 1947 and 1955, he was unlucky to be scrapping at the same time as outstanding ringmen such as Willie Pep and Sandy Saddler. However, when Saddler was inducted into the US army, he became world "interim" champion on defeating Ray Famechon in February 1953 and held the title until losing to Teddy "Red Top" Davis in November 1954. Was one of the most feared and avoided fighters of his day, beating Lew Jenkins, Bobby Bell, Terry Young, Orlando Zulueta, Teddy Davis, Charley Riley, Lulu Perez and two men well known over here in Danny Webb and Aaron Joshua, among many others, before being forced to retire due to failing health.

BLAKE Johnny *Born* Chelsea, London, 26 October, 1912. *Died* 20 July, 1994. A pro between 1937 and 1949, he met Ernie Woodman four times, winning two, losing one and drawing the other. Beat Ted Barter, Johnny Jenkins, Charlie Webster, Joe Kelt, Mossy Condon, George Howard, Jack Milburn, Dick Johnson, Dave McCleave and Battling Jo Jo. Also met Freddie Mills, Dick Turpin, Albert Finch, Ginger Sadd, Jack Powell, "Battling" Charlie Parkin, Reg Spring, Bob Cleaver and Ron Grogan. Another fine middleweight who came from Chelsea was Billy Bird. They met twice, Johnny winning one with the other being drawn. A bricklayer by trade, he and wife Helen had nine children and had been married for 60 years.

BODDINGTON Arthur *Died* 31 January, 1994. Popular boxer who tackled the best, beating top men like Nel Tarleton (1926), and meeting world champions, Frankie Genaro, Emile Pladner and Al Brown. Was a member of Northampton Ex-Boxers' Association.

BRATTON Johnny *Born* Little Rock, Arkansas, USA, 9 September, 1927. *Died* August, 1993. *Pro* 1944-1955. Won the vacant NBA welterweight title by beating Charlie Fusari (1951), but was defeated by Kid Gavilan for the vacant world title (1951). Although again beaten by Gavilan for the latter's world title (1953), among his victims were Freddie Dawson, Willie Joyce, Joe Brown, Gene Hairston, Lester Felton, Bobby Dykes, Livio Minelli, Pierre Langlois, Laurent Dauthuille, Del Flanagan, Joe Miceli, Tuzo Portuguez and Danny Womber.

BURNS Sam *From* London *Died* May, 1994 aged 80. Last surviving member of the Jack Solomons' team, which included Nat Seller and Dave Edgar. Started as copy-boy for the London Evening News and as a journalist wrote on boxing and racing for the *Sporting Life*. Later employed in the box-office at Earls Court, he tried promoting, but settled as a top manager, looking after Bobby Neill, Eddie Thomas, Tony Sibson, Chris and Kevin Finnegan. However, his most satisfying feat was in guiding Terry Downes to the world middleweight title (1961). Became general manager of the William Hill organisation. In the later years suffered from Parkinson's Disease.

CAMPBELL Johnny *From* Birkenhead. *Died* 2 May, 1994, aged 89. Father was a scrap dealer and Johnny was out with a pony and cart from the age of 13. When he was 17 his passage was paid (£22) to seek fame and fortune in America, where he watched the Dempsey-Firpo fight, but after his father died in 1929, Johnny returned home. In September 1939 he built a gym in his yard and opened it as the Provincial ABC, where he produced stars like Joe Bygraves and Pat McAteer. When both turned pro, Johnny managed them. He also managed Wally Thom, Les McAteer and Johnny Cooke, whom manager Johnny described as "the greatest of them all. He never gave me a single headache" and when Johnny Cooke retired in 1971, he decided to call it a day also. Countless boxers had

passed through his hands, and his Whetstone Lane gym became famous. He owned a flourishing scrap and car spares business, a beautiful home in Bidston Village, and he and his wife Mary had four sons and three daughters.

CAMPBELL Martin *Born* Wishaw, 2 December, 1966. *Died* February, 1994. Turned pro in 1988 with Alex Morrison, having represented Scotland as an amateur while with Springfield Boys ABC. Only had three fights as a professional, winning just one and had recently made a comeback to the ring. Died at his home in tragic circumstances.

CARRINGTON Johnny *Born* Nottingham, 5 October, 1928. *Died* 10 September, 1993. *Pro* 1947-1952. Beat Ricky McCullough, Tony Brazil, Johnny Hudson, Stan Parkes, Cliff Anderson, Owen Trainor, Allan Buxton, Ralph Moss, Billy Dixon, Jackie Ryder, Chris Jenkins, Teddy Larkham, Billy Cunningham and Ivor Simpson and averaged 20 bouts per year throughout his career. Was a member of Nottingham Ex-Boxers' Association.

CLARKE Peter *From* Liverpool. *Died* 20 March, 1994. A member of St Peters ABC, he turned pro in the early 1930s. Had around 100 bouts and opponents included Tony Butcher, Tom Bailey, Tommy Hyams, Jim Learoyd, Harry Mizler, Kid Farlo, Norman Snow, Alby Day and Dick Corbett. Also trained with world champion, Freddie Miller, when he came to Britain to fight Nel Tarleton. Affectionately known as "Jimmy Cagney" because of his bouncy walk, he was a member of Merseyside EBA.

CORBETT 111 Young *Born* Raffaele Capabianca Giordano in Protenza, Italy, 27 May, 1905. *Died* July, 1993. Raised in California, he took the ringname Corbett, thus following in the footsteps of the former featherweight champion, and emulated his hero when winning the world welterweight title from Jackie Fields in February 1933. However, he was not destined to hold the championship belt for long, just over three months to be precise, before being kayoed inside a round by the hard-hitting Jimmy McLarnin. In a pro career that was launched in 1919 and ended in 1942, he lost only 11 times in 151 bouts and defeated past and future world champions such as Young Jack Thompson, Ceferino Garcia, Mickey Walker, Gus Lesnevich, Billy Conn and Fred Apostoli, prior to calling it a day.

COX Bill London. *Died* 27 December, 1993. Assistant Secretary of the Amateur Boxing Association (1975), he was appointed Executive Officer (1979), but resigned after ten months. Later elected ABA Chairman (1992), although unable to complete his term of office following the re-organisation of the ABA into a Limited Company. Served 27 years with Repton ABC, and was a referee and judge, representing the ABA on the international front at the AIBA and EABA.

CRASTER Harry *Born* Middlesbrough 29 September, 1915. *Died* 10 September, 1993. *Pro* 1929-1942. Won the Northern Area lightweight title by beating Jimmy Stewart (1937), for which he was awarded a Boxing News Certificate of Merit. Beat Marcel Cerdan on a disqualification in the latter's first contest in Britain (1939), and defeated Billy Charlton, Joe Baldasara, Jack Lewis, Billy Quinlan, Douglas Parker, Sonny Lee. Met Arthur Danahar three times (lost all three), Harry Mizler (won one lost one), Lefty Flynn (won one, lost one, drew two) and was outpointed by Jimmy Walsh, Ernie Roderick, and Jack "Kid" Berg. Later he was posted to Egypt as a Sergeant PTI, linking up with Terry Allen. Standing only 5ft 5in., and having put on two stones, he decided to retire, coaching the boys at Bede College (Durham University) for six years. Following that, he became a driver in the United Bus Company until retiring in 1982.

CUMMINGS Tommy Leicester. *Died* 14 July, 1994, aged 78. *Pro* 1945-1950. Beaten by Owen Johnson for the North Midlands Area featherweight title (1950), but defeated Jackie Turpin, Johnny Kent, Arthur Dykes, Alf Clark, Billy Daniels, Ernie Ormerod, Stan Mace and Gerry Speers. Fought Ken Diston three times, winning one and loosing the other two and also met Freddie King, Bobby Boland, Jimmy Webster, Peter Fay and Danny O'Sullivan. A Member of Leicester EBA, he was also vice-president of Bournemouth EBA.

DOCHERTY Paddy *Died* May, 1994, aged 84 in Glasgow. Turned pro in 1931 and met world featherweight champion Benny Lynch seven times between 1931 and 1933, winning two, losing three, with two draws. Also fought Jim Campbell, Jim Maharg, Jim Brady, Freddie Tennant and Boy McIntosh. His real name was Paddy Reilly.

DOCHERTY Sammy *From* Glasgow. *Died* 1994, aged 73. Top Scottish promoter in the 1950s and 1960s, helping the careers of champions like Peter Keenan and Freddie Gilroy, he also managed former world champion, John Caldwell. Had the knack of staging highly entertaining contests such as Danny "Bang Bang" Womber v Bob Frost amd Willie Toweel v Guy Gracia and hosted outstanding outdoor shows at Firhill Stadium featuring Peter Keenan. Retired in 1968 to live at Girvan on the Ayrshire coast.

DUFFETT Frank *Born* Camberwell, London, 16 January, 1913. *Died* 3 November, 1993. His father, Fred Duffett, ran a gym used by all the top boxers over the years and that was where Frank learned about coaching and training. In 1920 he joined Lynn ABC, coaching there for over 50 years. He guided among others, Terry Waller, who won five ABA titles, and Billy Knight, who won three ABA titles, plus a Commonwealth Games Gold Medal. Frank also worked with many professional champions, such as Freddie Mills, Len Harvey, Paddy Maguire, John and Pat McCormack and, in particular, Wally Lesley's stable, which included Dick Richardson and Johnny Lewis. Among his business interests was the Ampro Sports shop near Waterloo Station. Awarded the British Empire Medal

in 1992, Frank was also a member of the London Ex-Boxers' Association, winning the Joe Bromley Award by the Boxing Writers' Club for oustanding services to the sport.

FITZHUGH Sid *From* Little Broughton, Salford. *Died* 20 January, 1994, in his late 80s. At the age of 18 he joined the 2nd Dragoon Guards, being posted to India, where he won Army titles at lightweight and welter. In 1936, he arranged a few fights for local pros in Northampton and, when one dropped out, Sid took his place, and was outpointed by former Army champion, Vic Jones. Hardly surprising when it was noted that Sid was conceding a stone in weight. Continued as a pro, and in 1938 he was outpointed by Dick Turpin. His best win came againsed Canadian, Joe Gollob, whom he stopped after coming in as a sub at the Devonshire Club, on New Year's Day, 1939. The same year he beat Cyril Johnson, Sam Smithson ans drew with heavyweight, Dave Lapping. On Army reserve and called up for World War ii, he was posted to palestine, where he met his manager George Biddles. Sid was secretary and vice-president of Northampton EBA.

FOSTER Bob *Born* Covent Garden, 6 April, 1923. *Died* 20 January, 1994. Won Schools and London Federation titles and at 17 boxed against Army champion, Bombardier Merryfield, who played the part of "Uncle Albert" in the popular TV series Only Fools and horses. Served in the Royal Air Force, turning pro in 1946 and beating men of the class of Bob Frost, Bert Middleton, Ken West, George Barker, Harry Brown, Harry Warner, Roy Davies and Joe Corcoran, befor retiring in 1952.

FREEMAN Bert "Kid" *Died* 2 September, 1994, aged 84. Turned pro 1930 and won the Kent flyweight title (1930) and then the county featherweight title (1933). For this he was presented with a Silver Belt, which he was proud to display whenever the occasion arose. Among his victims were Bugler Lake, British, European and Empire champion, and he also met the South African champion, Johnny Holt, with almost half of his 80 bouts staged at the Rochester Casino. A founder-member of Kent EBA, later becoming a vice-president, he was an "ever-present" at their monthly meetings, and, in July 1994, was presented with an engraved goblet in recognition of his services to boxing and, in particular, to Kent EBA.

GEE George *Died* March 1994. A former West of England featherweight champion, in 1936 he went seven rounds in Plymouth with Jackie Wilson. The American, who went on to win the world (NBA) title two years later, was in Britain on a barnstorming tour which took in 12 fights against some of the best man the country had on offer, with only Ronnie James able to lower his colours.

HARPER Danny *Born* Barnsley, 18 October, 1967. *Died* September, 1993. Promising young welterweight who turned pro in September 1992 and had won two and drawn one in his four contests to date. Managed by Keith Tate, Danny had previously boxed for Grimethorpe ABC and competed in the Yorkshire and Humberside ABA semi-finals in 1992.

JENKINS Richie *Died* 1994, aged 59. Boxed as a pro from 1953 until 1955 and beat Roy Paine, Cliff Giles, Sid Hiom and Laurie McShane. As an amateur, he won schools, and Welsh titles, representing England and the ABA in internationals during 1951-52, against USA, Italy and Denmark (twice), winning three out of four.

KELLY Chris *From* Liverpool. *Died* September, 1993, aged 65. Had a handful of bouts for Kensington BC before being granted a pro licence in 1944 at the age of 16 years and two months. Retired in 1953 after 75 contests, having beaten Jimmy Green, Joe Carr, Tommy Proffitt, Denny Dawson, Jackie Horseman, Freddie Hicks, Tom Bailey, Jackie Lucraft, Johnny Molloy, Charlie White and Tony Hardwick.

KILIMANJARO Proud *Born* Zimbabwe. *Died* 1994. Real name Proud Chinembiri. Turning pro in 1981, he won the Zimbabwean heavyweight title the following year and two fights later was crowned African champion when beating Adamah Nelson (1982). Disappointed on his first trip to England, when losing to Hughroy Currie on points (1985), and as ABU champion he came back to challenge Horace Notice for the Commonwealth title in March, 1987. His luck was still out as he was stopped in the eighth round by the hard-hitting Notice. After that, it was a downhill slope and as to the nature of his death, apart from a one-line entry in a boxing paper announcing it, the writer can add nothing further.

LARTY Eddie "Zulu Kid" *Born* Ghana, 17 April, 1923. *Died* 30 July, 1994. Came to Merseyside in the late 1940s with Roy Ankrah and other countrymen from what was then the Gold Coast, of which Eddie was featherweight champion. His career was unfortunately shortened because of blindness, due to running into a lampost on a misty training run in Switzerland. Beat Jackie Ryan, Jackie Molloy, drew with Johnny Martin and also met George Stewart and Bernard Pugh. After Stopping Ron Gladwell in two rounds at Northampton in 1949, he was asked if he would box again the same night as Lionel Binney's opponant had not turned up. Eddie agreed, and stopped Binney inside two rounds. More recently, the Left-Hook Club of Liverpool organised a testimonial night in his honour. Served in Burma with the Royal West African Frontier Force during World War II.

LYONS Paddy *Born* Dewsbury, 1919, *Died* 1994. Turned pro in 1939 and retired in 1945 after winning the Northern Area middleweight title by beating "Battling" Charlie Parkin. Also defeated Jack McKnight, Dave McCleave, Ted Barter, Paddy Roche, Johnny Downes and Billy Mawson.

McCULLOUGH Ricky *Born* Belfast, 12 July, 1926. *Died* January, 1994. *Pro* 1946-1953. Beat Gerry Smyth to win the Northern Ireland lightweight title (June 1953), losing it in a return (September 1953). Also defeated Bertie Conn, Stan Skinkiss, Cliff Anderson, Gordon Goodman, Ronnie Gill, Allan Buxton, Ben Duffy and Laurie Buxton. Settled in London and attended a few meetings of the London Ex-Boxers' Association.

McDERMOTT Gerry *Born* Screen, Co. Sligo, Ireland, 29 May, 1923. *Died* 24 January, 1994. As a pro between 1943 and 1952 he beat Dennis Powell, Bill Brennan, Matt Hardy and George Dawson and became Eire heavyweight champion. Had several jobs, including painter and decorator, bouncer and electrical storeman at Times Newspapers, where he remained for 20 years. In 1971 he contracted a muscle wasting disease, and for two years, couldn't eat, swallow or talk. By some miracle he pulled through, but was unable to do any heavy work. However, he did work again until retiring at 63. Sadly, as his condition deteriorated, he was confined to a wheelchair, then to bed. When his lungs were infected, he was rushed to Queens Square Hospital, where he died six days later.

McLEAVY Johnny *Born* Dagenham. *Died* at the end of 1993. An Army representative at heavyweight, where he was in the shadows of future British and European champion, Johnny Gardner, on coming out of the armed service in 1949 he immediately turned pro. McLeavy was a good test for any aspiring youngster, having 23 contests, of which he won 12 and drew two, before retiring in 1955, after being stopped in the fourth round by another future European titleholder, Dick Richardson.

Phil Martin holds the BBBoC "Special Award" for services to boxing Harry Goodwin

MARTIN Phil Manchester. *Born* 5 April, 1950. *Died* 27 May, 1994. Real name Phil Adelegun. *Pro* 1974-1978. In a career that took in 20 contests, Phil won the vacant Central Area light-heavyweight title by beating Pat Thompson (1975), but was beaten by Tim Wood for the vacant British title (April, 1976) and by Bunny Johnson in a final eliminator for the British title (December, 1976). Turning to training and managing, he took over a run-down building and made it a gym, which eventually became known as Champs Camp. Anyone could visit the gym, amateurs, pros, and, with those who were neither, were made welcome. Phil said he wanted to keep youngsters off the streets, and give them a purpose in life. This proved so successful that he produced four champions, Paul Burke, Maurice Core, Frank Grant and Carl Thompson, at the same time. Earlier this year, the Board of Control gave him the Special Award for outstanding services to the sport at their annual dinner. He had known about his cancer condition for quite a while, but kept going right up to the end. No one ever made a bigger contribution to boxing.

MASTRO Earl *Born* Chicago, USA, 5 February, 1908. *Died* January, 1994. An Italian-American, whose real name was Verle Maestro, he was a crack featherweight of the late 1920s, boxing as a pro between 1926-1931. Fought his way to a shot at the world title in 1931, but was outpointed by "Battling" Battalino and retired. Managed by Art Winch and Sam Pian, Earl beat Fidel la Barba, Kid Francis, Eddie Shea, Young Nationalista, Gregorio Vidal, Bud Taylor and Santiago Zorilla, in a career that saw him retire at his peak rather than succumb to less talented men.

MILLS Ernie *Born* London. *Died* 16 January, 1994, aged 88. As an amateur he boxed for Lynn ABC before turning pro in 1923. In beating Arthur Cunningham, Jimmy Welsh, Johnny Gordon, George Swinbourne, Harry Pullen, Teddy Duffy, Wally Milsom, Jimmy Lawrence, Ernie Jeal, Johnny Whyman and Tommy Mitchell and also going 15 rounds with Arthur Boddington, his pro career lasted until 1934. On retiring, Ernie trained the boys at the Lynn along with Frank Duffett and later looked after Tommy Daly's pro stable. The father of former leading amateur, Lenny Mills, now a London Ex-boxers' Association committee member, he was also a member of LEBA.

MOGARD Don New Brunswick, Canada. *Born* 12 August, 1925. *Died* 4 June, 1994. Was the first man to go the full distance with Rocky Marciano (ten rounds). Never saw a boxing ring until he joined the Canadian Air Force (1943), where at Mountain View Airport, a bombing and gunnery training centre, he met PTI Corporal Vic Bagnato, who had been a good amateur with two brothers then boxing in the pro ranks. After demob (1946), Don went to see Vic in Toronto, and started his pro career there. Went to Paterson, New Jersey, where he linked up with "Squire" Bill Daly and Lee Savold and from December 1947, Don won 14 successive bouts before losing to world title contender, Roland Lastarza. In 1949, he came to Britain with Bill Daly, Savold and Frankie Cortese, just after the Marciano bout and beat Paddy Slavin, Gerry McDermott, Frank Bell and met Jack London and Don Cockell. When Daly returned to the United States with Ray Wilding and Charles Henry, Don stayed in Britain with wife Barbara. In 1951, Don was outpointed by Albert Finch, and retired to join the Post Office. A modest man, he never went out of his way to reveal that he had settled in Britain and it wasn't until former Walworth middleweight, Ron King, who lived

near Don, mentioned to Solly Cantor at Tommy McGovern's funeral that Don was here, that Solly brought it to our notice. Almost immediately, Don and Ron were made members of the London Ex-boxers' Association, thus joining Solly. In 1990, Don and Solly were inducted into the Canadian "Hall of Fame", something which Don said made him very proud. He once made the remark: "We have a few holidays in Canada, but when we get back to England we are home."

MORRISON Gordon Sheffield. *Born* 12 February, 1931. *Died* 31 October, 1993. Pro 1950-1952. Beat Patsy Griffith, Vic Levers and Harry Cook, all in one round. Also defeated Fred Evans. Started boxing at Hillsborough Boys Club, winning a NCB title and the Army lightweight championship during his time in the amateur ranks. A butcher by trade, he was treasurer and later chairman of Sheffield EBA and a member of London EBA, whose president, Jack Powell, also came from Sheffield.

MOUNSEY BILLY Preston. *Died* October, 1993. Pro 1929-1939. Started as a flyweight and finished as a middleweight. Beat "Battling" Jim Hayes, Bert Chambers, Chick Duggan and Johnny Blake.

NELSON Bob Liverpool. *Died* February, 1994, aged 81. Beat Ernie Roderick (1934), Paddy Bennett, Stan Quinn, Ted Moran, "Battling" McCormick and George Boyce. Also met Cock Moffitt and Paddy McGrath. Claiming never to have been knocked out, he boxed many times at the old Liverpool Stadium. Later became a member of Merseyside EBA.

O'GARA Johnny *Died* 22 May, 1994, aged 68. Came from Yorkshire to Aylesham, Kent, after World War II to reside with his uncle, Albert Cooper, and to work at Snowdown Colliery. Albert's friend, Mickey Worton, a veteran booths' fighter, set up a gym in the front room of his house in King's Road, and taught Johnny the basics of the noble art. He turned pro in 1947 under manager Les Roberts and numbered among his victims, Jimmy Daly, Billy Cook, Cliff Wilson, Les Yates, Tommy Williams, Buddy Yasmin, Jimmy Cardew, Wally Basquille, Ken Diston, Alf Clarke and Joe Walsh. Also met Freddie King and Peter Fay, but, handicapped by back injuries, he retired in 1950. He was also a fine athlete, running the mile for Snowdown Colliery and taking part in local track meetings. Eventually, Johnny returned to Yorkshire, living at Kirkburton, near Huddersfield, and continued his work as a miner, before finishing as an overman.

PEARCE Jimmy Middlesbrough. *Died* June, 1994, aged 66. Turned pro in 1948 and won the Central Area flyweight title by beating Jeff Oscroft (1951), but was beaten by Terry Allen in final eliminator for the British flyweight title (1952). Beat Vic Herman, Sid Hiom, Jimmy Gill, Johnny Black, Henry Carpenter, Norman Tennant, Glyn David and Paddy Hardy. When he was 13 he was riding on the crossbar of his friend's bike, when they went down a steep hill and ran into a lorry. His friend was killed, and it was thought that Jimmy's leg might have to be amputated. Fortunately, it was saved, but because of the injury he was rejected by the Army and instead, joined the Merchant Navy. He always considered the highlight of his career was in winning a *Boxing News* Certificate of Merit for beating Henry Carpenter. Also presented with a gold tie-pin by former world champion, Jimmy Wilde, during World War II.

PERKINS Doug "Smiler" Ipswich. *Died* 10 March, 1994, aged 76. A short pro career was highlighted when winning an 8st competition at Clacton, around 1936, but a scarcity of flyweight opponents led to his retiring to train amateurs at Ipswich Boys Club, a job he did for over 20 years. During the last war, he served with the 58th Royal Artillery, and was continually excused parades because he stood only 4ft 8in. Became secretary of Ipswich EBA, and when attending functions, his party-piece was singing *The Kid's Last Fight*.

POMPHREY Albert "Tiger" Bristol. *Died* March, 1994, aged 81. Reputed to have had in the region of 200 bouts, he beat Roy Lock and met Bert Kirby, Hal Bagwell and Charlie Thomas.

QUIROZ Francisco *Born* Moca, Dominican Republic, 4 June, 1957. *Died* May, 1993. Turned pro in 1978 and, after 20 contests of which he had won just eight, while suffering nine losses in a row, he was fortunate to get a crack at Lupe Madera's WBA light-flyweight title. Astounding his critics, he knocked the Mexican out in the ninth on 19 May, 1984 and then successfully defended his laurels against Victor Acosta, before being outscored over 15 rounds by Joey Olivo. There was to be no more title glory and one fight later, a points defeat at the hands of Agustin Garcia, he announced his retirement from the ring.

RALPH Johnny Maritzburg, Natal, South Africa. *Born* 1925. *Died* 16 October, 1993. Was in the Services from 1942 to 1945, boxing in Cairo, Alexandria and Naples, and on demob in 1946 he turned pro. Won the South African heavyweight title by beating Nick Wolmarans, also beating Tommy Bensch, Joe Foord, Jack Kukard, Ken Shaw, Alf Gallagher and Stephane Olek. His last two bouts were in Johannesburg, when stopped by Freddie Mills (1948) and Bruce Woodcock (1949). Soon after the Woodcock fight, Johnny married Enid Stephenson. On the day following the wedding, they were involved in a car accident which claimed one life and Johnny and Enid were both badly injured. A steel plate was inserted in his broken leg, and although he trained hard for a long time the injury prevented him from ever boxing again.

RILEY Ronnie Preston. *Died* 3 September, 1993, aged 63. Pro 1946-1961. Won Central Area middleweight title by beating Johnny Cunningham (1960), but never defended. In beating men such as Brian McTigue, Phil Mellish, Danny O'Brien, George Casson, Bert Middleton, George Roe and Jackie Whitehouse, he was known as "The Fighting Plumber". Later became president of Preston Ex-Boxers' Association.

ROSTRON Joe *From* Heywood. *Born* 15 February, 1910. *Died* December, 1993. Never an amateur, Joe made his pro debut at Manchester Free Trade Hall when he was 13 and while working in the gents' outfitters department of the Co-operative Society, he was allowed time off for training and actual contests. In 1930, he came in as a substitute against Jock McAvoy and outpointed the Rochdale man. Later that year there was a return, but with Joe handicapped by an injured hand, he lost on points. Also beat Glen Moody, Archie Sexton, "Battling" Charlie Parkin, George Gordon, Jack Lord, Fred Shaw and Charlie McDonald, losing only ten in over a 100 fights. After retiring in 1933, he joined the Nottingham City Police as boxing instructor. In 1942 he volunteered for flying duties with the RAF, but after a week was transferred to the Army School of Physical Training and qualified as a Sergeant PTI. After the war, Joe became a publican at Derby, moving to the Royal British Legion as steward, thence to Blackpool's Huntsman Hotel as bar manager and worked for Qualcast for ten years after the family moved back to Derby. In 1959 was appointed a Board of Control referee. In later years he was resident at the Littleover Nursing Home, Derby, but loved to correspond, sending and receiving letters from many of his old friends and opponents, his handwriting being well-nigh perfect.

SCALZO Petey *Born* New York City, USA, 1 August, 1917. *Died* June, 1993. A former NBA featherweight champion, his pro career spanned 1936-1943 and took in 111 contests, of which he lost just 15. Unable to get a crack at the title after a two round kayo win over Joey Archibald in December 1938, he was proclaimed champion by the NBA in May 1940 and successfully defended against Bobby Poison Ivy and Phil Zwick, before falling victim to Richie Lemos in July 1941. His career then plummeted downhill with only ten wins in the next 19 fights and, following a sixth round knockout at the hands of future lightweight champion, Bob Montgomery, he called it a day.

SHARKEY Jack *Born* 26 October, 1902, Bingham, New York. *Died* August, 1994. Real name Joseph Paul Cukoschay. Pro 1924-1936. Joined US Navy at age of 17, after running away from home. At 21 he was ashore in Boston when he walked into a gym and persuaded a promoter that he had a good fight record. He changed his name, taking Jack from Dempsey and Sharkey from Tom of that ilk, and was discharged from the Navy to take up a pro career. When Gene Tunney was world heavyweight champion, Jack was matched with Dempsey, but was stopped in round seven (1927). He then stopped Tommy Loughran in a fight billed for "the vacant American heavyweight title", but it meant nothing. By then, Tunney had retired, and Sharkey was matched with Max Schmeling for the vacant world title (1930). This became the only title fight in that division to end in a disqualification. In round four, Schmeling received a low blow, his manager jumped into the ring screaming "foul" and, after some time, Sharkey was officially ruled out. He then outpointed Primo Carnera (1931) and the following year outscored Schmeling in a return world title fight, holding it for just over a year, before being kayoed by Carnera. After defeats by King Levinsky and Loughran he was inactive for two years, until coming back to stop Unknown Winston (1935), lose and draw against Tony Shucco and outpoint Phil Brubaker. He was then stopped by Joe Louis (1936). Having just 55 bouts in 12 years, Sharkey was known as the "Boston Gob" because of his Navy service and where he had most of his early fights. Elected to the Boxing Hall Of Fame in 1980.

SILKSTONE Tony *Born* Leeds 2 March, 1968. *Died* April, 1994, in a drowning tragedy. Was stopped by Bradley Stone in a final eliminator for the inaugural British super-bantamweight title (1993). A pro between 1990 and 1994, he won 13 fights in a row before losing to Stone, which turned out to be his last contest. Tony's father boxed as Young Silky, and won the Central Area lightweight title by beating Gerry McBride (1970), before losing it to Gary Yean (1971). He also fought for the Central Area Junior lightweight title, losing to Gerry McBride (1969).

SIMPKIN Bob *From* Bridlington. *Died* December, 1993, aged 80. Pro 1930-1940. Met Alban Mulrooney, Les Ward, "Battling" Charlie Parkin, Dai Jones, Butcher Gascoigne, Tommy Smith and Jack McKnight.

SLACK George *From* Doncaster. *Died* 29 June, 1993, aged 88. Pro 1924-1937. Won the Northern Area heavyweight title by beating Guardsman Gater (1932). After losing the title to Bob Carvill (1933), he regained it from the latter (1934), before successfully defending it against Alf Robinson (1934) and Carvill (1935). He never lost the title in the ring. Met all the top heavyweights of that period, including Len Harvey, Jack Petersen, Charlie Smith, Jack Doyle, Larry Gains and Don McCorkindale. Among his victims were Jack Pettifer, Tony Arpino, Dick Bartlett, Bobby Shields, Don Shortland, Jack London, Jack Stanley, Bill Hudson, Steve McCall, Alf Luxton and Alex Bell.

SPRING Reg *From* Southall. *Died* August, 1993, aged 69. Pro 1946-1952. Known as "Buster" and a former schoolboy champion, he won South-East Area light-heavyweight title by beating Al Marson (1949), before losing it to Mark Hart (1949). Beat Don Cockell, Johnny Williams, Ernie Woodman, Tony Lord, Johnny Blake and Paddy Roche and sparred regularly with Freddie Mills. Worked for most of his life at EMI, Hayes, and enjoyed long bike rides until his illness.

STONE Bradley *Born* Mile End, London, 27 May, 1970. *Died* 28 April, 1994, two days after he was stopped in round ten of a scheduled twelve-rounder at York Hall, Bethnal Green, in a bout for the inaugural British super-bantamweight title. A pro from 1990, as an amateur, Bradley reached the London ABA featherweight final (1989). He left a professional record of 20 bouts, 17 wins (seven inside schedule), one draw and two defeats.

Bradley Stone (left) appears to have the upper hand over his rival, Richie Wenton, during their contest for the inaugural British super-bantamweight title   Les Clark

THOMAS Charlie *From* Marylebone, London. *Born* 28 March, 1914. *Died* 1 June, 1994. Pro 1931-1938. At the same school as "Nipper" Pat Daly, in Richmond Street, he won ten bouts as an amateur before George Rodham took him to Professor Andrew Newton's gym. As a pro he boxed often, including over 30 bouts in 1932, and was managed by Andy Newton, the son of the Professor. Beat Harry Barnes, "Nipper" Fred Morris, Jimmy Roberts, Jack Hinfin, Johnny Ryan, Jackie Stayton and Jack Bishop and also met Jack Gubbins, Al Capone, Len Beynon, Johnny Holt, Willie Smith, Ernie Laxton, Herbie Hill and Billy Walker. Retired because of persistent hand injuries, becoming a demolition foreman during World War II and a member of the Home Guard. Later, when working as a street trader, a bus struck his barrow and injured his spine, producing an arthritic condition. In the late 1980s he had a slight stroke, followed by blood clots in his right leg. Although was pronounced cured by a by-pass operation, he had further leg problems in later years, and amputation was talked about. This Charlie refused, but, unfortunately, he became confined to a wheel-chair. In 1971 he was a founder-member of the London Ex-Boxers' Association, and a vice-president. A cheerful cockney character, he was known as Charlie "The Bell", which he rang to restore order at LEBA meetings.

TODD Jock *From* Ayr. *Died* July, 1994. Pro 1946-1951. Beaten by Bert Gilroy for the Scottish light-heavyweight title (1949), but defeated Hugh McDonald, Tommy Caswell, Matt Locke, Billy Mawson, Jackie Moran, Paddy Roche, Eddie Donaldson and Tug Fawcett. Also met Garnett Denny, Charel Baert, Elfryn Morris, Alf Hines and Jackie Wilson.

TREADAWAY Jack *From* Sutton, Surrey. *Died* 4 July, 1993, aged 79. As a top class amateur who never turned pro, he was ABA bantamweight champion (1932), ABA featherweight champion (1934 and 1936) and reached the quarter-final stages of 1936 Olympic Games, before being outpointed by German, Josef Miner. Also represented Britain in the American Golden Gloves during his distinguished career.

WALCOTT "Jersey" Joe *Born* Merchantville, New Jersey, USA, 31 January, 1914. *Died* 26 February, 1994. Real name Arnold Raymond Cream. A high school graduate, on moving to Camden, NJ, his earliest recorded fight was in 1930, but he probably began earlier. Started his rise to fame in 1945 when he beat Steve Dudas, Joe Baksi, Jimmy Bivins and Lee Oma. Although he lost to Joey Maxim and Elmer Ray, he beat them in return bouts. Beaten by Joe Louis for the World heavyweight title (1947), in spite of flooring the champion, he was given a return in 1948, but was again defeated. When Louis gave up the title, Walcott met Ezzard Charles for the vacant crown, the latter winning on points (1949), and despite losing again to Charles in (1951), later that year, he stopped his three-time rival to win the title. Lost the crown to Rocky Marciano (1952), and was again beaten by Marciano, this time in one round (1953). Retired to go into the motel business, also becoming a parole officer and eventually sheriff of Camden. Had a good part in the Bub Shulberg movie, *The Harder They Fall*.

WANGILA Robert *Born* Kenya. *Died* 24 July, 1994, aged 26, following a stoppage defeat against David Gonzales in Las Vegas. He had collapsed in the dressing room after the fight and succumbed following a vain attempt to remove a blood clot from the brain. As a top Kenyan amateur, Wagila (Napunyi) had won the Olympic welterweight title at Seoul in 1988, but never attained his full potential as a pro. Joining the paid ranks, after moving to the States in 1989, he never really got over a six-round stoppage defeat at the hands of Eric Hernandez in July, 1990, and later suffered further inside the distance defeats against Buck Smith, Will Hernandez and Troy Waters. His death was the first in Nevada since that of the unfortunate South Korean, Deuk-Koo Kim, in 1982.

WARD Fred *From* Ashton-under-Lyne. *Born* 3 September, 1898. *Died* 24 July, 1993. At the age of ten his father bought him a set of boxing gloves and when old enough he sparred at the local gyms. An apprentice moulder at Jones' Sewing Machines factory in Audenshaw, he joined the Army in 1916, and made his pro debut the same year. Ace record compiler, Vic Hardwicke, traced a contest at the Alhambra, Openshaw, on 6 December that year, showing Fred knocking out Young Brierly in two rounds. During his war service, Fred was trained by the great champion, Johnny Basham. After the war, Fred continued his boxing career, and also became a steeplejack. His firm were not keen on him boxing, so he used assumed names, beating Jack Terral, J. Deane, Walt Len Aston, Tom Massey, Len Evans, Johnny Wright and Billy Gibbons, among many others. Retired in 1925 and became a cornerman. Fred was present at the first-ever meeting of an Ex-Boxers' Association, the Oldham, Ashton & Manchester EBA, in 1951. Although the title was changed to the Ex-Boxers' Association of Great Britain and eventually disbanded, it was revived in 1968 as the Manchester & District EBA, later changed again to Manchester EBA. Fred was a member throughout and, up to the time of his death, was generally regarded as the oldest surviving ex-boxer, certainly the oldest member of an EBA. Before the war, he had great hopes of his protege, Jack Davies, but the latter was killed in a Japanese POW Camp in 1943. Never married, he retained his interest in boxing and other sports, and was a familiar figure at the local park, where he enjoyed watching the bowls.

WARNER Jim London. *Died* December, 1993, aged 82. As a trainer at New Enterprise ABC, he guided Mickey Pye, Jimmy Anderson and Dave Parris among others and, in the pro ranks, he was responsible for Johnny Barclay's stable for 20 years. Helped Clyde Ruan to win the Southern Area featherweight title and progress to British and European title fights against Barry McGuigan.

WEBB Freddie *Born* Belfast, September, 1925. *Died* 21 December, 1993. Pro 1944-1953. Real name Frederick Rea. Won the Northern Ireland middleweight title by beating Jackie Wilson (1949), for which he was awarded a *Boxing News* Certificate of Merit. He lost the title in a return with Wilson (1951), but beat Joe Quinn, Dave Warnock, Billy Black, Jackie Brown, Bert Chambers, Billy Stevens, Jim Doran, Billy Kelly, Teddy Dexter, Brian McTigue and Frankie Cortese. Was employed by the Belfast Corporation Cleansing Department all his working life.

WILLIAMS Ike *Born* 2 August, 1923. *Died* Los Angeles, USA, 5 September, 1994. Turning pro in 1940, he won the NBA lightweight championship in 1945, knocking out Juan Zurita inside two rounds, and unified the title when he kayoed Bob Montgomery in the seventh on 4 August, 1947. One of the best fighters of the post-war era, he missed nobody. British champion, Ronnie James, was dispatched on a wet night at Ninian Park (1946), and prior to losing his title to Jimmy Carter in 1951, wins over Enrique Bolanos (three times), Beau Jack, Jesse Flores, Freddie Dawson and Montgomery, ensured his grip on the 135 lbs division for over six years. Although continuing his ring career until 1955, he was a shell of the once great fighter he assuredly was. In 153 contests, he won 123 (60 inside the distance) and drew five, beating men of the class of Willie Roache, Gene Burton, Slugger White, Sammy Angott, Lulu Constantino, Dave Castilloux, Willie Joyce, Maxie Berger, Johnny Bratton, Bobby Ruffin, Ralph Zannelli, Tippy Larkin, Tony Pellone, Livio Minelli, Kid Gavilan, Lester Felton, Charley Salas and Fitzie Pruden, to name but a few. In an era when the "mob" controlled boxing in America, and he was managed by the infamous "Blinky" Palermo, Williams showed courage beyond the call of duty when attempting to get a boxers' union off the ground and, although unsuccessful, will be remembered just as much for that as for his greatness in the ring.

Leading BBBoC License Holders: Names and Addresses

Licensed Promoters

Billy Aird
The Golden Gloves
346 Seaside
Eastbourne
East Sussex BN22 7RJ

Michael Andrew
38 Kennedy Avenue
Laindon West
Basildon
Essex

Jack Bishop
76 Gordon Road
Fareham
Hampshire PO16 7SS

Fred Boustead
46 Coombe Lane
St Marychurch
Torquay
Devon TQ2 8DY

Teresa Breen
31 Penlan Road
Treboeth
Swansea

Pat Brogan
112 Crewe Road
Haslington
Crewe
Cheshire

Harry Burgess
25 Calthorpe Street
London WC1X 0JX

Bruce Burrows
126 Ferndale Road
Swindon
Wiltshire

Roy Cameron
5 Birbeck Road
Acton
London W3 6BG

Carlton Carew
18 Mordaunt Street
Stockwell
London SW9 9RB

Champion Enterprises
Frank Maloney
84 Green Lanes
London N16

Eva Christian
80 Alma Road
Plymouth
Devon PL3 4HU

Thomas Cooper
Pen Prys Farm
Bryn
Llanelli
Dyfed

Pat Cowdell
129a Moat Road
Oldbury
Warley
West Midlands

John Cox
11 Fulford Drive
Links View
Northampton

Dragon Boxing Promotions
Dai Gardiner &
Kevin Hayde
93 St Mary's Street
Cardiff
South Wales
CF1 1DW

Eastwood Promotions
Bernard Eastwood
Eastwood House
2-4 Chapel Lane
Belfast 1
Northern Ireland

Christine Edwards
44 The Fairway
Westella
Near Hull
Humberside

James Evans
88 Windsor Road
Bray
Berkshire

Evesham Sporting Club
Mike Goodall
Schiller
Gibbs Lane
Offenham
Evesham

Norman Fawcett
4 Wyndsak Place
Gosforth
Newcastle upon Tyne

Douglas Firkin-Flood
Stockport Road West
Bredbury
Stockport
Cheshire SK6 2AR

John Forbes
5 Durham Road
Sedgefield
Stockton on Tees
Cleveland TS21 3DW

Joe Foster
4 Denham Avenue
Fulwell
Sunderland

Joe Frater
The Cottage
Main Road
Grainthorpe
Louth
Lincolnshire

Dai Gardiner
13 Hengoed Hall Drive
Cefn Hengoed
Hengoed
Mid Glamorgan
CF8 7JW

Anthony Gee
35 Greville Street
Hatton Garden
London EC1

Harold Gorton
Gorton House
4 Hollius Road
Oldham
Lancashire

Ron Gray
Ingrams Oak
19 Hatherton Road
Cannock
Staffordshire

Johnny Griffin
98 Stonehill Avenue
Birstall
Leicester

Clive Hall
23 Linnett Drive
Barton Seagrave
Kettering
Northamptonshire

David Harris
16 Battle Crescent
St Leonards on Sea
Sussex

Brian Hearn
12 Newnham Road
Colebrook
Plympton
Devon PL7 4AW

Dennis Hobson
The Lodge
Stone Lane
Woodhouse
Sheffield
Yorkshire
S13 7BR

Steve Holdsworth
85 Sussex Road
Watford
Hertfordshire
WD2 5HR

Harry Holland
12 Kendall Close
Feltham
Middlesex

Terry Holland
29/31 Orchard Road
Stevenage
Hertfordshire
SG1 3HE

Alan Honniball
83 Russell Drive
Mudeford
Dorset

Hull & District Sporting Club
Mick Toomey
25 Purton Grove
Bransholme
Hull HU7 4QD

Alma Ingle
26 Newman Road
Wincobank
Sheffield S9 1LP

K K Promotions
Ken Whitney
22 Oundle Road
Weldon
Corby
Northamptonshire

John Levine
38 St Vincent Road
Westcliff on Sea
Essex S50 7PR

McKenzie Promotions
85-87 High Street
South Norwood
London SE25 6NA

Owen McMahon
3 Atlantic Avenue
Belfast BT15 2HN

McMahon Promotions
17c Lewisham Park
London SE13 6QZ
and
60 Stapleton Road
Easton
Bristol

Matchroom
Barry Hearn
10 Western Road
Romford
Essex RM1 3JT

Midland Sporting Club
D. L. Read
Ernest & Young
Windsor House
3 Temple Row
Birmingham B2 5LA

Katherine Morrison
5 Abercromby Drive
Glasgow G40

National Promotions
Mickey Duff
National House
60-66 Wardour Street
London W1V 3HP

Noble Art Promotions
Greg Steene
22 Welbeck Street
London W1M 7PG

North Staffs Sporting Club
J Baddeley
29 Redwood Avenue
Stone
Staffordshire ST15 0DB

North-West Promotions
Pat Dwyer
93 Keir Hardie Avenue
Bootle
Liverpool 20
Merseyside

Michael O'Brien
39 Clydesdale Mount
Byker
Newcastle upon Tyne
NE6 2EN

Steve Pollard
269 Hessle Road
Hull
East Yorkshire
HU3 4BE

Queensberry Sporting Club
1 Concorde Drive
5c Business Centre
Clevedon
Avon BS21 6UH

Ringmaster Productions
Alan Lacey
Rococo House
281 City Road
London EC1V 1LA

Gus Robinson
Stranton House
Westview Road
Hartlepool
TS24 0BB

Round One Boxing Promotions
Dave Furneaux
251 Embankment Road
Prince Rock
Plymouth
Cornwall
PL4 9JH

Christine Rushton
20 Alverley Lane
Balby
Doncaster
Yorkshire
DN4 9AS

Chris Rustage
Riverside House
St Simon Street
Salford
Manchester
M3 7ET

St Andrews Sporting Club
Tommy Gilmour
Anderson Suite
Forte Crest Hotel
Bothwell Street
Glasgow
G2 7EN

Chris Sanigar
147 Two Mile Hill Road
Kingswood
Bristol
Avon
BS15 1BH

Mike Shinfield
126 Birchwood Lane
Somercotes
Derbyshire
DE55 4NF

Brian Snagg
The Heath Hotel
Green Hill Road
Allerton
Liverpool

Jack Solomons Sporting Club
High Beech
Hayway
Rushden
Northamptonshire

John Spensley
The Black Swan Hotel
Tremholme Bar
Near Stokesley
North Yorkshire
DL6 3JY

Sporting Club of Wales
Paul Boyce
79 Church Street
Britton Ferry
Neath
SA11 2TU

Tara Promotions
Jack Doughty
Grains Road
Shaw
Oldham
Lancashire
OL2 8JB

Team Promotions
David Gregory
Contract House
Split Crow Road
Gateshead
Tyne and Wear

Jack Trickett
Acton Court Hotel
187 Buxton Road
Stockport
Cheshire

Uppercut Promotions
Arthur Urry
26 Nella Road
London W6

Carl van Bailey
Merrimead Farm
Five Bridges
Cullompton
Devon
EX15 1QP

Stephen Vaughan
43-45 Pembroke Place
Liverpool
L3 5PH

Brian Walker
52 Cardiff Street
Aberdare
Wales

Frank Warren
Centurion House
Bircherley Green
Hertford
Hertfordshire
SG14 1AP

Winning Combination
Annette Conroy
144 High Street East
Sunderland
Tyne and Wear
SR1 2BL

Wolverhampton Sporting Club
Centre City Tower
7 Hill Street
Birmingham
B5 4UU

Yorkshire Executive Sporting Club
John Celebanski
87 Crowtree Lane
Allerton
Bradford
Yorkshire
BD8 0AN

Licensed Managers

Billy Aird
The Golden Gloves
346 Seaside
Eastbourne
East Sussex BN22 7RJ

Isola Akay
129 Portnall Road
Paddington
London W9 3BN

John Ashton
557 Nottingham Road
Lower Somercotes
Derbyshire
DE55 4NQ

Mike Atkinson
9 Tudor Road
Ainsdale
Southport
Lancashire PR8 2RU

Don Austin
14 Winchat Road
Broadwaters
Thamesmead
London SE28 0DZ

Billy Ball
6 Copse Close
Marlow
Buckinghamshire
SL7 2NY

Johnny Barclay
3 Newall Close
The Furlongs
Turnfurlong Lane
Aylesbury
Buckinghamshire
HP21 7FE

Mike Barrett
PO Box 1230
London SW7 4QZ

Nat Basso
38 Windsor Road
Prestwich
Lancashire
M25 8FF

Bob Batey
243 Ladykirk Road
Newcastle upon Tyne
NE4 8AL

John Baxter
6 Havencrest Drive
Leicester
LE5 2AG

Lance Billany
32 Beaconsfield
Carrs Meadow
Withernsea
North Humberside
HU19 2EP

Jack Bishop
76 Gordon Road
Fareham
Hampshire PO16 7SS

Abner Blackstock
23 Alice Street
Pill
Newport
Gwent
South Wales

Gerald Bousted
69 Queensway
Chelston
Torquay
Devon TQ2 6BP

George Bowes
24 St Mawes Close
Throston Grange
Hartlepool
Cleveland

Paul Boyce
Brynamlwg
2 Pant Howell Ddu
Ynysmerdy
Briton Ferry
Neath SA11 2TU

David Bradley
Dallicote Cottage
Worfield
Shropshire WV15 5PC

Colin Breen
31 Penlan Road
Treboeth
Swansea
West Glamorgan

Mike Brennan
2 Canon Avenue
Chadwell Heath
Romford
Essex

Fred Britton
71 Henrietta Street
Leigh
Lancashire WN7 1LH

Pat Brogan
112 Crewe Road
Haslington
Cheshire

Michael Brooks
114 Gildane
Orchard Park Estate
Hull HU6 9AY

Dick Brownson
Armada House
Marine Parade
Instow
North Devon EX39 4JJ

Harry Burgess
25 Calthorpe Street
London WC1X 0JX

Winston Burnett
6 Faber Way
City Gardens
Sloper Road
Grangetown
Cardiff CF1 8DN

Paddy Byrne
70 Benfield Way
Portslade by Sea
Sussex BN4 2DL

Pat Byrne
11 Cadman Close
Bedworth
Warwickshire
CV12 8PD

Trevor Callighan
40 Prescott Street
Halifax
West Yorkshire
HX1 2QW

Ernie Cashmore
18 North Drive
Handsworth
Birmingham
B20 8SX

John Celebanski
87 Crowtree Lane
Allerton
Bradford BD8 0AN

Michael Chapman
9 Mill Lane
Farington
Moss
Lancashire PR5 3PS

Nigel Christian
80 Alma Road
Plymouth
Devon PL3 4HU

Peter Coleman
29 The Ring Road
Leeds
Yorkshire LS14 1NH

Roger Colson
63 Amwell Street
Roseberry Avenue
London EC1

William Connelly
72 Clincart Road
Mount Florida
Glasgow G42

Tommy Conroy
144 High Street East
Sunderland
Tyne and Wear

George Cooper
16 Robin Hood Green
St Mary Cray
Orpington
Kent

Michael Copp
62 Fleet Street
Swansea
West Glamorgan

Pat Cowdell
129a Moat Road
Oldbury
Warley
West Midlands
B68 8EE

John Cox
11 Fulford Drive
Links View
Northampton NN2 7NX

Jimmy Cresswell
3 Williamson Street
Clydebank G81 2AS

Bingo Crooks
37 Helming Drive
Danehust Estate
Wolverhampton
West Midlands
WV1 2AF

David Davies
10 Bryngelli
Carmel
Llanelli
Dyfed SA14 7EL

Glyn Davies
63 Parc Brynmawr
Felinfoel
Llanelli
Dyfed SA15 4PG

Ronnie Davies
3 Vallensdean Cottages
Hangleton Lane
Portslade
Sussex

John Davison
31 Wishaw Rise
Lemington
Newcastle upon Tyne
NE15 7LL

Brendan Devine
12 Birkdale Close
Clubmoor
Liverpool L6 0DL

Michael Donovan
8 Sefton Road
Walton
Liverpool L9 2BP

Jack Doughty
Lane End Cottage
Golden Street
Shaw
Lancashire OL2 8LY

Shaun Doyle
15 Jermyn Croft
Dodworth
Barnsley
South Yorkshire
S75 3LR

Phil Duckworth
The Shepherd
96 Pontefract Lane
Leeds
Yorkshire LS9 6TG

Mickey Duff
National House
60-66 Wardour Street
London W1V 3HP

Pat Dwyer
93 Keir Hardie Avenue
Bootle
Liverpool 20
Merseyside L20 0DN

Bernard Eastwood
Eastwood House
2-4 Chapel Lane
Belfast 1
Northern Ireland

George Evans
14 Donald Street
Abercanaid
Merthyr Tydfil
Glamorgan

Greg Evans
21 Portman Road
Liverpool
Merseyside L15 2HH

Jack Evans
Morlee House
Hanbury Road
Pontypool
Monmouth

Michael Fawcett
44 Rawstone Walk
Plaistow
London E13

Norman Fawcett
4 Wyndsak Place
Gosforth
Newcastle upon Tyne

Colin Flute
84 Summerhill Road
Coseley
West Midlands
WV14 8RE

Dai Gardiner
13 Hengoed Hall Drive
Cefn Hengoed
Mid Glamorgan

John Gaynor
7 Westhorne Fold
Counthill Drive
Brooklands Road
Crumpsall
Manchester
M8 6JN

Danny Gill
8 Whitehouse Street
Coseley
West Midlands
WV14 8HE

Tommy Gilmour
Forte Crest Hotel
Bothwell Street
Glasgow
G2 7EN

Lee Graham
17 Felday Road
Lewisham
London
SE13 7HQ

Ron Gray
Ingrams Oak
19 Hatherton Road
Cannock
Staffordshire

Dave Gregory
10 Mill Farm Road
Hamsterley Mill
Nr Rowlands Gill
Tyne & Wear

Johnny Griffin
98 Stonehill Avenue
Birstall
Leicestershire

Harry Griver
187 Redbridge Lane
East
Redbridge
Essex IG4 5DF

Dick Gunn
43 Moray Avenue
Hayes
Middlesex OB3 2AY

Carl Gunns
Flat 2
Heathcliffe
469 Loughborough
Road
Birstall
Leicester LE4 0DS

Frank Harrington
178 Kingsway
Heysham
Lancashire LA3 2EG

David Harris
16 Battle Crescent
St Leonards on Sea
Sussex

Harold Hayes
16 Hyland Crescent
Warmsworth
Doncaster
South Yorkshire
DN4 9JS

Teddy Haynes
The Henry Cooper
516 Old Kent Road
London SE1 5BA

Geoff Hayward
51 Derby Avenue
Tettenhall
Wolverhampton
West Midlands
WV6 9JR

Patrick Healy
1 Cranley Buildings
Brookes Market
Holborn
London EC1

Barry Hearn
Matchroom
10 Western Road
Romford
Essex RM1 3JT

George Hill
52 Hathaway
Marton
Blackpool
Lancashire
FY4 4AB

Mick Hill
35 Shenstone House
Aldrington Road
London SW16 1TL

Clive Hogben
44 Polwell Lane
Barton Seagrave
Kettering
Northamptonshire
NN15 6UA

Steve Holdsworth
85 Sussex Road
Watford
Hertfordshire
WD2 5HR

Harry Holland
12 Kendall Close
Feltham
Middlesex

Gordon Holmes
New Cottage
Watton Road
Hingham
Norfolk NR9 4NN

Lloyd Honeyghan
22 Risborough
Deacon Way
Walworth Road
London SE17

Brendan Ingle
26 Newman Road
Wincobank
Sheffield S9 1LP

Derek Isaamen
179 Liverpool Road
South
Maghill
Liverpool L31 8AA

Mike Jacobs
KOPRO
The Penthouse Suite
Duke Street House
50 Duke Street
London W1M 5DS

Colin Jones
1 Brookfield Close
Penyrheol
Gorseinon
Swansea SA4 2GW

Richard Jones
1 Churchfields
Croft
Warrington
Cheshire WA3 7JR

Duncan Jowett
Cedarhouse
Caplethill Road
Paisley
Strathclyde
Scotland

Billy Kane
17 Bamburn Terrace
Byker
Newcastle upon Tyne
NE6 2GH

Johnny Kramer
115 Crofton Road
Plaistow
London E13

Terry Lawless
4 Banyards
Off Nelmes Way
Emerson Park
Hornchurch
Essex

Buddy Lee
The Walnuts
Roman Bank
Leverington
Wisbech
Cambridgeshire

Brian Lynch
53 Hall Lane
Upminster
Essex

Pat Lynch
Gotherinton
68 Kelsey Lane
Balsall Common
Near Coventry
West Midlands

Glenn McCrory
Holborn
35 Station Road
Stanley
Co Durham DH9 0JL

Bobby McEwan
302 Langside Road
Glasgow

Clinton McKenzie
2 Wisbourgh Road
South Croydon
Surrey CR2 0DR

Jim McMillan
21 Langcliffe Road
Preston
Lancashire PR2 6UE

Frank Maloney
Champion Enterprises
84 Green Lanes
London N16

Dennie Mancini
16 Rosedew Road
Off Fulham Palace Road
London W6 9ET

Terry Marsh
141 Great Gregorie
Basildon
Essex

Gary Mason
Unit 12
Canada House
Blackburn Road
West Hampstead
London NW6

Arthur Melrose
33 Easterhill Street
Glasgow G32 8LN

Tommy Miller
128 Clapton Mount
King Cross Road
Halifax
West Yorkshire

Achille Mitchell
54 Portland Avenue
Gravesend
Kent

Glyn Mitchell
28 Furneaux Road
Milehouse
Plymouth
Devon

Carl Moorcroft
108 Stuart Road
Crosby
Liverpool 23

Alex Morrison
39 Armour Street
Glasgow G33 5EX

James Murray
87 Spean Street
Glasgow G44 4DS

Herbert Myers
The Lodge
Lower House Lane
Burnley
Lancashire

David Nelson
29 Linley Drive
Stirchley Park
Telford
Shropshire TF3 1RQ

Paul Newman
8 Teg Close
Downs Park Estate
Portslade
Sussex BN41 2GZ

Gary Nickels
11 St Andrews Drive
Highgrove Gardens
Stevenage
Hertfordshire SG1 4UY

Norman Nobbs
364 Kings Road
Kingstanding
Birmingham B44 0UG

Bob Paget
8 Masterman House
New Church Road
London SE5 7HU

George Patrick
84 Wooler Road
Edmonton
London N18 2JS

Billy Pearce
Flat C
36 Courtfield Gardens
South Kensington
London SW5 0PT

Terry Petersen
54 Green Leafe Avenue
Wheatley Hills
Doncaster
South Yorkshire
DN2 5RF

Steve Pollard
35 Gorthorpe
Orchard Park Estate
Hull HU6 9EY

John Pook
75 Stapley Road
Hove
Sussex

Ricky Porter
73 County Road
Swindon
Wiltshire

Dean Powell
10 Cuddington
Deacon Way
Heygate Estate
Walworth
London SE17 1SP

Dennis Read
65 Bridle Road
Shirley
Croydon
Surrey

Glyn Rhodes
8 Valentine Crescent
Shine Green
Sheffield S5 0NW

Ken Richardson
15 East Walk
North Road Estate
Retford
Nottinghamshire
DN22 7YF

Fred Rix
14 Broom Road
Shirley
Croydon
Surrey CR0 8NE

Gus Robinson
Stranton House
Westview Road
Hartlepool TS24 0BB

John Rushton
20 Alverley Lane
Balby
Doncaster DN4 9AS

Joe Ryan
22a Glenarm Road
Clapton
London E5 0LZ

Kevin Sanders
19 Whittington
Off Parnwell Way
Peterborough
Cambridgeshire

Chris Sanigar
147 Two Mile Hill Road
Kingswood
Bristol BS15 1BH

Eric Secombe
11 Joseph Trotter Close
Myddleton Street
Finsbury
London EC1

Kevin Sheehan
84 Amesbury Circus
Bells Lane Estate
Nottingham NG8 6DH

Mike Shinfield
126 Birchwood Lane
Somercotes
Derbyshire DE55 4NE

Steve Sims
9 High Street
Newport
Gwent

Len Slater
78 Sutcliffe Avenue
Nunsthorpe
Grimsby
Lincolnshire

Andy Smith
Valandra
19 St Audreys Lane
St Ives
Cambridgeshire

Darkie Smith
21 Northumberland House
Gaisford Street
London NW5

John Smith
6 Kildare Road
Chorlton
Manchester
M21 1YR

Brian Snagg
The Heath Hotel
Green Hill Road
Allerton
Liverpool

Les Southey
Oakhouse
Park Way
Hillingdon
Middlesex

John Spensley
The Black Swan Hotel
Tremholme Bar
Near Stokesley
North Yorkshire
DL6 3JY

Ken Squires
27 University Close
Syston
Leicestershire
LE7 8AY

Greg Steene
11 Whitcomb Street
London WC2H 7HA

Norrie Sweeney
3 Saucehill Terrace
Paisley
Scotland PA2 6SY

Wally Swift
Grove House
54 Grove Road
Knowle
Solihull
West Midlands
B93 0PJ

Amos Talbot
70 Edenfield Road
Rochdale OL11 5AE

Keith Tate
214 Dick Lane
Tyersal
Bradford BD4 8JH

Glenroy Taylor
95 Devon Close
Perivale
Middlesex

Eddie Thomas
Runnington
Penydarren Park
Merthyr Tydfil
Mid Glamorgan

Jimmy Tibbs
44 Gylingdune Gardens
Seven Kings
Essex

Terry Toole
8 Conningsby Gardens
South Chingford
London E4 9BD

Mick Toomey
25 Purton Grove
Bransholme
Hull HU7 4QD

Jack Trickett
Acton Court Hotel
187 Buxton Road
Stockport
Cheshire

Noel Trigg
Waterford
The Bridge
Bettws Lane
Newport NP9 6AB

Frankie Turner
Matchroom
10 Western Road
Essex RM1 3JT

Bill Tyler
Northcroft House
Chorley
Lichfield
Staffordshire WS13 8DL

Danny Urry
26 Nella Road
Hammersmith
London W6

Stephen Vaughan
43-45 Pembroke Place
Liverpool L3 5PH

Alan Walker
47 Consett Road
Castleside
Consett
Durham DH8 9QL

Frank Warren
Centurion House
Bircherley Green
Hertford
Hertfordshire
SG14 1AP

Robert Watt
32 Dowanhill Street
Glasgow G11

Gordon White
34 Gaskell Street
London
SW4 6NS

Ken Whitney
22 Oundle Road
Weldon
Northamptonshire

William Wigley
4 Renfrew Drive
Wollaton
Nottinghamshire
NG8 2FX

Mick Williamson
34a St Marys Grove
Cannonbury
London N1

Tex Woodward
Spanorium Farm
Berwick Lane
Compton Greenfield
Bristol
BS12 3RX

Licensed Matchmakers

Nat Basso
38 Windsor Road
Prestwich
Lancashire
M25 8FF

Harry Burgess
25 Calthorpe Street
London WC1

Paddy Byrne
70 Benfield Way
Portslade by Sea
Sussex BN4 2DL

David Davies
10 Byrngelli
Carmel
Llanelli
Dyfed
SA14 7EL

Glyn Davies
63 Parc Brynmawr
Felinfoel
Llanelli
Dyfed SA15 4PG

David Davis
179 West Heath Road
Hampstead
London NW3

Mickey Duff
National House
60-66 Wardour Street
London W1 3HP

Ernie Fossey
26 Bell Lane
Brookmans Park
Hertfordshire

John Gaynor
7 Westhorne Fold
Counthill Drive
Brooklands Road
Crumpsall
Manchester M8 6JN

Tommy Gilmour
Fort Crest Hotel
Bothwell Street
Glasgow G2 7EN

Ron Gray
Ingrams Oak
19 Hatherton Road
Cannock
Staffordshire

Patrick Healy
1 Cranley Buildings
Brookes Market
Holborn
London EC1

Steve Holdsworth
85 Sussex Road
Watford
Herts
WD2 5HR

Terry Lawless
4 Banyards
Off Nelmes Way
Emerson Park
Hornchurch
Essex

Graham Lockwood
106 Burnside Avenue
Skipton
N. Yorkshire
BD23 2OB

Frank Maloney
Champion Enterprises
84 Green Lanes
London N16

Dennie Mancini
16 Rosedew Road
Off Fulham Palace Road
Hammersmith
London W6 9ET

Tommy Miller
128 Clapton Mount
King Cross Road
Halifax
West Yorkshire

Chris Moorcroft
17 Cambrian Drive
Prostatyn
Clwyd LL19 9RN

Alex Morrison
39 Armour Street
Glasgow G33 5EX

Gary Nickels
11 St Andrews Drive
Highgrove Gardens
Stevenage
Hertfordshire
SG1 4UY

Norman Nobbs
364 Kings Road
Kingstanding
Birmingham B44 0UG

Ricky Porter
Angelique Guest House
73 County Road
Swindon
Wiltshire

Dean Powell
10 Cuddington
Deacon Way
Heygate Estate
Walworth
London SE17 1SP

Len Slater
78 Sutcliffe Avenue
Nunsthorpe
Grimsby
Lincolnshire

Darkie Smith
21 Northumberland House
Gaisford Street
London NW5

Terry Toole
8 Conningsby Gardens
South Chingford
London E4 9BD

Frank Turner
Matchroom
10 Western Road
Romford
Essex RM1 3JT

Licensed Referees

Class 'B'

Kenneth Curtis	Southern Area
Teddy Gardner	Southern Area
Keith Garner	Central Area
Mark Green	Southern Area
Rudi Harders	Welsh Area
Jeffrey Hinds	Southern Area
Al Hutcheon	Scottish Area
David Irving	Northern Ireland
Ian John-Lewis	Southern Area
Marcus McDonnell	Southern Area
Terry O'Connor	Midlands Area
Roy Snipe	Central Area
Grant Wallis	Western Area
Gerald Watson	Northern Area

Class 'A'

Ivor Bassett	Welsh Area
Arnold Bryson	Northern Area
Phil Cowsill	Central Area
Richard Davies	Southern Area
Roddy Evans	Welsh Area
Anthony Green	Central Area
Ron Hackett	Central Area
Michael Heatherwick	Welsh Area
Brian Hogg	Central Area
Wynford Jones	Welsh Area
Denzil Lewis	Western Area
Len Mullen	Scottish Area
James Pridding	Midlands Area
Reg Thompson	Southern Area
Lawrence Thompson	Northern Area
Anthony Walker	Southern Area
Barney Wilson	Northern Ireland

Class 'A' Star

John Coyle	Midlands Area
Roy Francis	Southern Area
John Keane	Midlands Area
Adrian Morgan	Welsh Area
Larry O'Connell	Southern Area
Dave Parris	Southern Area
Billy Rafferty	Scottish Area
Paul Thomas	Midlands Area
Mickey Vann	Central Area

Licensed Timekeepers

Alan Archbold	Northern Area
Roy Bicknell	Midlands Area
Roger Bowden	Western Area
John Breward	Northern Area
Neil Burder	Welsh Area
Ivor Campbell	Welsh Area
Frank Capewell	Central Area
Robert Edgeworth	Southern Area
Harold Elliott	Northern Ireland
Harry Foxall	Midlands Area
Eric Gilmour	Scottish Area
Brian Heath	Midlands Area
Ken Honiball	Western Area

Lewis G. Hubbard	Southern Area
Winston Hughes	Midlands Area
Albert Kelleher	Northern Area
Michael McCann	Southern Area
Peter McCann	Southern Area
Norman Maddox	Midlands Area
Gordon Pape	Welsh Area
Daniel Peacock	Southern Area
Barry Pinder	Central Area
Raymond Preston	Western Area
Raymond Rice	Southern Area
Tommy Rice	Southern Area
Colin Roberts	Central Area
James Russell	Scottish Area
Nick White	Southern Area
Geoffrey Williams	Southern Area

Licensed Inspectors

Alan Alster	Central Area
Michael Barnett	Central Area
Don Bartlett	Midlands Area
Jeffrey Bowden	Western Area
John Braley	Midlands Area
Fred Breyer	Southern Area
David Brown	Western Area
Ray Chichester	Welsh Area
Geoff Collier	Midlands Area
John Crowe	Midlands Area
Jaswinder Dhaliwal	Midlands Area
Les Dean	Midlands Area
Robert Edgar	Central Area
Phil Edwards	Central Area
Kevin Fulthorpe	Welsh Area
Bob Galloway	Southern Area
John Hall	Central Area
Richard Hingston	Western Area
Jonathan Hooper	Western Area
Freddie King	Southern Area
Bob Lonkhurst	Southern Area
Ken Lyas	Southern Area
Tom McElkinney	Northern Area
Stuart Meiklejohn	Central Area
David Ogilvie	Northern Area
Charlie Payne	Southern Area
Fred Potter	Northern Area
Les Potts	Midlands Area
Ron Pudney	Southern Area
Ken Rimmington	Southern Area
John S. Shaw	Western Area
Bert Smith	Western Area
Charlie Thurley	Southern Area
John Toner	Northern Ireland
David Underwood	Midlands Area
David Venn	Northern Area
Ernie Wallis	Welsh Area
P. J. White	Southern Area
Billy Wilkins	Welsh Area
Clive Williams	Western Area
Geoff Williams	Midlands Area
Harry Woods	Scottish Area

Licensed Ringwhips

Bob Ainsley-Matthews	Southern Area
George Andrews	Central Area
Robert Brazier	Southern Area
Albert Brewer	Southern Area
Steve Butler	Central Area
Theodore Christian	Western Area
John Davis	Southern Area
Ernie Draper	Southern Area
Colin Gallagher	Central Area
Danny Gill	Midlands Area
Chris Gilmore	Scottish Area
Mike Goodall	Midlands Area
Simon Goodall	Midlands Area
Peter Gray	Midlands Area
Arran Lee Grinnell	Midlands Area
David Hall	Central Area
Thomas Hallett	Northern Area
John Hardwick	Southern Area
Keith Jackson	Midlands Area
Philip Keen	Central Area
Fred Little	Western Area
Alun Martin	Welsh Area
James McGinnis	Scottish Area
Tommy Miller (Jnr)	Central Area
Linton O'Brien	Northern Area
Dennis Pinching	Southern Area
Sandy Risley	Southern Area
John Vary	Southern Area
Paul Wainwright	Northern Area
James Wallace	Scottish Area
James Whitelaw	Scottish Area
John Whitelaw	Scottish Area

Boxers' Record Index